THE PHILOSOPHY OF LAW

Classic and Contemporary Readings with Commentary

THE PHILOSOPHY OF LAW

**Classic and Contemporary Readings
with Commentary**

Frederick Schauer
John F. Kennedy School of Government
Harvard University

Walter Sinnott-Armstrong
Dartmouth College

New York   Oxford
OXFORD UNIVERSITY PRESS

For Virginia, a great teacher — FS

For Alice, a great inspiration — WSA

Oxford University Press, Inc., publishes works that further Oxford University's
objective of excellence in research, scholarship, and education.

Oxford New York
Auckland Cape Town Dar es Salaam Hong Kong Karachi
Kuala Lumpur Madrid Melbourne Mexico City Nairobi
New Delhi Shanghai Taipei Toronto

With offices in
Argentina Austria Brazil Chile Czech Republic France Greece
Guatemala Hungary Italy Japan Poland Portugal Singapore
South Korea Switzerland Thailand Turkey Ukraine Vietnam

Published by Oxford University Press, Inc.
198 Madison Avenue, New York, New York 10016
http://www.oup.com

Oxford is a registered trademark of Oxford University Press

ISBN 978-0-19-515512-9

The philosophy of law is exciting. It is exciting to philosophers and philosophy students because the concrete cases and practical concerns of the law bring the abstract theories of philosophy down to earth and show how philosophical views affect real people. Law provides a kind of experiential test for philosophical theories. The philosophy of law is also exciting to legal scholars and law students because it brings out the general principles and presuppositions behind the law. Philosophy then provides critical methods for assessing laws. Indeed, the philosophy of law is exciting to anyone interested in our society, not only because our culture is so legalistic, but also because debates in the philosophy of law parallel and illuminate many of our current social tensions.

The study of the philosophy of law has developed considerably in recent years. Critical legal studies, feminist legal theory, critical race theory, the law and economics movement, communitarianism, and the new conservatism have all raised questions about almost everything that used to be taken for granted in the law. Recent years have seen new versions of retributivism and of the insanity defense, new kinds of civil disobedience, and new demands for equality by women, homosexuals, and other disadvantaged groups. And, because in the United States so many legal issues of legal philosophy become constitutional cases in the Supreme Court, the changes in the Court since the Warren era have brought about new perspectives on issues of the philosophy of law.

In order to capture this excitement and these developments, we have gathered some of the most important classic texts, a wide range of contemporary theoretical innovations, and many of the best-known recent court cases. Many aspects of these materials set our collection apart from previous anthologies in the philosophy of law. We have balanced selection from law journals and philosophy journals. Almost all contemporary movements, covering the full political and theoretical spectrum, are represented. We have also included numerous cases at various judicial levels, including part of a transcript of a trial (of John Hinckley). We have selected topics that we expect to hold the most interest for students, such as hate speech regulations, equality for homosexuals, rape, the insanity defense, and capital punishment. We even have a chapter on evidence and procedure, topics that rarely make it into books on the philosophy of law despite their obvious relevance to many legal issues and their great interest to epistemologists and philosophers of science.

Because these materials often presuppose background knowledge that students lack, we have provided extensive introductions that will make the most profound writings comprehensible to virtually all undergraduates in philosophy and political science and to law students as well. Although the introductions present philosophical arguments that can themselves be the subject of class discussion, they were designed to be used as background reading, thereby freeing up class time for more informed discussion of cases, primary readings, and problems of special interest.

Because the philosophy of law is intrinsically interdisciplinary, we think it is helpful that the editors represent different disciplines. Frederick Schauer is a law professor who specializes in constitutional law and jurisprudence and whose work in the philosophy of law has focused on rules, rights, legal positivism, and legal interpretation. Walter Sinnott-Armstrong is a philosopher with a specialty in moral theory, whose work in the philosophy of law has been most involved with moral questions surrounding punishment, responsibility, supposed obligations to obey the law, and constitutional interpretation. By combining our perspectives, this anthology is designed to embody the intersection of philosophy and law that is at the heart of the subject.

This anthology is unified by a concern with the relationship between morality and law. Chapter 1 looks at classic and contemporary theories about the nature of law and particularly at how law may differ from morality. Chapter 2 discusses methods and sources of legal reasoning and asks whether judges should base their decisions on their moral beliefs. Chapter 3 addresses the issue of when it is morally wrong to break the law. Chapter 4 compares legal rights with moral rights and asks when, if ever, morality should be enforced by law. Chapter 5 looks at moral theories of justice and their implications for the law of equal protection. Chapter 6 includes theories about the moral justification of legal punishment. Chapter 7 emphasizes the question of whether individuals should be held legally responsible when they are not morally responsible. Chapter 8 raises issues about evidence and procedure that pervade the law in ways that distinguish law from morality. This emphasis on law's relationships to morality should stimulate interest not only in students who plan to enter some legal profession but also in anyone who must deal with law in everyday life; that is to say, everyone.

This anthology was developed in several stages. First, in order to find out what instructors want to teach, we sent a preliminary table of contents to many philosophers of law and asked for their comments. The number of responses was overwhelming. We could not, of course, incorporate every suggestion, but many improvements resulted from helpful feedback. For guidance at this stage, we are grateful to the following people:

David Averbuck
   (Sonoma State University)
Harold A. Bassford
   (Atkinson College)
Bernard Baumrin
   (City University of New York)

Rodger Beehler
   (University of Victoria)
Raymond A. Belliotti
   (State University of New York—Fredonia)
Theodore M. Benditt
   (University of Alabama—Birmingham)

Luther J. Binkley
  (*Franklin and Marshall College*)
James B. Brady
  (*State University of New York–Buffalo*)
David Brink
  (*University of California at San Diego*)
Jovan Brkic
  (*North Dakota State University*)
Richard Bronaugh
  (*University of Western Ontario*)
Scott Brophy
  (*Hobart and William Smith Colleges*)
Daniel Brudney
  (*University of Chicago*)
Keith Burgess-Jackson
  (*University of Texas-Arlington*)
Richard W. Burgh
  (*Rider College*)
John R. Carnes
  (*University of Colorado–Boulder*)
Charles R. Carr
  (*Arkansas State University*)
John Robert Cassidy
  (*Ramapo College of New Jersey*)
Andrew Christie
  (*University of New Hampshire*)
Robert Paul Churchill
  (*George Washington University*)
Robert L. Cunningham
  (*University of San Francisco*)
Randall R. Curren
  (*University of Rochester*)
Michael Davis
  (*Illinois Institute of Technology*)
Elliot Dorff
  (*University of Judaism*)
James F. Doyle
  (*University of Missouri–St. Louis*)
Gerald Dworkin
  (*University of Illinois–Chicago*)
Frank K. Fair
  (*Sam Houston State University*)
Michael A. Foley
  (*Marywood College*)
Leslie Francis
  (*University of Utah*)
Peter A. French
  (*Trinity University*)
Michel Giroux
  (*Campus Notre Dame de Foy*)

John Hasnas
  (*Georgetown University*)
Mark Hebért
  (*Austin College*)
Hilde Hein
  (*College of the Holy Cross*)
H. Hamner Hill
  (*Southeast Missouri State University*)
Roscoe E. Hill
  (*University of Denver*)
Douglas Husak
  (*Rutgers University*)
Ginger O. Justus
  (*Belmont University*)
John Kleinig
  (*City University of New York*)
Ron Koshoshek
  (*University of Wisconsin–Eau Claire*)
Barbara Levenbook
  (*North Carolina State University*)
J. Ralph Lindgren
  (*Lehigh University*)
Anthony J. Lisska
  (*Denison University*)
Don Loeb
  (*University of Vermont*)
David Lyons
  (*Cornell University*)
Joseph Martire
  (*Southwest Missouri State University*)
Eugene Mayers
  (*California State University–Hayward*)
Joan McGregor
  (*Arizona State University*)
Ronald Moore
  (*University of Washington*)
Mario Morelli
  (*Western Illinois University*)
Daniel O. Nathan
  (*Texas Tech University*)
Hans Oberdiek
  (*Swarthmore College*)
Michael Otsuka
  (*University of California–Los Angeles*)
Paul O. Otubusin
  (*Calumet College of St. Joseph*)
Richard Parker
  (*California State University–Chico*)
Stanley L. Paulson
  (*Washington University*)

Leon Pearl
(*Hofstra University*)
Cliff Perry
(*Auburn University*)
Gerald Postema
(*University of North Carolina*)
George Rainbolt
(*Oberlin College*)
A. S. Rosenbaum
(*Cleveland State University*)
Stephen C. Rowntree
(*Loyola University*)
George Schedler
(*Southern Illinois University*)
James Schofield
(*Onondaga Community College*)
David Seligman
(*Western Maryland College*)
Roger A. Shiner
(*University of Alberta–Edmonton*)
Christine T. Sistare
(*Muhlenberg College*)
M. B. E. Smith
(*Smith College*)

Aaron Snyder
(*University of Wisconsin*)
Howard T. Sprow
(*Union University*)
Bonnie Steinbock
(*State University of New York–Albany*)
Peter Suber
(*Earlham College*)
Paul Sukys
(*North Central Technical College*)
Adelaide Thomason
(*College of New Rochelle*)
Julie C. Van Camp
(*California State University–Long Beach*)
Harold T. Walsh
(*Michigan State University*)
Carl Wellman
(*Washington University*)
Burleigh T. Wilkins
(*University of California–Santa Barbara*)
Kenneth Winston
(*Wheaton College*)
Daniel E. Wueste
(*Clemson University*)

We also learned from our reviewers that many teachers want discussion questions, suggestions for further reading, and detailed introductions to provide background for students. So we added numerous discussion questions after each reading and several suggestions for further reading at the end of each chapter. Professor Schauer then wrote the introductions to Chapters 1, 2, 4, and 8, and Professor Sinnott-Armstrong wrote the introductions to Chapters 3, 5, 6, and 7. These introductions benefited greatly from comments by Michael Davis (Illinois Institute of Technology), Frank K. Fair (Sam Houston State University), Michael A. Foley (Marywood College), Ron Koshoshek (University of Wisconsin–Eau Claire), and Aaron Snyder (University of Wisconsin). We also received help with our introductions from several friends and colleagues including Walter Armstrong, Jr., Ted Brader, Susan Brison, Ann Bumpus, Robert Fogelin, Bernard Gert, and Chris Timmel.

Dartmouth's philosophy librarian, Bill Fontaine, aided us greatly in compiling the anthology, as did three extraordinary student assistants: Malia Brink, Robert Geisler, and Chris Timmel. Support was also provided by the Joan Shorenstein Center on the Press, Politics, and Public Policy, John F. Kennedy School of Government, Harvard University. Finally, we owe a debt of gratitude to Jeff Beckham, Claire Brantley, and David Tatom at Harcourt Brace College Publishers for their encouragement and patience.

TABLE of CONTENTS

<table>
<tr><td>CHAPTER 2 LEGAL REASONING</td><td align="right">117</td></tr>
</table>

INTRODUCTION   117

CHAPTER 8 LEGAL PROCEDURE AND EVIDENCE   929

INTRODUCTION   929

THE PHILOSOPHY OF LAW

Classic and Contemporary Readings with Commentary

CHAPTER 1

WHAT IS LAW?

INTRODUCTION

This book is an introduction to the study of the philosophy of law. But just what is it that we will be studying? Why is studying the philosophy of law different from studying law? What exactly do we do when we study the philosophy of something? And even if we know what it is to study the philosophy of something, what is the something that we call "law"? Thus both of the key terms in the name of the topic—"philosophy" and "law"—cry out for further explanation. Although a book on the philosophy of law might not be the best place to explore the complex question of what philosophy is, dealing with the question of what law is seems an obvious starting point. Indeed, questions about the philosophical dimensions of some institution or practice or phenomenon are often phrased, in part, as "What is . . . ?" questions. Aesthetics, the philosophy of art, is often concerned with the questions of just what art *is*, and what distinguishes a work of art from something else. When those who study the philosophy of art ask what makes a painting by Rembrandt a work of art, they are puzzled by why a Rembrandt painting so clearly qualifies as art, but why the designs we draw when sitting in a boring lecture do not. Similarly, philosophers of science on occasion ask, "What is science?", and the difference between science and the philosophy of science lies partly in the difference between "What is science?", a philosophical question, and "What is photosynthesis?", a scientific question. Much the same can be said about the philosophy of social science, the philosophy of literature, the philosophy of education, and the philosophy of history.

So too with the philosophy of law. Consider the difference between "Is smoking marijuana a crime in Michigan?", which is a question about the law, and "What is a crime?", which because of its depth and abstraction is much more a question of the philosophy of law. And so an enduring question of legal philosophy, and the one that is the subject of this chapter, can be phrased simply as the question, "What is law?". Yet when we ask that question, deeper problems may lurk beneath the surface. When we ask what law is, we think something more important is at stake than when we ask what dentistry is, and that is not because law is more important than dentistry, or lawyers more important than dentists. Rather, it is that there are serious questions about what law might *not* be. The English ordinary language philosopher J. L. Austin[1] suggested that we can often understand what a word means by examining its opposite in some context, as when we understand better what "real" means by trying to figure out the sense in which something might not be real. Thus, to use Austin's example, a "real" duck is different from a dummy duck, a toy duck, a picture of a duck, and so on. Thus we know what "real" means in some context by knowing what the user of the word means to *exclude*.[2]

In much the same way, therefore, a person who wants to know what law is might be just as interested in what law is not. There might be certain things that someone using the word "law" intends to exclude. When we say that decisions of the Attorney General of the United States should be guided only by the law, we may want to distinguish law from politics. When we observe that it is immoral to join the Ku Klux Klan even though it is legal in the United States to do so, we may wish to distinguish law from morality. In other contexts we may wish to distinguish the norms of law from social norms of etiquette, honor, and the like. If we respond to the question "What is law?" with the question "Why do you want to know?", we may discover that the central questions about the nature or essence or definition of law are in fact questions seeking to distinguish the legal domain from other domains. Then we might look carefully at whether the distinction is sound, and what turns on drawing it.

Yet perhaps there is even less to the matter than this. In the 1940s the English legal philosopher Glanville Williams[3] suggested that the question "What is law?" is merely a semantic question about the definition of terms. For example, people often ask whether international law, which has rules but little in the way of enforcement, and which does not emanate out of a sovereign state with sovereign powers, is "really" law or not. But Williams did not see this as a particularly useful question. Better to talk about just what international law *is*, he thought, and focus on the ways in which it is different from or similar to other normative systems, without becoming preoccupied with what we call any or all of those systems. "Law" is just a word, he argued, and a linguistic community can choose to apply it or not as it wishes. Whether international law, for example, is "properly" called law or not is just a matter of linguistic stipulation. Arguing about what that stipulation should be, about what institutions should be *called*, he maintained, distracted us from more important questions about how institutions operated and how they should be designed.[4]

---

[1] J. L. Austin lived from 1911–1960, spent most of his philosophical career at Oxford, and made major contributions to the philosophy of language. He is not to be confused with the philosopher of law John Austin, who lived in the nineteenth century, and whose work we will consider later in this chapter.

[2] *Sense and Sensibilia* (Oxford University Press, 1962), p. 70.

[3] Williams, born in 1909, has spent most of his academic career at the University of London and Cambridge University. He is best known for his contributions to the theory of criminal law.

[4] Glanville Ll. Williams, "International Law and the Controversy Concerning the Word 'Law'," in Peter Laslett, ed., *Philosophy, Politics and Society* (Oxford: Basil Blackwell, 1956), pp. 142 ff.

Yet as the English philosopher of law H. L. A. Hart has argued,[5] this approach to the question "What is law?" may leave too much unanswered. First, the question itself may be shorthand for a number of more important ones about the distinction (if any) between law and morality, about the relation (if any) between law and rules, and about the sources on which judges rely in making their decisions. Moreover, the word "law," Hart argued, is like most other terms in containing a core of settled meaning and a fringe of debatable applications. We know, for instance, to take one of Hart's most famous examples, that cars and trucks are "vehicles," and that these are in most contexts the core and noncontroversial applications of the word "vehicle." But when we consider bicycles, or roller skates, or baby carriages, we might argue about whether they are properly called "vehicles" or not. It is precisely this uncertainty about the application of the term that causes these to be fringe (or penumbral) rather than core applications of the word "vehicle." And so too with the word "law." Just because there are fringe cases of "law" such as "international law" and "customary law," in which we can argue about whether a term is properly or improperly applied (as when we argue about whether handcrafts are really art, or whether sociology is really science), does not mean that there are not core or central cases of law. And thus although Hart opened his book by suggesting that the "What is law?" question is often the surrogate for other and deeper questions, he also believed that there were central and philosophically interesting cases of "law," with much of the remainder of his book, parts of which are included in this chapter, devoted to exploring what features characterized the central cases of law.

Let us think a bit further about what we are trying to do when we seek to *define* or understand the *concept* of law. In the 1950s Hart and his American contemporary Lon Fuller[6] engaged in a famous debate in the pages of the *Harvard Law Review* about the perennial question whether there was a necessary connection between law and morality, a question we consider both in this chapter and in Chapter 2. Fuller maintained, in a variation on the natural law position examined in the next section of this chapter, that consistency with certain moral norms was a necessary condition for the existence of law. To Fuller, failure to adhere to this belief (that certain kinds of moral failings would make law simply impossible) could result, as it did in Nazi Germany, in all of the positive associations of the word "law" being attached to quite wicked legal systems. Fuller therefore believed that the word "law" should be withheld from application to such evil legal systems just because of the moral importance of not attaching the positive emotive associations of the word "law" to something

---

[5]H. L. A. Hart, *The Concept of Law* (Oxford: Clarendon Press, 1961), pp. 1–2. Hart (1907–1993), whose work we consider in depth in this chapter and at various other places throughout this book, was a practicing lawyer for nine years and then spent the remainder of his life at Oxford, where he became one of the most influential legal philosophers of the twentieth century.

[6]Fuller lived from 1902–1978, and was for much of his career Carter Professor of General Jurisprudence at the Harvard Law School, where he made important contributions to contract law as well as to the philosophy of law.

deserving no such implicit approval.[7] Hart, however, articulating what has come to be taken as one of the central tenets of legal positivism, the subject of Section 3 of this chapter, urged the separation of the concept of law from the concept of morality. Hart of course did not believe that laws *should* be immoral, but he maintained that the features that made some norm or some system a *legal* one were not moral features, and that as a consequence the existence of law was independent of the morality of particular laws or of the entire legal system. This approach, Hart argued, was more likely than Fuller's approach to foster resistance to wicked legal systems. Hart maintained that if people came to believe that attaching the word "law" to some system entailed no moral approval whatsoever, we would be better able to separate the existence of a legal system from its evaluation, and thus better able to see wicked legal systems for just what they are. These people thus would recognize the importance of engaging in their own moral determinations of what to do, when to follow the law, and when to disobey it.[8]

Although Hart and Fuller disagreed about whether the concept of law *should* be understood as necessarily incorporating moral criteria of some kind, the most important thing here is to observe that they agreed about what kind of question they were debating. For both Fuller and Hart the topic of their debate was a moral one, to be decided by moral criteria. What looked like a definitional or conceptual question was in fact a moral one. In other words, the question of the definition or understanding of the concept of law was to be decided instrumentally, according to which conception would better serve the agreed moral goal of discouraging citizens from obeying morally iniquitous laws just because they were law. Indeed, thirty years later the Scottish legal philosopher Neil Mac-Cormick (1928–   ), siding with Hart's position within the debate, made it very clear that the view that law should not be understood as necessarily incorporating morality was itself a moral view based instrumentally on an assessment of which approach would better serve certain moral goals.[9]

But is this the right way to think about identifying the concept of law or defining the word "law"? After all, when we ask what words like "medicine" or "science" mean, or when we try to find out what is at the core of the concepts of medicine or science, we do not immediately think that we should then try to answer this question in light of what it would be morally good for the concepts of medicine or science to be. Why should the concept of law be any different? Thus many theorists have thought it peculiar to debate questions about the nature of law in such explicitly instrumental moral terms. The American law professor

---

[7]Lon L. Fuller, "Positivism and Fidelity to Law—A Reply to Professor Hart," *Harvard Law Review*, vol. 71 (1958), pp. 630 ff. Fuller's position was more complex than the simple description just given. Unlike some of the traditional natural law theorists, Fuller did not believe that substantive morality was a necessary condition for legality. Rather, he believed that procedural morality (publishing the laws, not punishing retroactively, and so on) was a necessary condition for legality, in part because procedural morality was highly conducive to substantive morality.

[8]H. L. A. Hart, "Positivism and the Separation of Law and Morals," *Harvard Law Review*, vol. 71 (1958), pp. 593 ff.

[9]Neil MacCormick, "A Moralistic Case for A-Moralistic Law?", *Valparaiso University Law Review*, vol. 20 (1985), pp. 1 ff.

Philip Soper (1942–   ), for example, objects to the idea of choosing a legal theory on moral grounds and argues that law exists in the world. Thus to Soper the job of a theorist is trying to give the picture of law that is right, and not the picture of law that would best serve certain moral goals. Consequently the definition of the concept of law is, for Soper, an ontological and not a normative question. That is, it is a question about what *is*, about the nature of what exists in the world and not about what should be. Our job, Soper argues, is to look for what law is, and not for what it would be morally good for it to be.[10]

To this it might be responded, however, that law's ontological status is not the same as that of a natural kind like carbon or an artifact like a bus. So although we might try to figure out what carbon *is*, independent of what we would like carbon to be, and to identify the existing extensions of the word "bus" without engaging in deep moral argument, the same approach might be odd for things like law. Law is, after all, a social construct not existing in the pre–human world, and most elements of legal systems do not exist in the physical world the way buses do. Because of this, it could be argued, it remains open to us to construct it as we will and to understand it as we will. So even if there are natural kinds and other phenomena that pre–exist human categorization, law may not be one of them. Therefore it remains not only open but also desirable to understand (and therefore to define) the phenomenon of law in ways that will best serve moral purposes.

Even if Soper is right, and Hart, Fuller, and MacCormick are wrong, and even if we therefore take the task of defining law as one more of discovery than of normative construction, there is still the question of just what it is that we are looking for when we are trying to answer the "What is law"? question. The contemporary American legal and moral philosopher Jules Coleman (1947–   ) maintains that we are trying to determine what is true about the concept of law in all *possible* legal systems in all possible worlds. Thus for him the inquiry into the nature of law is fundamentally conceptual and not empirical. For Coleman the conceptual possibility that law could exist without a connection with morality would be sufficient to rebut the claim that there is a *necessary* connection between law and morality. Therefore, even if morality were in fact a criterion for legal validity in all existing legal systems, the claim of a necessary connection between the two could still be false.[11] Coleman and others consequently see the task of answering the "What is law?" question as a task far removed from asking descriptive empirical questions about what happens contingently to be true about the particular legal systems with which we are most familiar.

Yet asking that kind of conceptual or analytic question is not the only way to inquire into the nature of law. When Ronald Dworkin[12] and others seek to examine

---

[10]Philip Soper, "Choosing a Legal Theory on Moral Grounds," in Jules Coleman and Ellen Frankel Paul, eds., *Philosophy and Law* (Oxford: Basil Blackwell, 1987), pp. 31 ff.

[11]Jules L. Coleman, "Rules and Social Facts," *Harvard Journal of Law and Public Policy*, vol. 14 (1991), pp. 703 ff.; and also his "Negative and Positive Positivism," in Jules L. Coleman, *Markets, Morals and the Law* (Cambridge: Cambridge University Press, 1988), pp. 3 ff.

[12]Ronald Dworkin (1931–   ), an American, is H.L.A. Hart's successor as Professor of Jurisprudence at Oxford University. We consider Dworkin's work extensively in this chapter and in Chapter 2.

what "law" means, their inquiries appear to be a blend of the descriptive and the conceptual. Less concerned about what might be true about all possible legal systems in all possible worlds, Dworkin wants to know about the operation of law and legal norms in the legal systems we know best. We learn much about the concept of law, his work suggests, by actually looking at the practices and styles of discourse and justification and argument of real lawyers and real judges in real legal systems. Dworkin's work, therefore, focuses on modern western legal systems, and he makes no claim to be talking about the full universe of actual or possible legal systems. In pursuing this investigation, Dworkin returns to what is probably the most enduring of the dimensions of the "What is law?" question, and one that will occupy a significant portion of this chapter. This is the question of what, if anything, separates the rules, principles, norms, commands, and maxims that we call "law" from all of the other rules, principles, norms, commands, and maxims that generally seek to control our behavior. Is there a difference worth talking about between the legal requirement in the Equal Protection Clause of the Fourteenth Amendment to the Constitution of the United States, which says that a state shall not "deny to any person within its jurisdiction the equal protection of the laws," and the moral requirement that governments shall treat all of their citizens equally? Although it is plain from its wording that the Equal Protection Clause incorporates moral values, what is the significance of the fact that these moral values have been set down in a written constitution or in some other piece of "hard law"? If the Fourteenth Amendment were to be repealed, or if (as was the case prior to 1868) the Equal Protection Clause had never existed, would it be legally wrong (as well as morally wrong) for governments to treat their citizens unequally? If so, would judges have operated within their legitimate authority in striking down statutes that denied equality to all citizens? Or is it the case that regardless of the moral stature of the requirement that states treat their citizens equally, it was lawful for states to treat their citizens unequally before 1868? And if it was lawful, even if immoral, for states to treat their citizens unequally prior to 1868, would a judge of the time have been acting illegitimately—outside of his authority—in refusing to enforce a law that required unequal treatment? In order to answer these questions, we must answer the question of how the rules and principles *of the law* relate to moral and political rules that would govern our lives and behavior even were there no formal legal system at all.

Dworkin's subtle and complex answers to these questions return consistently to the *judge* as the central actor in legal theory. If there is a strong difference between legal and other norms, then, Dworkin supposes, we would see it reflected in judicial behavior, and in judges' use of norms found in books of statutes and regulations and court cases, and conversely in judges' refusal to use norms, however morally desirable, that they could not find in the law books. But if we see, however, as a contingent empirical matter, that judges are actually making their decisions by recourse to a largely undifferentiated set of legal, political, social, and moral norms, then the answer to the "What is law?" question may not yield some plainly identifiable subset of the larger set of a society's social norms. More to the point, therefore, for Dworkin and others the question "What is law?" is partly a function of the answer to the "What do judges do?" question. For Dworkin this is also closely related to the "What *should* judges do?" question, and Dworkin's mythical judge Hercules is intended not so much to describe an actual judge as to picture a judge being all that a judge can be. Still, for Dworkin as well as for others, when we find out what judges (and other so–called legal officials) do and should do in actual legal systems, we will have given as much of an answer to the "What is law?" question as it is possible or desirable to give.

1.1 THE THEORY OF NATURAL LAW

INTRODUCTION

From the beginning laws have told us not to kill, not to steal, and, sometimes, not to lie. Yet it is usually morally as well as legally wrong to kill, to steal, and to lie. Even were there no laws at all, killing would usually be (or always be, to some) morally wrong. And if it is morally wrong to kill, then what does the fact that killing is illegal as well as immoral tell us about the nature of law? Does law exist just to enforce moral norms? If so, how are we to understand laws that enforce immoral norms, such as the American fugitive slave laws that existed prior to the Civil War, and that required people in all states to return escaped slaves to their owners (a case and commentary about these laws is presented later in this chapter). Were these laws not "really" law because the norms they sought to enforce failed all tests of morality? And what of genuine moral norms that might not be written down in law books? The Constitution of the United States does not specify, in so many words, that there is a right to privacy. Does that lack of specification in positive law mean that a right to privacy is not part of the Constitution even if there is a moral right to privacy? And does that mean that law-enforcing officials act wrongly in enforcing such a moral right? Or instead is the written Constitution just a human attempt, admittedly imperfect, to capture some deeper or higher law, so that the judge who enforces a constitutional right to privacy is not violating the Constitution, but rather just enforcing a deeper sense of the "real" Constitution?

These are the kinds of questions that have traditionally been the concern of the perspective known as *natural law*. Although one can find traces in Aristotle and in some of the writings of the Stoics, the position we now know as natural law has its earliest extended explication in Cicero's (106–43 B.C.) *De Legibus* (*The Laws*). Cicero was not concerned with the power of judges, but he was concerned with trying to explain the nature of law in relation to morality. In doing so he saw law and morality as one. Law to Cicero was the product of the Gods, the highest form of human reason. Thus, Cicero says that:

> Law is the highest reason, implanted in nature, which commands what ought to be done and forbids the opposite. This reason, when firmly fixed and fully developed in the human mind, is Law. . . . Law is intelligence, whose natural function it is to command right conduct and forbid wrongdoing. . . . For as [the most learned men] have attributed the idea of fairness to the word law, so we have given it the idea of selection, though both ideas properly belong to Law. Now if this is correct,

. . . then the origin of Justice is to be found in Law, for Law is a natural force; it is the mind and reason of the intelligent man, the standard by which Justice and Injustice are measured. But since our whole discussion has to do with the reasoning of the populace, it will sometimes be necessary to speak in the popular manner, and give the name of law to that which in written form decrees whatever it wishes, either by command or prohibition. But in determining what Justice is, let us begin with that supreme Law which had its origin, ages before any written law existed or any State had been established.[13]

Thus Law, with a capital "L," was to Cicero decidedly not a product of human action. Instead Law was the product of God, to be found, by definition, in the best of human reason. As a result, although it is important that states have institutions reflecting Law—reflecting the distinction between the just and the unjust—it is not the fact of human creation but the fact of consistency with the proper standards of justice that makes something Law. Thus to Cicero we have human laws to *realize* the higher moral norms that are the true law. Law consequently stems from morality and is inseparable from it.

But consider what follows from this view. If morality is the source of all law, then things that look like law—enacted by legislatures, or enforced by courts, and written down in lawbooks—might not really be law at all. And this is the position Cicero took, arguing that an unjust law, although it might be thought of as a law by the populace, is not in fact a genuine Law. Thus, Cicero argued that, for example, "a law of personal exception," a law that "penalized particular individuals," was "unjust" and thus not a law at all. "For this reason Lucius Cotta, a man of great talent and the highest wisdom, was all the more surely correct in his opinion with reference to [the case in which Cicero himself had been banished] that no legal action at all had really been taken against me. . . . From this he concluded that I needed no law to repeal what had never been legally enacted against me."[14] Consequently, Cicero saw compliance with certain morally guided principles as a necessary condition for the existence of real law.[15] If I build a car but it does not run, is it really a car, or is it just something that resembles a car? Cicero saw moral correctness as the purpose of law in the same way we might see driveability as the purpose of a car. If a non-driveable car is no car at all, then an immoral law is no law at all, or so Cicero maintained. Similarly, consider whether a hammer with a paper head is really a tool. For Cicero moral purpose was an essential feature of law, just as certain properties are essential to, say, humanity. A lifelike dummy such as we might find in a wax museum might fool someone who didn't look carefully, but that does not make the dummy a person. And this is what not only Cicero, but later thinkers in the natural law tradition, argued with respect to the idea of law. The views of the greatest of all natural law

[13]Cicero, *De Legibus* (C. W. Keyes, trans., Cambridge, Massachusetts: Harvard University Press, Loeb Classical Library, 1928), Book 1, section 6.

[14]Book III, section 19

[15]Cicero also saw compliance with these moral principles as sufficient for Law, so that all natural moral requirements were also Legal requirements.

thinkers, Saint Thomas Aquinas, are more complex and will be considered later. But a more straightforward natural law view, similar to that of Cicero, is represented by people like the great English theorist and legal commentator William Blackstone (1723–1780). Blackstone maintained that human laws are but realizations of God's law, the moral laws of nature. Thus things that look like laws, but in fact contradict God's law, are for Blackstone, as for Cicero, simply not laws at all. The very idea of law, Blackstone and some others in the natural law tradition have argued, has a moral criterion, and something that is not moral is not a valid law, as when Blackstone says that "no human laws are of any validity, if contrary to" natural law.[16] We might, according to Blackstone, call an immoral law a law (just like Cicero said that the populace might refer to all written directives as laws), but we are mistaken in doing so, having confused the false (invalid) law with a real law just as someone may occasionally think that a wax mannequin is a real person.

Blackstone was not only concerned with recognizing that immoral laws were not really law at all. Indeed, at other times Blackstone was quite willing to draw a distinction between human laws, laws that were laws even if immoral, and natural laws, which might or might not be realized in human laws. Still, once it becomes clear that things like constitutions and statutes and regulations and court cases are but the realization of a higher law, then it is a mistake not only when statutes enacted by fallible human beings try to enforce what is not moral, but also when they fail to enforce what *is* moral. In Blackstone's view, law existed in nature and not exclusively in the books labelled "The Laws of England." A judge or other official who therefore enforced the laws of nature that had not yet been enacted into statutes was doing nothing wrong. Accordingly, when judges reached conclusions not previously reflected in human law, they were still declaring the law, putting into concrete form the law that had been there all along, rather than making new law. Hence, to Blackstone and others, a judge, in going beyond the law in the books, was recognizing that there was more to law than what appeared in those books, and was thus acting in furtherance of and not contrary to the law.

Perhaps ironically in light of his views about natural law as a source of law, Blackstone is now remembered less as a legal theorist than as a cataloguer and systematizer of, and commentator on, the enacted or judge-made concrete law. Nevertheless, Blackstone's importance as a commentator on the positive law has caused him to be identified with two of the central positions in the natural law tradition. One is the idea of morality as a necessary criterion for the existence of valid law, such that immoral laws were simply not valid laws at all, and immoral legal systems were not valid legal systems. And the other was the idea of human law as the realization of higher moral law, such that the higher but unwritten moral law was just as much law as that which happened to be enacted by legislatures or decided by judges. But one of the reasons we now pay less attention to Blackstone as a legal theorist is that his arguments for understanding law as

---

[16]William Blackstone, *Commentaries on the Laws of England,* vol. 1, p. 44.

natural law were sketchy, contained at various places in a four-volume work devoted primarily to descriptions of and commentaries on specific areas of law and concrete legal doctrines.

Nowadays when we think of the natural law tradition we think most often of Saint Thomas Aquinas (1225–1274), in part because his writings on natural law were much more extensive and sophisticated than those of Blackstone and Cicero. Unlike Cicero in his less guarded passages, and perhaps unlike Blackstone, Aquinas saw clearly the distinction between higher law and human law. Similarly, he appreciated the distinction between moral soundness and legal validity. But we associate Aquinas centrally with the natural law tradition in part also because the Thomistic natural law tradition has become a central thesis of Catholic theology. Yet it is a mistake, albeit one commonly made, to assume that the natural law tradition has a necessary connection with Catholicism, or indeed even with religion in a formal sense. Aquinas's basic arguments about the nature of law, and about the relation of law with morality, are not dependent on particular views about the sources or substantive content of that morality. If there can be a secular morality antecedent to human laws and concrete human institutions, the basic principles of the natural law tradition can be considered even apart from their location within the traditions of Catholic theology. And thus the "higher law" tradition of John Locke, a substantial influence on American constitutionalism and the concept of constitutional rights, remains a worthwhile reminder of the danger of confusing the structure of the natural law position with the substantive moral views with which the natural law position is most commonly associated. As long as one believes that there are moral requirements that are logically antecedent to enacted human laws—that murder would be wrong even if the laws against it were to be repealed, and that it makes sense to say that the fugitive slave laws were immoral even for the states in which they were enacted— then the starting point of the natural law tradition must be taken seriously. It takes more argument than this to establish a relationship between the immoral and the illegal. Still, the point that written-down law may be incomplete, and the point that written-down law may be so immoral as not to count as law at all, are ones that are plausibly related to the view that morality precedes and is higher than human law. In considering the views of Aquinas, therefore, consider how they might be applicable across the range of moral beliefs, and then consider whether his arguments about the relationship of law to morality are sound. So too with more modern writers in the natural law tradition, of whom the English legal philosopher John Finnis (1942–   ) is the most prominent example. And then compare Lon Fuller, who wrote in the natural law tradition, but who believed that the moral criteria for law were not so much substantive as procedural. Is Fuller's position a natural law view at all, or is he more different from than similar to central natural law figures like Cicero, Aquinas, Finnis, and Blackstone?

SUMMA THEOLOGIAE

THOMAS AQUINAS

QUESTION 90

Law is a rule and measure of acts, whereby man is induced to act or is restrained from acting; for *lex [law]* is derived from *ligare [to bind]*, because it binds one to act. Now the rule and measure of human acts is the reason, which is the first principle of human acts. . . . For it belongs to the reason to direct to the end, which is the first principle in all matters of action, according to [Aristotle]. . . . Reason has its power of moving from the will, . . . for it is due to the fact that one wills the end, that the reason issues its commands as regards things ordained to the end. But in order that the volition of what is commanded may have the nature of law, it needs to be in accord with some rule of reason. And in this sense is to be understood the saying that the will of the sovereign has the force of law; or otherwise the sovereign's will would savor of lawlessness rather than of law.

[Now] the first principle in practical matters, which are the object of the practical reason, is the last end: and the last end of human life is happiness or beatitude. . . . Consequently, law must . . . concern itself mainly with the order that is in beatitude. Moreover, since every part is ordained to the whole as the imperfect to the perfect, and since one man is a part of the perfect community, law must . . . concern itself properly with the order directed to universal happiness. Therefore Aristotle mentions both happiness and the body politic, since he says that we call those legal matters *just which are adapted to produce and preserve happiness and its parts for the body politic.*

Now in every genus, that which belongs to it chiefly is the principle of the others, and the others belong to that genus according to some order towards that thing. Thus fire, which is chief among hot things, is the cause of heat in mixed bodies, and these are said to be hot in so far as they have a share of fire. Consequently, since law is chiefly ordained to the common good, any other precept in regard to some individual work must . . . be devoid of the nature of law, save in so far as it regards the common good. Therefore every law is ordained to the common good.

Just as nothing stands firm with regard to the speculative reason except that which is traced back to the first indemonstrable principles, so nothing stands firm with regard to the practical reason, unless it be directed to the last end which is the common good. Now whatever stands to reason in this sense has the nature of a law.

[A] private person cannot lead another to virtue efficaciously; for he can only advise, and if his advice be not taken, it has no coercive power, such as the law should have, in order to prove an efficacious inducement to virtue. . . . But this coercive power is vested in the whole people or in some public personage, to whom it belongs to inflict penalties. . . . Therefore the framing of laws belongs to him alone.

[A] law is imposed on others as a rule and measure. Now a rule or measure is imposed by being applied to those who are to be ruled and measured by it. Therefore, in order that a law obtain the binding force which is proper to a law, it must . . . be applied to the men

Selections from Thomas Aquinas, *Summa Theologiae*, Part II (London: Fathers of the English Dominican Province, trans., 1915), Questions 90, 91, 94, 95, 96

who have to be ruled by it. But such application is made by its being made known to them by promulgation. Therefore promulgation is necessary for law to obtain its force.

Thus, . . . Law is nothing else than an ordinance of reason for the common good, promulgated by him who has the care of the community.

The natural law is promulgated by the very fact that God instilled it into man's mind so as to be known by him naturally. . . . The promulgation that takes place in the present extends to future time by reason of the durability of written characters, by which means it is continually promulgated.

QUESTION 91

Every act of reason and will in us is based on that which is according to nature. . . . For every act of reasoning is based on principles that are known naturally, and every act of appetite in respect of the means is derived from the natural appetite in respect of the last end. Accordingly, the first direction of our acts to their end must . . . be through the natural law.

[Augustine] distinguishes two kinds of law, the one eternal, the other temporal, which he calls human. . . . Just as in the speculative reason, from naturally known indemonstrable principles we draw the conclusions of the various sciences, the knowledge of which is not imparted to us by nature, but acquired by the efforts of reason, so too it is that from the precepts of the natural law, as from common and indemonstrable principles, the human reason needs to proceed to the more particular determination of certain matters. These particular determinations, devised by human reason, are called human laws, provided that the other essential conditions of law be observed.

QUESTION 94

[The] precepts of the natural law are to the practical reason what the first principles of

demonstrations are to the speculative reason, because both are self-evident principles. . . . Now as *being* is the first thing that falls under the apprehension absolutely, so *good* is the first thing that falls under the apprehension of the practical reason, which is directed to action (since every agent acts for an end, which has the nature of good). Consequently, the first principle in the practical reason is one founded on the nature of the good, viz., that *good is that which all things seek after.* Hence this is the first precept of law, that *good is to be promoted, and evil is to be avoided.* All other precepts of the natural law are based on this; so that all things which the practical reason naturally apprehends as man's good belong to the precepts of the natural law under the form of things to be done or avoided.

QUESTION 95

[As] Augustine says, *that which is not just seems to be no law at all.* Hence the force of a law depends on the extent of its justice. Now in human affairs a thing is said to be just from being right, according to the rule of reason. But the first rule of reason is the law of nature. . . . Consequently, every human law has just so much of the nature of law as it is derived from the law of nature. But if in any point it departs from the law of nature, it is no longer law but a perversion of law.

[The] common principles of the natural law cannot be applied to all men in the same way because of the great variety of human affairs; and hence arises the diversity of positive laws among various people. . . . In this respect, there are various human laws according to the various forms of government. . . . Tyrannical government, which is altogether corrupt, . . . has no corresponding law.

QUESTION 96

The natural law is a participation in us of the eternal law, while human law falls short of the eternal law. For Augustine says, *The law which is framed for the government of states allows and leaves unpunished many things that are punished by divine providence. Nor, if this law does not attempt to do everything, is this a reason why it should be blamed for what it does.* Therefore, human law likewise does not prohibit everything that is forbidden by the natural law.

[Laws] framed by man are either just or unjust. If they be just, they have the power of binding the conscience from the eternal law whence they are derived. . . . On the other hand, laws may be unjust in two ways: first,

by being contrary to human good, . . . as when an authority imposes on his subjects burdensome laws, conducive, not to the common good, but rather to his own cupidity or vainglory. . . . Such are acts of violence rather than laws, because, as Augustine says, *a law that is not just seems to be no law at all.* Therefore, such laws do not bind in conscience. . . .

Secondly, laws may be unjust through being opposed to the divine good. . . . Laws of this kind must in no way be observed, because . . . *we ought to obey God rather than men.*

QUESTIONS FOR DISCUSSION

1. What, according to Aquinas, is the purpose of law?

2. What does Aquinas mean by "promulgation"? Does he think that natural law needs to be promulgated? Human law? What does Aquinas see as the purpose in promulgating laws?

3. How does Aquinas distinguish between natural law and human law? Does Aquinas believe that natural law is binding? Does he believe that human law is binding? What does he mean by "binding"?

4. Does Aquinas agree with Cicero that a human law that violates natural law is not a law at all? Does Aquinas agree with Blackstone that a human law that violates natural law is not a *valid* law?

NATURAL LAW AND NATURAL RIGHTS

JOHN FINNIS

What are *principles of natural law*? The sense that the phrase 'natural law' has in this book can be indicated in the following rather bald assertions, formulations which will seem per-

haps empty or question-begging until explicated in Part Two: There is (i) a set of basic practical principles which indicate the basic forms of human flourishing as goods to be

Selection from John Finnis, *Natural Law and Natural Rights* (Oxford: Clarendon Press, 1980), Chapter II

pursued and realized, and which are in one way or another used by everyone who considers what to do, however unsound his conclusions; and (ii) a set of basic methodological requirements of practical reasonableness (itself one of the basic forms of human flourishing) which distinguish sound from unsound practical thinking and which, when all brought to bear, provide the criteria for distinguishing between acts that (always or in particular circumstances) are reasonable-all-things-considered (and not merely relative-to-a-particular purpose) and acts that are unreasonable-all-things-considered, i.e. between ways of acting that are morally right or morally wrong—thus enabling one to formulate (iii) a set of general moral standards.

To avoid misunderstandings about the scope of our subject-matter in this book, I should add here that the principles of natural law, thus understood, are traced out not only in moral philosophy or ethics and individual conduct, but also in political philosophy and jurisprudence, in political action, adjudication, and the life of the citizen. For those principles justify the exercise of authority in community. They require, too, that that authority be exercised, in most circumstances, according to the manner conveniently labelled the Rule of Law, and with due respect for the human rights which embody the requirements of justice, and for the purpose of promoting a common good in which such respect for rights is a component. More particularly, the principles of natural law explain the obligatory force (in the fullest sense of 'obligation') of positive laws, even when those laws cannot be deduced from those principles. And attention to the principles, in the context of these explanations of law and legal obligation, justifies regarding certain positive laws as radically defective, *precisely as laws*, for want of conformity to those principles.

My present purpose, however, is not to anticipate later chapters, but to make some preliminary clarifications. A first essential distinction is that between a theory, doctrine, or account and the subject-matter of that theory, doctrine, or account. There can be a history of theories, doctrines, and accounts of matters that have no history. And principles of natural law, in the sense formulated in the two preceding paragraphs, have no history.

Since I have yet to show that there are indeed any principles of natural law, let me put the point conditionally. Principles of this sort would hold good, as principles, however extensively they were overlooked, misapplied, or defied in practical thinking, and however little they were recognized by those who reflectively theorize about human thinking. That is to say, they would 'hold good' just as the mathematical principles of accounting 'hold good' even when, as in the medieval banking community, they are unknown or misunderstood. So there could be a history of the varying extent to which they have been used by people, explicitly or implicitly, to regulate their personal activities. And there could be a history of varying extent to which reflective theorists have acknowledged the sets of principles as valid or 'holding good'. And there could be a history of the popularity of the various theories offered to explain the place of those principles in the whole scheme of things. But of natural law itself there could, strictly speaking, be no history.

Natural law could not rise, decline, be revived, or stage 'eternal returns'. It could not have historical achievements to its credit. It could not be held responsible for disasters of the human spirit or atrocities of human practice.

But there is a history of the opinions or set of opinions, theories, and doctrines which assert that there are principles of natural law, a history of origins, rises, declines and falls, revivals and achievements, and of historical responsibilities. Anyone who thinks there really are no such principles will consider that a book about natural law must be a book about mere opinions, and that the principal interest of those opinions is their historical causes and effects. But anyone who considers that there are principles of natural law, in the sense already outlined, ought to see the importance of maintaining a distinction between discourse about natural law and discourse about a doctrine or doctrines of natural law. Unhappily, people often fail to maintain the distinction.

This is a book about natural law. It expounds or sets out a theory of natural law, but is not *about* that theory. Nor is it about other theories. It refers to other theories only to illuminate the theory expounded here, or to explain why some truths about natural law have at various times and in various ways been overlooked or obscured. The book does not enter into discussions about whether natural law doctrines have exerted a conservative or radical influence on Western politics, or about the supposed psychological (infantile) origins of such doctrines, or about the claim that some or all specific natural law doctrines are asserted hypocritically, arrogantly, or as a disguise or vehicle for expressions of ecclesiastical faith. For none of these discussions has any real bearing on the question whether there is a natural law and, if so, what its content is. Equally irrelevant to that question is the claim that disbelief in natural law yields bitter fruit. Nothing in this book is to be interpreted as either advancing or denying such claims; the book simply prescinds from all such matters.

■ ■ ■

The preceding section treated theories of natural law as theories of the rational foundations for moral judgment, and this will be the primary focus of subsequent sections of this chapter. But in the present section I consider the more restricted and juristic understanding of 'natural law' and 'natural law doctrine(s)'.

Here we have to deal with the image of natural law entertained by jurists such as Kelsen, Hart, and Raz. This image should be reproduced in their own words, since they themselves scarcely identify, let alone quote from, any particular theorist as defending the view that they describe as the view of natural law doctrine. Joseph Raz usefully summarizes and adopts Kelsen's version of this image:

> Kelsen correctly points out that according to natural law theories there is no specific notion of legal validity. The only concept of validity is validity according to natural law, i.e., moral validity. Natural lawyers can only judge a law as morally valid, that is, just or morally invalid, i.e., wrong. They cannot say of a law that it is legally valid but morally wrong. If it is wrong and unjust, it is also invalid in the only sense of validity they recognize.

In his own terms, Raz later defines 'Natural Law theorists' as 'those philosophers who think it a criterion of adequacy for theories of law that they show . . . that it is a necessary truth that every law has moral worth'.

For my part, I know of no philosopher who fits, or fitted, such a description, or who would be committed to trying to defend that sort of theoretical or meta-theoretical proposal.

■ ■ ■

The image of natural law theory which we have just been dealing with is closely related, in the mind of Kelsen, with another image. For Kelsen says it is a 'cardinal point of the historical doctrine of natural law . . . over two thousand years' that it attempts 'to found positive law upon a natural law delegation'. So far, so good (though the formulation is not classical). But Kelsen regards the attempt as 'logically impossible', on the ground that such a delegation would entail ascribing legal validity to norms not because of their justice but because of their origination by the delegate; and this in turn would entail, he says, that the delegate could override and 'replace' the natural law, 'in view of the fact that positive law is not, on principle, subject to limitations of . . . its . . . material validity.' The *non sequitur* is Kelsen's, I am afraid, and is not in his sources; the 'principle' to which he appeals is a mere *petitio principii*. If we may translate the relevant portion of, for example, Thomas Aquinas's theory into Kelsenian terminology (as far as possible), it runs as follows: The legal validity (in the focal, moral sense of 'legal validity') of positive law is derived from its rational connection with (i.e. derivation from) natural law, and this connection holds good, normally, if and only if (i) law originates in a way which is legally valid (in the specially restricted, purely legal sense of 'legal validity') and (ii) the law is not materially unjust either in its content or in relevant circumstances of its positing. Aquinas's discussion of these points is under-elaborated, in relation to the modern jurisprudential debate. But it avoids the self-contradiction and/or vacuity of which Kelsen accuses it. To delegate is not to delegate unconditionally.

In view of the foregoing, it is not surprising to find Kelsen propagating another misleading, and not uncommon, image of natural law juristic theory:

> The natural-law teachers contend, in a version which has remained a stereotype from the church fathers down to Kant, that positive law derives its entire validity from natural law; it is essentially a mere emanation of natural law; the making of statutes or of decisions does not freely create, it merely reproduces the true law which is already somehow in existence. . . .

Positive law, he says, is thus treated as a mere 'copy' of natural law. But all this is travesty. We may refer again to Thomas Aquinas—as always, not because there is any presumption that whatever he asserts is true, but simply because he is unquestionably a paradigm 'natural law theorist' and dominates the period 'from the church fathers down to Kant,' by synthesizing his patristic and early medieval predecessors and by fixing the vocabulary and to some extent the doctrine of later scholastic and, therefore, early modern thought. Now Aquinas indeed asserts that positive law derives its validity from natural law; but in the very same breath he shows how it is *not* a mere emanation from or copy of natural law, and how the legislator enjoys all the creative freedom of an architect: the analogy is Aquinas's. Aquinas thinks that positive law is needed for two reasons, of which one is that the natural law 'already somehow in existence' does *not* itself provide all or even most of the solutions to the co-ordination problems of communal life. On any reasonable view, Aquinas's clear elaborations of these points (based on a hint from Aristotle) must be considered one of the more successful parts of his not always successful work on natural law.

Finally we may note that the other of the two justifications for constructing a system of positive law to supplement the 'natural' requirements of morality, according to Aquinas (who gives this justification a perhaps excessive prominence), is the need for compulsion, to force selfish people to act reasonably. How strange, then, to read Kelsen finding yet another 'necessary contradiction between positive and natural law', this time 'because the one is a coercive order, while the other, ideally, is not only non-coercive, but actually has to forbid any coercion among men. This, alas, is yet another distorted image; a sound theory of natural law is an attempt to express reflectively the requirements and ideals of practical reasonableness, not of idealism.

QUESTIONS FOR DISCUSSION

1. In challenging others he believes have misinterpreted the natural law tradition, Finnis says that "to delegate is not to delegate unconditionally." What does he mean by this, and how is it relevant to thinking about the natural law idea?

2. If Finnis is right in rejecting views about natural law associated with, for example, Cicero, then what is *his* version of the natural law position?

3. What, according to Finnis, makes a law valid?

4. Does Finnis think that all laws should be obeyed? Does he think that all valid laws should be obeyed? Why or why not?

THE MORALITY OF LAW

LON FULLER

[Let us] begin with a fairly lengthy allegory. It concerns the unhappy reign of a monarch who bore the convenient, but not very imaginative and not even very regal sounding name of Rex.

EIGHT WAYS TO FAIL TO MAKE LAW

Rex came to the throne filled with the zeal of a reformer. He considered that the greatest failure of his predecessors had been in the field of law. For generations the legal system had known nothing like a basic reform. Procedures of trial were cumbersome, the rules of law spoke in the archaic tongue of another age, justice was expensive, the judges were slovenly and sometimes corrupt. Rex was resolved to remedy all this and to make his name in history as a great lawgiver. It was his unhappy fate to fail in this ambition. Indeed, he failed spectacularly, since not only did he not succeed in introducing the needed reforms, but he never even succeeded in creating any law at all, good or bad.

His first official act was, however, dramatic and propitious. Since he needed a clean slate on which to write, he announced to his subjects the immediate repeal of all existing law, of whatever kind. He then set about drafting a new code. Unfortunately, trained as a lonely prince, his education had been very defective. In particular he found himself incapable of making even the simplest generalizations. Though not lacking in confidence when it came to deciding specific controversies, the effort to give articulate reasons for any conclusion strained his capacities to the breaking point.

Becoming aware of his limitations, Rex gave up the project of a code and announced to his subjects that henceforth he

Selections from Lon Fuller, *The Morality of Law* (New Haven: Yale University Press, revised edition, 1969)

would act as a judge in any disputes that might arise among them. In this way under the stimulus of a variety of cases he hoped that his latent powers of generalization might develop and, proceeding case by case, he would gradually work out a system of rules that could be incorporated in a code. Unfortunately the defects in his education were more deep-seated than he had supposed. The venture failed completely. After he had handed down literally hundreds of decisions neither he nor his subjects could detect in those decisions any pattern whatsoever. Such tentatives toward generalization as were to be found in his opinions only compounded the confusion, for they gave false leads to his subjects and threw his own meager powers of judgment off balance in the decision of later cases.

After this fiasco Rex realized it was necessary to take a fresh start. His first move was to subscribe to a course of lessons in generalization. With his intellectual powers thus fortified, he resumed the project of a code and, after many hours of solitary labor, succeeded in preparing a fairly lengthy document. He was still not confident, however, that he had fully overcome his previous defects. Accordingly, he announced to his subjects that he had written out a code and would henceforth be governed by it in deciding cases, but that for an indefinite future the contents of the code would remain an official state secret, known only to him and his scrivener. To Rex's surprise this sensible plan was deeply resented by his subjects. They declared it was very unpleasant to have one's case decided by rules when there was no way of knowing what those rules were.

Stunned by this rejection Rex undertook an earnest inventory of his personal strengths and weaknesses. He decided that life had taught him one clear lesson, namely, that it is easier to decide things with the aid of hindsight than it is to attempt to foresee and control the future. Not only did hindsight make

it easier to decide cases, but—and this was of supreme importance to Rex—it made it easier to give reasons. Deciding to capitalize on this insight, Rex hit on the following plan. At the beginning of each calendar year he would decide all the controversies that had arisen among his subjects during the preceding year. He would accompany his decisions with a full statement of reasons. Naturally, the reasons thus given would be understood as not controlling decisions in future years, for that would be to defeat the whole purpose of the new arrangement, which was to gain the advantages of hindsight. Rex confidently announced the new plan to his subjects, observing that he was going to publish the full text of his judgements with the rules applied by him, thus meeting the chief objection to the old plan. Rex's subjects received this announcement in silence, then quietly explained through their leaders that when they said they need to know the rules, they meant they needed to know them *in advance* so they could act on them. Rex muttered something to the effect that they might have made that point a little clearer, but said he would see what could be done.

Rex now realized that there was no escape from a published code declaring the rules to be applied in future disputes. Continuing his lessons in generalization, Rex worked diligently on a revised code, and finally announced that it would shortly be published. This announcement was received with universal gratification. The dismay of Rex's subjects was all the more intense, therefore, when his code became available and it was discovered that it was truly a masterpiece of obscurity. Legal experts who studied it declared that there was not a single sentence in it that could be understood either by an ordinary citizen or by a trained lawyer. Indignation became general and soon a picket appeared before the royal palace carrying a sign that read, "How can anybody follow a rule that nobody can understand?"

The code was quickly withdrawn. Recognizing for the first time that he needed assistance, Rex put a staff of experts to work on a revision. He instructed them to leave the substance untouched, but to clarify the expression throughout. The resulting code was a model of clarity, but as it was studied it became apparent that its new clarity had merely brought to light that it was honeycombed with contradictions. It was reliably reported that there was not a single provision in the code that was not nullified by another provision inconsistent with it. A picket again appeared before the royal residence carrying a sign that read, "This time the king made himself clear—in both directions."

Once again the code was withdrawn for revision. By now, however, Rex had lost his patience with his subjects and the negative attitude they seemed to adopt toward everything he tried to do for them. He decided to teach them a lesson and put an end to their carping. He instructed his experts to purge the code of contradictions, but at the same time to stiffen drastically every requirement contained in it and to add a long list of new crimes. Thus, where before the citizen summoned to the throne was given ten days in which to report, in the revision the time was cut to ten seconds. It was made a crime, punishable by ten years' imprisonment, to cough, sneeze, hiccough, faint or fall down in the presence of the king. It was made treason not to understand, believe in, and correctly profess the doctrine of evolutionary, democratic redemption.

When the new code was published a near revolution resulted. Leading citizens declared their intention to flout its provisions. Someone discovered in an ancient author a passage that seemed apt: "To command what cannot be done is not to make law; it is to unmake law, for a command that cannot be obeyed serves no end but confusion, fear and chaos." Soon this passage was being quoted in a hundred petitions to the king.

The code was again withdrawn and a staff of experts charged with the task of revision. Rex's instructions to the experts were that whenever they encountered a rule requiring an impossibility, it should be revised to make compliance possible. It turned out that to accomplish this result every provision in the code had to be substantially rewritten. The final result was, however, a triumph of draftsmanship. It was clear, consistent with itself, and demanded nothing of the subject that did not lie easily within his powers. It was printed and distributed free of charge on every street corner.

However, before the effective date for the new code had arrived, it was discovered that so much time had been spent in successive revisions of Rex's original draft, that the substance of the code had been seriously overtaken by events. Ever since Rex assumed the throne there had been a suspension of ordinary legal processes and this had brought about important economic and institutional changes within the country. Accommodation to these altered conditions required many changes of substance in the law. Accordingly as soon as the new code became legally effective, it was subjected to a daily stream of amendments. Again popular discontent mounted; an anonymous pamphlet appeared on the streets carrying scurrilous cartoons of the king and a leading article with the title: "A law that changes every day is worse than no law at all."

Within a short time this source of discontent began to cure itself as the pace of amendment gradually slackened. Before this had occurred to any noticeable degree, however, Rex announced an important decision. Reflecting on the misadventures of his reign, he concluded that much of the trouble lay in bad advice he had received from experts. He accordingly declared he was reassuming the judicial power in his own person. In this way he could directly control the application of the new code and insure his country against another crisis. He began to spend practically all of his time hearing and deciding cases arising under the new code.

As the king proceeded with this task, it seemed to bring to a belated blossoming his long dormant powers of generalization. His opinions began, indeed, to reveal a confident and almost exuberant virtuosity as he deftly distinguished his own previous decisions, exposed the principles on which he acted, and laid down guide lines for the disposition of future controversies. For Rex's subjects a new day seemed about to dawn when they could finally conform their conduct to a coherent body of rules.

This hope was, however, soon shattered. As the bound volumes of Rex's judgments became available and were subjected to closer study, his subjects were appalled to discover that there existed no discernible relation between those judgments and the code they purported to apply. Insofar as it found expression in the actual disposition of controversies, the new code might just as well not have existed at all. Yet in virtually every one of his decisions Rex declared and redeclared the code to be the basic law of his kingdom.

Leading citizens began to hold private meetings to discuss what measures, short of open revolt, could be taken to get the king away from the bench and back on the throne. While these discussions were going on Rex suddenly died, old before his time and deeply disillusioned with his subjects.

The first act of his successor, Rex II, was to announce that he was taking the powers of government away from the lawyers and placing them in the hands of psychiatrists and experts in public relations. This way, he explained, people could be made happy without rules.

THE CONSEQUENCES OF FAILURE

Rex's bungling career as legislator and judge illustrates that the attempt to create and maintain a system of legal rules may miscarry in at least eight ways; there are in this enterprise, if you will, eight distinct routes to disaster. The first and most obvious lies in a failure to achieve rules at all, so that every issue must be decided on an ad hoc basis. The other routes are: (2) a failure to publicize, or at least to make available to the affected party, the rules he is expected to observe; (3) the abuse of retroactive legislation, which not only cannot itself guide action, but undercuts the integrity of rules prospective in effect, since it puts them under the threat of retrospective change; (4) a failure to make rules understandable; (5) the enactment of contradictory rules or (6) rules that require conduct beyond the powers of the affected party; (7) introducing such frequent changes in the rules that the subject cannot orient his action by them; and, finally, (8) a failure of congruence between the rules as announced and their actual administration.

A total failure in any one of these eight directions does not simply result in a bad system of law; it results in something that is not properly called a legal system at all, except perhaps in the Pickwickian sense in which a void contract can still be said to be one kind of contract. Certainly there can be no rational ground for asserting that a man can have a moral obligation to obey a legal rule that does not exist, or is kept secret from him, or that came into existence only after he had acted, or was unintelligible, or was contradicted by another rule of the same system, or commanded the impossible, or changed every minute. It may not be impossible for a man to obey a rule that is disregarded by those charged with its administration, but at some point obedience becomes futile—as futile, in fact, as casting a vote that will never be counted. As the sociologist Simmel has observed, there is a kind of reciprocity between government and the citizen with respect to the observance of rules. Government says to the citizen in effect, "These are the rules we expect you to follow. If you follow them, you have our assurance that they are the rules that will be applied to your conduct." When this bond of reciprocity is finally and completely ruptured by government, nothing is left on which to ground the citizen's duty to observe the rules.

The citizen's predicament becomes more difficult when, though there is no total failure in any direction, there is a general and drastic deterioration in legality, such as occurred in Germany under Hitler. A situation begins to develop, for example, in which though some laws are published, others, including the most important, are not. Though most laws are prospective in effect, so free a use is made of retrospective legislation that no law is immune to change ex post facto if it suits the convenience of those in power. For the trial of criminal cases concerned with loyalty to the regime, special military tribunals are established and these tribunals disregard, whenever it suits their convenience, the rules that are supposed to control their decisions. Increasingly the principal object of government seems to be, not that of giving the citizen rules by which to shape his conduct, but to frighten him into impotence. As such a situation develops, the problem faced by the citizen is not so simple as that of a voter who knows with certainty that his ballot will not be counted. It is more like that of the voter who knows that the odds are against his ballot being counted at all, and that if it is counted, there is a good chance that it will be counted for the side against which he actually voted. A citizen in this predicament has to decide for himself whether to stay with the system and cast his ballot as a kind of symbolic act expressing the hope of a better day. So it was with the German citizen under Hitler faced with deciding whether he had an obligation to obey such portions of the laws as the Nazi terror had left intact.

In situations like these there can be no simple principle by which to test the citizen's obligation of fidelity to law, any more than there can be such a principle for testing his right to engage in a general revolution. One thing is, however, clear. A mere respect for constituted authority must not be confused with fidelity to law. Rex's subjects, for example, remained faithful to him as king throughout his long and inept reign. They were not faithful to his law, for he never made any.

THE ASPIRATION TOWARD PERFECTION IN LEGALITY

So far we have been concerned to trace out eight routes to failure in the enterprise of creating law. Corresponding to these are eight kinds of legal excellence toward which a system of rules may strive. What appear at the lowest level as indispensable conditions for the existence of law at all, become, as we ascend the scale of achievement, increasingly demanding challenges to human capacity. At the height of the ascent we are tempted to imagine a utopia of legality in which all rules are perfectly clear, consistent with one another, known to every citizen, and never retroactive. In this utopia the rules remain constant through time, demand only what is possible, and are scrupulously observed by courts, police, and everyone else charged with their administration. For reasons that I shall advance shortly, this utopia, in which all eight of the principles of legality are realized to perfection, is not actually a useful target for guiding the impulse toward legality; the goal of perfection is much more complex. Nevertheless it does suggest eight distinct standards by which excellence in legality may be tested.

In expounding in my first chapter the distinction between the morality of duty and that of aspiration, I spoke of an imaginary scale that starts at the bottom with the most obvious and essential moral duties and ascends upward to the highest achievements open to man. I also spoke of an invisible pointer as marking the dividing line where the pressure of duty leaves off and the challenge of excellence begins. The inner morality of law, it should now be clear, presents all of these aspects. It too confronts us with the problem of knowing where to draw the boundary below which men will be condemned for failure, but can expect no praise for success, and above which they will be admired for success and at worst pitied for the lack of it.

In applying the analysis of the first chapter to our present subject, it becomes essential to consider certain distinctive qualities of the inner morality of law. In what may be called the basic morality of social life, duties that run toward other persons generally (as contrasted with those running toward specific individuals) normally require only forbearances, or as we say, are negative in nature: Do not kill, do not injure, do not deceive, do not defame, and the like. Such duties lend themselves with a minimum of difficulty to formalized definition. That is to say, whether we are concerned with legal or moral duties, we are able to develop standards which designate with some precision—though it is never complete—the kind of conduct that is to be avoided.

The demands of the inner morality of the law, however, though they concern a relationship with persons generally, demand more than forbearances; they are, as we loosely say, affirmative in nature: make the law known, make it coherent and clear, see that your decisions as an official are guided by it, etc. To meet these demands human energies must be directed toward specific kinds of achievement and not merely warned away from harmful acts.

Because of the affirmative and creative quality of its demands, the inner morality of law lends itself badly to realization through duties, whether they be moral or legal. No matter how desirable a direction of human effort may appear to be, if we assert there is a duty to pursue it, we shall confront the responsibility of defining at what point that duty has been violated. It is easy to assert that the legislator has a moral duty to make his laws clear and understandable. But this remains at best an exhortation unless we are prepared to define the degree of clarity he must attain in order to discharge his duty. The notion of subjecting clarity to quantitative measure presents obvious difficulties. We may content ourselves, of course, by saying that the legislator has at least a moral duty to try to be clear. But this only postpones the difficulty, for in some situations nothing can be more baffling than to attempt to measure how vigorously a man intended to do that which he has failed to do. In the morality of law, in any event, good intentions are of little avail, as King Rex amply demonstrated. All of this adds up to the conclusion that the inner morality of law is condemned to remain largely a morality of aspiration and not of duty. Its primary appeal must be to a sense of trusteeship and to the pride of the craftsman.

To these observations there is one important exception. This relates to the desideratum of making the laws known, or at least making them available to those affected by them. Here we have a demand that lends itself with unusual readiness to formalization. A written constitution may prescribe that no statute shall become law until it has been given a specified form of publication. If the courts have power to effectuate this provision, we may speak of a legal requirement for the making of law. But a moral duty with respect to publication is also readily imaginable. A custom, for example, might define what kind of promulgation of laws is expected, at the same time leaving unclear what consequences attend a departure from the accepted mode of publication. A formalization of the desideratum of publicity has obvious advantages over uncanalized efforts, even when they are intelligently and conscientiously pursued. A formalized standard of promulgation not only tells the lawmaker where to publish his laws; it also lets the subject—or a lawyer representing his interests—know where to go to learn what the law is.

One might suppose that the principle condemning retroactive laws could also be very readily formalized in a simple rule that no such law should ever be passed, or should be valid if enacted. Such a rule would, however, disserve the cause of legality. Curiously, one of the most obvious seeming demands of legality—that a rule passed today should govern what happens tomorrow, not what happened yesterday—turns out to present some of the most difficult problems of the whole internal morality of law.

With respect to the demands of legality other than promulgation, then, the most we can expect of constitutions and courts is that they save us from the abyss; they cannot be expected to lay out very many compulsory steps toward truly significant accomplishment.

■ ■ ■

LEGAL MORALITY AND NATURAL LAW

[An important] task is to relate what I have called the internal morality of the law to the ages-old tradition of natural law. Do the principles expounded in my second chapter represent some variety of natural law? The answer is an emphatic, though qualified, yes.

What I have tried to do is to discern and articulate the natural laws of a particular kind of human undertaking, which I have described as "the enterprise of subjecting human conduct to the governance of rules." These natural laws have nothing to do with any "brooding omnipresence in the skies." Nor have they the slightest affinity with any such proposition as that the practice of contraception is a violation of God's law. They remain entirely terrestrial in origin and application. They are not "higher" laws; if any metaphor of elevation is appropriate they

should be called "lower" laws. They are like the natural laws of carpentry, or at least those laws respected by a carpenter who wants the house he builds to remain standing and serve the purpose of those who live in it.

Though these natural laws touch one of the most vital of human activities they obviously do not exhaust the whole of man's moral life. They have nothing to say on such topics as polygamy, the study of Marx, the worship of God, the progressive income tax, or the subjugation of women. If the question be raised whether any of these subjects, or others like them, should be taken as objects of legislation, that question relates to what I have called the external morality of law.

As a convenient (though not wholly satisfactory) way of describing the distinction of being taken we may speak of a procedural, as distinguished from a substantive natural law. What I have called the internal morality of law is in this sense a procedural version of natural law, though to avoid misunderstanding the word "procedural" should be assigned a special and expanded sense so that it would include, for example, a substantive accord between official action and enacted law. The term "procedural" is, however, broadly appropriate as indicating that we are concerned, not with the substantive aims of legal rules, but with the ways in which a system of rules for governing human conduct must be constructed and administered if it is to be efficacious and at the same time remain what it purports to be.

In the actual history of legal and political thinking what association do we find between the principles I have expounded in my second chapter and the doctrine of natural law? Do those principles form an integral part of the natural law tradition?

With respect to thinkers associated with the natural law tradition, [their] chief concern is with what I have called substantive natural law, with the proper ends to be sought through legal rules. When they treat of the demands of legal morality it is, I believe, usually in an incidental way, though occasionally one aspect of the subject will receive considerable elaboration. Aquinas is probably typical in this respect. Concerning the need for general rules (as contrasted with a case-by-case decision of controversies) he develops a surprisingly elaborate demonstration, including an argument that wise men being always in short supply it is a matter of economic prudence to spread their talents by putting them to work to draft general rules which lesser men can then apply. On the other hand, in explaining why Isidore required laws to be "clearly expressed" he contents himself with saying that this is desirable to prevent "any harm ensuing from the law itself."

With writers of all philosophic persuasions it is, I believe, true to say that when they deal with problems of legal morality it is generally in a casual and incidental way. The reason for this is not far to seek. Men do not generally see any need to explain or to justify the obvious. It is likely that nearly every legal philosopher of any consequence in the history of ideas has had occasion to declare that laws ought to be published so that those subject to them can know what they are. Few have felt called upon to expand the argument for this proposition or to bring it within the cover of any more inclusive theory. . . .

To the generalization that in the history of political and legal thought the principles of legality have received a casual and incidental treatment—such as befits the self-evident—there is one significant exception. This lies in a literature that arose in England during the seventeenth century, a century of remonstrances, impeachments, plots and civil war, a period during which existing institutions underwent a fundamental reexamination.

It is to this period that scholars trace the "natural law foundations" of the American Constitution. Its literature—curiously embodied chiefly in the two extremes of anonymous pamphlets and judicial utterances—was intensely and almost entirely concerned with problems I have regarded as those of the internal morality of law. It spoke of repugnancies, of laws impossible to be obeyed, of parliaments walking contrary to their own laws before they have repealed them. The most famous pronouncement to come down from that great period is that of Coke in *Dr. Bonham's Case.*

Henry VIII had given to the Royal College of Physicians (in a grant later confirmed by Parliament) broad powers to license and regulate the practice of medicine in London. The College was granted the right to try offenses against its regulations and to impose fines and imprisonments. In the case of a fine, one half was to go to the King, the other half to the College itself. Thomas Bonham, a doctor of medicine of the University of Cambridge, undertook the practice of medicine in London without the certificate of the Royal College. He was tried by the College, fined and later imprisoned. He brought suit for false imprisonment.

In the course of Coke's judgment upholding Bonham's cause, this famous passage appears:

> The censors [of the Royal College] cannot be judges, ministers and parties; judges to give sentence or judgment; ministers to make summons; and parties to have the moiety of the forfeiture, *quia aliquis non debet esse Judes in propria causa, imo iniquum est aliquem suae rai esse judicem;* and one cannot be Judge and attorney for any of the parties. . . . And it appears in our books, that in many cases, the common law will control Acts of Parliament, and sometimes adjudge them to be utterly void: for when an Act of Parliament is against common right and reason, or repugnant, or impossible to be performed, the common law will control it, and adjudge such Act to be void.

Today this pronouncement is often regarded as the quintessence of the natural law point of view. Yet notice how heavily it emphasizes procedures and institutional practices. Indeed, there is only one passage that can be said to relate to substantive rightness or justice, that speaking of parliamentary acts "against common right and reason." Yet by "common right" Coke may very well have had in mind rights acquired through the law and then taken away by law, the kind of problem, in other words, often presented by retrospective legislation. It may seem odd to speak of repugnant statutes in a context chiefly concerned with the impropriety of a man's acting as judge in his own cause. Yet for Coke there was here a close association of ideas. Just as legal rules can be repugnant to one another, so institutions can be repugnant. Coke and his associates on the bench strove to create an atmosphere of impartiality in the judiciary, in which it would be unthinkable that a judge, say, of Common Pleas should sit in judgment of his own case. Then came the King and Parliament sticking an ugly, incongruous finger into this effort, creating a "court" of physicians for judging infringements of their own monopoly and collecting half the fines for themselves. When Coke associated this legislative indecency with repugnancy he was not simply expressing his distaste for it; he meant that it contradicted essential purposive efforts moving in an opposite direction.

The view, common among modern scholars, that in the quoted passage Coke betrays a naive faith in natural law, tells us little that will help us understand the intellectual climate of the seventeenth century. It tells us a great deal about our own age, an age that in some moods at least thinks itself capable of believing that no appeal to man's nature, or to the nature of things, can ever be more than a cover for subjective preference, and that under the rubric "subjective preference" must be listed indifferently propositions as far apart as that laws ought to be clearly expressed and that the only just tax is one that makes the citizen pay the exact equivalent of what he himself receives from government.

Those who actually created our republic and its Constitution were much closer in their thinking to the age of Coke than they are to ours. They, too, were concerned to avoid repugnancies in their institutions and to see to it that those institutions should suit the nature of man. Hamilton rejected the "political heresy" of the poet who wrote:

For forms of government let fools contest—
That which is best administered is best.

In supporting the power of the judiciary to declare acts of Congress unconstitutional Hamilton pointed out that the judiciary can never be entirely passive toward legislation; even in the absence of a written constitution judges are compelled, for example, to develop some rule for dealing with contradictory enactments, this rule being derived not "from any positive law, but from the nature and reason of the thing."

A continuing debate in this country relates to the question whether in interpreting the Constitution the courts should be influenced by considerations drawn from "natural law." I suggest that this debate might contribute more to a clarification of issues if a distinction were taken between a natural law of substantive ends and a natural law concerned with procedures and institutions. It should be confessed, however, that the term "natural law" has been so misused on all sides that it is difficult to recapture a dispassionate attitude toward it.

What is perfectly clear is that many of the provisions of the Constitution have the quality I have described as that of being blunt and incomplete. This means that in one way or another their meaning must be filled out. Surely those whose fate in any degree hinges on the creative act of interpretation by which this meaning is supplied, as well as those who face the responsibility of the interpretation itself, must wish that it should proceed on the most secure footing that can be obtained, that it should be grounded insofar as possible in the necessities of democratic government and of human nature itself.

I suggest that this ideal lies most nearly within our reach in the area of constitutional law concerned with what I have called the internal morality of the law. Within this area, interpretation can often depart widely from the explicit words of the Constitution and yet rest secure in the conviction that it is faithful to an intention implicit in the whole structure of our government. There is, for example, no explicit prohibition in the Constitution of vague or obscure legislation. Yet I doubt if anyone could regard as a judicial usurpation the holding that a criminal statute violates "due process of law" if it fails to give a reasonably clear description of the act it prohibits. When one reflects on the problems of drafting a constitution the justification for this holding becomes obvious. If an express provision directed against vague laws were included in the Constitution, some standard, explicit or tacit, would have to determine what degree of obscurity should vitiate. This standard would have to run in quite general terms. Starting with the premise that law governs and judges men's actions by general rules, any criminal statute ought to be sufficiently clear to serve the double purpose of giving to the citizen an adequate warning of the nature of the act prohibited and of providing adequate guidelines for adjudication in accordance with law. If one wished to summarize all this in a phrase, it would be hard to find a better expression than "due process of law."

QUESTIONS FOR DISCUSSION

1. Fuller lists eight "desiderata" of law. He then claims that these are each necessary for the existence of law. Why does Fuller think they are necessary rather than merely desirable? Does he think they are also *sufficient* for the existence of law?

2. What is the difference between an "internal" and an "external" moral requirement? Why is an internal requirement a "moral" requirement? What is the relationship, according to Fuller, between the internal requirements and substantive morality?

3. How is Fuller's position different from the natural law positions of Aquinas and Finnis? How is it similar?

4. In "Positivism and Fidelity to Law—A Reply to Professor Hart," *Harvard Law Review*, vol. 71 (1958), pp. 138 ff., Fuller made the empirical claim in support of his internal morality of law that "coherence and goodness have more affinity than coherence and evil. . . . I also believe that when men are compelled to explain and justify their decisions, the effect will generally be to pull those decisions toward goodness, by whatever standards of ultimate goodness there are." Do you think that Fuller is correct in believing that compliance with internal morality will increase the likelihood of observance of substantive morality?

5. If a statute were to be passed by a legislature prohibiting interracial marriage (see the Supreme Court case of *Loving v. Virginia*, 388 U.S. 1 [1967]), would it be a law? Should a judge enforce the statute? What is the connection between the two questions?

SUGGESTIONS FOR FURTHER READING

A good modern commentary on Aquinas is Thomas E. Davitt, "Law as a Means to an End—Thomas Aquinas," *Vanderbilt Law Review* vol. 14 (1960), pp. 65 ff. Another is D. J. O'Connor, *Aquinas and Natural Law* (London: Macmillan 1967). An important twentieth century natural law theory is Jean Dabin, *General Theory of Law*, in *Legal Philosophies of Lask, Radbruch, and Dabin*, K. Wilks, trans. (Cambridge: Harvard University Press, 1950). For a more general treatment of natural law, a relatively modern classic is A. P. d'Entreves, *Natural Law* (London: Hutchinson, second edition revised, 1979). A good historical study is Otto Gierke, *Natural Law and the Theory of Society 1500–1800* (E. Barker, trans., Cambridge: Cambridge University Press, 1950). On the relationship, discussed by Fuller, between natural law theory and American constitutional law, an important series of articles is Thomas Grey, "Do We Have an Unwritten Constitution?", *Stanford Law Review*, vol. 27 (1975), pp. 703 ff.; Thomas Grey, "Origins of the Unwritten Constitution: Fundamental Law in American Revolutionary Thought," *Stanford Law Review*, vol. 30 (1978), pp. 843 ff.

LEGAL POSITIVISM 1.2

INTRODUCTION

Central to the natural law idea, in all of its variations, is the view that the concept of law has some type of a necessary connection with some type of morality. Whether it be the form of natural law theory that holds that conformity with moral standards is a necessary condition for something being law, or the form maintaining only that law exists, possibly imperfectly, as the realization of moral norms, law and morality are in natural law theory inextricably linked. Yet the enduring challenge to natural law theory has denied that there is a necessary connection between law and morality. Although there are large variations, the common term for accounts of law denying the necessity of a law–morality connection is *legal positivism*.

Legal positivism is so named because it starts with the premise that neither law nor legal systems have any natural or essential connections with morality. Rather, laws and legal systems are *posited* by human beings. Law, to the positivist, is simply a social fact, although what kind of social fact it is has been the subject of much controversy. Still, once we understand law as nothing other than a human creation, legal positivists say, we can also understand why to the positivist there is no *necessary* connection between law and morality. This claim, however, is easy to caricature in a misleading way. Legal positivists certainly admit that law is frequently the vehicle for the enforcement or realization of morally desirable norms. The legal positivist does not deny that laws against murder, rape, and theft, for example, stem from and enforce moral norms. And legal positivists acknowledge equally willingly that legal norms and legal systems should seek to realize the good and discourage the bad. The legal positivist can believe that the Fugitive Slave Laws are immoral and should be repealed, and can even believe that immoral laws should not be obeyed. But legal positivists also stress the importance of distinguishing between is and ought. What legal systems ought to be or ought to do is not the same as what legal systems in fact are. Thus it is a central feature of legal positivism to recognize that something can *be* a legal system while still falling far short, morally, of what a legal system ought to be. To the positivist the legal system of Nazi Germany was no less law just because it was both substantively wicked and procedurally authoritarian. And to the legal positivist the apartheid laws of South Africa were still laws, monuments to the conceptual and empirical difference between the laws we have and the laws we ought to have.

If there is, according to the positivist, no necessary connection between law and morality, then the essence of the idea of law must be found in some feature that is not reducible to or derived from moral values. Until recently this feature was one closely associated with the sovereign power of the state. In *Leviathan*,

Thomas Hobbes (1588–1679), himself perhaps more properly associated with the natural law tradition, saw law as the device by which the sovereign power secured the obedience of the sovereign's subjects, and thus a central feature of law was the command from sovereign to subject. This command theory of law, according to which law is identified not by its substantive moral content but by the presence of commands from sovereign to subject, was more fully developed by the English Utilitarians, particularly Jeremy Bentham (1748–1832) and his friend and associate John Austin (1790–1859). Bentham, who viewed the idea of natural rights as "nonsense upon stilts," was, not surprisingly, hostile to the natural law tradition. Moreover, Bentham was above all a progressive legal reformer. Consequently, it was important for him to understand the difference between what the law is and what the law ought to be. As a reformer, he wanted a way of identifying even (and maybe especially) those laws that were in need of reform (which included most of them, according to Bentham). So for Bentham it was crucial to be able to identify law in a way that did not itself involve moral evaluation, because he wanted a way of identifying all law, the better to find the subjects for what he took to be, from his utilitarian perspective, morally necessary reform.

Following Hobbes, Bentham thus associated law with sovereign power, but he did so in a work—*Of Laws in General*—that was unpublished and not discovered in Bentham's papers until 1945.[17] Before this work came to light, most of what was known about Bentham's views about the nature of law were known through the writings of John Austin. With the discovery and publication of *Of Laws in General*, scholars now recognize that many of the ideas long associated with Austin were in fact Bentham's, but in some sense the "damage" was already done. Austin is still most commonly associated with the connection between the idea of law and the idea of sovereignty. He is also given credit (or blame) for the so-called "command theory," pursuant to which law is defined simply as the general commands of the sovereign, and the sovereign is defined as that power with the ability to secure, and that in fact secures, habitual obedience from its subjects without in turn being habitually obedient to anyone else. As the selection that follows shows, therefore, the concepts of sovereignty, command, and obedience, none of which necessarily involve morality, are central to Austinian legal positivism.

Although it is possible to apply an Austinian conception of law to modern democratic states, Austin's views about sovereignty and commands seem to fit somewhat more comfortably with a more vertical sovereign–subject model of political organization. For Austin, the sovereign was something like a king, whose commands were to be obeyed by his subjects. This model of sovereign and subject, however, does not appear to resemble the contemporary democratic state. When we think of laws as at least partially created by or authorized by the same people who are then to follow them, Austin's picture seems overly simplistic, and other versions of positivism may be more appealing. The work of the great Austrian legal philosopher Hans Kelsen (1881–1973), for example, stressed the relationship between one legal rule (or norm) and another. The source of legal authority for

---

[17]The current authoritative edition is Jeremy Bentham, *Of Laws in General*, H. L. A. Hart, ed., (London: Athlone Press, 1970).

Kelsen was not a sovereign like a king or queen, but rather just another legal rule creating or granting that authority. As the title of his major work—*The Pure Theory of Law*[18]—indicates, Kelsen, like other positivists, sought to separate the concept of law from the concept of morality. Kelsen departed from Austin and other early positivists, however, in seeing the nature of law as existing in a hierarchy of authorizations. Consider the idea of a *valid* law. Legal officials make *valid* legal decisions, Kelsen argued, because they are authorized to do so by legal norms, and those legal norms are themselves made *valid* by higher legal norms, which are made valid by even higher legal norms, and so on, until there are no more norms left in this hierarchy. At that point, Kelsen argued, we merely posit or stipulate the existence of a master norm, the basic norm (or *Grundnorm*, in German), which is the understanding that enables us to grasp the idea of a legal system. The *Grundnorm* was to Kelsen like the transcendental understanding of Kant, the idea that enabled us to make sense of the idea of a legal system. All of this is somewhat obscure, but the central point is that the very idea of legal *validity* requires some standard distinguishing the valid from the invalid, a standard that could itself be validated by still other standards until this hierarchy of justification ran out.

Similar ideas about legal validity were developed in a much more accessible way by H. L. A. Hart. Like Kelsen, Hart focused on the idea of legal validity, because the key to distinguishing a valid from an invalid law was also the key to distinguishing law from everything else. To Hart, rules were identifiable as law (as legal rules rather than some other kind of rule) not necessarily because they emanated out of the commands of a sovereign, as Bentham and Austin supposed. Hart argued that a rule became a valid legal rule when it fell within a *rule of recognition,* a rule that did not itself regulate conduct, but told us which laws were valid and which were not. Various provisions of Article I of the United States Constitution, for example, are rules of recognition. They tell us that laws passed by a majority of Congress and signed by the President are valid federal laws, and conversely that laws not signed by the President (unless a veto is overridden) or laws not coming within one of the powers enumerated in Article I, section 8 are not valid federal laws. A rule of recognition in the Constitution, the Supremacy Clause of Article VI, also tells us that the laws made by the United States according to the Constitution are superior in cases of conflict to the laws of the states. To identify law according to the idea of a rule of recognition, therefore, one looks not to higher morality, but to the rules of recognition of a given society to determine which laws are valid and which are not.[19]

---

[18]Hans Kelsen, *Pure Theory of Law* (Max Knight, trans., Berkeley: University of California Press, 1967). Kelsen's other major works on legal philosophy are *General Theory of Law and State* (A. Wedberg trans., Cambridge, Massachusetts: Harvard University Press, 1949) and the first (and quite different) version of *Pure Theory of Law,* published as *Introduction to The Problems of Legal Theory* (Bonnie Litschewski Paulson and Stanley L. Paulson, trans., Oxford: Clarendon Press, 1992).

[19]It is important to stress that a rule of recognition might, contingently, require reference to higher moral law. The equal protection clause of the Fourteenth Amendment can be read as saying that no state law is valid law unless it comports with inherently moral ideas and ideals of equality, and in this respect the Equal Protection Clause is different from those provisions—like the provisions of Article I, section 8 empowering Congress to "coin Money" and "establish Post Offices"—whose criteria for recognition of validity incorporate no moral standards.

As with Kelsen, Hart recognized that this process at some point runs out. Although we may know which laws are valid laws by referring to Article I of the United States Constitution, how do we know that Article I of the Constitution is valid? And if we answer, too quickly, that it is valid because various provisions of the Constitution, such as those on initial ratification and subsequent amendment, make it so, then the easy rejoinder is to ask how we know that *those* provisions are legally valid. Here again Hart parts company with Austin. When rules of recognition run out, Hart says, we look to the *ultimate rule of recognition*. The ultimate rule of recognition is not a rule of law at all, but instead it is what tells us, for example, that the United States Constitution and not the Articles of Confederation, or the Declaration of Independence, or the Mayflower Compact, or even the Canadian Charter of Rights and Freedoms, is the place to look to determine legal validity. But this is so, Hart argues, not because there is some deeper or higher rule of recognition telling us in the United States to look to the Constitution of the United States and not to the Mayflower Compact or the Canadian Charter of Rights and Freedoms. It is because it is simply accepted, *as a social fact*, that the Constitution of the United States is the master legal document within this society. The ultimate rule of recognition cannot, therefore, be (legally) valid or not. It just is. The very idea of *legal* validity presupposes a standard that exists within law. Law itself cannot therefore be legally valid or invalid. Its existence is determined outside of law, and this is why the ultimate rule of recognition is itself a matter of social fact and not of law. Thus a central theme in Hart's version of positivism, as the reading indicates, is to locate the essence of law in a certain set of features about what societies have in fact done, rather than in a more formal and more abstract notion of sovereignty.

THE PROVINCE OF JURISPRUDENCE DETERMINED AND THE USES OF THE STUDY OF JURISPRUDENCE

JOHN AUSTIN

LECTURE I

The matter of jurisprudence is positive law: law, simply and strictly so called: or law set by political superiors to political inferiors.

But positive law (or law, simply and strictly so called) is often confounded with objects to which it is related by *resemblance*, and with objects to which it is related in the way of

John Austin, *The Province of Jurisprudence Determined and the Uses of the Study of Jurisprudence* (H.L.A. Hart, ed., London: Weidenfeld & Nicolson, 1954), selections from Lectures I, V, and VI.

analogy: with objects which are *also* signified, *properly* and *improperly*, by the large and vague expression *law*. . . .

A law, in the most general and comprehensive acceptation in which the term, in its literal meaning, is employed, may be said to be a rule laid down for the guidance of an intelligent being by an intelligent being having power over him. Under this definition are concluded, and without impropriety, several species. It is necessary to define accurately the line of demarcation which separates these species from one another, as much mistiness and intricacy has been infused into the science of jurisprudence by their being confounded or not clearly distinguished. In the comprehensive sense above indicated, or in the largest meaning which it has, without extension by metaphor or analogy, the term *law* embraces the following objects:—Laws set by God to his human creatures, and laws set by men to men. The whole or a portion of the laws set by God to men is frequently styled the law of nature, or natural law: being, in truth, the only natural law of which it is possible to speak without a metaphor, or without a blending of objects which ought to be distinguished broadly. But, rejecting the appellation Law of Nature as ambiguous and misleading, I name those laws or rules, as considered collectively or in a mass, the *Divine law*, or the *law of God*.

Laws set by men to men are of two leading or principal classes: classes which are often blended, although they differ extremely; and which, for that reason, should be severed precisely, and opposed distinctly and conspicuously.

Of the laws or rules set by men to men, some are established by *political* superiors, sovereign and subject: by persons exercising supreme and subordinate *government*, in independent nations, or independent political societies. The aggregate of the rules thus established, or some aggregate forming a portion of that aggregate, is the appropriate matter of jurisprudence, general or particular. To the aggregate of the rules thus established, or to some aggregate forming a portion of that aggregate, the term *law*, as used simply and strictly, is exclusively applied. But, as contradistinguished to *natural* law, or to the law of *nature* (meaning, by those expressions, the law of God), the aggregate of the rules, established by political superiors, is frequently styled *positive* law, or law existing *by position*. As contradistinguished to the rules which I style *positive morality*, and on which I shall touch immediately, the aggregate of the rules, established by political superiors, may also be marked commodiously with the name of *positive law*. For the sake, then, of getting a name brief and distinctive at once, and agreeably to frequent usage, I style that aggregate of rules, or any portion of that aggregate, *positive law*: though rules, which are *not* established by political superiors, are also *positive*, or exist *by position*, if they be rules or laws, in proper signification of the term.

Though *some* of the laws or rules, which are set by men to men, are established by political superiors, *others* are *not* established by political superiors, or are *not* established by political superiors, in that capacity or character.

Closely analogous to human laws of this second class, are a set of objects frequently but *improperly* termed *laws*, being rules set and enforced by *mere opinion*, that is, by the opinions or sentiments held or felt by an indeterminate body of men in regard to human conduct. Instances of such a use of the term *law* are the expressions—'The law of honor,' 'The law set by fashion,' and rules of this species constitute much of what is usually termed 'International law.'

The aggregate of human laws properly so called belonging to the second of the classes above mentioned, with the aggregate of objects *improperly* but by *close analogy* termed laws, I place together in a common class, and denote them by the term *positive morality*. The name *morality* severs them from *positive law*, while the epithet *positive* disjoins them from the *law of God*. And to the end of obviating confusion, it is necessary or expedient that they *should* be disjoined from the latter by that distinguishing epithet. For the name *morality* (or *morals*), when standing unqualified or alone, denotes indifferently either of the following objects: namely, positive morality *as it is*, or without regard to its merits; and positive morality *as it would be*, if it conformed to the law of God, and were, therefore, deserving of *approbation*.

Every *law* or *rule* (taken with the largest signification which can be given to the term *properly*) is a *command*. Or, rather, laws or rules, properly so called, are a *species* of commands.

Now, since the term *command* comprises the term *law*, the first is the simpler as well as the larger of the two. But, simple as it is, it admits of explanation. And, since it is the *key* to the sciences of jurisprudence and morals, its meaning should be analyzed with precision. . . .

If you express or intimate a wish that I shall do or forbear from some act, and if you will visit me with an evil in case I comply not with your wish, the *expression* or *intimation* of your wish is a *command*. A command is distinguished from other significations of desire, not by the style in which the desire is signified, but by the power and the purpose of the party commanding to inflict an evil or pain in case the desire be disregarded. If you cannot or will not harm me in case I comply not with your wish, the expression of your wish is not a command, although you utter your wish in imperative phrase. If you are able and willing to harm me in case I comply not with your wish, the expression of your wish amounts to a command, although you are prompted by a spirit of courtesy to utter it in the shape of a request. . . .

Being liable to evil from you if I comply not with a wish which you signify, I am

bound or *obliged* by your command, or I lie under a *duty* to obey it. If, in spite of that evil in prospect, I comply not with the wish which you signify, I am said to disobey your command, or to violate the duty which it imposes.

Command and duty are, therefore, correlative terms: the meaning denoted by each being implied or supposed by the other. Or (changing the expression) wherever a duty lies, a command has been signified; and whenever a command is signified, a duty is imposed.

Concisely expressed, the meaning of the correlative expressions is this. He who will inflict an evil in case his desire be disregarded, utters a command by expressing or intimating his desire: He who is liable to the evil in case he disregard the desire, is bound or obliged by the command.

The evil which will probably be incurred in case a command be disobeyed or (to use an equivalent expression) in case a duty be broken, is frequently called a *sanction*, or an *enforcement of obedience*. Or (varying the phrase) the command or the duty is said to be *sanctioned* or *enforced* by the chance of incurring the evil. . . .

It appears, then, from what has been premised, that the ideas or notions comprehended by the term *command* are the following. 1. A wish or desire conceived by a rational being, that another rational being shall do or forbear. 2. An evil to proceed from the former, and to be incurred by the latter, in case the latter comply not with the wish. 3. An expression or intimation of the wish by words or other signs.

It also appears from what has been premised, that *command*, *duty*, and *sanction* are inseparably connected terms: that each embraces the same ideas as the others, though each denotes those ideas in a peculiar order or series. . . .

Commands are of two species. Some are *laws* or *rules*. The others have not acquired an appropriate name, nor does language afford an expression which will mark them briefly and precisely. I must, therefore, note them as well as I can by the ambiguous and inexpressive name of '*occasional* or *particular* commands.'

The term *laws* or *rules* being not unfrequently applied to occasional or particular commands, it is hardly possible to describe a line of separation which shall consist in every respect with established forms of speech. But the distinction between laws and particular commands may, I think, be stated in the following manner.

By every command, the party to whom it is directed is obliged to do or to forbear.

Now where it obliges *generally* to acts or forbearances of a *class*, a command is a law or rule. But where it obliges to a *specific* act or forbearance, or to acts or forbearances which it determines *specifically* or *individually*, a command is occasional or particular. In other words, a class or description of acts is determined by a law or rule, and acts of that class or description are enjoined or forbidden generally. But where a command is occasional or particular, the act or acts, which the command enjoins or forbids, are assigned or determined by their specific or individual natures as well as by the class or description to which they belong.

The statement which I have given in abstract expressions I will now endeavor to illustrate by apt examples.

If you command your servant to go on a given errand, or *not* to leave your house on a given evening, or to rise at such an hour on such a morning, or to rise at that hour during the next week or month, the command is occasional or particular. For the act or acts enjoined or forbidden are specially determined or assigned.

But if you command him *simply* to rise at that hour, or to rise at that hour *always* or to rise at that hour *till further orders*, it may be said, with propriety, that you lay down a *rule* for the guidance of your servant's conduct. For no specific act is assigned by the command, but the command obliges him generally to acts of a determined class.

If a regiment be ordered to attack or defend a post, or to quell a riot, or to march from their present quarters, the command is occasional or particular. But an order to exercise daily till further orders shall be given would be called a *general* order, and *might* be called a rule. . . .

According to the line of separation which I have now attempted to describe, a law and a particular command are distinguished thus:—Acts or forbearances of a *class* are enjoined *generally* by the former. Acts *determined specifically*, are enjoined or forbidden by the latter. . . .

Most, indeed, of the laws which are established by political superiors, or most of the laws which are simply and strictly so called, oblige generally the members of the political community, or oblige generally persons of a class. To frame a system of duties for every individual of the community, were simply impossible: and if it were possible, it were utterly useless. Most of the laws established by political superiors are, therefore, *general* in a twofold manner: as enjoining or forbidding generally acts of kinds or sorts; and as binding the whole community, or, at least, whole classes of its members. . . .

It appears, from what has been premised, that a law, properly so called, may be defined in the following manner.

A law is a command which obliges a person or persons.

But, as contradistinguished or opposed to an occasional or particular command, a law is a command which obliges a person or persons, and obliges *generally* to acts or forbearances of a *class*.

In language more popular but less distinct and precise, a law is a command which obliges a person or persons to a *course* of conduct.

Laws and other commands are said to proceed from *superiors*, and to bind or oblige *inferiors*. . . .

But, taken with the meaning wherein I here understand it, the term *superiority* signifies *might*: the power of affecting others with evil or pain, and of forcing them, through fear of that evil, to fashion their conduct to one's wishes.

For example, God is emphatically the *superior* of Man. For his power of affecting us with pain, and of forcing us to comply with his will, is unbounded and resistless.

To a limited extent, the sovereign One or Number is the superior of the subject or citizen: the master, of the slave or servant: the father, of the child. In short, whoever can *oblige* another to comply with his wishes, is the *superior* of that other, so far as the ability reaches: The party who is obnoxious to the impending evil, being, to that same extent, the *inferior*.

LECTURE VI

I shall finish . . . by explaining the marks or characters which distinguish positive laws, or laws strictly so called. And, in order to [offer] an explanation of the marks which distinguish positive laws, I shall analyze the expression *sovereignty*, the correlative expression *subjection*, and the inseparably connected expression *independent political society*. With the ends or final causes for which governments *ought* to exist, or with their different degrees of fitness to attain or approach those ends, I have no concern. I examine the notions of *sovereignty* and *independent political society*, in order that I may finish the purpose to which I have adverted above: in order that I may distinguish completely the appropriate province of jurisprudence from the regions which lie upon its confines, and by which it is encircled. It is necessary that I should examine those notions, in order that I may finish that purpose. For the essential difference of a positive law (or the difference that severs it from a law

which is not a positive law) may be stated thus. Every positive law, or every law simply and strictly so called, is set by a sovereign person, or a sovereign body of persons, to a member or members of the independent political society wherein that person or body is sovereign or supreme. Or (changing the expression) it is set by a monarch, or sovereign number, to a person or persons in a state of subjection to its author. Even though it sprung directly from another fountain or source, it *is* a positive law, or a law strictly so called, by the institution of that present sovereign in the character of political superior. . . .

The superiority which is styled sovereignty, and the independent political society which sovereignty implies, is distinguished from other superiority, and from other society, by the following marks or characters:—
1. The *bulk* of the given society are in a *habit* of obedience or submission to a *determinate* and *common* superior: let that common superior be a certain individual person, or a certain body or aggregate of individual persons.
2. That certain individual, or that certain body of individuals, is *not* in a habit of obedience to a determinate human superior. Laws (improperly so called) which opinion sets or imposes, may permanently affect the conduct of that certain individual or body. To express or tacit commands of other determinate parties, that certain individual or body may yield occasional submission. But there is no determinate person, or determinate aggregate of persons, to whose commands, express or tacit, that certain individual or body renders habitual obedience.

Or the notions of sovereignty and independent political society may be expressed concisely thus.—If a *determinate* human superior, *not* in a habit of obedience to a like superior, receive *habitual* obedience from the *bulk* of a given society, that determinate superior is sovereign in that society, and the society (including the superior) is a society political and independent.

To that determinate superior, the other members of the society are *subject:* or on that determinate superior, the other members of the society are *dependent.* The position of its other members towards that determinate superior, is *a state of subjection,* or *a state of dependence.* The mutual relation which subsists between that superior and them, may be styled *the relation of sovereign and subject,* or *the relation of sovereignty and subjection.* . . .

Since every actual society is inadequately instructed or enlightened, the habitual obedience to its government which is rendered by the bulk of the community, is partly the consequence of custom: They partly pay that obedience to that present or established government, because they, and perhaps their ancestors, have been in a habit of obeying it. Or the habitual obedience to the government which is rendered by the bulk of the community, is partly the consequence of prejudices: meaning by 'prejudices,' opinions and sentiments which have no foundation whatever in the principle of general utility. . . .

But though that habitual obedience is partly the consequence of custom, or though that habitual obedience is partly the consequence of prejudices, it partly arises from a reason bottomed in the principle of utility. It partly arises from a perception, by the generality or bulk of the community, of the expediency of political government: or (changing the phrase) it partly arises from a preference, by the generality or bulk of the community, of any government to anarchy. . . .

[In every society political and independent, the actual positive law is a creature of the actual sovereign. Although it was positive law under foregoing sovereigns, it is positive law presently, or *is* positive law, through the power and authority of the present supreme government.]

It follows from the foregoing analysis, that the duties of the subjects towards the sovereign government, with the duties of the sovereign government towards the subjects, originate respectively in three several sources: namely, the Divine law (as indicated by the principle of utility), positive law, and positive morality. And, to my understanding, it seems that we account sufficiently for the origin of those obligations, when we simply refer them to those their obvious fountains. . . .

LECTURE V

Positive laws, or laws strictly so called, are established directly or immediately by authors of three kinds:—by monarchs, or sovereign bodies, as supreme political superiors: by men in a state of subjection, as subordinate political superiors: by subjects, as private persons, in pursuance of legal rights. But every positive law, or every law strictly so called, is a direct or circuitous command of a monarch or sovereign number in the character of political superior: that is to say, a direct or circuitous command of a monarch or sovereign number to a person or persons in a state of subjection to its author. And being a *command* (and therefore flowing from a *determinate* source), every positive law is a law proper, or a law properly so called. . . .

In consequence of the frequent coincidence of positive law and morality, and of positive law and the law of God, the true nature and fountain of positive law is often absurdly mistaken by writers upon jurisprudence. Where positive law has been fashioned on positive morality, or where positive law has been fashioned on the law of God, they forget that the copy is the creature of the sovereign, and impute it to the author of the model. . . .

Note—on the prevailing tendency to confound what is with what ought to be law or morality, that is, 1st to confound positive law with the science of legislation, and positive morality with deontology; and 2ndly, to confound positive law with positive morality, and both with legislation and deontology.

The existence of law is one thing; its merit or demerit is another. Whether it be or be not is one enquiry; whether it be or be not conformable to an assumed standard, is a different enquiry. A law, which actually exists, is a law, though we happen to dislike it, or though it vary from the text, by which we regulate our approbation and disapprobation. This truth, when formally announced as an abstract proposition, is so simple and glaring that it seems idle to insist upon it. But simple and glaring as it is, when enunciated in abstract expressions the enumeration of the instances in which it has been forgotten would fill a volume.

Sir William Blackstone, for example, says in his 'Commentaries,' that the laws of God are superior in obligation to all other laws; that no human laws should be suffered to contradict them; that human laws are of no validity if contrary to them; and that all valid laws derive their force from that Divine original.

Now, he *may* mean that all human laws ought to conform to the Divine laws. If this be his meaning, I assent to it without hesitation. The evils which we are exposed to suffer from the hands of God as a consequence of disobeying His commands are the greatest evils to which we are obnoxious; the obligations which they impose are consequently paramount to those imposed by any other laws, and if human commands conflict with the Divine law, we ought to disobey the command which is enforced by the less powerful sanction; this is implied in the term *ought*: the proposition is identical, and therefore perfectly indisputable—it is our interest to choose the smaller and more uncertain evil, in preference to the greater and surer. If this be Blackstone's meaning, I assent to his proposition, and have only to object to it, that it tells us just nothing. Perhaps, again, he means that human lawgivers are themselves obliged by the Divine laws to fashion the laws which they impose by that ultimate standard, because if they do not, God will

punish them. To this also I entirely assent: for if the index to the law of God be the principle of utility, that law embraces the whole of our voluntary actions in so far as motives applied from without are required to give them a direction conformable to the general happiness.

But the meaning of this passage of Blackstone, if it has a meaning, seems rather to be this: that no human law which conflicts with the Divine law is obligatory or binding; in other words, that no human law which conflicts with the Divine law *is a law*, for a law without an obligation is a contradiction in terms. I suppose this to be his meaning, because when we say of any transaction that it is invalid or void, we mean that it is not binding: as, for example, if it be a contract, we mean that the political law will not lend its sanction to enforce the contract.

Now, to say that human laws which conflict with the Divine law are not binding, that is to say, are not laws, is to talk stark nonsense. The most pernicious laws, and therefore those which are most opposed to the will of God, have been and are continually enforced as laws by judicial tribunals. Suppose an act innocuous, or positively beneficial, be prohibited by the sovereign under the penalty of death; if I commit this act, I shall be tried and condemned, and if I object to the sentence, that it is contrary to the law of God, who has commanded that human lawgivers shall not prohibit acts which have no evil consequences, the Court of Justice will demonstrate the inconclusiveness of my reasoning by hanging me up, in pursuance of the law of which I have impugned the validity. An exception, demurrer, or plea, founded on the law of God was never heard in a Court of Justice, from the creation of the world down to the present moment.

But this abuse of language is not merely puerile, it is mischievous. When it is said that a law ought to be disobeyed, what is meant is that we are urged to disobey it by motives more cogent and compulsory than those by which it is itself sanctioned. If the laws of God are certain, the motives which they hold out to disobey any human command which is at variance with them are paramount to all others. But the laws of God are not always certain. All divines, at least all reasonable divines, admit that no scheme of duties perfectly complete and unambiguous was ever imparted to us by revelation. As an index to the Divine will, utility is obviously insufficient. What appears pernicious to one person may appear beneficial to another. And as for the moral sense, innate practical principles, conscience, they are merely convenient cloaks for ignorance or sinister interest: they mean either that I hate the law to which I object and cannot tell why, or that I hate the law, and that the cause of my hatred is one which I find it incommodious to avow. If I say openly, I hate the law, *ergo*, it is not binding and ought to be disobeyed, no one will listen to me; but by calling my hate my conscience or my moral sense, I urge the same argument in another and more plausible form: I seem to assign a reason for my dislike, when in truth I have only given it a sounding and specious name. In times of civil discord the mischief of this detestable abuse of language is apparent. In quiet times the dictates of utility are fortunately so obvious that the anarchical doctrine sleeps, and men habitually admit the validity of laws which they dislike. To prove by pertinent reasons that a law is pernicious is highly useful, because such process may lead to the abrogation of the pernicious law. To incite the public to resistance by determinate views of *utility* may be useful, for resistance, grounded on clear and definite prospects of good, is sometimes beneficial. But to proclaim generally that all laws which are pernicious or contrary to the will of God are void and not to be tolerated, is to preach anarchy, hostile and perilous as much to wise and benign rule as to stupid and galling tyranny. . . .

QUESTIONS FOR DISCUSSION

1. How does Austin distinguish laws *properly so called* from laws *improperly so called?* Why does he do so?

2. How does Austin define a *command?* What makes someone *bound* or *obliged* to follow a command? To Austin is there a difference between being obliged to follow a command and having a *duty* to follow the command? What is the role of *sanctions* in all of this?

3. What do you think that Austin gains from his system of classification? What do you think he loses?

4. Identify specifically where and how Austin diverges from the natural law tradition.

5. In a section of *The Concept of Law* not included here, H. L. A. Hart objects to Austin's preoccupation with sanctions, claiming that there is more to law than the "gunman writ large." Do you agree with Hart that Austin misses something when he puts the threat of sanctions imposed by force at the center of a legal system? If so, what do you think Austin misses?

THE CONCEPT OF LAW

H . L . A .   H A R T

CHAPTER V

It is, of course, possible to imagine a society without a legislature, courts or officials of any kind. Indeed, there are many studies of primitive communities which not only claim that this possibility is realized but depict in detail the life of a society where the only means of social control is that general attitude of the group towards its own standard modes of behavior in terms of which we have characterized rules of obligation. A social structure of this kind is often referred to as one of 'custom'; but we shall not use this term, because it often implies that the customary rules are very old and supported with less social pressure than other rules. To avoid these implications we shall refer to such a social structure as one of primary rules of obligation. If a society is to live by such primary rules alone, there are certain conditions which, granted a few of the most obvious truisms about human nature and the world we live in, must clearly be satisfied. The first of these conditions is that the rules must contain in some form restrictions on the free use of violence, theft, and deception to which human beings are tempted but which they must, in general, repress, if they are to coexist in close proximity to each other. Such rules are in fact always found in the primitive societies of which we have knowledge, together with a variety of others imposing on individuals various positive duties to perform services or make contributions to the common life. Secondly, though such a society may exhibit the tension, already described, between those who accept the rules and those who reject the rules except where fear of social pressure induces them to conform, it is plain that the latter cannot be more than a minority, if so loosely organized a society of persons, approximately equal in physical strength, is to endure: for otherwise those who reject the rules would have too little social pressure to fear. This too is confirmed by what we know of primitive communities where, though there are dissidents and malefactors, the majority live by the rules seen from the internal point of view.

More important for our present purpose is the following consideration. It is plain that only a small community closely knit by ties of kinship, common sentiment, and belief, and placed in a stable environment, could live successfully by such a régime of unofficial rules. In any other conditions such a simple form of social control must prove defective and will require supplementation in different ways. In the first place, the rules by which the group lives will not form a system, but will simply be a set of separate standards, without any identifying or common mark, except of course that they are the rules which a particular group of human beings accepts. They will in this respect resemble our own rules of etiquette. Hence if doubts arise as to what the rules are or as to the precise scope of some given rule, there will be no procedure for settling this doubt, either by reference to an authoritative text or to an official whose declarations on this point are authoritative. For, plainly, such a procedure and the acknowledgement of either authoritative text

H. L. A. Hart, *The Concept of Law* (Oxford: Clarendon Press, 1961), selections from Chapters V and VI or persons involve the existence of rules of a type different from the rules of obligation or duty which *ex hypothesi* are all that the group has. This defect in the simple social structure of primary rules we may call its *uncertainty*.

A second defect is the *static* character of the rules. The only mode of change in the rules known to such a society will be the slow process of growth, whereby courses of conduct once thought optional become first habitual or usual, and then obligatory, and the converse process of decay, when deviations, once severely dealt with, are first tolerated and then pass unnoticed. There will be no means, in such a society, of deliberately adapting the rules to changing circumstances, either by eliminating old rules or introducing new ones: for, again, the possibility of doing this presupposes the existence of rules of a different type from the primary rules of obligation by which alone the society lives. In an extreme case the rules may be static in a more drastic sense. This, though never perhaps fully realized in any actual community, is worth considering because the remedy for it is something very characteristic of law. In this extreme case, not only would there be no way of deliberately changing the general rules, but the obligations which arise under the rules in particular cases could not be varied or modified by the deliberate choice of any individual. Each individual would simply have fixed obligations or duties to do or abstain from doing certain things. It might indeed very often be the case that others would benefit from the performance of these obligations; yet if there are only primary rules of obligation they would have no power to release those bound from performance or to transfer to others the benefits which would accrue from performance. For such operations of release or transfer create changes in the initial positions of individuals under the primary rules of obligation, and for these operations to be possible there must be rules of a sort different from the primary rules.

The third defect of this simple form of social life is the *inefficiency* of the diffuse social pressure by which the rules are maintained. Disputes as to whether an admitted rule has or has not been violated will always occur and will, in any but the smallest societies, continue interminably, if there is no agency specially empowered to ascertain finally, and authoritatively, the fact of violation. Lack of such final and authoritative determinations is to be distinguished from another weakness associated with it. This is the fact that punishments for violations of the rules, and other forms of social pressure involving physical effort or the use of force, are not administered by a special agency but are left to the individuals affected or to the group at large. It is obvious that the waste of time involved in the group's unorganized efforts to catch and punish offenders, and the smoldering vendettas which may result from self help in the absence of an official monopoly of 'sanctions', may be serious. The history of law does, however, strongly suggest that the lack of official agencies to determine authoritatively the fact of violation of the rules is a much more serious defect; for many societies have remedies for this defect long before the other.

The remedy for each of these three main defects in this simplest form of social structure consists in supplementing the *primary* rules of obligation with *secondary* rules which are rules of a different kind. The introduction of the remedy for each defect might, in itself, be considered a step from the pre-legal into the legal world; since each remedy brings with it many elements that permeate law: certainly all three remedies together are enough to convert the régime of primary rules into what is indisputably a legal system. We shall consider in turn each of these remedies and show why law may most illuminatingly be characterized as a union of primary rules of obligation with such secondary rules. Before we do this, however, the following general points should be noted. Though the remedies consist in the introduction of rules which are certainly different from each other, as well as from the primary rules of obligation which they supplement, they have important features in common and are connected in various ways. Thus they may all be said to be on a different level from the primary rules, for they are all *about* such rules; in the sense that while primary rules are concerned with the actions that individuals must or must not do, these secondary rules are all concerned with the primary rules themselves. They specify the ways in which the primary rules may be conclusively ascertained, introduced, eliminated, varied, and the fact of their violation conclusively determined.

The simplest form of remedy for the *uncertainty* of the régime of primary rules is the introduction of what we shall call a 'rule of recognition'. This will specify some feature or features possession of which by a suggested rule is taken as a conclusive affirmative indication that it is a rule of the group to be supported by the social pressure it exerts. The existence of such a rule of recognition may take any of a huge variety of forms, simple or complex. It may, as in the early law of many societies, be no more than that an authoritative list or text of the rules is to be found in a written document or carved on some public monument. No doubt as a matter of history this step from the pre-legal to the legal may be accomplished in distinguishable stages, of which the first is the mere reduction to writing of hitherto unwritten rules. This is not itself the crucial step, though it is a very important one: what is crucial is the acknowledgement of reference to the writing or inscription as *authoritative*, i.e. as the *proper* way of disposing of doubts as to the existence of the rule. Where there is such an acknowledgement there is a very simple form of secondary rule: a rule for conclusive identification of the primary rules of obligation.

In a developed legal system the rules of recognition are of course more complex; instead of identifying rules exclusively by reference to a text or list they do so by reference to some general characteristic possessed by the primary rules. This may be the fact of their having been enacted by a specific body, or their long customary practice, or their relation to judicial decisions. Moreover, where more than one of such general characteristics are treated as identifying criteria, provision may be made for their possible conflict by their arrangement in an order of superiority, as by the common subordination of custom or precedent to statute, the latter being a 'superior source' of law. Such complexity may make the rules of recognition in a modern legal system seem very different from the simple acceptance of an authoritative text: yet even in this simplest form, such a rule brings with it many elements distinctive of law. By providing an authoritative mark it introduces, although in embryonic form, the idea of a legal system: for the rules are now not just a discrete unconnected set but are, in a simple way, unified. Further, in the simple operation of identifying a given rule as possessing the required feature of being an item on an authoritative list of rules we have the germ of the idea of legal validity.

The remedy for the *static* quality of the régime of primary rules consists in the introduction of what we shall call 'rules of change'. The simplest form of such a rule is that which empowers an individual or body of persons to introduce new primary rules for the conduct of the life of the group, or of some class within it, and to eliminate old rules. . . . Such rules of change may be very simple or very complex: the powers conferred may be unrestricted or limited in various ways: and the rules may, besides specifying the persons who are to legislate, define in more or less rigid terms the procedure to be followed in legislation. Plainly, there will be a very close connection between the rules of change and the rules of recognition: for where the former exists the latter will necessarily incorporate a reference to legislation as an identifying feature of the rules, though it need not refer to all the details of procedure involved in legislation. . . .

The third supplement to the simple régime of primary rules, intended to remedy the *inefficiency* of its diffused social pressure, consists of secondary rules empowering individuals to make authoritative determinations of the question whether, on a particular occasion, a primary rule has been broken. The minimal form of adjudication consists in such determinations, and we shall call the secondary rules which confer the power to make them 'rules of adjudication'. Besides identifying the individuals who are to adjudicate, such rules will also define the procedure to be followed. Like the other secondary rules these are on a different level from the primary rules: though they may be reinforced by further rules imposing duties on judges to adjudicate, they do not impose duties but confer judicial powers and a special status on judicial declarations about the breach of obligations. Again these rules, like the other secondary rules, define a group of important legal concepts: in this case the concepts of judge or court, jurisdiction and judgment. Besides these resemblances to the other secondary rules, rules of adjudication have intimate connections with them. Indeed, a system which has rules of adjudication is necessarily also committed to a rule of recognition of an elementary and imperfect sort. This is so because, if courts are empowered to make authoritative determinations of the fact that a rule has been broken, these cannot avoid being taken as authoritative determinations of what the rules are. So the rule which confers jurisdiction will also be a rule of recognition, identifying the primary rules through the judgments of the courts and these judgments will become a 'source'

of law. It is true that this form of rule of recognition, inseparable from the minimum form of jurisdiction, will be very imperfect. Unlike an authoritative text or a statute book, judgments may not be couched in general terms and their use as authoritative guides to the rules depends on a somewhat shaky inference from particular decisions, and the reliability of this must fluctuate both with the skill of the interpreter and the consistency of the judges.

It need hardly be said that in few legal systems are judicial powers confined to authoritative determinations of the fact of violation of the primary rules. Most systems have, after some delay, seen the advantages of further centralization of social pressure; and have partially prohibited the use of physical punishments or violent self help by private individuals. Instead they have supplemented the primary rules of obligation by further secondary rules, specifying or at least limiting the penalties for violation, and have conferred upon judges, where they have ascertained the fact of violation, the exclusive power to direct the application of penalties by other officials. These secondary rules provide the centralized official 'sanctions' of the system.

If we stand back and consider the structure which has resulted from the combination of primary rules of obligation with the secondary rules of recognition, change and adjudication, it is plain that we have here not only the heart of a legal system, but a most powerful tool for the analysis of much that has puzzled both the jurist and the political theorist.

Not only are the specifically legal concepts with which the lawyer is professionally concerned, such as those of obligation and rights, validity and source of law, legislation and jurisdiction, and sanction, best elucidated in terms of this combination of elements. The concepts (which bestride both law and political theory) of the state, of authority, and of an official require a similar analysis if the obscurity which still lingers about them is to be dissipated. The reason why an analysis in these terms of primary and secondary rules has this explanatory power is not far to seek. Most of the obscurities and distortions surrounding legal and political concepts arise from the fact that these essentially involve reference to what we have called the internal point of view: the view of those who do not merely record and predict behaviour conforming to rules, but *use* the rules as standards for the appraisal of their own and others' behaviour. This requires more detailed attention in the analysis of legal and political concepts than it has usually received. Under the simple régime of primary rules the internal point of view is manifested in its simplest form, in the use of those rules as the basis of criticism, and as the justification of demands for conformity, social pressure, and punishment. Reference to this most elementary manifestation of the internal point of view is required for the analysis of the basic concepts of obligation and duty. With the addition to the system of secondary rules, the range of what is said and done from the internal point of view is much extended and diversified. With this extension comes a whole set of new concepts and they demand a reference to the internal point of view for their analysis. These include the notions of legislation, jurisdiction, validity and, generally, of legal powers, private and public. There is a constant pull towards an analysis of these in the terms of ordinary or 'scientific', fact-stating or predictive discourse. But this can only reproduce their external aspect: to do justice to their distinctive, internal aspect we need to see the different ways in which the law-making operations of the legislator, the adjudication of a court, the exercise of private or official powers, and other 'acts-in-the-law' are related to secondary rules.

In the next chapter we shall show how the ideas of the validity of law and sources of law, and the truths latent among the errors of the doctrines of sovereignty may be rephrased and clarified in terms of rules of recognition. But we shall conclude this chapter with a warning: though the combination of primary and secondary rules merits, because it explains many aspects of law, the central place assigned to it, this cannot by itself illuminate every problem. The union of primary and secondary rules is at the center of a legal system; but it is not the whole, and as we move away from the center we shall have to accommodate, in ways indicated in later chapters, elements of a different character.

CHAPTER VI

According to the [Austinian theory], the foundations of a legal system consist of the situation in which the majority of a social group habitually obey the orders backed by threats of the sovereign person or persons, who themselves habitually obey no one. This social situation is, for this theory, both a necessary and a sufficient condition of the existence of law. We have already exhibited in some detail the incapacity of this theory to account for some of the salient features of a modern municipal legal system: yet nonetheless, as its hold over the minds of many thinkers suggests, it does contain, though in a blurred and misleading form, certain truths about certain important aspects of law. These truths can, however, only be clearly presented, and their importance rightly assessed, in terms of the more complex social situation where a secondary rule of recognition is accepted and used for the identification of primary rules of obligation. It is this situation which deserves, if anything does, to be called the foundations of a legal system. In this chapter we shall discuss various elements of this situation which have received only partial or misleading expression in the theory of sovereignty and elsewhere.

Wherever such a rule of recognition is accepted, both private persons and officials are provided with authoritative criteria for identifying primary rules of obligation. The criteria so provided may, as we have seen, take any one or more of a variety of forms: these include reference to an authoritative text; to legislative enactment; to customary practice; to general declarations of specified persons, or to past judicial decisions in particular cases. . . .

In the day–to–day life of a legal system its rule of recognition is very seldom expressly formulated as a rule; though occasionally, courts in England may announce in general terms the relative place of one criterion of law in relation to another, as when they assert the supremacy of Acts of Parliament over other sources or suggested sources of law. For the most part the rule of recognition is not stated, but its existence is *shown* in the way in which particular rules are identified, either by courts or other officials or private persons or their advisers. There is, of course, a difference in the use made by courts of the criteria provided by the rule and the use of them by others: for when courts reach a particular conclusion on the footing that a particular rule has been correctly identified as law, what they say has a special authoritative status conferred on it by other rules. In this respect, as in many others, the rule of recognition of a legal system is like the scoring rule of a game. In the course of the game the general rule defining the activities which constitute scoring (runs, goals, & c.) is seldom formulated; instead it is *used* by officials and players in identifying the particular phases which count towards winning. Here too, the declarations of officials (umpire or scorer) have a special authoritative status attributed to them by other rules. Further, in both cases there is the possibility of a conflict between these author-itative applications of the rule and the general understanding of what the rule plainly requires according to its terms. This, as we shall see later, is a complication which must be catered for in any account of what it is for a system of rules of this sort to exist.

The use of unstated rules of recognition, by courts and others, in identifying particular rules of the system is characteristic of the internal point of view. Those who use them in this way thereby manifest their own acceptance of them as guiding rules and with this attitude there goes a characteristic vocabulary different from the natural expressions of the external point of view. Perhaps the simplest of these is the expression, 'It is the law that . . .', which we may find on the lips not only of judges, but of ordinary men living under a legal system, when they identify a given rule of the system. This, like the expression 'Out' or 'Goal', is the language of one assessing a situation by reference to rules which he in common with others acknowledges as appropriate for this purpose. This attitude of shared acceptance of rules is to be contrasted with that of an observer who records *ab extra* the fact that a social group accepts such rules but does not himself accept them. The natural expression of this external point of view is not 'It is the law that . . .' but 'In England they recognize as law . . . whatever the Queen in Parliament enacts . . . .' The first of these forms of expression we shall call an *internal statement* because it manifests the internal point of view and is naturally used by one who, accepting the rule of recognition and without stating the fact that it is accepted, applies the rule in recognizing some particular rule of the system as valid. The second form of expression we shall call an *external statement* because it is the natural language of an external observer of the system who, without himself accepting its rule of recognition, states the fact that others accept it.

If this use of an accepted rule of recognition in making internal statements is understood and carefully distinguished from an external statement of fact that the rule is accepted, many obscurities concerning the notion of legal 'validity' disappear. For the word 'valid' is most frequently, though not always, used, in just such internal statements, applying to a particular rule of a legal system, an unstated but accepted rule of recognition. To say that a given rule is valid is to recognize it as passing all the tests provided by the rule of recognition and so as a rule of the system. We can indeed simply say that the statement that a particular rule is valid means that it satisfies all the criteria provided by the rule of recognition. This is incorrect only to the extent that it might obscure the internal character of such statements; for, like the cricketers' 'Out', these statements of validity normally apply to a particular case a rule of recognition accepted by the speaker and others, rather than expressly state that the rule is satisfied.

Some of the puzzles connected with the idea of legal validity are said to concern the relation between the validity and the 'efficacy' of law. If by 'efficacy' is meant the fact that a rule of law which requires certain behaviour is obeyed more often than not, it is plain that there is no necessary connection between the validity of any particular rule and *its* efficacy, unless the rule of recognition of the system includes among its criteria, as some do, the provision (sometimes referred to as a rule of obsolescence) that no rule is to count as a rule of the system if it has long ceased to be efficacious. . . .

One who makes an internal statement concerning the validity of a particular rule of a system may be said to *presuppose* the truth of the external statement of fact that the system is generally efficacious. For the normal use of internal statements is in such a context of general efficacy. It would however be wrong to say that statements of validity 'mean' that the system is generally efficacious. For though it is normally pointless or idle to talk of the validity of a rule of a system which has never established itself or has been discarded, none the less it is not meaningless nor is it always pointless. One vivid way of teaching Roman Law is to speak *as if* the system were efficacious still and to discuss the validity of particular rules and solve problems in their terms; and one way of nursing hopes for the restoration of an old social order destroyed by revolution, and rejecting the new, is to cling to the criteria of legal validity of the old régime. This is implicitly done by the White Russian who still claims property under some rule of descent which was a valid rule of Tsarist Russia.

The rule of recognition providing the criteria by which the validity of other rules of the system is assessed is in an important sense, which we shall try to clarify, an *ultimate* rule: and where, as is usual, there are several criteria ranked in order of relative subordination and primacy one of them is *supreme*. These ideas of the ultimacy of the rule of recognition and the supremacy of one of its criteria merit some attention. It is important to disentangle them from the theory, which we have rejected, that somewhere in every legal system, even though it lurks behind legal forms, there must be a sovereign legislative power which is legally unlimited.

Of these two ideas, supreme criterion and ultimate rule, the first is the easiest to define. We may say that a criterion of legal validity or source of law is supreme if rules identified by reference to it are still recognized as rules of the system, even if they conflict with rules identified by reference to the other criteria, whereas rules identified by reference to the latter are not so recognized if they conflict with the rules identified by reference to the supreme criterion. A similar explanation in comparative terms can be given of the notions of 'superior' and 'subordinate' criteria which we have already used.

It is plain that the notions of a superior and a supreme criterion merely refer to a *relative* place on a scale and do not import any notion of legally *unlimited* legislative power. Yet 'supreme' and 'unlimited' are easy to confuse—at least in legal theory. One reason for this is that in the simpler forms of legal system the ideas of ultimate rule of recognition, supreme criterion, and legally unlimited legislature seem to converge. For where there is a legislature subject to no constitutional limitations and competent by its enactment to deprive all other rules of law emanating from other sources of their status as law, it is part of the rule of recognition in such a system that enactment by that legislature is the supreme criterion of validity. This is, according to constitutional theory, the position in the United Kingdom. But even systems like that of the United States in which there is no such legally unlimited legislature may perfectly well contain an ultimate rule of recognition which provides a set of criteria of validity, one of which is supreme. This will be so, where the legislative competence of the ordinary legislature is limited by a constitution which contains no amending power, or places some clauses outside the scope of that power. Here there is no legally unlimited legislature, even in the widest interpretation of 'legislature'; but the system of course contains an ultimate rule of recognition and, in the clauses of its constitution, a supreme criterion of validity.

The sense in which the rule of recognition is the *ultimate* rule of a system is best understood if we pursue a very familiar chain of legal reasoning. If the question is raised whether some suggested rule is legally valid, we must, in order to answer the question, use a criterion of validity provided by some other rule. Is this purported by-law of the Oxfordshire County Council valid? Yes: because it was made in exercise of the powers conferred, and in accordance with the procedure specified, by a statutory order made by the Minister of Health. At this first stage the statutory order provides the criteria in terms of which the validity of the by-law is assessed. There may be no practical need to go farther; but there is a standing possibility of doing so. We may query the validity of the statutory order and assess its validity in terms of the statute empowering the minister to make such orders. Finally when the validity of the statute has been queried and assessed by reference to the rule that what the Queen in Parliament enacts is law, we are brought to a stop in inquiries concerning validity: for we have reached a rule which, like the intermediate statutory order and statute, provides criteria for the assessment of the validity of other rules; but it is also unlike them in that there is no rule providing criteria for the assessment of its own legal validity.

There are, indeed, many questions which we can raise about this ultimate rule. We can ask whether it is the practice of courts, legislatures, officials, or private citizens in England actually to use this rule as an ultimate rule of recognition. Or has our process of legal reasoning been an idle game with the criteria of validity of a system now discarded? We can ask whether it is a satisfactory form of legal system which has such a rule at its root. Does it produce more good than evil? Are there prudential reasons for supporting it? Is there a moral obligation to do so? These are plainly very important questions; but, equally plainly, when we ask them about the rule of recognition, we are no longer attempting to answer the same kind of question about it as those which we answered about other rules with its aid. When we move from saying that a particular enactment is valid, because it satisfies the rule that what the Queen in Parliament enacts is law, to saying that in England this last rule is used by courts, officials, and private persons as the ultimate rule of recognition, we have moved from an internal statement of law asserting the validity of a rule of the system to an external statement of fact which an observer of the system might make even if he did not accept it. So too when we move from the statement that a particular enactment is valid, to the statement that the rule of recognition of the system is an excellent one and the system based on it is one worthy of support, we have moved from a statement of legal validity to a statement of value. . . .

In the simple system of primary rules of obligation sketched in the last chapter, the assertion that a given rule existed could only be an external statement of fact such as an observer who did not accept the rules might make and verify by ascertaining whether or not, as a matter of fact, a given mode of behaviour was generally accepted as a standard and was accompanied by those features which, as we have seen, distinguish a social rule from mere convergent habits. It is in this way also that we should now interpret and verify the assertion that in England a rule—though not a legal one—exists that we must bare the head on entering a church. If such rules as these are found to exist in the actual practice of a social group, there is no separate question of their validity to be discussed, though of course their value or desirability is open to question. Once their existence has been established as a fact we should only confuse matters by affirming or denying that they were valid or by saying that 'we assumed' but could not show their validity. Where, on the other hand, as in a mature legal system, we have a system of rules which includes a rule of recognition so that the status of a rule as a member of the system now depends on whether it satisfies certain criteria provided by the rule of recognition, this brings with it a new application of the word 'exist'. The statement that a rule exists may now no longer be what it was in the simple case of customary rules—an external statement of the *fact* that a certain mode

of behaviour was generally accepted as a standard in practice. It may now be an internal statement applying an accepted but unstated rule of recognition and meaning (roughly) no more than 'valid given the system's criteria of validity'. In this respect, however, as in others a rule of recognition is unlike other rules of the system. The assertion that it exists can only be an external statement of fact. For whereas a subordinate rule of a system may be valid and in that sense 'exist' even if it is generally disregarded, the rule of recognition exists only as a complex, but normally concordant, practice of the courts, officials, and private persons in identifying the law by reference to certain criteria. Its existence is a matter of fact. . . .

There are therefore two minimum conditions necessary and sufficient for the existence of a legal system. On the one hand those rules of behaviour which are valid according to the system's ultimate criteria of validity must be generally obeyed, and, on the other hand, its rules of recognition specifying the criteria of legal validity and its rules of change and adjudication must be effectively accepted as common public standards of official behaviour by its officials. The first condition is the only one which private citizens *need* satisfy: they may obey each 'for his part only' and from any motive whatever; though in a healthy society they will in fact often accept these rules as common standards of behaviour and acknowledge an obligation to obey them, or even trace this obligation to a more general obligation to respect the constitution. The second condition must also be satisfied by the officials of the system. They must regard these as common standards of official behaviour and appraise critically their own and each other's deviations as lapses. Of course it is also true that besides these there will be many primary rules which apply to officials in their merely personal capacity which they need only obey.

QUESTIONS FOR DISCUSSION

1. How specifically does Hart's position differ from Austin's? What turns on the difference?

2. How does Hart define a *primary rule*? How does he define a *secondary rule*? What is the difference? Can you give your own examples of primary and secondary rules?

3. What to Hart is the relationship between law and a *legal system*? Why is it important to define *legal system*?

4. Hart argues that all mature legal systems have an ultimate rule of recognition, even if it is nowhere written down in one place. How would you describe the ultimate rule of recognition for the United States?

5. Unlike Austin, Hart does not explicitly (at least here) take issue with natural law theory. Still, Hart is classed as a legal positivist and not classed with the natural law theorists. Why do you think that is so?

SUGGESTIONS FOR FURTHER READING

A good modern analysis of Austin's work is W.L. Morrison, *John Austin* (Stanford: Stanford University Press, 1984). Austin is defended against Hart in Robert N. Moles, *Definition and Rule in Legal Theory: A Reassessment of H.L.A. Hart and the Positivist Tradition* (Oxford: Basil Blackwell, 1987). Most of H.L.A. Hart's other works are collected in *Essays in Jurisprudence and Philosophy* (Oxford: Clarendon Press, 1983) and *Essays on Bentham: Jurisprudence and Political Theory* (Oxford: Clarendon Press, 1982). A new edition of *The Concept of Law*, published (Oxford: Clarendon Press) in 1994, contains Hart's replies to critics. Books on Hart's legal theory include Neil MacCormick, *H.L.A. Hart* (London: Edward Arnold, 1981), Michael Martin, *The Legal Philosophy of H.L.A. Hart* (Philadelphia: Temple University Press, 1987), Ruth Gavison, ed., *Issues in Contemporary Legal Philosophy: The Influence of H.L.A. Hart* (Oxford: Clarendon Press, 1987) and P.M.S. Hacker and J. Raz, eds., *Law, Morality, and Society: Essays in Honour of H.L.A. Hart* (Oxford: Clarendon Press, 1977). Among the leading modern positivists and their works are David Lyons, *Ethics and the Rule of Law* (Cambridge: Cambridge University Press, 1984); Neil MacCormick, *Legal Reasoning and Legal Theory* (Oxford: Clarendon Press, 1978); Joseph Raz, *The Concept of a Legal System* (Oxford: Clarendon Press, 1970) and *The Authority of Law: Essays on Law and Morality* (Oxford: Clarendon Press, 1979). A good collection of contemporary positivist perspectives is Robert George, ed., *The Autonomy of Law: Essays on Legal Positivism* (Oxford: Clarendon Press, 1994).

1.3 LEGAL REALISM AND CRITICAL LEGAL STUDIES

INTRODUCTION

Theories of natural law and theories of legal positivism have both seemed to many people to be excessively removed from the realities of legal life. If we want to find out what law is, these people say, we should look to what legal officials—primarily, albeit not exclusively, judges—actually *do*. After all, what point is there in trying to determine what law is except as some guide to what *we* should do? Or at least that is where the great American Supreme Court Justice Oliver Wendell Holmes, Jr. (1841–1935, and the son of the poet and literary figure Dr. Oliver Wendell Holmes), who had earlier written about the nature of law, suggested we go when inquiring into what law is all about. Holmes, therefore, sought to define law as the prediction of what legal officials would do, because the "bad man," as Holmes put it, was most interested in finding out what the law would do to him, and thus was most interested in seeing law as it was likely to be applied to his actions by actual legal officials. Thus Holmes said things like: "a legal duty so called is nothing but a prediction that if a man does or omits certain things he will be made to suffer in this or that way by judgment of the court;—and so of a legal right."[20] And, similarly, "If you want to know the law and nothing else, you must look at it as a bad man, who cares only for the material consequences which such knowledge enables him to predict, not as a good one, who finds his reasons for conduct, whether inside the law or outside of it, in the vaguer sanctions of conscience." And, perhaps most famously, "The prophecies of what the courts will do . . . are what I mean by law."

Because of Holmes's focus on what officials would actually do, theorists following in his footsteps, many of whom called themselves Legal Realists,[21] often seemed explicitly uninterested in the *philosophy* of law and much more interested in empirical examination of how law in fact operated in specific legal systems. Yet underneath the empirical inquiry was a philosophical position about the nature of law, and that philosophical position is worth taking seriously in its own right.

[20]Oliver Wendell Holmes, Jr., "The Path of the Law," *Harvard Law Review*, vol. 10 (1897), pp. 457 ff.

[21]There is *no* relationship between Legal Realism and various philosophical positions that go by the name of "realism," such as moral realism and scientific realism and metaphysical realism. Indeed, you may be able to see after consideration of the material that follows why Legal Realism and all of these other realisms are in some ways exactly opposed to each other.

So suppose, in the manner of Holmes and others such as John Chipman Gray,[22] we try to locate law in what judges do. We might then ask why judges do what they do. What leads them to decide in one way and not another? And of course the standard picture is that judges consult a set of rules, the rules that Hart would say are the ones recognized as legally valid by a valid rule of recognition. Having consulted these valid rules, the standard picture continues, judges then decide the issue before them in the way indicated by the legal rules. But what if, as an empirical matter, this is rarely true? What if judges reached their decisions in some other way? It might then turn out that what started out as an empirical challenge brought to light a whole new conception of the very idea of law. What if, as the Texas trial and appellate Judge Joseph C. Hutcheson, Jr. (1879–1974) argued (and reported) in 1929, judges first came to a "hunch" about the correct result, and then looked for the *rationalization* from the legal rules to support the result that they had reached on other grounds?[23] And then what if, as then-lawyer and later-federal judge Jerome Frank (1889–1957) argued in 1930 in *Law and the Modern Mind*,[24] and Columbia law professor Karl Llewellyn (1893–1962) argued at about the same time in *The Bramble Bush*,[25] it turned out as a contingent empirical matter that in some legal systems (such as the legal system of the United States) there were enough legal rules going in enough different directions that judges could usually find some legal rule to support whatever result they decided, *on other grounds*, to be the result they wanted to reach? What if, therefore, law turned out to be able to justify whatever result the judge thought best for his or her own reasons?

If Hutcheson, Frank, Llewellyn, and others are right as an empirical matter about the ready availability of legal rules to rationalize the results that judges choose to reach on other grounds, then the inquiry turns to the other grounds on which judges might actually base their decisions. Frank, greatly influenced by theories of psychoanalysis (he also underwent analysis), thought the answer lay in the psychological preconceptions and attitudes of the judge. Judges, even though they might not recognize it, are often inclined to favor some people over some others, or might just have, as Hutcheson argued, some intuitive sense of who ought to win in a certain case on its own particular facts. Llewellyn also stressed something he called a judge's "situation sense," and he and others looked as well for less psychological explanations. Many of the Legal Realists consequently saw judges as people who were trying to make policy. They decided cases, therefore, again not by *applying* settled legal rules, but by deciding, not

[22]John Chipman Gray, *The Nature and Sources of Law* (R. Gray, ed., 2d ed., New York: Macmillan, 1921). Gray, who lived from 1839 to 1915, was a Boston lawyer and a professor at the Harvard Law School. His most famous observation was that things like statutes were only *sources* of law, with only judicial decisions being the law itself.

[23]Joseph C. Hutcheson, Jr., "The Judgment Intuitive: The Function of the 'Hunch' in Judicial Decision," *Cornell Law Quarterly*, vol. 14 (1929), pp. 274 ff.

[24]Jerome N. Frank, *Law and the Modern Mind* (New York: Brentano, 1930). See selection in Section 2.3.

[25]Karl Llewellyn, *The Bramble Bush: Some Lectures on Law and Its Study* (New York: Columbia University School of Law, 1930). See selections later in this section.

unlike a legislator or a bureaucrat, what the best policy would be. Only after deciding on the best policy would they look for a legal rule to dress up the policy decision, and, again as a contingent empirical matter, at least in the United States they would usually find what they were looking for.

Now consider what this says about the nature of law. If judges are deciding cases based on their own psychology, or based on what they think is the best policy decision, then in an important way the domain of law may not be distinct from other domains. Although most of the Legal Realists distanced themselves from natural law theories because they saw themselves as interested more in policy than in eternal morality, and because they did not think there was an overarching essential nature of law at all, they also tended to diverge in outlook from one of the basic tenets of legal positivism. This tenet is that law is, in theory, a limited domain, created and described by what Hart called the rules of recognition. To the positivist, not every source of value or decision counts as law, but only those sources specifically recognized as law by the rule of recognition. But if, as the Realists often argued, judges were actually using *everything* to reach their decisions, then what is the point of saying that law is defined by a rule of recognition that distinguishes law from non-law? Nothing in the Legal Realist perspective directly contradicts this aspect of legal positivism, but if, having distinguished law from non-law, it turns out that judges use non-law at least as much as (if not more than) they use the law, then what is the point of drawing the distinction? We might also distinguish, the Legal Realists could say, between laws that begin with the letters "A," "B," and "C" from all other laws. This would be a real distinction, but it would serve no point because it would have no bearing on the practice of legal decision makers.

The empirical claim that lies at the heart of Legal Realism could, of course, be false. It could be false because judges consulted and were guided by the law prior to deciding how the case should come out, and it could be false because even if judges first thought about how they wanted the case to come out, it might be the case that a large number of outcomes could not be rationalized in light of existing legal rules. American judges sometimes say that an opinion "won't write," by which they mean that having tentatively decided how they want to come out, they cannot find a persuasive justification, supported by legal rules, principles, and precedents, to support their tentative decision. But how often this happens is not only an empirical question, but one that may have a substantial effect on just how we understand the very idea of law. Indeed, this question is the one that best enables us to understand the perspective offered here by Duncan Kennedy. Kennedy (1942–), a professor at the Harvard Law School, is one of the founding members of the Critical Legal Studies movement, a movement that, in part, carries on the agenda and tradition of Legal Realism. Many members of the Critical Legal Studies movement diverge from Legal Realism in being more inclined to see politics or ideology, where the Legal Realists saw psychology or social policy, as the empirically dominant motivator of judicial decisions. Although Critical Legal Studies is also noteworthy for the way in which it has exposed the political presuppositions lying behind seemingly neutral legal procedures and for representing a challenge from the Left to what it sees as the essentially conservative tendencies of most legal practice, our greatest concern here is with its interesting twist on Legal Realism. In an important article entitled "Legal Formality," for example, Kennedy points out that it is a contingent fact about American law that judges, without being subject to impeachment or much criticism, can at least sometimes make decisions contrary to the clear indications of settled legal rules.[26] And if they can thus go above or around what appears to be the law, and if they can do this based on a full range of social, moral, ideological, economic, and political factors, then this has a profound influence on our understanding of the very nature of law. After all, if judges can override the law in the service of (to the positivist) non-legal factors in one case out of a hundred, then in one hundred cases out of a hundred judges must decide if this is the case in which the law (in the positivist sense) will not control. And thus, following the Realist tradition, Kennedy sees the idea of a distinct domain of the legal as empirically and conceptually misguided, a position we see in more refined form in the excerpt that follows.

[26]Duncan Kennedy, "Legal Formality," *Journal of Legal Studies*, vol. 2 (1973), pp. 251 ff.

THE BRAMBLE BUSH, A REALISTIC JURISPRUDENCE, AND THE COMMON LAW TRADITION

KARL LLEWELLYN

FROM *THE BRAMBLE BUSH*

What, then, is this law business about? It is about the fact that our society is honeycombed with disputes. Disputes actual and potential; disputes to be settled and disputes to be prevented; both appealing to law, both making up the business of the law. But obviously those which most violently call for attention are the actual disputes, and to these our first attention must be directed. Actual disputes call for somebody to do something about them. First, so that there may be peace, for the disputants; for other persons whose ears and toes disputants are disturbing. And secondly, so that the dispute may really be put at rest, which means, so that a solution may be achieved which, at least in the main, is bearable to the parties and not disgusting to the lookers-on. This doing of something about disputes, this doing of it

Karl Llewellyn, *The Bramble Bush: Some Lectures on Law and Its Study* (New York: Columbia University School of Law, 1930)
Karl Llewellyn, "A Realistic Jurisprudence: The Next Step," *Columbia Law Review*, vol. 30 (1930), pp. 431 ff.
Karl Llewellyn, *The Common Law Tradition: Deciding Appeals* (Boston: Little, Brown, 1960)

reasonably, is the business of law. And the people who have the doing in charge, whether they be judges or sheriffs or clerks or jailers or lawyers, are officials of the law. *What these officials do about disputes is, to my mind, the law itself.*

There are not so many, I think, who would agree with me in thus regarding law. It is much more common to approach the law as *being a set of rules of conduct,* and most thinkers would say rules of *external* conduct to distinguish them from the rules of morality: be good, sweet maid, and let who will be clever. And most of the thinkers would probably say rules *enforced by external constraint,* to distinguish them not only from rules of morality, but also from some phases of custom, such as wearing ties and Paris garters. And many thinkers would add, rules *laid down by the state,* in order to distinguish them from the commands of a father, or the regulations of a university, or the compulsion to be a Democrat in Georgia. Most thinkers, too, would take these rules as *addressed to the man on the street* and as telling him what to do and what not to do. To most thinkers, I say, *rules* are the heart of law, and the arrangement of rules in orderly coherent system is the business of the legal scholar, and argument in terms of rules, the drawing of a neat solution from a rule to fit the case in hand—that is the business of the judge and of the advocate.

All of which seems to me rather sadly misleading. There is indeed much, in some parts of law, to be said for this view that "rules laid down *for* conduct" are the focus, quite *apart from disputes.* Rules that everyone's income tax return must be made out on the same type of form do not look to disputes so much as to convenience of administration. Rules as to fencing elevator shafts look primarily to avoiding not disputes, but injuries. And indeed it may properly be said that as civilization grows more complex there is a widening slice of law in which disputes as such sink out of sight, and the focus of law

becomes the arrangement or rearrangement of business or conduct to get things done more quickly, more easily, more safely. It may properly be said that in many such cases there is not even (as there is in requiring travel on the left side of the road or on the right; or in fixing *the* one effective form for validating will or deed) a purpose of dispute-avoidance running *beside* the purpose of convenience. It may properly be said, finally, that even where the purpose clearly is dispute-avoidance, that purpose in turn often sinks into the background, and men talk about contracts, and trusts, and corporations, as if these things existed in themselves, instead of being the shadows cast across the front stage by the movements of the courts unheeded in the rear. All of this, however, goes not so much to the importance of "rules" as to the *non-exclusive* importance of disputes. Whether about disputes, or about when wills are valid, or about the form for income tax reports, we come back always to one common feature: The main thing is what officials are going to *do*. . . . And *rules*, in all of this, are important to you so far as they help you see or predict what judges will do or so far as they help you get judges to do something. That is their importance. That is all their importance, except as pretty playthings.

FROM "A REALISTIC JURISPRUDENCE"
The difficulty in framing any concept of "law" is that there are so many things to be included, and the things to be included are so unbelievably different from each other. Perhaps it is possible to get them all under one verbal roof. But I do not see what you have accomplished if you do. For a concept, as I understand it, is built for a purpose. It is a thinking tool. It is to make your data more manageable in doing something, in getting somewhere with them. And I have not yet met the job, or heard of it, to which all the data that associate themselves with this

loosest of suggestive symbols, "law," are relevant at once. We do and have too many disparate things and thinkings to which we like to attach that name. . . .

So that I am not going to attempt a definition of law. Not anybody's definition; much less my own. A definition both excludes and includes. It marks out a field. It makes some matters fall inside the field; it makes some fall outside. And the exclusion is almost always rather arbitrary. I have no desire to exclude anything from matters legal. In one aspect law is as broad as life, and for some purposes one will have to follow life pretty far to get the bearings of the legal matters one is examining. . . .

When men talk or think about law, they talk and think about *rules*. "Precepts" as used by Pound, for instance, I take to be roughly synonymous with rules and principles, the principles being wider in scope and proportionately vaguer in connotation, with a tendency toward idealization of some portion of the *status quo* at any given time. And I think you will find as you read Pound that the precepts are *central* to his thinking about law. Along with rules and principles—along with precepts proper, may I say?—he stresses for instance "standards" as a part of the subject matter of law. These standards seem to be those vague but useful pictures with which one approaches a wide and varied field of conduct to measure the rights of a particular situation: a conception of what a reasonable man would do in the circumstances, or of what good faith requires, and similar pictures. They differ from rules, though not from principles, partly in their vagueness; they differ from both in being not propositions in themselves, but normative approaches to working out the application of some one *term* in a major proposition. The principle, let us say, would read: a man must answer for what good faith requires. But a standard (like a concept; like any class-term, loose or sharp) functions chiefly or exclusively as *part* of a

precept. Consequently, it belongs in much the same world. It, too, *centers* on precepts. But Pound mentions more as law than precepts and standards. Along with the standards he stresses also ideals as to "the end" of law. These I take to be in substance standards on a peculiarly vague and majestic scale; standards, perhaps, to be applied to rules rather than to individual transactions. Finally, he stresses—and we meet here a very different order of phenomena—"the traditional techniques of developing and applying" precepts. Only a man gifted with insight would have added to the verbal formulae and verbalized (though vague) conceptual pictures thus far catalogued, such an element of *practices*, of habits and techniques of action, of *behavior*. But only a man partially caught in the traditional precept-thinking of an age that is passing would have focussed that behavior on, have given it a major reference to, have belittled its importance by dealing with it as a phase of, those merely verbal formulae: precepts. I have no wish to argue the point. It will appeal, or it will not, and argument will be of little service. But not only this particular bit of phrasing (which might be accidental), but the use made in Pound's writings of the idea, brings out vigorously the limitations of rules, of precepts, of *words*, when made the focus, the *center of reference*, in thinking about law. . . .

"Rules" is a term sufficiently ambiguous. A rule may be prescriptive: "this is what *ought* to be; what the judges *ought* to do in such cases." Or it may be descriptive: "this is what is; what the judges *actually* do in such cases." Or it may be both at once: "this is *both* what they do *and* what they ought to do." And when theorists discuss, they will move from one of these meanings into another without notice, and with all and any gradations of connotations. In the particular case of rules "of law" a further ambiguity affects the word "rule": whether descriptive or prescriptive, there is little effort to make out *whose* action and *what* action is prescribed or described. The statement "this is the rule" typically means: "I find this formula of words in authoritative books." Does this connote: *"Courts are actually proceeding* according to this formula"; or "Courts always rehearse this formula in this connection"? Does it connote: *"People* are conducting themselves in the light of this formula"; or even "People are conducting themselves as this formula suggests that they ought to"? The theorist will rarely trouble to tell you how many (if any) of these connotations are implicit in his statement: "this is the rule." But he will reason, on the next page, from some one of such implications. Which means: confusion, profuse and inevitable.

The confusion is stirred blacker with the concept "right" poured in. "Right" adds nothing to descriptive power. But it gives a specious appearance of substance to prescriptive rules. They seem to be *about* some *thing*. So that to clothe one's statement about what rules of law are in terms of rights, is to double the tendency to disregard the limitations actually put on rules or rights by practice and by remedies. At the vital core of thought about law, at the very place where one thought impinges on another, or where one part of law impinges on another, one sees the impingement in terms of idealized some-things which may not, which mostly *do* not, accurately reflect men's actions. In terms of words, and not in terms of conduct; in terms of what *apparently* is understandable without checking up in life. So that one makes the assumption—without the urge to inquiry—that one is dealing with reality when he talks of rights, and proceeds to use these unchecked words for further building.

There is another confusion, found in dealing with rules, and strengthened by the associated idea of rights, within the field of doctrine itself. Having come to regard words as sound bases for further thinking, the tendency is well nigh inevitable to simplify the

formulations more and more: to rub out of the formulations even the discrepancies in paper doctrine which any growing system of law contains in heaping measure; doubly so because the word "rights" introduces *sub rosa* at this point the additional notion of "rightness" (in the sense of what ought to be)—before which unwanted discrepancies must fall. I am speaking here of the effects of the idea of rightness on the rejection of some of the existent purely doctrinal materials in favor of other equally doctrinal materials, the case of conflicts in and within legal doctrine—a matter of vast concern to a lawyer, though commonly enough of no great moment to a political scientist.

But the same tendency carries over quite as well into the confusion of legal with non-legal materials, where it concerns political scientist and lawyer in common; and here the idea of "rights" seems to be the heavy tool of confusion, with no help at all from the idea of "rules." "Right" eternally suggests its connotation of inherent "rightness"—social, political, economic, and especially moral. It takes more careful self-analysis than most have been interested in giving to keep the *non-legal* "right" (which was a reason for claiming or striving toward or awarding a legal right) distinguished from the "legal right" which was conceived, I take it, as something not quite a mere description of an available remedy.

What now, is the place of rules and rights, under such an approach? To attempt their excision from the field of law would be to fly in the face of fact. I should like to begin by distinguishing real "rules" and rights from paper rules and rights. The former are conceived in terms of behavior; they are but other names, convenient shorthand symbols, for the remedies, the actions of the courts. They are descriptive, not prescriptive, except in so far as there may commonly be implied that courts *ought* to continue in their practices. "Real rules," then, if I had my way with words, would by legal scientists be called the practices of the courts, and not "rules" at all. And for such *scientists* statements of "rights" would be statements of likelihood that in a given situation a certain type of court action loomed in the offing. Factual terms. No more. This use of "rights," at least, has already considerable standing among the followers of Hohfeld. This concept of "real rule" has been gaining favor since it was first put into clarity by Holmes. "Paper rules" are what have been treated, traditionally, as rules of law: the accepted *doctrine* of the time and place—what the books there say "the law" is. The "real rules" and rights—"what the courts will do in a given case, and nothing more pretentious"—are then predictions. They are, I repeat, on the level of isness and not of oughtness; they seek earnestly to go no whit, in their suggestions, beyond the remedy actually available. Like all shorthand symbols, they are dangerous in connotation, when applied to situations which are not all quite alike. But their intent and effort is to describe. And one can adapt for them Max Weber's magnificent formulation in terms of probability: a right (or practice, or "real rule") exists *to the extent that* a likelihood exists that *A* can induce a court to squeeze, out of *B*, *A's* damages; more: *to the extent that* the likely collections will cover *A's* damage. In this aspect *substantive* rights and "rules," as distinct from [procedural ones], simply disappear—on the descriptive level. The measure of a "rule," the measure of a right, becomes what can be done about the situation. *Accurate* statement of a "real rule" or of a right includes all procedural limitations on what can be done about the situation. What is left, in the realm of *description*, are at the one end the facts, the groupings of conduct (and demonstrable expectations [and/or needs]) which may be claimed to constitute an interest; and on the other the practices of courts in their effects upon the conduct and expectations of the laymen in question. Facts, in the world of is-

ness, to be compared directly with other facts, also in the world of isness. . . .

Are "rules of law" in the accepted sense eliminated in such a course of thought? Somewhat obviously not. Whether they be pure paper rules, or are the accepted patter of the law officials, they remain present, and their presence remains an actuality—an actuality of importance—but an actuality whose *precise* importance, whose bearing and influence become clear. First of all they appear as what they are: rules of authoritative ought, addressed *to* officials, telling *officials* what the *officials* ought to do. To which telling the officials either pay no heed at all (the pure paper rule; the dead-letter statute; the obsolete case) or listen partly (the rule "construed" out of recognition; the rule to which lipservice chiefly is paid, while practice runs another course) or listen with all care (the rule with which the official practice pretty accurately coincides). I think that every such official precept-on-the-books (statute, doctrine laid down in the decision of a court, administrative regulation) tacitly contains an element of pseudodescription along with its statement of what officials ought to do; a tacit statement that officials do act according to the tenor of the rule; a tacit prediction that officials will act according to its tenor. Neither statement nor prediction is often true *in toto*. And the first point of the approach here made is skepticism as to the truth of either in any case in hand. Yet it is an accepted convention to act and talk as if this statement and prediction were most solemn truth: a tradition marked peculiarly among the legal profession when engaged officially. It is indeed of first importance to remember that such a tradition contains a tendency to verify itself. But no more so than to remember that such a tendency is no more powerful than its opposite: that other tendency to move quietly into falsifying the prediction in fact, while laying on an ointment of conventional words to soothe such as wish to believe the prediction has worked out.

FROM *THE COMMON LAW TRADITION*

2. Legal Doctrine

(a) It is understood and accepted that the context for seeing and discussing the question to be decided is to be set by and in a body of legal doctrine; and that where there is no real room for doubt, that body is to control the deciding; that where there is real room for doubt, that body of doctrine is nonetheless to guide the deciding; and that even when there is deep trouble, the deciding should strive to remain moderately consonant with the language and also with the spirit of some part of that body of doctrine.

That body, of course, includes not merely the very elaborate body of recorded directions which we know as rules of law,

whether gathered and phrased in unchanging rigor (e.g., statutes) or scattered and loosely phrased in case law style. The body includes also the accepted lines of organizing and seeing these materials: concepts, "fields" of law with their differential importance, pervading principles, living ideals, tendencies, constellations, tone.

(b) *Per contra*, in any case at all decently handled below and also worth appealing, either interpretation of language or the sizing up of the facts, or the choice open as among available divergent premises or tendencies in our multiwayed legal scheme, or the like, will allow a fair technical case to be made either way or a third or fourth other way, *if one looks at the authorities taken alone. . . .*
[For example,]

Canons of Construction

Thrust	But	Parry
1. A statute cannot go beyond its text.		1. To effect its purpose a statute may be implemented beyond its text.
2. Statutes in derogation of the common law will not be extended by construction.		2. Such acts will be liberally construed if their nature is remedial.
3. Statutes are to be read in the light of the common law and a statute affirming a common law rule is to be construed in accordance with the common law.		3. The common law gives way to a statute which is inconsistent with it and when a statute is designed as a revision of a whole body of law applicable to a given subject it supersedes the common law.
4. Where a foreign statute which has received construction has been adopted, previous construction is adopted too.		4. It may be rejected where there is conflict with the obvious meaning of the statute or where the foreign decisions are unsatisfactory in reasoning or where the foreign interpretation is not in harmony with the spirit or policy of the laws of the adopting state.

■ ■ ■

Thrust	But	Parry
12. If language is plain and unambiguous it must be given effect.		12. Not when literal interpretation would lead to absurd or mischievous consequences or thwart manifest purpose.
13. Words and phrases which have received judicial construction before enactment are are to be understood according to that construction.		13. Not if the statute clearly requires them to have a different meaning.

QUESTIONS FOR DISCUSSION

1. Llewellyn's "thrust but parry" shows that there are often respectable legal arguments that can be made on both sides of the same case. Assuming he is right, what do you think brought about this state of affairs?

2. Llewellyn sees courts as policymakers. What kinds of policies should courts make? What kinds of "jobs," to use Llewellyn's term, are courts and judges likely to be good at?

3. Elsewhere, Llewellyn emphasized that "common sense" and "situation sense" played a major role in legal decision making. What is common sense? Is it always a good thing? Is it always a good thing for judges to use it?

4. In what is taken as somewhat of a slogan representing Legal Realism, Chief Justice Charles Evan Hughes of the United States Supreme Court is alleged to have said, "The Constitution is what the judges say it is." Consider the response of H. L. A. Hart, from *The Concept of Law*, pp. 132 ff:

[The] mistake becomes immediately apparent when we consider how the judge's own statement that a particular rule is valid functions in judicial decision; for, though here too, in making such a statement, the judge presupposes but does not state the general efficacy of the system, he plainly is not concerned to predict his own or others' official action. His statement that a rule is valid is an internal statement recognizing that the rule satisfies the tests for identifying what is to count as law in his court, and constitutes not a prophecy of but part of the *reason* for his decision. . . .

It may seem strange that the contention that rules have a central place in the structure of a legal system could ever be seriously doubted. Yet 'rule-skepticism', or the claim that talk of rules is a myth, cloaking the truth that law consists simply of the decisions of courts and the prediction of them, can make a powerful appeal to a lawyer's candor. Stated in an unqualified general form, so as to embrace both secondary and primary rules, it is indeed quite incoherent; for the assertion that there are decisions of courts cannot consistently be combined with the denial that there are any rules at all. This

is so because, as we have seen, the existence of a court entails the existence of secondary rules conferring jurisdiction on a changing succession of individuals and so making their decisions authoritative. . . .

The [most] interesting form of rule-skepticism [rests] on the fact that the decision of a court has a unique position as something authoritative, and in the case of supreme tribunals, final. This form of the theory, to which we shall devote the next section, is implicit in Bishop Hoadly's famous phrase echoed so often by Gray in *The Nature and Sources of Law*, 'Nay whoever hath an absolute authority to interpret any written or spoken laws it is he who is the lawgiver to all intents and purposes and not the person who first wrote or spake them.' . . .

A supreme tribunal has the last word in saying what the law is and, when it has said it, the statement that the court was 'wrong' has no consequences within the system: no one's rights or duties are thereby altered. The decision may, of course, be deprived of legal effect by legislation, but the very fact that resort to this is necessary demonstrates the empty character, so far as the law is concerned, of the statement that the court's decision was wrong.

Consideration of these facts makes it seem pedantic to distinguish, in the case of a supreme tribunal's decisions, between their finality and infallibility. This leads to another form of the denial that courts in deciding are ever bound by rules: 'The law (or the constitution) is what the courts say it is.'

The most interesting and instructive feature of this form of the theory is its exploitation of the ambiguity of such statements as 'the law (or the constitution) is what the courts say it is', and the account which the theory must, to be consistent, give of the relation of non-official statements of law to the official statements of a court. To understand this ambiguity, we shall turn aside to consider its analogue in the case of a game. Many competitive games are played without an official scorer: notwithstanding their competing interests, the players succeed tolerably well in applying the scoring rule to particular cases; they usually agree in their judgments, and unresolved disputes may be few. Before the institution of an official scorer, a statement of the score made by a player represents, if he is honest, an effort to assess the progress of the game by reference to the particular scoring rule accepted in that game. Such statements of the score are internal statements applying the scoring rule, which though they presuppose that the players will, in general, abide by the rules and will object to their violation, are not statements or predictions of these facts.

Like the changes from a régime of custom to a mature system of law, the addition to the game of secondary rules providing for the institution of a scorer whose rulings are final, brings into the system a new kind of internal statement; for unlike the players' statements as to the score, the scorer's determinations are given, by secondary rules, a status which renders them unchallengeable. In *this* sense it is true that for the purposes of the game 'the score is what the scorer says it is'. But it is important to see that the scoring *rule* remains what it was before and it is the scorer's duty to apply it as best he can. 'The score is what the scorer says it is' would be false if it meant that there was no rule for scoring save what the scorer in his discretion chose to apply. There might indeed be a game with such a rule, and some amusement might be found in playing it if the scorer's discretion were exercised with some regularity; but it would be a different game. We may call such a game the game of 'scorer's discretion'.

It is plain that the advantages of quick and final settlement of disputes, which a scorer brings, are purchased at a price. The institution of a scorer may face the players with a predicament: the wish that the game should be regulated, as before, by the scoring rule and the wish for final authoritative decisions as to its application, where it is doubtful, may turn out to be conflicting aims. The scorer may make honest mistakes, be drunk or may wantonly violate his duty to apply the scoring rule to the best of his ability. He may for any of these reasons record a 'run' when the batsman has never moved. Provision may be made for correcting his rulings by appeal to a higher authority: but this must end somewhere in a final, authoritative judgment, which will be made by fallible human beings and so will carry with it the same risk of honest mistake, abuse, or violation. It is impossible to provide by rule for the correction of the breach of every rule.

The risk inherent in setting up an authority to make final authoritative applications of rules may materialize in any sphere. Those that might materialize in the humble sphere of a game are worth consideration, since they show, in a particularly clear fashion, that some of the inferences drawn by the rule-skeptic ignore certain distinctions which are necessary for the understanding of this form of authority wherever it is used. When an official scorer is established and his determinations of the score are made final, statements as to the score made by the players or other non–officials have no status within the game; they are irrelevant to its result. If they happen to coincide with the scorer's statement, well and good; if they conflict, they must be neglected in computing the result. But these very obvious facts would be distorted if the players' statements were classified as predictions of the scorer's rulings, and it would be absurd to explain the neglect of these statements, when they conflicted with the scorer's rulings, by saying that they were predictions of those rulings which had turned out to be false. The player, in making his own statements as to the score after the introduction of an official scorer, is doing what he did before: namely, assessing the progress of the game, as best he can, by reference to the scoring rule. This, too, is what the scorer himself, so long as he fulfills the duties of his position, is also doing. The difference between them is not that one is predicting what the other will say, but that the players' statements are unofficial

applications of the scoring rule and hence have no significance in computing the result; whereas the scorer's statements are authoritative and final. It is important to observe that if the game played were 'scorer's discretion' then the relationship between unofficial and official statements would necessarily be different: the players' statements not only *would* be a prediction of the scorer's rulings but *could* be nothing else. For in that case 'the score is what the scorer says it is' would itself be the scoring *rule*; there would be no possibility of the players' statements being merely unofficial versions of what the scorer does officially. Then the scorer's rulings would be both final and infallible—or rather the question whether they were fallible or infallible would be meaningless; for there would be nothing for him to get 'right' or 'wrong'. But in an ordinary game 'the score is what the scorer says it is' is not the scoring rule: it is a rule providing for the authority and finality of his application of the scoring rule in particular cases.

EDITOR'S NOTE: Now consider the following, from the revised edition of Llewellyn's *The Bramble Bush*:

Correcting an error: "What these officials do about disputes . . ."

On the old page 3 and on the present page 12 appear the words: *"What these officials do about disputes is, to my mind, the law itself."*

These words express a deep and often sad truth for any counsellor: he can get for his client what he can actually get, and no more. They express a deeper and often even sadder truth for any litigant: "rights" which cannot be realized are worse than useless; they are traps of delay, expense and heartache. The words pose the problem of reform of institutions and press upon us the eternal problem of the need for personnel careful, upright, wise. They signal the possibility of differential favoritism and prejudice on the one hand; the possibility, on the other, of

much good being brought out of an ill–designed and limping machinery of measures. In so far the words are useful words, and true ones, and I have let them stand.

They are, however, unhappy words when not more fully developed, and they are plainly at best a very partial statement of the whole truth. For it is clear that one office of law is to control officials in some part, and to guide them even in places where no thoroughgoing control is possible, or is desired. And it is clear that guidance and control for action and by others than the actor cannot be had out of the very action sought to be controlled or guided. Moreover, no man sees law whole who ever forgets that one inherent drive which is a living part of even the most wrongheaded and arbitrary legal system is a drive–patent or latent, throbbing or faint–pulsed, impatient or sluggish, but always present—to make the system, its detail and its officials more closely realize an ideal of justice. That drive works in ways so complex and varied as to be but dimly suggested in "what these officials do," in regard to any given occasion. Thus the words

fail to take proper account either of the office of the institution of law as an instrument for conscious shaping or of the office and work of that institution as a machinery of sometimes almost unconscious questing for the ideal; and the words therefore need some such expansion and correction as the foregoing.

Does Llewellyn in effect concede Hart's point? If Hart is right, what is the most plausible version of Legal Realism?

FREEDOM AND CONSTRAINT IN ADJUDICATION: A CRITICAL PHENOMENOLOGY

DUNCAN KENNEDY

This paper attempts to describe the process of legal reasoning as I imagine I might do it if I were a judge assigned a case that initially seemed to present a conflict between "the law" and "how–I–want–to–come–out." Such a description, if at all true to experience, may be helpful in assessing the various claims about and images of law that figure in jurisprudential, political, and social theoretical discussion. . . .

The judge is a federal district court judge in Boston. I'm more a ruling class elite type than a local politician or notable type, which is why I chose the federal forum. But what's most important is that the judge is responsible for deciding this case, rather than a party or an observer or an advocate. I am going to

be looking at law as a person who will have to apply it, interpret it, change it, defy it, or whatever. I will do this in the context of the legal and lay community that follows what federal district court judges do, and with the possibility of appeal always present to my mind.

The more complex conditions of this inquiry have to do with the polarity between my initial impression of "the law" and my initial sense of how–I–want–to–come–out. How–I–want–to–come–out might be based on my having been bribed and wanting to keep my bargain, or on a sense of what decision would be popular with my community (legal or local), or on what I thought the appeals court would likely do in the case of an appeal. It

Duncan Kennedy, excerpt from "Freedom and Constraint in Adjudication: A Critical Phenomenology," *Journal of Legal Education*, vol. 36 (1986), pp. 518 ff.

might be based on a sense that the equities of this particular case are peculiar because they favor an outcome different from what the law requires, even though the law is basically a very good one, and even though it was on balance a good decision to frame it so inflexibly that it couldn't adjust to take account of these particular equities.

Or it might be that I disagree with the way the law here resolves the problem of exceptional situations, believing that it could have been crafted to be flexible to take care of this case. Or it could be that I see the law here as "unfair" in the sense that, taking the rest of the system at face value, it would be better to change this rule. This rule might be an anomaly. (Later I will take up the question of the rules about the judge changing the rules.)

Instead of any of these objections, imagine that I think the rule that seems to apply is bad because it strikes the wrong balance between two identifiable conflicting groups, and does so as part of a generally unjust overall arrangement that includes many similar rules, all of which ought in the name of justice to change. I mean to suggest a "political" objection to the law, and a how-I-want-to-come-out that is part of a general plan of opposition.

Again, the experience of legality may well be different according to the character of the "I want" that opposes "the law." All I insist on is this: it is useless to discuss the conflict of "personal preference vs. law" without specifying what kind of preference we are dealing with.

■ ■ ■

Here's what I mean by my initial impression that the law requires a particular outcome. Suppose there is a strike of union bus drivers going on in Boston. The company hires nonunion drivers and sets out to resume service. On the first day union members lie down in the street outside the bus station to prevent the buses from passing.

They do not disturb the general flow of traffic, and they are nonviolent. The local police arrest them and cart them off, but this takes hours. They are charged with disturbing the peace and obstructing a public way (misdemeanors) and released on light bail. The next day other union members obstruct, with similar results. The buses run, but only late and amid a chaotic jumble. The company goes into federal court for an injunction against the union tactic.

When I first think about this case, not being a labor law expert, but having some general knowledge, I think, "there is no way they will be able to get away with this. The rule of law is going to be that workers cannot prevent the employer from making use of the buses during the strike. The company will get its injunction."

I disagree with this imagined rule. I don't think management should be allowed to operate the means of production [m.o.p.] with substitute labor during a strike. I think there should be a rule that until the dispute has been resolved, neither side can operate the m.o.p. without the permission of the other (barring various kinds of extraordinary circumstances). This view is part of a general preference for transforming the current modes of American economic life in a direction of greater worker self-activity, worker control and management of enterprise, in a decentralized setting that blurs the lines between "owner" and "worker," and "public" and "private" enterprise.

My feeling that the law is against me in this case is a quick intuition about the way things have to be. I haven't actually read any cases or articles that describe what the employer can and can't do with the m.o.p. during a strike. I vaguely remember *In Dubious Battle*, a Steinbeck classic I read when I was 16. But I would bet money that some such rule exists.

If there is a rule that the employer can do what he wants with the m.o.p., I think it will probably turn out to be true that there is relief in federal court (under the rubric of unfair labor practices?). If relief is available, I have a strong feeling that the workers threaten irreparable injury to the employer, so that he can show the various things usually required to justify an injunction. But I also vaguely remember that federal courts aren't supposed to issue injunctions in labor disputes.

There is lots of uncertainty here. I am not sure that a federal district court has jurisdiction under the labor law statutes to intervene on the employer's behalf when the local authorities are already enforcing the local general law about obstructing public ways. I am not sure that if there is a basis for federal intervention an injunction is appropriate. I will have to look into all these things before I'm at all sure how this case will or should come out.

On the other hand, I am quite sure the employer can use the m.o.p. as he pleases. And I am quite, quite sure that if there is such a rule, then the workers have violated it here. I am sure that what I mean by the rule is that the employer has both a privilege to act and a right to protection against interference, and that what the workers did here *was* interference.

Since the supposed rule of law that I don't like won't get applied so as to lead to an injunction unless all the uncertainties are resolved against the workers, I do not yet confront a direct conflict between the law and how–I–want–to–come–out. But I already have the feeling of "the law" as a constraint on me. It's time to ask what that means.

■ ■ ■

The initial apparent objectivity of the objectionable rule. I use the word objectivity here to indicate that from my point of view the *application of the rule to this case* feels like a nondiscretionary, necessary, compulsory procedure. I can no more deny that, if there is such a rule, the workers have violated it, than I can deny that I am at this minute in

Cambridge, Massachusetts, sitting on a chair, using a machine called a typewriter. The rule just applies itself. What I *meant* by interfering with the owner's use of the m.o.p. was workers lying down in the street when the employer tries to drive the buses out to resume service during the strike. I'm sure from the description that the workers actually intended to do exactly what the rule says they have no right to do.

Note that this sense of objectivity is internal—it's what happens in my head. But the minute I begin to think about the potential conflict between the law and how–I–want–to–come–out a quite different question will arise. How will other people see this case, supposing that the preliminary hurdles are overcome?

Sometimes it will seem to me that everyone (within the relevant universe) will react to this case as one to which the rule applies. I imagine them going through the same process I did, and it is instantly obvious that they too will see the workers as having violated the rule. If this happens, the rule application acquires a double objectivity. The reaction of other people is an anticipated fact like my anticipation that the sun will rise tomorrow or that this glass will break if I drop it on the floor.

It is important not to mush these forms of objectivity together. It is possible for me to see the case as "not clearly governed by the rule" when I do my interior rule application, but to anticipate that the relevant others will see it as "open and shut." And it is possible for me to see it as clear but to anticipate that others will see it as complex and confusing.

■ ■ ■

The next thing that happens is that I set to work on the problem of this case. I already have, as part of my life as I've lived it up to this moment, a set of intentions, a life-project as a judge, that will orient me among the many possible attitudes I could take to this work.

It so happens that I see myself as a political activist, someone with the "vocation of social transformation," as Roberto Unger put it. I see the set of rules in force as chosen by the people who had the power to make the choices in accord with their views on morality and justice and their own self-interest. And I see the rules as remaining in force because victimized groups have not had the political vision and energy and raw power to change them. I see myself as a focus of political energy for change in an egalitarian, communitarian, decentralized, democratic socialist direction (which doesn't mean these slogans are any help in figuring out what the hell to do in any particular situation).

■ ■ ■

Given my general orientation, the work I am going to do in this case will have two objectives, which may or may not conflict. I want these specific workers to get away with obstructing the buses, and I want to move the law as much as possible in the direction of allowing workers a measure of legally legitimated control over the disposition of the m.o.p. during a strike.

If my only objective were to avoid an injunction against lying down in front of the buses during this strike, I would be tempted toward a strategy that would allow me to avoid altogether the apparent legal rule forbidding worker interference. I could just delay, in the hope that the workers will win the strike before I'm forced to rule. I could focus on developing a new version of the facts, and hope to deny the injunction on that basis, or I could look for a "technicality" having no apparent substantive relevance (e.g., the statute of frauds, a mistake in the caption of a pleading).

On a more substantive level, I could put my energy into researching the issues of federal jurisdiction and the appropriateness of an injunction. Here, if the effort paid off, I might be able to move the law in a way favorable to workers in general, even though the move wouldn't formally address worker control over the m.o.p. during a strike.

But the strategy I want to discuss here is that of frontal assault on the application of the rule that the workers can't obstruct the company's use of the m.o.p. If this strategy succeeds, the result will be both to get the workers off in this case *and* to accomplish my law reform objective. There will be a small reduction in employers' power to invoke the state apparatus, a change that will be practically useful in future legal disputes over strikes. And the mantle of legal legitimacy will shift a little, from all out endorsement of management prerogatives to a posture that legitimates, to some degree, workers' claims to rights over the m.o.p.

■ ■ ■

What I see as interesting about the situation as I have portrayed it up to this point is that we are not dealing with a "case governed by a rule," but rather with a perception that a rule probably governs, and that applying the rule will very likely produce a particular (pro–employer) result. The judge is neither free nor bound. I don't see it that way from inside the situation. From inside the situation, the question is, Where am I going to deploy the resources I have available for this case? The issue is how should I direct my *work* to bring about an outcome that accords with my sense of justice. My situation as a judge (initial perceived conflict between "the law" and how–I–want–to–come–out) is thus quite like that of a lawyer who is brought a case by a client and on first run-through is afraid the client will lose. The question is, Will this first impression hold up as I set to work to develop the best possible case on the other side?

Having to work to achieve an outcome is in my view fundamental to the situation of the judge. It is neither a matter of being bound nor a matter of being free. Or, you could say that the judge is both free *and* bound—free to deploy work in any direction but limited by the pseudo–objectivity of the rule–as–applied, which he may or may not be able to overcome.

■ ■ ■

Isn't what I am doing illegitimate, from the standpoint of legality right from the start? One could argue that since I think the law favors the company I have no business trying to develop the best possible case for the union. But this misunderstands the rules of the game of legality. All members of the community know that one's initial impression that a particular rule governs and that when applied to the facts it yields X result is *often* wrong. That's what makes law such a trip. What at first looked open and shut is ajar, and what looked vague and altogether indeterminate abruptly reveals itself to be quite firmly settled under the circumstances.

So it is an important part of the role of judges and lawyers to test whatever conclusions they have reached about "the correct legal outcome" by trying to develop the best possible argument on the other side. In my role as an activist judge I am simply doing what I'm supposed to when I test my first impression against the best pro–union argument I can develop.

If I manage to develop a legal argument against the injunction, the ideal of impartiality requires me to test that argument in turn against a newly worked–out best counter–argument in favor of the company. Eventually, my time will run out, and I'll just have to decide.

What would betray legality would be to adopt the wrong attitude at the *end* of the reasoning process, when I've reached a conclusion about "what the law requires" and found it still conflicts with how–I–want–to–come–out.

For the moment, I'm free to play around.

■ ■ ■

The euphoric moment in which I conceive legal reasoning as "playing around with the rule" doesn't last long. What follows is panic as I rack my brain for any way around the overwhelming sense that if the rule is "workers can't interfere with the owner's use of the m.o.p. during a strike," then I cannot do anything for the union. I am ashamed of this panic. It's not just that I'm not coming up with anything; I also feel that I *should* be coming up with something. It's a disgrace—it shows I lack legal reasoning ability. I feel like a fool for trumpeting the indeterminacy of doctrine and claiming to be a manipulative whiz.

As my panic deepens, I begin to consider alternatives. If I can't mount an attack on the rule–as–applied, maybe I will have to research the earlier contract between the union and the bus company. I have a strong feeling that contracts are manipulable if one applies concepts like good faith, implication of terms, and the public interest, all relevant here. Maybe I'll have to try to "read something in." But this approach is clearly less good than going right for the rule itself.

Then I start thinking about the federal injunction aspect of the case, as opposed to the labor tort aspect. I'm sure that the combination of the 1930s anti–injunction statute with federal court injunctive enforcement of at least some terms in collective bargaining agreements (after *Lincoln Mills*? I can't quite remember) must have made a total hash of the question of when federal courts will grant injunctions. If only I could worry just about *that*, I bet I could easily come up with a good pro–worker argument. But that move is also less good than going for the rule.

Then there are the really third–rate solutions based on the hope that the facts will turn out to be at least arguably different than they seemed to be when I first heard about the case, and that the company's lawyers will make a stupid technical mistake.

■ ■ ■

All the while I'm desperately racking my brains. I think I have good maxims for legal reasoning, but what are they? The rule represents a compromise between two conflicting policies, so there must be a gray area where the terms of the compromise are not clear. But this case seems clear. There are *always* exceptions to the rule. But I can't think of any here.

When an idea starts to come, it just comes, little by little getting clearer, as I work to tease it out, flesh it out, add analogies. Here it is:

Of course (oh, how I love to feel that reassuring "of course" tripping off my tongue at the beginning of an argument), it is not *literally* true that the workers are forbidden from "interfering with the owners' use of the m.o.p. during a strike." They can picket and use all kinds of publicity measures to dissuade people from riding the company's buses.

Here I begin to lose my grip again. Lying down in the roadway is a far cry from picketing, which doesn't interfere at all *physically* with the company's use of the buses and is after all justified as an exercise of First Amendment rights. This exception won't do me any good.

After more false leads and panic (I try manipulating the concept of "owner" to get the workers a piece of the action but that tactic just seems to push me into the inferior implied contract route) I come back to my exception. The workers did lie down in the street to block the buses, but they did not intend to and did not in fact use force to prevent them from rolling. After all, they submitted peacefully to arrest. And the press was everywhere. Obviously the worker on the ground *could not have* physically prevented the bus from rolling, because it could have rolled right over him.

Still, on those two days of lie-ins the company failed to resume service in the fashion it had planned. The workers did physically obstruct the owner's use of the m.o p. and were delighted to do so. The disruption wasn't just a side effect.

On the other hand, maybe I can argue that the demonstration was a symbolic protest, an attempt to (a) exert moral suasion on the company by impressing it with the extreme feeling of the workers and their willingness to take risks, their sense that the company is theirs as much as management's and (b) a gesture toward the public through the media.

I will emphasize the non-violent civil disobedience aspects: a physical tactic that *could not in fact* have prevented the use of the m.o.p. by the company, and submission to arrest.

I could hold that because of these factors there should be no federal labor law injunctive remedy beyond what is accorded under state law (narrow version). Or that this demonstration is the exercise of First Amendment rights, so that injunction of a non-violent civil disobedient protest would be an unconstitutional restriction of expression, even though it is of course perfectly permissible for the state to arrest the demonstrators and subject them to its normal criminal process (broad version).

By this time, I'm getting high. I have no idea whether this line of argument will work. I have even lost track of exactly how this argument can be brought to bear in the employer's federal court action for an injunction. (This is probably because I've gotten into an argument on the merits before clarifying in my own mind what the basis of federal jurisdiction may be, and before getting into the anti-injunction Wagner Act issue.) But I am nonetheless delighted. My heart lifts because it seems that the work of legal reasoning within my pro-worker project is paying off.

■ ■ ■

The question is not whether my initial off-the-wall legal intuitions turn out to be right. They *may* eventually generate at least superficially plausible legal arguments. But maybe it will turn out that the law is so well settled in another direction that I will have to abandon them and try something else the minute I get out *Gorman on Labor Law* and *Prosser on Torts.* Legal reasoning is a kind of work with a purpose, and here the purpose is to make the case come out the way my sense of justice tells me it ought to, in spite of what seems at first like the *resistance* or *opposition* of "the law."

■ ■ ■

The metaphor of a physical medium does not help us solve the problem of just how constraining the law is. All it does is suggest that we should understand both freedom and constraint as aspects of the experience of work—chosen project constrained by material properties of the medium—rather than thinking in the back of our mind of a transcendentally free subject who "could do anything," contrasted with a robot programmed by the law.

One might accept the notion that legal argument is manipulation of the legal materials understood as a medium and still believe that the medium constrains very tightly. An absolutely basic question is whether there are some outcomes that you just can't reach so long as you obey the internal rules of the game of legal reasoning. These would be "things you just can't make with bricks," or silk purses you can't make with this particular sow's ear.

For the moment, make any assumption you want as to how tightly the medium constrains the message. Perhaps there is only one correct legal result in most cases, or perhaps there are some results that you simply can't reach through correct legal reasoning, or perhaps there will be a legally plausible course of reasoning to justify any result that you might want to reach.

What I want to ask is how, rather than how tightly law constrains, when we understand it as a medium through which my liberal activist judge–self pursues social justice. When we are clearer about this it will be

time to ask, first, whether it is even (or sometimes, or always) possible in the last analysis to have a conflict between the law and how–I–want–to–come–out, and, if so, what the ethics of the conflict may be.

■ ■ ■

I dealt here with a case in which my initial apprehension was that the law was clear against the workers, but I was able to undermine the perceived objectivity of the rule (at least in a preliminary way). That was an example among many possible of how an initial apprehension of ruledness can dissolve. Sometimes I approach the field in an agnostic frame of mind, and just can't figure out what the rule is supposed to be; sometimes I can't decide whether the facts are such that the outcome specified by the rule is triggered or not. Sometimes it seems there are several possible answers to the question and I don't have any feeling about which is correct. Sometimes I'm initially quite sure what the rule is and how to apply it but a conversation with another person who has reached a different set of conclusions leaves me feeling neither that I was "right" nor that she was "right," but rather that the rule was in fact hopelessly ambiguous or internally contradictory all along.

If you tell me that there is always a right answer to a legal problem, I will answer with these cases in which my experience was that the law was indeterminate, or that I gave it its determinate shape as a matter of my free ethical or political choice. It is true that when we are unselfconsciously applying rules together, we have an unselfconscious experience of social objectivity. We know what is going to happen next by mentally applying the rule as others will, and then they apply the rule and it comes out the way we thought it would. But this is not in fact objectivity, and it is *always* vulnerable to different kinds of disruption—intentional and accidental—that suddenly disappoint our expectations of consensus and make people question their own sanity and that of others. This vulnerability of the field, its plasticity, its instability, are just as essential to it as we experience it as its sporadic quality of resistance.

The rule may at any given moment appear objective; but at the next moment it may appear manipulable. It is not, *as I apprehend it from within the practice of legal argument,* essentially one thing or the other.

If this is what it is like to ask [about] the nature of law from within the practice of legal argument, then the answer to the question must come from outside that practice. All over the United States and indeed all over the world there are professors of jurisprudence who think they possess professional knowledge of the nature of law. Where are they getting it from? For my own part, I think their answers to questions like those I have been addressing are just made up out of whole cloth. Show me your ground before you pretend to be moving the earth.

QUESTIONS FOR DISCUSSION

1. In a footnote, Kennedy describes himself as carrying on, in this article, "an extension of the legal realist project." How does Kennedy's perspective seem similar to that of the Realists? How does it seem different?

2. How does Kennedy as judge decide how he would like the case to come out? How might other judges make the same decision?

3. Is Kennedy's claim a descriptive one about American law, or a conceptual claim about the nature of law? What is the difference, and why might it matter?

SUGGESTIONS FOR FURTHER READING

An excellent analysis of Legal Realism is William Twining, *Karl Llewellyn and the Realist Movement* (London: Weidenfeld and Nicolson, 1973). Also useful is W.E. Rumble, *American Legal Realism: Skepticism, Reform, and the Legal Process* (Ithaca: Cornell University Press, 1968). A more historical approach is Laura Kalman, *Legal Realism at Yale* (Chapel Hill: University of North Carolina Press, 1986). A lively version of the central Realist claims, but less subtle than Llewellyn, is Jerome Frank, *Law and the Modern Mind* (New York: Brentano's, 1930). Many of Llewellyn's shorter works are collected in *Jurisprudence: Realism in Theory and Practice* (Chicago: University of Chicago Press, 1962).

On Critical Legal Studies, an important collection of articles is in "Critical Legal Studies Symposium," *Stanford Law Review,* vol. 36 (1984), pp. 1 ff. One of the most prominent Critical Legal Studies theorists is Roberto Unger. On the relationship between Critical Legal Studies and some of the themes of this chapter, see Unger's *The Critical Legal Studies Movement* (Cambridge: Harvard University Press, 1986). Unger's most important works are *Knowledge and Politics* (New York: The Free Press, 1975) and *Law in Modern Society* (New York: The Free Press, 1976). For a sympathetic overview of many Critical Legal Studies themes, see Mark Kelman, *A Guide to Critical Legal Studies* (Cambridge: Harvard University Press, 1987). An excellent analysis and critique is Andrew Altman, *Critical Legal Studies: A Liberal Critique* (Princeton: Princeton University Press, 1990).

1.4 RONALD DWORKIN AND LAW AS INTEGRITY

INTRODUCTION

Recall from the introduction to this chapter that it is not always clear why we ask the question, "What is Law?"; that it is not always clear that we should be asking it; and that it is not always clear what we are doing when we try to answer that question. Let us consider again one tradition sketched by Jules Coleman in an important article entitled "Negative and Positive Positivism."[27] Coleman says that when we ask about the nature or definition of law, we are trying to understand the *concept* of law in its deepest sense. When we do this, Coleman goes on, we are thus trying to see what might be true of the concept of law in all possible legal systems in all possible worlds. The inquiries are analytic and conceptual, rather than empirical or contingent. This is certainly the kind of inquiry that much of the natural law tradition sees itself as pursuing, and this is what Coleman sees as his own agenda in making the case for legal positivism and against natural law. For Coleman it is crucially (and morally) important to see that law is a human creation, and that all of the dimensions of law, especially its connection with morality, are human artifacts. In making the case for legal positivism, Coleman therefore seeks to deny the natural law claim that there is a necessary connection between law and morality in all possible legal systems in all possible worlds. This logically leaves open the possibility that there is a necessary connection between law and morality in some legal systems. Indeed, it leaves open the possibility that there is, but as a contingent empirical fact and not as a conceptual truth, a necessary connection between law and morality in all legal systems of which we are aware. Coleman wants to show that the concept of law itself is a morally thin one, and that we ought to confront our moral questions directly and not in the guise of definitions of law.

Not everyone sees the enterprise of legal philosophy in the same way that Coleman does, however. Ronald Dworkin, among the most important of contemporary legal philosophers, studiously attempts to avoid giving a formal definition of the concept of law. Dworkin is much more concerned with understanding how law operates, and what law is, in the legal systems with which we are most familiar. Behind this seemingly modest goal, however, is a profound challenge to legal positivism, albeit one that can be understood best by understanding first

---

[27]Jules Coleman, "Negative and Positive Positivism," in *Markets, Morals and the Law* (Cambridge: Cambridge University Press, 1988), pp. 3 ff.

that the questions that concern Dworkin are not the ones that concern Coleman. Somewhat in the tradition of the Legal Realists, although often with starkly different conclusions, Dworkin focuses on the judge and uses judicial decisions in actual legal systems as his way of challenging the legal positivist picture of law as demarcated by a set of primary rules identified by secondary rules of recognition. Like the Legal Realists, and like Duncan Kennedy's "A Critical Phenomenology . . .", Dworkin challenges the dominance of formal or paper legal rules within judicial decision making. But unlike the Realists and unlike Critical Legal Studies, Dworkin does not take the relative absence of formal rule–based legal constraint as suggesting a relative lack of constraint at all. Rather, Dworkin sees the constraint both in the methods of the judge and in the full array of society's previous political as well as legal decisions. His focus on interpretation, reflected most prominently in *Law's Empire*, is Dworkin's way simultaneously of rejecting a rule-based picture of law without rejecting the idea that judges are different from other kinds of official decision makers.

What intrigues Dworkin, as the following selections and cases indicate, are the sources on which judges draw in making their decisions. Under the legal positivist picture as set out primarily by Hart, cases often lie within the core of a settled rule (as with the ordinary private automobile coming within the core of the "No Vehicles in the Park" rule) or lie within the fringe or penumbra of a rule (as with roller skates, bicycles, and baby carriages). Hart admits that the rules recognized by a rule of recognition cannot help us very much in deciding cases lying within the penumbra, and certainly not in deciding cases lying within some court's jurisdiction but as to which there is no rule at all (or two rules directly contradicting each other). In such cases positivists like Hart say that the judge, if she is to decide the case at all, must then exercise her *discretion*. Because the law has "run out," the judge, when she is exercising her discretion in such cases, is simply and unashamedly making new law. If, based on the same kinds of considerations and facts used by legislators, the judge were to decide that bicycles were to be considered vehicles, then the judge would have made new law to that effect. If the decision stated clearly that bicycles were now to be considered vehicles, and if the decision were to be followed by other judges, then the effect of this decision would be for the future to take one class of cases out of the penumbra of this rule and place it into the core. Under the positivist picture, therefore, there are easy cases within the core, in which legal officials apply the rules. And there are also hard cases outside of the core, in which legal officials exercise discretion and in the process make new rules and new law.

Yet this classic positivist picture strikes Dworkin as simply empirically false. Consider *Riggs v. Palmer* and *Henningsen v. Bloomfield Motors*, both described at length by Dworkin in "The Model of Rules." In both of these cases it appears as if the facts fell within the core of a legal rule recognized by a rule of recognition. In *Riggs*, for example, the grandson who killed his grandfather in order to get his inheritance more quickly did not present a fringe or penumbral case. Instead, the Statute of Wills, read literally, made it clear that the grandson would inherit, the murder notwithstanding. Yet the judges did not follow the literal reading of the Statute of Wills, but instead reached the opposite result, not by consulting another rule, but by consulting a larger, broader, and more amorphous *principle*. Although some principles might be recognized by legal rules of recognition, not all of them have been, and it is Dworkin's central attack on positivism that the principles that judges might use to set aside even settled rules of law are not only the principles that we could find in law books, but the full range of principles available in a society's political culture. If that is so, then there is little, if any, connection between the rules recognized by a rule of recognition and the realities of judicial practice, for judges are not in fact, in any case, limited to the rules recognized by a rule of recognition in reaching their decisions.

Defenders of legal positivism have questioned whether Dworkin's quasi-empirical account, even if true, constitutes an attack on positivism at all. The ultimate rule of recognition in some societies, theorists like Coleman and the American moral and legal philosopher David Lyons (1935–   ) argue,[28] might recognize as legal rules all of the moral principles that Dworkin discusses. Indeed, the ultimate rule of recognition might even empower judges to use all of the moral principles of which they are aware in deciding cases. This would still be consistent with the positivist perspective, they argue, because this empowerment would be a product of a social decision, a continent fact about some societies and not a necessary feature of the concept of law. We might have a legal system in which judges were empowered to decide only according to a narrower class of legal rules—the kinds found in lawbooks published by recognized legal publishers—but this would still be a legal system. Dworkin, they say, has confused the contingent features of American (and perhaps English) law with necessary truths about the very concept of law.

"But what's the point?" Dworkin might respond. If it turns out that judges, the prototypical legal officials, are not restricted to *legal* norms in some system, then in that system positivism is best thought of as false, rather than a theoretical construct allowing an essentially infinite range of legal systems. If judges are not restricted to the law in lawbooks, but can look at a much larger collection of moral and political values, then why be concerned about the difference between what is in the lawbooks and what is not? Positivism thus might be correct, Dworkin could respond, as a denial of the natural law claim that there is a necessary connection between law and morality in all possible legal systems in all possible worlds. But when we get back to this planet, there are more important issues than just challenging this version of the natural law position. That is why, Dworkin could continue, there is a more down-to-earth version of legal positivism, one that sees legal rules as a subset of and not congruent with the total set of all moral and social norms and sees the rules recognized by rules of recognition as actually dominating legal decision making. That is a more important positivist claim, Dworkin could say, but that claim turns out to be false.

So if judges draw on sources other than individual rules, how do they make their decisions? Here Dworkin famously challenges the positivist vision of judges as exercising discretion when the rules do not control. Rather, if we examine ac-

[28]David Lyons, "Principles, Positivism, and Legal Theory," *Yale Law Journal*, vol. 87 (1977), pp. 415 ff.

tual legal practice we do not see lawyers arguing that it would be good policy for a case to be decided in such and such a way. Instead they argue that their clients have a *right* that a case be decided in their favor, not just that it would be wise public policy for that to be the result. Moreover, when judges decide cases they do not make their decisions sound like decisions of policy. Indeed, if they did, it would seem unfair that their policy decisions were applied retroactively to the parties then before the court. So we see judges saying that Mary Smith won because she had a pre-existing legal right to win, and that pre-existing legal right explains why it is not unfair to apply that result even to John Jones, the loser in that very case.

In the very cases in which the positivist claims there is discretion, therefore, Dworkin says that there is, in theory, a *right answer*. This claim of Dworkin's is often misunderstood, however. Dworkin is not claiming that we can easily read the right answer off of noncontroversial materials. Instead, he argues that the very nature of legal argument and legal practice, including the practice of retro-active application of results even when it seems that the law has changed, pre-supposes the existence of a right answer in theory and presupposes that judges reaching conclusions, including conclusions not explicitly reached before, still un-derstand themselves as having discovered the law rather than as having made it. Dworkin often makes this point through his mythical judge Hercules. Dworkin uses Hercules not to describe the typical American judge, but rather to portray what the best judges aspire to, in Dworkin's view. Hercules is thus someone seek-ing, as the following readings indicate, to come up with the single best interpreta-tion of society's past political decisions (some, but not all, of which look very much like formal law). Having come up with this best interpretation, Hercules then applies it to the case at hand. This decision may be controversial, but it is the act of trying to come up with the best interpretation of past political deci-sions, just like the act of trying to come up with the best interpretation of a work of art or literature, that lies at the center of the "One Right Answer" thesis.

In his most recent work Dworkin has developed further the interpretive methods that judges can, often do, and at their best should, use in reaching their conclusions. The excerpt that follows from *Law's Empire* shows Dworkin arguing that legal decision making is essentially an interpretive act. Judges according to this account interpret the full range of a society's previous political decisions, in-cluding but not limited to the decisions reached by courts. Having done this, they then try to weave these past political decisions into a coherent "story," and then make a decision in the current case that attempts to make the "story" told by the previous decisions the "best it can be." In reading Dworkin's account, consider the question what "data" the judge is interpreting, because this is the issue that con-nects Dworkin's focus on interpretation with his earlier challenges to legal posi-tivism. And consider as well the analogy between interpreting law and interpreting art, literature, and history. Is the analogy close? Should it be?

TAKING RIGHTS SERIOUSLY

RONALD DWORKIN

THE MODEL OF RULES I

2. Positivism

Positivism has a few central and organizing propositions as its skeleton, and though not every philosopher who is called a positivist would subscribe to these in the way I present them, they do define the general position I want to examine. These key tenets may be stated as follows:

(a) The law of a community is a set of special rules used by the community directly or indirectly for the purpose of determining which behavior will be punished or coerced by the public power. These special rules can be identified and distinguished by specific criteria, by tests having to do not with their content but with their *pedigree* or the manner in which they were adopted or developed. These tests of pedigree can be used to distinguish valid legal rules from spurious legal rules (rules which lawyers and litigants wrongly argue are rules of law) and also from other sorts of social rules (generally lumped together as 'moral rules') that the community follows but does not enforce through public power.

(b) The set of these valid legal rules is exhaustive of 'the law', so that if someone's case is not clearly covered by such a rule (because there is none that seems appropriate, or those that seem appropriate are vague, or for some other reason) then that case cannot be decided by 'applying the law.' It must be decided by some official, like a judge, 'exercising his discretion,' which means reaching beyond the law for some other sort of standard to guide him in manufacturing a fresh legal rule or supplementing an old one.

(c) To say that someone has a 'legal obligation' is to say that his case falls under a valid legal rule that requires him to do or to forbear from doing something. (To say he has a legal right, or has a legal power of some sort, or a legal privilege or immunity, is to assert, in a shorthand way, that others have actual or hypothetical legal obligations to act or not to act in certain ways touching him.) In the absence of such a valid legal rule there is no legal obligation; it follows that when the judge decides an issue by exercising his discretion, he is not enforcing a legal right as to that issue.

This is only the skeleton of positivism. The flesh is arranged differently by different positivists, and some even tinker with the bones. Different versions differ chiefly in their description of the fundamental test of pedigree a rule must meet to count as a rule of law. . . .

3. Rules, Principles, and Policies

I want to make a general attack on positivism, and I shall use H. L. A. Hart's version as a target, when a particular target is needed. My strategy will be organized around the fact that when lawyers reason or dispute about legal rights and obligations, particularly in those hard cases when our problems with these concepts seem most acute, they make use of standards that do not function as rules, but operate differently as principles, policies, and other sorts of standards. Positivism, I

Selections from Chapters 2 ("The Model of Rules I") and 4 ("Hard Cases") of Ronald Dworkin, *Taking Rights Seriously* (Cambridge: Harvard University Press, 1977)

shall argue, is a model of and for a system of rules, and its central notion of a single fundamental test for law forces us to miss the important roles of these standards that are not rules.

I just spoke of 'principles, policies, and other sorts of standards'. Most often I shall use the term 'principle' generically, to refer to the whole set of these standards other than rules; occasionally, however, I shall be more precise, and distinguish between principles and policies. Although nothing in the present argument will turn on the distinction, I should state how I draw it. I call a 'policy' that kind of standard that sets out a goal to be reached, generally an improvement in some economic, political, or social feature of the community (though some goals are negative, in that they stipulate that some present feature is to be protected from adverse change). I call a 'principle' a standard that is to be observed, not because it will advance or secure an economic, political, or social situation deemed desirable, but because it is a requirement of justice or fairness or some other dimension of morality. Thus the standard that automobile accidents are to be decreased is a policy, and the standard that no man may profit by his own wrong a principle. The distinction can be collapsed by construing a principle as stating a social goal (i.e., the goal of a society in which no man profits by his own wrong), or by construing a policy as stating a principle (i.e., the principle that the goal the policy embraces is a worthy one) or by adopting the utilitarian thesis that principles of justice are disguised statements of goals (securing the greatest happiness of the greatest number). In some contexts the distinction has uses which are lost if it is thus collapsed.

My immediate purpose, however, is to distinguish principles in the generic sense from rules, and I shall start by collecting some examples of the former. The examples I offer are chosen haphazardly; almost any case in a law school casebook would provide examples that would serve as well. In 1889 a New York court, in the famous case of *Riggs v. Palmer*, had to decide whether an heir named in the will of his grandfather could inherit under that will, even though he had murdered his grandfather to do so. The court began its reasoning with this admission: 'It is quite true that statutes regulating the making, proof and effect of wills, and the devolution of property, if literally construed, and if their force and effect can in no way and under no circumstances be controlled or modified, give this property to the murderer.' But the court continued to note that 'all laws as well as all contracts may be controlled in their operation and effect by general, fundamental maxims of the common law. No one shall be permitted to profit by his own fraud, or to take advantage of his own wrong, or to found any claim upon his own iniquity, or to acquire property by his own crime.' The murderer did not receive his inheritance.

In 1960, a New Jersey court was faced, in *Henningsen v. Bloomfield Motors, Inc.*, with the important question of whether (or how much) an automobile manufacturer may limit his liability in case the automobile is defective. Henningsen had bought a car, and signed a contract which said that the manufacturer's liability for defects was limited to 'making good' defective parts—'this warranty being expressly in lieu of all other warranties, obligations or liabilities.' Henningsen argued that, at least in the circumstances of his case, the manufacturer ought not to be protected by this limitation, and ought to be liable for the medical and other expenses of persons injured in a crash. He was not able to point to any statute, or to any established rule of law, that prevented the manufacturer from standing on the contract. The court nevertheless agreed with Henningsen. At various points in the court's argument the following appeals to standards are made: (a) '[W]e must keep in mind the general principle that, in the absence of fraud, one who does not choose to read a contract before signing it cannot later relieve himself of its burdens. (b) 'In applying that principle, the basic tenet of freedom of competent parties to contract is a factor of importance.' (c) 'Freedom of contract is not such an immutable doctrine as to admit of no qualification in the area in which we are concerned.' (d) 'In a society such as ours, where the automobile is a common and necessary adjunct of daily life, and where its use is so fraught with danger to the driver, passengers and the public, the manufacturer is under a special obligation in connection with the construction, promotion and sale of his cars. Consequently, the courts must examine purchase agreements closely to see if consumer and public interests are treated fairly.' (e) '[I]s there any principle which is more familiar or more firmly embedded in the history of Anglo-American law than the basic doctrine that the courts will not permit themselves to be used as instruments of inequity and injustice?' (f) 'More specifically the courts generally refuse to lend themselves to the enforcement of a 'bargain' in which one party has unjustly taken advantage of the economic necessities of other . . . .'

The standards set out in these quotations are not the sort we think of as legal rules. They seem very different from propositions like 'The maximum legal speed on the turnpike is sixty miles an hour' or 'A will is invalid unless signed by three witnesses'. They are different because they are legal principles rather than legal rules.

The difference between legal principles and legal rules is a logical distinction. Both sets of standards point to particular decisions about legal obligation in particular circumstances, but they differ in the character of the direction they give. Rules are applicable in an all-or-nothing fashion. If the facts a rule stipulates are given, then either the rule

is valid, in which case the answer it supplies must be accepted, or it is not, in which case it contributes nothing to the decision.

This all-or-nothing is seen most plainly if we look at the way rules operate, not in law, but in some enterprise they dominate—a game, for example. In baseball a rule provides that if the batter has had three strikes, he is out. An official cannot consistently acknowledge that this is an accurate statement of a baseball rule, and decide that a batter who has had three strikes is not out. Of course, a rule may have exceptions (the batter who has taken three strikes is not out if the catcher drops the third strike). However, an accurate statement of the rule would take this exception into account, and any that did not would be incomplete. If the list of exceptions is very large, it would be too clumsy to repeat them each time the rule is cited; there is, however, no reason in theory why they could not all be added on, and the more that are, the more accurate is the statement of the rule.

If we take baseball as a model we find that rules of law, like the rule that a will is invalid unless signed by three witnesses, fit the model well. If the requirement of three witnesses is a valid legal rule, then it cannot be that a will has been signed by only two witnesses and is valid. The rule might have exceptions, but if it does then it is inaccurate and incomplete to state the rule so simply, without enumerating the exceptions. In theory, at least, the exceptions could all be listed, and the more of them that are, the more complete is the statement of the rule.

But this is not the way the sample principles in the quotations operate. Even those which look most like rules do not set out legal consequences that follow automatically when the conditions provided are met. We say that our law respects the principle that no man may profit from his own wrong, but we do not mean that the law never permits a man to profit from wrongs he commits. In fact, people often profit, perfectly legally, from their legal wrongs. The most notorious case is adverse possession—if I trespass on your land long enough, some day I will gain a right to cross your land whenever I please. There are many less dramatic examples. If a man leaves one job, breaking a contract, to take a much higher paying job, he may have to pay damages to his first employer, but he is usually entitled to keep his new salary. If a man jumps bail and crosses state lines to make a brilliant investment in another state, he may be sent back to jail, but he will keep his profits.

We do not treat these—and countless other counter-instances that can easily be imagined—as showing that the principle about profiting from one's wrongs is not a principle of our legal system, or that it is incomplete and needs qualifying exceptions. We do not treat counter-instances as exceptions (at least not exceptions in the way in which a catcher's dropping the third strike is an exception) because we could not hope to capture these counter-instances simply by a more extended statement of the principle. They are not, even in theory, subject to enumeration, because we would have to include not only these cases (like adverse possession) in which some institution has already provided that profit can be gained through a wrong, but also those numberless imaginary cases in which we know in advance that the principle would not hold. Listing some of these might sharpen our sense of the principle's weight (I shall mention that dimension in a moment), but it would not make for a more accurate or complete statement of the principle.

A principle like 'No man may profit from his own wrong' does not even purport to set out conditions that make its application necessary. Rather, it states a reason that argues in one direction, but does not neces-sitate a particular decision. If a man has or is about to receive something, as a direct result of something illegal he did to get it, then that is a reason which the law will take into account in deciding whether he should keep it. There may be other principles or policies arguing in the other direction—a policy of securing title, for example, or a principle limiting punishment to what the legislature has stipulated. If so, our principle may not prevail, but that does not mean that it is not a principle of our legal system, because in the next case, when these contravening considerations are absent or less weighty, the principle may be decisive. All that is meant, when we say that a particular principle is a principle of our law, is that the principle is one which officials must take into account, if it is relevant, as a consideration inclining in one direction or another.

The logical distinction between rules and principles appears more clearly when we consider principles that do not even look like rules. Consider the proposition, set out under '(d)' in the excerpts from the *Henningsen* opinion, that 'the manufacturer is under a special obligation in connection with the construction, promotion and sale of his cars'. This does not even purport to define the specific duties such a special obligation entails, or to tell us what rights automobile consumers acquire as a result. It merely states—and this is an essential link in the *Henningsen* argument—that automobile manufacturers must be held to higher standards than other manufacturers, and are less entitled to rely on the competing principle of freedom of contract. It does not mean that they may never rely on that principle, or that courts may rewrite automobile purchase contracts at will; it means only that if a particular clause seems unfair or burdensome, courts have less reason to enforce the clause than if it were for the purchase of neckties. The 'special obligation' counts in favor, but

does not in itself necessitate, a decision refusing to enforce the terms of an automobile
purchase contract.

This first difference between rules and
principles entails another. Principles have a
dimension that rules do not—the dimension
of weight or importance. When principles
intersect (the policy of protecting automobile
consumers intersecting with principles of
freedom of contract, for example), one who
must resolve the conflict has to take into account the relative weight of each. This cannot be, of course, an exact measurement, and
the judgment that a particular principle or
policy is more important than another will
often be a controversial one. Nevertheless, it
is an integral part of the concept of a principle that it has this dimension, that it makes
sense to ask how important or how weighty
it is.

Rules do not have this dimension. We
can speak of rules as being *functionally* important or unimportant (the baseball rule
that three strikes are out is more important
than the rule that runners may advance on a
balk, because the game would be much
more changed with the first rule altered than
the second). In this sense, one legal rule may
be more important than another because it
has a greater or more important role in regulating behavior. But we cannot say that one
rule is more important than another within
the system of rules, so that when two rules
conflict one supersedes the other by virtue
of its greater weight. . . .

4. Principles and the Concept of Law

Once we identify legal principles as separate sorts of standards, different from legal
rules, we are suddenly aware of them all
around us. Law teachers teach them, lawbooks cite them, legal historians celebrate
them. But they seem most energetically at
work, carrying most weight, in difficult lawsuits like *Riggs* and *Henningsen*. In cases like
these, principles play an essential part in ar-

guments supporting judgments about particular legal rights and obligations. After the
case is decided, we may say that the case
stands for a particular rule (e.g., the rule that
one who murders is not eligible to take
under the will of his victim). But the rule
does not exist before the case is decided; the
court cites principles as its justification for
adopting and applying a new rule. In *Riggs*,
the court cited the principle that no man
may profit from his own wrong as a background standard against which to read the
statute of wills and in this way justified a
new interpretation of that statute. In *Henningsen*, the court cited a variety of intersecting principles and policies as authority for a
new rule respecting manufacturer's liability
for automobile defects.

An analysis of the concept of legal obligation must therefore account for the important role of principles in reaching particular
decisions of law. There are two very different
tacks we might take:

(a) We might treat legal principles the
way we treat legal rules and say that some
principles are binding as law and must be
taken into account by judges and lawyers
who make decisions of legal obligation. If we
took this tack, we should say that in the
United States, at least, the 'law' includes
principles as well as rules.

(b) We might, on the other hand, deny
that principles can be binding the way some
rules are. We would say, instead, that in
cases like *Riggs* or *Henningsen* the judge
reaches beyond the rules that he is bound to
apply (reaches, that is, beyond the 'law') for
extra-legal principles he is free to follow if
he wishes.

One might think that there is not much
difference between these two lines of attack,
that it is only a verbal question of how one
wants to use the word 'law'. But that is a
mistake, because the choice between these
two accounts has the greatest consequences
for an analysis of legal obligation. It is a

choice between two *concepts* of a legal principle, a choice we can clarify by comparing it to a choice we might make between two concepts of a legal rule. We sometimes say of someone that he 'makes it a rule' to do something, when we mean that he has chosen to follow a certain practice. We might say that someone has made it a rule, for example, to run a mile before breakfast because he wants to be healthy and believes in a regimen. We do not mean, when we say this, that he is *bound* by the rule that he must run a mile before breakfast, or even that he regards it as binding upon him. Accepting a rule as binding is something different from making it a rule to do something. If we use Hart's example again, there is a difference between saying that Englishmen make it a rule to see a movie once a week, and saying that the English have a rule that one must see a movie once a week. The second implies that if an Englishman does not follow the rule, he is subject to criticism or censure, but the first does not. The first does not exclude the possibility of a *sort* of criticism—we can say that one who does not see movies is neglecting his education—but we do not suggest that he is doing something wrong *just* in not following the rule.

If we think of the judges of a community as a group, we could describe the rules of law they follow in these two different ways. We could say, for instance, that in a certain state the judges make it a rule not to enforce wills unless there are three witnesses. This would not imply that the rare judge who enforces such a will is doing anything wrong just for that reason. On the other hand we can say that in that state a rule of law requires judges not to enforce such wills; this does imply that a judge who enforces them is doing something wrong. Hart, Austin and other positivists, of course, would insist on this latter account of legal rules; they would not at all be satisfied with the 'make it a rule' account. It is not a verbal

question of which account is right. It is a question of which describes the social situation more accurately. Other important issues turn on which description we accept. If judges simply 'make it a rule' not to enforce certain contracts, for example, then we cannot say, before the decision, that anyone is 'entitled' to that result, and that proposition cannot enter into any justification we might offer for the decision.

The two lines of attack on principles parallel these two accounts of rules. The first tack treats principles as binding upon judges, so that they are wrong not to apply the principles when they are pertinent. The second tack treats principles as summaries of what most judges 'make it a principle' to do when forced to go beyond the standards that bind them. The choice between these approaches will affect, perhaps even determine, the answer we can give to the question whether the judge in a hard case like *Riggs* or *Henningsen* is attempting to enforce pre-existing legal rights and obligations. If we take the first tack, we are still free to argue that because such judges are applying binding legal standards they are enforcing legal rights and obligations. But if we take the second, we are out of court on that issue, and we must acknowledge that the murderer's family in *Riggs* and the manufacturer in *Henningsen* were deprived of their property by an act of judicial discretion applied *ex post facto*. This may not shock many readers—the notion of judicial discretion has percolated through the legal community—but it does illustrate one of the most nettlesome of the puzzles that drive philosophers to worry about legal obligation. If taking property away in cases like these cannot be justified by appealing to an established obligation, another justification must be found, and nothing satisfactory has yet been supplied.

In my skeleton diagram of positivism, previously set out, I listed the doctrine of judicial discretion as the second tenet. Positivists hold that when a case is not covered by a clear rule, a judge must exercise his discretion to decide that case by what amounts to a fresh piece of legislation. There may be an important connection between this doctrine and the question of which of the two approaches to legal principles we must take. We shall therefore want to ask whether the doctrine is correct, and whether it implies the second approach, as it seems on its face to do. En route to these issues, however, we shall have to polish our understanding of the concept of discretion. I shall try to show how certain confusions about that concept and in particular a failure to discriminate different senses in which it is used, account for the popularity of the doctrine of discretion. I shall argue that in the sense in which the doctrine does have a bearing on our treatment of principles, it is entirely unsupported by the arguments the positivists use to defend it.

5. Discretion

The concept of discretion was lifted by the positivists from ordinary language, and to understand it we must put it back in *habitat* for a moment. What does it mean, in ordinary life, to say that someone 'has discretion?' The first thing to notice is that the concept is out of place in all but very special contexts. For example, you would not say that I either do or do not have discretion to choose a house for my family. It is not true that I have 'no discretion' in making that choice, and yet it would be almost equally misleading to say that I do have discretion. The concept of discretion is at home in only one sort of context; when someone is in general charged with making decisions subject to standards set by a particular authority. It makes sense to speak of the discretion of a sergeant who is subject to orders of superiors, or the discretion of a sports official or contest judge who is governed by a

rule book or the terms of the contest. Discretion, like the hole in a doughnut, does not exist except as an area left open by a surrounding belt of restriction. It is therefore a relative concept. It always makes sense to ask, 'Discretion under which standards?' or 'Discretion as to which authority?' Generally the context will make the answer to this plain, but in some cases the official may have discretion from one stand-point though not from another.

Like almost all terms, the precise meaning of 'discretion' is affected by features of the context. The term is always colored by the background of understood information against which it is used. Although the shadings are many, it will be helpful for us to recognize some gross distinctions.

Sometimes we use 'discretion' in a weak sense, simply to say that for some reason the standards an official must apply cannot be applied mechanically but demand the use of judgment. We use this weak sense when the context does not already make that clear, when the background our audience assumes does not contain that piece of information. Thus we might say, 'The sergeant's orders left him a great deal of discretion', to those who do not know what the sergeant's orders were or who do not know something that made those orders vague or hard to carry out. It would make perfect sense to add, by way of amplification, that the lieutenant had ordered the sergeant to take his five most experienced men on patrol but that it was hard to determine which were the most experienced.

Sometimes we use the term in a different weak sense, to say only that some official has final authority to make a decision and cannot be reviewed and reversed by any other official. We speak this way when the official is part of a hierarchy of officials structured so that some have higher authority but in which the patterns of authority are different for different classes of decision. Thus we might say that in baseball certain decisions, like the decision whether the ball or the runner reached second base first, are left to the discretion of the second base umpire, if we mean that on this issue the head umpire has no power to substitute his own judgment if he disagrees.

I call both of these senses weak to distinguish them from a stronger sense. We use 'discretion' sometimes not merely to say that an official must use judgment in applying the standards set him by authority, or that no one will review that exercise of judgment, but to say that on some issue he is simply not bound by standards set by the authority in question. In this sense we say that a sergeant has discretion who has been told to pick any five men for patrol he chooses or that a judge in a dog show has discretion to judge airedales before boxers if the rules do not stipulate an order of events. We use this sense not to comment on the vagueness or difficulty of the standards, or on who has the final word in applying them, but on their range and the decisions they purport to control. If the sergeant is told to take the five most experienced men, he does not have discretion in this strong sense because that order purports to govern his decision. The boxing referee who must decide which fighter has been the more aggressive does not have discretion, in the strong sense, for the same reason.

If anyone said that the sergeant or the referee had discretion in these cases, we should have to understand him, if the context permitted, as using the term in one of the weak senses. Suppose, for example, the lieutenant ordered the sergeant to select the five men he deemed most experienced, and then added that the sergeant had discretion to choose them. Or the rules provided that the referee should award the round to the more aggressive fighter, with discretion in selecting him. We should have to under-

stand these statements in the second weak sense, as speaking to the question of review of the decision. The first weak sense—that the decisions take judgment—would be otiose, and the third, strong sense is excluded by the statements themselves.

We must avoid one tempting confusion. The strong sense of discretion is not tantamount to license, and does not exclude criticism. Almost any situation in which a person acts (including those in which there is no question of decision under special authority, and so no question of discretion) makes relevant certain standards of rationality, fairness, and effectiveness. We criticize each other's acts in terms of these standards, and there is no reason not to do so when the acts are within the center rather than beyond the perimeter of the doughnut of special authority. So we can say that the sergeant who was given discretion (in the strong sense) to pick a patrol did so stupidly or maliciously or carelessly, or that the judge who had discretion in the order of viewing dogs made a mistake because he took boxers first although there were only three airedales and many more boxers. An official's discretion means not that he is free to decide without recourse to standards of sense and fairness, but only that his decision is not controlled by a standard furnished by the particular authority we have in mind when we raise the question of discretion. Of course this latter sort of freedom is important; that is why we have the strong sense of discretion. Someone who has discretion in this third sense can be criticized, but not for being disobedient, as in the case of the soldier. He can be said to have made a mistake, but not to have deprived a participant of a decision to which he was entitled, as in the case of a sports official or contest judge.

We may now return, with these observations in hand, to the positivists' doctrine of judicial discretion. That doctrine argues that if a case is not controlled by an established rule, the judge must decide it by exercising discretion. We want to examine this doctrine and to test its bearing on our treatment of principles; but first we must ask in which sense of discretion we are to understand it.

Some [Legal Realists] argue that judges always have discretion, even when a clear rule is in point, because judges are ultimately the final arbiters of the law. This doctrine of discretion uses the second weak sense of that term, because it makes the point that no higher authority reviews the decisions of the highest court. It therefore has no bearing on the issue of how we account for principles, any more than it bears on how we account for rules.

The positivists do not mean their doctrine this way, because they say that a judge has no discretion when a clear and established rule is available. If we attend to the positivists' arguments for the doctrine we may suspect that they use discretion in the first weak sense to mean only that judges must sometimes exercise judgment in applying legal standards. Their arguments call attention to the fact that some rules of law are vague (Professor Hart, for example, says that all rules of law have 'open texture'), and that some cases arise (like *Henningsen*) in which no established rule seems to be suitable. [However, the] proposition that when no clear rule is available discretion in the sense of judgment must be used is a tautology. . . .

It therefore seems that positivists, at least sometimes, take their doctrine in the third, strong sense of discretion. In that sense it is nothing less than a restatement of our second approach. It is the same thing to say that when a judge runs out of rules he has discretion, in the sense that he is not bound by any standards from the authority of law, as to say that the legal standards judges cite other than rules are not binding on them.

So we must examine the doctrine of judicial discretion in the strong sense. (I shall henceforth use the term 'discretion' in that sense.) Do the principles judges cited in cases like *Riggs* or *Henningsen* control their decisions, as the sergeant's orders to take the most experienced men or the referee's duty to choose the more aggressive fighter control the decisions of these officials? What arguments could a positivist supply to show that they do not?

(1) A positivist might argue that principles cannot be binding or obligatory. That would be a mistake. It is always a question, of course, whether any particular principle is *in fact* binding upon some legal official. But there is nothing in the logical character of a principle that renders it incapable of binding him. Suppose that the judge in *Henningsen* had failed to take any account of the principle that automobile manufacturers have a special obligation to their consumers, or the principle that the courts seek to protect those whose bargaining position is weak, but had simply decided for the defendant by citing the principle of freedom of contract without more. His critics would not have been content to point out that he had not taken account of considerations that other judges have been attending to for some time. Most would have said that it was his duty to take the measure of these principles and that the plaintiff was entitled to have him do so. We mean no more, when we say that a *rule* is binding upon a judge, than that he must follow it if it applies, and that if he does not he will on that account have made a mistake.

It will not do to say that in a case like *Henningsen* the court is only 'morally' obligated to take particular principles into account, or that it is 'institutionally' obligated, or obligated as a matter of judicial 'craft', or something of that sort. The question will still remain why this type of obligation (what-

ever we call it) is different from the obligation that rules impose upon judges, and why
it entitles us to say that principles and policies are not part of the law but are merely
extra-legal standards 'courts characteristically use'.

(2) A positivist might argue that even
though some principles are binding, in the
sense that the judge must take them into account, they cannot determine a particular
result. This is a harder argument to assess
because it is not clear what it means for a
standard to 'determine' a result. Perhaps it
means that the standard *dictates* the result
whenever it applies so that nothing else
counts. If so, then it is certainly true that the
individual principles do not determine results, but that is only another way of saying
that principles are not rules. Only rules dictate results, come what may. When a contrary result has been reached, the rule has
been abandoned or changed. Principles do
not work that way; they incline a decision
one way, though not conclusively, and they
survive intact when they do not prevail. This
seems no reason for concluding that judges
who must reckon with principles have discretion because a set of principles *can* dictate
a result. If a judge believes that principles he
is bound to recognize point in one direction
and that principles pointing in the other
direction, if any, are not of equal weight,
then he must decide accordingly, just as he
must follow what he believes to be a binding rule. He may, of course, be wrong in his
assessment of the principles, but he may also
be wrong in his judgment that the rule is
binding. The sergeant and the referee, we
might add, are often in the same boat. No
one factor dictates which soldiers are the
most experienced or which fighter the more
aggressive. These officials must make judgments of the relative weights of these various factors; they do not on that account
have discretion.

(3) A positivist might argue that principles cannot count as law because their authority, and even more so their weight, are
congenitally *controversial*. It is true that generally we cannot *demonstrate* the authority or
weight of a particular principle as we can
sometimes demonstrate the validity of a rule
by locating it in an act of Congress or in the
opinion of an authoritative court. Instead,
we make a case for a principle, and for its
weight, by appealing to an amalgam of practice and other principles in which the implications of legislative and judicial history
figure along with appeals to community
practices and understandings. There is no litmus paper for testing the soundness of such
a case—it is a matter of judgment, and reasonable men may disagree. But again this
does not distinguish the judge from other
officials who do not have discretion. The
sergeant has no litmus paper for experience,
the referee none for aggressiveness. Neither
of these has discretion, because he is bound
to reach an understanding, controversial or
not, of what his orders or the rules require,
and to act on that understanding. That is the
judge's duty as well. . . .

These are the most obvious of the arguments a positivist might use for the doctrine
of discretion in the strong sense, and for the
second approach to principles. I shall mention one strong counter-argument against
that doctrine and in favor of the first approach. Unless at least some principles are
acknowledged to be binding upon judges,
requiring them as a set to reach particular
decisions, then no rules, or very few rules,
can be said to be binding upon them either.

In most American jurisdictions, and now
in England also, the higher courts not infrequently reject established rules. Common
law rules—those developed by earlier court
decisions—are sometimes overruled directly,
and sometimes radically altered by further
development. Statutory rules are subjected

to interpretation and reinterpretation, sometimes even when the result is not to carry out what is called the 'legislative intent.' If courts had discretion to change established rules, then these rules would of course not be binding upon them, and so would not be law on the positivists' model. The positivist must therefore argue that there are standards, themselves binding upon judges, that determine when a judge may overrule or alter an established rule, and when he may not.

When, then, is a judge permitted to change an existing rule of law? Principles figure in the answer in two ways. First, it is necessary, though not sufficient, that the judge find that the change would advance some principle, which principle thus justifies the change. In *Riggs* the change (a new interpretation of the statute of wills) was justified by the principle that no man should profit from his own wrong; in *Henningsen* the previously recognized rules about automobile manufacturers' liability were altered on the basis of the principles I quoted from the opinion of the court.

But not any principle will do to justify a change, or no rule would ever be safe. There must be some principles that count and others that do not, and there must be some principles that count for more than others. It could not depend on the judge's own preferences amongst a sea of respectable extra-legal standards, any one in principle eligible, because if that were the case we could not say that any rules were binding. We could always imagine a judge whose preferences amongst extra-legal standards were such as would justify a shift or radical reinterpretation of even the most entrenched rule.

Second, any judge who proposes to change existing doctrine must take account of some important standards that argue against departures from established doctrine, and these standards are also for the most part principles. They include the doctrine of 'legislative supremacy', a set of principles that require the courts to pay a qualified deference to the acts of the legislature. They also include the doctrine of precedent, another set of principles reflecting the equities and efficiencies of consistency. . . .

6. The Rule of Recognition

This discussion was provoked by our two competing accounts of legal principles. We have been exploring the second account, which the positivists seem to adopt through their doctrine of judicial discretion, and we have discovered grave difficulties. It is time to return to the fork in the road. What if we adopt the first approach? What would the consequences of this be for the skeletal structure of positivism? Of course we should have to drop the second tenet, the doctrine of judicial discretion (or, in the alternative, to make plain that the doctrine is to be read merely to say that judges must often exercise judgment). Would we also have to abandon or modify the first tenet, the proposition that law is distinguished by tests of the sort that can be set out in a master rule like Professor Hart's rule of recognition? If principles of the *Riggs* and *Henningsen* sort are to count as law, and we are nevertheless to preserve the notion of a master rule for law, then we must be able to deploy some test that all (and only) the principles that do count as law meet. Let us begin with the test Hart suggests for identifying valid *rules* of law, to see whether these can be made to work for principles as well.

Most rules of law, according to Hart, are valid because some competent institution enacted them. Some were created by a legislature, in the form of statutory enactments. Others were created by judges who formulated them to decide particular cases, and thus established them as precedents for the future. But this test of pedigree will not work for the *Riggs* and *Henningsen* principles. The origin of these as legal principles lies not in a particular decision of some legislature or court, but in a sense of appropriateness developed in the profession and the public over time. Their continued power depends upon this sense of appropriateness being sustained. If it no longer seemed unfair to allow people to profit by their wrongs, or fair to place special burdens upon oligopolies that manufacture potentially dangerous machines, these principles would no longer play much of a role in new cases, even if they had never been overruled or repealed. (Indeed, it hardly makes sense to speak of principles like these as being 'overruled' or 'repealed'. When they decline they are eroded, not torpedoed.)

True, if we were challenged to back up our claim that some principle is a principle of law, we would mention any prior cases in which that principle was cited, or figured in the argument. We would also mention any statute that seemed to exemplify that principle (even better if the principle was cited in the preamble of the statute, or in the committee reports or other legislative documents that accompanied it). Unless we could find some such institutional support, we would probably fail to make out our case, and the more support we found, the more weight we could claim for the principle.

Yet we could not devise any formula for testing how much and what kind of institutional support is necessary to make a principle a legal principle, still less to fix its weight at a particular order of magnitude. We argue for a particular principle by grappling with a whole set of shifting, developing and interacting standards (themselves principles rather than rules) about institutional responsibility, statutory interpretation, the persuasive force of various sorts of precedent, the relation of all these to contemporary moral practices, and hosts of other such standards. We could not bolt all of these together into a single 'rule', even a complex one, and if we could the result would bear little relation to

Hart's picture of a rule of recognition, which is the picture of a fairly stable master rule specifying 'some feature or features possession of which by a suggested rule is taken as a conclusive affirmative indication that it is a rule. . . .'

Moreover, the techniques we apply in arguing for another principle do not stand (as Hart's rule of recognition is designed to) on an entirely different level from the principles they support. Hart's sharp distinction between acceptance and validity does not hold. If we are arguing for the principle that a man should not profit from his own wrong, we could cite the acts of courts and legislatures that exemplify it, but this speaks as much to the principle's acceptance as its validity. (It seems odd to speak of a principle as being valid at all, perhaps because validity is an all–or–nothing concept, appropriate for rules, but inconsistent with a principle's dimension of weight.) If we are asked (as we might well be) to defend the particular doctrine of precedent, or the particular technique of statutory interpretation, that we used in this argument, we should certainly cite the practice of others in using that doctrine or technique. But we should also cite other general principles that we believe support that practice, and this introduces a note of validity into the chord of acceptance. We might argue, for example, that the use we make of earlier cases and statutes is supported by a particular analysis of the point of the practice of legislation or the doctrine of precedent, or by the principles of democratic theory, or by a particular position on the proper division of authority between national and local institutions, or something else of that sort. Nor is this path of support a one–way street leading to some ultimate principle resting on acceptance alone. Our principles of legislation, precedent, democracy, or federalism might be challenged too; and if they were we should argue for them, not only in terms of practice, but in terms of each other and in terms of the implications of trends of judicial and legislative decisions, even though this last would involve appealing to those same doctrines of interpretation we justified through the principles we are now trying to support. At this level of abstraction, in other words, principles rather hang together than link together.

So even though principles draw support from the official acts of legal institutions, they do not have a simple or direct enough connection with these acts to frame that connection in terms of criteria specified by some ultimate master rule of recognition. . . .

I conclude that if we treat principles as law we must reject the positivists' first tenet, that the law of a community is distinguished from other social standards by some test in the form of a master rule. We have already decided that we must then abandon the second tenet—the doctrine of judicial discretion—or clarify it into triviality. What of the third tenet, the positivists' theory of legal obligation?

This theory holds that a legal obligation exists when (and only when) an established rule of law imposes such an obligation. It follows from this that in a hard case—when no such established rule can be found—there is no legal obligation until the judge creates a new rule for the future. The judge may apply that new rule to the parties in the case, but this is *ex post facto* legislation, not the enforcement of an existing obligation.

The positivists' doctrine of discretion (in the strong sense) required this view of legal obligation, because if a judge has discretion there can be no legal right or obligation—no entitlement—that he must enforce. Once we abandon that doctrine, however, and treat principles as law, we raise the possibility that a legal obligation might be imposed by a constellation of principles as well as by an established rule. We might want to say that a legal obligation exists whenever the case

supporting such an obligation, in terms of binding legal principles of different sorts, is stronger than the case against it. . . .

HARD CASES

2. The Rights Thesis

A. Principles and policies

Theories of adjudication have become more sophisticated, but the most popular theories still put judging in the shade of legislation. The main outlines of this story are familiar. Judges should apply the law that other institutions have made; they should not make new law. That is the ideal, but for different reasons it cannot be realized fully in practice. Statutes and common law rules are often vague and must be interpreted before they can be applied to novel cases. Some cases, moreover, raise issues so novel that they cannot be decided even by stretching or reinterpreting existing rules. So judges must sometimes make new law, either covertly or explicitly. But when they do, they should act as deputy to the appropriate legislature, enacting the law that they suppose the legislature would enact if seized of the problem.

That is perfectly familiar, but there is buried in this common story a further level of subordination not always noticed. When judges make law, so the expectation runs, they will act not only as deputy to the legislature but as a deputy legislature. They will make law in response to evidence and arguments of the same character as would move the superior institution if it were acting on its own. This is a deeper level of subordination, because it makes any understanding of what judges do in hard cases parasitic on a prior understanding of what legislators do all the time. This deeper subordination is thus conceptual as well as political.

In fact, however, judges neither should be nor are deputy legislators, and the familiar assumption, that when they go beyond political decisions already made by someone else they are legislating, is misleading. It misses the importance of a fundamental distinction within political theory, which I shall now introduce in a crude form. This is the distinction between arguments of principle on the one hand and arguments of policy on the other.

Arguments of policy justify a political decision by showing that the decision advances or protects some collective goal of the community as a whole. The argument in favor of a subsidy for aircraft manufacturers, that the subsidy will protect national defense, is an argument of policy. Arguments of principle justify a political decision by showing that the decision respects or secures some individual or group right. The argument in favor of anti–discrimination statutes, that a minority has a right to equal respect and concern, is an argument of principle. These two sorts of argument do not exhaust political argument. Sometimes, for example, a political decision, like the decision to allow extra income tax exemptions for the blind, may be defended as an act of public generosity or virtue rather than on grounds of either policy or principle. But principle and policy are the major grounds of political justification. . . .

B. Principles and democracy

The familiar story, that adjudication must be subordinated to legislation, is supported by two objections to judicial originality. The first argues that a community should be governed by men and women who are elected by and responsible to the majority. Since judges are, for the most part, not elected, and since they are not, in practice, responsible to the electorate in the way legislators are, it seems to compromise that proposition when judges make law. The second argues that if a judge makes new law and applies it retroactively in the case before him, then the losing

party will be punished, not because he violated some duty he had, but rather a new duty created after the event.

These two arguments combine to support the traditional ideal that adjudication should be as unoriginal as possible. But they offer much more powerful objections to judicial decisions generated by policy than to those generated by principle. The first objection, that law should be made by elected and responsible officials, seems unexceptionable when we think of law as policy; that is, as a compromise among individual goals and purposes in search of the welfare of the community as a whole. It is far from clear that interpersonal comparisons of utility or preference, through which such compromises might be made objectively, make sense even in theory; but in any case no proper calculus is available in practice. Policy decisions must therefore be made through the operation of some political process designed to produce an accurate expression of the different interests that should be taken into account. The political system of representative democracy may work only indifferently in this respect, but it works better than a system that allows nonelected judges, who have no mail bag or lobbyists or pressure groups, to compromise competing interests in their chambers.

The second objection is also persuasive against a decision generated by policy. We all agree that it would be wrong to sacrifice the rights of an innocent man in the name of some new duty created after the event; it does, therefore, seem wrong to take property from one individual and hand it to another in order just to improve overall economic efficiency.

[But] suppose, on the other hand, that a judge successfully justifies a decision in a hard case [on] grounds not of policy but of principle. [The] two arguments just described would offer much less of an objection to the decision. The first is less relevant when a court judges principle, because an argument of principle does not often rest on assumptions about the nature and intensity of the different demands and concerns distributed throughout the community. On the contrary, an argument of principle fixes on some interest presented by the proponent of the right it describes, an interest alleged to be of such a character as to make irrelevant the fine discriminations of any argument of policy that might oppose it. A judge who is insulated from the demands of the political majority whose interests the right would trump is, therefore, in a better position to evaluate the argument.

The second objection to judicial originality has no force against an argument of principle. If the plaintiff has a right against the defendant, then the defendant has a corresponding duty, and it is that duty, not some new duty created in court, that justifies the award against him. Even if the duty has not been imposed upon him by explicit prior legislation, there is, but for one difference, no more injustice in enforcing the duty than if it had been. . . .

5. Legal Rights

We might do well to consider how a philosophical judge might develop, in appropriate cases, theories of what legal principles require. We shall find that he would construct these theories in the same manner as a philosophical referee would construct the character of a game. I have invented, for this purpose, a lawyer of superhuman skill, learning, patience and acumen, whom I shall call Hercules. I suppose that Hercules is a judge in some representative American jurisdiction. I assume that he accepts the main uncontroversial constitutive and regulative rules of the law in his jurisdiction. He accepts, that is, that statutes have the general power to create and extinguish legal rights, and that judges have the general duty to fol-

low earlier decisions of their court or higher courts whose rationale, as lawyers say, extends to the case at bar. . . .

Hercules must suppose that it is understood in his community, though perhaps not explicitly recognized, that judicial decisions must be taken to be justified by arguments of principle rather than arguments of policy. He now sees that the familiar concept used by judges to explain their reasoning from precedent, the concept of certain principles that underlie or are embedded in the common law, is itself only a metaphorical statement of the rights thesis. He may henceforth use that concept in his decisions of hard common law cases. [It] provides a question—What set of principles best justifies the precedents?—that builds a bridge between the general justification of the practice of precedent, which is fairness, and his own decision about what that general justification requires in some particular hard case.

Hercules must now develop his concept of principles that underlie the common law by assigning to each of the relevant precedents some scheme of principle that justifies the decision of that precedent. He will now discover a further important difference between this concept and the concept of statutory purpose that he used in statutory interpretation. In the case of statutes, he found it necessary to choose some theory about the purpose of the particular statute in question, looking to other acts of the legislature only insofar as these might help to select between theories that fit the statute about equally well. But if the gravitational force of precedent rests on the idea that fairness requires the consistent enforcement of rights, then Hercules must discover principles that fit, not only the particular precedent to which some litigant directs his attention, but all other judicial decisions within his general jurisdiction and, indeed, statutes as well, so far as these must be seen to be generated by principle rather than policy. He does not satisfy his duty to show that his decision is consistent with established principles, and therefore fair, if the principles he cites as established are themselves inconsistent with other decisions that his court also proposes to uphold.

You will now see why I called our judge Hercules. He must construct a scheme of abstract and concrete principles that provides a coherent justification for all common law precedents and, so far as these are to be justified on principle, constitutional and statutory provisions as well. We may grasp the magnitude of this enterprise by distinguishing, within the vast material of legal decisions that Hercules must justify, a vertical and a horizontal ordering. The vertical ordering is provided by distinguishing layers of authority; that is, layers at which official decisions might be taken to be controlling over decisions made at lower levels. In the United States the rough character of the vertical ordering is apparent. The constitutional structure occupies the highest level, the decisions of the Supreme Court and perhaps other courts interpreting that structure the next, enactments of the various legislatures the next and decisions of the various courts developing the common law different levels below that. Hercules must arrange justification of principle at each of these levels so that the justification is consistent with principles taken to provide the justification of higher levels. The horizontal ordering simply requires that the principles taken to justify a decision at one level must also be consistent with the justification offered for other decisions at that level.

QUESTIONS FOR DISCUSSION

1. What is Dworkin's distinction between a rule and a principle? Is the distinction sound? Can you think of counter-examples? How much of Dworkin's attack on positivism depends on the distinction?

2. Now that you have read H. L. A. Hart and know something about legal positivism, do you think that Dworkin's characterization of legal positivism is accurate? What could Hart say in response to Dworkin?

3. Which of the varieties of *discretion* do you think best characterizes the positivist view of what judges do when there is no settled law? What does Dworkin mean when he says that judges do not exercise discretion?

4. Does Dworkin think there is a difference between legal principles, political principles, and moral principles? If so, what is it? Do you agree?

5. In "Hard Cases," Dworkin describes the "rights thesis" as maintaining, in part, that judges do and should enforce rights and not make decisions of policy. Do you think the rights thesis is accurate as a description? What would Llewellyn and Kennedy think? Do you agree with the rights thesis as a norm? Why or why not?

6. Dworkin claims that legal positivism is mistaken, but he does not subscribe to a "natural law" position. Are there similarities between Dworkin's views and the natural law views considered earlier, such as those of Aquinas, Finnis, and Fuller? What are the differences? (On this question, see also Dworkin's "Natural Law Revisited," excerpted in Chapter 2).

LAW'S EMPIRE

RONALD DWORKIN

Mrs. McLoughlin's husband and four children were injured in an automobile accident in England at about 4 P.M. on October 19, 1973. She heard about the accident at home from a neighbor at about 6 P.M. and went immediately to the hospital, where she learned that her daughter was dead and saw the serious condition of her husband and other children. She suffered nervous shock and later sued the defendant driver, whose negligence had caused the accident, as well as other parties who were in different ways involved, for compensation for her emotional injuries. Her lawyer pointed to several earlier decisions of English courts awarding compensation to people who had suffered emotional injury on seeing serious injury to a close relative. But in all these cases the plaintiff had either been at the scene of the accident or had arrived within minutes. In a 1972 case, for example, a wife recovered—won compensation—for emotional injury; she had come upon the body of her husband immediately after his fatal accident. In 1967 a man who was not related to any of the victims of a train crash worked for hours trying to rescue victims and suffered nervous shock from the experience. He was allowed to recover. Mrs. McLoughlin's lawyer relied on these cases as precedents, decisions which had made it part of the law that people in her position are entitled to compensation. . . .

The judge before whom Mrs. McLoughlin first brought her suit, the trial judge, decided that the precedents her lawyer cited, about others who had recovered compensa-

tion for emotional injury suffered when they saw accident victims, were distinguishable because in all those cases the shock had occurred at the scene of the accident while she was shocked some two hours later and in a different place. Of course not every difference in the facts of two cases makes the earlier one distinguishable: no one could think it mattered if Mrs. McLoughlin was younger than the plaintiffs in the earlier cases.

The trial judge thought that suffering injury away from the scene was an important difference because it meant that Mrs. Mc-Loughlin's injury was not "foreseeable" in the way that the injury to the other plaintiffs had been. Judges in both Britain and America follow the common law principle that people who act carelessly are liable only for reasonably foreseeable injuries to others, injuries a reasonable person would anticipate if he reflected on the matter. The trial judge was bound by the doctrine of precedent to recognize that emotional injury to close relatives at the scene of an accident is reasonably foreseeable, but he said that injury to a mother who saw the results of the accident later is not. So he thought he could distinguish the putative precedents in that way and decided against Mrs. McLoughlin's claim.

She appealed his decision to the next highest court in the British hierarchy, the Court of Appeals. That court affirmed the trial judge's decision—it refused her appeal and let his decision stand—but not on the argument he had used. The Court of Appeals said it *was* reasonably foreseeable that a mother would rush to the hospital to see her

Ronald Dworkin, *Law's Empire* (Cambridge: Harvard University Press, 1986), selection from Chapter 7 ("Integrity and Law") and Chapter 11 ("Law Beyond Law")

injured family and that she would suffer emotional shock from seeing them in the condition Mrs. McLoughlin found. That court distinguished the precedents not on that ground but for the very different reason that what it called "policy" justified a distinction. The precedents had established liability for emotional injury in certain restricted circumstances, but the Court of Appeals said that recognizing a larger area of liability, embracing injuries to relatives not at the scene, would have a variety of adverse consequences for the community as a whole. It would encourage many more lawsuits for emotional injuries, and this would exacerbate the problem of congestion in the courts. It would open new opportunities for fraudulent claims by people who had not really suffered serious emotional damage but could find doctors to testify that they had. It would increase the cost of liability insurance, making it more expensive to drive and perhaps preventing some poor people from driving at all. The claims of those who had suffered genuine emotional injury away from the scene would be harder to prove, and the uncertainties of litigation might complicate their condition and delay their recovery.

Mrs. McLoughlin appealed the decision once more, to the House of Lords, which re-. versed the Court of Appeals and ordered a new trial. The decision was unanimous, but their lordships disagreed about what they called the true state of the law. Several of them said that policy reasons, of the sort described by the Court of Appeals, might in some circumstances be sufficient to distinguish a line of precedents and so justify a judge's refusal to extend the principle of those cases to a larger area of liability. But they did not think these policy reasons were of sufficient plausibility or merit in Mrs. McLoughlin's case. They did not believe that the risk of a "flood" of litigation was sufficiently grave, and they said the courts should be able to distinguish genuine from fraudulent claims even among those whose putative injury was suffered several hours after the accident. They did not undertake to say when good policy arguments might be available to limit recovery for emotional injury; they left it an open question, for example, whether Mrs. McLoughlin's sister in Australia (if she had one) could recover for the shock she might have in reading about the accident weeks or months later in a letter.

Two of their lordships took a very different view of the law. They said it would be wrong for courts to deny recovery to an otherwise meritorious plaintiff for the *kinds* of reasons the Court of Appeals had mentioned and which the other law lords had said might be sufficient in some circumstances. The precedents should be regarded as distinguishable, they said, only if the moral *principles* assumed in the earlier cases for some reason did not apply to the plaintiff in the same way. And once it is conceded that the damage to a mother in the hospital hours after an accident is reasonably foreseeable to a careless driver, then no difference in moral principle can be found between the two cases. Congestion in the courts or a rise in the price of automobile liability insurance, they said, however inconvenient these might be to the community as a whole, cannot justify refusing to enforce individual rights and duties that have been recognized and enforced before. They said these were the wrong sorts of arguments to make to judges as arguments of law, however cogent they might be if addressed to legislators as arguments for a change in the law. (Lord Scarman's opinion was particularly clear and strong on this point.) The argument among their lordships revealed an important difference of opinion about the proper role of considerations of policy in deciding what result parties to a lawsuit are entitled to have. ■ ■ ■

INTEGRITY AND INTERPRETATION

The adjudicative principle of integrity instructs judges to identify legal rights and duties, so far as possible, on the assumption that they were all created by a single author—the community personified—expressing a coherent conception of justice and fairness. We form our third conception of law, our third view of what rights and duties flow from past political decisions, by restating this instruction as a thesis about the grounds of law. According to law as integrity, propositions of law are true if they figure in or follow from the principles of justice, fairness, and procedural due process that provide the best constructive interpretation of the community's legal practice. Deciding whether the law grants Mrs. McLoughlin compensation for her injury, for example, means deciding whether legal practice is seen in a better light if we assume the community has accepted the principle that people in her position are entitled to compensation.

INTEGRITY AND HISTORY

History matters in law as integrity: very much but only in a certain way. Integrity does not require consistency in principle over all historical stages of a community's law; it does not require that judges try to understand the law they enforce as continuous in principle with the abandoned law of a previous century or even a previous generation. It commands a horizontal rather than vertical consistency of principle across the range of the legal standards the community now enforces. It insists that the law—the rights and duties that flow from past collective decisions and for that reason license or require coercion—contains not only the narrow explicit content of these decisions but also, more broadly, the scheme of principles necessary to justify them. History matters because that scheme of principle must justify the standing as well as the content of these past decisions. Our justification for treating the Endangered Species Act as law, unless

and until it is repealed, crucially includes the fact that Congress enacted it, and any justification we supply for treating that fact as crucial must itself accommodate the way we treat other events in our political past.

Law as integrity, then, begins in the present and pursues the past only so far as and in the way its contemporary focus dictates. It does not aim to recapture, even for present law, the ideals or practical purposes of the politicians who first created it. It aims rather to justify what they did (sometimes including, as we shall see, what they said) in an overall story worth telling now, a story with a complex claim: that present practice can be organized by and justified in principles sufficiently attractive to provide an honorable future. Law as integrity deplores the mechanism of the older "law is law" view as well as the cynicism of the newer "realism." It sees both views as rooted in the same false dichotomy of finding and inventing law. When a judge declares that a particular principle is instinct in law, he reports not a simple-minded claim about the motives of past statesmen, a claim a wise cynic can easily refute, but an interpretive proposal: that the principle both fits and justifies some complex part of legal practice, that it provides an attractive way to see, in the structure of that practice, the consistency of principle integrity requires. Law's optimism is in that way conceptual; claims of law are endemically constructive, just in virtue of the kind of claims they are. This optimism may be misplaced: legal practice may in the end yield to nothing but a deeply skeptical interpretation. But that is not inevitable just because a community's history is one of great change and conflict. An imaginative interpretation can be constructed on morally complicated, even ambiguous terrain.

THE CHAIN NOVEL

[We] can usefully compare the judge deciding what the law is on some issue [with] the literary critic teasing out the various dimensions of value in a complex play or poem.

Judges, however, are authors as well as critics. A judge deciding *McLoughlin* adds to the tradition he interprets; future judges confront a new tradition that includes what he has done. Of course literary criticism contributes to the traditions of art in which authors work; the character and importance of that contribution are themselves issues in critical theory. But the contribution of judges is more direct, and the distinction between author and interpreter more a matter of different aspects of the same process. We can find an even more fruitful comparison between literature and law, therefore, by constructing an artificial genre of literature that we might call the chain novel.

In this enterprise a group of novelists writes a novel *seriatum*; each novelist in the chain interprets the chapters he has been given in order to write a new chapter, which is then added to what the next novelist receives, and so on. Each has the job of writing his chapter so as to make the novel being constructed the best it can be, and the complexity of this task models the complexity of deciding a hard case under law as integrity. The imaginary literary enterprise is fantastic but not unrecognizable. Some novels have actually been written in this way, though mainly for a debunking purpose, and certain parlor games for rainy weekends in English country houses have something of the same structure. Television soap operas span decades with the same characters and some minimal continuity of personality and plot, though they are written by different teams of authors even in different weeks. In our example, however, the novelists are expected to take their responsibilities of continuity more seriously; they aim jointly to create, so far as they can, a single unified novel that is the best it can be.

Each novelist aims to make a single novel of the material he has been given,
what he adds to it, and (so far as he can control this) what his successors will want to be able to add. He must try to make this the best novel it can be construed as the work of a single author rather than, as is the fact, the product of many different hands. That calls for an overall judgment on his part, or a series of overall judgments as he writes and rewrites. He must take up some view about the novel in progress, some working theory about its characters, plot, genre, theme, and point, in order to decide what counts as continuing it and not as beginning anew. If he is a good critic, his view of these matters will be complicated and multifaceted, because the value of a decent novel cannot be captured from a single perspective. He will aim to find layers and currents of meaning rather than a single, exhaustive theme. We can, however, in our now familiar way give some structure to any interpretation he adopts, by distinguishing two dimensions on which it must be tested. The first is what we have been calling the dimension of fit. He cannot adopt any interpretation, however complex, if he believes that no single author who set out to write a novel with the various readings of character, plot, theme, and point that interpretation describes could have written substantially the text he has been given. That does not mean his interpretation must fit every bit of the text. It is not disqualified simply because he claims that some lines or tropes are accidental, or even that some events of plot are mistakes because they work against the literary ambitions the interpretation states. But the interpretation he takes up must nevertheless flow throughout the text; it must have general explanatory power, and it is flawed if it leaves unexplained some major structural aspect of the text, a subplot treated as having great dramatic importance or a dominant and repeated metaphor. If no interpretation can be found that is not flawed in that way, then the chain novelist will not be able fully to

meet his assignment; he will have to settle for an interpretation that captures most of the text, conceding that it is not wholly successful. Perhaps even that partial success is unavailable; perhaps every interpretation he considers is inconsistent with the bulk of the material supplied to him. In that case he must abandon the enterprise, for the consequence of taking the interpretive attitude toward the text in question is then a piece of internal skepticism: that nothing can count as continuing the novel rather than beginning anew.

He may find, not that no single interpretation fits the bulk of the text, but that more than one does. The second dimension of interpretation then requires him to judge which of these eligible readings makes the work in progress best, all things considered. At this point his more substantive aesthetic judgments, about the importance or insight or realism or beauty of different ideas the novel might be taken to express, come into play. But the formal and structural considerations that dominate on the first dimension figure on the second as well, for even when neither of two interpretations is disqualified out of hand as explaining too little, one may show the text in a better light because it fits more of the text or provides a more interesting integration of style and content. . . .

SCROOGE

We can expand this abstract description of the chain novelist's judgment through an example. Suppose you are a novelist well down the chain. Suppose Dickens never wrote *A Christmas Carol,* and the text you are furnished, though written by several people, happens to be the first part of that short novel. You consider these two interpretations of the central character: Scrooge is inherently and irredeemably evil, an embodiment of the untarnished wickedness of human nature freed from the disguises of convention he rejects; or Scrooge is inherently good but

progressively corrupted by the false values and perverse demands of high capitalist society. Obviously it will make an enormous difference to the way you continue the story which of these interpretations you adopt. If you have been given almost all of *A Christmas Carol* with only the very end to be written— Scrooge has already had his dreams, repented, and sent his turkey—it is too late for you to make him irredeemably wicked, assuming you think, as most interpreters would, that the text will not bear that interpretation without too much strain. I do not mean that no interpreter could possibly think Scrooge inherently evil after his supposed redemption. Someone might take that putative redemption to be a final act of hypocrisy, though only at the cost of taking much else in the text not at face value. This would be a poor interpretation, not because no one could think it a good one, but because it is in fact, on all the criteria so far described, a poor one.

But now suppose you have been given only the first few sections of *A Christmas Carol.* You find that neither of the two interpretations you are considering is decisively ruled out by anything in the text so far; perhaps one would better explain some minor incidents of plot that must be left unconnected on the other, but each interpretation can be seen generally to flow through the abbreviated text as a whole. A competent novelist who set out to write a novel along either of the lines suggested could well have written what you find on the pages. In that case you have a further decision to make. Your assignment is to make of the text the best it can be, and you will therefore choose the interpretation you believe makes the work more significant or otherwise better. That decision will probably (though not inevitably) depend on whether you think that real people somewhat like Scrooge are born bad or are corrupted by capitalism. But it will depend on much else as well, because your aesthetic convictions are not so simple as to make only this aspect of a novel relevant to its overall success. Suppose you think that one interpretation integrates not only plot but image and setting as well; the social interpretation accounts, for example, for the sharp contrast between the individualistic fittings and partitions of Scrooge's countinghouse and the communitarian formlessness of Bob Cratchit's household. Now your aesthetic judgment—about which reading makes the continuing novel better as a novel—is itself more complex because it must identify and trade off different dimensions of value in a novel. Suppose you believe that the original sin reading is much the more accurate depiction of human nature, but that the sociorealist reading provides a deeper and more interesting formal structure for the novel. You must then ask yourself which interpretation makes the work of art better on the whole. You may never have reflected on that sort of question before—perhaps the tradition of criticism in which you have been trained takes it for granted that one or the other of these dimensions is the more important—but that is no reason why you may not do so now. Once you make up your mind you will believe that the correct interpretation of Scrooge's character is the interpretation that makes the novel better on the whole, so judged.

This contrived example is complex enough to provoke the following apparently important question. Is your judgment about the best way to interpret and continue the sections you have been given of *A Christmas Carol* a free or a constrained judgment? Are you free to give effect to your own assumptions and attitudes about what novels should be like? Or are you bound to ignore these because you are enslaved by a text you cannot alter? The answer is plain enough: neither of these two crude descriptions—of total creative freedom or mechani-

cal textual constraint—captures your situation, because each must in some way be qualified by the other. You will sense creative freedom when you compare your task with some relatively more mechanical one, like direct translation of a text into a foreign language. But you will sense constraint when you compare it with some relatively less guided one, like beginning a new novel of your own. . . .

Law as integrity asks a judge deciding a common-law case like *McLoughlin* to think of himself as an author in the chain of common law. He knows that other judges have decided cases that, although not exactly like his case, deal with related problems; he must think of their decisions as part of a long story he must interpret and then continue, according to his own judgment of how to make the developing story as good as it can be. (Of course the best story for him means best from the standpoint of political morality, not aesthetics.) We can make a rough distinction once again between two main dimensions of this interpretive judgment. The judge's decision—his postinterpretive conclusions—must be drawn from an interpretation that both fits and justifies what has gone before, so far as that is possible. But in law as in literature the interplay between fit and justification is complex. Just as interpretation within a chain novel is for each interpreter a delicate balance among different types of literary and artistic attitudes, so in law it is a delicate balance among political convictions of different sorts; in law as in literature these must be sufficiently related yet disjoint to allow an overall judgment that trades off an interpretation's success on one type of standard against its failure on another. I must try to exhibit that complex structure of legal interpretation, and I shall use for that purpose an imaginary judge [Hercules] of superhuman intellectual power and patience who accepts law as integrity.

SIX INTERPRETATIONS

Hercules must decide *McLoughlin*. Both sides in that case cited precedents; each argued that a decision in its favor would count as going on as before, as continuing the story begun by the judges who decided those precedent cases. Hercules must form his own view about that issue. Just as a chain novelist must find, if he can, some coherent view of character and theme such that a hypothetical single author with that view could have written at least the bulk of the novel so far, Hercules must find, if he can, some coherent theory about legal rights to compensation for emotional injury such that a single political official with that theory could have reached most of the results the precedents report.

He is a careful judge, a judge of method. He begins by setting out various candidates for the best interpretation of the precedent cases even before he reads them. Suppose he makes the following short list: (1) No one has a moral right to compensation except for physical injury. (2) People have a moral right to compensation for emotional injury suffered at the scene of an accident against anyone whose carelessness caused the accident but have no right to compensation for emotional injury suffered later. (3) People should recover compensation for emotional injury when a practice of requiring compensation in their circumstances would diminish the overall costs of accidents or otherwise make the community richer in the long run. (4) People have a moral right to compensation for any injury, emotional or physical, that is the direct consequence of careless conduct, no matter how unlikely or unforeseeable it is that that conduct would result in that injury. (5) People have a moral right to compensation for emotional or physical injury that is the consequence of careless conduct, but only if that injury was reasonably foreseeable by the person who acted carelessly. (6) People have a moral right to compensation for reasonably foreseeable injury but not in circumstances when recognizing such a right would impose massive and destructive financial burdens on people who have been careless out of proportion to their moral fault.

These are all relatively concrete statements about rights and, allowing for a complexity in (3) we explore just below, they contradict one another. No more than one can figure in a single interpretation of the emotional injury cases. (I postpone the more complex case in which Hercules constructs an interpretation from competitive rather than contradictory principles, that is, from principles that can live together in an overall moral or political theory though they sometimes pull in different directions.) Even so, this is only a partial list of the contradictory interpretations someone might wish to consider; Hercules chooses it as his initial short list because he knows that the principles captured in these interpretations have actually been discussed in the legal literature. It will obviously make a great difference which of these principles he believes provides the best interpretation of the precedents and so the nerve of his postinterpretive judgment. If he settles on (1) or (2), he must decide for Mr. O'Brian; if on (4), for Mrs. McLoughlin. Each of the others requires further thought, but the line of reasoning each suggests is different. (3) invites an economic calculation. Would it reduce the cost of accidents to extend liability to emotional injury away from the scene? Or is there some reason to think that the most efficient line is drawn just between emotional injuries at and those away from the scene? (5) requires a judgment about foreseeability of injury, which seems to be very different, and (6) a judgment both about foreseeability and the cumulative risk of financial responsibility if certain injuries away from the scene are included.

Hercules begins testing each interpretation on his short list by asking whether a single political official could have given the verdicts of the precedent cases if that official were consciously and coherently enforcing the principles that form the interpretation. He will therefore dismiss interpretation (1) at once. No one who believed that people never have rights to compensation for emotional injury could have reached the results of those past decisions cited in *McLoughlin* that allowed compensation. Hercules will also dismiss interpretation (2), though for a different reason. Unlike (1), (2) fits the past decisions; someone who accepted (2) as a standard would have reached these decisions, because they all allowed recovery for emotional injury at the scene and none allowed recovery for injury away from it. But (2) fails as an interpretation of the required kind because it does not state a principle of justice at all. It draws a line that it leaves arbitrary and unconnected to any more general moral or political consideration.

What about (3)? It might fit the past decisions, but only in the following way. Hercules might discover through economic analysis that someone who accepted the economic theory expressed by (3) and who wished to reduce the community's accident costs would have made just those decisions. But it is far from obvious that (3) states any principle of justice or fairness. . . .

Interpretations (4), (5), and (6) do, however, seem to pass these initial tests. The principles of each fit the past emotional injury decisions, at least on first glance, if only because none of these precedents presented facts that would discriminate among them. Hercules must now ask, as the next stage of his investigation, whether any one of the three must be ruled out because it is incompatible with the bulk of legal practice more generally. He must test each interpretation against other past judicial decisions, beyond those involving emotional injury, that might be thought to engage them. Suppose he discovers, for example, that past decisions provide compensation for physical injury caused by careless driving only if the injury was reasonably foreseeable. That would rule out interpretation (4) unless he can find some principled distinction between physical and emotional injury that explains why the conditions for compensation should be more restrictive for the former than the latter, which seems extremely unlikely.

Law as integrity, then, requires a judge to test his interpretation of any part of the great network of political structures and decisions of his community by asking whether it could form part of a coherent theory justifying the network as a whole. No actual judge could compose anything approaching a full interpretation of all of his community's law at once. That is why we are imagining a Herculean judge of superhuman talents and endless time. But an actual judge can imitate Hercules in a limited way. He can allow the scope of his interpretation to fan out from the cases immediately in point to cases in the same general area or department of law, and then still farther, so far as this seems promising. In practice even this limited process will be largely unconscious: an experienced judge will have a sufficient sense of the terrain surrounding his immediate problem to know instinctively which interpretation of a small set of cases would survive if the range it must fit were expanded.

Suppose a modest expansion of Hercules' range of inquiry does show that plaintiffs are denied compensation if their physical injury was not reasonably foreseeable at the time the careless defendant acted, thus ruling out interpretation (4). But this does not eliminate either (5) or (6). He must expand his survey further. He must look also to cases involving economic rather than physical or emotional injury, where damages are potentially very great: for example, he must look to cases in which professional advisers like surveyors or accountants are sued for losses others suffer through their negligence. Interpretation (5) suggests that such liability might be unlimited in amount, no matter how ruinous in total, provided that the damage is foreseeable, and (6) suggests, on the contrary, that liability is limited just because of the frightening sums it might otherwise reach. If one interpretation is uniformly contradicted by cases of that sort and finds no support in any other area of doctrine Hercules might later inspect, and the other is confirmed by the expansion, he will regard the former as ineligible, and the latter alone will have survived. But suppose he finds, when he expands his study in this way, a mixed pattern. Past decisions permit extended liability for members of some professions but not for those of others, and this mixed pattern holds for other areas of doctrine that Hercules, in the exercise of his imaginative skill, finds pertinent.

The contradiction he has discovered, though genuine, is not in itself so deep or pervasive as to justify a skeptical interpretation of legal practice as a whole, for the problem of unlimited damages, while important, is not so fundamental that contradiction within it destroys the integrity of the larger system. So Hercules turns to the second main dimension, but here, as in the chain-novel example, questions of fit surface again, because an interpretation is *pro tanto* more satisfactory if it shows less damage to integrity than its rival. He will therefore consider whether interpretation (5) fits the expanded legal record better than (6). But this cannot be a merely mechanical decision; he cannot simply count the number of past decisions that must be conceded to be "mistakes" on each interpretation. For these numbers may reflect only accidents like the number of cases that happen to have come to court and not been settled before verdict. He must take into account not only the numbers of decisions counting for each interpretation, but whether the decisions expressing one principle seem more important or fundamental or wide-ranging than the decisions expressing the other. Suppose in-

terpretation (6) fits only those past judicial decisions involving charges of negligence against one particular profession—say, lawyers—and interpretation (5) justifies all other cases, involving all other professions, and also fits other kinds of economic damage cases as well. Interpretation (5) then fits the legal record better on the whole, even if the number of cases involving lawyers is for some reason numerically greater, unless the argument shifts again, as it well might, when the field of study expands even more.

■ ■ ■

EPILOGUE: WHAT IS LAW?

Law is an interpretive concept. Judges should decide what the law is by interpreting the practice of other judges deciding what the law is. General theories of law, for us, are general interpretations of our own judicial practice. We rejected conventionalism [positivism], which finds the best interpretation in the idea that judges discover and enforce special legal conventions, and pragmatism [realism], which finds it in the different story of judges as independent architects of the best future, free from the inhibiting demand that they must act consistently in principle with one another. I urged the third conception, law as integrity, which unites jurisprudence and adjudication. It makes the content of law depend not on special conventions or independent crusades but on more refined and concrete interpretations of the same legal practice it has begun to interpret.

These more concrete interpretations are distinctly legal because they are dominated by the adjudicative principle of inclusive integrity. Adjudication is different from legislation, not in some single, univocal way, but as the complicated consequence of the dominance of that principle. We tracked its impact by acknowledging the stronger force of integrity in adjudication that makes it sovereign over judgments of law, though not inevitably over the verdicts of courts, by noticing how legislation invites judgments of policy that adjudication does not, by observing how inclusive integrity enforces distinct judicial constraints of role. Integrity does not enforce itself: judgment is required. That judgment is structured by different dimensions of interpretation and different aspects of these. We noticed how convictions about fit contest with and constrain judgments of substance, and how convictions about fairness and justice and procedural due process contest with one another. The interpretive judgment must notice and take account of these several dimensions; if it does not, it is incompetent or in bad faith, ordinary politics in disguise. But it must also meld these dimensions into an overall opinion: about which interpretation, all things considered, makes the community's legal record the best it can be from the point of view of political morality. So legal judgments are pervasively contestable.

That is the story told by law as integrity. I believe it provides a better account of our law than conventionalism or pragmatism on each of the two main dimensions of interpretation, so no trade-off between these dimensions is necessary at the level at which integrity competes with other conceptions. Law as integrity, that is, provides both a better fit with and a better justification of our legal practice as a whole. I argued the claim of justification by identifying and studying integrity as a distinct virtue of ordinary politics, standing beside and sometimes conflicting with the more familiar virtues of justice and fairness. We should accept integrity as a virtue of ordinary politics because we should try to conceive our political community as an association of principle; we should aim at this because, among other reasons, that conception of community offers an attractive basis for claims of political legitimacy in a community of free and independent people who disagree about political morality and wisdom.

I argued the first claim—that law as integrity provides an illuminating fit with our legal practice—by showing how an ideal judge committed to law as integrity would decide three types of hard cases: at common law, under statutes, and, in the United States, under the Constitution. I made Hercules decide the several cases I offered as working examples in Chapter 1, and my claims of fit can be checked by comparing his reasoning with the kind of arguments that seemed appropriate to lawyers and judges on both sides of those cases. But this is too limited a test to be decisive; law students and lawyers will be able to test the illuminating power of law as integrity against a much wider and more varied experience of law at work.

Have I said what law is? The best reply is: up to a point. I have not devised an algorithm for the courtroom. No electronic magician could design from my arguments a computer program that would supply a verdict everyone would accept once the facts of the case and the text of all past statutes and judicial decisions were put at the computer's disposal. But I have not drawn the conclusion many readers think sensible. I have not said that there is never one right way, only different ways, to decide a hard case. On the contrary, I said that this apparently worldly and sophisticated conclusion is either a serious philosophical mistake, if we read it as a piece of external skepticism, or itself a contentious political position resting on dubious political convictions if we treat it, as I am disposed to do, as an adventure in global internal skepticism.

I described the nested interpretive questions a judge should put to himself and also the answers I now believe he should give to the more abstract and basic of these. I carried the process further in some cases, into the capillaries as well as the arteries of decision, but only as example and not in more detail than was needed to illustrate the character of the decisions judges must make. Our main concern has been to identify the branching points of legal argument, the points where opinion divides in the way law as integrity promises. For every route Hercules took from that general conception to a particular verdict, another lawyer or judge who began in the same conception would find a different route and end in a different place, as several of the judges in our sample cases did. He would end differently because he would take leave of Hercules, following his own lights, at some branching point sooner or later in the argument.

The question how far I have succeeded in showing what law is is therefore a distinct question for each reader. He must ask how far he would follow me along the tree of argument, given the various interpretive and political and moral convictions he finds he has after the reflection I have tried to provoke. If he leaves my argument early, at some crucial abstract stage, then I have largely failed for him. If he leaves it late, in some matter of relative detail, then I have largely succeeded. I have failed entirely, however, if he never leaves my argument at all.

What is law? Now I offer a different kind of answer. Law is not exhausted by any catalogue of rules or principles, each with its own dominion over some discrete theater of behavior. Nor by any roster of officials and their powers each over part of our lives. Law's empire is defined by attitude, not territory or power or process. We studied that attitude mainly in appellate courts, where it is dressed for inspection, but it must be pervasive in our ordinary lives if it is to serve us well even in court. It is an interpretive, self-reflective attitude addressed to politics in the broadest sense. It is a protestant attitude that makes each citizen responsible for imagining what his society's public commitments to principle are, and what these commitments require in new circumstances. The protestant character of law is confirmed, and the creative role of private decisions acknowledged, by the backward-looking, judgmental nature of judicial decisions, and also by the regulative assumption that though judges must have the last word, their word is not for that reason the best word. Law's attitude is constructive: it aims, in the interpretive spirit, to lay principle over practice to show the best route to a better future, keeping the right faith with the past. It is, finally, a fraternal attitude, an expression of how we are united in community though divided in project, interest, and conviction. That is, anyway, what law is for us: for the people we want to be and the community we aim to have.

QUESTIONS FOR DISCUSSION

1. What does Dworkin mean by "integrity"? Is there a relationship between what he means by "integrity" and what we mean when we say that a person has integrity?

2. Why does Dworkin think that integrity in his sense is a good thing? Why might integrity in Dworkin's sense not be good?

3. Are there differences between writing a chain novel and deciding a case in court that Dworkin ignores? What are they, and how might they argue against Dworkin's conclusions?

4. How would you decide the *McLoughlin* case? Why?

5. If Dworkin were forced to give a definition of "law," what do you think it would be?

PLAYING BY THE RULES

FREDERICK SCHAUER

For generations legal theorists have been debating the conceptual validity, descriptive accuracy, and normative desirability of a perspective on law known as *positivism*, which under one view is the systemic embodiment of a rule-based perspective on normative systems. Discussions of legal positivism often counterpoise that perspective with one known as 'natural law', and the central tenet of positivism is consequently taken to be its denial of any necessary connection between law and morality. From Austin and Bentham to Hart and Kelsen to MacCormick and Raz, prominent positivists have offered a perspective on legal systems that maintains that the identification of a legal norm, and the designation of it as legal, are logically independent of the substantive moral content of that norm. At this point, however, confusion sets in unless we distinguish two quite different conceptions of positivism.

One conception of positivism [denies] that positivism is a descriptive claim, and maintains instead that it is a conceptual claim about the idea of law, such that what is or is not law in a community is a social fact about that community. Under this view, what Coleman calls 'the separability thesis', positivism is correct as long as a community *could* establish as law a set of norms or decision-making process not dependent for its status as law on its moral correctness. The separability thesis is the claim that there exists at least one conceivable rule of recognition (and therefore one possible legal system) that does not specify truth as a moral principle among the truth conditions for any proposition of law'. But

pursuant to this account of positivism a community could also establish as its law not only a set of norms dependent on moral correctness, but could even make its set of legal norms totally congruent with its set of moral norms. As long as the determination is made by the community, as long as it is a question itself of social fact, then there remains no *necessary* connection between law and morality.

This conceptual account of positivism may well be correct, and in fact I believe it is, but whether it is or not has very little connection with an account of rules. If positivism maintains only that what is law and what is not is determined by social fact and not necessarily by moral argument, then similarly a community decision to take as its law the *ad hoc* decisions of one person would also be sufficient for it to be so. And if such an extreme version of rule-free decision-making satisfies the conditions for law, then it is clear that nothing about rules has much bearing one way or another on the soundness of the positivist thesis as a non-descriptive metaphysical or conceptual account of the nature of law.

Under another understanding of positivism, however, one defended (in a more extreme form than is relevant here) by Raz and attacked by Dworkin, positivism is a descriptive claim about extensional divergence between a community's law and its morality, such that for positivism to be descriptively correct the rule of recognition in any community (if the descriptive claim is taken to be universal) or some community (if the descriptive claim is only about one community)

Frederick Schauer, *Playing By the Rules: A Philosophical Examination of Rule-Based Decision Making in Law and in Life* (Oxford: Clarendon Press, 1991), selection from Chapter 8 ("Rules and Law")

must demarcate that community's law from its morality. Under this view (and I have no cause here to argue which view is a better account of positivism), one seeing positivism as descriptive rather than conceptual account, a community whose law and morality are congruent is not a community whose legal system is accurately *described* as positivistic.

From the perspective of this understanding of what positivism purports to claim, positivism is descriptively accurate in any community in which the set of legal norms is not congruent with the set of moral norms. Now, however, the emphasis on morality is distracting. In this descriptive rather than conceptual debate about positivism, morality is but an example of a larger universe of the 'non-legal'. Although those who subscribe to this version of what questions positivism seeks to address and what answers it gives to them do maintain that the core of positivism consists of its denial of a conceptual or necessary connection between the status of a rule as a rule of law and the moral desirability of that rule, they would, if asked, maintain with equivalent fervor the denial of a conceptual connection between the status of a rule as a rule of law and, say, its political feasibility, its aesthetic or literary appeal, or its economic viability. Just as this understanding of positivism maintains that a morally iniquitous law can still be a law, so too does it (or would it) maintain that both economically silly and politically disastrous laws are still laws.

Little point would be served here by trying to resolve the debate between which of these accounts of positivism is sounder. I want to assume the soundness of the latter account of what positivism claims (which is not to assume that the claim is correct), but that is consistent with the former account, addressing a quite different question, also being sound. But nothing here turns on the assumption, and readers who resist it can substitute a word other than 'positivism' for the claim of extensional divergence that grounds what is to follow. Still, under the assumption that positivism is about the *idea* of recognition (rather than 'rule' of recognition, which may impose an unnecessary constraint) in the Hartian sense, the heart of positivism lies not in something special about the law/morality distinction, but in the concept of *systemic isolation*. To the positivist there can be systems whose norms are identified by reference to some identifier that can distinguish *legal* norms from other norms, such as those of politics, morality, economics, or etiquette. This identifier, which Hart refers to as the 'rule of recognition' and Dworkin labels a 'pedigree', picks out legal norms from the universe of norms, and thus provides a test for legal validity. If a norm is so selected, it is a valid legal norm, notwithstanding its moral repugnance, economic inconsistency, or political folly.

Once we see that positivism is about normative systems smaller than and distinguishable from the entire normative universe, we can agree that a positivist system is in many respects the systemic analogue of a rule. Just as rules commit decision-making to a truncated array of relevant decisional factors, so too does positivism commit decision-making to a truncated array of norms. And just as this narrowing of the potentially relevant may in the case of individual rules generate an answer that is, all things considered, the wrong answer, so too may decision-making solely according to the norms picked out by the rule of recognition be the wrong answer from the perspective of the background justifications for the legal system as a whole. A positivist view of a legal system takes the legal system as a whole to be the instantiation of its background justification (justice, or order, or whatever), and, in rule-like fashion, treats that instantiation as entrenched against efforts to view it as merely transparent to the justifications for the system itself.

We are now in a position to understand Ronald Dworkin's powerful attack on positivism. If we look at real legal systems, he claims, we often see that the results indicated by application of the pedigreed rule are morally, socially, economically, or politically undesirable. Consider again *Riggs v. Palmer*, the case of the murdering heir. *Riggs*, to repeat, was not a hard case in the sense of presenting events not covered by existing rules. The existing rules, rules whose validity could be ascertained by recourse to a Hartian rule of recognition, *did* provide an answer. It was just that that answer was morally uncomfortable, and what positivism cannot explain is when and how, as in *Riggs*, the answer generated by positivism is rejected by recourse to norms not themselves identified or identifiable by a rule of recognition. Positivism, of course, does not maintain a strong thesis of exclusivity. Nothing about positivism compels the idea that only legally pedigreed rules should guide judicial decisions. But positivism does seem committed to the weaker thesis that *if* there is a legally pedigreed rule that applies to the case at hand, then it should be employed to produce the result. If legal decision-makers may disregard the result generated by the legally recognized rule, then there seems little point in the idea of a rule of recognition at all.

But even this view might be stronger than positivism needs. That is, it could be said that what happened in *Riggs* was simply that non-legal norms trumped the legal, in the same way that positivist theory allows the citizen to refuse to obey morally reprehensible laws. Positivism is about legal validity and not about ultimate action, and nothing in positivism commits any decision-maker, including a judge in a court of law, to treating positivistic norms as the exclusive input into decision-making.

Such a solution to *Riggs*, however logically impeccable it might be, would seem to the Dworkinian as experientially impoverished. If it turns out that judges, the archetypal legal actors, are with some frequency deciding cases according to norms other than legal norms, then what purpose is served by identifying the subset that we would call 'legal'?

Some defenders of positivism have attempted to respond to Dworkin's challenge in a different way, noting the way in which the trumping norm in *Riggs*, that no man may profit from his own wrong, is itself a legal norm, pedigreed as valid in its own right by a rule of recognition. If that is so, then nothing about Riggs calls positivism into question, and Riggs is but an example of the fact that the rule of recognition may recognize rules of priority allowing such general and distant rules (what Dworkin calls 'principles') to trump less general and more locally applicable rules.

Yet even this response can be met by cases such as *Henningsen v. Bloomfield Motors*. What makes *Henningsen* important is not that it too, as in *Riggs*, set aside what seemed prior to the case to be the answer generated by the positivistically recognized rules. What cases like *Henningsen* show us is that no answer generated by the set of positivistically pedigreed norms is immune from rejection in the service of norms not so pedigreed. However possible it might be to argue that *Riggs* set aside the positive law in the name of other positive law, the same cannot be said of *Henningsen*, where the positive law was set aside in the name of moral and social principles not previously incorporated within the legal system. And if positive law is always capable of being set aside in the name of non-pedigreed values, then even a decision not to set aside the positive law involves a decision, *en passant*, that the positive law is consistent with those larger values. The result of this, a result inconsistent with the positivist picture, is that legal results are *always* a function not only of pedigreed norms, but of non-pedigreed and non-pedigreeable ones as well.

Riggs, *Henningsen*, and related cases cannot be taken to have refuted positivism, however, but only to have refuted the proposition that positivism accurately describes the legal system of the United States or the legal system of any other country in which similar examples can be found. Imagine a system, however, in which (a) a master rule of recognition pedigreed a limited number of rules; (b) all decision-makers within the system were instructed to make decisions according to and only according to those pedigreed rules; and (c) a default (or closure) rule specified the result to be reached in all cases not covered by one of the pedigreed rules. In such a system, a positivistic explanation appears to be sound, and we can thus see that positivism as a descriptive thesis is flawed not conceptually (unless taken to be a claim about all legal systems, rather than about possible legal systems), but only empirically. Few legal systems resemble this stylized model, but there is no logical reason why they could not.

That real systems have departed from this model should come as no surprise. It is characteristic of legal systems that the matters with which they deal are important, in a way that the rule systems of chess and cricket are not. The outcome of a legal decision may make a litigant a prince or a pauper, famous or infamous, a success or a failure. And when the litigants for whom such consequences attach are standing before the legal decision-maker, the pressure to reach the correct result, rather than the substantively incorrect result generated by faithful application of the rules, is likely to be enormous. Moreover, law does not just stand there to be watched. We expect people to obey its mandates, even when they disagree. In some systems, most notably and most extremely the United States, the system is also entrusted with the power to make decisions with profound moral, political, and economic effects. Is it any wonder, then, that such a system would be uncomfortable with a decision, however justified by reference only to a particular rule, that seemed incorrect in light of all morally, socially, and politically relevant considerations? And if a society desires a system in which respect and accuracy are more important than predictability, stability, or even decision-maker disability, then might not the virtues of ruleness be sacrificed with some frequency to the goals of reaching the best answer?

Yet even within a system recognizing that the large and distant must occasionally trump the small and local, the virtues associated with rules seem still to persist. We cannot and do not expect individuals incessantly to be calculating the likelihood that 55 miles per hour may under some circumstances mean something else. Or maybe we do expect citizens to engage in such calculations, but we are confident that these calculations will be so intuitive and usually so coincident with the locally generated answer that the calculating citizen need not be paralyzed by uncertainty.

This confidence exists, however, precisely because the local does have a priority. That priority is not absolute, as cases such as *Riggs* and *Henningsen* show us, but it can be and is a priority none the less. And if in fact there is a priority for the result generated by a limited and pedigreeable set of rules, what emerges is a system that might best be described as *presumptive positivism*. Such a theory would explain not only why Riggs's grandson did not inherit, but also why a host of almost but not quite as unworthy beneficiaries *do* inherit. It could explain not only why the document that Henningsen and Bloomfield Motors signed did not control when Henningsen brought suit, but also why what people sign most often does control. And more broadly, it would explain why lawyers and judges devote so much time to learning and referring to legal rules. Were those rules to be but one type of a much larger array of types of considerations to be considered in a more holistic decisional mode, we would be at a loss to explain the proportional dominance of those rules in legal decision-making, and puzzled about the justification for institutions such as law schools, bar examinations, and the West Publishing Company [a leading publisher of law books].

Thus, presumptive positivism is a descriptive claim about the status of a set of pedigreed norms within the universe of reasons for decision employed by the decision-makers within some legal system. In saying that this pedigreed set has presumptive but not absolute force, I do not mean to rely on the strictly epistemic sense of 'presumptive' that one finds, for example, in the law of evidence. Often when we employ a presumption, we presume the existence of some fact from the existence of some other fact, and thus the existence of the presumed fact is a product of uncertainty about the actual state of affairs. Presumptions, like the presumption of innocence or the presumption of paternity, serve primarily as substantively skewed accommodations to epistemic uncertainty.

By contrast, my use of 'presumptive' refers generally to the force possessed by a rule, and more specifically to a degree of force such that the rule is to be applied unless particularly exigent reasons can be supplied for not applying it. When used this way, there is nothing necessarily epistemic about the idea of a presumption, and the idea is only a way of describing a degree of strong but overridable priority within a normative universe in which conflicting norms might produce mutually exclusive results. We might prefer the norms emanating from one source to those emanating from another for epistemic reasons, but the same preference might instead emerge from any of a number of non-epistemic reasons for allocating jurisdiction in one way rather than another. When, for example, in American constitutional law a distinction drawn by government on the basis of race is taken to be unconstitutional unless the state can show a 'compelling interest' in drawing such

a distinction, the status of the racial distinction can properly be described as 'presumptively unconstitutional', despite the fact that the reasons for creating that status are not epistemic. It is not that the state is taken to know less about some factual matter, but rather that various non-epistemic considerations make some governmental decisions impermissible (rather than erroneous) except in the gravest of emergencies.

A similar notion of presumptiveness undergirds presumptive positivism. Presumptive positivism is a way of describing the interplay between a pedigreed subset of rules and the full (and non-pedigreeable) normative universe, such that the former is treated by certain decision-makers as presumptively controlling in this not-necessarily-epistemic sense of presumptive. As a result, these decision-makers override a rule within the pedigreed subset not when they believe that the rule has produced an erroneous or suboptimal result in this case, no matter how well grounded that belief, but instead when, and only when, the reasons for overriding are perceived by the decision-maker to be particularly strong. . . .

[Perhaps now] we can reconcile the opposing observations in the dispute about positivism. On the one hand, positivists observe that most of the things people call laws exist in a moderately limited collection of books, that lawyers refer to a moderately limited collection of sources with remarkable frequency, and that it does not seem all that difficult in most easy cases to figure out what the law requires. But in other cases, Dworkin and others observe, norms that in no way constitute such a closed set seem to control, even when a norm that is legal in the narrow sense goes in the opposite direction. But if presumptive positivism is correct, then both observations are correct. In most cases, the result generated by the most locally applicable and pedigreed rule controls. But in every case that rule will be tested against a larger and unpedigreeable set of considerations, and the rule will be set aside when the result it indicates is egregiously at odds with the result that is indicated by this larger and more morally acceptable set of values. Whether we call this array of overriding factors 'law' or not is a dispute that is to some extent terminological. It is also a dispute, however, that goes to the rhetoric of legality, to the extent to which legal decision-makers relying on a

non-pedigreeable universe of social norms shall when doing so be buttressed by the connotations of deduction, constraint, and limited domain suggested by the word 'law'. I will explore this question no further here, and conclude this chapter only with the descriptive assertion that presumptive positivism may be the most accurate picture of the place of rules within many modern legal systems.

QUESTIONS FOR DISCUSSION

1. What do you think Schauer means by a "rule"? Is his conception of a rule the same as that of Dworkin in *Taking Rights Seriously*?

2. When Schauer talks about "presumptive positivism," is his understanding of positivism the same as Hart's? As Coleman's? As Dworkin's? Or is it a new one entirely?

3. What does Schauer mean by a "presumption"? When might the presumption be overcome? What makes Schauer's view a critique of Dworkin? Is it also a critique of Hart?

4. If there is an empirical disagreement between Schauer and Dworkin, what methods might we use to resolve it or to establish that one is right and the other wrong?

SUGGESTIONS FOR FURTHER READING

Ronald Dworkin's works on the philosophy of law are contained in *Taking Rights Seriously* (Cambridge: Harvard University Press, 1977), *A Matter of Principle* (Cambridge: Harvard University Press, 1986), and *Law's Empire* (Cambridge: Harvard University Press, 1987). Much of the most important commentary on Dworkin is collected in Marshall Cohen, ed., *Ronald Dworkin and Contemporary Jurisprudence* (Totowa, N.J.: Rowman & Allanheld, 1984). A recent book-length analysis and critique of Dworkin is Stephen Guest, *Ronald Dworkin* (Stanford: Stanford University Press, 1992). On the interpretive themes in *Law's Empire* and elsewhere in legal theory, a useful recent addition to the literature is Andrei Marmor, *Interpretation and Legal Theory* (Oxford: Clarendon Press, 1992). A collection of early critiques of Dworkin is found in Symposium, "Taking Dworkin Seriously," *Social Theory and Practice*, vol. 5 (1980), pp. 267 ff.

CASE STUDY: THE FUGITIVE SLAVE LAWS

INTRODUCTION

Throughout this chapter we have seen various theoretical perspectives on the relationship between positive law in the narrowest sense—the rules of law found in lawbooks—and a range of larger social, political, and moral considerations. This relationship is likely to be overlooked when the positive law coincides with these various other factors. When both morality and the positive law point in the same direction, as with, for example, laws against child abuse, there is less occasion to focus specifically on the law–morality relationship. When morality and positive law point in opposite directions, however, we can see much more clearly the issues that have preoccupied the theorists featured in this chapter. For when morality commands what the positive law forbids, or when morality forbids what the positive law commands, questions about the nature and status of law cannot be avoided.

A historically important example of this divergence between morality and the specific rules of law found in lawbooks is the case of the Fugitive Slave Laws. The first of such laws, a federal statute passed in 1793, required that all slaves be returned to their owners, even if they had escaped to a state in which slavery was prohibited. A similar statute was again passed in 1850. Shortly thereafter, Thomas Sims, a slave in Savannah, Georgia, stowed away on a ship to Massachusetts. He was discovered in Boston within months after his arrival, however, and was subsequently arrested. In the midst of great public controversy, and elaborate legal strategies designed to prevent Sims from being returned to slavery in Georgia, Sims' lawyers argued both that the Fugitive Slave Law of 1850 was unconstitutional and that the Massachusetts judges should not become the instruments for Sims' return to slavery. In two separate proceedings, however, one before the United States Fugitive Slave Commission and one before the Supreme Judicial Court of Massachusetts, the courts rejected these arguments and ordered Sims returned to slavery in Georgia.

SLAVERY IN THE COURTROOM

PAUL FINKELMAN

Because this was the first extensive examination of the Act of 1850, Rantoul [Sims' lawyer] presented a detailed attack on the constitutionality of the statute. He argued (1) that the commissioner exercised what was essentially a judicial power, yet was—as Rantoul thought—unconstitutionally selected so could not function in his position: (2) that the procedure was "a suit between the claimant and the captive, involving an alleged right of property on one hand, and the right of personal liberty on the other, and that either party therefore is entitled to a trial by jury," but since the law did not allow for such a trial, it was unconstitutional; (3) that the evidence of Sims's status taken down in Georgia before a state court was unacceptable in a federal hearing because "Congress having no power to confer upon State Courts or magistrates, judicial authority" could not pass such a law; (4) that the evidence collected in Georgia was "incompetent" because "the captive was not represented at the taking thereof, and had no opportunity for cross-examination"; and (5) that Congress was not authorized by the Constitution to pass the act of 1850.

Rantoul supported his assertions with a lengthy and detailed analysis of various sections of the Constitution, previous court decisions, various federal statutes, and numerous treatises, including Story's *Commentaries* and Coke's *Institutes*. His strongest arguments centered on the judicial nature of the hearing and the need for a jury trial. Citing *Prigg v. Pennsylvania*, 41 U.S. (16 Pet.) 539 (1842), Rantoul showed that U.S. Supreme Court Justice Joseph Story believed "that where a *claim* is made by the owner . . . capable of being recognized, and asserted by proceedings before a court of justice, between parties adverse to each other, it constitutes *in the strictest sense* a controversy between the parties, and is *a case* 'arising under the Constitution' of the United States; within the EXPRESS delegation of JUDICIAL POWER given by that instrument". From this declaration in *Prigg*, Rantoul argued that only a judge, appointed properly under Article III of the Constitution, could hear a case involving the rendition of a fugitive slave.

Rantoul also became involved in a heated argument with [Commissioner] Curtis over the right of the fugitive to a trial either before or after rendition. He argued that the master could take Sims anywhere he chose, once he left Massachusetts, and thus deny him a trial on his right to freedom. Curtis, however, asserted that a certificate of removal required that the alleged slave be taken to the state from which he allegedly escaped, and in that state he could have a trial on the merits of his claim. Rantoul presented a long and elaborate argument on this issue, while Curtis often interrupted him to disagree. Clearly, despite the logic of his argument, Rantoul was unable to convince Curtis that the alleged slave could not expect to get a fair hearing elsewhere to his claim to freedom, and thus the hearing before the commissioner constituted a final decision on the matter. (The fact that when Sims arrived in Georgia he was immediately whipped in public and then sent to be a laborer suggested the factual strength of Rantoul's position.)

Report of proceedings before the Fugitive Slave Commission, from Paul Finkelman, *Slavery in the Courtroom: An Annotated Bibliography of American Cases* (Washington: Library of Congress, 1985)

Rantoul's argument took up most of Monday and part of Tuesday. Despite his extensive references and citations, he complained that the twenty-four-hour period he was allowed was not enough time to adequately support his arguments. It seems clear from the nature of Rantoul's argument and the dialogue between Curtis and Rantoul that the commissioner was bent on ensuring that this hearing be summary.

Charles G. Loring began his closing argument with the same complaints enunciated by Rantoul. Loring was absent from town when Sims was arrested and on the first day of the hearing, and he was annoyed and complains throughout his argument that Curtis would not delay the hearing in "a case of vast importance, involving the first principles of civil liberty and personal security under the laws and Constitution of the United States [and] . . . nothing else than a question of personal liberty between a man claiming to be a freeman, and another man claiming to seize and carry him away as his bound slave."

Many of the arguments presented by Loring were echoes of theories introduced by Rantoul. But, unlike Rantoul, Loring seems to have explicitly attempted to draw Curtis into the argument and to personalize the issues. Loring presented "the idea that your handwriting may consign that man to endless slavery!" Curtis responded, "That I cannot believe." Loring answered: "I submit to you with perfect confidence, that your decree to deliver the prisoner places his liberty for ever in the power of the claimant." Loring continued in great detail, with Curtis interrupting, asking questions, and at one point even asking Loring: "Will you pause for a moment? I want to get this point very distinctly." Loring attempted to show the rendition of an alleged fugitive is not the same as the extradition of an alleged criminal. His argument rested essentially on the unconstitutionality of the 1850 act and on the moral onus he attempted to place on Curtis.

Even though he allowed only limited time to Sims's attorneys to prepare their case, Commissioner Curtis himself took two days to prepare his opinion in the case and delivered it three days after closing arguments. In it he refused every objection raised by Rantoul and Loring. He also indicated his displeasure at their attempts to put him in a morally ambiguous position. During the arguments the difference in fees for the commissioner ($5 if he found against and $10 if he found in favor of the claimant) was declared to "be humiliating to this Court." Curtis noted in his opinion that "if the learned counsel supposed that the sum of five dollars was likely to influence my judgment upon any question in this case, he did right in reminding me that the Statute provides for a compensation," but Curtis declared he was not obligated to accept any compensation, and implying that he would not in fact do so, he saw "no cause for humiliation." He also showed evident distaste for the attempt "to increase to the utmost intensity the responsibility of acting" in a manner that "will send this man to perpetual slavery." Curtis stated he would not be influenced by these considerations. In a long opinion he declared there was conclusive evidence that Sims was the slave of James Potter of Georgia, that the commissioner was not acting as a judge but was simply returning a claimed fugitive and that the act of 1850 was constitutional. Seeing no reason not to, he then issued a certificate of removal to Potter's agent.

As the first important and intensive investigation of the meaning of the 1850 act, this case was extremely important and influential. This pamphlet allowed both antislavery lawyers and other federal commissioners to read the arguments and opinion in this case. The arguments of Rantoul and Loring would be copied, added to, and refined by other antislavery lawyers in the next decade. Similarly, various commissioners would borrow from Curtis to refute such arguments.

THE OFFICIAL REPORT OF THE CASE BEFORE CHIEF JUSTICE LEMUEL SHAW OF THE SUPREME JUDICIAL COURT OF MASSACHUSETTS

THOMAS SIMS' CASE, 7 CUSHING 285, MARCH 1851.

"This is a petition for a writ of *habeas corpus* to bring the petitioner before this court, with a view to his discharge from imprisonment. . . . We are then to examine the petition, accompanied as it is, by a copy of the warrant under which the marshal of the district claims to hold the petitioner, and the return thereon. It appears that the petitioner has been arrested and is claimed as a fugitive from labor, [from the state of Georgia] upon a warrant, issued by . . . a commissioner of the circuit court of the United States, in pursuance of a law of the United States, and that the deputy marshal has returned the warrant to the commissioner who issued it, and has the body of the petitioner before the commissioner for the purposes expressed in the warrant. It is now argued, that the whole proceeding . . . is unconstitutional and void; because, although the act of congress of 1850, c. 60, (9 U.S. Stat. at Large, 462), has provided for, and directed this course of proceeding, yet that the statute itself is void, because congress had no power, by the constitution of the United States, to pass such a law, and confer such an authority. . . . The subject matter of this act is the return and restoration of fugitive slaves, designated in the constitution as persons held to service or labor in one state under the laws thereof, escaping into another. The whole provision, art. 4 sect. 2, is as follows: 'No person held to service or labor in one state under the laws thereof, escaping into another, shall, in consequence of any law or regulation therein, be discharged from such service or labor, but shall be delivered up on claim of the party to whom such service or labor may be due.' . . . It is necessary to refer briefly to the circumstances under which the constitution was made, and the great social and political objects and purposes, which the people had in adopting it. . . . These North American provinces, when they became independent of . . . Great Britain, regarded themselves and were regarded, as sovereign states; . . . with the usual powers of . . . exercising an exclusive control and jurisdiction over all persons and subjects within their respective territories. In some of the states, large numbers of slaves were held; in others a few only; but some, it is believed, in all except Massachusetts, in which slavery was considered as abolished, by the constitution of 1780. So long as the states remained sovereign, they could assert their rights in regard to fugitive slaves by war or treaty, and, therefore, before renouncing and surrendering such sovereignty, some substitute, in the nature of a treaty or compact, must necessarily be devised and agreed to. The clause above cited from the constitution seems to have been, in character, precisely such a treaty. But the right, thus secured by the constitution to the slave owner, is limited by it, and cannot be extended, by implication or construction, a line beyond the precise *casus foederis*. The fugitive must not only owe service or labor in another state, but he must have escaped from it. This is the extent of the right of the master. It is founded in the compact, and limited by the compact. But the constitution itself did not profess or propose to direct, in detail, how the rights, privileges, benefits and immunities, intended to be declared and secured by it, should be practically carried into effect; this was left to be done by laws to be passed by the legislature, and applied by the judiciary, for the establishment of which full provision was at the same time made. It was, as we believe, under this view of the right of regaining specifically the custody of one from whom service or labor is due by the laws of one state, and who has escaped into another, and under this view of the powers of the general government, and the duty of congress, that the law of February 12, 1793, was passed (I U.S. Stat. at Large, 302). The constitutionality of the act of 1793, came directly before this court, and was argued and decided in 1823. . . . [Another] case came before the supreme court of the United States, in 1842, in which the point in question was fully discussed and deliberately settled. *Prigg v. Pennsylvania*, 16 Pet. 539. There was some difference of opinion among the judges upon minor points, but not, it is believed, upon the con-stitutionality of the act of congress of 1793, and especially of that part of it which confers an authority on circuit and district judges, to take a summary jurisdiction, in the manner provided by the act of 1793. We have thought it important thus to inquire into the validity and constitutionality of the act of 1793, because it appears to be decisive of that in question. In the only particular in which the constitutionality of the act of congress of 1850 is now called in question, that of 1793 was obnoxious to the same objection, viz., that of authorizing a summary proceeding before officers and magistrates not qualified under the constitution to exercise the judicial powers of the general government. On the whole, we consider that the question raised by the petitioner, and discussed in the argument before us, is settled by a course of legal decisions which we are bound to respect, and which we regard as binding and conclusive upon this court. I have, therefore, to state, in behalf of the court, under the weighty responsibility which rests upon us, and as the unanimous opinion of the court, that the writ of *habeas corpus* prayed for cannot be granted."

JUSTICE ACCUSED

ROBERT M. COVER

Samuel Sewall, Robert Rantoul, and Richard Henry Dana began the legal attack on the act. All three were competent lawyers who had imbibed the stern Massachusetts legal positivism of Story and Shaw. Sewall was a Garrisonian; Rantoul was a Jacksonian Ben-thamite of strong antislavery views; Dana was a former Whig Free-Soiler of generally conservative views. For very different reasons none of these three men would have been capable of the kind of argument that Birney or Chase or Jolliffe could make. They

Robert M. Cover, *Justice Accused: Antislavery and the Judicial Process* (New Haven: Yale University Press, 1975)

would have choked on the suggestion that the Constitution somehow has a necessary relationship to what is right.

A writ of habeas corpus was sought on behalf of Sims from Chief Justice Shaw. Shaw finally conceded that the state court had jurisdiction to entertain the petition for the writ. This result was in keeping with the general antebellum view of state habeas corpus jurisdiction. Rantoul delivered the principal argument against the constitutionality of the act before the Massachusetts court. Like a good craftsman, he steered away from the arguments that had already been rejected under the 1793 act. Instead, he argued first that the Act of 1850 purported to vest judicial power in an officer who was not a judge within the meaning of Article III. For the commissioner was not appointed for a tenure of good behavior and with no diminution in salary. Second, he argued that the fee differential denied due process to the alleged fugitive, as it made the commissioner an interested party in the outcome.

Shaw's opinion in *Sims* was a telling blow to the legal strategy of antislavery. He did reach the merits of the suit, but declined, in an elaborate opinion, to even let the writ of habeas corpus issue. He asserted that no court should issue the writ if it appeared on the face of the petition that the prisoner would have to be remanded. Since the petition of Sims showed his restraint for purpose of the rendition process under the Act of 1850, Shaw held that his remand would be immediately necessary should the writ issue. He reached that conclusion by holding the act free of all constitutional doubt. Moreover, he rested his conclusion on precedent decided with respect to the Act of 1793, holding the differences between the acts irrelevant for purposes of the constitutional questions presented. Shaw's decision in effect closed the doors of the Massachusetts state courts to any collateral attacks on renditions. This consequence meant that the only remaining tribunal was the commissioner himself from whom no ap-

peal was provided. In *Sims* the commissioner, in an elaborate opinion, upheld the act, his own authority, and the rendition of Sims. By dint of military might, Sims was returned.

The furor over the *Sims* case had immediate and important consequences for the Massachusetts judiciary. In 1853 a constitutional convention was held. For the first time in Massachusetts, a serious proposal for an elected judiciary was put forward. It was handily defeated. But a remarkable feature of both the defense of and attack on the independence of the judiciary was the use of *Sims's Case* and the fugitive problem as support for their assumed position. As defender of judicial independence, Dana argued, "Take the fugitive slave law. Suppose the court equally divided upon that subject. A new judge is to be elected. . . . The votes will be given for principles and not men." But for Mr. French of New Bedford, supporting an elected judiciary, the loss of a good man for the bench was less important than the loss of justice caused by a too independent court:

> We have been told that every citizen however humble, may come before our courts, and spread out his case and demand his rights, I stand here and tell you, that a free citizen of Mass.—as free Mr. Pres., as either you or I—has failed to be protected by the judiciary. . . . But I do stand here to say that I heard the claim for a writ of habeas corpus in the case of Thomas Sims . . . and it failed to induce the supreme judges to issue the writ and thus secure to that citizen his inalienable rights. Now Sir, I would like to have judges elected by the people that they may not be so independent of them, so that if another case upon the writ of habeas corpus similar to the one to which I have referred should come up before them, they will be dependent enough to listen favorably to argument. . . .

Mr. French, however, was not as sensitive to the formal issue as he might have been. Richard Henry Dana, one of Sims's counsel, strongly supported the maintenance of an independent judiciary. He felt that the fugitive's interest lay with the system that would best preserve a courageous and intelligent judiciary. The coincidence of popular passion with moral right in the *Sims* Case was by no means clear and, in any event, not inevitable.

The convention of 1853 implicitly rejected the notion that a judge ought to perform his tasks with an eye to the morality of the majority. But Dana's suggestion that an independent and high-minded judge was the fugitive's best refuge was simply whistling in the dark. The list of independent and high-minded judges who upheld the Act of 1850 began to lengthen: McLean in Ohio and Michigan; Kane in Pennsylvania; Grier in Pennsylvania; Miller in Wisconsin; Conkling in New York; Woodbury and Curtis in Massachusetts; and, of course, as always, Shaw. More and more, it appeared the question ought not to be put, "How should a judge of integrity decide these cases?" but rather "how can a man of integrity judge these cases?"

■ ■ ■

The narrative of fugitive slave cases in this chapter makes clear that the interplay of antislavery demand and judicial "cannot" was seldom on the simple level of "what is the law?" The antislavery bar sought doctrinal growth, minimally. The utopians sought constitutional upheaval. Both practitioners and utopians seemed to tread the line of demanding conscious disregard of role limits. The judicial responses to these demands, insofar as they went beyond refusal, appealed to one or more of four justifications for role fidelity.

The most extreme justification asserted that ordered society itself depended on judicial adherence to positive law, constitutional limits. Thus, McLean's assertion that disregard of these limits "would undermine and overturn the social compact." The terms of ordered society embrace fidelity to the limits and conditions on which power is conferred.

A second, somewhat more common, justification for "cannot" is that of "separation of powers": "It is for the people . . . and their representatives . . . to consider the laws of nature." Now, the "social compact" justification may be used (as it was by McLean) in conjunction with the separation of powers. But the judge may appeal to separation of powers as a self-evident, presumably acceptable, argument, without in turn justifying it with the social compact. He may consider the principle of distribution of sovereignty a desirable end, in itself, regardless of whether sanctioned as one of the terms of the original agreement.

A third justification of judicial role fidelity—in particular with regard to the Fugitive Slave Law—was "union." I have already noted the common view of the Fugitive Slave clause as a basic part of the constitutional bargain. I think it fair to say that not a little of this vision was a reading of the problems of the present backward into history. As the fugitive issue was one of the great issues for compromise or adjustment in 1850, it was seen as one of the great issues of 1787.

Finally, a few judges justified their adherence to role limits by stressing their oath to support the Constitution. The oath was entitled to respect because it was a solemn, consensual undertaking on their part, and because it was a legitimate requirement for the exercise of delegated power.

When Story pointed to the Constitution as the only legitimate source of his judicial obligation, he evoked all four of these justifications. The Constitution derived its moral authority from its character as a substantially democratic and consensual arrangement of a polity. In its wisdom, it preserved limited spheres for the various branches of government. And, it embraced the agreed upon terms for cementing the Union. Story, like all other judges, was sworn to uphold it. Thus, the word "constitution" was a remarkably powerful shorthand—a symbol that evoked all of the relevant values on the side of judicial fidelity to law.

■ ■ ■

The preceding chapters have described a variety of contexts in which antislavery judges decided cases amidst claims that the morality of slavery be considered as a major factor in the decision. Usually these claims were put forward directly by the parties or their representatives. Few of the men who made such claims and none of the judges who heard them, however, thought that consideration of the morality of slavery alone would suffice to reach a decision. Most of the actors assumed that in many cases an antislavery result could be achieved only with some stretching or reconstruction of formal principles. By formal principles I mean: (1) those governing the role of the judge, his place vis-à-vis other lawmaking bodies, his subordination to precedent, statute, Constitution; (2) the hierarchical character of the judicial system and the respect due to both the decrees and the precedents of higher tribunals and especially the Supreme Court; (3) the standards of professional responsibility, articulated more often in schools, treatises, and controversy literature than in decisions and statutes; (4) the sense of the judicial craft.

Both the judges and the men who addressed them understood that these formal constraints were independently justifiable in terms of interests they served. Therefore, the judge's problem in any case where some impact on the formal apparatus could be expected, was never a single-dimensioned moral question—is slavery or enslavement, or rendition to slavery, morally justified or reprehensible? [R]ather, the issue was whether the moral values served by antislavery (the substantive moral dimension) outweighed interests and values served by fidelity to the formal system when such values seemed to block direct application of the moral or natural law proposition.

I shall designate choices between these two sets of values as "moral-formal decisions." By this designation I do not mean to

imply that there is no moral dimension to fidelity to formal principles or to the content of the principles themselves. In a sense the moral-formal decision was a moral-moral decision—a decision between the substantive moral propositions relating to slavery and liberty and the moral ends served by the formal structure as a whole, by fidelity to it, or by some relevant particular element of it. Thus, the legal actor did not choose between liberty and slavery. He had to choose between liberty and ordered federalism; between liberty and consistent limits on the judicial function; between liberty and fidelity to public trust; between liberty and adherence to the public corporate undertakings of nationhood; or, as some of the judges would have it, between liberty and the viability of the social compact. Moreover individual cases seldom presented the choice between universal liberty and total destruction of the competing values underlying the formal restraints. Rather, they presented choices between incremental furtherance of liberty and marginal vitiation of these values.

Because of the difficulties inherent in making the sorts of choices outlined above, many antislavery advocates either argued that the relevant choice point be shifted to the decision of entering or remaining within the formal structures, or that moral imperatives be translated into legal ones. By deciding to act as insurgent rather than judge, a man could avoid confronting many of the formal issues involved in the judicial choice. He need not have worried about considerations of constitutional limits on judicial lawmaking, whether deemed to have emerged out of considerations of federalism or of separation of powers. Moreover, even his obligations of fidelity to decisions and processes of the majority were of a different and lesser character as citizen than as magistrate. To act as insurgent was to assume a role the ethic of which was compatible with an antislavery stance amidst a proslavery legal system. This decision thus eliminated the tension of moral–formal conflict.

The alternative course of working within the formal system to translate moral imperatives into legal ones led to a constant battle over the formal principles. Instead of arguing about slavery, the antislavery man found himself arguing about state court habeas corpus jurisdiction; the appellate authority of the United States Supreme Court over state court decisions; the proper bounds of judicial interpretation; and the deference due to imperfectly articulated legislative policy. Such sidetracks could be avoided only by asserting an alternative formal (legal) principle that either maintained the identity of moral and legal imperatives through requiring the law to conform to some "natural law," or presumed the identity of law and morality subject only to explicit defeasance by express legislative action. As I have shown, such natural law constructs bore little relation to the uses to which "nature" had been put in slave law for more than a half-century and conflicted directly with the dominant jurisprudential and constitutional assumptions of the profession. . . .

Whenever judges confronted the moral-formal dilemma, they almost uniformly applied the legal rules. Moreover, they seemed very reluctant to resort to, and thus legitimate, substantial doctrinal innovations that might have made certain cases less a choice between law and morality and more a choice between alternative legal formulations. Furthermore, even as they opted for role fidelity and noninnovative behavior, these judges accompanied their decisions with striking manifestations of at least one of three related responsibility-mitigation mechanisms: (1) Elevation of the formal stakes (sometimes combined with minimization of the moral stakes). (2) Retreat to a mechanistic formalism. (3) Ascription of responsibility elsewhere. While all three of these are related and, indeed, may be viewed as different perspectives on a single phenomenon, it is useful to treat them separately. The more aggravated the conflict between moral and formal demands on the judge, the more pronounced these effects seem to be.

QUESTIONS FOR DISCUSSION

1. What would Austin have said was "the law" that should control Chief Justice Shaw's decision? Hart? Dworkin? Kennedy?

2. Would Cicero have said that the Fugitive Slave Law was not really "law"? Aquinas? Finnis? Fuller?

3. Cover (1941–1986, and Professor of Law at the Yale Law School at the time he wrote this book) says that Shaw's opinion is an example of "positivism." What does he mean by "positivism"? How is Cover's conception of positivism related to Hart's or Austin's?

4. Would any of the theorists you have read in this chapter have reached the same result as Curtis and Shaw? Which ones, and why? How would the theorists who reached a different result have justified their decisions?

5. Did the existence of prior judicial decisions upholding and enforcing the Fugitive Slave Laws make a difference to Curtis and Shaw? Should it have?

CHAPTER 2

LEGAL REASONING

INTRODUCTION

A large part (some philosophers would say the most important part) of philosophy is the study of reasoning. Not surprisingly, therefore, a large part of the philosophy of law is the study of reasoning in the law. What kinds of arguments do lawyers make, and how do judges reach their decisions? Are there considerations that are legitimately used outside of legal argument but not inside? Conversely, are there factors that count in legal argument but not elsewhere? And what distinguishes a good legal argument from a bad one?

In order to confront any of these questions, we must take on the overriding issue in the study of legal reasoning—is *legal* reasoning distinct from reasoning? Is there good *legal* reasoning or is there simply good reasoning? Are there methods of analysis unique to the legal system? That there are such distinct methods of legal reasoning has been a common claim made by or about the legal system for generations. This is perhaps best demonstrated by the claim of law schools that they teach their students to "think like lawyers." But the claim that there is something teachable called "thinking like a lawyer" does not usually imply that lawyers systematically reason better (or worse) than other people. Instead it is a claim that there are methods of analysis and reasoning employed in the legal system that are different from those employed in other decision-making environments.

One possible distinction between legal reasoning and ordinary reasoning is the emphasis in legal reasoning on the application of written-down legal rules, including the legal rules found in constitutions, statutes, regulations, and other formal codes. A common mode of reasoning in the law starts with a particular set of facts—former President Ronald Reagan is, hypothetically, considering running for a third term as President of the United States—and a legal text—the Twenty-second Amendment to the Constitution, providing that no one may hold the office of President "more than twice." The question then arises whether the set of facts of Ronald Reagan's holding a third term falls within that prohibition. In this case, it quite clearly does. The facts fall under, or are *subsumed* under, the legal rule.

Of course, not all cases involving the application of legal codes are this simple. Problems of vagueness and ambiguity, among others, often make the issue of legal interpretation substantially more difficult than it is in the simple example we have just used. Frequently the constitutional provision, for example, is not as plain as is the Twenty-second Amendment. For example, the Constitution prohibits Congress from "abridging the freedom of speech," precludes states from "deny[ing] to any person . . . the equal protection of the laws," and bars "unreasonable searches and seizures." In these examples, complex questions arise about the methods that legal decision makers do or should employ in determining whether some act counts as an abridgement of the freedom of speech, or a denial of the equal protection of the laws, or an unreasonable search or seizure. The same problems arise with statutes. When we must decide whether bicycles are "vehicles" for purposes of the "No vehicles in the park" rule, we confront difficulties we did not confront when considering whether privately owned automobiles may, as part of a drive for pleasure, be allowed in the park.

Issues of statutory or code interpretation are often complex and often raise interesting philosophical questions. The first section of this chapter will be devoted to many of these issues. Still, claims about the supposed distinctiveness of legal reasoning are rarely made in the context of these kinds of legal and judicial tasks. After all, ordinary people interpret statutes and regulations all the time, not only when they fill out their tax returns, but also when they decide what to do when faced with signs that say things like "Stop," "Speed Limit 35," and "Adults Only." So, although there are ways in which lawyers focus more systematically on such matters and deal with complications generally not a concern in everyday life, there does not appear to be anything especially distinctive to law about this form of reasoning.

It is important to note that when lawyers and judges *do* focus on cases of statutory or code interpretation, the cases they handle are likely to be unusual. When cases are really *easy*, there is often no need to consult a lawyer, and no need to go to court. Ronald Reagan might have wanted to serve a third term, but the language of the Twenty–second Amendment is so clear that Reagan could recognize for himself that it would be hopeless even to try to argue for the legal permissibility of a third term. So if people rarely go to court when their "case" falls clearly within an easily understood law, this says a great deal about the cases that *do* wind up in court, or even wind up in a lawyer's office. The cases that go to the lawyers, and the cases that go to court, are rarely the easy ones. Because people simply follow the law in most of the truly easy cases, the cases that involve lawyers and judges are generally ones in which both sides believe they have a chance to win. This idea, which economists call the "selection effect,"[1] puts the task of lawyers and judges in perspective. The selection effect warns us that it is often a mistake to generalize about how law or legal rules operate from the distorted sample of cases that winds up in court, and the even more distorted sample that winds up in an appellate court. Thus one possibility is that legal reasoning about statutes is distinctive only because the legal system systematically deals with hard rather than routine cases of statutory interpretation.

Another candidate for the distinctiveness of legal reasoning comes up not with respect to statutes or other formal codes. Often the claim of the distinctive

---

[1] See George L. Priest and William Klein, "The Selection of Disputes for Litigation," *Journal of Legal Studies*, vol. 13 (1984), pp. 1 ff.

nature of legal reasoning is made in the context of what is sometimes called *common law reasoning, reasoning from precedent,* or *reasoning by analogy.* There are differences among these three concepts, but there are also things they share in common. The basic idea is that in the legal system judges make decisions, and then judges in subsequent cases make decisions that are expected to take account of what the judges have done in previous cases. Recall from Chapter 1 the case of *Riggs v. Palmer,* discussed in the Dworkin reading, in which the grandson who murdered his grandfather claimed that he was nevertheless entitled to inherit his grandfather's property. The New York Court of Appeals (New York's highest court) rejected this claim, relying on the principle that "no man may profit from his own wrong." In subsequent and similar cases, then, New York judges would be expected to *follow* the decision in *Riggs v. Palmer.* So suppose it turned out that a week after the decision in *Riggs v. Palmer,* a virtually identical New York case (lawyers would call it a case "on all fours") arose involving a grandson who poisoned his grandfather in order to claim his inheritance. If that happened, Judge Gray, who in his dissent in *Riggs v. Palmer* made it clear that he thought that the grandson should have been allowed his inheritance, would nevertheless have been expected to follow the precedent set a week earlier, and thus to decide against the grandson.

Cases that are so identical to an earlier case do not occur that often. More commonly, what it is to follow a case is not so simple a matter. If in some future case a grandson killed his grandfather negligently in a farm accident rather than intentionally with poison, may he still collect his inheritance under his grandfather's will? The question would not involve interpreting the text of a statute, but deciding the effect of a requirement to follow the previous case. Indeed, the idea of "the common law" is that in common law countries like England and the United States, judges often develop entire areas of law—like contracts and torts—entirely by judicial decision, without there ever being a statutory text to interpret (as there was in *Riggs v. Palmer*). But even though there was initially the Statute of Wills to interpret in the first case, that would not be the most important issue in the second. In the second case the attention would be focused on the relationship between the second case and the first judicial decision, that is, *Riggs v. Palmer.* Is the second case—negligent killing—sufficiently like the first case—intentional killing—or are the differences between negligence and intent relevant? And what makes a similarity or a difference relevant or irrelevant? These are the questions we will take up in considering how reasoning from precedent and reasoning by analogy operate; and these are the questions that will determine how, if at all, this form of reasoning differs from reasoning in everyday life.

Although reasoning from statutes and reasoning from precedent appear to be different, they are similar in an important way. As the American legal philosopher Richard Wasserstrom (1932–   ) has explained,[2] both methods involve the same kind of deference or obedience to the *past.* In both forms of decision making there

---

[2]Richard A. Wasserstrom, *The Judicial Decision: Toward a Theory of Legal Justification* (Stanford: Stanford University Press, 1961).

is an expectation that the decision maker will not simply reach the conclusion that she thinks best, but will instead follow the legal *authority*. Maybe it would be good for the country if Ronald Reagan were to run for a third term. But even if that is what the legal decision maker believes, she is expected to subjugate her own judgment to that of the people who wrote and ratified the Twenty-second Amendment in 1951, most of whom are now dead, most of whom had thought of Ronald Reagan (if at all) only as an actor, and none of whom had much of an idea of what the world would be like in, say, 1996. In the same way Judge Gray in the hypothetical second case is expected to subjugate his own judgment to that of Judge Earl, even though he thought a week ago that Judge Earl was wrong and Judge Gray probably still thinks the same thing. Is a form of reasoning that gives this kind of control to past decision makers to be applauded or condemned? Is it rational? Is it moral? If a judge thinks that a precedent is morally wrong, is it immoral as well as irrational for her to decide against her own best moral judgment? If not, why not?[5]

These questions about a form of decision making that compels obedience to the past are more important than many people realize, perhaps because many people like to say that they are following rules or following precedents when all they are doing is what they actually think is the right thing to do. But when we say that a judge should follow a precedent, we mean, as with the hypothetical negligent killing case just described, that a judge should do what some previous judge did, even if this judge thinks the previous judge was wrong. Imagine this approach applied to logic! The very kind of reasoning that the legal system celebrates is often treated in books on informal logic as a fallacy, because the fact that a decision has been made is not itself a reason to believe in the soundness of the decision. Yet the law requires judges to do just what the strictures of good reasoning often tell other people not to do. Is this an accurate picture of legal reasoning? If so, are there good reasons why the legal system celebrates it?

The concluding section of this chapter will take up a number of critical challenges to the traditional picture of legal reasoning. The foremost of these comes from the Legal Realists, who appeared briefly in Chapter 1 as the proponents of a view about law that focused on predictions of judicial decisions, and who also saw judicial decisions as based less on the application of "recognized" rules than the standard legal positivist picture would suppose. The second part of this claim is directly relevant to the issues we take up in this chapter, because the Legal Realists would claim that judges do not reason *from* statutes or precedents, but rather reason just the way all of the rest of us do, by deciding what to do based on an "all things considered" judgment of what is the best decision under the circumstances. Only after they have come to that conclusion, the Legal Realists maintained, do they look for a statute or a precedent to support the conclusion

---

[5]An important discussion of the morality and rationality of relying on rules and precedent is contained in the works of the English legal, political, and moral theorist Joseph Raz (1938–). In particular, see his *Practical Reason and Norms* (Princeton: Princeton University Press, 1990) and *The Authority of Law* (Oxford: Clarendon Press, 1978).

they have reached on other grounds, and, at least in American law, they are usually able to find what they are looking for.

The critique of the standard picture of legal reasoning is even more extreme in some of the writings of the proponents of Critical Legal Studies. Just as various perspectives in the interpretation of art or literature have maintained that texts are what we make them, that texts can be almost anything we want them to be, and that it is the interpreter and not the text that matters most, so theorists like Mark Tushnet, whose arguments are presented in this chapter, maintain that the same applies to law. Are judges bound by the "intentions of the framers" of the Constitution, as some would say they are and should be, or is history something that we *make* rather than find? Thus the question is not whether as a normative matter judges should follow the original intentions of the framers. It is whether it is possible for them to do so even if they wanted to, or even if society attempted to make them do so. So too with textual interpretations. When we interpret a text, do we take something out of it, or do we instead, as many modern thinkers believe, impose something on it? If the latter is true, then what does that say about what judges do, and what does that say about the entire traditional picture of how the process of legal reasoning operates? Thus the various critical challenges connect the themes of this chapter with the themes of Chapter 1. The very definition of law is closely related to what lawyers and judges do. If they do nothing distinctive from other decision makers, as the various critical challenges maintain, then the idea of law as a distinct domain is in jeopardy as well. If, however, there is something distinctive about what lawyers and judges do, then a positivist conception of law as a limited and distinct domain becomes much more plausible.

2.1 THE INTERPRETATION OF LEGAL TEXTS

INTRODUCTION

Recall from Chapter 1 the example used by H. L. A. Hart of the "No Vehicles in the Park" sign. Hart used this sign as an example of the kind of statutory or regulatory text that legal interpreters confront all the time, involving some clear cases at the core, and some difficult cases at the fringe, or penumbra. A local ordinance prohibiting people from keeping "livestock" (but not pets) on their property would plainly prohibit people from keeping a herd of commercial cattle in the backyard, and equally plainly not prohibit them from having a canary as a pet. But what if someone has two pet pigs? That case is more problematic, lying within the uncertain territory between the clear inclusions and the clear exclusions.

Yet what makes these clear cases so clear? In Chapter 1 we discussed the famous debate between H. L. A. Hart and Lon Fuller about the moral merits and demerits of legal positivism, but in the same articles Hart and Fuller also debated the questions of legal interpretation that interest us here.[4] In drawing his distinction between core and fringe cases, Hart appeared to suggest that the ordinary linguistic meaning of the text of a rule determined which cases were clear and which not. What made the case of the automobile a core case under the "No vehicles in the park" was just that an automobile is a clear example of the proper use of the word "vehicle."

To this Fuller objected. As in much of his work, Fuller was concerned with *purpose*, and he saw Hart's approach as insufficiently mindful of the importance of purpose in legal interpretation. To make his point Fuller asked us to imagine a statue, erected by a veterans' group as a war memorial, that incorporated a fully functioning military truck. Surely, Fuller maintained, the truck that was part of the statue was a vehicle, and just as surely, Fuller went on, it would be absurd to exclude the truck just because of a literal and acontextual reading of the word "vehicle." We must always look to the purpose of the law, he claimed, and once we did that, we would see that we could never claim to have identified an easy or core case just by consulting the words of the statute.

The debate between Hart and Fuller, as further described and analyzed in the selection "Formalism" by Frederick Schauer, was thus about both the possibility

---

[4]H. L. A. Hart, "Positivism and the Separation of Law and Morals," *Harvard Law Review*, vol. 71 (1958), pp. 593 ff.; Lon L. Fuller, "Positivism and Fidelity to Law—A Reply to Professor Hart," *Harvard Law Review*, vol. 71 (1958), pp. 630 ff.

and desirability of interpreting legal texts according to the plain or ordinary or literal meaning of the words in the text. Fuller's position, focusing on purpose, calls forth a range of related debates about the use of original legislative intent in statutory interpretation, and about the use of the original framers' intent in constitutional interpretation. It is important to note, however, that *intent* and *purpose* are not the same thing. If a rule prohibited automobiles, motorcycles, and musical instruments, but not electric golf carts and artists with easels, we might say that the rule itself had the purpose of lessening noise, and we would have determined the purpose just by reasoning inductively from the more specific things the statute included. This method is not the same as trying to interpret a law by looking at the intentions of those who actually wrote the law, or those who actually voted in favor of it, at least *if* intentions are conscious mental states. Suppose we just had the original "No vehicles in the park" rule. *Why* do you think it was enacted? Perhaps in order to decrease noise. Perhaps to increase safety. Perhaps to protect the environment. All of these *purposes* (and more) are possible, but we might be able to decide among them by finding out what the people who made the rule actually *intended.* Maybe they would just tell us. Or maybe they would have written down their goal, as is often the case when legislatures produce what is called a *legislative history.* So we might actually find out that the writers of the rule wanted to prevent noise. If that is so, and if we think that what they thought is important,[5] then we would know that bicycles and baby carriages, no noisier than pedestrians, would not be within the rule. And we would know that motor scooters would clearly be within the rule, even though we would not have been so sure if we looked only at the text.

Yet Fuller's point was not just that purpose or intent could help us in the fringe. His point was that we could not even know what was the core and what was the fringe, what was inside the law and what was outside, without consulting the purpose or the intent. So he would say that the vehicle/statue, even though clearly within the literal meaning of the words, was not really within the rule. Do you think he would also say that a marching band, not within the words but within the purpose of preventing noise, was to be excluded from the park? Are there differences between the two cases? In the real case that inspired the example, *McBoyle v. United States,*[6] Justice Holmes wrote an opinion involving a law that made it a federal crime to transport a stolen vehicle across state lines. The case involved an airplane, which was then a sufficiently new form of transportation (the case was decided in 1931, and the statute was written in 1919) that it was not clearly a vehicle. Holmes said that criminal laws like this must be interpreted narrowly, and thus concluded that an airplane was not a vehicle for purposes of this law.

But why should those who interpret laws be bound by what people long ago wrote, or by what people long ago intended? The world changes, and it might be

---

[5]For a defense of why original intent is important, see the Bork article in this chapter, and the discussion of *Wallace v. Jaffree* in Chapter 4.

[6]283 U.S. 25 (1931).

sensible for those in charge of interpreting laws to try to make sure that the law changes to keep up with changes in the world. Especially when the words used are vague, there is likely to be a strong desire to change the interpretation of those words as times change, or an equally strong desire to interpret the words according to contemporary social, moral, or political values. When the First Amendment to the Constitution, prohibiting Congress from "abridging . . . the freedom of speech, or of the press," was adopted, the drafters wanted to protect political and religious speeches, books, and newspapers from governmental repression. Should the First Amendment apply to cable television? Video games? What about the Fourteenth Amendment, which prevents states from denying to their citizens the "equal protection of the laws." We know it was intended primarily for the benefit of newly freed slaves, and we know that it was directed at the problem of racial discrimination. Should it now be applied to sex discrimination? Discrimination on the basis of sexual orientation? Why or why not? (On some of these problems, see Chapter 5.) And what about the provision in the Constitution setting the minimum age to be President at thirty-five? When that provision was adopted in 1787, the life span of the average person was about forty-six. Now it is well over seventy. Should that make a difference in interpreting the requirement that Presidents be thirty-five or older?

FORMALISM

FREDERICK SCHAUER

With accelerating frequency, legal decisions and theories are condemned as "formalist" or "formalistic." But what *is* formalism, and what is so bad about it? Even a cursory look at the literature reveals scant agreement on what it is for decisions in law, or perspectives on law, to be formalistic, except that whatever formalism is, it is not good. Few judges or scholars would describe themselves as formalists, for a congratulatory use of the word "formal" seems almost a linguistic error. Indeed, the pejorative connotations of the word "formalism," in concert with the lack of agreement on the word's descriptive content, make it tempting to conclude that "formalist" is the adjective used to describe any judicial decision, style of legal thinking, or legal theory with which the user of the term disagrees.

Yet this temptation should be resisted. There *does* seem to be descriptive content in the notion of formalism, even if there are widely divergent uses of the term. At the heart of the word "formalism" in many of its numerous uses, lies the concept of decisionmaking according to *rule*. Formalism is the way in which rules achieve their "ruleness" precisely by doing what is supposed to be the failing of formalism: screening off from a decisionmaker

Excerpts from Frederick Schauer, "Formalism," *Yale Law Journal*, vol. 97 (1989), pp. 509 ff.

factors that a sensitive decisionmaker would otherwise take into account. Moreover, it appears that this screening off takes place largely through the force of the language in which rules are written. Thus the tasks performed by rules are tasks for which the primary tool is the specific linguistic formulation of a rule. As a result, insofar as formalism is frequently condemned as excessive reliance on the language of a rule, it is the very idea of decisionmaking by rule that is being condemned, either as a description of how decisionmaking can take place or as a prescription for how decisionmaking should take place.

Once we disentangle and examine the various strands of formalism and recognize the way in which formalism, rules, and language are conceptually intertwined, it turns out that there is something, indeed much, to be said for decision according to rule—and therefore for formalism. . . .

■ ■ ■

Is it possible for written norms to limit the factors that a decisionmaker considers? At first glance, the answer to this question seems to be "no." Language is both artificial and contingent and therefore appears insufficiently rigid to limit the choices of the human actors who have created it. The word "cat," for example, could have been used to refer to canines, and the English language could have followed the language of the Eskimos in having several different words to describe the varieties of snow. Yet this answer confuses the long-term mobility of language with its short-term plasticity, and is a conclusion comparable to taking the ponderous progress of a glacier as indicating that it will move if we put our shoulders against it and push. Of course language is a human creation, and of course the rules of language are contingent, in the sense that they could have been different. It is also beyond controversy that the rules of language reflect a range of political, social, and cultural factors that are hardly *a priori*. But this artificiality and contingency does not deny the short-term, or even intermediate-term, noncontingency of

meaning. If I go to a hardware store and request a hammer, the clerk who hands me a screwdriver has made a mistake, even though it is artificial, contingent, and possibly temporary that the word "hammer" represents hammers and not screwdrivers. . . .

The questions about the possibility of linguistic constraint can be clarified by considering again the rule prohibiting vehicles in the park. [Let us look] at the central applications—whether cars and trucks are excluded. Hart assumed that, whatever else the rule did, it excluded cars and trucks. This was the rule's "core" of settled meaning and application. Against this, Fuller offered the example of a statue of a truck created as a war memorial by a group of patriotic citizens. According to Fuller, the example challenges the idea that a rule will have a settled core of meaning which can be applied without looking at the rule's purpose. Fuller argues that it cannot be determined whether the truck, which is a perfectly functional vehicle, falls into the rule's periphery or core unless one considers the purpose of the rule. Fuller's challenge is ambiguous, however; there are three variant interpretations of his challenge to the theory of linguistic constraint. One interpretation of Fuller's challenge is that legal systems necessarily incorporate rule-avoiding norms. . . . Legal systems must provide some escape route from the occasional absurdity generated by literal application because applying the literal meaning of a rule can at times produce a result which is plainly silly, clearly at odds with the purpose behind the regulation, or clearly inconsistent with any conception of wise policy. Insofar as a legal system offers its decisionmakers no legitimate escape from unreasonable consequences literally indicated by the system's norms, the system is much less a *legal* system, or is at least not a legal system worthy of that name. This argument, however, asserts a normative point about how legal systems should operate, rather than any necessary truth about how the norms themselves operate. Moreover, the argument itself admits the potential binding authority of rules: If rules require an escape route to avoid the consequences of literal application, then it must be that literal application can generate answers different from those which a decision-maker would otherwise choose. Thus, this interpretation fails to challenge the possibility of linguistic constraint; it merely points out the undesirability of employing it too rigorously in certain domains.

Alternatively, Fuller might be arguing that legal systems necessarily require the interpretation of regulatory language in light of the purpose of the regulation. As with the first interpretation of the challenge, however, this interpretation focuses on whether a rule should bind, and it leaves the claims of linguistic determinacy untouched. We still can imagine a system in which decisionmakers do not interpret clear regulatory language according to its purpose if its purpose diverges from the regulatory language. The outcome in some instances might seem absurd, but it is question-begging to use the existence of the absurd result as an attack on the possibility of a core of literal meaning.

Finally, Fuller might be interpreted as making a point about language itself: He might be arguing that meaning cannot be severed from the speaker's purpose and that meaning must be a function of the specific context in which words are used. Fuller's argument that the idea of literal meaning is incoherent, an argument also made by other critics, reveals a mistaken view of the nature of language. Fuller and his followers fail to distinguish the possibility and existence of meaning from the *best* or *fullest* meaning that might be gleaned from a given communicative context. In conversation, I am assisted in determining what a speaker intends for me to understand by a number of contextual cues, including inflection, pitch, modulation, and body language, as well as by the circumstances surrounding the conversation. That such contextual cues assist my understanding, however, does not imply that the words, sentences, and paragraphs used by the speaker have *no* meaning without those cues. The "no vehicles in the park" rule clearly points to the exclusion of

the statue from the park even if we believe that the exclusion is unnecessary from the point of view of the statute's purpose.

If I come across an Australian newspaper from 1827, I can read it because I understand, acontextually, the meaning of most of the words and sentences in that newspaper, even though with better historical understanding I might understand *more* of what was written by a colony of transported English convicts. This example does not demonstrate that language is unchanging, nor that language can be perfectly understood without attention to context, but rather that some number of linguistic conventions, or rules of language, are known and shared by all people having competence in the English language. Linguistic competence in a given language involves understanding some number of rules also understood by others who are linguistically competent in the same language. When individuals understand the same rules, they convey meaning by language conforming to those rules. Members of the community of English speakers, for example, possess shared understandings that enable them to talk to all other members of the community.

Among the most remarkable features of language is its compositional nature, i.e., the way in which we comprehend sentences we have never heard before. We can do this because rules, unspecified and perhaps unspecifiable, allow us to give meaning to certain marks and certain noises without having to inspect the thought processes of the speaker or the full context in which words appear. Words communicate meaning at least partially independently of the speaker's intention. When the shells wash up on the beach in the shape of C–A–T, I think of small house pets and not of frogs or Oldsmobiles precisely because those marks, themselves, convey meaning independently of what might have been meant by any speaker. Of course there can never be *totally* acontextual meaning. The community of speakers of the English language is itself a context. Yet meaning can be "acontextual" in the sense that that meaning draws on no other context besides those understandings shared among virtually all speakers of English.

Given that the meaning of words may be acontextually derived from our understandings of language, the central question becomes whether enough of these understandings exist to create the possibility of literal language. In other words, we must ask whether words have sufficient acontextual import so that communication can take place among speakers of English in such a way that at least a certain limited range of meaning, if not one and only one meaning, will be shared by all or almost all speakers of English. The answer to this question is clearly "yes." As with the shells that washed up on the beach in the shape of C–A–T, words strung together in sentences point us toward certain meanings on the basis of our shared understandings. At times these sentences may be descriptive, but at other times these comprehensible sentences may be general prescriptions—rules. Because we understand the rules of language, we understand the language of rules. Contextual understanding might be necessary to determine whether a given application does or does not serve the purposes of a rule's framers. Yet the rule itself communicates meaning as well, although that meaning might depart from the purposes behind the rule or from the richer understanding to be harvested from considering a wider range of factors than the rule's words. That we might learn more from considering additional factors or from more fully understanding a speaker's intentions does not mean that we learn nothing by consulting the language of rules themselves.

■ ■ ■

The language in which a rule is written and the purpose behind that rule can diverge precisely because that purpose is plastic in a way that literal language is not. Purpose cannot be reduced to any one canonical formulation, for when purpose is set down canonically, that canonical formulation of purpose may frustrate the purpose itself. It is because purpose is not reduced to a concrete set of words that it retains its sensitivity to novel cases, to bizarre applications, and to the complex unfolding of the human experience. Thus, for the recourse to purpose to "solve" the problem of formalism, the purpose must not be imprisoned in the rigidity of words. This unrigidified purpose can be explained, clarified, and enriched as new examples and applications come to our attention. The purpose behind the "No vehicles in the park" regulation is not embarrassed by the statue of the truck exactly because purpose can bend to the circumstances of the moment in a way that language, with its acontextual autonomy of meaning, cannot. In contrast, the term "vehicles," at least at the core, literally refers to vehicles, if it turns out that the prohibition of some vehicles does not serve the purpose of the regulation, then the embarrassment is unavoidable. . . .

The view that rules should be interpreted to allow their purposes to trump their language in fact collapses the distinction between a rule and a reason, and thus loses the very concept of a rule. Rules are by definition general. They gather numerous known and unknown particulars under headings such as "vehicles," "punishment," "dogs," and "every person who is directly or indirectly the beneficial owner of more than 10 per centum of any class of any [registered] equity security (other than an exempted security)." After identifying a category of items or events to which the rule applies, in the *protasis*, rules then prescribe what shall be done with these particulars in the *apodosis*. Occasionally, however, not all of the particulars comprising the rule's category of coverage are suitable for the prescribed treatment; the generalizations that are a necessary part of any rule treat all members of the class in a manner that may be appropriate only for *most* members of the class. What, then, is to happen when a case arises in which the generalization does not apply to this particular? When a rule's prescribed treatment is unsuitable, if the decisionmaker were to ignore the rule, the rule would not be a real rule providing a reason for decision but would be a mere rule of thumb, defeasible when purposes behind the rule would not be served. If every application that would not serve the reason behind the rule were jettisoned from the coverage of the rule, then the decision procedure would be identical to one applying reasons directly to individual cases, without the mediation of rules. Under such a model, rules are superfluous except as predictive guides, for they lack any normative power of their own. By contrast, if in cases in which the particular application would not serve the reasons behind the rule, the rule nevertheless provides its own reason for deciding the case according to the rule, the rule itself has a normative force that provides for action or decision.

In summary, it is exactly a rule's rigidity, even in the face of applications that would ill serve its purpose, that renders it a rule. This rigidity derives from the language of the rule's formulation, which prevents the contemplation of every fact and principle relevant to a particular application of the rule. To be formalistic in Llewellyn's sense is to be governed by the rigidity of a rule's formulation; yet this governance by rigidity is central to the constraint of regulative rules. Formalism in this sense is therefore indistinguishable from "rulism," for what makes a regulative rule a rule, and what distinguishes it from reason, is precisely the unwillingness to pierce the generalization even in cases in which the generalization appears to the decisionmaker to be inapposite. A rule's acontextual rigidity is what makes it a rule. . . .

Thus, the essential equivalency of formalism and "ruleness" is before us. Viewing formalism as merely rule-governed decisionmaking does not make it desirable. Yet recognizing the way in which formalism is merely a way of describing the process of taking rules seriously allows us to escape the epithetical mode and to confront the critical question of formalism: What, if anything, is good about the unwillingness to go beneath the rule and apply its purpose, or the purposes behind that purpose, directly to the case before the decisionmaker? . . .

The simple answer to this question, and perhaps also the correct one, is "nothing." Little about decision constrained by the rigidity of rules seems intrinsically valuable. Once we understand that rules get in the way, that they gain their ruleness by cutting off access to factors that might lead to the best resolution in a particular case, we see that rules function as impediments to optimally sensitive decisionmaking. Rules doom decisionmaking to mediocrity by mandating the inaccessibility of excellence.

Nor is there anything essentially *just* about a system of rules. We have scarce reason to believe that rule–based adjudication is more likely to be just than are systems in which rules do not block a decisionmaker, especially a just decisionmaker, from considering every reason that would assist her in reaching the best decision. Insofar as factors screened from consideration by a rule might in a particular case turn out to be those necessary to reach a just result, rules stand in the way of justice in those cases and thus impede optimal justice in the long term. We equate Solomon's wisdom with justice not because Solomon followed the rules in solving the dispute over the baby but because Solomon came up with exactly the right solution for that case. We frequently laud not history's rule followers, but those whose abilities at particularized decisionmaking transcend the inherent limitations of rules.

Still, that rules may be in one sense unjust, or even that they may be inappropriate in much of what we call a legal system, does not mean there is nothing to be said for rules. One of the things that can be said for rules is the value variously expressed as predictability or certainty. But if we pursue the predictability theme, we see that what most arguments for ruleness share is a focus on disabling certain classes of decisionmakers from making certain kinds of decisions. Predictability follows from the decision to treat all instances falling within some accessible category in the same way. It is a function of the way in which rules decide ahead of time how *all* cases within a class will be determined.

[P]redictability comes only at a price. Situations may arise in which putting this particular into that category seems just too crude—something about this particular makes us desire to treat it specially. *This* vehicle is merely a statue, emits no fumes, makes no noise, and endangers no lives; it ought to be treated differently from those vehicles whose characteristics mesh with the purpose behind the rule. Serving the goal of predictability, however, requires that we ignore this difference, because to acknowledge this difference is also to create the power— the *jurisdiction*—to determine whether this vehicle or that vehicle actually serves the purpose of the "no vehicles in the park" rule. It is the jurisdiction to determine that only some vehicles fit the purpose of the rule that undermines the confidence that *all* vehicles will be prohibited. No longer is it the case that anything that is a *vehicle*, a moderately accessible category, is excluded. Instead, the category is now that of *vehicles whose prohibition will serve the purposes of the "no vehicles in the park" rule*, a potentially far more controversial category.

Thus, the key to understanding the relationship of ruleness to predictability is the idea of decisional jurisdiction. The issue is not whether the statue serves the purpose of the "no vehicles in the park" rule. It is whether giving some decisionmaker jurisdiction to determine what the rule's purpose is (as well as jurisdiction to determine whether some item fits that purpose) injects a possibility of variance substantially greater than that involved in giving a decisionmaker jurisdiction solely to determine whether some particular is or is not a vehicle. Note also that the jurisdictional question has a double aspect. When we grant jurisdiction we are first concerned with the range of equally correct decisions that might be made in the exercise of that jurisdiction. If there is no authoritative statement of the purpose behind the "no

vehicles in the park" rule, granting jurisdiction to determine that purpose would allow a decisionmaker to decide whether the purpose is to preserve quiet, to prevent air pollution, or to prevent accidents, and each of these determinations would be equally correct. In addition to increasing the range of correct decisions, however, certain grants of jurisdiction increase the likelihood of erroneous determinations. Compare "No vehicles in the park" with "The park is closed to vehicles whose greatest horizontal perimeter dimension, when added to their greatest vertical perimeter dimension, exceeds the lesser of (a) sixty-eight feet, six inches and (b) the greatest horizontal perimeter dimension, added to the greatest vertical perimeter dimension, of the average of the largest passenger automobile manufactured in the United States by the three largest automobile manufacturers in the preceding year." The second adds no inherent variability, but it certainly compounds the possibility of decisionmaker error. Creating the jurisdiction to determine whether the purposes of a rule are served undermines predictability by allowing the determination of any of several possible purposes; in addition, the creation of that jurisdiction engenders the possibility that those who exercise it might just get it wrong.

With these considerations in mind, let us approach formalism in a new light. Consider some of the famous marchers in formalism's parade of horribles, examples such as . . . Fuller's statue of the truck in the park and the poor Bolognese surgeon who, having opened the vein of a patient in the course of performing an emergency operation outdoors, was prosecuted for violating the law prohibiting "drawing blood in the streets." Each of these examples reminds us that cases may arise in which application of the literal meaning of words produces an absurd result. But now we can recast the question, for we must consider not only whether the result was absurd in these cases but also whether a particular decisionmaker should be empowered to determine absurdity. Even in cases as extreme as these, formalism is only superficially about rigidity and absurdity. More fundamentally, it is about power and its allocation.

Formalism is about power, but is also about its converse—modesty. To be formalistic as a decisionmaker is to say that something is not my concern, no matter how compelling it may seem. When this attitude is applied to the budget crisis or to eviction of the starving, it seems objectionable. But when the same attitude of formalism requires judges to ignore the moral squalor of the Nazis or the Ku Klux Klan in First Amendment cases, or the guilt of the defendant in Fourth Amendment cases, or the wealth of the plaintiff who seeks to recover for medical expenses occasioned by the defendant's negligence, it is no longer clear that refusal to take all factors into account is condemnable.

QUESTIONS FOR DISCUSSION

1. Schauer thinks we can interpret laws according to their "literal meaning." What does he think a "literal meaning" is? Is this the same as plain meaning? As ordinary meaning? Is there such a thing as literal meaning? Can meaning be determined apart from context?

2. Schauer argues that sometimes it might be the right thing to reach an "absurd" result. What does he mean by "absurd"? Why does he think it is sometimes right for judges to reach an absurd conclusion? Is this an absurd view?

3. What is it that makes the view that Schauer calls "formalism" formal? Think about formality in other contexts. When is it good? When is it bad?

HOME BUILDING AND LOAN ASSOCIATION V. BLAISDELL
290 U.S. 398 (1934)

From the dissenting opinion of Justice SUTHERLAND:

The whole aim of construction, as applied to a provision of the Constitution, is to discover the meaning, to ascertain and give effect to the intent, of its framers and the people who adopted it. The necessities which gave rise to the provision, the controversies which preceded, as well as the conflicts of opinion which were settled by its adoption, are matters to be considered to enable us to arrive at a correct result. The history of the times, the state of things existing when the provision was framed and adopted, should be looked to in order to ascertain the mischief and the remedy. As nearly as possible we should place ourselves in the condition of those who framed and adopted it. . . .

GOVERNMENT BY JUDICIARY

RAOUL BERGER

Why is the "original intention" so important? The answer was long since given by Madison: if "the sense in which the Constitution was accepted and ratified by the Nation . . . be not the guide in expounding it, there can be no security for a consistent and stable government more than for a faithful exercise of its powers." A judicial power to revise the Constitution transforms the bulwark of our liberties into a parchment barrier. This it was that caused Jefferson to say, "Our peculiar security is in the possession of a written constitution. Let us not make it a blank paper by construction." Given a system founded on a dread of power, with "limits" to fence it about, those who demand compliance with those limits (pursuant to the counsel of four or five early State constitutions) are not to be charged with invoking the shades of the Framers in order to satisfy "the need for certainty. . . . If we pretend that the framers had a special sort of wisdom, then perhaps we do not have to think too hard about how to solve pressing social problems." The issue rather is whether solution of those "pressing social problems" was confided to the judiciary.

Effectuation of the draftsman's intention is a long-standing rule of interpretation in the construction of all documents—wills, contracts, statutes—and although today such rules are downgraded as "mechanical" aids, they played a vastly more important role for the Founders. Hamilton, it will be recalled, averred: "To avoid arbitrary discretion in the courts, it is indispensable that they should be bound down by *strict rules* and precedents, which serve to define and point out their duty in every particular case that comes before them." That Hamilton was constrained thus to reassure the ratifiers testifies to prevailing distrust of unbounded judicial interpretive discretion. Some fifty years later, Justice Joseph Story, perhaps the greatest scholar who sat on the Supreme Court, emphasized that such rules provided a "fixed standard" for interpretation, without which a "fixed Constitution" would be forever unfixed. The Constitution, in short, was written against a background of interpretive presuppositions that assured the Framers their design would be effectuated.

From Raoul Berger, *Government by Judiciary: The Transformation of the Fourteenth Amendment* (Cambridge: Harvard University Press, 1977)

THE TEMPTING OF AMERICA

ROBERT BORK

What was once the dominant view of constitutional law—that a judge is to apply the Constitution according to the principles intended by those who ratified the document—is now very much out of favor among the theorists of the field. In the legal academies in particular, the philosophy of original understanding is usually viewed as thoroughly passé, probably reactionary, and certainly—the most dreaded indictment of all—"outside the mainstream." That fact says more about the lamentable state of the intellectual life of the law, however, than it does about the merits of the theory.

In truth, only the approach of original understanding meets the criteria that any theory of constitutional adjudication must meet in order to possess democratic legitimacy. Only that approach is consonant with the design of the American Republic.

THE CONSTITUTION AS LAW: NEUTRAL PRINCIPLES

When we speak of "law," we ordinarily refer to a rule that we have no right to change except through prescribed procedures. That statement assumes that the rule has a meaning independent of our own desires. Otherwise there would be no need to agree on procedures for changing the rule. Statutes, we agree, may be changed by amendment or repeal. The Constitution may be changed by amendment pursuant to the procedures set out in article V. It is a necessary implication of the prescribed procedures that neither statute nor Constitution should be changed by judges. Though that has been done often enough, it is in no sense proper.

What is the meaning of a rule that judges should not change? It is the meaning understood at the time of the law's enactment. Though I have written of the understanding of the ratifiers of the Constitution, since they enacted it and made it law, that is actually a shorthand formulation, because what the ratifiers understood themselves to be enacting must be taken to be what the public of that time would have understood the words to mean. It is important to be clear about this. The search is not for a subjective intention. If someone found a letter from George Washington to Martha telling her that what he meant by the power to lay taxes was not what other people meant, that would not change our reading of the Constitution in the slightest. Nor would the subjective intentions of all the members of a ratifying convention alter anything. When lawmakers use words, the law that results is what those words ordinarily mean. If Congress enacted a statute outlawing the sale of automatic rifles and did so in the Senate by

From Robert H. Bork, *The Tempting of America: The Political Seduction of the Law* (New York: The Free Press, 1990)[7]

[7]Robert Bork (1929–) was a Professor of Law at the Yale Law School. In 1972 he became Solicitor General of the United States (the government's chief lawyer before the Supreme Court), and in this capacity was the one who, on behalf of Richard Nixon, fired Archibald Cox as special prosecutor investigating Watergate. Bork later became a judge of the United States Court of Appeals for the District of Columbia, and in 1986 was nominated by President Reagan to serve on the Supreme Court. The hearings before the Senate were televised, and Bork's views about constitutional interpretation were challenged. By a narrow vote the Senate refused to give its "advice and consent" to the nomination, and thus Bork never served on the Supreme Court.

a vote of 51 to 49, no court would overturn a conviction because two senators in the majority testified that they really had intended only to prohibit the *use* of such rifles. They said "sale" and "sale" it is. Thus, the common objection to the philosophy of original understanding—that Madison kept his notes of the convention at Philadelphia secret for many years—is off the mark. He knew that what mattered was public understanding, not subjective intentions. Madison himself said that what mattered was the intention of the ratifying conventions. His notes of the discussions at Philadelphia are merely evidence of what informed public men of the time thought the words of the Constitution meant. Since many of them were also delegates to the various state ratifying conventions, their understanding informed the debates in those conventions. As Professor Henry Monaghan of Columbia has said, what counts is what the public understood. Law is a public act. Secret reservations or intentions count for nothing. All that counts is how the words used in the Constitution would have been understood at the time. The original understanding is thus manifested in the words used and in secondary materials, such as debates at the conventions, public discussion, newspaper articles, dictionaries in use at the time, and the like. Almost no one would deny this; in fact almost everyone would find it obvious to the point of thinking it fatuous to state the matter—except in the case of the Constitution. Why our legal theorists make an exception for the Constitution is worth exploring.

The search for the intent of the lawmaker is the everyday procedure of lawyers and judges when they must apply a statute, a contract, a will, or the opinion of a court. To be sure, there are differences in the way we deal with different legal materials, which was the point of John Marshall's observation in *McCulloch v. Maryland* that "we must never forget, that it is *a constitution* we are expounding." By that he meant that narrow, legalistic reasoning was not to be applied to the document's broad provisions, a

document that could not, by its nature and uses, "partake of the prolixity of a legal code." But he also wrote there that it was intended that a provision receive a "fair and just interpretation," which means that the judge is to interpret what is in the text and not something else. And, it will be recalled, in *Marbury v. Madison* Marshall placed the judge's power to invalidate a legislative act upon the fact that the judge was applying the words of a written document. Thus, questions of breadth of approach or of room for play in the joints aside, lawyers and judges should seek in the Constitution what they seek in other legal texts: the original meaning of the words.

We would at once criticize a judge who undertook to rewrite a statute or the opinion of a superior court, and yet such judicial rewriting is often correctable by the legislature or the superior court, as the Supreme Court's rewriting of the Constitution is not. At first glance, it seems distinctly peculiar that there should be a great many academic theorists who explicitly defend departures from the understanding of those who ratified the Constitution while agreeing, at least in principle, that there should be no departure from the understanding of those who enacted a statute or joined a majority opinion. A moment's reflection suggests, however, that Supreme Court departures from the original meaning of the Constitution are advocated *precisely because* those departures are not correctable democratically. The point of the academic exercise is to be free of democracy in order to impose the values of an elite upon the rest of us.

If the Constitution is law, then presumably its meaning, like that of all other law, is the meaning the lawmakers were understood to have intended. If the Constitution is law, then presumably, like all other law, the meaning the lawmakers intended is as binding upon judges as it is upon legislatures and executives. There is no other sense in which the Constitution can be what article VI proclaims it to be: "Law." It is here that the concept of neutral principles, which Wechsler said were essential if the

Supreme Court was not to be a naked power organ, comes into play. Wechsler, it will be recalled, in expressing his difficulties with the decision in *Brown v. Board of Education*, said that courts must choose principles which they are willing to apply neutrally, apply, that is, to all cases that may fairly be said to fall within them. This is a safeguard against political judging. No judge will say openly that any particular group or political position is always entitled to win. He will announce a principle that decides the case at hand, and Wechsler had no difficulty with that if the judge is willing to apply the same principle in the next case, even if it means that a group favored by the first decision is disfavored by the second. That was precisely what Arthur M. Schlesinger, Jr., said that the Black–Douglas wing of the Court was unwilling to do. Instead, it pretended to enunciate principles but in fact warped them to vote for interest groups.

The Court cannot, however, avoid being a naked power organ merely by practicing the neutral application of legal principle. The Court can act as a legal rather than a political institution only if it is neutral as well in the way it derives and defines the principles it applies. If the Court is free to choose any principle that it will subsequently apply neutrally, it is free to legislate just as a political body would. Its purported resolution of the Madisonian dilemma is spurious, because there is no way of saying that the correct spheres of freedom have been assigned to the majority and the minority. Similarly, if the Court is free to define the scope of the principle as it sees fit, it may, by manipulating the principle's breadth, make things come out the way it wishes on grounds that are not contained in the principle it purports to apply. Once again, the Madisonian dilemma is not resolved correctly but only according to the personal preferences of the Justices. The philosophy of original understanding is capable of supplying neutrality in all three respects—in deriving, defining, and applying principle.

NEUTRALITY IN THE DERIVATION OF PRINCIPLE

When a judge finds his principle in the Constitution as originally understood, the problem of the neutral derivation of principle is solved. The judge accepts the ratifiers' definition of the appropriate ranges of majority and minority freedom. The Madisonian dilemma is resolved in the way that the founders resolved it, and the judge accepts the fact that he is bound by that resolution as law. He need not, and must not, make unguided judgments of his own.

This means, of course, that a judge, no matter on what court he sits, may never create new constitutional rights or destroy old ones. Any time he does so, he violates not only the limits to his own authority but, and for that reason, also violates the rights of the legislature and the people. To put the matter another way, suppose that the United States, like the United Kingdom, had no written constitution and, therefore, no law to apply to strike down acts of the legislature. The U.S. judge, like the U.K. judge, could never properly invalidate a statute or an official action as unconstitutional. The very concept of unconstitutionality would be meaningless. The absence of a constitutional provision means the absence of a power of judicial review. But when a U.S. judge is given a set of constitutional provisions, then, as to anything not covered by those provisions, he is in the same position as the U.K. judge. He has no law to apply and is, quite properly, powerless. In the absence of law, a judge is a functionary without a function. . . .

NEUTRALITY IN THE DEFINITION OF PRINCIPLE

The neutral definition of the principle derived from the historic Constitution is also crucial. The Constitution states its principles in majestic generalities that we know cannot be taken as sweepingly as the words alone might suggest. The first amendment states that "Congress shall make no law . . . abridging the freedom of speech," but no one has ever supposed that Congress could not make some speech unlawful or that it could not make all speech illegal in certain places, at certain times, and under certain circumstances. Justices Hugo Black and William O. Douglas often claimed to be first amendment absolutists, but even they would permit the punishment of speech if they thought it too closely "brigaded" with illegal action. From the beginning of the Republic to this day, no one has ever thought Congress could not forbid the preaching of mutiny on a ship of the Navy or disruptive proclamations in a courtroom. . . .

Thus, once a principle is derived from the Constitution, its breadth or the level of generality at which it is stated becomes of crucial importance. The judge must not state the principle with so much generality that he transforms it. The difficulty in finding the proper level of generality has led some critics to claim that the application of the original understanding is actually impossible. That sounds fairly abstract, but an example will make clear both the point and the answer to it.

In speaking of my view that the fourteenth amendment's equal protection clause requires black equality, Dean Paul Brest said:

The very adoption of such a principle, however, demands an arbitrary choice among levels of abstraction. Just what is "the general principle of equality that applies to all cases"? Is it the "core idea of *black* equality" that Bork finds in the original understanding (in which case Alan Bakke [a white who sued because a state medical school gave preference in admissions to other races] did not state a constitutionally cognizable claim), or a broader principle of "*racial* equality" (so that, depending on the precise content of the principle, Bakke might have a case after all), or is it a still broader principle of equality that encompasses discrimination on the basis of gender (or sexual orientation) as well? . . .

. . . The fact is that all adjudication requires making choices among the levels of generality on which to articulate principles, and all such choices are inherently non-neutral. No form of constitutional decisionmaking can

be salvaged if its legitimacy depends on satisfying Bork's requirements that principles be "neutrally derived, defined and applied."

If Brest's point about the impossibility of choosing the level of generality upon neutral criteria is correct, we must either resign ourselves to a Court that is a "naked power organ" or require the Court to stop making "constitutional" decisions. But Brest's argument seems to me wrong, and I think a judge committed to original understanding can do what Brest says he cannot. We may use Brest's example to demonstrate the point.

The role of a judge committed to the philosophy of original understanding is not to "*choose* a level of abstraction." Rather, it is to find the meaning of a text—a process which includes finding its degree of generality, which is part of its meaning—and to apply that text to a particular situation, which may be difficult if its meaning is unclear. With many if not most textual provisions, the level of generality which is part of their meaning is readily apparent. The problem is most difficult when dealing with the broadly stated provisions of the Bill of Rights. It is to the latter that we confine discussion here. In dealing with such provisions, a judge should state the principle at the level of generality that the text and historical evidence warrant. The equal protection clause was adopted in order to protect the freed slaves, but its language, being general, applies to all persons. As we might expect, and as Justice Miller found in the *Slaughter-House Cases*, the evidence of what the drafters, the Congress that proposed the clause, and the ratifiers understood themselves to be requiring is clearest in the case of race relations. It is there that we may begin in looking for evidence of the level of generality intended. Without meaning to suggest what the historical evidence in fact shows, let us assume we find that the ratifiers intended to guarantee that blacks should be treated by law no worse than whites, but that it is unclear whether whites were intended to be protected from discrimination in favor of blacks.

On such evidence, the judge should protect only blacks from discrimination, and Alan Bakke would not have had a case. The reason is that the next higher level of generality above black equality, which is racial equality, is not shown to be a constitutional principle, and therefore there is nothing to be set against a current legislative majority's decision to favor blacks. Democratic choice must be accepted by the judge where the Constitution is silent. The test is the reasonableness of the distinction, and the level of generality chosen by the ratifiers determines that. If the evidence shows the ratifiers understood racial equality to have been the principle they were enacting, Bakke would have a case. In cases concerning gender and sexual orientation, however, interpretation is not additionally assisted by the presence of known intentions. The general language of the clause, however, continues to subject such cases to the test of whether statutory distinctions are reasonable. Sexual differences obviously make some distinctions reasonable while others have no apparent basis. That has, in fact, been the rationale on which the law has developed. Society's treatment of sexual orientation is based upon moral perceptions, so that it would be difficult to say that the various moral balances struck are unreasonable.

Original understanding avoids the problem of the level of generality in equal protection analysis by finding the level of generality that interpretation of the words, structure, and history of the Constitution fairly supports. This is a solution generally applicable to all constitutional provisions as to which historical evidence exists. There is, therefore, a form of constitutional decisionmaking that satisfies the requirement that principles be neutrally defined. . . .

NEUTRALITY IN THE APPLICATION OF PRINCIPLE

The neutral or nonpolitical application of principle [is] a requirement, like the others, addressed to the judge's integrity. Having derived and defined the principle to be applied, he must apply it consistently and without regard to his sympathy or lack of sympathy with the parties before him. This does not mean that the judge will never change the principle he has derived and defined. Anybody who has dealt extensively with law knows that a new case may seem to fall within a principle as stated and yet not fall within the rationale underlying it. As new cases present new patterns, the principle will often be restated and redefined. There is nothing wrong with that; it is, in fact, highly desirable. But the judge must be clarifying his own reasoning and verbal formulations and not trimming to arrive at results desired on grounds extraneous to the Constitution. This requires a fair degree of sophistication and self-consciousness on the part of the judge. The only external discipline to which the judge is subject is the scrutiny of professional observers who will be able to tell over a period of time whether he is displaying intellectual integrity.

QUESTIONS FOR DISCUSSION

1. Sutherland, Berger, and Bork argue that the Constitution should be interpreted according to the intentions of its drafters. What arguments do they offer for this conclusion? Are those arguments sound?

2. Do Berger and Bork confront the question of what to do when the literal meaning of the text and the evidence of original intentions of the drafters point in opposite directions? What do you think they would do?

3. What do Sutherland, Berger, and Bork mean by "intentions"? Do they distinguish intentions from purposes?

THE MISCONCEIVED QUEST FOR THE ORIGINAL UNDERSTANDING

PAUL BREST

By "originalism" I mean the familiar approach to constitutional adjudication that accords binding authority to the text of the Constitution or the intentions of its adopters. [The] most widely accepted justification for originalism is simply that the Constitution is the supreme law of the land. The Constitution manifests the will of the sovereign citizens of the United States— "we the people" assembled in the conventions and legislatures that ratified the Constitution and its amendments. The interpreter's task is to ascertain their will. Originalism may be supported by more instrumental rationales as well: Adherence to the text and original understanding arguably constrains the discretion of decisionmakers and assures that the Constitution will be interpreted consistently over time.

The most extreme forms of originalism are "strict textualism" (or literalism) and "strict intentionalism." A strict textualist purports to construe words and phrases very narrowly and precisely. For the strict intentionalist, "the whole aim of construction, as applied to a provision of the Constitution, is . . . to ascertain and give effect to the intent of its framers and the people who adopted it."

Much of American constitutional interpretation rejects strict originalism in favor of what I shall call "moderate originalism." The text of the Constitution is authoritative but many of its provisions are treated as inherently open-textured. The original understanding is also important, but judges are more concerned with the adopters' general purposes than with their intentions in a very precise sense.

Some central doctrines of American constitutional law cannot be derived even by moder-ate originalist interpretation, but depend, instead, on what I shall call "nonoriginalism." The modes of nonoriginalist adjudication defended in this article accord the text and original history presumptive weight, but do not treat them as authoritative or binding. The presumption is defeasible over time in the light of changing experiences and perceptions.

Textualism takes the language of a legal provision as the primary or exclusive source of law (a) because of some definitional or supralegal principle that only a written text can impose constitutional obligations, or (b) because the adopters intended that the Constitution be interpreted according to a textualist canon, or (c) because the text of a provision is the surest guide to the adopters' intentions. . . .

By contrast to the textualist, the intentionalist interprets a provision by ascertaining the intentions of those who adopted it. The text of the provision is often a useful guide to the adopters' intentions, but the text does not enjoy favored status over other sources. . . .

■ ■ ■

1. WHO ARE THE ADOPTERS?

The adopters of the Constitution of 1787 were some portion of the delegates to the Philadelphia Convention and majorities or supermajorities of the participants in the ratifying conventions in nine states. For all but one amendment to the Constitution, the adopters were two-thirds or more of the members of each House of Congress and at least a majority of the legislators in [three-fourths] of the state legislatures.

For a textual provision to become part of the Constitution the requisite number of

Paul Brest, "The Misconceived Quest for the Original Understanding" *Boston University Law Review*, vol. 60 (1980), pp. 204 ff. Brest (1940–) is Dean and Professor of Law at the Stanford Law School.

persons in each of these bodies must have assented to it. Likewise, an intention can only become binding—only become an institutional intention—when it is shared by at least the same number and distribution of adopters. (Hereafter, I shall refer to this number and distribution as the "adopters.")

If the only way a judge could ascertain institutional intent were to count individual intention-votes, her task would be impossible even with respect to a single multimember lawmaking body, and a fortiori where the assent of several such bodies were required. Therefore, an intentionalist must necessarily use circumstantial evidence to deduce a collective or general intent.

Interpreters often treat the writings or statements of the framers of a provision as evidence of the adopters' intent. This is a justifiable strategy for the moderate originalist who is concerned with the framers' intent on a relatively abstract level of generality—abstract enough to permit the inference that it reflects a broad social consensus rather than notions peculiar to a handful of the adopters. It is a problematic strategy for the strict originalist.

As the process of adoption moves from the actual framers of a constitutional amendment to the members of Congress who proposed it to the state legislators who ratified it, the amount of thought given the provision surely diminishes—especially if it is relatively technical or uncontroversial, or one of several of disparate provisions (*e.g.*, the Bill of Rights) adopted simultaneously. This suggests that there may be instances where a framer had a determinate intent but other adopters had no intent or an indeterminate intent. For example, suppose that the framers of the commerce clause considered the possibility that economic transactions taking place within the confines of a state might nonetheless affect interstate commerce in such a way as to come within the clause, and that they intended the clause to cover such transactions. But suppose that most of the delegates to the ratifying conventions did not conceive of this

possibility and that either they "did not intend" that the clause encompass such transactions or else their intentions were indeterminate. Under these circumstances, what is the institutional intent, *i.e.*, the intent of the provision?

If the intent of the framers is to be attributed to the provision, it must be because the other adopters have in effect delegated their intention-votes to the framers. Leaving aside the question whether the adopters-at-large had any thoughts at all concerning this issue of delegation, consider what they might have desired if they had thought about it. Would they have wanted the framers' intentions to govern without knowing what those intentions were? The answers might well differ depending on whether the adopters had "no intent" or "indeterminate intent."

A delegate to a ratifying convention might well want his absence of intention (*i.e.*, "no-intent") regarding wholly intrastate transactions to be treated as a vote against the clause's encompassing such transactions (*i.e.*, "intent-not"): Since no-intent is the intentionalist equivalent of no-text, to accede to the framers' unknown intentions would be tantamount to blindly delegating to them the authority to insert textual provisions in the Constitution.

Where the framers intend that the activity be covered by the clause, and the adopters' intentions are merely indeterminate, the institutional intent is ambiguous. One adopter might wish his indeterminate intent to be treated as "no intent." Another adopter might wish to delegate his intention-vote to those whose intent is determinate. Yet another might wish to delegate authority to decisionmakers charged with applying the provision in the future. Without knowing more about the mindsets of the actual adopters of particular constitutional provisions, one would be hard-pressed to choose among these.

2. THE ADOPTERS' INTERPRETIVE INTENT

The intentionalist interpreters' first task must be to determine the interpretive intentions of the adopters of the provision before her—that is the canons by which the adopters intended their provisions to be interpreted. The practice of statutory interpretation from the 18th through at least the mid-19th century suggests that the adopters assumed—if they assumed anything at all—a mode of interpretation that was more textualist than intentionalist. The plain meaning rule was frequently invoked: judicial recourse to legislative debates was virtually unknown and generally considered improper. Even after references to extrinsic sources became common, courts and commentators frequently asserted that the plain meaning of the text was the surest guide to the intent of the adopters.

This poses obvious difficulties for an intentionalist whose very enterprise is premised on fidelity to the original understanding.

3. THE INTENDED SPECIFICITY OF A PROVISION

I now turn to an issue that lies at the intersection of what I have called interpretive and substantive intent: How much discretion did an adopter intend to delegate to those charged with applying a provision? Consider, for example, the possible intentions of the adopters of the cruel and unusual punishment clause of the eighth amendment. They might have intended that the language serve only as a shorthand for the Stuart tortures which were their exemplary applications of the clause. Somewhat more broadly, they might have intended the clause to be understood to incorporate the principle of *ejusdem generis*—to include their exemplary applications and other punishments that they found or would have found equally repugnant.

What of instances where the adopters' substantive intent was indeterminate—where even if they had adverted to a proposed application they would not have been certain how the clause should apply? Here it is plausible that—if they *had* a determinate interpretive intent—they intended to delegate to future decisionmakers the authority to apply the clause in light of the general principles underlying it. To use

Ronald Dworkin's terms, the adopters would have intended future interpreters to develop their own "conceptions" of cruel and unusual punishment within the framework of the adopters' general "concept" of such punishments.

What of a case where the adopters viewed a certain punishment as not cruel and unusual? This is not the same as saying that the adopters "intended not to prohibit the punishment." For even if they expected their laws to be interpreted by intentionalist canons, the adopters may have intended that their own views not always govern. Like parents who attempt to instill values in their child by both articulating and applying a moral principle, they may have accepted, or even invited, the eventuality that the principle would be applied in ways that diverge from their own views. The adopters may have understood that, even as to instances to which they believe the clause ought or ought not to apply, further thought by themselves or others committed to its underlying principle might lead them to change their minds. Not believing in their own omniscience or infallibility, they delegated the decision to those charged with interpreting the provision. If such a motivation is plausible with respect to applications of the clause in the adopters' contemporary society, it is even more likely with respect to its application by future interpreters, whose understanding of the clause will be affected by changing knowledge, technology, and forms of society.

The extent to which a clause may be properly interpreted to reach outcomes different from those actually contemplated by the adopters depends on the relationship between a general principle and its exemplary applications. A principle does not exist wholly independently of its author's subjective, or his society's conventional exemplary applications, and is always limited to some extent by the applications they found conceivable. Within these fairly broad limits, however, the adopters may have intended their examples to constrain more or less. To the intentionalist interpreter falls the unenviable task of ascertaining, for each provision, how much more or less.

■ ■ ■

The interpreter's task as historian can be divided into three stages or categories. First, she must immerse herself in the world of the adopters to try to understand constitutional concepts and values from their perspective. Second, at least the intentionalist must ascertain the adopters' interpretive intent and the intended scope of the provision in question. Third, she must often "translate" the adopters' concepts and intentions into our time and apply them to situations that the adopters did not foresee.

The first stage is common to originalists of all persuasions. Although the textualist's aim is to understand and apply the language of a constitutional provision, she must locate the text in the linguistic and social contexts in which it was adopted. . . . The intentionalist would ideally count the intention-votes of the individual adopters. In practice, she can at best hope to discover a consensus of the adopters as manifested in the text of the provision itself, the history surrounding its adoption, and the ideologies and practices of the time.

The essential difficulty posed by the distance that separates the modern interpreter from the objects of her interpretation has been succinctly stated by Quentin Skinner in addressing the analogous problem facing historians of political theory:

> [I]t will never in fact be possible simply to study what any given classic writer has *said* . . . without bringing to bear some of one's own expectations about what he must have been saying. . . . [T]hese models and preconceptions in terms of which we unavoidably organize and adjust our perceptions and thoughts will themselves tend to act as determinants of what we think or perceive. We must classify in order to understand, and we can only classify the unfamiliar in terms of the familiar. The perpetual danger, in our attempts to enlarge

our historical understanding, is thus that our expectations about what someone must be saying or doing will themselves determine that we understand the agent to be doing something which he would not—or even could not—himself have accepted as an account of what he *was* doing.

To illustrate the problem of doing original history with even a single example would consume more space than I wish to here. Instead, I suggest that a reader who wants to get a sense of the elusiveness of the original understanding study some specific areas of constitutional history, reading both works that have been well received, and also the controversy surrounding some of those that have not.

The intentionalist interpreter must next ascertain the adopters' interpretive intent and the intended breadth of their provisions. That is, she must determine what the adopters intended future interpreters to make of their substantive views. Even if she can learn how the adopters intended contemporary interpreters to construe the Constitution, she cannot assume they intended the same canons to apply one or two hundred years later. Perhaps they wanted to bind the future as closely as possible to their own notions. Perhaps they intended a particular provision to be interpreted with increasing breadth as time went on. Or—more likely than not—the adopters may have had no intentions at all concerning these matters.

For purposes of analytic clarity I have distinguished between (1) the adopters' interpretive intent and the intended scope of a provision and (2) their substantive intent concerning the application of the provision. If interpretive intent and intended scope can be ascertained at all, they may instruct the interpreter to adopt different canons of interpretation than she would prefer. Under these circumstances, the intentionalist interpreter may wish to ignore these intentions and limit her inquiry to the adopters' substantive intentions. Leaving aside the normative difficulty of such selective infidelity, this is a problematic strategy: To be a coherent theory of interpretation, intentionalism must distinguish between the adopters' personal *views* about an issue and their *intentions* concerning its constitutional resolution. And it is only by reference to their interpretive intent and the intended scope of a provision that this distinction can be drawn.

The interpreter's final task is to translate the adopters' intentions into the present in order to apply them to the question at issue. Consider, for example, whether the cruel and unusual punishment clause of the eighth amendment prohibits the imposition of the death penalty today. The adopters of the clause apparently never doubted that the death penalty was constitutional. But was death the same event for inhabitants of the American colonies in the late 18th century as it is two centuries later? Death was not only a much more routine and public phenomenon then, but the fear of death was more effectively contained within a system of religious belief. Twentieth-century Americans have a more secular cast of mind and seem less willing to accept this dreadful, forbidden, solitary, and shameful event. The interpreter must therefore determine whether we view the death penalty with the same attitude—whether of disgust or ambivalence—that the adopters viewed their core examples of cruel and unusual punishment.

Intentionalist interpretation frequently requires translations of this sort. For example, to determine whether the commerce clause applies to transactions taking place wholly within the boundaries of one state, or whether the first amendment protects the mass media, the interpreter must abstract the adopters' concepts of federalism and freedom of expression in order to find their analogue in our contemporary society with its different technology, economy, and systems of communication. The alternative would be to limit the application of constitutional provisions to the particular events and transactions with which the adopters were familiar. Even if such an approach were coherent, however, it would produce results that even a strict intentionalist would likely reject: Congress could not regulate any item of commerce or any mode of transportation that did not exist in 1789; the first amendment would not protect any means of communication not then known.

However difficult the earlier stages of her work, the interpreter was only trying to understand the past. The act of translation required here is different in kind, for it involves the counterfactual and imaginary act of projecting the adopters' concepts and attitudes into a future they probably could not have envisioned. When the interpreter engages in this sort of projection, she is in a fantasy world more of her own than of the adopters' making.

QUESTIONS FOR DISCUSSION

1. What does Brest mean by "textualism"? Is it the same as what Schauer means by "formalism"?

2. What is Brest's argument against intentionalism? Is his argument sound? If his argument is sound, then what is an intention? How would Bork or Berger best respond to Brest's argument?

3. In a later portion, Brest summarizes his argument by saying that historical knowledge is "indeterminate and contingent." What do you think he means? Is he right?

NATURAL LAW REVISITED

RONALD DWORKIN

Everyone likes categories, and legal philosophers like them very much. So we spend a good deal of time, not all of it profitably, labeling ourselves and the theories of law we defend. One label, however, is particularly dreaded: no one wants to be called a natural lawyer. Natural law insists that what the law is depends in some way on what the law should be. This seems metaphysical or at least vaguely religious. In any case it seems plainly wrong. If some theory of law is shown to be a natural law theory, therefore, people can be excused if they do not attend to it much further.

In the past several years, I have tried to defend a theory about how judges should decide cases that some critics (though not all) say is a natural law theory and should be rejected for that reason. I have of course made the pious and familiar objection to this charge, that it is better to look at theories than labels. But since labels are so much a part of our common intellectual life it is almost as silly to flee as to hurl them. If the crude description of natural law I just gave is correct, that any theory which makes the content of law sometimes depend on the correct answer to some moral question is a natural law theory, then I am guilty of natural law. I am not now interested, I should add, in whether this crude characterization is historically correct, or whether it succeeds in distinguishing natural law from positivist theories of law. My present concern is rather this: Suppose this is natural law. What in the world is wrong with it?

I shall start by giving the picture of adjudication I want to defend a name, and it is a name which accepts the crude characterization. I shall call this picture naturalism. According to

naturalism, judges should decide hard cases by interpreting the political structure of their community in the following, perhaps special way: by trying to find the best *justification* they can find, in principles of political morality, for the structure as a whole, from the most profound constitutional rules and arrangements to the details of, for example, the private law of tort or contract. Suppose the question arises for the first time, for example, whether and in what circumstances careless drivers are liable, not only for physical injuries to those whom they run down, but also for any emotional damage suffered by relatives of the victim who are watching. According to naturalism, judges should then ask the following questions of the history (including the contemporary history) of their political structure. Does the best possible justification of that history suppose a principle according to which people who are injured emotionally in this way have a right to recover damages in court? If so, what, more precisely, is that principle? Does it entail, for example, that only immediate relatives of the person physically injured have that right? Or only relatives on the scene of the accident, who might themselves have suffered physical damage?

Of course a judge who is faced with these questions in an actual case cannot undertake anything like a full justification of all parts of the constitutional arrangement, statutory system and judicial precedents that make up his "law." I had to invent a mythical judge, called Hercules, with superhuman powers in order even to contemplate what a full justification of the entire system would be like. Real judges can attempt only what we might call a partial justification of the

Excerpt from Ronald Dworkin, "Natural Law Revisited," *University of Florida Law Review*, vol. 34 (1982), pp. 165 ff.

law. They can try to justify, under some set of principles, those parts of the legal background which seem to them immediately relevant, like, for example, the prior judicial decisions about recovery for various sorts of damage in automobile accidents. Nevertheless it is useful to describe this as a partial justification—as a part of what Hercules himself would do—in order to emphasize that, according to this picture, a judge should regard the law he mines and studies as embedded in a much larger system, so that it is always relevant for him to expand his investigation by asking whether the conclusions he reaches are consistent with what he would have discussed had his study been wider.

It is obvious why this theory of adjudication invites the charge of natural law. It makes each judge's decision about the burden of past law depend on his judgment about the best political justification of that law, and this is of course a matter of political morality. Before I consider whether this provides a fatal defect in the theory, however, I must try to show how the theory might work in practice. It may help to look beyond law to other enterprises in which participants extend a discipline into the future by re-examining its past. This process is in fact characteristic of the general activity we call interpretation, which has a large place in literary criticism, history, philosophy and many other activities. Indeed, the picture of adjudication I have just sketched draws on a sense of what interpretation is like in these various activities, and I shall try to explicate the picture through an analogy to literary interpretation. I shall, however, pursue that analogy in a special context designed to minimize some of the evident differences between law and literature, and so make the comparison more illuminating.

[EDITOR'S NOTE: Here Dworkin sets forth the interpretive methodology refined in *Law's Empire*, including the chain novel and *Christmas Carol* examples. This material can be found in Section 1.4.]

Any naturalist judge's working approach to interpretation will recognize [the] distinction between two "dimensions" of interpretations of the prior law, and so we might think of such a theory as falling into two parts. One part refines and develops the idea that an interpretation must fit the data it interprets. This part takes up positions on questions like the following. How many decisions (roughly) can an interpretation set aside as mistakes, and still count as an interpretation of the string of decisions that includes those "mistakes?" How far is an interpretation better if it is more consistent with later rather than earlier past decisions? How far and in what way must a good interpretation fit the opinions judges write as well as the decisions they make? How far must it take account of popular morality contemporary with the decisions it offers to interpret? A second part of any judge's tacit theory of interpretation, however, will be quite independent of these "formal" issues. It will contain the substantive ideals of political morality on which he relies in deciding whether any putative interpretation is to be preferred because it shows legal practice to be better as a matter of substantive justice. Of course, if any working approach to interpretation has these two parts, then it must also have principles that combine or adjudicate between them.

This account of the main structure of a working theory of interpretation has heuristic appeal. It provides judges, and others who interpret the law, with a model they might use in identifying the approach they have been using, and self-consciously to inspect and improve that model. A thoughtful judge might establish for himself, for example, a rough "threshold" of fit which any interpretation of data must meet in order to be "acceptable" on the dimension of fit, and then suppose that if more than one interpretation of some part of the law meets this threshold, the choice among these should be made, not through further and more precise comparisons between the two along that dimension, but by choosing the interpretation which is "substantively" better, that is, which better promotes the political ideals he thinks correct. Such a judge might say, for example, that since both the foreseeability and the area–of–physical–risk interpretations rise above the threshold of fit with the emotional damage cases I mentioned earlier, foreseeability is better *as an interpretation* because it better accords with the "natural" rights of people injured in accidents.

The practical advantages of adopting such a threshold of fit are plain enough. A working theory need specify that threshold in only a rough and impressionistic way. If two interpretations both satisfy the threshold, then, as I said, a judge who uses such a theory need make no further comparisons along that dimension in order to establish which of them in fact supplies the "better" fit, and he may therefore avoid many of the difficult and perhaps arbitrary decisions about better fit that a theory without this feature might require him to make. But there are nevertheless evident dangers in taking the device too seriously, as other than a rule–of–thumb practical approach. A judge might be tricked into thinking that these two dimensions of interpretations are in some way deeply competitive with one another, that they represent the influence of two different and sometimes contradictory ambitions of adjudication.

He will then worry about those inevitable cases in which it is unclear whether some substantively attractive interpretation does indeed meet the threshold of fit. He will think that in such cases he must define that threshold, not impressionistically, as calling for a "decent" fit, but precisely, perhaps everything will then turn on whether that interpretation in fact just meets or just fails the crucial test. This rigid attitude toward the heuristic distinction would miss the point that any plausible theory of interpretation, in law as in literature, will call for some cross influence between the level of fit at which the threshold is fixed and the substantive issues involved. If an interpretation of some string of cases is far superior "substantively" it may be given the benefit of a less stringent test of fit for that reason.

For once again the underlying issue is simply one of comparing two pictures of the judicial past to see which offers a more attractive picture, from the standpoint of political morality, overall. The distinction between the dimensions of fit and substance is a rough distinction in service of that issue. The idea of a threshold of fit, and therefore of a lexical ordering between the two dimensions, is simply a working hypothesis, valuable so far as the impressionistic characterization of fit on which it depends is adequate, but which must be abandoned in favor of a more sophisticated and piecemeal analysis when the occasion demands.

Of course the moment when more sophisticated analysis becomes necessary, because the impressionistic distinction of the working theory no longer serves, is a moment of difficulty calling for fresh political judgments that may be hard to make. Suppose a judge faces, for the first time, the possibility of overruling a narrow rule followed for some time in his jurisdiction. Suppose, for example, that the courts have consistently held, since the issue was first raised, that lawyers may not be sued in negligence. Our judge believes that this rule is wrong and unjust, and that it is inconsistent in principle with the general rule allowing actions in negligence against other professional people like doctors and accountants. Suppose he can nevertheless find some putative principle, in which others find though he does not, which would justify the distinction the law has drawn. Like the principle, for example, that lawyers owe obligations to the courts or to abstract justice, it would be unfair to impose on them any legal obligation of due care to their clients. He must ask whether the best interpretation of the past includes *that* principle in spite of the fact that he himself would reject it.

Neither answer to this question will seem wholly attractive to him. If he holds that the law does include this putative principle, then this argument would present the law, including the past decisions about suits against lawyers as coherent; but he would then expose what he would believe to be a flaw in the substantive law. He would be supposing that the law includes a principle he believes is wrong, and therefore has no place in a just and wise system. If he decides that the law does not include the putative principle, on the other hand, then he can properly regard this entire line of cases about actions against lawyers as mistakes, and ignore or overrule them; but he then exposes a flaw in the record of a different sort, namely that past judges have acted in an unprincipled way, and a demerit in his own decision, that it treats the lawyer who loses the present case differently from how the judges have treated other lawyers in the past. He must ask which is, in the end, the greater of these flaws; which way of reading the record shows it, in the last analysis, in the better and which in the worse light.

It would be absurd to suppose that all the lawyers and judges of any common law community share some set of convictions from which a single answer to that question could be deduced. Or even that many lawyers or judges would have ready at hand some convictions of their own which could supply an answer without further ado. But it is nevertheless possible for any judge to confront issues like these in a principled way, and this is what naturalism demands of him. He must accept that in deciding one way rather than another about the force of a line of precedents, for example, he is developing a working theory of legal interpretation in one rather than another direction and this must seem to him the right direction as a matter of political principle, not simply an appealing direction for the moment because he likes the answer it recommends in the immediate case before him. Of course there is, in this counsel, much room for deception, including self-deception. But in most cases it will be possible for judges to recognize when they have submitted some issue to the discipline this description requires and also to recognize when some other judge has not.

Let me recapitulate. Interpretation is not a mechanical process. Nevertheless, judges can form working styles of interpretation, adequate for routine cases, and ready for refinement when cases are not routine. These working styles will include what I called formal features. They will set out, impressionistically, an ac-

count of fit, and may characterize a threshold of fit an interpretation must achieve in order to be eligible. But they will also contain a substantive part, formed from the judge's background political morality, or rather that part of his background morality which has become articulate in the course of his career. Sometimes this heuristic distinction between fit and substantive justice, as dimensions of a successful interpretation, will itself seem problematic, and a judge will be forced to elaborate that distinction by reflecting further on the full set of the substantive and procedural political rights of citizens a just legal system must respect and serve. In this way any truly hard case develops as well as engages a judge's style of adjudication. . . .

I have been describing naturalism as a theory about how judges should decide cases. It is of course a further question whether American (or any other) judges actually do decide cases that way. I shall not pursue that further question now. Instead, I want to consider certain arguments that I expect will be made against naturalism simply as a recommendation. In fact, many of the classical objections to "natural law" theories are objections to such theories as models for, rather than descriptions of, judicial practice. I shall begin with what might be called the skeptical attack.

I put my description of naturalism in what might be called a subjective mode. I described the question which, according to naturalism, judges should put to themselves and answer from their own convictions. Someone is bound to object that, although each judge can answer these questions for himself, different judges will give different answers, and no single answer can be said to be *objectively* right. "There are as many different 'best' interpretations as there are interpreters, he will say, because no one can offer any argument in favor of one interpretation over another, except that it strikes him as the best, and it will strike some other interpreter as the worst. No doubt judges (as well as many other people) would deny this. They think their opinions can have some objective standing, that they can be either true or false. But this is delusion merely."

What response can naturalism, as I have described it, make to this sceptical challenge? We must begin by asking what kind of scepticism is in play. I have in mind a distinction which, once again, might be easier to state if we return to a literary analogy. Suppose we are studying Hamlet and the question is put by some critic whether, before the play begins, Hamlet and Ophelia have been lovers. This is a question of interpretation, and two critics who disagree might present arguments trying to show why the play is, all things considered, more valuable as a work of art on one or the other understanding about Hamlet and Ophelia. But plainly a third position is possible. Someone might argue that it makes no difference to the importance or value of the play which of these assumptions is made about the lovers, because the play's importance lies in a humanistic vision of life and fate, not in any detail of plot or character whose reading would be affected by either assumption. This third position argues that the right answer to this particular question of interpretation is only that there is no right answer; that there is no "best" interpretation of the sexual relationship between Hamlet and Ophelia, only "different" interpretations, because neither interpretation would make the play more or less valuable as a work of art. This might strike you (it does me) as exactly the right position to take on this particular issue. It is, in a sense, a sceptical position, because it denies "truth" both to the proposition that Hamlet slept with Ophelia, and to the apparently contrary proposition that he did not. But if this is scepticism, it is what he might call *internal* scepticism. It does not challenge the idea that good arguments can in principle be found for one interpretation of Hamlet rather than another. On the contrary it *relies* on an interpretive argument—that the value of the play lies in a dimension that does not intersect the sexual question—in order to reach its "sceptical" position on that question.

Contrast the position of someone who says that no one interpretation of any work of art could ever succeed in showing it to be either really better or really worse, because there is not and cannot be any such thing as "value" in art at all. He means that there is something very wrong with the enterprise of interpretation (at least as I have described it) as a whole, not simply with particular issues or arguments within it. Of course he may have arguments for his position, or think he has; but these will not be arguments that, like the arguments of the internal sceptic, explicitly assume a positive theory of the value of art in general or of a particular work of art. They will be a priori, philosophical arguments attempting to show that the very idea of value in art is a deep mistake, that people who say they find a work of art "good" or "valuable" are not describing any objective property, but only expressing their own subjective reaction. This is *external* scepticism about art, and about interpretation in art.

If a lawyer says that no one interpretation of the legal record can be "objectively" the correct interpretation, he might have external scepticism in mind. He might mean that if two judges disagree about the "correct" interpretation of the emotional damages cases, because they hold different theories of what a just law of negligence would be like, their disagreement is for that reason alone merely "subjective," and neither side can be "objectively" right. I cannot consider, in this essay, the various arguments that philosophers have offered for external scepticism about political morality. The best of these arguments rely on a general thesis of philosophy that might be called the "demonstrability hypothesis." This holds that no proposition can be true unless the means exist, at least in principle, to demonstrate its truth through arguments to everyone who understands the language and is rational. If the demonstrability hypothesis is correct, then external scepticism is right about a great many human enterprises and activities; perhaps about all of them, including the activities we call scientific. I know of no good reason to accept the demonstrability hypothesis (it is at least an embarrassment that this hypothesis cannot itself be demonstrated in the sense it requires) and I am not myself an external sceptic. But rather than pursue the question of the demonstrability hypothesis, I shall change the subject.

Suppose you are an external sceptic about justice and other aspects of political morality. What follows about the question of how judges should decide cases? About whether naturalism is better than other (more conservative or more radical) theories of adjudication? You might think it follows that you should take no further interest in these questions at all. If so, I have some sympathy with your view. After all, you believe, on what you take to be impressive philosophical grounds, that no way of deciding cases at law can really be thought to be any better than any other, and that no way of interpreting legal practice can be preferred to any other on rational grounds. The "correct" theory of what judges should do is only a matter of what judges feel like doing, or of what they believe will advance political causes to which they happen to be drawn. The "correct" interpretation of legal practice is only a matter of reading legal history so that it appeals to you, or so that you can use it in your own political interests. If you are convinced of these externally sceptical propositions, you might well do better to take up the interesting questions raised by certain sociologists of law—questions about the connection between judges' economic class and the decisions they are likely to reach, for example. Or to take up the study of strategies for working your will on judges if you ever come to argue before them, or on other judges if you ever join the bench yourself. Your external scepticism might well persuade you to take up these "practical" questions and set aside the "theoretical" questions you have come to see as meaningless.

But it is worth noticing that philosophers who say they are external sceptics rarely draw that sort of practical conclusion for themselves. Most of them seem to take a rather different line, which I do not myself fully understand, but which can, I think, fairly be represented as fol-

lows. External scepticism is not a position within an enterprise, but about an enterprise. It does not tell us to stop making the kinds of arguments we are disposed to make and accept and act on within morality or politics, but only to change our beliefs about what we are doing when we act this way. Imagine that some chessplayers thought that chess was an "objective" battle between forces of light and darkness, so that when black won good had triumphed in some metaphysical sense. External sceptics about chess would reject this view, and think that chess was entertainment merely; but they would not thereupon cease playing chess or play it any differently from their deluded fellow players. So external sceptics about political morality will still have opinions and make arguments about justice; they will simply understand, in their philosophical moments, that when they do this they are not discovering timeless and objective truths.

If you are an external sceptic who takes this attitude, you will have driven a wedge between your external scepticism and any judgments you might make about how judges should decide cases, in general, or about what the best justification is of some part of the law, in particular. You will have your own opinions about these matters, which you will express in arguments or, if you are an academic lawyer, in law review articles or, if you are a judge, in your decisions. You may well come to believe that the best interpretation of the emotional damages cases shows them to be grounded in the principle of foreseeability, for example. When you retreat to your philosophical study, you will have a particular view about the opinions you expressed or exhibited while you were "playing the game." You will believe that your opinions about the best justification of the emotional damage cases were "merely" subjective opinions (whatever that means) with no basis in any "objective" reality. But this does not itself provide any argument in favor of *other* opinions about the best interpretation. In particular, it does not provide any argument in favor of the *internally* sceptical opinion that no interpretation of the accident cases is best.

Of course your external scepticism leaves you free to take up that internally sceptical position if you believe you have good internal arguments for it. Suppose you are trying to decide whether the best interpretation of the emotional damage cases lies in the principle that people in the area of physical risk may recover for emotional damage, or the broader principle that anyone whose emotional damage was foreseeable may recover. After the most diligent search and reflection asking yourself exactly the questions naturalism poses, you may find that the case for neither of these interpretations seems to you any stronger than the case for the other. I think this is very unlikely, but that is beside the present point, which is only that it is possible. You would be internally sceptical, in this way, about any uniquely "correct" interpretation of this group of cases; but you would have supplied an affirmative argument, beginning in your naturalistic theory, for that internally sceptical conclusion. It would not have mattered whether you were an external sceptic, who nevertheless "played the game" as a naturalist, or an external "believer" who thought that naturalism was stitched into the fabric of the universe. You would have reached the same internally sceptical conclusion, on these assumed beliefs and facts, in either case.

What is, then, the threat that external scepticism poses to naturalism? It is potentially very threatening indeed, not only to naturalism, but to all its rival theories of adjudication as well. It may persuade you to try to have nothing to do with morality or legal theory at all, though I do not think you will succeed in giving up these immensely important human activities. If this very great threat fails (as it seems to have failed for almost all external sceptics) then no influence remains. For in whatever spirit you do enter any of these enterprises—however firmly your fingers may be crossed—the full range of positions within the enterprise is open to you on equal terms. If you end in some internally

sceptical position of some sort, this will be because of the internal power of the arguments that drove you there, not because of your external sceptical credentials.

We must now consider another possibility. The sceptical attack upon naturalism may in fact consist, not in the external scepticism I have been discussing, but in some global form of internal scepticism. I just conceded the possibility that we might find reason for internal scepticism about the best interpretation of some particular body of law. Suppose we had reasons to be internally sceptical about the best interpretation of any and all parts of the law? It is hard to imagine the plausible arguments that would bring us to that conclusion, but not hard to imagine how someone with bizarre views might be brought to it. Suppose one holds that all morality rests on God's will, and had just decided that there is no God. Or he believes that only spontaneous and unreflective decisions can have moral value, and that no judicial decision can either be spontaneous or encourage spontaneity. These would be arguments not rejecting the idea or sense of morality, as in the case of external scepticism, but employing what the author takes to be the best conception of morality in service of a wholesale internally sceptical position. If this position were in fact the right view to take up about political morality, then it would always be wrong to suppose that one interpretation of past judicial decisions was better than another, at least in cases when both passed the threshold test of fit. Naturalism would therefore be a silly theory to recommend to judges. So the threat of [internal] scepticism, it materializes, is in fact much greater than the threat of [external] scepticism. But (as the examples I chose may have suggested) I cannot think of any plausible arguments for global internal scepticism about political morality.

Of course, nothing in this short discussion disputes the claim, which is plainly true, that different judges hold different political moralities, and will therefore disagree about the best justification of the past. Or the claim, equally true, that there will be no way for any side in such disagreements to prove that it is right and its opponents are wrong. The demonstrability thesis (as I said) argues from these undeniable facts to general external scepticism. But even if we reject that thesis, as I do, the bare fact of disagreement may be thought to support an independent challenge of naturalism, which

does not depend on either external or internal scepticism. For it may be said that whether or not there is an objectively right answer to the question of justification, it is unfair that the answer of one judge be accepted as final when he has no way to prove, as against those who disagree, that his position is better. This is part of the argument from democracy....

QUESTIONS FOR DISCUSSION

1. What is the dimension of fit? What is the dimension of substance? How are they related to each other?

2. Consider Dworkin's analogy between interpreting law and interpreting a work of literature, such as the example of the *Christmas Carol* found in Section 1.4. Why does Dworkin use the analogy? How can it be instructive? How might it be misleading?

3. What does Dworkin mean by internal skepticism? What does he mean by external skepticism? What are his arguments against the skeptical challenges? Are you persuaded?

4. Does Dworkin think there is a difference between the best answer and a right answer? Does Dworkin think there is a difference between the right answer and what someone believes to be the right answer?

UNITED STATES V. LOCKE

471 U.S. 89 (1985)

Justice MARSHALL delivered the opinion of the Court.

Section 314 of the [Federal Land Policy and Management] Act establishes a federal recording system that is designed both to rid federal lands of stale mining claims and to provide federal land managers with up-to-date informa-

tion that allows them to make informed land management decisions. For claims located before FLPMA's enactment, the federal recording system imposes two general requirements. First, the claims must initially be registered with the [Bureau of Land Management] by filing, within three years of FLPMA's enactment, a copy of the official record of the notice or certificate of location. Second, in the year of the initial recording, and "prior to December 31" of every year after that, the claimant must file with state officials and with BLM a notice of intention to hold the claim, an affidavit of assessment work performed on the claim, or a detailed reporting form. Section 314(c) of the Act provides that failure to comply with either of these requirements "shall be deemed conclusively to constitute an abandonment of the mining claim . . . by the owner."

The second of these requirements—the annual filing obligation—has created the dispute underlying this appeal. Appellees, four individuals engaged "in the business of operating mining properties in Nevada," purchased in 1960 and 1966 10 unpatented mining claims on public lands near Ely, Nevada. These claims were major sources of gravel and building material: the claims are valued at several million dollars, and, in the 1979–1980 assessment year alone, appellees' gross income totaled more than $1 million. Throughout the period during which they owned the claims, appellees complied with annual state–law filing and assessment work requirements. In addition, appellees satisfied FLPMA's initial recording requirement by properly filing with BLM a notice of location, thereby putting their claims on record for purposes of FLPMA.

At the end of 1980, however, appellees failed to meet on time their first annual obligation to file with the Federal Government. After allegedly receiving misleading information from a BLM employee, appellees waited until December 31 to submit to BLM the annual notice of intent to hold or proof of assessment work performed required under § 314(a) of FLPMA. As noted above, that section requires these documents to be filed annually "prior to December 31." . . . Thus, appellees' filing was one day too late.

This fact was brought painfully home to appellees when they received a letter from the BLM Nevada State Office informing them that their claims had been declared abandoned and

void due to their tardy filing. In many cases, loss of a claim in this way would have minimal practical effect; the claimant could simply locate the same claim again and then rerecord it with BLM. In this case, however, relocation of appellees' claims [was] prohibited by the Common Varieties Act of 1955; that Act prospectively barred location of the sort of minerals yielded by appellees' claims. Appellees' mineral deposits thus [reverted] to the Government.

Before the District Court, appellees asserted that the § 314(a) requirement of a filing "prior to December 31 of each year" should be construed to require a filing "on or before December 31." Thus, appellees argued, their December 31 filing had in fact complied with the statute, and the BLM had acted ultra vires in voiding their claims. . . .

It is clear to us that the plain language of the statute simply cannot sustain the gloss appellees would put on it. As even counsel for appellees conceded at oral argument, § 314(a) "is a statement that Congress wanted it filed by December 30th. I think that is a clear statement. . . ." While we will not allow a literal reading of a statute to produce a result "demonstrably at odds with the intentions of its drafters," with respect to filing deadlines a literal reading of Congress' words is generally the only proper reading of those words. To attempt to decide whether some date other than the one set out in the statute is the date actually "intended" by Congress is to set sail on an aimless journey, for the purpose of a filing deadline would be just as well served by nearly any date a court might choose as by the date Congress has in fact set out in the statute.

The notion that a filing deadline can be complied with by filing sometime after the deadline falls due is, to say the least, a surprising notion, and it is a notion without limiting principle. If 1–day late filings are acceptable, 10–day late filings might be equally acceptable, and so on in a cascade of exceptions that would engulf the rule erected by the filing deadline; yet regardless of where the cutoff line is set, some individuals will always fall just on the other side of it. Filing deadlines, like statutes of limitations, necessarily operate harshly and arbitrarily with respect to individuals who fall just on the other side of them, but if the concept of a filing deadline is to have any content, the deadline must be enforced.

Justice STEVENS, with whom Justice BRENNAN joins, dissenting.

The Court's opinion is contrary to the intent of Congress, engages in unnecessary constitutional adjudication, and unjustly creates a trap for unwary property owners. First, the choice of the language "prior to December 31" when read in context in 43 U.S.C. § 1744(a) is, at least, ambiguous, and, at best, the consequence of a legislative *accident*, perhaps caused by nothing more than the unfortunate fact that Congress is too busy to do all of its work as carefully as it should. In my view, Congress actually intended to authorize an annual filing at any time prior to the close of business on December 31st, that is, prior to the end of the calendar year to which the filing pertains. Second, even if Congress irrationally intended that the applicable deadline for a calendar year should end *one day before* the end of the calendar year that has been recognized since the amendment of the Julian Calendar in 8 B.C., it is clear that appellees have substantially complied with the requirements of the statute. . . .

LEGAL FORMALISM, LEGAL REALISM, AND THE INTERPRETATION OF STATUTES AND THE CONSTITUTION

RICHARD POSNER

The major premise of a syllogism is a definition (like "All men are mortal"), or, what is the same thing, a rule (e.g., the perfect-tender rule), or, what is again the same thing, a concept (e.g., negligence, which stated as a rule or definition is "All persons are prima facie liable for accidents resulting from their failure to take due care, i.e., the cost-justified level of care"). The common law, like the system of real numbers, is a conceptual system—not a textual one. The concepts of negligence, of consideration, of reliance, are not tied to a particular verbal formulation, but can be restated in whatever words seem clearest in light of current linguistic conventions. Common law is thus unwritten law in a profound sense. There are more or less

Richard A. Posner, "Legal Formalism, Legal Realism, and the Interpretation of Statutes and the Constitution," *Case Western Reserve University Law Review*, vol. 37 (1987), pp. 179 ff.[8]

[8]Richard Posner (1939–   ) was for many years Professor of Law at the University of Chicago. Considered one of the founders of the Law and Economics movement, he is now a judge of the United States Court of Appeals for the Seventh Circuit. See also the reading in Section 2.3.

influential statements of every doctrine but none is authoritative in the sense that the decision of a new case must be tied to the statement, rather than to the concept of which the statement is one of an indefinite number of possible formulations.

Considering the importance that the common law attaches to decision in accordance with precedent, it may seem odd to divorce common law from the verbal formulas in the judicial opinions that create it. A common law doctrine, however, is no more textual than Newton's universal law of gravitation. The doctrine is inferred from a judicial opinion, or more commonly a series of judicial opinions, but it is not those opinions, just as Newton's law is learned from a text but is not the text itself. Decision according to precedent means decision according to the doctrines of the common law, not according to specific verbal expressions of those doctrines.

Statutory and constitutional law differs fundamentally from common law in that every statutory and constitutional text—the starting point for decision, and in that respect (but that respect only) corresponding to judicial opinions in common law decisionmaking—is in some important sense not to be revised by the judges. They cannot treat the statute as a stab at formulating a concept which they are free to rewrite in their own words. This might seem to entail just that formalist reasoning in statutory or constitutional law would be deduction from a text and therefore would be possible as long as the text was as precise as a common law concept. But there is no such thing as deduction from a text. No matter how clear the text seems, it must be interpreted (or decoded) like any other communication, and interpretation is neither logical deduction nor policy analysis. The terms formalism and realism as I have defined them thus have no application to statutory or constitutional law, except, as I have said, when the framers' command is simply that the judges go out and make common law.

A conclusion obtained by deduction is already contained in the premises in the sense that the only materials used to obtain the conclusion are the premises themselves and the rules of logic. But meaning cannot be extracted from a text merely by taking the language of the text and applying the rules of logic to it. All sorts of linguistic and cultural tools must be brought to bear on even the simplest text to get meaning out of it. This is not to suggest that all texts are ambiguous. A text is clear if all or most persons, having the linguistic and cultural competence assumed by the authors of the text, would agree on its meaning. Most texts are clear in this sense, which is the only sense that captures the meaning of the word "clear" as applied to texts.

I shall illustrate the distinction between logic and interpretation by reference to the clearest of constitutional provisions—the provision that fixes thirty-five years as the age of eligibility for the Presidency. It might seem that if the question were whether X, who is thirty-two years old, is eligible to be President, the answer would involve an application of formalist reasoning: one must be at least thirty-five to be eligible, X is not thirty-five, therefore X is not eligible. But the answer is open to attack along the following lines: the framers may not have intended to set a rigid limitation; they may have meant that the candidate must either be thirty-five years old or be at least as mature as the average thirty-five year old; they might have countenanced a change if life expectancy changed. The attack is, as we shall see, very weak, but the only point I want to make here is that it cannot be repelled by formal logic. The legal task in this case is not to make deductions from a definition—it is not to apply a rule—it is to do something prior, to interpret a text. The proper riposte to the attempted "deconstruction" of the age thirty-five provision is not that the attempt is illogical or is bad public policy but that the meaning of the text is clear. We do not decide the clarity of texts, or decode communications generally, by syllogistic reasoning or appeals to policy (though logic and policy may enter indirectly, as we shall see). If a message is unclear we ask the sender to repeat or amplify it until we no longer doubt what he meant to say. We do not use that approach to solve a mathematical problem or to decide what course of action will best promote the public welfare.

Consulting post-enactment legislative history, and even hearing testimony by legislators in cases in which the meaning of legislation is contested, are methods by which courts sometimes try to get legislatures, in effect, to repeat unclear messages. These methods have plenty of problems, and I don't mean by mentioning them to endorse them, but they do serve to show that the enactment of legislation is a method of communication with judges, in a way that the statement of a common law doctrine is not. If we are puzzled about the formulation of the doctrine of consideration in some opinion, we are not likely to feel an urge to ask the author of the opinion what he meant. This is because we are always free to reformulate the doctrine in a way that will describe the underlying concept more accurately.

The idea of legislation as communication may seem to have no utility beyond showing the fatuity and confusion of applying the terms legal formalism and legal realism to the interpretation of legislation. For most of the time it is impossible to ask the legislature to repeat an unclear message. But by considering what the possible responses are to an unclear message when the sender cannot be queried about his intended meaning, we shall see that the notion of legislation as communication has considerable utility. One possible response of the receiver is to ignore the message, and this might seem the appropriate posture for a court faced with an enactment whose meaning, with respect to the case at hand, cannot be deciphered. Yet that kind of response can be profoundly unresponsive. Suppose the commander of the lead platoon in an attack finds his way blocked by an unexpected enemy pillbox. He has two choices: go straight ahead at the pillbox, or try to bypass it to the left. He ra-

dios the company commander for instructions. The commander replies, "Go—"; but the rest of the message is garbled. When the platoon commander radios back for clarification, he is unable to get through. If the platoon commander decides that, not being able to receive an intelligible command, he should do nothing until communications can be restored, his decision will be wrong. For it is plain from the part of the message that was received that the company commander wanted him to get by the enemy pillbox, either by frontal attack or by bypassing it. And surely the company commander would have preferred the platoon commander to decide by himself which course to follow rather than to do nothing and let the attack fail. For the platoon commander to take the position that he may do nothing, just because the communication was garbled, would be an irresponsible "interpretation."

The situation with regard to legislative interpretation is analogous. In our system of government the framers of statutes and constitutions are the superiors of the judges. The framers communicate orders to the judges through legislative texts (including, of course, the Constitution). If the orders are clear, the judges must obey them. Often, however, because of passage of time and change of circumstance the orders are unclear and normally the judges cannot query the framers to find out what the order means. The judges are thus like the platoon commander in my example. It is irresponsible for them to adopt the attitude that if the order is unclear they will refuse to act. They are part of an organization, an enterprise— the enterprise of governing the United States— and when the orders of their superiors are unclear, this does not absolve them from responsibility for helping to make the enterprise succeed. The platoon commander will ask himself, if he is a responsible officer: what would the company commander have wanted me to do if communications failed? Judges should ask themselves the same type of question when the "orders" they receive from the framers of statutes and constitutions are unclear: what would the framers have wanted us to do in this case of failed communication? The question is often difficult to answer, but it is the right question to frame the interpretive issue in cases where the enactment is unclear. . . .

I am naturally more interested in the unclear cases of interpretation than the clear ones. But it is important to insist that there are clear cases, though they are underrepresented both in appellate opinions and in academic debate. The age thirty-five case is easy, although no text is really "clear on its face." The provision is profoundly unclear to a person who does not know English; and if it is still in force in a thousand years, it may be as unclear as Anglo-Saxon or Old English is to us. In India, where the official language is English but age is measured from conception rather than birth, it would mean something different from what it means to us. It would mean something different in a society that did not record the date of birth. A text is clear only by virtue of linguistic and cultural competence. What makes the age thirty-five provision clear is that American lawyers recognize it as part of a family of rules that establish arbitrary eligibility dates in preference to making eligibility turn on uncertain qualitative judgments. Legislatures set eighteen or twenty-one years as the age of majority rather than provide that one is legally an adult when one is mature. They also refuse to allow precocious twelve-year-olds to take the driving test. If eligibility for the Presidency were not fixed at a definite age, there would be great difficulty in determining in advance of the election who is eligible; after the election it's too late. When all these considerations are taken into account, as can be done only by people living in a certain kind of society (e.g., one where the date of birth is recorded and age is measured in years from that date), the age thirty-five provision becomes clear.

We shall see later that provisions that seem equally clear "on their face" may become unclear when the various contextual considerations that

we use in decoding messages are taken into account. But the present point is that the rejection of formalism as a method of statutory interpretation doesn't condemn us to universal skepticism about the possibility of interpretation. Interpretation is no less a valid method of acquiring knowledge because it necessarily ranges beyond the text. No text is clear except in terms of a linguistic and cultural environment, but it doesn't follow that no text is clear. The relevant environment, and its bearing on the specific interpretive question, may be clear.

Nevertheless, it is true that many statutory and constitutional texts, including the most illustrious and also many that seem clear "on their face" (a pernicious usage), are unclear in the sense of my hypothetical company commander's order. But the lack of clarity does not entitle the court to say that it will not apply the text until the authors rewrite it. The court still has the duty to interpret, which requires, as I have suggested, figuring out what outcome will best advance the program or enterprise set on foot by the enactment. This conclusion is entailed by my assumption that the best way to look at the relationship between legislatures (or the adopters of the Constitution and its amendments) and courts is as superior and subordinate officers, with the former often being unable to communicate clearly with the latter. . . .

United States v. Locke is another hard case that seemed easy to the Justices, though this time to only six of them. *Locke* involved a federal statute requiring a firm that has an unpatented mining claim on federal public lands to reregister the claim annually, "prior to December 31." Claims not reregistered in time are forfeited. Mines are frequently abandoned; the requirement of annual registration provides an easy means of determining abandonment. The plaintiffs in *Locke* filed on December 31, and the government declared the plaintiffs' mine forfeited. The Supreme Court upheld this determination.

The decision is impeccable as a matter of lexicography: "prior to December 31" means no later than December 30. It seems more than probable, however, that the statute contains a drafting error and that what Congress meant was that you must file before the end of the year, i.e., on or before December 31. Further evidence of inadvertence in the use of "prior to" is that the same section of the statute distinguishes between claims "located prior to October 21, 1976" and claims "located after October 21, 1976," thus leaving a void for claims located on October 21, 1976—if "prior to" is read literally. No one has ever suggested a reason why Congress might have wanted the filings made before December 31. It is not enough to say that all deadlines are arbitrary and that if the plaintiffs in *Locke* had won, then the next plaintiff would file on January 1 and say that his filing was timely too. The end of the year is a natural and common deadline and is almost certainly what Congress intended, so a claim filed on January 1 would be too late. Anyone familiar with the workings of the legislative process knows how easily drafting errors are made and how frequently they escape notice. The statute as drafted by Congress and as enforced by the Supreme Court became a trap for the unwary, destroying valuable property rights (and thereby precipitating a constitutional controversy which the plaintiffs also lost) because of a natural and harmless inadvertence. Nor is there any reason to think the trap was set by some interest group. No purpose, whether self-interested or public-interested, can be ascribed to the December 30 deadline. Finally, no one relied on the December 30 deadline, as by snapping up the "abandoned" Locke mining claim.

What makes the case appear difficult rather than plainly incorrect, is that the plaintiff seems not to have been asking the Supreme Court to interpret an ambiguity or fill in a gap, but to rewrite clear statutory language. The language is clear, however, only if significant contextual circumstances are ignored. The Court's approach was analogous to that of a platoon commander who (in a variant of my previous example), having received an order that is clear, but also clearly erroneous because of a mistake in transmission, nevertheless carries out the order as received, rather than trying to determine what response would advance the common enterprise.

Is my preferred interpretation of *Locke* consistent with refusing to read the Constitution's age thirty-five requirement nonliterally? I think so. As I said before, the framers' selection of a fixed age for eligibility, like a legislature's selection of a fixed age to denote the assumption of adult rights and responsibilities (or a fixed period for a statute of limitations), reflects a preference for a definite rule over a standard uncertain in application. To interpret age thirty-five to mean as mature as the average thirty-five year old would thus undo a choice deliberately made by the framers. The Federal Land Policy and Management Act of 1976 also reflects a preference for a fixed deadline but not necessarily for a fixed deadline of December 30 rather than December 31. Congress (by which I mean those members who took an interest in this provision of the Act) almost certainly thought it was making December 31 the deadline, even though it said December 30.

QUESTIONS FOR DISCUSSION

1. Who has the better argument, Justice Marshall or Judge Posner? Why? How would Brest decide *Locke*? Schauer? Bork? Dworkin?

2. Does Judge Posner confuse what Congress meant with what it said? Does Justice Marshall think that words can be interpreted without reference to their context? Is he right?

3. Posner thinks that Justice Marshall was being "wooden" and "unimaginative." What might Justice Marshall say in response?

BRAY V. ALEXANDRIA WOMEN'S HEALTH CLINIC

113 S. Ct. 753 (1993)

Justice SCALIA delivered the opinion of the Court.

This case presents the question whether the first clause 42 U.S.C. § 1985(3)—the surviving version of § 2 of the Civil Rights Act of 1871—provides a federal cause of action against persons obstructing access to abortion clinics. Respondents are clinics that perform abortions, and organizations that support legalized abortion and that have members that may wish to use abortion clinics. Petitioners are Operation Rescue, an unincorporated association whose members oppose abortion, and six individuals. Among its activities, Operation Rescue organizes antiabortion demonstrations in which participants trespass on, and obstruct general access to, the premises of abortion clinics. The individual petitioners organize and coordinate these demonstrations.

Respondents sued to enjoin petitioners from conducting demonstrations at abortion clinics in the Washington, D.C., metropolitan area. Following an expedited trial, the District Court ruled that petitioners had violated § 1985(3)* by conspiring to deprive women seeking abortions of their right to interstate travel. . . .

Our precedents establish that in order to prove a private conspiracy in violation of the first clause of § 1985(3), a plaintiff must show, *inter alia,* (1) that "some racial, or perhaps otherwise class–based, invidiously discriminatory animus [lay] behind the conspirators' action," *Griffin v. Breckenridge,* 403 U.S. 88 (1971), and (2) that the conspiracy "aimed at interfering with rights" that are "protected against private, as well as official, encroachment," *Carpenters v. Scott,*

463 U.S. 825 (1983). We think neither showing has been made in the present case.

In *Griffin* this Court held that § 1985(3) reaches not only conspiracies under color of state law, but also purely private conspiracies. In finding that the text required that expanded scope, however, we recognized the "constitutional shoals that would lie in the path of interpreting § 1985(3) as a general federal tort law." That was to be avoided, we said, "by requiring, as an element of the cause of action, the kind of invidiously discriminatory motivation stressed by the sponsors of the limiting amendment,"—citing specifically Representative Shellabarger's statement that the law was restricted "'to the prevention of deprivations which shall attack the equality of rights of American citizens; that any violation of the right, the *animus* and effect of which is to strike down the citizen, to the end that he may not enjoy equality of rights as contrasted with his and other citizens' rights, shall be within the scope of the remedies. . . .'" quoting Cong.Globe, 42d Cong., 1st Sess., App. 478 (1871). We said that "[t]he language [of § 1985(3)] requiring intent to deprive of *equal* protection, or *equal* privileges and immunities, means that there must be some racial, or perhaps otherwise class–based, invidiously discriminatory animus behind the conspirators' action."

We have not yet had occasion to resolve the "perhaps"; only in *Griffin* itself have we addressed and upheld a claim under § 1985(3), and that case involved race discrimination. Respondents assert that there qualifies alongside race discrimination, as an "otherwise class–based, invidiously discriminatory animus" covered by the 1871 law, opposition to abortion. Neither common sense nor our precedents support this.

Respondents' contention, however, is that the alleged class-based discrimination is directed not at "women seeking abortion" but at women in general. We find it unnecessary to decide whether *that* is a qualifying class under § 1985(3), since the claim that petitioners' opposition to abortion reflects an animus against women in general must be rejected. We do not think that the "animus" requirement can be met only by maliciously motivated, as opposed to assertedly benign (though objectively invidious), discrimination against women. It does demand, however, at least a purpose that focuses upon women *by reason of their sex*—for example (to use an illustration of assertedly benign discrimination), the purpose of "saving" women *because they are women* from a combative, aggressive profession such as the practice of law. The record in this case does not indicate that petitioners' demonstrations are motivated by a purpose (malevolent *or* benign) directed specifically at women as a class; to the contrary, the District Court found that petitioners define their "rescues" not with reference to women, but as physical intervention "'between abortionists and the innocent victims,'" and that "all [petitioners] share a deep commitment to the goals of stopping the practice of abortion and reversing its legalization." Given this record, respondents' contention that a class-based animus has been established can be true only if one of two suggested propositions is true: (1) that opposition to abortion can reasonably be presumed to reflect a sex-based intent, or (2) that intent is irrelevant, and a class-based animus can be determined solely by effect. Neither proposition is supportable.

As to the first: Some activities may be such an irrational object of disfavor that, if they are targeted, and if they also happen to be engaged in exclusively or predominantly by a particular class of people, an intent to disfavor that class can readily be presumed. A tax on wearing yarmulkes is a tax on Jews. But opposition to voluntary abortion cannot possibly be considered such an irrational surrogate for opposition to (or paternalism towards) women. Whatever one thinks of abortion, it cannot be denied that there are common and respectable reasons for opposing it, other than hatred of or condescension toward (or indeed any view at all concerning) women as a class—as is evident from the fact that men and women are on both sides of the issue, just as men and women are on both sides of the petitioners' unlawful demonstrations.

Respondents' case comes down, then, to the proposition that intent is legally irrelevant; that since voluntary abortion is an activity engaged in only by women, to disfavor it is *ipso facto* to discriminate invidiously against women as a class. Our cases do not support that proposition. . . .

The nature of the "invidiously discriminatory animus" *Griffin* had in mind is suggested both by the language used in that phrase ("invidious . . . [t]ending to excite odium, ill will, or envy; likely to give offense; esp., unjustly and irritatingly discriminating," Webster's Second International Dictionary 1306 (1954)) and by the company in which the phrase is found ("there must be *some racial, or perhaps otherwise class-based*, invidiously discriminatory animus," *Griffin*). Whether one agrees or disagrees with the goal of preventing abortion, that goal in itself (apart from the use of unlawful means to achieve it, which is not relevant to our discussion of animus) does not remotely qualify for such harsh description, and for such derogatory association with racism. To the contrary, we have said that "a value judgment favoring childbirth over abortion" is proper and reasonable enough to be implemented by the allocation of public funds, and Congress itself has, with our approval, discriminated against abortion in its provision of financial support for medical procedures. This is not the stuff out of which a § 1985(3) "invidiously discriminatory animus" is created.

Justice STEVENS, with whom Justice BLACKMUN joins, dissenting.

After the Civil War, Congress enacted legislation imposing on the Federal Judiciary the responsibility to remedy both abuses of power by persons acting under color of state law and lawless conduct that state courts are neither fully competent, nor always certain, to prevent. The Ku Klux Klan Act of 1871, was a response to the massive, organized lawlessness that infected our Southern States during the post Civil War era. When a question concerning this statute's coverage arises, it is appropriate to consider whether the controversy has a purely local character or the kind of federal dimension that gave rise to the legislation.

It is unfortunate that the Court has analyzed this case as though it presented an abstract question of logical deduction rather than a question concerning the exercise and allocation of power in our federal system of government. The Court ignores the obvious (and entirely constitutional) congressional intent behind § 1985(3) to protect this Nation's citizens from what amounts to the theft of their constitutional rights by organized and violent mobs across the country. . . .

The text of the statute makes plain the reasons Congress considered a federal remedy for such conspiracies both necessary and appropriate. In relevant part the statute contains two independent clauses which I separately identify in the following quotation:

"If two or more persons in any State or Territory conspire or go in disguise on the highway or on the premises of another, [first] for the purpose of depriving, either directly or indirectly, any person or class of persons of the equal protection of the laws, or of equal privileges and immunities under the laws; or [second] for the purpose of preventing or hindering the constituted authorities of any State or Territory from giving or securing to all persons within such State or Territory the equal protection of the laws; . . . in any case of conspiracy set forth in this section, if one or more persons engaged therein do, or cause to be done, any act in furtherance of the object of such conspiracy, whereby another is injured in his person or property, or deprived of having and exercising any right or privilege of a citizen of the United States, the party so injured or deprived may have an action for the recovery of damages occasioned by such injury or deprivation, against any one or more of the conspirators." 42 U.S.C. § 1985(3).

The plain language of the statute is surely broad enough to cover petitioners' conspiracy. Their concerted activities took place on both the public "highway" and the private "premises of another." The women targeted by their blockade fit comfortably within the statutory category described as "any person or class of persons." Petitioners' interference with police protection of women seeking access to abortion clinics "directly or indirectly" deprived them of equal protection of the laws and of their privilege of engaging in lawful travel. Moreover, a literal reading of the second clause of the statute describes petitioners' proven "purpose of preventing or hindering the constituted authorities of any State or Territory" from securing "to all persons within such State or Territory the equal protection of the laws."

No one has suggested that there would be any constitutional objection to the application of this statute to petitioners' nationwide conspiracy; it is obvious that any such constitutional claim would be frivolous. Accordingly, if, as it sometimes does, the Court limited its analysis to the statutory text, it would certainly affirm the judgment of the Court of Appeals. For both the first clause and the second clause of § 1985(3) plainly describe petitioners' conspiracy.

NOTE

*42 U.S.C. § 1985(3): *"Conspiracy to interfere with civil rights.* [If] two or more persons in any State or Territory conspire or go in disguise on the highway or on the premises of another, for the purpose of depriving, either directly or indirectly, any person or class of persons of the equal protection of the laws, or of equal privileges and immunities under the laws; [the] party so injured or deprived may have an action for the recovery of damages occasioned by such injury or deprivation, against any one or more of the conspirators."

NATIONAL ORGANIZATION FOR WOMEN V. SCHEIDLER

114 S.Ct. 832 (1994)

Chief Justice REHNQUIST delivered the opinion of the Court.

We are required once again to interpret the provisions of the Racketeer Influenced and Corrupt Organizations (RICO) chapter of the Organized Crime Control Act of 1970 (OCCA), Pub. L. 91–452, Title IX, 84 Stat. 941, as amended, 18 U. S. C. §§1961–1968 (1988 ed. and Supp. IV). Section 1962(c) prohibits any person associated with an enterprise from conducting its affairs through a pattern of racketeering activity. We granted certiorari to determine whether RICO requires proof that either the racketeering enterprise or the predicate acts of racketeering were motivated by an economic purpose. We hold that RICO requires no such economic motive.

I

Petitioner National Organization For Women, Inc. (NOW) is a national nonprofit organization that supports the legal availability of abortion. . . . Respondents are a coalition of antiabortion groups called the Pro–Life Action Network (PLAN), Joseph Scheidler and other individuals and organizations that oppose legal abortion, and a medical laboratory that formerly provided services to the two petitioner health centers. . . .

Petitioners alleged that respondents conspired to use threatened or actual force, violence or fear to induce clinic employees, doctors, and patients to give up their jobs, give up their economic right to practice medicine, and give up their right to obtain medical services at the clinics. Petitioners claimed that this conspiracy "has injured the business and/or property interests of the [petitioners]." According to the amended complaint, PLAN constitutes the alleged racketeering "enterprise" for purposes of § 1962(c).

[We] turn to the question of whether the racketeering enterprise or the racketeering predicate acts must be accompanied by an underlying economic motive. Section 1962(c) makes it unlawful "for any person employed by or associated with any enterprise engaged in, or the activities of which affect, interstate or foreign commerce, to conduct or participate, directly or indirectly, in the conduct of such enterprise's affairs through a pattern of racketeering activity or collection of unlawful debt." Section 1961(1) defines "pattern of racketeering activity" to include conduct that is "chargeable" or "indictable" under a host of state and federal laws. RICO broadly defines "enterprise" in § 1961(4) to "includ[e] any individual, partnership, corporation, association, or other legal entity, and any union or group of individuals associated in fact although not a legal entity." Nowhere in either § 1962(c), or in the RICO definitions in § 1961, is there any indication that an economic motive is required.

The phrase "any enterprise engaged in, or the activities of which affect, interstate or foreign commerce" comes the closest of any language in subsection (c) to suggesting a need for an economic motive. Arguably an enterprise engaged in interstate or foreign commerce would have a profit-seeking motive, but the language in § 1962(c) does not stop there; it includes enterprises whose activities "affect" interstate or foreign commerce. Webster's Third New International Dictionary 35 (1969) defines "affect" as "to have a detrimental influence on—used especially

in the phrase *affecting commerce.*" An enterprise surely can have a detrimental influence on interstate or foreign commerce without having its own profit-seeking motives. . . .

QUESTIONS FOR DISCUSSION

1. Does Justice Scalia in *Bray* base his decision on the text of Section 1985(3)? On its purpose? On the intentions of Congress in passing it? On something else?

2. What is the basis for Justice Stevens' dissent? Identify as precisely as you can his disagreement with the majority.

3. Justice Scalia voted with the unanimous Supreme Court in the *NOW* case. What might make his opinions in the two cases consistent?

4. How does Chief Justice Rehnquist define the word "enterprise"? Where does he get the definition? Does it sound right to you? If it does not, how might such a difference be resolved?

5. If an interpreter were concerned only with the text of the statute, how would she decide the two cases? If an interpreter were concerned only with original intentions, how would she decide the two cases? How do you think Dworkin would decide the two cases?

SUGGESTIONS FOR FURTHER READING

Various methods of interpretation are presented, contrasted, and criticized in Brian Bix, *Law, Language, and Legal Determinacy* (Oxford: Clarendon Press, 1993), and Andrei Marmor, *Interpretation and Legal Theory* (Oxford: Clarendon Press, 1993). On differing approaches in different countries, see P.S. Atiyah and R.S. Summers, *Form and Substance in Anglo-American Law: A Comparative Study of Legal Reasoning, Legal Theory and Legal Institutions* (Oxford: Clarendon Press, 1987); D. Neil MacCormick and Robert S. Summers, *Interpreting Statutes: A Comparative Study* (Aldershot, UK: Dartmouth Publishing, 1991). On questions of legal reasoning in the context of interpreting the United States Constitution, see Philip Bobbitt, *Constitutional Interpretation* (Oxford: Basil Blackwell, 1991); Stephen R. Munzer and James Nickel, "Does the Constitution Mean What It Always Meant?", *Columbia Law Review*, vol. 77 (1977), pp. 1029 ff.; Frederick Schauer, "An Essay on Constitutional Language," *UCLA Law Review*, vol. 29 (1982), pp. 797 ff. A critical survey of various forms of constitutional reasoning is in Philip Bobbitt, *Constitutional Fate: Theory of the Constitution* (Oxford: Oxford University Press, 1982). Important collections of articles on constitutional interpretation are Susan Brison and Walter Sinnott-Armstrong, eds., *Contemporary Perspectives on Constitutional Interpretation* (Boulder, Colo.: Westview Press, 1993); John H. Garvey and T. Alexander Aleinikoff, eds., *Modern Constitutional Theory: A Reader* (St. Paul, Minn.: West Publishing Company, 1994). For various attempts to apply the perspectives of Wittgenstein to questions of legal reasoning and legal language, see Dennis Patterson, ed., *Wittgenstein and Legal Theory* (Boulder, Colo.: Westview Press, 1992).

REASONING FROM 2.2
PRECEDENT

INTRODUCTION

In many legal systems, in fact in most non-English-speaking countries, the basic mode of legal reasoning traces its roots to Roman law. The method is one of interpreting a formal code covering, in theory, all legal topics. Although any code will obviously contain gaps, vagueness, and ambiguity, the basic task of the interpreter is to interpret a formal code of laws, just like in the previous section we saw interpreters trying to interpret provisions of the Constitution and state and federal statutes.

In countries whose legal system derives from English law, however, including most of the English-speaking world, the basic method is different. Entire areas or topics of law, such as contracts, torts, and much of property law, were developed not as interpretations of some text, but by judges in a "case-by-case" manner. As judges faced new situations, they developed new rules and principles, and over time there developed bodies of law whose content is determined not by looking at a formal code, but by looking at the collection of judicial decisions. In the United States, most of the state law of contracts and torts was developed in this manner.

In a code system, or, as it is more commonly called, a *civil law* system, stability and consistency are secured by the relatively fixed nature of the codes themselves. Judges are thus less concerned with being consistent with what other judges have done, and more concerned with trying to be faithful to the code itself. In *common law* jurisdictions, however, there is no fixed code, and stability comes from the principle that judges are expected to follow precedent—they are expected to decide cases in the same way that previous judges have decided them, even if they themselves disagree with those decisions.

Although it is often true that one case is pretty much exactly like another, it is also commonly true, especially in appellate courts, that there are differences between the current case and any case that a judge might locate. Even if the judge acknowledges that she is "bound" to follow the previous case, it is not clear what that means when the current case is in some respects different from the earlier case. It is frequently said that in such cases the judge tries to draw an "analogy" between the case before her and some previous case, but it is worth thinking carefully about just what it is to draw an analogy. What kind of reasoning is analogical reasoning, and is it different from or similar to other kinds of reasoning? What enables us to say that something is "similar" to something else? Is a blue shirt similar to a blue car? Is it similar to a red shirt? These may seem like strange questions, but this kind of problem arises very frequently in the law, where the case now before the judge is similar in some respects to one previous case, and similar in other respects to another. When the two previous cases indicate the opposite result in the pending case, the judge must decide which analogy is closer or better. Proponents of analogical reasoning say that it is possible to do this. Those who do not believe that there is a distinct method of reasoning by analogy admit that judges in common law systems do and must draw analogies. They contend, however, that this is not a distinct mode of reasoning. Rather, the judges are just creating some rule, and then fitting the present case within the rule they have created.

Even though reasoning from precedent originates with the idea of judges developing entire areas of law, precedential reasoning is also important in other areas. Any time a court interprets a statute, or a constitutional provision, its interpretations themselves carry precedential weight, and are treated as sources of law by other courts. As a practical matter, therefore, court cases interpreting particular provisions present the same issues about legal reasoning that are presented by court cases simply developing some area of the common law.

Although reasoning from a rule and reasoning from precedent are similar in that both require the decision maker to respect *authority*, the question of authority, especially the authority of the past, is especially obvious when we are thinking about precedent. Why is it that one judge should be bound by what some other judge happens to have done in the past? When we expect one judge to be bound by the judge of a *higher* court (what we might call *vertical* precedent), we can pretty well understand the arguments from higher authority that justify this practice. But when, as is the case in common law systems, we also expect judges to be bound by their *own* past decisions, or by decisions in the past by the same court (*horizontal* precedent, often called *stare decisis*, meaning "it is decided"), the reasons for doing so are less obvious. Not only, as noted before (p. 120), does this seem like bad logic, but it is not a practice normally expected of all official decision makers. If a President of the United States agrees with his predecessor about, say, welfare policy, or how much of the Gross National Product to spend on national defense, then there is no problem. But if a President disagrees with his predecessor on these matters, we do not expect him to follow what his predecessor has done just for the sake of precedent, or just for the sake of consistency. Yet that is what we appear to demand of our judges in common law systems.

Most of the arguments for taking precedent seriously are arguments about the importance of treating consistency as itself valuable. These arguments in turn rest on the importance to many people of being able to determine in advance what the law is, and to rely on what they believe the law to be in planning their lives and their business transactions. Justice Brandeis perhaps put it best, saying that "in most matters it is more important that the applicable rule of law be settled than that it be settled right."[9] Or as an English judge put it much earlier, it is "better that the law should be certain than that every judge should speculate upon improvements."[10] It is worth thinking carefully about these claims, for the

---

[9]Burnet v. Coronado Oil & Gas Co., 285 U.S. 393, 406 (1932) (Brandeis, J., dissenting).
[10]Sheddon v. Goodrich, 8 Ves. 481, 32 Eng. Rep. 441 (1803).

implication is that there are values in reliance, predictability, and consistency that may be more important than reaching the correct decision.[11]

Somewhat different from arguments for reliance, consistency, and predictability are arguments from stability for stability's sake. When legal systems and their rules do not change, they may secure a permanence that is independently desirable. Perhaps the most sophisticated form of this argument is Dworkin's view of law as integrity (see Chapter 1.4). Part of this claim is that the law should have integrity over time, and that there are strong reasons why political communities should try to make their political (and legal) decisions coherent over time. Indeed, it is possible that to Dworkin this sense of integrity and coherence over time (and over space as well) is what *defines* a political community. But even if we do not accept the claim in exactly this version, it is still the case that a commonly argued reason for following precedent is that it helps us to respect and to share the experiences and decisions of the past and, similarly, helps us to make decisions knowing that the decisions that we make today will be respected tomorrow. Although we might not see the value of this in all walks of life, and for all decisions, it is possible that law and the legal system are the special repositories of the values of stability and coherence, while other branches of government might be more focused on the importance of flexibility and change. If that is so, then it might explain why precedent seems especially important in legal decision making, and often especially unimportant in other forms of decision making.

[11]For a more extended discussion of these values, see Frederick Schauer, *Playing By the Rules: A Philosophical Examination of Rule-Based Decision-Making in Law and in Life* (Oxford: Clarendon Press, 1991), Chapter 7

ON ANALOGICAL REASONING

CASS R. SUNSTEIN

Outside of law, analogical reasoning often helps to inform our judgments. I have a German shepherd dog who is gentle with children. When I see another German shepherd dog, I assume that he, too, will be gentle with children. I have a Toyota Camry that starts even on cold days in winter. I assume that my friend's Toyota Camry will start on cold winter days as well. This kind of thinking has a simple structure: (1) A has characteristic X; (2) B shares that

Cass R. Sunstein, "On Analogical Reasoning," *Harvard Law Review*, vol. 106 (1992), pp. 741 ff.[12]

[12]Cass Sunstein (1954–   ), a professor at the University of Chicago Law School, writes about constitutional law, administrative law, environmental law, and legal theory.

characteristic; (3) *A* also has characteristic *Y*; (4) Because *A* and *B* share characteristic *X*, we conclude what is not yet known, that *B* shares characteristic *Y* as well.

This is a usual form of reasoning in daily life, but it will readily appear that it does not guarantee truth. The existence of one or many shared characteristics does not mean that all characteristics are shared. Some German shepherd dogs are not gentle with children. Some Toyota Camrys do not start on cold days in winter. For analogical reasoning to work well, we have to say that the relevant, known similarities give us good reason to believe that there are further similarities and thus help to answer an open question. Of course this is not always so. At most, analogical thinking can give rise to a judgment about probabilities, and often these are of uncertain magnitude.

Analogical reasoning has a similar structure in law. Consider some examples. We know that an employer may not fire an employee for refusing to commit perjury; it is said to follow that an employer is banned from firing an employee for filing a workers' compensation claim. We know that a speech by a member of the Ku Klux Klan, advocating racial hatred, cannot be regulated unless it is likely to incite, and is directed to inciting, imminent lawless action; it is said to follow that the government cannot forbid the Nazis to march in Skokie, Illinois. We know that there is no constitutional right to welfare, medical care, or housing; it is said to follow that there is no constitutional right to government protection against domestic violence.

From a brief glance at these examples, we can get a sense of the characteristic form of analogical thought in law. The process appears to work in four simple steps: (1) Some fact pattern *A* has a certain characteristic *X*, or characteristics *X*, *Y*, and *Z*; (2) Fact pattern *B* differs from *A* in some respects but shares characteristic *X*, or characteristics *X*, *Y*, and *Z*; (3) The law treats *A* in a certain way; (4) Because *B* shares certain characteristics with *A*, the law should treat *B* the same way. For example, someone asking for protection against domestic violence is requesting affirmative government assistance, just like someone asking the government for medical care; it is said to "follow" from the medical care case that there is no constitutional right to protection against domestic violence.

As in the nonlegal examples, it should readily appear that analogical reasoning does not guarantee good outcomes or truth. For analogical reasoning to operate properly, we have to know that *A* and *B* are "relevantly" similar, and that there are not "relevant" differences between them. Two cases are always different from each other along some dimensions. When lawyers say there are no relevant differences, they mean that any differences between the two cases either (a) do not make a difference in light of the relevant precedents, which foreclose certain possible grounds for distinction, or (b) cannot be fashioned into the basis for a distinction that is genuinely principled. A claim that one case is genuinely analogous to another—that it is "apposite" or cannot be "distinguished"—is parasitic on conclusion (a) or (b), and either of these must of course be justified.

The major challenge facing analogical reasoners is to decide when differences are relevant. To make this decision, they must investigate cases with care in order to develop governing principles. The judgment that a distinction is not genuinely principled requires a substantive argument of some kind. For example, one difference between the Nazi march and the Klan speech is that the Nazi Party is associated with the Holocaust. This is indeed a difference, but American law currently deems it irrelevant. It appears unprincipled—or excessively ad hoc—for the states to ban prohibitions on political speech except when the speaker is associated with the Holocaust. As we will see, analogical reasoning goes wrong when there is an inadequate inquiry into the matter of relevant differences and governing principles. But what are the defining characteristics of a competent lawyer's inquiry into analogies?

In law, analogical reasoning has four different but overlapping features: *principled consistency; a focus on particulars; incompletely theorized judgments; and principles operating at a low or intermediate level of abstraction.* Taken in concert, these features produce both the virtues and the vices of analogical reasoning in law.

First, and most obviously, judgments about specific cases must be made consistent with one another. A requirement of coherence, or principled consistency, is a hallmark of analogical reasoning (as it is of reasoning of almost all sorts). It follows that in producing the necessary consistency, some principle, harmonizing seemingly disparate outcomes, will be invoked to explain the cases.

Second, analogical reasoning focuses on particulars, and it develops from concrete controversies. Holmes put it this way: a common law court "decides the case first and determines the principle afterwards." Ideas are developed from the details, rather than imposed on them from above. In this sense, analogical reasoning, unlike many forms of reasoning, is a version of "bottom-up" thinking.

Despite the focus on particulars, the analogizer's description of a particular holding inevitably has some general theoretical components. One cannot even characterize one's convictions about a case without using abstractions, and without taking a position on competing abstractions. We cannot fully describe the outcome in case *X* if we do not know something about the reasons that count in its favor. We cannot say whether decided case *X* has anything to do with undecided case *Y* unless we are able to abstract, a bit, from the facts and holding of case *X*. The key point is that analogical reasoning involves a process in which principles are developed with constant reference to particular cases.

Third, analogical reasoning operates without a comprehensive theory that accounts for the particular outcomes it yields. The judgments that underlie convictions about, or holdings in, the relevant case are incompletely theorized, in the sense that they are unaccom-

panied by a full apparatus to explain the basis for those judgments. Lawyers might firmly believe, for example, that the Constitution does not create a right to welfare or that the state cannot regulate political speech without a showing of immediate and certain harm. But it is characteristic of reasoning by analogy, as I understand it here, that lawyers are not able to explain the basis for these beliefs in much depth or detail, or with full specification of the theory that accounts for those beliefs. Lawyers (and almost all other people) typically lack any large-scale theory. They reason anyway, and their reasoning is often analogical.

Finally, analogical reasoning produces principles that operate at a low or intermediate level of abstraction. If we say that the state cannot ban a Nazi march, we might mean that the state cannot stop political speech without showing that the speech poses a clear and immediate harm. This is a principle, and it does involve a degree of abstraction from the particular case; but it does not entail any high-level theory about the purposes of the free speech guarantee or about the relation between the citizen and the state. Analogical reasoning usually operates without express reliance on any general principles about the right or the good. Some such principles may of course be an implicit or even necessary basis for decision, but the lawyer who engages in analogical reasoning is not self-conscious about them.

Reasoning by analogy, understood in light of these four characteristics, is the mode through which the ordinary lawyer typically operates. He has no abstract theory to account for his convictions, or for what he knows to be the law. But he knows that these are his convictions, or that this is the law, and he is able to bring that knowledge to bear on undecided cases. For guidance, he looks to areas in which his judgment is firm. Analogical reasoning thus works when an incompletely theorized judgment about case *X* is invoked to come to terms with case *Y*, which bears much (but not all) in common with case *X*, and in which there is as yet no judgment at all.

QUESTIONS FOR DISCUSSION

1. How does Sunstein define "analogy"? Would he distinguish analogical reasoning from the rule-based reasoning discussed in the previous section? How?

2. What sources does Sunstein suggest that judges do or should use in drawing analogies?

3. Sunstein says that analogical reasoning "involves a process in which principles are developed with constant reference to particular cases." What does he mean? How does he think that judgments about the particular cases are reached?

CONSTRAINED BY PRECEDENT

LARRY ALEXANDER

The first model of precedent following is what I call the natural model. Under this model the court in deciding a case gives prior judicial decisions the weight that those decisions carry independently of any formal requirement that precedent be followed. In other words, the constrained court looks to the "precedential" effects of the prior decision and assigns them a moral weight, which it then factors into its overall decisionmaking calculus.

To understand the natural model better, let us look at an instance of nonlegal decision-making where the model clearly does operate. Suppose that when my daughter reaches the age of thirteen, she requests permission from me to attend a rock concert. I weigh the possible risks involved in her going and the potential benefits to her and to our relationship and I decide to grant her permission to go. When my son reaches the age of thirteen and also

seeks permission to attend a rock concert, he predictably will cite my previous decision granting permission to his sister as a reason for a decision in his favor, a reason in addition to the risks and benefits I would normally consider. The natural model of precedent requires that I give the previous decision its true weight as an independent reason.

The natural model would have the same features in the legal system. In the precedent case, which I am assuming is not governed by any statute or constitutional provision that speaks to its substantive merits, and which I shall also assume is not itself governed by an applicable precedent case, the court—which I shall hereafter call the "precedent court"—will assess the reasons why the dispute should be resolved in one party's favor or the other's. Those reasons might primarily be the parties' relative moral desert or some other deontologi-

Larry Alexander, "Constrained by Precedent," *Southern California Law Review*, vol. 63 (1989), pp. 1 ff. Alexander (1943–) is Professor of Law at the University of San Diego.

cal consideration—a sort of "What if these parties were alone on a desert island?" inquiry. Alternatively, those reasons might primarily be the social consequences of the alternative decisions. Although it is interesting to reflect upon how a court should resolve a dispute in the absence of controlling statutory rules or precedent, we do not need to assume anything beyond the fact that the precedent court does in fact resolve the dispute based on reasons—deontological, consequentialist, or some mixture—that it believes correct political/moral theory approves.

The important point here is that once the precedent court decides the case, the existence of that decision can be invoked as an independent reason for subsequent courts to decide "similar" disputes in the same way. This is true even in the absence of a formal practice of precedent following. Similarly, my decision to allow my daughter to attend a rock concert at age thirteen can (and will) be invoked by my son as a reason for permitting him to attend a rock concert at the same age. The earlier decision is invoked as a reason for a similar decision, a reason that did not exist in the precedent case and that is to be added to the other reasons for such a decision. More precisely, the precedent decision gives rise to reasons for a similar decision, such as equality and reliance, that did not exist in the precedent case.

Moreover, even if the subsequent court—which I shall hereafter call the "constrained court"—believes the precedent case was decided incorrectly because the balance of reasons favored the losing party, the constrained court might believe that the new reasons generated by the precedent decision tip the balance in favor of the party who would have lost had the constrained court decided the precedent case. Similarly, I might decide that although I should not have let my daughter attend the rock concert, and should not let my son attend were this my first decision on the point, the decision in my daughter's case now tips the balance of reasons in favor of permitting my son to go.

I suspect that we all recognize the natural model, if not in the legal system, at least in other areas of our lives. But how can a past decision that we now believe was incorrect convert a present decision that would otherwise be incorrect into a correct decision? The arguments on behalf of following incorrect decisions on the natural model of precedent boil down to two reasons: furthering equality of treatment and respecting justified expectations on which people have relied.

It is easy to see why one might argue that equality supports the constrained court's decision that, but for the precedent court's decision, would be incorrect. If I tell my son that I will not permit him to attend the rock concert and that I should not have permitted his sister to go, he predictably will claim that I have not treated him equally with respect to her. By saying so, he will be making more than the obvious descriptive point that my treatment of his sister and him with respect to attending rock concerts at age thirteen is dissimilar. Rather, he will be making the normative claim that such dissimilarity in treatment is wrong in the absence of countervailing considerations of substantial moral weight. In other words, he will be asserting that the value of equality is a sufficiently weighty reason in support of letting him go to the concert that it tips the balance of reasons in his favor.

The role of the justified reliance argument in support of a decision in favor of the present analog to the party who won in the precedent case is also fairly easy to understand. Even if there is no formal requirement that courts follow precedent, people frequently will look to judicial decisions and the expressed reasons on which they are based in order to predict how their contemplated courses of action will be treated by the courts should a legal dispute arise. Similarly, my son may undertake action based upon his reasonable expectation that because I allowed his sister to attend a rock concert at age thirteen, I will allow him to do the same. These expectations become reasons that may justify decisions that would otherwise (in the absence of the expectations) be regarded as erroneous. . . .

In one sense, the natural model of precedent is not a model of precedential constraint at all. The constrained court need do nothing more than decide the case before it as it believes is morally correct, even if it knows that the precedent court would strongly disagree with its decision. What is morally correct, of course, will be a function of facts about the parties and the world. Importantly, these facts might include the equality and reliance effects of earlier court decisions. This same concern for equality of treatment, however, might also arise from a decision by a court inferior in rank to the constrained court or from a decision by a nonjudicial official or body. Likewise, people may have present expectations that should be given weight by the constrained court even though they are not based on the decisions of precedent courts and perhaps not based on the decisions of any courts. Thus, equality and reliance concerns founded on an earlier decision within the jurisdiction by a court of equal or superior rank are simply items that the constrained court must factor into its deliberations along with many other relevant considerations, including not only constitutional, statutory, and other authoritative rules beyond the power of the constrained court to affect but also equality and reliance concerns traceable to sources other than precedent decisions. It is perhaps misleading, therefore, to label the method of the natural model of precedent as precedent following at all. . . .

The second model of precedential constraint is the rule model of precedent. Under the rule model, the precedent court has authority not only to decide the case before it but also to promulgate a general rule binding on courts of subordinate and equal rank. The rule will operate like a statute and will, like a statute, have a canonical formulation.

Versions of the rule model can vary along two dimensions. First, they can vary according to the strength by which the precedent court's rule binds the constrained court. On some versions, the constraint may be absolute, like that of a statute or constitutional rule on a court. On those versions, the constrained court may never overrule a precedent rule. On other versions, the constraint may be much weaker. On no version, however, is a constrained court as free to disregard a precedent rule as it is on the natural model. The constrained court cannot decide to overrule merely because, having weighed equality and reliance against the advantages of a different rule or decision, it has found the balance slightly tilted in favor of the latter.

The second dimension along which versions of the rule model vary is in their methodologies for identifying the precedent rule. Some versions try to locate a statement of a canonical rule in the opinion of the precedent court. Other versions look for rules that the precedent court implicitly as well as explicitly used as necessary steps in reaching its decision or facts that it deemed material to its decision. On all versions of the rule model, however, the identification of the rule must meet three conditions. First, the rule must have a canonical formulation, even if that canonical formulation does not appear in the original opinion, such as, "Whenever facts A, B, and C, and not fact D, decide for P." Second, the rule must be treated as separate from the reasoning that led to its adoption by the precedent court; it is only the rule, and not the reasoning, that binds the constrained court. Third, the formulation of the rule must be fixed at the time of the precedent decision; that is, it must not be dependent on what any court other than the precedent court did.

As long as these three conditions are met, coupled with the condition that the constraint be greater than under the natural model of precedent, we are dealing with the rule model. Thus, issues such as whether an announced rule can be a precedent when the precedent court (mistakenly) reached a decision opposite from that which its rule dictates or, relatedly, whether rules intended to apply prospectively only can be binding are issues that arise within the rule model of precedent. The resolution of these questions as well as the resolution of the general debate over how to identify the precedent rule do not affect the general points that I wish to make about the rule model. If the model is otherwise attractive, however, their resolution will become necessary.

The rule model of precedent has several advantages over the natural model. If one considers equality to be a value supporting precedential constraint—a value that I, for one, discount heavily—then the rule model has the advantage of providing access to all the facts of the precedent case relevant to equality. All one needs to know about the precedent case is its rule, which establishes the relevant criteria of equal treatment.

The most important advantage of the rule model, however, is that lower courts (and people in general) derive much more guidance from constraining general rules than they do from constraining particular decisions, even when the particular decisions take the value of rules into account. In claiming this, I am making three assumptions. First, I am assuming a practice of precedent following, precedent here consisting of the rules laid down in precedent cases—that is at least moderately strong. In other words, the constrained court cannot overrule the precedent merely because it can think of a rule that is slightly superior to the precedent court's rule. The rule model collapses into the natural model if the precedent can be so easily overruled. The advantage that the rule model provides in terms of guidance does not require that precedential constraint be absolute, but it does require that it be greater than zero.

Second, I am assuming that rules provide greater predictability than do other factors to which people might resort in order to predict courts' decisions—factors such as the judges' politics, economic class, and so forth.

Third, I am assuming that an improvement in legal predictability can be a net gain in terms of whatever political morality we hold, even when it comes at the cost of setbacks under that same political morality in particular cases and to particular litigants. This assumption holds up, I believe, despite its paradoxical quality, at least for any political morality that seems at all plausible.

Finally, there is one additional "advantage" of the rule model: the third model of precedential constraint, the result model, is undesirable and perhaps incoherent. Therefore, it is not a tenable alternative to the rule model. . . .

Many readers will feel that I have as yet failed to describe the model of precedential constraint with which they are most familiar. Like Goldilocks and the bowls of porridge and beds, they will complain that the natural model of precedent is too weak to capture their sense of how precedents operate and that the rule model of precedent is too strong. I have not described a model that is "just right."

The third model of precedential constraint appears to meet this complaint. It seems stronger than the natural model in that an incorrect decision has more power to constrain subsequent courts than just reliance or equality values would explain. Yet it also seems weaker than the rule model in that the precedent court's stated rule is not itself binding.

The simplest formulation of the pure result model is as follows: To follow precedent, a constrained court must decide its case for the party analogous to the winner in the precedent case if the constrained case is as strong or stronger a case for that result than the precedent case was for its result. The constrained court must do so even if under the natural model it would have decided its case differently and regardless of any rule stated in the precedent case. Conversely, however, the constrained court may depart from the precedent court's result if the constrained case is a weaker case for that result than was the precedent case, even when the stated rule of the precedent case covers the constrained case and demands a similar result. Put differently, under the pure result model the constrained court must depart from what the natural model requires if and only if its case is an a fortiori case for the same (incorrect) result as in the precedent case.

This formulation of the pure result model of precedent can be presented schematically as follows: Assume that the relevant facts of the precedent case are A, B, C, and D and the precedent court holds for P, declaring as its rule that in all cases of A and B, the decision must be for P. In the constrained case the facts are A, B, C, and E (rather than D) plus N, the natural weight (equality and reliance) of the precedent case. If the absence of D and the presence of E and N make the constrained case a weaker case for P than the precedent case, the constrained court may ignore the rule of the precedent case ("if A and B, decide for P") and decide against P. On the other hand, if the presence of E is a stronger reason for deciding for P than was the presence of D, then even if the constrained court believes that, giving precedent its natural weight, P ought not prevail, the pure result model of precedent constrains it to decide in favor of P.

The a fortiori case formulation of the pure result model of precedent is a way of giving meaning to the injunction "treat like cases alike." That injunction is either empty, because all cases are alike in some respects and not in others, or it translates into "reach the same result as in the precedent case in any case that is as or more morally compelling for the result reached in the precedent case than was the precedent case itself, even if that result is not on balance compelling in either case." In other words, a case is "like" the precedent case if the facts point at least equally as strongly toward a decision analogous to the decision in the precedent case.

A problem with the pure result model is that it requires the constrained court to have access to those facts of the precedent case that bear on the constrained court's assessment of whether its case is or is not [controlled by] precedent. The precedent court might be quite obliging and recite volumes of facts in its opinion regardless of *its* view of their relevance. On the other hand, the precedent court may believe that its case and future cases should be governed by a very broad rule, which in turn may lead it to recite only those facts pertinent to the rule and only at the level of generality at which the rule operates. For example, it may reveal only that defendant is a promisor and plaintiff a promisee if it believes that the appropriate rule is that all promises should be legally enforced.

The problem raised by a spare recitation of facts characterized at a high level of generality is that it seriously impedes the constrained court's determination of whether the constrained case is an a fortiori case or is instead distinguishable on its facts from the precedent case. If all the constrained court knows about the precedent case is that the plaintiff was a promisee, the defendant was a promisor, and the plaintiff won, then if it believes its plaintiff-promisor should not win (in the absence of the precedent case), it will be unable to determine whether its case is factually different from the precedent case in a way that supports the defendant (that is, that it is not an a fortiori case for the plaintiff).

If this lack of access to the facts of the precedent case causes the constrained court to follow the precedent decision and to decide, contrary to its natural model judgment, for the party analog to who won in the precedent case, the pure result model of precedent all but collapses into the rule model. At least it does so if the precedent court is clever and reveals only that the facts picked out by its rule obtain. In other words, the advantage that the pure result model purports to have over the rule model—the absence of judicial legislation—is quite fragile and easily defeated by a clever court.

Thus, the pure result model is, because of lack of direct access to the facts of the precedent case, threatened with collapse into either the rule model or the natural model. Neither of these models, however, is hampered by the problem of the precedent court's characterization of the facts of the precedent case. The rule model clearly is not; the natural model merely asks the constrained court to do the best it can with whatever facts it has. On the natural model, limitations on the constrained court's knowledge about the facts of the precedent case are no more significant than other limitations on its information about the world, limitations that are the hallmark of the human condition generally.

QUESTIONS FOR DISCUSSION

1. What does Alexander mean by the "natural model" of precedent? The "rule model"? The "result model"?

2. Is Alexander's result model similar to Sunstein's conception of reasoning by analogy? How are they similar or different? What would Alexander say about Sunstein's claims about analogical reasoning?

3. Why does Alexander believe that the rule model is superior to the natural model? Where does Alexander think that the rules in the rule model come from?

4. Does Alexander think that constraint by precedent is a good thing? Why? Do you? Why?

DONOGHUE V. STEVENSON

1932 S.C. 31
(House of Lords)[13]

By an action brought in the Court of Session the appellant, who was a shop assistant, sought to recover damages from the respondent, who was a manufacturer of aerated waters, for injuries she suffered as a result of consuming part of the contents of a bottle of ginger-beer which had been manufactured by the respondent, and which contained the decomposed remains of a snail. The appellant by her condescendence averred that the bottle of ginger-beer was purchased for the appellant by a friend in a café at Paisley, which was occupied by one Minchella, that the bottle was made of dark opaque glass and that the appellant had no reason to suspect

---

[13]This version of the case is as edited in William Twining and David Miers, *How to Do Things With Rules*, second edition (London: Weidenfeld and Nicolson, 1982), pp. 54–58. Case citations have been left in for illustrative purposes. Note also that in English cases, such as this one, no opinion is designated as *the* majority opinion, or opinion of the court. Rather, each judge writes an opinion (or gives a "speech"), and the *ratio decidendi* of the case is the reasoning shared in common by a majority of the judges hearing the case.

that it contained anything but pure ginger-beer; that the said Minchella poured some of the ginger-beer out into a tumbler, and that the appellant drank some of the contents of the tumbler; that her friend was then proceeding to pour the remainder of the contents of the bottle into a tumbler when a snail, which was in a state of decomposition, floated out of the bottle; that as a result of the nauseating sight of the snail in such circumstances, and in consequence of the impurities in the ginger-beer which she had already consumed the appellant suffered from shock and severe gastro-enteritis. The appellant further averred that the ginger-beer was manufactured by the respondent to be sold as a drink to the public (including the appellant); that it was bottled by the respondent and labelled by him with a label bearing his name; and that the bottles were thereafter sealed with a metal cap by the respondent. She further averred that it was the duty of the respondent to provide a system of working his business which would not allow snails to get into his ginger-beer bottles and that it was also his duty to provide an efficient system of inspection of the bottles before the ginger-beer was filled into them, and that he had failed in both these duties and had so caused the accident. . . .

1932. May 26, *Lord Buckmaster* (dissenting). My Lords, the facts of this case are simple. On August 26, 1928, the appellant drank a bottle of ginger-beer, manufactured by the respondent which a friend had brought from a retailer and given to her. The bottle contained the decomposed remains of a snail which were not, and could not be, detected until the greater part of the contents of the bottle had been consumed. As a result she alleged, and at this stage her allegations must be accepted as true, that she suffered from shock and severe gastro-enteritis. She accordingly instituted the proceedings against the manufacturer which have given rise to this appeal.

The foundation of her case is that the respondent, as the manufacturer of an article intended for consumption and contained in a receptacle which prevented inspection, owed a duty to her as consumer of the article to take care that there was no noxious element in the goods, that he neglected such duty and is consequently liable for any damage caused by such neglect. After certain amendments, which are now immaterial, the case came before the Lord Ordinary, who rejected the plea in law of the respondent and allowed a proof. His interlocutor was recalled by the Second Division of the Court Session, from whose judgment this appeal has been brought. . . .

Now the common law must be sought in law books by writers of authority and in judgments of the judges entrusted with its administration. The law books give no assistance, because the work of living authors however deservedly eminent, cannot be used as authority, though the opinions they express may demand attention; and the ancient books do not assist. I turn, therefore to the decided cases to see if they can be construed so as to support the appellant's case. One of the earliest is the case of *Langridge v. Levy* ((1837) 2 M. & W. 519). It is a case often quoted and variously explained. There a man sold a gun which he knew was dangerous for the use of the purchaser's son. The gun exploded in the son's hands, and he was held to have a right of action in tort against the gunmaker. How far it is from the present case can be seen from the judgment of Parke B., who, in delivering the judgment of the Court, used these words: 'We shall pause before we make a precedent by our decision which would be an authority for an action against the vendors, even of such instruments and articles as are dangerous in themselves at the suit of any person whomsoever into whose hands they might happen to pass, and who should be injured thereby'. . . .

The case of *Langridge v. Levy* therefore, can be dismissed from consideration with the comment that it is rather surprising it has so often been cited for a proposition it cannot support.

The case of *Winterbottom v. Wright* ((1842) 10 M. & W. 109) is on the other hand, an authority that is closely applicable. Owing to negligence in the construction of a carriage it broke down, and a stranger to the manufacture and sale sought to recover damages for injuries which he alleged were due to negligence in the work, and it was held that he had no cause of action either in tort or arising out of contract. This case seems to me to show that the manufacturer of any article is not liable to a third party injured by negligent construction, for there can be nothing in the character of a coach to place it in a special category. It may be noted, also, that in this case Alderson B. said: 'The only safe rule is to confine the right to recover to those who enter into the contract, if we go one step beyond that, there is no reason why we should not go fifty.' . . .

Of the remaining cases, *George v. Skivington* ((1869) L.R. 5 Ex. 1) is the one nearest to the present, and without that case, and the statement of Cleasby B. in *Francis v. Cockrell* ((1870) L.R. 5 Q.B. 501) and the dicta of Brett M.R., in *Heaven v. Pender* ((1883) 11 Q.B.D. 503) the appellant would be destitute of authority. *George v. Skivington* related to the sale of a noxious hairwash, and a claim made by a person who had not bought it but who had suffered from its use, based on its having been negligently compounded, was allowed. It is remarkable that *Langridge v. Levy* was used in support of the claim and influenced the judgment of all the parties to the decision. Both Kelly C.B. and Pigott B. stressed the fact that the article had been purchased to the knowledge of the defendant for the use of the plaintiff, as in *Langridge v. Levy*, and Cleasby B., who, realizing that *Langridge v. Levy* was decided on the ground of fraud, said: 'Substitute the word "negligence" for "fraud" and the analogy between *Langridge v. Levy* and this case is complete.' It is unnecessary to point out too emphatically that such a substitution cannot possibly be made. No action based on fraud can be supported by mere proof of negligence.

I do not propose to follow the fortunes of *George v. Skivington*; few cases can have lived so dangerously and lived so long. Lord Sumner, in the case of *Blacker v. Lake & Elliot Ltd* ((1912) 106 L.T. 533) closely examines its history, and I

agree with his analysis. He said that he could not presume to say that it was wrong, but he declined to follow it on the ground which is, I think, firm that it was in conflict with *Winterbottom v. Wright*.

Lord Atkin. My Lords, the sole question for determination in this case is legal: Do the averments made by the pursuer in her pleading, if true, disclose a cause of action? I need not restate the particular facts. The question is whether the manufacturer of an article of drink sold by him to a distributor, in circumstances which prevent the distributor or the ultimate purchaser or consumer from discovering by inspection any defect, is under any legal duty to the ultimate purchaser or consumer to take reasonable care that the article is free from defect likely to cause injury to health. I do not think a more important problem has occupied your Lordships in your judicial capacity: important both because of its bearing on public health and because of the practical test which it applies to the system under which it arises. . . .

At present I content myself with pointing our that in English law there must be, and is, some general conception of relations giving rise to a duty of care, of which the particular cases found in the books are but instances. The liability for negligence, whether you style it such or treat it as in other systems as a species of 'culpa', is no doubt based upon a general public sentiment of moral wrongdoing for which the offender must pay. But acts or omissions which any moral code would censure cannot in a practical world be treated so as to give a right to every person injured by them to demand relief. In this way rules of law arise which limit the range of complainants and the extent of their remedy. The rule that you are to love your neighbour becomes in law, you must not injure your neighbour; and the lawyer's question, Who is my neighbour? receives a restricted reply. You must take reasonable care to avoid acts or omissions which you can reasonably foresee would be likely to injure your neighbour. Who, then in law is my neighbour? The answer seems to be—persons who are so closely and directly affected by my act that I ought reasonably to have them in contemplation as being so affected when I am directing my mind to the acts or omissions which are called in question. . . .

There will no doubt arise cases where it will be difficult to determine whether the contemplated relationship is so close that the duty arises. But in the class of case now before the Court I cannot conceive any difficulty to arise. A manufacturer puts up an article of food in a container which he knows will be opened by the actual consumer. There can be no inspection by any purchaser and no reasonable preliminary inspection by the consumer. Negligently, in the course of preparation, he allows the contents to be mixed with poison. It is said that the Law of England and Scotland is that the poisoned consumer has no remedy against the negligent manufacturer. If this were the result of the authorities, I should consider the result a grave defect in the law. . . .

There are other instances than of articles of food and drink where goods are sold intended to be used immediately by the consumer, such as many forms of goods sold for cleaning purposes, where the same liability must exist. The doctrine supported by the decision below would not only deny a remedy to the consumer who was injured by consuming bottled beer or chocolates poisoned by the negligence of the manufacturer, but also to the user of what should be a harmless proprietary medicine, an ointment, a soap, a cleaning fluid or cleaning powder. I confine myself to articles of common household use, where every one, including the manufacturer knows that the articles will be used by other persons than the actual ultimate purchaser—namely, by members of his family and his servants, and in some cases his guests. I do not think so ill of our jurisprudence as to suppose that its principles are so remote from the ordinary needs of civilized society and the ordinary claims it makes upon its members as to deny a legal remedy where there is so obviously a social wrong.

It now becomes necessary to consider the cases which have been referred to in the Courts below as laying down the proposition that no duty to take care is owed to the consumer in such a case as this.

In *Winterbottom v. Wright* it is to be observed that no negligence apart from breach of contract was alleged—in other words, no duty was alleged other than the duty arising out of the contract; it is not stated that the defendant knew, or ought to have known, of the latent defect. The argument of the defendant was that, on the face of the declaration, the wrong arose merely out of the breach of a contract, and that only a party to the contract could sue. The Court of Exchequer adopted that view, as clearly appears from the judgments of Alderson and Rolfe BB. There are dicta by Lord Abinger which are too wide as to an action of negligence being confined to cases of breach of a public duty. The actual decision appears to have been manifestly right; no duty to the plaintiff arose out of the contract; and the duty of the defendant under the contract with the Postmaster-General to put the coach in good repair could not have involved such direct relations with the servant of the persons whom the Postmaster-General employed to drive the coach as would give rise to a duty of care owed to such servant. . . .

My Lords, if your Lordships accept the view that this pleading discloses a relevant cause of action you will be affirming the proposition that by Scots and English law alike a manufacturer of products, which he sells in such a form as to show that he intends them to reach the ultimate consumer in the form in which they left him with no reasonable possibility of intermediate examination, and with the knowledge that the absence of reasonable care in the preparation or putting up of the products will result in an injury to the consumer's life or property, owes a duty to the consumer to take that reasonable care.

It is a proposition which I venture to say no one in Scotland or England who was not a lawyer would for one moment doubt. It will be an advantage to make it clear that the law in this matter, as in most others, is in accordance with sound common sense. I think that this appeal should be allowed.

Appeal allowed.

QUESTIONS FOR DISCUSSION

Bearing in mind Sunstein's description of analogical reasoning, and Alexander's contrast between three models of precedent, what is the best way of describing the defendant in *Donoghue v. Stevenson*:

1. A Scottish manufacturer of ginger-beer in opaque bottles?
2. A manufacturer of aerated water?
3. A manufacturer of consumable products?
4. A manufacturer of products?
5. A person who, in the course of trade, puts goods into circulation?
6. A person who puts into circulation a potentially harmful item?
7. A person who puts someone else in danger?

What led you to choose one description rather than another? What kinds of cases would follow from *Donoghue v. Stevenson* under each of these descriptions?

PLANNED PARENTHOOD OF SOUTHEASTERN PENNSYLVANIA V. CASEY

112 S.Ct. 2791 (1992)

[EDITOR'S NOTE: This 1992 Supreme Court case considered the issue of abortion and addressed the status of *Roe v. Wade*, the 1973 case in which the Supreme Court had held that the Constitution contained a right to privacy, and that the right to privacy included the right of a woman, under most circumstances, to have an abortion without interference from the state. We will take up privacy and other aspects of abortion in Chapter 4. Here the question is about the status in 1992 of the 1973 case. In the 1992 case, involving restrictions on abortion that stopped short of a total prohibition, some of the Justices argued that *Roe v. Wade* should be overruled. Others argued that it should be followed because of its precedential force. And others argued that it should be modified. The following debate took place in this context.]

Justices O'CONNOR, KENNEDY and SOUTER:

[While] we appreciate the weight of the arguments made on behalf of the State in the case before us, arguments which in their ultimate formulation conclude that Roe should be overruled, the reservations any of us may have in reaffirming the central holding of Roe are outweighed by the explication of individual liberty we have given combined with the force of stare decisis. We turn now to that doctrine.

A. The obligation to follow precedent begins with necessity, and a contrary necessity marks its outer limit. With Cardozo, we recognize that no judicial system could do society's work if it eyed each issue afresh in every case that raised it. The Nature of the Judicial Process 149 (1921). Indeed, the very concept of the rule of law [requires] such continuity over time that a respect for precedent is, by definition, indispensable. At the other extreme, a different necessity would make itself felt if a prior judicial ruling should come to be seen so clearly as error that its enforcement was for that very reason doomed.

Even when the decision to overrule a prior case is not [virtually] foreordained, [the] rule of stare decisis is not an "inexorable command," and certainly it is not such in every constitutional case, Burnet v. Coronado Oil Gas Co., 285 U.S. 393 (1932) (Brandeis, dissenting). Rather, when this Court reexamines a prior holding, its judgment is customarily informed by a series of prudential and pragmatic considerations designed to test the consistency of overruling a prior decision with the ideal of the rule of law, and to gauge the respective costs of reaffirming and overruling a prior case. Thus, for example, we may ask whether the rule has proved to be intolerable simply in defying practical workability; whether the rule is subject to a kind of reliance that would lend a special hardship to the consequences of overruling and add in-

equity to the cost of repudiation; whether related principles of law have so far developed as to have left the old rule no more than a remnant of abandoned doctrine; or whether facts have so changed or come to be seen so differently, as to have robbed the old rule of significant application or justification.

So in this case we may inquire whether Roe's central rule has been found unworkable; whether the rule's limitation on state power could be removed without serious inequity to those who have relied upon it or significant damage to the stability of the society governed by the rule in question; whether the law's growth in the intervening years has left Roe's central rule a doctrinal anachronism discounted by society; and whether Roe's premises of fact have so far changed in the ensuing two decades as to render its central holding somehow irrelevant or unjustifiable in dealing with the issue it addressed.

1. Although Roe has engendered opposition, it has in no sense proven "unworkable," representing as it does a simple limitation beyond which a state law is unenforceable. While Roe has [required] judicial assessment of [laws] affecting the exercise of the choice guaranteed against government infringement, and although the need for such review will remain as a consequence of today's decision, [these] determinations fall within judicial competence.

2. The inquiry into reliance counts the cost of a rule's repudiation as it would fall on those who have relied reasonably on the rule's continued application. Since the classic case for weighing reliance heavily in favor of following the earlier rule occurs in the commercial context, where advance planning of great precision is most obviously a necessity, it is no cause for surprise that some would find no reliance worthy of consideration in support of Roe. [Abortion] is customarily chosen as an unplanned

response to the consequence of unplanned activity or to the failure of conventional birth control, and except on the assumption that no intercourse would have occurred but for Roe's holding, such behavior may appear to justify no reliance claim. [This] argument would be premised on the hypothesis that reproductive planning could take virtually immediate account of any sudden restoration of state authority to ban abortions. To eliminate the issue of reliance that easily, however, one would need to limit cognizable reliance to specific instances of sexual activity. But to do this would be simply to refuse to face the fact that for two decades of economic and social developments, people have organized intimate relationships and made choices that define their views of themselves and their places in society, in reliance on the availability of abortion in the event that contraception should fail. The ability of women to participate equally in the economic and social life of the Nation has been facilitated by their ability to control their reproductive lives. [While] the effect of reliance on Roe cannot be exactly measured, neither can the certain cost of overruling Roe for people who have ordered their thinking and living around that case be dismissed.

3. No evolution of legal principle has left Roe's doctrinal footings weaker than they were in 1973. No development of constitutional law since the case was decided has [left] Roe behind as a mere survivor of obsolete constitutional thinking. [The] Roe Court itself placed its holding in the succession of cases most prominently exemplified by Griswold. When it is so seen, Roe is clearly in no jeopardy, since subsequent [developments] have neither disturbed, nor do they threaten to diminish, the scope of recognized protection accorded to the liberty relating to intimate relationships, the family, and decisions about whether or not to beget or bear a child. Roe, however, may be seen not only as an exemplar of Griswold liberty but as a rule (whether or not mistaken) of personal autonomy and bodily integrity, with doctrinal affinity to cases

recognizing limits on governmental power to mandate medical treatment or to bar its rejection. If so, our cases since Roe accord with Roe's view that a State's interest in the protection of life falls short of justifying any plenary override of individual liberty claims.

[Nor] will courts building upon Roe be likely to hand down erroneous decisions as a consequence. Even on the assumption that the central holding of Roe was in error, that error would go only to the strength of the state interest in fetal protection, not to the recognition afforded [the] woman's liberty. [The] soundness of this prong of [Roe] is apparent from a consideration of the alternative. If indeed the woman's interest in deciding whether to bear and beget a child had not been recognized as in Roe, the State might as readily restrict a woman's right to choose to carry a pregnancy to term as to terminate it, to further asserted state interests in population control, or eugenics, for example. Yet Roe has been sensibly relied upon to counter any such suggestions.

4. [Time] has overtaken some of Roe's factual assumptions: advances in maternal health care allow for abortions safe to the mother later in pregnancy than was true in 1973, and advances in neonatal care have advanced viability to a point somewhat earlier. But these facts go only to the scheme of time limits on the realization of competing interests, and [have] no bearing on the [central] holding that viability marks the earliest point at which the State's interest in fetal life is constitutionally adequate to justify a legislative ban on nontherapeutic abortions. The soundness or unsoundness of that constitutional judgment in no sense turns on whether viability occurs at approximately 28 weeks, as was usual at the time of Roe; at 23 to 24 weeks, as it sometimes does today, or at some moment even slightly earlier in pregnancy, as it may if fetal respiratory capacity can somehow be enhanced in the future. Whenever it may occur, the attainment of viability may continue to serve as the critical fact, just as it has done since Roe; [no] change

in Roe's factual underpinning has left its central holding obsolete, and none supports an argument for overruling it.

5. The sum of the precedential inquiry to this point shows Roe's underpinnings unweakened in any way affecting its central holding. While it has engendered disapproval, it has not been unworkable. An entire generation has come of age free to assume Roe's concept of liberty in defining the capacity of women to act in society, and to make reproductive decisions; no erosion of principle going to liberty or personal autonomy has left Roe's central holding a doctrinal remnant; Roe portends no developments at odds with other precedent for the analysis of personal liberty; and no changes of fact have rendered viability more or less appropriate as the point at which the balance of interests tips. Within the bounds of normal stare decisis analysis, [the] stronger argument is for affirming Roe's central holding, with whatever degree of personal reluctance any of us may have, not for overruling it.

B. In a less significant case, stare decisis analysis [would] stop at the point we have reached. But the sustained and widespread debate Roe has provoked calls for some comparison between that case and others of comparable dimension that have responded to national controversies and taken on the impress of the controversies addressed. Only two such decisional lines from the past century present themselves for examination, and in each instance the result reached by the Court accorded with the principles we apply today.

The first example is that line of cases identified with Lochner v. New York. [The] Lochner decisions were exemplified by Adkins v. Children's Hospital, in which this Court held it to be an infringement of constitutionally protected liberty of contract to require the employers of adult women to satisfy minimum wage standards. Fourteen years later, West Coast Hotel v. Parrish signalled the demise of Lochner by overruling Adkins. In the meantime, the Depression had come and, with it, the

lesson that seemed unmistakable to most people by 1937, that the interpretation of contractual freedom protected in Adkins rested on fundamentally false factual assumptions about the capacity of a relatively unregulated market to satisfy minimal levels of human welfare. [The] facts upon which the earlier case had premised a constitutional resolution of social controversy had proved to be untrue, and history's demonstration of their untruth not only justified but required the new choice of constitutional principle that West Coast Hotel announced.

[The] second comparison that 20th century history invites is with the cases employing the separate-but-equal rule. [They] began with Plessy v. Ferguson (1896), holding that legislatively mandated racial segregation in public transportation works no denial of equal protection. [The] Plessy Court considered "the underlying fallacy of the plaintiff's argument to consist in the assumption that the enforced separation of the two races stamps the colored race with a badge of inferiority. If this be so, it is not by reason of anything found in the act, but solely because the colored race chooses to put that construction upon it." Whether, as a matter of historical fact, the Justices in the Plessy majority believed this or not, this understanding of the implication of segregation was the stated justification for the Court's opinion. But this understanding of the facts and the rule it was stated to justify were repudiated in Brown v. Bd. of Educ. (1954). The Court in Brown [observed] that whatever may have been the understanding in Plessy's time of the power of segregation to stigmatize those who were segregated with a "badge of inferiority," it was clear by 1954 that legally sanctioned segregation had just such an effect, to the point that racially separate [facilities] were deemed inherently unequal. Society's understanding of the facts upon which a constitutional ruling was sought in 1954 was thus fundamentally different from the basis claimed for the decision in 1896. While we think Plessy was wrong the day it was decided, we must also recognize that the Plessy Court's explanation for its decision was so clearly at odds with the facts apparent to the Court in 1954 that the decision to reexamine Plessy was on this ground alone not only justified but required.

West Coast Hotel and Brown each rested on facts, or an understanding of facts, changed from those which furnished the claimed justifications for the earlier constitutional resolutions. [In] constitutional adjudication as elsewhere in life, changed circumstances may impose new obligations, and the thoughtful part of the Nation could accept each decision to overrule a prior case as a response to the Court's constitutional duty. Because the case before us presents no such occasion it could be seen as no such response. Because neither the factual underpinnings of Roe's central holding nor our understanding of it has changed (and because no other indication of weakened precedent has been shown), the Court could not pretend to be reexamining the prior law with any justification beyond a present doctrinal disposition to come out differently from the Court of 1973. To overrule prior law for no other reason than that would run counter to the view [that] a decision to overrule should rest on some special reason over and above the belief that a prior case was wrongly decided. [As Justice Stewart said in 1974], "A basic change in the law upon a ground no firmer than a change in our membership invites the popular misconception that this institution is little different from the two political branches of the Government. No misconception could do more lasting injury to this Court and to the system of law which it is our abiding mission to serve".

C. [As] Americans of each succeeding generation are rightly told, the Court cannot buy support for its decisions by spending money and, except to a minor degree, it cannot independently coerce obedience to its decrees. The Court's power lies, rather, in its legitimacy, a product of substance and perception that shows itself in the people's acceptance of the Judiciary as fit to determine what the Nation's law means and to declare what it demands. The underlying substance of this legitimacy is of course the warrant for the Court's decisions in the Constitution and the lesser sources of legal principle on which the Court draws. But even when justification is furnished by apposite legal principle, something more is required. Because not every conscientious claim of principled justification will be accepted as such, the justification claimed must be beyond dispute. The Court must take care to speak and act in ways that allow people to accept its decisions on the terms the Court claims for them, as grounded truly in principle, not as compromises with social and political pressures having, as such, no bearing on the principled choices that the Court is obliged to make. Thus, the Court's legitimacy depends on making legally principled decisions under circumstances in which their principled character is sufficiently plausible to be accepted by the Nation.

The need for principled action to be perceived as such is implicated to some degree whenever [any appellate court] overrules a prior case. [In] two circumstances, however, the Court would almost certainly fail to receive the benefit of the doubt in overruling prior cases. There is, first, a point beyond which frequent overruling would overtax the country's belief in the Court's good faith. Despite the variety of reasons that may inform and justify a decision to overrule, we cannot forget that such a decision is usually perceived (and perceived correctly) as [a] statement that a prior decision was wrong. There is a limit to the amount of error that can plausibly be imputed to prior courts. If that limit should be exceeded, disturbance of prior rulings would be taken as evidence that justifiable reexamination of principle had given way to drives for particular results in the short term. The legitimacy of the Court would fade with the frequency of its vacillation.

That first circumstance can be described as hypothetical; the second is to the point here and now. Where, in the performance of its judicial duties, the Court decides a case in such a way as to resolve the sort of intensely divisive controversy reflected in Roe and those rare, comparable cases, its decision has a dimension that the resolution of the normal case does not carry. It is the dimension present whenever the Court's interpretation of the Constitution calls the contending sides of a national controversy to end their national division by accepting a common mandate rooted in the Constitution. The Court is not asked to do this very often, having thus addressed the Nation only twice in our lifetime, in [Brown] and Roe. But when the Court does act in this way, its decision requires an equally rare precedential force to counter the inevitable efforts to overturn it and to thwart its implementation. Some of those efforts may be mere unprincipled emotional reactions; others may proceed from principles worthy of profound respect. But whatever the premises of opposition may be, only the most convincing justification under accepted standards of precedent could suffice to demonstrate that a later decision overruling the first was anything but a surrender to political pressure, and an unjustified repudiation of the principle on which the Court staked its authority in the first instance. So to overrule under fire in the absence of the most compelling reason to reexamine a watershed decision would subvert the Court's legitimacy beyond any serious question. The country's loss of confidence in the judiciary would be underscored by an equally certain and equally reasonable condemnation for another failing in overruling unnecessarily and under pressure. Some cost will be paid by anyone who approves or implements a constitutional decision where it is unpopular, or who refuses to work to undermine the decision or to force its reversal. The price may be criticism or ostracism, or it may be violence. An extra price will be paid by those who themselves disapprove of the decision's results when viewed outside of constitutional terms, but who nevertheless struggle to accept it, because they respect the rule of law. To all those

who will be so tested by following, the Court implicitly undertakes to remain steadfast, lest in the end a price be paid for nothing. The promise of constancy, once given, binds its maker for as long as the power to stand by the decision survives and the understanding of the issue has not changed so fundamentally as to render the commitment obsolete.

[Like] the character of an individual, the legitimacy of the Court must be earned over time. So, indeed, must be the character of a Nation of people who aspire to live according to the rule of law. Their belief in themselves as such a people is not readily separable from their understanding of the Court invested with the authority to decide their constitutional cases and speak before all others for their constitutional ideals. If the Court's legitimacy should be undermined, then, so would the country be in its very ability to see itself through its constitutional ideals. The Court's concern with legitimacy is not for the sake of the Court but for the sake of the Nation.

[The] Court's duty in the present case is clear. In 1973, it confronted the already-divisive issue of governmental power to limit personal choice to undergo abortion, for which it provided a new resolution based on the [Fourteenth] Amendment. Whether or not a new social consensus is developing on that issue, its divisiveness is no less today than in 1973, and pressure to overrule the decision, like pressure to retain it, has grown only more intense. A decision to overrule Roe's essential holding under the existing circumstances would address error, if error there was, at the cost of [profound] and unnecessary damage to the Court's legitimacy, and to the Nation's commitment to the rule of law. It is therefore imperative to adhere to the essence of Roe's original decision, and we do so today. . . .

The Court is unquestionably correct in concluding that the doctrine of stare decisis has controlling significance in a case of this kind, notwithstanding an individual justice's concerns about the merits. The central holding of

Roe has been "part of our law" for almost two decades. It was a natural sequel to the protection of individual liberty established in Griswold. The societal costs of overruling Roe at this late date would be enormous. Roe is an integral part of a correct understanding of both the concept of liberty and the basic equality of men and women. . . .

Chief Justice REHNQUIST:

The joint opinion cannot bring itself to say that Roe was correct as an original matter, but the authors are of the view that "the immediate question is not the soundness of Roe's resolution of the issue, but the precedential force that must be accorded to its holding." Instead of claiming that Roe was correct as a matter of original constitutional interpretation, the opinion therefore contains an elaborate discussion of stare decisis. This discussion of the principle of stare decisis appears to be almost entirely dicta, because the joint opinion does not apply that principle in dealing with Roe. Roe decided that a woman had a fundamental right to an abortion. The joint opinion rejects that view. Roe decided that abortion regulations were to be subjected to "strict scrutiny." [The] joint opinion rejects that view. Roe analyzed abortion regulation under a rigid trimester framework. [The] joint opinion rejects that framework.

Stare decisis is defined in Black's Law Dictionary as meaning "to abide by, or adhere to, decided cases." Whatever the "central holding" of Roe that is left after the joint opinion finishes dissecting it is surely not the result of that principle. While purporting to adhere to precedent, the joint opinion instead revises it. Roe continues to exist, but only in the way a storefront on a western movie set exists: a mere facade to give the illusion of reality. Decisions following Roe [are] frankly overruled in part under the "undue burden" standard.

[Authentic] principles of stare decisis do not require that any portion of [Roe] be kept intact. [Erroneous] decisions in [constitutional] cases are uniquely durable, because correction through legislative action, save for constitutional amendment, is impossible. [Our] constitutional watch does not cease merely because we have spoken before on an issue; when it becomes clear that a prior constitutional interpretation is unsound we are obliged to reexamine the question. The joint opinion discusses several stare decisis factors which, it asserts, point toward retaining a portion of Roe. Two of these factors are that the main "factual underpinning" of Roe has remained the same, and that its doctrinal foundation is no weaker now than it was in 1973. Of course, what might be called the basic facts which gave rise to Roe have remained the same—women become pregnant, there is a point somewhere, depending on medical technology, where a fetus becomes viable, and women give birth to children. But this is only to say that the same facts which gave rise to Roe will continue to give rise to similar cases. It is not a reason, in and of itself, why those cases must be decided in the same incorrect manner as was the first case to deal with the question.

The joint opinion also points to reliance interests [to] explain why precedent must be followed for precedent's sake. Certainly where reliance is truly at issue, as in the case of judicial decisions that have formed the basis for private decisions, "[c]onsiderations in favor of stare decisis are at their acme." Payne v. Tennessee, (1991). But [any] traditional notion of reliance is not applicable here. [The] joint opinion thus turns to what can only be described as an unconventional—and unconvincing—notion of reliance, a view based on the surmise that the availability of abortion since Roe has led to "two decades of economic and social developments" that would be undercut if the error of Roe were recognized. The joint opinion's assertion [is] undeveloped and totally conclusory. In fact, one can not be sure to what economic and social developments the opinion is referring. Surely it is dubious to suggest that women have reached their "places in society" in reliance upon Roe, rather than as a result of their determination to obtain higher education and compete with men in the job market, and of society's increasing recognition of their ability to fill positions that were previously thought to be reserved only for men. In the end, having failed to put forth any evidence to prove any true reliance, the joint opinion's argument is based solely on generalized assertions about the national psyche, on a belief that the people of this country have grown accustomed to the Roe decision over the last 19 years and have "ordered their thinking and living around" it. As an initial matter, one might inquire how the joint opinion can view the "central holding" of Roe as so deeply rooted in our constitutional culture, when it so casually uproots and disposes of that same decision's trimester framework. Furthermore, at various points in the past, the same could have been said about this Court's erroneous decisions that the Constitution allowed "separate but equal" treatment of minorities, or that "liberty" under the Due Process Clause protected "freedom of contract." The "separate but equal" doctrine lasted 58 years after Plessy, and Lochner's protection of contractual freedom lasted 32 years. However, the simple fact that a generation or more had grown used to these major decisions did not prevent the Court from correcting its errors in those cases, nor should it prevent us [here].

Apparently realizing that conventional stare decisis principles do not support its position, the joint opinion advances a belief that retaining a portion of Roe is necessary to protect the "legitimacy" of this Court. Because the Court must take care to render decisions "grounded truly in principle," and not simply as political and social compromises, the joint opinion properly declares it to be this Court's duty to ignore the public criticism and protest that may arise as a result of a decision. Few would quarrel with this statement, although it may be doubted that Members of this Court, holding their tenure as they do during constitutional "good behavior," are at all likely to be intimidated by such public protests.

But the joint opinion goes on to state that when the Court "resolve[s] the sort of intensely divisive controversy reflected in Roe and those rare, comparable cases," its decision is exempt from reconsideration under established principles of stare decisis in constitutional cases. [This] is a truly novel principle, one which is contrary to both the Court's historical practice and to the Court's traditional willingness to tolerate criticism of its opinions. Under this principle, when the Court has ruled on a divisive issue, it is apparently prevented from overruling that decision for the sole reason that it was incorrect, unless opposition to the original decision has died away.

[The] joint opinion picks out and discusses two prior rulings it believes are of the "intensely divisive" variety, and concludes that they are of comparable divisiveness. It appears very odd indeed that the joint opinion chooses as benchmarks two cases in which the Court chose not to adhere to erroneous constitutional precedent, but instead enhanced its stature by acknowledging and correcting its error, apparently in violation of the joint opinion's "legitimacy" principle. One might also wonder how it is that the joint opinion puts these, and not others, in the "intensely divisive" category, and how it assumes that these are the only two lines of cases of comparable dimension to Roe. There is no reason to think that either Plessy or Lochner produced the sort of public protest when they were decided that Roe did. There were undoubtedly large segments of the bench and bar who agreed with the dissenting views in those cases, but surely that cannot be what the Court means when it uses the term "intensely divisive," or many other cases would have to be added to the list. In terms of public protest, however, Roe, so far as we know, was unique. But just as the Court should not respond to that sort of protest by retreating from the decision simply to allay the concerns of the protesters, it should likewise not respond by determining to adhere to the decision at all costs lest it seem to be retreating under fire. Public protests should not alter the normal application of stare decisis, lest perfectly lawful protest activity be penalized by the Court itself.

Taking the joint opinion on its own terms, we doubt that its distinction between Roe, on the one hand, and Plessy and Lochner, on the other, withstands analysis. The joint opinion acknowledges that the Court improved its stature by overruling Plessy on a deeply divisive issue. And our decision in West Coast Hotel [was] rendered at a time when Congress was considering President Roosevelt's proposal to "reorganize" this Court and enable him to name six additional Justices in the event that any member of the Court over the age of 70 did not elect to retire. It is difficult to imagine a situation in which the Court would face more intense opposition to a prior ruling than it did at that time, and, under the general principle proclaimed in the joint opinion, the Court seemingly should have responded to this opposition by stubbornly refusing to reexamine the Lochner rationale, lest it lose legitimacy by appearing to "overrule under fire." The joint opinion agrees that the Court's stature would have been seriously damaged if in Brown and West Coast Hotel it had dug in its heels and refused to apply normal principles of stare decisis to the earlier decisions. But the opinion contends that the Court was entitled to overrule Plessy and Lochner in those cases, despite the existence of opposition to the original decisions, only because both the Nation and the Court had learned new lessons in the in-

terim. This is at best a feebly supported, post hoc rationalization. [For] example, the opinion asserts that the Court could justifiably overrule its decision in Lochner only because the Depression had convinced "most people" that constitutional protection of contractual freedom contributed to an economy that failed to protect the welfare of all. Surely the joint opinion does not mean to suggest that people saw this Court's failure to uphold minimum wage statutes as the cause of the Great Depression! In any event, the Lochner Court did not base its rule upon the policy judgment that an unregulated market was fundamental to a stable economy; it simply believed, erroneously, that "liberty" under the Due Process Clause protected the "right to make a contract." Nor is it the case that the people of this Nation only discovered the dangers of extreme laissez faire economics because of the Depression. State laws regulating maximum hours and minimum wages were in existence well before that time. [These] statutes were indeed enacted because of a belief on the part of their sponsors that "freedom of contract" did not protect the welfare of workers, demonstrating that that belief manifested itself more than a generation before the Great Depression. Whether "most people" had come to share it in the hard times of the 1930's is [entirely] speculative. The crucial failing at that time was not that workers were not paid a fair wage, but that there was no work available at any wage.

When the Court finally recognized its error in West Coast Hotel, it did not engage in the post hoc rationalization that the joint opinion attributes to it; it did not state that Lochner had been based on an economic view that had fallen into disfavor, and that it therefore should be overruled. [The] theme of the opinion is that the Court had been mistaken as a matter of constitutional law when it embraced "freedom of contract" 32 years previously.

The joint opinion also agrees that the Court acted properly in rejecting the doctrine of "separate but equal" in Brown. In fact, the opinion lauds Brown in comparing it to Roe. This is strange, in that under the opinion's "legitimacy" principle the Court would seemingly have been forced to adhere to its erroneous decision in Plessy because of its "intensely divisive" character. To us, adherence to Roe today under the guise of "legitimacy" would seem to resemble more closely adherence to Plessy on the same ground. Fortunately, the Court did not choose that option in Brown, and instead frankly repudiated Plessy. The joint opinion concludes that such repudiation was justified only because of newly discovered evidence that segregation had the effect of treating one race as inferior to another. But it can hardly be argued that this was not urged upon those who decided Plessy, as Justice Harlan observed in his dissent that the law "puts the brand of servitude and degradation upon a large class of our fellow citizens, our equals before the law." [The] same arguments made before the Court in Brown were made in Plessy as well. The Court in Brown simply recognized, as Justice Harlan had recognized beforehand, that the Fourteenth Amendment does not permit racial segregation. The rule of Brown is not tied to popular opinion about the evils of segregation; it is a judgment that the Equal Protection Clause does not permit racial segregation, no matter whether the public might come to believe that it is beneficial.

[There] is also a suggestion in the joint opinion that the propriety of overruling a "divisive" decision depends in part on whether "most people" would now agree that it should be overruled. Either the demise of opposition or its progression to substantial popular agreement apparently is required to allow the Court to reconsider a divisive decision. How such agreement would be ascertained, short of a public opinion poll, the joint opinion does not say. But surely even

the suggestion is totally at war with the idea of "legitimacy" in whose name it is invoked. The Judicial Branch derives its legitimacy, not from following public opinion, but from deciding by its best lights whether legislative enactments [comport] with the Constitution.

[There] are other reasons why the joint opinion's discussion of legitimacy is unconvincing as well. In assuming that the Court is perceived as "surrender[ing]" to political pressure" when it overrules a controversial decision, the joint opinion forgets that there are two sides to any controversy. The joint opinion asserts that [the] Court must refrain from overruling a controversial decision lest it be viewed as favoring those who oppose the decision. But a decision to adhere to prior precedent is subject to the same criticism, for in such a case one can easily argue that the Court is responding to those who have demonstrated in favor of the original decision. The decision in Roe has engendered large demonstrations, including repeated marches on this Court and on Congress, both in opposition to and in support of that opinion. A decision either way can therefore be perceived as favoring one group or the other. But this perceived dilemma arises only if one assumes [that] the Court should make its decisions with a view toward speculative public perceptions. If one assumes instead [that] the Court's legitimacy is enhanced by faithful interpretation of the Constitution irrespective of public opposition, such self-engendered difficulties may be put to one side. . . .

Justice SCALIA:
Beyond [a] brief summary of the essence of my position, I will not swell the United States Reports with repetition of what I have said before; and applying the rational basis test, I would uphold the Pennsylvania statute in its entirety. I must, however, respond to a few of the more outrageous arguments in today's opinion, which it is beyond human nature to leave unanswered. I shall

discuss each of them under quotation from the Court's opinion to which they pertain.

"The inescapable fact is that adjudication of substantive due process claims may call upon the Court in interpreting the Constitution to exercise that same capacity which by tradition courts always have exercised: reasoned judgment."

Assuming that the question before us is to be resolved at such a level of philosophical abstraction, in such isolation from the traditions of American society, as by simply applying "reasoned judgment," I do not see how that could possibly have produced the answer the Court arrived at in Roe. Today's opinion describes the methodology of Roe, quite accurately, as weighing against the woman's interest the State's "important and legitimate interest in protecting the potentiality of human life." But "reasoned judgment" does not begin by begging the question, as Roe unquestionably did by assuming that what the State is protecting is the mere "potentiality of human life." The whole argument of abortion opponents is that what the Court calls the fetus and what others call the unborn child is a human life. Thus, whatever answer Roe came up with after conducting its "balancing" is bound to be wrong, unless it is correct that the human fetus is in some critical sense merely potentially human. There is of course no way to determine that as a legal matter; it is in fact a value judgment. Some societies have considered newborn children not yet human, or the incompetent elderly no longer so.

The authors of the joint opinion [do] not squarely contend that Roe was a correct application of "reasoned judgment"; merely that it must be followed, because of stare decisis. But in their exhaustive discussion of all the factors that go into the determination of when stare decisis should be observed and when disregarded, they never mention "how

wrong was the decision on its face?" Surely, if "[t]he Court's power lies . . . in its legitimacy, a product of substance and perception," the "substance" part of the equation demands that plain error be acknowledged and eliminated. Roe was plainly wrong—even on the Court's methodology of "reasoned judgment," and even more so (of course) if the proper criteria of text and tradition are applied. The emptiness of the "reasoned judgment" that produced Roe is displayed in plain view by the fact that, after more than 19 years of effort by some of the brightest (and most determined) legal minds in the country, after more than 10 cases upholding abortion rights in this Court, and after dozens upon dozens of amicus briefs submitted in this and other cases, the best the Court can do to explain how it is that the word "liberty" must be thought to include the right to destroy human fetuses is to rattle off a collection of adjectives that simply decorate a value judgment and conceal a political choice. The right to abort, we are told, inheres in "liberty" because it is among "a person's most basic decisions"; it involves a "most intimate and personal choic[e];" it is "central to personal dignity and autonomy"; it "originate[s] within the zone of conscience and belief"; it is "too intimate and personal" for state interference; it reflects "intimate views" of a "deep, personal character"; it involves "intimate relationships," and notions of "personal autonomy and bodily integrity"; and it concerns a particularly "important decisio[n]." But it is obvious to anyone applying "reasoned judgment" that the same adjectives can be applied to many forms of conduct that this Court [has] held are not entitled to constitutional protection—because, like abortion, they are forms of conduct that have long been criminalized in American society. Those adjectives might be applied, for example, to homosexual sodomy, polygamy, adult incest, and suicide, all of which are equally "intimate" and "deep[ly] personal" decisions involving "personal autonomy and bodily integrity," and all of which can constitutionally be proscribed because it is our unquestionable constitutional tradition that they are proscribable. It is not reasoned judgment that supports the Court's decision; only personal predilection. Justice Curtis's warning is as timely today as it was 135 years ago: "[W]hen a strict interpretation of the Constitution, according to the fixed rules which govern the interpretation of laws, is abandoned, and the theoretical opinions of individuals are allowed to control its meaning, we have no longer a Constitution; we are under the government of individual men, who for the time being have power to declare what the Constitution is, according to their own views of what it ought to mean." Dred Scott v. Sandford, 19 How. 393 (1857) (Curtis, J., dissenting).

> "While we appreciate the weight of the arguments . . . that Roe should be overruled, the reservations any of us may have in reaffirming the central holding of Roe are outweighed by the explication of individual liberty we have given combined with the force of stare decisis."

The Court's reliance upon stare decisis can best be described as contrived. It insists upon the necessity of adhering not to all of Roe, but only to what it calls the "central holding." It seems to me that stare decisis ought to be applied even to the doctrine of stare decisis, and I confess never to have heard of this new, keep-what-you-want-and-throw-away-the-rest version. I wonder whether, as applied to Marbury v. Madison, [the] new version of stare decisis would be satisfied if we allowed courts to review the constitutionality of only those statutes that (like the one in Marbury) pertain to the jurisdiction of the courts. I am certainly not in a good position to dispute that the Court has saved the "central holding" of Roe, since to do that effec-

tively I would have to know what the Court has saved, which in turn would require me to understand (as I do not) what the "undue burden" test means. I must confess, however, that I have always thought, and I think a lot of other people have always thought, that the arbitrary trimester framework [was] quite as central to Roe as the arbitrary viability test which the Court today retains. It seems particularly ungrateful to carve the trimester framework out of the core of Roe, since its very rigidity (in sharp contrast to the utter indeterminability of the "undue burden" test) is probably the only reason the Court is able to say [that] Roe "has in no sense proven unworkable." I suppose the Court is entitled to call a "central holding" whatever it wants to call a "central holding"—which is, come to think of it, perhaps one of the difficulties with this modified version of stare decisis. . . .

It is particularly difficult, in the circumstances of the present decision, to sit still for the Court's lengthy lecture upon the virtues of "constancy," of "remain[ing] steadfast," of adhering to "principle." Among the five Justices who purportedly adhere to Roe, at most three agree upon the principle that constitutes adherence (the joint opinion's "undue burden" standard)—and that principle is inconsistent with Roe. To make matters worse, two of the three, in order thus to remain steadfast, had to abandon previously stated positions. It is beyond me how the Court expects these accommodations to be accepted "as grounded truly in principle, not as compromises with social and political pressures having, as such, no bearing on the principled choices that the Court is obliged to make." The only principle the Court "adheres" to, it seems to me, is the principle that the Court must be seen as standing by Roe. That is not a principle of law (which is what I thought the Court was talking about), but a principle of Realpolitik—and a wrong one at that.

I cannot agree with, indeed I am appalled by, the Court's suggestion that the decision whether to stand by an erroneous constitutional decision must be strongly influenced—against overruling, no less—by the substantial and continuing public opposition the decision has generated. The Court's judgment that any other course would "subvert the Court's legitimacy" must be another consequence of reading the error–filled history book that described the deeply divided country brought together by Roe. In my history-book, the Court was covered with dishonor and deprived of legitimacy by Dred Scott v. Sandford, an erroneous (and widely opposed) opinion that it did not abandon, rather than by West Coast Hotel, which produced the famous "switch in time" from the Court's erroneous (and widely opposed) constitutional opposition to the social measures of the New Deal.

But whether it would "subvert the Court's legitimacy" or not, the notion that we would decide a case differently from the way we otherwise would have in order to show that we can stand firm against public disapproval is frightening. It is a bad enough idea, even in the head of someone like me, who believes that the text of the Constitution, and our traditions, say what they say and there is no fiddling with them. But when it is in the mind of a Court that believes the Constitution has an evolving meaning; that the Ninth Amendment's reference to "othe[r]" rights is not a disclaimer, but a charter for action; and that the function of this Court is to "speak before all others for [the people's] constitutional ideals" unrestrained by meaningful text or tradition—then the notion that the court must adhere to a decision for as long as the decision faces "great opposition" and the Court is "under fire" acquires a character of almost czarist arrogance. We are offended by these marchers who descend upon us, every year on the anniversary of Roe, to protest our saying that the Constitution requires what our society has never thought the Constitution requires. These people who refuse to

be "tested by following" must be taught a lesson. We have no Cossacks, but at least we can stubbornly refuse to abandon an erroneous opinion that we might otherwise change—to show how little they intimidate us. Of course, as the Chief Justice points out, we have been subjected to what the Court calls "political pressure" by both sides of this issue. Maybe today's decision not to overrule Roe will be seen as buckling to pressure from that direction. Instead of engaging in the hopeless task of predicting public perception—a job not for lawyers but for political campaign managers—the Justices should do what is legally right by asking two questions: (1) Was Roe correctly decided? (2) Has Roe succeeded in producing a settled body of law? If the answer to both questions is no, Roe should undoubtedly be overruled.

In truth, I am as distressed as the Court is—and expressed my distress several years ago, see Webster—about the "political pressure" directed to the Court: the marches, the mail, the protests aimed at inducing us to change our opinions. How upsetting it is, that so many of our citizens (good people, not lawless ones, on both sides of this abortion issue, and on various sides of other issues as well) think that we Justices should properly take into account their views, as though we were engaged not in ascertaining an objective law but in determining some kind of social consensus. The Court would profit, I think, from giving less attention to the fact of this distressing phenomenon, and more attention to the cause of it. That cause permeates today's opinion: a new mode of constitutional adjudication that relies not upon text and traditional practice to determine the law, but upon what the Court calls "reasoned judgment," which turns out to be nothing but philosophical predilection and moral intuition. All manner of "liberties," the Court tells us, inhere in the Constitution and are enforceable by this Court—not just those mentioned in the text or established in the traditions of our society. Why even the Ninth Amendment [is,] despite our contrary understanding for almost 200 years, a literally boundless source of additional, unnamed, unhinted-at "rights," definable and enforceable by us, through "reasoned judgment."

What makes all this relevant to the bothersome application of "political pressure" against the Court are the twin facts that the American people love democracy and the American people are not fools. As long as this Court thought (and the people thought) that we Justices were doing essentially lawyers' work up here—reading text and discerning our society's traditional understanding of that text—the public pretty much left us alone. Texts and traditions are facts to study, not convictions to demonstrate about. But if in reality our process of constitutional adjudication consists primarily of making value judgments; if we can ignore a long and clear tradition clarifying an ambiguous text, [if our] pronouncement of constitutional law rests primarily on value judgments, then a free and intelligent people's attitude towards us can be expected to be (ought to be) quite different. The people know that their value judgments are quite as good as those taught in any law school—maybe better. If [the] "liberties" protected by the Constitution are [undefined] and unbounded, then the people should demonstrate, to protest that we do not implement their values instead of ours. Not only that, but confirmation hearings for new Justices should deteriorate into question-and-answer sessions in which Senators go through a list of their constituents' most favored and most disfavored alleged constitutional rights, and seek the nominee's commitment to support or oppose them. Value judgments, after all, should be voted on, not dictated; and if our Constitution has somehow accident[al]ly committed them to the Supreme Court, at least we can have a sort of plebiscite each time a new nominee to that body is put forward.

QUESTIONS FOR DISCUSSION

1. Justice Scalia argues here and elsewhere that reliance on precedent in constitutional cases is unwise, because it perpetuates past mistakes. What is his argument? Do you agree?

2. The plurality opinion of Justices O'Connor, Kennedy, and Souter places great weight on the idea of legitimacy. What do the Justices in the plurality mean by "legitimacy"? How do they think this relates to following precedent?

3. Are the Justices in the plurality successful in distinguishing the cases in which precedent should be followed from the cases in which precedent should be overruled? Why or why not? How do they draw the distinction?

SUGGESTIONS FOR FURTHER READING

The classic defense of the use of analogical reasoning in American law is Edward Levi, *An Introduction to Legal Reasoning* (Chicago: University of Chicago Press, 1948). Another American classic is Benjamin N. Cardozo, *The Nature of the Judicial Process* (New Haven: Yale University Press, 1949). The best account of traditional practice is Rupert Cross and J. W. Harris, *Precedent in English Law* (Oxford: Clarendon Press, Fourth Edition, 1990). For an approach similar to Alexander's, see Frederick Schauer, "Precedent," *Stanford Law Review*, vol. 39 (1987), pp. 571 ff. Among the better analyses of legal reasoning, the methods of the common law, and the place of precedent are Melvin Aron Eisenberg, *The Nature of the Common Law* (Cambridge: Harvard University Press, 1988); Guido Calabresi, *A Common Law for the Age of Statutes* (Cambridge: Harvard University Press, 1982); Karl N. Llewellyn, *The Case Law System in America* (Chicago: University of Chicago Press, Paul Gewirtz, ed., Michael Ansaldi, trans., 1989); Neil MacCormick, *Legal Reasoning and Legal Theory* (Oxford: Clarendon Press, 1978); William Twining, ed., *Legal Theory and Common Law* (Oxford: Basil Blackwell, 1986) (in this volume, see especially A.W.B. Simpson, "The Common Law and Legal Theory"). An excellent introduction to the concepts of legal reasoning is Steven J. Burton, *An Introduction to Law and Legal Reasoning* (Boston: Little, Brown, 1985).

2.3 CRITICAL PERSPECTIVES ON LEGAL REASONING

INTRODUCTION

In Chapter 1 we introduced the basic ideas of the Legal Realists. Although the Legal Realist perspective was important in considering a number of questions about the nature of law, the ideas of the Realists are even more relevant as we take up the question of legal reasoning. Now that we have seen the standard picture of legal reasoning, we can better understand the Legal Realist challenge to it.

In the context of thinking about reasoning by applying written-down rules, the Realists believed that decision makers, especially judges deciding hard cases, initially make an "all things considered" judgment about who ought to win. This preliminary judgment, which (the Realists believed) takes into account the full range of moral, political, social, psychological, and economic factors, is hardly arbitrary, or at least need not be arbitrary. It does, however, focus on the best result for *this* case and this case alone. In this respect the decision of the judge is, to many of the Legal Realists, much like the decision of Solomon in the biblical story about the two women who claimed that the same baby was their child. By proposing that the baby be cut in half as a way of determining the identity of the real mother, Solomon was not following a precedent or following a preexisting rule. Rather, he was using what Llewellyn called "situation sense," using his best judgment to come up with the best solution for *this* case.

A similar picture of situation-sensitive adjudication, without the constraints of rules or precedent, can be seen in the decision-making procedures of the q'adi, the "trial" judge under Islamic law. Some would just call this "common sense," or "good judgment." But whatever the name, the Legal Realist idea is that judges usually try to reach the best judgment for the case before them, a judgment that is not itself guided by pre-existing legal rules or precedents. Having reached this situation-specific judgment, the Realists contend, the judge *then* rationalizes the decision in terms of some legal rule. To the Legal Realist, rules serve not as sources of guidance, but as vehicles of legitimation, rationalization, or justification of decisions reached on other grounds.

The Realists recognized that making their conclusions appear legally legitimate was a practical necessity for most judges. The Realists did not believe that very many judges could get away with saying, in the manner of some parents, "because I said so." Nor did the Realists believe that judges could justify their decisions as pure policy judgments, even if that is what they were. Rather, the Realists acknowledged that legal decision makers were in practice required to come up with some law-like justification for the result that they had reached. The Realists believed, however, that this was not hard to do. First of all, the Realists recognized that most situations presented to judges are highly complex. This means that there are numerous different facts, and numerous different ways of characterizing those facts. If there were one rule for cars and another rule for dogs, then a case involving a car and a dog could be characterized as a car case or as a dog case depending on whether the car rule or the dog rule was most consistent with the result that the judge had decided to reach. To give a more concrete example, consider the issue of sexual harassment. Suppose the male workers at a factory post pornographic pictures all around the workplace and around the workers' lunchroom. The female workers claim that this creates a "hostile and intimidating workplace environment" in violation of federal law. The male workers claim that to punish them (or the employer) for this activity is a violation of the First Amendment right to freedom of speech. The case is thus *both* a sexual harassment case and a free speech case, and it is the Realists' point that a judge will characterize it as a free speech case if he has decided on other grounds that the female workers should lose, and will characterize it as a sexual harassment case if he has decided, again on other grounds (such as what he believes about sexual harassment), that the female workers should win.

In addition to the possibility of multiple characterizations of the same set of facts, the Realists also relied on the frequency that multiple rules or precedents, not all consistent with each other, could be applied to the same characterization of the same facts. Because common law systems develop incrementally, and because statutes are drafted by different people at different times, there are often conflicting rules at the same time. It might be the case, for example, that a diligent researcher could discover one "recognized" legal rule that allowed someone like Mrs. Donoghue to recover damages against a bottler, and another that disallowed virtually the same suit. This would be rare in a civil law system where comprehensive codes govern, in theory, all transactions. It is far from rare in a common law system, however, where statutes and regulations are developed less systematically, and where many legal rules come from precedents that are also developed in a more haphazard manner. As long as conflicting legal rules exist, not only can judges frequently select a characterization of the facts that would lead to the result that they wanted to reach on other grounds, but they can also select among some number of rules in order to accomplish the same end.

The Realist challenge is particularly powerful in the context of rules with comparatively indeterminate content. The Sherman Antitrust Act, for example, prohibits "contracts, combinations, and conspiracies in restraint of trade." Much of the law of "insider trading" in the United States is based on a rule that does little more than prohibit "devices or artifices to defraud." And in the context of the Constitution, the words alone give little assistance when we are trying to figure out what counts as an "unreasonable" search and seizure, a denial of "due process of law," a deprivation of the "equal protection of the laws," or a "cruel and unusual punishment." Moreover, often the legislative intent is of less assistance than we might suppose, even were we to believe that in all such cases the legislative intent should control. Just as Antonio in *The Merchant of Venice* observes that "Yea, Bassanio, even the Devil can cite scripture to his purpose," so too is it often the case that among hundreds or thousands of pages of legislative history there will be something to support almost all plausible positions, even positions opposed to each other.

Much the same applies to statutory purposes as well. Without the benefit of actual legislative history, for example, the "No vehicles in the park" law can be said to have the purpose of preventing noise, protecting pedestrian safety, and preserving recreational space, all of which are compatible with the language of the rule. If we combine this potential multiplicity of purposes with what we have already seen, we can then say that legal *indeterminacy* exists when there is either: (1) vagueness or (2) contradictory rules, with respect to: (a) the words of a rule; (b) the intentions of a rule's drafters; (c) the possible purposes of a rule or; (d) the precedents that interpret or create the rule. The full range of this complexity demonstrates the numerous possibilities of indeterminacy that provide the foundation of the Legal Realist argument.

In the context of reasoning from *precedent*, the Realist challenge is likely to seem particularly compelling. It is rare for specific statutes or regulations to conflict with each other, but overwhelmingly common for lawyers to be able to find precedents to support almost any proposition they wish to advance. To the Realist the judge is essentially like a lawyer. Just as a lawyer takes her client's position and preferred outcome and then goes to look (usually successfully, according to the Realists) for cases to support it, so too judges, according to the Realists, do essentially the same thing. The only difference is that lawyers take their positions from their clients, while judges take them from the results that they have decided on non-legal grounds would be the ones that they want to reach.

Legal Realism flourished in the United States in the 1930s and 1940s. Justice Douglas, a member of the United States Supreme Court from 1939 to 1975, who had earlier been a professor at the Columbia Law School, and who wrote the opinion invalidating an anti-contraceptive statute in *Griswold v. Connecticut*,[14] was one of the most prominent of the Realists. More recently, Realist ideas have been advanced with somewhat different twists. We saw one in the reading from Duncan Kennedy in Chapter 1. Other members of the Critical Legal Studies movement, such as Mark Tushnet in one of the following readings, often make even stronger claims about the inherent indeterminacy of law based on claims about the indeterminacy of language or the indeterminacy of historical inquiry. An important strand of feminist jurisprudence, represented in the article by Martha Minow and Elizabeth Spelman, emphasizes the importance of context, and in doing so emphasizes, as did many of the Realists, the importance of looking not exclusively to formal and generalizing rules, but to all of the relevant features of a particular case. And although it is often the case that Law and Economics adopts different political positions from these adopted by Critical Legal Studies or feminist jurisprudence, some members of the Law and Economics movement, most notably Judge Posner, have what they describe as a "pragmatic" approach to decision making that pays little attention to the formal characteristics of legal rules. Indeed, as the selections that follow indicate, Judge Posner believes quite strongly that there is nothing distinctive about legal reasoning at all.

---

[14]Discussed in the section on the right to privacy in Chapter 4 of this book.

LAW AND THE MODERN MIND

JEROME FRANK

Lawyers and judges purport to make large use of precedents; that is, they purport to rely on the conduct of judges in past cases as a means of procuring analogies for action in new cases. But since what was actually decided in the earlier cases is seldom revealed, it is impossible, in a real sense, to rely on these precedents. What the courts in fact do is to manipulate the language of former decisions. They could approximate a system of real precedents only if the judges, in rendering those former decisions, had reported with fidelity the precise steps by which they arrived at their decisions. The paradox of the situation is that, granting there is value in a system of precedents, our present use of illusory precedents makes the employment of real precedents impossible.

The decision of a judge after trying a case is the product of a unique experience. "Of the many things which have been said of the mystery of the judicial process," writes Yntema, "the most salient is that *decision is reached after an emotive experience in which principles and logic play a secondary part*. The function of juristic logic and the principles which it employs seem to be like that of language, to describe the event which has already transpired. These considerations must reveal to us the impotence of general principles to control decision. Vague because of their generality, they mean nothing save what they suggest in the organized experience of one who thinks them, and, because of their vagueness, they only remotely compel the organization of that expe-

rience. The important problem . . . is not the formulation of the rule but the ascertainment of the cases to which, and the extent to which, it applies. And this, even if we are seeking uniformity in the administration of justice, will lead us again to the circumstances of the concrete case. . . . The reason why the general principle cannot control is because it does not inform. . . . It should be obvious that when we have observed a recurrent phenomenon in the decisions of the courts, we may appropriately express the classification in a rule. But the rule will be only a mnemonic device, a useful but hollow diagram of what has been. It will be intelligible only if we *relive again the experience of the classifier."*

The rules a judge announces when publishing his decision are, therefore, intelligible only if one can relive the judge's unique experience while he was trying the case—which, of course, cannot be done. One cannot even approximate that experience as long as opinions take the form of abstract rules applied to facts formally described. Even if it were desirable that, despite its uniqueness, the judge's decision should be followed, as an analogy, by other judges while trying other cases, this is impossible when the manner in which the judge reached his judgment in the earlier case is most inaccurately reported, as it now is. You are not really applying his decision as a precedent in another case unless you can say, in effect, that, having relived his experience in the earlier case, you believe that he would have thought his

From Jerome Frank, *Law and the Modern Mind* (New York: Brentano's, 1930), Chapter 14[15]

[15]Jerome Frank (1888–1962) was one of the most strident of the Realists. Having been psychoanalyzed himself, he attributed much of judicial decision to psychological motivations of which judges were themselves unaware. A New York lawyer at the time he wrote *Law and the Modern Mind,* he served for many years as a judge of the United States Court of Appeals for the Second Circuit.

decision applicable to the facts of the other case. And as opinions are now written, it is impossible to guess what the judge did experience in trying a case. The facts of all but the simplest controversies are complicated and unlike those of any other controversy; in the absence of a highly detailed account by the judge of how he reacted to the evidence, no other person is capable of reproducing his actual reactions. The rules announced in his opinions are therefore often insufficient to tell the reader why the judge reached his decision. . . .

Every lawyer of experience comes to know (more or less unconsciously) that in the great majority of cases, the precedents are none too good as bases of prediction. Somehow or other, there are plenty of precedents to go around. A recent writer, a believer in the use of precedents, has said proudly that "it is very seldom indeed that a judge cannot find guidance of some kind, direct or indirect, in the mass of our reported decisions—by this time a huge accumulation of facts as well as rules." In plain English, as S. S. Gregory or Judge Hutcheson would have put it, a court can usually find earlier decisions which can be made to appear to justify almost any conclusion.

What has just been said is not intended to mean that most courts arrive at their conclusions arbitrarily or apply a process of casuistical deception in writing their opinions. The process we have been describing involves no insincerity or duplicity. The average judge sincerely believes that he is using his intellect as "a cold logic engine" in applying rules and principles derived from the earlier cases to the objective facts of the case before him.

A satirist might indeed suggest that it is regrettable that the practice of precedent-mongering does not involve *conscious* deception, for it would be comparatively easy for judges entirely aware of what they were doing, to abandon such conscious deception and to report accurately how they arrived at their decisions. Unfortunately, most judges have no such awareness. Worse than that, they are not even aware that they are not aware. Judges Holmes, Cardozo,

Hand, Hucheson, Lehman and a few others have attained the enlightened state of awareness of their unawareness. A handful of legal thinkers off the bench have likewise come to the point of noting the ignorance of all of us as to just how decisions, judicial or otherwise, are reached. Until many more lawyers and judges become willing to admit that ignorance which is the beginning of wisdom and from that beginning work forward painstakingly and consciously, we shall get little real enlightenment on that subject.

Perhaps one of the worst aspects of rule-fetishism and veneration for what judges have done in the past is that the judges, in writing their opinions, are constrained to think of themselves altogether too much as if they were addressing posterity. Swayed by the belief that their opinions will serve as precedents and will therefore bind the thought processes of judges in cases which may thereafter arise, they feel obliged to consider excessively not only what has previously been said by other judges but also the future effect of those generalizations which they themselves set forth as explanations of their own decisions. When publishing the rules which are supposed to be the core of their decisions, they thus feel obligated to look too far both backwards and forwards. Many a judge, when unable to find old word-patterns which will fit his conclusions, is overcautious about announcing a so-called new rule for fear that, although the new rule may lead to a just conclusion in the case before him, it may lead to undesirable results in the future—that is, in cases not then before the court. Once trapped by the belief that the announced rules are the paramount thing in the law, and that uniformity and certainty are of major importance and are to be procured by uniformity and certainty in the phrasing of rules, a judge is likely to be affected, in determining what is fair to the parties in the unique situation before him, by consideration of the possible, yet scarcely imaginable, bad effect of a just opinion in the instant case on possible unlike cases which may later be brought into court. He then refuses to do justice in the case on trial because he fears that "hard cases make bad laws." And thus arises what may aptly be called "injustice according to law."

Such injustice is particularly tragic because it is based on a hope doomed to futility, a hope of controlling the future. Of course, present problems will be clarified by reference to future ends; but ends, although they have a future bearing, must obtain their significance in present consequences, otherwise those ends lose their significance. For it is the nature of the future that it never arrives. If all decisions are to be determined with reference to a time to come, then the law is indeed chasing a will-o'-the-wisp. "Yesterday today was tomorrow." To give too much attention to the future is to ignore the problem which is demanding solution today. Any future, when it becomes the present, is sure to bring new complicating and individualized problems. "Future problems" can never be solved. There is much wisdom in Valéry's reference to the "anachronism of the future."

Indeed, alleged interest in the future may be a disguise for too much devotion to the past, and a means of avoiding the necessity for facing unpleasant risks in the present. If the decision of a particular case takes the form of the enunciation of a rule with emphasis on its future incidence, the tendency will be to connect the past by smooth continuities with the future, and the consequence will be an overlooking of the distinctive novelties of the present. There will be undue stress on past, habitual ways of doing things.

What is more significant is that this regard for the future serves also to conceal that factor in judging which is most disturbing to the rule-minded—the personality of the judge. Thus in a recent book the author finds an advantage in the technique of abstract logic which judges purport to employ in that it requires the judges to "raise their minds above the facts of the immediate case before them and subordinate their feelings and impressions to a process of intricate abstract reasoning. *One danger in the administration of justice is that the necessities of the future and the interest of parties not before the court may be sacrificed in favor of present litigants.* . . . Nothing is so effective to prevent this outcome as that judges should approach the decision of a controversy with minds directed to considerations having no connection with the immediate situation or interest in the parties. Judges are human instruments, with prejudices, passions, and weaknesses. As it is, they often decide a new point or a doubtful point, ignore a principle, narrow a rule, or explain a concept under the influence of these human limitations. But this influence is enormously diminished by the necessity of centering their attention on a mass of considerations which lie outside the color of the case at bar; and by the habit of coming at every question from the angle of a dry and abstract logic."

It might be more accurately said that the influence of this point of view promotes judicial self-delusion and produces that ineffectual suppression of the judge's personality which leads to the indirect, unobserved and harmful effects of his personality on judicial decisions.

Present problems should be worked out with reference to present events. We cannot rule the future. We can only imagine it in terms of the present. And the way to do that is as thoroughly as possible to know the present.

QUESTIONS FOR DISCUSSION

1. Does Frank believe that the situation he describes is necessarily the case, or just an empirically contingent claim? Why might this make a difference?

2. Is Frank's claim descriptive or normative? Does he think that the manipulation of precedent is a good thing?

3. Could Frank make the same claim about statutory law that he makes about case law? Why or why not?

FOLLOWING THE RULES LAID DOWN: A CRITIQUE OF INTERPRETIVISM AND NEUTRAL PRINCIPLES

MARK TUSHNET

The rule of law, according to the liberal conception, is meant to protect us against the exercise of arbitrary power. The theory of neutral principles asserts that a requirement of consistency, the core of the ideal of the rule of law, places sufficient bounds on judges to reduce the risk of arbitrariness to an acceptable level. The question is whether the concepts of neutrality and consistency can be developed in ways that are adequate for the task. My discussion examines various candidates for a definition of neutrality, beginning with a crude definition and moving toward more sophisticated ones. Yet each candidate suffers from similar defects: each fails to provide the kinds of constraints on judges that liberalism requires. Some candidates seek to limit the results judges might reach, others the methods they may use. The supposed substantive bounds that consistency imposes on judges, however, are either empty or parasitic on other substantive theories of constitutional law, and the methodological bounds are either empty or dependent on a sociology of law that undermines liberalism's assumptions about society.

Robert Bork's version of neutral principles theory would require that decisions rest on principles that are neutral in content and in application. Bork's formulation may be an attempt to generalize Wechsler's definition, which characterizes neutrality as judicial indifference to who the winner is. For Wechsler, such indifference was a matter of judicial willingness to apply the present case's rule in the next case as well, regardless of whether the beneficiary in the later case was less attractive than the earlier winner in ways not made relevant by the rule itself. Neutral content for Bork might mean a similar indifference, but not within the case: the principle governing the case should be developed in a form that employs only general terms and that avoids any express preference for any named groups. This outcome, however, is impossible. We might coherently require that rules not use proper names, but there is no principled way to distinguish between the general terms that in effect pick out specific groups or individuals and those that are "truly" general. Any general term serves to identify some specific group; hence if the notion of content

Mark Tushnet, "Following the Rules Laid Down: A Critique of Interpretivism and Neutral Principles," *Harvard Law Review*, vol. 96 (1983), pp. 781 ff. Tushnet (1945–   ) is Professor of Law at Georgetown University.

neutrality is to make any sense, it must depend on a prior understanding of which kinds of distinctions are legitimately "neutral" and which are not. The demand for neutrality in content thus cannot provide an independent criterion for acceptable decisions.

Standing alone, the theory that principles must be neutral in content cannot constrain judicial discretion. But it could be coupled with some other theory—such as interpretivism, [or] a moral philosophy. When coordinated with some such substantive theory, the demand for neutral principles stipulates that a decision is justified only if the principles derived from the other theory are neutrally applied. Yet to require neutral application of the principles of the other theory is merely to apply those principles in given cases; the requirement of content neutrality adds nothing.

If neutrality is to serve as a meaningful guide, it must be understood not as a standard for the content of principles, but rather as a constraint on the process by which principles are selected, justified, and applied. Thus, the remaining candidate explications of neutrality all focus on the judicial process and the need for "neutral *application*." This focus transfers our attention from the principles themselves to the judges who purport to use them.

■ ■ ■

1. *Prospective Application.*—What then are methodologically neutral principles? To Wechsler, such principles are identified primarily by a forward-looking aspect: a judge who invokes a principle in a specific instance commits himself or herself to invoking it in future cases that are relevantly identical. For example, a judge who justifies the holding in *Brown v. Board of Education* that segregated schools are unconstitutional by invoking the principle that the state may not take race into account in any significant policy decision is thereby also committed to holding state–developed affirmative action programs unconstitutional. The judge's interior monologue involves specifying the principle

about to be invoked, imagining future cases and their proper resolution, determining whether those cases are different from the present one in any ways that the proposed principle itself says are relevant, and asking whether the principle yields the proper results.

There are two levels of problems with the idea that commitment to prospective neutral application constrains judicial choices. First, there are two features of our judicial institutions that dissipate any constraining force that the demand for prospective neutrality may impose. Second, there is a conceptual problem that robs the very idea of prospective neutrality of any normative force.

(a) *Institutional Problems.*—The first institutional problem is that Supreme Court decisions are made by a collective body, which is constrained by a norm of compromise and cooperation. Suppose that in case 1 Justices M, N, and O have taken neutral principles theory to heart and believe that the correct result is justified by principle A. Justices P, Q, R, and S have done likewise but believe that the same result is justified by principle B. Justices T and V, who also accept principle A but believe it inapplicable to case 1, dissent. The four-person group gains control of the writing of the opinion, and the three others who agree with the result accede to the institutional pressure for majority decisions and join an opinion that invokes principle B. Now case 2 arises. Justices T and V are convinced that, because case 2 is relevantly different from case 1, principle A should be used. They join with Justices M, N, and O and produce a majority opinion invoking principle A. If principle B were used, the result would be different; thus, there are four dissenters.

Kent Greenawalt has argued that neutral principles theory is required to acknowledge that neutrality sometimes must yield to other considerations, such as the institutional pressure for majority decisions. If the norm of compromise is thought to authorize submersion of individual views in the selection of principles, we could not charge anyone with prospective nonneutrality in the handling of case 1. When case 2 subsequently arises, however, it would be odd—and ultimately destructive of the willingness to compromise—to demand that Justices *M, N,* and *O* follow principle *B* to a result that they, on principled grounds, believe wrong. But at the same time, to allow a judge criticized for nonneutrality to reply that in the particular situation neutrality had to yield to more pressing circumstances is to give the game of theory away. If we allow neutrality to yield to the institutional need here (a need that is quite weak—we all can live with fragmented Courts and decisions), a sufficiently pressing need will likely be available to justify virtually any deviation from neutrality.

A second institutional problem is that prospective neutrality involves unreasonable expectations concerning the capacities of judges. Every present case is connected to every conceivable future case, in the sense that a skilled lawyer can demonstrate how the earlier case's principles ought to affect (although perhaps not determine) the outcome in any later case. In these circumstances, neutral application means that each decision constrains a judge in every future decision; the import of the prospective approach is that, the first time a judge decides a case, he or she is to some extent committed to particular decisions for the rest of his or her career.

There are two difficulties here. First, even if we confine our attention to cases in the same general area as the present one, this formulation of the neutrality requirement is obviously too stringent. We cannot and should not expect judges to have fully elaborated theories of race discrimination in their first cases, much less theories of gender, illegitimacy, and other modes of discrimination as well. Second, to the extent that perceptions of connections vary with skill, the theory has the curious effect of constraining only the better judges. The less skilled judge will not think to test a principle developed in a race-discrimination case against

gender-discrimination or abortion cases; a more skilled judge will.

Wechsler responded to these difficulties by relaxing the requirement: the judge must test the principle against "applications that are now foreseeable," and must either agree with the result in such applications or be able to specify a relevant difference between the cases. But now the judge charged with nonneutrality will often be able to defend by saying that he or she simply had not foreseen the case at hand when the prior one was decided. That defense may lead us to conclude that the judge is not terribly competent, but it defeats the charge of nonneutrality.

(b) *Conceptual Difficulty.*—The third, largely conceptual difficulty with the theory of neutral principles was foreshadowed by the example of a case whose result could be justified by either of two principles. Neutral application requires that we be able to identify *the* principle that justified the result in case 1 in order to be sure that it is neutrally applied in case 2. This requirement, however, cannot be fulfilled, because there are always a number of justificatory principles available to make sense of case 1 and a number of techniques to select the "true" basis of case 1. Of course, the opinion in case 1 will articulate a principle that purports to support the result. But the thrust of introductory law courses is to show that the principles offered in opinions are never good enough. And this indefiniteness bedevils—and liberates—not only the commentators and the lawyers and judges subsequently dealing with the decision; it equally affects the author of the opinion.

. . . At the moment a decision is announced, we cannot identify the principle that it embodies. Even when we take account of the language of the opinion, each decision can be traced to many different possible principles, and we often learn the justifying principle of case 1 only when a court in case 2 states it. . . . The theory of neutral principles thus loses almost all of its constraining force when neutrality has a prospective meaning. What is left is something like a counsel to judges that they be sincere within the limits of their ability. But this formulation hardly provides a reassuring constraint on judicial willfulness.

2. *Retrospective Application.*—Although Wechsler framed the neutral principles theory in prospective terms, it might be saved by recasting it in retrospective terms. The theory would then impose as a necessary condition for justification the requirement that a decision be consistent with the relevant precedents. This tack links the theory to general approaches to precedent-based judicial decisionmaking in nonconstitutional areas. It also captures the natural way in which we raise questions about neutrality. The prospective theory requires that we pose hypothetical future cases, apply the principle, and ask whether the judges really meant to resolve the hypothetical cases as the principle seems to require. Because the hypothetical cases have not arisen, we cannot know the answer; we can do little more than raise our eyebrows, as Wechsler surely did, and emphasize the "really" as we ask the question in a skeptical tone.

In contrast, the retrospective theory encourages concrete criticism. . . . We need only compare case 2, which is now decided, with case 1 to see if a principle from case 1 has been neutrally applied in case 2. But if the retrospective demand is merely that the opinion in case 2 deploy some reading of the earlier case from which the holding in case 2 follows, the openness of the precedents means that the demand can always be satisfied. And if the demand is rather that the holding be derived from the principles actually articulated in the relevant precedents, differences between case 2 and the precedents will inevitably demand a degree of reinterpretation of the old principles. New cases always present issues different from those settled by prior cases. Thus, to decide a new case, a judge must take some liberties with the old principles, if they are to be applied at all. There is, however, no principled way to determine

how many liberties can be taken; hence this second reading of the retrospective approach likewise provides no meaningful constraints.

The central problem here is that, given the difficulty of isolating a single principle for which a given precedent stands, we lack any criteria for distinguishing between cases that depart from and those that conform to the principles of their precedents. In fact, any case can compellingly be placed in either category. . . .

3. *The Craft Interpretation.*—This critique of the retrospective-application interpretation points the way to a more refined version—what I will term the craft interpretation—of the calls of the neutral principles theorists for retrospective consistency. The failings of this final alternative bring out the underlying reasons that the demand for consistency cannot do the job expected of it.

The preceding discussion has reminded us that each decision reworks its precedents. A decision picks up some threads that received little emphasis before, and places great stress on them. It deprecates what seemed important before by emphasizing the factual setting of the precedents. The techniques are well known; indeed, learning them is at the core of a good legal education. But they are techniques. This recognition suggests that we attempt to define consistency as a matter of craft. When push comes to shove, in fact, adherents of neutral principles simply offer us lyrical descriptions of the sense of professionalism in lieu of sharper characterizations of the constraints on judges. Charles Black, for example, attempts to resolve the question whether law can rely on neutral principles by depicting "the art of law" living between the two poles of subjective preference and objective validation in much the same way that "the art of music has its life somewhere between traffic noise and a tuning fork—more disciplined by far than the one, with an unfathomably complex inner discipline of its own, far richer than the other, with inexhaustible variety of resource." The difficulty then is to specify the limits to permissible craftiness. One limit may be that a judge cannot lie about the precedents—for example, by grossly mischaracterizing the facts. And Black adds that "decision [must] be taken in knowledge of and with consideration of certainly known facts of public life," such as the fact that segregation necessarily degrades blacks. But these limits are clearly not terribly restrictive, and no one has suggested helpful others.

If the craft interpretation cannot specify limits to craftiness, another alternative is to identify some decisions that are within and some that are outside the limits in order to provide the basis for an inductive and intuitive generalization. As the following discussion indicates, however, it turns out that the limits of craft are so broad that in any interesting case any reasonably skilled lawyer can reach whatever result he or she wants. The craft interpretation thus fails to constrain the results that a reasonably skilled judge can reach, and leaves the judge free to enforce his or her personal values, as long as the opinions enforcing those values are well written. Such an outcome is inconsistent with the requirements of liberalism in that, once again, the demand for neutral principles fails in any appreciable way to limit the possibility of judicial tyranny. . . .

We can now survey our progress in the attempt to define "neutral principles." Each proposed definition left us with judges who could enforce their personal values unconstrained by the suggested version of the neutrality requirement. Some of the more sophisticated candidates, such as the craft interpretation, seemed plausible because they appealed to an intuitive sense that the institution of judging involves people who are guided by and committed to general rules applied consistently. But the very notions of generality and consistency can be specified only by reference to an established institutional setting. We can know what we mean by "acting consistently" only if we understand the institution of judging in our society. Thus, neutral principles theory proves

unable to satisfy its demand for rule-guided judicial decisionmaking in a way that can constrain or define the judicial institution; in the final analysis, it is the institution—or our conception of it—that constrains the concept of rule-guidedness.

Consider the following multiple choice question: "Which pair of numbers comes next in the series 1, 3, 5, 7? (a) 9, 11; (b) 11, 13; (c) 25, 18." It is easy to show that any of the answers is correct. The first is correct if the rule generating the series is "list the odd numbers"; the second is correct if the rule is "list the odd prime numbers"; and the third is correct if a more complex rule generates the series. Thus, if asked to follow the underlying rule—the "principle" of the series—we can justify a tremendous range of divergent answers by constructing the rule so that it generates the answer that we want. As the legal realists showed, this result obtains for legal as well as mathematical rules. The situation in law might be thought to differ, because judges try to articulate the rules they use. But even when an earlier case identifies the rule that it invokes, only a vision of the contours of the judicial role constrains judges' understanding of what counts as applying the rule. Without such a vision, there will always be a diversity of subsequent uses of the rule that could fairly be called consistent applications of it.

There is, however, something askew in this anarchic conclusion. After all, we know that no test maker would accept (c) as an answer to the mathematical problem; and indeed we can be fairly confident that test makers would not include both (a) and (b) as possible answers, because the underlying rules that generate them are so obvious that they make the question fatally ambiguous. Another example may sharpen the point. The examination for those seeking driver's licenses in the District of Columbia includes this question: "What is responsible for most automobile accidents? (a) The car; (b) the driver, (c) road conditions." Anyone who does not know immediately that the answer is (b) does not understand what the testing enterprise is all about.

In these examples, we know something about the rule to follow only because we are familiar with the social practices of intelligence testing and drivers' education. That is, the answer does not follow from a rule that can be uniquely identified without specifying something about the substantive practices. Similarly, although we can, as I have argued elsewhere, use standard techniques of legal argument to draw from the decided cases the conclusion that the Constitution requires socialism, we know that no judge will in the near future draw that conclusion. But the failure to reach that result is not ensured because the practice of "following rules" or neutral application of the principles inherent in the decided cases precludes a judge from doing so. Rather, it is ensured because judges in contemporary America are selected in a way that keeps them from thinking that such arguments make sense. This branch of the argument thus makes a sociological point about neutral principles. Neither the principles nor any reconstructed version of a theory that takes following rules as its focus can be neutral in the sense that liberalism requires, because taken by itself, an injunction to follow the rules tells us nothing of substance. If such a theory constrains judges, it does so only because judges, before they turn to the task of finding neutral principles for the case at hand, have implicitly accepted some image of what their role in shaping and applying rules in controverted cases ought to be.

There is something both odd and important here. The theory of neutral principles is initially attractive because it affirms the openness of the courts to all reasonable arguments drawn from decided cases. But if the courts are indeed open to such arguments, the theory allows judges to do whatever they want. If it is only in consequence of the pressures exerted by a highly developed, deeply entrenched, homeostatic social structure that judges seem to eschew conclusions grossly at odds with the values of liberal capitalism, sociological analysis ought to destroy the attraction of neutral principles theory. Principles are "neutral" only in the sense that they are, as a matter of contingent fact, unchallenged, and the contingencies have obvious historical limits.

QUESTIONS FOR DISCUSSION

1. Does Tushnet accurately characterize Bork's position? Do Bork and Tushnet mean the same thing by "neutrality"?

2. What is the point of Tushnet's example of the question about "which pair of numbers comes next in the series"? Could "Cleveland, Newark, Bombay" be the numbers that come next in the series 1, 3, 5, 7? If not, why not? Does this say anything about Tushnet's argument?

3. Why is it that "the driver" is the correct answer to the driving test question? What do you think Tushnet's point is in using this example?

4. What do you think that Legal Realists like Jerome Frank and Mark Tushnet would say about the opinion in *Planned Parenthood* in Section 2.2? What methods would they use to decide the case?

IN CONTEXT

MARTHA MINOW AND ELIZABETH SPELMAN

What do people mean when they say, "You must see it in context"? Often, such a statement arises in a moment of judgment or decision. Or it can arise in a moment of misunderstanding. In everyday conversation people call upon context when a question arises about the meaning of someone's statement or action. In contemporary political philosophy and legal theory, demands for "contextual" analysis appear in works by people claiming the name pragmatist and in other works by people calling themselves feminists. As we turn to address the meaning of "context" in these contexts, we are pointedly aware of a plausible question likely to occur to a sensitive reader: What is the context for our inquiry?

So let's start over. Welcome to our context. Though we do not wish to claim that our contexts are thoroughly known to us (or to you, whether or not you share them), we feel particularly obliged, in the context of an essay on context, to situate our concern about it. On reflection, we realize that we have been using the phrase "in context" for most of our lives. But we note with considerable interest how, in recent years, we have begun depending increasingly upon it. In our writing and our teaching, we find ourselves insisting on the importance of the context in which someone lived, the context in which something was said, the context in which a problem arose, the context in which someone proposes a response to it, and the context in which some comment or idea made or did not make sense. This heightened concern about context is not, we dare to hope, simply a case of academic flu, even though the current ubiquity of the phrase "in context" suggests the possibility of unthinking conceptual contagion.

We have been deliberate, moreover, in addressing context in some of our recent work. One of us (Minow) has emphasized the importance of context in describing the workings of "the dilemma of difference": when people have suffered harmful discrimination based on traits of race, sex, or disability, remedies can be sought by rejecting lines of difference and focusing on the similarities between the favored and unfavored groups. But other harms may be incurred unless certain differences are recognized in contexts in which those differences continue to carry significance. For example, to satisfy the definition of a "family" for residential zoning restrictions, persons with mental disabilities who plan to live together as a group should not be burdened by a rule treating them differently from others who can also be described as living together in a group. On the other hand, persons with mental handicaps should be able to claim relevant differences from others in order to receive special services tailored to meet their needs. Thus, just treatment of all people requires us to recognize relevant differences in different contexts.

The other of us (Spelman) has insisted that gender identity and gender relations exist and cannot be understood apart from racial and class identity, and racial and class relations. Race and class privilege are furthered when people ignore or deny the fact that what are presented as examinations of women's experiences "as women" are in fact studies of the experiences of women of a particular race and class. In a context in which racial and class dif-

Martha Minow and Elizabeth Spelman, "In Context," *Southern California Law Review*, vol. 63 (1990), pp. 1597ff. Minow (1954–) is Professor of Law at the Harvard Law School. Spelman is Professor of Philosophy at Smith College.

ferences among women are significant, analyses of gender that treat it as if it were separable from race and class in effect serve racial and class domination.

In addition, in an essay we jointly authored, we argued that justice is more likely to be served when judges attend to the specific contexts in which their judgments are rendered. We identified as relevant the perspectives and relative positions of power of all the parties in a lawsuit, including the judge; we also identified the actual effects of the judicial decision as an important feature of the context. We have also been mindful of the claims appearing in judicial opinions and scholarly commentary that attention to context marks the beginning of a precipitous slide down that slippery slope of "case-by-case" treatment; a descent that, so the worry goes, inexorably plops one into the muck of relativism.

If context occasions such debate, what does it mean? Our sense that it is high time to make context itself a subject of scrutiny is confirmed by a recent book we found after writing the first draft of this paper. Ben-Ami Scharfstein writes in the opening pages of *The Dilemma of Context:* "[T]he very commonness of the [importance of context] makes it the more striking that so little thought has been devoted to context in itself." Similarly, Stephen Toulmin has recently argued for renewed interest in context. He suggests that Montaigne and other sixteenth century philosophers emphasized particularity and promoted tolerant, practical forms of reason. Yet, maintains Toulmin, Descartes and others rejected contextual approaches as partly to blame for religious wars that divided Europe. Descartes in particular devised a philosophical method seeking logical certainty even if his culture and his senses misled him. Toulmin is especially effective in reminding readers that theories that seek to remove moral and epistemological claims from the cultural situation and perceptions of a particular person are nevertheless themselves products of historically specific circumstances;

understanding those circumstances can help us make deliberate choices about the kinds of theories to adopt as our own.

One more quite local pin on the butterfly of context is Thomas Grey's recent essay on legal pragmatism. Grey explains that pragmatists—referring to the school of North American philosophical thought associated with C. S. Peirce, William James, and John Dewey—"treated thinking as contextual and situated." Thinking is something particular people do as they try to resolve specific problems in specific situations. The significance of context, particularity, and situated perspectives to the tasks of knowing and judging appears in many of the contributions to this symposium.

In this Article, our emphasis on context is not simply a focus upon the particularity of persons, places, and problems. We could identify for analysis particular people in particular situations trying to solve particular problems without specifying the historical and cultural identities of the people, places, and problems. For example, one could, as Kant did, describe someone—a very particular, singular someone—facing a specific dilemma in this way: As a rational being, wondering whether it is permissible to lie in order to make a profit on a sale, one asks whether one can universalize the maxim of one's intended action. For Kant, the relevant specificity of the person and problem involved consists simply in being numerically different from other rational beings facing other instances of the same problem.

In contrast, we mean to signal with "context" a readiness, indeed an eagerness, to recognize patterns of differences that have been used historically to distinguish among people, among places, and among problems. This focus distinguishes our interest from what was probably a more common usage of "context" by the early pragmatists. Dewey, for example, stressed individual uniqueness when he looked to context; he maintained that perhaps the highest calling of our reason and intelligence was figuring out what to do when confronting moral problems. Dewey said that each moral problem "is a unique situation having its own irreplaceable good." Dewey was responding to the tradition characterized by Kant's celebration of the capacity of practical reason to enable us to figure out what to do despite being "[i]nexperienced in the course of the world, incapable of being prepared for its contingencies." William James seemed to think human beings blessed with both Kantian and Deweyan versions of rationality and identified the real problem as figuring out how and when to use each: "Life is one long struggle between conclusions based on abstract ways of conceiving cases, and opposite conclusions prompted by our intuitive perception of them as individual facts."

It is not the familiar competition between the universal and the particular that motivates our interest in context. Like others concerned with the failures of abstract, universal principles to resolve problems, we emphasize "context" in order to expose how apparently neutral and universal rules in effect burden or exclude anyone who does not share the characteristics of privileged, white, Christian, able-bodied, heterosexual, adult men for whom those rules were actually written. It is the particular particularities associated with legacies of power and oppression that we mean to highlight by the interest in context. In so doing, we aim to question the distinction between abstraction and context, while also paying attention to the risk that calling our concerns "contextual" in fact may bury them and remove their political implications. Yet, we are equally interested in the charge that an emphasis on context undermines capacities for political, moral, and legal judgments.

Therefore, we will first examine several persistent uses of the phrase "in context"—uses that provide clues to the goals behind a turn to context. We then turn to examples of theorists calling for context. This will lead us to articulate objections to the move to context that we have heard or can imagine. We will respond to those objections in the context of a contemporary social problem: the role of children as witnesses in prosecutions of child abuse.

■ ■ ■

We have noticed three contrasting uses of the phrase "in context" in contemporary theoretical debates. The first refers to the historical and social situation of writers and thinkers, such as the drafters of the United States Constitution. By calling for an examination of their context, critics seek to challenge the claim that the texts stand free of the situation in which they were produced, or to challenge the asserted universality of the norms and rules they articulate. The reference to the context of the drafters is not designed to reduce the texts to the identities and self-interests of the drafters, but is posed as an effort to render comprehensible the contrast between the drafters' language of universality and the particular, and at times discriminatory, effects of their words as applied.

A second possible meaning of the phrase "in context" in contemporary debates over political philosophy and legal theory focuses on the context of the reader or critic who examines texts and understands them within a context not envisioned by the author. For example, Joyce Appelby has written evocatively of the contests in constitutional interpretation between those who defend "a conservative, sometimes literal, reading of the Constitution and those articulating a more radical, underlying meaning." She argues that the Constitution represents a victory by some interests over others, but that its language permits, or succumbs to, continued struggle by the "disinherited" to replace Biblical and common law traditions with legal rights against hierarchy. Based on their own experiences, however, white women, people of color, members of religious and ethnic minorities, and others who have been "disinherited" by prevailing legal and cultural documents may nonetheless claim authority to use those very documents and argue for social and political change.

Yet the phrase "in context" can also carry a third meaning. Here, especially when addressing actions and decisions, people emphasize "context" in order to highlight the importance of the particular details of a problem. For example, as one philosopher maintained, "Ethical problems arise in the changing contexts of persons and events within which we live. We make our choices and act . . . in situation. [We must be] sensitive to the special characteristics and requirements of each problematic situation, to the distinctive needs of the persons involved." Moral decisions cannot be reached adequately by simply figuring out which moral rule applies to the situation at hand; that situation is too specific and its particularities are too numerous and too complex to be covered by a rule whose very abstractness has been made possible by erasing contextual details.

All three meanings of context are illustrated in recent judicial debates over the constitutionality of a community's decision to display on public property a creche and a Menorah during the holiday season. A majority of the Supreme Court concluded, without a majority opinion, that displaying the creche violated the establishment clause, while displaying the Menorah, in conjunction with the Christmas tree, would not violate that provision of the Constitution. Amid sharply differing opinions, the Justices also disagreed about which contexts should be germane to their decision: the context of the drafters of the Constitution, the contemporary context in which new readers bring new interpretations to the Constitution's language, or the particular, detailed contexts of the fact situation at issue and the historical and social setting in which it arose.

The historical context of those who drafted the governing law received attention in Justice Stevens's opinion; the opinion explored the historical backdrop for the Congressional debate in 1789 over several drafts of language for the establishment clause. Justice Stevens also looked to definitions of terms found in dictionaries of the time. Similarly, Justice Kennedy considered both the historic practice of public displays commemorating religious holidays at the time the establishment clause was written, and the more general historic practices and understandings about establishment of religion prevailing at that time.

In contrast, Justice Blackmun's opinion explicitly rejected evidence of the meaning of the establishment clause of the first amendment at the time of its adoption in favor of interpretations used in the late twentieth century. Thus, Justice Blackmun's opinion adopts the second conception of context and explicitly looks to situations and applications that would not have been contemplated or endorsed by the authors of the Constitution's text.

The third meaning of context, pointing to the particular details of the problem at hand as the critical focus for decisionmaking, also appears in many of the opinions in the case. Justice Blackmun's opinion analyzes the constitutional question as dependent on the setting in which the creche appears and the context in which the Menorah is displayed. No doubt for that reason, the opinion explores in specific detail the practice of displaying a creche in the county courthouse in Allegheny County, the location of this display in relation to the physical layout of the building, the county's decision to add a Menorah to the display, and the place of the Menorah in Jewish tradition and Jewish law. Photographs of the displays are appended to his opinion.

Justice O'Connor's opinion emphasizes the tradition of case-specific decisionmaking and resistance to any fixed rule in applying the establishment clause. Her opinion also looks to social and historical context in concluding that a Christmas tree can be reasonably seen as a secular symbol, while a Chanukah Menorah is more aptly known as a central religious symbol in a religious holiday. In addition, several of the Justices demanded that both symbols be examined in the context of their joint display, for that context could alter the meaning of either of them if displayed alone.

Each of the three meanings of context implies opposition to decision or interpretation removed from context. Indeed, some arguments against contextual decisionmaking of any sort suggest a contrast between abstraction and context. Arguments over context, however, may wrongly imply that we can ever escape context. We will argue instead that we are always in some context, as are the texts that we read, their authors and readers, our problems, and our efforts to achieve solutions. Typically, therefore, when people advocate looking or deciding "in context," they advocate a switch from one context to another—from one level of analysis to another, or from a focus on one set of traits or concerns to a focus on another set. In many contemporary arguments for context, what people in fact urge is greater attention to factors of race, gender, or class. Perhaps paradoxically, then, the call for context represents a call to consider societal structures of power that extend far beyond the particularities of a given situation. The call for context itself tacitly signals both that the selection of some context is unavoidable, if only by default, and that the selection of one context over another implies a preference for one set of analytic categories rather than another. Against the background assumptions of liberal political and legal theory that treat principles as universal and the individual self as the proper unit of analysis, a call for contextual interpretation may well defend switching from one set of analytic categories to another that may only seem more "contextual" because it emphasizes group-based traits of individuals. In the late twentieth century in the United States, those who urge contextual interpretation often point to the harmful effects of legacies of exclusion based on race, gender, class, or other group traits. They imply new normative directions for legal and political life. . . .

The move to context, then, is an attempt to shift the location of significance: writers emphasizing context have done so out of a sense that the significance of particular facts about persons and events was being obscured by the processes of abstraction necessary for the formulation of general empirical statements or universally applicable moral rules. Those focusing on the forest cannot see the trees.

■ ■ ■

A [reason] for rejecting the distinction between abstraction and contextualism also provides a response to the charge that contextual approaches undermine the possibility of moral judgments beyond the particular situation at hand. The call to look at context typically represents a call to focus on some previously neglected features. It does not, however, mean focusing on all possible features. As human beings, we simply cannot hold in our heads all possible sensory inputs. Thus, we may say "don't forget the historical context," but we do not then mean, "don't forget to look at all possible features of the historical moment and its place in the chronology of history." Perhaps even more obviously, many calls to look at context specifically refer to the traits of race, gender, and class that have been ignored by a more general statement. Thus, once the pretended distinction between context and abstraction is discarded, the important question becomes which context should matter, what traits or aspects of the particular should be addressed, how wide should the net be cast in collecting the details, and what scale should be used to weigh them? Whether you prefer to be called a contextualist or a devotee of principled reason, you make choices about what features of context to address.

It is for this reason that contextualists do not merely address each situation as a unique one with no relevance for the next one. As Virginia Held puts it, "Morality, which ought to guide us in all contexts, ought to guide us differently in different contexts." The basic norm of fairness—treat like cases alike—is fulfilled, not undermined, by attention to what particular traits make one case like, or unlike, another. Here, a useful contrast can be drawn between the notions of universality and generality. Both "Thou Shall Not Kill" and "Thou Shall Not Kill Except in Self-Defense" have a universal form: they are meant to apply to everyone—their form tells us "This means YOU, whoever you are." So however "Thou Shall Not Kill" and "Thou Shall Not Kill Except in Self-Defense" differ, both make unconditional demands on everyone—their form is meant to tell us that they apply to us whatever our particular historical and personal condition happens to be. There are no exceptions in the scope of their applicability to human beings.

But they are different, of course. The first says that all acts of killing are forbidden to all human beings; the second says that some acts of killing are not forbidden to all such beings. "Thou Shall Not Kill" is more general than "Thou Shall Not Kill Except in Self-Defense," in the sense that the scope of forbidden acts is broader in the first case than in the second. "Thou Shall Not Kill Except in Self-Defense" specifies that some acts of killing are not forbidden.

"Thou Shall Not Kill Except in Self-Defense" is a position no less *principled*—in the sense of determining similar outcomes for similar cases—than "Thou Shall Not Kill" just be-cause it builds in a certain kind of exception. What determines whether one holds a principled position in this sense is whether one applies it to all situations so specified and not how those situations are specified.

The degree of specificity does not alter the fact of principle nor the injunction of universal application. This would hold even if the norm read, "Thou Shall Not Kill Except If Thy Name Be Rambo And Thy Motives Be Inspiring to a Public Composed of Teenagers." Just in case there happens to be more than one person named Rambo, this rule would apply to more than one case; it is universal with respect to the situation so specified and its form reveals this intent to assure universal applicability. When a rule specifies a context, it does not undermine the commitment to universal application to the context specified; it merely identifies the situations to be covered by the rule.

[If] we are no longer distracted by a confusion between the universal and the general, we avoid the mistaken view that increased attention to specific circumstances undermines commitments to universal normative judgments. And if we are no longer besieged by a simplistic distinction between context and abstraction, we may have to speak with more cumbersome phrases, but we can respond without difficulty to the objections raised against "contextual" approaches.

QUESTIONS FOR DISCUSSION

1. How do Minow and Spelman define "context"? Are there other possible definitions?

2. Is deciding cases "in context" always a good thing? Do Minow and Spelman believe it is always a good thing? When might it not be?

3. When they are talking about "particulars," what distinguishes Minow and Spelman from Jerome Frank?

4. Why do Minow and Spelman believe that an increased attention to context will help those who traditionally have been oppressed?

ECONOMIC ANALYSIS OF LAW

RICHARD POSNER

The efficiency theory of the common law is not that *every* common law doctrine and decision is efficient. That would be completely unlikely, given the difficulty of the questions that the law wrestles with and the nature of judges' incentives. The theory is that the common law is best (not perfectly) explained as a system for maximizing the wealth of society. Statutory or constitutional as distinct from common law fields are less likely to promote efficiency, yet even they as we shall see are permeated by economic concerns and illuminated by economic analysis.

But, it may be asked, do not the lawyer and the economist approach the same case in such different ways as to suggest a basic incompatibility between law and economics? X is shot by a careless hunter, Y. The only question in which the parties and their lawyers are interested and the only question decided by the judge and jury is whether the cost of the injury should be shifted from X to Y, whether it is "just" or "fair" that X should receive compensation. X's lawyer will argue that it is just that X be compensated since Y was at fault and X blameless. Y's lawyer may argue that X was also careless and hence that it would be just for the loss to remain on X. Not only are justice and fairness not economic terms, but the economist is not (one might think) interested in the one question that concerns the victim and his lawyer: Who should bear the costs of *this* accident? To the economist, the accident is a closed chapter. The costs that it inflicted are sunk. The economist is interested in methods of preventing future accidents (that are not cost-justified) and thus reducing the sum of accident and accident-prevention costs, but the parties to the litigation have no interest in the future. Their concern is limited to the financial consequences of a past accident.

This dichotomy, however, is overstated. The decision in the case will affect the future and so it should interest the economist, because it will establish or confirm a rule for the guidance of people engaged in dangerous activities. The decision is a warning that if one behaves in a certain way and an accident results, he will have to pay a judgment (or will be unable to obtain a judgment, if the victim). By thus altering the prices that confront people, the warning may affect their behavior and therefore accident costs.

Conversely, the judge (and hence the lawyers) cannot ignore the future. Since any ruling of law will constitute a precedent, the judge must consider the probable impact of alternative rulings on the future behavior of people engaged in activities that give rise to the kind of accident involved in the case before him. If, for example, judgment is awarded to the defendant on the ground that he is a "deserving," albeit careless, fellow, the decision will encourage similar people to be careless, a type of costly behavior.

Once the frame of reference is thus expanded beyond the immediate parties to the case, justice and fairness assume broader meanings than what is just or fair as between this plaintiff and this defendant. The issue becomes what is a just and fair result for a *class* of activities, and it cannot be sensibly resolved without consideration of the impact of alternative rulings on the frequency of accidents and the cost

Richard Posner, *Economic Analysis of Law* (Boston: Little, Brown, 1986)

of accident precautions. The legal and economic approaches are not so divergent after all. The economic approach to law, both in its normative and in its positive aspects, has aroused considerable antagonism, especially, but not only, among academic lawyers who dislike the thought that the law might be economics.

The most frequent criticism is that the normative underpinnings of the economic approach are so repulsive that it is inconceivable that the legal system would (let alone should) embrace them. This criticism may appear to confound positive and normative analysis, but it does not. Law embodies and enforces fundamental social norms, and it would be surprising to find that those norms were inconsistent with the society's ethical system. But is the Kaldor–Hicks concept of efficiency really so at variance with that system? [Provided] only that this concept is a component, though not necessarily the only or most important one, of our ethical system, it may be the one that dominates the law as administered by the courts because of the courts' inability to promote other goals effectively. And so long as efficiency is any sort of value in our ethical system, two normative uses of economics mentioned earlier—to clarify value conflicts and to point the way toward reaching given social ends by the most efficient path—are untouched by the philosophical debate. . . .

Another common criticism of the "new" law and economics—although it is perhaps better described as a reason for the distaste with which the subject is regarded in some quarters—is that it manifests a conservative political bias. We shall see that its practitioners have found, for example, that capital punishment has a deterrent effect, legislation designed to protect consumers frequently ends up hurting them, no-fault automobile insurance is probably inefficient, and securities regulation may be a waste of time. Findings such as these indeed provide ammunition to the supporters of capital punishment and the opponents of the other policies

mentioned. Yet economic research that provides support for liberal positions is rarely said to exhibit political bias. For example, the theory of public goods could be viewed as one of the ideological underpinnings of the welfare state but is not so viewed; once a viewpoint becomes dominant, it ceases to be perceived as having an ideological character. The criticism also overlooks a number of findings of economic analysts of law . . . —concerning right to counsel and standard of proof in criminal cases, bail, products liability, application of the First Amendment to broadcasting, social costs of monopoly, damages in personal-injury cases, and many others—that support liberal positions.

The economic approach to law is also criticized for ignoring "justice." In evaluating this criticism, one must distinguish between different meanings of the word. Sometimes it means distributive justice, which is the proper degree of economic equality. Although economists cannot tell society what that degree is, they have much to say that is highly relevant to the debate over inequality—about the actual amounts of inequality in different societies and in different periods, about the difference between real economic inequality and inequalities in pecuniary income that merely offset cost differences or reflect different positions in the life cycle, and about the costs of achieving greater equality.

A second meaning of justice, perhaps the most common, is efficiency. We shall see, among many other examples, that when people describe as unjust convicting a person without a trial, taking property without just compensation, or failing to make a negligent automobile driver answer in damages to the victim of his negligence, this means nothing more pretentious than that the conduct wastes resources. Even the principle of unjust enrichment can be derived from the concept of efficiency. And with a little reflection, it will come as no surprise that in a world of scarce resources waste should be regarded as immoral.

But there is more to notions of justice than a concern with efficiency. It is not obviously inefficient to allow suicide pacts; to allow private discrimination on racial, religious, or sexual grounds; to permit killing and eating the weakest passenger in the lifeboat in circumstances of genuine desperation; to force people to give self-incriminating testimony; to flog prisoners; to allow babies to be sold for adoption; to allow the use of deadly force in defense of a purely property interest; to legalize blackmail; or to give convicted felons a choice between imprisonment and participation in dangerous medical experiments. Yet all of these things offend the sense of justice of many (some almost all) modern Americans, and all are to a greater or lesser (usually greater) extent illegal. An effort will be made in this book to explain some of these prohibitions in economic terms, but most cannot be; there is more to justice than economics, a point the reader should keep in mind in evaluating normative statements in this book. There may well be definite although wide boundaries on both the explanative and reformative power of economic analysis of law. Always, however, economics can provide value clarification by showing the society what it must give up to achieve a noneconomic ideal of justice. The demand for justice is not independent of its price.

THE ECONOMIC NATURE AND FUNCTION OF CRIMINAL LAW

The types of wrongful conduct examined in previous chapters, mainly torts and breaches of contract, subject the wrongdoer to having to pay money damages to his victim, or sometimes to being prohibited on pain of contempt from continuing or repeating the wrong (i.e., enjoined)—but in either case only if the victim sues. But crimes are prosecuted by the state, and the criminal is forced to pay a fine to the state or to undergo a nonpecuniary sanction such as being imprisoned. For now our interest is in why there should be distinctive sanctions, sought by the state, for some types of wrongdoing and what substantive doctrines such sanctions entail.

There are five principal types of wrongful conduct made criminal in our legal system.

1. Intentional torts, examined in the last chapter, that represent a pure coercive transfer either of wealth or utility from victim to wrongdoer. Murder, robbery, burglary, larceny, rape, assault and battery, mayhem, false pretenses, and most other common law crimes (i.e., crimes punishable under the English common law) are essentially instances of such intentional torts as assault, battery, trespass, and conversion, although we shall see that the state-of-mind and injury requirements for the criminal counterpart of the intentional tort sometimes differ. Here, however, are two somewhat more problematic examples of crime.

(1) *Counterfeiting.* This can be viewed as a form of theft by false pretenses, the false pretense being that the payor is paying with legal tender. If the counterfeiting is discovered, the victim is whoever ends up holding the worthless currency. If it is not discovered, the loss is more widely diffused. Since the amount of money in circulation is now larger than it was before the counterfeiting relative to the total stock of goods in society, everyone's money is worth less (inflation); everyone but the counterfeiter is a loser. In addition to this coerced transfer, counterfeiting imposes the usual deadweight costs (such as?).

(2) *Rape.* Suppose a rapist derives extra pleasure from the coercive character of his act. Then there would be no market substitute for rape and it could be argued therefore that rape is not a pure coercive transfer and should not be punished criminally. But the argument would be weak:

(a) Given that there are heavy penalties for rape, the rapes that take place—that have not been deterred—may indeed be weighted toward a form of rape for which there are no consensual substitutes; it does not follow that the rape that is deterred is generally of this character. The prevention of rape is essential to protect the marriage market and more generally to se-cure property rights in women's persons. Al-lowing rape would be the equivalent of communalizing property rights in women. More generally, crimes of passion bear the same relation to informal markets in human relations as acquisitive crimes such as theft, and murder for gain, bear to explicit markets: They bypass them, which reduces efficiency.

(b) Allowing rape would lead to heavy ex-penditures on protecting women, as well as ex-penditures on overcoming those protections. The expenditures would be largely offsetting, and to that extent socially wasted.

(c) Given the economist's definition of value, the fact that the rapist cannot find a consensual substitute does not mean that he values the rape more than the victim disvalues it. There is a difference between a coerced transaction that has no consensual substitute and a coerced transaction necessary to over-come the costs of a consensual transaction.

Now back to our typology.

2. Other coerced transfers, such as price fixing and tax evasion, the wrongfulness of which may not have been recognized at com-mon law.

3. Voluntary, and therefore presumptively value maximizing, exchanges incidental to ac-tivities that the state has outlawed. Examples of such exchanges are prostitution, selling pornog-raphy, selling babies for adoption, selling regu-lated transportation services at prices not listed in the carrier's published tariffs, and trafficking in narcotics.

4. Certain menacing but nontortious preparatory acts, such as unsuccessfully at-tempting or conspiring to murder someone where the victim is not injured and the ele-ments of a tortious attempt are not present (as they would not be if, for example, the victim did not know of the attempt at the time it was made).

5. Conduct that if allowed would compli-cate other forms of common law regulation. Examples are leaving the scene of an accident and fraudulently concealing assets from a judgment creditor.

Why, though, cannot all five categories be left to the tort law? An answer leaps to mind for categories 3 and 4: No one is hurt. But this is a superficial answer; we could allow whomever the law was intended to protect to sue for puni-tive damages. A better answer is that detection is difficult where there is no victim to report the wrongdoing and testify against the wrongdoer. This answer is not complete. Punitive damages can be adjusted upward to take account of the difficulty of detection; in principle this device could take care of category 5 crimes as well. But (as we shall see) the higher the optimal level of punitive damages, the less likely it is that they will be a feasible sanction. Another question about categories 3 and 4, however, is, why pun-ish acts that don't hurt anybody? For category 3 the answer lies outside of economics; it is diffi-cult for an economist to understand why, if a crime is truly "victimless," the criminal should be punished. (Of course, ostensibly victimless crimes may, like other contractual exchanges, have third party effects; the sale of liquor to a drunk driver is an example.) For category 4 the answer is bound up with the question—to which we can now turn—why tort law is not ad-equate to deal with categories 1 and 2 (coerced transfers in violation of common law or statu-tory principles).

We know from the last chapter that the proper sanction for a pure coercive transfer such as theft is something greater than the law's estimate of the victim's loss—the extra something being designed to confine transfers to the market whenever market transaction costs are not prohibitive. We can be more pre-cise: The extra something should be the differ-ence between the victim's loss and the injurer's gain, and then some.

To illustrate, suppose B has a jewel worth $1,000 to him but $10,000 to A, who steals it ("converts" it, in tort parlance). We want to channel transactions in jewelry into the mar-ket, and can do this by making sure that the coerced transfer is a losing proposition to A. Making A liable to pay damages of $10,000 will almost do this, but not quite; A will be indifferent between stealing and buying, so he might just as well steal as buy. (How will attitude toward risk affect his choice?) So let us add something on, and make the damages $11,000. But of course the jewel might be worth less to A than to B (A is not planning to pay for it, after all), in which event a smaller fine would do the trick of deterring A. If the jewel were worth only $500 to him, damages of $501 should be enough. But as a court can't determine subjective values, it probably will want to base damages on the market value of the thing in question and then add on a hefty bonus (just how hefty is examined in the next section of this chapter) to take account of the possibility that the thief may place a higher subjective value on the thing.

In the case of crimes that cause death or even just a substantial risk of death, optimal damages will often be astronomical. A normal person will demand an extremely large amount of money to assume a substantial risk of immediate death—an infinite amount, if the probability is one. Even when a person sets out deliberately to kill another, the probability of death is significantly less than one. But it is much higher than in most accident cases. And we know that the relation between risk and compensation is not linear. If A will accept $1 in compensation for a .0001 chance of being accidentally killed by B, it does not follow that he will demand only $10,000 to let B murder him.

In figuring optimal damages for pure coercive transfers, moreover, we have ignored the problem of concealment. Accidents, being a by-product of lawful, public activities, usually are difficult to conceal; breaches of contract usually are impossible to conceal. But when the tortfeasor's entire purpose is to take something of value from someone else, he will naturally try to conceal what he is doing, and will often succeed. The formula for deciding how much to award in

damages if the probability that the tortfeasor will actually be caught and forced to pay the damages is less than one is $D = L/p$, where D is the optimal damage award, L is the harm caused by the tortfeasor in the case in which he is caught (including any adjustment to discourage bypassing the market by coercing wealth transfers), and p is the probability of being caught and made to pay the optimal damage award. If $p = 1$, L and D are the same amount. But if, for example, $L = \$10,000$ and $p = .1$, meaning that nine times out of ten the tortfeasor escapes the clutches of the law, then D, the optimal penalty, is $100,000. Only then is the expected penalty cost to the prospective tortfeasor (pD) equal to the harm of his act (L).

Once the damages in the pure coercive transfer case are adjusted upward to discourage efforts to bypass the market, to recognize the nonlinear relationship between risk of death and compensation for bearing the risk, and to correct for concealment, it becomes apparent that the optimal damages will often be very great—greater, in many cases, than the tortfeasor's ability to pay. Three responses are possible, all of which society uses. One is to impose disutility in nonmonetary forms, such as imprisonment or death. Another is to reduce the probability of concealment by maintaining a police force to investigate crimes. A third, which involves both the maintenance of a police force and the punishment of preparatory acts (category 4), is to prevent criminal activity before it occurs. If public policing is more efficient than private, the state is in the enforcement picture and has a claim to any monetary penalties imposed. Hence these penalties are paid to the state as fines, rather than to the victims of crime as damages. The victims can seek damages if the crime is also a tort, whether common law or statutory.

In cases where tort remedies are an adequate deterrent, because optimal tort damages, including any punitive damages, are within the ability to pay of the potential defendant, there is no need to invoke criminal penalties, which, as explained below, are costlier than civil penalties even when just a fine is imposed. The criminal (= tortious) conduct probably will be deterred; and if for reasons explained in the last chapter it is not even though the tort remedy is set at the correct level and there is no solvency problem to interfere with it, there still is no social gain from using the criminal sanction (why not?). Although in some cases, notably antitrust and securities cases, affluent defendants are both prosecuted criminally and sued civilly, criminal sanctions generally are reserved, as theory predicts, for cases where the tort remedy bumps up against a solvency limitation.

This means that the criminal law is primarily designed for the nonaffluent; the affluent are kept in line by tort law. This suggestion is not refuted by the fact that fines are a common criminal penalty. Fines are much lower than the corresponding tort damage judgments, and this for two reasons. The government invests resources in raising the probability of criminal punishment above that of a tort suit, which makes the optimal fine lower than the punitive damages that would be optimal in the absence of such an investment. And a fine is a more severe punishment than its dollar cost. Every criminal punishment imposes some nonpecuniary disutility in the form of a stigma, enhanced by such rules as forbidding a convicted felon to vote. There is no corresponding stigma to a tort judgment.

OPTIMAL CRIMINAL SANCTIONS

In order to design a set of optimal criminal sanctions, we need a model of the criminal's behavior. The model can be very simple: A person commits a crime because the expected benefits of the crime to him exceed the expected costs. The benefits are the various tangible (in the case of crimes of pecuniary gain) or intangible (in the case of so-called crimes of passion) satisfactions from the criminal act. The costs include various out-of-pocket expenses (for guns, burglar tools, masks, etc.), the opportunity costs of the criminal's time, and the expected costs of criminal punishment. The last of these costs will be the focus of our analysis, but it is well to mention the others in order to bring out the possibility of controlling the level of criminal activity other than simply by the amount of law enforcement activity and the severity of punishment. For example, the benefits of theft, and hence its incidence, might be reduced by a redistribution of wealth away from the wealthy. Similarly, the opportunity costs of crime could be increased, and thus the incidence of crime reduced, by reducing unemployment, which would increase the gains from lawful work. The out-of-pocket expenses of crime could also be increased, for example by imposing a heavy tax on handguns.

The notion of the criminal as a rational calculator will strike many readers as highly unrealistic, especially when applied to criminals having little education or to crimes not committed for pecuniary gain. But the test of a theory is not the realism of its assumptions but its predictive power. A growing empirical literature on crime has shown that criminals respond to changes in opportunity costs, in the probability of apprehension, in the severity of punishment, and in other relevant variables as if they were indeed the rational calculators of the economic model—and this regardless of whether the crime is committed for pecuniary gain or out of passion, or by well educated or poorly educated people.

We saw earlier that the criminal sanction ought to be so contrived that the criminal is made worse off by committing the act. But now a series of qualifications has to be introduced. Suppose I lose my way in the woods and, as an alternative to starving, enter an unoccupied cabin and steal a trivial amount of food which I find there. Do we really want to make the punishment for this theft death, on the theory that the crime saved my life, and therefore no lesser penalty would deter? Of course not. The problem is that while the law of theft generally punishes takings in settings of low transaction costs, in this example the costs of transacting with the absent owner of the cabin are prohibitive. One approach would be to define theft so as to exclude such examples; and there is in fact in the criminal law a defense of necessity that probably could be invoked successfully in this example. But [the] costs of attempting so detailed a specification of the crime might be very great, and the alternative is to employ a more general, albeit somewhat overinclusive, definition but set the expected punishment cost at a level that will not deter the occasional crime that is value maximizing.

There is a related reason for putting a ceiling on criminal punishments such that not all crimes are deterred. If there is a risk either of accidental violation of the criminal law (and there is, for any crime that involves an element of negligence or strict liability) or of legal error, a very severe penalty will induce people to forgo socially desirable activities at the borderline of criminal activity. For example, if the penalty for driving more than 55 m.p.h. were death, people would drive too slowly (or not at all) to avoid an accidental violation or an erroneous conviction. True, if the category of criminal acts is limited through the concept of intentionality and through defenses such as necessity to cases where, in Hand Formula terms, there is a very great disparity between B and PL, the risk of either accident or error will be slight and the legal system can feel freer in setting heavy penalties. But not totally free; if the consequences of error are sufficiently enormous, even a very slight risk of error will generate avoidance measures that may be socially very costly. And as there are costs of underinclusion if the requirements of proof of guilt are set very high, it may make sense to make proof easier but at the same time to make the penalty less severe in order to reduce the costs of avoidance and error.

Once the expected punishment cost for a crime is determined, it becomes necessary to choose a combination of probability and sever-

ity of punishment that will impose that cost on the would-be offender. Let us begin with fines. An expected punishment cost of $1,000 can be imposed by combining a fine of $1,000 with a probability of apprehension and conviction of 1, a fine of $10,000 with a probability of .1, a fine of $1 million with a probability of .001, etc. If the costs of collecting fines are assumed to be zero regardless of the size of the fine, the most efficient combination is a probability arbitrarily close to zero and a fine arbitrarily close to infinity. For while the costs of apprehending and convicting criminals rise with the probability of apprehension—higher probabilities imply more police, prosecutors, judges, defense attorneys, etc. (because more criminals are being apprehended and tried) than when the probability of apprehension is very low—the costs of collecting fines are by assumption zero regardless of their size. Thus every increase in the size of the fine is costless, while every corresponding decrease in the probability of apprehension and conviction, designed to offset the increase in the fine and so maintain a constant expected punishment cost, reduces the costs of enforcement—to the vanishing point if the probability of apprehension and conviction is reduced arbitrarily close to zero.

There are, however, several problems with the assumption that the cost of the fine is unrelated to the size of the fine.

1. If criminals (or some of them) are risk averse, an increase in the fine will not be a costless transfer payment. The reason why, in our model, the only cost of a fine is the cost of collecting it and not the dollar amount of the fine itself is that either the fine is not paid (because the crime is deterred) or, if paid, it simply transfers an equal dollar amount from the criminal to the taxpayer. But for criminals who are risk averse, every reduction in the probability of apprehension and conviction, and corresponding increase in the fine for those who are apprehended and convicted, imposes a disutility not translated into revenue by the state. Thus, the real social cost of fines increases for risk-averse criminals as the fine increases. Nor

is this effect offset by the effect on risk-preferring criminals, even if there are as many of them as there are risk-averse criminals. To the extent that a higher fine with lower probability of apprehension and conviction increases the utility of the risk preferrer, the fine has to be put up another notch to make sure that it deters, which makes things even more painful for the risk averse.

2. The stigma effect of a fine (as of any criminal penalty), noted earlier, is not transferred either.

3. The tendency in the model is to punish all crimes by a uniformly severe fine. This, however, eliminates marginal deterrence—the incentive to substitute less for more serious crimes. If robbery is punished as severely as murder, the robber might as well kill his victim to eliminate a witness. Thus, one cost of increasing the severity of punishment of a crime is to reduce the incentive to substitute that crime for a more serious one. If it were not for considerations of marginal deterrence, more serious crimes might not always be punishable by more severe penalties than less serious ones. Of course, marginal deterrence would be uninteresting if all crimes were deterred. And even if all are not (why not, from an economic standpoint?), marginal deterrence involves a tradeoff that may not be worth making. Suppose we want to reduce the number of murders committed in the course of robberies. One way might be to make robbery punishable by death. This would violate the principles of marginal deterrence and would increase the probability that, if a robbery were committed, someone would be murdered in the course of it. But it would reduce the probability that the robbery would be committed in the first place. If the robbery rate was very sensitive to the severity of the punishment, the total number of murders committed during robberies might fall (because there were so many fewer robberies), even though robbers' incentive to kill was greater.

4. Limitations of solvency make the cost of collecting fines rise with the size of the fine—and, for most criminal offenders, to become prohibitive rather quickly. The problem is so acute that the costs of collecting fines would often be prohibitive even if the probability of punishment were one and fines correspondingly much smaller than in the model. This explains the heavy reliance in all criminal justice systems on nonpecuniary sanctions, of which imprisonment is the most common today. Imprisonment imposes pecuniary costs on the violator by reducing his income during the period of confinement and, in many cases, by reducing his earning capacity after release as well (the criminal record effect). It also imposes nonpecuniary costs on people—the vast majority—who prefer living outside of prison.

Since fines and imprisonment are simply different ways of imposing disutility on violators, the Supreme Court is wrong to regard a sentence that imposes a fine but provides for imprisonment if the defendant cannot or will not pay the fine as discriminating against the poor. A rate of exchange can be found that equates, for a given individual, a number of dollars with a number of days in jail. But maybe the Court's real objection is to the fact that most criminal statutes establish a rate of exchange highly favorable to people who have assets. Five hundred dollars is a milder sanction than 100 days in jail (*Williams v. Illinois*), even for people of low income; it is a trivial sanction for other people—those most likely to be able to pay the fine in lieu of serving a jail term.

From an economic standpoint, the use of fines should be encouraged relative to imprisonment. Not only does imprisonment generate no revenue for the state, as fines do, but the social costs of imprisonment exceed those of collecting fines from solvent defendants. There is the expense of constructing, maintaining, and operating prisons (only partly offset by the savings in living expenses on the outside that the criminal would incur if he were not in prison), the loss of the incarcerated individual's lawful production (if any) during the period while he is in prison, the disutility of imprisonment to him (which generates no corresponding benefit to the state, as a fine does), and the impairment of his productivity in legitimate activities after release. Since the forgone income from lawful employment is an opportunity cost of crime, a reduction in the prisoner's lawful earnings prospects reduces the costs of criminal activity to him and thereby increases the likelihood that he will commit crimes after his release. But imprisonment yields one benefit that a fine does not: It prevents the criminal from committing crimes (at least outside of prison!) for as long as he is in prison.

Much can be done to make alternative punishments to imprisonment effective. Fines can be made payable in installments. They can be made proportionate to and payable out of earnings, rather than being a fixed dollar amount. Exclusion from particular occupations can be used as a sanction. Freedom of action can be (and nowadays often is) restricted in ways that permit productive activity, such as by imprisonment at night and on weekends only. But some of these methods are not entirely free from the drawbacks of imprisonment. A fine payable in installments or proportionate to future earnings would reduce the offender's income from lawful activity and therefore also his incentive to choose it over criminal activity, as would exclusion from an occupation.

Nevertheless more white collar crimes—financial, nonviolent crimes committed by middle class people, such as price fixing, tax evasion, securities fraud, and bribery—probably could be punished exclusively by fines. The fact that many of these crimes are less grave than crimes of violence and that many of these criminals are far more solvent than violent criminals suggests that it often would be possible to set a realistic (i.e., a collectable) fine that imposed on the criminal a net disutility equal to that of the normally very short prison sentences that are imposed for these crimes, even when the stigma effect of imprisonment is

added to the more tangible deprivations. (Any criminal punishment has some stigma effect.) This might of course require much higher fines than we have been accustomed to—although times are changing. Even so, our analysis of the nonlinear relationship between compensation demanded and risk of death implies that even very large financial crimes are less costly than almost all crimes of violence that create a significant probability of death.

Thus no white collar crime is apt to approach murder in gravity. Moreover, even prolonged incarceration may not impose on the murderer costs equal to those of the victim, which may truly be infinite. This suggests a possible economic justification for capital punishment of murder, which imposes on the convicted murderer a cost roughly commensurate with the cost of his conduct. It might seem that the important thing is not that the punishment for murder equal the cost to the victim but that it be high enough to make murder not pay—and surely imprisonment for the remainder of one's life would cost the murderer more than the murder could possibly have gained him. But this analysis implicitly treats the probability of apprehension and conviction as one. If it is less than one, as of course it is, the murderer will not be comparing the gain from the crime with the cost if he is caught and sentenced; he will be comparing it with the cost of the sentence discounted by the probability that he will be caught and sentenced.

This argument for capital punishment is not conclusive. Because the penalty is so severe, and irreversible, the cost of mistaken imposition is very high and therefore substantially greater resources are invested in the litigation of a capital case. The additional resources may not be justified if the incremental deterrent effect of capital punishment compared with long prison terms is small. But there is evidence that it is substantial.

Capital punishment is also supported (although equivocally) by considerations of marginal deterrence, which requires as big a spread as possible between the punishments for the least and most serious crimes. If the maximum punishment for murder is life imprisonment, we may not want to make armed robbery also punishable by life imprisonment. But if we therefore step down the maximum punishment for armed robbery from life to 20 years, we shall not be able to punish some lesser crime by 20 years. It does not follow, however, that capital punishment should be the punishment for *simple* murder. For if it is, then we have the problem of marginally deterring the multiple murderer. Maybe capital punishment should be reserved for him, so that murderers have a disincentive to kill witnesses to the murder. An important application of this point is to prison murders. If a prisoner is serving life for murder, he has no disincentive not to kill in prison, unless prison murder is punishable by death.

Problems of this sort vexed medieval thinkers. Because most medieval people believed in an afterlife, capital punishment was not so serious a punishment in those days as it is in our modern, and (it had seemed until recently) increasingly secular, world. In an effort to make capital punishment a more costly punishment, horrible methods of execution (e.g., drawing and quartering) were prescribed for particularly serious crimes, such as treason. Boiling in oil, considered more horrible than hanging or beheading, was used to punish murder by poisoning; since poisoners were especially difficult to apprehend in those times, a heavier punishment than that prescribed for ordinary murderers was (economically) indicated.

If (coming back to modern times) we must continue to rely heavily on imprisonment as a criminal sanction, there is an argument—subject to caveats that should be familiar by now to the reader, based on risk aversion, overinclusion, avoidance and error costs, and (possibly) marginal deterrence—for combining heavy prison terms for convicted criminals with low probabilities of apprehension and conviction. Con-

sider the choice between combining a .1 probability of apprehension and conviction with a 10 year prison term and a .2 probability of apprehension and conviction with a 5 year term. Under the second approach twice as many individuals are imprisoned but for only half as long, so the total costs of imprisonment will be similar under the two approaches. But the costs of police, court officials, etc. are clearly less under the first approach, since the probability of apprehension and conviction (and hence the number of prosecutions) is only half as great. Although more resources will be devoted to a trial where the possible punishment is greater, these resources will be incurred in fewer trials because fewer people will be punished. And notice that this variant of our earlier model of high fines and trivial probabilities of apprehension and conviction corrects the most serious problem with that model—that of solvency.

But isn't a system under which probabilities of punishment are low unfair because it creates ex post inequality among offenders? Many go scot-free; others serve longer prison sentences than they would if more offenders were caught. To object to this result, however, is like saying that all lotteries are unfair because, ex post, they create wealth differences among the players. In an equally significant sense both the criminal justice system that creates low probabilities of apprehension and conviction and the lottery are fair so long as the ex ante costs and benefits are equalized among the participants. This ignores risk aversion, however, which if prevalent will add to the social costs of the low probability approach. Moreover, a prison term is lengthened, of course, by adding time on to the end of it, and if the criminal has a significant discount rate, the added years may not create a substantial added disutility. At a discount rate of 10 percent, a prison term of 10 years imposes a disutility only 6.1 times the disutility of a one year sentence, and a sentence of 20 years increases this figure to only 8.5 (the corresponding figures for a 5 percent discount rate are 7.7 and 12.5).

QUESTIONS FOR DISCUSSION

1. What does Posner mean by "economic analysis of law"? How is economic reasoning different from other kinds of reasoning?

2. Does Posner believe that judges should decide cases according to an economic analysis? If not, could he? Do you? What would an economic analysis of *Riggs v. Palmer* (p. 75) look like? What result would it produce?

3. Under Posner's account, is there any difference between legal reasoning and good reasoning?

SUGGESTIONS FOR FURTHER READING

On Legal Realism, two good historical introductions are Laura Kalman, *Legal Realism at Yale, 1927–60* (Chapel Hill: University of North Carolina Press, 1986), and Wilfred E. Rumble, *American Legal Realism: Skepticism, Reform, and the Judicial Process* (Ithaca, N.Y.: Cornell University Press, 1968). Many of the important articles are collected in William W. Fisher III, Morton J. Horwitz, and Thomas A. Reed, eds., *American Legal Realism* (New York: Oxford University Press, 1933). An insightful combination of philosophical and historical perspectives is William Twining, *Karl Llewellyn and the Realist Movement* (London: Weidenfeld and Nicolson, 1973). On Critical Legal Studies, see David Kairys, ed., *The Politics of Law* (New York: Pantheon, 1982); Mark Kelman, *A Guide to Critical Legal Studies* (Cambridge: Harvard University Press, 1988); Duncan Kennedy, "Legal Formality," *Journal of Legal Studies*, vol. 2 (1973), pp. 351 ff.; Joseph Singer, "The Player and the Cards: Nihilism and Legal Theory," *Yale Law Journal*, vol. 94 (1984), pp. 13 ff.; Mark Tushnet, *Red, White, and Blue: A Critical Analysis of Constitutional Law* (Cambridge: Harvard University Press, 1988); Mark Tushnet, "Critical Legal Studies: An Introduction to Its Origins and Underpinnings," *Journal of Legal Education*, vol. 36 (1986), pp. 505 ff.; Roberto Unger, *The Critical Legal Studies Movement* (Cambridge: Harvard University Press, 1986). An intelligent critique is Andrew Altman, *Critical Legal Studies: A Liberal Critique* (Princeton: Princeton University Press, 1990). Important works of feminist jurisprudence include Katharine T. Bartlett, "Feminist Legal Methods," *Harvard Law Review*, vol. 103 (1990), pp. 829 ff.; Catharine MacKinnon, *Toward a Feminist Theory of the State* (Cambridge: Harvard University Press, 1989); Martha Minow, "The Supreme Court, 1986 Term: Foreword: Justice Engendered," *Harvard Law Review*, vol. 101 (1987), pp. 10 ff; Margaret Jane Radin, "The Pragmatist and the Feminist," *Southern California Law Review*, vol. 63 (1990), pp. 1699 ff.; Robin West, "Jurisprudence and Gender," *University of Chicago Law Review*, vol. 55 (1988), pp. 1 ff. In recent years Richard Posner's perspective has embedded his law and economics approach into a larger "pragmatism." See Richard A. Posner, *The Problems of Jurisprudence* (Cambridge: Harvard University Press, 1990). On law and economics, see Guido Calabresi, *The Costs of Accidents: A Legal and Economic Analysis* (Cambridge: Harvard University Press, 1970); Richard A. Posner, *The Economics of Justice* (Cambridge: Harvard University Press, 1983). For critical engagement with the economic approach, see Jules L. Coleman, *Markets, Morals and the Law* (Cambridge: Cambridge University Press, 1988).

CHAPTER 3

THE MORAL
FORCE OF LAW

INTRODUCTION

Many issues in the philosophy of law concern relations between law and morality. Discussions of the nature of law and legal reasoning often focus on the question of whether judges should use moral values to reach legal decisions (see
Chapters 1–2). Legal moralists and their opponents debate whether legislators
should use laws to force citizens to behave morally (see Chapter 4). Yet another
relation between law and morality applies to citizens who are neither judges nor
legislators nor any other kind of official. The issue is: Do ordinary citizens have a
moral obligation to obey the law?

It is common to assume that citizens have a moral obligation to obey most
laws. However, this issue is less clear when laws are bad. In the days of slavery,
for example, some people helped slaves escape. Did these people have a moral
obligation to obey slavery laws? A similar issue arises today when citizens hide
illegal immigrants from authorities because they think these immigrants should
be allowed to stay in the United States.

Even when laws are good and are admitted to be good, it is still not always
clear that citizens have a moral obligation to obey them. There is a stop sign behind my office at the exit of one parking lot leading into another. It is a good idea
to have a stop sign there, for it is busy during the day. But when I work very late, I
can easily see that nobody else is around. Why shouldn't I just drive through the
stop sign when I know that there is no danger? In this case, my only reason to
break the law is my own interest in getting home earlier, but other cases involve
moral reasons to break good laws. Imagine a mother who gets lost on a winter
camping trip. Her child is starving and freezing, and she can keep the child alive
only by breaking into a deserted cabin and taking the food locked inside. Laws
against theft and breaking and entering are good laws, but does the mother have
an obligation not to break in and take the food in these special circumstances?

This issue also arises for public officials. A police officer might not be able to
catch a dangerous criminal without obtaining evidence in some way that is illegal. Courts will throw out the conviction if they find out that the evidence was
obtained illegally, but there might be little or no chance that anyone will discover
or prove any illegality. Does the police officer have a moral obligation to obey the

law anyway? Similarly, if a secondary rule of our legal system requires lower court judges to follow clear precedents by the U.S. Supreme Court, do lower court judges have a moral obligation to follow such precedents? In the days of slavery, again, judges who opposed slavery laws had to decide whether to return run-away slaves to their angry masters and punish those who helped them escape (see Section 1.5). A similar issue arises today when a lower court judge believes that capital punishment is immoral in circumstances where higher courts have declared it constitutional (see Section 6.6). Does the judge have a moral obligation to follow the higher court precedents?

Whenever laws tell people what to do, people have to ask whether they should obey those laws. One way to answer this question is to break it into two parts. First, is there a moral obligation to obey the law? Second, what kinds of reasons can justify violating that obligation? The first question will be addressed in Section 3.1, and the second question will be addressed in Section 3.2.

IS THERE A **3.1**
MORAL OBLIGATION
TO OBEY THE LAW?

INTRODUCTION

One thing is clear. There is always a *legal* obligation to obey the law. All this means is that it is always illegal to disobey the law. It also seems that it is often, but not always, in one's *self-interest* to obey the law, if only because lawbreakers are often punished. Of course, criminals sometimes feel sure that they will not be caught, and sometimes they are right. If you can steal a car or cheat on your taxes with no danger of being caught or suffering any other harm as a result, then you have no prudential reason to obey the law. But you still might have a *moral* reason to obey the law, and that is the issue here.

To say that there is a moral obligation to obey the law is not to say that it is always morally wrong to break the law. Almost nobody thinks that. Recall the lost mother who must break into a cabin and steal food in order to save her child's life. Even if her breaking, entering, and stealing are illegal, they are still not immoral, because they are justified by stronger moral reasons. There might be *some* moral obligation to obey the law, but it need not always be the *strongest* moral reason.

To say that there is a moral obligation to obey the law, then, is just to say that it *would* be morally wrong to break the law if one had no adequate reason to break the law. On this picture, obligations are like forces. Just as forces can be overpowered by conflicting forces but still determine the movement of objects when there are no conflicting forces, so obligations can be overridden by conflicting reasons but still determine what is wrong when there are no conflicting reasons. Such obligations are often described as *prima facie* (which translates as "on first appearance") in order to signal that they might be overridden.

Moral obligations range from strong to weak. The strength of an obligation depends on what kinds of reasons are adequate to justify violating the obligation. When a reason justifies violating an obligation, the reason overrides the obligation, so the strength of an obligation depends on how much it takes to override it. Regardless of strength, the initial question is whether there is *any* prima facie moral obligation to obey the law.

There is clearly at least sometimes some prima facie moral obligation to obey the law. Regardless of the law, there is a moral obligation not to rape, so there is a moral obligation not to do acts that violate laws against rape. Similarly for murder, theft, and all acts that are *mala in se* (which translates as "wrong in it-self"), or immoral independent of the law. What is not so clear is whether the law ever or always creates a moral obligation where none existed previously. If the bare fact that an act is illegal creates a prima facie moral obligation not to do that act, then this obligation arises for every law as such. So the controversial question is whether there is *always* a prima facie moral obligation to obey every law.

One's answer to this question depends on one's view of the nature of law. If, as on some natural law theories (see Section 1.1), immoral laws are not valid as laws, and if immoral laws are the only cases where there seems to be no prima facie moral obligation to obey the law, then such natural law theories seem to imply that there is such an obligation for every valid law. The story is not so sim-ple, since some laws (such as parking regulations) are neither immoral nor based directly on morality, so the acts they forbid are called *mala prohibita* (which trans-lates as "wrong by virtue of being prohibited"). These laws are valid, even on nat-ural law theories, so natural law theories still need to show why there is a prima facie moral obligation to obey such laws.

This task is even harder for other theories of law, such as legal realism and legal positivism. Legal realists (Section 1.3) claim that law is just what judges de-cide, and legal positivists (Section 1.2) see laws either as commands of a sovereign or as rules that conform to official conventions. Judges and legislators are, accord-ing to their critics, just a bunch of rich old people who got lucky and grabbed power. If so, why must anyone obey them? Under such theories, it would take a strong argument to establish a prima facie moral obligation to obey every law.

This might seem to be a disadvantage for legal realism and positivism. Some theorists claim that legal realism and positivism are inadequate just because they cannot explain why there is a general prima facie moral obligation to obey every law. This was one of Lon Fuller's criticisms of legal positivism (see Section 1.1). Re-alists and positivists can respond in two ways. They can try to show that there is a general prima facie moral obligation to obey the law even on a realist or posi-tivist conception of the law. Or they can admit that there is no general moral obligation to obey every law under their theories, and then argue that this is not a problem, since there really is no such general obligation. Either way, we can test these theories about the nature of law by evaluating their implications for moral obligations to obey the law.

In order to do so, we must first determine whether there really is a prima facie moral obligation to obey every law. Some think this obligation is intuitively obvious, but others think it is obvious that there is no such obligation. In the face of such controversy, the only way to determine whether such an obligation exists is to look at the arguments for and against it.

ARGUMENTS BASED ON CONSEQUENCES

The first kind of argument claims that disobeying the law has bad *consequences*, and that is why there is a prima facie moral obligation to obey the law. The basic idea is simple, but there are many ways to base obligations on consequences.

Traditional act–utilitarians claim that the right act is always the one that causes "the greatest good for the greatest number." One need not agree that overall consequences are the *only* source of moral reasons in order to think that overall consequences are *one* source of moral obligations. If so, one still accepts

> *The Overall Theory*: A person has a prima facie moral obligation to do an act if that act has better overall consequences than any alternative.

On this theory, there is not always a moral obligation to obey the law. Suppose that the mother who is lost on a winter camping trip cannot keep her child alive except by stealing food. Also suppose that the mother will not be caught, and the food is not needed by the owner or anyone else. Then stealing the food has the best consequences overall. So this theft does not violate any moral obligation based on the overall theory, even if theft does violate the law.

Stealing the food still has *some* bad consequences. The owner loses property as well as the ability to use the food. So there would be a prima facie moral obligation not to steal the food on a second theory:

> *The Harm Theory*: A person has a prima facie moral obligation to do an act if not doing that act would cause some harm to someone.

This move seems natural because our question is not about overall or overriding obligations but is instead just about prima facie obligations.

However, the harm theory does not yield even a prima facie moral obligation to obey the law in *every* case. Recall the stop sign behind my office. If I run it when nobody else is around, nobody will be harmed. Then there is not a prima facie moral obligation to obey this law based on the harm theory.

It is common to respond that, even when breaking a law does not harm any specific individual, it still harms the legal system or society. This creates an obligation to obey the law according to a third theory:

> *The Social Harm Theory*: A person has a prima facie moral obligation to do an act if not doing that act would cause some harm to someone or to society.

How could breaking the law harm society without harming any specific individual? The idea seems to be that lawbreaking creates disrespect for the law and sets a bad example, so other people become more likely to break the law in harmful situations, even if we cannot yet specify which individuals will be harmed. However, if nobody else ever finds out that I ran the stop sign (or that the lost mother stole the food), these secret acts cannot have such bad effects on other people or on society. Lawbreaking still might build bad habits in the person who breaks the law. Just as smoking makes people smoke, so stealing and running stop signs might make people more likely to break the law again, even in situations where it is harmful. Such bad habits should be avoided, but there is no reason to think that every illegal act creates bad habits in its agent. When none of these harms occurs, there is no moral obligation to obey the law based on the social harm theory.

There is still some risk of harm in such cases. Running stop signs always creates *some* danger, because there is some chance that I am wrong to think that the parking lot is deserted. This is enough for a prima facie moral obligation to obey the law on a fourth theory:

> *The Risk Theory*: A person has a prima facie moral obligation to do an act if not doing that act causes some risk of harm to someone or to society.

On this theory, the only cases with no moral obligation to obey the law are cases where breaking the law does not cause any risk of any harm. Such cases are rare, but they do occur. Suppose that the speed limit on a crowded highway is 55 miles per hour, but everyone else is driving at 75 miles per hour. If I drive at 55 miles per hour, then other cars will repeatedly change lanes and pass me. Such quick maneuvering on a crowded highway will create more risk of an accident for me and for others than if I speed up. In these circumstances, breaking the law actually reduces the risk of harm, so there is no moral obligation to obey the law based on the risk theory.

Even if every act did create risk, the risk theory would prove too much. Careful driving under normal circumstances creates some risk of harm, but careful, normal driving does not seem to violate any moral obligation. The risk theory is only about prima facie obligations, so it does not imply that normal driving is morally wrong, but it is still unsatisfying to say that every act (or almost every act) violates a prima facie moral obligation. What we want is a theory that reveals something special about lawbreaking that puts illegal acts in a different moral class from legal acts. Driving at 65 miles per hour violates a moral obligation on the risk theory just as much when it is legal as when it is illegal, if the risk is the same. So the risk theory fails to draw any moral distinction between legal acts and illegal acts.

This puts consequentialists in a dilemma. If they do not base prima facie moral obligations on risks, then they cannot get a prima facie moral obligation to obey every law. But if they do base prima facie moral obligations on risks, then they imply prima facie moral obligations even where there seem to be none. It is hard to see how consequentialists can formulate a theory that both is plausible and also yields a prima facie moral obligation to obey the law in every case.

Consequentialists still might be able to defend a prima facie moral obligation to obey every law if they turn to *rule utilitarianism*. Instead of judging particular acts directly by the consequences of those acts, rule utilitarians judge acts by general rules, and they justify rules by the consequences of obeying or accepting those rules. One version of rule utilitarianism is:

> *The General Obedience Theory*: A person has a prima facie moral obligation to do an act if and only if not doing that act would violate a rule that it would be disastrous for people to disobey generally.

This theory is supposed to capture the basic idea behind the common retort: "What if everybody did that?"[1]

The general obedience theory might seem to yield a prima facie moral obligation to obey the law. It would be disastrous if people generally violated the law, including killing, raping, stealing, and so on. That is supposed to justify the rule "Obey the law" and thereby to imply a general obligation to obey every law.

The general obedience theory faces several problems. The most important one here is to locate the right *level of generality*. We can't answer the question "What would happen if everybody did that?" unless we know what "that" refers to. The rule utilitarian argument about the law assumes that "did that" refers to "broke the law," and that the justified rule is:

The Unqualified Rule: Obey the law.

Society probably would be worse off if people generally disobeyed the unqualified rule "Obey the law" than if people generally obeyed the unqualified rule "Obey the law." Even so, these are not the only options. People could obey the law under some but not all circumstances, which amounts to obeying a rule with exceptions. Here is one example:

The Qualified Rule: Obey the law except when disobeying the law has better overall consequences.

Universal obedience to the qualified rule would create more utility than universal obedience to the unqualified rule, since the only acts that obey the qualified rule but disobey the unqualified rule are illegal acts that have better overall consequences. When we ask, "What would happen if everyone broke the law only when disobedience has better overall consequences?", the answer is "Society would be better off." Thus, the qualified rule rather than the unqualified rule is the one that is justified and the one that determines prima facie moral obligations according to the general obedience theory. Consequently, this version of rule utilitarianism does not yield any moral obligation to obey every law.

The problem with the qualified rule is practical: people often make mistakes about which act has the best consequences, so they will mistakenly cause a lot of harm if they believe that they are morally permitted to disobey the law whenever disobedience has better consequences. Because of such mistakes, a society might be worse off if its members consciously use the qualified rule in deciding what to do and in judging other people, and if they teach the qualified rule to their children. The unqualified rule seems to function better in these roles, because it leaves less room for error.

---

[1] This kind of theory is developed by Marcus Singer, *Generalization in Ethics* (New York: Atheneum, 1971). The implications of Singer's views for law are discussed by M.B.E. Smith, "Is there a Prima Facie Obligation to Obey the Law?", *Yale Law Journal* vol. 82 (1972). Many of my points in the text are derived from Smith and from David Lyons, *Forms and Limits of Utilitarianism* (Oxford: Clarendon, 1965).

This practical problem is the basis for a new version of rule utilitarianism. Instead of asking, "What would happen if everyone did that?", this new kind of rule utilitarianism asks, "What would happen if everyone believed that everyone is allowed to do that?" More precisely,

> *The General Acceptance Theory:* A person has a moral obligation to do an act if and only if not doing that act would violate a rule that it would be best for people to accept generally.[2]

When is a rule accepted generally? On one view, a person *accepts* a rule when she feels a certain reluctance to violate it, when she uses it consciously in reaching decisions and in judging other people's acts, and when she teaches it to her children. From another perspective, a person accepts a rule when he believes that he has a general prima facie moral obligation to obey the rule. A rule is then accepted *generally* (or publicly) when almost everyone in a society accepts the rule and knows that others also accept it. According to the general acceptance theory, our moral obligations are then determined by which rules would function best in this social role.

This kind of theory is supposed to yield a prima facie moral obligation to obey every law. If people generally accept the qualified rule "Obey the law except when disobedience has better consequences," then they will be less reluctant to break the law when they think that disobedience has better consequences, so they will be more likely to cause harm when they are mistaken about what has the best consequences. In contrast, accepting the unqualified rule "Obey the law" will make people more reluctant to break the law and less likely to make harmful mistakes. So it would be best for society to accept generally the unqualified rule "Obey the law." This implies a prima facie moral obligation to obey every law, according to the general acceptance theory.

Although this argument is forceful, it is not clear that general acceptance of "Obey the law" really is best. If people accept this unqualified rule, then they probably will be less likely to disobey the law when this would cause harm, but they will *also* be less likely to disobey the law in cases where disobeying it has better consequences. Sometimes we want people to feel free to break the law in order to improve other people's lives, their own lives, society, or even the law itself. It is not clear which kind of case is more common or more important, so it is not clear that general acceptance of the unqualified rule "Obey the law" really does have the best consequences overall.

Furthermore, even if people do not generally accept "Obey the law," they still might not be much more likely to disobey the law. If disobedience is punished, then people have personal reasons not to disobey the law. People also have

---

[2]This kind of theory is developed by Richard Brandt in many places, including "Toward a Credible Utilitarianism," in *Morality and the Language of Conduct*, ed. H. N. Castañeda and G. Nakhnikian (Detroit: Wayne State University Press, 1963) and by Bernard Gert, *Morality* (New York: Oxford University Press, 1988). The implications of Brandt's views for the law are discussed in Smith, "Is there a Prima Facie Obligation to Obey the Law?" Gert's views are defended against Smith by Michael Davis in "Smith, Gert, and Obligation to Obey the Law," *Southern Journal of Philosophy*, vol. 20 (1982), pp. 139-152.

moral reasons not to disobey laws that forbid acts that are immoral independent of the law. This makes it doubtful that harmful disobedience would become widespread even if people did not generally accept "Obey the law" as a separate moral rule. If not, this new version of rule utilitarianism also fails to justify a prima facie moral obligation to obey every law.

Thus, it is hard to see how a prima facie moral obligation to obey every law could be based on consequences alone. If there is such a universal obligation, this is a problem for consequentialists, who claim that every moral obligation is based on consequences alone. But consequentialists can respond by denying that there is any prima facie moral obligation to obey *every* law. Consequentialists can still hold that there is a prima facie obligation to obey the law in *most* cases, since most lawbreaking does cause some harm (or unusual risk). And consequentialists can still say a great deal about *when* there really are prima facie moral obligations to obey the law, and also about *who* has these obligations and *how strong* these obligations are. This approach might even capture every moral obligation that really exists, if there is no better reason to believe in a prima facie obligation to obey every law.

ARGUMENTS BASED ON THE PAST

This limited result will not satisfy those who believe in a prima facie moral obligation to obey every law, so they will need to find a different kind of argument. Instead of looking forward to future consequences, they might look back at the past and, in particular, at the benefits that the law confers on citizens.

The first argument of this kind appeals to *gratitude*. Children owe a debt of gratitude for all that their parents gave them and did for them. This debt seems to create a prima facie moral obligation to obey their parents in many cases. If your father cooks your favorite dinner for you, and he asks you to wash the dishes, you should not refuse, unless you have a good reason. Cases like this suggest that people have a prima facie moral obligation not only to feel grateful but also to do something to show gratitude to their benefactors.

This general obligation seems to extend to the government insofar as it has helped its citizens in the past.[3] Good governments usually do protect their citizens from crime as well as from attack by foreign powers, they regulate traffic and commerce in beneficial ways, and they set up "safety nets" of welfare programs that provide security even when they are not used. These benefits and others are supposed to show that citizens have a moral obligation to be grateful to their governments, at least if those governments are not too bad.

Governments and parents differ, however, in many ways. Children do not pay taxes to their parents, but many citizens do pay taxes to their government. Taxes make government services seem less like gifts and more like payouts by insurance companies. Moreover, most parents help their children out of love for the individual child and not out of self-interest. In contrast, politicians rarely have in

---

[3] See Plato, *Crito* 50d, 51cd.

mind the interest of an individual citizen, and politicians who benefit citizens typically do so at least partly to stay in office, which gives them both power and pay. It is not at all clear that an individual owes a debt of gratitude to someone who acts out of self-interest without thinking of that individual. If not, then gratitude cannot be the basis for a prima facie moral obligation to obey every law.

Gratitude still might be the basis for *some* moral obligations to obey *some* laws, and it might affect the strength of such obligations. Children who have received more from their parents seem to have a stronger obligation of gratitude to obey their parents. Similarly, to the extent that a moral obligation to obey the law is based on gratitude, that obligation seems stronger for those who have received more from the government. This seems to include public officials who get salaries from the government, the poor who get welfare, the rich and famous who get extra police protection, and so on. Their greater debts of gratitude might show that these people have greater moral obligations to obey some laws than if they had received less from the government.

Partly to avoid the limits on gratitude, some philosophers base a moral obligation to obey the law on a *social contract* or promise. In order to generate an obligation to obey every law, the promise must be a promise to obey every law, good or bad.

But who promises to obey every law? There are explicit promises of obedience in some societies and by some people in our society. When officials are sworn into office, and when new citizens are naturalized, they often promise to uphold the Constitution. These promises might create general moral obligations for these people to obey every law. Even if so, however, most ordinary citizens never promise to obey the law. The pledge of allegiance to the flag is not a promise to obey every law. Indeed, many would refuse to promise complete obedience, unless coerced.

In response, it is often said that citizens make some kind of *tacit* promise to obey the law. The notion of a tacit promise is not clear, but one model is consent by silence.[4] At the end of a committee meeting, the chairman says, "If there are no objections, we will all meet here again next Tuesday." In this situation, silence signals a promise. This is supposed to resemble the tacit promise to obey the law. No public official ever says, "If you do not promise to obey the law, speak now," but there are supposed to be other signs of tacit consent.

It is often claimed that *residence* signals consent. Plato's Socrates started this tradition when he had the state say, "if any one of you stands his ground, when he can see how we administer justice and the rest of our public organization, we hold that by doing so he has in fact undertaken to do anything that we tell him."[5] The problem with this argument is that people often cannot change countries without leaving behind many of the things that are most valuable to them, such as their friends, their homes, and so on. When there is such great personal cost for refusing to make a promise, the promise is coerced, and coerced promises are not morally

---

[4]Cf. A. John Simmons, "Tacit Consent and Political Obligation," *Philosophy and Public Affairs*, vol. 5 (Spring 1976), pp. 274–291.

[5]Plato, *Crito* 51e.

binding.[6] Just imagine someone who says, "If you don't agree to obey me, I will keep you away from your friends and your immovable possessions." An agreement made under such coercion would not be binding, even if it were explicit.

It is also said, for example, that *voting* signals a tacit promise to obey the law,[7] but similar problems arise. It is not so costly to give up voting, but most people do not see voting as promising to obey the law, and an *unconscious* promise is not morally binding. So we need a better reason to hold that citizens tacitly promise to obey the law.

Even though the argument from a social contract or promise cannot ground a moral obligation for everyone to obey every law, it still might justify a more limited moral obligation in some cases. Tacit promises can be binding when they are made knowingly without coercion. And people who explicitly promise to obey the law, such as government officials, soldiers, and naturalized citizens, thereby gain a prima facie moral obligation to obey the law. So there might be some reason to think that these people have more moral obligation to obey the law than those of us who have made no such promise.

The next argument applies a principle of *fairness* that was proposed by H. L. A. Hart, a professor of jurisprudence at Oxford University, and developed by John Rawls, a professor of philosophy at Harvard University (see later reading). In Rawls' version, the principle claims that one has a prima facie moral obligation to obey the rules of a cooperative enterprise that: (1) is just and mutually beneficial, (2) would fail without obedience by almost everyone, (3) requires some sacrifice, and (4) has been obeyed by others, if one (5) has accepted benefits from the enterprise and (6) can benefit from the enterprise without obeying its rules. Rawls argues that these conditions are often met by legal systems, and then people have a prima facie moral obligation based on fair play to obey the law.

Even if it works, the argument from fairness does not yield a general obligation to obey every law. It does not apply to unjust legal systems. It does not even seem to apply to all laws in just legal systems. Several of these limitations are discussed later in this section by John Simmons, a philosophy professor at the University of Virginia.

Rawls himself recognizes some of these limits. He says that obligations differ from duties in that "obligations are normally the consequence of voluntary acts of persons." The principle of fairness gives rise to obligations because it requires a voluntary act of acceptance of benefits. However, not everyone has accepted the

[6]Thomas Hobbes, *Leviathan*, ed. M. Oakeshott (New York: Collier Books, 1962), p. 110, claims that some coerced promises are morally binding. However, the only convincing examples depend on an antecedent authority, such as when a judge says to a criminal, "If you don't promise to meet your parole officer each week, I will sentence you to jail." The argument from tacit social contract cannot assume any antecedent authority without begging the question.

[7]E.g., J. Plamenatz, *Man and Society* (New York: McGraw-Hill, 1963), and A. Gewirth, "Political Justice," in *Social Justice*, ed. R. Brandt (Englewood Cliffs, N.J.: Prentice-Hall, 1962). Both are criticized in Smith, "Is there a Prima Facie Obligation to Obey the Law?"

benefits in any way that creates a moral obligation, and some people have received very few benefits. Rawls concludes that

> only the more favored members of society are likely to have a clear political obligation as opposed to a political duty. They are better situated to win public office and find it easier to take advantage of the political system. And having done so, they have acquired an obligation owed to citizens generally to uphold the just constitution. But members of subjected minorities, say, who have a strong case for civil disobedience will not generally have a political obligation of this sort.[8]

One might conclude that there is no moral reason to obey every law, but only a moral obligation when and to the extent that the principle of fairness and other principles apply.

However, instead of giving up, Rawls tries to cover all laws with a new kind of moral reason, which he calls a *natural duty*.

> From the standpoint of the theory of justice, the most important natural duty is that to support and to further just institutions. This duty has two parts: first, we are to comply with and to do our share in just institutions when they exist and apply to us; and second, we are to assist in the establishment of just arrangements when they do not exist, at least when this can be done with little cost to ourselves. It follows that if the basic structure of society is just, or as just as it is reasonable to expect in the circumstances, everyone has a natural duty to do what is required of him.[9]

Rawls justifies this natural duty by arguing that it would be chosen by all rational people under conditions of impartiality.[10] The crucial difference between this natural duty and the moral obligations due to fairness is that the natural duty does not depend on any voluntary act, so it applies equally to the rich and the poor, to officials and ordinary citizens. Those who also have moral obligations to obey the law are "bound even more tightly to the scheme of just institutions,"[11] but the natural duty to support just institutions is supposed to give everyone a prima facie moral reason to obey every law within a just system.

The main problem with this argument lies in its assumption that obedience to the law is always the best way to support and further just institutions. Sometimes, however, lawbreaking has no effect on just institutions. If I run a stop sign when there is no danger, and if nobody ever discovers my transgression, then I don't harm the legal system or any other just institution.

Moreover, when a mostly just legal system includes some unjust laws, the overall system might be supported and furthered by violating the unjust laws. Until 1954, segregation laws often required African-Americans to sit in the back of the bus. Openly violating such unjust laws might sometimes be the best way

---

[8]John Rawls, *A Theory of Justice* (Cambridge: Harvard University Press, 1971), p. 376.

[9]Rawls, *A Theory of Justice*, p. 334.

[10]Rawls, *A Theory of Justice*, pp. 335–336.

[11]Rawls, *A Theory of Justice*, p. 344.

to get rid of them and thereby to make the whole legal system more just and more stable. Rawls could respond that every open violation of the law carries some risk of harm to the legal system as a whole. However, obeying an unjust law might create even more risk in the long run, and not all risks create moral obligations anyway (see the previous discussion of social harm and risk). So the natural duty to support just institutions does not yield a prima facie moral obligation to obey every law, even in a just system.

There still might be some other argument for a prima facie moral obligation to obey every law. But even if there is no such general obligation, certain people still might have moral obligations to obey certain laws. This raises new questions: *Who* has a prima facie moral obligation to obey *which* laws? Are some of these obligations *stronger* than others? These more specific questions can be answered by considering such factors as harms, risks, gratitude, promises, fairness, and justice in particular kinds of cases.

LEGAL OBLIGATION
AND THE DUTY OF FAIR PLAY

JOHN RAWLS

1. The subject of law and morality suggests many different questions. In particular, it may consider the historical and sociological question as to the way and manner in which moral ideas influence and are influenced by the legal system; or it may involve the question whether moral concepts and principles enter into an adequate definition of law. Again, the topic of law and morality suggests the problem of the legal enforcement of morality and whether the fact that certain conduct is immoral by accepted precepts is sufficient to justify making that conduct a legal offense. Finally, there is the large subject of the study of the rational principles of moral criticism of legal institutions and the moral grounds of our acquiescence in them. I shall be concerned solely with a frag-

ment of this last question: with the grounds for our moral obligation to obey the law, that is, to carry out our legal duties and to fulfill our legal obligations. My thesis is that the moral obligation to obey the law is a special case of the prima facie duty of fair play.

I shall assume, as requiring no argument, that there is, at least in a society such as ours, a moral obligation to obey the law, although it may, of course, be overridden in certain cases by other more stringent obligations. I shall assume also that this obligation must rest on some general moral principle; that is, it must depend on some principle of justice or upon some principle of social utility or the common good, and the like. Now, it may appear to be a truism, and let us suppose it is, that a moral

John Rawls, "Legal Obligation and the Duty of Fair Play," in Sidney Hook, ed., *Law and Philosophy* (New York: New York University Press, 1964), pp. 3–18.

obligation rests on some moral principle. But I mean to exclude the possibility that the obligation to obey the law is based on a special principle of its own. After all, it is not, without further argument, absurd that there is a moral principle such that when we find ourselves subject to an existing system of rules satisfying the definition of a legal system, we have an obligation to obey the law; and such a principle might be final, and not in need of explanation, in the way in which the principles of justice or of promising and the like are final. I do not know of anyone who has said that there is a special principle of legal obligation in this sense. Given a rough agreement, say, on the possible principles as being those of justice, of social utility, and the like, the question has been on which of one or several is the obligation to obey the law founded, and which, if any, has a special importance. I want to give a special place to the principle defining the duty of fair play.

2. In speaking of one's obligation to obey the law, I am using the term "obligation" in its more limited sense, in which, together with the notion of a duty and of a responsibility, it has a connection with institutional rules. Duties and responsibilities are assigned to certain positions and offices, and obligations are normally the consequence of voluntary acts of persons, and while perhaps most of our obligations are assumed by ourselves, through the making of promises and the accepting of benefits, and so forth, others may put us under obligation to them (as when on some occasion they help us, for example, as children). I should not claim that the moral grounds for our obeying the law is derived from the duty of fairplay except insofar as one is referring to an obligation in this sense. It would be incorrect to say that our duty not to commit any of the legal offenses, specifying crimes of violence, is based on the duty of fair play, at least entirely. These crimes involve wrongs as such, and with such offenses, as with the vices of cruelty and greed, our doing them is wrong independently

of there being a legal system the benefits of which we have voluntarily accepted.

I shall assume several special features about the nature of the legal order in regard to which a moral obligation arises. In addition to the generally strategic place of its system of rules, as defining and relating the fundamental institutions of society that regulate the pursuit of substantive interests, and to the monopoly of coercive powers, I shall suppose that the legal system in question satisfies the concept of the *rule of law* (or what one may think of as justice as regularity). By this I mean that its rules are public, that similar cases are treated similarly, that there are no bills of attainder, and the like. These are all features of a legal system insofar as it embodies without deviation the notion of a public system of rules addressed to rational beings for the organization of their conduct in the pursuit of their substantive interests. This concept imposes, by itself, no limits on the *content* of legal rules, but only on their regular administration. Finally, I shall assume that the legal order is that of a constitutional democracy: that is, I shall suppose that there is a constitution establishing a position of equal citizenship and securing freedom of the person, freedom of thought and liberty of conscience, and such political equality as in suffrage and the right to participate in the political process. Thus I am confining discussion to a legal system of a special kind, but there is no harm in this.

3. The moral grounds of legal obligation may be brought out by considering what at first seem to be two anomalous facts: first, that sometimes we have an obligation to obey what we think, and think correctly, is an unjust law; and second, that sometimes we have an obligation to obey a law even in a situation where more good (thought of as a sum of social advantages) would seem to result from not doing so. If the moral obligation to obey the law is founded on the principle of fair play, how can one become bound to obey an unjust law, and what is there about the principle that explains the grounds for forgoing the greater good?

It is, of course, a familiar situation in a constitutional democracy that a person finds himself morally obligated to obey an unjust law. This will be the case whenever a member of the minority, on some legislative proposal, opposes the majority view for reasons of justice. Perhaps the standard case is where the majority, or a coalition sufficient to constitute a majority, takes advantage of its strength and votes in its own interests. But this feature is not essential. A person belonging to the minority may be advantaged by the majority proposal and still oppose it as unjust, yet when it is enacted he will normally be bound by it.

Some have thought that there is ostensibly a paradox of a special kind when a citizen, who votes in accordance with his moral principles (conception of justice), accepts the majority decision when he is in the minority. Let us suppose the vote is between two bills, A and B each establishing an income tax procedure, rates of progression, or the like, which are contrary to one another. Suppose further that one thinks of the constitutional procedure for enacting legislation as a sort of machine that yields a result when the votes are fed into it— the result being that a certain bill is enacted. The question arises as to how a citizen can accept the machine's choice, which (assuming that B gets a majority of the votes) involves thinking that B ought to be enacted when, let us suppose, he is of the declared opinion that A ought to be enacted. For some the paradox seems to be that in a constitutional democracy a citizen is often put in a situation of believing that both A and B should be enacted when A and B are contraries: that A should be enacted because A is the best policy, and that B should be enacted because B has a majority—and moreover, and this is essential, that this conflict is different from the usual sort of conflict between prima facie duties.

There are a number of things that may be said about this supposed paradox, and there are several ways in which it may be resolved, each of which brings out an aspect of the situation.

But I think the simplest thing to say is to deny straightway that there is anything different in this situation than in any other situation where there is a conflict of prima facie principles. The essence of the matter seems to be as follows: (1) Should A or B be enacted and implemented, that is, administered? Since it is supposed that everyone accepts the outcome of the vote, within limits, it is appropriate to put the enactment and implementation together. (2) Is A or B the best policy? It is assumed that everyone votes according to his political opinion as to which is the best policy and that the decision as to how to vote is not based on personal interest. There is no special conflict in this situation: the citizen who knows that he will find himself in the minority believes that, taking into account only the relative merits of A and B as prospective statutes, and leaving aside how the vote will go, A should be enacted and implemented. Moreover, on his own principles he should vote for what he thinks is the best policy, and leave aside how the vote will go. On the other hand, given that a majority will vote for B, B should be enacted and implemented, and he may know that a majority will vote for B. These judgments are relative to different principles (different arguments). The first is based on the person's conception of the best social policy; the second is based on the principles on which he accepts the constitution. The real decision, then, is as follows: A person has to decide, in each case where he is in the minority, whether the nature of the statute is such that, given that it will get, or has got, a majority vote, he should oppose its being implemented, engage in civil disobedience, or take equivalent action. In this situation he simply has to balance his obligation to oppose an unjust statute against his obligation to abide by a just constitution. This is, of course, a difficult situation, but not one introducing any deep logical paradox. Normally, it is hoped that the obligation to the constitution is clearly the decisive one.

Although it is obvious, it may be worthwhile mentioning, since a relevant feature of voting will be brought out, that the result of a vote is that a rule of law is enacted, and although given the fact of its enactment, everyone agrees that it should be implemented, no one is required to believe that the statute enacted represents the best policy. It is consistent to say that another statute would have been better. The vote does not result in a statement to be believed: namely, that B is superior, on its merits, to A. To get this interpretation one would have to suppose that the principles of the constitution specify a device which gathers information as to what citizens think should be done and that the device is so constructed that it always produces from this information the morally correct opinion as to which is the best policy. If in accepting a constitution it was so interpreted, there would, indeed, be a serious paradox: for a citizen would be torn between believing, on his own principles, that A is the best policy, and believing at the same time that B is the best policy as established by the constitutional device, the principles of the design of which he accepts. This conflict could be made a normal one only if one supposed that a person who made his own judgment on the merits was always prepared to revise it given the opinion constructed by the machine. But it is not possible to determine the best policy in this way, nor is it possible for a person to give such an undertaking. What this misinterpretation of the constitutional procedure shows, I think, is that there is an important difference between voting and spending. The constitutional procedure is not, in an essential respect, the same as the market: Given the usual assumptions of perfect competition of price theory, the actions of private persons spending according to their interests will result in the best situation, as judged by the criterion of Pareto. But in a perfectly just constitutional procedure, people voting their political opinions on the merits of policies may or may not reflect the best policy. What this misinterpretation brings out, then, is that when citizens vote for policies on their merits, the constitutional procedure cannot be viewed as acting as the market does, even under ideal conditions. A constitutional procedure does not reconcile differences of opinion into an opinion to be taken as true—this can only be done by argument and reasoning—but rather it decides whose opinion is to determine legislative policy.

4. Now to turn to the main problem, that of understanding how a person can properly find himself in a position where, by his own principles, he must grant that, given a majority vote, B should be enacted and implemented even though B is unjust. There is, then, the question as to how it can be morally justifiable to acknowledge a constitutional procedure for making legislative enactments when it is certain (for all practical purposes) that laws will be passed that by one's own principles are unjust. It would be impossible for a person to undertake to change his mind whenever he found himself in the minority; it is not impossible, but entirely reasonable, for him to undertake to abide by the enactments made, whatever they are, provided that they are within certain limits. But what more exactly are the conditions of this undertaking?

First of all, it means, as previously suggested, that the constitutional procedure is misinterpreted as a procedure for making legal rules. It is a process of social decision that does not produce a statement to be believed (that B is the best policy) but a rule to be followed. Such a procedure, say involving some form of majority rule, is necessary because it is certain that there will be disagreement on what is the best policy. This will be true even if we assume, as I shall, that everyone has a similar sense of justice and everyone is able to agree on a certain constitutional procedure as just. There will be disagreement because they will not approach issues with the same stock of information, they will regard different moral features of situations as carrying different weights, and so on. The acceptance of a constitutional procedure is, then, a necessary political device to decide between conflicting legislative proposals. If one thinks of the constitution as a fundamental part of the scheme of social cooperation, then one can say that if the constitution is just, and if one has accepted the benefits of its working and intends to continue doing so, and if the rule enacted is within certain limits, then one has an obligation, based on the principle of fair play, to obey it when it comes one's turn. In accepting the benefits of a just constitution one becomes bound to it, and in particular one becomes bound to one of its fundamental rules: given a majority vote in behalf of a statute, it is to be enacted and properly implemented.

The principle of fair play may be defined as follows. Suppose there is a mutually beneficial and just scheme of social cooperation, and that the advantages it yields can only be obtained if everyone, or nearly everyone, cooperates. Suppose further that cooperation requires a certain sacrifice from each person, or at least involves a certain restriction of his liberty. Suppose finally that the benefits produced by cooperation are, up to a certain point, free: that is, the scheme of cooperation is unstable in the sense that if any one person knows that all (or nearly all) of the others will continue to do their part, he will still be able to share a gain from the scheme even if he does not do his part. Under these conditions a person who has accepted the benefits of the scheme is bound by a duty of fair play to do his part and not to take advantage of the free benefit by not cooperating. The reason one must abstain from this attempt is that the existence of the benefit is the result of everyone's effort, and prior to some understanding as to how it is to be shared, if it can be shared at all, it belongs in fairness to no one. (I return to this question below.)

Now I want to hold that the obligation to obey the law, as enacted by a constitutional procedure, even when the law seems unjust to us, is a case of the duty of fair play as defined. It is, moreover, an obligation in the more limited sense in that it depends upon our having accepted and our intention to continue accepting the benefits of a just scheme of cooperation that the constitution defines. In this sense it de-

pends on our own voluntary acts. Again, it is an obligation owed to our fellow citizens generally: that is, to those who cooperate with us in the working of the constitution. It is not an obligation owed to public officials, although there may be such obligations. That it is an obligation owed by citizens to one another is shown by the fact that they are entitled to be indignant with one another for failure to comply. Further, an essential condition of the obligation is the justice of the constitution and the general system of law being roughly in accordance with it. Thus the obligation to obey (or not to resist) an unjust law depends strongly on there being a just constitution. Unless one obeys the law enacted under it, the proper equilibrium, or balance, between competing claims defined by the constitution will not be maintained. Finally, while it is true enough to say that the enactment by a majority binds the minority, so that one may be bound by the acts of others, there is no question of their binding them in conscience to certain beliefs as to what is the best policy, and it is a necessary condition of the acts of others binding us that the constitution is just, that we have accepted its benefits, and so forth.

5. Now a few remarks about the principles of a just constitution. Here I shall have to presuppose a number of things about the principles of justice. In particular, I shall assume that there are two principles of justice that properly apply to the fundamental structure of institutions of the social system and, thus, to the constitution. The first of these principles requires that everyone have an equal right to the most extensive liberty compatible with a like liberty for all; the second is that inequalities are arbitrary unless it is reasonable to expect that they will work out for everyone's advantage and provided that the positions and offices to which they attach or from which they may be gained are open to all. I shall assume that these are the principles that can be derived by imposing the constraints of morality upon rational and mutually self-interested persons when

they make conflicting claims on the basic form of their common institutions: that is, when questions of justice arise.

The principle relevant at this point is the first principle, that of equal liberty. I think it may be argued with some plausibility that it requires, where it is possible, the various equal liberties in a constitutional democracy. And once these liberties are established and constitutional procedures exist, one can view legislation as rules enacted that must be ostensibly compatible with both principles. Each citizen must decide as best he can whether a piece of legislation, say the income tax, violates either principle; and this judgment depends on a wide body of social facts. Even in a society of impartial and rational persons, one cannot expect agreement on these matters.

Now recall that the question is this: How is it possible that a person, in accordance with his own conception of justice, should find himself bound by the acts of another to obey an unjust law (not simply a law contrary to his interests)? Put another way: Why, when I am free and still without my chains, should I accept certain a priori conditions to which any social contract must conform, a priori conditions that rule out all constitutional procedures that would decide in accordance with my judgment of justice against everyone else? To explain this (Little has remarked),[1] we require two hypotheses: that among the very limited number of procedures that would stand any chance of being established, none would make my decision decisive in this way; and that all such procedures would determine social conditions that I judge to be better than anarchy. Granting the second hypothesis, I want to elaborate on this in the following way: the first step in the explanation is to derive the principles of justice that are to apply to the basic form of the social system and, in particular, to the constitution. Once we have these principles, we see that no just constitutional procedure would make my judgment as to the best policy decisive (would make me a dictator in Arrow's sense).[2] It is not simply that,

among the limited number of procedures actually possible as things are, no procedure would give me this authority. The point is that even if such were possible, given some extraordinary social circumstances, it would not be just. (Of course it is not possible for everyone to have this authority.) Once we see this, we see how it is possible that within the framework of a just constitutional procedure to which we are obligated, it may nevertheless happen that we are bound to obey what seems to us to be and is an unjust law. Moreover, the possibility is present even though everyone has the same sense of justice (that is, accepts the same principles of justice) and everyone regards the constitutional procedure itself as just. Even the most efficient constitution cannot prevent the enactment of unjust laws if, from the complexity of the social situation and like conditions, the majority decides to enact them. A just constitutional procedure cannot foreclose all injustice; this depends on those who carry out the procedure. A constitutional procedure is not like a market reconciling interests to an optimum result.

6. So far I have been discussing the first mentioned anomaly of legal obligation, namely, that though it is founded on justice, we may be required to obey an unjust law. I should now like to include the second anomaly: that we may have an obligation to obey the law even though more good (thought of as a sum of advantages) may be gained by not doing so. The thesis I wish to argue is that not only is our obligation to obey the law a special case of the principle of fair play, and so dependent upon the justice of the institutions to which we are obligated, but also the principles of justice are absolute with respect to the principle of utility (as the principle to maximize the net sum of advantages). By this I mean two things. First, unjust institutions cannot be justified by an appeal to the principle of utility. A greater balance of net advantages shared by some cannot justify the injustice suffered by others; and where unjust institutions are tolerable it is because a certain degree of injustice sometimes cannot be

avoided, that social necessity requires it, that there would be greater injustice otherwise, and so on. Second, our obligation to obey the law, which is a special case of the principle of fair play, cannot be overridden by an appeal to utility, though it may be overridden by another duty of justice. These are *sweeping* propositions and most likely false, but I should like to examine them briefly.

I do not know how to establish these propositions. They are not established by the sort of argument used above to show that the two principles, previously mentioned, are the two principles of justice, that is, when the subject is the basic structure of the social system. What such an argument might show is that, if certain natural conditions are taken as specifying the concept of justice, then the two principles of justice are the principles logically associated with the concept when the subject is the basic structure of the social system. The argument might prove, if it is correct, that the principles of justice are incompatible with the principle of utility. The argument might establish that our intuitive notions of justice must sometimes conflict with the principle of utility. But it leaves unsettled what the more general notion of right requires when this conflict occurs. To prove that the concept of justice should have an absolute weight with respect to that of utility would require a deeper argument based on an analysis of the concept of right, at least insofar as it relates to the concepts of justice and utility. I have no idea whether such an analysis is possible. What I propose to do instead is to try out the thought that the concept of justice does have an absolute weight, and to see whether this suggestion, in view of our considered moral opinions, leads to conclusions that we cannot accept. It would seem as if to attribute to justice an absolute weight is to interpret the concept of right as requiring that a special place be given to persons capable of a sense of justice and to the principle of their working out together, from an initial position of equality, the form of their common institu-

tions. To the extent that this idea is attractive, the concept of justice will tend to have an absolute weight with respect to utility.

7. Now to consider the two anomalous cases. First: In the situation where the obligation requires obedience to an unjust law, it *seems* true to say that the obligation depends on the principle of fair play and, thus, on justice. Suppose it is a matter of a person being required to pay an income tax of a kind that he thinks is unjust, not simply by reference to his interests. He would not want to try to justify the tax on the ground that the net gain to certain groups in society is such as to outweigh the injustice. The natural argument to make is to his obligation to a just constitution.

But in considering a particular issue, a citizen has to make two decisions: how he will vote (and I assume that he votes for what he thinks is the best policy, morally speaking), and, in case he should be in the minority, whether his obligation to support, or not obstruct, the implementation of the law enacted is not overridden by a stronger obligation that may lead to a number of courses including civil disobedience. Now in the sort of case imagined, suppose there is a real question as to whether the tax law should be obeyed. Suppose, for example, that it is framed in such a way that it seems deliberately calculated to undermine unjustly the position of certain social or religious groups. Whether the law should be obeyed or not depends, if one wants to emphasize the notion of justice, on such matters as (1) the justice of the constitution and the real opportunity it allows for reversal; (2) the depth of the injustice of the law enacted; (3) whether the enactment is actually a matter of calculated intent by the majority and warns of further such acts; and (4) whether the political sociology of the situation is such as to allow of hope that the law may be repealed. Certainly, if a social or religious group reasonably (not irrationally) and correctly supposes that a permanent majority, or majority coalition, has deliberately set out to undercut its basis and that there is no chance of successful constitutional resistance, then the obligation to obey that particular law (and perhaps other laws more generally) ceases. In such a case a minority may no longer be obligated by the duty of fair play. There may be other reasons, of course, at least for a time, for obeying the law. One might say that disobedience will not improve the justice of their situation or of their descendants' situation; or that it will result in injury and harm to innocent persons (that is, members not belonging to the unjust majority). In this way, one might appeal to the balance of justice, if the principle of not causing injury to the innocent is a question of justice; but, in any case, the appeal is not made to the greater net balance of advantages (irrespective of the moral portion of those receiving them). The thesis I want to suggest then, is that in considering whether we are obligated to obey an unjust law, one is led into no absurdity if one simply throws out the principle of utility altogether, except insofar as it is included in the general principle requiring one to establish the most efficient just institutions.

Second: Now the other sort of anomaly arises when the law is just and we have a duty of fair play to follow it, but a greater net balance of advantages could be gained from not doing so. Again, the income tax will serve to illustrate this familiar point: The social consequences of any one person (perhaps even many people) not paying his tax are unnoticeable, and let us suppose zero in value, but there is a noticeable private gain for the person himself, or for another to whom he chooses to give it (the institution of the income tax is subject to the first kind of instability). The duty of fair play binds us to pay our tax, nevertheless, since we have accepted, and intend to continue doing so, the benefits of the fiscal system to which the income tax belongs. Why is this reasonable and not a blind following of a rule, when a greater net sum of advantages is possible?—because the system of cooperation consistently followed by everyone else itself produces the advantages generally enjoyed and in the

case of a practice such as the income tax there is no reason to give exemptions to anyone so, that they might enjoy the possible benefit. (An analogous case is the moral obligation to vote and so to work the constitutional procedure from which one has benefited. This obligation cannot be overridden by the fact that our vote never makes a difference in the outcome of an election; it may be overridden, however, by a number of other considerations, such as a person being disenchanted with all parties, being excusably uninformed, and the like.)

There are cases, on the other hand, where a certain number of exemptions can be arranged for in a just or fair way; and if so, the practice, including the exemptions, is more efficient, and when possible it should be adopted (waiving problems of transition) in accordance with the principle of establishing the most efficient just practice. For example, in the familiar instance of the regulation to conserve water in a drought, it might be ascertained that there would be no harm in a certain extra use of water over and above the use for drinking. In this case some rotation scheme can be adopted that allots exemptions in a fair way, such as houses on opposite sides of the street being given exemptions on alternate days. The details are not significant here. The main idea is simply that if the greater sum of advantages can effectively and fairly be distributed amongst those whose cooperation makes these advantages possible, then this should be done. It would indeed be irrational to prefer a lesser to a more efficient just scheme of cooperation; but this fact is not to be confused with justifying an unjust scheme by its greater efficiency or excusing ourselves from a duty of fair play by an appeal to utility. If there is no reason to distribute the possible benefit, as in the case of the income tax, or in the case of voting, or if there is no way to do so that does not involve such problems as excessive costs, then the benefit should be foregone. One may disagree with this view, but it is not irrational, not a matter of rule worship: it is, rather, an appeal to the duty of fair play, which requires one to abstain from an advantage that cannot be distributed fairly to those whose efforts have made it possible. That those who make the efforts and undergo the restrictions of their liberty should share in the benefits produced is a consequence of the assumption of an initial position of equality, and it falls under the second principle. But the question of distributive justice is too involved to go into here. Moreover, it is unlikely that there is any substantial social benefit for the distribution of which some fair arrangement cannot be made.

8. To summarize, I have suggested that the following propositions may be true:

First, that our moral obligation to obey the law is a special case of the duty of fair play. This means that the legal order is construed as a system of social cooperation to which we become bound because: first, the scheme is just (that is, it satisfies the two principles of justice), and no just scheme can ensure against our ever being in the minority in a vote; and second, we have accepted, and intend to continue to accept, its benefits. If we failed to obey the law, to act on our duty of fair play, the equilibrium between conflicting claims, as defined by the concept of justice, would be upset. The duty of fair play is not, of course, intended to account for its being wrong for us to commit crimes of violence, but it is intended to account, in part, for the obligation to pay our income tax, to vote, and so on.

Second, I then suggested that the concept of justice has an absolute weight with respect to the principle of utility (not necessarily with respect to other moral concepts). By that I meant that the union of the two concepts of justice and utility must take the form of the principle of establishing the most efficient just institution. This means that an unjust institution or law cannot be justified by an appeal to a greater net sum of advantages, and that the duty of fair play cannot be analogously overridden. An unjust institution or law or the overriding of the duty of fair play can be justified only by a greater balance of justice. I know of no way to prove this proposition. It is not proved by the analytic argument to show that the principles of justice are indeed the principles of justice. But I think it may be shown that the principle to establish the most efficient just institutions does not lead to conclusions counter to our intuitive judgments and that it is not in any way irrational. It is, moreover, something of a theoretical simplification, in that one does not have to balance justice against utility. But this simplification is no doubt not a real one, since it is as difficult to ascertain the balance of justice as anything else.

NOTES

[1]The metaphor of being free and without one's chains is taken from I. M. D. Little's review of K. Arrow's book *Social Choice and Individual Values*, (New York, 1951) which appeared in *Journal of Political Economy*, LX (1952). See p. 431. My argument follows his in all essential respects, the only addition being that I have introduced the concept of justice in accounting for what is, in effect, Arrow's non–dictatorship condition.

[2]See Arrow, *opus cit. supra*.

QUESTIONS FOR DISCUSSION

1. Rawls lists several conditions that are supposed to be necessary for the principle of fairness to apply. Explain why Rawls sees each condition as necessary. Do you agree that each condition is necessary? Why or why not?

2. Do you agree that it is always unfair not to pay taxes that you are legally required to pay? Why or why not?

3. Does Rawls' principle of fair play imply that every citizen has the same moral obligation to obey the law? Why or why not?

4. Suppose there is a law against gambling, even in private. Bernie's benefits from private gambling do not depend on other people refraining from private gambling. He might even prefer it if other people gambled more, since then he would have more people to play with and to win money from. Thus, his benefits from disobedience do not depend on others' obedience and sacrifice. Does Rawls' argument from fairness imply a moral obligation for Bernie not to gamble? Do you think that Bernie has any moral obligation not to gamble? Why or why not?

5. In Rawls' view, did African-Americans during the 1940s have prima facie moral obligations to obey laws that required them to sit at the back of the bus? Do you think that they had such an obligation? Why or why not?

6. Does Rawls' argument from fairness imply that homosexuals have a prima facie moral obligation to obey laws against sodomy? Do you think that homosexuals have this obligation? Why or why not? Does your answer depend on your views of whether sodomy is immoral independent of the law? Does your answer depend on your views about the nature of law?

THE PRINCIPLE OF FAIR PLAY

A. JOHN SIMMONS

I

The traditional consent theory account of political obligation can be understood as advancing two basic claims. (1) All or most citizens, at least within reasonably just political communities, have political obligations (that is, moral obligations or duties to obey the law and support the political institutions of their countries of residence). (2) All political obligations are grounded in personal consent (express or tacit). Today most political philosophers (and nonphilosophers, I suspect) are still prepared to accept (1). But (2) has been widely rejected largely because it entails, in conjunction with (1), that

all or most of us have undertaken political obligations by *deliberate consensual acts*. And this seems not even approximately true. If it is not true, then (1) requires a defense employing a more complex account of special rights and obligations than the one offered by consent theory.

One popular way of defending (1) relies on what has been called "the principle of fair play" (or "the principle of fairness").[1] Advocates of this principle argue that promises and deliberate consent are not the only possible grounds of special rights and obligations; the acceptance of benefits within certain sorts of cooperative schemes, they maintain, is by itself sufficient to

A. John Simmons, "The Principle of Fair Play," *Philosophy and Public Affairs*, vol. 8, no. 4 (1979), pp. 307–337. Copyright © 1979 by Princeton University Press.

generate such rights and obligations. It is these arguments I want to examine.

. . . [R]egardless of the advantages this account may have over the consent-theory account, it surely falls short on one score. Consent is a *clear* ground of obligation. If we are agreed on anything concerning moral requirements, it is that promising and consenting generate them. In specifying a different ground of obligation, the account using the principle of fair play draws away from the paradigm of acts that generate obligations. And to those who are strongly wedded to this paradigm of consent, such as Robert Nozick, the principle of fair play may seem a sham.

IV

In Chapter 5 of *Anarchy, State, and Utopia*, Nozick argues against accepting the principle of fair play as a valid moral principle, not just in political settings, but in any settings whatsoever. He begins by describing a cooperative scheme of the sort he thinks Hart and Rawls have in mind, and then suggests that benefaction within that scheme may *not* bind one to do one's part:

> Suppose some of the people in your neighborhood (there are 364 other adults) have found a public address system and decide to institute a system of public entertainment. They post a list of names, one for each day, yours among them. On his assigned day (one can easily switch days) a person is to run the public address system, play records over it, give news bulletins, tell amusing stories he has heard, and so on. After 138 days on which each person has done his part, your day arrives. Are you obligated to take your turn? You *have* benefited from it, occasionally opening your window to listen, enjoying some music or chuckling at someone's funny story. The other people *have* put themselves out. But must you answer the call when it is your turn to do so? As it stands, surely not. Though you benefit from

the arrangement, you may know all along that 364 days of entertainment supplied by others will not be worth your giving up *one* day. You would rather not have any of it and not give up a day than have it all and spend one of your days at it. Given these preferences, how can it be that you are required to participate when your scheduled time comes?[13]

On the basis of this example and others, Nozick concludes that we are never bound to cooperate in such contexts (unless we have given our consent to be constrained by the rules of the cooperative scheme).

Now, to be fair, Nozick does not simply pick the weakest form of the principle of fair play and then reject it for its inadequacy in hard cases; he has, in fact, a suggestion for improving the principle in response to the cases he describes. Having noticed, I suppose, that the case described above favors his conclusions largely because of the negligible value of the benefits received, Nozick suggests that "at the very least one wants to build into the principle of fairness the condition that the benefits to a person from the actions of others are greater than the cost to him of doing his share" (Nozick, p. 94). There is certainly something right about this; something like this must be built into the idea of a useful cooperative scheme. On the other hand, we can imagine a defender of the principle saying "if you weren't prepared to do your part you ought not to have taken *any* benefits from the scheme, no matter how insignificant." Nozick, of course, has more to say on this point, and so do I.

Even if we do modify the principle with this condition, however, Nozick has other arguments against it. "The benefits might only barely be worth the costs to you of doing your share, yet others might benefit from *this* institution much more than you do; they all treasure listening to the public broadcasts. As the person least benefited by the practice, are you obligated to do an equal amount for it?" (Nozick, p. 94). The understood answer is no, but we might agree with this answer without agreeing that it tells against the principle. For if we understand that "doing one's part" or "doing one's fair share" is not necessarily "doing an equal part," but rather "doing a part proportionate to the part of the benefits received," then the one who benefits least from a cooperative scheme will *not* be bound to share equally in the burdens of cooperation. [I]f we accept [this interpretation], Nozick's PA system example may no longer seem so troublesome. For we might be willing to admit that the individual in question, because he benefited so little, was bound to cooperate but not to the same extent as others who benefit more from the scheme. Would being obligated to do one's part in the PA scheme seem quite so objectionable if one's part was only, say, an hour's worth of broadcasting, as opposed to that of the PA enthusiasts, whose parts were one and a half days of broadcasting? There are, perhaps, not clear answers to these questions.

But surely the defender of the principle of fair play will have more fundamental objections to Nozick's case than these. In the first place, the individual in Nozick's PA example does not seem to be a *participant* in the scheme in the sense that Hart and Rawls may have in mind. While he does live in the neighborhood within which the scheme operates, and he does benefit from it, he is still very much of an "innocent bystander." The PA system scheme has been built up around him in such a way that he could not escape its influence. And, of course, the whole force of Nozick's example lies in our feeling that others ought not to be able to *force* any scheme they like upon us, with the attendant obligations. The PA case would be precisely such a case of "forced" obligation. So naturally we may find Nozick's criticism of the principle of fair play convincing, if we believe the principle to entail that we *do* have obligations under the PA scheme.

But it seems clear that Hart and Rawls did not mean for the principle to apply to such cases of "innocent bystanders" (though admit-

tedly neither emphasizes the point). Nozick's case seems to rest on a reading of the principle which runs contrary to the spirit of their remarks, a reading according to which the principle binds everyone who benefits from a cooperation scheme, regardless of their relations to it. And Nozick is surely right that a moral principle which had those results *would* be an outrageous one. People who have no significant relationship at all with some cooperative scheme may receive incidental benefits from its operation. Thus, imagine yourself a member of some scheme which benefits you immensely by increasing your income. Your friends and relatives may benefit incidentally from the scheme as well if, say, you now become prone to send them expensive presents. But the suggestion that their benefiting in this way obligates them to do their part in the scheme is absurd.

Hart and Rawls can most fairly be read as holding that only beneficiaries who are also participants (in some significant sense) are bound under the principle of fair play. And on this reading, of course, Nozick's PA system example does not seem to be a case to which the principle applies; the individual in question is not a participant in the scheme, having had nothing to do with its institution, and having done nothing to lead anyone to believe that he wished to become involved in the scheme. The example, then, cannot serve as a counterexample to Hart's principle. In fact, all of Nozick's examples in his criticisms of Hart are examples in which an "outsider" has some benefit thrust on him by some cooperative scheme to which he is in no way tied (see Nozick's "street-sweeping," "lawn-mowing," and "book-thrusting" examples, pp. 94–95). But if I am right, these examples do not tell against the principle of fair play, since the benefits accruing to "outsiders" are not thought by Hart and Rawls to bind under that principle.

The problem of specifying who are "outsiders," and consequently whose benefits will count, is a serious one, especially in the political applications of the principle. And it seems that the problem may provide ammunition for a serious counterattack by someone such as Nozick against the principle of fair play. We have maintained, remember, that only "participants" or "insiders" in the cooperative scheme are candidates for being obligated under the principle to do their share in cooperating. Those "outsiders" who benefit from the scheme's operation are not bound under the principle of fair play. But how exactly do we differentiate between these outsiders and the insiders? What relationship must hold between an individual and a cooperative scheme for him to be said to be a participant in some significant sense?

This is a hard question to answer, but we have already considered some cases where an individual is *not* a participant in the right sense. Thus, merely being a member of some group, other members of which institute a scheme, is not enough to make one a participant or an "insider." Although Nozick's man is a "member" of an identifiable group, namely his neighborhood, this "membership" does not suffice to make him a participant in any scheme his neighbors dream up. Normally, we would want to say that for an individual to be a real participant in a cooperative scheme, he must have either (1) pledged his support or tacitly agreed to be governed by the scheme's rules, or (2) played some active role in the scheme after its institution. It is not enough to be associated with the "schemers" in some vague way to make one an "insider" or a participant; one must go out and do things to become a participant and to potentially be bound under the principle of fair play. . . .

For Rawls and Hart, the principle of fair play accounts for the obligations of those whose active role in the scheme consists of accepting the benefits of its workings. One becomes a participant in the scheme precisely by accepting the benefits it offers; the other ways in which one can become a participant are not important to considerations of fair play. And individuals who have merely *received* benefits

from the scheme have the same status relative to it as those who have been unaffected by the scheme; they are not in any way bound to do their part in the scheme unless they have independently undertaken to do so. If, as I've suggested, the acceptance of benefits constitutes the sort of "participation" in a scheme with which Rawls and Hart are concerned, we can understand why neither Rawls nor Hart specifically limits the application of the principle to *participants* in the scheme. This limitation has already been accomplished by making obligation conditional on the acceptance of benefits. This means, of course, that the principle cannot be read as the outrageous one which requires anyone at all who benefits from the scheme to do his part in it. . . .

The reading of the principle which I have given obviously places a very heavy load on the notion of "acceptance," a notion to which we have as yet given no clear meaning (and Rawls and Hart certainly give us no help on this count). It is not at all easy to distinguish in practice between benefits that have been accepted and those that have only been received, although some cases seem clearly to fall on the "merely received" side. Thus, benefits we have actively resisted getting, and those which we have gotten unknowingly or in ways over which we have had no control at all, seem clearly *not* to be benefits we have accepted. To have accepted a benefit, I think, we would want to say that an individual must either (1) have tried to get (and succeeded in getting) the benefit, or (2) have taken the benefit willingly and knowingly.

Consider now Nozick's example of the program that involves "thrusting books" into unsuspecting people's houses. Clearly the benefits in question are merely received, not accepted. "One cannot," Nozick writes, "whatever one's purposes, just act so as to give people benefits and then demand (or seize) payment. Nor can a group of persons do this" (p. 95). I am suggesting that, on the contrary, the principle of fair play does *not* involve justifying this sort of behavior; people are only bound under the principle when they have accepted benefits.

Nozick's first-line example, the PA scheme, however, is slightly more difficult. For here the benefits received are not forced upon you, as in the "book-thrusting" case, or gotten in some other way which is outside your control. Rather, the benefits are what I will call "open"; while they can be avoided, they cannot be avoided without considerable inconvenience. Thus, while I can avoid the (questionable) benefits the PA system provides by remaining indoors with the windows closed, this is a considerable inconvenience. The benefits are "open" in the sense that I cannot avoid receiving them, even if I want to, without altering my life style (economists often have such benefits in mind in speaking of "public goods"). Many benefits yielded by cooperative schemes (in fact most benefits, I should think) are "open" in this way. A neighborhood organization's program to improve the neighborhood's appearance yields benefits which are "open." And the benefits of government are mostly of this sort. The benefits of the rule of law, protection by the armed forces, pollution control, and so on can be avoided only by emigration.

We can contrast these cases of "open" benefits with benefits that are only "readily available." If instead of a PA system, Nozick's group had decided to rent a building in the middle of town in which live entertainment was continuously available to neighborhood members, the benefits of the scheme would only be "readily available." A good example of the distinction under consideration would be the distinction between two sorts of police protection, one sort being an "open" benefit, the other being only "readily available." Thus, the benefits which I receive from the continuous efforts of police officers to patrol the streets, capture criminals, and eliminate potential threats to my safety, are benefits which are "open." They can be avoided only by leaving the area which the police force protects. But I may also request *special* protection by the police, if I fear for my life,

say, or if I need my house to be watched while I'm away. These benefits are "readily available." Benefits which are "readily available" can be easily avoided without inconvenience.

Now I think that clear cases of the acceptance of benefits, as opposed to receipt, will be easy to find where benefits which are only "readily available" are concerned. Getting these benefits will involve going out of one's way, making some sort of effort to get the benefit, and hence there will generally be no question that the benefit was accepted in the sense we have described. The principle of fair play seems most clearly to apply in cases such as these. These will be cases where our actions may obviously fall short of constituting *consent* to do our part in the scheme in question, but where our acceptance of benefits binds us to do our part because of considerations of fair play. When we accept benefits in such cases, it may be necessary that we be aware that the benefits in question *are* the fruits of a cooperative scheme, in order for us to be willing to ascribe any obligations of fair play; but it will *not* be necessary that some express or tacit act of consent have been performed.

The examples of "open" benefits are, of course, harder to handle. Nozick's comments seem quite reasonable with respect to them. For surely it is very implausible to suggest that if we are unwilling to do our part, we must alter our life styles in order to avoid enjoying these benefits. As Nozick suggests, there is surely no reason why, when the street-sweeping scheme comes to your town, you must "imagine dirt as you traverse the street, so as not to benefit as a free rider" (p. 94). Nozick's comments here do not, however, strike against the principle of fair play in any obvious way. For as I have interpreted it, the principle does not apply to cases of mere receipt of benefits from cooperative schemes; and the cases where the benefits are "open" in this way seem to be cases of mere receipt of benefits. Certainly it would be peculiar if a man, who by simply going about his business in a normal fashion benefited unavoidably from some cooperative scheme, were told that he had voluntarily accepted benefits which generated for him a special obligation to do his part.

This problem of "acceptance" and "open benefits" is a serious one, and there are real difficulties involved in solving it. It may look, for instance, as if I am saying that a genuine acceptance of open benefits is impossible. But I would not want to be pushed so far. It seems to me that it is possible to accept a benefit which is (in one sense) unavoidable; but it is not at all the *normal* case that those who receive open benefits from a scheme have also accepted those benefits. In the case of benefits which are only "readily available," receipt of the benefits is generally *also* acceptance. But this is not so in the case of open benefits. I suggested earlier that accepting a benefit involved either (1) trying to get (and succeeding in getting) the benefit, or (2) taking the benefit willingly and knowingly. Getting benefits which are "readily available" normally involves (1) trying to get the benefit. It is not clear, however, how one would go about *trying* to get an open benefit which is not distributed by request, but is rather received by everyone involved, whether they want it or not. If open benefits can be accepted, it would seem that method (2) of accepting benefits is the way in which this is normally accomplished. We can take the open benefits which we receive willingly and knowingly. But doing so involves a number of restrictions on our attitudes toward and beliefs about the open benefits we receive. We cannot, for instance, regard the benefits as having been forced upon us against our will, or think that the benefits are not worth the price we must pay for them. And taking the benefits "knowingly" seems to involve an understanding of the status of those benefits relative to the party providing them. Thus, in the case of open benefits provided by a cooperative scheme, we must understand that the benefits *are* provided by the cooperative scheme in order to accept them.

The necessity of satisfying such conditions, however, seems to significantly reduce the number of individuals who receive open benefits, who can be taken to have *accepted* those benefits. And it will by no means be a standard case in which all beneficiaries of a cooperative scheme's workings have accepted the benefits they receive.

I recognize, of course, that problems concerning "acceptance" remain. But even if they did not, my reading of the principle of fair play, as binding only those who have accepted benefits, would still face difficulties. The fact remains that we *do* criticize persons as "free riders" (in terms of fair play) for not doing their part, even when they have *not* accepted benefits from a cooperative scheme. We often criticize them merely because they *receive* benefits without doing their part in the cooperative scheme. Let us go back to Nozick's neighborhood and imagine another, more realistic cooperative scheme in operation, this one designed to beautify the neighborhood by assigning to each resident a specific task involving landscaping or yard work. Home owners are required to care for their yards and to do some work on community property on weekends. There are also a number of apartments in the neighborhood, but because the apartment grounds are cared for by the landlords, apartment dwellers are expected only to help on community property (they are expected to help because even tenants are granted full community membership and privileges; and it is reasoned that all residents have an equal interest in the neighborhood's appearance, at least during the time they remain). Two of these apartment dwellers, Oscar and Willie, refuse to do their part in the scheme. Oscar refuses because he hates neatly trimmed yards, preferring crabgrass, long weeds, and scraggly bushes. The residents do not feel so bad about Oscar (although they try to force him out of the neighborhood), since he does not seem to be benefiting from their efforts without putting out. He hates what they are doing to the neighborhood. Willie, however, is another case altogether. He values a neat neighborhood as much as the others; but he values his spare time more than the others. While he enjoys a beautiful neighborhood, the part he is expected to play in the cooperative scheme involves too much of his time. He makes it clear that he would prefer to have an ugly neighborhood to joining such a scheme.

So while the others labor to produce an almost spotless neighborhood, Willie enjoys the benefits resulting from their efforts while doing nothing to help. And it seems to me that Willie is *just* the sort of person who would be accused by the neighborhood council of "free riding," of unfairly benefiting from the cooperative efforts of others; for he receives exactly the same benefits as the others while contributing nothing. Yet Willie has not accepted the benefits in question, for he thinks that the price being demanded is too high. He would prefer doing without the benefits to having the benefits and the burdens.

So it looks as if the way in which we have filled out the principle of fair play is not entirely in accord with some common feelings about matters of fair play; for these common feelings do not seem to require acceptance of benefits within the scheme, as our version of the principle does. It is against these "ordinary feelings about fair play" (and not against the "filled–out" principle we have been describing), I think, that Nozick's arguments, and the "Nozickian" arguments suggested, strike most sharply.

But Willie's position is *not* substantially different from that of the salesman, Sam, whose sole territory is the neighborhood in question. Sam works eight hours every day in the neighborhood, enjoying its beauty, while Willie (away at work all day) may eke out his forty weekly hours of enjoyment if he stays home on weekends. Thus, Sam and Willie receive substantially the same benefits. Neither Sam nor Willie has done anything at all to ally himself with the cooperative scheme, and neither has "accepted" the fruits of that scheme. Willie is a "member" of the community only because the council voted to award "membership" to tenants, and he has made no commitments. To make the parallel complete, we can even sup-

pose that Sam, beloved by all the residents, is named by the council an "honorary member." But if the neighborhood council accused Sam, the salesman, of "free riding" and demanded that *he* work on community property, their position would be laughable. Why, though, should Willie, who is like Sam in all important respects, be any *more* vulnerable to such accusations and demands?

The answer is that he is *not* any more vulnerable; if ordinary feelings about obligations of fair play insist that he is more vulnerable, those feelings are mistaken. But in fairness to Nozick, the way that Hart and Rawls phrase their account of the principle of fair play *does* sometimes look as if it expresses those (mistaken) feelings about fair play. As Rawls states it,

> The main idea is that when a number of persons engage in a mutually advantageous cooperative venture according to rules, and thus restrict their liberty in ways necessary to yield advantages for all, those who have submitted to these restrictions have a right to a similar acquiescence on the part of those who have benefited from their submission. We are not to gain from the cooperative labors of others without doing our fair share.[14]

This certainly looks like a condemnation of Willie's actions. Of course, the way in which Rawls fills out this idea, in terms of accepting benefits and taking advantage of the scheme, points in quite a different direction; for on the "filled–out" principle, Willie is not bound to cooperate, and neither is the salesman.

It looks, then, as if we have a choice to make between a general principle (which binds all beneficiaries of a scheme) which is *very* implausible, and a more limited principle which is more plausible. I say that we have a choice to make simply because it seems clear that the limited principle is much more limited than either Hart or Rawls realized. For if my previous suggestions were correct, participants in cooperative schemes which produce "open" benefits will not always have a right to cooperation on the part of those who benefit from their labors. And this does not look like a result that either Hart or Rawls would be prepared to accept. Perhaps it is, after all, just the result Nozick wished to argue for.

V

When we move to political communities the "schemes of social cooperation" with which we will be concerned will naturally be schemes on a rather grand scale. . . . While it is clear that at least most citizens in most states *receive* benefits from the workings of their legal and political institutions, how plausible is it to say that they have voluntarily *accepted* those benefits? Not, I think, very plausible. The benefits in question have been mentioned before: the rule of law, protection by armed forces, pollution control, maintenance of highway systems, avenues of political participation, and so on. But these benefits are what we have called "open" benefits. It is precisely in cases of such "open" benefits that it is least plausible to suggest that benefits are being *accepted* by most beneficiaries. It will, of course, be difficult to be certain about the acceptance of benefits in actual cases; but on any natural understanding of the notion of "acceptance," our having accepted open benefits involves our having had certain attitudes toward and beliefs about the benefits we have received (as noted in Section IV). Among other things, we must regard the benefits as flowing from a cooperative scheme rather than seeing them as "free" for the taking. And we must, for instance, think that the benefits we receive are worth the price we must pay for them, so that we would take the benefits if we had a choice between taking them (with the burdens involved) or leaving them. These kinds of beliefs and attitudes are necessary if the benefaction is to be plausibly regarded as constituting voluntary participation in the cooperative scheme.

But surely most of us do not have these requisite attitudes toward or beliefs about the

benefits of government. At least many citizens barely notice (and seem disinclined to think about) the benefits they receive. And many more, faced with high taxes, with military service which may involve fighting in foreign "police actions," or with unreasonably restrictive laws governing private pleasures, believe that the benefits received from governments are not worth the price they are forced to pay. While such beliefs may be false, they seem nonetheless incompatible with the "acceptance" of the open benefits of government. Further, it must be admitted that, even in democratic political communities, these benefits are commonly regarded as purchased (with taxes) from a central authority, rather than as accepted from the cooperative efforts of our fellow citizens. We may feel, for instance, that if debts are owed at all, they are owed not to those around us, but to our government. Again, these attitudes seem inconsistent with the suggestion that the open benefits are accepted, in the strict sense of "acceptance." Most citizens will, I think, fall into one of these two classes: those who have not "accepted" because they have not taken the benefits (with accompanying burdens) willingly, and those who have not "accepted" because they do not regard the benefits of government as the products of a cooperative scheme. But if most citizens cannot be thought to have voluntarily accepted the benefits of government from the political cooperative scheme, then the fair-play account of political obligation will not be suitably general in its application, even within democratic states. And if we try to make the account more general by removing the limitations set by our strict notion of "acceptance," we open the floodgates and turn the principle of fair play into the "outrageous" principle discussed earlier. We seem forced by such observations to conclude that citizens generally in no actual states will be bound under the principle of fair play. . . .

These brief remarks all point toward the conclusion that at very best the principle of fair play can hope to account for the political obligations of only a very few citizens in a very few actual states; it is more likely, however, that it accounts for no such obligations at all. While we have seen that the principle does not "collapse" into a principle of consent, we have also seen that in an account of political obligation, the principle has very little to recommend it, either as a supplement to, or a replacement for, principles of fidelity and consent. In particular, the main advantage which the fair–play account was thought to have over consent theory's account, namely, an advantage in *generality*, turns out to be no advantage at all.

NOTES
¹These are John Rawls' two names for the principle, from "Legal Obligation and the Duty of Fair Play," *Law and Philosophy*, ed. S. Hook (New York: New York University Press, 1964) and *A Theory of Justice* (Cambridge: Harvard University Press, 1971). The same principle was alluded to by C. D. Broad in "On the Function of False Hypotheses in Ethics," *International Journal of Ethics* 26 (April 1916), and developed by H.L.A. Hart ["Are There Any Natural Rights?" *Philosophical Review* 64 (April 1955), p. 185].
¹³Robert Nozick, *Anarchy, State, and Utopia* (New York: Basic Books, 1974), p. 93. Citations of Nozick in the text refer to this work.
¹⁴Rawls, *A Theory of Justice*, p. 112.

QUESTIONS FOR DISCUSSION

1. How exactly does the argument from fairness differ from the argument from tacit consent, according to Simmons?

2. What is the difference between "open" benefits and "readily available" benefits that are not open, according to Simmons? List three examples of each kind. Does the acceptance of open benefits create any prima facie moral obligations? Why or why not? Does the acceptance of readily available benefits that are not open create any prima facie moral obligations? Why or why not?

3. In Nozick's entertainment cooperative, discussed by Simmons, would it be unfair for you to refuse to entertain those who entertained you? Do you have a prima facie moral obligation to entertain them? Why or why not?

4. Does Simmons end up in the same position as Nozick? Why or why not?

5. In his last section, Simmons claims that the argument from fairness does not apply to most ordinary citizens in modern states. Why does he think this? Do you agree? Why or why not?

6. Does every driver always have a prima facie moral obligation to stay within the speed limit? Why or why not? Be sure to consider whether violations of such laws cause harm or risk.

7. Do women who want abortions have a prima facie moral obligation to obey laws against abortion? Why or why not?

8. If a police officer believes that abortion is murder and supports protests at abortion clinics, does the police officer have a moral obligation to stop abortion protesters when ordered to do so and when the protesters break the law?

9. The law requires employers to pay social security tax for home workers who earn more than $50 per month. Suppose Kim cleans Zoë's house once a

week for $20, but Kim does not want Zoë to pay her social security, either because Kim does not think that it is worth the trouble or because Kim does not want her income reported to the IRS. Does Zoë have a moral obligation to pay Kim's social security anyway? Why or why not? If Zoë does not pay Kim's social security, is this an adequate reason to reject her nomination to a political office, such as attorney general? To refuse to hire her as a police officer? As a town clerk? As a public school teacher? Why? (Compare the Zoë Baird case in 1993.)

10. Many commercial videotapes start with a warning, such as "Licensed for private home exhibition only. Any public performance, copying, or other use is strictly prohibited." Do you have a moral obligation not to copy a rented videotape so that you can watch the movie again later as often as you want? Why or why not? Is this case significantly different from copying computer software without permission? Does it matter whether the person who would profit if you obeyed the law is already rich?

11. Do public officials have stronger obligations to obey the law than private citizens? Why (and which officials) or why not?

12. Do police officers have a prima facie moral obligation not to obtain evidence illegally? When, if ever, are they morally justified in violating that obligation?

SUGGESTIONS FOR FURTHER READING

An excellent survey and critique of various arguments for an obligation to obey the law is John Simmons, *Moral Principles and Political Obligations* (Princeton: Princeton University Press, 1979). Briefer surveys can be found in M.B.E. Smith, "Is There a Prima Facie Obligation to Obey the Law?", *Yale Law Journal*, vol. 82 (1972); Joel Feinberg, "Civil Disobedience in the Modern World" in *Humanities in Society*, vol. 2, no. 1 (Winter 1979), pp. 37–60; and Kent Greenawalt, *Conflicts of Law and Morality* (New York: Oxford University Press, 1987), Chapter II. Smith's arguments against a prima facie moral obligation to obey all laws are criticized in Michael Davis, "Smith, Gert, and Obligation to Obey the Law," *Southern Journal of Philosophy*, vol. 20 (1982), pp. 139–152. Rawls' argument from fairness is discussed in Part I of Sidney Hook, ed., *Law and Philosophy* (New York: New York University Press, 1964). An argument from gratitude is defended by A.D.M. Walker, "Political Obligation and the Argument from Gratitude," *Philosophy and Public Affairs*, vol. 17, no. 3 (Summer 1988), pp. 191–211, with criticisms by George Klosko and a reply by Walker in *Philosophy and Public Affairs*, vol. 18, no. 4 (Fall 1989), pp. 352–364. On differences in strength between the obligations of officials and ordinary citizens, see Gerald Postema, "Coordination and Convention at the Foundation of Law," *Journal of Legal Studies*, vol. 11 (1982), pp. 165–203. For a discussion of authority from the perspective of the authority, see Frederick Schauer, "The Questions of Authority," *Georgetown Law Journal*, vol. 81 (1992), pp. 95–115. See also Donald Regan, "Law's Halo," in *Philosophy and Law*, eds. Jules Coleman and Ellen Frankel Paul (Oxford: Basil Blackwell, 1987), pp. 15–30.

3.2 CIVIL DISOBEDIENCE

INTRODUCTION

Even if there is no general moral obligation to obey *all* laws, there still are prima facie moral obligations to obey *many* laws. These obligations are *prima facie* because they are not so strong that they always override other reasons. Sometimes there seems to be an adequate justification for violating a law even when there is a prima facie moral obligation to obey that law. But when?

This issue is raised by civil disobedience. In the 1840s, Henry David Thoreau refused to pay his poll tax as a protest against the government's war with Mexico, its support for slavery in southern states, and its violations of rights of Native Americans.[12] If Thoreau had a prima facie moral obligation to pay his poll tax, did he also have an adequate moral justification for refusing to pay the tax in these circumstances? On December 1, 1955, in Montgomery, Alabama, Rosa Parks sat in the front of a bus, knowing that it was illegal for African–Americans to sit there. If Parks had a prima facie moral obligation to obey that law, was she justified in sitting there anyway? More recently, when Operation Rescue protesters trespass in order to block access to abortion clinics, its members seem to have prima facie moral obligations to obey trespass laws, but do they also have an adequate justification for breaking those laws? What about supporters of ACT UP who block traffic as a protest against the lack of government action on AIDS?

This issue of the justifiability of civil disobedience will be approached in two steps. First, what is civil disobedience? Second, when is civil disobedience justified?

WHAT IS CIVIL DISOBEDIENCE?

The best place to begin is John Rawls' definition of civil disobedience as "a public, nonviolent, and conscientious act contrary to law usually done with the intent to bring about a change in the policies or laws of the government." (p. 260) Each term in this definition contrasts civil disobedience with similar acts that are not civil disobedience according to Rawls.

The central requirement is that civil disobedience must be *contrary to law*, although Rawls sometimes says instead that it must be "thought to be contrary to law."[13] It is not civil disobedience to demonstrate with a permit, to lobby against a

---

[12]Thoreau defends his protest in "Civil Disobedience," which is reprinted in many places, including Hugo Adam Bedau, ed., *Civil Disobedience in Focus* (New York: Routledge, 1991).

[13]Rawls, *A Theory of Justice*, p. 365. This qualification is important, for example, in classifying acts intended to test whether laws are constitutional.

bill, or to work in a political campaign against an incumbent in order to change a specific law or policy. Even when demonstrators walk onto private property without permission, this is probably not civil disobedience if they do not know that they are trespassing.

Intended legal violations are still not civil disobedience unless their motivation is *conscientious*. Tax evasion for personal gain is not civil disobedience. Not even every conscientious legal violation counts as civil disobedience for Rawls. He adds that civil disobedience must be *political* in three ways. First, civil disobedience must be political in its *justification:* "it is justified by moral principles which define a conception of civil society and the public good." (pp. 260–1) This seems to exclude acts based solely on personal moral principles or on religious principles, so it might exclude some protests against abortion. Second, civil disobedience must be political in its *audience.* According to Rawls, the civilly disobedient person must be "addressing the sense of justice of the majority." (p. 261) Third, civil disobedience is usually political in its *goal,* for it is "usually done with the intent to bring about a change in the policies or laws of the government." (p. 260) So it is not standard civil disobedience when Jehovah's Witnesses refuse to salute the flag despite a law requiring them to do so, if they are not trying to change the law.[14] And protests against companies or universities are at least not typical of civil disobedience, although they still might be justified.

The aim of civil disobedience supports Rawls' requirement that civil disobedience be *public,* since one usually cannot appeal to the majority and change government laws and policies in secret. However, when people helped slaves escape to the north in the 1850s, part of their aim was to end slavery by making it more difficult and costly, but they tried to keep their specific activities secret, at least from the government and slaveowners. Such secret conscientious illegal opposition to law does not count as civil disobedience for Rawls.

Finally, Rawls does not count anything as civil disobedience unless it is *nonviolent*. This excludes violent acts of revolution, terrorism, assassination, sabotage, and rioting. Rawls' claim is not that violence can never be justified. His point is just that a violent act should not be classified as civil disobedience. The rationale is that violent acts are not civil, so they cannot be civil disobedience.

With all of these restrictions, Rawls' definition specifies a very narrow class of acts. Rawls admits that it is more common to define civil disobedience more broadly by dropping some of his restrictions.[15] Nonetheless, he adopted his narrower definition because he wanted to make generalizations about every act in his narrower class that might not apply to other acts under a wider definition. All illegal protests raise the same basic question of when one is justified in breaking the law, but different illegal protests get justified in very different ways. That is why it is important to specify the range of acts being discussed when one talks about civil disobedience. We will focus on civil disobedience under Rawls' narrower definition, unless otherwise indicated.

---

[14]This law was upheld in *Minersville School District v. Gobitis* 310 U.S. 586 (1940), which was reversed in *West Virginia State Board of Education v. Barnette* 319 U.S. 624 (1943).

[15]John Rawls, *A Theory of Justice,* p. 368.

WHEN IS CIVIL DISOBEDIENCE JUSTIFIED?

Some people, including Plato's Socrates and Hobbes, have argued that civil disobedience is never morally justified. The main argument for this position is that civil disobedience violates the law, and there is a moral obligation to obey the law. Even if there is no general moral obligation to obey every law, acts of civil disobedience are defined as public, so they almost always cause some harm or inconvenience, or at least some risk of harming the legal system and society. So civil disobedience almost always violates a prima facie moral obligation.

Nonetheless, this general obligation is just prima facie, so this argument alone is not enough to show that civil disobedience is always morally wrong overall. People who commit civil disobedience usually think that they have a moral justification for breaking the law, because the opposed law or policy is immoral. When they are right, moral reasons conflict, so we need to ask whether the prima facie moral obligation to obey the law is stronger or weaker than the moral reasons to disobey the law.

One could claim that the moral obligation to obey the law is always stronger or is always weaker than the moral reasons to disobey the law. But few people adopt these absolute positions. To most people, the moral obligation to obey the law seems stronger in some cases, but the moral reason to break the law seems stronger in others. If so, the crucial questions are: *when* is one moral reason stronger, and when is civil disobedience morally justified?

One answer is provided by act utilitarianism. Act utilitarians claim that any act, including civil disobedience, is morally justified if and only if it creates the greatest good for the greatest number. Under this theory, we need to ask how likely civil disobedience is to succeed in changing the law it opposes, how bad that law is, how likely civil disobedience is to harm innocent bystanders or to create a harsh backlash by opponents, whether the protesters will be punished and how much, whether there is a less dangerous way to change the law, and so on. These questions will not be easy to answer, but act utilitarianism does at least specify which factors determine whether or not a particular act of civil disobedience is morally justified.[16]

A different intermediate approach attempts to spell out general conditions that civil disobedience must meet in order to be morally justified. These restrictions contrast with utilitarianism if they allow that civil disobedience is not always justified when it would maximize utility. The most detailed theory of this kind comes from John Rawls in the reading later in this section. Rawls claims that an act of civil disobedience in a nearly just society is justified (and not morally wrong) when and only when all of the following conditions are met:

(1) *Last Resort:* all reasonable legal means were tried.

(2) *Substance:* the act opposes an injustice that is both substantial and clear.

---

[16]For a discussion of civil disobedience from a generally utilitarian perspective, see Peter Singer, *Practical Ethics* (New York: Cambridge University Press, 1979), Chapter 9.

(3) *Fairness:* the agent is willing to give everyone else a right to commit similar acts in similar circumstances.

(4) *Success:* the act is not too likely to fail.[17]

The last condition is not very controversial. It would be silly, for example, to hijack or even stow away on Air Force One as a protest against the government's policy of letting the President have his own plane. This protest has no real chance of changing the policy, and it is very likely to get one jailed or killed. Of course, there will be important disputes about which protests are *too* likely to fail. But Rawls is not saying that civil disobedience should never be risky at all. The point of the success condition is just that there are limits. Even act utilitarians should accept that.

The *fairness* condition, (3), is more controversial. Rawls imagines a situation where many groups suffer the same degree of injustice. Then he asks, "What would happen if they all were allowed to commit civil disobedience?" If many of them would commit civil disobedience when allowed, and if so much disobedience would undermine the entire government, and if that would be undesirable to these groups, then Rawls claims that none of the groups is justified in committing civil disobedience. The basic reason is that it is unfair to allow one group to commit civil disobedience when other groups are not allowed to do similar acts in similar situations. However, it is not clear when situations really are similar. The group that acts first might not be in the same situation as the others if the first act of civil disobedience makes it more risky for the later groups to commit civil disobedience, as is the case when many such acts would undermine the government. If so, any of the groups can justifiably commit civil disobedience if it acts first. So it is not clear that Rawls' condition of fairness really rules out many, if any, acts of civil disobedience.

The condition of *last resort*, (1), might seem less controversial. Rawls does not require legal means to be exhausted. All he requires is that "standard" legal means were tried "in good faith." Elsewhere he explains that this condition requires only that "further attempts may reasonably be thought fruitless."[18] Of course, there will be disputes about when legal means have been tried in good faith and when it is reasonable to give up on legal means. The latter problem is central to *Walker v. Birmingham* (later in this section). But Rawls again is just pointing out that one should not resort to civil disobedience *too* soon.

Nonetheless, Ronald Dworkin has argued against the condition of last resort for one kind of civil disobedience.[19] Civil disobedience is *integrity-based* when the agent's "personal integrity, his conscience, forbids him to obey" the law. For example, "Someone who believes it is deeply wrong to deny help to an escaped

---

[17]In *A Theory of Justice,* p. 375, Rawls adds that the act also must not cause too much harm to innocent third parties.

[18]Rawls, *A Theory of Justice,* p. 373.

[19]The following quotations are from Ronald Dworkin, "Civil Disobedience and Nuclear Protest," in *A Matter of Principle* (Cambridge: Harvard University Press, 1985), pp. 107–108.

slave who knocks at his door, and even worse to turn him over to the authorities, thinks the Fugitive Slave Act requires him to behave in an immoral way." Similarly, some Jehovah's Witnesses and their children see it as deeply immoral for the children to obey a law requiring them to salute the flag in school. For such integrity-based civil disobedience, Dworkin argues that a plausible theory

> could not, for example, add the further and tempting qualification that a citizen must have exhausted the normal political process so long as this offers any prospect of reversing the political decision he opposes. Integrity-based civil disobedience is typically a matter of urgency. The Northerner who is asked to hand over a slave to the slave-catcher, even the schoolchild asked once to salute the flag, suffers a final loss if he obeys, and it does not much help him if the law is reversed soon after.

The point is that, even if legal means would change a law, they would also take time, and one should not be required to do what one sees as deeply immoral while waiting for the law to change. Rawls might respond that the illegal acts in Dworkin's examples are not civil disobedience on his narrow definition, either because they are not public or because they are not aimed at changing the law. However, if the schoolchild refuses publicly, and if part of his aim is to change the law, then his refusal fits Rawls' definition of civil disobedience, and the school child still seems justified in refusing to salute without trying legal means first.

The most complex and controversial condition of all is that of *substance*, (2). The basic argument for this condition is that civil disobedience works only by appealing to the majority's sense of justice, but the majority probably will not sense an injustice unless it is made clear, and will not bother to change it unless it is substantial, so civil disobedience is not likely to work unless the opposed injustice is both "substantial and clear."

Controversy comes when we ask which injustices are substantial and clear. Rawls' answer is that the clearest injustices will be "serious" violations of his first principle (which requires the greatest equal basic liberty) and of the second part of his second principle (which requires equality of opportunity). Injustice is usually obvious when people are denied basic liberties, such as the right to vote, own property, or practice religion, and when they are denied opportunities, such as holding government offices. In contrast, it is hard to determine long-term effects of social and economic inequalities, so it is hard to know when a law or policy violates the first part of Rawls' second principle, which rules out economic and social inequalities that are not "to everyone's advantage." Rawls concludes that civil disobedience is more likely to be justified when the opposed injustice is a violation of equal liberty or equal opportunity.

These generalizations have many exceptions. It is not always clear when the first principle is violated. There are serious disputes about whether electoral districts are drawn so that people have "equal" voting power,[20] and about how much freedom of speech is the "most" that is compatible with a similar liberty for

---

[20]See Lani Guinier, *The Tyranny of the Majority* (New York: Free Press, 1994).

others (see Section 4.3). It is also not clear whether the costs of elections unjustly deny poor people an equal opportunity to win government offices. Moreover, it is not always hard to tell that an economic policy disadvantages a certain group, including the worst-off. Some taxes are obviously regressive, for example. Rawls' general condition of substance (2) still might be right, but his further specific claims about which kinds of injustice meet this condition are at best rough approximations.

There are also problems for the condition of substance itself. There seem to be two main reasons for limiting civil disobedience to clear injustices. One is that too many people would commit civil disobedience if it were allowed for injustices that are not clear. This argument forgets, however, that civil disobedience carries personal risks that will deter many people. These risks make it doubtful that anarchy would result if people were allowed to use civil disobedience against injustices that are substantial but not so clear.[21]

The second reason for limiting civil disobedience to clear injustices is that the purpose of civil disobedience is to persuade the majority, but the majority will not be persuaded if the injustice is not clear to them. In Rawls' view, civil disobedience does not change laws or policies by coercion or by making the laws or policies too costly to maintain. Instead, civil disobedience is supposed to appeal to the majority's sense of justice. However, Peter Singer (see later reading) argues that civil disobedience can also be justified as a way to get the majority to change its prior conception of justice. This suggests that the injustice need not be clear to the majority before the civil disobedience occurs. If not, then the unclarities surrounding abortion, for example, do not show that civil disobedience in protests against abortion is unjustified (although these protests might be wrong for other reasons).

Singer also asks why the appeal must be to *justice* rather than to some other area of morality. For example, Rawls denies that cruelty to animals is a matter of justice even if it is immoral. But if an animal rights group blocks the entrance to a laboratory that experiments on animals, it would be unconvincing to argue that their civil disobedience is morally wrong because experiments on animals are not unjust, even though they are immoral in another way. The same might be said of civil disobedience against environmental abuses and even against nuclear weapons and nuclear power. If these policies are opposed not because they are unfair to any specific group, but instead because they are dangerous to everyone, then what these protesters oppose might not best be described as an injustice.[22] Nonetheless, these causes still might seem important enough to justify civil disobedience in some cases. If so, Rawls' condition of substance is too restrictive.

Finally, Rawls does not say that *violent* illegal acts cannot be justified. He simply does not call them civil disobedience. But others have argued that violent disobedience is never justified, so this claim is worth considering.

[21]This point is made by Vinit Haksar, *Civil Disobedience, Threats and Offers* (Delhi: Oxford University Press, 1986), pp. 24–25.

[22]See Ronald Dworkin's discussion of policy-based civil disobedience in "Civil Disobedience and Nuclear Protest."

What is violence? The clearest examples are sudden positive acts that intentionally cause bodily harm, such as hitting someone. Harm to property also counts, such as beating the windshield of a Mercedes with a golf club.

Apart from extreme pacifists, everyone admits that violence is morally permitted in some situations, such as self-defense. So why should violence always be wrong in conscientious disobedience? The idea might be that such disobedience is supposed to persuade the majority, but violence will only produce a backlash and harden the majority against the protesters. However, this is not always true. Violence might be necessary to capture attention, and the opposed injustice might be obvious once the majority pays attention. Even if violence is inappropriate for persuasion, violent protests still might change the law by making the law too costly to maintain. This might be enough to justify violent conscientious disobedience if its goal is to change the law "by any means necessary," as Malcolm X said.

Although violence can work, it does cause harm, and it creates risks of more violence. But this shows only that there is a prima facie moral obligation not to resort to violence unless necessary. This obligation might be overridden sometimes. Just as violence in self-defense can sometimes be justified, John Morreall argues,

> The same would hold true for the slaveowner chasing a runaway slave in the United States of the 1850s. If he has almost caught up with the slave, and my engaging him in a fistfight would give the slave the few precious minutes he needs to get away again, then I would be perfectly justified in grabbing the man and knocking him to the ground to give the slave the time he needs. The law says that I must help slaveowners capture their runaway slaves, the slaveowner may claim; he may also claim that he has a right to his own bodily security. But, obviously, both the law, because it is immoral, and his right to bodily security, because it has been superceded by the slave's right to be free, are not morally binding on me.[23]

This is not a case of civil disobedience under Rawls' narrow definition, because it is not a public appeal to the community's sense of justice. However, the scenario described by Morreall could take place in the context of such an appeal; for example, in a public march by slaves to trains that will take them to freedom. Besides, Morreall's main point is that the moral obligation not to be violent can be overridden in special circumstances by more pressing needs. That point applies to civil disobedience as well:

> A more recent example might be the case of civil disobedients' pouring blood on draft files in protest of the Vietnam war. The government's right not to have its records damaged, though it may hold in most cases, has simply been superseded in this case. The right which people in Vietnam have to life takes precedence over the U.S. government's right to property.[24]

---

[23]John Morreall, "The Justifiability of Violent Civil Disobedience," *Canadian Journal of Philosophy*, vol. 6 (1976), p. 42.

[24]John Morreall, "The Justifiability of Violent Civil Disobedience," p. 43.

Of course, this destruction of property might not do any good. It might even increase the danger to other people, such as South Vietnamese and U.S. troops in Vietnam. So it is not obvious that this act of civil disobedience is justified. Nonetheless, such an act *might* prevent more harm and rights violations, so it *might* be justified, despite its violent nature. This possibility is enough to raise serious doubts about any claim that violent conscientious disobedience can *never* be justified.

SHOULD JUSTIFIED CIVIL DISOBEDIENCE BE PUNISHED?

When one person commits civil disobedience, other people, especially government officials, must decide how to respond. Prosecutors must decide whether to prosecute. When they do, judges and juries must decide whether to find protesters guilty, whether to punish them, and how much.

Most people agree that someone who commits *unjustified* civil disobedience should be punished. But there is less agreement about whether someone who commits *justified* civil disobedience should be punished. That depends on the purpose of punishment.

One of the main theories of punishment is retributivism (Section 6.4). Most traditional retributivists hold that punishment should be proportionate to moral guilt. If so, no punishment is appropriate when civil disobedience is morally justified if moral justification excludes moral guilt. However, one might argue that civil disobedience still includes *some* moral guilt when it violates a prima facie moral obligation to obey the law. Besides, other retributivists insist that punishment is justified not by moral guilt, but merely by the fact that a law was broken. So some retributivists can justify punishment for civil disobedience, even when it is morally justified.

The other main theory of punishment is utilitarianism (Section 6.3). Many utilitarians emphasize deterrence of crime as a goal of punishment, but society might not want to deter civil disobedience when it is necessary to stop a substantial and clear injustice. Justified civil disobedience has too many benefits to society for utilitarians to want to deter it completely. However, utilitarians also might argue that punishment is necessary to make people careful not to resort to civil disobedience too quickly. If people believe that they can publicly disobey bad laws with no personal cost, they might be more likely to commit civil disobedience in situations where it is not justified and where it is harmful.

In addition, people who commit civil disobedience sometimes *want* to be punished in order to further their cause. Punishment often brings publicity and sympathy. The courage to accept punishment can impress uncommitted onlookers and win them over to one's side. This was recognized by one Mississippi sheriff who refused to arrest Martin Luther King, Jr., so as to rob King of this benefit of his illegal protest. A different reason for accepting punishment is that many people who commit civil disobedience want to express their respect for the legal system as a whole. Unlike revolutionaries, people who commit civil disobedience usually do not want to overthrow the entire government. They oppose only certain laws or policies. Breaking the law and then accepting punishment can express this tension between respecting the system and opposing part of it.

These conflicting considerations make it difficult to formulate hard and fast rules about when, if ever, justified civil disobedience should be punished. Part of the problem is that we need to make distinctions among kinds of civil disobedience.

First, direct civil disobedience is importantly different from indirect civil disobedience. Civil disobedience is *direct* when it violates the very law that is opposed. Rosa Parks engaged in direct civil disobedience when she sat in the front of the bus, because she opposed the law that prohibited her from sitting in the front of the bus, among other segregation laws. In contrast, civil disobedience is *indirect* when it violates a law different from the law or policy that it opposes. A protester who illegally parks in the entrance to a nuclear power plant or abortion clinic engages in indirect civil disobedience, since the protest is not against parking regulations.

This distinction affects the justifiability of punishment. Someone who commits direct civil disobedience does not want to express respect for *that* law. When direct civil disobedience is justified, the violated law is unjust, and it seems unfair to punish someone for violating an unjust law. It is not even clear that there is a prima facie moral obligation to obey the unjust law. In contrast, it is easier to justify punishment for acts of indirect civil disobedience, since everyone respects the law that is violated, and few deny that there is a prima facie obligation to obey *that* law even in those circumstances. We still would not want to inflict so much punishment that it would deter anyone from ever committing indirect civil disobedience, for such civil disobedience can help society. But some punishment does seem appropriate even for justified indirect civil disobedience.

Ronald Dworkin emphasizes a second useful distinction.[25] Some acts of direct civil disobedience violate the rights of other people. For example, Alabama Governor George Wallace stood in the doorway of a school in order to prevent African-American children from entering the school. He was violating the very court order that he opposed, so his civil disobedience was direct. And his act violated the rights of school children to enter that school and receive an equal education. In contrast, Dworkin argues that other kinds of direct civil disobedience do *not* violate the rights of any specific individual. His example is people who publicly refused to report for the draft during the Vietnam War. Given the size and structure of the military, one individual's failure to report did not significantly affect anyone else's chances of being drafted or sent to Vietnam, so no individual's rights were violated. Of course, there will be disputes about when someone's rights are violated. Nonetheless, the point here is that, when direct civil disobedience does violate another individual's rights, it is easier to justify punishing the civilly disobedient person, because a failure to punish would be a failure to protect the affected individual's rights. This argument for punishment does not apply when civil disobedience does not violate any individual's rights, so there is less to lose by showing mercy and restraint in punishment.

Finally, acts of civil disobedience are done under different circumstances with different effects. Not every act of civil disobedience leads to widespread

---

[25]Ronald Dworkin, "Civil Disobedience," in *Taking Rights Seriously* (Cambridge: Harvard University Press, 1978), pp. 206–222.

disobedience. But there might be unstable emergency situations where acts of civil disobedience, if not punished, will become widespread enough to undermine the entire government. In such circumstances, civil disobedience should be punished to prevent governmental collapse, *if* the government is worth protecting.

Overall, then, it seems reasonable to conclude that we should punish justified civil disobedience roughly when the civil disobedience is indirect or violates an individual's rights or when failure to punish is likely to lead to disaster. These conditions are vague and probably incomplete, but they are intended only as a guide to further discussion.

THE JUSTIFICATION OF CIVIL DISOBEDIENCE

JOHN RAWLS

I. INTRODUCTION

I should like to discuss briefly, and in an informal way, the grounds of civil disobedience in a constitutional democracy. Thus, I shall limit my remarks to the conditions under which we may, by civil disobedience, properly oppose legally established democratic authority; I am not concerned with the situation under other kinds of government nor, except incidentally, with other forms of resistance. My thought is that in a reasonably just (though of course not perfectly just) democratic regime, civil disobedience, when it is justified, is normally to be understood as a political action which addresses the sense of justice of the majority in order to urge reconsideration of the measures protested and to warn that in the firm opinion of the dissenters the conditions of social cooperation are not being honored. This characterization of civil disobedience is intended to apply to dissent on fundamental questions of

internal policy, a limitation which I shall follow to simplify our question.

II. THE SOCIAL CONTRACT DOCTRINE

It is obvious that the justification of civil disobedience depends upon . . . the conception of justice which is the basis of a theory of political obligation. I believe that the appropriate conception, at least for an account of political obligation in a constitutional democracy, is that of the social contract theory from which so much of our political thought derives. If we are careful to interpret it in a suitably general way, I hold that this doctrine provides a satisfactory basis for political theory, indeed even for ethical theory itself, but this is beyond our present concern.[1] The interpretation I suggest is the following: that the principles to which social arrangements must conform, and in particular the principles of justice, are those which free and rational men would agree to in an original

John Rawls, "The Justification of Civil Disobedience," in Hugo Bedau, ed., *Civil Disobedience: Theory and Practice* (New York: Pegasus, 1969), pp. 240–255

position of equal liberty; and similarly, the principles which govern men's relations to institutions and define their natural duties and obligations are the principles to which they would consent when so situated. . . .

I believe that as a consequence of the peculiar nature of the original position there would be an agreement on the following two principles for assigning rights and duties and for regulating distributive shares as these are determined by the fundamental institutions of society: first, each person is to have an equal right to the most extensive liberty compatible with a like liberty for all; second, social and economic inequalities (as defined by the institutional structure or fostered by it) are to be arranged so that they are both to everyone's advantage and attached to positions and offices open to all. In view of the content of these two principles and their application to the main institutions of society, and therefore to the social system as a whole, we may regard them as the two principles of justice. Basic social arrangements are just insofar as they conform to these principles, and we can, if we like, discuss questions of justice directly by reference to them. But a deeper understanding of the justification of civil disobedience requires, I think, an account of the derivation of these principles provided by the doctrine of the social contract. Part of our task is to show why this is so.

III. THE GROUNDS OF COMPLIANCE WITH AN UNJUST LAW

. . . The principles of justice provide a criterion for the laws desired; the problem is to find a set of political procedures that will give this outcome. I shall assume that, at least under the normal conditions of a modern state, the best constitution is some form of democratic regime affirming equal political liberty and using some sort of majority (or other plurality) rule. Thus it follows that on the contract theory a constitutional democracy of some sort is required by the principles of justice. . . .

The difficulty is that we cannot frame a procedure which guarantees that only just and effective legislation is enacted. Thus even under a just constitution unjust laws may be passed and unjust policies enforced. Some form of the majority principle is necessary but the majority may be mistaken, more or less willfully, in what it legislates. In agreeing to a democratic constitution (as an instance of imperfect procedural justice) one accepts at the same time the principle of majority rule. Assuming that the constitution is just and that we have accepted and plan to continue to accept its benefits, we then have both an obligation and a natural duty (and in any case the duty) to comply with what the majority enacts even though it may be unjust. In this way we become bound to follow unjust laws, not always, of course, but provided the injustice does not exceed certain limits. . . .

[T]here is, of course, no corresponding obligation or duty to regard what the majority enacts as itself just. The right to make law does not guarantee that the decision is rightly made; and while the citizen submits in his conduct to the judgment of democratic authority, he does not submit his judgment to it.[2] And if in his judgment the enactments of the majority exceed certain bounds of injustice, the citizen may consider civil disobedience. For we are not required to accept the majority's acts unconditionally and to acquiesce in the denial of our and others' liberties; rather we submit our conduct to democratic authority to the extent necessary to share the burden of working a constitutional regime, distorted as it must inevitably be by men's lack of wisdom and the defects of their sense of justice.

IV. THE PLACE OF CIVIL DISOBEDIENCE IN A CONSTITUTIONAL DEMOCRACY

We are now in a position to say a few things about civil disobedience. I shall understand it to be a public, nonviolent, and conscientious act contrary to law usually done with the intent to bring about a change in the policies or laws of the government.[3] Civil disobedience is a political act in the sense that it is an act justified by moral principles which define a conception of civil society and the public good. It rests, then, on political conviction as opposed to a search for self or group interest; and in the case of a constitutional democracy, we may assume that this conviction involves the conception of justice (say that expressed by the contract doctrine) which underlies the constitution itself. That is, in a viable democratic regime there is a common conception of justice by reference to which its citizens regulate their political affairs and interpret the constitution. Civil disobedience is a public act which the dissenter believes to be justified by this conception of justice and for this reason it may be understood as addressing the sense of justice of the majority in order to urge reconsideration of the measures protested and to warn that, in the sincere opinion of the dissenters, the conditions of social cooperation are not being honored. For the principles of justice express precisely such conditions, and their persistent and deliberate violation in regard to basic liberties over any extended period of time cuts the ties of community and invites either submission or forceful resistance. By engaging in civil disobedience a minority leads the majority to consider whether it wants to have its acts taken in this way, or whether, in view of the common sense of justice, it wishes to acknowledge the claims of the minority.

Civil disobedience is also civil in another sense. Not only is it the outcome of a sincere conviction based on principles which regulate civic life, but it is public and nonviolent, that is, it is done in a situation where arrest and punishment are expected and accepted without resistance. In this way it manifests a respect for legal procedures. Civil disobedience expresses disobedience to law within the limits of fidelity to law, and this feature of it helps to establish in the eyes of the majority that it is indeed conscientious and sincere, that it really is meant to address their sense of justice.[4] Being completely open about one's acts and being willing to accept the legal consequences of one's conduct is a bond given to make good one's sincerity, for that one's deeds are consci-

entious is not easy to demonstrate to another or even before oneself. No doubt it is possible to imagine a legal system in which conscientious belief that the law is unjust is accepted as a defense for noncompliance, and men of great honesty who are confident in one another might make such a system work. But as things are such a scheme would be unstable; we must pay a price in order to establish that we believe our actions have a moral basis in the convictions of the community.

The nonviolent nature of civil disobedience refers to the fact that it is intended to address the sense of justice of the majority and as such it is a form of speech, an expression of conviction. To engage in violent acts likely to injure and to hurt is incompatible with civil disobedience as a mode of address. Indeed, an interference with the basic rights of others tends to obscure the civilly disobedient quality of one's act. Civil disobedience is nonviolent in the further sense that the legal penalty for one's action is accepted and that resistance is not (at least for the moment) contemplated. Nonviolence in this sense is to be distinguished from nonviolence as a religious or pacifist principle. While those engaging in civil disobedience have often held some such principle, there is no necessary connection between it and civil disobedience. For on the interpretation suggested, civil disobedience in a democratic society is best understood as an appeal to the principles of justice, the fundamental conditions of willing social cooperation among free men, which in the view of the community as a whole are expressed in the constitution and guide its interpretation. Being an appeal to the moral basis of public life, civil disobedience is a political and not primarily a religious act. It addresses itself to the common principles of justice which men can require one another to follow and not to the aspirations of love which they cannot. Moreover by taking part in civilly disobedient acts one does not foreswear indefinitely the idea of forceful resistance; for if the appeal against injustice is repeatedly denied, then the majority has declared its intention to invite submission or resistance and the latter may conceivably be justified even in a democratic regime. We are not required to acquiesce in the crushing of fundamental liberties by democratic majorities which have shown themselves blind to the principles of justice upon which justification of the constitution depends.

V. THE JUSTIFICATION OF CIVIL DISOBEDIENCE

So far we have said nothing about the justification of civil disobedience, that is, the conditions under which civil disobedience may be engaged in consistent with the principles of justice that support a democratic regime. Our task is to see how the characterization of civil disobedience as addressed to the sense of justice of the majority (or to the citizens as a body) determines when such action is justified.

First of all, we may suppose that the normal political appeals to the majority have already been made in good faith and have been rejected, and that the standard means of redress have been tried. Thus, for example, existing political parties are indifferent to the claims of the minority and attempts to repeal the laws protested have been met with further repression since legal institutions are in the control of the majority. While civil disobedience should be recognized, I think, as a form of political action within the limits of fidelity to the rule of law, at the same time it is a rather desperate act just within these limits, and therefore it should, in general, be undertaken as a last resort when standard democratic processes have failed. In this sense it is not a normal political action. When it is justified there has been a serious breakdown; not only is there grave injustice in the law but a refusal more or less deliberate to correct it.

Second, since civil disobedience is a political act addressed to the sense of justice of the majority, it should usually be limited to substantial and clear violations of justice and preferably to those which, if rectified, will establish a basis for doing away with remaining injustices. For this reason there is a presumption in favor of restricting civil disobedience to violations of the first principle of justice, the principle of equal liberty, and to barriers which contravene the second principle, the principle of open offices which protects equality of opportunity. It is not, of course, always easy to tell whether these principles are satisfied. But if we think of them as guaranteeing the fundamental equal political and civil liberties (including freedom of conscience and liberty of thought) and equality of opportunity, then it is often relatively clear whether their principles are being honored. After all, the equal liberties are defined by the visible structure of social institutions; they are to be incorporated into the recognized practice, if not the letter, of social arrangements. When minorities are denied the right to vote or to hold certain political offices, when certain religious groups are repressed and others denied equality of opportunity in the economy, this is often obvious and there is no doubt that justice is not being given. However, the first part of the second principle which requires that inequalities be to everyone's advantage is a much more imprecise and controversial matter. Not only is there a problem of assigning it a determinate and precise sense, but even if we do so and agree on what it should be, there is often a wide variety of reasonable opinion as to whether the principle is satisfied. The reason for this is that the principle applies primarily to fundamental economic and social policies. The choice of these depends upon theoretical and speculative beliefs as well as upon a wealth of concrete information, and all of this mixed with judgment and plain hunch, not to mention in actual cases prejudice and self-interest. Thus unless the laws of taxation are clearly designed to attack a basic equal liberty, they should not be protested by civil disobedience; the appeal to justice is not sufficiently clear and its resolution is best left to the political process. But violations of the equal liberties that define the common status of citizenship are another matter.

The deliberate denial of these more or less over any extended period of time in the face of normal political protest is, in general, an appropriate object of civil disobedience. We may think of the social system as divided roughly into two parts, one which incorporates the fundamental equal liberties (including equality of opportunity) and another which embodies social and economic policies properly aimed at promoting the advantage of everyone. As a rule civil disobedience is best limited to the former where the appeal to justice is not only more definite and precise, but where, if it is effective, it tends to correct the injustices in the latter.

Third, civil disobedience should be restricted to those cases where the dissenter is willing to affirm that everyone else similarly subjected to the same degree of injustice has the right to protest in a similar way. That is, we must be prepared to authorize others to dissent in similar situations and in the same way, and to accept the consequences of their doing so. Thus, we may hold, for example, that the widespread disposition to disobey civilly clear violations of fundamental liberties more or less deliberate over an extended period of time would raise the degree of justice throughout society and would insure men's self-esteem as well as their respect for one another. Indeed, I believe this to be true, though certainly it is partly a matter of conjecture. As the contract doctrine emphasizes, since the principles of justice are principles which we would agree to in an original position of equality when we do not know our social position and the like, the refusal to grant justice is either the denial of the other as an equal (as one in regard to whom we are prepared to constrain our actions by principles which we would consent to) or the manifestation of a willingness to take advantage of natural contingencies and social fortune at his expense. In either case, injustice invites submission or resistance; but submission arouses the contempt of the oppressor and confirms him in his intention. If straightway,

after a decent period of time to make reasonable political appeals in the normal way, men were in general to dissent by civil disobedience from infractions of the fundamental equal liberties, these liberties would, I believe, be more rather than less secure. Legitimate civil disobedience properly exercised is a stabilizing device in a constitutional regime, tending to make it more firmly just.

Sometimes, however, there may be a complication in connection with this third condition. It is possible, although perhaps unlikely, that there are so many persons or groups with a sound case for resorting to civil disobedience (as judged by the foregoing criteria) that disorder would follow if they all did so. There might be serious injury to the just constitution. Or again, a group might be so large that some extra precaution is necessary in the extent to which its members organize and engage in civil disobedience. Theoretically the case is one in which a number of persons or groups are equally entitled to and all want to resort to civil disobedience, yet if they all do this, grave consequences for everyone may result. The question, then, is who among them may exercise their right, and it falls under the general problem of fairness. I cannot discuss the complexities of the matter here. Often a lottery or a rationing system can be set up to handle the case; but unfortunately the circumstances of civil disobedience rule out this solution. It suffices to note that a problem of fairness may arise and that those who contemplate civil disobedience should take it into account. They may have to reach an understanding as to who can exercise their right in the immediate situation and to recognize the need for special constraint.

The final condition, of a different nature, is the following. We have been considering when one has a right to engage in civil disobedience, and our conclusion is that one has this right should three conditions hold: when one is subject to injustice more or less deliberate over an extended period of time in the face of normal political protests; where the injustice is a clear violation of the liberties of equal citizenship; and provided that the general disposition to protest similarly in similar cases would have acceptable consequences. These conditions are not, I think, exhaustive but they seem to cover the more obvious points; yet even when they are satisfied and one has the right to engage in civil disobedience, there is still the different question of whether one should exercise this right, that is, whether by doing so one is likely to further one's ends. Having established one's right to protest one is then free to consider these tactical questions. We may be acting within our rights but still foolishly if our action only serves to provoke the harsh retaliation of the majority; and it is likely to do so if the majority lacks a sense of justice, or if the action is poorly timed or not well designed to make the appeal to the sense of justice effective. It is easy to think of instances of this sort, and in each case these practical questions have to be faced. From the standpoint of the theory of political obligation we can only say that the exercise of the right should be rational and reasonably designed to advance the protester's aims, and that weighing tactical questions presupposes that one has already established one's right, since tactical advantages in themselves do not support it.

VI. CONCLUSION: SEVERAL OBJECTIONS CONSIDERED

In a reasonably affluent democratic society justice becomes the first virtue of institutions. Social arrangements irrespective of their efficiency must be reformed if they are significantly unjust. No increase in efficiency in the form of greater advantages for many justifies the loss of liberty of a few. That we believe this is shown by the fact that in a democracy the fundamental liberties of citizenship are not understood as the outcome of political bargaining nor are they subject to the calculus of social interests. Rather these liberties are fixed points which serve to limit political transactions and which determine the scope of calculations of social advantage. It

is this fundamental place of the equal liberties which makes their systematic violation over any extended period of time a proper object of civil disobedience. For to deny men these rights is to infringe the conditions of social cooperation among free and rational persons, a fact which is evident to the citizens of a constitutional regime since it follows from the principles of justice which underlie their institutions. The justification of civil disobedience rests on the priority of justice and the equal liberties which it guarantees.

It is natural to object to this view of civil disobedience that it relies too heavily upon the existence of a sense of justice. Some may hold that the feeling for justice is not a vital political force, and that what moves men are various other interests, the desire for wealth, power, prestige, and so on. Now this is a large question the answer to which is highly conjectural and each tends to have his own opinion. But there are two remarks which may clarify what I have said: first, I have assumed that there is in a constitutional regime a common sense of justice the principles of which are recognized to support the constitution and to guide its interpretation. In any given situation particular men may be tempted to violate these principles, but the collective force in their behalf is usually effective since they are seen as the necessary terms of cooperation among free men; and presumably the citizens of a democracy (or sufficiently many of them) want to see justice done. Where these assumptions fail, the justifying conditions for civil disobedience (the first three) are not affected, but the rationality of engaging in it certainly is. In this case, unless the cost of repressing civil dissent injures the economic self–interest (or whatever) of the majority, protest may simply make the position of the minority worse. No doubt as a tactical matter civil disobedience is more effective when its appeal coincides with other interests, but a constitutional regime is not viable in the long run without an attachment to the principles of justice of the sort which we have assumed.

Then, further, there may be a misapprehension about the manner in which a sense of justice manifests itself. There is a tendency to think that it is shown by professions of the relevant principles together with actions of an altruistic nature requiring a considerable degree of self-sacrifice. But these conditions are obviously too strong, for the majority's sense of justice may show itself simply in its being unable to undertake the measures required to suppress the minority and to punish as the law requires the various acts of civil disobedience. The sense of justice undermines the will to uphold unjust institutions, and so a majority despite its superior power may give way. It is unprepared to force the minority to be subject to injustice. Thus, although the majority's action is reluctant and grudging, the role of the sense of justice is nevertheless essential, for without it the majority would have been willing to enforce the law and to defend its position. Once we see the sense of justice as working in this negative way to make established injustices indefensible, then it is recognized as a central element of democratic politics.

Finally, it may be objected against this account that it does not settle the question of who is to say when the situation is such as to justify civil disobedience. And because it does not answer this question, it invites anarchy by encouraging every man to decide the matter for himself. Now the reply to this is that each man must indeed settle this question for himself, although he may, of course, decide wrongly. This is true on any theory of political duty and obligation, at least on any theory compatible with the principles of a democratic constitution. The citizen is responsible for what he does. If we usually think that we should comply with the law, this is because our political principles normally lead to this conclusion. There is a presumption in favor of compliance in the absence of good reasons to the contrary. But because each man is responsible and must decide for himself as best he can whether the

circumstances justify civil disobedience, it does not follow that he may decide as he pleases. It is not by looking to our personal interests or to political allegiances narrowly construed, that we should make up our mind. The citizen must decide on the basis of the principles of justice that underlie and guide the interpretation of the constitution and in the light of his sincere conviction as to how these principles should be applied in the circumstances. If he concludes that conditions obtain which justify civil disobedience and conducts himself accordingly, he has acted conscientiously and perhaps mistakenly, but not in any case at his convenience.

In a democratic society each man must act as he thinks the principles of political right require him to. We are to follow our understanding of these principles, and we cannot do otherwise. There can be no morally binding legal interpretation of these principles, not even by a supreme court or legislature. Nor is there any infallible procedure for determining what or who is right. In our system the Supreme Court, Congress, and the President often put forward rival interpretations of the Constitution.[5] Although the Court has the final say in settling any particular case, it is not immune from powerful political influence that may change its reading of the law of the land. The Court presents its point of view by reason and argument; its conception of the Constitution must, if it is to endure, persuade men of its soundness. The final court of appeal is not the Court, or Congress, or the President, but the electorate as a whole. The civilly disobedient appeal in effect to this body. There is no danger of anarchy as long as there is a sufficient working agreement in men's conceptions of political justice and what it requires. That men can achieve such an understanding when the essential political liberties are maintained is the assumption implicit in democratic institutions. There is no way to avoid entirely the risk of divisive strife. But if legitimate civil disobedience seems to threaten civil peace, the responsibility falls not so much on those who protest as upon

those whose abuse of authority and power justifies such opposition.

NOTES

[1]By the social contract theory I have in mind the
doctrine found in Locke, Rousseau, and Kant. I have
attempted to give an interpretation of this view in
[the reading in Section 5.2.]

[2]On this point see A. E. Murphy's review of Yves
Simon's *The Philosophy of Democratic Government* (1951) in
the *Philosophical Review* (April, 1952).

[3]Here I follow H. A. Bedau's definition of civil disobedience. See his "On Civil Disobedience," *Journal of Philosophy* (October, 1961).

[4]For a fuller discussion of this point to which I am
indebted, see Charles Fried, "Moral Causation," *Harvard Law Review* (1964).

[5]For a presentation of this view to which I am indebted, see A. M. Bickel, *The Least Dangerous Branch* (Indianapolis, 1962), especially Chapters 5 and 6.

QUESTIONS FOR DISCUSSION

1. Which of the following acts count as civil disobedience under Rawls'
   definition?
   (a) David knows that his boss is part of a large group that is going to lie
   down in the entrance to a military base as a protest against an ongoing
   war. David does not care about the war, but he lies down in the entrance
   with the others, because he wants to get in good with his boss. (Must we
   know an individual's motives or aims to know whether his act is civil
   disobedience?)
   (b) A member of a radical group robs a bank to get money for the group.
   (Is this act political in Rawls' sense?)
   (c) Protesters lie down in the entrance to a military base in protest against
   a war on an Arab country. They base their act on personal pacifism, which
   they do not think other people must accept. What if they are guided by
   specifically Islamic principles? (Are these acts political in the way Rawls
   requires?)
   (d) Phyllis blocks access to an abortion clinic because she believes that
   abortion is immoral. She believes this because of her religious views. (Is her
   act political?)
   (e) An environmental activist puts metal spikes into trees and warns loggers. The spikes do not hurt the trees, but trees with spikes cannot be made
   into lumber without risk to equipment, to loggers, and to sawmill workers.
   (Is spiking violent?)
   (f) A protester hijacks an airplane with a toy gun. (Is this violent?)
   (g) Official U. S. policy in 1994 does not allow military personnel to declare
   publicly that they are homosexuals. Suppose some military personnel think
   this restriction is unconstitutional, so they announce their homosexuality
   just to force courts to say whether the restriction is constitutional. (Is this
   act contrary to law, or thought to be so? Does it matter what the courts
   decide?)

2. Rawls sees civil disobedience as an "expression of conviction," but Brian
   Barry asks, "Why, then, bother to break the law at all? As far as I can see
   from Rawls' account, any form of self-injury would do as well to make it

known that one believed strongly in the injustice of a certain law; public self–immolation or, if that seemed too extreme, making a bonfire of one's best clothes would be as good as law breaking."[26] How could Rawls best respond? Is lawbreaking a better form of expression than publicly burning clothes? Why or why not?

3. Suppose that ten groups are subject to similar injustices. Each would be justified in committing civil disobedience if the others did not. But if all were allowed to commit civil disobedience, they all would do so, and that would cause anarchy and disaster. Does this make it wrong for any of them to commit civil disobedience? How would you solve this problem?

4. Do you agree with Rawls that civil disobedience should be limited to clear and substantial injustices? To violations of equal liberty and equal opportunity? Why or why not?

[26] *A Liberal Theory of Justice* (Oxford: Clarendon Press, 1973), p. 153.

DEMOCRACY AND DISOBEDIENCE

PETER SINGER

This is an appropriate point at which to consider the theory of civil disobedience proposed by John Rawls in his much discussed book, *A Theory of Justice*.[1] According to Rawls, civil disobedience is an act which 'addresses the sense of justice of the community and declares that in one's considered opinion the principles of social co-operation among free and equal men are not being respected.'[2] Civil disobedience is here regarded as a form of address, or an appeal. It should, he says, be non-violent and refrain from hurting or interfering with others because violence or interference tends to obscure the fact that what is being done is a form of address. While civil disobedience may 'warn and admonish, it is not it-self a threat.' Similarly, to show sincerity and general fidelity to law, one should be completely open about what one is doing, willing to accept the legal consequences of one's act.

I am . . . in agreement with Rawls on the main point: limited disobedience, far from being incompatible with a genuinely democratic form of government, can have an important part to play as a justifiable form of protest. There are, however, some features of Rawls's position which I cannot accept. These features derive from the theory of justice which is the core of the book. The reader may have noticed that the sentence I quoted above contains a reference to 'the sense of justice of the community' and to

Peter Singer, *Democracy and Disobedience* (Oxford: Clarendon Press, 1973), pp. 86–92.

the 'principles of social co-operation among free and equal men.' Rawls's justification of civil disobedience depends heavily on the idea that a community has a sense of justice which is a single sense of justice on which all can agree, at least in practice if not in all theoretical details. It is the violation of this accepted basis of society which legitimates disobedience. To be fair to Rawls, it must be said that he is not maintaining that men ever do or did get together and agree on a sense of justice, and on the principles of social co-operation. Rather the idea is that a basically just society will have a sense of justice that corresponds to the principles that free and equal men would have chosen, had they met together to agree, under conditions designed to ensure impartiality, to abide by the basic principles necessary for social co-operation. It should also be said that Rawls does not maintain that every society in fact has such a sense of justice, but he intends his theory of disobedience to apply only to those that do. (As an aside, he suggests that the wisdom of civil disobedience will be problematic when there is no common conception of justice, since disobedience may serve only to rouse the majority to more repressive measures.)⁵

This is not the place to discuss Rawls's theory of justice as a whole. I want to discuss only its application to our topic. From his view that civil disobedience is justified by 'the principles of justice which regulate the constitution and social institutions generally', Rawls draws the consequence that 'in justifying civil disobedience one does not appeal to principles of personal morality or to religious doctrines . . . Instead one invokes the commonly shared conception of justice which underlies the political order.'⁴

Even bearing in mind that this is intended to apply only to societies in which there is a common conception of justice, one can see that this is a serious limitation on the grounds on which disobedience can be justified. I shall suggest two ways in which this limitation could be unreasonable.

Firstly, if disobedience is an appeal to the community, why can it only be an appeal which invokes principles which the community already accepts? Why could one not be justified in disobeying in order to ask the majority to alter or extend the shared conception of justice? Rawls might think that it could never be necessary to go beyond this shared conception, for the shared conception is broad enough to contain all the principles necessary for a just society. Disobedience, he would say, can be useful to ensure that society does not depart too seriously from this shared conception, but the conception itself is unimpeachable. The just society, on this view, may be likened to a good piece of machinery: there may occasionally be a little friction, and some lubrication will then be necessary but the basic design needs no alteration.

Now Rawls can, of course, make this true by definition. We have already seen that he intends his theory of disobedience to apply only to societies which have a common conception of justice. If Rawls means by this that his theory applies only when the shared conception of justice encompasses all the legitimate claims that anyone in the society can possibly make, then it follows that no disobedience which seeks to extend or go beyond the shared conception of justice can be legitimate. Since this would follow simply in virtue of how Rawls had chosen to use the notion of a shared conception of justice, however, it would be true in a trivial way, and would be utterly unhelpful for anyone wondering whether he would be justified in disobeying in an actual society.

If Rawls is to avoid this trivializing of his position it would seem that he must be able to point to at least some societies which he thinks have an adequate sense of justice. This course would invite our original question: why will disobedience be justified only if it invokes this particular conception of justice? This version of the theory elevates the conception of justice at present held by some society or societies into a standard valid for all time. Does any existing society have a shared conception of justice which cannot conceivably be improved? Maybe we cannot ourselves see improvements in a particular society's conception of justice, but we surely cannot rule out the possibility that in time it may appear defective, not only in its application, but in the fundamentals of the conception itself. In this case, disobedience designed to induce the majority to rethink its conception of justice might be justified.

I cannot see any way in which Rawls can avoid one or other of these difficulties. Either his conception of justice is a pure ideal, in which case it does not assist our real problems, or it unjustifiably excludes the use of disobedience as a way of making a radical objection to the conception of justice shared by some actual society.

Rawls's theory of civil disobedience contains a second and distinct restriction on the grounds of legitimate disobedience. As we have seen, he says that the justification of disobedience must be in terms of justice, and not in terms of 'principles of personal morality or religious doctrine'. It is not clear exactly what this phrase means, but since Rawls opposes it to 'the commonly shared conception of justice which underlies the political order' we may take it to include all views that are not part of this shared conception. This makes it a substantial restriction, since according to Rawls there are important areas of morality which are outside the scope of justice. The theory of justice is, he says, 'but one part of a moral view'.[5] As an example of an area of morality to which justice is inapplicable, Rawls instances our relations with animals. It is, he says, wrong to be cruel to animals, although we do not owe them justice. If we combine this view with the idea that the justification of civil disobedience must be in terms of justice, we can see that Rawls is committed to holding that no amount of cruelty to animals can justify disobedience. Rawls would no doubt admit that severe and widespread cruelty to animals would be a great moral evil, but his position requires him to say that the licensing, or even the promotion of such cruelty by a government (perhaps to amuse the public, or as is more likely nowadays, for experimental purposes) could not possibly justify civil disobedience, whereas something less serious would justify disobedience if it were contrary to the shared conception of justice. This is a surprising and I think implausible conclusion. A similar objection could be made in respect of any other area of morality which is not included under the conception of justice. Rawls does not give any other examples, although he suggests (and it is implied by his theory of justice) that our dealings with permanent mental defectives do not come under the ambit of justice.[6]

So far I have criticized Rawls's theory of disobedience because of certain restrictions it places on the kind of reason which can justify disobedience. My final comment is different. Rawls frequently writes as if it were a relatively simple matter to determine whether a majority decision is just or unjust. This, coupled with his view that the community has a common conception of justice, leads him to underestimate the importance of a settled, peaceful method of resolving disputes. It could also lead one to the view that there are cases in which the majority is clearly acting beyond its powers, that is, that there are areas of life in which the decision-procedure is entirely without weight, for instance, if it tries to restrict certain freedoms. . . . Consider the following passage:

> It is assumed that in a reasonably just democratic regime there is a public conception of justice by reference to which citizens regulate their political affairs and interpret the constitution. The persistent and deliberate violation of the basic principles of this conception over any extended period of time, especially the infringement of the fundamental equal liberties, invites either submission or resistance. By engaging in civil disobedience a minority forces the majority to consider whether it wishes to have its actions construed in this way, or whether, in view of the common sense of justice, it wishes to acknowledge the legitimate claims of the minority.[7]

There will, of course, be some instances in a society when the actions of the majority can only be seen as a deliberate violation for selfish ends of basic principles of justice. Such actions do 'invite submission or resistance'. It is a mistake, though, to see these cases as in any way typical of those disputes which lead people to ask whether disobedience would be justified. Even when a society shares a common conception of justice, it is not likely to agree on the application of this conception to particular cases. Rawls admits that it is not always clear when the principles of justice have been violated, but he thinks it is often clear, especially when the principle of equal liberty (for Rawls the first principle of justice) is involved. As examples, he suggests that a violation of this principle can clearly be seen when 'certain religious groups are repressed' and when 'certain minorities are denied the right to vote or to hold office . . .'[8] These cases appear straightforward, but are they? Timothy Leary's League for Spiritual Discovery claimed to be a religious group using the drug LSD as a means of exploring ultimate spiritual reality. At least three other groups—the Neo-American Church, the Church of the Awakening, and the Native American Church—have used hallucinogenic drugs as part of religious ceremonies. Of these groups, only the last has legal permission to do so. Is freedom of worship being denied to the others? When is a group a religious group? There are similar problems about denying minorities the vote. Is the denial of the vote to children a violation of equal liberty? Or to convicted prisoners? It may seem obvious to us that these are legitimate exceptions, but then it seemed obvious to many respectable citizens a hundred years ago that blacks and women should not have the vote, and it seemed obvious to Locke that the suppression of atheism and Roman Catholicism were quite compatible with the principle of religious toleration.

When we go beyond religious persecution and the denial of voting rights, it is even easier to find complex disputes on which sincere disagreement over the justice of an action is likely to occur. Many of the issues which have led to civil disobedience in recent years have been of this more complex kind. This is why I do not think it helpful to assume that most issues arise from deliberate disregard of some common principles, or to try to specify limits, whether in the form of rights or of principles of justice, on what the majority can legitimately do.

NOTES

[1]Clarendon Press, Oxford, 1972. The theory of civil disobedience is to be found in ch. 6, mostly in sects. 55, 57, and 59.

[2]Ibid., p. 364.

[3]Ibid., p. 386–7.

[4]Ibid., p. 365.

[5]Ibid., p. 512.

[6]Ibid., p. 510.

[7]Ibid., p. 365–6.

[8]Ibid., p. 372.

QUESTIONS FOR DISCUSSION

1. What are Singer's main criticisms of Rawls? How could Rawls best respond?

2. The British Animal Liberation Front (ALF) releases caged animals and damages equipment in animal experiment laboratories and fur farms. Can these acts ever be justified according to Rawls? According to Singer? According to you? Why or why not?

3. Is a moral rebel ever justified in committing civil disobedience when she knows that the majority will see her acts as unjust and the law she opposes as just? If so, when? If not, why not?

WALKER V. BIRMINGHAM

388 U.S. 307 (1966)

Mr. Justice STEWART delivered the opinion of the Court.

On Wednesday, April 10, 1963, officials of Birmingham, Alabama, filed a bill of complaint in a state circuit court asking for injunctive relief against 139 individuals and two organizations. The bill and accompanying affidavits stated that during the preceding seven days:

> "[R]espondents [had] sponsored and/or participated in and/or conspired to commit and/or to encourage and/or to participate in certain movements, plans or projects commonly called 'sit-in' demonstrations, 'kneel-in' demonstrations, mass street parades, trespasses on private property after being warned to leave the premises by the owners of said property, congregating in mobs upon the public streets and other public places, unlawfully picketing private places of business in the City of Birmingham, Alabama; violation of numerous ordinances and statutes of the City of Birmingham and State of Alabama...."

It was alleged that this conduct was "calculated to provoke breaches of the peace," "threaten[ed] the safety, peace and tranquility of the City," and placed "an undue burden and strain upon the manpower of the Police Department."

The bill stated that these infractions of the law were expected to continue and would "lead to further imminent danger to the lives, safety, peace, tranquility and general welfare of the people of the City of Birmingham," and that the "remedy by law [was] inadequate." The circuit judge granted a temporary injunction as prayed in the bill, enjoining the petitioners from, among other things, participating in or encouraging mass street parades or mass processions without a permit as required by a Birmingham ordinance.

Five of the eight petitioners were served with copies of the writ early the next morning. Several hours later four of them held a press conference. There a statement was distributed, declaring their intention to disobey the injunction because it was "raw tyranny under the guise of maintaining law and order."[1] At this press conference one of the petitioners stated: "That they had respect for the Federal Courts, or Federal Injunctions, but in the past the State Courts had favored local law enforcement, and if the police couldn't handle it, the mob would."

That night a meeting took place at which one of the petitioners announced that "[i]njunction or no injunction we are going to march tomorrow." The next afternoon, Good Friday, a large crowd gathered in the vicinity of Sixteenth Street and Sixth Avenue North in Birmingham. A group of about 50 or 60 proceeded to parade along the sidewalk while a crowd of 1,000 to 1,500 onlookers stood by, "clapping, and hollering, and [w]hooping." Some of the crowd followed the marchers and spilled out into the street. At least three of the petitioners participated in this march.

Meetings sponsored by some of the petitioners were held that night and the following night, where calls for volunteers to "walk" and go to jail were made. On Easter Sunday, April 14, a crowd of between 1,500 and 2,000 people congregated in the midafternoon in the vicinity of Seventh Avenue and Eleventh Street North in Birmingham. One of the petitioners was seen organizing members of the crowd in formation. A group of about 50, headed by three other petitioners, started down the sidewalk two abreast. At least one other petitioner was among the marchers. Some 300 or 400 people from among the onlookers followed in a crowd that occupied the entire width of the street and overflowed onto the sidewalks. Violence occurred. Members of the crowd threw rocks that injured a newspaperman and damaged a police motorcycle.

The next day the city officials who had requested the injunction applied to the state circuit court for an order to show cause why the petitioners should not be held in contempt for violating it. At the ensuing hearing the petitioners sought to attack the constitutionality of the injunction on the ground that it was vague and overbroad, and restrained free speech. They also sought to attack the Birmingham parade ordinance upon similar grounds, and upon the further ground that the ordinance had previously been administered in an arbitrary and discriminatory manner.

The circuit judge refused to consider any of these contentions, pointing out that there had been neither a motion to dissolve the injunction, nor an effort to comply with it by applying for a permit from the city commission before engaging in the Good Friday and Easter Sunday parades. Consequently, the court held that the only issues before it were whether it had jurisdiction to issue the temporary injunction, and whether thereafter the petitioners had knowingly violated it. Upon these issues the court found against the petitioners, and imposed upon each of them a sentence of five days in jail and a $50 fine, in accord with an Alabama statute.

The Supreme Court of Alabama affirmed. . . .

In the present case, . . . [w]e are asked to say that the Constitution compelled Alabama to allow the petitioners to violate this injunction, to organize and engage in these mass street parades and demonstrations, without any previous effort on their part to have the injunction dissolved or modified, or any attempt to secure

a parade permit in accordance with its terms. . . . [W]e cannot accept the petitioner's contentions in the circumstances of this case.

Without question the state court that issued the injunction had, as a court of equity, jurisdiction over the petitioners and over the subject matter of the controversy. And this is not a case where the injunction was transparently invalid or had only a frivolous pretense to validity. We have consistently recognized the strong interest of state and local governments in regulating the use of their streets and other public places. . . .

The generality of the language contained in the Birmingham parade ordinance upon which the injunction was based would unquestionably raise substantial constitutional issues concerning some of its provisions. . . . The petitioners, however, did not even attempt to apply to the Alabama courts for an authoritative construction of the ordinance. . . .

The breadth and vagueness of the injunction itself would also unquestionably be subject to substantial constitutional question. But the way to raise that question was to apply to the Alabama courts to have the injunction modified or dissolved. The injunction in all events clearly prohibited mass parading without a permit, and the evidence shows that the petitioners fully understood that prohibition when they violated it. . . .

This case would arise in quite a different constitutional posture if the petitioners, before disobeying the injunction, had challenged it in the Alabama courts, and had been met with delay or frustration of their constitutional claims. But there is no showing that such would have been the fate of a timely motion to modify or dissolve the injunction. . . .

The rule of law that Alabama followed in this case reflects a belief that in the fair administration of justice no man can be judge in his own case, however exalted his station, however righteous his motives, and irrespective of his race, color, politics, or religion. This Court cannot hold that the petitioners were constitutionally free to ignore all the procedures of the law and carry their battle to the streets. One may sympathize with the petitioners' impatient commitment to their cause. But respect for judicial process is a small price to pay for the civilizing hand of law, which alone can give abiding meaning to constitutional freedom.

Affirmed.

Mr. Justice BRENNAN, with whom THE CHIEF JUSTICE, Mr. Justice DOUGLAS, and Mr. Justice FORTAS, join, dissenting.

. . . . It is said that petitioners should have sought to dissolve the injunction before conducting their processions. That argument is plainly repugnant to the principle that First Amendment freedoms may be exercised in the face of legislative prior restraints, and *a fortiori* of *ex parte* restrains broader than such legislative restraints, which may be challenged in any subsequent proceeding for their violation. But at all events, prior resort to a motion to dissolve this injunction could not be required because of the complete absence of any time limits on the duration of the *ex parte* order. . . . Even the Alabama Supreme Court's Rule 47 leaves the timing of full judicial consideration of the validity of the restraint to that court's untrammeled discretion.

The shifting of the burden to petitioners to show the lawfulness of their conduct prior to engaging in enjoined activity also is contrary to the principle, settled by Speiser v. Randall, 357 U.S. 513, 526, that

"The man who knows that he must bring forth proof and persuade another of the lawfulness of his conduct necessarily must steer far wider of the unlawful zone than if the State must bear these burdens . . . . In practical operation, therefore, this procedural device must necessarily produce a result which the State could not command directly. It can only result in a deterrence of speech which the Constitution makes free."

NOTE

[1]The Statement distributed by petitioners read:

"In our struggle for freedom we have anchored our faith and hope in the rightness of the Constitution and the moral laws of the universe.

"Again and again the Federal judiciary has made it clear that the priviledges [sic] guaranteed under the First and the Fourteenth Amendments are to [sic] sacred to be trampled upon by the machinery of state government and police power. In the past we have abided by Federal injunctions out of respect for the forthright and consistent leadership that the Federal judiciary has given in establishing the principle of integration as the law of the land.

"However we are now confronted with recalcitrant forces in the Deep South that will use the courts to perpetuate the unjust and illegal system of racial separation.

"Alabama has made clear its determination to defy the law of the land. Most of its public officials, its legislative body and many of its law enforcement agents have openly defied the desegration [sic] decision of the Supreme Court. We would feel morally and legal [sic] responsible to obey the injunction if the courts of Alabama applied equal justice to all of its citizens. This would be sameness made legal. However the ussuance [sic] of this injunction is a blatant of *difference* made *legal*.

"Southern law enforcement agencies have demonstrated now and again that they will utilize the force of law to misuse the judicial process.

"This is raw tyranny under the guise of maintaining law and order. We cannot in all good conscience obey such an injunction which is an unjust, undemocratic and unconstitutional misuse of the legal process.

"We do this not out of any desrespect [sic] for the law but out of the highest respect for *the* law. This is not an attempt to evade or defy the law or engage in chaotic anarchy. Just as in all good conscience we cannot obey unjust laws, neither can we respect the unjust use of the courts.

"We believe in a system of law based on justice and morality. Out of our great love for the Constitution of the U.S. and our desire to purify the judicial system of the state of Alabama, we risk this critical move with an awareness of the possible consequences involved."

Appendix B to Opinion of the Court, 388 U.S. at 323–24.

QUESTIONS FOR DISCUSSION

1. Was the march under consideration in *Walker v. Birmingham* an act of civil disobedience? Why or why not?

2. Is the march morally justified according to Rawls' conditions? In your own opinion? Why or why not?

3. What legal means did the marchers in *Walker v. Birmingham* try before their march? What legal steps could they have taken that they did not take? Should they have tried these other legal means first? Why or why not?

4. Should the marchers in *Walker v. Birmingham* have been punished? Why or why not?

5. Operation Rescue (founded by Randall Terry) and Rescue America are two groups that practice civil disobedience against abortion. Operation Rescue pledges non–violence, but its members are commonly arrested for trespass, disorderly conduct, and resisting arrest. Their most famous protest was their "Summer of Mercy" campaign in Wichita, Kansas (population 300,000), between July 15 and August 25, 1991. About 25,000 attended rallies, and 2,600 (about half from Wichita) were arrested for their protests against Wichita's three abortion clinics, including Women's Health Care Services, where George Tiller was one of the few doctors known to perform late–term abortions. Six thousand pro–choice supporters also came to defend the abortion clinics. The following list describes some tactics of these antiabortion groups (gathered from a variety of sources). Which of these acts, if any, are civil disobedience? Assuming that you believe a human fetus has a right to life from the moment of conception, which of these acts, if any, are morally justified? Why?

(a) They surround, show pictures to, and scream at women who approach abortion clinics, presumably to get abortions.

(b) They surround and block access to abortion clinics.

(c) They trespass on the property of abortion clinics in open violation of orders by owners, by police, and by courts.

(d) They storm barricades set up to prevent trespassing.

(e) They chain themselves to clinic doors.

(f) They descend on communities in large numbers with the intention of flooding and breaking their criminal justice systems.

(g) They bring children to their protests.

(h) They take itsy–bitsy baby steps (the "Wichita Baby Walk") when police order them to get into police buses. It took some protesters 30 minutes or more to walk to the bus.

(i) They resist arrest and give pseudonyms to the police.

(j) They establish "crisis pregnancy" centers that purport to offer abortions but instead confront women with films and lectures intended to frighten them away from getting abortions.

(k) They publicize both work and home phone numbers of judges and other officials who oppose them, and then they encourage people to flood

those telephones with calls. (They defend this as an exercise of their First Amendment right "to petition the Government for a redress of grievances.")
(l)   They stalk doctors who perform abortions and other clinic personnel (their so-called No-Place-to-Hide campaign).
(m) They are suspected of sending death threats to opponents.
(n) They are suspected of supporting butyric acid attacks and bombings of abortion clinics, gunfire at a Michigan Planned Parenthood office, and arson at clinics in Texas and Florida.
(o) Dr. David Gunn was murdered by an individual at a Pensacola abortion clinic during a demonstration run by Rescue America. Dr. John Bayard Britton and his bodyguard were shot to death in the parking lot of a Pensacola abortion clinic, allegedly by an abortion protester, in July 1994.

6. The AIDS Coalition to Unleash Power (ACT UP) is a group of AIDS activists. The following list describes some of the things they have done (gathered from a variety of sources). Which of these acts, if any, are civil disobedience? Which, if any, are morally justified? Why?
(a) "In a demonstration in March, 1989, 5,000 people met at City Hall and blocked peak-hour traffic to protest the city's hospital crisis."[27]
(b) Burroughs Wellcome manufactures the AIDS drug AZT. When AZT first came out in 1987, a year's supply cost $10,000, but the price was reduced 20 percent after protests. "In April 1989, in an abortive bid to lower the price further, members of ACT UP infiltrated the company's headquarters in Research Triangle Park, North Carolina. . . . The protestors bolted themselves inside one of the company's offices and convened a press conference by telephone. Five months later, ACT UP staged one of its most daring and widely publicized coups. [Peter] Staley and six other members put on business suits and forged identification badges, then slipped onto the trading floor of the New York Stock Exchange. They chained themselves to a banister, unravelled a banner that said SELL WELLCOME, set off miniature foghorns, and stopped trading on the floor for the first time in its history. . . . Five days later, Burroughs Wellcome announced a second 20% reduction in the price of AZT."[28]
(c) "Cardinal O'Connor [is] an advocate of Operation Rescue and an opponent of education about condoms, not just in Roman Catholic *and* public schools but also in shelters for people with AIDS." The Cardinal was the target of a protest at St. Patrick's Cathedral on December 10, 1989, by 5,000 members and supporters of ACT UP and WHAM! (Women's Health Action and Mobilization, a reproductive rights group), 111 of which were arrested. "[J]ust as the cardinal began his sermon, the protestors staged a 'die-in.' Some lay down along the nave and chained themselves to the pews,

[27]*New York,* Nov. 12, 1990, p. 70.
[28]*New York,* Nov. 12, 1990, pp. 70–71.

blowing whistles and shouting slogans, such as 'Pro-choice is pro-life' and 'Condoms save lives.' Worshipers were aghast as uniformed police walked in with walkie-talkies and wire cutters and proceeded to handcuff the demonstrators and haul them out on stretchers. Everything returned to normal for a while . . . [but] then came communion. . . . As ACT UP's Tom Keane, a lapsed Catholic, recalls it, he 'scrunched' a consecrated communion wafer in his hand, dropped it to the floor, and mumbled, 'Opposing safe-sex education is murder.' . . . He was removed by police and charged with disrupting a religious service, disorderly conduct, and resisting arrest."[29]

(d) "ACT UP and Queer Nation [a gay rights group] believe that the lurid new movie 'Basic Instinct' is anti-homosexual. . . . Last year in San Francisco, ACT UP and Queer Nation disrupted filming of "Instinct" in an attempt to censor the script. Paint was splattered on sets, whistles were blown, and drivers were induced to honk car horns in an effort to ruin the sound track. Shortly afterward, Ray Chalker, owner of a gay bar and publisher of a gay newspaper, was punished for renting the bar to the film company as a site. The bar was picketed, his answering machine jammed with threatening calls; Super Glue was poured into the locks of his home, and his car was vandalized."[30]

(e) In a protest against Stephen Joseph, New York City health commissioner, "ACT UP tossed paint on his residence, occupied his office, harrassed his family with phone calls, shouted down his public speeches, and hounded him for weeks everywhere he went, even in restaurants."[31]

7. Find out what Greenpeace does to protest environmental abuses. Do they commit civil disobedience? Which of their acts are justified? Why?

8. Suppose a convicted murderer is sentenced to death, but a district court judge declares the sentence unconstitutional, because she believes that the death penalty is immoral, even though she knows that the Supreme Court has found it constitutional in similar cases. Does this judge's act count as civil disobedience? Is it morally justified? Why or why not?

9. Should the fact that someone has engaged in civil disobedience in the past be a reason to reject his or her nomination to the Supreme Court? To the position of Attorney General? To the position of Director of the Park Service? Why or why not?

10. When, if ever, should people who commit civil disobedience be punished? Should they be punished as much as other people who break the same laws but not for conscientious reasons? Why or why not?

[29]*New York*, Nov. 12, 1990, pp. 72–73.

[30]John Leo, *U.S. News & World Report*, April 6, 1992.

[31]John Leo, *U.S. News & World Report*, July 9, 1990.

SUGGESTIONS FOR FURTHER READING

Classic and contemporary writings on civil disobedience are usefully collected with further bibliography in Hugo Bedau, ed., *Civil Disobedience in Focus* (London and New York: Routledge, 1991). Clear and lively discussions from a utilitarian perspective can be found in Peter Singer, *Democracy and Disobedience* (Oxford: Clarendon Press, 1973) and *Practical Ethics* (Cambridge: Cambridge University Press, 1979), Chapter 9. Two good recent monographs are Kent Greenawalt, *Conflicts of Law and Morality* (New York: Oxford University Press, 1987) and Vinit Haksar, *Civil Disobedience, Threats and Offers: Ghandi and Rawls* (Delhi: Oxford University Press, 1986). For classic arguments against civil disobedience, see Thomas Hobbes, *Leviathan*, ed. M. Oakeshott (New York: Collier Books, 1962). On punishment for civil disobedience, see Ronald Dworkin, "Civil Disobedience," in *Taking Rights Seriously* (Cambridge: Harvard University Press, 1978), pp. 206–222; and Daniel M. Farrell, "Paying the Penalty: Justifiable Civil Disobedience and the Problem of Punishment," *Philosophy and Public Affairs*, vol. 6, no. 2 (Winter 1977), pp. 165–184. For useful distinctions among kinds of civil disobedience, see Ronald Dworkin, "Civil Disobedience and Nuclear Protest," in *A Matter of Principle* (Cambridge: Harvard University Press, 1985), pp. 104–116.

CHAPTER 4

THE STRUCTURE AND CONTENT OF RIGHTS

INTRODUCTION

Especially in the United States, law often appears to be centrally about the *rights* that people have. There are constitutional rights, such as the right to free speech, the right to freedom of religion, the right to keep and bear arms, the right to be free from being forced to testify against yourself, the right to be represented by a lawyer if you are charged with a crime, and the right to the equal protection of the laws. There are also rights not explicitly set out as such in the text of the Constitution—the right to privacy, the right to vote, and the right to travel are important examples—but which through a continuing process of judicial interpretation have attained the status of enforceable constitutional rights. And when we talk about what constitutional rights we do or should have, we often make reference to background political and moral rights, such as the right to own property, or the right to personal liberty. Indeed, to many people the rights set forth in the Constitution are but the concrete versions of deep *human rights* or *natural rights,* rights that would exist even were there no Constitution.

Although constitutional rights are important, it is a mistake to suppose that the only rights we have are constitutional rights. When a state legislature by statute or a city council by ordinance says that all restaurants shall have a no-smoking section, these political bodies have then created a legal right to sit in a no-smoking section of a restaurant.[1] This right is enforceable by legal instrumentalities—courts and police officers, for example. And the legal right created by positive law then justifies the claim that a person's legal rights have been violated when a restaurant says that it does not have a no-smoking section. Yet this legal right is a creature of a statute or an ordinance, and not of the Constitution. The right, as a legal right, would not exist unless the state legislature or the city council created it. Similarly, there is a legal right to drive a car in New Jersey for people over the age of seventeen, and a legal right to drive a car in Michigan for people over the age of sixteen, but residents of New Jersey between the ages of

---

[1] The statement in the text is a bit of an over-simplification, since the right would not ordinarily give someone a seat if the no-smoking section were full, for example. The question of what a right-holder actually "gets" will be taken up shortly.

sixteen and seventeen have not been deprived of any legal rights that they had prior to or independent of state statutes just because they are unable to drive lawfully in New Jersey, even though they could if they were residents of Michigan. Here legal rights are created by state statutes, and the fact that some statutes create broader legal rights than others is not itself necessarily a *deprivation* of any rights. Again, therefore, we use the language of legal rights, and demand the recognition and enforcement of legal rights, even when constitutional rights are not involved.

The fact that there are rights all around us is for some people a source of pride. For others, however, it is a reason for concern. Those who celebrate a culture of rights see rights as the protectors of individual dignity in an increasingly impersonal world, and see rights as the way in which people are shielded against what John Stuart Mill and Alexis de Tocqueville called the "tyranny of the majority." Indeed, say the people who celebrate a culture of rights, the increasing prevalence throughout the world of ideas of human rights is a sign of increasing moral sensibility. When we recognize that people have rights in addition to interests, and when we recognize that the rights people have are more important than the interests that people might serve, so it is said, we have taken a big step forward. A society with rights, they say, is simply better than a society without them.

Others, however, are not so sure. Some of these people are skeptical of a culture of rights in general, fearing that rights get in the way of serving the public interest, or the general welfare. When Jeremy Bentham referred to natural rights as "nonsense upon stilts,"[2] he was not only expressing skepticism about the very idea that there could be rights other than those created by positive law. He was also, although less obviously, expressing a normative point—that rights conflict with a pure act–utilitarianism. Under that view, every decision of policy should be based on selecting the policy that secures the greatest good for the greatest number. If rights could get in the way of maximizing utility, as we will see that they often do, then for the thoroughgoing utilitarian rights are much more to be bemoaned than celebrated.

The argument that increased attention to rights comes at the expense of the general welfare is also reflected in contemporary political argument. For example, military officers complain that the right of the press to report on military actions while they are taking place makes it harder to wage war successfully. Police officers complain that the rights of suspects or defendants, for example their right to have a lawyer present at questioning or their right to make the police obtain a warrant before conducting a search, make it harder to control crime. Welfare agencies complain that the right of people to hearings before their benefits may be reduced draws scarce resources away from needed uses and reallocates those resources to bureaucracy and administration. Teachers object to the idea of students' rights, arguing that students' rights of free speech, or rights to hearings before being suspended, get in the way of the best education for all. Finally, many

---

[2]For an illuminating collection of background materials, see Jeremy Waldron, *Nonsense upon Stilts: Bentham, Burke, and Marx on the Rights of Man* (London: Methuen, 1987).

citizens say that the right to possess weapons increases the amount of violent crime and thus decreases everyone's security.

A different form of objection to a culture of rights, however, focuses not on the very idea of rights, but instead on an increasing tendency to characterize all desires and all interests as rights.[3] Rights to free speech, freedom of religion, and racial equality, it is said, are genuinely important and need to be protected both legally and politically. But, it is argued, we devalue the rhetoric of rights, and dilute the force of a claim of right, once we start talking about and protecting the rights of smokers, the rights of people who want to play video games, and the rights of those who wish to swim in the nude at a national park. If every interest is a right, if every desire is a right, so the argument goes, then we have lost the central feature of rights—something that must be recognized even if it is not at the moment the optimal policy to do so. Moreover, as Mary Ann Glendon argues, rights protect the individual against the demands of the common good. When we become too preoccupied with rights, therefore, we may be too little concerned with the common life that holds a society together.

■ ■ ■

The existence of a culture of rights, and controversies about its desirability, thus suggest the importance of trying to see just what rights *are* and why they are important. That is the topic of this chapter, whose goal is to take on a number of different questions about the idea of rights.

Especially in a book on the philosophy of law, an important topic is the relationship between legal rights and other kinds of rights. Many people believe, for example, that Jeremy Bentham was wrong to claim that the idea of natural rights was nonsense upon stilts. They believe that there are moral rights antecedent to particular laws and to particular legal or political cultures. This belief, central to the entire non–utilitarian tradition in moral philosophy, maintains that certain actions are morally wrong even if good consequences would be produced by engaging in them. It also maintains that people's moral rights are thus violated when certain things are done to them, regardless of whether the actions are taken in accordance with the law or in violation of it. Although the positive law in much of the United States now permits discrimination on the basis of sexual orientation, for example, many people believe that those who are so discriminated against have had their moral and political rights violated. They further argue that the law should be changed to prohibit discrimination on the basis of sexual orientation, not to create new rights, but to ensure that the law protects the moral rights we have independent of the law. This, they argue, is in the spirit of the American tradition, which sees rights as something that governments protect, not create. A good example of this, they say, is the recognition of "inalienable rights" in the Declaration of Independence. So too, they argue, is seeing rights as antecedent to or independent of positive law consistent with the idea of human rights in international relations. When we condemn another nation for violating

---

[2]The most prominent contemporary example of this argument is Mary Ann Glendon, *Rights Talk: The Impoverishment of Political Discourse* (New York: The Free Press, 1991).

the human rights of its citizens by, for example, torturing them, or refusing to allow them to practice their religion, we do not care if the torture was permitted by the domestic law of the country of which they are citizens. Often we do not even care if some formal treaty or convention or United Nations resolution has defined the action as a violation of human rights. We call them *human* rights, so the argument goes, just because the rights are things we possess because we are human, and not because we are citizens of this country or that, and not because we are citizens of a country that happens to have signed a particular international convention.

Thus a central question about the nature of rights is the relationship between legal rights and moral rights. Things get more complicated still when we introduce the idea of *political* rights—rights that may pre-exist the positive law of particular societies, but that are derived from the political presuppositions of that society and not necessarily from ideas about humanity applicable to all societies and all political cultures. Some people might say, for example, that there is a political right to choose leaders in all societies that think of themselves as democracies, but that this is a political right and not a moral right because there is nothing immoral about a monarchy or theocracy. Others would disagree, of course, but the idea is only that we can imagine rights that are antecedent to positive law but still not universal in the way that we think of moral or human rights as being universal.

A related cluster of questions, applicable to moral, political, and legal rights, concerns the *structure* of rights. In any of these domains—legal, moral, and political—just what *is* a right, and what does one actually have when one has a right? Relatedly, is there just one relationship that is properly characterized as a right, or does the word "right" encompass a number of different relationships? Some people say that a person suspected of a crime has a *privilege* against self-incrimination. Typically, the Registry of Motor Vehicles reminds us that driving is not a right but a *privilege*. What is going on here? Are rights different from privileges, as the Registry of Motor Vehicles would have us believe, or is the word "privilege" almost a synonym for the word "right," as might be suggested by the fact that just as many people refer to the *right* against self-incrimination as refer to the privilege against self-incrimination?

The questions of terminology become even more complex when we think of *freedom* and *liberty*. Again, are the words "freedom" and "liberty" just synonyms for the word "right," or is there a difference among the three? Like the word "right," is it possible that the words "liberty" and "freedom" can refer to a number of different ideas. When President Franklin Delano Roosevelt referred, famously, to the Four Freedoms—Freedom to Speak, Freedom of Belief, Freedom from Want, and Freedom from Fear—was he giving four different examples of the same kind of relationship? Or might there be something quite different between, for example, the Freedom to Speak and Freedom from Want? If a government wanted to guarantee the freedom of speech, what would it have to do? Would it be sufficient for the government to refrain from interfering with people who wanted to speak, or would the government have to provide the opportunities to speak? Would the government have to provide people to listen? And consider the related right of freedom of the press, and the famous statement made close to a hundred years ago by the prominent journalist A. J. Liebling when he said that "freedom of the press is for the man who owns one." Does this mean that people with fewer resources have fewer rights, or is there a difference between a right and the ability to exercise it?

Thus another central question in rights theory is one of distinguishing between what are often called *positive* and *negative* rights, or freedoms, or liberties. Negative rights are rights to be free from some kind of interference, and thus my right to freedom of speech is preserved as long as no one keeps me from speaking, even if I am not a good speaker, and even if I have few opportunities to speak. Positive rights, on the other hand, relate closely to abilities, or opportunities. A positive freedom to speak would require someone to give the speaker the opportunity to speak, just as a positive freedom from want would require someone to provide for people the material resources such that they would no longer be needy.

Related to questions about positive and negative rights are questions about the people, or institutions, that rights protect against. If a police officer, as an employee of the government, breaks into a house without a search warrant or without "probable cause," the homeowner's rights under the Fourth Amendment to the Constitution have been violated. But if a private individual, like a neighbor, with no connection to the government, breaks into the same house looking for the same articles, no constitutional rights, at least in the United States, have been violated. That is because in the United States constitutional rights ordinarily protect only against governmental entities and not against other sorts of institutions. The private individual who breaks into a home, or the private school teacher who searches a student's locker, or the corporation that fires an employee for speaking out against the company, or the newspaper editor who refuses to publish a reporter's story because the editor does not like the reporter, have in the United States violated no one's constitutional rights, because only governments can do that. But is this limitation to government wrongs a necessary feature of constitutional law, or only a contingent feature of American constitutional law? Perhaps the relationship with government is something about all rights, or about certain rights, such that they are necessarily rights against government only?

■ ■ ■

Although much of this chapter will accordingly focus on the concept and structure of rights and on the relationships among constitutional, legal, political, and moral rights, the chapter will also look at particular rights and the controversies that have surrounded them. Some of these controversies are about the very existence of the rights themselves, especially at the "prelegal" level. For example, there is no question that in American law there are constitutional rights to freedom of speech and freedom of the press, because the First Amendment to the Constitution explicitly provides that "Congress shall make no law ... abridging the freedom of speech, or of the press." But what if the Constitution contained no such language? What if it were like the Australian Constitution, which has no bill of rights at all? Or what if, like in Great Britain, New Zealand, and Israel, there were no written constitution whatsoever? Is there a right to free speech in those countries? If so, what kind? More to the point, if you were asked to draft the constitution for a new country, would you include a right to free speech? In order to answer this question, you would have to figure out whether there was a pre-legal moral or political right to free speech, or whether it would be good policy for there to be a legal right to free speech, for only if one or the other were the case would it be a good idea for your new constitution to protect it. To decide whether a constitution *should* protect a right to free speech, therefore, it would be necessary to determine, as a question of moral and political philosophy or as a question of policy, but not as a question of positive law, whether there *was* a right to free speech.

Thinking pre-legally about specific rights is important not only because such thinking is important in deciding what rights should be contained in constitutions, or in international treaties, or in other pieces of positive law. It is important also because in many cases questions remain about the existence of such rights even where there is already a written constitution or similar document. Consider again the right to privacy. Although the right to privacy is explicitly mentioned in the Constitution of the state of Alaska, the right to privacy is not explicitly mentioned in the Constitution of the United States. Still, as we explored in Chapter 1, it may be permissible in some systems, including the United States, for judges to recognize or to create rights not explicitly mentioned in a constitution or similar item of positive law.

Once we recognize the power of judges to create or recognize rights not explicitly set forth in the written Constitution, we still have much work to do. After all, not all rights are equally important, and not all claims of right are equally sound. That there is a right to free speech does not mean that there must be a right to drive an automobile. In order to determine, for example, whether judges should recognize or create a right to privacy, or recognize or create a fetus's right to life, we again have to think pre-legally about the existence or status of such rights. Those who think, for example, that the Constitution should (or does) recognize a right of a woman to have an abortion, but that the Constitution should not (or does not) recognize a fetus's right to life, must provide some basis for believing that the one right exists while the other does not. It is just for that reason that exploring the nature of specific rights is as important as exploring the idea of the concept of rights itself.

Even when specific rights are found in a legal document, they are often phrased in general terms. The United States Constitution, for example, protects the "free exercise [of religion]" and the right to be free from "cruel and unusual punishment." But what kinds of activities do these rights cover? Is the right to be free from cruel and unusual punishment violated when a judge requires people convicted of driving under the influence of alcohol to put on their car a bumper sticker saying "I was convicted of DUI"? Is the right to the free exercise of one's religion violated when the government prohibits animal sacrifice but one's religion requires that animals be sacrificed as an offering to God? Does the right to free speech include the right of tobacco companies to advertise cigarettes? In order to answer these questions about the scope of these rights, it is necessary to examine the particular rights politically and philosophically, since little in the typically vague statements in formal legal documents gets us very far in thinking about difficult questions about application.

Even when some activity is within the scope of a right, it is often necessary to confront cases when rights conflict with each other, or when it is argued that a right is overridden by some sufficiently weighty interest—whether a right or not. When reporters disclose in a newspaper report of a trial the previous convictions of someone then on trial, the right to freedom of the press conflicts with the defendant's right to a fair trial. When a person refers to another person by use of a racial or religious epithet, the right to free speech may conflict with the right to equality. When a person refuses to let people of other races into his home, the right to equality may conflict with the right to own property. And when society prohibits parents from refusing, for religious reasons, to allow their children to have blood transfusions, the right to freedom of religion conflicts with interests in avoiding unnecessary suffering, illness, or death. In all of these cases we confront issues not only about particular rights, but also about the nature and structure of rights. This constant conjunction of substantive and structural features of rights will be a recurring theme of the writings and commentary in this chapter.

4.1 THE STRUCTURE OF RIGHTS

INTRODUCTION

As Americans we have a right to free speech, but what do we have when we have it? Commonly we think this means the government cannot prevent us from, or punish us for, speaking. But the government can and does punish people for committing perjury, disclosing military secrets, defrauding their employers, misrepresenting by false advertising the characteristics of products they sell, and engaging in other unlawful activities that take place largely by speaking. Although it is generally understood in the United States that it would be an infringement of the right to free speech for the government to imprison someone for criticizing the President of the United States, does the right to free speech protect an employee of General Motors against being fired for criticizing the president of General Motors? Does a television newscaster like Dan Rather have a greater right to free speech than the person on the street because Rather has the ability to speak to so many more people?

Questions like these illustrate the importance of commencing a study of rights with an inquiry into the structure of rights. Just what is a right, and what does a person have when she has one? As some of the examples just given demonstrate, this is hardly an easy question, and it is hardly one that has produced much agreement. Still, a good place to start is with an examination of the contributions of Wesley Newcomb Hohfeld,[4] whose analysis of the concept of rights has had an enduring effect. Hohfeld's own exposition, however, primarily contained in two long law review articles,[5] is often obscure, frequently lacking the clarity he urged on others. It is best, therefore, to summarize the basic ideas, ideas that will reappear at numerous points throughout this chapter.

Hohfeld started with the insight that the word "right" was used to refer to numerous different relationships. He believed that great confusion came from using the same word to refer to what were in fact several different concepts. Hohfeld sought to cure this confusion not only by giving each distinct relationship a separate name, but also by identifying the components of the relationship. Thus for Hohfeld the central idea was that of a right as a *relationship*, and, more particularly, a two-party relationship. When one person, A, has a right to something, there is at least one other person, B, whose status is implicated because of A's

---

[4]Hohfeld (1879–1918) was a Professor of Law at the Stanford and Yale Law Schools.

[5]"Some Fundamental Legal Conceptions as Applied in Judicial Reasoning," *Yale Law Journal*, vol. 23 (1913), pp. 16 ff; "Fundamental Conceptions as Applied in Judicial Reasoning," *Yale Law Journal*, vol. 26 (1917), pp. 710 ff.

right. This can be made more clear by examining each of Hohfeld's four types of right.

The first type of right was what Hohfeld called a *claim*, or a right in the strict sense. Here the two-party relationship is most obvious, for *A* has a claim when and only when *B* has a duty. For example, suppose that *A* and *B* enter into a contract and according to the contract *A* will give *B* a car, and *B* in exchange will give *A* $5,000. *A* then gives *B* the car. At that time, according to the law of contracts, *B* has a *duty* to give *A* the $5,000, and *A* has a claim against *B* that *B* perform that duty. The claim of *A* and the duty of *B* are thus the two parts of the two-party relationship, and in Hohfeld's terminology *B*'s duty is the *correlative* of *A*'s claim. Similarly, in the context of public law rather than private law, the Social Security laws create duties on the part of government to give certain people money under certain conditions, and when we refer to "rights under the Social Security laws" we refer to a person's *claim* against the government that is the correlative of the government's *duty* to pay a certain amount of money under the conditions specified in the Social Security Act.

Although Hohfeld believed that a claim was a right in the strict sense, it is central to Hohfeld's insight that not all rights are claims. His second kind of right was what he called a *privilege*, and what is perhaps now more commonly referred to as a *liberty*. Consider the right to free speech. A right like the right to free speech was to Hohfeld a privilege because a person who has a right to free speech has a privilege, or liberty, to speak, and also a privilege, or a liberty, not to speak. In this sense a liberty is an area in which it is not wrong to act, and not wrong not to act, depending on the preferences of the holder of the privilege. When we say that someone has a privilege against self-incrimination, we mean that the person may choose to make statements that incriminate him, but may also choose not to make statements that incriminate him.

The correlative of a liberty, to Hohfeld, was "no-claim" on the part of someone else. Thus, *A* has a liberty of speech with respect to *B* if *B* has no claim on *A* that *A* speak or not speak, and thus a liberty is just the opposite of a duty. When *A* is not under a duty to *B*, then *A* has a liberty with respect to *B*, and *B* has no claim (the opposite of a claim) with respect to *A*.

Commonly, liberties are connected with and supported by claims.[6] The liberty of speech protected by the First Amendment is in part the absence of a claim on the part of government that a person speak or not speak, but that liberty is supported by a duty on the part of government not to interfere with a person's speaking. This duty on the part of the government thus also creates a claim on the part of a speaker, which the speaker can use in court to enforce the government's duty not to interfere with a person's speech. The "right" to free speech, therefore, is in fact at least the conjunction of: (1) the privilege that is the correlative of the government's lack of a claim against citizens that they speak or not

---

[6]This is why Judith Jarvis Thomson, in *The Realm of Rights* (Cambridge: Harvard University Press, 1991), pp. 53–56, resists treating "privilege" and "liberty" as synonymous. For her the word "liberty" is best reserved for the conjunction of a privilege and a claim.

speak; and (2) the claim that is the correlative of the government's duty not to interfere with a person's speaking or not speaking.

To be distinguished from both a claim and a liberty (or privilege) is Hohfeld's third type of right, a *power*. A power is the ability to change the legal status of another person, so that when *A* has what is called a *power of attorney* with respect to *B*, that means that *A*, usually as a result of some document signed by *B*, can now make commitments on behalf of *B* that will as a result change *B*'s legal condition or status. The two-person relationship in the case of a power is thus the relationship between the holder of a power and the person whose status can be changed as a result of the exercise of that power. The correlative of a power is a *liability*, because, when *A* has a power with respect to *B*, then *B* is liable to have her status changed as a result of *A*'s action. I am liable to lose a great deal of money, for example, if I give a legal power to a bad attorney.

Finally, the fourth type of right to Hohfeld was an *immunity*, which is just the opposite of a liability. *A* has an immunity from *B* just when *B* has no power over *A*, and thus the correlative of an immunity is a *disability*. When *A* has an immunity, then *B* is under a disability, which is just the opposite of a power. When an accomplice to a crime is given an immunity from prosecution in order to get him to testify in court (and thus to waive his privilege against self-incrimination), the witness is then immune from the prosecutor's power to prosecute, and the prosecutor is disabled by no longer having the power to prosecute that accomplice.

Hohfeld's exact scheme has been contested ever since it was first introduced. Some scholars have questioned whether all of Hohfeld's distinctions are sound. Is there a difference, for example, between an immunity and a liberty? Others have noted that some of Hohfeld's formal categories have less significance than others. If a liberty is almost always supported by a claim, as in the free speech example, then what is the point of distinguishing between the two?

Controversy about the details of the Hohfeldian approach have not, however, lessened the importance of the two basic ideas introduced by Hohfeld: (1) the word "right" encompasses several quite different relationships (including, possibly, some not on Hohfeld's own list); and (2) each of these relationships can be captured by focusing on a two-party relationship, where one party has some version of a right, and some other party has the status that is the *correlative* of the right. An understanding of these two fundamental points in Hohfeld's broad message enables us to think of rights not in isolation, but in terms both of the right-holder and of someone standing in a relationship with the right-holder. Freedom of speech, for example, may turn out to be a liberty with respect to the state but not a liberty with respect to a non-governmental employer. There is nothing illogical, therefore, in saying that the right to free speech gives a person a liberty with respect to the government, a claim to enforce the government's duty not to interfere with speech, and (possibly) an immunity from government action with respect to speech; but neither a liberty, a claim, nor an immunity with respect to private employers. If a person makes a speech criticizing the President of the United States, and as a result is fired by her (non-governmental) employer, this does not mean she has no right to free speech. It means only that she has a cluster of free speech rights against the government, but none against her employer. We may believe that this is normatively wrong as a matter of substance—that it would be better if there were rights against private employers similar to those against the government—but Hohfeld helps us to see why it is not incoherent as a matter of logic.

Hohfeld was concerned primarily with the kind of rights that exist in areas of private law such as contracts, torts, property, wills, and trusts. His approach does provide useful clarification and background when we consider moral rights, human rights, natural rights, and constitutional rights, but none of these were Hohfeld's direct concern. These kinds of rights have, however, been the primary concern of most contemporary philosophical writing about rights, and the selections that follow all focus on one or another of these kinds of rights. In considering these readings, try to bear in mind Hohfeld's warning about the dangers of not being clear about the different types of rights, and try to consider as well the relationship between the accounts of each of these authors and the account offered by Hohfeld.

THE NATURE AND VALUE OF RIGHTS

JOEL FEINBERG

I would like to begin by conducting a thought experiment. Try to imagine Nowheresville—a world very much like our own except that no one, or hardly any one (the qualification is not important), has *rights*. If this flaw makes Nowheresville too ugly to hold very long in contemplation, we can make it as pretty as we wish in other moral respects. We can, for example, make the human beings in it as attractive and virtuous as possible without taxing our conceptions of the limits of human nature. In particular, let the virtues of moral sensibility flourish. Fill this imagined world with as much benevolence, compassion, sympathy, and pity as it will conveniently hold without strain.

Now we can imagine men helping one another from compassionate motives merely, quite as much [as] or even more than they do in our actual world from a variety of more complicated motives.

■■■

So much for the imaginary "world without rights." If some of the moral concepts and practices I have allowed into that world do not sit well with one another, no matter. Imagine Nowheresville with all of these practices if you can, or with any harmonious subset of them, if you prefer. The important thing is not what I've let into it, but what I have kept out. The remainder of this paper will be devoted to an

Joel Feinberg, "The Nature and Value of Rights," *Journal of Value Inquiry*, vol. 4 (1970), pp. 243 ff.

analysis of what precisely a world is missing when it does not contain rights and why that absence is morally important.

The most conspicuous difference, I think, between the Nowheresvillians and ourselves has something to do with the activity of *claiming*. Nowheresvillians, even when they are discriminated against invidiously, or left without the things they need, or otherwise badly treated, do not think to leap to their feet and make righteous demands against one another though they may not hesitate to resort to force and trickery to get what they want. They have no notion of rights, so they do not have a notion of what is their due; hence they do not claim before they take. The conceptual linkage between personal rights and claiming has long been noticed by legal writers and is reflected in the standard usage in which "claim-rights" are distinguished from other mere liberties, immunities, and powers, also sometimes called "rights," with which they are easily confused. When a person has a legal claim-right to X, it must be the case (i) that he is at liberty in respect to X, i.e. that he has no duty to refrain from or relinquish X, and also (ii) that his liberty is the ground of other people's *duties* to grant him X or not to interfere with him in respect to X. Thus, in the sense of claim-rights, it is true by definition that rights logically entail other people's duties. The paradigmatic examples of such rights are the creditor's right to be paid a debt by his debtor, and the landowner's right not to be interfered with by anyone in the exclusive occupancy of his land. The creditor's right against his debtor, for example, and the debtor's duty to his creditor, are precisely the same relation seen from two different vantage points, as inextricably linked as the two sides of the same coin.

And yet, this is not quite an accurate account of the matter, for it fails to do justice to the way claim-rights are somehow prior to, or more basic than, the duties with which they are necessarily correlated. If Nip has a claim-right against Tuck, it is because of this fact that Tuck has a duty to Nip. It is only because

something from Tuck is *due* Nip (directional element) that there is something Tuck *must* do (modal element). This is a relation, moreover, in which Tuck is bound and Nip is free. Nip not only has a right, but he can choose whether or not to exercise it, whether to claim it, whether to register complaints upon its infringement, even whether to release Tuck from his duty, and forget the whole thing. If the personal claim-right is also backed up by criminal sanctions, however, Tuck may yet have a duty of obedience to the law from which no one, not even Nip, may release him. He would even have such duties if he lived in Nowheresville; but duties subject to acts of claiming, duties derivative from and contingent upon the personal rights of others, are unknown and undreamed of in Nowheresville.

Many philosophical writers have simply identified rights with claims. The dictionaries tend to define "claims," in turn as "assertions of right," a dizzying piece of circularity that led one philosopher to complain, "We go in search of rights and are directed to claims, and then back again to rights in bureaucratic futility." What then is the relation between a claim and a right?

As we shall see, a right is a kind of claim, and a claim is "an assertion of right," so that a formal definition of either notion in terms of the other will not get us very far. Thus if a "formal definition" of the usual philosophical sort is what we are after, the game is over before it has begun, and we can say that the concept of a right is a "simple, undefinable, unanalysable primitive." Here as elsewhere in philosophy this will have the effect of making the commonplace seem unnecessarily mysterious. We would be better advised, I think, not to attempt definition of either "right" or "claim," but rather to use the idea of a claim in informal elucidation of the idea of a right. This is made possible by the fact that *claiming* is an elaborate sort of rule-governed *activity*. A claim is that which is claimed, the object of the act of claiming. . . . If we concentrate on the whole activity of claiming, which is public, familiar, and open to our observation, rather than on its upshot alone, we may learn more about the generic nature of rights than we could ever hope to learn from a formal definition, even if one were possible. Moreover, certain facts about rights more easily, if not solely, expressible in the language of claims and claiming are essential to a full understanding not only of what rights are, but also why they are so vitally important.

Let us begin then by distinguishing between: (i) making claim to . . . , (ii) claiming that . . . , and (iii) having a claim. One sort of thing we may be doing when we claim is to *make claim to something*. This is "to petition or seek by virtue of supposed right; to demand as due." Sometimes this is done by an acknowledged right-holder when he serves notice that he now wants turned over to him that which has already been acknowledged to be his, something borrowed, say, or improperly taken from him. This is often done by turning in a chit, a receipt, an I.O.U., a check, an insurance policy, or a deed, that is, a *title* to something currently in the possession of someone else. On other occasions, making claim is making application for titles or rights themselves, as when a mining prospector stakes a claim to minimal rights, or a householder to a tract of land in the public domain, or an inventor to his patent rights. In the one kind of case, to make claim is to exercise rights one already has by presenting title; to the other kind of case it is to apply for the title itself, by showing that one has satisfied the conditions specified by a rule for the ownership of title and therefore that one can demand it as one's due.

Generally speaking, only the person who has a title or who has qualified for it, or someone speaking in his name, can make claim to something as a matter of right. It is an important fact about rights (or claims), then, that they can be claimed only by those who have them. Anyone can claim, of course, *that* this umbrella is yours, but only you or your representative can actually claim the umbrella. If Smith owes

Jones five dollars, only Jones can claim the five dollars as his own, though any bystander can *claim that* it belongs to Jones. One important difference then between *making legal claim to* and *claiming that* is that the former is a legal performance with direct legal consequences whereas the latter is often a mere piece of descriptive commentary with no legal force. Legally speaking, *making claim to* can itself make things happen. This sense of "claiming," then, might well be called "the performative sense." The legal power to claim (performatively) one's right or the things to which one has a right seems to be essential to the very notion of a right. A right to which one could not make claim (i.e. not even for recognition) would be a very "imperfect" right indeed!

Claiming that one has a right (what we can call "propositional claiming" as opposed to "performative claiming") is another sort of thing one can do with language, but it is not the sort of doing that characteristically has legal consequences. To claim that one has rights is to make an assertion that one has them, and to make it in such a manner as to demand or insist that they be recognized. In this sense of "claim" many things in addition to rights can be claimed, that is, many other kinds of proposition can be asserted in the claiming way. I can claim, for example, that you, he, or she has certain rights, or that Julius Caesar once had certain rights; or I can claim that certain statements are true, or that I have certain skills, or accomplishments, or virtually anything at all. I can claim that the earth is flat. What is essential to *claiming that* is the manner of assertion. One can assert without even caring very much whether anyone is listening, but part of the point of propositional claiming is to *make sure* people listen. When I claim to others that I know something, for example, I am not merely asserting it, but rather [, as G. J. Warnock says,] "obtruding my putative knowledge upon their attention, demanding that it be recognized, that appropriate notice be taken of it by those concerned. . . ." Not every truth is properly assertable, much less claimable, in every context. To claim that something is the case in circumstances that justify no more than calm assertion is to behave like a boor. (This kind of boorishness, I might add, is probably less common in Nowheresville.) But not to claim in the appropriate circumstance that one has a right is to be spiritless or foolish. A list of "appropriate circumstances" would include occasions when one is challenged, when one's possession is denied, or seems insufficiently acknowledged or appreciated; and of course even in these circumstances, the claiming should be done only with an appropriate degree of vehemence.

Even if there are conceivable circumstances in which one would admit rights diffidently, there is no doubt that their characteristic use and that for which they are distinctively well suited, is to be claimed, demanded, affirmed, insisted upon. They are especially sturdy objects to "stand upon," a most useful sort of moral furniture. Having rights, of course, makes claiming possible; but it is claiming that gives rights their special moral significance. This feature of rights is connected in a way with the customary rhetoric about what it is to be a human being. Having rights enables us to "stand up like men," to look others in the eye, and to feel in some fundamental way the equal of anyone. To think of oneself as the holder of rights is not to be unduly but properly proud, to have that minimal self-respect that is necessary to be worthy of the love and esteem of others. Indeed, respect for persons (this is an intriguing idea) may simply be respect for their rights, so that there cannot be the one without the other; and what is called "human dignity" may simply be the recognizable capacity to assert claims. To respect a person then, or to think of him as possessed of human dignity, simply *is* to think of him as a potential maker of claims. Not all of this can be packed into a definition of "rights"; but these are *facts* about the possession of rights that argue well their supreme moral importance. More than anything else I am

going to say, these facts explain what is wrong with Nowheresville.

We come now to the third interesting employment of the claiming vocabulary, that involving not the verb "to claim" but the substantive "a claim." What is it to *have a claim* and how is this related to rights? I would like to suggest that *having a claim consists in being in a position to claim, that is, to make claim to or claim that.* If this suggestion is correct it shows the primacy of the verbal over the nominative forms. It links claims to a kind of activity and obviates the temptation to think of claims as *things,* on the model of coins, pencils, and other material possessions which we can carry in our hip pockets. To be sure, we often make or establish our claims by presenting titles, and these typically have the form of receipts, tickets, certificates, and other pieces of paper or parchment. The title, however, is not the same thing as the claim; rather it is the evidence that establishes the claim as valid. On this analysis, one might have a claim without ever claiming that to which one is entitled, or without even knowing that one has the claim; for one might simply be ignorant of the fact that one is in a position to claim; or one might be unwilling to exploit that position for one reason or another, including fear that the legal machinery is broken down or corrupt and will not enforce one's claim despite its validity.

Nearly all writers maintain that there is some intimate connection between having a claim and having a right. Some identify right and claim without qualification; some define "right" as justified or justifiable claim, others as recognized claim, still others as valid claim. My own preference is for the latter definition. Some writers, however, reject the identification of rights with valid claims on the ground that all claims as such are valid, so that the expression "valid claim" is redundant. These writers, therefore, would identify rights with claims *simpliciter.* But this is a very simple confusion. All claims, to be sure, are *put forward* as justified, whether they are justified in fact or not. A claim conceded even by its maker to have no validity is not a claim at all, but a mere demand. The highwayman, for example, *demands* his victim's money; but he hardly makes claim to it as rightfully his own.

But it does not follow from this sound point that it is redundant to qualify claims as justified (or as I prefer, valid) in the definition of a right; for it remains true that not all claims put forward as valid really are valid; and only the valid ones can be acknowledged as rights.

If having a valid claim is not redundant, i.e. if it is not redundant to pronounce *another's* claim valid, there must be such a thing as having a claim that is not valid. What would this be like? One might accumulate just enough evidence to argue with relevance and cogency that one has a right (or ought to be granted a right), although one's case might not be overwhelmingly conclusive. In such a case, one might have strong enough argument to be entitled to a hearing and given fair consideration. When one is in this position, it might be said that one "has a claim" that deserves to be weighed carefully. Nevertheless, the balance of reasons may turn out to militate against recognition of the claim, so that the claim, which one admittedly had, and perhaps still does, is not a valid claim or right. "Having a claim" in this sense is an expression very much like the legal phrase "having a *prima facie* case." A plaintiff establishes a *prima facie* case for the defendant's liability when he establishes grounds that will be sufficient for liability unless outweighed by reasons of a different sort that may be offered by the defendant. Similarly, in the criminal law, a grand jury returns an indictment when it thinks that the prosecution has sufficient evidence to be taken seriously and given a fair hearing, whatever countervailing reasons may eventually be offered on the other side. That initial evidence, serious but not conclusive, is also sometimes called a *prima facie* case. In a parallel "*prima facie* sense" of "claim,"

having a claim to X is not (yet) the same as having a right to X, but is rather having a case of at least minimal plausibility that one has a right to X, a case that does establish a right, not to X, but to a fair hearing and consideration. Claims, so conceived, differ in degree: some are stronger than others. Rights, on the other hand, do not differ in degree; no one right is more of a right than another.

Another reason for not identifying rights with claims *simply* is that there is a well-established usage in international law that makes a theoretically interesting distinction between claims and rights. Statesmen are sometimes led to speak of "claims" when they are concerned with the natural needs of deprived human beings in conditions of scarcity. Young orphans *need* good upbringings, balanced diets, education, and technical training everywhere in the world; but unfortunately there are many places where these goods are in such short supply that it is impossible to provision all who need them. If we persist, nevertheless, in speaking of these needs as constituting rights and not merely claims, we are committed to the conception of a right which is an entitlement *to* some good, but not a valid claim *against* any particular individual; for in conditions of scarcity there may be no determinate individuals who can plausibly be said to have a duty to provide the missing goods to those in need. J. E. S. Fawcett therefore prefers to keep the distinction between claims and rights firmly in mind. "Claims," he writes, "are needs and demands in movement, and there is a continuous transformation, as a society advances [towards greater abundance] of economic and social claims into civil and political rights . . . and not all countries or all claims are by any means at the same stage in the process." The manifesto writers on the other side who seem to identify needs, or at least basic needs, with what they call "human rights," are more properly described, I think, as urging upon the world community the moral principle that *all* basic human needs ought to be recognized as *claims* (in the customary *prima facie* sense) worthy of sympathy and serious consideration right now, even though, in many cases, they cannot yet plausibly be treated as *valid* claims, that is, as grounds of any other people's duties. . . .

Still for all of that, I have a certain sympathy with the manifesto writers, and I am even willing to speak of a special "manifesto sense" of "right," in which a right need not be correlated with another's duty. Natural needs are real claims if only upon hypothetical future beings not yet in existence. I accept the moral principle that to have an unfulfilled need is to have a kind of claim against the world, even if against no one in particular. A natural need for some good as such, like a natural desert, is always a reason in support of a claim to that good. A person in need, then, is always "in a position" to make a claim, even when there is no one in the corresponding position to do anything about it. Such claims, based on need alone, are "permanent possibilities of rights," the natural seed from which rights grow. When manifesto writers speak of them as if already actual rights, they are easily forgiven, for this is but a powerful way of expressing the conviction that they ought to be recognized by states here and now as potential rights and consequently determinants of *present* aspirations and guides to *present* policies. That usage, I think, is a valid exercise of rhetorical licence.

I prefer to characterize rights as valid claims rather than justified ones, because I suspect that justification is rather too broad a qualification. "Validity," as I understand it, is justification of a peculiar and a narrow kind, namely justification within a system of rules. A man has a legal right when the official recognition of his claim (as valid) is called for by the governing rules. This definition, of course, hardly applies to moral rights, but that is not because the genus of which moral rights are a species is something other than *claims*. A man has a moral right when he has a claim the recognition of which is called for—not (necessarily) by legal rules—but by moral principles, or the principles of an enlightened conscience. . . .

In brief conclusion: To have a right is to have a claim against someone whose recognition as valid is called for by some set of governing rules or moral principles. To have a *claim* in turn, is to have a case meriting consideration, that is, to have reasons or grounds that put one in a position to engage in performative and propositional claiming. The activity of claiming, finally, as much as any other thing, makes for self-respect and respect for others, gives a sense to the notion of personal dignity, and distinguishes this otherwise morally flawed world from the even worse world of Nowheresville.

QUESTIONS FOR DISCUSSION

1. What does Feinberg mean by a "claim"? Does Feinberg define "claim" in the same way as Hohfeld? If not, what is the difference?

2. Feinberg says that there is a way in which claims are "prior to, or more basic than" duties. What does he mean by this? Is this inconsistent with Hohfeld? Is Feinberg right?

3. Feinberg says that it is not redundant to talk of an "invalid claim." Give an example of an invalid claim. Could Hohfeld imagine an invalid claim?

HARD CASES

RONALD DWORKIN

Arguments of principle are arguments intended to establish an individual right; arguments of policy are arguments intended to establish a collective goal. Principles are propositions that describe rights; policies are propositions that describe goals. But what are rights and goals and what is the difference? It is hard to supply any definition that does not beg the question. It seems natural to say, for example, that freedom of speech is a right, not a goal, because citizens are entitled to that freedom as a matter of political morality, and that increased munitions manufacture is a goal, not a right, because it contributes to collective welfare, but no particular manufacturer is entitled to a government contract. This does not improve our understanding, however, because the concept of entitlement uses rather than explains the concept of a right.

In this chapter I shall distinguish rights from goals by fixing on the distributional character of claims about rights, and on the force of these claims, in political argument, against competing claims of a different distributional character. I shall make, that is, a formal distinction that does not attempt to show which rights men and women actually have, or indeed that they have any at all. It rather provides a guide for discovering which rights a particular political theory supposes men and women to have. The formal distinction does suggest, of course, an approach to the more fundamental question: it suggests that we discover what rights people actually have by looking for arguments that would justify claims having the appropriate distributional character. But the distinction does not itself supply any such arguments.

I begin with the idea of a political aim as a generic political justification. A political theory takes a certain state of affairs as a political aim if, for that theory, it counts in favor of any political decision that the decision is likely to advance, or to protect, that state of affairs, and counts against the decision that it will retard or endanger it. A political right is an individuated political aim. An individual has a right to some opportunity or resource or liberty if it counts in favor of a political decision that the decision is likely to advance or protect the state of affairs in which he enjoys the right, even when no other political aim is served and some political aim is disserved thereby, and counts against that decision that it will retard or endanger that state of affairs, even when some other political aim is thereby served. A goal is a nonindividuated political aim, that is, a state of affairs whose specification does not in this way call for any particular opportunity or resource or liberty for particular individuals.

Collective goals encourage trade-offs of benefits and burdens within a community in order to produce some overall benefit for the community as a whole. Economic efficiency is a collective goal: it calls for such distribution of opportunities and liabilities as will produce the greatest aggregate economic benefit defined in some way. Some conception of equality may also be taken as a collective goal; a community may aim at a distribution such that maximum wealth is no more than double minimum wealth, or, under a different conception, so that no racial or ethnic group is much worse off than other groups. Of course, any collective goal will suggest a particular distribution, given

Ronald Dworkin, "Hard Cases," from *Taking Rights Seriously* (Cambridge: Harvard University Press, 1977)

particular facts. Economic efficiency as a goal will suggest that a particular industry be subsidized in some circumstances, but taxed punitively in others. Equality as a goal will suggest immediate and complete redistribution in some circumstances, but partial and discriminatory redistribution in others. In each case distributional principles are subordinate to some conception of aggregate collective good, so that offering less of some benefit to one man can be justified simply by showing that this will lead to a greater benefit overall.

Collective goals may, but need not, be absolute. The community may pursue different goals at the same time, and it may compromise one goal for the sake of another. It may, for example, pursue economic efficiency, but also military strength. The suggested distribution will then be determined by the sum of the two policies, and this will increase the permutations and combinations of possible trade-offs. In any case, these permutations and combinations will offer a number of competing strategies for serving each goal and both goals in combination. Economic efficiency may be well served by offering subsidies to all farmers, and to no manufacturers, and better served by offering double the subsidy to some farmers and none to others. There will be alternate strategies of pursuing any set of collective goals, and, particularly as the number of goals increases, it will be impossible to determine in a piecemeal or case-by-case way the distribution that best serves any set of goals. Whether it is good policy to give double subsidies to some farmers and none to others will depend upon a great number of other political decisions that have been or will be made in pursuit of very general strategies into which this particular decision must fit.

Rights also may be absolute: a political theory which holds a right to freedom of speech as absolute will recognize no reason for not securing the liberty it requires for every individual; no reason, that is, short of impossibility. Rights may also be less than absolute; one

principle might have to yield to another, or even to an urgent policy with which it competes on particular facts. We may define the weight of a right, assuming it is not absolute, as its power to withstand such competition. It follows from the definition of a right that it cannot be outweighed by all social goals. We might, for simplicity, stipulate not to call any political aim a right unless it has a certain threshold weight against collective goals in general; unless, for example, it cannot be defeated by appeal to any of the ordinary routine goals of political administration, but only by a goal of special urgency. Suppose, for example, some man says he recognizes the right of free speech, but adds that free speech must yield whenever its exercise would inconvenience the public. He means, I take it, that he recognizes the pervasive goal of collective welfare, and only such distribution of liberty of speech as that collective goal recommends in particular circumstances. His political position is exhausted by the collective goal; the putative right adds nothing and there is no point to recognizing it as a right at all.

■ ■ ■

I must call attention to the fact, familiar to philosophers, but often ignored in political debate, that the word 'right' has different force in different contexts. In most cases when we say that someone has 'right' to do something, we imply that it would be wrong to interfere with his doing it, or at least that some special grounds are needed for justifying any interference. I use this strong sense of right when I say that you have the right to spend your money gambling, if you wish, though you ought to spend it in a more worthwhile way. I mean that it would be wrong for anyone to interfere with you even though you propose to spend your money in a way that I think is wrong.

There is a clear difference between saying that someone has a right to do something in this sense and saying that it is the 'right' thing for him to do, or that he does no 'wrong' in doing it. Someone may have the right to do something that is the wrong thing for him to do, as might be the case with gambling. Conversely, something may be the right thing for him to do and yet he may have no right to do it, in the sense that it would not be wrong for someone to interfere with his trying. If our army captures an enemy soldier, we might· say that the right thing for him to do is to try to escape, but it would not follow that it is wrong for us to try to stop him. Wc might admire him for trying to escape, and perhaps even think less of him if he did not. But there is no suggestion here that it is wrong of us to stand in his way; on the contrary, if we think our cause is just, we think it right for us to do all we can to stop him.

Ordinarily this distinction, between the issues of whether a man has a right to do something and whether it is the right thing for him to do, causes no trouble. But sometimes it does, because sometimes we say that a man has a right to do something when we mean only to deny that it is the wrong thing for him to do. Thus we say that the captured soldier has a 'right' to try to escape when we mean, not that we do wrong to stop him, but that he has no duty not to make the attempt. We use 'right' this way when we speak of someone having the 'right' to act on his own principles, or the 'right' to follow his own conscience. We mean that he does no wrong to proceed on his honest convictions, even though we disagree with these convictions, and even though, for policy or other reasons, we must force him to act contrary to them.

Suppose a man believes that welfare payments to the poor are profoundly wrong, because they sap enterprise, and so declares his full income-tax each year but declines to pay half of it. We might say that he has a right to refuse to pay, if he wishes, but that the Government has a right to proceed against him for the full tax, and to fine or jail him for late payment if that is necessary to keep the collection system working efficiently. We do not take this

line in most cases; we do not say that the ordinary thief has a right to steal, if he wishes, so long as he pays the penalty. We say a man has the right to break the law, even though the State has a right to punish him, only when we think that, because of his convictions, he does no wrong in doing so. . . .

I said that in the United States citizens are supposed to have certain fundamental rights against their Government, certain moral rights made into legal rights by the Constitution. If this idea is significant, and worth bragging about, then these rights must be rights in the strong sense I just described. The claim that citizens have a right to free speech must imply that it would be wrong for the Government to stop them from speaking, even when the Government believes that what they will say will cause more harm than good. The claim cannot mean, on the prisoner-of-war analogy, only that citizens do no wrong in speaking their minds, though the Government reserves the right to prevent them from doing so.

This is a crucial point, and I want to labour it. Of course a responsible government must be ready to justify anything it does, particularly when it limits the liberty of its citizens. But normally it is a sufficient justification, even for an act that limits liberty, that the act is calculated to increase what the philosophers call general utility—that it is calculated to produce more over-all benefit than harm. So, though the New York City government needs a justification for forbidding motorists to drive up Lexington Avenue, it is sufficient justification if the proper officials believe, on sound evidence, that the gain to the many will outweigh the inconvenience to the few. When individual citizens are said to have rights against the Government, however, like the right of free speech, that must mean that this sort of justification is not enough. Otherwise the claim would not argue that individuals have special protection against the law when their rights are in play, and that is just the point of the claim.

Not all legal rights, or even Constitutional rights, represent moral rights against the Government. I now have the legal right to drive either way on Fifty-seventh Street, but the Government would do no wrong to make that street one-way if it thought it in the general interest to do so. I have a Constitutional right to vote for a congressman every two years, but the national and state governments would do no wrong if, following the amendment procedure, they made a congressman's term four years instead of two, again on the basis of a judgment that this would be for the general good.

But those Constitutional rights that we call fundamental like the right of free speech, are supposed to represent rights against the Government in the strong sense; that is the point of the boast that our legal system respects the fundamental rights of the citizen. If citizens have a moral right of free speech, then governments would do wrong to repeal the First Amendment that guarantees it, even if they were persuaded that the majority would be better off if speech were curtailed.

I must not overstate the point. Someone who claims that citizens have a right against the Government need not go so far as to say that the State is *never* justified in overriding that right. He might say, for example, that although citizens have a right to free speech, the Government may override that right when necessary to protect the rights of others, or to prevent a catastrophe, or even to obtain a clear and major public benefit (though if he acknowledged this last as a possible justification he would be treating the right in question as not among the most important or fundamental). What he cannot do is to say that the Government is justified in overriding a right on the minimal grounds that would be sufficient if no such right existed. He cannot say that the Government is entitled to act on no more than a judgment that its act is likely to produce, overall, a benefit to the community. That admission would make his claim of a right pointless, and would show him to be using some sense of 'right' other than the strong sense necessary to give his claim the political importance it is normally taken to have.

QUESTIONS FOR DISCUSSION

1. Elsewhere Dworkin has described rights as "trumps." How does this metaphor relate to his argument here? What are rights trumps *of*?

2. Can Dworkin's rights ever be overridden? If so, by what? Does Dworkin think that rights can be overridden by other rights? Do you? Can you think of any example of a right that is properly overridden by another right? Can you think of any example of a right being overridden by "utility" or "policy" or the "general welfare"?

3. Does Dworkin purport to analyze all of Hohfeld's different kinds of rights? If not, then which ones?

4. Is Dworkin's account of rights compatible with Feinberg's? How are they similar, and how are they different?

5. Does Dworkin believe that rights can be exercised wrongly? Do you? If so, give an example of a wrongful exercise of a right, and explain what "right" and "wrong" mean in this context.

SOME RUMINATIONS ON RIGHTS

JUDITH JARVIS THOMSON

Suppose that someone has a right that such and such shall not be the case. I shall say that we infringe a right of his if and only if we bring about that it is the case. I shall say that we violate a right of his if and only if *both* we bring about that it is the case *and* we act wrongly in so doing. The difference I have in mind comes out in the following case, which I shall call A:

(A) There is a child who will die if he is not given some drug in the near future. The only bit of that drug which can be obtained for him in the near future is yours. You are out of town, and hence cannot be asked for consent within the available time. You keep your supply of the drug in a locked box on your back porch.

In this case the box is yours, you have a right that it not be broken into without your consent; since the drug is yours, you have a right that it shall not be removed and given to someone without your consent. So if we break into the box, remove the drug, and feed it to the child, we thereby infringe a number of rights of yours. But I take it that a child's life being at stake, we do not act wrongly if we go ahead; that is, though we infringe a number of your rights, we violate none of them.

It might be said that we do violate one or more of your rights if we go ahead, but that our act, though wrongful, is excusable. In other words, although we act wrongly if we go ahead, we are not to be blamed for doing so. It is true that for clarity about rights we need, and do not have, a general account of when one should say "a nonwrongful infringement of a right" and when one should instead say "a wrongful, but

excusable, infringement of a right." I think (but without great confidence) that the difference lies in this: The former may not be said where, and the latter may only be said where the agent ought not act or ought not have acted. If so, then the proposal we are considering is false: For it surely is plain that a third party would not speak truly if he said to us, given we are in (A): "You ought not go ahead."

In any case, the proposal in a certain sense hangs in midair. What I have in mind is this. It is presumably agreed universally that if we go ahead in (A), we are not to be blamed, punished, scolded, or the like, for doing so. Now the question is: Why? One possible answer is: If we go ahead in (A) we do not act wrongly, and that is why we are not to be blamed for doing so. That this is my answer shows itself in the paragraph in which I first set out (A). But how is a proponent of the proposal we are now considering to answer? On his view, we act wrongly if we go ahead; what, on his view, is the reason why we are not to be blamed for doing so? There are cases in which there is an answer to an analogous question. Thus if I break your box in a rage which you provoked, then I acted wrongly, but perhaps excusably, and the reason why I am not to be blamed (if I am not) is at hand: you yourself provoked the rage out of which I acted. Again, a reason why I am not to be blamed in another case might be: I was not fully aware of what I was doing; or I was so frantic with worry I could not think clearly; or I was so frantic with worry, nothing else seemed to matter. If (A) had read: "*Our* child will die if he is not given . . . ," then there might have been a toehold for an answer of

Judith Jarvis Thomson, "Some Ruminations on Rights," *Arizona Law Review*, vol. 19 (1977), pp. 45 ff.

the kind just pointed to. But (A) says: "There is a child who will die if he is not given . . . ," and it is possible to suppose that we go ahead in (A)—break the box, and give the drug to the child—calmly, coolly, carefully weighing all the relevant considerations. If so, just what is a proponent of the proposal we are now considering to give as an answer to the question of why we are not to be blamed for doing so?

So I shall simply assume that this proposal is false, and I shall take it, then, that while we infringe some of your rights if we go ahead, we do not violate them.

A second way of responding to what I said of our act if we go ahead in (A) is this: True, we violate no rights if we go ahead, but we also infringe no rights if we go ahead. What I have in mind is the possibility of saying that you do not have either of the rights it might have been thought you had—that you do not have a right that your box not be broken into without your consent, and that you do not have a right that your drug not be removed and given to someone without your consent—on the ground that it is morally permissible for us to go ahead in (A). What rights do you have over your box and drug on this view? Well, I suppose it would be said that what you have is at most a right that your-box-not-be-broken-into-and-your-drug-not-taken-without-your-consent-when-there-is-no-child-who-needs-that-drug-for-life. The inclination to take, everywhere, either the view discussed just above, or the view indicated here, is the inclination to regard all rights as "absolute." That is, it is the inclination to take it that if a man has a right that such and such shall not be the case, then if we bring about that it is the case, we act wrongly in so doing. As the point might be put, every infringing of a right is a violation of a right. So if a man really does have a right that such and such shall not be the case (as it might be, that his drug not be removed from his box), then we act at best excusably if we bring about that it is the case—as in the view discussed just above. If we do not act wrongly in bringing it

about, then he did not really have a right that it not come about, but at most a right that it-not-come-about-when-the-circumstances-are-so-and-so, as in the view indicated here.

It seems to me, however, that you do have a right that your box not be broken into without your consent and a right that your drug not be removed and given to someone without your consent, and that what shows this is the fact that if we go ahead in (A)—break into your box and give some of the drug to the child—we shall have later to pay you some, if not all, of the cost we imposed on you by doing so. We shall have to pay some, if not all, of the cost of repairing or replacing the box and of replacing the drug we removed. You may reject payment: you may say, on your return, that, the circumstances having been what they were, all is well, and that you do not mind bearing the costs yourself. But we must at least offer. If you had no right that we not do these things without your consent, why would we have to pay you some of the costs we imposed on you by doing them?

It is sometimes said that if we go ahead in (A) we shall have to *compensate* you for the costs we imposed on you by doing so, and that *that* is what shows that we infringed some of your rights by going ahead—for compensation is repayment for a wrong. But I think that this is not a good way to put the point, and will bring out my reason for thinking so later.

In any case, it seems to me we do well to agree that rights are not all absolute: There are rights which can be infringed without being violated. In particular, it seems to me that if we go ahead in (A), we infringe some of your property rights, but do not violate any of them.

What people who would agree with me on this matter would say is this: If we go ahead in (A), we will infringe your property rights, but we would not violate them, since those rights are "overridden" by the fact that the child will die if we do not go ahead.

A more *stringent* right than your property rights over your box and drug might not have been overridden by this fact. For example, if it had been necessary for the saving of the child's life that we kill you, then it would not have been morally permissible that we go ahead. Your right to not be killed is considerably more stringent than any of your property rights, and would not have been overridden by the child's need.

The question just how stringent our several rights are is obviously a difficult one. It does not even seem to be obvious that there is any such thing as *the* degree of stringency of any given right. Perhaps a right may be more or less stringent, as the rightholder's circumstances vary, and also, in the case of special rights, as the means by which he acquired the right vary. One thing only is plain: Only an absolute right is infinitely stringent. For only an absolute right is such that every possible infringement of it is a violation of it. Indeed, we may re-express the thesis that all rights are absolute as follows: all rights are infinitely stringent.

There are passages in *Anarchy, State, and Utopia* which suggest that Robert Nozick thinks all rights are infinitely stringent. He says: "[O]ne might place [rights] as side constraints upon the actions to be done: don't violate constraints C. The rights of others determine the constraints upon your actions. . . . The side-constraint view forbids you to violate these moral constraints in the pursuit of your goals." If you use "violate" in the way I suggested we should use it, this "side-constraint view" does not amount to much—under that reading of the term, all Nozick says is that we may not wrongly infringe a right. Of course we may not. But I think he does not mean so to use the term "violate," in this passage at any rate. I think that in this passage all he means by it is "infringe." Thus I think that we are to take this "side-constraint view" to say that we may not ever infringe a right. Accordingly, every infringing of a right is wrong. Compare what Nozick says a few pages on:

A specific side constraint upon action toward others expresses the fact that others

may not be used in the specific ways the side constraint excludes. Side constraints express the inviolability of others, in the ways they specify. These modes of inviolability are expressed by the following injunction: "Don't use people in specified ways."

Now Nozick does not in fact say that his view is the "side-constraint view," so interpreted, but he implies that it is. Certainly his thesis about redistribution suggests it: for according to that thesis it is not morally permissible to tax people for the purpose of redistribution, however dire the human need which makes redistribution seem called for, and if dire human need does not override a right, what on earth would?

There are also passages which suggest that Nozick thinks that rights *may* be overrideable, and thus not infinitely stringent, though very stringent all the same. He says that it is an open question "whether these side constraints are absolute, or whether they may be violated in order to avoid catastrophic moral horror." Catastrophic moral horror is pretty horrible moral horror; so even if rights are overrideable, as the passage suggests is possible, it is likely to be a rare occasion on which they are overridden. Unfortunately, Nozick leaves the question unanswered; he says it "is one I hope largely to avoid."

There are also passages which suggest that Nozick thinks that some rights at least are overrideable even where catastrophic moral horror is not in the offing. In the course of a discussion of what may be done to animals, he asks: "Can't one save 10,000 animals from excruciating suffering by inflicting some slight discomfort on a person who did not cause the animals' suffering?" And he adds: "One may feel the side constraint is not absolute when it is *people* who can be saved from excruciating suffering. So perhaps the side constraint also relaxes, though not as much, when animals' suffering is at stake." Of course Nozick does not *say* the side constraint relaxes when animals' suffering is at stake, but he seems to think so, and it would surely be mad to think it did not. Well, perhaps

10,000 animals suffering excruciating pain counts as catastrophic moral horror. But does it require 10,000 of them, in excruciating pain, to override your right to not be caused some slight discomfort? I take it you have a right to not be pinched without your consent. But surely we can pinch you without your consent, if doing so is required to save even one cow from excruciating suffering. Indeed I should have thought we could do so if doing so is required to save just one cow from suffering which is considerably less than excruciating.

This wobbling about the degree of stringency of rights makes a reader feel nervous. It also makes it very unclear just how Nozick is to get from his starting point, which is that we have rights, to his thesis that a government which imposes taxes for the purpose of redistribution violates the rights of its citizens. I am inclined to think that what happens is this: At the outset, he is unclear what degree of stringency should be assigned to rights (and hopes to avoid having to take a stand on the matter), but by the time he gets to government, all is forgotten, and rights—at any rate, property rights—are infinitely stringent. It is my impression that his argument for his thesis rests entirely on the supposition that they are.

But surely it is plain as day that property rights are not infinitely stringent. It hardly needs argument to show they are not. In any case, the fact that it is morally permissible for us to go ahead in (A) would show—if it needed showing—that they are not.

Consider now case (B), which is in an interesting way different from (A):

(B) There is a child who will die if he is not given some drugs in the future. The only bit of that drug which can be obtained for him in the near future is yours. You are out of town, so we telephone you to ask. You refuse consent. You keep your supply of the drug in a locked box on your back porch.

"They did it without Jones' consent" covers two interestingly different kinds of cases: In the one kind, they were unable to get Jones' con-

sent because he was not available to be asked for his consent; in the other kind, they were unable to get Jones' consent because he refused to give it. In the latter kind of case they acted, not merely without Jones' consent, but against his wishes. (A) is a case of the first kind; we cannot reach you to ask for consent. (B) is a case of the second kind; if we go ahead in (B) we act, not merely without your consent, but against your wishes. I said it is morally permissible for us to go ahead in (A); is it morally permissible for us to go ahead in (B)?

The fact is that our going ahead in (B)—our breaking into the box and removing the drug to give it to the child—seems morally suspect in a way in which our going ahead in (A) does not. Why? And should it?

Anyone who thinks that it is morally permissible for us to go ahead in (A) but not in (B) must think that there is at least a good chance that in (A), you would give consent if we were able to reach you to ask for consent. Surely if it were known that if we were to ask for consent in (A) you would refuse to give it, then it would be no better to go ahead in (A) than it is to go ahead in (B). For then (A) too would be a case in which going ahead would be acting against your wishes—though not against any wish that was in fact given expression.

Anyone who thinks that it is not morally permissible for us to go ahead in (B) must think that the box and the drug in it are in some way very important to you—that you place a very high value on the box not being broken into, and on the drug not being taken away from you. Suppose, however, that there is a toothpick on your desk, and it is in no way special to you. By virtue of some peculiarity in nature, we can save a life if we snap it in two. We ask if we can, but you are feeling refractory and say "No." Can we not go ahead and snap it in two, despite your expressed wish that we not do so? By contrast, suppose what is on your desk is the last remaining photograph of your dead mother, and what we need to do to save the life is to burn it. Well, some people would say we can go ahead all the same. Suppose that what we need to do is to destroy *all* the now existing beautiful works of art, and that their owners (individuals, museums, governments) say, "Alas no, we are very sorry, but no." Could we go ahead all the same?

If (X), "The box and drug are, at most, of little value to you," is true, then we may surely go ahead in both (A) and (B). If (X) is true and we are in (A), then in the absence of information to the contrary, we shall rightly assume you would consent if we were able to ask. But even if we have information to the effect that you would not consent—even if we were in (B) instead of (A)—it is morally permissible for us to go ahead all the same. Why? Because if (X) is true, then it would be indecent for you to refuse consent in (A), and it is indecent for you to refuse consent in (B). I said you might be feeling refractory; alternatively, you might think: "What is that child to me?" There are other possible sources of refusal, but none of them bears looking at.

What if, instead, (Y), "The box and drug are of immense value to you," is true? Some would say we can go ahead all the same. I feel considerable sympathy for this view, but I do not hold it myself. It seems to me that if (Y) is true, we may not go ahead in (B), and in the absence of reason to think you would consent despite the truth of (Y), we may not go ahead in (A) either. I hope that when I first produced (A) above, your intuition agreed with mine; if so, I think that was because you were assuming that nothing so strong as (Y) was true. Why may we not go ahead if (Y) is true? It is not morally splendid to value bits of property more than human lives; but if there are some which you do—and this for no morally suspect reason—then it seems to me that there are cases, and that this is one of them, in which we must withdraw.

There are all manner of possibilities between (X) and (Y), but it is not necessary for our purposes that we attend to them.

It is also not necessary for our purposes that we attend to a very interesting question which is raised by consideration of the difference (which I take there to be) between what we may do if (X) is true and what we may do if (Y) is true, but I suggest we have a brief look at it all the same. What I have in mind is the question in precisely what way the difference between (X) and (Y) makes such a difference. One way of explaining it is this: If (Y) is true, then your rights that your box not be broken and drug not be taken are more stringent than they would be if (X) were true. More generally, that

(T) The stringency of A's right that x not be broken and y not be taken away from him varies with the degree to which he values x's not being broken and y's not being taken away from him.

If so, then more is required to override your rights over your box and drug if (Y) is true than is required to override them if (X) is true. In particular, the fact that a human life may be saved by going ahead overrides your rights if (X) is true, but not if (Y) is true.

I think, myself, that this is how we should explain the difference (which I take there to be) between what we may do if (X) is true and what we may do if (Y) is true. Indeed, I think we should adopt (T). But the question whether or not (T) is true is very important for the logic of rights; and so it should be noticed that there is yet another way of explaining the difference even if (T) is rejected. What might be said is this: The stringency of your rights that your box not be broken and your drug not be taken is no greater whether (Y) is true or (X) is true; and these rights are overridden by the fact that a human life may be saved by going ahead. But if (Y) is true, then it is less likely, perhaps even impossible, that we are going to be able to reimburse you for all of the costs we impose on you by going ahead; and if we take "immense" *very* seriously, it is less likely, perhaps even impossible, that we are even going to be able to pay you a meaningful part of those costs. Now it will be remembered that I said earlier that if we go ahead in (A) we are going to have to pay you some, if not all, of the costs we impose on you by going ahead. This means that you have a right, not merely that your-box-not-be-broken-and-drug-taken-without-consent, but also that your-box-not-be-broken-and-drug-taken-without-consent-without-reimbursement-for-some-if-not-all-of-the-cost-imposed-by-the-breaking-and-taking. The former, simpler right is overridden by the fact that a human life may be saved by going ahead; the latter, more complex, right is more stringent, and is not overridden by this fact—indeed, it would be violated if we went ahead without reimbursing you. If (X) is true we can easily make the required payment; but if (Y) is true we cannot. So if (X) is true we may go ahead without violating any right of yours, for we can pay later; but if (Y) is true, then if we go ahead we shall violate, not the simpler right, but the more complex one, for we cannot pay later. And *that* is why we may go ahead if (X) is true, but not if (Y) is.

QUESTIONS FOR DISCUSSION

1. Is Thomson offering an analysis of legal rights or of moral rights? Does her analysis apply to both?
2. What is Thomson's distinction between infringing a right and violating a right? Can you give an example of a justified infringement of the right to free speech? Of a violation of the right to free speech?
3. Some philosophers, including Joel Feinberg, write about *prima facie* rights, rights that are capable of being overridden. How does this relate to Thomson's analysis?
4. Does Thomson think there can be absolute rights? Can you give an example of an absolute right? Does Thomson think there can be *weak* rights? Do you? Can you give an example?

CRAIG V. BOREN

429 U.S. 190 (1976)

Mr. Justice BRENNAN delivered the opinion of the Court.

The interaction of two sections of an Oklahoma statute prohibits the sale of "non-intoxicating" 3.2% beer to males under the age of 21 and to females under the age of 18. The question [is] whether such a gender-based differential constitutes a denial to males 18–20 years of age of [equal protection].

We accept for purposes of discussion the District Court's identification of the objective underlying [the law] as the enhancement of traffic safety. Clearly, the protection of public health and safety represents an important function of state and local governments. However, appellees' statistics in our view cannot support the conclusion that the gender-based distinction closely serves to achieve that objective and therefore the distinction cannot withstand equal protection challenge. The appellees introduced a variety of statistical surveys. First, an analysis of arrest statistics for 1973 demonstrated that 18–20-year-old male arrests for "driving under the influence" and "drunkenness" substantially exceeded female arrests for that same age period. Similarly, youths aged 17–21 were found to be overrepresented among those killed or injured in traffic accidents, with males again numerically exceeding females in this regard. Third, a random roadside survey in Oklahoma City revealed that young males were more inclined to drive and drink beer than were their female counterparts. Fourth, [FBI] nationwide statistics exhibited a notable increase in arrests for "driving under the influence." Finally, statistical evidence gathered in other jurisdictions [was] offered to corroborate Oklahoma's experience by indicating the pervasiveness of youthful participation in motor vehicle accidents following the imbibing of [alcohol]. Even were this statistical evidence accepted as accurate, it nevertheless offers only a weak answer to the equal protection question presented here. The most focused and relevant of the statistical surveys, arrests of 18–20-year-olds for alcohol-related driving offenses, exemplifies the ultimate unpersuasiveness of this evidentiary record. Viewed in terms of the correlation between sex and the actual activity that Oklahoma seeks to regulate—driving while under the influence of alcohol—the statistics broadly establish that .18% of females and 2% of males in that age group were arrested for that offense. While such a disparity is not trivial in a statistical sense, it hardly can form the basis for employment of a gender line as a classifying device. Certainly if maleness is to serve as a proxy for drinking and driving, a correlation of 2% must be considered an unduly tenuous "fit."

Indeed, prior cases have consistently rejected the use of sex as a decisionmaking factor even though the statutes in question certainly rested on far more predictive empirical relationships than this.

Moreover, the statistics exhibit a variety of other shortcomings that seriously impugn their value to equal protection analysis. Setting aside the obvious methodological problems, the surveys do not adequately justify the salient features of Oklahoma's gender-based traffic-safety law. None purports to measure the use and dangerousness of 3.2% beer as opposed to alcohol [generally]. Moreover, many of the studies, while graphically documenting the unfortunate increase in driving while under the influence of alcohol, make no effort to relate their findings to age-sex differentials as involved here. [There] is no reason to belabor this line of analysis. It is unrealistic to expect either members of the judiciary or state officials to be well versed in the rigors of experimental or statistical technique. But this merely illustrates that proving broad sociological propositions by statistics is a dubious business, and one that inevitably is in tension with the normative philosophy that underlies [equal protection]. Suffice to say that the showing offered by the appellees does not satisfy us that sex represents a legitimate, accurate proxy for the regulation of drinking and driving. In fact, when it is further recognized that Oklahoma's statute prohibits only the selling of 3.2% beer to young males and not their drinking the beverage once acquired (even after purchase by their 18–20-year-old female companions), the relationship between gender and traffic safety becomes far too tenuous to satisfy the requirement that the gender-based difference be substantially related to achievement of the [statutory objective].

[Social science] studies that have uncovered quantifiable differences in drinking tendencies dividing along both racial and ethnic lines strongly suggest the need for application of [equal protection] in preventing discriminatory treatment that almost certainly would be perceived as invidious. In sum, the principles embodied in [equal protection] are not to be rendered inapplicable by statistically measured but loose-fitting generalities concerning the drinking tendencies of aggregate groups. We conclude that [this] gender-based differential [is] a denial of [equal protection to males aged 18–20].

QUESTIONS FOR DISCUSSION

1. Assuming that men between the ages of eighteen and twenty-one are in fact more likely than women of the same age to drive while intoxicated, would Oklahoma's distinction be legitimate in a world without rights?
2. What is the right involved in *Craig v. Boren*? What is the effect of recognition of the right?
3. Justice Brennan says that the use of "statistics" is "in tension with the normative philosophy that underlies" the Equal Protection Clause of the Fourteenth Amendment. What does he mean? How might this relate to Dworkin's distinction between rights and goals? To Nozick's (as set out by Thomson) idea of rights as side constraints?

SUGGESTIONS FOR FURTHER READING

Dworkin's views on rights appear throughout *Taking Rights Seriously* (Cambridge: Harvard University Press, 1977), and also in various essays in *A Matter of Principle* (Cambridge: Harvard University Press, 1986). A number of Thomson's articles on rights are collected in *Rights, Restitution, and Risk: Essays in Moral Theory* (Cambridge: Harvard University Press, 1986), but her most recent and comprehensive treatment is in *The Realm of Rights* (Cambridge: Harvard University Press, 1990). Feinberg's views are expanded somewhat in *Social Philosophy* (Englewood Cliffs, New Jersey: Prentice-Hall, 1973). Other important articles include T.M. Scanlon, "Rights, Goals and Fairness," in Stuart Hampshire, ed., *Public and Private Morality* (Cambridge: Cambridge University Press, 1978), pp. 93 ff.; Alan Gewirth, "Are There Any Absolute Rights?", *The Philosophical Quarterly*, vol. 17 (1980), pp. 165 ff. On specific issues about the structure of rights, see Robert Nozick, "Moral Complications and Moral Structures," *Natural Law Forum*, vol. 13 (1968), pp. 1 ff.; Frederick Schauer, "Can Rights Be Abused?", *The Philosophical Quarterly*, vol. 31 (1981), pp. 216 ff.; Frederick Schauer, "A Comment on the Structure of Rights," *Georgia Law Review*, vol. 27 (1993), pp. 415 ff. A valuable overview of modern perspectives is Rex Martin and James Nickel, "Recent Work on the Concept of Rights," *American Philosophical Quarterly*, vol. 17 (1980), pp. 165 ff. Among the important books on rights are Richard Flathman, *The Practice of Rights* (Cambridge: Cambridge University Press, 1976); Charles Fried, *Right and Wrong* (Cambridge: Harvard University Press, 1978); Alan R. White, *Rights* (Oxford: Clarendon Press, 1984). Useful collections include R.G. Frey, ed., *Utility and Rights* (Minneapolis: University of Minnesota Press, 1984); David Lyons, ed., *Rights* (Belmont, California: Wadsworth Publishing Co., 1979); Michael J. Meyer and W.A. Parent, eds., *The Constitution of Rights: Human Dignity and American Values* (Ithaca, New York: Cornell University Press, 1992).

THE RIGHT TO LIBERTY 4.2

INTRODUCTION

As many of the previous readings make clear, the concept of rights in modern constitutional democracies is closely related to rights against the government, or rights not to have government do certain things to people. Thus, the common conception of a right to free speech is a right as a shield against government interference with speaking. Similarly, the right to privacy would ordinarily be understood as the right to have government refrain from interfering with certain activities or invading certain space. The right to privacy is thus the correlative of the government's duty to refrain from interfering or invading in certain ways.

All of this typifies a conception of rights commonly called a *negative* one. Thus, negative rights, or negative freedom, or negative liberty (all three are commonly used to refer to the same idea) refer to a freedom *from* a certain kind of interference, typically (although not necessarily) a certain kind of interference with action or choice by the government. A person has the negative liberty of speech insofar as the state is under a duty not to interfere with her speaking by imprisoning her or fining her for her speech; a person has the negative freedom of religion (or right to freedom of religion, or right to religious liberty) to the extent that the state is under a duty not to impose substantial barriers to religious choices or religious practices; and a person has the negative right to privacy when the state is under a duty not to intrude on those choices or spaces that are encompassed by the right.

Yet in many cases mere non-interference by the state, or indeed mere noninterference by anyone, is insufficient for some activity actually to take place. Consider the negative right to freedom of the press. According to the traditional conception of this negative right, the government may not require newspapers and other publications to be licensed; it may not fine or imprison publishers or editors or reporters for what they write in newspapers and other publications or require the preapproval of written materials; and it may not, by physical force or otherwise, close down newspapers, magazines, and book publishers.

Still, for many people this negative freedom may not actually produce the *ability* to publish a newspaper, a magazine, or a book. To do so requires money, space, and certain talents, and many people lack one or more of these. For the person with no money but a desire to publish a newspaper, the negative right to publish a newspaper will be of little consequence in enabling her actually to publish the newspaper. The negative right, many people have argued, is of little use without the conditions for its exercise; and the conditions for its exercise cannot be guaranteed simply by guaranteeing the negative right to be free from some sort of external interference.

Those who take this position commonly draw a contrast between negative rights, freedoms, or liberties, on the one hand, and *positive* rights, or positive freedom, or positive liberty, on the other. A positive right, it is argued, is the right against some person or institution that that person or institution provide, in an affirmative or positive way, the conditions that will make the exercise of the negative right "meaningful." Insofar as there were a positive right to freedom of the press, to continue the example, there would be a right, perhaps against the state, to enforce the state's duty to provide the resources (money, paper, ink, printing presses) such that people would have the ability to operate a press.

A positive right to freedom of the press is not something that people commonly propose, but there are other positive rights that are more frequently urged. When people argue that there is, or should be, a right to education, or a right to shelter, they are not arguing that the government should refrain from interfering with people getting their own education with their own resources, or that government not tear down people's houses. Rather, they are arguing that government has a positive duty to provide education, or shelter, and that a person's positive right against the government is the correlative of this duty on the part of the state. Those who claim a right to health care do not claim that government should refrain from interfering with the ability of people to use their own resources to buy whatever health care they wish. Instead, they claim that the state has obligations actually to provide that health care, and not just avoid interfering with its provision by others.

The Constitution of the United States is a good example of a document that is almost exclusively concerned with negative and not positive rights. Its focus is on freedom *from* and not freedom *to*. Indeed, the courts have generally rejected arguments to interpret some of the negative rights in the Constitution as having a positive dimension as well. Consider again the freedom of the press protected by the First Amendment. There is no doubt that it protects reporters from being fined or imprisoned for what they write, and it protects newspapers against licensing and judicial injunctions that would prevent publication. But reporters have also argued that freedom of the press is not just a negative right against government interference; it is also a positive right to *access* to certain sources of information. Reporters have argued, for example, that the constitutional right to freedom of the press requires government to give them certain documents, or to allow them access to certain meetings or to certain military installations. In general, however, the courts have rejected these claims. Although there are frequently statutes, such as the Freedom of Information Act and various state "sunshine" or "open meeting" laws, which grant enforceable statutory rights to documents and to meetings, these statutes supplement rather than enforce constitutional rights. The constitutional right to freedom of the press, the courts have held, is like most other American constitutional rights—largely negative and not positive. By granting protection against government but not access to it, and by granting a right against government but not necessarily the ability to exercise it, the First Amendment is typical of American constitutional rights in operating only as a "shield" and not as a "sword."

Not all constitutions take the same approach. The Constitution of West Virginia does create a positive right to an education, and the new constitutions in South Africa and much of Eastern Europe contain various positive rights to food, shelter, education, and health care. Whether these rights will turn out to be enforceable in practice remains to be seen. It is, after all, easier for courts, the common determiners of rights, to prohibit state action than to require it, especially when the state action requires the expenditure of funds, and when the expenditure of funds may require raising additional taxes. Still, the basic distinction between positive and negative rights remains important, both philosophically and in practical application. If there is a right to an abortion, for example, is that only the negative right against state interference with abortions, or is it as well a positive right to government funding for abortions? As a matter of American constitutional law, the courts have held that it is only the former and not the latter,[7] but this remains a hotly contested issue.

■ ■ ■

If we turn our attention away from the distinction between positive and negative liberties and focus primarily on the negative liberties, there remain numerous questions. Perhaps the most important of these is the initial question whether there is a *right* to liberty, even as a negative right only, in the first instance. Some would argue that there is, and we see this in quite different versions in John Stuart Mill's *On Liberty* (1859) and in more recent works such as Robert Nozick's *Anarchy, State, and Utopia* (1974). Although there are many differences between Mill and Nozick, some of which will be explored later in this chapter, they share the common belief that there is a background negative right to liberty, the consequence of which is that they both believe that any government action interfering with an individual's liberty to do whatever she pleases must bear a burden of justification. For both Mill and Nozick the baseline or background principle is "no interference." Thus one way of characterizing their position is that they believe there is a general right to liberty, which the state may override only when it shows that interference is *necessary* to serve certain purposes.

Still, there remains much controversy, which we will explore in this chapter, about the *kinds* of reasons that might be sufficient to override a general right to liberty. Least controversial is the *harm principle*, which says that liberty may be restricted in order to prevent harm to others. But it is controversial whether the harm principle extends to government actions that would prevent harm to the individual himself (*legal paternalism*), as when the state requires the use of seatbelts and motorcycle helmets, and restricts the use of harmful substances such as narcotic drugs. It is also controversial whether the harm principle, regardless of whether it includes or excludes paternalism, is exclusive. Libertarians such as John Stuart Mill and Robert Nozick believe that some version of the harm principle constitutes the exclusive justification for restricting individual liberty. Others, such as Joel Feinberg, believe that the harm principle must be supplemented by

---

[7]*Harris v. McRae*, 448 U.S. 297 (1980); *Maher v. Roe*, 432 U.S. 464 (1977).

an *offense principle*, according to which liberty may be restricted not only to prevent harm, but also non–harmful offense, as when the government prohibits people from engaging in sexual intercourse in public parks or on public streets. And still others, such as Patrick Devlin, believe that liberty may be restricted not only to prevent harm and offense, but also (*legal moralism*) to protect public moral values.

Although a belief in a general right to liberty is common, it is by no means universal. A thoroughgoing act–utilitarian would have no need for such principles or presumptions. Indeed, even many non–utilitarians who do believe in the existence of rights do not believe that there is a general right to liberty. Ronald Dworkin, for example, argues that in the absence of specific rights the state can and should make its decisions simply on the utilitarian basis of maximizing the general welfare.[8] If maximizing the general welfare requires restricting people's general freedom of action, so be it, Dworkin would argue. Only when maximizing the general welfare interferes with rights more specific than a general right to liberty, such as a right to free speech, or a right to freedom of religion, or a right to equal concern and respect (the right that Dworkin believes generates all the others), will there be a "trump" (to use his term) or a "side constraint" (to use Robert Nozick's) on the pursuit of the general welfare.

[8]Ronald Dworkin, "What Rights Do We Have?", in *Taking Rights Seriously* (London: Duckworth, 1977), pp. 266 ff.

■ The Harm Principle

ON LIBERTY

JOHN STUART MILL

The object of this Essay is to assert one very simple principle, as entitled to govern absolutely the dealings of society with the individual in the way of compulsion and control, whether the means used be physical force in the form of legal penalties, or the moral coercion of public opinion. That principle is, that the sole end for which mankind are warranted, individually or collectively, in interfering with the liberty of action of any of their number, is self-protection. That the only purpose for which power can be rightfully exercised over any member of a civilized community, against his will, is to prevent harm to others. His own good, either physical or moral, is not a sufficient warrant. He cannot rightfully be compelled to do or forbear because it will be better for him to do so, because it will make him

John Stuart Mill, *On Liberty* (1859), selection from Chapter 1

happier, because, in the opinions of others, to do so would be wise, or even right. These are good reasons for remonstrating with him, or reasoning with him, or persuading him, or entreating him, but not for compelling him, or visiting him with any evil in case he do otherwise. To justify that, the conduct from which it is desired to deter him must be calculated to produce evil to some one else. The only part of the conduct of any one, for which he is amenable to society, is that which concerns others. In the part which merely concerns himself, his independence is, of right, absolute. Over himself, over his own body and mind, the individual is sovereign.

It is, perhaps hardly necessary to say that this doctrine is meant to apply only to human beings in the maturity of their faculties. We are not speaking of children, or of young persons below the age which the law may fix as that of manhood or womanhood. Those who are still in a state to require being taken care of by others, must be protected against their own actions as well as against external injury. For the same reason, we may leave out of consideration those backward states of society in which the race itself may be considered as in its nonage. The early difficulties in the way of spontaneous progress are so great, that there is seldom any choice of means for overcoming them; and a ruler full of the spirit of improvement is warranted in the use of any expedients that will attain an end, perhaps otherwise unattainable. Despotism is a legitimate mode of government in dealing with barbarians, provided the end be their improvement, and the means justified by actually effecting that end. Liberty, as a principle, has no application to any state of things anterior to the time when mankind have become capable of being improved by free and equal discussion. Until then, there is nothing for them but implicit obedience to an Akbar or a Charlemagne, if they are so fortunate as to find one. But as soon as mankind have attained the capacity of

being guided to their own improvement by conviction or persuasion (a period long since reached in all nations with whom we need here concern ourselves), compulsion, either in the direct form or in that of pains and penalties for non-compliance, is no longer admissible as a means to their own good, and justifiable only for the security of others.

It is proper to state that I forego any advantage which could be derived to my argument from the idea of abstract right, as a thing independent of utility. I regard utility as the ultimate appeal on all ethical questions; but it must be utility in the largest sense, grounded on the permanent interests of man as. a progressive being. Those interests, I contend, authorise the subjection of individual spontaneity to external control, only in respect to those actions of each, which concern the interest of other people. If any one does an act hurtful to others, there is a *prima facie* case for punishing him, by law, or, where legal penalties are not safely applicable, by general disapprobation. There are also many positive acts for the benefit of others, which he may rightfully be compelled to perform; such as to give evidence in a court of justice; to bear his fair share in the common defence, or in any other joint work necessary to the interest of the society of which he enjoys the protection; and to perform certain acts of individual beneficence, such as saving a fellow-creature's life, or interposing to protect the defenceless against ill-usage, things which whenever it is obviously a man's duty to do, he may rightfully be made responsible to society for not doing. A person may cause evil to others not only by his actions but by his inaction, and in either case he is justly accountable to them for the injury. The latter case, it is true, requires a much more cautious exercise of compulsion than the former. To make any one answerable for doing evil to others is the rule; to make him answerable for not preventing evil is, comparatively speaking, the exception. Yet there are many cases clear enough and grave enough to justify that exception. In all things which regard the external relations of the individual, he is *de jure* amenable to those whose interests are concerned, and, if need be, to society as their protector. There are often good reasons for not holding him to the responsibility; but these reasons must arise from the special expediencies of the case: either because it is a kind of case in which he is on the whole likely to act better, when left to his own discretion, than when controlled in any way in which society have it in their power to control him; or because the attempt to exercise control would produce other evils, greater than those which it would prevent. When such reasons as these preclude the enforcement of responsibility, the conscience of the agent himself should step into the vacant judgment seat, and protect those interests of others which have no external protection; judging himself all the more rigidly, because the case does not admit of his being made accountable to the judgment of his fellow–creatures.

But there is a sphere of action in which society, as distinguished from the individual, has, if any, only an indirect interest; comprehending all that portion of a person's life and conduct which affects only himself, or if it also affects others, only with their free, voluntary, and undeceived consent and participation. When I say only himself, I mean directly, and in the first instance; for whatever affects himself, may affect others *through* himself; and the objection which may be grounded on this contingency, will receive consideration in the sequel. This, then, is the appropriate region of human liberty. It comprises, first, the inward domain of consciousness; demanding liberty of conscience in the most comprehensive sense; liberty of thought and feeling; absolute freedom of opinion and sentiment on all subjects, practical or speculative, scientific, moral, or theological. The liberty of expressing and publishing opinions may seem to fall under a different principle, since it belongs to that part of the conduct of an individual which concerns

other people; but, being almost of as much importance as the liberty of thought itself, and resting in great part on the same reasons, is practically inseparable from it. Secondly, the principle requires liberty of tastes and pursuits; of framing the plan of our life to suit our own character; of doing as we like, subject to such consequences as may follow: without impediment from our fellow creatures, so long as what we do does not harm them, even though they should think our conduct foolish, perverse, or wrong. Thirdly, from this liberty of each individual, follows the liberty, within the same limits, of combination among individuals; freedom to unite, for any purpose not involving harm to others: the persons combining being supposed to be of full age, and not forced or deceived.

No society in which these liberties are not, on the whole, respected, is free, whatever may be its form of government; and none is completely free in which they do not exist absolute and unqualified. The only freedom which deserves the name, is that of pursuing our own good in our own way, so long as we do not attempt to deprive others of theirs, or impede their efforts to obtain it. Each is the proper guardian of his own health, whether bodily, or mental and spiritual. Mankind are greater gainers by suffering each other to live as seems good to themselves, than by compelling each to live as seems good to the rest.

Though this doctrine is anything but new, and, to some persons, may have the air of a truism, there is no doctrine which stands more directly opposed to the general tendency of existing opinion and practice. Society has expended fully as much effort in the attempt (according to its lights) to compel people to conform to its notions of personal as of social excellence. The ancient commonwealths thought themselves entitled to practise, and the ancient philosophers countenanced, the regulation of every part of private conduct by public authority, on the ground that the State had a deep interest in the whole bodily and mental discipline of every one of its citizens; a mode of thinking which may have been admissible in small republics surrounded by powerful enemies, in constant peril of being subverted by foreign attack or internal commotion, and to which even a short interval of relaxed energy and self-command might so easily be fatal that they could not afford to wait for the salutary permanent effects of freedom. In the modern world, the greater size of political communities, and, above all, the separation between spiritual and temporal authority (which placed the direction of men's consciences in other hands than those which controlled their worldly affairs), prevented so great an interference by law in the details of private life; but the engines of moral repression have been wielded more strenuously against divergence from the reigning opinion in self-regarding, than even in social matters; religion, the most powerful of the elements which have entered into the formation of moral feeling, having almost always been governed either by the ambition of a hierarchy, seeking control over every department of human conduct, or by the spirit of Puritanism. And some of those modern reformers who have placed themselves in strongest opposition to the religions of the past, have been noway behind either churches or sects in their assertion of the right of spiritual domination: M. Comte, in particular, whose so-

cial systems, as unfolded in his *Système de Politique Positive*, aims at establishing (though by moral more than by legal appliances) a despotism of society over the individual, surpassing anything contemplated in the political ideal of the most rigid disciplinarian among the ancient philosophers.

Apart from the peculiar tenets of individual thinkers, there is also in the world at large an increasing inclination to stretch unduly the powers of society over the individual, both by the force of opinion and even by that of legislation; and as the tendency of all the changes taking place in the world is to strengthen society, and diminish the power of the individual, this encroachment is not one of the evils which tend spontaneously to disappear, but, on the contrary, to grow more and more formidable. The disposition of mankind, whether as rulers or as fellow-citizens, to impose their own opinions and inclinations as a rule of conduct on others, is so energetically supported by some of the best and by some of the worst feelings incident to human nature, that it is hardly ever kept under restraint by anything but want of power; and as the power is not declining, but growing, unless a strong barrier of moral conviction can be raised against the mischief, we must expect, in the present circumstances of the world, to see it increase.

QUESTIONS FOR DISCUSSION

1. Why does Mill believe that harm to others is the only basis for governmental interference? What does he mean when he says that he will forgo an argument "from the idea of abstract right"? Does Mill in fact forgo it?

2. How does Mill define "harm"? Does Mill believe that government may legitimately try to prevent all harms? If not, which ones?

3. Mill says his argument applies as well to "the moral coercion of public opinion." What does he mean? How might you distinguish this form of coercion from official state coercion?

LIBERTY, EQUALITY, FRATERNITY

JAMES FITZJAMES STEPHEN

There is hardly anything in [On Liberty] which can properly be called proof as distinguished from enunciation or assertion of the general principles quoted. I think, however, that it will not be difficult to show that the principle stands in much need of proof. In order to make this clear it will be desirable in the first place to point out the meaning of the word liberty according to principles which I think are common to Mr Mill and to myself. I do not think Mr Mill would have disputed the following statement of the theory of human actions. All voluntary acts are caused by motives. All motives may be placed in one of two categories—hope and fear, pleasure and pain. Voluntary acts of which hope is the motive are said to be free. Voluntary acts of which fear is the motive are said to be done under compulsion, or omitted under restraint. A woman marries. This in every case is a voluntary action. If she regards the marriage with the ordinary feelings and acts from the ordinary motives, she is said to act freely. If she regards it as a necessity, to which she submits in order to avoid greater evil, she is said to act under compulsion and not freely.

If this is the true theory of liberty—and, though many persons would deny this, I think they would have been accepted by Mr Mill—the propositions already stated will in a condensed form amount to this: 'No one is ever justified in trying to affect any one's conduct by exciting his fears, except for the sake of self-protection;' or, making another substitution which he would also approve—'It can never promote the general happiness of mankind that the conduct of any persons should be affected by an appeal to their fears, except in the cases excepted.'

Surely these are not assertions which can be regarded as self-evident, or even as otherwise than paradoxical. What is all morality, and what are all existing religions in so far as they aim at affecting human conduct, except an appeal either to hope or fear, and to fear far more commonly and far more emphatically than to hope? Criminal legislation proper may be regarded as an engine of prohibition unimportant in comparison with morals and the forms of morality sanctioned by theology. For one act from which one person is restrained by the fear of the law of the land, many persons are restrained from innumerable acts by the fear of the disapprobation of their neighbours, which is the moral sanction; or by the fear of punishment in a future state of existence, which is the religious sanction; or by the fear of their own disapprobation, which may be called the conscientious sanction, and may be regarded as a compound case of the other two. Now, in the innumerable majority of cases, disapprobation, or the moral sanction, has nothing whatever to do with self-protection. The religious sanction is by its nature independent of it. Whatever special forms it may assume, the fundamental condition of it is a being intolerant of evil in the highest degree, and inexorably determined to punish it wherever it exists, except upon certain terms. I do not say

James FitzJames Stephen, *Liberty, Equality, Fraternity* (1873)[9]

---

[9]Sir James FitzJames Stephen (1829–1894) was a prominent English criminal lawyer and then judge. *Liberty, Equality, Fraternity* was a broad-based critique of democratic secularism, of which the response to Mill was only a part.

that this doctrine is true, but I do say that no one is entitled to assume it without proof to be essentially immoral and mischievous. Mr Mill does not draw this inference, but I think his theory involves it, for I know not what can be a greater infringement of his theory of liberty, a more complete and formal contradiction to it, than the doctrine that there are a court and a judge in which, and before whom, every man must give an account of every work done in the body, whether self-regarding or not. According to Mr Mill's theory, it ought to be a good plea in the day of judgment to say 'I pleased myself and hurt nobody else.' Whether or not there will ever be a day of judgment is not the question, but upon his principles the conception of a day of judgment is fundamentally immoral. A God who punished any one at all, except for the purpose of protecting others, would, upon his principles, be a tyrant trampling on liberty.

The application of the principle in question to the moral sanction would be just as subversive of all that people commonly regard as morality. The only moral system which would comply with the principle stated by Mr Mill would be one capable of being summed up as follows: 'Let every man please himself without hurting his neighbour;' and every moral system which aimed at more than this, either to obtain benefits for society at large other than protection against injury or to do good to the persons affected, would be wrong in principle. This would condemn every existing system of morals. Positive morality is nothing but a body of principles and rules more or less vaguely expressed, and more or less left to be understood, by which certain lines of conduct are forbidden under the penalty of general disapprobation, and that quite irrespectively of self-protection. Mr Mill himself admits this to a certain extent. In the early part of his fourth chapter he says that a man grossly deficient in the qualities which conduce to his own good is 'necessarily and properly a subject of distaste, or in extreme cases even of contempt,' and he enumerates various inconveniences to which this would expose such a person. He adds, however: 'The inconveniences which are strictly inseparable from the unfavourable judgment of others are the only ones to which a person should ever be subjected for that portion of his conduct and character which concerns his own good, but which does not affect the interests of others in their relation with him.' This no doubt weakens the effect of the admission; but be this how it may, the fact still remains that morality is and must be a prohibitive system, one of the main objects of which is to impose upon every one a standard of conduct and of sentiment to which few persons would conform if it were not for the constraint thus put upon them. In nearly every instance the effects of such a system reach far beyond anything that can be described as the purposes of self-protection.

Mr Mill's system is violated not only by every system of theology which concerns itself with morals, and by every known system of positive morality, but by the constitution of human nature itself. There is hardly a habit which men in general regard as good which is not acquired by a series of more or less painful and laborious acts. The condition of human life is such that we must of necessity be restrained and compelled by circumstances in nearly every action of our lives. Why, then, is liberty, defined as Mr Mill defines it, to be regarded as so precious? What, after all, is done by the legislator or by the person who sets public opinion in motion to control conduct of which he disapproves—or, if the expression is preferred, which he dislikes—which is not done for us all at every instant of our lives by circumstances? The laws which punish murder or theft are substitutes for private vengeance, which, in the absence of law, would punish those crimes more severely, though in a less regular manner. If there were laws which punished incontinence, gluttony, or drunkenness, the same might be said of them. Mr Mill admits in so many words that there are 'inconveniences which are strictly inseparable from the unfavourable judgment of others.' What is the distinction in principle between such inconveniences and similar ones organized, defined, and inflicted upon proof that the circumstances which call for their infliction exist? This organization, definition, and procedure make all the difference between the restraints which Mr Mill would permit and the restraints to which he objects. I cannot see on what the distinction rests. I cannot understand why it must always be wrong to punish habitual drunkenness by fine, imprisonment, or deprivation of civil rights, and always be right to punish it by the infliction of those consequences which are 'strictly inseparable from the unfavourable judgment of others.' It may be said that these consequences follow, not because we think them desirable, but in the common order of nature. This answer only suggests the further question, whether nature is in this instance to be regarded as a friend or as an enemy? Every reasonable man would answer that the restraint which the fear of the disapprobation of others imposes on our conduct is the part of the constitution of nature which we could least afford to dispense with. But if this is so, why draw the line where Mr Mill draws it? Why treat the penal consequences of disapprobation as things to be minimized and restrained within the narrowest limits? What 'inconvenience,' after all, is 'strictly inseparable from the unfavourable judgment of others'? If society at large adopted fully Mr Mill's theory of liberty, it would be easy to diminish very greatly the inconveniences in question. Strenuously preach and rigorously practise the doctrine that our neighbour's private character is nothing to us, and the number of unfavourable judgments formed, and therefore the number of inconveniences inflicted by them, can be reduced as much as we please, and the province of liberty can be enlarged in a corresponding ratio. Does any reasonable man wish for this? Could anyone desire gross licentiousness, monstrous extravagance, ridiculous vanity, or the like, to be

unnoticed, or, being known, to inflict no inconveniences?

If, however, the restraints on immorality are the main safeguards of society against influences which might be fatal to it, why treat them as if they were bad? Why draw so strongly marked a line between social and legal penalties? Mr Mill asserts the existence of the distinction in every form of speech. He makes his meaning perfectly clear. Yet from one end of his essay to the other I find no proof and no attempt to give the proper and appropriate proof of it. His doctrine could have been proved if it had been true. It was not proved because it was not true.

■ ■ ■

Not only is an appeal to facts and experience opposed to Mr Mill's principle, but his essay contains exceptions and qualifications which are really inconsistent with it. He says that his principle 'is meant to apply to human beings only in the maturity of their faculties,' and, he adds, 'we may leave out of account those backward states of society in which the race itself may be considered in its nonage.' Despotism, he says, 'is a legitimate mode of government in dealing with barbarians, provided the end be their improvement, and the means justified by actually effecting that end. Liberty as a principle has no application to any state of things anterior to the time when mankind have become capable of being improved by free and equal discussion. Until then there is nothing for them but implicit obedience to an Akbar or a Charlemagne if they are so fortunate as to find one. But as soon as mankind have attained the capacity of being guided to their own improvement by conviction or persuasion (a period long since reached in all nations with whom we need here concern ourselves), compulsion is no longer admissible as a means to their own good, and is justifiable only for the security of others.'

It seems to me that this qualification either reduces the doctrine qualified to an empty commonplace which no one would care to dispute, or makes an incredible assertion about the state of human society. No one, I suppose, ever denied either in theory or in practice that there is a sphere within which the tastes of people of mature age ought not to be interfered with, and within which differences must be regarded as natural and inevitable—in which better or worse means that which the individual prefers or dislikes. On the other hand, no one ever suggested that it was or could be good for anyone to be compelled to do what he did not like, unless the person compelling was not only stronger but wiser than the person compelled, at all events in reference to the matter to which the compulsion applied. . . .

[T]here is no principle on which the cases in which Mr Mill admits the justice of legal punishment can be distinguished from those in which he denies it. The principle is that private vices which are injurious to others may justly be punished, if the injury be specific and the persons injured distinctly assignable, but not otherwise. If the question were as to the possibility in most cases of drawing an indictment against such persons I should agree with him. Criminal law is an extremely rough engine, and must be worked with great caution; but it is one thing to point out a practical difficulty which limits the application of a principle and quite another to refute the principle itself. Mr Mill's proviso deserves attention in considering the question whether a given act should be punished by law, but he applies it to 'the moral coercion of public opinion,' as well as to legal coercion, and to this the practical difficulty which he points out does not apply. A set of young noblemen of great fortune and hereditary influence, the representatives of ancient names, the natural leaders of the society of large districts, pass their whole time and employ all their means in gross debauchery. Such people are far more injurious to society than common pickpockets, but Mr Mill says that if any one having the opportunity of making them ashamed of themselves uses it in order to coerce them into decency, he sins against liberty, unless their example does assignable harm to specific people. It might be right to say, 'You, the Duke of A, by extravagantly keeping four mistresses—to wit, B and C in London, and D and E in Paris—set an example which induced your friend F to elope with Mrs G at _____ on _____, and you are a great blackguard for your pains, and all the more because you are a duke.' It could never be right to say, 'You, the Duke of A, are scandalously immoral and ought to be made to smart for it, though the law cannot touch you.' The distinction is more likely to be overlooked than to be misunderstood.

■ ■ ■

The object of morally intolerant legislation . . . is to establish, to maintain, and to give power to that which the legislator regards as a good moral system or standard. . . . I think that this object is good if and in so far as the system so established and maintained is good. How far any particular system is good or not is a question which probably does not admit of any peremptory final decision; but I may observe that there are a considerable number of things which appear good and bad, though no doubt in different degrees, to all mankind. For the practical purpose of legislation refinements are of little importance. In any given age and nation virtue and vice have meanings which for that purpose are quite definite enough.

■ ■ ■

If this is so, the only remaining questions will be as to the efficiency of the means at the disposal of society for this purpose, and the cost of their application. Society has at its disposal two great instruments by which vice may be prevented and virtue promoted—namely, law and public opinion; and law is either criminal or civil. The use of each of these instruments is subject to certain limits and conditions, and the wisdom of attempting to make men good either by Act of Parliament or by the action of public opinion depends entirely upon the degree in which those limits and conditions are recognized and acted upon.

First, I will take the case of criminal law. What are the conditions under which and the limitations within which it can be applied with success to the object of making men better? In considering this question it must be borne in mind that criminal law is at once by far the most powerful and by far the roughest engine which society can use for any purpose. Its power is shown by the fact that it can and does render crime exceedingly difficult and dangerous. Indeed, in civilized society it absolutely prevents avowed open crime committed with the strong hand, except in cases where crime rises to the magnitude of civil war. Its roughness hardly needs illustration. It strikes so hard that it can be enforced only on the gravest occasions, and with every sort of precaution against abuse or mistake. Before an act can be treated as a crime, it ought to be capable of distinct definition and of specific proof, and it ought also to be of such a nature that it is worthwhile to prevent it at the risk of inflicting great damage, direct and indirect, upon those who commit it. These conditions are seldom, if ever, fulfilled by mere vices. It would obviously be impossible to indict a man for ingratitude or perfidy. Such charges are too vague for specific discussion and distinct proof on the one side, and disproof on the other. Moreover, the expense of the investigations necessary for the legal punishment of such conduct would be enormous. It would be necessary to go into an infinite number of delicate and subtle inquiries which would tear off all privacy from the lives of a large number of persons. These considerations are, I think, conclusive reasons against treating vice in general as a crime.

The excessive harshness of criminal law is also a circumstance which very greatly narrows the range of its application. It is the *ratio ultima* of the majority against persons whom its application assumes to have renounced the common bonds which connect men together. When a man is subjected to legal punishment, society appeals directly and exclusively to his fears. It renounces the attempt to work upon his affections or feelings. In other words, it puts itself into distinct, harsh, and undisguised opposition to his wishes; and the effect of this will be to make him rebel against the law. The violence of the rebellion will be measured partly by the violence of the passion the indulgence of which is forbidden, and partly by the degree to which the law can count upon an ally in the man's own conscience. A law which enters into a direct contest with a fierce imperious passion, which the person who feels it does not admit to be bad, and which is not directly injurious to others, will generally do more harm than good; and this is perhaps the principal reason why it is impossible to legislate directly against unchastity, unless it takes forms which every one regards as monstrous and horrible. The subject is not one for detailed discussion, but any one who will follow out the reflections which this hint suggests will find that they supply a striking illustration of the limits which the harshness of criminal law imposes upon its range.

If we now look at the different acts which satisfy the conditions specified, it will, I think, be found that criminal law in this country actually is applied to the suppression of vice and so to the promotion of virtue to a very considerable extent; and this I say is right.

The punishment of common crimes, the gross forms of force and fraud, is no doubt ambiguous. It may be justified on the principle of self protection, and apart from any question as to their moral character. It is not, however, difficult to show that these acts have in fact been forbidden and subjected to punishment not only because they are dangerous to society, and so ought to be prevented, but also for the sake of gratifying the feeling of hatred—call it revenge, resentment, or what you will—which the contemplation of such conduct excites in healthily constituted minds. If this can be shown, it will follow that criminal law is in the nature of a persecution of the grosser forms of vice, and an emphatic assertion of the principle that the feeling of hatred and the desire of vengeance above-mentioned are important elements of human nature which ought in such cases to be satisfied in a regular public and legal manner.

■ ■ ■

I now pass to the manner in which civil law may and does, and as I say properly, promote virtue and prevent vice. This is a subject so wide that I prefer indicating its nature by a few illustrations to attempting to deal with it systematically. It would, however, be easy to show that nearly every branch of civil law assumes the existence of a standard of moral good and evil which the public at large have an interest in maintaining, and in many cases enforcing—a proceeding which is diametrically opposed to Mr Mill's fundamental principles.

■ ■ ■

Perhaps the most pointed of all illustrations of the moral character of civil law is to be found in the laws relating to marriage and inheritance. They all proceed upon an essentially moral theory as to the relation of the sexes. Take the case of illegitimate children. A bastard is *filius nullius*—he inherits nothing, he has no claim on his putative father. What is all this except the expression of the strongest possible determination on the part of the Legislature to recognize, maintain, and favour marriage in every possible manner as the foundation of civilized society? It has been plausibly maintained that these laws bear hardly upon bastards, punishing them for the sins of their parents. It is not necessary to my purpose to go into this, though it appears to me that the law is right. I make the remark merely for the sake of showing to what lengths the law does habitually go for the purpose of maintaining the most important of all moral principles, the principle upon which one great department of it is entirely founded. It is a case in which a good object is promoted by efficient and adequate means.

■ ■ ■

I have now said what I had to say about liberty, and I may briefly sum up the result. It is that, if the word 'liberty' has any definite sense attached to it, and if it is consistently used in that sense, it is almost impossible to make any true general assertion whatever about it, and quite impossible to regard it either as a good thing or a bad one. If, on the other hand, the word is used merely in a general popular way without attaching any distinct signification to it, it is easy to make almost any general assertion you please about it; but these assertions will be incapable of either proof or disproof as they will have no definite meaning. Thus the word is either a misleading appeal to passion, or else it embodies or rather hints at an exceedingly complicated assertion, the truth of which can be proved only by elaborate historical investigations.

QUESTIONS FOR DISCUSSION

1. What does Stephen believe the purpose of the state to be? How does this differ from Mill? Does Stephen disagree with Mill's harm principle, or does he just disagree on what is to count as a harm? Is it possible that the two only disagree about the utility of using *law* for certain purposes?

2. Stephen argues that Mill's concession about immature individuals and societies is fatal to his whole argument. How might Mill respond?

3. When the government forces people to pay taxes to fund schools, libraries, and museums, does this support Stephen's argument? Why or why not?

■ Offense

OFFENSE TO OTHERS

JOEL FEINBERG

Passing annoyance, disappointment, disgust, embarrassment, and various other disliked conditions such as fear, anxiety, and minor ("harmless") aches and pains, are not in themselves necessarily harmful. Consequently, no matter how the harm principle is mediated, it will not certify as legitimate those interferences with the liberty of some citizens that are made for the sole purpose of preventing such unpleasant states in others. For convenience I will use the word "offense" to cover the whole miscellany of universally disliked mental states and not merely that species of the wider genus that are offensive in a strict and proper sense. If the law is justified, then, in using its coercive methods to protect people from mere offense, it must be by virtue of a separate and distinct legitimizing principle, which we can label "the offense principle" and formulate as follows: *It is always a good reason in support of a proposed criminal prohibition that it would probably be an effective way of preventing serious offense (as opposed to injury or harm) to persons other than the actor, and that it is probably a necessary means to that end* (i.e., there is probably no other means that is equally effective at no greater cost to other values). The principle asserts, in effect, that the prevention of offensive conduct *is* properly the state's business.

Like the word "harm", the word "offense" has both a general and a specifically normative sense, the former including in its reference any or all of a miscellany of disliked mental states (disgust, shame, hurt, anxiety, etc.), and the lat-ter referring to those states only when caused by the wrongful (right-violating) conduct of others. Only the latter sense—wrongful offense—is intended in the offense principle as we shall understand it. In this respect there is a parallel with the harm principle. We can also use the verb "to offend" meaning "to cause another to experience a mental state of a universally disliked kind (e.g., disgust, shame)." The offense principle then cites the need to prevent some people from *wrongfully offending* (offending and wronging) others as a reason for coercive legislation. Finally, the word "offense" in the strict and proper sense it bears in ordinary language is specific in a different way. Whereas "offense" in the sense of the offense principle specifies an objective condition—the unpleasant mental state must be caused by conduct that really is wrongful—"offense" in the strict sense of ordinary language specifies a subjective condition—the offending act must be taken by the offended person to wrong him whether in fact it does or not. In the strict and narrow sense, I am offended (or "take offense") when (a) I suffer a disliked state, and (b) I attribute that state to the wrongful conduct of another, and (c) I *resent* the other for his role in causing me to be in the state. The sense of grievance against the other or resentment of him for wronging me in this way is a phenomenological component of the unpleasant experience itself, an element that actually reenforces and magnifies its unpleasantness. If I am disgusted by the sight of a hospital patient's bloody wounds, the experience

Joel Feinberg, *Offense to Others* (New York: Oxford University Press, 1985), selection from Chapter 1

is one of that miscellany of disliked states I call "offended states of mind in the broad sense," but I can hardly resent the poor fellow for his innocent role in causing me to suffer that state of mind, and indeed there may be nobody to resent, in which case I do not "take offense," which is to say I am not offended in the strict and narrow sense.

The offense principle requires that the disliked state of mind (offense in the broad sense) be produced wrongfully by another party, but not that it be an offense in the strict sense of ordinary language. The victim may not know, or may not care, that another has wrongfully caused his unease, and therefore his unpleasant state of mind will not contain the element of resentment, and thus will not be offense in the strict sense. The offense principle as we shall interpret it then applies to offended states in either the broad or the strict sense—that is either with or without resentment—when these states are in fact wrongfully produced in violation of the offended party's rights. It is necessary that there *be* a wrong, but not that the victim *feel* wronged. And there will always be a wrong whenever an offended state (in the generic sense) is produced in another without justification or excuse.

Since I shall be defending a highly restricted version of the offense principle in this chapter, I should begin with some important disclaimers. To begin with, *offense is surely a less serious thing than harm.* That comparative value judgment seems to me self-evident, yet not simply true by definition. It is possible to deny it without contradiction if only because offense is not strictly commensurable with harm. It is a misconception to think of offenses as occupying the lower part of the same scale as harms; rather offenses are a different sort of thing altogether, with a scale all of their own. Yet most people after reflection will probably acknowledge that a person is not treated as badly, other things being equal, when he is merely offended as when he is harmed. We may (at most) be inclined to rank extreme offenses as

greater wrongs to their victims than trifling harms, but perhaps that is because they may become so offensive as to be actually harmful, in a minor sort of way. (At any rate the comparison of extreme offense with minor harm is the only place controversy could reasonably arise over the relative seriousness of offenses and harms.) Continued extreme offense [can] *cause* harm to a person who becomes emotionally upset over the offense, to the neglect of his real interests. But the offended mental state in itself is not a condition of harm. From the moral point of view, considered in its own nature (apart from possible causal linkages to harmful consequences), it is a relatively trivial thing.

It follows from this evident but unprovable truth that the law should not treat offenses as if they were as serious, by and large, as harms. It should not, for example, attempt to control offensiveness by the criminal law when other modes of regulation can do the job as efficiently and economically. For the control of uncommon and transitory forms of offensiveness, for example, reliance can be placed on individual suits for injunctions, or by court orders initiated by police to cease and desist on pain of penalty, or by licensing procedures that depend on administrative suspension of license as a sanction. These alternatives would not entirely dispense with the need for punishment (which is almost always a disproportionately greater evil to the offender than offended mental states are to his "victims"), but punishment would be reserved as a back-up threat, not inflicted for offending others so much as for defying authority by persisting in prohibited conduct. It may well be that the ordinary criminal law need not concern itself at all with defining crimes of offensiveness, even though offensiveness is the sort of evil it could in principle be used legitimately to combat. It is more likely, however, that for various practical reasons, reliance on injunctions, administrative orders, and license withdrawals would be insufficient to control *all* properly prohibitable offensive conduct. In some cases, we can know very well in advance that conduct of a certain kind will offend; that is, we don't have to wait for the particular circumstances to decide the question. Moreover, in some cases there will not be time to get an injunction or administrative hearing. By the time that sort of relief is forthcoming, the annoyance has come and gone, and the offense, such as it is, already committed.

Even if there must be defined crimes with specified penalties for purely offensive conduct, however, the penalties should be light ones: more often fines than imprisonment, but when imprisonment, it should be measured in days rather than months or years. Where crimes are divided into the categories of misdemeanor and felony, purely offensive crimes should always be misdemeanors, never felonies. Where penal codes follow the American Law Institute model in dividing offenses into felonies, misdemeanors, petty misdemeanors, and "violations," harmlessly offensive conduct at its worst should be a petty misdemeanor, but typically only a violation—a status it would share with traffic and parking violations, various illegal sales, and unintentional violations of health or safety codes. When a given crime is both harmful and offensive the punishment can properly be severe, but legislators and judges should make it clear that the severity of the punishment is primarily a function of the harmfulness (or dangerousness) of the criminal act, not a reaction to its offensiveness. The state should punish a very harmful or dangerous but only routinely offensive crime much more severely than a crime that is greatly offensive but harmful or dangerous only to a minor degree.

■ ■ ■

A RIDE ON THE BUS

There is a limit to the power of abstract reasoning to settle questions of moral legitimacy. The question raised by this chapter is whether there are any human experiences that are harmless in themselves yet so unpleasant that we can rightly demand legal protection from them even at the cost of other persons' liberties. The best way to deal with that question at the start is to engage our imaginations in the inquiry, consider hypothetically the most offensive experiences we can imagine, and then sort them into groups in an effort to isolate the kernel of the offense in each category. Accordingly, this section will consist of a number of vividly sketched imaginary tales, and the reader is asked to project himself into each story and determine as best he can what his reaction would be. In each story the reader should think of himself as a passenger on a normally crowded public bus on his way to work or to some important appointment in circumstances such that if he is forced to leave the bus prematurely, he will not only have to pay another fare to get where he is going, but he will probably be late, to his own disadvantage. If he is not exactly a captive on the bus, then, he would nevertheless be greatly inconvenienced if he had to leave the bus before it reached his destination. In each story, another passenger, or group of passengers, gets on the bus, and proceeds to cause, by their characteristics or their conduct, great offense to *you*. The stories form six clusters corresponding to the kind of offense caused.

A. Affronts to the senses

Story 1. A passenger who obviously hasn't bathed in more than a month sits down next to you. He reeks of a barely tolerable stench. There is hardly room to stand elsewhere on the bus and all other seats are occupied.

Story 2. A passenger wearing a shirt of violently clashing orange and crimson sits down directly in your forward line of vision. You must keep your eyes down to avoid looking at him.

Story 3. A passenger sits down next to you, pulls a slate tablet from his brief case, and proceeds to scratch his fingernails loudly across the slate, sending a chill up your spine and making your teeth clench. You politely ask him to stop, but he refuses.

Story 4. A passenger elsewhere in the bus turns on a portable radio to maximum volume. The sounds it emits are mostly screeches, whistles, and static, but occasionally some electronically amplified rock and roll music blares through.

B. Disgust and revulsion

Story 5. This is much like story 1 except that the malodorous passenger in the neighboring seat continually scratches, drools, coughs, farts, and belches.

Story 6. A group of passengers enters the bus and shares a seating compartment with you. They spread a table cloth over their laps and proceed to eat a picnic lunch that consists of live insects, fish heads, and pickled sex organs of lamb, veal, and pork, smothered in garlic and onions. Their table manners leave almost everything to be desired.

Story 7. Things get worse and worse. The itinerant picnickers practice gluttony in the ancient Roman manner, gorging until satiation and then vomiting on to their table cloth. Their practice, however, is a novel departure from the ancient custom in that they eat their own and one another's vomit along with the remaining food.

Story 8. A coprophagic sequel to story 7.

Story 9. At some point during the trip the passenger at one's side quite openly and nonchalantly changes her sanitary napkin and drops the old one into the aisle.

C. Shock to moral, religious, or patriotic sensibilities

Story 10. A group of mourners carrying a coffin enters the bus and shares a seating compartment with you. Although they are all dressed in black their demeanor is by no means funereal. In fact they seem more angry than sorrowful, and refer to the deceased as "the old bastard," and "the bloody corpse." At one point they rip open the coffin with hammers and proceed to smash the corpse's face with a series of hard hammer blows.

Story 11. A strapping youth enters the bus and takes a seat directly in your line of vision. He is wearing a T–shirt with a cartoon across his chest of Christ on the cross. Underneath the picture appear the words "Hang in there, baby!"

Story 12. After taking the seat next to you a passenger produces a bundle wrapped in a large American flag. The bundle contains, among other things, his lunch, which he proceeds to eat. Then he spits into the star-spangled corner of the flag and uses it first to clean his mouth and then to blow his nose. Then he uses the main striped part of the flag to shine his shoes.

D. Shame, embarrassment (including vicarious embarrassment), and anxiety

Story 13. The passenger who takes the seat directly across from you is entirely naked. On one version of the story, he or she is the same sex as you; on the other version of the story, he or she is the opposite sex.

Story 14. The passenger in the previous story proceeds to masturbate quietly in his or her seat.

Story 15. A man and woman, more or less fully clothed to start, take two seats directly in front of you, and then begin to kiss, hug, pet, and fondle one another to the accompaniment of loud sighs and groans of pleasure. They continue these activities throughout the trip.

Story 16. The couple of the previous story, shortly before the bus reaches their destination, engage in acts of mutual masturbation, with quite audible instructions to each other and other sound effects.

Story 17. A variant of the previous story which climaxes in an act of coitus, somewhat acrobatically performed as required by the crowded circumstances.

Story 18. The seat directly in front of you is occupied by a youth (of either sex) wearing a T-shirt with a lurid picture of a copulating couple across his or her chest.

Story 19. A variant of the previous story in which the couple depicted is recognizable (in virtue of conventional representations) as Jesus and Mary.

Story 20. The couple in stories 15–17 perform a variety of sadomasochistic sex acts with appropriate verbal communications ("Oh, that hurts so sweet! Hit me again! Scratch me! Publicly humiliate me!").

Story 21. The two seats in front of you are occupied by male homosexuals. They flirt and tease at first, then kiss and hug, and finally perform mutual fellatio to climax.

Story 22. This time the homosexuals are both female and they perform cunnilingus.

Story 23. A passenger with a dog takes an aisle seat at your side. He or she keeps the dog calm at first by petting it in a familiar and normal way, but then petting gives way to hugging, and gradually goes beyond the merely affectionate to the unmistakably erotic, culminating finally with oral contact with the canine genitals.

E. Annoyance, boredom, frustration

Story 24. A neighboring passenger keeps a portable radio at a reasonably low volume, and the sounds it emits are by no means offensive to the senses. Nor is the content of the program offensive to the sensibilities. It is, however, a low quality "talk show"

which you find intensely boring, and there is no possible way for you to disengage your attention.

Story 25. The two seats to your left are occupied by two persons who put on a boring "talk show" of their own. There is no way you can avoid hearing every animated word of their inane conversation, no way your mind can roam to its own thoughts, problems, and reveries.

Story 26. The passenger at your side is a friendly bloke, garrulous and officious. You quickly tire of his conversation and beg leave to read your newspaper, but he persists in his chatter despite repeated requests to desist. The bus is crowded and there are no other empty seats.

F. Fear, resentment, humiliation, anger (from empty threats, insults, mockery, flaunting, or taunting)

Story 27. A passenger seated next to you reaches into a military kit and pulls out a "hand grenade" (actually only a realistic toy), and fondles and juggles it throughout the trip to the accompaniment of menacing leers and snorts. Then he pulls out a (rubber) knife and "stabs" himself and others repeatedly to peals of maniacal laughter. He turns out to be harmless enough. His whole intent was to put others in apprehension of harm.

Story 28. A passenger sits next to you wearing a black arm band with a large white swastika on it.

Story 29. A passenger enters the bus straight from a dispersed street rally. He carries a banner with a large and abusive caricature of the Pope and an anti-Catholic slogan. (You are a loyal and pious Catholic.)

Story 30. Variants of the above. The banner displays a picture of a black according to some standard offensive stereotype (Step 'n Fetchit, Uncle Tom, etc.) with an insulting caption, or a picture of a sneering, sniveling, hook–nosed Fagin or Shylock, with a scurrilous anti–Jewish caption, or a similar offensive denunciation or lampooning of groups called "Spicks," "Dagos," "Polacks", etc.

Story 31. Still another variant. A counter-demonstrator leaves a feminist rally to enter the bus. He carries a banner with an offensive caricature of a female and the message, in large red letters: "Keep the bitches barefoot and pregnant."

QUESTIONS FOR DISCUSSION

1. How does Feinberg distinguish between harm and offense? Do you agree with the distinction? If not, do you think that offensive conduct is harmful or harmless?

2. What is Feinberg's justification for restricting conduct that is offensive but not harmful? Do you agree with him?

3. Try to "take" Feinberg's "Ride on the Bus." As you do so, think about what makes each example different from the one that preceded it. Then consider which of the activities you would prohibit, and why.

NEW ENGLAND NATURIST ASSOCIATION V. LARSEN

692 F. Supp. (D.R.I. 1988)

New England Naturist Association, Inc. (the "Association") is a non-business corporation chartered under the laws of the State of Rhode Island. Its principal purpose is to provide activities for persons interested in nudism. For many years, its members have regularly gathered during the summer months at Moonstone Beach to swim, sunbathe, and otherwise share their mutual interest in nudism. The individual plaintiffs include members and officers of the Association and non-members who frequent the beach to swim and sunbathe while attired in swimsuits. The defendants are officials of the Fish and Wildlife Service ("FWS") of the United States Department of the Interior who are charged with responsibility for managing the Trustom Pond National Wildlife Refuge (the "Refuge") on which most of Moonstone Beach is located.

The Refuge is located in the Town of South Kingstown, Rhode Island. Initially, it consisted of 365 acres of land that was donated to FWS in 1974. Subsequent donations and purchases have expanded its size to approximately 641 acres. It is composed primarily of grassy sand dunes, marsh land, and ponds. Because of these features, the Refuge is a prime nesting area for several species of birds, including the Piping Plover and the Least Tern, which lay their eggs in the sand during the spring and, together with their fledglings, feed along the shore during the summer months. The southerly border of the Refuge abuts the waters of Block Island Sound and consists of an expanse of sand approximately 120 feet wide and more than 7,000 feet long which is known as Moonstone Beach. The beach runs in an east–west direction and is intersected near its easterly end by a 30 foot right-of-way known as Moonstone Beach Road which provides members of the public with access to the shore.

For many years, the public has used Moonstone Beach for sunbathing and swimming. Many of those using it, including members of the Association, have engaged in those activities unencumbered by bathing suits. By tacit agreement, the nudists have confined their activities to an area segregated from that frequented by their attired brethren.

In 1983, FWS became concerned that human activities on the beach might be having adverse effects upon the reproductive activities of the Least Tern and the Piping Plover. In particular, FWS feared that the activities of bathers were destroying nests, inhibiting mating, and that refuse left by bathers was attracting predators. Accordingly, FWS partitioned the westerly portion of the beach by erecting 4,000 linear feet of fence along a line parallel to and above the shoreline.

In January of 1986, FWS's concern was further heightened by the Plover's official designation as a "threatened species" under the Endangered Species Act ("ESA"), 16 U.S.C. §§ 1531 et seq., which required FWS to do everything in its power to protect the species. This development, together with the donation of additional beach front property to the east of Moonstone Beach Road, caused FWS to extend the fence an additional 750 feet leaving approximately 1550 feet at the east end of the beach for public use.

By 1987, FWS still was not satisfied with the balance it had attempted to strike between public enjoyment of the beach and the needs of the Plovers. That dissatisfaction was reinforced by the findings of a study conducted by the Service's Piping Plover Recovery Team to the effect that the proximity of humans interfered with the Plover's reproductive activities and that the section of Moonstone Beach still used by bathers encompassed a very desirable nesting area.

Accordingly, FWS developed a Master Plan for management of the Refuge which proposed, among other things, to further restrict public use of Moonstone Beach during the Plover's nesting season (i.e., April 1–August 31). The plan also proposed breaching the sand dune between Trustom Pond and Block Island Sound to improve feeding opportunities for the Plover, removing vegetation on the back side of the dune to encourage nesting activities, constructing an artificial island in Trustom Pond to further encourage nesting, and seeking an agreement with the State of Rhode Island to prohibit public use of the intertidal zone adjacent to the Refuge during the nesting season.

A draft Environmental Assessment ("EA") outlining the anticipated environmental effects of the plan and several alternative courses of action was circulated by FWS for public comment. In January of 1988, a final environmental assessment was prepared. It discussed the comments received in response to the draft and included a finding that preparation of a full-blown Environmental Impact Statement ("EIS") was not required because the environmental effects of the proposed plan were not significant.

Several months later, FWS erected a fence excluding the public from an area extending the entire length of the beach and bounded on the South by a line ranging from 57 to 83 feet above the mean high-water line. Plaintiffs, thereupon, commenced this action for a declaration of their right to use Moonstone Beach and for an injunction prohibiting defendants from interfering with that right. The arguments they make in support of their position may be summarized as follows:

1. Defendants had no authority to erect the fence in question because it encompasses a portion of the intertidal zone which is owned by the State of Rhode Island and held in trust for the use of its citizens.

2. Prohibiting the plaintiffs from sunbathing nude within the fenced portion of Moonstone Beach constitutes a violation of their rights under the First, Fifth, and Ninth Amendments to the United States Constitution.

3. Defendants acted unlawfully in erecting a fence without first filing a determination, pursuant to the Coastal Zone Management Act ("CZMA"), that such action was consistent with Rhode Island's Coastal Zone Management Program.

4. Defendants acted unlawfully in erecting a fence without first filing an EIS pursuant to the National Environmental Policy Act ("NEPA"), and the fence seems to afford a more than ample margin for possible error. Nor is there any suggestion that the fence impedes public access to or from the shoreline along Moonstone Beach Road. In fact, FWS's own environmental assessment acknowledges its lack of authority to prevent public use of the intertidal zone adjacent to the Refuge or to impede access along the right–of–way. Consequently, it appears that the fenced area is clearly on federally owned property; and, therefore, plaintiffs' assertion that FWS lacks dominion over it is without merit.

The plaintiffs' Constitutional arguments are difficult to address because the nature of the rights they assert is not precisely defined. The gist of their contention seems to be that since they used the portion of Moonstone Beach in question in the past; and, since they gathered there to share their common interest in nudism, their activities constitute an exercise of their associational and property rights which are protected by the First Amendment and the due process guarantee of the Fifth Amendment. The applicability of the Ninth Amendment is more difficult to discern. The plaintiffs have failed to articulate any basis for bringing their conduct under the protective umbrella of that

Amendment nor have they cited any authority holding that nude sunbathing, particularly on a public beach, is one of the rights contemplated by it.

The case law on this subject has uniformly rejected arguments that nude sunbathing on a public beach is Constitutionally protected either as a mode of expression, or as a privacy right. In short, while nudity in the privacy of one's own property and nudity in the context of artistic expression may be protected, it seems clear that nude sunbathing on a public beach is not a right of Constitutional dimension.

It is even clearer that nudity does not confer a license to sunbathe on a beach that has been closed to the public. In this case, it is not nude sunbathing that has been banned on Moonstone Beach. What has been prohibited is *any* use of the disputed area. The uncontradicted evidence is that the prohibition has been applied uniformly both to those wearing bathing suits and to nudists. There is no evidence even remotely suggesting that defendants' actions were aimed directly or indirectly at nudists. In fact, the evidence establishes that plaintiffs remain free to associate and sunbathe on the portion of the Refuge beach that has not been fenced.

Consequently, the issue in this case is not whether the plaintiffs have a Constitutionally protected right to sunbathe in the nude or to associate with other nudists but rather whether they have a Constitutionally protected right to do so *on that portion of the beach from which the public, in general, has been excluded.* In answering that question, the plaintiffs cannot be considered as standing on any different footing than any other members of the public. The fact that some of the plaintiffs prefer to sunbathe in the nude or associate with others sharing that preference doesn't confer on them any greater right to use the beach than those who choose to wear bathing suits. The question, in either case, is whether the defendants' actions have deprived sunbathers, in general, of a legally recognized right to use the area in question.

The plaintiffs are unable to identify any such right. They cite the fact that they have used Moonstone "since time immemorial" but fail to demonstrate any legal right flowing from such past use. Plaintiffs also assert that Art. I, § 17 of the Rhode Island Constitution confers on them a right to use the area in question. However, as previously noted, that right extends only to the area below the mean high-tide line and recognized points of access thereto. The area from which these plaintiffs have been excluded fits neither description. Moreover, it is part of a federal wildlife refuge and the reason for excluding them is FWS's belief that such action is necessary to preserve the nesting habitat of a threatened species that ESA requires them to do everything in their power to protect.

There is certainly some room for disagreement as to whether the measures adopted by FWS strike a perfect balance between the competing interests of sunbathers and Plovers. Nevertheless, as long as the agency's action was not irrational or was not arbitrary, capricious or an abuse of its discretion, that is a determination for the agency to make. Here, the Court cannot characterize the defendants' actions as any of those things. While FWS cannot guarantee that those actions will increase the number of Plovers, it concluded, after considerable study, that its action would significantly improve conditions by increasing the nesting area and reducing human interference with the reproductive process. Further, FWS estimates that such action would increase the birth rate of young Plovers from 3–4 to 3–14 annually.

In sum, the Court finds that barring the plaintiffs from the area in question has not infringed upon any associational right, property right or other Constitutionally recognized right secured to them by the First, Fifth, and/or Ninth Amendments and it was not arbitrary, capricious or an abuse of FWS's discretion.

QUESTIONS FOR DISCUSSION

1. What in your view is the *best* justification for prohibiting public nudity? Is that justification sufficient to allow prohibition?
2. If it is not morally justified to prohibit public nudity, does such a prohibition violate the Constitution? Why or why not?

■ Paternalism

ON LIBERTY

JOHN STUART MILL

[N]either one person, nor any number of persons, is warranted in saying to another human creature of ripe years, that he shall not do with his life for his own benefit what he chooses to do with it. He is the person most interested in his own well-being: the interest which any

John Stuart Mill, *On Liberty* (1859), selection from Chapters 4 and 5.

other person, except in cases of strong personal attachment, can have in it, is trifling, compared with that which he himself has; the interest which society has in him individually (except as to his conduct to others) is fractional, and altogether indirect; while with respect to his own feelings and circumstances, the most ordinary man or woman has means of knowledge immeasurably surpassing those that can be possessed by anyone else. The interference of society to overrule his judgment and purposes in what only regards himself must be grounded on general presumptions; which may be altogether wrong, and even if right, are as likely as not to be misapplied to individual cases, by persons no better acquainted with the circumstances of such cases than those are who look at them merely from without. In this department, therefore, of human affairs, individuality has its proper field of action. In the conduct of human beings towards one another it is necessary that general rules should for the most part be observed, in order that people may know what they have to expect; but in each person's own concerns his individual spontaneity is entitled to free exercise. Considerations to aid his judgment, exhortations to strengthen his will, may be offered to him, even obtruded on him, by others: but he himself is the final judge. All errors which he is likely to commit against advice and warning are far outweighed by the evil of allowing others to constrain him to what they deem his good.

I do not mean that the feelings with which a person is regarded by others ought not to be in any way affected by his self-regarding qualities or deficiencies. This is neither possible nor desirable. . . . Though doing no wrong to anyone, a person may so act as to compel us to judge him, and to feel him, as a fool, or as a being of an inferior order; and since this judgment and feeling are a fact which he would prefer to avoid, it is doing him a service to warn him of it beforehand, as of any other disagreeable consequence to which he exposes himself. It would be well, indeed, if this good office were much more freely rendered than the common notions of politeness at present permit, and if one person could honestly point out to another that he thinks him in fault, without being considered unmannerly or presuming. We have a right, also, in various ways, to act upon our unfavorable opinion of anyone, not to the oppression of his individuality, but in the exercise of ours. We are not bound, for example, to seek his society; we have a right to avoid it (though not to parade the avoidance), for we have a right to choose the society most acceptable to us. We have a right, and it may be our duty, to caution others against him, if we think his example or conversation likely to have a pernicious effect on those with whom he associates. We may give others a preference over him in optional good offices, except those which tend to his improvement. In these various modes a person may suffer very severe penalties at the hands of others for faults which directly concern only himself; but he suffers these penalties only in so far as they are natural and, as it were, the spontaneous consequences of the faults themselves, not because they are purposely inflicted on him for the sake of punishment. A person who shows rashness, obstinacy, self-conceit—who cannot live within moderate means—who cannot restrain himself from hurtful indulgences—who pursues animal pleasures at the expense of those of feeling and intellect—must expect to be lowered in the opinion of others, and to have a less share of their favorable sentiments; but of this he has no right to complain, unless he has merited their favor by special excellence in his social relations, and has thus established a title to their good offices, which is not affected by his demerits towards himself.

What I contend for is, that the inconveniences which are strictly inseparable from the unfavorable judgment of others, are the only ones to which a person should ever be subjected for that portion of his conduct and character which concerns his own good, but which does not affect the interest of others in their relations with him. . . .

The right inherent in society, to ward off crimes against itself by antecedent precautions, suggests the obvious limitations to the maxim, that purely self-regarding misconduct cannot properly be meddled with in the way of prevention or punishment. Drunkenness, for example, in ordinary cases, is not a fit subject for legislative interference; but I should deem it perfectly legitimate that a person, who had once been convicted of any act of violence to others under the influence of drink, should be placed under a special legal restriction, personal to himself; that if he were afterwards found drunk, he should be liable to a penalty, and that if when in that state he committed another offence, the punishment to which he would be liable for that other offence should be increased in severity. The making himself drunk, in a person whom drunkenness excites to do harm to others, is a crime against others. So, again, idleness, except in a person receiving support from the public, or except when it constitutes a breach of contract, cannot without tyranny be made a subject of legal punishment; but if, either from idleness or from any other avoidable cause, a man fails to perform his legal duties to others, as for instance to support his children, it is no tyranny to force him to fulfil that obligation, by compulsory labour, if no other means are available.

Again, there are many acts which, being directly injurious only to the agents themselves, ought not to be legally interdicted, but which, if done publicly, are a violation of good manners, and coming thus within the category of offences against others, may rightly be prohibited. Of this kind are offences against decency; on which it is unnecessary to dwell, the rather as they are only connected indirectly with our subject, the objection to publicity being equally strong in the case of many actions not in themselves condemnable, nor supposed to be so.

There is another question to which an answer must be found, consistent with the principles which have been laid down. In cases of personal conduct supposed to be blameable, but which respect for liberty precludes society from preventing or punishing, because the evil directly resulting falls wholly on the agent; what the agent is free to do, ought other persons to be equally free to counsel or instigate? This question is not free from difficulty. The case of a person who solicits another to do an act is not strictly a case of self-regarding conduct. To give advice or offer inducements to any one is a social act, and may, therefore, like actions in general which affect others, be supposed amenable to social control. But a little reflection corrects the first impression, by showing that if the case is not strictly within the definition of individual liberty, yet the reasons on which the principle of individual liberty is grounded are applicable to it. If people must be allowed, in whatever concerns only themselves, to act as seems best to themselves, at their own peril, they must equally be free to consult with one another about what is fit to be so done; to exchange opinions, and give and receive suggestions. Whatever it is permitted to do, it must be permitted to advise to do. The question is doubtful only when the instigator derives a personal benefit from his advice; when he makes it his occupation, for subsistence or pecuniary gain, to promote what society and the State consider to be an evil. Then, indeed, a new element of complication is introduced; namely, the existence of classes of persons with an interest opposed to what is considered as the public weal, and whose mode of living is grounded on the counteraction of it. Ought this to be interfered with, or not? Fornication, for example, must be tolerated, and so must gambling; but should a person be free to be a pimp, or to keep a gambling-house? The case is one of those which lie on the exact boundary line between two principles, and it is not at once apparent to which of the two it properly belongs. There are arguments on both sides. On the side of toleration it may be said that the fact of following anything as an occupation, and living or profiting by the practice of it, cannot make that criminal which would otherwise be admissible; that the act should either be consistently permitted or consistently prohibited; that if the principles which we have hitherto defended are true, society has no business, *as* society, to decide anything to be wrong which concerns only the individual; that it cannot go beyond dissuasion, and that one person should be as free to persuade as another to dissuade. In opposition to this it may be contended, that although the public, or the State, are not warranted in authoritatively deciding, for purposes of repression or punishment, that such or such conduct affecting only the interests of the individual is good or bad, they are fully justified in assuming, if they regard it as bad, that its being so or not is at least a disputable question: That, this being supposed, they cannot be acting wrongly in endeavouring to exclude the influence of solicitations which are not disinterested, of instigators who cannot possibly be impartial—who have a direct personal interest on one side, and that side the one which the State believes to be wrong, and who confessedly promote it for personal objects only. There can surely, it may be urged, be nothing lost, no sacrifice of good, by so ordering matters that persons shall make their election, either wisely or foolishly, on their own prompting, as free as possible from the arts of persons who stimulate their inclinations for interested purposes of their own. Thus (it may be said) though the statutes respecting unlawful games are utterly indefensible—though all persons should be free to gamble in their own or each other's houses, or in any place of meeting established by their own subscriptions, and

open only to the members and their visitors—yet public gambling-houses should not be permitted. It is true that the prohibition is never effectual, and that whatever amount of tyrannical power may be given to the police, gambling-houses can always be maintained under other pretences; but they may be compelled to conduct their operations with a certain degree of secrecy and mystery, so that nobody knows anything about them but those who seek them; and more than this society ought not to aim at. There is considerable force in these arguments. I will not venture to decide whether they are sufficient to justify the moral anomaly of punishing the accessary, when the principal is (and must be) allowed to go free, of fining or imprisoning the procurer, but not the fornicator—the gambling-house keeper, but not the gambler. Still less ought the common operations of buying and selling to be interfered with on analogous grounds. Almost every article which is bought and sold may be used in excess, and the sellers have a pecuniary interest in encouraging that excess; but no argument can be founded on this, in favour, for instance, of the Maine Law; because the class of dealers in strong drinks, though interested in their abuse, are indispensably required for the sake of their legitimate use. The interest, however, of these dealers in promoting intemperance is a real evil, and justifies the State in imposing restrictions and requiring guarantees which, but for that justification, would be infringements of legitimate liberty.

PATERNALISM

GERALD DWORKIN

By paternalism I shall understand roughly the interference with a person's liberty of action justified by reasons referring exclusively to the welfare, good, happiness, needs, interests or values of the person being coerced. One is always well advised to illustrate one's definitions

Gerald Dworkin, "Paternalism," *The Monist,* vol. 56 (1972), pp. 1 ff.

by examples, but it is not easy to find 'pure' examples of paternalistic interferences. For almost any piece of legislation is justified by several different kinds of reasons, and even if historically a piece of legislation can be shown to have been introduced for purely paternalistic motives, it may be that advocates of the legislation with an anti–paternalistic outlook can find sufficient reasons justifying the legislation without appealing to the reasons which were originally adduced to support it. Thus, for example, it may be that the original legislation requiring motorcyclists to wear safety helmets was introduced for purely paternalistic reasons. But the Rhode Island Supreme Court recently upheld such legislation on the grounds that it was 'not persuaded that the legislature is powerless to prohibit individuals from pursuing a course of conduct which could conceivably result in their becoming public charges', thus clearly introducing reasons of a quite different kind. Now I regard this decision as being based on reasoning of a very dubious nature, but it illustrates the kind of problem one has in finding examples. The following is a list of the kinds of interferences I have in mind as being paternalistic.

(1) Laws requiring motorcyclists to wear safety helmets when operating their machines.

(2) Laws forbidding persons from swimming at a public beach when lifeguards are not on duty.

(3) Laws making suicide a criminal offence.

(4) Laws making it illegal for women and children to work at certain types of jobs.

(5) Laws regulating certain kinds of sexual conduct, e.g., homosexuality between consenting adults in private.

(6) Laws regulating the use of certain drugs which may have harmful consequences to the user but do not lead to antisocial conduct.

(7) Laws requiring a license to engage in certain professions, with those not receiving a license subject to fine or jail sentence if they do engage in the practice.

(8) Laws compelling people to spend a specified fraction of their income on the purchase of retirement annuities (Social Security).

(9) Laws forbidding various forms of gambling (often justified on the grounds that the poor are more likely to throw away their money on such activities than the rich who can afford to).

(10) Laws regulating the maximum rates of interest for loans.

(11) Laws against duelling.

We might begin looking for principles governing the acceptable use of paternalistic power in cases where it is generally agreed that it is legitimate. Even Mill intends his principles to be applicable only to mature individuals, not those in what he calls 'non–age.' What is it that justifies us in interfering with children? The fact that they lack some of the emotional and cognitive capacities required in order to make fully rational decisions. It is an empirical question to just what extent children have an adequate conception of their own present and future interests, but there is not much doubt that there are many deficiencies. For example, it is very difficult for a child to defer gratification for any considerable period of time. Given these deficiencies and given the very real and permanent dangers that may befall the child, it becomes not only permissible but even a duty of the parent to restrict the child's freedom in various ways. There is, however, an important moral limitation on the exercise of such parental power which is provided by the notion of the child eventually coming to see the correctness of his parent's interventions. Parental paternalism may be thought of as a wager by the parent on the child's subsequent recognition of the wisdom of the restrictions. There is an emphasis on what could be called future-oriented consent—on what the child will come to welcome, rather than on what he does welcome.

The essence of this idea has been incorporated by idealist philosophers into various types of 'real-will' theory as applied to fully adult persons. Extensions of paternalism are argued for by claiming that in various respects, chronologically mature individuals share the same deficiencies in knowledge, capacity to think rationally, and the ability to carry out decisions that children possess. Hence in interfering with such people we are in effect doing what they would do if they were fully rational. Hence we are not really opposing their will, hence we are not really interfering with their freedom. The dangers of this move have been sufficiently exposed by Berlin in his *Two Concepts of Liberty*. I see no gain in theoretical clarity nor in practical advantage in trying to pass over the real nature of the interferences with liberty that we impose on others. Still, the basic notion of consent is important and seems to me the only acceptable way of trying to delimit an area of justified paternalism.

Let me start by considering a case where the consent is not hypothetical in nature. Under certain conditions it is rational for an individual to agree that others should force him to act in ways which, at the time of action, the individual may not see as desirable. If, for example, a man knows that he is subject to breaking his resolves when temptation is present, he may ask a friend to refuse to entertain his requests at some later stage.

A classical example is given in the *Odyssey* when Odysseus commands his men to tie him to the mast and refuse all future orders to be set free, because he knows the power of the Sirens to enchant men with their songs. Here we are on relatively sound ground in later refusing Odysseus's request to be set free. He may even claim to have changed his mind, but since it is just such changes that he wished to guard against we are entitled to ignore them.

A process analogous to this may take place on a social rather than individual basis. An electorate may mandate its representatives to pass legislation which, when it comes time to 'pay the price', may be unpalatable. I may believe that a tax increase is necessary to halt inflation though I may resent the lower pay cheque each month. However, in both this case and that of Odysseus the measure to be enforced is specifically requested by the party involved and at some point in time there is genuine consent and agreement on the part of those persons whose liberty is infringed. Such is not the case for the paternalistic measures we have been speaking about. What must be involved here is not consent to specific measures, but rather consent to a system of government, run by elected representatives, with an understanding that they may act to safeguard our interests in certain limited ways.

I suggest that since we are all aware of our irrational propensities, deficiencies in cognitive and emotional capacities and avoidable and unavoidable ignorance, it is rational and prudent for us to in effect take out 'social insurance policies.' We may argue for and against proposed paternalistic measures in terms of what fully rational individuals would accept as forms of protection. Now, clearly since the initial agreement is not about specific measures, we are dealing with a more-or-less blank cheque and therefore there have to be carefully defined limits. What I am looking for are certain kinds of conditions which make it plausible to suppose that rational men could reach agreement to limit their liberty even when other men's interests are not affected.

Of course, as in any kind of agreement schema, there are great difficulties in deciding what rational individuals would or would not accept. Particularly in sensitive areas of personal liberty, there is always a danger of the dispute over agreement and rationality being a disguised version of evaluative and normative disagreement.

Let me suggest types of situations in which it seems plausible to suppose that fully rational individuals would agree to having paternalistic restrictions imposed upon them. It is reasonable to suppose that there are 'goods' such as health which any person would want to have in order to pursue his own good—no matter how that good is conceived. This is an argument that is used in connection with compulsory education for children, but it seems to me that it can be extended to other goods which have this character. Then one could agree that the attainment of such goods should be promoted even when not recognized to be such, at the moment, by the individuals concerned.

An immediate difficulty that arises stems from the fact that men are always faced with competing goods and that there may be reasons why even a value such as health—or indeed life—may be overridden by competing values. Thus the problem with the Jehovah's Witness and blood transfusions. It may be more important for him to reject 'impure substances' than to go on living. The difficult problem that must be faced is whether one can give sense to the notion of a person irrationally attaching weights to competing values.

Consider a person who knows the statistical data on the probability of being injured when not wearing seat belts in an automobile and knows the types and gravity of the various injuries. He also insists that the inconvenience attached to fastening the belt every time he gets in and out of the car outweighs for him the possible risks to himself. I am inclined in this case to think that such a weighing is irrational. Given his life-plans which we are assuming are those of the average person, his interests and commitments already undertaken, I think it is safe to predict that we can find inconsistencies in his calculations at some point. I am assuming that this is not a man who for some conscious or unconscious reasons is trying to injure himself, nor is he a man who just likes to 'live dangerously'. I am assuming that he is like us in all the relevant respects but just puts an enormously high negative value on in-

convenience—one which does not seem comprehensible or reasonable.

It is always possible, of course, to assimilate this person to creatures like myself. I also neglect to fasten my seat belt and I concede such behaviour is not rational, but not because I weigh the inconvenience differently from those who fasten the belts. It is just that having made (roughly) the same calculation as everybody else, I ignore it in my actions. [Note: a much better case of weakness of the will than those usually given in ethics texts.] A plausible explanation for this deplorable habit is that although I know in some intellectual sense what the probabilities and risks are, I do not fully appreciate them in an emotionally genuine manner.

We have two distinct types of situation in which a man acts in a non-rational fashion. In one case he attaches incorrect weights to some of his values; in the other he neglects to act in accordance with his actual preferences and desires. Clearly there is a stronger and more persuasive argument for paternalism in the latter situation. Here we are really not—by assumption—imposing a good on another person. But why may we not extend our interference to what we might call evaluative delusions? After all, in the case of cognitive delusions we are prepared, often, to act against the expressed will of the person involved. If a man believes that when he jumps out the window he will float upwards—Robert Nozick's example—would we not detain him, forcibly if necessary? The reply will be that this man doesn't wish to be injured, and if we could convince him that he is mistaken as to the consequences of his action he would not wish to perform the action. But part of what is involved in claiming that a man who doesn't fasten his seat belts is attaching an irrational weight to the inconvenience of fastening them is that if he were to be involved in an accident and severely injured, he would look back and admit that the inconvenience wasn't as bad as all that. So there is a sense in which if I could convince him of the consequences of his action he also would not wish to continue his present course of action. Now the notion of consequences being used here is covering a lot of ground. In one case it's being used to indicate what will or can happen as a result of a course of action, and in the other it's making a prediction about the future evaluation of the consequences—in the first sense—of a course of action. And whatever the difference between facts and values—whether it be hard and fast or soft and slow—we are genuinely more reluctant to consent to interferences where evaluative differences are the issue. Let me now consider another factor which comes into play in some of these situations which may make an important difference in our willingness to consent to paternalistic restrictions.

Some of the decisions we make are of such a character that they produce changes which are in one or another way irreversible. Situations are created in which it is difficult or impossible to return to anything like the initial state at which the decision was made. In particular, some of these changes will make it impossible to continue to make reasoned choices in the future. I am thinking specifically of decisions which involve taking drugs that are physically or psychologically addictive and those which are destructive of one's mental and physical capacities.

I suggest we think of the imposition of paternalistic interferences in situations of this kind as being a kind of insurance policy which we take out against making decisions which are far reaching, potentially dangerous and irreversible. Each of these factors is important. Clearly there are many decisions we make that are relatively irreversible. In deciding to learn to play chess I could predict, in view of my general interest in games, that some portion of my free time was going to be pre-empted and that it would not be easy to give up the game once I acquired a certain competence. But my whole life style was not going to be jeopardized in an extreme manner. Further, it might be argued that even with addictive drugs such as heroin one's normal life-plans would not be seriously interfered with if an inexpensive and adequate supply were readily available. So this type of argument might have a narrower scope than appears to be the case at first.

A second class of cases concerns decisions which are made under extreme psychological and sociological pressures. I am not thinking here of the making of the decision as being something one is pressured into—e.g., a good reason for making duelling illegal is that unless this is done many people might have to manifest their courage and integrity in ways in which they would rather not do so—but rather of decisions such as that to commit suicide which are usually made at a point where the individual is not thinking clearly and calmly about the nature of his decision. In addition, of course, this comes under the previous heading of all-too-irrevocable decisions. Now there are practical steps which a society could take if it wanted to decrease the possibility of suicide—for example, not paying social security benefits to the survivors or, as religious institutions do, not allowing such persons to be buried with the same status as natural deaths. I think we may count these as interferences with the liberty of persons to attempt suicide, and the question is whether they are justifiable.

Using my argument schema the question is whether rational individuals would consent to such limitations. I see no reason for them to consent to an absolute prohibition, but I do think it is reasonable for them to agree to some kind of enforced waiting period. Since we are all aware of the possibility of temporary states, such as great fear or depression, that are inimical to the making of well-informed and rational decisions, it would be prudent for all of us if there were some kind of institutional arrangement whereby we were restrained from making a decision which is (all too) irreversible.

What this would be like in practice is difficult to envisage, and it may be that if no practical arrangements were feasible then we would have to conclude that there should be no restriction at all on this kind of action. But we might have a 'cooling off' period, in much the same way that we now require couples who file for divorce to go through a waiting period. Or, more farfetched, we might imagine a Suicide Board composed of a psychologist and another member picked by the applicant. The Board would be required to meet and talk with the person proposing to take his life, though its approval would not be required.

A third class of decisions—these classes are not supposed to be disjoint—involves dangers which are not either sufficiently understood or appreciated correctly by the persons involved. Let me illustrate, using the example of cigarette smoking, a number of possible cases.

(1) A man may not know the facts—e.g., smoking between 1 and 2 packs a day shortens life expectancy 6.2 years, the costs and pain of the illness caused by smoking, etc.

(2) A man may know the facts, wish to stop smoking, but not have the requisite will power.

(3) A man may know the facts but not have them play the correct role in his calculation because, say, he discounts the danger psychologically because it is remote in time and/or inflates the attractiveness of other consequences of his decision which he regards as beneficial.

In case 1 what is called for is education, the posting of warnings, etc. In case 2 there is no theoretical problem. We are not imposing a good on someone who rejects it. We are simply using coercion to enable people to carry out their own goals. [Note: There obviously is a difficulty in that only a subclass of individuals affected wish to be prevented from doing what they are doing.] In case 3 there is a sense in which we are imposing a good on someone since, given his current appraisal of the facts, he doesn't wish to be restricted. But in another sense we are not imposing a good since what is being claimed—and what must be shown or at least argued for—is that an accurate accounting on his part would lead him to reject his current course of action. Now we all know that such cases exist, that we are prone to disregard dangers that are only possibilities, that immediate pleasures are often magnified and distorted.

If in addition the dangers are severe and far-reaching, we could agree to allow the state a certain degree of power to intervene in such situations. The difficulty is in specifying in advance, even vaguely, the class of cases in which intervention will be legitimate.

A related difficulty is that of drawing a line so that it is not the case that all ultra-hazardous activities are ruled out, e.g., mountain climbing, bull fighting, sports car racing, etc. There are some risks—even very great ones—which a person is entitled to take with his life.

A good deal depends on the nature of the deprivation—e.g., does it prevent the person from engaging in the activity completely or merely limit his participation?—and how important to the nature of the activity is the absence of restriction when this is weighed against the role that the activity plays in the life of the person. In the case of automobile seat belts, for example, the restriction is trivial in nature, interferes not at all with the use or enjoyment of the activity, and does, I am assuming, considerably reduce a high risk of serious injury. Whereas, for example, making mountain climbing illegal completely prevents a person from engaging in an activity which may play an important role in both his life and his conception of the person he is.

In general the easiest cases to handle are those which can be argued about in the terms which Mill thought to be so important—a concern not just for the happiness or welfare, in some broad sense, of the individual, but rather a concern for the autonomy and freedom of the person. I suggest that we would be most likely to consent to paternalism in those instances in which it preserves and enhances for the individual his ability to rationally consider and carry out his own decisions.

I have suggested in this essay a number of types of situations in which it seems plausible that rational men would agree to granting the legislative powers of a society the right to impose restrictions on what Mill calls 'self-regarding' conduct. However, rational men knowing something about the resources of ignorance, ill will and stupidity available to the lawmakers of a society—a good case in point is the history of drug legislation in the United States—will be concerned to limit such intervention to a minimum. I suggest in closing two principles designed to achieve this end.

In all cases of paternalistic legislation there must be a heavy and clear burden of proof placed on the authorities to demonstrate the exact nature of the harmful effects (or beneficial consequences) to be avoided (or achieved) and the probability of their occurrence. The burden of proof here is twofold—what lawyers distinguish as the burden of going forward and the burden of persuasion. That the authorities have the burden of going forward means that it is up to them to raise the question and bring forward evidence of the evils to be avoided. Unlike the case of new drugs where the manufacturer must produce some evidence that the drug has been tested and found not harmful, no citizen has to show with respect to self-regarding conduct that it is not harmful or promotes his best interests. In addition, the nature and cogency of the evidence for the harmfulness of the course of action must be set at a high level. To paraphrase a formulation of the burden of proof for criminal proceedings—better ten men ruin themselves than one man be unjustly deprived of liberty.

Finally, I suggest a principle of the least restrictive alternative. If there is an alternative way of accomplishing the desired end without restricting liberty, then although it may involve great expense, inconvenience, etc., the society must adopt it.

QUESTIONS FOR DISCUSSION

1. Should one be free to sell oneself into slavery? Why or why not?

2. How does Mill's objection to paternalistic laws relate to his requirement that laws should prevent harm? Do paternalistic laws prohibit harmless actions?

3. When does Dworkin think that paternalism is justified? Do you agree?

4. Is there a difference between laws requiring drivers to wear seat belts and a law requiring motorcyclists to wear helmets? What might it be?

5. Many pregnant women say that they would like to go through labor and delivery without anesthesia because they want to be fully conscious for delivery and post-delivery. Suppose that some of these women will ask for anesthesia during delivery despite their earlier intention to do without it, but that many subsequently regret that their request for anesthesia was granted. It is therefore proposed that women be allowed to authorize the hospital to ignore a request for anesthesia unless the health of the mother or baby is in danger. Should such a policy be adopted?

■ Moralism

THE ENFORCEMENT OF MORALS

PATRICK DEVLIN

The Report of the Committee on Homosexual Offences and Prostitution, generally known as the Wolfenden Report, is recognized to be an excellent study of two very difficult legal and social problems. But it has also a particular claim to the respect of those interested in jurisprudence; it does what law reformers so rarely do; it sets out clearly and carefully what in relation to its subjects it considers the function of the law to be. Statutory additions to the criminal law are too often made on the simple principle that 'there ought to be a law against it'. The greater part of the law relating to sexual offences is the creation of statute and it is difficult to ascertain any logical relationship between it and the moral ideas which most of us uphold. Adultery, fornication, and prostitution are not, as the Report points out, criminal offences: homosexuality between males is a criminal offence, but between females it is not. Incest was not an offence until it was declared so by statute only fifty years ago. Does the legislature select these offences haphazardly or are there some principles which can be used to determine what part of the moral law should be embodied in the criminal? There is, for example, being now considered a proposal to make A.I.D., that is, the practice of artificial insemination of a woman with the seed of a man who is not her husband, a criminal offence; if, as is usually the case, the woman is married, this is in substance, if not in form, adultery. Ought it to be made punishable when adultery is not?

This sort of question is of practical importance, for a law that appears to be arbitrary and illogical, in the end and after the wave of moral indignation that has put it on the statute book subsides, forfeits respect. As a practical question it arises more frequently in the field of sexual morals than in any other, but there is no special answer to be found in that field. The inquiry must be general and fundamental. What is the connection between crime and sin and to what extent, if at all, should the criminal law of England concern itself with the enforcement of morals and punish sin or immorality as such?

■ ■ ■

It is true that for many centuries the criminal law was much concerned with keeping the peace and little, if at all, with sexual morals. But it would be wrong to infer from that that it had no moral content or that it would ever have tolerated the idea of a man being left to judge for himself in matters of morals. The criminal law of England has from the very first concerned itself with moral principles. A simple way of testing this point is to consider the attitude which the criminal law adopts towards consent.

Subject to certain exceptions inherent in the nature of particular crimes, the criminal law has never permitted consent of the victim to be used as a defence. In rape, for example, consent negatives an essential element. But consent of the victim is no defence to a charge of murder.

Patrick Devlin, *The Enforcement of Morals* (Oxford: Oxford University Press, 1965)

It is not a defence to any form of assault that the victim thought his punishment well deserved and submitted to it; to make a good defence the accused must prove that the law gave him the right to chastise and that he exercised it reasonably. Likewise, the victim may not forgive the aggressor and require the prosecution to desist; the right to enter a *nolle prosequi* belongs to the Attorney–General alone.

Now, if the law existed for the protection of the individual, there would be no reason why he should avail himself of it if he did not want it. The reason why a man may not consent to the commission of an offence against himself beforehand or forgive it afterwards is because it is an offence against society. It is not that society is physically injured; that would be impossible. Nor need any individual be shocked, corrupted, or exploited; everything may be done in private. Nor can it be explained on the practical ground that a violent man is a potential danger to others in the community who have therefore a direct interest in his apprehension and punishment as being necessary to their own protection. That would be true of a man whom the victim is prepared to forgive but not of one who gets his consent first; a murderer who acts only upon the consent, and maybe the request, of his victim is no menace to others, but he does threaten one of the great moral principles upon which society is based, that is, the sanctity of human life. There is only one explanation of what has hitherto been accepted as the basis of the criminal law and that is that there are certain standards of behaviour or moral principles which society requires to be observed; and the breach of them is an offence not merely against the person who is injured but against society as a whole.

Thus, if the criminal law were to be reformed so as to eliminate from it everything that was not designed to preserve order and decency or to protect citizens (including the protection of youth from corruption), it would overturn a fundamental principle. It would also

end a number of specific crimes. Euthanasia or the killing of another at his own request, suicide, attempted suicide, and suicide pacts, duelling, abortion, incest between brother and sister, are all acts which can be done in private and without offence to others and need not involve the corruption or exploitation of others. Many people think that the law on some of these subjects is in need of reform, but no one hitherto has gone so far as to suggest that they should all be left outside the criminal law as matters of private morality. They can be brought within it only as a matter of moral principle. It must be remembered also that although there is much immorality that is not punished by the law, there is none that is condoned by the law. The law will not allow its processes to be used by those engaged in immorality of any sort. For example, a house may not be let for immoral purposes; the lease is invalid and would not be enforced. But if what goes on inside there is a matter of private morality and not the law's business, why does the law inquire into it all?

I think it is clear that the criminal law as we know it is based upon moral principle. In a number of crimes its function is simply to enforce a moral principle and nothing else. The law, both criminal and civil, claims to be able to speak about morality and immorality generally. Where does it get its authority to do this and how does it settle the moral principles which it enforces? Undoubtedly, as a matter of history, it derived both from Christian teaching. But [the] law can no longer rely on doctrines in which citizens are entitled to disbelieve. It is necessary therefore to look for some other source.

In jurisprudence, as I have said, everything is thrown open to discussion and, in the belief that they cover the whole field, I have framed three interrogatories addressed to myself to answer:

1. Has society the right to pass judgment at all on matters of morals? Ought there, in other words, to be a public morality, or are morals always a matter for private judgment?

2. If society has the right to pass judgment, has it also the right to use the weapon of the law to enforce it?

3. If so, ought it to use that weapon in all cases or only in some; and if only in some, on what principles should it distinguish?

I shall begin with the first interrogatory and consider what is meant by the right of society to pass a moral judgment, that is, a judgment about what is good and what is evil. The fact that a majority of people may disapprove of a practice does not of itself make it a matter for society as a whole. Nine men out of ten may disapprove of what the tenth man is doing and still say that it is not their business. There is a case for a collective judgment (as distinct from a large number of individual opinions which sensible people may even refrain from pronouncing at all if it is upon somebody else's private affairs) only if society is affected. Without a collective judgment there can be no case at all for intervention. Let me take as an illustration the Englishman's attitude to religion as it is now and as it has been in the past. His attitude now is that a man's religion is his private affair; he may think of another man's religion that it is right or wrong, true or untrue, but not that it is good or bad. In earlier times that was not so; a man was denied the right to practise what was thought of as heresy, and heresy was thought of as destructive of society.

The language used in the passages I have quoted from the Wolfenden Report suggests the view that there ought not to be a collective judgment about immorality *per se*. Is this what is meant by 'private morality' and 'individual freedom of choice and action'? Some people sincerely believe that homosexuality is neither immoral nor unnatural. Is the 'freedom of choice and action' that is offered to the individual, freedom to decide for himself what is moral or immoral, society remaining neutral; or is it freedom to be immoral if he wants to be? The language of the Report may be open to question, but the conclusions at which the Committee arrive answer this question unambiguously. If society is not prepared to say that homosexuality is morally wrong, there would be no basis for a law protecting youth from 'corruption' or punishing a man for living on the 'immoral' earnings of a homosexual prostitute, as the Report recommends. This attitude the Committee make even clearer when they come to deal with prostitution. In truth, the Report takes it for granted that there is in existence a public morality which condemns homosexuality and prostitution. What the Report seems to mean by private morality might perhaps be better described as private behaviour in matters of morals.

This view—that there is such a thing as public morality—can also be justified by *a priori* argument. What makes a society of any sort is community of ideas, not only political ideas but also ideas about the way its members should behave and govern their lives; these latter ideas are its morals. Every society has a moral structure as well as a political one: or rather, since that might suggest two independent systems, I should say that the structure of every society is made up both of politics and morals. Take, for example, the institution of marriage. Whether a man should be allowed to take more than one wife is something about which every society has to make up its mind one way or the other. In England we believe in the Christian idea of marriage and therefore adopt monogamy as a moral principle. Consequently the Christian institution of marriage has become the basis of family life and so part of the structure of our society. It is there not because it is Christian. It has got there because it is Christian, but it remains there because it is built into the house in which we live and could not be removed without bringing it down. The great majority of those who live in this country accept it because it is the Christian idea of marriage and for them the only true one. But a non–Christian is bound by it, not because it is part of Christianity but because, rightly or wrongly, it has been adopted by the society in which he lives. It would be useless for him to stage a debate designed to prove that polygamy was theologically more correct and socially preferable; if he wants to live in the house, he must accept it as built in the way in which it is.

We see this more clearly if we think of ideas or institutions that are purely political. Society cannot tolerate rebellion; it will not allow argument about the rightness of the cause. Historians a century later may say that the rebels were right and the Government was wrong and a percipient and conscientious subject of the State may think so at the time. But it is not a matter which can be left to individual judgment.

The institution of marriage is a good example for my purpose because it bridges the division, if there is one, between politics and morals. Marriage is part of the structure of our society and it is also the basis of a moral code which condemns fornication and adultery. The institution of marriage would be gravely threatened if individual judgments were permitted about the morality of adultery; on these points there must be a public morality. But public morality is not to be confined to those moral principles which support institutions such as marriage. People do not think of monogamy as something which has to be supported because our society has chosen to organize itself upon it; they think of it as something that is good in itself and offering a good way of life and that it is for that reason that our society has adopted it. I return to the statement that I have already made, that society means a community of ideas; without shared ideas on politics, morals, and ethics no society can exist. Each one of us has ideas about what is good and what is evil; they cannot be kept private from the society in which we live. If men and women try to create a society in which there is no fundamental agreement about good and evil they will fail; if, having based it on common agreement, the agreement goes, the society will disintegrate. For society is not something that is kept together physically; it is held by the invisible bonds of common thought. If the bonds were too far relaxed the members would drift apart. A common morality is part of the bondage. The bondage is part of the price of society; and mankind, which needs society, must pay its price

■ ■ ■

I think, therefore, that it is not possible to set theoretical limits to the power of the State to legislate against immorality. It is not possible to settle in advance exceptions to the general rule or to define inflexibly areas of morality into which the law is in no circumstances to be allowed to enter. Society is entitled by means of its laws to protect itself from dangers, whether from within or without. Here again I think that the political parallel is legitimate. The law of treason is directed against aiding the king's enemies and against sedition from within. The justification for this is that established government is necessary for the existence of society and therefore its safety against violent overthrow must be secured. But an established morality is as necessary as good government to the welfare of society. Societies disintegrate from within more frequently than they are broken up by external pressures. There is disintegration when no common morality is observed and history shows that the loosening of moral bonds is often the first stage of disintegration, so that society is justified in taking the same steps to preserve its moral code as it does to preserve its government and other essential institutions. The suppression of vice is as much the law's business as the suppression of subversive activities; it is no more possible to define a sphere of private morality than it is to define one of private subversive activity. It is wrong to talk of private morality or of the law not being concerned with immorality as such or to try to set rigid bounds to the part which the law may play in the suppression of vice. There are no theoretical limits to the power of the State to legislate against treason and sedition, and likewise I think there can be no theoretical limits to legislation against immorality. You may argue that if a man's sins affect only himself it cannot be the concern of society. If he chooses to get drunk every night in the privacy of his own home, is any one except himself the worse for it? But suppose a quarter or a half of the population got drunk every night, what sort of society would it be? You cannot set a theoretical limit to the number of people who can get drunk before society is entitled to legislate against drunkenness. The same may be said of gambling. The Royal Commission on Betting, Lotteries, and Gaming took as their test the character of the citizen as a member of society. They said: 'Our concern with the ethical significance of gambling is confined to the effect which it may have on the character of the gambler as a member of society. If we were convinced that whatever the degree of gambling this effect must be harmful we should be inclined to think that it was the duty of the State to restrict gambling to the greatest extent practicable.'

In what circumstances the State should exercise its power is the third of the interrogatories I have framed. But before I get to it I must raise a point which might have been brought up in any one of the three. How are the moral judgments of society to be ascertained? By leaving it until now, I can ask it in the more limited form that is now sufficient for my purpose. How is the law-maker to ascertain the moral judgments of society? It is surely not enough that they should be reached by the opinion of the majority; it would be too much to require the individual assent of every citizen. English law has evolved and regularly uses a standard which does not depend on the counting of heads. It is that of the reasonable man. He is not to be confused with the rational man. He is not expected to reason about anything and his judgment may be largely a matter of feeling. It is the viewpoint of the man in the street—or to use an archaism familiar to all lawyers—the man in the Clapham omnibus. He might also be called the right-minded man. For my purpose I should like to call him the man in the jury box, for the moral judgment of society must be something about which any twelve men or women drawn at random might after discussion be expected to be unanimous. This was the standard the judges applied in the days before Parliament was as active as it is now and when they laid down rules of public policy. They did not think of themselves as making law but simply as stating principles which every right-minded person would accept as valid. It is what Pollock called 'practical morality', which is based not on theological or philosophical foundations but 'in the mass of continuous experience half-consciously or unconsciously accumulated and embodied in the morality of common sense'. He called it also 'a certain way of thinking on questions of morality which we expect to find in a reasonable civilized man or a reasonable Englishman, taken at random'.

Immorality then, for the purpose of the law, is what every right-minded person is presumed to consider to be immoral. Any immorality is capable of affecting society injuriously and in effect to a greater or lesser extent it usually does; this is what gives the law its *locus standi*. It cannot be shut out. But—and this brings me to the third question—the individual has a *locus standi* too; he cannot be expected to surrender to the judgment of society the whole conduct of his life. It is the old and familiar question of striking a balance between the rights and interests of society and those of the individual. This is something which the law is constantly doing in matters large and small. To take a very down-to-earth example, let me consider the right of the individual whose house adjoins the highway to have access to it; that means in these days the right to have vehicles stationary in the highway, sometimes for a considerable time if there is a lot of loading or unloading. There are many cases in which the courts have had to balance the private right of access against the public right to use the highway without obstruction. It cannot be done by carving up the highway into public and private areas. It is done by recognizing that each have rights over the whole; that if each were to exercise their rights to the full, they would come into conflict; and therefore that the rights of each must be curtailed so as to ensure as far as possible that the essential needs of each are safeguarded.

I do not think that one can talk sensibly of a public and private morality any more than one can of a public or private highway. Morality is a sphere in which there is a public interest and a private interest, often in conflict, and the problem is to reconcile the two. This does not mean that it is impossible to put forward any general statements about how in our society the balance ought to be struck. Such statements cannot of their nature be rigid or precise; they would not be designed to circumscribe the operation of the law-making power but to guide those who have to apply it. While every decision which a court of law makes when it balances the public against the private interest is an *ad hoc* decision, the cases contain statements of principle to which the court should have regard when it reaches its deci-

sion. In the same way it is possible to make general statements of principle which it may be thought the legislature should bear in mind when it is considering the enactment of laws enforcing morals.

■ ■ ■

This indicates a general sentiment that the right to privacy is something to be put in the balance against the enforcement of the law. Ought the same sort of consideration to play any part in the formation of the law? Clearly only in a very limited number of cases. When the help of the law is invoked by an injured citizen, privacy must be irrelevant; the individual cannot ask that his right to privacy should be measured against injury criminally done to another. But when all who are involved in the deed are consenting parties and the injury is done to morals, the public interest in the moral order can be balanced against the claims of privacy. The restriction on police powers of investigation goes further than the affording of a parallel; it means that the detection of crime committed in private and when there is no complaint is bound to be rather haphazard and this is an additional reason for moderation. These considerations do not justify the exclusion of all private immorality from the scope of the law. I think that, as I have already suggested, the test of 'private behaviour' should be substituted for 'private morality' and the influence of the factor should be reduced from that of a definite limitation to that of a matter to be taken into account. Since the gravity of the crime is also a proper consideration, a distinction might well be made in the case of homosexuality between the lesser acts of indecency and the full offence, which on the principles of the Wolfenden Report it would be illogical to do.

LAW, LIBERTY, AND MORALITY

H. L. A. HART

When we turn [to] the positive grounds held to justify the legal enforcement of morality it is important to distinguish a moderate and an extreme thesis, though critics of Mill have sometimes moved from one to the other without marking the transition. Lord Devlin seems to me to maintain, for most of his essay, the moderate thesis and Stephen the extreme one.

According to the moderate thesis, a shared morality is the cement of society; without it there would be aggregates of individuals but no society. "A recognized morality" is, in Lord Devlin's words, "as necessary to society's existence as a recognized government," and though a particular act of immorality may not harm or endanger or corrupt others nor, when done in private, either shock or give offence to others, this does not conclude the matter. For we must not view conduct in isolation from its effect on the moral code: if we remember this, we can see that one who is "no menace to others" nonetheless may by his immoral conduct "threaten one of the great moral principles on which society is based." In this sense the breach of moral principle is an offence "against society as a whole," and society may use the law to preserve its morality as it uses it to safeguard anything else essential to its existence. This is why "the suppression of vice is as much the law's business as the suppression of subversive activities."

By contrast, the extreme thesis does not look upon a shared morality as of merely instrumental value analogous to ordered government, and it does not justify the punishment of immorality as a step taken, like the punishment of treason, to preserve society from dissolution or collapse. Instead, the enforcement of morality is regarded as a thing of value, even if immoral acts harm no one directly, or indirectly by weakening the moral cement of society. I do not say that it is possible to allot to one or other of these two theses every argument used, but they do, I think, characterise the main critical positions at the root of most arguments, and they incidentally exhibit an ambiguity in the expression "enforcing morality as such." Perhaps the clearest way of distinguishing the two theses is to see that there are always two levels at which we may ask whether some breach of positive morality is harmful. We may ask first, Does this act harm anyone independently of its repercussion on the shared morality of society? And secondly we may ask, Does this act affect the shared morality and thereby weaken society? The moderate thesis requires, if the punishment of the act is to be justified, an affirmative answer at least at the second level. The extreme thesis does not require an affirmative answer at either level.

Lord Devlin appears to defend the moderate thesis. I say "appears" because, though he says that society has the right to enforce a morality as such on the ground that a shared morality is essential to society's existence, it is not at all clear that for him the statement that immorality jeopardizes or weakens society is a statement of empirical fact. It seems sometimes to be an *a priori* assumption, and sometimes a necessary truth and a very odd one. The most important indication that this is so is that,

H. L. A. Hart, *Law, Liberty, and Morality* (Oxford: Oxford University Press, 1963)

apart from one vague reference to "history" showing that "the loosening of moral bonds is often the first stage of disintegration," no evidence is produced to show that deviation from accepted sexual morality, even by adults in private, is something which, like treason, threatens the existence of society. No reputable historian has maintained this thesis, and there is indeed much evidence against it. As a proposition of fact it is entitled to no more respect than the Emperor Justinian's statement that homosexuality was the cause of earthquakes. Lord Devlin's belief in it, and his apparent indifference to the question of evidence, are at points traceable to an undiscussed assumption. This is that all morality—sexual morality together with the morality that forbids acts injurious to others such as killing, stealing, and dishonesty—forms a single seamless web, so that those who deviate from any part are likely or perhaps bound to deviate from the whole. It is of course clear (and one of the oldest insights of political theory) that society could not exist without a morality which mirrored and supplemented the law's proscription of conduct injurious to others. But there is again no evidence to support, and much to refute, the theory that those who deviate from conventional sexual morality are in other ways hostile to society.

There seems, however, to be central to Lord Devlin's thought something more interesting, though no more convincing, than the conception of social morality as a seamless web. For he appears to move from the acceptable proposition that *some* shared morality is essential to the existence of any society to the unacceptable proposition that a society is identical with its morality as that is at any given moment of its history, so that a change in its morality is tantamount to the destruction of a society. The former proposition might be even accepted as a necessary rather than an empirical truth depending on a quite plausible definition of society as a body of men who hold certain moral views in common. But the latter proposition is absurd. Taken strictly, it would prevent us saying that the morality of the given society had changed, and would compel us instead to say that one society had disappeared and another one taken its place. But it is only on this absurd criterion of what it is for the same society to continue to exist that it could be asserted without evidence that any deviation from a society's shared morality threatens its existence.

It is clear that only this tacit identification of a society with its shared morality supports Lord Devlin's denial that there could be such a thing as private immorality and his comparison of sexual immorality, even when it takes place "in private," with treason. No doubt it is true that if deviations from conventional sexual morality are tolerated by the law and come to be known, the conventional morality might change in a permissive direction, though this does not seem to be the case with homosexuality in those European countries where it is not punishable by law. But even if the conventional morality did so change, the society in question would not have been destroyed or "subverted." We should compare such a development not to the violent overthrow of government but to a peaceful constitutional change in its form, consistent not only with the preservation of a society but with its advance.

■ ■ ■

The extreme thesis has many variants, and it is not always clear which of them its advocates are concerned to urge. According to some variants, the legal enforcement of morality is only of instrumental value: it is merely a means, though an indispensable one, for preserving morality, whereas the preservation of morality is the end, valuable in itself, which justifies its legal enforcement. According to other variants, there is something intrinsically valuable in the legal enforcement of morality. What is common to all varieties of the extreme thesis is that, unlike the moderate thesis, they do not hold the enforcement of morality or its preservation to be valuable merely because of their beneficial consequences in securing the existence of society.

It is to be observed that Lord Devlin hovers somewhat ambiguously between one form of the extreme thesis and the moderate thesis. For if we interpret his crucial statement that the preservation of a society's morality is necessary for its existence as a statement of fact (as the analogy with the suppression of treason suggests we should), then the continued existence of society is something distinguishable from the preservation of its morality. It is, in fact, a desirable consequence of the preservation of its morality, and, on the assumption that the enforcement of morality is identical with or required for its preservation, this desirable consequence justifies the enforcement of morality. So interpreted, Lord Devlin is an advocate of the moderate thesis and his argument is a utilitarian one. The objection to it is that his crucial statement of fact is unsupported by evidence; it is Utilitarianism without benefit of facts. If, on the other hand, we interpret his statement that any immorality, even in private, threatens the existence of society, not as an empirical statement but as a necessary truth (as the absence of evidence suggests we should), then the continued existence of a society is not something different from the preservation of its morality; it is identical with it. On this view the enforcement of morality is not justified by its valuable consequences in securing society from dissolution or decay. It is justified simply as identical with or required for the preservation of the society's morality. This is a form of the extreme thesis, disguised only by the tacit identification of a society with its morality which I criticised.

■ ■ ■

Stephen is, I think, a more consistent defender of certain forms of the extreme thesis than Lord Devlin is of the moderate one.

It is important for the understanding of Stephen's views on the legal enforcement of morality to notice that he, like Lord Devlin, assumes that the society to which his doctrine is to apply is marked by a considerable degree of moral solidarity, and is deeply disturbed by infringements of its moral code. Just as for Lord Devlin the morality to be enforced by law must be "public," in the sense that it is generally shared and identifiable by the triple marks of "intolerance, indignation, and disgust," so for Stephen "you cannot punish anything which public opinion as expressed in the common practice of society does not strenuously and unequivocally condemn . . . To be able to punish a moral majority must be overwhelming." It is possible that in mid-Victorian England these conditions were satisfied in relation to "that considerable number of acts" which according to Stephen were treated as crimes merely because they were regarded as grossly immoral. Perhaps an "overwhelming moral majority" then actually did harbour the healthy desire for revenge of which he speaks and which is to be gratified by the punishment of the guilty. But it would be sociologically naïve to assume that these conditions obtain in contemporary England at least as far as sexual morality is concerned. The fact that there is lip service to an official sexual morality should not lead us to neglect the possibility that in sexual, as in other matters, there may be a number of mutually tolerant moralities, and that even where there is some homogeneity of practice and belief, offenders may be viewed not with hatred or resentment but with amused contempt or pity.

In a sense, therefore, Stephen's doctrine, and much of Lord Devlin's, may seem to hover in the air above the *terra firma* of contemporary social reality; it may be a well-articulated construction, interesting because it reveals the outlook characteristic of the English judiciary but lacking application to contemporary society.

BOWERS V. HARDWICK

478 U.S. 186 (1986)

Justice WHITE delivered the opinion of the Court.

[Respondent, an adult male, was charged with violating Georgia's sodomy law by committing a sexual act with another adult male in his own bedroom. The law defines sodomy as committing or submitting to "any sexual act involving the sex organs of one person and the mouth or anus of another." After the prosecutor chose not to present the case to a grand jury, the respondent sued in federal court to challenge the constitutionality of the law. The trial court rejected the claim, but the Court of Appeals reversed, relying on earlier cases protecting contraception and abortion. The Court of Appeals held that the law "violated respondent's fundamental rights because his homosexual activity is a private and intimate association that is beyond the reach of state regulation." The Supreme Court reversed that judgment.]

This case does not require a judgment on whether laws against sodomy between consenting adults in general, or between homosexuals in particular, are wise or desirable. [The] issue presented is whether the Federal Constitution confers a fundamental right upon homosexuals to engage in sodomy and hence invalidates the laws of the many States that still make such conduct illegal and have done so for a very long time. The case also calls for some judgment about the limits of the Court's role in carrying out its constitutional mandate.

We first register our disagreement with the Court of Appeals [that] the Court's prior cases have construed the Constitution to confer a right of privacy that extends to homosexual sodomy and for all intents and purposes have decided this case. . . .

Precedent aside, however, respondent would have us announce [a] fundamental right to engage in homosexual sodomy. This we are quite unwilling to do. It is true that despite the language of the [Due Process Clauses] which appears to focus only on the processes by which life, liberty, or property is taken, the cases are legion in which those Clauses have been interpreted to have substantive [content]. Striving to assure itself and the public that announcing rights not readily identifiable in the Constitution's text involves much more than the imposition of the Justices' own choice of values on the States and the Federal Government, the Court has sought to identify the nature of the rights qualifying for heightened judicial protection. In [Palko v. Connecticut] it was said that this category includes those fundamental liberties that are "implicit in the concept of ordered liberty," such that "neither liberty nor justice would exist if [they] were sacrificed." A different description of fundamental liberties appeared in [Moore v. East Cleveland], where they are characterized as those liberties that are "deeply rooted in this Nation's history and tradition."

It is obvious to us that neither of these formulations would extend a fundamental right to homosexuals to engage in acts of consensual sodomy. Proscriptions against that conduct have ancient roots. Sodomy was a criminal offense at common law and was forbidden by the laws of the original thirteen States when they ratified the Bill of Rights. In 1868, when the Fourteenth Amendment was ratified, all but 5 of the 37 States in the Union had criminal sodomy laws. In fact, until 1961, all States outlawed sodomy, and today, 24 States and the District of Columbia continue to provide criminal penalties for sodomy performed in private and between consenting adults. Against this background, to claim that a right to engage in such conduct is "deeply rooted in this Nation's history and tradition" or "implicit in the concept of ordered liberty" is, at best, facetious.

Nor are we inclined to take a more expansive view of our authority to discover new fundamental rights imbedded in the Due Process Clause. The Court is most vulnerable and comes nearest to illegitimacy when it deals with judge-made constitutional law having little or no cognizable roots in the language or design of the Constitution. That this is so was painfully demonstrated by the face-off between the Executive and the Court in the 1930's, which resulted in the repudiation of much of the substantive gloss that the Court had placed on [due process]. There should be, therefore, great resistance to expand the substantive reach of those Clauses, particularly if it requires redefining the category of rights deemed to be fundamental. Otherwise, the Judiciary necessarily takes to itself further authority to govern the country without express constitutional authority. The claimed right pressed on us today falls far short of overcoming this resistance.

Respondent, however, asserts that the result should be different where the homosexual conduct occurs in the privacy of the home. He relies on Stanley v. Georgia, where the Court held that the First Amendment prevents conviction for possessing and reading obscene material in the privacy of his home. [Stanley] did protect conduct that would not have been protected outside the home, and it partially prevented the enforcement of state obscenity laws; but the decision was firmly grounded in the First Amendment. The right pressed upon us here has no similar support in the text of the Constitution, and it does not qualify for recognition under the prevailing principles for construing the Fourteenth Amendment. Its limits are also difficult to discern. Plainly enough, otherwise illegal conduct is not always immunized whenever it occurs in the home. Victimless crimes, such as the possession and use of illegal drugs, do not escape the law where they are committed at home. Stanley itself recognized that its holding offered no protection for the possession in the home of drugs, firearms, or stolen goods. And if respondent's submission is limited to the voluntary sexual conduct between consenting adults, it would be difficult, except by fiat, to limit the claimed right to homosexual conduct while leaving exposed to prosecution adultery, incest, and other sexual crimes even though they are committed in the home. We are unwilling to start down that road.

Even if the conduct at issue here is not a fundamental right, respondent asserts that there must be a rational basis for the law and that there is none in this case other than the presumed belief of a majority of the electorate in Georgia that homosexual sodomy is immoral and unacceptable. This is said to be an inadequate rationale to support the law. The law, however, is constantly based on notions of morality, and if all laws representing essentially moral choices are to be invalidated under the Due Process Clause, the courts will be very busy indeed. Even respondent makes no such claim, but insists that majority sentiments about the morality of homosexuality should be declared inadequate. We do not agree, and are unpersuaded that the sodomy laws of some 25 States should be invalidated on this basis.

[Reversed.]

Chief Justice BURGER, concurring.

I join the Court's opinion, but I write separately to underscore my view that in constitutional terms there is no such thing as a fundamental right to commit homosexual sodomy. As the Court notes, the proscriptions against sodomy have very "ancient roots." Decisions of individuals relating to homosexual conduct have been subject to state intervention throughout the history of Western Civilization. Condemnation of those practices is firmly rooted in Judeao–Christian [sic] moral and ethical standards. Homosexual sodomy was a capital crime under Roman law. During the English Reformation, [the] first English statute criminalizing sodomy was passed. Blackstone described "the infamous crime against nature" as an offense of "deeper malignity" than rape, an heinous act "the very mention of which is a disgrace to human nature," and "a crime not fit to be named." The common law of England, including its prohibition of sodomy, became the received law of Georgia and the other Colonies. In 1816 the Georgia Legislature passed the statute at issue [here]. To hold that the act of homosexual sodomy is somehow protected as a fundamental right would be to cast aside millennia of moral teaching. This is essentially not a question of personal "preferences" but rather of the legislative authority of the State. I find nothing in the Constitution depriving a State of the power to enact the statute challenged here.

Justice POWELL, concurring.

[I] agree with the Court that there is no fundamental right—i.e., no substantive right under the Due Process Clause such as that claimed by [respondent]. This is not to suggest, however, that respondent may not be protected by the Eighth Amendment of the Constitution. The Georgia statute at issue in this case authorizes a court to imprison a person for up to 20 years for a single private, consensual act of sodomy. In my view, a prison sentence for such conduct—certainly a sentence of long duration—would create a serious Eighth Amendment [issue]. In this case however, respondent has not been tried, much less convicted and sentenced. Moreover, respondent has not raised the Eighth Amendment issue [below].

Justice BLACKMUN, with whom Justice BRENNAN, Justice MARSHALL, and Justice STEVENS join, dissenting.

This case is no more about "a fundamental right to engage in homosexual sodomy" as the Court purports to declare, than [Stanley] was about a fundamental right to watch obscene movies. Rather, this case is about "the most comprehensive of rights and the right most valued by civilized men," namely, "the right to be let alone." [I] believe we must analyze respondent's claim in the light of the values that underlie the constitutional right to privacy. If that right means anything, it means that, before Georgia can prosecute its citizens for making choices about the most intimate aspects of their lives, it must do more than assert that the choice they have made is an " 'abominable crime not fit to be named among Christians.' "

[In] construing the right to privacy, the Court has proceeded along two somewhat distinct, albeit complementary, lines. First, it has recognized a privacy interest with reference to certain decisions that are properly for the individual to make. Second, it has recognized a privacy interest with reference to certain places without regard for the particular activities in which the individuals who occupy them are engaged. The case before us implicates both the decisional and the spatial aspects of the right to privacy.

The Court concludes today that none of our prior cases dealing with various decisions that individuals are entitled to make free of governmental interference "bears any resemblance to the claimed constitutional right of homosexuals to engage in acts of sodomy that is asserted in this case." While it is true that these cases may be characterized by their connection to protection of the family, the Court's conclusion that they extend no further than this boundary ignores the warning in [Moore] against "clos[ing] our eyes to the basic reasons why certain rights associated with the family have been accorded shelter under [due process]." We protect those rights not because they contribute, in some direct and material way, to the general public welfare, but because they form so central a part of an individual's life.

Only the most willful blindness could obscure the fact that sexual intimacy is "a sensitive, key relationship of human [existence]." [The] fact that individuals define themselves in a significant way through their intimate sexual relationships with others suggests, in a Nation as diverse as ours, that there may be many "right" ways of conducting those relationships, and that much of the richness of a relationship will come from the freedom an individual has to *choose* the form and nature of these intensely personal bonds. [The] Court claims that its decision today merely refuses to recognize a fundamental right to engage in homosexual sodomy; what the Court really has refused to recognize is the fundamental interest all individuals have in controlling the nature of their intimate associations with others. [Moreover, the] behavior for which Hardwick faces prosecution occurred in his own home, a place to which the Fourth Amendment attaches special significance. [The] Court's interpretation of the pivotal case of [Stanley] is entirely unconvincing. [Stanley did not rest entirely on the First Amendment.] Rather, the Stanley Court anchored its holding in the Fourth Amendment's special protection for the individual in his home. [Indeed,] the right of an individual to conduct intimate relationships in the intimacy of his or her own home seems to me to be the heart of the Constitution's protection of privacy.

The Court's failure to comprehend the magnitude of the liberty interests at stake in this case leads it to slight the question whether petitioner, on behalf of the State, has justified Georgia's infringement on these interests. I believe that neither of the two general justifications [that] petitioner has advanced warrants dismissing respondent's challenge for failure to state a claim.

First, petitioner asserts that the acts made criminal by the statute may have serious adverse consequences for "the general public health and welfare," such as spreading communicable diseases or fostering other criminal activity. Inasmuch as this case was dismissed by the District Court on the pleadings, it is not surprising that the record before us is barren of any evidence to support petitioner's claim. In light of the state of the record, I see no justification for the Court's attempt to equate the private, consensual sexual activity at issue here with the 'possession in the home of drugs, firearms, or stolen goods,' to which Stanley refused to extend its protection.

[The] core of petitioner's defense of [the law], however, is that respondent and others who engage in the [conduct] interfere with Georgia's exercise of the "'right of the Nation and of the States to maintain a decent society.'" Essentially, petitioner argues, and the Court agrees, that the fact that acts described in [the law] "for hundreds of years, if not thousands, have been uniformly condemned as immoral" is a sufficient reason to permit a State to ban them today. The assertion that "traditional Judeo-Christian values proscribe" the conduct involved cannot provide an adequate justification for [the law]. That certain, but by no means all, religious groups condemn the behavior at issue gives the State no license to impose their judgments on the entire citizenry. The legitimacy of secular legislation depends instead on whether the State can advance some justification for its law beyond its conformity to religious doctrine.

[Nor] can [the law] be justified as a "morally neutral" exercise of Georgia's power to "protect the public environment." Certainly, some private behavior can affect the fabric of society as a whole. [But the Court fails] to see the difference between laws that protect public sensibilities and those that enforce private morality. Statutes banning public sexual activity are entirely consistent with protecting the individual's liberty interest in decisions concerning sexual relations: the same recognition that those decisions are intensely private which justifies protecting them from governmental interference can justify protecting individuals from unwilling exposure to the sexual activities of others. But the mere fact that intimate behavior may be punished when it takes place in public cannot dictate how States can regulate intimate behavior that occurs in intimate places. [This] case involves no real interference with the rights of others, for the mere knowledge that other individuals do not adhere to one's value system cannot be a legally cognizable interest, let alone an interest that can justify invading the houses, hearts, and minds of citizens who choose to live their lives [differently].

Justice STEVENS, with whom Justice BRENNAN and Justice MARSHALL join, dissenting.

Like the statute that is challenged in this case, the rationale of the Court's opinion applies equally to the prohibited conduct regardless of whether the parties who engage in it are married or unmarried, or are of the same or different sexes. Sodomy was condemned as an odious and sinful type of behavior during the formative period of the common law. That condemnation was equally damning for heterosexual and homosexual sodomy. Moreover, it provided no special exemption for married couples. [Because] the Georgia statute expresses the traditional view that sodomy is an immoral kind of conduct regardless of the identity of the persons who engage in it, I believe that a proper analysis of its constitutionality requires consideration of two questions: First, may a State totally prohibit the described conduct by means of a neutral law applying without exception to all persons subject to its jurisdiction? If not, may the State save the statute by announcing that it will only enforce the law against homosexuals? The two questions merit separate discussion.

I. Our prior cases make two propositions abundantly clear. First, the fact that the governing majority in a State has traditionally viewed a particular practice as immoral is not a sufficient reason for upholding a law prohibiting the practice; neither history nor tradition could save a law prohibiting miscegenation from constitutional attack. Second, individual decisions by married persons, concerning the intimacies of their physical relationship, even when not intended to produce offspring, are a form of "liberty" protected by [due process.] Moreover, this protection extends to intimate choices by unmarried as well as married persons. [The] essential "liberty" that animated the development of the law in our cases surely embraces the right to engage in sexual nonreproductive conduct that others may consider offensive or immoral. Paradoxical as it may seem, our prior cases thus establish that a State may not prohibit sodomy within "the sacred precincts of marital bedrooms," or, indeed, between unmarried heterosexual adults.

II. If the Georgia statute cannot be enforced as it is written—if the conduct it seeks to prohibit is a protected form of liberty for the vast majority of Georgia's citizens—the State must assume the burden of justifying a selective application of its law. Either the persons to whom Georgia seeks to apply its statute do not have the same interest in "liberty" that others have, or there must be a reason why the State may be permitted to apply a generally applicable law to certain persons that it does not apply to others.

The first possibility is plainly unacceptable. Although the meaning of the principle that "all men are created equal" is not always clear, it surely must mean that every free citizen has the same interest in "liberty" that the members of the majority share. From the standpoint of the individual, the homosexual and the heterosexual have the same interest in deciding how he will live his own life, and, more narrowly, how he will conduct himself in his personal and voluntary associations with his companions. State intrusion into the private conduct of either is equally burdensome.

The second possibility is similarly unacceptable. A policy of selective application must be supported by a neutral and legitimate interest—something more substantial than a habitual dislike for, or ignorance about, the disfavored group. Neither the State nor the Court has identified any such interest in this case. The Court has posited as a justification for the Georgia statute "the presumed belief of a majority of the electorate in Georgia that homosexual sodomy is immoral and unacceptable." But the Georgia electorate has expressed no such belief—instead, its representatives enacted a law that presumably reflects the belief that *all sodomy* is immoral and unacceptable. Unless the Court is prepared to conclude that such a law is constitutional, it may not rely on the work product of the Georgia Legislature to support its holding. For the Georgia statute does

not single out homosexuals as a separate class meriting special disfavored [treatment].

Both the Georgia statute and the Georgia prosecutor [because of nonenforcement of the law in this case and in earlier decades] completely fail to provide the Court with any support for the conclusion that homosexual sodomy, *simpliciter*, is considered unacceptable conduct in that State, and that the burden of justifying a selective application of the generally applicable law has been [met].

QUESTIONS FOR DISCUSSION

1. Does the Supreme Court in *Bowers* address the question of whether the regulation of homosexual sodomy is desirable? If not, why not?

2. What is the moral relevance of the fact that twenty-four states and the District of Columbia outlawed homosexual sodomy at the time of the *Bowers* decision? What is the constitutional relevance of the same fact? Would Devlin find this fact morally relevant? Would Hart?

3. What is the relevance of the Court's discussion of whether the conduct in *Bowers* is a "fundamental right"? What kind of right is the Court talking about? Would the discussion of rights look the same in a legislative debate as it did in the Supreme Court?

4. How much of Devlin's argument rests on empirical premises? How much of Hart's critique of Devlin rests on empirical premises? Do Hart and Devlin have a philosophical disagreement? If so, what is it?

5. Do you think that Georgia relied in *Bowers* on a version of what Hart calls the "moderate thesis"? The "extreme thesis"? Would it have made any difference to Justice White or Chief Justice Burger?

SUGGESTIONS FOR FURTHER READING

The literature on Mill's *On Liberty* is voluminous. Many of the important commentaries are collected in J. B. Schneewind, *Mill: Collection of Critical Essays* (London: Macmillan, 1968), and in the Norton Critical Edition (David Spitz, ed., New York: W. W. Norton, 1975) of *On Liberty*. On questions of positive and negative liberty, the classic work is Isaiah Berlin, *Four Essays On Liberty* (Oxford: Oxford University Press, 1969). Also useful are Lawrence Crocker, *Positive Liberty: An Essay in Normative Political Philosophy* (The Hague: Martinus Nijhoff, 1980), and Gerald MacCallum, Jr., "Negative and Positive Freedom," *Philosophical Review*, vol. 76 (1967), pp. 318 ff. Gerald Dworkin, ed., *Morality, Harm and the Law* (Boulder, Colorado: Westview Press, 1993) collects a number of useful articles on harm, offense, paternalism, and moralism. Joel Feinberg, *The Moral Limits of the Criminal Law* (4 volumes) (New York: Oxford University Press, 1984, etc.) is a magisterial explication of the positions that Feinberg has developed over the years about the appropriate uses of law with respect to harm, offense, and morality. A good summary of various positions can be found in William A. Parent, "Recent Work on the Concept of Liberty," *American Philosophical Quarterly*, vol. 11 (1974), pp. 156 ff.

4.3 A RIGHT TO FREE SPEECH

INTRODUCTION

The right to free speech is perhaps the most important, or in any event the most widely discussed, of the *specific* rights that are commonly recognized in most western democracies. Unlike a general right to liberty, a right to free speech does not purport to encompass the full range of human conduct, but only some narrower class of conduct. Indeed, in some sense the very phrase "free speech" is a misnomer, or at the very least a potentially misleading label. It is misleading because no one would maintain that the right to free speech covers all activities that would count as "speech" in ordinary language. The issue here is not the question of when free speech rights may be overridden. It is that free speech rights do not even include all speech in the first instance. A vast range of human activities (for example, making contracts, placing bets, and telling customers about the mileage on a used car) involve speech, but do not even come close to the kinds of activities that a right to free speech is all about. Unlike paradigm cases of free speech such as political argument, the speech that is the basis for making contracts, bets, and warranties is not shielded from otherwise permissible state control by a specific principle of free speech. A company would be laughed out of court if it tried to argue that it could not be held liable for its written factual statements about the quality of the products it sold because those representations were immunized from liability by the principle of free speech.

Thus, it is important to distinguish the name of a right—"free speech"—from the right that the name is the name of. This not only applies when the name is over-inclusive—when the right does not include activities that might be encompassed by the ordinary meaning of the words in the right's name. It also applies when the name is under-inclusive—when there are activities encompassed by the right that are beyond the plausible scope of the ordinary meaning of the right's name. Protest armbands, oil paintings, and photographs, for example, could only with a great stretch properly be called "speech." Yet most armbands, oil paintings, and photographs are typically protected by a right to free speech.

Although the right to free speech is narrower than a right to liberty, it is from this very narrowness that the right to free speech commonly derives its strength. In order to understand this, we must initially note the traditional distinction, central to Mill's position, between self-regarding conduct (conduct affecting only the person who engages in the conduct) and other-regarding conduct (conduct affecting others). Although this distinction is itself controversial (does *any* conduct affect only the person engaging in it?), that controversy is not directly relevant here. Even if there is a distinction between self-regarding and other-regarding conduct, we know that speech often harms others, and thus we know that speech, whether harmful or helpful to others, typically falls on the other-regarding and not on the self-regarding side of that divide. People ordinarily talk for the purpose of affecting others in some way, and restrictions on speech are typically based on the effects that the speech is thought to have. When people argue that depictions of violence ought to be restricted because those depictions have some effect on the number of actual acts of violence, they make the same kind of argument as those who would restrict other harmful forms of conduct. When people propose that racial epithets be restricted, they base their proposals on what they perceive to be the harm or the regulable offense of those epithets. When we see the ways in which words can injure reputations (would you rather be punched in the arm or have someone tell all of your friends that you are a child molester?), or invade privacy (would you rather be kicked in the shins or have a picture of you urinating posted all over campus?), we can understand the impact of words and pictures, an impact that sometimes can be greater than a physical impact.

Thus there are two possible responses to an argument for restricting a communication on the grounds that the communicative act will produce the kinds of consequences otherwise sufficient to justify control. One is to deny that those consequences are as they are claimed to be, either by denying the causal relationship between the communicative act and the consequence itself, or by denying that the consequence of speech is itself a proper subject of control. Maybe there is no relationship between depictions of violence and acts of violence, in which case there is no justification for restricting the depictions, just as there is no justification for restricting any other exercise of personal liberty without some showing of negative consequences. Similarly, maybe offensive words should not be restricted just because offensive conduct should not be restricted. Perhaps, therefore, the consequences claimed are not in fact sufficient to justify a restriction even apart from the fact that those consequences, whatever they are, are the consequences of a speech act.

This argument, it can be seen, does not rely on anything about the "speechness" of the act, but only on the fact that speech acts, like other acts, may at times fail to produce the consequences that would justify restriction of an actor's (and therefore a speaker's) liberty. There is a quite different type of argument, however: an argument that even if the consequences produced by a speech act would *otherwise* be sufficient to justify restriction, those consequences are not sufficient in this instance because there is a *right to* free speech that prevents restriction even if the conditions for restriction of an act of any other kind would otherwise be satisfied.

Much of the theory of free speech has been devoted to this latter variety of argument. Given that the right to free speech frequently protects speech not because it is harmless, but despite the harm it may cause, what justifies this special treatment? Why should speech acts of a certain variety have a degree of immunity from otherwise prevailing principles of liberty and its restriction? That is the central question in the philosophical examination of freedom of speech, and that is the question that pervades all of the material that follows.

ON LIBERTY

JOHN STUART MILL

If all mankind minus one were of one opinion, and only one person were of the contrary opinion, mankind would be no more justified in silencing that one person, than he, if he had the power, would be justified in silencing mankind. Were an opinion a personal possession of no value except to the owner; if to be obstructed in the enjoyment of it were simply a probate injury, it would make some difference whether the injury was inflicted only on a few persons or on many. But the peculiar evil of silencing the expression of an opinion is, that it is robbing the human race; posterity as well as the existing generation; those who dissent from the opinion, still more than those who hold it. If the opinion is right, they are deprived of the opportunity of exchanging error for truth: if wrong, they lose, what is almost as great a benefit, the clearer perception and livelier impression of truth, produced by its collision with error.

It is necessary to consider separately these two hypotheses, each of which has a distinct branch of the argument corresponding to it. We can never be sure that the opinion we are endeavouring to stifle is a false opinion; and if we were sure, stifling it would be an evil still.

First: the opinion which it is attempted to suppress by authority may possibly be true. Those who desire to suppress it, of course deny its truth; but they are not infallible. They have no authority to decide the question for all mankind, and exclude every other person from the means of judging. To refuse a hearing to an opinion, because they are sure that it is false, is to assume that *their* certainty is the same thing as *absolute certainty*. All silencing of discussion is an assumption of infallibility. Its condemnation may be allowed to rest on this common argument, not the worse for being common.

Unfortunately for the good sense of mankind, the fact of their fallibility is far from carrying the weight in their practical judgment which is always allowed to it in theory; for while every one well knows himself to be fallible, few think it necessary to take any precautions against their own fallibility, or admit the supposition that any opinion, of which they feel very certain, may be one of the examples of the error to which they acknowledge themselves to be liable. Absolute princes, or others who are accustomed to unlimited deference, usually feel this complete confidence in their own opinions on nearly all subjects. People more happily situated, who sometimes hear their opinions disputed, and are not wholly unused to be set right when they are wrong, place the same unbounded reliance only on such of their opinions as are shared by all who surround them, or to whom they habitually defer; for in proportion to a man's want of confidence in his own solitary judgment, does he usually repose, with implicit trust, on the infallibility of "the world" in general. And the world, to each individual, means the part of it with which he comes in contact; his party, his sect, his church, his class of society; the man may be called by comparison, almost liberal and large-minded to whom it means anything so comprehensive as his own country or his own age. Nor is his faith in this collective authority at all shaken by his being aware that other ages, countries, sects, churches, classes, and parties have thought, and even now think,

John Stuart Mill, *On Liberty* (1859), selections from Chapter 2

the exact reverse. He devolves upon his own world the responsibility of being in the right against the dissentient worlds of other people; and it never troubles him that mere accident has decided which of these numerous worlds is the object of his reliance, and that the same causes which make him a Churchman in London, would have made him a Buddhist or a Confucian in Pekin. Yet it is as evident in itself, as any amount of argument can make it, that ages are no more infallible than individuals; every age having held many opinions which subsequent ages have deemed not only false but absurd; and it is as certain that many opinions now general will be rejected by future ages, as it is that many, once general, are rejected by the present.

The objection likely to be made to this argument would probably take some such form as the following. There is no greater assumption of infallibility in forbidding the propagation of error, than in any other thing which is done by public authority on its own judgment and responsibility. Judgment is given to men that they may use it. Because it may be used erroneously, are men to be told that they ought not to use it at all? To prohibit what they think pernicious, is not claiming exemption from error, but fulfilling the duty incumbent on them, although fallible, of acting on their conscientious conviction. If we were never to act on our opinions, because those opinions may be wrong, we should leave all our interests uncared for, and all our duties unperformed. An objection which applies to all conduct can be no valid objection to any conduct in particular. It is the duty of governments, and of individuals, to form the truest opinions they can; to form carefully, and never impose them upon others unless they are quite sure of being right. But when they are sure (such reasoners may say), it is not conscientiousness but cowardice to shrink from acting on their opinions, and allow doctrines which they honestly think dangerous to the welfare of mankind, either in this life or in another, to be

scattered abroad without restraint, because other people, in less enlightened times, have persecuted opinions now believed to be true. Let us take care, it may be said, not to make the same mistake: but government and nations have made mistakes in other things, which are not denied to be fit subjects for the exercise of authority: they have laid on bad taxes, made unjust wars. Ought we therefore to lay on no losses, and, under whatever provocation, make no wars? Men and governments, must act to the best of their ability. There is no such thing as absolute certainty, but there is assurance sufficient for the purposes of human life. We may, and must, assume our opinion to be true for the guidance of our own conduct: and it is assuming no more when we forbid bad men to pervert society by the propagation of opinions which we regard as false and pernicious.

I answer, that it is assuming very much more. There is the greatest difference between presuming an opinion to be true, because, with every opportunity for contesting it, it has not been refuted, and assuming its truth for the purpose of not permitting its refutation. Complete liberty of contradicting and disproving our opinion is the very condition which justifies us in assuming its truth for purposes of action; and on no other terms can a being with human faculties have any rational assurance of being right.

When we consider either the history of opinion, or the ordinary conduct of human life, to what is it to be ascribed that the one and the other are no worse than they are? Not certainly to the inherent force of the human understanding; for, on any matter not self-evident, there are ninety-nine persons totally incapable of judging of it for one who is capable; and the capacity of the hundredth person is only comparative; for the majority of the eminent men of every past generation held many opinions now known to be erroneous, and did or approved numerous things which no one will now justify. Why is it, then, that there is on the whole 🌢 preponderance among mankind of rational opinions and rational conduct? If there really is this preponderance—which there must be unless human affairs are, and have always been, in an almost desperate state—it is owing to a quality of the human mind, the source of everything respectable in man either as an intellectual or as a moral being, namely, that his errors are corrigible. He is capable of rectifying his mistakes, by discussion and experience. Not by experience alone. There must be discussion, to show how experience is to be interpreted. Wrong opinions and practices gradually yield to fact and argument; but facts and arguments, to produce any effect on the mind, must be brought before it. Very few facts are able to tell their own story, without comments to bring out their meaning. The whole strength and value, then, of human judgment, depending on the one property, that it can be set right when it is wrong, reliance can be placed on it only when the means of setting it right are kept constantly at hand. In the case of any person whose judgment is really deserving of confidence, how has it become so? Because he has kept his mind open to criticism on his opinions and conduct. Because it has been his practice to listen to all that could be said against him; to profit by as much of it as was just, and expound to himself, and upon occasion to others, the fallacy of what was fallacious. Because he has felt, that the only way in which a human being can make some approach to knowing the whole of a subject, is by hearing what can be said about it by persons of every variety of opinion, and studying all modes in which it can be looked at by every character of mind. No wise man ever acquired his wisdom in any mode but this; nor is it in the nature of human intellect to become wise in any other manner. The steady habit of correcting and completing his own opinion by collating it with those of others, so far from causing doubt and hesitation in carrying it into practice, is the only stable foundation for a just reliance on it: for, being cognisant of all that can, at least obviously, be said against him, and having taken up his position against all gainsayers—knowing that he has sought for objections and difficulties, instead of avoiding them, and has shut out no light which can be thrown upon the subject from any quarter—he has a right to think his judgment better than that of any person, or any multitude, who have not gone through a similar process.

It is not too much to require that what the wisest of mankind, those who are best entitled to trust their own judgment, find necessary to warrant their relying on it, should be submitted to by that miscellaneous collection of a few wise and many foolish individuals, called the public. The most intolerant of churches, the Roman Catholic Church, even at the canonisation of a saint, admits, and listens patiently to, a "devil's advocate." The holiest of men, it appears, cannot be admitted to posthumous honours, until all that the devil could say against him is known and weighed. If even the Newtonian philosophy were not permitted to be questioned, mankind could not feel as complete assurance of its truth as they now do. The beliefs which we have most warrant for have no safeguard to rest on, but a standing invitation to the whole world to prove them unfounded. If the challenge is not accepted, or is accepted and the attempt fails, we are far enough from certainty still; but we have done the best that the existing state of human reason admits of; we have neglected nothing that could give the truth a chance of reaching us: if the lists are kept open, we may hope that if there be a better truth, it will be found when the human mind is capable of receiving it; and in the meantime we may rely on having attained such approach to truth as is possible in our own day. This is the amount of certainty attainable by a fallible being, and this the sole way of attaining it.

■ ■ ■

Let us now pass to the second division of the argument, and dismissing the supposition that any of the received opinions may be false, let us assume them to be true, and examine into the worth of the manner in which they are likely to be held, when their truth is not freely and openly canvassed. However unwillingly a person who has a strong opinion may admit the possibility that his opinion may be false, he ought to be moved by the consideration that, however true it may be, if it is not fully, frequently, and fearlessly discussed, it will be held as a dead dogma, not a living truth.

There is a class of persons (happily not quite so numerous as formerly) who think it enough if a person assents undoubtingly to what they think true, though he has no knowledge whatever of the grounds of the opinion, and could not make a tenable defence of it against the most superficial objections. Such persons, if they can once get their creed taught from authority, naturally think that no good, and some harm, comes of its being allowed to be questioned. Where their influence prevails, they make it nearly impossible for the received opinion to be rejected wisely and considerately, though it may still be rejected rashly and ignorantly; for to shut out discussion entirely is seldom possible, and when it once gets in, beliefs not grounded on conviction are apt to give way before the slightest semblance of an argument. Waiving, however, this possibility—assuming that the true opinion abides in the mind, but abides as a prejudice, a belief independent of, and proof against, argument—this is not the way in which truth ought to be held by a rational being. This is not knowing the truth. Truth, thus held, is but one superstition the more, accidentally clinging to the words which enunciate a truth.

If the intellect and judgment of mankind ought to be cultivated, a thing which Protestants at least do not deny, on what can these faculties be more appropriately exercised by any one, than on the things which concern him so much that it is considered necessary for him to hold opinions on them? If the cultivation of the understanding consists in one thing more than in another, it is surely in learning the grounds of one's own opinions. Whatever

people believe, on subjects on which it is of the first importance to believe rightly, they ought to be able to defend against at least the common objections. But, some one may say, "Let them be *taught* the grounds of their opinions. It does not follow that opinions must be merely parroted because they are never heard controverted. Persons who learn geometry do not simply commit the theorems to memory, but understand and learn likewise the demonstrations; and it would be absurd to say that they remain ignorant of the grounds of geometrical truths, because they never hear any one deny, and attempt to disprove them." Undoubtedly: and such teaching suffices on a subject like mathematics, where there is nothing at all to be said on the wrong side of the question. The peculiarity of the evidence of mathematical truths is that all the argument is on one side. There are no objections, and no answers to objections. But on every subject on which difference of opinion is possible, the truth depends on a balance to be struck between two sets of conflicting reasons. Even in natural philosophy, there is always some other explanation possible of the same facts; some geocentric theory instead of heliocentric, some phlogiston instead of oxygen; and it has to be shown why that other theory cannot be the true one: and until this is shown, and until we know how it is shown, we do not understand the grounds of our opinion. But when we turn to subjects infinitely more complicated, to morals, religion, politics, social relations, and the business of life, three fourths of the arguments for every disputed opinion consist in dispelling the appearances which favour some opinion different from it. The greatest orator, save one, of antiquity, has left it on record that he always studied his adversary's case with as great, if not still greater, intensity than even his own. What Cicero practised as the means of forensic success requires to be imitated by all who study any subject in order to arrive at the truth. He who knows only his own side of the case, knows little of that. His reasons may be good, and no one may have been able to refute them. But if he is equally unable to refute the reasons on the opposite side; if he does not so much as know what they are, he has no ground for preferring either opinion. The rational position for him would be suspension of judgment, and unless he contents himself with that, he is either led by authority, or adopts, like the generality of the world, the side to which he feels most inclination. Nor is it enough that he should hear the arguments of adversaries from his own teachers, presented as they state them, and accompanied by what they offer as refutations. That is not the way to do justice to the arguments, or bring them into real contact with his own mind. He must be able to hear them from persons who actually believe them; who defend them in earnest, and do their very utmost for them. He must know them in their most plausible and persuasive form; he must feel the whole force of the difficulty which the true view of the subject has to encounter and dispose of; else he will never really possess himself of the portion of truth which meets and removes the difficulty. Ninety-nine in a hundred of what are called educated men are in this condition; even of those who can argue fluently for their opinions. Their conclusion may be true, but it might be false for anything they know: they have never thrown themselves into the mental position of those who think differently from them, and considered what such persons may have to say; and consequently they do not, in any proper sense of the word, know the doctrine which they themselves profess. They do not know those parts of it which explain and justify the remainder; the considerations which show that a fact which seemingly conflicts with another is reconcilable with it, or that, of two apparently strong reasons, one and not the other ought to be preferred. All that part of the truth which turns the scale, and decides the judgment of a completely informed mind, they are strangers to; nor is it ever really known, but to those who have attended equally and impartially to both sides, and endeavoured to see the reasons of both in the strongest light. So essential is this discipline to a real understanding of moral and human subjects, that if opponents of all important truths do not exist, it is indispensable to imagine them, and supply them with the strongest arguments which the most skillful devil's advocate can conjure up.

■ ■ ■

It still remains to speak of one of the principal causes which make diversity of opinion advantageous, and will continue to do so until mankind shall have entered a stage of intellectual advancement which at present seems at an incalculable distance. We have hitherto considered only two possibilities: that the received opinion may be false, and some other opinion, consequently, true; or that, the received opinion being true, a conflict with the opposite error is essential to a clear apprehension and deep feeling of its truth. But there is a commoner case than either of these; when the conflicting doctrines, instead of being one true and the other false, share the truth between them; and the nonconforming opinion is needed to supply the remainder of the truth, of which the received doctrine embodies only a part. Popular opinions, on subjects not palpable to sense, are often true, but seldom or never the whole truth. They are a part of the truth; sometimes a greater, sometimes a smaller part, but exaggerated, distorted, and disjointed from the truths by which they ought to be accompanied and limited. Heretical opinions, on the other hand, are generally some of these suppressed and neglected truths, bursting the bonds which kept them down, and either seeking reconciliation with the truth contained in the common opinion, or fronting it as enemies, and setting themselves up, with similar exclusiveness, as the whole truth. The latter case is hitherto the most frequent, as, in the human mind, one-sidedness has always been the rule, and many-sidedness the exception. Hence, even in revolutions of opinion, one part of the truth usually sets while another rises. Even progress which ought to super-add, for the most part only substitutes, one partial and incomplete truth for another, improvement consisting chiefly in this, that the new fragment of truth is more wanted, more adapted to the needs of the time, than that which it displaces. Such being the partial character of prevailing opinions, even when resting on a true foundation, every opinion which embodies somewhat of the portion of truth which the common opinion omits, ought to be considered precious, with whatever amount of error and confusion that truth may be blended. No sober judge of human affairs will feel bound to be indignant because those who force on our notice truths which we should otherwise have overlooked, overlook some of those which we see. Rather, he will think that so long as popular truth is one-sided, it is more desirable than otherwise that unpopular truth should have one-sided assertors too; such being usually the most energetic, and the most likely to compel reluctant attention to the fragment of wisdom which they proclaim as if it were the whole.

■ ■ ■

We have now recognised the necessity to the mental well-being of mankind (on which all their other well-being depends) of freedom of opinion, and freedom of the expression of opinion, on four distinct grounds; which we will now briefly recapitulate.

First, if any opinion is compelled to silence, that opinion may, for aught we can certainly know, be true. To deny this is to assume our own infallibility.

Secondly, though the silenced opinion be an error, it may, and very commonly does, contain a portion of truth; and since the general or prevailing opinion on any subject is rarely or never the whole truth, it is only by the collision of adverse opinions that the remainder of the truth has any chance of being supplied.

Thirdly, even if the received opinion be not only true, but the whole truth; unless it is suffered to be, and actually is, vigorously and earnestly contested, it will, by most of those who receive it, be held in the manner of a prejudice, with little comprehension or feeling of its rational grounds. And not only this, but, fourthly, the meaning of the doctrine itself will be in danger of being lost, or enfeebled, and deprived of its vital effect on the character and conduct; the dogma becoming a mere formal profession, inefficacious for good, but cumbering the ground, and preventing the growth of any real and heartfelt conviction, from reason or personal experience.

QUESTIONS FOR DISCUSSION

1. As we have seen (in Section 4.2), Mill argued in Chapter 1 of *On Liberty* that self-regarding conduct should not be restricted. Why does Mill argue that thought and discussion should not be restricted? What is the relationship between this argument and the conclusion in Chapter 1?
2. Mill argues that challenges to received opinions should be allowed when the received opinion is true, when it is false, and when it is partly true. What arguments does Mill use in each case? How do they relate to each other?
3. Mill contends that freedom to contradict an opinion "is the very condition which justified us in assuming its truth for purposes of action; and on no other terms can a being with human faculties have any rational assurance of being right." Does this seem right to you? Why or why not?
4. At the beginning of Chapter 3 of *On Liberty*, Mill gives the following famous example: "An opinion that corn-dealers are starvers of the poor, or that

private property is robbery, ought to be unmolested when simply circulated through the press, but may justly incur punishment when delivered orally to an excited mob assembled before the house of a corn–dealer, or when handed about among the same mob in the form of a placard." What is the point of this example? Why would Mill allow the restriction? Would you allow it? Why or why not? Would you allow right–to–life protesters to picket or demonstrate outside an abortion clinic? (On this, see the Supreme Court case of *Masden v. Women's Health Clinic. Inc.*, 114 S. Ct. 2516 [1994].)

A THEORY OF FREEDOM OF EXPRESSION

THOMAS SCANLON

The doctrine of freedom of expression is generally thought to single out a class of 'protected acts' which it holds to be immune from restrictions to which other acts are subject. In particular, on any very strong version of the doctrine there will be cases where protected acts are held to be immune from restriction despite the fact that they have as consequences harms which would normally be sufficient to justify the imposition of legal sanctions. It is the existence of such cases which makes freedom of expression a significant doctrine and which makes it appear, from a certain point of view, an irrational one. . . .

Suppose some misanthropic inventor were to discover a simple method whereby anyone could make nerve gas in his kitchen out of gasoline, table salt, and urine. It seems just as clear to me that he could be prohibited by law from passing out his recipe on handbills or broadcasting it on television as that he could be prohibited from passing out free samples of his product in aerosol cans or putting it on sale

at Abercrombie & Fitch. In either case his action would bring about a drastic decrease in the general level of personal safety by radically increasing the capacity of most citizens to inflict harm on each other. The fact that he does this in one case through an act of expression and in the other through some other form of action seems to me not to matter.

It might happen, however, that a comparable decrease in the general level of personal safety could be just as reliably predicted to result from the distribution of a particularly effective piece of political propaganda which would undermine the authority of the government, or from the publication of a theological tract which would lead to a schism and a bloody civil war. In these cases the matter seems to me to be entirely different, and the harmful consequence seems clearly not to be a justification for restricting the acts of expression.

What I conclude from this is that the distinction between expression and other forms of action is less important than the distinction be-

Thomas Scanlon, "A Theory of Freedom of Expression," *Philosophy and Public Affairs*, vol. 1 (1971), pp. 203 ff. Scanlon (1941–) is Professor of Philosophy at Harvard University.

tween expression which moves others to act by pointing out what they take to be good reasons for action and expression which gives rise to action by others in other ways, e.g., by providing them with the means to do what they wanted to do anyway. This conclusion is supported, I think, by our normal views about legal responsibility.

If I were to say to you, an adult in full possession of your faculties, 'What you ought to do is rob a bank', and you were subsequently to act on this advice, I could not be held legally responsible for your act, nor could my act legitimately be made a separate crime. This remains true if I supplement my advice with a battery of arguments about why banks should be robbed or even about why a certain bank in particular should be robbed and why you in particular are entitled to rob it. It might become false—what I did might legitimately be made a crime—if certain further conditions held: for example, if you were a child, or so weak-minded as to be legally incompetent, and I knew this or ought to have known it; or if you were my subordinate in some organization and what I said to you was not advice but an order, backed by the discipline of the group; or if I went on to make further contributions to your act, such as aiding you in preparations or providing you with tools or giving you crucial information about the bank.

The explanation for these differences seems to me to be this. A person who acts on reasons he has acquired from another's act of expression acts on what *he* has come to believe and has judged to be a sufficient basis for action. The contribution to the genesis of his action made by the act of expression is, so to speak, superseded by the agent's own judgment. This is not true of the contribution made by an accomplice, or by a person who knowingly provides the agent with tools (the key to the bank) or with technical information (the combination of the safe) which he uses to achieve his ends. Nor would it be true of my contribution to your act if, instead of providing you with reasons for thinking bank robbery a good thing, I issued or-

ders or commands backed by threats, thus changing your circumstances so as to *make* it a (comparatively) good thing for you to do.

I will now state the principle of freedom of expression. . . . The principle, which seems to me to be a natural extension of the thesis Mill defends in Chapter II of *On Liberty*, and which I will therefore call the Millian Principle, is the following:

There are certain harms which, although they would not occur but for certain acts of expression, nonetheless cannot be taken as part of a justification for legal restrictions on these acts. These harms are: (a) harms to certain individuals which consist in their coming to have false beliefs as a result of those acts of expression; (b) harmful consequences of acts performed as a result of those acts of expression, where the connection between the acts of expression and the subsequent harmful acts consists merely in the fact that the act of expression led the agents to believe (or increased their tendency to believe) these acts to be worth performing.

■ ■ ■

I would like to believe that the general observance of the Millian Principle by governments would, in the long run, have more good consequences than bad. But my defense of the principle does not rest on this optimistic outlook. The Millian Principle, as a general principle about how governmental restrictions on the liberty of citizens may be justified, is a consequence of the view, coming down to us from Kant and others, that a legitimate government is one whose authority citizens can recognize while still regarding themselves as equal, autonomous, rational agents. Thus, while it is not a principle about legal responsibility, the Millian Principle has its origins in a certain view of human agency from which many of our ideas about responsibility also derive.

■ ■ ■

To regard himself as autonomous in the sense I have in mind a person must see himself as sovereign in deciding what to believe and in weighing competing reasons for action. He must apply to these tasks his own canons of rationality, and must recognize the need to defend his beliefs and decisions in accordance with these canons. . . . An autonomous person cannot accept without independent consideration the judgment of others as to what he should believe or what he should do. He may rely on the judgment of others, but when he does so he must be prepared to advance independent reasons for thinking their judgment likely to be correct, and to weigh the evidential value of their opinion against contrary evidence.

The requirements of autonomy as I have so far described them are extremely weak. They are much weaker than the requirements Kant draws from essentially the same notion, in that being autonomous in my sense (like being free in Hobbes's) is quite consistent with being subject to coercion with respect to one's actions. A coercer merely changes the considerations which militate for or against a certain course of action; weighing these conflicting considerations is still up to you.

An autonomous man may, if he believes the appropriate arguments, believe that the state has a distinctive right to command him. That is, he may believe that (within certain limits, perhaps) the fact that the law requires a certain action provides him with a very strong reason for performing that action, a reason which is quite independent of the consequences, for him or others, of his performing it or refraining. How strong this reason is—what, if anything, could override it—will depend on his view of the arguments for obedience to law. What is essential to the person's remaining autonomous is that in any given case his mere recognition that a certain action is required by law does not settle the question of whether he will do it. That question is settled only by his own decision, which may take into account his current assessment of the general case for obedience and the exceptions it admits, consideration of his other duties and obligations, and his estimate of the consequences of obedience and disobedience in this particular case.

Thus, while it is not obviously inconsistent with being autonomous to recognize a special obligation to obey the commands of the state, there are limits on the *kind* of obligation which autonomous citizens could recognize. In particular, they could not regard themselves as being under an "obligation" to believe the decrees of the state to be correct, nor could they concede to the state the right to have its decrees obeyed without deliberation. The Millian Principle can be seen as a refinement of these limitations.

The apparent irrationality of the doctrine of freedom of expression derives from its apparent conflict with the principle that it is the prerogative of a state—indeed, part of its duty to its citizens—to decide when the threat of certain harms is great enough to warrant legal action, and when it is, to make laws adequate to meet this threat. (Thus Holmes's famous reference to "substantive evils that Congress has a right to prevent.") Obviously this principle is not acceptable in the crude form in which I have just stated it; no one thinks that Congress can do *anything* it judges to be required to save us from "substantive evils." The Millian Principle specifies two ways in which this prerogative must be limited if the state is to be acceptable to autonomous subjects. The argument for the first part of the principle is as follows.

The harm of coming to have false beliefs is not one that an autonomous man could allow the state to protect him against through restrictions on expression. For a law to provide such protection it would have to be in effect and deterring potential misleaders while the potentially misled remained susceptible to persuasion by them. In order to be protected by such a law a person would thus have to concede to the state the right to decide that certain views were false and, once it had so decided, to prevent him from hearing them advocated even if he might wish to. The conflict between doing this and remaining autonomous would be direct if a person who authorized the state to protect him in this way necessarily also bound himself to accept the state's judgment about which views were false. . . .

The argument for the second half of the Millian Principle is parallel to this one. What must be argued against is the view that the state, once it has declared certain conduct to be illegal, may when necessary move to prevent that conduct by outlawing its advocacy. The conflict between this thesis and the autonomy of citizens is . . . slightly oblique. Conceding to the state the right to use this means to secure compliance with its laws does not immediately involve conceding to it the right to require citizens to believe that what the law says ought not to be done ought not to be done. Nonetheless it is a concession that autonomous citizens could not make, since it gives the state the right to deprive citizens of the grounds for arriving at an independent judgment as to whether the law should be obeyed.

These arguments both depend on the thesis that to defend a certain belief as reasonable a person must be prepared to defend the grounds of his belief as not obviously skewed or otherwise suspect. There is a clear parallel between this thesis and Mill's famous argument that if we are interested in having truth prevail we should allow all available arguments to be heard. But the present argument does not depend, as Mill's may appear to, on an empirical claim that the truth is in fact more likely to win out if free discussion is allowed. Nor does it depend on the perhaps more plausible claim that, given the nature of people and governments, to concede to government the power in question would be an outstandingly poor strategy for bringing about a situation in which true opinions prevail.

It is quite conceivable that a person who recognized in himself a fatal weakness for certain kinds of bad arguments might conclude that everyone would be better off if he were to rely entirely on the judgment of his friends in certain crucial matters. Acting on this conclusion, he might enter into an agreement, subject to periodic review by him, empowering them to shield him from any sources of information likely to divert him from their counsel on the matters in question. Such an agreement is not obviously irrational, nor, if it is entered into voluntarily, for a limited time, and on the basis of the person's own knowledge of himself and those he proposes to trust, does it appear to be inconsistent with his autonomy. The same would be true if the proposed trustees were in fact the authorities of the state. But the question we have been considering is quite different: Could an autonomous individual regard the state as having, not as part of a special voluntary agreement with him but as part of its normal powers qua state, the power to put such an arrangement into effect without his consent whenever *it* (i.e., the legislative authority) judged that to be advisable? The answer to this question seems to me to be quite clearly no.

■ ■ ■

The Millian Principle is obviously incapable of accounting for all of the cases that strike us as infringements of freedom of expression. On the basis of this principle alone we could raise no objection against a government that banned all parades or demonstrations (they interfere with traffic), outlawed posters and handbills (too messy), banned public meetings of more than ten people (likely to be unruly), and restricted newspaper publication to one page per week (to save trees). Yet such policies surely strike us as intolerable. That they so strike us is a reflection of our belief that free expression is a good which ranks above the maintenance of absolute peace and quiet, clean streets, smoothly flowing traffic, and rock-bottom taxes.

Thus there is a part of our intuitive view of freedom of expression which rests upon a balancing of competing goods. By contrast with the Millian Principle, which provides a single defense for all kinds of expression, here it does not seem to be a matter of the value to be placed on expression (in general) as opposed to other goods. The case seems to be different for, say, artistic expression than for the discussion of scientific matters, and different still for expression of political views.

Within certain limits, it seems clear that the value to be placed on having various kinds of expression flourish is something which should be subject to popular will in the society in question. The limits I have in mind here are, first, those imposed by considerations of distributive justice. Access to means of expression for whatever purposes one may have in mind is a good which can be fairly or unfairly distributed among the members of a society, and many cases which strike us as violations of freedom of expression are in fact instances of distributive injustice. This would be true of a case where, in an economically inegalitarian society, access to the principal means of expression was controlled by the government and auctioned off by it to the highest bidders, as is essentially the case with broadcasting licenses in the United States today....

QUESTIONS FOR DISCUSSION

1. Scanlon refers to his autonomy justification for freedom of speech as "Millian." Why does Scanlon think there is a right to free speech? How does Scanlon's account relate to Mill's?

2. Scanlon argues that the state should allow people to urge violation of the law. Why? What is the strongest argument against Scanlon's position about this?

3. Consider Scanlon's "nerve gas" example. Why does Scanlon think the distribution of the recipe can be prohibited? Is there an argument the other way? Should books explaining in detail various methods of suicide be restricted? The ways of processing heroin? The best way to sexually molest young children?

FREE SPEECH: A PHILOSOPHICAL ENQUIRY

FREDERICK SCHAUER

Stipulating that increased knowledge is a valuable end does not help to answer the central question—does granting a special liberty of discussion and communication aid us in reaching that end? Is the marketplace of ideas more likely to lead to knowledge than to error, ignorance, folly, or nonsense?

To many people this question answers itself. They assert that free and open discussion of ideas is the only rational way of achieving

Frederick Schauer, *Free Speech: A Philosophical Enquiry* (Cambridge: Cambridge University Press, 1982), selections from Chapters 2, 3, 4

knowledge, and they assume that the mere assertion of this proposition is proof of its truth. This is of course unsatisfactory. Without a causal link between free speech and increased knowledge the argument from truth must fail. Examining this link is the primary purpose of this chapter.

One way of avoiding the difficult task of establishing this connexion between discussion and knowledge is by *defining* truth in terms of the process of discussion; that is, define truth as that which survives the process of open discussion. Whatever is rejected after full, open enquiry is, by definition, false, wrong, or unwise. Whatever is agreed or accepted is, conversely, true, good, or sound. One might call this a consensus theory of truth. Under this theory there is no test of truth other than the *process* by which opinions are accepted or rejected.

When truth is defined in this way, the 'marketplace of ideas' metaphor is most apt, because the economic analogy is strongest. Under the purest theory of a free market economy the worth of goods is determined solely by the value placed on them by operation of the market. The value of an object is what it will fetch in a free market at leisurely sale. Similarly, the consensus or 'survival' theory of truth holds that truth is determined solely by the value that ideas or opinions are given in the intellectual marketplace. Under this view the results are defined by the process through which those results are produced. The goal is then not so much the search for knowledge as it is the search for rational thinking. Given this definition of truth, knowledge flows from rational thinking as a matter of logical necessity. The argument substitutes a tautology for the problematic causal link between discussion and knowledge. Since the result is defined by the process, it is the process and not the result that matters.

This is a consummate sceptical argument, and it is no surprise that its pardigmatic ex-

pression ('the best test of truth is the power of the thought to get itself accepted in the competition of the market') comes from Holmes, whose scepticism pervades all his writings. If we reject the possibility of attaining objective knowledge, and reject as unsatisfactory any method of discovering truth, defining truth as a process rather than a standard becomes compelling.

The survival theory of truth is alluringly uncomplicated; but as the basis for the principle of free speech it suffers from crippling weaknesses. Foremost among these weaknesses is that the argument begs the question. If truth is defined by reference to and in terms of a process, then why is the process of open discussion preferable to any other process, such as random selection or authoritarian fiat? Why is open discussion taken to be the only rational method of enquiry?

The survival theory, in refusing to acknowledge independent criteria for truth, provides no guidance for preferring one method of decision to any other. The survival theory does not purport to demonstrate *why* open discussion leads to knowledge, because it rejects any objective test of truth. Moreover, the survival theory does not tell us why open discussion leads to more desirable results of any kind. Thus the theory prompts us to ask why we should prefer rational thinking to any other form of thinking. But then the theory *defines* rationality as willingness to participate in open discussion and receptiveness to a variety of ideas. The survival theory thereby skirts the entire question by assuming open enquiry as valuable *a priori*. But we are still left with no criteria for evaluating whether this method of enquiry is better than any other. By taking open enquiry as sufficient *ex hypothesi*, the survival or consensus theory provides no assistance in answering the question of why free discussion should be preferred.

In his essay *On Liberty*, Mill suggests a version of the survival theory of truth in referring to the complete liberty to contradict a proposition as 'the very condition which justifies us in assuming its truth for purposes of action'. Perhaps rational assurance flows more easily from hearing opposing views. Perhaps freedom of contradiction is an important consideration in assuming the truth of any proposition. But that does not transform freedom to contradict into a sufficient condition, or even a necessary condition, for truth. We presuppose, at the very least, independent criteria of verifiability and falsifiability. Geoffrey Marshall has noted in response to Mill's argument that we should still have rational assurance 'that the Earth is roundish' even 'if the Flat Earth Society were an illegal organization'. In those circumstances we would certainly want to look closely at why the contrary view was banned, so as more carefully to scrutinize the received view. But the very fact of allowing the expression of the opposing opinion is not what provides us with our assurance about the shape of the Earth.

The consensus theory seems slightly less bizarre in the context of ethical rather than factual or scientific propositions. But even with respect to ethics, a consensus theory incorporates a strange and unacceptably extreme subjectivism. If we define moral truth as what in fact survives, then we are committed to saying that Nazism was 'right' in Germany in the 1930s, and that slavery was equally 'correct' or 'wise' in parts of the United States prior to the Civil War. Nor is it satisfactory to respond by saying that these were not fully open systems, and that only propositions arising out of open systems can properly be recognized as sound. If that were the case, then any prevailing American view on anything in the last thirty years would have been correct, because there has been virtually unlimited freedom of discussion in the United States during that time.

A form of subjectivism that defines truth solely in terms of the strength of an opinion in the marketplace of ideas is so totally at odds with the idea of truth embodied in our language of evaluation as to be virtually useless. A theory of majority rule for truth distorts out of all recognition our use of words like 'true', 'good', 'sound', or 'wise'. Subjectivism may argue for greater freedom of speech, but not in a way related to the argument from truth. I will return to this theme in later chapters, but we can confidently pass over the consensus theory here. Defining truth (and, in turn, knowledge) solely in terms of a process answers none of the important questions about free speech. If free speech is justified because it defines the process that produces knowledge, and if that knowledge is in turn defined by the very same process, we are saying nothing at all. It is entirely possible that the process of open discussion is the best way of arriving at knowledge. But this is the causal link that the survival theory of truth fails even to address.

■ ■ ■

Mill, Popper, and their followers have refined the argument from truth by explaining how knowledge is more likely to be gained in a society in which all views can be freely expressed. But they have still neglected the critical question—does truth, when articulated, make itself known? Does truth prevail when placed side-by-side with falsity? Does knowledge triumph over ignorance? Are unsound policies rejected when sound policies are presented? The question is whether the theory accurately portrays reality. It does not follow as a matter of logical entailment that truth will be accepted and falsehood rejected when both are heard. There must be some justification for assuming this to be an accurate description of the process, and such a justification is noticeably absent from all versions of the argument from truth. . . .

It is hardly surprising that the search for truth was so central in the writings of Milton, Locke, Voltaire, and Jefferson. They placed their faith in the ability of reason to solve problems and distinguish truth from falsehood. They had confidence in the reasoning power of *all* people, if only that power were allowed to flourish. The argument from truth is very much a child of the Enlightenment, and of the optimistic view of the rationality and perfectibility of humanity it embodied. But the naiveté of the Enlightenment has since been largely discredited by history and by contemporary insights of psychology. People are not nearly so rational as the Enlightenment assumed, and without this assumption the empirical support for the argument from truth evaporates. . . .

I do not mean to be taken as saying that falsity, ignorance, or evil have inherent power over truth, knowledge, or goodness. Rather, I mean only to deny the reverse—that truth has inherent ability to gain general acceptance. The argument from truth must demonstrate either that true statements have some intrinsic property that allows their truth to be universally apparent, or that empirical evidence supports the belief that truth will prevail when matched against falsehood. The absence of such a demonstration, in the face of numerous counter-examples, is the most prominent weakness of the argument from truth. History provides too many examples of falsity triumphant over truth to justify the assertion that truth will inevitably prevail. Mill noted that 'the dictum that truth always triumphs over persecution is one of those pleasant falsehoods which men repeat after one another till they pass into commonplaces, but which all experience refutes'. My point is that, *contra* Mill, the point would be the same if we removed the persecution and instead let truth battle with falsehood rather than the forces of oppression. Mill's assumption that the removal of persecution will allow truth to triumph in all cases is every bit as much a 'pleasant falsehood'.

■ ■ ■

The argument from democracy as understood today was most prominently articulated by Alexander Meiklejohn. Meiklejohn was much taken with the notion of self-government, and consequently was strongly influ-

enced by the institution of the town meeting, a form of government prevalent in small towns in New England. Under a town meeting form of government, all major decisions are taken by the entire adult population assembled together. It is self-government in the purest form. A key feature of the town meeting is that there are no government officials in the sense of political leaders; there is only a moderator whose sole function is to organize the meeting and enforce the rules of order. Members of the population propose ideas, debate those ideas, and then adopt or reject them by vote of all the people.

Meiklejohn saw all democracies as New England town meetings writ large. His thesis extended the ideal of popular sovereignty embodied in the town meeting to the larger and more complex republic. To Meiklejohn the size and complexity of the modern state did not diminish the theoretical absolute sovereignty of the populace. As final decision-making authority rests in the people who attend the town meeting, so does that same authority rest in the people who populate the more cumbersome modern state. As the essential feature of the town meeting is the open debate and public deliberation that precedes any decision, so also is open debate and public deliberation an intrinsic and indispensable feature of any society premised on the principle of self-government.

The argument from democracy is composed of two critical elements that support a principle of free speech. The first is the necessity of making all relevant information available to the sovereign electorate so that they, in the exercise of their sovereign powers, can decide which proposals to accept and which proposals to reject. Because the people are the ones who make the decisions, the people are the ones who need to receive all material information before making any decision. Although a restriction on the general liberty of the individual would not necessarily affect the democratic governmental process, a circumscription of speech would limit the information available to those making the decisions, impair the deliberative process, and thereby directly erode the mechanism of self-government. Because we cannot vote intelligently without full information, it is argued, denying access to that information is as serious an infringement of the fundamental tenets of democracy as would be denying the right to vote.

Second, freedom of speech is perceived as the necessary consequence of the truism that if the people as a whole are sovereign, then governmental officials must be servants rather than rulers. This in turn generates several more specific foundations for freedom of speech. It reminds us that, in a democracy, our leaders are in office to serve the wishes of the people. Freedom of speech is a way for the people to communicate those wishes to the government. . . .

The argument from democracy pivots on the particular conception of democracy from which it was spawned. The entire argument is generated by the single principle of a sovereign electorate. Paradoxically, the same concept of sovereignty that provides the foundation for the argument from democracy also exposes the argument's most prominent weaknesses.

If the people collectively are in fact the sovereign, and if that sovereign has the unlimited powers normally associated with sovereignty, then acceptance of this view of democracy compels acceptance of the power of the sovereign to restrict the liberty of speech just as that sovereign may restrict any other liberty. Moreover, there is no reason to say that the sovereign may not entrust certain individuals with certain powers. The power to delegate authority is implicit in the unlimited power that sovereignty connotes. But if the people may entrust Jones with the exclusive obligation and authority to round up all stray dogs, why may it not entrust Brown with the exclusive obligation and authority to determine truth or falsity, or to exercise a power of censorship over publications?

■ ■ ■

Treating freedom of speech as a primary good suggests that we should be looking not at freedom of speech but rather at freedom of *expression*. References to 'freedom of expression' are as common as references to 'freedom of speech'. 'Freedom of expression' is protected by the European Convention on Human Rights, and 'freedom of expression' is the term most commonly used in academic writing about the subject. 'Expression' avoids the strictly oral connotations of 'speech', and thus 'expression' may be preferable because it more clearly includes writing and pictures. Or, the preference may be explained solely by the fact that 'expression' is the longer word. But if 'expression' is anything more than a synonym for 'communication', a view of speech as expression must be derived chiefly from the naturalistic concepts that constitute the subject of this chapter. We must consider whether freedom of speech is something more than the freedom to communicate.

Much of the unfortunate confusion of freedom of speech with freedom of expression can be traced to the fact that 'expression' can have two quite different meanings, meanings that are often uncritically interchanged in this context.

First, 'expression' can mean communication, requiring both a communicator and a recipient of the communication. For example, if my new colour television set insists on presenting its offerings solely in black and white, it would be quite natural to say that I would *express* my dissatisfaction to the manager of the store where I bought the television set. If someone is a good public speaker, we may say that he *expresses* himself well. If someone's prose style is ambiguous and ungrammatical, we are likely to say that he cannot *express* himself in writing. In this sense the word 'expression' could easily be replaced by the word 'communication' without any significant change in meaning (except to the extent that to express oneself well in speaking or writing implies a certain elegance of style that is not suggested by the word 'communication').

On the other hand, the word 'expression' can also be used to describe certain activities not involving communication. This is the other meaning of 'expressing', or 'expressing oneself', a meaning that generates the locution 'self-expression'. For example, my reaction to the absence of colour on my new colour television set might be to throw a paperweight at the television screen. In that case I could be said to be *expressing* anger, or *expressing* hostility. I would be *expressing myself*, although there was no communication. 'Expression', on the one hand, can refer to communication, and, on the other hand, it can refer to any external manifestation of inner feeling. The existence of these two senses of the word 'expression' has created confusion about just what it is that freedom of speech is intended to protect.

The confusion is compounded because communicating, the first sense of 'expression', is one very important way of 'expressing oneself' in the second sense of 'expression'. Artists, poets and novelists, for example, are expressing themselves in the sense that they are doing something that is an extension of their emotions, and at the same time they are expressing their ideas and their emotions *to* viewers and readers. One who protested against the war in Vietnam by shouting obscene epithets at public officials might both have been expressing his own anger (which does not require a listener), and at the same time have been communicating a message of objection to government policy. Although in this book I am (I hope) expressing my ideas to the reader, I am also expressing myself in the second sense by choosing to write it. Moreover, I am expressing myself in this second sense by choosing to be an academic rather than a farmer, a postman, or a neurosurgeon, and by choosing to reside in Williamsburg rather than in Rangoon. Some choices, of course, are consequent upon (or derivative from) other choices and may therefore be less expressive or not expressive at all. My choice of residence may be a primary choice, in

which case it would be a form of expression, or it may on the other hand be the only place in which I can practise my chosen profession, in which case it would be derivative from a form of expression. I am not arguing that *every* intentional act is necessarily a form of expression (although that is not an implausible position), but only that the range of expressive activity is broad, and that 'expression' in this sense is very different from 'expression' in the communicative sense. The problem occurs when we try to separate these meanings of 'expression', and when we look at the relation of the two meanings to the principle of freedom of speech.

It is certainly possible to argue that a free speech principle is in fact a free expression principle, encompassing other forms of self-expression as well as communication. But if we look closely at this argument, we discover that there emerges no Free Speech Principle at all, because we must conclude that there is nothing special about speech. My mode of dress is usually a form of self-expression, as is the length of my hair and the style in which I wear it. Both my choice of occupation and residence are frequently ways of expressing myself. Choosing to drive a Ford or a Mini might not be an obvious form of self-expression, but choosing a Ferrari or an Hispano-Suiza most certainly is. If I have beaten this point beyond submission, it is only to emphasize that self-expression is an unworkably amorphous concept, subtracting far more than it adds to any sensible view of what free speech means.

Speech as communication is of course a method of self-expression, but the concept of self-expression is not helpful to an analysis of free speech. When speech is considered merely as one form of self-expression, nothing special is said about speech. Because virtually any activity may be a form of self-expression, a theory that does not isolate speech from this vast range of other conduct causes freedom of speech to collapse into a principle of general liberty. If the Free Speech Principle is derived from the value of self-expression, then any of the foregoing examples would be included within the Free Speech Principle. Any form of voluntary conduct may be to the actor a form of self-expression, and we are left with only a justification for a broad and undifferentiated principle of general liberty. Unless we can derive an argument for freedom of speech that is independent of the arguments for general personal freedom, there is little need to emphasize free speech. True, we might refer to free speech as a more concrete example of an abstract principle, but if that is all we are doing we have lost the special force of a Free Speech Principle. We might reject the existence of a Free Speech Principle, but accepting it is inconsistent with treating free speech merely as an instance of freedom of self-expression. If, as in the self-expression model, freedom of speech is coextensive with freedom of action, the state is no less constrained in dealing with speech than it is in dealing with any other form of human activity. In Robert Nozick's utopia this might be of little consequence, but existing states assert and exercise greater authority over the individual than Nozick would concede to be legitimate. Real states restrict action quite frequently, and often quite legitimately. If freedom of speech is freedom of self-expression, anyone who has conceded some of his freedom of action must, *pro tanto*, have conceded his freedom of speech. If there is an independent principle of free speech, this is an unnecessary concession.

QUESTIONS FOR DISCUSSION

1. What is the Argument from Truth? How does it relate to the "marketplace of ideas"? How does the marketplace of ideas relate to any other marketplace?

2. How does the Argument from Democracy relate to the Argument from Truth? What kinds of speech would be covered by the Argument from Democracy?

3. Does Schauer believe that self-expression should be protected? Do you? Why? Is this a free speech argument or a liberty argument? Why does it make a difference?

■ Case Study: Pornography

INTRODUCTION

A definitional preliminary—In considering the following materials on pornography and obscenity, it is important not to be confused by the definitions. The word "obscene" traditionally refers to something that is vile or disgusting, and need not refer to sex at all. The law of obscenity, however, is a body of law that has prohibited the distribution of highly sexually explicit materials, and has done so on the basis that the supporters of such laws consider those materials to be vile or disgusting. Obscenity law, therefore, is aimed at only a subset of what might be considered "obscene" in ordinary language, and is aimed at a subset that not all would agree deserves to be called "obscene." By contrast, the word "pornography," which in Greek means "the writing of harlots," refers traditionally to highly sexually explicit materials intended to produce sexual stimulation. More recently, however, the word "pornography" has taken on a different definition, and is often restricted, as it is in the subsequent Catharine MacKinnon reading, to highly sexually explicit material that promotes sexual violence against women. In considering the material that follows, try to avoid being misled by this confusing array of definitions.

PARIS ADULT THEATRE I V. SLATON

413 U.S. 49 (1973)

[EDITOR'S NOTE: This was a Georgia civil proceeding to enjoin the showing of two allegedly obscene films at two "adult" theaters. At a trial before a judge, the evidence consisted primarily of the films and of photographs of the entrance to the theaters. As described by the Chief Justice, these photographs "show a conventional, inoffensive theatre entrance, without any pictures, but with signs indicating that the theatres exhibit 'Atlanta's Finest Mature Feature Films.' On the door itself is a sign saying: 'Adult Theatre—You must be 21 and able to prove it. If viewing the nude body offends you, Please Do Not Enter.' (Two state investigators who saw the films testified that the signs did not indicate "the full nature of what was shown. In particular, nothing indicated that the films depicted—as they did—scenes of simulated fellatio, cunnilingus, and group sex intercourse.") The trial judge dismissed the complaint. He held the showing of obscene films permissible where there was "requisite notice to the public" and "reasonable protection against the exposure of these films to mi-

nors." The Georgia Supreme Court reversed, and the case went to the Supreme Court.]

■ ■ ■

Mr. Chief Justice BURGER delivered the opinion of the [Court].

We categorically disapprove the theory [that] obscene, pornographic films acquire constitutional immunity from state regulation simply because they are exhibited for consenting adults only. [Although] we have often pointedly recognized the high importance of the state interest in regulating the exposure of obscene materials to juveniles and unconsenting adults, this Court has never declared these to be the only legitimate state interests permitting regulation of obscene material. [In] particular, we hold that there are legitimate state interests at stake in stemming the tide of commercialized obscenity, even assuming it is feasible to enforce effective safeguards against exposure to juveniles and to passersby. [These] include the interest of the public in the quality of life and the total community environment, the tone of commerce in the great city centers, and, possibly, the public safety itself. The Hill–Link Minority Report of the Commission on Obscenity and Pornography indicates that there is at least an arguable correlation between obscene material and crime. Quite apart from sex crimes, however, there remains one problem of large proportions aptly described by Professor Bickel: "It concerns the tone of the society, the mode, or to use terms that have perhaps greater currency, the style and quality of life, now and in the future. A man may be entitled to read an obscene book in his room, or expose himself indecently there. [We] should protect his privacy. But if he demands a right to obtain the books and pictures he wants in the market, and to foregather in public places—discreet, if you will, but accessible to all—with others who share his tastes, *then to grant him his right is to affect the world about the rest of us, and to impinge on other privacies.* Even supposing that each of us can, if he wishes, effectively avert the eye and stop the ear (which, in truth, we cannot), what is commonly read and seen and heard and done intrudes upon us all, want it or not." As Mr. Chief Justice Warren stated, there is a "right of the Nation and of the States to maintain a decent society."

But, it is argued, there is no scientific data which conclusively demonstrate that exposure to obscene materials adversely affects men and women or their society. It is [urged] that, absent such a demonstration, any kind of state regulation is "impermissible." We reject this argument. It is not for us to resolve empirical uncertainties underlying state legislation, save in the exceptional case where that legislation plainly impinges upon rights protected by the Constitution itself. [Although] there is no conclusive proof of a connection between antisocial behavior and obscene material, the legislature of Georgia could quite reasonably determine that such a connection does or might exist. In deciding Roth, this Court implicitly accepted that a legislature could legitimately act on such a conclusion to protect *"the social interest in order and morality."*

From the beginning of civilized societies, legislators and judges have acted on various unprovable assumptions. If we accept the unprovable assumption that a complete education requires certain books and the well nigh universal belief that good books, plays, and art lift the spirit, improve the mind, enrich the human personality and develop character, can we then say that a state legislature may not act on the corollary assumption that commerce in obscene books, or public exhibitions focused on obscene conduct, have a tendency to exert a corrupting and debasing impact leading to antisocial behavior? [The sum of experience] affords an ample basis for legislatures to conclude that a sensitive, key relationship of human existence, central to family life, community welfare, and the development of human personality, can be debased and distorted by crass commercial exploitation of sex. Nothing in the Constitution prohibits a State from reaching such a conclusion and acting on it legislatively simply because there is no conclusive evidence or empirical [data].

It is asserted, however, that standards for evaluating state commercial regulations are inapposite in the present context, as state regulation of access by consenting adults to obscene material violates the constitutionally protected right to privacy enjoyed by petitioners' customers. [I]t is unavailing to compare a theater open to the public for a fee, with the private home of [Stanley] and the marital bedroom of [Griswold]. [Nothing] in this Court's decisions intimates that there is any "fundamental" privacy right "implicit in the concept of ordered liberty" to watch obscene movies in places of public accommodation. [The] idea of a "privacy" right and a place of public accommodation are, in this context, mutually exclusive. Conduct or depictions of conduct that the state police power can prohibit on a public street do not become automatically protected by the Constitution merely because the conduct is moved to a bar or a "live" theatre stage, any more than a "live" performance of a man and woman locked in a sexual embrace at high noon in Times Square is protected by the Constitution because they simultaneously engage in a valid political dialogue. [We also] reject the claim that [Georgia] is here attempting to control the minds or thoughts of those who patronize theaters. [Where] communication of ideas, protected by the First Amendment, is not involved, or the particular privacy of the home protected by Stanley, or any of the other "areas or zones" of constitutionally protected privacy, the mere fact that, as a consequence, some human "utterances" or "thoughts" may be incidentally affected does not bar the State from acting to protect legitimate state interests. [Finally, for] us to say that our Constitution incorporates the proposition that conduct involving consenting adults only is always beyond state regulation, is a step we are unable to take. [We] hold that the States have a legitimate interest in regulating commerce in obscene material and in regulating exhibition of obscene material in places of public accommodation, including so-called "adult" theaters from which minors are [excluded].

Vacated and remanded.

Mr. Justice BRENNAN, with whom Mr. Justice STEWART and Mr. Justice MARSHALL join, dissenting.

[I] am convinced that the approach initiated 16 years ago in [Roth], and culminating in the Court's decision today, cannot bring stability to this area of the law without jeopardizing fundamental First Amendment values, and I have concluded that the time has come to make a significant departure from that approach. [The] essence of our problem in the obscenity area is that we have been unable to provide "sensitive tools" to separate obscenity from other sexually oriented but constitutionally protected speech, so that efforts to suppress the former do not spill over into the

suppression of the latter. [I] am reluctantly forced to the conclusion that none of the available formulas, including the one announced today, can reduce the vagueness [of our obscenity standards] to a tolerable level. The vagueness of the standards in the obscenity area produces a number of separate problems, [including a] lack of fair notice, [a] chill on protected expression, and [a severe] stress [on] the state and federal judicial machinery.

In short, while I cannot say that the interest of the State—apart from the question of juveniles and unconsenting adults—are trivial or nonexistent, I am compelled to conclude that these interests cannot justify the substantial damage to constitutional rights and to this Nation's judicial machinery that inevitably results from state efforts to bar the distribution even of unprotected material to consenting adults. I would hold, therefore, that at least in the absence of distribution to juveniles or obtrusive exposure to unconsenting adults, the [First Amendment prohibits governments] from attempting wholly to suppress sexually oriented materials on the basis of their allegedly "obscene" contents. Nothing in this approach precludes [governments] from taking action to serve what may be strong and legitimate interests through regulation of the manner of distribution of sexually oriented material. [I] do not pretend to have found a complete and infallible [answer]. Difficult questions must still be faced, notably in the areas of distribution to juveniles and offensive exposure to unconsenting adults. Whatever the extent of state power to regulate in those areas, it should be clear that the view I espouse today would introduce a large measure of clarity to this troubled area, would reduce the institutional pressure on this Court and the rest of the State and Federal Judiciary, and would guarantee fuller freedom of expression while leaving room for the protection of legitimate governmental [interests].

PORNOGRAPHY, CIVIL RIGHTS, AND "SPEECH"

CATHARINE MACKINNON

In pornography, there it is, in one place, all of the abuses that women had to struggle so long even to begin to articulate, all the *unspeakable* abuse: the rape, the battery, the sexual harassment, the prostitution, and the sexual abuse of children. Only in the pornography it is called something else: sex, sex, sex, sex, and sex, respectively. Pornography sexualizes rape, battery, sexual harassment, prostitution, and child sexual abuse; it thereby celebrates, promotes, authorizes, and legitimizes them. More generally, it eroticizes the dominance and submission that is the dynamic common to them all. It makes hierarchy sexy and calls that "the truth about sex" or just a mirror of reality. Through this process, pornography constructs what a woman is as what men want from sex. This is what the pornography means.

■ ■ ■

Pornography constructs what a woman is in terms of its view of what men want sexually, such that acts of rape, battery, sexual harassment, prostitution, and sexual abuse of children become acts of sexual equality. Pornography's world of equality is a harmonious and balanced place. Men and women are perfectly complementary and perfectly bipolar. Women's desire to be fucked by men is equal to men's desire to fuck women. All the ways men love to take and violate women, women love to be taken and violated. The women who most love this are most men's equals, the most liberated; the most participatory child is the most grown-up, the most

equal to an adult. Their consent merely expresses or ratifies these preexisting facts.

The content of pornography is one thing. There, women substantively desire dispossession and cruelty. We desperately want to be bound, battered, tortured, humiliated, and killed. Or, to be fair to the soft core, merely taken and used. This is erotic to the male point of view. Subjection itself with self-determination ecstatically relinquished is the content of women's sexual desire and desirability. Women are there to be violated and possessed, men to violate and possess us either on screen or by camera or pen on behalf of the consumer. On a simple descriptive level, the inequality of hierarchy, of which gender is the primary one, seems necessary for the sexual arousal to work. Other added inequalities identify various pornographic genres or sub-themes, although they are always added through gender: age, disability, homosexuality, animals, objects, race (including anti-semitism), and so on. Gender is never irrelevant.

What pornography *does* goes beyond its content: It eroticizes hierarchy, it sexualizes inequality. It makes dominance and submission sex. Inequality is its central dynamic; the illusion of freedom coming together with the reality of force is central to its working. Perhaps because this is a bourgeois culture, the victim must look free, appear to be freely acting. Choice is how she got there. Willing is what she is when she is being equal. It seems

Catharine MacKinnon, "Pornography, Civil Rights, and 'Speech'," *Harvard Civil Rights—Civil Liberties Law Review*, vol. 20 (1985), pp. 1 ff., and Catharine MacKinnon, *Feminism Unmodified: Discourses on Life and Law* (Cambridge: Harvard University Press, 1987), pp. 163 ff.

equally important that then and there she actually be forced and that forcing be communicated on some level, even if only through still photos of her in postures of receptivity and access, available for penetration. Pornography in this view is a form of forced sex, a practice of sexual politics, an institution of gender inequality.

From this perspective, pornography is neither harmless fantasy nor a corrupt and confused misrepresentation of an otherwise natural and healthy sexual situation. It institutionalizes the sexuality of male supremacy, fusing the erotization of dominance and submission with the social construction of male and female. To the extent that gender is sexual, pornography is part of constituting the meaning of that sexuality. Men treat women as who they see women as being. Pornography constructs who that is. Men's power over women means that the way men see women defines who women can be. Pornography is that way. Pornography is not imagery in some relation to a reality elsewhere constructed. It is not a distortion, reflection, projection, expression, fantasy, representation, or symbol either. It is a sexual reality.

■ ■ ■

In this approach, the experience of the (overwhelmingly) male audiences who consume pornography is therefore not fantasy or simulation or catharsis but sexual reality, the level of reality on which sex itself largely operates. Understanding this dimension of the problem does not require noticing that pornography models are real women to whom, in most cases, something real is being done; nor does it even require inquiring into the systematic infliction of pornography and its sexuality upon women, although it helps. The way in which the pornography itself provides what those who consume it want matters. Pornography *participates* in its audience's eroticism through creating an accessible sexual object, the possession and consumption of which *is* male sexuality, as socially constructed; to be

consumed and possessed as which, *is* female sexuality, as socially constructed; and pornography is a process that constructs it that way.

The object world is constructed according to how it looks with respect to its possible uses. Pornography defines women by how we look according to how we can be sexually used. Pornography codes how to look at women, so you know what you can do with one when you see one. Gender is an assignment made visually, both originally and in everyday life. A sex object is defined on the basis of its looks, in terms of its usability for sexual pleasure, such that both the looking—the quality of the gaze, including its point of view—and the definition according to use become eroticized as part of the sex itself. This is what the feminist concept "sex object" means. In this sense, sex in life is no less mediated than it is in art. One could say men have sex with *their image* of a woman. It is not that life and art imitate each other; in this sexuality, they *are* each other.

To give a set of rough epistemological translations, to defend pornography as consistent with the equality of the sexes is to defend the subordination of women to men as sexual equality. What in the pornographic view is love and romance looks a great deal like hatred and torture to the feminist. Pleasure and eroticism become violation. Desire appears as lust for dominance and submission. The vulnerability of women's projected sexual availability, that acting we are allowed (i.e. asking to be acted upon), is victimization. Play conforms to scripted roles. Fantasy expresses ideology, *is* not exempt from it. Admiration of natural physical beauty becomes objectification. Harmlessness becomes harm. Pornography is a harm of male supremacy made difficult to see because of its pervasiveness, potency, and, principally, because of its success in making the world a pornographic place. Specifically, its harm cannot be discerned, and will not be addressed, if viewed and approached neutrally, because it *is* so much of "what is." In other words, to the extent pornography succeeds in constructing social reality, it becomes invisible as harm. If we live in a world that pornography creates through the power of men in a male dominated situation the issue is not what the harm of pornography is, but how that harm is to become visible.

■ ■ ■

Obscenity, in this light, is a moral idea; an idea about judgments of good and bad. Pornography, by contrast, is a political practice, a practice of power and powerlessness. Obscenity is ideational and abstract; pornography is concrete and substantive. The two concepts represent two entirely different things. Nudity, excess of candor, arousal or excitement, prurient appeal, illegality of the act depicted, and unnaturalness or perversion are all qualities that bother obscenity law when sex is depicted or portrayed. Sex forced on real women so that it can be sold at a profit to be forced on other real women; women's bodies trussed and maimed and raped and made into things to be hurt and obtained and accessed and this presented as the nature of women in a way that is acted on and acted out over and over; the coercion that is visible and the coercion that has become invisible—this and more bothers feminists about pornography. Obscenity as such probably does little harm. Pornography is integral to attitudes and behaviors of violence and discrimination which define the treatment and status of half the population.

■ ■ ■

At the request of the city of Minneapolis, Andrea Dworkin and I conceived and designed a local human rights ordinance in accordance with our approach to the pornography issue. We define pornography as a practice of sex discrimination, a violation of women's civil rights, the opposite of sexual equality. Its point is to hold accountable, to those who are injured, those who profit from and benefit from that injury. It means that women's injury—our damage, our pain, our enforced inferiority—

should outweigh their pleasure and their profits, or sex equality is meaningless.

We define pornography as the graphic sexually explicit subordination of women through pictures or words that also includes women dehumanized as sexual objects, things, or commodities, enjoying pain or humiliation or rape, being tied up, cut up, mutilated, bruised, or physically hurt, in postures of sexual submission or servility or display, reduced to body parts, penetrated by objects or animals, or presented in scenarios of degradation, injury, torture, shown as filthy or inferior, bleeding, bruised, or hurt in a context that makes these conditions sexual. Erotica, defined by distinction as not this, might be sexually explicit materials premised on equality. We also provide that the use of men, children or transsexuals in the place of women is pornography. The definition is substantive in that it is sex-specific, but it covers everyone in a sex-specific way, so is gender neutral in overall design.

To define pornography as a practice of sex discrimination combines a mode of portrayal that has a legal history—the sexually explicit—with an active term central to the inequality of the sexes—subordination. Among other things, subordination means to be placed in a position of inferiority or loss of power, or to be demeaned or denigrated. To be someone's subordinate is the opposite of being their equal. The definition does not include all sexually explicit depictions *of* the subordination of women. That is not what it says. It says, this which *does* that: the sexually explicit which subordinates women. To these active terms to capture what the pornography *does*, the definition adds a list of what it must also contain. This list, from our analysis, is an exhaustive description of what must be in the pornography for it to do what it does behaviorally. Each item in the definition is supported by experimental, testimonial, social, and clinical evidence. We made a legislative choice to be exhaustive and specific and concrete rather than conceptual and general, to minimize problems of chilling effect, making it hard to guess wrong, thus making self-censor-ship less likely, but encouraging (to use a phrase from discrimination law) voluntary compliance, knowing that if something turns up that is not on the list, the law will not be expansively interpreted.

■ ■ ■

Although police have known it for years, reported cases are increasingly noting the causal role of pornography in some sexual abuse. In a recent Minnesota case, a fourteen-year-old girl on a bicycle was stopped with a knife and forced into a car. Her hands were tied with a belt, she was pushed to the floor and covered with a blanket. The knife was then used to cut off her clothes, and fingers and a knife were inserted into her vagina. Then the man had her dress, drove her to a gravel pit, ordered her to stick a safety pin into the nipple of her left breast, and forced her to ask him to hit her. After hitting her, he forced her to commit fellatio and to submit to anal penetration, and made her use a cigarette to burn herself on her breast and near her pubic area. Then he defecated and urinated on her face, forced her to ingest some of the excrement and urine and made her urinate into a cup and drink it. He took a string from her blouse and choked her to the point of unconsciousness, leaving burn marks on her neck, and after cutting her with his knife in a couple of places, drove her back to where he had gotten her and let her go. The books that were found with this man were: *Violent Stories of Kinky Humiliation, Violent Stories of Dominance and Submission*—you think feminists made up these words?—*Bizarre Sex Crimes, Shamed Victims*, and *Water Sports Fetish, Enemas and Golden Showers*. The Minnesota Supreme Court said "It appears that in committing these various acts, the defendant was giving life to some stories he had read in various pornographic books."

■ ■ ■

Now I'm going to talk about causality in its narrowest sense. Recent experimental research on pornography shows that the materials cov-ered by our definition cause measurable harm to women through increasing men's attitudes and behaviors of discrimination in both violent and nonviolent forms. Exposure to some of the pornography in our definition increases normal men's immediately subsequent willingness to aggress against women under laboratory conditions. It makes normal men more closely resemble convicted rapists attitudinally, although as a group they don't look all that different from them to start with. It also significantly increases attitudinal measures known to correlate with rape and self-reports of aggressive acts, measures such as hostility toward women, propensity to rape, condoning rape, and predicting that one would rape or force sex on a woman if one knew one would not get caught. This latter measure, by the way, begins with rape at about a third of all men and moves to half with "forced sex."

■ ■ ■

For those of you who still think pornography is only an idea, consider the possibility that obscenity law got one thing right. Pornography is more act-like than thought-like. The fact that pornography, in a feminist view, furthers the idea of the sexual inferiority of women, which is a political idea, doesn't make the pornography itself into a political idea. One can express the idea a practice embodies. That does not make that practice into an idea. Segregation expresses the idea of the inferiority of one group to another on the basis of race. That does not make segregation an idea. A sign that says "Whites Only" is only words. Is it therefore protected by the first amendment? Is it not an act, a practice, of segregation because of the inseparability of what it means from what it does? *Law* is only words.

The issue here is whether the fact that the central link in the cycle of abuse that *I* have connected is words and pictures will immunize that entire cycle, about which we cannot do anything without doing something about the pornography.

AMERICAN BOOKSELLERS ASSOCIATION, INC. V. HUDNUT

771 F.2d 323 (7th Cir. 1985)

EASTERBROOK, Circuit Judge [for the court]

Indianapolis enacted an ordinance defining "pornography" as a practice that discriminates against women. "Pornography" is to be redressed through the administrative and judicial methods used for other discrimination. The City's definition of "pornography" is considerably different from "obscenity," which the Supreme Court has held is not protected by the First Amendment.

["Pornography"] under the ordinance is "the graphic sexually explicit subordination of women, whether in pictures or in words, that also includes one or more of the following:

(1) Women are presented as sexual objects who enjoy pain or humiliation; or

(2) Women are presented as sexual objects who experience sexual pleasure in being raped; or

(3) Women are presented as sexual objects tied up or cut up or mutilated or bruised or physically hurt, or as dismembered or truncated or fragmented or severed into body parts; or

(4) Women are presented as being penetrated by objects or animals; or

(5) Women are presented in scenarios of degradation, injury, abasement, torture, shown as filthy or inferior, bleeding, bruised, or hurt in a context that makes these conditions sexual; or

(6) Women are presented as sexual objects for domination, conquest, violation, exploitation, possession, or use, or through postures or positions of servility or submission or display."

Indianapolis Code § 16-3(q). The statute provides that the "use of men, children, or transsexuals in the place of women in paragraphs (1) through (6) above shall also constitute pornography under this section." The ordinance as passed in April 1984 defined "sexually explicit" to mean actual or simulated intercourse or the uncovered exhibition of the genitals, buttocks or anus. An amendment in June 1984 deleted this provision, leaving the term undefined.

[We] do not try to balance the arguments for and against an ordinance such as this. The ordinance discriminates on the ground of the content of the speech. Speech treating women in the approved way—in sexual encounters "premised on equality"—is lawful no matter how sexually explicit. Speech treating women in the disapproved way—as submissive in matters sexual or as enjoying humiliation—is unlawful no matter how significant the literary, artistic, or political qualities of the work taken as a whole. The state may not ordain preferred viewpoints in this way. The Constitution forbids the state to declare one perspective right and silence opponents. [Under] the First Amendment the government must leave to the people the evaluation of ideas. Bald or subtle, an idea is as powerful as the audience allows it to be. A belief may be pernicious—the beliefs of Nazis led to the death of millions, those of the Klan to the repression of millions. A pernicious belief may prevail. Totalitarian governments today rule much of the planet, practicing suppression of billions and spreading dogma that may enslave others. One of the things that separates our society from theirs is our absolute right to propagate opinions that the government finds wrong or even hateful.

The ideas of the Klan may be propagated. Communists may speak freely and run for office. The Nazi Party may march through a city with a large Jewish population. People may criticize the President by misrepresenting his positions, and they have a right to post their misrepresentations on public property. People may teach religions that others despise. People may seek to repeal laws guaranteeing equal opportunity in employment or to revoke the constitutional amendments granting the vote to blacks and women. They may do this because "above all else, the First Amendment means that government has no power to restrict expression because of its message [or] its ideas. . . ." Police Department v. Mosley.

Under the ordinance graphic sexually explicit speech is "pornography" or not depending on the perspective the author adopts. Speech that "subordinates" women and also, for example, presents women as enjoying pain, humiliation, or rape, or even simply presents women in "positions of servility or submission or display" is forbidden, no matter how great the literary or political value of the work taken as a whole. Speech that portrays women in positions of equality is lawful, no matter how graphic the sexual content. This is thought control. It establishes an "approved" view of women, of how they may react to sexual encounters, of how the sexes may relate to each other. Those who espouse the approved view may use sexual images; those who do not, may not.

Indianapolis justifies the ordinance on the ground that pornography affects thoughts. Men who see women depicted as subordinate are more likely to treat them so. Pornography is an aspect of dominance. It does not persuade people so much as change them. It works by socializing, by establishing the expected and the permissible. In this view pornography is not an idea; pornography is the injury.

There is much to this perspective. Beliefs are also facts. People often act in accordance with the images and patterns they find around them. People raised in a religion tend to accept the tenet of that religion, often without independent examination. People taught from birth that black people are fit only for slavery rarely rebelled against that creed; beliefs coupled with the self-interest of the masters established a social structure that inflicted great harm while enduring for centuries. Words and images act at the level of the subconscious before they persuade at the level of the conscious. Even the truth has little chance unless a statement fits within the framework of beliefs that may never have been subjected to rational study.

Therefore we accept the premises of this legislation. Depictions of subordination tend to perpetuate subordination. The subordinate status of women in turn leads to affront and lower pay at work, insult and injury at home, battery and rape on the streets.* In the language of the legislature, "[p]ornography is central in creating and maintaining sex as a basis of discrimination. Pornography is a systematic practice of exploitation and subordination based on sex which differentially harms women. The bigotry and contempt it produces, with the acts of aggression it fosters, harm women's opportunities for equality and rights [of all kinds]."

Yet this simply demonstrates the power of pornography as speech. All of these unhappy effects depend on mental intermediation. Pornography affects how people see the world, their fellows, and social relations. If pornography is what pornography does, so is other speech. Hitler's orations affected how some Germans saw Jews. Communism is a world view, not simply a *Manifesto* by Marx and Engels or a set of speeches. Efforts to suppress communist speech in the United States were based on the belief that the public acceptability of such ideas would increase the likelihood of totalitarian government. [Many] people believe that the existence of television, apart from the content of specific programs, leads to intellectual laziness, to a penchant for violence, to many other ills. The Alien and Sedition Acts passed during the administration of John Adams rested on a sincerely held belief that disrespect for the government leads to social collapse and revolution—a belief with support in the history of many nations. Most governments of the world act on this empirical regularity, suppressing critical speech. In the United States, however, the strength of the support for this belief is irrelevant. Seditious libel is protected speech unless the danger is not only grave but also imminent.

Racial bigotry, anti-semitism, violence on television, reporters' biases—these and many more influence the culture and shape our socialization. None is directly answerable by more speech, unless that speech too finds its place in the popular culture. Yet all is protected as speech, however insidious. Any other answer leaves the government in control of all of the institutions of culture, the great censor and director of which thoughts are good for us.

Sexual responses often are unthinking responses, and the association of sexual arousal with the subordination of women therefore may have a substantial effect. But almost all cultural stimuli provoke unconscious responses. Religious ceremonies condition their participants. Teachers convey messages by selecting what not to cover; the implicit message about what is off limits or unthinkable may be more powerful than the messages for which they present rational argument. Television scripts contain unarticulated assumptions. People may be conditioned in subtle ways. If the fact that speech plays a role in a process of conditioning were enough to permit governmental regulation, that would be the end of freedom of speech.

It is possible to interpret the claim that the pornography is the harm in a different way. Indianapolis emphasizes the injury that models in pornographic films and pictures may suffer. The record contains materials depicting sexual torture, penetration of women by red–hot irons and the like. These concerns have nothing to do with written materials subject to the statute, and physical injury can occur with or without the "subordination" of women. As we discuss in Part IV [omitted here], a state may make injury in the course of producing a film unlawful independent of the viewpoint expressed in the film.

The more immediate point, however, is that the image of pain is not necessarily pain. In *Body Double*, a suspense film directed by Brian DePalma, a woman who has disrobed and presented a sexually explicit display is murdered by an intruder with a drill. The drill runs through the woman's body. The film is sexually explicit and a murder occurs—yet no one believes that the actress suffered pain or died. In *Barbarella* a character played by Jane Fonda is at times displayed in sexually explicit ways and at times shown "bleeding, bruised, [and] hurt in a context that makes these conditions sexual"—and again no one believes that Fonda was actually tortured to make the film. In *Carnal Knowledge* a woman grovels to please the sexual whims of a character played by Jack Nicholson; no one believes that there was a real sexual submission, and the Supreme Court held the film protected by the First Amendment. And this works both ways. The description of women's sexual domination of men in *Lysistrata* was not real dominance. Depictions may affect slavery, war, or sexual roles, but a book about slavery is not itself slavery, or a book about death by poison a murder.

Much of Indianapolis's argument rests on the belief that when speech is "unanswerable," and the metaphor that there is a "marketplace of ideas" does not apply, the First Amendment does not apply either. The metaphor is honored; Milton's *Aeropagitica* and John Stuart Mill's *On Liberty* defend freedom of speech on the ground that the truth will prevail, and many of the most important cases under the First Amendment recite this position. The Framers undoubtedly believed it. As a general matter it is true. But the Constitution does not make the dominance of truth a necessary condition of freedom of speech. To say that it does would be to confuse an outcome of free speech with a necessary condition for the application of the amendment.

A power to limit speech on the ground that truth has not yet prevailed and is not likely to prevail implies the power to declare truth. At some point the government must be able to say (as Indianapolis has said): "We know what the truth is, yet a free exchange of speech has not driven out falsity, so that we must now prohibit falsity." If the government may declare the truth, why wait for the failure of speech? Under the First Amendment, however, there is no such thing as a false idea, Gertz v. Robert Welch, Inc., 418 U.S. 323 (1974), so the government may not restrict speech on the ground that in a free exchange truth is not yet dominant.

At any time, some speech is ahead in the game; the more numerous speakers prevail. Supporters of minority candidates may be forever "excluded" from the political process because their candidates never win, because few people believe their positions. This does not mean that freedom of speech has failed. . . .

[The] definition of "pornography" is unconstitutional. [No] amount of struggle with particular words and phrases in this ordinance can leave anything in effect. The district court came to the same conclusion. Its judgment is therefore [Affirmed.]

NOTE

*[In] saying that we accept the finding that pornography as the ordinance defines it leads to unhappy consequences, we mean only that there is evidence to this effect, that this evidence is consistent with much human experience, and that as judges we must accept the legislative resolution of such disputed empirical questions. . . . [Footnote by Judge Easterbrook.]

WOMEN AND PORNOGRAPHY

RONALD DWORKIN

People once defended free speech to protect the rights of firebrands attacking government, or dissenters resisting an established church, or radicals campaigning for unpopular political causes. Free speech was plainly worth fighting for, and it still is in many parts of the world where these rights hardly exist. But in America now, free-speech partisans find themselves defending mainly racists shouting "nigger" or Nazis carrying swastikas or—most often—men looking at pictures of naked women with their legs spread open.

Conservatives have fought to outlaw pornography in the United States for a long time: for decades the Supreme Court has tried, though without much success, to define a limited category of "obscenity" that the Constitution allows to be banned. But the campaign for outlawing all forms of pornography has been given new and fiercer form, in recent years, by

Ronald Dworkin, "Women and Pornography," *The New York Review of Books,* October 21, 1993, p. 26 ff.

the feminist movement. It might seem odd that feminists have devoted such energy to that campaign: other issues, including abortion and the fight for women's equality in employment and politics, seem so much more important. No doubt mass culture is in various ways an obstacle to sexual equality, but the most popular forms of that culture—the view of women presented in soap operas and commercials, for example—are much greater obstacles to that equality than the dirty films watched by a small minority.

But feminists' concentration on pornography nevertheless seems easy to explain. Pornographic photographs, films, and videos are the starkest possible expression of the idea feminists most loathe: that women exist principally to provide sexual service to men. Advertisements, soap operas, and popular fiction may actually do more to spread that idea in our culture, but pornography is the rawest, most explicit symbol of it. Like swastikas and burning crosses, pornography is deeply offensive in itself, whether or not it causes any other injustice or harm. It is also particularly vulnerable politically: the religious right supports feminists on this issue, though on few others, so feminists have a much greater chance to win political campaigns for censorship than any of the other campaigns they fight.

And pornography seems vulnerable on principle as well. The conventional explanation of why freedom of speech is important is Mill's theory that truth is most likely to emerge from a "marketplace" of ideas freely exchanged and debated. But most pornography makes no contribution at all to political or intellectual debate: it is preposterous to think that we are more likely to reach truth about anything at all because pornographic videos are available. So liberals defending a right to pornography find themselves triply on the defensive: their view is politically weak, deeply offensive to many women, and intellectually doubtful. Why, then should we defend pornography? Why should

we care if people can no longer watch films of people copulating for the camera, or of women being whipped and enjoying it? What would we lose, except a repellent industry?

In the most interesting parts of *Only Words*, [Catharine] MacKinnon offers a new argument that is [designed] to transcend mere repulsion. She says that the way in which pornography is offensive—that it portrays women as submissive victims who enjoy torture and mutilation—contributes to the unequal opportunities of women in American society, and therefore contradicts the values meant to be protected by the equal protection clause. She concedes, for the sake of this argument, that in spite of its minimal contribution to intellectual or political debate, pornography is protected under the First Amendment. But that First Amendment protection must be balanced, she says, against the Fourteenth Amendment's requirement that people be treated equally. "The law of equality and the law of freedom of speech are on a collision course in this country," she says, and she argues that the balance, which has swung too far toward liberty, must now be redressed.

The censorship of pornography, she says, should be regarded as like other kinds of government action designed to create genuine equality of opportunity. It is now accepted by almost everyone that government may properly prohibit discrimination against blacks and women in employment and education, for example. But such discrimination may take the form, not merely of refusing them jobs or university places, but of subjecting those who do manage to find jobs or places to an environment of insult and prejudice that makes work or education less attractive or even impossible. Government prohibits racial or sexual harassment at work—it punishes employers who subject blacks to racial insult or women to sexual pressures, in spite of the fact that these objectionable practices are carried out through speech—and many universities have adopted "speech codes" that prohibit racial insults in classrooms or on campus.

Banning or punishing pornography, MacKinnon suggests, should be regarded as a more general remedy of the same kind. If pornography contributes to the general subordination of women by picturing them as sexual or servile objects, as she believes it does, then eliminating pornography can also be defended as serving equality of opportunity even though it restricts liberty. The "egalitarian" argument for censorship is in many ways like the "silencing" argument [the argument that the presence of pornography diminishes speech by silencing the speech of women] I described earlier: it supposes not that pornography significantly increases sexual crimes of violence, but that it works more insidiously to damage the standing and power of women within the community. But the "egalitarian" argument is in two ways different and apparently more cogent.

First, it claims not a new and paradoxical conflict within the idea of liberty, as the silencing argument does, but a conflict between liberty and equality, two ideals that many political philosophers think are often in conflict. Second, it is more limited in its scope. The "silencing" argument supposes that everyone—the bigot and the creationist as well the social reformer—has a right to whatever respectful attention on the part of others is necessary to encourage him to speak his mind and to guarantee that he will be correctly understood; and that is absurd. The "egalitarian" argument, on the contrary, supposes only that certain groups—those that are victims of persisting disadvantage in our society—should not be subject to the kind of insult, harassment, or abuse that has contributed to that disadvantage.

But the "egalitarian" argument is nevertheless much broader and more dangerous in its scope than might first appear. The analogies MacKinnon proposes—to sexual harassment laws and university speech codes—are revealing, because though each of these forms of reg-

ulation might be said to serve a general egalitarian purpose, they are usually defended on much more limited and special grounds. Laws against sexual harassment are designed to protect women not from the diffuse effects of whatever derogatory opinions about them are part of the general culture, but from direct sexual taunts and other degrading language in the workplace. University speech codes are defended on a different ground: they are said to serve an educational purpose by preserving the calm and reflective atmosphere of mutual respect and of appreciation for a diversity of cultures and opinions that is essential for effective teaching and research.

I do not mean that such regulations raise no problems about free speech. They do. Even if university speech codes, for example, are enforced fairly and scrupulously (and in the charged atmosphere of university politics they often are not) they sometimes force teachers and students to compromise or suppress their opinions by erring on the side of safety, and some speech codes may actually be unconstitutional. I mean only that constraints on speech at work and on the campus can be defended without appealing to the frightening principle that considerations of equality require that some people not be free to express their tastes or convictions or preferences anywhere. MacKinnon's argument for banning pornography from the community as a whole does presuppose this principle, however, and accepting her argument would therefore have devastating consequences.

Government could then forbid the graphic or visceral or emotionally charged expression of any opinion or conviction that might reasonably offend a disadvantaged group. It could outlaw performances of *The Merchant of Venice*, or films about professional women who neglect their children, or caricatures or parodies of homosexuals in nightclub routines. Courts would have to balance the value of such expression, as a contribution to public debate or learning, against the damage it might cause to the standing or sensibilities of its targets. MacKinnon thinks that pornography is different from other forms of discriminatory or hostile speech. But the argument she makes for banning it would apply to much else. She pointedly declares that freedom of speech is respected too much by Americans and that the Supreme Court was right in 1952 when it sustained a prosecution of anti-Semitic literature—a decision it has since abandoned—and wrong in 1978 when it struck down an ordinance banning a Nazi march in Illinois.

So if we must make the choice between liberty and equality that MacKinnon envisages—if the two constitutional values really are on a collision course—we should have to choose liberty because the alternative would be the despotism of thought-police.

But is she right that the two values do conflict in this way? Can we escape despotism only by cheating on the equality the Constitution also guarantees? The most fundamental egalitarian command of the Constitution is for equality throughout the political process. We can imagine some compromises of political equality that would plainly aid disadvantaged groups—it would undoubtedly aid blacks and women, for example, if citizens who have repeatedly expressed racist or sexist or bigoted views were denied the vote altogether. That would be unconstitutional, of course; the Constitution demands that everyone be permitted to play an equal part in the formal process of choosing a president, a Congress, and other officials, that no one be excluded on the ground that his opinions or tastes are too offensive or unreasonable or despicable to count.

Elections are not all there is to politics, however. Citizens play a continuing part in politics between elections, because informal public debate and argument influences what responsible officials—and officials anxious for re-election—will do. So the First Amendment contributes a great deal to political equality: it insists that just as no one may be excluded from the vote because his opinions are despicable, so no one may be denied the right to speak or write or broadcast because what he will say is too offensive to be heard.

That amendment serves other goals as well, of course: free speech helps to expose official stupidity and corruption, and it allows vigorous public debate that sometimes generates new ideas and refutes old ones. But the First Amendment's egalitarian role is independent of these other goals; it forbids censoring cranks or neo-Nazis not because anyone thinks that their contributions will prevent corruption or improve public debate, but just because equality demands that everyone, no matter how eccentric or despicable, have a chance to influence policies as well as elections. Of course it does not follow that government will in the end respect everyone's opinion equally, or that official decisions will be equally congenial to all groups. Equality demands that everyone's opinion be given a chance for influence, not that anyone's opinion will triumph or even be represented in what government eventually does.

The First Amendment's egalitarian role is not confined, however, to political speech. People's lives are affected not just by their political environment—not just by what their presidents and legislators and other public officials do—but even more comprehensively by what we might call their moral environment. How others treat me—and my own sense of identity and self-respect—are determined in part by the mix of social conventions, opinions, tastes, convictions, prejudices, life styles, and cultures that flourish in the community in which I live. Liberals are sometimes accused of thinking that what people say or do or think in private has no impact on anyone except themselves, and that is plainly wrong. Someone to whom religion is of fundamental importance, for example, will obviously lead a very different and perhaps more satisfying life in a community in which most other people share his convictions than in a dominantly secular society of atheists for whom his beliefs are laughable superstitions. A woman who believes that explicit sexual material degrades her will likely lead a very different, and no doubt more satisfying, life among people who also despise pornography than in a community where others, including other women, think it liberating and fun.

Exactly because the moral environment in which we all live is in good part created by others, however, the question of who shall have the power to help shape that environment, and how, is of fundamental importance, though it is often neglected in political theory. Only one answer is consistent with the ideals of political equality: that no one may be prevented from influencing the shared moral environment, through his own private choices, tastes, opinions, and example, just because these tastes or opinions disgust those who have the power to shut him up or lock him up. Of course, the ways in which anyone may exercise that influence must be limited in order to protect the security and interests of others. People may not try to mold the moral climate by intimidating women with sexual demands or by burning a cross on a black family's lawn, or by refusing to hire women or blacks at all, or by making their working conditions so humiliating as to be intolerable.

But we cannot count, among the kinds of interests that may be protected in this way, a right not to be insulted or damaged just by the fact that others have hostile or uncongenial tastes, or that they are free to express or indulge them in private. Recognizing that right would mean denying that some people—those whose tastes these are—have any right to participate in forming the moral environment at all. Of course it should go without saying that no one has a right to *succeed* in influencing others through his own private choices and tastes. Sexists and bigots have no right to live in a community whose ideology or culture is even

partially sexist or bigoted: they have no right to any proportional representation for their odious views. In a genuinely egalitarian society, however, those views cannot be locked out, in advance, by criminal or civil law: they must instead be discredited by the disgust, outrage, and ridicule of other people.

MacKinnon's "egalitarian" argument for censorship is important mainly because it reveals the most important reason for resisting her suggestions, and also because it allows us to answer her charge that liberals who oppose her are crypto-pornographers themselves. She thinks that people who defend the right to pornography are acting out of self-interest, not principle—she says she has been driven to the conclusion that "speech *will* be defined so that men can have their pornography." That charge is based on the inadequacy of the conventional explanation, deriving from John Stuart Mill, that pornography must be protected so that truth may emerge. What is actually at stake in the argument about pornography, however, is not society's chance to discover truth, but its commitment to the very ideal of equality that MacKinnon thinks underrated in the American community. Liberals defend pornography, though most of them despise it, in order to defend a conception of the First Amendment that includes, as at least one of its purposes, protection of equality in the processes through which the moral as well as the political environment is formed. First Amendment liberty is not equality's enemy, but the other side of equality's coin.

MacKinnon is right to emphasize the connection between the fight over pornography and the larger, more general and important, argument about the freedom of Americans to say and teach what others think politically incorrect. She and her followers regard freedom of speech and thought as an elitist, inegalitarian ideal that has been of almost no value to women, blacks, and others without power; they say America would be better off if it demoted that ideal as many other nations have. But most of her constituents would be appalled if this denigration of freedom should escape from universities and other communities where their own values about political correctness are now popular and take root in the more general political culture. Local majorities may find homosexual art or feminist theater just as degrading to women as the kind of pornography MacKinnon hates, or radical or separatist black opinion just as inimical to racial justice as crude racist epithets.

That is an old liberal warning—as old as Voltaire—and many people have grown impatient with it. They are willing to take that chance, they say, to advance a program that seems overwhelmingly important now. Their impatience may prove fatal for that program rather than essential to it, however. If we abandon our traditional understanding of equality for a different one that allows a majority to define some people as too corrupt or offensive or radical to join in the informal moral life of the nation, we will have begun a process that ends, as it has in so many other parts of the world, in making equality something to be feared rather than celebrated, a mocking, "correct" euphemism for tyranny.

■ Case Study: Hate Speech

COLLIN V. SMITH
578 F.2d 1197 (7th Cir. 1978)

PELL, Circuit Judge.

Plaintiff-appellee, the National Socialist Party of America (NSPA) is a political group described by its leader, plaintiff-appellee Frank Collin, as a Nazi party. Among NSPA's more controversial and generally unacceptable beliefs are that black persons are biologically inferior to white persons, and should be expatriated to Africa as soon as possible; that American Jews have "inordinate political and financial power" in the world and are "in the forefront of the international Communist revolution." NSPA members affect a uniform reminiscent of those worn by members of the German Nazi Party during the Third Reich, and display a swastika thereon and on a red, white, and black flag they frequently carry.

The Village of Skokie, Illinois, a defendant-appellant, is a suburb north of Chicago. It has a large Jewish population, including as many as several thousand survivors of the Nazi holocaust in Europe before and during World War II. Other defendants-appellants are Village officials.

When Collin and NSPA announced plans to march in front of the Village Hall in Skokie on May 1, 1977, Village officials responded by obtaining in state court a preliminary injunction against the demonstration. The injunction was subsequently reversed first in part, and then in its entirety. On May 2, 1977, the Village enacted three ordinances to prohibit demonstrations such as the one Collin and NSPA had threatened.

Collin and NSPA applied for a permit to march on July 4, 1977, which was denied. The permit application stated that the march would last about a half hour, and would involve 30 to 50 demonstrators wearing uniforms including swastikas and carrying a party banner with a swastika and placards with statements thereon such as "White Free Speech," "Free Speech for the White Man," and "Free Speech for White America." A single file sidewalk march that would not disrupt traffic was proposed, without speeches or the distribution of handbills or literature. Counsel for the Village advises us that the Village does not maintain that Collin and NSPA will behave other than as described in the permit application(s).

The conflict underlying this litigation has commanded substantial public attention, and engendered considerable and understandable emotion. We would hopefully surprise no one by confessing personal views that NSPA's beliefs and goals are repugnant to the core values held generally by residents of this country, and, indeed, to much of what we cherish in civilization. As judges sworn to defend the Constitution, however, we cannot decide this or any case on that basis. Ideological tyranny, no matter how worthy its motivation, is forbidden as much to appointed judges as to elected legislators.

The record in this case contains the testimony of a survivor of the Nazi holocaust in Europe. Shortly before oral argument in this case, a lengthy and highly publicized citizenship revocation trial of an alleged Nazi war criminal was held in a federal court in Chicago, and in the week immediately after argument here, a four-part "docudrama" on the holocaust was nationally televised and widely observed. We cannot then be unmindful of the horrors associated with the Nazi regime of the Third Reich, with which to some real and apparently intentional degree appellees associate themselves. Nor does the record allow us to ignore the certainty that appellees know full well that, in light of their views and the historical associations they would bring with them to Skokie, many people would find their demonstration extremely mentally and emotionally disturb-ing, or the suspicion that such a result may be relished by appellees.

But our task here is to decide whether the First Amendment protects the activity in which appellees wish to engage, not to render moral judgment on their views or tactics. No authorities need be cited to establish the proposition, which the Village does not dispute, that First Amendment rights are truly precious and fundamental to our national life. Nor is this truth without relevance to the saddening historical images this case inevitably arouses. It is, after all, in part the fact that our constitutional system protects minorities unpopular at a particular time or place from governmental harassment and intimidation, that distinguishes life in this country from life under the Third Reich.

We may agree with the district court that

if any philosophy should be regarded as completely unacceptable to civilized society, that of plaintiffs, who, while disavowing on the witness stand any advocacy of genocide, have nevertheless deliberately identified themselves with a regime whose record of brutality and barbarism is unmatched in modern history, would be a good place to start.

But there can be no legitimate start down such a road.

Under the First Amendment there is no such thing as a false idea. However pernicious an opinion may seem, we depend for its correction not on the conscience of judges and juries but on the competition of other ideas. Gertz v. Robert Welch [U.S. Sup.Ct., 1974].

In the words of Justice Jackson, "every person must be his own watchman for truth, because the forefathers did not trust any government to separate the true from the false for us." The asserted falseness of Nazi dogma, and, indeed, its general repudiation, simply do not justify its suppression.

It would be grossly insensitive to deny, as we do not, that the proposed demonstration would seriously disturb, emotionally and mentally, at least some, and probably many of the Village's residents. The problem with engrafting an exception on the First Amendment for such situations is that they are indistinguishable in principle from speech that "invite[s] dispute . . . induces a condition of unrest, creates dissatisfaction with conditions as they are, or even stirs people to anger." Yet these are among the "high purposes" of the First Amendment.

It is said that the proposed march is not speech, or even "speech plus," but rather an invasion, intensely menacing no matter how peacefully conducted. The Village's expert psychiatric witness, in fact, testified that the effect of the march would be much the same regardless of whether uniforms and swastikas were displayed, due to the intrusion of self-proclaimed Nazis into what he characterized as predominately [sic] Jewish "turf." There is room under the First Amendment for the government to protect targeted listeners from offensive speech, but only when the speaker intrudes on the privacy of the home, or a captive audience cannot practically avoid exposure.

This case does not involve intrusion into people's homes. There *need be* no captive audience, as Village residents may, if they wish, simply avoid the Village Hall for thirty minutes on a Sunday afternoon, which no doubt would be their normal course of conduct on a day when the Village Hall was not open in the regular course of business. Absent such intrusion or captivity, there is no justifiable substantial privacy interest to save [the ordinance] from constitutional infirmity, when it attempts, by fiat, to declare the entire Village, at all times, a privacy zone that may be sanitized from the offensiveness of Nazi ideology and symbols.

CAMPUS ANTIRACISM RULES: CONSTITUTIONAL NARRATIVES IN COLLISION

RICHARD DELGADO

Persons tend to react to the problem of racial insults in one of two ways. On hearing that a university has enacted rules forbidding certain forms of speech, some will frame the issue as a first amendment problem: the rules limit speech, and the Constitution forbids official regulation of speech without a very good reason. If one takes that starting point, several consequences follow. First, the burden shifts to the other side to show that the interest in protecting members of the campus community from insults and name-calling is compelling enough to overcome the presumption in favor of free speech. Further, there must be no less

Richard Delgado, "Campus Antiracism Rules: Constitutional Narratives in Collision," *Northwestern University Law Review,* vol. 85 (1991), pp. 343 ff.

onerous way of accomplishing that objective. Moreover, some will worry whether the enforcer of the regulation will become a censor, imposing narrow-minded restraints on campus discussion. Some will also be concerned about slippery slopes and line-drawing problems: if a campus restricts this type of expression, might the temptation arise to do the same with classroom speech or political satire in the campus newspaper?

Others, however, will frame the problem as one of protection of equality. They will ask whether an educational institution does not have the power, to protect core values emanating from the thirteenth and fourteenth amendments, to enact reasonable regulations aimed at assuring equal personhood on campus. If one characterizes the issue *this* way, other consequences follow. Now, the defenders of racially scathing speech are required to show that the interest in its protection is compelling enough to overcome the preference for equal personhood; and we will want to be sure that this interest is advanced in the way least damaging to equality. There are again concerns about the decisionmaker who will enforce the rules, but from the opposite standpoint: the enforcer of the regulation must be attuned to the nuances of insult and racial supremacy at issue, for example by incorporating multi-ethnic representation into the hearing process. Finally, a different set of slopes will look slippery. If we do *not* intervene to protect equality here, what will the next outrage be?

The legal analysis, therefore, leads to opposite conclusions depending on the starting point. But there is an even deeper indeterminacy: both sides invoke different narratives to rally support. Protectors of the first amendment see campus antiracism rules as parts of a much longer story: the centuries-old struggle of Western society to free itself from superstition and enforced ignorance. The tellers of this story invoke martyrs like Socrates, Galileo, and Peter Zenger, and heroes like Locke, Hobbes, Voltaire, and Hume who fought for the right of free expression. They conjure up struggles against official censorship, book burning, witch trials, and communist blacklists. Compared to that richly textured, deeply stirring account, the minority-protector's interest in freeing a few (supersensitive?) individuals from momentary discomfort looks thin. A textured, historical account is pitted against a particularized, slice-of-life, dignitary one.

Those on the minority-protection side invoke a different, and no less powerful, narrative. They see a nation's centuries-long struggle to free itself from racial and other forms of tyranny, including slavery, lynching, Jim Crow laws, and "separate-but-equal" schools. They conjure up different milestones—Lincoln's Emancipation Proclamation, *Brown v. Board of Education;* they look to different heroes—Martin Luther King, the early Abolitionists, Rosa Parks, and Cesar Chavez, civil rights protestors who put their lives on the line for racial justice. Arrayed against that richly textured historical account, the racist's interest in insulting a person of color face-to-face looks thin.

One often hears that the problem of campus antiracism rules is that of balancing free speech and equality. But more is at stake. Each side wants not merely to have the balance struck in its favor; each wants to impose its own understanding of what is at stake. Minority protectors see the injury of one who has been subject to a racial assault as not a mere isolated event, but as part of an interrelated series of acts, by which persons of color are subordinated, and which will follow the victim wherever she goes. First amendment defenders see the wrong of silencing the racist as much more than a momentary inconvenience: protection of his right to speak is part of the never-ending vigilance necessary to preserve freedom of expression in a society that is too prone to balance it away.

My view is that both stories are equally valid. Judges and university administrators have no easy, a priori way of choosing between them, of privileging one over the other. They could coin an exception to free speech, thus giving primacy to the equal protection values at stake. Or, they could carve an exception to equality, saying in effect that universities may protect minority populations except where this abridges speech. Nothing in constitutional or moral theory requires one answer rather than the other. Social science, case law, and the experience of other nations provide some illumination. But ultimately, judges and university administrators must *choose.*

IF HE HOLLERS LET HIM GO: REGULATING RACIST SPEECH ON CAMPUS

CHARLES LAWRENCE

Face-to-face racial insults, like fighting words, are undeserving of first amendment protection for two reasons. The first reason is the immediacy of the injurious impact of racial insults. The experience of being called "nigger," "spic," "Jap," or "kike" is like receiving a slap in the face. The injury is instantaneous. There is neither an opportunity for intermediary reflection on the idea conveyed nor an opportunity for responsive speech. The harm to be avoided is both clear and present. The second reason that racial insults should not fall under protected speech relates to the purpose underlying the first amendment. If the purpose of the first amendment is to foster the greatest amount of speech, then racial insults disserve that purpose. Assaultive racist speech functions as a preemptive strike. The racial invective is experienced as a blow, not a proffered idea, and once the blow is struck, it is unlikely that dialogue will follow. Racial insults are undeserving of first amendment protection because the perpetrator's intention is not to discover truth or initiate dialogue but to injure the victim.

The fighting words doctrine anticipates that the verbal "slap in the face" of insulting words will provoke a violent response with a resulting breach of the peace. When racial insults are hurled at minorities, the response may be silence or flight rather than a fight, but the preemptive effect on further speech is just as complete as with fighting words. Women and minorities often report that they find themselves speechless in the face of discriminatory verbal attacks. This inability to respond is not the result of oversensitivity among these groups, as some individuals who oppose protective regulation have argued. Rather, it is the product of several factors, all of which reveal the non-speech character of the initial preemptive verbal assault. The first factor is that the visceral emotional response to personal attack precludes speech. Attack produces an instinctive, defensive psychological reaction. Fear, rage, shock, and flight all interfere with any reasoned response. Words like "nigger," "kike," and "faggot" produce physical symptoms that temporarily disable the victim, and the perpetrators often use these words with the intention of producing this effect. Many victims do not find words of response until well after the assault when the cowardly assaulter has departed.

A second factor that distinguishes racial insults from protected speech is the preemptive nature of such insults—the words by which to respond to such verbal attacks may never be forthcoming because speech is usually an inadequate response. When one is personally attacked with words that denote one's subhuman status and untouchability, there is little (if anything) that can be said to redress either the emotional or reputational injury. This is particularly true when the message and meaning of the epithet resonates with beliefs widely held in society. This preservation of widespread beliefs is what makes the face-to-face racial attack more likely to preempt speech than are other fighting words. The racist name-caller is accompanied by a cultural chorus of equally demeaning speech and symbols.

The subordinated victim of fighting words also is silenced by her relatively powerless position in society. Because of the significance of

power and position, the categorization of racial epithets as "fighting words" provides an inadequate paradigm; instead one must speak of their "functional equivalent." The fighting words doctrine presupposes an encounter between two persons of relatively equal power who have been acculturated to respond to face-to-face insults with violence. The fighting words doctrine is a paradigm based on a white male point of view. In most situations, minorities correctly perceive that a violent response to fighting words will result in a risk to their own life and limb. Since minorities are likely to lose the fight, they are forced to remain silent and submissive. This response is most obvious when women submit to sexually assaultive speech or when the racist name-caller is in a more powerful position—the boss on the job or the mob. . . . Less obvious, but just as significant, is the effect of pervasive racial and sexual violence and coercion on individual members of subordinated groups who must learn the survival techniques of suppressing and disguising rage and anger at an early age.

REGULATING RACIST SPEECH ON CAMPUS: A MODEST PROPOSAL?

NADINE STROSSEN

Because civil libertarians have learned that free speech is an indispensable instrument for the promotion of other rights and freedoms—including racial equality—we fear that the movement to regulate campus expression will

undermine equality, as well as free speech. Combating racial discrimination and protecting free speech should be viewed as mutually reinforcing, rather than antagonistic, goals. A diminution in society's commitment to racial

Nadine Strossen, "Regulating Racist Speech on Campus: A Modest Proposal?", *Duke Law Journal*, vol. 1990, pp. 484 ff.

equality is neither a necessary nor an appropriate price for protecting free speech. Those who frame the debate in terms of this false dichotomy simply drive artificial wedges between would-be allies in what should be a common effort to promote civil rights and civil liberties.

■ ■ ■

In the recent wave of college crackdowns on racist and other forms of hate speech, examples abound of attempts to censor speech conveying ideas that clearly play a legitimate role in academic discourse, although some of us might find them wrongheaded or even odious. For example, the University of Michigan's anti-hate speech policy could justify attacks on author Salman Rushdie because his book, *The Satanic Verses*, was offensive to Muslims.

In addition to their chilling effect on the ideas and expressions of university community members, policies that bar hate speech could engender broader forms of censorship. As noted by Professor William Cohen of Stanford Law School, an anti-hate speech rule such as the one adopted by his university "purports to create a personal right to be free from involuntary exposure to any form of expression that gives certain kinds of offense." Therefore, he explains, such a rule "could become a sword to challenge assigned readings in courses, the showing of films on campus, or the message of certain speakers."

The various proposed campus hate speech regulations, including the Stanford code that Professor Lawrence endorses, are inconsistent with current Supreme Court doctrine prescribing permissible limits on speech. More importantly, they jeopardize basic free speech principles. Whereas certain conduct may be regulable, speech that advocates such conduct is not, and speech may not be regulated on the basis of its content, even if many of us strongly disagree with—or are repelled by—that content.

Civil libertarians, scholars, and judges consistently have distinguished between speech advocating unlawful conduct and the unlawful conduct itself. Although this distinction has been drawn in numerous different factual settings, the fundamental underlying issues always are the same. For example, within recent years, some pro-choice activists have urged civil libertarians and courts to make an exception to free speech principles in order to restrain the expressive conduct of anti-abortion activists. Instead, civil libertarians have persuaded courts to prohibit assaults, blockages of clinic entrances, trespasses, and other illegal conduct by anti-choice activists. Similarly, civil libertarians and courts have rejected pleas by some feminists to censor pornography that reflects sexist attitudes. Instead, civil libertarians have renewed their efforts to persuade courts and legislatures to invalidate sexist actions. A decade ago, civil libertarians and several courts—including the Supreme Court—rejected the plea of Holocaust survivors in Skokie, Illinois to prohibit neo-Nazis from demonstrating. Instead, civil libertarians successfully have lobbied for the enactment and enforcement of laws against anti-Semitic vandalism and other hate-inspired conduct.

A pervasive weakness in Professor Lawrence's analysis is his elision of the distinction between racist speech, on the one hand, and racist conduct, on the other. It is certainly true that racist speech, like other speech, may have some causal connection to conduct. As Justice Holmes observed, "[e]very idea is an incitement" to action. However, as Justice Holmes also noted, to protect speech that advocates conduct you oppose does not "indicate that you think the speech impotent, . . . or that you do not care wholeheartedly for the result." Rather, this protection is based on the critical distinction between speech that has a direct and immediate link to unlawful conduct and all other speech, which has less direct and immediate links. In Holmes' immortal words:

[W]e should be eternally vigilant against attempts to check the expression of opinions that we loathe and believe to be fraught with death, unless they so imminently threaten immediate interference with the lawful and pressing purposes of the law that an immediate check is required to save the country. . . . Only the emergency that makes it immediately dangerous to leave the correction of evil counsels to time warrants making any exception to the sweeping command, "Congress shall make no law . . . abridging the freedom of speech."

It is impossible to draw a bright line between speech and conduct. It also may be difficult to determine whether certain speech has a sufficiently tight nexus to conduct to justify regulating that speech. Professor Lawrence, however, abandons the attempt to make any such distinctions at all. He treats even the most extreme, blatant discriminatory conduct as speech, including slavery itself. Although undoubtedly harmful, the utterance of disparaging remarks cannot be equated fairly with the systematic denial of all rights to a group of human beings. Professor Lawrence recognizes this and appropriately chides anyone who insists that *all* racist conduct that includes an expressive component should be treated alike—namely, as protected speech. However, Professor Lawrence himself engages in precisely the same kind of oversimplification when he suggests that all conduct with an expressive component—which, in his view, includes *all* racist conduct and *all* racist speech—should be treated alike, namely, as *unprotected* speech. Those of us who reject either extreme as unreasonably rigid should join forces in undertaking the essential, albeit difficult, task of line-drawing.

It is important to place the current debate about campus racist speech in the context of earlier efforts to censor other forms of hate speech, including sexist and anti-Semitic speech. Such a broadened perspective suggests that consistent principles should be applied each time the issue resurfaces in any guise. Every person may find one particular type of speech especially

odious and one message that most sorely tests his or her dedication to free speech values. But for each person who would exclude racist speech from the general proscription against content-based speech regulations, recent experience shows that there is another who would make such an exception only for anti-choice speech, another who would make it only for sexist speech, another who would make it only for anti-Semitic speech, another who would make it only for flag desecration, and so on.

The recognition that there is no principled basis for curbing speech expressing some particular ideas is reflected in the time-honored prohibition on any content-based or viewpoint-based regulations. As stated by Professor Tribe, "If the Constitution forces government to allow people to march, speak and write in favor of peace, brotherhood, and justice, then it must also require government to allow them to advocate hatred, racism, and even genocide."

The position stated by Professor Tribe is not just the traditional civil libertarian view, but it also is the law of the land. The courts consistently have agreed with civil libertarian claims that the first amendment protects the right to engage in racist and other forms of hate speech. Why is this so, and should it be so? Professor Lawrence rightly urges us to take a fresh look at this issue, no matter how well-settled it is as a matter of law. I have taken that invitation seriously and reflected long and hard upon his thought-provoking article and the questions it presents. Having done so, however, I conclude that the courts and traditional civil libertarians are correct in steadfastly rejecting laws that create additional new exceptions to free speech protections for racist expression.

To attempt to craft free speech exceptions only for racist speech would create a significant risk of a slide down the proverbial "slippery slope." To be sure, lawyers and judges are capable of—indeed, especially trained in—drawing distinctions between similar situations. Therefore, I agree with Professor Lawrence and other critics of the absolutist position that slippery slope dangers should not be exaggerated. It is probably hyperbole to contend that if we ever stepped off the mountaintop where all speech is protected regardless of its content, then inevitably we would end up in the abyss where the government controls all our words. On the other hand, critics of absolutism should not minimize the real danger: We would have a difficult time limiting our descent to a single downward step by attempting to prohibit only racist expression on campus. Applicable rules and supporting rationales would need to be crafted carefully to distinguish this type of speech from others.

First, we must think hard about the groups that should be protected. Should we regulate speech aimed only at racial and ethnic groups, as the University of Texas is considering? Or should we also bar insults of religious groups, women, gays and lesbians, individuals with disabilities, Vietnam War veterans, and so on, as do the rules adopted by Stanford and the University of Michigan? As the committee that formulated the University of Texas's proposed rule pointed out, each category requires a separate evaluation, since each "raise[s] different policy and legal concerns." Therefore, we should not play fast and loose with the first amendment by casually expanding the categories of proscribed hate speech.

Second, we must carefully define proscribable harassing speech to avoid encompassing the important expression that inevitably is endangered by any hate speech restriction. Censorial consequences could result from many proposed or adopted university policies, including the Stanford code, which sanctions speech intended to "insult or stigmatize" on the basis of race or other prohibited grounds. For example, certain feminists suggest that all heterosexual sex is rape because heterosexual men are aggressors who operate in a cultural climate of pervasive sexism and violence against women. Aren't these feminists insulting or stigmatizing heterosexual men on the basis of their sex and sexual orientation? And how about a Holocaust survivor who blames all ("Aryan") Germans for their collaboration during World War II? Doesn't this insinuation insult or stigmatize on the basis of national and ethnic origin? And surely we can think of numerous other examples that would have to give us pause.

■ ■ ■

An exaggerated concern with racist speech creates a risk of elevating symbols over substance in two problematic respects. First, it may divert our attention from the causes of racism to its symptoms. Second, a focus on the hateful message conveyed by particular speech may distort our view of fundamental neutral principles applicable to our system of free expression generally. We should not let the racist veneer in which expression is cloaked obscure our recognition of how important free expression is and of how effectively it has advanced racial equality.

UWM POST, INC. V. BOARD OF REGENTS OF UNIVERSITY OF WISCONSIN

774 F. Supp. 1163 (E.D. Wis. 1991)

WARREN, Senior District Judge

In May of 1988, the Board of Regents adopted "Design for Diversity," a plan to increase minority representation, multi-cultural understanding and greater diversity throughout the University of Wisconsin System's 26 campuses. Design for Diversity responded to concerns over an increase in incidents of discriminatory harassment.

For example, several highly publicized incidents involving fraternities occurred at the University of Wisconsin—Madison. In May of 1987, a fraternity erected a large caricature of a black Fiji Islander as a party theme. Later that year, there was a fight with racial overtones between members of two fraternities. In October of 1988, a fraternity held a "slave auction" at which pledges in black face performed skits parroting black entertainers.

Design for Diversity directed each of the UW System's institutions to prepare nondiscriminatory conduct policies. In addition, pursuant to the plan, the Board of Regents approved its "Policy and Guidelines on Racist and Discriminatory Conduct," which stated the Board's general policy against discrimination and provided guidance to the individual campuses in developing their own non-discrimination policies. Finally, the Board established a working group to draft amendments to the student conduct code, Chapter UWS 17, to implement its policy system-wide. With the help of UW-Madison Law School Professors Gordon Baldwin, Richard Delgado

and Ted Finman, the group developed a proposed rule based, in part, on a policy being developed simultaneously at the UW-Madison.

The UW Rule provides:

UWS 17.06 Offenses defined. The university may discipline a student in nonacademic matters in the following situations. . . .

(2)(a) For racist or discriminatory comments, epithets or other expressive behavior directed at an individual or on separate occasions at different individuals, or for physical conduct, if such comments, epithets or other expressive behavior or physical conduct intentionally:

1. Demean the race, sex, religion, color, creed, disability, sexual orientation, national origin, ancestry or age of the individual or individuals; and

2. Create an intimidating, hostile or demeaning environment for education, university-related work, or other university-authorized activity.

(b) Whether the intent required under par. (a) is present shall be determined by consideration of all relevant circumstances.

(c) In order to illustrate the types of conduct which this subsection. is designed to cover, the following examples are set forth. These examples are not meant to illustrate the only situations or types of conduct intended to be covered.

1. A student would be in violation if:

a. He or she intentionally made demeaning remarks to an individual based on that person's ethnicity, such as name calling, racial slurs, or "jokes"; and

b. His or her purpose in uttering the remarks was to make the educational environment hostile for the person to whom the demeaning remark was addressed.

2. A student would be in violation if: a. He or she intentionally placed visual or written material demeaning the race or sex of an individual in that person's university living quarters or work area; and

b. His or her purpose was to make the educational environment hostile for the person in whose quarters or work area the material was placed.

3. A student would be in violation if he or she seriously damaged or destroyed private property of any member of the university community or guest because of that person's race, sex, religion, color, creed, disability, sexual orientation, national origin, ancestry or age.

4. A student would not be in violation if, during a class discussion, he or she expressed a derogatory opinion concerning a racial or ethnic group. There is no violation, since the student's remark was addressed to the class as a whole, not to a specific individual. Moreover, on the facts as stated, there seems no evidence that the student's purpose was to create a hostile environment.

Thus, in order to be regulated under the UW Rule, a comment, epithet or other expressive behavior must:

(1) Be racist or discriminatory;

(2) Be directed at an individual;

(3) Demean the race, sex, religion, color, creed, disability, sexual orientation, national origin, ancestry or age of the individual addressed; and

(4) Create an intimidating, hostile or demeaning environment for education, university-related work, or other university-authorized activity.

In addition to the rule, the UW System issued and circulated to its students and faculty a brochure which explains the rule and provides guidance as to its scope and application. This guide provides some illustrations of situations where the UW Rule applies and does not apply:

Question 1. In a class discussion concerning women in the workplace, a male student states his belief that women are by nature better equipped to be mothers than executives, and thus should not be employed in upper level management positions. Is this statement actionable under proposed UWS 17.06(2)?

Answer: No. The statement is an expression of opinion, contains no epithets, is not directed to a particular individual, and does not, standing alone, evince the requisite intent to demean or create a hostile environment.

Question 2. A student living in the University dormitory continually calls a black student living on his floor "nigger" whenever they pass in the hallway. May the university take action against the name-caller?

Answer: Yes. The word "nigger" is an epithet, and is directed specifically at an individual. Its use and continuous repetition demonstrate the required intent on the part of the speaker to demean the individual and create a hostile living environment for him.

Question 3. Two university students become involved in an altercation at an off-campus bar. During the fight one student used a racial epithet to prolong the dispute. May the university invoke a disciplinary action?

Answer: Perhaps. Use of the epithet, and its direction to an individual suggests a potential violation of proposed UWS 17.06(2); however, because the episode occurred off campus, the intent to create a hostile environment for university-authorized activities would be difficult to demonstrate. Additional facts would have to be developed if disciplinary action were to be pursued.

Question 4. A group of students disrupts a university class shouting discriminating epithets. Are they subject to disciplinary action under the provisions related to regulation of expressive behavior?

Answer: Perhaps. It is clear that the students are subject to disciplinary action for disrupting a class under existing UWS 17.06(1)(c)3. The question is whether they also violated the newly created provision concerning expressive behavior, because they shouted epithets while in the course of other misconduct. If the epithets were directed to individuals within class, and were intended to demean them and create an intimidating environment, then the behavior might also be in violation of the provision concerning expressive misconduct.

Question 5. A faculty member, in a genetics class discussion, suggests that certain racial groups seem to be genetically pre-disposed to alcoholism. Is this statement subject to discipline under Chapter UWS 17?

Answer: No. A faculty member is in no case subject to discipline under Chapter UWS 17, since that chapter applies only to students. This situation would not warrant disciplinary action under any other policy, either, since it is protected expression of an idea.

To date, at least nine students have been sanctioned under the UW Rule:

(1) The University of Wisconsin—Parkside found that a student used inappropriate language when he called another student "Shakazulu." The university found that the student entered the other student's bedroom area as an uninvited guest and proceeded to use inappropriate language and that later there was a confrontation between the student and residents of the apartment. The student was placed on probation and required to consult with an alcohol abuse counselor and to "plan a project in conjunction with the Center for Education and Cultural Advancement to help sensitize [himself] to the issues of diversity."

(2) The University of Wisconsin—Eau Claire found that plaintiff John Doe violated the UW Rule by yelling epithets loudly at a woman for approximately ten minutes, calling her a "fucking bitch" and "fucking cunt." Plaintiff John Doe was responding to statements the woman made in a university newspaper about the athletic department. The university placed the student on probation for a semester and required him to perform twenty hours of community service at a shelter for abused women.

(3) The University of Wisconsin—Oshkosh disciplined a student for angrily telling an Asian-American student: "It's people like you— that's the reason this country is screwed up" and "you don't belong here." The student also stated that "Whites are always getting screwed by minorities and some day the Whites will take over." The University placed the student on probation for seven months and required him to participate in alcohol abuse assessment and treatment.

(4) The University of Wisconsin—Stevens Point found that a student harassed a Turkish-American student by impersonating an immigration official and demanding to see immigration documents. The student signed a "No Contest Agreement" admitting violations of the rule as well as violations of UWS 17.06(4) (conduct obstructing a university official) and his university housing contract. The university placed the student on probation for eight months.

(5) The University of Wisconsin—Stout charged a student involved in a physical altercation with two residence hall staff members with calling one of them a "piece of shit nigger" and the other a "South American immigrant." The student waived a formal hearing and accepted a seven-month suspension.

(6) The University of Wisconsin—Eau Claire disciplined a student under the UW Rule for sending a message that stated, "Death to all Arabs!! Die Islamic scumbags!" on a university computer system to an Iranian faculty member. The university formally reprimanded the student and placed him on probation for the remainder of the semester.

(7) The University of Wisconsin—Stevens Point brought a disciplinary action under the UW Rule against a student who stole a TYME automatic bank teller card and access number belonging to his dormitory roommate, who is Japanese. The student acknowledged that he had stolen the TYME card, that he had twice in-

tercepted and opened the Japanese student's correspondence from the bank and that he had successfully withdrawn $60.00 from the Japanese student's bank account using the TYME card and personal identification number he had stolen. The student also admitted that he was motivated by his resentment that his roommate is Japanese and does not speak English well. The student signed a no contest agreement, acknowledging that he had violated the UW Rule as well as other provisions of the student conduct code. The student was placed on probation [and] required to take a course in ethics or East Asian history and to make restitution.

(8) The University of Wisconsin—Oshkosh disciplined a female student under the UW Rule for referring to a black female student as a "fat-ass nigger" during an argument. The university found that the student violated the rule and another provision of the student code. The student, who was already on disciplinary probation, was required to view a video on racism and write an essay and a letter of apology and was reassigned to another residence hall.

(9) The University of Wisconsin—River Falls disciplined a male student under the UW Rule for yelling at a female student in public, "you've got nice tits." The university placed the student on probation for the remainder of his enrollment at the university and required him to apologize to the female student, to refrain from any further contact with her and to obtain psychological counseling.

■ ■ ■

The Board [asserts] that the regulated speech lacks First Amendment value because it is unlikely to form any part of a dialogue or exchange of views and because it does not provide an opportunity for a reply. In *American Booksellers*, the Seventh Circuit addressed and rejected these arguments.

> Much of [defendant's] argument rests on the belief that when speech is "unanswerable," and the metaphor that there is a "marketplace of ideas" does not apply, the

First Amendment does not apply either. The metaphor is time honored; Milton's *Aeropagitica* and John Stewart Mill's *On Liberty* defend freedom of speech on the ground that the truth will prevail, and many of the most important cases under the First Amendment recite this position. The Framers undoubtedly believed it. As a general matter it is true. But the Constitution does not make the dominance of truth a necessary condition of freedom of speech. To say that it does would be to confuse an outcome of free speech with a necessary condition for the application of the amendment.

The Board states that the prohibited speech constitutes a kind of verbal assault on the addressee. However, the Supreme Court has already performed a balancing test with respect to speech which inflicts injury and has found it to be worthy of First Amendment protection. Accordingly, it would be improper for this Court to find the speech regulated by the UW Rule unprotected based upon its assaultive characteristics.

Finally, the Board argues that the prohibited discriminatory speech lacks First Amendment value because of its tendency to incite reaction. While the Board is correct that the discriminatory speech prohibited by the UW Rule may in many circumstances tend to incite violent reaction, the rule prohibits speech regardless of its tendency to do this. . . . The Supreme Court has clearly defined the category of speech which is unprotected due to its tendency to incite violent reaction. This category of speech is limited to speech which by its very utterance tends to incite an immediate breach of the peace. It would be improper for this Court to expand the Supreme Court's definition of fighting words to include speech which does and speech which does not tend to incite violent reaction.

The founding fathers of this nation produced a remarkable document in the Constitution but it was ratified only with the promise of the Bill of Rights. The First Amendment is central to our concept of freedom. The God–given "unalienable rights" that the infant nation rallied to in the Declaration of Independence can be preserved only if their application is rigorously analyzed.

The problems of bigotry and discrimination sought to be addressed here are real and truly corrosive of the educational environment. But freedom of speech is almost absolute in our land and the only restriction the fighting words doctrine can abide is that based on the fear of violent reaction. Content-based prohibitions such as that in the UW Rule, however well intended, simply cannot survive the screening which our Constitution demands.

SUGGESTIONS FOR FURTHER READING

On the philosophical dimensions of freedom of speech, see Frederick Schauer, *Free Speech: A Philosophical Enquiry* (Cambridge: Cambridge University Press, 1982), critically evaluating traditional defenses of freedom of speech; R. Kent Greenawalt, *Speech, Crime, and the Uses of Language* (New York: Oxford University Press, 1989), philosophically analyzing the distinction between language triggering the idea of free speech and language as to which free speech concerns remain properly absent; and a number of books offering particular theories about why (and what) free speech is protected, including C. Edwin Baker, *Human Liberty and Freedom of Speech* (New York: Oxford University Press, 1989); Lee Bollinger, *The Tolerant Society: Free Speech and Extremist Speech in America* (New York: Oxford University Press, 1986); Robert Ladenson, *A Philosophy of Free Expression and Its Constitutional Applications* (Totowa, New Jersey: Rowman and Littlefield, 1983); Steven Shiffrin, *The First Amendment, Democracy, and Romance* (Cambridge: Harvard University Press, 1990); Cass Sunstein, *Democracy and the Problem of Free Speech* (New York: Viking, 1993). A more skeptical look is Stanley Fish, *There's No Such Thing as Free Speech . . . And It's a Good Thing Too* (New York: Oxford University Press, 1994). Useful collections include Fred Berger, ed., *Freedom of Expression* (Belmont, California: Wadsworth, 1980); Judith Lichtenberg, ed., *Democracy and the Mass Media* (Cambridge: Cambridge University Press, 1990). Among the important contemporary philosophical articles are Alvin I. Goldman, "Epistemic Paternalism: Communication Control in Law and Society," *Journal of Philosophy*, vol. 88 (1991), pp. 113 ff.; Robert Post, "Managing Deliberation: The Quandary of Democratic Dialogue," *Ethics*, vol. 103 (1993), pp. 654 ff.; Joseph Raz, "Free Expression and Personal Identification," *Oxford Journal of Legal Studies*, vol. 11 (1991), pp. 304 ff.; Frederick Schauer, "The Phenomenology of Speech and Harm," *Ethics*, vol. 103 (1993), pp. 635 ff. On pornography, Catharine MacKinnon's views are collected in the essays in her *Feminism Unmodified: Discourses on Life and Law* (Cambridge: Harvard University Press, 1987), and updated and expanded in *Only Words* (Cambridge: Harvard University Press, 1993). An extended defense of the constitutionality of the ordinance struck down in *Hudnut* is Cass R. Sunstein, "Pornography and the First Amendment," *Duke Law Journal*, vol. 1986, pp. 589 ff. On the argument that pornography silences women, see Frank I. Michelman, "Conceptions of Democracy in American Constitutional Argument: The Case of Pornography Regulation," *Tennessee Law Review*, vol. 56 (1989), pp. 291 ff.; Melinda Vadas, "A First Look at the Pornography/Civil Rights Ordinance: Could Pornography Be the Subordination of Women?," *Journal of Philosophy*, vol. 84 (1987), pp. 487 ff. On the empirical evidence about harm and conceptions of causation lying behind it, see Frederick Schauer, "Causation Theory and the Causes of Sexual Violence," *American Bar Foundation Research Journal*, vol. 1987, pp. 737 ff. Ronald

Dworkin's views are also found in his "Do We Have a Right to Pornography?," in *A Matter of Principle* (Cambridge: Harvard University Press, 1985), pp. 335 ff.; "The Coming Battle Over Free Speech," *The New York Review of Books*, June 11, 1992; "Two Concepts of Liberty," *The New York Review of Books*, August 15, 1991. A response to Dworkin is Rae Langton, "Whose Right?: Ronald Dworkin, Women, and Pornographers," *Philosophy and Public Affairs*, vol. 19 (1990), pp. 311 ff. The libertarian position is also developed in David A. J. Richards, "Free Speech and Obscenity Law: Toward a Moral Theory of the First Amendment," *University of Pennsylvania Law Review*, vol. 123 (1974), pp. 45 ff.; David A. J. Richards, "Pornography Commissions and the First Amendment: On Constitutional Values and Constitutional Facts," *Maine Law Review*, vol. 39 (1987), pp. 275 ff. Scanlon's views are modified in his "Freedom of Expression and Categories of Expression," *University of Pittsburgh Law Review*, vol. 40 (1979), pp. 519 ff.

THE RIGHT TO PRIVACY 4.4

INTRODUCTION

In the contemporary United States there is widespread agreement that there is a right to privacy, and that this is a good thing. But once we get beyond that generality, agreement breaks down. One reason for this is that even beyond the questions about rights in general, there is a particular ambiguity about the right to privacy, for the phrase "right to privacy" encompasses an especially diverse collection of relationships. Consider first the Fourth Amendment to the Constitution, which protects private property by prohibiting "unreasonable searches and seizures." This kind of right to privacy, the privacy of physical space (we might call it *spatial privacy*) is also protected by the Third Amendment to the Constitution, which prohibits the quartering of troops in private homes, and by various common law and statutory rights aimed at giving people some space in which they can be secure against physical intrusions.

Compare this, however, with the right that was the subject of a famous law review article more than a hundred years ago. In "The Right to Privacy,"[10] Louis Brandeis, later to become a Justice of the Supreme Court of the United States, and his law partner, Charles Warren, argued that a woman whose picture had been used as part of an advertisement without her permission ought to be entitled to recover tort damages against the advertiser for wrongfully using the picture of her for their own commercial purposes. This interest in controlling your own personality and image, they argued, was deserving of legal protection, and so they urged recognition of what they called "the right to privacy." In the ensuing century, courts expanded on this theme, and now the tort of invasion of privacy, protecting the *right* to privacy, includes not only the wrongful appropriation for commercial purposes of an image, but also the unreasonable disclosure of personal facts about an individual, as when a newspaper publishes embarrassing facts or photographs about a private individual, or when a newspaper or television station discloses the identity of a rape victim without her permission. In some cases this activity is protected by countervailing constitutional rights to freedom of speech and freedom of the press. Even when the right is thus overridden by other rights, however, there remains the basic idea that there is a version of the right to privacy, one we might call *informational privacy*, quite different from the spatial right to privacy protected by the Fourth Amendment, that protects the ability of an individual to control the dissemination of certain information about himself. Thus, when people fear that the proliferation of data banks

[10]*Harvard Law Review*, vol. 4 (1890), pp. 466 ff.

with information about all of us threatens our right of privacy, they call upon rights similar to those first addressed by Brandeis and Warren, and later protected both by statute and by common law.

There is yet another right going by the name of "the right to privacy." This is the right, one we can call *personal privacy*, to be free from governmental interference in making certain choices commonly argued to be "personal." This right to personal privacy is the topic of much of this section. The right to have an abortion unconstrained by government, the right to purchase contraceptives unconstrained by government, and the right to engage in self-regarding conduct unconstrained by government, for example, are often characterized as instances of a "right to privacy." John Stuart Mill's arguments in Chapter 1 of *On Liberty* (see Section 4.2), therefore, are arguments that often reappear in constitutionalized form in the name of "the right to privacy."

In reading the materials that follow, consider whether the privacy here is related to various other rights going by the same name, or whether the same word is being used for rights having quite little in common. Consider as well how some of these issues might be discussed differently if the "right to privacy" was mentioned as explicitly in the Constitution as are the rights to freedom of speech, freedom of the press, and freedom of religion.

GRISWOLD V. CONNECTICUT

381 U.S. 479 (1965)

Mr. Justice DOUGLAS delivered the opinion of the Court.

Appellant Griswold is Executive Director of the Planned Parenthood League of Connecticut. Appellant Buxton is a licensed physician and a professor at the Yale Medical School who served as Medical Director for the [League]. They gave information, instruction, and medical advice to *married persons* as to the means of preventing conception. [Fees] were usually charged, although some couples were serviced free. [The] constitutionality [of two Connecticut provisions] is involved. [One] provides: "Any person who uses any drug, medicinal article or instrument for the purpose of preventing con-

ception shall be fined not less than fifty dollars or imprisoned not less than sixty days nor more than one year or [both]." [The other] provides: "Any person who assists, abets, counsels, causes, hires or commands another to commit any offense may be prosecuted and punished as if he were the principal offender." The appellants were found guilty as accessories and fined $100 each, against the claim that the accessory statute as so applied violated the 14th Amendment. [The state appellate courts affirmed.]

[We] are met with a wide range of questions that implicate the Due Process Clause of the 14th Amendment. Overtones of some arguments suggest that *Lochner v. New York*, 198 U.S.

45, should be our guide. But we decline that invitation. We do not sit as a super-legislature to determine the wisdom, need, and propriety of laws that touch economic problems, business affairs, or social conditions. This law, however, operates directly on an intimate relation of husband and wife and their physician's role in one aspect of that relation.

The association of people is not mentioned in the Constitution nor in the Bill of Rights. The right to educate a child in a school of the parents' choice—whether public or private or parochial—is also not mentioned. Nor is the right to study any particular subject or any foreign language. Yet the First Amendment has been construed to include certain of those rights. [The] State may not, consistently with the spirit of the First Amendment, contract the spectrum of available knowledge. The right of freedom of speech and press includes not only the right to utter or to print, but the right to distribute, the right to receive, the right to read [and] freedom of inquiry, freedom of thought, and freedom to [teach]. Without those peripheral rights the specific rights would be less secure. In NAACP v. Alabama, we protected the "freedom to associate and privacy in one's association," noting that freedom of association was a peripheral First Amendment right. Disclosure of membership lists of a constitutionally valid association, we held, was invalid. In other words, the First Amendment has a penumbra where privacy is protected from governmental intrusion. In like context, we have protected forms of "association" that are not political in the customary sense but pertain to the social, legal, and economic benefit of the members. [The right of association], while it is not expressly included in the First Amendment, [is] necessary in making the express guarantees fully meaningful.

The foregoing cases suggest that specific guarantees in the Bill of Rights have penumbras, formed by emanations from those guarantees that help give them life and substance. Various guarantees create zones of privacy. The right of association contained in the penumbra

of the First Amendment is one, as we have seen. The Third Amendment in its prohibition against the quartering of soldiers "in any house" in time of peace without the consent of the owner is another facet of that privacy. The Fourth Amendment explicitly affirms the "right of the people to be secure in their persons, houses, papers, and effects against unreasonable searches and seizures." The Fifth Amendment in its Self-Incrimination Clause enables the citizen to create a zone of privacy which government may not force him to surrender to his detriment. The Ninth Amendment provides: "The enumeration in the Constitution, of certain rights, shall not be construed to deny or disparage others retained by the people." The Fourth and Fifth Amendments protect against all governmental invasions "of the sanctity of a man's home and the privacies of life." We recently referred [to] the Fourth Amendment as creating a "right to privacy, no less important than any other right carefully and particularly reserved to the people." We have had many controversies over these penumbral rights of "privacy and repose." These cases bear witness that the right of privacy which presses for recognition here is a legitimate one.

The present case, then, concerns a relationship lying within the zone of privacy created by several fundamental constitutional guarantees. And it concerns a law which, in forbidding the *use* of contraceptives rather than regulating their manufacture or sale, seeks to achieve its goals by means having a maximum destructive impact upon that relationship. Such a law cannot stand in light of the familiar principle [that] a "governmental purpose to control or prevent activities constitutionally subject to state regulation may not be achieved by means which sweep unnecessarily broadly and thereby invade the area of protected freedoms." Would we allow the police to search the sacred precincts of marital bedrooms for telltale signs of the use of contraceptives? The very idea is repulsive to the notions of privacy surrounding the marriage relationship.

We deal with a right of privacy older than the [Bill of Rights]. Marriage is a coming together for better or for worse, hopefully enduring, and intimate to the degree of being sacred. The association promotes a way of life, not causes; a harmony in living, not political faiths; a bilateral loyalty, not commercial or social projects. Yet it is an association for as noble a purpose as any involved in our prior decisions.

Reversed.

Mr. Justice GOLDBERG, whom The Chief Justice [WARREN] and Mr. Justice BRENNAN join, concurring [in the Court's opinion].

[Although] I have not accepted the view that "due process" as used in the 14th Amendment incorporates all of the first eight Amendments, [I] do agree that the concept of liberty protects those personal rights that are fundamental, and is not confined to the specific terms of the Bill of Rights. My conclusion [that liberty] embraces the right of marital privacy though that right is not mentioned explicitly in the Constitution is supported both by numerous decisions [and] by the language and history of the Ninth Amendment, [which] reveal that the Framers [believed] that there are additional fundamental rights, protected from governmental infringement, which exist alongside those fundamental rights specifically mentioned in the first [eight] amendments.

The Ninth Amendment reads, "The enumeration in the Constitution, of certain rights, shall not be construed to deny or disparage others retained by the people." [It] was proffered to quiet expressed fears that a bill of specifically enumerated rights could not be sufficiently broad to cover all essential rights and that the specific mention of certain rights would be interpreted as a denial that others were protected. [This] Court has had little occasion to interpret the Ninth Amendment, [but to] hold that a right so basic and fundamental and so deep–rooted in our society as the right of privacy in marriage may be infringed because that right is not guaranteed in so many words by the first eight amendments [is] to ignore the Ninth Amend-

ment and to give it no effect whatsoever. [I] do not mean to imply that the Ninth Amendment is applied against the States by the Fourteenth [nor] that the Ninth Amendment constitutes an independent source of rights protected from infringement by either the States or Federal Government. [Rather,] the Ninth Amendment simply lends strong support to the view that the "liberty" protected by the Fifth and [14th] Amendments [is] not restricted to rights specifically mentioned in the first eight amendments.

In determining which rights are fundamental, judges are not left at large to decide cases in light of their personal and private notions. Rather, they must look to the "traditions and [collective] conscience of our people" to determine whether a principle is "so rooted [there] as to be ranked as fundamental." [The] entire fabric of the Constitution and the purposes that clearly underlie its specific guarantees demonstrate that the rights to marital privacy and to marry and raise a family are of similar order and magnitude as the fundamental rights specifically protected. [The] logic of the dissents would sanction federal or state legislation that seems to me even more plainly unconstitutional than the statute before us. Surely the Government, absent a showing of a compelling subordinating state interest, could not decree that all husbands and wives must be sterilized after two children have been born to them. [If] upon a showing of a slender basis of rationality, a law outlawing voluntary birth control by married persons is valid, then, by the same reasoning, a law requiring compulsory birth control also would seem to be valid. In my view, however, both types of law would unjustifiably intrude upon rights of marital privacy which are constitutionally protected.

In a long series of cases this Court has held that where fundamental personal liberties are involved, they may not be abridged by the States simply on a showing that a regulatory statute has some rational relationship to the effectuation of a proper state purpose. "Where there is a significant encroachment upon personal liberty, the State may prevail only upon showing a subordinating interest which is compelling." The law must be shown "necessary, and not merely rationally related, to the accomplishment of a permissible state policy." The State, at most, argues that there is some rational relation between this statute and what is admittedly a legitimate subject of state concern—the discouraging of extramarital relations. It says that preventing the use of birth-control devices by married persons helps prevent the indulgence by some in such extramarital relations. The rationality of this justification is dubious, particularly in light of the admitted widespread availability to all persons [in] Connecticut, unmarried as well as married, of birth-control devices for the prevention of disease, as distinguished from the prevention of conception. But, in any event, it is clear that the state interest in safeguarding marital fidelity can be served by a more discriminately tailored statute, which does not, like the present one, sweep unnecessarily broadly, reaching far beyond the evil sought to be dealt with and intruding upon the privacy of all married couples. [Connecticut] does have statutes [which] prohibit adultery and fornication. These statutes demonstrate that means for achieving the same basic purpose of protecting marital fidelity are available to Connecticut without the need to "invade the area of protected freedoms." [Finally], it should be said of the Court's holding today that it in no way interferes with a State's proper regulation of sexual promiscuity or [misconduct]. In sum, I believe that the right of privacy in the marital relation is fundamental and basic—a personal right "retained by the people" within the meaning of the Ninth Amendment, [a right] which is protected by the Fourteenth Amendment from infringement by the [States].

Mr. Justice HARLAN, concurring in the judgment.

[I] find myself unable to join the Court's opinion [because] it seems to me to evince an approach [that] the Due Process Clause of the 14th Amendment does not touch this Connecticut statute unless the enactment is found to violate some right assured by the letter or penumbra of the Bill of Rights. [In] my view, the proper constitutional inquiry in this case is whether this Connecticut statute infringes the Due Process Clause of the 14th Amendment because the enactment violates basic values "implicit in the concept of ordered liberty." For reasons stated at length in my dissenting opinion in Poe v. Ullman [see the excerpts below], I believe that it does. While the relevant inquiry may be aided by resort to one or more of the provisions of the Bill of Rights, it is not dependent on them or any of their radiations. The Due Process Clause of the 14th Amendment stands, in my opinion, on its own bottom. [While] I could not more heartily agree that judicial "self restraint" is an indispensable ingredient of sound constitutional adjudication, I do submit that the formula suggested for achieving it is more hollow than real. "Specific" provisions of the Constitution, no less than "due process," lend themselves as readily to "personal" interpretations by judges whose constitutional outlook is simply to keep the Constitution in supposed "tune with the times." [Judicial self-restraint will be achieved] only by continual insistence upon respect for the teachings of history, solid recognition of the basic values that underlie our society, and wise application of the great roles that the doctrines of federalism and separation of powers have played [in] preserving American freedoms. Adherence to these principles will not, of course, obviate all constitutional differences of opinion among judges, nor should it. Their continued recognition will, however, go farther toward keeping most judges from roaming at large in the constitutional field than will the interpolation into the Constitution of an artificial and largely illusory restriction on the content of the Due Process Clause.

[EDITOR'S NOTE: Justice Harlan relied on his dissent in Poe v. Ullman, 367 U.S. 497 (1961), where he had elaborated his due process approach and had found the application of the Connecticut law unconstitutional. The Poe majority had failed to reach the merits: it had managed to dismiss the appeal on justiciability grounds. Excerpts from Justice Harlan's dissent in Poe follow:]

[I] believe that a statute making it a criminal offense for *married couples* to use contraceptives is an intolerable and unjustifiable invasion of privacy in the conduct of the most intimate concerns of an individual's personal life. [I] feel it desirable at the outset to state the framework of Constitutional principles in which I think the issue must be [judged]. [Through] the course of this Court's decisions, [due process] has represented the balance which our Nation, built upon postulates of respect for the liberty of the individual, has struck between that liberty and the demands of organized society. [The] balance of which I speak is the balance struck by this country, having regard to what history teaches are the traditions from which it developed as well as the traditions from which it broke. That tradition is a living thing. [The] full scope of the liberty guaranteed by the Due Process Clause cannot be found in or limited by the precise terms of the specific guarantees elsewhere provided in the Constitution. This "liberty" is not a series of isolated points picked out in terms of [such specific guarantees as speech and religion]. It is a rational continuum which, broadly speaking, includes a freedom from all substantial arbitrary impositions and purposeless restraints, . . . and which also recognizes [that] certain interests require particularly careful scrutiny of the state needs asserted to justify their abridgment.

It is argued by appellants that the judgment implicit in this statute—that the use of contraceptives by married couples is immoral—is an irrational one, that in effect it subjects them in a very important matter to the arbitrary whim of the legislature, and that it does so for no good purpose. [Yet] the very inclusion of the category of morality among state concerns indicates that society is not limited in its objects only to the physical well-being of the community, but has traditionally concerned itself with the moral soundness of its people as well. Indeed to attempt a line between public behavior and that which is purely consensual or solitary would be to withdraw from community concern a range of subjects with which every society in civilized times has found it necessary to

deal. The laws regarding marriage which provide both when the sexual powers may be used and the legal and societal context in which children are born and brought up, as well as laws forbidding adultery, fornication and homosexual practices which express the negative of the proposition, confining sexuality to lawful marriage, form a pattern so deeply pressed into the substance of our social life that any Constitutional doctrine in this area must build upon that basis. It is in this area of sexual morality, which contains many proscriptions of consensual behavior having little or no direct impact on others, that [Connecticut] has expressed its moral judgment that all use of contraceptives is improper. [Certainly], Connecticut's judgment is no more demonstrably correct or incorrect than are the varieties of judgment, expressed in law, on marriage and divorce, on adult consensual homosexuality, abortion, and sterilization, or euthanasia and suicide. If we had a case before us which required us to decide simply, and in abstraction, whether the moral judgment implicit in the application of the present statute to married couples was a sound one, the very controversial nature of these questions would, I think, require us to hesitate long before concluding that the Constitution precluded Connecticut from choosing as it has among these various views. [But we] are not presented simply with this moral judgment to be passed on as an abstract proposition. The secular state is not an examiner of consciences: it must operate in the realm of behavior, of overt actions, and where it does so operate, not only the underlying, moral purpose of its operations, but also the *choice of means* becomes relevant to any Constitutional judgment on what is [done].

Precisely what is involved here is this: the State is asserting the right to enforce its moral judgment by intruding upon the most intimate details of the marital relation with the full power of the criminal law. Potentially, this could allow the deployment of all the incidental machinery of the criminal law, arrests, searches and seizures; inevitably, it must mean at the very least the lodging of criminal charges, a public trial, and testimony as to the corpus delicti. Nor could any imaginable elaboration of presumptions, testimonial privileges, or other safeguards alleviate the necessity for testimony as to the mode and manner of the married couples' sexual relations, or at least the opportunity for the accused to make denial of the charges. In sum, the statute allows the State to enquire into, prove and punish married people for the private use of their marital intimacy.

The statute must pass a more rigorous Constitutional test than that going merely to the plausibility of its underlying rationale. This enactment involves what, by common understanding throughout the English-speaking world, must be granted to be a most fundamental aspect of "liberty," the privacy of the home in its most basic sense, and it is this which requires that the statute be subjected to "strict scrutiny." That aspect of liberty which embraces the concept of the privacy of the home receives explicit Constitutional protection at two places only [the Third and Fourth Amendments]. [It] is clear, of course, that [this] statute does not invade the privacy of the home in the usual sense, since the invasion involved [here] doubtless usually would [be] accomplished without any physical intrusion whatever into the home. What the statute undertakes to do, however, is to create a crime which is grossly offensive to this privacy, while the Constitution refers only to methods of ferreting out substantive [wrongs]. But such an analysis forecloses any claim to Constitutional protection against this form of deprivation of privacy, only if due process in this respect is limited to what is explicitly provided in the Constitution, divorced from the rational purposes, historical roots, and subsequent developments of the relevant provisions. [If] the physical curtilage of the home is protected, it is surely as a result of solicitude to protect the privacies of the life within. [The] home derives its pre-eminence as the seat of family life. And the integrity of that life is something so fundamental that it has been found to draw to its protection the principles of more than one explicitly

granted Constitutional right. Of [the] whole "private realm of family life" it is difficult to imagine what is more private or more intimate than a husband and wife's [marital relations].

Of course, [there] are countervailing considerations. [I]t would be an absurdity to suggest either that offenses may not be committed in the bosom of the family or that the home can be made a sanctuary for crime. The right of privacy [is] not an absolute. Thus, I would not suggest that adultery, homosexuality, fornication and incest are immune from criminal enquiry, however privately practiced. [But] not to discriminate between what is involved in this case and either the traditional offenses against good morals or crimes which, though they may be committed anywhere, happen to have been committed or concealed in the home, would entirely misconceive the argument that is being made. Adultery, homosexuality and the like are sexual intimacies which the State forbids altogether, but the intimacy of husband and wife is necessarily an essential and accepted feature of the institution of marriage, an institution which the State not only must allow, but which always it has fostered and protected. It is one thing when the State exerts its power either to forbid extra-marital sexuality altogether, or to say who may marry, but it is quite another when, having acknowledged a marriage and the intimacies inherent in it, it undertakes to regulate by means of the criminal law the details of that intimacy. In sum, [the] intrusion of the whole machinery of the criminal law into the very heart of marital privacy, requiring husband and wife to render account before a criminal tribunal of their uses of that intimacy, is surely a very different thing indeed from punishing those who establish intimacies which the law has always forbidden and which can have no claim to social protection.

[Since the law] marks an abridgment of important fundamental liberties, [it] will not do to urge in justification [simply] that the statute is rationally related to the effectuation of a proper state purpose. A closer scrutiny and stronger justification than that are required. Though the State has argued the Constitutional permissibility of the moral judgment underlying this statute, [its arguments do not] even remotely [suggest] a justification for the obnoxiously intrusive means it has chosen to effectuate that policy. [But] conclusive, in my view, is the utter novelty of this enactment. [No other State] has made the *use* of contraceptives a crime. [Though] undoubtedly the States [should] be allowed broad scope in experimenting, "There are limits to the extent to which a legislatively represented majority may [conduct] experiments at the expense of the dignity and personality" of the individual. In this instance these limits are, in my view, reached and [passed].

Mr. Justice WHITE, concurring in the judgment.

In my view this Connecticut law as applied to married couples deprives them of "liberty" without [due process]. Surely the right invoked in this case, to be free of regulation of the intimacies of the marriage relationship, "come[s] to this Court with a momentum for respect lacking when appeal is made to liberties which derive merely from shifting economic arrangements." The Connecticut [law] deals rather substantially with this relationship. [A] statute with these effects bears a substantial burden of justification when attacked under the 14th Amendment. [An] examination of the justification offered, however, cannot be avoided by saying that the Connecticut anti-use statute invades a protected area of privacy and association or that it demeans the marriage relationship. The nature of the right invaded is pertinent, to be sure, for statutes regulating sensitive areas of liberty [do] require "strict scrutiny" and "must be viewed in light of less drastic means for achieving the same basic purpose." [But] such statutes, if reasonably necessary for the effectuation of a legitimate and substantial state interest, and not arbitrary or capricious in application, are not [invalid].

There is no serious contention that Connecticut thinks the use of artificial or external methods of contraception immoral or unwise in itself, or that the anti-use statute is founded upon any policy of promoting population expansion. Rather, the statute is said to serve the State's policy against all forms of promiscuous or illicit sexual relationships, be they premarital or extramarital, concededly a permissible and legitimate legislative goal. [I] wholly fail to see how the ban on the use of contraceptives by married couples in any way reinforces the State's ban on illicit sexual relationships. [Perhaps] the theory is that the flat ban on use prevents married people from possessing contraceptives and without the ready availability of such devices for use in the marital relationship, there will be no or less temptation to use them in extramarital ones. This reasoning rests on the premises that married people will comply with the anti-use ban in regard to their marital relationship, notwithstanding total nonenforcement in this context and apparent nonenforcibility, but will not comply with criminal statutes prohibiting extramarital affairs and the anti-use statute in respect to illicit sexual relationships, a premise whose validity has not been demonstrated and whose intrinsic validity is not very evident. At most the broad ban is of marginal utility to the declared objective. A statute limiting its prohibition on use to persons engaging in the prohibited relationship would serve the end posited by Connecticut in the same way, and with the same effectiveness, or ineffectiveness, as the broad anti-use statute under attack in this case. I find nothing in this record justifying the sweeping scope of this statute, with its telling effect on the freedoms of [married persons].

Mr. Justice BLACK [joined by Justice STEWART] dissenting.

[The] law is every bit as offensive to me as it is to my Brethren [who], reciting reasons why it is offensive to them, hold it unconstitutional. [But] I cannot [join] their conclusion. [The] Court talks about a constitutional ["right of privacy"]. There are, of course, guarantees in certain specific constitutional provisions which are designed in part to protect privacy at certain times and places with respect to certain activities.

Such, for example, is the [Fourth Amendment]. But I think it belittles that Amendment to talk about it as though it protects nothing but "privacy." One of the most effective ways of diluting or expanding a constitutionally guaranteed right is to substitute for the crucial word or words of a constitutional guarantee another word or words, more or less flexible and more or less restricted in [meaning]. "Privacy" is a broad, abstract and ambiguous concept which can easily be shrunken in meaning but which can [also] easily be interpreted as a constitutional ban against many things other than searches and seizures. [I] get nowhere in this case by talk about a constitutional "right of privacy" as an emanation from one or more constitutional provisions. I like my privacy as well as the next one, but I am nevertheless compelled to admit that government has a right to invade it unless prohibited by some specific constitutional [provision].

This brings me to the arguments made by my Brothers Harlan, White and Goldberg. [I] discuss the due process and Ninth Amendment arguments together because on analysis they turn out to be the same thing—merely using different words to claim [the] power to invalidate any legislative act which the judges find irrational, unreasonable or offensive. [If] formulas based on "natural justice" [are] to prevail, they require judges to determine what is or is not constitutional on the basis of their own appraisal of what laws are unwise or unnecessary. The power to make such decisions is of course that of a legislative body. [I] do not believe that we are granted power [to] measure constitutionality by our belief that the legislation is arbitrary, capricious or unreasonable, or accomplishes no justifiable purpose, or is offensive to our own notions of "civilized standards of conduct."

My Brother Goldberg has adopted the recent discovery that the Ninth Amendment as well as the Due Process Clause can be used by this Court as authority to strike down all state legislation which this Court thinks violates "fundamental principles of liberty and justice," or is contrary to the "traditions and collective

conscience of our people." He also states [that] in making decisions on this basis judges will not consider "their personal and private notions." One may ask how they can avoid considering them. [The Framers did not give this Court] veto powers over [lawmaking]. Nor does anything in the history of the Amendment offer any support for such a shocking doctrine. [That] Amendment was passed [to] assure the people that the [Constitution] was intended to limit the Federal Government to the powers granted expressly or by necessary implication. [This] fact is perhaps responsible for the peculiar phenomenon that for a period of a century and a half no serious suggestion was ever made that the Ninth Amendment, enacted to protect state powers against federal invasion, could be used as a weapon of federal power to prevent state legislatures from passing laws they consider appropriate to govern [local affairs].

I realize that many good and able men have eloquently spoken and written [about] the duty of this Court to keep the Constitution in tune with the times. [I] reject that philosophy. The Constitution makers knew the need for change and provided for it [through the amendment process]. [The] Due Process Clause with an "arbitrary and capricious" or "shocking to the conscience" formula was liberally used by this Court to strike down economic legislation in the early decades of this century, threatening, many people thought, the tranquility and stability of the Nation. See, e.g., [Lochner]. That formula [is] no less dangerous when used to enforce this Court's views about personal rights than those about economic rights. I had thought that we had laid that formula, as a means for striking down state legislation, to rest. [Apparently] my Brethren have less quarrel with state economic regulations than former Justices of their persuasion had. But any limitation upon their using the natural law due process philosophy to strike down any state law, dealing with any activity whatever, will obviously be only self-imposed. [The] late Judge Learned Hand, after emphasizing his view that judges should not use the due process formula suggested in the concurring opinions today or any other formula like it to invalidate legislation offensive to their "personal preferences," made the statement, with which I fully agree, that: "For myself it would be most irksome to be ruled by a bevy of Platonic Guardians, even if I knew how to choose them, which I assuredly do not." So far as I am concerned, Connecticut's law as applied here is not forbidden by any provision of the Federal Constitution as that Constitution was [written].

Mr. Justice STEWART, whom Mr. Justice BLACK joins, dissenting.

[I] think this is an uncommonly silly law. [But] we are not asked in this case to say whether we think this law is unwise, or even asinine. We are asked to hold that it violates [the] Constitution. And that I cannot do. In the course of its opinion the Court refers to no less than six Amendments to the Constitution [but] does not say which of these Amendments, if any, it thinks is infringed by this Connecticut law. We *are* told that the Due Process Clause of the 14th Amendment is not, as such, the "guide" in this case. With that much I agree. [As] to the First, Third, Fourth, and Fifth Amendments, I can find nothing in any of them to invalidate this Connecticut [law]. [To] say that the Ninth Amendment has anything to do with this case is to turn somersaults with history. The Ninth Amendment, like its companion the Tenth, [was] simply to make clear that the adoption of the Bill of Rights did not alter the plan that the *Federal* Government was to be a government of express and limited powers. [What] provision of the Constitution, then, does make this state law invalid? The Court says it is the right of privacy "created by several fundamental constitutional guarantees." With all deference, I can find no such general right of privacy in the Bill of Rights, in any other part of the Constitution, or in any case ever before decided by this [Court].

■ Privacy as a Constitutional Right

INTERPRETATION AND
HISTORIOGRAPHY

DAVID A. J. RICHARDS

The idea of a written constitution does not arise in a historical and cultural vacuum. It is associated with deep currents in Western political and religious thought. The form of moral ideal to which both political and religious thought point is contractarian. Accordingly, when the greatest political theorist of this culture and period, John Locke, gives clear expression to the moral ideal of religious and political community underlying these developments, his highly abstract political theory is clearly contractarian. The interpretation of Locke's political theory and its actual historical influence on American political culture are complex matters. Critical historians of political theory make increasingly clear the religious roots of Locke's thought. The

David A. J. Richards, "Interpretation and Historiography," *Southern California Law Review,* vol. 56 (1985), pp. 490 ff.

general influence of contractarian thought on America may have been mediated more by Hutcheson and other moral sense theorists who, of course, incorporated and developed Locke's political ideas. The Lockean texts of central influence in the early eighteenth century in America appear to be his general epistemology and his arguments for religious toleration. Furthermore, the text of Locke's political theory (i.e., *The Second Treatise of Government*) appears as a central vehicle of American political thought only in the revolutionary period. Nonetheless, the critical historiography of this period confirms the pervasive contractarian nature of political thought, not always tied to specifically Lockean political texts, but implicit in other Lockean texts and other works that were read and that assume and elaborate Locke's thought.

The self-conception of the American Constitution as a written constitution cannot be given a historical sense if legal interpreters fail to take seriously the contractarian moral ideal of community that actuates it. The abortive republican ideals and conceptions of the Puritan Revolution that never took root in Britain permitted in America the remarkable opportunity of self-conscious political elaboration. The American Constitution is a historically remarkable attempt to use the best political theory and political science of the age, combined with a diverse practical experience of democratic self-rule, to give a written text of substantive and procedural constraints on and definitions of state power that would achieve in America what has never been achieved elsewhere: enduring republican government in a large territory. The Constitution, followed shortly by the Bill of Rights, is a self-conscious product of reflection on past republican experiments (Greece, Rome, the Florentine and Venetian republics, the Cromwellian commonwealth) and the republican political theory and science of their emergence, stability, and decline (Polybius, Machiavelli Guicciardini, Giannotti, Harrington, Locke, Sidney). The expression of such self-conscious reflection in the form of a written constitution takes its significance from a larger cultural and moral tradition, which conceives political legitimacy on a contractarian model of observance by the state of those predictable and orderly constraints that acknowledge and express the dignity of persons and citizens as free, rational, and equal. The written form of the constraints takes its moral life from a culture of widespread textual literacy, which recognizes in the substantive and procedural terms of the written constraints on state power the acknowledgment of one's own interpretive dignity as a free and rational person—thus, the focal significance in constitutional thought and practice, as I shall later elaborate, of the inalienable right to conscience.

Contractarian political theory may, I believe, deepen our understanding of these political traditions and the constitutional guarantees that they shape. Thus, in view of the primacy that the right to conscience has enjoyed in constitutional history, it should strike us that Rawls gives the argument for religious toleration central place in his argument for his first principle of justice (the principle of equal liberty). The argument for religious toleration is, Rawls argues, a kind of paradigm case, which can be suitably generalized to cover the other rights and liberties protected by the first principle. The priority accorded this argument is not, I believe, an expository convenience or accidentally connected to the structure of the underlying contractarian moral conception, as it might be in a comparable utilitarian argument. Rather, on a contractarian conception, the terms of the fundamentally regulative constitutional principles agreed to must dignify the nature of persons as free, rational, and equal. Accordingly, these principles and the constitutional guarantees that embody them must protect the inalienable right to conscience, for this right protects the very conditions of the freedom and rationality of the person. Thus, contractarian theory gives a deepened moral interpretation to the focal significance of the right to conscience in the historical elaboration of constitutional thought and practice. Recognition of this right to interpretive independence in basic questions of life's meaning is explicated as being at the core of the conception of persons as free, rational, and equal, which constitutional government dignifies and progressively elaborates.

This kind of illuminating convergence of political theory and constitutional interpretation has as an interpretive consequence that quite abstract philosophical reflection on relevant issues of justice in government may shape the terms of constitutional discourse. With respect to the religion guarantees of the first amendment, for example, quite abstract philosophical inquiry may usefully explicate the way in which the freedom and rationality of the person is best understood and, thus, the scope and meaning of the right to conscience. Such an inquiry would be, on the one hand, an abstract exercise in moral and political philosophy and, on the other, a searching inquiry into values and concepts implicit in our larger cultural and political history. As abstract normative philosophy, the agenda would include a philosophical psychology of the relations among will, desires, belief, and knowledge, a naturalized epistemology of epistemic rationality, a theory of practical rationality and its connections to epistemic rationality, an analysis of conceptions of freedom, and an account of moral ideals of the person and the unity of the self. As a form of political and cultural history, the same account would clarify and be clarified by the examination of deep metaphysical, epistemological, and moral shifts in Western thought. Some examples are the impact of voluntarist theology on the decline of metaphysical beliefs in the centrality to our personhood of contemplation of and regulation by "the great chain of being," and that theology's legitimation of an active scientific curiosity, the associated reintroduction and development of skeptical thought, its attack on Aristotelian certainty, and its stimulation of central scientific and philosophical interest in ways of knowing, and the associated political and religious defense of toleration, as in Bayle and Locke,

premised on both the new epistemology of experience (and the theory of common sense rationality, accessible to all, that it made possible) and a moral ideal of respect for the uncompromisable demands of one's own conscience. Such inquiries would illuminate the connections of constitutional traditions to the larger cultural traditions that they reflect. They would show the rich common discourse between philosophy and law, so deepening to both enterprises. For example, such an abstract exercise both in political philosophy and historical understanding would make possible a plausible theory of background rights, in Dworkin's sense, which would illuminate the meaning of the right to conscience as an abstract background right. This would enable constitutional theory to clarify how the religious clauses (free exercise and anti-establishment) should be understood and coordinated. We might, thus, advance discussion of what the underlying constitutional conception of neutrality, pervasive throughout the jurisprudence of the first amendment, should be taken to mean. Controversy over the proper historiography of the religion clauses might, thus, be resolved. Furthermore, intractable contemporary controversy over church–state relations might be clarified in ways that bring out the crucial significance of the antiestablishment principle as an expression of respect for the dignity of a free mind and person.

■ ■ ■

Controversy over the nature and application of the constitutional right to privacy has followed in the wake of each of the Supreme Court's decisions extending the right to the use of contraceptives, to the use of obscene materials in the home, and to the use of abortion services. My earlier remarks in defense of the interpretive legitimacy of the abstract intention approach to interpretation of the normative clauses of the Constitution argued that the maintenance of a continuous yet vital constitutional tradition in the United States has required the Supreme Court to interpret relevant constitutional text in terms of abstract background rights (equal liberties of religion and speech, equal treatment, cruel and unusual punishment, etc.). Continuity is insured by the common appeal to an abstract intention in different historical periods; vitality is insured by the Court's duty reasonably to articulate changes in the scope of application of the common concept in light of each generation's best arguments and experience about what should count as basic liberties of the person, or the demands of equality, or unjustly disproportionate punishment.

The constitutional right to privacy was elaborated by the Supreme Court consistent with this traditional approach to its interpretive task. There is a powerful historical argument that the generation who drafted and approved the Constitution and Bill of Rights thought of these documents as protecting not only enumerated rights, but unenumerated basic human rights as well. These documents were meant to embody such unenumerated basic rights both in the ninth amendment and in the privileges and immunities clause of article four. Certainly, later judicial traditions reflect and elaborate such an understanding. There can be little historical doubt that one such assumed basic human right was the natural right to marriage. Furthermore, there is quite good historical reason indeed to suppose that this right was thought of as one nonexclusive example of a more abstract background right of voluntary association. Because these understandings are appealed to by one or another of the clauses of the fourteenth amendment, the Supreme Court has quite properly deployed interpretations of the abstract right of voluntary association in its elaboration of the first amendment guarantees of liberty of religion and speech: the amendment is understood to protect, *inter alia*, rights to associate for various religious, political, philosophical, and other purposes. For the same reasons, the Court has properly elaborated a right to constitutional privacy originating precisely in the right to marriage, historically understood as one central example of the more abstract right to association. Consistent with the abstract nature of its background right, later cases have elaborated the right beyond intimate relations in marriage.

The principle of these cases rests on the vindication of a right of intimate association, the coercive prohibition of which by state laws cannot today satisfy their constitutionally required burden of justification. The contraception cases are, I believe, a clearly correct application of this principle. In *Griswold v. Connecticut*, for example, the state prohibition of the use of contraceptives in marriage limited the basic right of married couples to regulate the form of their sexual lives and their procreative consequences in forming new intimate relations with offspring. Such state prohibitions cannot today satisfy the constitutional burden of protecting the rights of other persons. On the contrary, legitimate state purposes of population control may thus be advanced. The prohibition could not reasonably be supposed to protect persons from self-destructive harms. In fact, contraceptive use in marriage has secured to couples the dignity of a deepened freedom and rationality of sexual expression in their intimate personal lives and greater control over their reproductive histories and other personal aims. Any residual justification of these laws appears to be grounded in an ideal linking sex with procreation and the associated ideal that sex without procreation is a kind of homicide. This argument cannot satisfy the constitutionally neutral burden of justification to the many reasonable persons who do not share these ideals.

Criminal prohibitions bearing on the right of constitutional privacy require a heavy burden of justification that can, in principle, be met. I assume there would be no constitutional objection to the application of neutral criminal statutes to intrafamilial murders, wife or husband beatings, or child abuse, no matter how rooted in intimate family life and sexuality. Nor should there be any objection to rape laws applicable to married or unmarried sexual intimacies. In these cases, the constitutional burden of justification is met. Countervailing rights of persons justify coercive interference into intimate relations. On the other hand, criminal prohibitions on the use of contraceptives could not meet this burden of justification. Countervailing rights were either too constitutionally nonneutral, controversial, or speculative to satisfy the burden required to abridge such intimately personal sexual matters.

The thought that arguments of countervailing rights here are nonneutral rests, in part, on arguments colored by the antiestablishment clause, which shows how the coherent integration of the meanings of seemingly disparate constitutional texts advances and deepens constitutional analysis. The kind of program for interpretation of the religious clauses, earlier sketched, may bear fruit here. For if the operative arguments for the criminalization of intimate association (a fundamental constitutional right) are associated with metaphysical and normative assumptions that many reasonable consciences do not entertain, the enforcement of such laws degrades the moral independence of free and rational persons to precisely the

kind of moral enslavement of conscience that the antiestablishment clause forbids.

For these reasons, the inference and elaboration of the constitutional right to privacy are consistent with both text (the ninth amendment, article four's privileges and immunities clause, and the privileges and immunities and due process clauses of the fourteenth amendment) and history. They are also supported by good arguments of political theory of the implicitly contractarian kind that underlies the constitutional right to privacy. Free and rational persons would preserve the dignity of a personal life from brutal and callous state manipulation ungrounded in the pursuit of neutral goods.

Arguments of these kinds explain the interpretive legitimacy of the right to constitutional privacy and can justify the Court's work in this area and clarify the incoherence of the Court's failure to extend the right further (to consensual adult sexual relations, for example). It suffices, however, for present purposes, to show how little substance there is in the so-called textual arguments against constitutional privacy as a general principle of our constitutional law.

NEUTRAL PRINCIPLES AND SOME FIRST AMENDMENT PROBLEMS

ROBERT BORK

The subject of the lengthy and often acrimonious debate about the proper role of the Supreme Court under the Constitution is one that preoccupies many people these days: when is authority legitimate? I find it conve-

nient to discuss that question in the context of the Warren Court and its works simply because the Warren Court posed the issue in acute form. The issue did not disappear along with the era of the Warren Court majorities, how-

Robert Bork, "Neutral Principles and Some First Amendment Problems," *Indiana Law Journal*, vol. 47, pp. 1 ff.

ever. It arises when any court either exercises or declines to exercise the power to invalidate any act of another branch of government. The Supreme Court is a major power center, and we must ask when its power should be used and when it should be withheld.

Our starting place, inevitably, is Professor Herbert Wechsler's argument that the Court must not be merely a "naked power organ," which means that its decisions must be controlled by principle. "A principled decision," according to Wechsler, "is one that rests on reasons with respect to all the issues in a case, reasons that in their generality and their neutrality transcend any immediate result that is involved."

Wechsler chose the term "neutral principles" to capsulate his argument, though he recognizes that the legal principle to be applied is itself never neutral because it embodies a choice of one value rather than another. Wechsler asked for the neutral application of principles, which is a requirement, as Professor Louis L. Jaffe puts it, that the judge "sincerely believe in the principle upon which he purports to rest his decision." "The judge," says Jaffe, "must believe in the validity of the reasons given for the decision at least in the sense that he is prepared to apply them to a later case which he cannot honestly distinguish." He must not, that is, decide lawlessly. But is the demand for neutrality in judges merely another value choice, one that is no more principled than any other? I think not, but to prove it we must rehearse fundamentals. This is familiar terrain but important and still debated.

The requirement that the Court be principled arises from the resolution of the seeming anomaly of judicial supremacy in a democratic society. If the judiciary really is supreme, able to rule when and as it sees fit, the society is not democratic. The anomaly is dissipated, however, by the model of government embodied in the structure of the Constitution, a model upon which popular consent to limited government by the Supreme Court also rests. This model we

may for convenience, though perhaps not with total accuracy, call "Madisonian."

A Madisonian system is not completely democratic, if by "democratic" we mean completely majoritarian. It assumes that in wide areas of life majorities are entitled to rule for no better reason [than] that they are majorities. We need not pause here to examine the philosophical underpinnings of that assumption since it is a "given" in our society; nor need we worry that "majority" is a term of art meaning often no more than the shifting combinations of minorities that add up to temporary majorities in the legislature. That majorities are so constituted is inevitable. In any case, one essential premise of the Madisonian model is majoritarianism. The model has also a counter-majoritarian premise, however, for it assumes there are some areas of life a majority should not control. There are some things a majority should not do to us no matter how democratically it decides to do them. These are areas properly left to individual freedom, and coercion by the majority in these aspects of life is tyranny.

Some see the model as containing an inherent, perhaps an insoluble, dilemma. Majority tyranny occurs if legislation invades the areas properly left to individual freedom. Minority tyranny occurs if the majority is prevented from ruling where its power is legitimate. Yet, quite obviously, neither the majority nor the minority can be trusted to define the freedom of the other. This dilemma is resolved in constitutional theory, and in popular understanding, by the Supreme Court's power to define both majority and minority freedom through the interpretation of the Constitution. Society consents to be ruled undemocratically within defined areas by certain enduring principles believed to be stated in, and placed beyond the reach of majorities by, the Constitution.

But this resolution of the dilemma imposes severe requirements upon the Court. For it follows that the Court's power is legitimate only if it has, and can demonstrate in reasoned opinions that it has, a valid theory, derived from the Constitution, of the respective spheres of majority and minority freedom. If it does not have such a theory but merely imposes its own value choices, or worse if it pretends to have a theory but actually follows its own predilections, the Court violates the postulates of the Madisonian model that alone justifies its power. It then necessarily abets the tyranny either of the majority or of the minority.

This argument is central to the issue of legitimate authority because the Supreme Court's power to govern rests upon popular acceptance of this model. Evidence that this is, in fact, the basis of the Court's power is to be gleaned everywhere in our culture. We need not canvass here such things as high school civics texts and newspaper commentary, for the most telling evidence may be found in the U.S. Reports. The Supreme Court regularly insists that its results, and most particularly its controversial results, do not spring from the mere will of the Justices in the majority but are supported, indeed compelled, by a proper understanding of the Constitution of the United States. Value choices are attributed to the Founding Fathers, not to the Court. The way an institution advertises tells you what it thinks its customers demand.

This is, I think, the ultimate reason the Court must be principled. If it does not have and rigorously adhere to a valid and consistent theory of majority and minority freedoms based upon the Constitution, judicial supremacy, given the axioms of our system, is, precisely to that extent, illegitimate. The root of its illegitimacy is that it opens a chasm between the reality of the Court's performance and the constitutional and popular assumptions that give it power.

I do not mean to rest the argument entirely upon the popular understanding of the Court's function. Even if society generally should ultimately perceive what the Court is in fact doing and, having seen, prove content to have major policies determined by the unguided discretion of judges rather than by elected representatives, a principled judge

would, I believe, continue to consider himself bound by an obligation to the document and to the structure of government that it prescribes. At least he would be bound so long as any litigant existed who demanded such adherence of him. I do not understand how, on any other theory of judicial obligation, the Court could, as it does now, protect voting rights if a large majority of the relevant constituency were willing to see some groups or individuals deprived of such rights. But even if I am wrong in that, at the very least an honest judge would owe it to the body politic to cease invoking the authority of the Constitution and to make explicit the imposition of his own will, for only then would we know whether the society understood enough of what is taking place to be said to have consented.

Judge J. Skelly Wright, in an argument resting on different premises, has severely criticized the advocates of principle. He defends the value-choosing role of the Warren Court, setting that Court in opposition to something he refers to as the "scholarly tradition," which criticizes that Court for its lack of principle. A perceptive reader, sensitive to nuance, may suspect that the Judge is rather out of sympathy with that tradition from such hints as his reference to "self-appointed scholastic mandarins."

The "mandarins" of the academy anger the Judge because they engage in "haughty derision of the Court's powers of analysis and reasoning." Yet, curiously enough, Judge Wright makes no attempt to refute the charge but rather seems to adopt the technique of confession and avoidance. He seems to be arguing that a Court engaged in choosing fundamental values for society cannot be expected to produce principled decisions at the same time. Decisions first, principles later. One wonders, however, how the Court or the rest of us are to know that the decisions are correct or what they portend for the future if they are not accompanied by the principles that explain and justify them. And it would not be amiss to point out that quite often the principles required of the Warren Court's decisions never did put in an appearance. But Judge Wright's main point appears to be that value choice is the most important function of the Supreme Court, so that if we must take one or the other, and apparently we must, we should prefer a process of selecting values to one of constructing and articulating principles. His argument, I believe, boils down to a syllogism. I. The Supreme Court should "protect our constitutional rights and liberties." II. The Supreme Court must "make fundamental value choices" in order to "protect our constitutional rights and liberties." III. Therefore, the Supreme Court should "make fundamental value choices."

The argument displays an all too common confusion. If we have constitutional rights and liberties already, rights and liberties specified by the Constitution, the Court need make no fundamental value choices in order to protect them, and it certainly need not have difficulty enunciating principles. If, on the other hand, "constitutional rights and liberties" are not in some real sense specified by the Constitution but are the rights and liberties the Court chooses, on the basis of its own values, to give to us, then the conclusion was contained entirely in the major premise, and the Judge's syllogism is no more than an assertion of what it purported to prove.

If I am correct so far, no argument that is both coherent and respectable can be made supporting a Supreme Court that "chooses fundamental values" because a Court that makes rather than implements value choices cannot be squared with the presuppositions of a democratic society. The man who understands the issues and nevertheless insists upon the rightness of the Warren Court's performance ought also, if he is candid, to admit that he is prepared to sacrifice democratic process to his own moral views. He claims for the Supreme Court an institutionalized role as perpetrator of limited coups d'etat.

Such a man occupies an impossible philosophic position. What can he say, for instance,

of a Court that does not share his politics or his morality? I can think of nothing except the assertion that he will ignore the Court whenever he can get away with it and overthrow it if he can. In his view the Court has no legitimacy, and there is no reason any of us should obey it. And, this being the case, the advocate of a value–choosing Court must answer another difficult question. Why should the Court, a committee of nine lawyers, be the sole agent of change? The man who prefers results to processes has no reason to say that the Court is more legitimate than any other institution. If the Court will not listen, why not argue the case to some other group, say the Joint Chiefs of Staff, a body with rather better means for implementing its decisions?

■ ■ ■

It follows that the choice of "fundamental values" by the Court cannot be justified. Where constitutional materials do not clearly specify the value to be preferred, there is no principled way to prefer any claimed human value to any other. The judge must stick close to the text and the history, and their fair implications, and not construct new rights. The [*Griswold* case] illustrates the point. The *Griswold* decision has been acclaimed by legal scholars as a major advance in constitutional law, a salutary demonstration of the Court's ability to protect fundamental human values. I regret to have to disagree, and my regret is all the more sincere because I once took the same position and did so in print. In extenuation I can only say that at the time I thought, quite erroneously, that new basic rights could be derived logically by finding and extrapolating a more general principle of individual autonomy underlying the particular guarantees of the Bill of Rights.

The Court's *Griswold* opinion, by Justice Douglas, and the array of concurring opinions, by Justices Goldberg, White and Harlan, all failed to justify the derivation of any principle used to strike down the Connecticut anti–contraceptive statute or to define the scope of the principle. Justice Douglas, to whose opinion I must confine myself, began by pointing out that "specific guarantees in the Bill of Rights have penumbras, formed by emanations from those guarantees that help give them life and substance." Nothing is exceptional there. In the case Justice Douglas cited, *NAACP v. Alabama*, the State was held unable to force disclosure of membership lists because of the chilling effect upon the rights of assembly and political action of the NAACP's members. The penumbra was created solely to preserve a value central to the first amendment, applied in this case through the fourteenth amendment. It had no life of its own as a right independent of the value specified by the first amendment.

But Justice Douglas then performed a miracle of transubstantiation. He called the first amendment's penumbra a protection of "privacy" and then asserted that other amendments create "zones of privacy." He had no better reason to use the word "privacy" than that the individual is free within these zones, free to act in public as well as in private. None of these penumbral zones—from the first, third, fourth or fifth amendments, all of which he cited, along with the ninth—covered the case before him. One more leap was required. Justice Douglas asserted that these various "zones of privacy" created an independent right of privacy, a right not lying within the penumbra of any specific amendment. He did not disclose, however, how a series of specified rights combined to create a new and unspecified right.

The *Griswold* opinion fails every test of neutrality. The derivation of the principle was utterly specious, and so was its definition. In fact, we are left with no idea of what the principle really forbids. Derivation and definition are interrelated here. Justice Douglas called the amendments and their penumbras "zones of privacy," though of course they are not that at all. They protect both private and public behavior and so would more properly be labelled "zones of freedom." If we follow Justice Douglas in his next step, these zones would then add up to an independent right of freedom, which

is to say, a general constitutional right to be free of legal coercion, a manifest impossibility in any imaginable society.

Griswold, then, is an unprincipled decision, both in the way in which it derives a new constitutional right and in the way it defines that right, or rather fails to define it. We are left with no idea of the sweep of the right of privacy and hence no notion of the cases to which it may or may not be applied in the future. The truth is that the Court could not reach its result in *Griswold* through principle. The reason is obvious. Every clash between a minority claiming freedom and a majority claiming power to regulate involves a choice between the gratifications of the two groups. When the Constitution has not spoken, the Court will be able to find no scale, other than its own value preferences, upon which to weigh the respective claims to pleasure. Compare the facts in *Griswold* with a hypothetical suit by an electric utility company and one of its customers to void a smoke pollution ordinance as unconstitutional. The cases are identical.

In *Griswold* a husband and wife assert that they wish to have sexual relations without fear of unwanted children. The law impairs their sexual gratifications. The State can assert, and at one stage in that litigation did assert, that the majority finds the use of contraceptives immoral. Knowledge that it takes place and that the State makes no effort to inhibit it causes the majority anguish, impairs their gratifications.

The electrical company asserts that it wishes to produce electricity at low cost in order to reach a wide market and make profits. Its customer asserts that he wants a lower cost so that prices can be held low. The smoke pollution regulation impairs his and the company's stockholders' economic gratifications. The State can assert not only that the majority prefer clean air to lower prices, but also that the absence of the regulation impairs the majority's physical and aesthetic gratifications.

Neither case is covered specifically or by obvious implication in the Constitution. Unless we can distinguish forms of gratification, the only course for a principled Court is to let the majority have its way in both cases. It is clear that the Court cannot make the necessary distinction. There is no principled way to decide that one man's gratifications are more deserving of respect than another's or that one form of gratification is more worthy than another. Why is sexual gratification more worthy than moral gratification? Why is sexual gratification nobler than economic gratification? There is no way of deciding these matters other than by reference to some system of moral or ethical values that has no objective or intrinsic validity of its own and about which men can and do differ. Where the Constitution does not embody the moral or ethical choice, the judge has no basis other than his own values upon which to set aside the community judgment embodied in the statute. That, by definition, is an inadequate basis for judicial supremacy. The issue of the community's moral and ethical values, the issue of the degree of pain an activity causes, are matters concluded by the passage and enforcement of the laws in question. The judiciary has no role to play other than that of applying the statutes in a fair and impartial manner.

One of my colleagues refers to this conclusion, not without sarcasm, as the "Equal Gratification Clause." The phrase is apt, and I accept it, though not the sarcasm. Equality of human gratifications, where the document does not impose a hierarchy, is an essential part of constitutional doctrine because of the necessity that judges be principled. To be perfectly clear on the subject, I repeat that the principle is not applicable to legislatures. Legislation requires value choice and cannot be principled in the sense under discussion. Courts must accept any value choice the legislature makes unless it clearly runs contrary to a choice made in the framing of the Constitution.

It follows, of course, that broad areas of constitutional law ought to be reformulated. Most obviously, it follows that substantive due process, revived by the *Griswold* case, is and always has been an improper doctrine. Substantive due process requires the Court to say, without guidance from the Constitution, which liberties or gratifications may be infringed by majorities and which may not. This means that *Griswold's* antecedents were also wrongly decided, *e.g.*, *Meyer v. Nebraska*, which struck down a statute forbidding the teaching of subjects in any language other than English; *Pierce v. Society of Sisters*, which set aside a statute compelling all Oregon school children to attend public schools; *Adkins v. Children's Hospital*, which invalidated a statute of Congress authorizing a board to fix minimum wages for women and children in the District of Columbia; and *Lochner v. New York*, which voided a statute fixing maximum hours of work for bakers. With some of these cases I am in political agreement, and perhaps *Pierce's* result could be reached on acceptable grounds, but there is no justification for the Court's methods. In *Lochner*, Justice Peckham, defending liberty from what he conceived as a mere meddlesome interference, asked, "[A]re we all . . . at the mercy of legislative majorities?" The correct answer, where the Constitution does not speak, must be "yes."

QUESTIONS FOR DISCUSSION

1. Does Richards' argument depend on the original intentions of the framers? If so, how?

2. Under Richards' view, can there be moral rights that are not constitutional rights? Can there be constitutional rights that are not moral rights? What would Richards say about a right contained in the constitutional text that

was immoral? What if the Constitution still specifically protected the ownership of slaves?

3. Does Bork think that there is a moral right to privacy? Would it matter
to him if there was? If he were a member of the Connecticut legislature,
do you think he would vote to repeal the prohibition on the use of contraceptives?

4. Is Justice Douglas's argument the same as Richards'? How are they similar,
and how are they different?

■ The Right to an Abortion

ROE V. WADE

410 U.S. 113 (1973)

Mr. Justice BLACKMUN delivered the opinion
of the Court.

[We] forthwith acknowledge our awareness
of the sensitive and emotional nature of the
abortion controversy, of the vigorous opposing
views, [and] of the deep and seemingly absolute
convictions that the subject inspires. [Our] task,
of course, is to resolve the issue by constitutional measurement, free of emotion and of
predilection. We seek earnestly to do this, and,
because we do, we have inquired into, and in
this opinion place some emphasis upon, medical and medical-legal history and what that
history reveals about man's attitudes toward
the abortion procedure over the centuries. [The]
principal thrust of appellant's attack on the
Texas statutes is that they improperly invade a
right, said to be possessed by the pregnant
woman, to choose to terminate her pregnancy.
[Before] addressing this claim, we feel it desirable briefly to survey, in several aspects, the history of abortion, for such insight as that history
may afford us.

[EDITOR'S NOTE: Justice Blackmun's review of that history is omitted. His survey began
with "ancient attitudes"—starting with "Persian
Empire abortifacients"—and continued through
"the Hippocratic Oath," "the common law," "English statutory law," and "American law," to the
positions of the American Medical, Public Health
and Bar Associations. After stating the possible
state interests in restricting abortions (summarized below), he continued:]

The Constitution does not explicitly mention any right of privacy. [But] the Court has
recognized that a right of personal privacy, or a
guarantee of certain areas or zones of privacy,
does exist under the Constitution. In varying
contexts, the Court or individual Justices have,
indeed, found at least the roots of that right in
the First Amendment; in the Fourth and Fifth
Amendments; in the penumbras of the Bill of

Rights [Griswold]; in the Ninth Amendment; or in the concept of liberty guaranteed [by] the 14th Amendment. These decisions make it clear that only personal rights that can be deemed "fundamental" or "implicit in the concept of ordered liberty" are included in this guarantee of personal privacy. They also make it clear that the right has some extension to activities relating to marriage, procreation, contraception, and family relationships.

This right of privacy, whether it be founded in the 14th Amendment's concept of personal liberty [as] we feel it is, or, as the District Court determined, in the [Ninth Amendment], is broad enough to encompass a woman's decision whether or not to terminate her pregnancy. The detriment that the State would impose upon the pregnant woman by denying this choice altogether is apparent. Specific and direct harm medically diagnosable even in early pregnancy may be involved. Maternity, or additional offspring, may force upon the woman a distressful life and future. Psychological harm may be imminent. Mental and physical health may be taxed by child care. There is also the distress, for all concerned, associated with the unwanted child, and there is the problem of bringing a child into a family already unable, psychologically and otherwise, to care for it. In other cases, as in this one, the additional difficulties and continuing stigma of unwed motherhood may be involved. All these are factors the woman and her responsible physician necessarily will consider in consultation.

On the basis of elements such as these, appellants and some amici argue that the woman's right is absolute and that she is entitled to terminate her pregnancy at whatever time, in whatever way, and for whatever reason she alone chooses. With this we do not agree. [The] Court's decisions recognizing a right of privacy also acknowledge that some state regulation in areas protected by that right is appropriate. [A] state may properly assert important interests in safeguarding health, in maintaining medical standards, and in protecting potential life. At some point in pregnancy, these respective interests become sufficiently compelling to sustain regulation of the factors that govern the abortion decision. The privacy right involved, therefore, cannot be said to be absolute. In fact, it is not clear to us that the claim asserted by some amici that one has an unlimited right to do with one's body as one pleases bears a close relationship to the right of privacy previously articulated in the Court's decisions. The Court has refused to recognize an unlimited right of this kind in the past. We, therefore, conclude that the right of personal privacy includes the abortion decision, but that this right is not unqualified and must be considered against important state interests in regulation. [Where] certain "fundamental rights" are involved, the Court has held that regulation limiting these rights may be justified only by a "compelling state interest" [and] that legislative enactments must be narrowly drawn to express only the legitimate state interests at stake. [Appellant claims] an absolute right that bars any state imposition of criminal penalties in the area. Appellee argues that the State's determination to recognize and protect prenatal life from and after conception constitutes a compelling state interest. [We] do not agree fully with either formulation.

A. The appellee and certain amici argue that the fetus is a "person" within the language and meaning of the 14th Amendment. [If so,] the appellant's case, of course, collapses, for the fetus' right to life is then guaranteed specifically by the Amendment. [The] Constitution does not define "person" in so many words. Section 1 of the 14th Amendment contains three references to "person." ["Person"] is used in other places in the Constitution. [But] in nearly all these instances, the use of the word is such that it has application only postnatally. None indicates, with any assurance, that it has any possible prenatal application. All this, together with our observation [that] throughout the major portion of the 19th century prevailing legal abortion practices were far freer than they are today, persuades us that the word "person," as used in the 14th Amendment, does not include the unborn. [We] pass on to other considerations.

B. The pregnant woman cannot be isolated in her privacy. She carries an embryo and, later, a [fetus]. The situation therefore is inherently different from marital intimacy, or bedroom possession of obscene material, or marriage, or procreation, or education. [I]t is reasonable and appropriate for a State to decide that at some point in time another interest, that of health of the mother or that of potential human life, becomes significantly involved. The woman's privacy is no longer sole and any right of privacy she possesses must be measured accordingly.

Texas urges that, apart from the 14th Amendment, life begins at conception and is present throughout pregnancy, and that, therefore, the State has a compelling interest in protecting that life from and after conception. We need not resolve the difficult question of when life begins. When those trained [in] medicine, philosophy, and theology are unable to arrive at any consensus, the judiciary, at this point in the development of man's knowledge, is not in a position to speculate as to the answer. It should be sufficient to note [the] wide divergence of thinking on this most sensitive and difficult question. [After reviewing a range of philosophical and religious beliefs, Justice Blackmun noted:] Physicians [have] tended to focus either upon conception, upon live birth, or upon the interim point at which the fetus becomes "viable," that is, potentially able to live outside the mother's womb, albeit with artificial aid. Viability is usually placed at about seven months (28 weeks) but may occur earlier, even at 24 weeks. [The modern official belief of the Catholic Church, recognizing the existence of life from the moment of conception,] is a view strongly held by many non-Catholics as well, and by many physicians. Substantial problems for precise definition of this view are posed, however, by new embryological data that purport to indicate that conception is a "process" over time, rather than an event, and by new medical techniques such as menstrual extraction, the "morning-after" pill, implantation of embryos, artificial insemination, and even artificial wombs. In areas other than criminal abortion, the law has been reluctant to endorse any theory that life, as we recognize it, begins before live birth or to accord legal rights to the unborn except in narrowly defined situations and except when the rights are contingent upon live birth. [Justice Blackmun noted illustrations in the law of torts and of inheritance.] In short, the unborn have never been recognized in the law as persons in the whole sense.

In view of all this, we do not agree that, by adopting one theory of life, Texas may override the rights of the pregnant woman that are at stake. We repeat, however, that the State does have an important and legitimate interest in preserving and protecting the health of the pregnant woman [and] that it has still *another* important and legitimate interest in protecting the potentiality of human life. These interests are separate and distinct. Each grows in substantiality as the woman approaches term and, at a point during pregnancy, each becomes "compelling."

With respect to [the] interest in the health of the mother, the "compelling" point, in the light of present medical knowledge, is at approximately the end of the first trimester. This is so because of the now established medical fact [that] until the end of the first trimester mortality in abortion is less than mortality in normal childbirth. It follows that, from and after this point, a State may regulate the abortion procedure to the extent that the regulation reasonably relates to the preservation and protection of maternal health. Examples of permissible state regulation in this area are requirements as to the qualifications of the person who is to perform the abortion; [as] to the facility in which the procedure is to be performed; and the like. This means, on the other hand, that, for the period of pregnancy prior to this "compelling" point, the attending physician, in consultation with his patient, is free to determine, without regulation by the State, that, in his medical judgment, the patient's pregnancy should be terminated. If that decision is reached, the judgment may be effectuated by an abortion free of interference by the State.

With respect to [the] interest in potential life, the "compelling" point is at viability. This is so because the fetus then presumably has the capability of meaningful life outside the mother's womb. State regulation protective of fetal life after viability thus has both logical and biological justifications. If the State is interested in protecting fetal life after viability, it may go so far as to proscribe abortion during that period, except when it is necessary to preserve the life or health of the mother.

Measured against these standards, [the Texas law] sweeps too broadly [and] cannot survive the constitutional attack made upon it here. To summarize and repeat: A state criminal abortion statute of the current Texas type, that excepts from criminality only a *life saving* procedure on behalf of the mother, without regard to pregnancy stage and without recognition of the other interests involved, is violative of [due process]. (a) For the stage prior to approximately the end of the first trimester, the abortion decision and its effectuation must be left to the medical judgment of the pregnant woman's attending physician. (b) For the stage subsequent to approximately the end of the first trimester, the State, in promoting its interest in the health of the mother, may, if it chooses, regulate the abortion procedure in ways that are reasonably related to maternal health. (c) For the stage subsequent to viability, the State in promoting its interest in the potentiality of human life may, if it chooses, regulate, and even proscribe, abortion except where it is necessary, in appropriate medical judgment, for the preservation of the life or health of the mother.

[This] holding, we feel, is consistent with the relative weights of the respective interests involved, with the lessons and examples of medical and legal history, with the lenity of the common law, and with the demands of the profound problems of the present day. The decision leaves the State free to place increasing restrictions on abortion as the period of pregnancy lengthens, so long as those restrictions are tailored to the recognized state interests. The decision vindicates the right of the physician to administer medical treatment according to his professional judgment up to the points where important state interests provide compelling justifications for intervention. Up to those points, the abortion decision in all its aspects is inherently, and primarily, a medical decision, and basic responsibility for it must rest with the [physician].

It is so ordered.

Mr. Justice STEWART, concurring.

In 1963, this Court, in Ferguson v. Skrupa, purported to sound the death knell for the doctrine of substantive due process. Barely two years later, in [Griswold], the Court held a Connecticut birth control law unconstitutional. In view of what had been so recently said in Skrupa, the Court's opinion in Griswold understandably did its best to avoid reliance on the Due Process Clause. [Yet], the Connecticut law did not violate [any] specific provision of the Constitution. So it was clear to me then, and it is equally clear to me now, that the Griswold decision can be rationally understood only as a holding that the Connecticut statute substantively invaded ["liberty"]. As so understood Griswold stands as one in a long line of pre-Skrupa cases decided under the doctrine of substantive due process, and I now accept it as such. [T]he "liberty" protected by the Due Process Clause of the 14th Amendment covers more than those freedoms explicitly named in the Bill of Rights. [As] recently as last Term, we recognized "the right of the *individual*, married or *single*, to be free from unwarranted governmental intrusion into matters so fundamentally affecting a person as the decision whether to bear or beget a child." That right necessarily includes the right of a woman to decide whether or not to terminate her [pregnancy]. It is evident that the Texas abortion statute infringes that right directly. [The] question then becomes whether the state interests advanced to justify this abridgment can survive the "particularly careful scrutiny" that the 14th Amendment here requires. The asserted state interests [are] legitimate objectives, amply sufficient to permit a State to regulate abortions as it does other surgical procedures, and perhaps sufficient to permit a State to regulate abortions more stringently or even to prohibit them in the late stages of pregnancy. But such legislation is not before us, and I think the Court today [has] demonstrated that these state interests cannot constitutionally support the broad abridgment of personal liberty worked by [the] Texas law. Accordingly, I join the Court's opinion holding that that law is invalid under [due process].

Mr. Justice DOUGLAS, concurring.

[These cases] involve the right of privacy. [The] Ninth Amendment obviously does not create federally enforceable rights [but] a catalogue of [the rights acknowledged by it] includes customary, traditional and time-honored rights, amenities, privileges, and immunities that come within the sweep of "the Blessings of Liberty" mentioned in the preamble to the Constitution. Many of them in my view come within the meaning of the term "liberty" as used in the 14th Amendment.

First is the autonomous control over the development and expression of one's intellect, interests, tastes, and personality. These are rights protected by the First Amendment and in my view they are [absolute]. *Second is freedom of choice in the basic decisions of one's life respecting marriage, divorce, procreation, contraception, and the education and upbringing of children.* These ["fundamental"] rights, unlike those protected by the First Amendment, are subject to some control by the [police power]. *Third is the freedom to care for one's health*

and person, freedom from bodily restraint or compulsion, freedom to walk, stroll, or loaf. These rights, though fundamental, are likewise subject to regulation on a showing of ["compelling state interest"]. [A] woman is free to make the basic decision whether to bear an unwanted child. [Childbirth] may deprive a woman of her preferred life style and force upon her a radically different and undesired future. [Such] reasoning is, however, only the beginning of the problem. The State has interests to protect. [Voluntary] abortion at any time and place regardless of medical standards would impinge on a rightful concern of society. The woman's health is part of that concern: as is the life of the fetus after quickening. These concerns justify the State in treating the procedure as [a medical one].

Mr. Justice WHITE, with whom Mr. Justice REHNQUIST joins, dissenting.

At the heart of the controversy in these cases are those recurring pregnancies that pose no danger whatsoever to the life or health of the mother but are nevertheless unwanted for any one or more of a variety of reasons—convenience, family planning, economics, dislike of children, the embarrassment of illegitimacy, etc. The common claim before us is that for any one of such reasons, or for no reason at all, and without asserting or claiming any threat to life or health, any woman is entitled to an abortion at her request if she is able to find a medical advisor willing to undertake [it]. The Court for the most part sustains this position: During the period prior to the time the fetus becomes viable, [the Constitution] values the convenience, whim or caprice of the putative mother more than the life or potential life of the fetus; the Constitution, therefore, guarantees the right to an abortion as against any state law or policy seeking to protect the fetus from an abortion not prompted by more compelling reasons of the mother. [I] dissent. I find nothing in the language or history of the Constitution to support the Court's judgment. The Court simply fashions and announces a new constitutional right for pregnant mothers and, with scarcely any reason or authority for its action, invests that right with sufficient substance to override most existing state abortion statutes. The upshot is that the people and the legislatures of the 50 States are constitutionally disentitled to weigh the relative importance of the continued existence and development of the fetus on the one hand against a spectrum of possible impacts on the mother on the other hand. As an exercise of raw judicial power, the Court perhaps has authority to do what it does today; but in my view its judgment is an improvident and extravagant exercise of the power of [judicial review].

Mr. Justice REHNQUIST, dissenting.

[I] have difficulty in concluding [that] the right of "privacy" is involved in this case. [Texas] bars the performance of a medical abortion by a licensed physician on a plaintiff such as Roe. A transaction resulting in an operation such as this is not "private" in the ordinary usage of that word. Nor is the "privacy" which the Court finds here even a distant relative of the [Fourth Amendment freedom from searches and seizures]. If the Court means by the term "privacy" no more than that the claim of a person to be free from unwanted state regulation of consensual transactions may be a form of "liberty" protected by the 14th Amendment, there is no doubt that similar claims have been upheld in our earlier decisions on the basis of that liberty. I agree [that "liberty"] embraces more than the rights found in the Bill of Rights. But that liberty is not guaranteed absolutely against deprivation, but only against deprivation without due process of law. The test traditionally applied in the area of social and economic legislation is whether or not a law such as that challenged has a rational relation to a valid state objective.

[If] the Texas statute were to prohibit an abortion even where the mother's life is in jeopardy, I have little doubt that such a statute would lack a rational relation to a valid state objective under the test stated in [Lee Optical]. But the Court's sweeping invalidation of any restrictions on abortion during the first trimester is impossible to justify under that [standard].

The Court eschews the history of the 14th Amendment in its reliance on the "compelling state interest" test. But the Court adds a new wrinkle to this test by transporting it from the legal considerations associated with [equal protection] to this case arising under [due process]. While the Court's opinion quotes from the dissent of Mr. Justice Holmes in [Lochner], the result it reaches is more closely attuned to the majority opinion of Mr. Justice Peckham in that case. As in Lochner and similar cases applying substantive due process standards to economic and social welfare legislation, the adoption of the compelling state interest standard will inevitably require this Court to examine the legislative policies and pass on the wisdom of these policies in the very process of deciding whether a particular state interest put forward may or may not be "compelling." The decision here to break the term of pregnancy into three distinct terms and to outline the permissible restrictions the State may impose in each one, for example, partakes more of judicial legislation than it does of a determination of the intent of the drafters of the 14th Amendment. The fact that a majority of the [States] have had restrictions on abortions for at least a century is a strong indication, it seems to me, that the asserted right to an abortion is not "so rooted in the traditions and conscience of our people as to be ranked as fundamental." Even today, when society's views on abortion are changing, the very existence of the debate is evidence that the "right" to an abortion is not so universally accepted as the appellants would have us believe. [By] the time of the adoption of the 14th Amendment in 1868, there were at least 36 laws enacted by state or territorial legislatures limiting abortion. [The] only conclusion possible from this history is that the drafters did not intend to have the 14th Amendment withdraw from the States the power to legislate with respect to this [matter].

THE ROOT AND BRANCH OF ROE V. WADE

JOHN NOONAN

By root I mean the jurisprudential source, by branch I mean the ultimate outcropping of the famous abortion rights case, *Roe v. Wade*. The root is of greater importance than the issue is. It reaches to every constitutional right and liberty. The branch illustrates what is possible once the law severs correspondence with reality.

Whoever has the power to define the bearer of constitutional rights has a power that can make nonsense of any particular constitutional right. That this power belongs to the state itself is a point of view associated in jurisprudence with Hans Kelsen. According to Kelsen a person is simply a construct of the law. As he expresses it in *The Pure Theory of Law*, even the apparently natural physical person is a construction of juristic thinking. In this account it appears that just as we personify a corporation for legal purposes so we personify natural physical beings. There are no independent, ontological existences to which we respond as persons. Personhood depends on recognition by the law.

A corollary of that position appears to be what has always seemed to me one of the most terrifying of legal propositions: there is no kind of human behavior that, because of its nature, could not be made into a legal duty corresponding to a legal right. When one thinks of the vast variety of human behavior it is at least startling to think that every variation could be converted into legal duties and legal rights. The proposition becomes terrifying when one thinks of Orwell's *1984* or the actual conduct of the Nazi regime from which Hans Kelsen himself eventually had to flee.

There is one massive phenomenon in the history of our country that might be invoked to support Kelsen's point of view. That phenomenon is the way a very large class of human beings were treated prior to the enactment of the thirteenth and fourteenth amendments. When one looks back at the history of 200 years of slavery in the United States, and looks back at it as a lawyer observing that lawyers had a great deal to do with the classifications that made the phenomenon possible, one realizes that the law, in fact, has been used to create legal rights and legal duties in relation to human behavior that should never have been given a legal form and a legal blessing. To put it bluntly, law was the medium and lawyers were the agents responsible for turning one class of human beings into property. The result was that the property laws of the different states made it smooth and easy to transfer ownership of these human beings. The property laws resolved the questions that occurred at those critical junctions where humanity asserted itself either in the birth of a child to a slave or the death of the owner of a slave. The only question left open for argument was whether the human beings classified as property were realty or personality. In the inheritance cases the slave child was treated like the issue of an animal, compared again and again in legal decisions to the issue of livestock.

John Noonan, "The Root and Branch of Roe v. Wade," Nebraska Law Review, vol. 63 (1984), pp. 668 ff.[11]

[11]John Noonan (1926–   ), now a judge of the United States Court of Appeals for the Ninth Circuit, was formerly Professor of Law at the University of California at Berkeley.

Gross characterization of human beings in terms that reduced them to animals, or real estate, or even kitchen utensils now may seem so unbelievable that we all can profess shock and amazement that it was ever done. Eminently respectable lawyers were able to engage in this kind of characterization—among them Thomas Jefferson, who co-authored the slave code of Virginia, and Abraham Lincoln who argued on behalf of a slave owner seeking to recover as his property a woman and her four children who had escaped to the free state of Illinois. Looking at such familiar examples and realizing how commonplace it was for lawyers to engage in this kind of fiction, we learn, I think, that law can operate as a kind of magic. All that is necessary is to permit legal legerdemain to create a mask obliterating the human person being dealt with. Looking at the mask—that is looking at the abstract category created by the law—is not to see the human reality on which the mask is imposed.

Masking of this kind even occurred in one case where the personhood of Blacks was put directly to the Supreme Court of the United States—*The Antelope*, a case that takes its name from a ship captured off the coast of Georgia in 1821. Aboard were 281 Africans about to be brought into the United States as slaves. Federal law made it a felony to import slaves and prescribed that the President should rescue any Africans found in that condition and arrange for them to return to Africa. President James Monroe was about to carry out this law when agents representing Spanish and Portuguese slave traders claimed in federal district court that the Africans were Spanish and Portuguese property. They alleged that their principals were trading peacefully off the coast of Africa when their property had been captured by pirates who then illegally attempted to bring the property into the United States. This illegality, they asserted, should not taint their title. Please give us back our property, they asked.

The United States District Attorney in Savannah, Richard Wylly Habersham, took the position that every one of the rescued African men and women was just as free as Americans would have been if they had been washed upon the shore of Algiers or Morocco and claimed by slave traders there. He put the argument directly to the district court that these were human beings that were not to be disposed of as property. The district judge disagreed as to the majority of persons before him and ordered them turned over to "their" owners; a small number, found to have come from an American ship, were freed. On appeal, the circuit court found the main problem to be how to distinguish between the Africans from the American ship and the Africans from the Spanish and Portuguese ships. The court resolved the problem by ordering a lottery to determine who was free, an eminently sensible solution if animals or other goods were being disposed of.

The main issues were put before the Supreme Court of the United States in 1825. One group of lawyers, led by Francis Scott Key, pointed to the human reality, arguing that here was flesh and blood, that these Africans could not be treated like things or disposed of by a game of chance. Another group of lawyers, led by Senator John MacPherson Berrien, argued just as earnestly that only property was before the Court. The Supreme Court found that some of the Africans were people and some of the Africans were property.

Three years later, after a period during which the status of which African was a person and which African was a thing was again litigated in the circuit court and the Supreme Court itself, 120 Africans were freed and thirty-seven became the property of Congressman Richard Henry Wilde of Georgia. Even with the most obvious kind of evidence before the Court as to the humanity of the class affected by the law, the justices of the Supreme Court had been capable of applying one category of law to one set of persons that left them free and another category—a mask—to a very similar group that left them enslaved in perpetuity.

A much more familiar case of the same kind is *Scott v. Sanford*. Here the black plaintiff attempted to assert his right to freedom in the federal court. The Supreme Court held that the federal statute that should have made him free was an interference with the property rights guaranteed by the Constitution to his owner. The Court applied the due process clause of the fifth amendment—gratuitously reading into this clause a concept of substantive due process—and held the statute invalid. The property mask dropped over Dred Scott was the means by which the Constitution was brought into play. As James Buchanan, the President at the time, happily put it, the Court had achieved "the final settlement" of the question of slavery in the Territories. It was a final settlement curiously like Adolph Hitler's "final solution" of "the Jewish question" in Germany.

Buchanan's description, of course, was inaccurate. The Supreme Court could not resolve an issue that so fundamentally divided the nation. The legal mask was shattered by the Civil War. The thirteenth and fourteenth amendments were adopted. The legal profession forgot about its participation in molding the mask that made slavery possible. It is only in our time that the analogy seems vital.

Kelsen's jurisprudence makes *The Antelope* and *Dred Scott* defensible decisions: according to it, there is nothing intrinsic in humanity requiring persons to be legally recognized as persons. The relevance of Kelsen's reasoning was acknowledged in a modern case, *Byrn v. New York City Health and Hospital Corporation*, decided a year before the Supreme Court decided *Roe v. Wade.* In *Byrn*, Robert Byrn was appointed guardian *ad litem* of an unborn child and asserted that child's constitutional right not to be aborted. His position was rejected by the majority of the Court of Appeals of New York, speaking through Judge Charles Breitel. Breitel quoted Kelsen explicitly to support his position that it was a policy determination of the state whether legal personality should be recognized or not. It was, Breitel stated "not true that the legal order corresponds to the natural order." Breitel did not go as far as Kelsen's statement that natural persons were juristic creations—Breitel seemed

to assume that there might be natural persons—but he left the recognition of natural persons to the legislature. As New York, at this time, had already enacted a fairly radical abortion law, he held that the legislature had conclusively made the decision that left the unborn child outside the class of recognized humanity.

The dissent, written by Judge Adrian Burke, objected to this jurisprudence. In Burke's view the reality of a person before the law was not dependent on a determination by the state. He contended that the state had no constitutional power to classify a group of living human beings as fit subjects for annihilation. He insisted that if the state could make that kind of classification, it became the source of all legal rights. He observed that all the protections of the Constitution meant nothing if you or your group could be classified by the state so that you fell outside the class of human beings protected by the Constitution.

Roe v. Wade itself, decided a year later, was profoundly ambivalent—indeed, to speak bluntly, it was schizoid in its approach to the power of the state to determine who was a person. The opinion was schizoid because the Court wanted to invoke rights that were not dependent on the state—the Court was trying to find a measure by which to invalidate state statutes. The precedents that the Court found to authorize it to act in this area of law were all cases that treated family rights as having a natural basis superior to the law of the state. The cases involved included *Meyer v. Nebraska* and *Pierce v. Society of Sisters*, recognizing a superior right of parents to educate their children; *Skinner v. Oklahoma*, recognizing that a man has a natural right to procreate and so cannot be arbitrarily sterilized by the state; *Loving v. Virginia*, where the natural right to marry was invoked in the course of invalidating a miscegenation statute; and *Griswold v. Connecticut*, where the rights of the married were also asserted, in this case to hold unconstitutional a statute prohibiting the use of contraceptives.

All of these cases rested on the supposition that the family rights being protected were those of persons, and that these persons could not be unmade at will by the state. The natural law fundament of these decisions was camouflaged by their being couched in constitutional language; but the constitutional content was derived from nowhere except the natural law as it had taken shape in the traditions of the United States. At the same time that it invoked such precedents in *Roe*, the Court, when treating of the unborn, felt free to impose its own notions of reality.

In one passage the Court spoke of the unborn before viability as "a theory of life," as though there were competing views as to whether life in fact existed before viability. The implication could also be found that there was no reality there in the womb but merely theories about what was there. The Court seemed to be uncertain itself and to take the position that if it were unsure, nobody else could be sure. In another passage the Court spoke of life in the womb up to birth as "potential life." This description was accurate if it meant there was existing life with a great deal of development yet to come, as one might say a 5-year-old is "potential life" meaning that he or she is only potentially what he or she will be at twenty-five. The Court's description was inaccurate if the Court meant to suggest that what was in the womb was pure potentiality, a zero that could not be protected by law. To judge from the weight the Court gave the being in the womb—found to be protectable in any degree only in the last two months of pregnancy—the Court itself must have viewed the unborn as pure potentiality or a mere theory before viability. The Court's opinion appeared to rest on the assumption that the biological reality could be subordinated or ignored by the sovereign speaking through the Court.

The conflict, visible in *Roe v. Wade* between a natural law response to human reality and a Kelsenite freedom in recognizing human reality, was resolved in the Kelsenite direction in the cases that followed. In *Doe v. Israel* the federal courts considered a statute recognizing the personhood of the unborn child in Rhode Island. The American Civil Liberties Union attacked the statute and persuaded the federal courts to hold it invalid. The courts actually took the position that Rhode Island's statute was frivolous, that a single federal judge could hold the statute invalid, and that the judge need not even hear the biological evidence supporting the statute. The Supreme Court had determined who was the bearer of rights. A federal judge now did not have to look at the physical realities. Evidence that the unborn were not zeros was not to be permitted.

■ ■ ■

[If the] state is the source of all parental rights, then the state must be able to curtail those rights and to take away its delegation of them. A state could refuse to delegate its right to education to the parents. Only by recognizing rights superior to the state did the natural law precedents invoked by *Roe v. Wade* have intelligibility.

The progeny of *Roe* have confirmed the Kelsenite reading of *Roe* that there is no reality that the sovereign must recognize unless the sovereign, acting through the agency of the Court, decides to recognize it. This view would be psychologically incomprehensible if we did not have the history of the creation of the institution of slavery by judges and lawyers. With that history we can see that intelligent and humane lawyers have been able to apply a similar approach to a whole class of beings that they could see that they were able to create a mask of legal concepts preventing humanity from being visible. A mask is a little easier to impose when the humanity concealed, being in the womb, is not even visible to the naked eye.

Kelsenite logic permits the judges at the apex of a system to dispense with correspondence to reality. The highest court is then free, within the limits that the society in which it functions will tolerate, to be inventive. It may, as the Supreme Court of the United States has sometimes thought, be constrained by the language of the Constitution and the purposes of its makers. Or, as has also sometimes happened, the Court, viewing itself as the final expounder of the Constitution's meaning, will exercise its inventiveness in creating new constitutional doctrine not dependent on text or purposes. Such doctrine—fantasy in the service of ideology—is "the branch" of *Roe v. Wade*. What then becomes possible was illustrated in 1983 by *Akron v. Akron Center for Reproductive Health*. In this case a whole set of constitutional requirements were created on behalf of the claims of an abortion clinic, named with Orwellian aptness, a center for "reproductive health."

In *Akron* the only justification that Justice Powell, writing for the Court, gave for the main holdings was *stare decisis—Roe v. Wade* would not be reexamined. He acknowledged that *stare decisis* "was perhaps never entirely persuasive on constitutional questions." In fact, *stare decisis* has "often" been rejected by the Court, reversing itself and discarding its own interpretation of the Constitution as mistaken. Still, Justice Powell made the case swing on the precedent, declaring roundly that *stare decisis* "is a doctrine that demands respect in a society governed by the rule of law. We respect it today, and reaffirm *Roe v. Wade*."

Looked at from one aspect this approach can be seen as ultimately subversive of *Roe v. Wade* itself. This approach called the Court back to a consideration of realities not controlled by judicial fiat. In a famous dissent, Justice Brandeis, arguing for overruling a line of bad constitutional precedents, declared that the Court should bring itself "into agreement with experience and with facts newly ascertained, so that its judicial authority may, as Mr. Chief Justice Taney said, 'depend altogether on the force of the reasoning by which it is supported.'" The roots of *Roe* are severed if the Court is willing to bring itself into agreement with experience and have its authority depend on the force of its reasoning.

In *Akron*, however, the Court, in general, held to the basic logic of *Roe* and discovered new dimensions of the Constitutional protection for abortion. The Akron ordinance required a person seeking an abortion to wait for twenty-four hours. Twenty-four hours was found to be too long. Justice Powell called it "arbitrary and inflexible." The requirement violated the Constitution.

In the so called "Abortion Funding Cases," Justice Powell, writing for the Court, had said the state had a traditional and judicially-recognizable interest in encouraging childbirth. The state's interest shrivelled to almost nothing when a mere twenty-four hour waiting period was too great a burden on the person seeking an abortion. Beyond any constitutional theory and beyond any jurisprudential considerations, the holding of *Akron* appeared to reflect a good deal of impatience with anything in the way of the victory of an ideology. Impatience was satisfied by constitutional inventiveness, unrestrained by the text or the purposes of the Constitution.

A further holding of *Akron* was that the city could not require that a physician give counselling to the abortion seeker; the most the law could require was that some "qualified" delegate of the doctor provide counselling. It was extraordinary that the Constitution could be found to speak so precisely as to what psychological advice could or could not be made available. The holding was also interestingly inconsistent with the general implication of *Roe v. Wade* as to the importance of the family physician. In *Roe* the physician was treated as an heroic figure, one on whom the abortion seeker could depend; but when an attempt was made to build upon this deference to the doctor in a way that the Court found restrictive of the abortion liberty, the Court's deference was swallowed up by its desire to extend the liberty as widely as possible.

Most strikingly of all, *Akron* held that there could not be a legal requirement that a woman seeking an abortion be informed that the being she wished put to death was a child, that the child was alive, and that the child was human. The Court treated this information as prejudicing the choice of whether to abort or not—as a kind of unfair interference with free choice. The ordinance was bad because it was designed "to influence the woman's informed choice between abortion and childbirth." The holding went beyond the Kelsenite jurisprudential root and any mainline theory of constitutional interpretation. It was, indeed, the invention of a kind of censorship by the Court itself.

The logic of *Akron* in this respect, if taken just a little further, is that a state university or a city high school should not be permitted to teach biology. The facts that would have been provided to a woman under the Akron ordinance are the same kind of facts that would be provided in a modern course in biology. Such a course would inform its students of the unique chromosomal composition of the child that distinguishes the child as male or female and as animal or human. If students looking at a genetic sample under the microscope could not recognize the number, the shape, and the bonding patterns of the chromosomes—if they could not say whether the genetic specimen came from a simian being or from a human being—they would fail the course. Information enabling them to answer correctly might also "influence" their choice of abortion or childbirth.

A final provision of the Akron ordinance was that "the remains of the unborn child" be "disposed in a humane and sanitary manner." The Sixth Circuit Court of Appeals found the word "humane" impermissibly vague in a criminal statute. The ordinance could, the court said, mean to "mandate some sort of 'decent burial' of an embryo at the earliest stages of formation. . . ." Justice Powell quoted this analysis and agreed; humane and sanitary burial was beyond the comprehension of a reasonable doctor.

In this conclusion one can observe in the most concrete way the Court's discomfort before reality. The Court cannot uphold a requirement of humane burial without conceding that the being who is to be buried is human. A mask has been placed over this being. Even death cannot remove the mask.

The Court's denial of reality stands in contrast with what Andre Gide has written on the humane burial of an unborn child:

When morning came, "get rid of that," I said naively to the gardener's wife when she finally came to see how everything was. Could I have supposed that those formless fragments, to which I turning away in disgust was pointing, could I have supposed that in the eyes of the Church they already represented the sacred human being they were being readied to clothe? O mystery of incarnation! Imagine then my stupor when some hours later I saw "it" again. The thing which for me already had no name in any language, now cleaned, adorned, beribboned, laid in a little cradle, awaiting the ritual entombment. Fortunately no one had been aware of the sacrilege I had been about to commit; I had already committed it in thought when I had said get rid of "that." Yes, very happily that ill-considered order had been heard by no one. And, I remained a long time musing before "it." Before that little face with the crushed forehead on which they had carefully hidden the wound. Before this innocent flesh which I, if I had been alone, yielding to my first impulse, would have consigned to the manure heap along with the afterbirth and which religious attentions had just saved from the void. I told no one then of what I felt. Of what I tell here. Was I to think that for a few moments a soul had inhabited this body? It has its tomb in Couvreville in that cemetery to which I wish not to return. Half a century has passed. I cannot truthfully say that I recall in detail that little face. No. What I remember exactly is my surprise, my sudden emotion, when confronted by its extraordinary beauty.

If the Court could respond to Gide and understand what humane and sanitary burial is, it might also perceive the reality of the extraordinary beauty of each human being put to death in the name of the abortion liberty and concealed from legal recognition by a jurisprudence that substitutes a judge's fiat for the truth.

REFLECTIONS ON SEX EQUALITY
UNDER LAW

CATHARINE MACKINNON

Grounding a sex equality approach to reproductive control requires situating pregnancy in the legal and social context of sex inequality and capturing the unique relationship between the pregnant woman and her fetus. The legal system has not adequately conceptualized pregnancy, hence the relationship between the fetus and the pregnant woman. This may be because the interests, perceptions, and experiences that have shaped the law have not included those of women. The social conception of pregnancy that has formed the basis for its legal treatment has not been from the point of view of the pregnant woman, but rather from the point of view of the observing outsider, gendered male. Traditionally, fetuses have not fared much better under this vantage point than have women. This may be changing at women's expense as increasingly, despite the explicit Supreme Court ruling to the contrary, the fetus becomes endowed with attributes of personhood. Men may more readily identify with the fetus than with the pregnant woman if only because all have been fetuses and none will ever be a pregnant woman.

Accordingly, the law of reproductive issues has implicitly centered on observing and controlling the pregnant woman and the fetus using evidence that is available from the outside. The point of these interventions is to control the woman through controlling the fetus. Technology, also largely controlled by men, has made it possible to view the fetus through ultrasound, fueling much of the present crisis in the legal status of the fetus by framing it as a free-floating independent entity rather than as connected with the pregnant woman. Much of the authority and persuasiveness of the ultrasound image derives from its presentation of the fetus from the standpoint of the outside observer, the so-called objective standpoint, so that it becomes socially experienced in these terms rather than in terms of its direct connection to the woman. Presenting the fetus from this point of view, rather than from that which is uniquely accessible to the pregnant woman, stigmatizes her unique viewpoint as subjective and internal. This has the epistemic effect of making the fetus more real than the woman, who becomes reduced to the "grainy blur" at the edge of the image.

The law of reproductive control has developed largely as a branch of the law of privacy, the law that keeps out observing outsiders. Sometimes it has. The problem is that while the private has been a refuge for some, it has been a hellhole for others, often at the same time. In gendered light, the law's privacy is a sphere of sanctified isolation, impunity, and unaccountability. It surrounds the individual in his habitat. It belongs to the individual with power. Women have been accorded neither individuality nor power. Privacy follows those with power wherever they go, like and as consent follows women. When the person with privacy is having his privacy, the person without power is tacitly imagined to be consenting. At whatever time and place man has privacy, woman wants to have happen, or lets happen, whatever he does to her. Everyone is implicitly equal in there. If the woman needs something—say, equality—to make these assumptions real, privacy law does nothing for her, and even ideologically undermines the state intervention that might provide the preconditions for its meaningful exercise. The private is a distinctive sphere of women's inequality to men. Because this has not been recognized, the doctrine of privacy has become the triumph of the state's abdication of women in the name of freedom and self-determination.

Theorized instead as a problem of sex inequality, the law of reproductive control would begin with the place of reproduction in the status of the sexes. A narrow view of women's "biological destiny" has confined many women to childbearing and childrearing and defined all women in terms of it, limiting their participation in other pursuits, especially remunerative positions with social stature. Women who bear children are constrained by a society that does not allocate resources to assist combining family needs with work outside the home. In the case of men, the two are traditionally tailored to a complementary fit, provided that a woman is available to perform the traditional role that makes that fit possible. Law has permitted women to be punished at work for their reproductive role. The option of pregnancy leave mandated by law was not even regarded as legal until recently; in the United States, it still is not required. When women begin to "show," they are often treated as walking obscenities unfit for public presentation. Inside the home, battering of women may increase during pregnancy. Pornography makes pregnancy into a sexual fetish, conditioning male sexual arousal to it, meaning targeting sexualized hatred against it. Whether or not women have children, they are disadvantaged by social norms that limit their options because of women's enforced role in childbearing and childrearing. For a woman who does become pregnant, these consequences occur even when a pregnancy is wanted.

Women often do not control the conditions under which they become pregnant; systematically denied meaningful control over the reproductive uses of their bodies through sex, it is exceptional when they do. Women are socially disadvantaged in controlling sexual access to their bodies through socialization to customs that define a woman's body as for sexual use by men. Sexual access is regularly forced or pressured or routinized beyond denial. Laws

against sexual assault provide little to no real protection. Contraception is inadequate or unsafe or inaccessible or sadistic or stigmatized. Sex education is often misleading or unavailable or pushes heterosexual motherhood as an exclusive life possibility and as the point of sex. Poverty and enforced economic dependence undermine women's physical integrity and sexual self-determination. Social supports or blandishments for women's self-respect are simply not enough to withstand all of this.

After childbirth, women tend to be the ones who are primarily responsible for the intimate care of offspring—their own and those of others. Social custom, pressure, exclusion from well-paying jobs, the structure of the marketplace, and lack of adequate daycare have exploited women's commitment to and caring for children and relegated women to this pursuit which is not even considered an occupation but an expression of the X chromosome. Women do not control the circumstances under which they rear children, hence the impact of those conditions on their own life chances. Men, as a group, are not comparably disempowered by the reproductive capacities. Nobody forces them to impregnate women. They are not generally required by society to spend their lives caring for children to the comparative preclusion of other life pursuits.

It is women who are caught, to varying degrees, between the reproductive consequences of sexual use and aggression on the one side and the economic and other consequences of the sex role allocations of labor in the market and family on the other. As a result of these conditions, women are prevented from having children they do want and forced to have children they do not want and cannot want because they are not in a position responsibly to care for them because they are women. This is what an inequality looks like.

Reproduction is socially gendered. Women are raped and coerced into sex. When conception results from rape or incest, it is a girl or a woman who was violated, shamed, and defiled in a way distinctively regarded as female. When a teenager gets pregnant because of ignorance or the negative social connotations of contraception, it is a young woman who is pregnant. When miscarriage results from physical assault, it is a woman who was beaten. When there is not enough money for another child or for an abortion, it is a woman who is forced to have a child she cannot responsibly care for. When a single parent is impoverished as a result of childbearing, usually that parent is female. When someone must care for the children, it is almost always a woman who does it, without her work being valued in terms of money or social status. Men, regardless of race, have not generally been sterilized without their knowledge and against their will, as have women of color. It has been held illegal to sterilize a male prisoner but legal to sterilize a mentally disabled woman. Those who have been defined and valued and devalued as breeders and body servants of the next generation are not usually men, except under circumstances recognized as slavery. The essential social function of nurturing new life has been degraded by being filled by women, as the women who fill it have been degraded by filling it. And it is women who, for reasons not always purely biological, may pay for giving birth with their lives.

■ ■ ■

[It is important to consider whether there is a] conflict between what is good for the woman and what is good for the fetus. Sometimes there is. Usually there is not, in large part because when there is, women tend to resolve it in favor of the fetus. Women may identify with the fetus because, like them, it is invisible, powerless, derivative, and silent. Grasping this unity in oppression, it has most often been women who have put the welfare of the fetus first, before their own. While most women who abort did not choose to conceive, many women who keep their pregnancies did not choose to conceive either. The priority women make of their offspring may be more true in the abortion context than it seems. Many women have abortions as a desperate act of love for their unborn children. Many women conceive in battering relationships; subjecting a child to a violent father is more than they can bear. When women in a quarter to a third of all American households face domestic violence, this motivation cannot be dismissed as marginal. Some women conceive in part to cement a relationship which dissolves or becomes violent when the man discovers the conception. Even where direct abuse is not present, sex inequality is. Many abortions occur because the woman needs to try to give herself a life. But many also occur because the woman faces the fact that she cannot give this child a life. Women's impotence to make this not so may make the decision tragic, but it is nonetheless one of absolute realism and deep responsibility as a mother.

Reproduction in the lives of women is a far larger and more diverse experience than the focus on abortion has permitted. The right to reproductive control I have in mind would include the abortion right but would not center on it. Women would have more rights when they carry a fetus: sex equality rights. Women who are assaulted and miscarry, women who are forced to have abortions and women who are denied abortions, women who are sterilized, and women who are negligently attended at birth all suffer deprivation of reproductive control. Under such circumstances, existing laws that regulate these areas should be interpreted consistent with constitutional sex equality mandates. If affirmative legislative pursuit of this principle were desired, this concept of reproductive control would encourage programs to support the fetus through supporting the woman, including guaranteed prenatal care, pregnancy leaves, and nutritional, alcohol, and drug counseling. If pursued in a context in which sexual coercion was effectively addressed, such programs would promote women's equality, not constitute inducements and pressures to succumb to women's subordinate roles. In this light, purported concern for the well-being of pregnant women and subsequently born children expressed by policing women's activities during pregnancy and forcing women to carry pregnancies to term is not only vicious and counterproductive, but unconstitutional.

Because the social organization of reproduction is a major bulwark of women's social inequality, any constitutional interpretation of a sex equality principle must prohibit laws, state policies, or official practices and acts that deprive women of reproductive control or punish women for their reproductive role or capacity. Existing examples include nonconsensual sterilization, forced obstetrical intervention, supervision of women's activities during pregnancy under the criminal law, and denials of abortion through criminalization or lack of public funding where needed. Women's right to reproductive control is a sex equality right because it is inconsistent with an equality mandate for the state, by law, to collaborate with or mandate social inequality on the basis of sex, as such legal incursions do. This is not so much an argument for an extension of the meaning of constitutional sex equality as a recognition that if it does not mean this, it does not mean anything at all.

Under this sex equality analysis, criminal abortion statutes of the sort invalidated in *Roe v. Wade* violate equal protection of the laws. They make women criminals for a medical procedure only women need, or make others criminals for performing a procedure on women that only women need, when much of the need for this procedure as well as barriers to access to it have been created by social conditions of sex inequality. Forced motherhood is sex inequality. Because pregnancy can be experienced only by women, and because of the unequal social predicates and consequences pregnancy has for women, any forced pregnancy will always deprive and hurt one sex only as a member of her gender. Just as no man will ever become pregnant, no man will ever need an abortion, hence be in a position to be denied one by law. On this level, only women can be disadvantaged, for a reason specific to sex, through state-mandated restrictions on abortion. The denial of funding for Medicaid abortions obviously violates this right. The Medicaid issue connects the maternity historically forced on African American women integral to their exploitation under slavery with the motherhood effectively forced on poor women, many of whom are Black, by deprivation of government funding for abortions. For those who have not noticed, the abortion right has already been lost: this was when.

PLANNED PARENTHOOD OF SOUTHEASTERN PENNSYLVANIA V. CASEY

112 S.Ct. 2791 (1992)

From the plurality opinion of Justices O'CONNOR, KENNEDY, and SOUTER:

[Time] has overtaken some of Roe's factual assumptions: advances in maternal health care allow for abortions safe to the mother later in pregnancy than was true in 1973, and advances in neonatal care have advanced viability to a point somewhat earlier. But these facts go only to the scheme of time limits on the realization of competing interests, and [have] no bearing on the [central] holding that viability marks the earliest point at which the State's interest in fetal life is constitutionally adequate to justify a legislative ban on nontherapeutic abortions. The soundness or unsoundness of that constitutional judgment in no sense turns on whether viability occurs at approximately 28 weeks, as was usual at the time of Roe, at 23 to 24 weeks, as it sometimes does today, or at some moment even slightly earlier in pregnancy, as it may if fetal respiratory capacity can somehow be enhanced in the future. Whenever it may occur, the attainment of viability may continue to serve as the critical fact, just as it has done since Roe; [no] change in Roe's factual underpinning has left its central holding obsolete, and none supports an argument for overruling it.

The sum of the precedential inquiry to this point shows Roe's underpinnings unweakened in any way affecting its central holding. While it has engendered disapproval, it has not been unworkable. An entire generation has come of age free to assume Roe's concept of liberty in defining the capacity of women to act in society, and to make reproductive decisions; no erosion of principle going to liberty or personal autonomy has left Roe's central holding a doctrinal remnant; Roe portends no developments at odds with other precedent for the analysis of personal liberty; and no changes of fact have rendered viability more or less appropriate as the point at which the balance of interests tips. Within the bounds of normal stare decisis analysis, [the] stronger argument is for affirming Roe's central holding, with whatever degree of personal reluctance any of us may have, not for overruling it.

■ ■ ■

[We] conclude that the basic decision in Roe was based on a constitutional analysis which we cannot now repudiate. The woman's liberty is not so unlimited, however, that from the outset the State cannot show its concern for the life of the unborn, and at a later point in fetal development the State's interest in life has sufficient force so that the right of the woman to terminate the pregnancy can be restricted.

That brings us [to] the point where much criticism has been directed at Roe, a criticism that always inheres when the Court draws a specific rule from what in the Constitution is but a general standard. We conclude, however, that the urgent claims of the woman to retain the ultimate control over her destiny and her body [require] us to perform that function. Liberty must not be extinguished for want of a line that is clear. And it falls to us to give some real substance to the woman's liberty to determine whether to carry her pregnancy to full term.

We conclude the line should be drawn at viability, so that before that time the woman has a right to choose to terminate her pregnancy. We adhere to this principle for two reasons. First [is] stare decisis. [Although] we must overrule those parts of Thornburgh and Akron I which [are] inconsistent with Roe's statement that the State has a legitimate interest in promoting the life or potential life of the unborn, the central premise of those cases represents an unbroken commitment [to] the essential holding of Roe.

[The] second reason is that the concept of viability [is] the time at which there is a realistic possibility of maintaining and nourishing a life outside the womb, so that the independent essence of the second life can [be] the object of state protection that now overrides the rights of the woman. [Legislatures] may draw lines which appear arbitrary without the necessity of offering a justification. But courts may not. We must justify the lines we draw. And there is no line other than viability which is more workable. [The] woman's right to terminate her pregnancy before viability is the most central principle of Roe.

[On] the other side of the equation is the interest of the State in the protection of potential life. [The] weight to be given this state interest, not the strength of the woman's interest, was the difficult question faced in Roe. We do not need to say whether each of us, had we been Members of the Court when the valuation of the State interest came before it as an original matter, would have concluded [that] its weight is insufficient to justify a ban on abortions prior to viability even when it is subject to certain exceptions. The [immediate] question is not the soundness of Roe's resolution of the issue, but the precedential force that must be accorded to its holding.

[Yet] it must be remembered that Roe speaks with clarity in establishing not only the woman's liberty but also the State's "important and legitimate interest in potential life." That portion of [Roe] has been given too little acknowledgment [in] subsequent cases [holding] that any regulation touching upon the abortion decision must survive strict scrutiny, to be sustained only if drawn in narrow terms to further a compelling state interest. [In] resolving this tension, we choose to rely upon Roe, as against the later cases. [The] trimester framework no doubt was erected to ensure that the woman's right to choose not become so subordinate to the State's interest in promoting fetal life that her choice exists in theory but not in fact. We do not agree, however, that the trimester approach is necessary to accomplish this objective.

[Though] the woman has a right to choose to terminate or continue her pregnancy before viability, it does not [follow] that the State is prohibited from taking steps to ensure that this choice is thoughtful and informed. Even in the earliest stages of pregnancy, the State may enact rules and regulations designed to encourage her to know that there are philosophic and social arguments of great weight that can be brought to bear in favor of continuing the pregnancy to full term and that there are procedures and institutions to allow adoption of unwanted children as well as a certain degree of state assistance if the mother chooses to raise the child herself.

[We] reject the trimester framework, which we do not consider to be part of the essential holding of Roe. Measures aimed at ensuring that a woman's choice contemplates the consequences for the fetus do not necessarily interfere with the right recognized in Roe, although those measures have been found to be inconsistent with the rigid trimester framework announced. [The] trimester framework suffers from these basic flaws: in its formulation it misconceives the nature of the pregnant woman's interest; and in practice it undervalues the State's interest in potential life.

[As] our jurisprudence relating to all liberties save perhaps abortion has recognized, not every law which makes a right more difficult to exercise is, ipso facto, an infringement of that right. Numerous forms of state regulation might have the incidental effect of increasing the cost or decreasing the availability of medical care, whether for abortion or any other medical procedure. The fact that a law which serves a valid purpose, one not designed to strike at the right itself, has the incidental effect of making it more difficult or more expensive to procure an abortion cannot be enough to invalidate it. Only where state regulation imposes an undue burden on a woman's ability to make this decision does the power of the State reach into the heart of the [protected] liberty.

[Roe] was express in its recognition of the State's "important and legitimate interest[s] in preserving and protecting the health of the pregnant woman [and] in protecting the potentiality of human life." The trimester framework, however, does not fulfill Roe's own promise that the State has an interest in protecting fetal life or potential life. Roe began the contradiction by using the trimester framework to forbid any regulation of abortion designed to advance that interest before viability. This [is incompatible] with the recognition that there is a substantial state interest in potential life throughout pregnancy. [Not] all burdens on the right to decide whether to terminate a pregnancy will be undue. In our view, the undue burden standard is the appropriate means of reconciling the State's interest with the woman's constitutionally protected liberty.

[Because] we set forth a standard of general application to which we intend to adhere, it is important to clarify what is meant by an undue burden. A finding of an undue burden is a shorthand for the conclusion that a state regulation has the purpose or effect of placing a substantial obstacle in the path of a woman seeking an abortion of a nonviable fetus. A statute with this purpose is invalid because the means chosen by the State to further the interest in potential life must be calculated to inform the woman's free choice, not hinder it. And a statute which [has] the effect of placing a substantial obstacle in the path of a woman's choice cannot be considered a permissible means of serving its legitimate ends. [In] our considered judgment, an undue burden is an unconstitutional burden. Understood another way, we answer the question, left open in previous opinions, [whether] a law designed to further the State's interest in fetal life which imposes an undue burden on the woman's decision before fetal viability could be constitutional. The answer is no.

Some guiding principles should emerge. What is at stake is the woman's right to make the ultimate decision, not a right to be insulated from all others in doing so. Regulations which do no more than create a structural mechanism by which the State, or the parent or guardian of a minor, may express profound respect for the life of the unborn are permitted, if they are not a substantial obstacle to the woman's exercise of the right to choose. Unless it has that effect on her right of choice, a state measure designed to persuade her to choose childbirth over abortion will be upheld if reasonably related to that goal. Regulations designed to foster the health of a woman seeking an abortion are valid if they do not constitute an undue burden.

Even when jurists reason from shared premises, some disagreement is inevitable. That is to be expected in the application of any legal standard which must accommodate life's complexity. We do not expect it to be otherwise with respect to the undue burden standard. We give this summary:

(a) To protect the central right recognized by Roe while at the same time accommodating the State's profound interest in potential life, we will employ the undue burden analysis as explained in this opinion. An undue burden exists, and therefore a provision of law is invalid, if its purpose or effect is to place a substantial obstacle in the path of a woman seeking an abortion before the fetus attains viability.

(b) We reject the rigid trimester framework of Roe. To promote the State's profound interest in potential life, throughout pregnancy the State may take measures to ensure that the woman's choice is informed, and measures designed to advance this interest will not be invalidated as long as their purpose is to persuade the woman to choose childbirth over abortion. These measures must not be an undue burden on the right.

(c) As with any medical procedure, the State may enact regulations to further the health or safety of a woman seeking an abortion. Unnecessary health regulations that have the purpose or effect of presenting a substantial obstacle to a woman seeking an abortion impose an undue burden on the right.

(d) Our adoption of the undue burden analysis does not disturb the central holding of Roe, and we reaffirm that holding. [A] State may not prohibit any woman from making the ultimate decision to terminate her pregnancy before viability.

(e) We also reaffirm Roe's holding that "subsequent to viability, the State in promoting its interest in the potentiality of human life may, if it chooses, regulate, and even proscribe, abortion except where it is necessary, in appropriate medical judgment, for the preservation of the life or health of the mother." . . .

From the dissenting opinion of Justice SCALIA:

The States may, if they wish, permit abortion-on-demand, but the Constitution does not require them to do so. The permissibility of abortion, and the limitations upon it, are to be resolved like most important questions in our democracy: by citizens trying to persuade one another and then voting. [The] Court is correct in adding the qualification that this "assumes a state of affairs in which the choice does not intrude upon a protected liberty,"—but the crucial part of that qualification is the penultimate word. A State's choice between two positions on which reasonable people can disagree is constitutional even when (as is often the case) it intrudes upon a "liberty" in the absolute sense. Laws against bigamy, for example—which entire societies of reasonable people disagree with—intrude upon men and women's liberty to marry and live with one another. But bigamy happens not to be a liberty specially "protected" by the Constitution.

That is, quite simply, the issue in this case: not whether the power of a woman to abort her unborn child is a "liberty" in the absolute sense; or even whether it is a liberty of great importance to many women. Of course it is both. The issue is whether it is a liberty protected by the Constitution. I am sure it is not. I reach that conclusion not because of anything so exalted as my views concerning the "concept of existence, of meaning, of the universe, and of the mystery of human life." Rather, I reach it for the same reason I reach the conclusion that bigamy is not constitutionally protected—because of two simple facts: (1) the Constitution says absolutely nothing about it, and (2) the longstanding traditions of American society have permitted it to be legally proscribed.

[But] the Court does not wish to be fettered by any such limitations on its preferences. The Court's statement that it is "tempting" to acknowledge the authoritativeness of tradition in order to "cur[b] the discretion of federal judges" is of course rhetoric rather than reality; no

government official is "tempted" to place restraints upon his own freedom of action, which is why Lord Acton did not say "Power tends to purify." The Court's temptation is in the quite opposite and more natural direction—towards systematically eliminating checks upon its own power; and it succumbs.

Beyond that brief summary of the essence of my position, I will not swell the United States Reports with repetition of what I have said before; and applying the rational basis test, I would uphold the Pennsylvania statute in its entirety. I must, however, respond to a few of the more outrageous arguments in today's opinion, which it is beyond human nature to leave unanswered. I shall discuss each of them under a quotation from the Court's opinion to which they pertain.

"The inescapable fact is that adjudication of substantive due process claims may call upon the Court in interpreting the Constitution to exercise that same capacity which by tradition courts always have exercised: reasoned judgment."

Assuming that the question before us is to be resolved at such a level of philosophical abstraction, in such isolation from the traditions of American society, as by simply applying "reasoned judgment," I do not see how that could possibly have produced the answer the Court arrived at in Roe. Today's opinion describes the methodology of Roe, quite accurately, as weighing against the woman's interest the State's "important and legitimate interest in protecting the potentiality of human life." But "reasoned judgment" does not begin by begging the question, as Roe unquestionably did by assuming that what the State is protecting is the mere "potentiality of human life." The whole argument of abortion opponents is that what the Court calls the fetus and what others call the unborn child is a human life. Thus, whatever answer Roe came up with after conducting its "balancing" is bound to be wrong, unless it is correct that the human fetus is in some critical sense merely potentially human. There is of course no way to determine that as a legal matter; it is in fact a value judgment. Some societies have considered newborn children not yet human, or the incompetent elderly no longer so.

The authors of the joint opinion [do] not squarely contend that Roe was a correct application of "reasoned judgment"; merely that it must be followed, because of stare decisis. But in their exhaustive discussion of all the factors that go into the determination of when stare decisis should be observed and when disregarded, they never mention "how wrong was the decision on its face?" Surely, if "[t]he Court's power lies . . . in its legitimacy, a product of substance and perception," the "substance" part of the equation demands that plain error be acknowledged and eliminated. Roe was plainly wrong—even on the Court's methodology of "reasoned judgment," and even more so (of course) if the proper criteria of text and tradition are applied. The emptiness of the "reasoned judgment" that produced Roe is displayed in plain view by the fact that, after more than 19 years of effort by some of the brightest (and most determined) legal minds in the country, after more than 10 cases upholding abortion rights in this Court, and after dozens upon dozens of amicus briefs submitted in this and other cases, the best the Court can do to explain how it is that the word "liberty" must

be thought to include the right to destroy human fetuses is to rattle off a collection of adjectives that simply decorate a value judgment and conceal a political choice. The right to abort, we are told, inheres in "liberty" because it is among "a person's most basic decisions"; it involves a "most intimate and personal choic[e]"; it is "central to personal dignity and autonomy"; it "originate[s] within the zone of conscience and belief"; it is "too intimate and personal" for state interference; it reflects "intimate views" of a "deep, personal character"; it involves "intimate relationships," and notions of "personal autonomy and bodily integrity"; and it concerns a particularly "important decisio[n]." But it is obvious to anyone applying "reasoned judgment" that the same adjectives can be applied to many forms of conduct that this Court [has] held are not entitled to constitutional protection—because, like abortion, they are forms of conduct that have long been criminalized in American society. Those adjectives might be applied, for example, to homosexual sodomy, polygamy, adult incest, and suicide, all of which are equally "intimate" and "deep[ly] personal" decisions involving "personal autonomy and bodily integrity," and all of which can constitutionally be proscribed because it is our unquestionable constitutional tradition that they are proscribable. It is not reasoned judgment that supports the Court's decision; only personal predilection.

QUESTIONS FOR DISCUSSION

1. If the Constitution explicitly protected the right to an abortion, what would Justices White and Rehnquist say? What would Justice Scalia say? What would Noonan say?

2. If the Constitution explicitly protected the right to life from the moment of conception, what would Justice Blackmun say? What would Justice O'Connor say? What would MacKinnon say?

3. How does MacKinnon's approach differ from the Court's in *Roe v. Wade*? If the Supreme Court had adopted MacKinnon's gender equality approach, do

you think Justices White, Rehnquist, and Scalia would still be dissenters? What would their dissents look like?

SUGGESTIONS FOR FURTHER READING

For legal/philosophical analyses of the concept of privacy, see Anita Allen, *Uneasy Access: Privacy for Women in a Free Society* (Totowa, New Jersey: Rowman and Allenheld, 1988); Charles Fried, "Privacy," *Yale Law Journal*, vol. 77 (1968), pp. 475 ff.; Tom Gerety, "Redefining Privacy," *Harvard Civil Rights—Civil Liberties Law Review*, vol. 12 (1977), pp. 233 ff.; H. J. McCloskey, "Privacy and the Right to Privacy," *Philosophy*, vol. 55 (1980), pp. 17 ff. Valuable collections on privacy include J. R. Pennock & J. W. Chapman, eds., *Privacy* (NOMOS XIII) (New York: Atherton Press, 1971); Ferdinand D. Schoeman, ed., *Philosophical Dimensions of Privacy* (Cambridge: Cambridge University Press, 1984). On privacy, personal autonomy, and constitutional theory, see David A. J. Richards, *Sex, Drugs, Death, and the Law: An Essay on Human Rights and Overcriminalization* (Totowa, New Jersey: Rowman and Littlefield, 1982). The classic article on abortion as a question of moral philosophy is Judith Jarvis Thomson, "A Defense of Abortion," *Philosophy and Public Affairs*, vol. 1 (1971), pp. 47 ff. See also Thomson's "The Right to Privacy," *Philosophy and Public Affairs*, vol. 4 (1975), pp. 295 ff. For a perspective similar to Thomson's in legal/constitutional context, see Donald H. Regan, "Rewriting Roe v. Wade," *Michigan Law Review*, vol. 77 (1979), pp. 1569 ff. On a gender equality approach to abortion, see (now Justice) Ruth Bader Ginsburg, "Some Thoughts on Autonomy and Equality in Relation to Roe v. Wade," *North Carolina Law Review*, vol. 63 (1985), pp. 375 ff. For arguments that abortion restrictions violate the religion clauses of the First Amendment, see Ronald Dworkin, "Unenumerated Rights:Whether and How *Roe* Should be Overruled" in *The Bill of Rights in the Modern State*, ed. G. Stone, R. Epstein, and C. Sunstein (Chicago: Univ. of Chicago Press, 1992), pp. 381–432; and *Life's Dominion* (New York: Knopf, 1993).

4.5 THE RIGHT TO RELIGIOUS FREEDOM

INTRODUCTION

In the United States the freedom of religion takes two forms. First, what is called the "Establishment Clause" of the First Amendment provides that "Congress shall make no law respecting an establishment of religion." This provision, held by the courts to apply to the states as well as to the federal government, at the very least prohibits the government from establishing the kind of official state church that exists in many countries, such as the Church of England in Great Britain, Judaism in Israel, and Islam in most of the countries of the Middle East. As interpreted by the courts, the Establishment Clause also prohibits the government from basing its policy decisions on explicitly religious considerations and from endorsing one religion over another, or endorsing religion over non-religion.[12]

Although the Establishment Clause aims at producing secular governmental decisions, and does so, at least historically, in the service of religious freedom, it is a *right* only in the sense that it creates the right not to have governmental decisions made on certain grounds, or the right not to have government engage in certain kinds of activities. A more direct right to religious freedom, however, is protected by another clause of the First Amendment, the one preventing Congress (and, again, the states) from "prohibiting the free exercise of [religion]." Here we have the kind of right resembling in structure constitutional rights to free speech and privacy, because here we have a negative right to be free from governmental interference in certain activities.

But which activities? One argument for a special right to freedom of religion is that people should not be forced to choose between the commands of their conscience and the commands of the state. Many commands of conscience, however, are not explicitly religious. Quakers believe all war to be wrong on religious grounds, and so refuse to serve in the military. Other people, however, believe that all war is wrong for secular moral reasons, and would also wish to refuse to serve in the military. Yet under the laws of the United States, Quakers and other religious objectors are exempt from military service, but equally sincere secular moral objectors are not exempt. This may, indirectly, be a function of the fact that both of the religion clauses in the First Amendment refer to "religion" as such,

---

[12]The Free Exercise Clause, discussed below, may also prevent government from endorsing non-religion over religion.

and this may explain a distinction between religious conscience and non-religious conscience.

As a philosophical question separate from the question of constitutional interpretation, it is not clear what the basis is for distinguishing the commands of religious conscience from the commands of non-religious personal morality. One common argument is that religious commands are commonly seen by believers as authoritative (a point stressed by John Garvey in the essay in this section), and thus it may strike us as wrong to require people to violate one authority in the service of another. But again the commands of secular morality commonly strike those who believe in them as the commands of moral authority, even if that authority is not in personal or God-like form. So perhaps what we think of as the right to freedom of religion is, as a philosophical but perhaps not as a formal legal matter, a right to freedom of conscience, of which the right to freedom of religious conscience is but a subset.

Whether we are considering a right to freedom of religion, specifically, or a right to freedom of conscience, more generally, there remain questions about what is covered by the right, questions that can be asked in terms of the recurring issue of *tolerance*. When we are asked to tolerate religions with which we disagree, or religious practices we think wrong, just what is it we are asked to do, or refrain from doing? Consider the question in a non-religious context. Suppose you like butter pecan ice cream but we like chocolate ripple and dislike butter pecan. We think your beliefs about ice cream flavors—your tastes, as we often say—are different, but we do not think them wrong. In this case we have little difficulty in *tolerating* your different but not wrong beliefs.

Suppose, now, however, that in addition to liking butter pecan ice cream you also believe that Frank Zappa was a more important figure in the history of music than Beethoven, and that Louisville is the capital of Kentucky. Here we think your beliefs are not just different, but wrong. Again, however, we tolerate your erroneous beliefs—we take no action against them, and would not wish the state to take any action against them—because we believe that little if any harm will come from your holding these mistaken beliefs. Here tolerance seems to be but an application of the harm principle discussed at the outset of this chapter. If we believe that the state (or anyone else with power) should not interfere with harmless activities then we will believe that the state should not interfere with harmless mistakes, whether of fact or of value. This would apply to religion as well, so if we believe that others' beliefs are harmlessly mistaken, then tolerance of mistaken beliefs will follow from acceptance of something like Mill's harm principle.

But now suppose you believe that women who say "no" mean "yes," that handling poisonous snakes is harmless (some people believe that snake-handling is commanded by the Bible, and believers occasionally lose their lives as a result of engaging in the practice), that blood transfusions are immoral (as the Jehovah's Witnesses believe), that separation of the races is commanded by God, or that prayer is better treatment than surgery for acute appendicitis. In all of these cases we again are convinced that your beliefs are mistaken, but no longer do we think they are harmlessly mistaken. We think that your beliefs (and the actions you might take in furtherance of them) are mistaken in a way that might cause harm to you or to others.

It is just at this point when the question of whether there is a *distinct* principle of tolerance, religious or otherwise, arises. Suppose you believe for religious reasons that handling poisonous snakes is harmless. The state, however, believes to the contrary, and seeks to prohibit you from handling poisonous snakes in pursuit of your beliefs. And suppose this is consistent with a general rejection of anti-paternalism. That is, the state also requires you to wear seat belts, requires you to wear a helmet when riding a bicycle or motorcycle, taxes cigarettes heavily, and prohibits you from using heroin and many other harmful narcotics. Now we can see where a principle of religious tolerance might make a difference, because now it is at least possible that a principle of religious tolerance might allow the snake handlers to jeopardize their own lives or health in circumstances in which the state would not otherwise be so tolerant of behavior harmful to the person engaging in the behavior. This is not yet to say that there *should be* such a principle. It is to say that if there were such a principle, this is what it would be like. It is to say as well that, although it is moderately easy to see why people should not be persecuted for their self-regarding beliefs that the state or the majority thinks mistaken, it is not as easy to see why beliefs or actions believed harmful (to self or others) by the state or the majority should be tolerated just because those harmful beliefs or actions are motivated by religious beliefs. As you consider the following readings, therefore, think carefully about what behavior the state is being asked to tolerate, then about what justifies the desire to control that behavior, and finally about what rights, if any, might prevent that control.

RELIGIOUS BELIEF AND PUBLIC MORALITY: A CATHOLIC GOVERNOR'S PERSPECTIVE

MARIO CUOMO

I would like to begin by drawing your attention to the title of this lecture: "Religious Belief and Public Morality: A Catholic Governor's Perspective." I was not invited to speak on "Church and State" generally. Certainly not "Mondale vs. Reagan." The subject assigned is difficult enough. I will not try to do more than I've been asked.

Mario Cuomo, "Religious Belief and Public Morality: A Catholic Governor's Perspective," *Notre Dame Journal of Law, Ethics & Public Policy*, vol. 1 (1984), pp. 13–31.

It's not easy to stay contained. Certainly, although everybody talks about a wall of separation between church and state, I've seen religious leaders scale that wall with all the dexterity of olympic athletes. In fact, I've seen so many candidates in churches and synagogues that I think we should change election day from Tuesdays to Saturdays and Sundays.

I am honored by this invitation, but the record shows that I am not the first Governor of New York to appear at an event involving Notre Dame. One of my great predecessors, Al Smith, went to the Army–Notre Dame football game each time it was played in New York.

His fellow Catholics expected Smith to sit with Notre Dame; protocol required him to sit with Army because it was the home team. Protocol prevailed. But not without Smith noting the dual demands on his affections. "I'll take my seat with Army," he said, "but I commend my soul to Notre Dame."

Today I'm happy to have no such problem: both my seat and my soul are with Notre Dame. And as long as Father McBrien doesn't invite me back to sit with him at the Notre Dame–St. John's basketball game, I'm confident my loyalties will remain undivided.

In a sense, it's a question of loyalty that Father McBrien has asked me here today to discuss. Specifically, must politics and religion in America divide our loyalties? Does the "separation between church and state" imply separation between religion and politics? Between morality and government? Are these different propositions? Even more specifically, what is the relationship of my Catholicism to my politics? Where does the one end and the other begin? Or are the two divided at all? And if they're not, should they be?

■ ■ ■

Hard questions.

No wonder most of us in public life—at least until recently—preferred to stay away from them, heeding the biblical advice that if "hounded and pursued in one city," we should flee to another.

Now, however, I think that it is too late to flee. The questions are all around us, and answers are coming from every quarter. Some of them have been simplistic, most of them fragmentary, and a few, spoken with a purely political intent, demagogic.

There has been confusion and compounding of confusion, a blurring of the issue, entangling it in personalities and election strategies, instead of clarifying it for Catholics, as well as others.

Today I would like to try to help correct that.

I can offer you no final truths, complete and unchallengeable. But it's possible this one effort will provoke other efforts—both in support and contradiction of my position—that will help all of us understand our differences and perhaps even discover some basic agreement.

In the end, I'm convinced we will all benefit if suspicion is replaced by discussion, innuendo by dialogue; if the emphasis in our debate turns from a search for talismanic criteria and neat but simplistic answers to an honest—more intelligent—attempt at describing the role religion has in our public affairs, and the limits placed on that role.

And if we do it right—if we're not afraid of the truth even when the truth is complex—this debate, by clarification, can bring relief to untold numbers of confused—even anguished—Catholics, as well as to many others who want only to make our already great democracy even stronger than it is.

I believe the recent discussion in my own State has already produced some clearer definition. In early summer, an impression was created in some quarters that official church spokespeople would ask Catholics to vote for or against specific candidates on the basis of their political position on the abortion issue. I was one of those given that impression. Thanks to the dialogue that ensued over the summer—only partially reported by the media—we learned that the impression was not accurate.

Confusion had presented an opportunity for clarification, and we seized it. Now all of us are saying one thing—in chorus—reiterating the statement of the National Conference of Catholic Bishops that they will not "take positions for or against political candidates" and that their stand on specific issues should not be perceived "as an expression of political partisanship."

Of course the bishops will teach—they must—more and more vigorously and more and more extensively. But they have said they will not use the power of their position, and the great respect it receives from all Catholics, to give an imprimatur to individual politicians or parties.

Not that they couldn't if they wished to— some religious leaders do; some are doing it at this very moment.

Not that it would be a sin if they did—God doesn't insist on political neutrality. But because it is the judgment of the bishops, and most of us Catholic lay people, that it is not wise for prelates and politicians to be tied too closely together.

I think that getting this consensus was an extraordinarily useful achievement.

Now, with some trepidation, I take up your gracious invitation to continue the dialogue in the hope that it will lead to still further clarification.

■ ■ ■

Let me begin this part of the effort by underscoring the obvious. I do not speak as a theologian; I do not have that competence. I do not speak as a philosopher; to suggest that I could, would be to set a new record for false pride. I don't presume to speak as a "good" person except in the ontological sense of that word. My principal credential is that I serve in a position that forces me to wrestle with the problems you've come here to study and debate.

I am by training a lawyer and by practice a politician. Both professions make me suspect in many quarters, including among some of my own co-religionists. Maybe there's no better illustration of the public perception of how politicians unite their faith and their profession than the story they tell in New York about "Fishhooks" McCarthy, a famous Democratic leader on the lower East Side, and right-hand man to Al Smith.

"Fishhooks," the story goes, was devout. So devout that every morning on his way to Tammany Hall to do his political work, he stepped into St. James Church on Oliver Street in downtown Manhattan, fell on his knees, and whispered the same simple prayer: "Oh, Lord, give me health and strength. We'll steal the rest."

■ ■ ■

"Fishhooks" notwithstanding, I speak here as a politician. And also as a Catholic, a lay person baptized and raised in the pre-Vatican II Church, educated in Catholic schools, attached to the Church first by birth, then by choice, now by love. An old-fashioned Catholic who sins, regrets, struggles, worries, gets confused and most of the time feels better after confession.

The Catholic Church is my spiritual home. My heart is there, and my hope.

There is, of course, more to being a Catholic than a sense of spiritual and emotional resonance. Catholicism is a religion of the head as well as the heart, and to be a Catholic is to say "I believe" to the essential core of dogmas that distinguishes our faith.

The acceptance of this faith requires a lifelong struggle to understand it more fully and to live it more truly, to translate truth into experience, to practice as well as to believe.

That's not easy: applying religious belief to everyday life often presents difficult challenges.

It's always been that way. It certainly is today. The America of the late twentieth century is a consumer society, filled with endless distractions, where faith is more often dismissed than challenged, where the ethnic and other loyalties that once fastened us to our religion seem to be weakening.

In addition to all the weaknesses, dilemmas and temptations that impede every pilgrim's progress, the Catholic who holds political office in a pluralistic democracy—who is elected to serve Jews and Muslims, atheists and Protestants, as well as Catholics—bears special responsibility. He or she undertakes to help create conditions under which *all* can live with a maximum of dignity and with a reasonable degree of freedom; where everyone who chooses may hold beliefs different from specifically Catholic ones—sometimes contradictory to them; where the laws protect people's right to divorce, to use birth control and even to choose abortion.

In fact, Catholic public officials take an oath to preserve the Constitution that guarantees this freedom. And they do so gladly. Not because they love what others do with their freedom, but because they realize that in guaranteeing freedom for all, they guarantee *our* right to be Catholics: *our* right to pray, to use the sacraments, to refuse birth control devices, to reject abortion, not to divorce and remarry if we believe it to be wrong.

The Catholic public official lives the political truth most Catholics through most of American history have accepted and insisted on: the truth that to assure our freedom we must allow others the same freedom, even if occasionally it produces conduct by them which we would hold to be sinful.

I protect my right to be a Catholic by preserving your right to believe as a Jew, a Protestant or non-believer, or as anything else you choose.

We know that the price of seeking to force our beliefs on others is that they might some day force theirs on us.

This freedom is the fundamental strength of our unique experiment in government. In the complex interplay of forces and considerations that go into the making of our laws and policies, its preservation must be a pervasive and dominant concern.

But insistence on freedom is easier to accept as a general proposition than in its applications to specific situations. There are other valid general principles firmly embedded in our Constitution, which, operating at the same time, create interesting and occasionally troubling problems. Thus, the same amendment of the Constitution that forbids the establishment of a State Church affirms my legal right to argue that my religious belief would serve well as an article of our universal public morality. I may use the prescribed processes of government—the legislative and executive and judicial processes—to convince my fellow citizens—Jews and Protestants and Buddhists and non-believers—that what I propose is as beneficial for them as I believe it is for me: that it is not just parochial or narrowly sectarian but fulfills a human desire for order, peace, justice, kindness, love, any of the values most of us agree are desirable even apart from their specific religious base or context.

I am free to argue for a governmental policy for a nuclear freeze not just to avoid sin but because I think my democracy should regard it as a desirable goal.

I can, if I wish, argue that the State should not fund the use of contraceptive devices not because the Pope demands it but because I think that the whole community—for the good of the whole community—should not sever sex from an openness to the creation of life.

And surely, I can, if so inclined, demand some kind of law against abortion not because my Bishops say it is wrong but because I think that the whole community, regardless of its religious beliefs, should agree on the importance of protecting life—including life in the womb, which is at the very least potentially human and should not be extinguished casually.

No law prevents us from advocating any of these things: I am free to do so.

So are the Bishops. And so is Reverend Falwell.

In fact, the Constitution guarantees my right to try. And theirs. And his.

But should I? Is it helpful? Is it essential to human dignity? Does it promote harmony and understanding? Or does it divide us so fundamentally that it threatens our ability to function as a pluralistic community?

When should I argue to make my religious value your morality? My rule of conduct your limitation?

What are the rules and policies that should influence the exercise of this right to argue and promote?

I believe I have a salvific mission as a Catholic. Does that mean I am in conscience required to do everything I can as Governor to translate *all* my religious values into the laws and regulations of the State of New York or the United States? Or be branded a hypocrite if I don't?

As a Catholic, I respect the teaching authority of the bishops.

But must I agree with everything in the bishops' pastoral letter on peace and fight to include it in party platforms?

And will I have to do the same for the forthcoming pastoral on economics even if I am an unrepentant supply sider?

Must I, having heard the Pope renew the Church's ban on birth control devices, veto the funding of contraceptive programs for non-Catholics or dissenting Catholics in my State?

I accept the Church's teaching on abortion. Must I insist you do? By law? By denying you Medicaid funding? By a constitutional amendment? If so, which one? Would that be the best way to avoid abortions or to prevent them?

These are only some of the questions for Catholics. People with other religious beliefs face similar problems.

■ ■ ■

Let me try some answers.

Almost all Americans accept some religious values as a part of our public life. We are a religious people, many of us descended from ancestors who came here expressly to live their religious faith free from coercion or repression. But we are also a people of many religions, with no established church, who hold different beliefs on many matters.

Our public morality, then—the moral standards we maintain for everyone, not just the ones we insist on in our private lives—depends on a consensus view of right and wrong. The values derived from religious belief will not—

and should not—be accepted as part of the public morality unless they are shared by the pluralistic community at large, by consensus.

That values happen to be religious values does not deny them acceptability as a part of this consensus. But it does not require their acceptability, either.

The agnostics who joined the civil rights struggle were not deterred because that crusade's values had been nurtured and sustained in black Christian churches. Those on the political left are not perturbed today by the religious basis of the clergy and lay people who join them in the protest against the arms race and hunger and exploitation.

The arguments start when religious values are used to support positions which would impose on other people restrictions they find unacceptable. Some people *do* object to Catholic demands for an end to abortion, seeing it as a violation of the separation of church and state. And some others, while they have no compunction about invoking the authority of the Catholic bishops in regard to birth control and abortion, might reject out of hand their teaching on war and peace and social policy.

Ultimately, therefore, the question "whether or not we admit religious values into our public affairs" is too broad to yield a single answer. "Yes," we create our public morality through consensus and in this country that consensus reflects to some extent religious values of a great majority of Americans. But "no," all religiously based values don't have an *a priori* place in our public morality.

The community must decide if what is being proposed would be better left to private discretion than public policy; whether it restricts freedoms, and if so to what end, to whose benefit; whether it will produce a good or bad result; whether overall it will help the community or merely divide it.

The right answers to these questions can be elusive. Some of the wrong answers, on the other hand, are quite clear. For example, there are those who say there is a simple answer to *all* these questions; they say that by history and practice of our people we were intended to be—and should be—a Christian country in law.

But where would that leave the non-believers? And whose Christianity would be law, yours or mine?

This "Christian nation" argument should concern—even frighten—two groups: non-Christians and thinking Christians.

I believe it does.

I think it's already apparent that a good part of this Nation understands—if only instinctively—that anything which seems to suggest that God favors a political party or the establishment of a state church, is wrong and dangerous.

Way down deep the American people are afraid of an entangling relationship between formal religions—or whole bodies of religious belief—and government. Apart from constitutional law and religious doctrine, there is a sense that tells us it's wrong to presume to speak for God or to claim God's sanction of our particular legislation and His rejection of all other positions. Most of us are offended when we see religion being trivialized by its appearance in political throw-away pamphlets.

The American people need no course in philosophy or political science or church history to know that God should not be made into a celestial party chairman.

To most of us, the manipulative invoking of religion to advance a politician or a party is frightening and divisive. The American people will tolerate religious leaders taking positions for or against candidates, although I think the Catholic bishops are right in avoiding that position. But the American people are leery about large religious organizations, powerful churches or synagogue groups engaging in such activities—again, not as a matter of law or doctrine, but because our innate wisdom and democratic instinct teaches us these things are dangerous.

■ ■ ■

Today there are a number of issues involving life and death that raise questions of public morality. They are also questions of concern to most religions. Pick up a newspaper and you are almost certain to find a bitter controversy over any one of them: Baby Jane Doe, the right to die, artificial insemination, embryos in vitro, abortion, birth control. . . . not to mention nuclear war and the shadow it throws across all existence.

Some of these issues touch the most intimate recesses of our lives, our roles as someone's mother or child or husband; some affect women in a unique way. But they are also public questions, for all of us.

Put aside what God expects—assume if you like there is no God—then the greatest thing still left to us is life. Even a radically secular world must struggle with the questions of when life begins, under what circumstances it can be ended, when it must be protected, by what authority; it too must decide what protection to extend to the helpless and the dying, to the aged and the unborn, to life in all its phases.

As a Catholic, I have accepted certain answers as the right ones for myself and my family, and because I have, they have influenced me in special ways, as Matilda's husband, as a father of five children, as a son who stood next to his own father's death bed trying to decide if the tubes and needles no longer served a purpose.

As a Governor, however, I am involved in defining policies that determine *other* people's rights in these same areas of life and death. Abortion is one of these issues, and while it is one issue among many, it is one of the most controversial and affects me in a special way as a Catholic public official.

So let me spend some time considering it.

I should start, I believe, by noting that the Catholic Church's actions with respect to the interplay of religious values and public policy make clear that there is no inflexible moral principle which determines what our *political* conduct should be. For example, on divorce and birth control, without changing its moral teaching, the Church abides the civil law as it now stands, thereby accepting—without making much of a point of it—that in our pluralistic society we are not required to insist that *all* our religious values be the law of the land.

Abortion is treated differently.

Of course there are differences both in degree and quality between abortion and some of the other religious positions the Church takes: abortion is a "matter of life and death," and degree counts. But the differences in approach reveal a truth, I think, that is not well enough perceived by Catholics and therefore still further complicates the process for us. That is, while we always owe our Bishops' words respectful attention and careful consideration, the question whether to engage the political system in a struggle to have it adopt certain articles of our belief as part of public morality, is not a matter of doctrine: it is a matter of prudential political judgment.

Recently, Michael Novak put it succinctly: "Religious judgment and political judgment are both needed," he wrote. "But they are not identical."

My church and my conscience require me to believe certain things about divorce, birth control and abortion. My church does not order me—under pain of sin or expulsion—to pursue my salvific mission according to a precisely defined political plan.

As a Catholic I accept the church's teaching authority. While in the past some Catholic theologians may appear to have disagreed on the morality of some abortions (it wasn't, I think, until 1869 that excommunication was attached to all abortions without distinction), and while some theologians still do, I accept the bishops' position that abortion is to be avoided.

As Catholics, my wife and I were enjoined never to use abortion to destroy the life we created, and we never have. We thought Church doctrine was clear on this, and—more than that—both of us felt it in full agreement with what our hearts and our consciences told us. For me life or fetal life in the womb should be protected, even if five of nine Justices of the Supreme Court and my neighbor disagree with me. A fetus is different from an appendix or a set of tonsils. At the very least, even if the argument is made by some scientists or some theologians that in the early stages of fetal development we can't discern human life, the full potential of human life is indisputably there. That—to my less subtle mind—by itself should demand respect, caution, indeed. . . . reverence.

But not everyone in our society agrees with me and Matilda.

And those who don't—those who endorse legalized abortions—aren't a ruthless, callous alliance of anti-Christians determined to overthrow our moral standards. In many cases, the proponents of legal abortion are the very people who have worked with Catholics to realize the goals of social justice set out in papal encyclicals: the American Lutheran Church, the Central Conference of American Rabbis, the Presbyterian Church in the United States, B'nai B'rith Women, the Women of the Episcopal Church. These are just a few of the religious organizations that don't share the Church's position on abortion.

Certainly, we should not be forced to mold Catholic morality to conform to disagreement by non-Catholics however sincere or severe their disagreement. Our bishops should be teachers not pollsters. They should not change what we Catholics believe in order to ease our consciences or please our friends or protect the Church from criticism.

But if the breadth, intensity and sincerity of opposition to church teaching shouldn't be allowed to shape our Catholic morality, it can't help but determine our ability—our realistic, political ability—to translate our Catholic morality into civil law, a law not for the believers who don't need it but for the disbelievers who reject it.

And it is here, in our attempt to find a political answer to abortion—an answer beyond our private observance of Catholic morality—that we encounter controversy within and without the Church over how and in what degree to press the case that our morality should be everybody else's, and to what effect.

I repeat, there is no Church teaching that mandates the best political course for making our belief everyone's rule, for spreading this part of our Catholicism. There is neither an encyclical nor a catechism that spells out a political strategy for achieving legislative goals.

And so the Catholic trying to make moral and prudent judgments in the political realm must discern which, if any, of the actions one could take would be best.

This latitude of judgment is not something new in the Church, not a development that has arisen only with the abortion issue. Take, for example, the question of slavery. It has been argued that the failure to endorse a legal ban on abortions is equivalent to refusing to support the cause of abolition before the Civil War. This analogy has been advanced by the bishops of my own state.

But the truth of the matter is, few if any Catholic bishops spoke for abolition in the years before the Civil War. It wasn't, I believe, that the bishops endorsed the idea of some humans owning and exploiting other humans; Pope Gregory XVI, in 1840, had condemned the slave trade. Instead it was a practical political judgment that the bishops made. They weren't hypocrites; they were realists. At the time, Catholics were a small minority, mostly immigrants, despised by much of the population, often vilified and the object of sporadic violence. In the face of a public controversy that aroused tremendous passions and threatened to break the country apart, the bishops made a pragmatic decision. They believed their opinion would not change people's minds. Moreover they knew that there were southern Catholics, even some priests, who owned slaves. They concluded that under the circumstances arguing for a constitutional amendment against slavery would do more harm than good, so they were silent. As they have been, generally, in recent years, on the question of birth control. And as the Church has been on even more controversial issues in the past, even ones that dealt with life and death.

What is relevant to this discussion is that the bishops were making judgments about translating Catholic teachings into public policy, not about the moral validity of the teachings. In so doing they grappled with the unique political complexities of their time. The decision they made to remain silent on a constitutional amendment to abolish slavery or on the repeal of the Fugitive Slave Law wasn't a mark of their moral indifference: it was a measured attempt to balance moral truths against political realities. Their decision reflected their sense of complexity, not their diffidence. As history reveals, Lincoln behaved with similar discretion.

The parallel I want to draw here is not between or among what we Catholics believe to be moral wrongs. It is in the Catholic response to those wrongs. Church teaching on slavery and abortion is clear. But in the application of those teachings—the exact way we translate them into action, the specific laws we propose, the exact legal sanctions we seek—there was and is no one, clear, absolute route that the Church says, as a matter of doctrine, we must follow.

The bishops' pastoral letter, "The Challenge of Peace," speaks directly to this point. "We recognize," the bishops wrote, "that the Church's teaching authority does not carry the same force when it deals with technical solutions involving particular means as it does when it speaks of principles or ends. People may agree in abhorring an injustice, for instance, yet sincerely disagree as to what practical approach will achieve justice. Religious groups are entitled as others to their opinion in such cases, but they should not claim that their opinions are the only ones that people of good will may hold."

With regard to abortion, the American bishops have had to weigh Catholic moral teaching against the fact of a pluralistic country where our view is in the minority, acknowledging that what is ideally desirable isn't always feasible, that there can be different political approaches to abortion besides unyielding adherence to an absolute prohibition.

This is in the American-Catholic tradition of political realism. In supporting or opposing specific legislation the Church in this country has never retreated into a moral fundamentalism that will settle for nothing less than total acceptance of its views.

Indeed, the bishops have already confronted the fact that an absolute ban on abortion doesn't have the support necessary to be placed in our Constitution. In 1981, they put aside earlier efforts to describe a law they could accept and get passed, and supported the Hatch Amendment instead.

Some Catholics felt the bishops had gone too far with that action, some not far enough. Such judgments were not a rejection of the bishops' teaching authority: the Bishops even disagreed among themselves. Catholics are allowed to disagree on these technical political questions without having to confess.

■ ■ ■

Respectfully, and after careful consideration of the position and arguments of the bishops, I have concluded that the approach of a constitutional amendment is not the best way for us to seek to deal with abortion.

I believe that legal interdicting of abortion by either the federal government or the individual states is not a plausible possibility and even if it could be obtained, it wouldn't work. Given present attitudes, it would be "Prohibition" revisited, legislating what couldn't be enforced and in the process creating a disrespect for law in general. And as much as I admire the bishops' hope that a constitutional amendment against abortion would be the basis for a full, new bill of rights for mothers and children, I disagree that this would be the result.

I believe that, more likely, a constitutional prohibition would allow people to ignore the causes of many abortions instead of addressing them, much the way the death penalty is used to escape dealing more fundamentally and more rationally with the problem of violent crime.

Other legal options that have been proposed are, in my view, equally ineffective. The Hatch Amendment, by returning the question of abortion to the states, would have given us a checkerboard of permissive and restrictive jurisdictions. In some cases people might have been forced to go elsewhere to have abortions and that might have eased a few consciences but it wouldn't have done what the Church wants to do—it wouldn't have created a deep-seated respect for life. Abortions would have gone on, millions of them.

Nor would a denial of medicaid funding for abortion achieve our objectives. Given *Roe v. Wade*, it would be nothing more than an attempt to do indirectly what the law says cannot be done directly; worse, it would do it in a way that would burden only the already disadvantaged. Removing funding from the medicaid program would not prevent the rich and middle classes from having abortions. It would not even assure that the disadvantaged wouldn't have them; it would only impose financial burdens on poor women who want abortions.

Apart from that unevenness, there is a more basic question. Medicaid is designed to deal with health and medical needs. But the arguments for the cutoff of medicaid abortion funds are not related to those needs. They are moral arguments. If we assume health and medical needs exist, our personal view of morality ought not to be considered a relevant basis for discrimination.

We must keep in mind always that we are a nation of laws—when we like those laws, and when we don't.

The Supreme Court has established a woman's constitutional right to abortion. The Congress has decided the federal government should not provide federal funding in the medicaid program for abortion. That, of course, does not bind states in the allocation of their own state funds. Under the law, the individual states need not follow the federal lead, and in New York I believe we cannot follow that lead. The equal protection clause in New York's Constitution has been interpreted by the courts as a standard of fairness that would preclude us from denying only the poor—indirectly, by a cutoff of funds—the practical use of the constitutional right given by *Roe v. Wade.*

In the end, even if after a long and divisive struggle we were able to remove all medicaid funding for abortion and restore the law to what it was—if we could put most abortions out of our sight, return them to the backrooms where they were performed for so long—I don't believe our responsibility as Catholics would be any closer to being fulfilled than it is now, with abortion guaranteed by the law as a woman's right.

The hard truth is that abortion isn't a failure of government. No agency or department of government forces women to have abortions, but abortion goes on. Catholics, the statistics show, support the right to abortion in equal proportion to the rest of the population. Despite the teaching in our homes and schools and pulpits, despite the sermons and pleadings of parents and priests and prelates, despite all the effort at defining our opposition to the sin of abortion, collectively we Catholics apparently believe—and perhaps act—little differently from those who don't share our commitment.

Are we asking government to make criminal what we believe to be sinful because we ourselves can't stop committing the sin?

The failure here is not Caesar's. This failure is our failure, the failure of the entire people of God.

Nobody has expressed this better than a bishop in my own state, Joseph Sullivan, a man who works with the poor in New York City, is resolutely opposed to abortion and argues, with his fellow bishops, for a change of law. "The major problem the Church has is internal," the Bishop said last month in reference to abortion. "How do we teach? As much as I think we're responsible for advocating public policy issues, our primary responsibility is to teach our own people. We haven't done that. We're asking politicians to do what we haven't done effectively ourselves."

I agree with the Bishop. I think our moral and social mission as Catholics must begin with the wisdom contained in the words "Physician, heal thyself." Unless we Catholics educate ourselves better to the values that define—and can ennoble—our lives, following those teachings better than we do now, unless we set an example that is clear and compelling, then we will never convince this society to change the civil laws to protect what we preach is precious human life.

Better than any law or rule or threat of punishment would be the moving strength of our own good example, demonstrating our lack of hypocrisy, proving the beauty and worth of our instruction.

We must work to find ways to avoid abortions without otherwise violating our faith. We should provide funds and opportunity for young women to bring their child to term, knowing both of them will be taken care of if that is necessary; we should teach our young men better than we do now their responsibilities in creating and caring for human life.

It is this duty of the Church to teach through its practice of love that Pope John Paul II has proclaimed so magnificently to all peoples, "The Church," he wrote in *Redemptor Hominis* (1979), "which has no weapons at her disposal apart from those of the spirit, of the word and of love, cannot renounce her proclamation of 'the word . . . in season and out of season.' For this reason she does not cease to implore . . . everybody in the name of God and in the name of man: Do not kill! Do not prepare destruction and extermination for each other! Think of your brothers and sisters who are suffering hunger and misery! Respect each one's dignity and freedom!"

The weapons of the word and of love are already available to us: we need no statute to provide them.

I am not implying that we should stand by and pretend indifference to whether a woman takes a pregnancy to its conclusion or aborts it. I believe we should in all cases try to teach a respect for life. And I believe with regard to abortion that, despite Roe v. Wade, *we can, in practical ways. Here, in fact, it seems to me that all of us can agree.*

Without lessening their insistence on a woman's right to an abortion, the people who call themselves "pro-choice" can support the development of government programs that present an impoverished mother with the full range of support she needs to bear and raise her children, to have a real choice. Without dropping their campaign to ban abortion, those who gather under the banner of "pro-life" can join in developing and enacting a legislative bill of rights for mothers and children, as the bishops have already proposed.

While we argue over abortion, the United States' infant mortality rate places us sixteenth among the nations of the world. Thousands of infants die each year because of inadequate medical care. Some are born with birth defects that, with proper treatment, could be prevented. Some are stunted in their physical and mental growth because of improper nutrition.

If we want to prove our regard for life in the womb, for the helpless infant—if we care about women having real choices in their lives and not being driven to abortions by a sense of helplessness and despair about the future of their child—then there is work enough for all of us. Lifetimes of it.

In New York, we have put in place a number of programs to begin this work, assisting women in giving birth to healthy babies. This year we doubled medicaid funding to private-care physicians for pre-natal and delivery services.

The state already spends 20 million dollars a year for prenatal care in out-patient clinics and for in-patient hospital care.

One program in particular we believe holds a great deal of promise. It's called "new avenues to dignity," and it seeks to provide a teenage mother with the special service she needs to continue with her education, to train for a job, to become capable of standing on her own, to provide for herself and the child she is bringing into the world.

My dissent, then, from the contention that we can have effective and enforceable legal prohibitions on abortion is by no means an argument for religious quietism, for accepting the world's wrongs because that is our fate as "the poor banished children of Eve."

■■■

Let me make another point.

Abortion has a unique significance but not a preemptive significance.

Apart from the question of the efficacy of using legal weapons to make people stop having abortions, we know our Christian responsibility doesn't end with any one law or amendment. That it doesn't end with abortion. Because it involves life and death, abortion will always be a central concern of Catholics. But so will nuclear weapons. And hunger and homelessness and joblessness, all the forces diminishing human life and threatening to destroy it. The "seamless garment" that Cardinal Bernardin has spoken of is a challenge to all Catholics in public office, conservatives as well as liberals.

We cannot justify our aspiration to goodness simply on the basis of the vigor of our demand for an elusive and questionable civil law declaring what we already know, that abortion is wrong.

Approval or rejection of legal restrictions on abortion should not be the exclusive litmus test of Catholic loyalty. We should understand that whether abortion is outlawed or not, our work has barely begun: the work of creating a society where the right to life doesn't end at the moment of birth; where an infant isn't helped into a world that doesn't care if it's fed properly, housed decently, educated adequately; where the blind or retarded child isn't condemned to exist rather than empowered to live.

■■■

The bishops stated this duty clearly in 1974, in their statement to the Senate Sub-Committee considering a proposed amendment to restrict abortions. They maintained such an amendment could not be seen as an end in itself. "We do not see a constitutional amendment as the final product of our commitment or of our legislative activity," they said. "It is instead the constitutional base on which to provide support and assistance to pregnant women and their unborn children. This would include nutritional, prenatal, child birth and post-natal care for the mother, and also nutritional and pediatric care for the child through the first year of life. . . . We believe that all of these should be available as a matter of right to all pregnant women and their children."

The bishops reaffirmed that view in 1976, in 1980, and again this year when the United States Catholic Committee asked Catholics to judge candidates on a wide range of issues—on abortion, yes; but also on food policy, the arms race, human rights, education, social justice and military expenditures.

The bishops have been consistently "pro-life" in the full meaning of that term, and I respect them for that.

■ ■ ■

The problems created by the matter of abortion are complex and confounding. Nothing is clearer to me than my inadequacy to find compelling solutions to all of their moral, legal and social implications. I—and many others like me—are eager for enlightenment, eager to learn new and better ways to manifest respect for the deep reverence for life that is our religion and our instinct. I hope that this public attempt to describe the problems as I understand them, will give impetus to the dialogue in the Catholic community and beyond, a dialogue which could show me a better wisdom than I've been able to find so far.

It would be tragic if we let that dialogue become a prolonged, divisive argument that destroys or impairs our ability to practice any part of the morality given us in the Sermon on the Mount, to touch, heal and affirm the human life that surrounds us.

We Catholic citizens of the richest, most powerful nation that has ever existed are like the stewards made responsible over a great household: from those to whom so much has been given, much shall be required. It is worth repeating that ours is not a faith that encourages its believers to stand apart from the world, seeking their salvation alone, separate from the salvation of those around them.

We speak of ourselves as a body. We come together in worship as companions, in the ancient sense of that word, those who break bread together, and who are obliged by the commitment we share to help one another, everywhere, in all we do, and in the process, to help the whole human family. We see our mission to be "the completion of the work of creation."

This is difficult work today. It presents us with many hard choices.

The Catholic Church has come of age in America. The ghetto walls are gone, our religion no longer a badge of irredeemable foreignness. This new-found status is both an opportunity and a temptation. If we choose, we can give in to the temptation to become more and more assimilated into a larger, blander culture, abandoning the practice of the specific values that made us different, worshipping whatever gods the marketplace has to sell while we seek to rationalize our own laxity by urging the political system to legislate on others a morality we no longer practice ourselves.

Or we can remember where we come from, the journey of two millennia, clinging to our personal faith, to its insistence on constancy and service and on hope. *We can live and practice the morality Christ gave us, maintaining His truth in this world, struggling to embody His love, practicing it especially where that love is most needed, among the poor and the weak and the dispossessed. Not just by trying to make laws for others to live by, but by living the laws already written for us by God, in our hearts and our minds.*

We can be fully Catholic; proudly, totally at ease with ourselves, a people in the world, transforming it, a light to this nation. Appealing to the best in our people not the worst. Persuading not coercing. Leading people to truth by love. And still, all the while, respecting and enjoying our unique pluralistic democracy. And we can do it even as politicians.

THE POPE'S SUBMARINE

JOHN GARVEY

The authoritativeness of the Church's teaching for ordinary Catholics depends in part on who the teacher is. Vatican II states that the highest authority resides in the college of bishops with the pope at their head. In the modern Church this is a lot of bishops, and they do not often get together. When they do (in an ecumenical council like Vatican II), they exercise their authority in a particularly "solemn way." Even when not gathered together the bishops can sometimes teach with the same authority, provided "they concur in a single viewpoint as the one which must be held conclusively." The pope can also act alone with an authority equivalent to that of an ecumenical council. He is, Vatican II observes, "the supreme teacher of the universal Church." Each of these actors (ecumenical council, the dispersed college of bishops, the pope) is thought to be capable of acting infallibly, though they seldom do so, and such action depends on other factors.

These are not the only Church officials capable of acting authoritatively. Individual bishops have jurisdiction over Church members within their territory. Their pronouncements are obligatory (though not infallible) in a sense which I will explore below. Groups of bishops may also gather together on a national or territorial basis to form episcopal conferences, a practice encouraged by Vatican II. The National Conference of Catholic Bishops is a fairly active example. These groups, like their members, can act authoritatively but not infallibly. Then there is a whole host of congregations, commissions, offices, and so on that make up the Vatican bureaucracy, and that function in ways not unlike the modern administrative state.

I need not detail the positions of all the various actors within the Church hierarchy to make my first point, which is simply that the authoritativeness of Church teaching varies with (among other things) the identity of the speaker. It also varies with the speaker's intention. The pope teaches infallibly only when "he proclaims *by a definitive act* some doctrine of faith or morals." The bishops do so only when "they concur in a single viewpoint *as the one which must be held conclusively.*" The principle is like the clear statement rule that we sometimes use in interpreting statutes: *Y* is understood to have acted with infallible authority only when it has made perfectly clear its intention to do so. And the significance of intentions is not confined to the question of infallibility. None of the many documents produced by Vatican II was meant to be definitive in that way. But they bear various titles intended to indicate the degree of authoritativeness attached to each: "dogmatic constitution," "pastoral constitution," "constitution," "decree," "declaration."

The authoritativeness of Church teaching thus varies with the speaker's office and intentions. It also varies with the subject matter. The idea is a familiar one to lawyers. The United States Supreme Court is often said to have ultimate authority to interpret the federal constitution, but it has no such authority with regard to state law. We sometimes express this by talking about the scope of its jurisdiction. So it is with the Church, whose jurisdiction is limited to matters of "faith or morals." Though it has sometimes pretended otherwise, for example, it has no brief explaining to us the proper form (monarchical, democratic) that civil government ought to take.

John Garvey, "The Pope's Submarine," *San Diego Law Review,* vol. 30 (1993), pp. 849 ff. (Garvey (1948–   ) is Professor of Law at Notre Dame University.

Even within the domain of faith and morals there is a great variety of issues, and the Church speaks with more authority on some of them than on others. There are, in the first place, those things said to be revealed in the gospel message (for example, that Jesus is God). Theologians say that these are the primary object of the Church's magisterium, things about which it can speak with most authority—at times infallibly. Then there is a range of other matters, more or less closely related to these, to which the Church can speak with diminishing degrees of authority (recognition of a Church council as ecumenical; canonization of saints; etc.). I do not want to dwell on these details, but only mention them to indicate how highly refined and variable is the notion of authority, and because they bear on my main interest, which is the deference due from observant Catholics to the Church's instructions on moral questions—abortion in particular. That is a subject on which various authorities within the Church have taught with a fairly consistent voice for a long time. The Second Vatican Council condemned the practice in the *Pastoral Constitution on the Church in the Modern World.* Pope Paul VI repeated this condemnation in his encyclical *Humanae Vitae.* The National Conference of Catholic Bishops has done the same on numerous occasions. So has the Congregation for the Doctrine of the Faith. Cardinal O'Connor and the bishop of Brooklyn have echoed these positions. What obligations do these teachings impose on Mr. Cuomo?

As a matter of Church law, Cuomo's obligations depend in part on whether the teachings of the pope and the council are supposed to be infallible, and that is an uncertain point. Neither the *Pastoral Constitution* nor the encyclical displays the kind of clear intention that accompanies infallible pronouncements. It may nonetheless be that papal and episcopal opinion on the subject merits that status because it has been so unanimous and so longstanding: I will assume that it does not, for the sake of making a point that can be applied more widely. Here is what Vatican II said about the appropriate response to noninfallible moral teachings:

> Bishops, teaching in communion with the Roman Pontiff, are to be respected by all as witnesses to divine and Catholic truth. In matters of faith and morals, the bishops speak in the name of Christ and *the faithful are to accept their teaching and adhere to it with a religious assent of soul. This religious submission of will and of mind* must be shown in a special way to the authentic teaching authority of the Roman Pontiff, even when he is not speaking ex cathedra.

All this talk so far, you might say, is beside the point, because Governor Cuomo concedes his obligation to conform (in mind and will) to the Church's teaching in his own life. He quarrels only with the Cardinal's assertion that he should make that teaching the law of the state of New York. What state officials must do in their official capacity, he contends, is a matter that is beyond the Church's jurisdiction.

Not quite. The Church acknowledges (though it has not always) that "Christ [gave it] no proper mission in the political, economic, or social order." But this does not mean everything that strict separationists might hope. The Church also rejects "the outmoded notion that 'religion is a purely private affair' or that 'the Church belongs in the sacristy.' Religion is relevant to the life and action of society." In particular it maintains that it "has the right to pass moral judgments, even on matters touching the political order, whenever basic personal rights or the salvation of souls make such judgments necessary." This of course entails that it should speak out on the issue of abortion, which it sees as involving both "personal rights" (of the fetus) and "salvation" (of those who procure and perform abortions). But there are several reasons why its teachings in this forum might be less authoritative than the model I have discussed above.

To begin with, of course, most citizens of the state are not members of the Church. Over them the Church has no authority at all, only such influence as the force of its arguments deserves. Cuomo is not exempt on that account, but it is a fact that bears on his obligations in a second way. It is no less true for Catholics than it is for others that duty is limited by possibility. Compromise is an unpleasant but necessary feature of political life. If the Governor finds it impossible to secure enactment of the Church's agenda, he can hardly be condemned for doing only what he can.

The need to compromise with nonmembers is not the only limit facing the observant Catholic politician. It is not self-evident that the full resources of the state should be used to enforce moral norms even in cases where a majority of the voters would stand for it. No one argues that Cuomo should work for passage of laws to enforce the moral norms (binding within the Church) against contraception and divorce. Consider the observation of Thomas Aquinas regarding the limits of law:

> Laws when they are passed should take account of the condition of the men who will be subject to them; for, as Isidore says: the law should be 'possible both with regard to nature and with regard to the custom of the country.' But capacity to act derives from habit, or interior disposition: not everything that is possible to a virtuous man is equally possible to one who lacks the habit of virtue. . . .
>
> Now human law is enacted on behalf of the mass of men, the majority of whom are far from perfect in virtue. For this reason human law does not prohibit every vice from which virtuous men abstain; but only the graver vices from which the majority can abstain; and particularly those vices which are damaging of others, and which, if they were not prohibited, would make it impossible for human society to endure: as murder, theft, and suchlike, which are prohibited by human laws.

The principal point here is that the moral law is a command of perfection that would land us all in jail were the state to enforce it to the letter. That would have disastrous implications for the Corrections budget. And it might mean that none of us would show up for work on Monday. There is also a subsidiary point which Aquinas overlooks, but which we who are more familiar with federal forms of government can more easily appreciate. There are any number of institutional problems connected with efforts by one legal authority to assimilate the regulatory law of another. It would be hard for the secular legal system to be sure that it correctly understood the corpus of Catholic moral rules. The borrowed norms might clash with existing New York law in ways too numerous to anticipate. The borrowed offenses might involve elements (e.g. questions about a sinner's mental state) that the existing secular law system (adversary procedure, rules of discovery, evidence, methods of trial and review) was incompetent to prove. (Remember that in the Catholic Church penitents confess their sins.) The burden of enforcing a supplementary set of norms might overload a justice system designed to do other work. And so on.

All of the reasons I have given so far are jurisdictional (the problem of nonmembers) or prudential (the need for compromise; the danger of pursuing perfection; the costs of assimilation). They do not go to the merits. By that I mean that they are consistent with saying that the Church rules would be best if we could have them. But that is not necessarily so. Consider the rules about economic due process. Although the Supreme Court asserts authority over constitutional questions, it gives great leeway to other branches on matters of business regulation. One common justification is that it knows little about business and economics, and the legislature (or the agency), so long as it stays within wide limits, is more likely to reach the right answer. Conservative Catholics make precisely the same point about the Catholic bishops' efforts in the economic realm. Though they say they are in complete agreement with the bishops' ultimate aims, they argue that we can get there faster by concentrating on production rather than (as the bishops naively do) distribution. I do not necessarily endorse this conclusion, but the method of argument is perfectly sensible. Moral questions arise in contexts that Church authorities will know little about, and in such cases other people might get to the right answer first.

The Church's authority over observant Catholic public officials is, then, qualified in a number of important ways. Let us consider what this might mean for the question of abortion. I should rather say questions, because there are many, and the answers differ. Consider first the precise issue for which *Roe v. Wade* is taken to stand: whether abortion is a fundamental human right protected by the Due Process Clause. That is a fairly abstract ethical proposition, unmixed with the kinds of contingencies that lead bishops astray. It is also obviously inconsistent with the Church's teaching that abortion is an "unspeakable crime." If we confine our attention to the simple question whether to recognize the right, there are few prudential reasons that would move one in sympathy with the Church's position to do so. It is difficult for me to see how Cuomo, if he accepts the Church's teaching about abortion, could agree with the Supreme Court's decision in *Roe.* But this is also an issue that he has no influence over. It can only be determined by the Supreme Court or by a constitutional amendment.

On the other hand, accepting the Church's teaching would not, I think, commit Cuomo to the proposition that New York should make procuring or performing an abortion a criminal offense. This is an issue, unlike the last, where enforcing the Church's position would control the behavior of nonmembers. That is not inherently improper; Cuomo routinely enforces the position of the Democratic Party against nonmembers. But it would lead non-Catholics to vote against him, and to undo any successes he had along this line. I am not convinced that Cuomo is morally obliged to pursue pyrrhic victories.

Quite apart from its effect on nonmembers, a criminal abortion law might entail very high enforcement costs. Proponents of abortion usually cite the example of Prohibition. The offense there is trivial but the point is not. If we had a high rate of illegal abortions and prosecuted violations vigorously we could put a lot of young women and doctors in jail. If doctors complied (I assume they would) and women continued to abort, they would run a new set of health risks. If juries balked at convicting (and they often would), we would encourage disrespect for the law and waste enforcement resources that we could employ elsewhere with more success (drunk drivers and drug dealers also kill people).

This is not to say that anti-abortion laws are, absolutely speaking, a bad idea—only that the government cannot successfully get too far out ahead of public opinion. I hasten to add that that has not been Cuomo's problem. I suspect that the people of New York are, if anything, more willing than he to accept some limitation on abortion rights. If that is so, the Governor could find common ground with Church nonmembers for doing something about the problem. And a law that had popular support would not entail the enforcement costs I have hypothesized. In short, I see no prudential reason that Cuomo can cite for declining to stand with at least one foot on his principles.

The third abortion question involved in Cuomo's case is the issue of government funding, which he supports. On this issue it is harder for the observant Catholic official to depart from the Church's teaching. It is not just a matter of declining for prudential reasons to enforce the moral law. Funding abortions actually promotes (what Cuomo concedes is) evil. And taxing Church members to raise the funds implicates them too. Cuomo argues that it is unjust to withhold funds because doing so leaves poor women worse off than rich ones. But if he is concerned about equalizing standards of living this is hardly the place to start.

I want to conclude this section with a few observations about the enforcement of Church authority. Suppose that the Governor publicly contradicts some authoritative teaching of the Church, or like Cuomo, affirms that he will obey in his personal life but takes an inconsistent political position. What sanctions are (from the Church's point of view) proper?

Under canon law, one who procures an abortion is subject to automatic excommunication. This means that she is unable to receive the sacraments, to participate in certain ways at mass and other public worship, and to hold any Church office or perform any official ecclesiastical function. The excommunication becomes effective without any trial, though this cannot happen inadvertently. The offender must know in advance not only about the gravity of the offense but also about the Church's punishment.

But that is not the offense that Catholic politicians are typically concerned with. Cuomo, for example, has rejected abortion as a possibility in his own life. His offense (if it is one) has been to support the actions of women who want to have abortions, by a course of official conduct (failure to promote regulation; approval of Medicaid funding) and public statements (his speech at Notre Dame). I have suggested that some, at least, of these activities are inconsistent with the Church's teaching on abortion, which Catholics are expected to heed. Canon 752 of the Code of Canon Law codifies the obligation to heed Church teaching and "to avoid whatever is not in harmony with that teaching." Canon 1371 deals with sanctions for violation of these obligations:

> The following are to be punished with a just penalty:
> 1 • . . . a person who teaches a doctrine condemned by the Roman Pontiff or by an ecumenical council or who pertinaciously rejects the doctrine mentioned in can. 752. . . .

What counts as a "just penalty" can vary. The local bishop seems to have considerable discretion, and the Code encourages him to proceed cautiously. Cardinal O'Connor suggested that excommunication was a possibility, but no American bishop has tried it. Bishop Maher in San Diego withheld communion (a less severe sanction) from Lucy Killea, a state senator who advocated abortion rights. O'Connor's Vicar and Bishop Daily of Brooklyn have barred Cuomo from speaking at parish churches.

These sanctions are intended to be coercive in the way that civil contempt is coercive: they aim at reformation of the offender's conduct. But they are effective only against religious believers. If I had no interest in participating in the religious life of the Catholic community, excommunication would not concern me. (It would be like being thrown out of the Book of the Month Club.) And once I was willing to sever my religious ties, the Church would have no independent source of leverage. It does not, for example, have control over its members' financial assets.

■ ■ ■

I now want to consider two situations that a Catholic politician like Cuomo might find himself in if he heeded religious authority in his public life. I want to observe in each case whether our liberal principles and our Constitution permit him to comply with the requirements of his faith. In Case One Cuomo heeds and is persuaded by the Church's epistemic authority and wants to act accordingly. In Case Two Cuomo is unconvinced by the Church's teaching but willing to submit to its practical authority. Case One does not present any problems for the observant politician; Case Two does.

Suppose first, then, that Cuomo believes that abortion is evil because human life begins at conception. This conviction is consistent with Catholic Church teaching, and Cuomo reached it in part because of the Church's persuasion and example. But it is like a proposition in geometry that Cuomo has worked out for himself: the teacher helped him to get it, but now he can kick away the props and get it himself. Or consider another simile:

> The alcoholic in the back row at the A.A. meeting does not go home and tell his wife

that the speaker said that anyone with his drinking behavior is a drunk. He says that his eyes were finally opened and now, with the speaker's help, he sees what everyone else but himself had long seen but he could not bear to see. The man says this as something he owes to a wise and helpful mentor, but now it is something he is vouching for himself.

The politician who holds this conviction in this way will not think that *Roe v. Wade* was right in saying that abortion is a fundamental right. Nor will he favor public funding of abortion (though he may have doubts about criminal penalties). Is there a problem with taking these positions on questions of public policy when the belief that underlies them had its origin in an exercise of religious authority?

No. In the first place, what else would we have Cuomo do? This is not a case where he can centrifuge his beliefs and separate the religious element. We sometimes ask juries to do that when hearsay evidence slips in. But here religious teaching is not a piece of evidence. It is a way of looking at the world that Cuomo has appropriated. He can no more set it aside than he can set aside his idea of color or shape in looking at a picture. We cannot ask him to act without reliance on his religious convictions, because he probably has no idea what he would do in that case. It would be like asking him how he would decide if he were someone else.

If we were determined to avoid any religious influence on politics we might then ask Cuomo to recuse himself from any decision involving abortion. But as Kent Greenawalt has pointed out, it is not clear why a liberal society would want to exclude all religious influence in a case like this. The question about the moral worth of the fetus is not one that anyone can answer on the basis of shared premises and publicly accessible reasons. So everyone who thinks about the question (and it is unavoidable in making abortion policy) will have to rely on some private or personal grounds.

Only a society actually hostile to religion would want to treat it worse than other kinds of 'personal' reasons.

Liberal principles, then, should not prevent Cuomo from acting on his religious belief about the morality of abortion. It would be both impossible and unfair to do so. As a matter of constitutional law, I think the case for Cuomo is even stronger, in large part because our Constitution does not rest entirely on liberal principles. The only conceivable constitutional objection would be that the Establishment Clause forbade public officials to act on beliefs that had religious origins. But this has the rules exactly backwards. I would argue not only that the Establishment Clause permits such action, but that the Free Exercise Clause positively encourages it.

That assertion requires a longer defense than I can make without changing the focus of this Article, so I will content myself with a sketch. I begin with the assumption that freedom of religion is a special form of protection for religious believers. From the Constitution's point of view, religious activity (ritual acts, the acquisition and propagation of religious knowledge, observance of moral obligations) is a good thing. The Free Exercise Clause encourages us to engage in it. There are several limits to our enthusiasm for such activity, but they do not stem from doubts about its worth. One is that we should not coerce people to perform ceremonies they do not believe in (prayer, worship, declarations of belief) because it is futile, or even counterproductive from a religious point of view, to do so. Another is that the best way for society to grasp religious truth is to allow free inquiry for everyone—atheists and agnostics as well as believers. A third is that religious compulsion can cause civil strife and leave everyone worse off.

Official action to limit abortions (by outright restrictions, or by withholding funds), even if it has its origin in religious conviction, does not transgress these limits. Restrictions may be coercive, but they do not force women to engage in religious activity or affirm a religious belief. Nor do they affect in any way the dissenter's ability to complain. And while they may cause contention, that alone is not enough for an Establishment Clause violation. (Some people were moved by religious principle to vote for the 1964 Civil Rights Act, and it caused contention.) This is an argument that relies on the lessons of history. And if history is to be our guide, the kind of contention we should fear results from a division along identifiably religious lines (Puritan/Baptist, Catholic/Protestant, Christian/Jew, Muslim/Baha'i) over indisputably religious questions.

Let me turn now to Case Two, which I view as more difficult. Suppose that Cuomo has listened attentively to the Church's teaching on abortion and has tried to come around to that point of view in his own mind, but he just does not get it. (He thinks that the fetus very early in pregnancy is like the very old person in a persistent vegetative state: we are not obliged to keep either one alive at great personal cost.) But as an observant Catholic he is aware that the Church asks its members to conform their conduct to its teaching (submission of will) even if they do not agree (submission of mind). It asserts practical as well as epistemic authority.

Suppose too that Cuomo is willing to comply with the Church's practical authority, for several reasons. One justification for the authority of the Catholic Church, as I explained in Part I, is that it promotes unity within the Church. Orthopraxy is a way of keeping faith with the religious community, and that might be important enough to Cuomo for him to act against his better judgment.

Cuomo might also be willing to conform his own behavior to the Church's teaching because of something like the service conception of authority. He is unable in his own mind to distinguish some cases of abortion and termination of life support. To that extent he does not agree with the Church's teaching. But his experience and his religious beliefs about God's guidance of his Church tell him that the

Church has a lower error rate than he does. In doing as the Church requires he trusts, though he is by no means convinced, that he will be doing the right thing.

Suppose further that in this case Cuomo is willing to obey Church teaching not just in his personal life (he would not urge his wife to have an abortion) but also in his public life (he follows the "Catholic line" in his political positions). As I explained in Part II, the Church's teaching authority in this area is qualified in numerous ways. But there are some points (like abortion funding) about which it is quite clear, and here Cuomo heeds what the Church has to say. Is there anything illiberal or unconstitutional in obedience to authority under these circumstances?

Unlike Case One, here it is possible for Cuomo to separate his religious from his secular convictions. Cuomo actually believes that there is nothing wrong with abortion under some circumstances. If you asked him he would tell you that. The reason he votes against abortion funding and publicly opposes *Roe v. Wade* is that he feels obligated to follow his Church's teaching. In asking Cuomo to set aside his religious beliefs, then, we would not be asking him to do the impossible. Would we be asking something that was unfair or otherwise improper?

Notice a second difference between this case and the last one. In Case One Cuomo could justify his public actions (e.g., a veto of abortion funding) in terms of harms, benefits, and reasons that all citizens should recognize. He would say that abortion takes innocent life which society should protect. And he would argue that our concept of rights cannot embrace actions so intrinsically evil. It is true that he came to believe these things by a specifically Catholic route, but other people have reached the same conclusions by other roads (some religious, some not), and there is nothing sectarian about saving lives.

In Case Two it is harder for Cuomo to point to a public benefit that justifies his actions. One reason he follows the 'Catholic line' is that orthopraxy promotes Church unity, and that is good for a variety of religious reasons. But there is no reason why non-Catholic citizens should care about the unity of Cuomo's Church. If Cuomo vetoes abortion funding or approves abortion restrictions solely for that reason, he puts the interest of his Church ahead of the public interest. That is troubling, both morally and constitutionally. As a moral matter, Cuomo is bound both by oath and by promise to represent all the citizens of New York and to uphold the Constitution. As a constitutional matter, the case I have so far put is one where he takes official action for the sole purpose of promoting the religious aims of his Church. That is certainly inconsistent with the [existing legal] rule against religious purposes. It is also an invitation to civil strife along religious lines in the classical form: Cuomo's action appeals just to Catholics, rests only on religious reasons, and imposes the costs on nonmembers.

What makes me most uncomfortable about this case, I think, is that it confirms the stereotype of Catholics as citizens with divided loyalties. Cuomo's sole reason for acting is that his Church has directed him to—and by 'his Church' I mean here the bishops and the pope. Locke said he would not extend toleration to churches whose members "pass into the allegiance and service of another prince." His sentiments are still in fashion. Twentieth-century Americans have been willing to "imagine the papal submarine ready to land the First Lord of its Admiralty in Chesapeake Bay when the White House is properly occupied." Part of my effort in this Article has been to show that this dilemma will rarely arise because: (i) Church authority is binding in varying degrees; (ii) politicians need not always implement Church teaching; (iii) people may quite properly act on religious beliefs in cases like Case One; and of course (iv) the Catholic Church, unlike other sovereigns, has no control over unwilling members. But the dilemma for the observant Catholic in Case Two is real. The solution is not, as Justice Brennan once suggested, to set aside his religious beliefs. It is to recuse himself, if that is possible, or resign if it is not.

WALLACE V. JAFFREE
472 U.S. 38 (1985)

Justice STEVENS delivered the opinion of the Court.

[T]he narrow question for decision is whether § 16-1-20.1, which authorizes a period of silence for "meditation or voluntary prayer," is a law respecting the establishment of religion within the meaning of the First Amendment.

Appellee Ishmael Jaffree is a resident of Mobile County, Alabama. On May 28, 1982, he filed a complaint on behalf of three of his minor children; two of them were second-grade students and the third was then in kindergarten [alleging] that two of the children had been subjected to various acts of religious indoctrination "from the beginning of the school year in September, 1981"; that the defendant teachers had "on a daily basis" led their classes in saying certain prayers in unison; that the minor children were exposed to ostracism from their peer group class members if they did not participate; and that Ishmael Jaffree had repeatedly but unsuccessfully requested that the devotional services be stopped.

The sponsor of the bill that became § 16-1-20.1, Senator Donald Holmes, inserted into the legislative record—apparently without dissent—a statement indicating that the legislation was an "effort to return voluntary prayer" to the public schools. Later Senator Holmes confirmed this purpose before the District Court. In response to the question whether he had any purpose for the legislation other than returning voluntary prayer to public schools, he stated, "No, I did not have no other purpose in mind." The State did not present evidence of *any* secular purpose.

The legislative intent to return prayer to the public schools is, of course, quite different from merely protecting every student's right to engage in voluntary prayer during an appropriate moment of silence during the school day. The 1978 statute already protected that right, containing nothing that prevented any student from engaging in voluntary prayer during a silent minute of meditation. The Legislature enacted § 16-1-20.1 despite the existence of § 16-1-20 for the sole purpose of expressing the State's endorsement of prayer activities for one minute at the beginning of each school day. The addition of "or voluntary prayer" indicates that the State intended to characterize prayer as a favored practice. Such an endorsement is not consistent with the established principle that the Government must pursue a course of complete neutrality toward religion.

The importance of that principle does not permit us to treat this as an inconsequential case involving nothing more than a few words of symbolic speech on behalf of the political majority. For whenever the State itself speaks on a religious subject, one of the questions that we must ask is "whether the Government intends to convey a message of endorsement or disapproval of religion." The well-supported concurrent findings of the District Court and the Court of Appeals—that § 16-1-20.1 was intended to convey a message of State-approval of prayer activities in the public schools—make it unnecessary, and indeed inappropriate, to evaluate the practical significance of the addition of the words "or voluntary prayer" to the statute. Keeping in mind, as we must, "both the fundamental place held by the Establishment Clause in our constitutional scheme and the myriad, subtle ways in which Establishment Clause values can be eroded," we conclude that § 16-1-20.1 violates the First Amendment.

The judgment of the Court of Appeals is affirmed.

Justice O'CONNOR, concurring in the judgment.

A state sponsored moment of silence in the public schools is different from state sponsored vocal prayer or Bible reading. First, a moment of silence is not inherently religious. Silence, unlike prayer or Bible reading, need not be associated with a religious exercise. Second, a pupil who participates in a moment of silence need not compromise his or her beliefs. During a moment of silence, a student who objects to prayer is left to his or her own thoughts, and is not compelled to listen to the prayers or thoughts of others.

It is difficult to discern a serious threat to religious liberty from a room of silence [sic], thoughtful schoolchildren. Even if a statute specifies that a student may choose to pray silently during a quiet moment, the State has not thereby encouraged prayer over other specified alternatives. Nonetheless, it is also possible that a moment of silence statute, either as drafted or as actually implemented, could effectively favor the child who prays over the child who does not. For example, the message of endorsement would seem inescapable if the teacher exhorts children to use the designated time to pray. Similarly, the face of the statute or its legislative history may clearly establish that it seeks to encourage or promote voluntary prayer over other alternatives, rather than merely provide a quiet moment that may be dedicated to prayer by those so inclined. The crucial question is whether the State has conveyed or attempted to convey the message that children should use the moment of silence for prayer.

Before reviewing Alabama's moment of silence law to determine whether it endorses prayer, some general observations on the proper scope of the inquiry are in order. First, the inquiry into the purpose of the legislature in enacting a moment of silence law should be deferential and limited. In determining whether the government intends a moment of silence statute to convey a message of endorsement or disapproval of religion, a court has no license to psychoanalyze the legislators. If a legislature expresses a plausible secular purpose for a moment of silence statute in either the text or the legislative history, or if the statute disclaims an intent to encourage prayer over alternatives during a moment of silence, then courts should generally defer to that stated intent. It is particularly troublesome to denigrate an expressed secular purpose due to postenactment testimony by particular legislators or by interested persons who witnessed the drafting of the statute. Even if the text and official history of a statute express no secular purpose, the statute should be held to have an improper purpose only if it is beyond purview that endorsement of religion or a religious belief "was and is the law's reason for existence." Since there is arguably a secular pedagogical value to a moment of silence in public schools, courts should find an improper purpose behind such a statute only if the statute on its face, in its official legislative history, or in its interpretation by a responsible administrative agency suggests it has the primary purpose of endorsing prayer.

Justice Rehnquist suggests that this sort of deferential inquiry into legislative purpose "means little," because "it only requires the legislature to express any secular purpose and omit all sectarian references." It is not a trivial matter, however, to require that the legislature manifest a secular purpose and omit all sectarian endorsements from its laws. That requirement is precisely tailored to the Establishment Clause's purpose of assuring that Government not intentionally endorse religion or a religious practice. It is of course possible that a legislature will enunciate a sham secular purpose for a statute. I have little doubt that our courts are capable of distinguishing a sham secular purpose from a sincere one. While the secular purpose requirement alone may rarely be determinative in striking down a statute, it nevertheless serves an important function. It reminds government that when it acts it should do so without endorsing a particular religious belief or practice that all citizens do not share.

Second, the effect of a moment of silence law is not entirely a question of fact: The relevant issue is whether an objective observer, acquainted with the text, legislative history, and implementation of the statute, would perceive it as a state endorsement of prayer in public schools. A moment of silence law that is clearly drafted and implemented so as to permit prayer, meditation, and reflection within the prescribed period, without endorsing one alternative over the others, should pass this test.

The analysis above suggests that moment of silence laws in many States should pass Establishment Clause scrutiny because they do not favor the child who chooses to pray during a moment of silence over the child who chooses to meditate or reflect. Alabama Code § 16-1-20.1 (Supp. 1984) does not stand on the same footing. However deferentially one examines its text and legislative history, however objectively one views the message attempted to be conveyed to the public, the conclusion is unavoidable that the purpose of the statute is to endorse prayer in public schools.

In finding that the purpose of Alabama Code § 16-1-20.1 is to endorse voluntary prayer during a moment of silence, the Court relies on testimony elicited from State Senator Donald G. Holmes during a preliminary injunction hearing. Senator Holmes testified that the sole purpose of the statute was to return voluntary prayer to the public schools. For the reasons expressed above, I would give little, if any, weight to this sort of evidence of legislative intent. Nevertheless, the text of the statute in light of its official legislative history leaves little doubt that the purpose of this statute corresponds to the purpose expressed by Senator Holmes at the preliminary injunction hearing. In light of the legislative history and the findings of the courts below, I agree with the Court that the State intended Alabama Code § 16-1-20.1 to convey a message that prayer was the endorsed activity during the state-prescribed moment of silence.

Chief Justice BURGER, dissenting.

The statute does not remotely threaten religious liberty; it affirmatively furthers the value of religious freedom and tolerance that the Establishment Clause was designed to protect. Without pressuring those who do not wish to pray, the statute simply creates an opportunity to think, to plan, or to pray if one wishes— as Congress does in providing chaplains and chapels. It accommodates the purely private, voluntary religious choices of the individual pupils who wish to pray while at the same time creating a time for nonreligious reflection for those who do not choose to pray. The statute also provides a meaningful opportunity for schoolchildren to appreciate the absolute constitutional right of each individual to worship and believe as the individual wishes. The statute "endorses" only the view that the religious observances of others should be tolerated and, where possible, accommodated. If the government may not accommodate religious needs when it does so in a wholly neutral and noncoercive manner, the "benevolent neutral-

ity" that we have long considered the correct constitutional standard will quickly translate into the "callous indifference" that the Court has consistently held the Establishment Clause does not require. The mountains have labored and brought forth a mouse.

Justice REHNQUIST, dissenting.

It is impossible to build sound constitutional doctrine upon a mistaken understanding of constitutional history, but unfortunately the Establishment Clause has been expressly freighted with Jefferson's misleading metaphor for nearly forty years. Jefferson's fellow Virginian James Madison, with whom he was joined in the battle for the enactment of the Virginia Statute of Religious Liberty of 1786, did play as large a part as anyone in the drafting of the Bill of Rights. During the ratification debate in the Virginia Convention, Madison had actually opposed the idea of any Bill of Rights. His sponsorship of the amendments in the House was obviously not that of a zealous believer in the necessity of the Religion Clauses, but of one who felt it might do some good, could do no harm, and would satisfy those who had ratified the Constitution on the condition that Congress propose a Bill of Rights. His original language "nor shall any national religion be established" obviously does not conform to the "wall of separation" between church and State idea which latter day commentators have ascribed to him.

It seems indisputable from these glimpses of Madison's thinking, as reflected by actions on the floor of the House in 1789, that he saw the amendment as designed to prohibit the establishment of a national religion, and perhaps to prevent discrimination among sects. He did not see it as requiring neutrality on the part of government between religion and irreligion. Thus the Court's opinion in *Everson*—while correct in bracketing Madison and Jefferson together in their exertions in their home state leading to the enactment of the Virginia Statute of Religious Liberty—is totally incorrect in suggesting that

Madison carried these views onto the floor of the United States House of Representatives when he proposed the language which would ultimately become the Bill of Rights.

In previous cases this Court has made the truly remarkable statement that "the views of Madison and Jefferson, preceded by Roger Williams came to be incorporated not only in the Federal Constitution but likewise in those of most of our States." On the basis of what evidence we have, this statement is demonstrably incorrect as a matter of history. And its repetition in varying forms in succeeding opinions of the Court can give it no more authority than it possesses as a matter of fact; *stare decisis* may bind courts as to matters of law, but it cannot bind them as to matters of history.

Notwithstanding the absence of an historical basis for this theory of rigid separation, the wall idea might well have served as a useful albeit misguided analytical concept, had it led this Court to unified and principled results in Establishment Clause cases. The opposite, unfortu-nately, has been true; our Establishment Clause cases have been neither principled nor unified.

If a constitutional theory has no basis in the history of the amendment it seeks to interpret, is difficult to apply and yields unprincipled results, I see little use in it.

The Framers intended the Establishment Clause to prohibit the designation of any church as a "national" one. The Clause was also designed to stop the Federal Government from asserting a preference for one religious denomination or sect over others. Given the "incorporation" of the Establishment Clause as against the States via the Fourteenth Amendment in *Everson*, States are prohibited as well from establishing a religion or discriminating between sects. As its history abundantly shows, however, nothing in the Establishment Clause requires government to be strictly neutral between religion and irreligion, nor does that Clause prohibit Congress or the States from pursuing legitimate secular ends through nondiscriminatory sectarian means.

EMPLOYMENT DIVISION, OREGON DEPT. OF HUMAN RESOURCES V. SMITH

494 U.S. 872 (1990)

Justice SCALIA delivered the opinion of the Court.

EDITOR'S NOTE: Smith and Black were fired by a private drug rehabilitation organiza-tion because they used peyote, a hallucinogen, at a ceremony of the Native American Church. Their applications for unemployment compensa-tion were denied under a state law disqualifying employees discharged for work–related "miscon-duct." When the case was first brought before the Supreme Court, the Court remanded for a determination of whether sacramental peyote use violates Oregon's criminal law. On remand, the Oregon court held that the criminal statute did apply to their conduct.]

. . . It is no more necessary to regard the collection of a general tax, for example, as "prohibiting the free exercise [of religion]" by those citizens who believe support of organized government to be sinful, than it is to regard the same tax as "abridging the freedom . . . of the press" of those publishing companies that must pay the tax as a condition of staying in business. It is a permissible reading of the text, in the one case as in the other, to say that if prohibiting the exercise of religion (or burdening the activity of printing) is not the object of the tax but merely the incidental effect of a generally applicable and otherwise valid provision, the First Amendment has not been offended.

Our decisions reveal that the latter reading is the correct one. We have never held that an individual's religious beliefs excuse him from compliance with an otherwise valid law prohibiting conduct that the State is free to regulate. On the contrary, the record of more than a century of our free exercise jurisprudence contradicts that proposition. . . .

The only decisions in which we have held that the First Amendment bars application of a neutral, generally applicable law to religiously motivated action have involved not the Free Exercise Clause alone, but the Free Exercise Clause in conjunction with other constitutional protections, such as freedom of speech and of the press, see Cantwell v. Connecticut (1940) (invalidating a licensing system for religious and charitable solicitations under which the administrator had discretion to deny a license to any cause he deemed nonreligious); Murdock v. Pennsylvania (1943) (invalidating a flat tax on solicitation as applied to the dissemination of religious ideas); or the right of parents, acknowledged in Pierce v. Society of Sisters (1925),

to direct the education of their children, see Wisconsin v. Yoder (invalidating compulsory school–attendance laws as applied to Amish parents who refused on religious grounds to send their children to school). Some of our cases prohibiting compelled expression, decided exclusively upon free speech grounds, have also involved freedom of religion. And it is easy to envision a case in which a challenge on freedom of association grounds would likewise be reinforced by Free Exercise Clause concerns.

■ ■ ■

Respondents argue that even though exemption from generally applicable criminal laws need not automatically be extended to religiously motivated actors, at least the claim for a religious exemption must be evaluated under the balancing test set forth in Sherbert v. Verner, 374 U.S. 398 (1963). Under the Sherbert test, governmental actions that substantially burden a religious practice must be justified by a compelling governmental interest. Applying that test we have, on three occasions, invalidated state unemployment compensation rules that conditioned the availability of benefits upon an applicant's willingness to work under conditions forbidden by his religion. We have never invalidated any governmental action on the basis of the Sherbert test except the denial of unemployment compensation. Although we have sometimes purported to apply the Sherbert test in contexts other than that, we have always found the test satisfied. In recent years we have abstained from applying the Sherbert test (outside the unemployment compensation field) at all. . . .

Even if we were inclined to breathe into Sherbert some life beyond the unemployment compensation field, we would not apply it to require exemptions from a generally applicable criminal law. The Sherbert test, it must be recalled, was developed in a context that lent itself to individualized governmental assessment of the reasons for the relevant conduct. [A] distinctive feature of unemployment compensation programs is that their eligibility criteria invite consideration of the particular circumstances behind an applicant's unemployment: "The statutory conditions [in Sherbert] provided that a person was not eligible for unemployment compensation benefits if, 'without good cause,' he had quit work or refused available work. The 'good cause' standard created a mechanism for individualized exemptions." [O]ur decisions in the unemployment cases stand for the proposition that where the State has in place a system of individual exemptions, it may not refuse to extend that system to cases of "religious hardship" without compelling reason.

Whether or not the decisions are that limited, they at least have nothing to do with an across-the-board criminal prohibition on a particular form of conduct. Although, as noted earlier, we have sometimes used the Sherbert test to analyze free exercise challenges to such laws, we have never applied the test to invalidate one. We conclude today that the sounder approach, and the approach in accord with the vast majority of our precedents, is to hold the test inapplicable to such challenges. . . . To make an individual's obligation to obey such a law contingent upon the law's coincidence with his religious beliefs, except where the State's interest is "compelling"—permitting him, by virtue of his beliefs, "to become a law unto himself"—contradicts both constitutional tradition and common sense.

Nor is it possible to limit the impact of respondents' proposal by requiring a "compelling state interest" only when the conduct prohibited is "central" to the individual's religion. It is no more appropriate for judges to determine the "centrality" of religious beliefs before applying a "compelling interest" test in the free exercise field, than it would be for them to determine the "importance" of ideas before applying the "compelling interest" test in the free speech field. . . .

If the "compelling interest" test is to be applied at all, then, it must be applied across the board, to all actions thought to be religiously commanded. Moreover, if "compelling interest"

really means what it says (and watering it down here would subvert its rigor in the other fields where it is applied), many laws will not meet the test. Any society adopting such a system would be courting anarchy, but that danger increases in direct proportion to the society's diversity of religious beliefs, and its determination to coerce or suppress none of them. . . . The rule respondents favor would open the prospect of constitutionally required religious exemptions from civic obligations of almost every conceivable kind—ranging from compulsory military service, to the payment of taxes, to health and safety regulation such as manslaughter and child neglect laws, compulsory vaccination laws, drug laws, and traffic laws. . . . The First Amendment's protection of religious liberty does not require this.

Values that are protected against government interference through enshrinement in the Bill of Rights are not thereby banished from the political process. Just as a society that believes in the negative protection accorded to the press by the First Amendment is likely to enact laws that affirmatively foster the dissemination of the printed word, so also a society that believes in the negative protection accorded to religious belief can be expected to be solicitous of that value in its legislation as well. It is therefore not surprising that a number of States have made an exception to their drug laws for sacramental peyote use. But to say that a nondiscriminatory religious-practice exemption is permitted, or even that it is desirable, is not to say that it is constitutionally required, and that the appropriate occasions for its creation can be discerned by the courts. It may fairly be said that leaving accommodation to the political process will place at a relative disadvantage those religious practices that are not widely engaged in; but that unavoidable consequence of democratic government must be preferred to a system in which each conscience is a law unto itself or in which judges weight the social importance of all laws against the centrality of all religious beliefs.

Justice O'CONNOR, concurring in the judgment.

The Court today gives no convincing reason to depart from settled First Amendment jurisprudence. There is nothing talismanic about neutral laws of general applicability or general criminal prohibitions, for laws neutral toward religion can coerce a person to violate his religious conscience or intrude upon his religious duties just as effectively as laws aimed at religion. Although the Court suggests that the compelling interest test, as applied to generally applicable laws, would result in a "constitutional anomaly," the First Amendment unequivocally makes freedom of religion, like freedom from race discrimination and freedom of speech, a "constitutional nor[m]," not an "anomaly." Nor would application of our established free exercise doctrine to this case necessarily be incompatible with our equal protection cases. We have in any event recognized that the Free Exercise Clause protects values distinct from those protected by the Equal Protection Clause. As the language of the Clause itself makes clear, an individual's free exercise of religion is a preferred constitutional activity. A law that makes criminal such an activity therefore triggers constitutional concern—and heightened judicial scrutiny—even if it does not target the particular religious conduct at issue. Our free speech cases similarly recognize that neutral regulations that affect free speech values are subject to a balancing, rather than categorical, approach. The Court's parade of horribles not only fails as a reason for discarding the compelling interest test, it instead demonstrates just the opposite: that courts have been quite capable of applying our free exercise jurisprudence to strike sensible balances between religious liberty and competing state interests.

Finally, the Court today suggests that the disfavoring of minority religions is an "unavoidable consequence" under our system of government and that accommodation of such religions must be left to the political process. In my view, however, the First Amendment was enacted precisely to protect the rights of those whose religious practices are not shared by the majority and may be viewed with hostility. The history of our free exercise doctrine amply demonstrates the harsh impact majoritarian rule has had on unpopular or emerging religious groups such as the Jehovah's Witnesses and the Amish. . . .

QUESTIONS FOR DISCUSSION

1. Consider Cuomo's arguments for separation of church and state. Are these arguments about *rights*? What rights are involved?

2. Garvey believes that Cuomo is sacrificing Catholic religious belief more than Cuomo admits. Why? According to Garvey, how is a good Catholic supposed to decide whether abortion is unjustified killing of a human being? Does Cuomo agree with this?

3. Whose rights are involved in the *Wallace* case? What are those rights?

4. What rights are involved in the *Smith* case? If you assume that peyote use is harmful to the user, what is the best argument against the result in *Smith*? Would you come to the same conclusion with respect to an animal cruelty law applied to a religion that believed in animal sacrifice? With respect to an anti-discrimination law applied to people who believed for sincere religious reasons that separation of the races was part of God's plan?

SUGGESTIONS FOR FURTHER READING

An important article on the history and original intentions of the religion clauses in the United States Constitution is Michael McConnell, "The Origins and Historical Understanding of Free Exercise of Religion," *Harvard Law Review*, vol. 103 (1990), pp. 1409 ff. A good collection of philosophical articles is J. Roland Pennock and John W. Chapman, eds., *Religion, Morality, and the Law* (NOMOS XXX) (New York: New York University Press, 1988). On the use of religious ideas in public decision making, see R. Kent Greenawalt, *Religious Convictions and Political Choice* (New York: Oxford University Press, 1988). A more secular perspective is reflected in John Rawls, *Political Liberalism* (New York: Columbia University Press, 1993). Religious toleration is explored insightfully in David A. J. Richards, *Toleration and the Constitution* (New York: Oxford University Press, 1986), and Nomi Maya Stolzenberg, "He Drew a Circle That Shut Me Out: Assimilation, Indoctrination, and the Paradox of a Liberal Education," *Harvard Law Review*, vol. 106 (1993), pp. 581 ff. Although not specifically about religion, no treatment of tolerance should ignore Robert Paul Wolff, Barrington Moore, and Herbert Marcuse, *A Critique of Pure Tolerance* (Boston: Beacon Press, 1969).

4.6 THE RIGHT TO PROPERTY

INTRODUCTION

We all think that we *own* things, like clothing, or books, or cars, or land. But what do we mean when we say we own something? What does it mean to say, "This is my *property*," or "Get off my *property*"? As with the right to privacy, property rights are of numerous varieties, and again the fundamental distinction is between those rights that are granted by law, on the one hand, and those moral or political or constitutional rights that restrict what the law properly may do, on the other.

With respect both to rights created by the law and rights that constrain the law, the right to property may not in fact be just one right. As to property rights created by the law, for example, the so-called right to property may simply be the shorthand expression we use to refer to a "bundle" of statutory or common law rights. Or, as Judith Jarvis Thomson puts it, the right to property may be a "cluster-right."[15] Thus when we say that we own a piece of property in Hanover, New Hampshire, or Cambridge, Massachusetts, we mean at least that the law of New Hampshire and the law of Massachusetts, as they now exist, give us various different legal rights. The law gives us claim-rights, in the Hohfeldian sense, to enforce the duty that everyone else has to stay off this land unless explicitly or implicitly invited. The tort called *trespass* is the name for this right, and we can sue for trespassing anyone who violates his or her duty to stay off of this land. In addition, we can, within various legal limits, exercise the *liberty* to do or not do certain things on our land. For example, our right to property often (subject to limitations imposed by zoning laws) includes the liberty to have or not to have a house on the property, and we are under no duty to anyone else to have or not to have a house on the land, and no one has any claim on us to enforce a duty regarding a house on the land, although we may be under a duty to the state to make sure that any house we build, if we choose to build one, conforms to certain zoning and related requirements. We also have the *power* to sell the land to someone else, or to give it to someone else, or to dispose of it in a will to anyone we choose. All of these (and other) statutory and common-law rights may, together, compose the right to property, and thus explain what we mean when we say that we *own* something.

In addition to such rights in positive statutory law or common law, however, the right to property may also refer to something superior to ordinary law. Suppose we were starting a new country, or, as is the case now in much of the world,

---

[15]*The Realm of Rights* (Cambridge, Massachusetts: Harvard University Press, 1990), pp. 55–60.

transforming the legal, constitutional, and political system of some country. Would we want to have the kinds of property rights that exist in countries like the United States? We might say that we would want to have these kinds of statutory and common law rights because having them would increase happiness, or efficiency, or productivity, or the general welfare, or utility. As some of the readings below indicate, a long tradition of utilitarian arguments in favor of recognition of rights to property is based on the claim that utility would be maximized by prohibiting courts or legislatures from taking certain kinds of actions that would diminish the legal rights that property owners had.

Not all of the arguments for the existence of a "pre-legal" right to private property are utilitarian ones, however. As the following readings indicate, many people, most famously John Locke in the seventeenth century and Robert Nozick in the twentieth, have argued that some right to private property is a *natural* or *human* right, just like the right to be free from torture, or the right to equality, or the right to freedom of religion, or (to some people) the right to freedom of speech. Even within the tradition of natural rights, however, it is controversial whether the right to private property is a natural right. Some people who believe that there *are* natural rights do not believe that the right to property is one of them. Conversely, others who believe that there is a natural or human right to private property may not believe that other rights, like the right to freedom of speech or freedom of the press, are natural rights. So it hardly follows from there being natural rights that the right to property is one of them, although there is certainly a tradition—from Locke to the present—that believes that the right to private property is one of the most important of the natural or human rights. The readings in this section explore the question whether there are rights to private property other than the legal rights created by positive law, and, if so, what kind of rights they are, and from where they come.

WHAT IS PRIVATE PROPERTY?

JEREMY WALDRON

As R. H. Tawney pointed out:

> It is idle . . . to present a case for or against private property without specifying the par-

ticular forms of property to which reference is made, and the journalist who says that 'private property is the foundation of civilization' agrees with Proudhon, who said it

Jeremy Waldron, "What Is Private Property?" *Oxford Journal of Legal Studies*, vol. 5 (1985), pp. 313 ff., and Jeremy Waldron, *The Right to Private Property* (Oxford: Oxford University Press, 1988). Waldron (1953–) is Professor of Jurisprudence and Social Policy at the University of California, Berkeley.

was theft, in this respect at least that, without further definition, the words of both are meaningless.

Many writers have argued that it is, in fact, impossible to define private property—that the concept itself defies definition. If those arguments can be sustained, then a work like this is misconceived. If private property is indefinable, it cannot serve as a useful concept in political and economic thought: nor can it be a point of interesting debate in political philosophy. Instead of talking about property systems, we should focus perhaps on the detailed rights that particular people have to do certain things with certain objects, rights which vary considerably from case to case, from object to object, and from legal system to legal system. But, if these sceptical arguments hold, we should abandon the enterprise of arguing about private property as such—of saying that it is, or is not, conducive to liberty, prosperity, or rights—because the term does not pick out any determinate institution for consideration.

Why has private property been thought indefinable? Consider the relation between a person (call her Susan) and an object (say, a motor car) generally taken to be her private property. The layman thinks of this as a two-place relation of ownership between a person and a thing: Susan owns that Porsche. But the lawyer tells us that legal relations cannot exist between people and Porsches, because Porsches cannot have rights or duties or be bound by or recognize rules. The legal relation involved must be a relation between persons—between Susan and her neighbours, say, or Susan and the police, or Susan and everyone else. But when we ask what this relation is, we find that the answer is not at all simple. With regard to Susan's Porsche, there are all sorts of legal relations between Susan and other people. Susan has a legal liberty to use it in certain ways; for example, she owes no duty to anyone to refrain from putting her houseplants in it. But that is true only of some of the ways that

the car could (physically) be used. She is not at liberty to drive it on the footpath or to drive it anywhere at a speed faster than 70 m.p.h. Indeed, she is not at liberty to drive it at all without a licence from the authorities. As well as her liberties, Susan also has certain rights. She has what Hohfeld called a 'claim-right' against everyone else (her neighbours, her friends, the local car thief, everyone in the community) that they should not use her Porsche without her permission. But Susan also owes certain duties to other people in relation to the vehicle. She must keep it in good order and see that it does not become a nuisance to her neighbours. She is liable to pay damages if it rolls into her neighbour's fence. These rights, liberties, and duties are the basic stuff of ownership. But legal relations can be changed, and, if Susan owns the Porsche, then *she* is in a position to change them. She has the power to sell it or give it to somebody else, in which case all the legal relations change: Susan takes on the duties (and limited rights) of a nonowner of the Porsche and someone else takes on the rights, liberties, duties, and powers of ownership. Or perhaps Susan lends or hires the car; that involves a temporary and less extensive change in legal relations. She can bequeath the car in her will so that someone else will take over her property rights when she dies. These are her powers to change her legal situation and that of others. She may also, in certain circumstances, have her own legal position altered in relation to the Porsche: for instance, she is liable to have the car seized in execution of a judgement summons for debt. All these legal relations are involved in what we might think of as a clear case, indeed a paradigm, of ownership. Private property, then, is not only not a simple relation between a person and a thing, it is not a simple relationship at all. It involves a complex bundle of relations, which differ considerably in their character and effect.

If that were all, there would be no problem of definition: private property would be a bundle of rights, but if it remained constant for all or most of the cases that we want to describe as private property, the bundle as a whole could be defined in terms of its contents. But, of course, it does not remain constant, and that is where the difficulties begin.

Each of the legal relations involved in Susan's ownership of the Porsche is not only distinct, but in principle separable, from each of the others. It is possible, for example, that someone has a liberty to use an automobile without having any of the other rights or powers which Susan has. Because they are distinct and separable, the component relations may be taken apart and reconstituted in different combinations, so that we may get smaller bundles of the rights that were involved originally in this large bundle we called ownership. But when an original bundle is taken apart like this and the component rights redistributed among other bundles, we are still inclined, in our ordinary use of these concepts, to say that one particular person—the holder of one of the newly constituted bundles—is the *owner* of the resource. If Susan leases the car to her friend Blair so that he has exclusive use of the Porsche in return for a cash payment, we may still say that Susan is really the car's owner even though she does not have many of the rights, liberties, and powers outlined in the previous paragraph. We say the same about landlords, mortgagors, and people who have conceded various encumbrances, like rights of way, over their real estate: they are still the owners of the pieces of land in question. But the legal position of a landlord is different from that of a mortgagor, different again from that of someone who has yielded a right of way, and different too from that of a person who has not redistributed any of the rights in his original bundle: depending on the particular transactions that have taken place, each has a different bundle of rights. If lay usage still dignifies them all with the title 'owner' of the land in question, we are likely to doubt whether the concept of ownership, and the concept of private property that goes with it, are doing very much work at all. The lawyer, certainly, who is concerned with

the day-to-day affairs of all these people, will not be interested in finding out which of them really counts as an owner. His only concern is with the detailed contents of the various different bundles of legal relations.

■ ■ ■

We owe to H. L. A. Hart the point that in jurisprudence, as in all philosophy, it is a mistake to think that particulars can be classified under general terms only on the basis of their possession of specified common features. But when jurists express doubts about the usefulness of general terms such as 'private property' or 'ownership', it is usually this sort of definition that they have in mind. They imply that if we are unable to specify necessary and jointly sufficient conditions which an institution must satisfy in order to be regarded as a system of private property, or which a legal relation must satisfy in order to be regarded as a relation of ownership, then those terms are to be regarded as ambiguous or confused and certainly as analytically unhelpful.

If Hart's point is accepted, however, this scepticism begins to seem a little premature. Conceptual definition is a complicated business and the idea that it always involves the precise specification of necessary and sufficient conditions must be regarded as naive and outdated. A term which cannot be given a watertight definition in analytic jurisprudence may nevertheless be useful and important for social and political theory; we must not assume in advance that the imprecision or indeterminacy which frustrates the legal technician is fatal to the concept in every context in which it is deployed.

■ ■ ■

The concept of property is the concept of a system of rules governing access to and control of material resources. Something is to be regarded as a material resource if it is a material object capable of satisfying some human need or want. In all times and places with which we are familiar, material resources are scarce relative to the human demands that are made on them. (Some, of course, are scarcer than others.)

Scarcity, as philosophers from Hume to Rawls have pointed out, is a presupposition of all sensible talk about property. If this assumption were ever to fail (as Marx believed it some day would) then the traditional problem of the nature and justification of rival types of property system would probably disappear. But so long as it obtains, individuals (either on their own or in groups) are going to disagree about who is to make which use of what. These disagreements are often serious because, in many cases, being able to make use of a resource that one wants is connected directly or indirectly with one's survival. A problem, then, which I shall call the problem of *allocation*, arises in any society which regards the avoidance of serious conflict as a matter of any importance. This is the problem of determining peacefully and reasonably predictably who is to have access to which resources for what purposes and when. The systems of social rules which I call property rules are ways of solving that problem.

The concept of property does not cover all rules governing the use of material resources, only those concerned with their allocation. Otherwise the concept would include almost all general rules of behaviour. (Since almost all human conduct involves the use of material resources, almost all rules about conduct can be related to resources in some way.) For example, most societies have rules limiting the use of weapons: they are not to be used to wound or kill people. Some jurists have suggested (in relation to private property systems) that rules prohibiting harmful use should be included among the standard incidents of ownership. (In our discussion of Susan and her Porsche, we suggested that speed restrictions might also be treated in this way.) Nothing much hangs on this, but I suspect a better approach is to treat prohibitions on harmful behaviour as general constraints on action, setting limits to what may be done in a given society. Then we can locate rules about property within those limits, as rules determining which (generally permissible) actions may be performed with which resources. As Nozick puts it, the rules of property

determine for each object at any time which individuals are entitled to realize which of the constrained set of options socially available with respect to that object at that time. So, for example, the rule that knives are not to be used murderously nor cars driven at a certain speed are not to be seen as property rules. They are part of the general background constraints on action which place limits on what anyone can do with any object whether it is his property— or something he has some sort of entitlement to use—or not. Once we have settled what the background rules of action are, we can then turn to the property rules. If a particular action, say, riding bicycles, is permitted by law, it does not follow that the law permits me to ride any bicycle I please. The specific function of property rules is to determine, once we have established that bicycles may be ridden, who is entitled to ride which bicycle and when.

■ ■ ■

I have defined property in terms of *material* resources, that is, resources like minerals, forests, water, land, as well as manufactured objects of all sorts. But sometimes we talk about objects of property which are not corporeal: intellectual property in ideas and inventions, reputations, stocks and shares, choses [sic] in action, even positions of employment. As we saw, this proliferation of different kinds of property object is one of the main reasons why jurists have despaired of giving a precise definition of ownership. I think there are good reasons for discussing property in material resources first before grappling with the complexities of incorporeal property.

■ ■ ■

I now want to say what distinguishes a system of *private* property from other types of property system. Some jurists give the impression that by making out a case for the establishment of some system of settled rules about material objects, they have thereby refuted socialism. This is a mistake. A socialist system, as much as a system of private property, is a system of rules governing access to and control of material objects. A case for private property must relate to what is distinctive about this type of system, and not merely to the concept of property rules, something to which socialists and capitalists have a common commitment. Marx, for example, regarded it as obvious that all forms of society require some system of property: 'That there can be no such thing as production, nor, consequently, society, where property does not exist in any form, is a tautology. . . . But it becomes ridiculous when from that one jumps at once to a definite form, e.g. private property'.

The definition of private property I shall give is abstract. But it has the advantage of separating the question of what sort of system private property is from any particular theory of how private property is to be defended.

In a system of private property, the rules governing access to and control of material resources are organized around the idea that resources are on the whole separate objects each assigned and therefore belonging to some particular individual.

This claim requires clarification. We need to know what it is for a system of property rules to be organized around an idea, and what exactly, in the case of private property, this organizing idea of *belonging* involves. Let me say something about the latter issue first.

The organizing idea of a private property system is that, in principle, each resource belongs to some individual. At its simplest and most abstract, the idea can be elucidated in the following way. Imagine that the material resources available for use in a society have been divided into discrete parcels (call each parcel an object), and that each object has the name of an individual member of the society attached to it. (There are many ways in which this division of resources and the allocation of names to objects could be made. I make no assumptions about the way in which these processes take place. Both are matters for a theory of distributive justice).

A private property system is one in which such a correlation is used as a basis for solving what we earlier called the problem of alloca-

tion. Each society faces the problem of determining which, among the many competing claims on the resources available for use in that society, are to be satisfied, when, by whom, and under what conditions. In a private property system, a rule is laid down that, in the case of each object, the individual person whose name is attached to that object is to determine how the object shall be used and by whom. His decision is to be upheld by the society as final. When something like the idea of a name/object correlation is used in this way as a basis for solving the problem of allocation, we may describe each such correlation as expressing the idea of *ownership* or *belonging*. 'Ownership', then, on my stipulation, is a term peculiar to systems of private property. The owner of a resource is simply the individual whose determination as to the use of the resource is taken as final in a system of this kind.

Clearly, this idea of ownership is a possible way of solving the problem of allocation. But everything would depend on whether people accepted it and were prepared to abide by its fundamental rule. Partly this would be a matter of the acceptability of the name/object correlation. People would not be happy with an arbitrary correlation or one which did not assign their name to any object worth using. That is a matter for the theory of justice. But there might also be controversies about the very idea of ownership. People might ask, 'Why should *one* individual be put in a specially privileged position with regard to a given resource? Why not insist that, for all resources (or at least all the most important resources), the claims of every citizen are to be treated on an equal basis? Or why not insist that resource use is to be determined in each instance by reference to collective aims of the society?' These questions constitute the ancient problem of the justification of private property. The definition of private property that I have given enables us to see, in the abstract, just what is at stake when these questions are asked. It enables us to see what is distinctive and controversial about private property.

UTILITY AND PROPERTY

ALAN RYAN

The simplest defence of the existence of property rights over external objects is directly utilitarian. Unless individuals had the right to appropriate, use, transfer and (perhaps) bequeath objects of value or interest, it would be impossible to use the raw materials provided by nature for anything other than the simplest sort of immediate consumption. The creation of such rights is, therefore, dictated by utility. Utilitarianism is a normative theory which holds that moral and legal rules are acceptable to the extent that their acceptance and enforcement promote happiness. It is hostile to doctrines of 'natural right', holding that legal rights must be a matter of positive law, and that 'moral rights' are explicable as liberties and powers which individuals *ought* to have in order to promote their most important interests. Although property rights are not the dictates of 'nature', what one might call the moral shadow of ownership—a presumption that an individual who has harmlessly acquired an object ought to be able to enjoy it undisturbed—is readily derived from utilitarian considerations, such as the thought that individuals have a right to security and autonomy, because the possession and enforcement of such a right is 'optimific'.

Characteristically, utilitarians have so taken for granted this simple moral point that they have been more anxious to insist on the difference between a simple moral presumption in favour of unmolested possession, and property rights in their full-fledged form. These latter are necessarily the creatures of the law. It is the question, 'what property rights ought the law to create and enforce?' that utilitarianism most naturally raises and most distinctively answers. Unsurprisingly, utilitarians have directed their attention to ownership as it is understood in modern European legal systems.

Ownership under a developed legal system has been well characterized by A. M. Honoré along the following lines: 'Ownership comprises the right to possess, the right to use, the right to manage, the right to the income of the thing, the right to the capital, the right to security, the rights or incidents of transmissibility and absence of term, the prohibition of harmful use, liability to execution, and the incident of residuarity: this makes eleven leading incidents.' It is to be noticed that our loose way of speaking of property as 'a bundle of rights' is inadequate to the extent that it excludes liability to execution—that is the vulnerability of property to being seized and sold in payment of one's debts; the notion of a bundle of *rights* also excludes prohibition of harmful use, but one might demur at including this as an incident of ownership without further ado. I am prohibited from using *anyone's* knife to stab you in the chest, so many harmful uses are prohibited without reference to ownership, whereas liability to execution is very much part of ownership. What attaches to ownership is less the prohibition of harmful use than liability for injuries *caused by* my property in the absence of human criminality—if a slate blows off the roof of my house and strikes you it is to me you will look for compensation. One might say that the price of sovereignty over one's possessions is responsibility for their misdeeds.

A legal order recognizes ownership in the full modern sense when all these rights and

Alan Ryan, "Utility and Property," from *Property* (Minneapolis: University of Minnesota Press, 1987), pp. 53 ff. Ryan is Professor of Politics at Princeton University.

duties are assigned to a single person. If they are split up and assigned to different people, or if some do not exist at all, it is a pre- or post-modern system. Simple societies often treat the community or the extended family as the bearer of the right of residuarity—that is, when all lesser rights have lapsed, the object returns to the family rather than to a particular individual; the communist society of the future envisaged by Marx will not have the same notion of rights as ourselves, but will certainly spread these incidents over several persons and institutions. The utilitarian defence of property in any form is thus the defence of the legal recognition of ownership as an instrument in promoting the greatest happiness. The defence of exactly this conception of ownership is a defence of attaching all these incidents to one person; a utilitarian critique of this conception condemns these arrangements as less than optimific. It has been suggested that it makes no sense to ask whether ownership ought to be recognized; if ownership is defined as *all* relations between persons with respect to things, then there is something to be said for the view that all societies must have some use for ownership, and the only question is what sort of ownership they ought to recognize. But it is an exaggeration. Persons could relate to one another with respect to things without ownership entering into the matter. The hunters who allow the man who kills the beast they chase to take the first piece of meat from it neither claim ownership of the beast for themselves nor confer it on the successful hunter. It is analytically more sensible to distinguish claims made to ownership or on the basis of ownership from all other claims on things. You may have good reason to use my bicycle, perhaps that you are in a hurry to perform some good; but your relation to me over the bicycle is not a matter of ownership, whereas my having the right to accept or reject your claims to its use is a matter of ownership.

The economic theory of property rights makes the twin claims that in order to put any resource to best use, it is optimific to make sure that somebody owns it in the full liberal sense, and that the legal recognition of property rights has evolved under the impulse of pressures towards efficiency through a process parallel to that of natural selection. First, however, we must concentrate on the main outlines of the utilitarian theory itself. The background assumptions of the utilitarian defence of property are that nature is niggardly, men demanding, labour disagreeable, and anxiety even worse. We thus need to devise ways of making nature yield as much as she can, with the minimum expenditure of effort; we cannot do without rules of mine and thine because most men are of limited altruism and some will try to take the fruits of another man's efforts if they are not prevented. And even if men were not disposed to try to seize the results of other men's efforts, property rights would still be useful because of the way they solve problems of coordination between cooperators. If you and I know who has what claims over the various factors that would have to go into making some novel useful object, we can organize its creation because we can decide who is to have what share of the benefits it yields, and know whose say-so is decisive in allowing us to employ the various factors which enter into making it.

Property satisfies the need for security, and allows the natural incentive to labour to succeed—we are impelled to labour by the mere desire to stay alive, but no man will sow where another may reap in his stead; by guaranteeing that we may call our own our own, rules of ownership ensure that our desire for well-being will lead us to work. Equally, the enforcement of freely made contracts serves the same ends; if I have what will do you more good than it does me and you have what will do me more good than it does you, exchange is the way forward. Direct barter is clumsy, and that indicates the need for money. Money is what Marx termed 'the universal equivalent', allowing the utility of exchange to be realized without needless physical movement of goods.

The argument runs swiftly and smoothly. What it does not do is distinguish very readily between the need for *property* and the need for *private* property. Would utility be best served by, for instance, leaving the right to the capital in the hands of families and only the income in the hands of particular individuals? There is no difficulty in effecting something analogous when an estate descends by will; it is not uncommon for the widow or widower to receive an income for life while the capital itself belongs to her or his children. Would it be intolerably cumbersome if individuals had to secure family assent to plans for investment? It probably would be, so if we think economic growth more important than family authority, we shall think the modern system of ownership superior to its rivals. If we think the side-effects of leaving investment decisions in private hands are excessively disagreeable in various ways— environmentally intolerable, prone to lead to massive concentrations of economic power in too few hands, or whatever—we may look for non-ownership based ways of controlling them, or for forms of social ownership which will secure such control while remaining more flexible and less lethargic than pre-modern family ownership. The question is always the same: what system of ownership would be optimific? The response will therefore vary according to our sociological hunches about the side-effects of different allocations of rights, as well as according to our views about what contributes most to human happiness.

In the same spirit, we may ask whether it is the best possible arrangement to allow owners to be 'without term' where entities like land are concerned. Perhaps land generally, or some land in particular, ought only to be held on something like a leasehold, the land reverting to the community or some body representing the community, after that time. What if we faced a new territory which we hoped to see occupied and cultivated? We might think that one possibility was to allow people to acquire any amount of land so long as they could bring

it under cultivation, and to grant them a shorthold, of, say, a dozen years, at the end of which time they might simply hand it back, and use their savings to buy some smaller quantity outright, or be required to sell it back at some settled price. Why might we do this? If we wished to spread the ownership of land around the population, but wanted to get as much into cultivation as possible and as fast as possible, we might think this route better than allowing unlimited or limited freehold acquisition.

The argument in favour of something nearer our own system of indeterminate ownership is that it allows us to buy and sell a clearer and less encumbered title. If the law permits a single person, so to speak, to collect all the incidents of ownership in his or her hands, then individuals may, as the French Code puts it, deal with things in the most absolute manner permitted by the law. Moreover, this will permit the owner to erect all sorts of subsidiary rights on top of his ownership. The owner who can raise a loan on the security of his land may if he is rational and efficient employ the money so raised to increase his income well beyond what is needed to repay the loan. It evidently promotes the general happiness that he should be able to do so; the law therefore ought to recognize mortgages. But only if the owner's powers of disposal of the land are complete will the prospective lender be happy with the security offered; so we have here an argument for unencumbered, nondetermining ownership from which lesser interests may be carved.

The argument needs many further refinements before it becomes persuasive. For instance, nothing has yet been said about the range of things that can become the object of ownership. In many societies, men have been able to own slaves, and in many others, offices such as judgeships or military commissions have been bought and sold. Some writers, for instance Hegel, have suggested that there is some sort of logical contradiction in the idea that such things can be owned. Ownership, they say, is ownership of *things*, objects which have no wills of their own; to claim to own a person is absurd, because persons are by definition beings with wills and perspectives of their own, subjects not objects. Ownership of offices is not absurd in the same way, but is none the less irrational. The essence of an office is public service and the logic of access to it is competence in doing that office's duties. Purchase assimilates it to what is properly bought and sold at will, and used without inhibition for the owner's own good.

The utilitarian cannot accept such an outlook. Property is the creature of the law, and if the law creates slaves and creates property rights in offices, then people just do own slaves and colonelcies. The argument against such forms of property is not that there is something conceptually amiss, but that they are condemned by the principle of utility. Slavery is very much disliked by slaves; even where slaves are well-fed, comfortable and even the possessors of great power—under the Roman Empire some slaves became what later ages would have described as senior civil servants— no free man would change places with them. There is thus a strong prima facie case against slavery. Strong though it is, it can be overridden; Mill thought ancient society could have taken no steps forward without the existence of slavery, and was half-inclined to justify it on such (Aristotelian) terms. But in the modern world it would plainly be intolerable. It is, so to speak, a bonus for utilitarian criticisms of slavery that slavery is also an inefficient way of organizing production. Free labour has always been much more efficient.

What is noticeable about the utilitarian condemnation of slavery, however, is what it leaves out; utilitarians cannot simply denounce slavery as a violation of human rights or of a man's 'property in his own person' in the way natural rights theorists can. It is not that slavery is only 'extrinsically' bad, for it is quite clear that it is in itself a miserable condition; rather, its intrinsic badness can in principle, though only rarely in practice, be overridden by a sufficient addition to human happiness, a claim that believers in natural rights cannot accept.

The case against property in government offices or military ranks is less contentious. It simply appeals to the evident inefficiency of a method of recruitment which depends on ability to pay rather than on some objective test of capacity. The flexibility of utilitarian arguments on this sort of issue is very considerable; we may consider the effects of changing from purchase to appointment on merit in terms of its effect on morale, or on 'raw' efficiency of performance; we may consider the questions of how far the holders of these abusive forms of property are entitled to compensation, balancing the need to preserve the security of property rights and justice between owners against the need to abolish abuses at a reasonable price. Even in the case of the abolition of slavery, the least defensible of all forms of ownership, the utilitarian may—and nineteenth-century utilitarians did— argue that the individual slave-owner had acquired a piece of property legitimate at the time, and should therefore be compensated for being expropriated.

It is characteristic of utilitarian arguments that they are reversible; that is, since all justification rests on a consideration of consequences, a reconsideration of consequences will force a reconsideration of what is being justified. Moreover the malleability of human reactions allows utilitarians to ask whether the attitudes whose gratification or frustration determines how much happiness an institution produces are more or less the effects of the institution in question. Expectations are crucial in utilitarian arguments over property rights. Gratified expectation is a great source of happiness; property is founded in and gives rise to expectation. It is thus capable of giving great happiness and it can be a source of great misery if expectations are frustrated. So it is important to know whether expectations can be reshaped or attached to new entities without too much trouble. We may often be optimistic. Thus, a colonel who is looking forward to passing on his colonelcy to his son gets pleasure from the expectation, but he might get even more pleasure from the knowledge that his son's promotion was due to his merits. Again, the particular pleasure we get from thinking of our property in the hands of our children may attach just as readily to the house he can buy with the compensation he gets when he is 'bought out' as it now does to the colonelcy.

Utilitarian arguments provide good, but lukewarm defences of private property, and by the same token provide good but lukewarm defences of public ownership, too. Since property rights are to be justified in terms of general benefit, due attention being paid to the importance of individual security and freedom of thought and action, the ownership of anything beyond consumer goods and the like is a matter of convenience; moreover, given the 'bundle of rights and liabilities' conception of ownership, utilitarians are happy to envisage ownership being broken up, so that control over the capital may be separated from the right to income, and residuary rights be detached from current control. This is anticipated in the complicated arrangements which underpin leasehold ownership of residential property in England and Wales, and in the relations of shareholders to the companies they own but by no means control. The utilitarian cannot accommodate Hegel's thought that the human will is essentially individual and property therefore essentially private property, nor the Marxian counter that production is essentially social and property therefore essentially social and all pre-communist societies an aberration sustained by brute force and ideological deception. Property may be more or less private or more or less public; there is only one question worth asking—'what rights over the resources for production and consumption ought we to recognize, and in whose hands should we vest them?'

THE LOCKEAN THEORY OF RIGHTS

A. JOHN SIMMONS

There has been no more widespread or enduring intuition about property rights than that labor in creating or improving a thing gives one special claim to it. We feel that those who innocently work to discover, make, or usefully employ some unowned good ought to be allowed to keep it (if in so doing they harm no others), that it would be wrong for others to take it away. It is the strength of this intuition that keeps alive the interest in Locke's labor theory of property acquisition, despite generations of criticism of Locke's arguments. However badly he defends his views, we might say, surely Locke is on to something. It is not just law or convention or agreement that gives laborers special claim to the fruits of their labors. There is something natural about this claim, something it would be somehow wrong for law to contradict.

A. John Simmons, *The Lockean Theory of Rights* (Princeton: Princeton University Press, 1992), selections from Chapter 5 (Property Rights). Simmons is Professor of Philosophy at the University of Virginia.

Locke's theory of property exploits fully this intuition of "naturalness" in the relation between labor and property. The "property" of which Locke writes in chapter 5 of the *Second Treatise* is a moral, not a legal or civil, ownership, and this moral relation is conceived of by Locke as a natural relation in the strongest possible sense—it is sanctioned by natural law and presupposes no agreements or conventions. Remember that for Locke a right is a natural right if its binding force is nonconventional and it could be possessed in the state of nature. Locke's property is not only a natural right in this sense, but a *nonconsensual* natural right. His theory can thus be usefully contrasted not only with natural right theories in which property is a consensual right (e.g., the compact theories), but also with all conventionalist accounts (like Hume's) and all accounts on which property can only be a civil, legal, or political right (such as the theories of Hobbes and the later positivists). Property is for Locke neither just a useful arrangement for the division of goods on which humankind informally settled nor a right created solely by civil law. For if property is a consensual, conventional, or legal notion, the rules of property can change as consent, conventions, and laws change, making our rights in effect subject to whatever constraints society deems proper. Our property is then not secure (defeating part of the point of having civil society). Locke's need for a natural, nonconsensual ground of private property rights, then, was clear; and labor seemed, then as now, an obvious choice.

Labor is not, of course, the only ground of private property allowed by Locke. It is the sole ground of *original* exclusive property rights, the way in which something previously unowned can become owned. Chapter 5 of the *Second Treatise* is concerned primarily with the defense of a theory of original appropriation, so naturally labor is the central concept at work there. But once a property has been established by labor, subsequent title to that property can be acquired in a variety of ways (not prominently discussed in chapter 5): (1) *inheritance* can give subsequent title, either consensually (as in inheritance based on spousal contract) or "naturally" (as in filial inheritance); (2) *need* can give title to the surplus of another's property (3) one may acquire title to another's property as *reparation for injuries* done to one by that person. The right to take reparation is part of each person's natural executive right, based on the forfeiture of rights suffered by wrongdoers; (4) *alienation* of property rights (by gift, sale, or trade, for example) can also give subsequent title to what was first acquired by labor. Thus, common libertarian summaries of Locke's position are misleading when they suggest that while original property rights rest on nonconsensual grounds (i.e., labor), subsequent rights are based on consent. For Locke accepts at least three nonconsensual bases for subsequent rights: filial status, need, and forfeiture.

In addition to these ways of creating property in external goods, each person for Locke is *born* to a right with regard to external goods. What I have called "the right of self-government" includes for Locke the rights to preserve and control one's own life; and these rights entail a moral power (and consequent liberty) to make property in unowned (common) nature by one's labor, as well as a claim right not to be excluded by the efforts of others from taking by labor one's fair share of the resources given in common to mankind by God. Thus, each person "begins" with a "right to property" (the morally protected power to create property in up-to-a-fair-share of common nature), but not with a right in any particular external goods. Particular exclusive rights (to *this* apple or *that* piece of land) arise only from labor (on unowned nature) or from one of the four grounds of subsequent title mentioned above, not directly from any "grant from God."

■ ■ ■

Assuming that Locke means by property (all or some of) our rights over things (internal or external), we have still not been sufficiently precise in specifying the content of Locke's concept of property. For to say that I have a right over something is not to say precisely what *kind* of moral control over the thing I possess. My rights over different things (or different kinds of things) may consist of quite different ranges of constituent or component rights (claims, powers, or liberties). It has now become a commonplace, for instance, to observe that property is best thought of as a bundle or cluster of constituent rights, rights that are logically separable and are often separated in fact in existing systems of property. The result is the possibility (and actuality) of a wide range of forms of property or ownership, depending on which constituent rights make up the bundle that comprises the "property right" in some particular instance, system, or society. We can, for instance, contrast the rights that make up the classical paradigm of modern (capitalist) private property, with the rights at issue in "the new property," feudal dominion, or (more communal) property in many tribal societies. A well-known article on ownership distinguishes eleven leading "incidents" of the liberal concept of "full ownership." Among these are the constituent rights to possess, use, and manage the thing, rights to the income, to capital, to security, transmissibility, and absence of term in one's possession of it. It is probably fair to say that the central constituents of standard instances of property are the rights to use the thing, to alienate it, to exclude others from using it, and to nonexpropriation of it. But it seems reasonable to ask at this point to what extent *Locke's* concept of property conforms to such "standard" cases—that is, what are the constituent rights that make up Lockean property?

It is clear that property rights in Locke cannot amount to absolute rights over a thing,

for Locke accepts many limits on our use of property. Nor, I think, can Locke's property even be the "full ownership" Honoré describes (which, of course, includes prohibitions on harmful uses of property), for Locke allows (among other things) that property in external goods must continue to be used by the owner, else it returns to common and may be taken by another (contrary to the "full ownership" rights to the capital and to absence of term). Indeed, it may be difficult to specify any *one* set of constituent rights in which property consists for Locke at all. For while it seems likely that Locke would accept the modern view of property as a bundle of rights, he might well insist that property consists in different component rights depending on the *kind* of property in question. The law of nature that defines our rights, remember, commands the best preservation of mankind, and it seems natural to argue that which *kind* of property (e.g., in our selves, our land, our artefacts [sic], etc.) is at issue will bear importantly on the question of what extent of control over the thing will best facilitate mankind's preservation. Nonetheless, Locke clearly seems to have in mind at least certain rights as necessary components of all kinds of property. The rights to possess, use, and manage the thing, to exclude others (at least where they have no prior or more weighty title—as the needy do to our surplus goods), and to security or nonexpropriation (similarly qualified) seem to be essential constituents of all property for Locke. Similarly, some rights that make sense only with respect to external goods (such as transmissibility) seem uncontroversial as features of Lockean property. Beyond this, however, the question of the precise content of property for Locke becomes more difficult to determine.

PENN CENTRAL TRANSPORTATION CO. V. CITY OF NEW YORK

438 U.S. 104 (1978)

Justice BRENNAN delivered the opinion of the Court.

[EDITOR'S NOTE: Following refusal of the New York City Landmarks Preservation Commission to approve plans for construction of 50-story office building over Grand Central Terminal, which had been designated a "landmark," the terminal owner filed a taking challenge to the landmarks preservation law.]

Before considering appellants' specific contentions, it will be useful to review the factors that have shaped the jurisprudence of the Fifth Amendment injunction "nor shall private property be taken for public use, without just compensation." The question of what constitutes a "taking" for purposes of the Fifth Amendment has proved to be a problem of considerable difficulty. While this Court has recognized that the "Fifth Amendment's guarantee . . . [is] designed to bar Government from forcing some people alone to bear public burdens which, in all fairness and justice, should be borne by the public as a whole," this Court, quite simply, has been unable to develop any "set formula" for determining when "justice and fairness" require that economic injuries caused by public action be compensated by the government, rather than remain disproportionately concentrated on a few persons. Indeed, we have frequently observed that whether a particular restriction will be rendered invalid by the government's failure to pay for any losses proximately caused by it depends largely "upon the particular circumstances [in that] case."

In engaging in these essentially ad hoc, factual inquiries, the Court's decisions have identified several factors that have particular significance. The economic impact of the regulation on the claimant and, particularly, the extent to which the regulation has interfered with distinct investment-backed expectations are, of course, relevant considerations. So, too, is the character of the governmental action. A "taking" may more readily be found when the interference with property can be characterized as a physical invasion by government, than when interference arises from some public program adjusting the benefits and burdens of economic life to promote the common good.

"Government hardly could go on if to some extent values incident to property could not be diminished without paying for every such change in the general law," and this Court has accordingly recognized, in a wide variety of contexts, that government may execute laws or programs that adversely affect recognized economic values. Exercises of the taxing power are one obvious example. A second are the decisions in which this Court has dismissed "taking" challenges on the ground that, while the challenged government action caused economic harm, it did not interfere with interests that were sufficiently bound up with the reasonable expectations of the claimant to constitute "property" for Fifth Amendment purposes.

More importantly for the present case, in instances in which a state tribunal reasonably concluded that "the health, safety, morals, or general welfare" would be promoted by prohibiting particular contemplated uses of land, this Court has upheld land-use regulations that destroyed or adversely affected recognized real property interests. Zoning laws are, of course, the classic example.

Zoning laws generally do not affect existing uses of real property, but "taking" challenges have also been held to be without merit in a wide variety of situations when the challenged governmental actions prohibited a beneficial use to which individual parcels had previously been devoted and thus caused substantial individualized harm. *Miller v. Schoene*, 276 U.S. 272 (1928), is illustrative. In that case, a state entomologist, acting pursuant to a state statute, ordered the claimants to cut down a large number of ornamental red cedar trees because they produced cedar rust fatal to apple trees cultivated nearby. . . . The Court held that the State might properly make "a choice between the preservation of one class of property and that of the other" and since the apple industry was important in the State involved, concluded that the State had not exceeded "its constitutional powers by deciding upon the destruction of one class of property [without compensation] in order to save another which, in the judgment of the legislature, is of greater value to the public."

Again, Hadacheck v. Sebastian, 239 U.S. 394 (1915), upheld a law prohibiting the claimant from continuing his otherwise lawful business of operating a brickyard in a particular physical community on the ground that the legislature had reasonably concluded that the presence of the brickyard was inconsistent with neighboring uses.

■ ■ ■

In contending that the New York City law has "taken" their property in violation of the Fifth and Fourteenth Amendments, appellants make a series of arguments, which, while tailored to the facts of this case, essentially urge that any substantial restriction imposed pursuant to a landmark law must be accompanied by just compensation if it is to be constitutional.

Before considering these, we emphasize what is not in dispute. Because this Court has recognized, in a number of settings, that States and cities may enact land-use restrictions or controls to enhance the quality of life by preserving the character and desirable aesthetic features of a city, appellants do not contest that New York City's objective of preserving structures and areas with special historic, architectural, or cultural significance is an entirely permissible governmental goal. . . . Finally, appellants do not challenge any of the specific factual premises of the decision below. They accept for present purposes both that the parcel of land occupied by Grand Central Terminal must, in its present state, be regarded as capable of earning a reasonable return, and that the transferable development rights afforded appellants by virtue of the Terminal's designation as a landmark are valuable, even if not as valuable as the rights to construct above the Terminal. In appellants' view none of these factors derogate from their claim that New York City's law has effected a "taking."

They first observe that the airspace above the Terminal is a valuable property interest. They urge that the Landmarks Law has deprived them of any gainful use of their "air rights" above the Terminal and that, irrespective of the value of the remainder of their parcel, the city has "taken" their right to this superadjacent airspace, thus entitling them to "just compensation" measured by the fair market value of these air rights.

■ ■ ■

"Taking" jurisprudence does not divide a single parcel into discrete segments and attempt to determine whether rights in a particular segment have been entirely abrogated. In deciding whether a particular governmental action has effected a taking, this Court focuses rather both on the character of the action and on the nature and extent of the interference with rights in the parcel as a whole—here, the city tax block designated as the "landmark site."

Secondly, appellants, focusing on the character and impact of the New York City law, argue that it effects a "taking" because its operation has significantly diminished the value of the Terminal site. Appellants concede that the decisions sustaining other land-use regulations, which, like the New York City law, are reasonably related to the promotion of the general welfare, uniformly reject the proposition that diminution in property value, standing alone, can establish a "taking," and that the "taking" issue in these contexts is resolved by focusing on the uses the regulations permit. Appellants, moreover, also do not dispute that a showing of diminution in property value would not establish a "taking" if the restriction had been imposed as a result of historic-district legislation, but appellants argue that New York City's regulation of individual landmarks is fundamentally different from zoning or from historic-district legislation because the controls imposed by New York City's law apply only to individuals who own selected properties.

Stated baldly, appellants' position appears to be that the only means of ensuring that selected owners are not singled out to endure financial hardship for no reason is to hold that any restriction imposed on individual landmarks pursuant to the New York City scheme is a "taking" requiring the payment of "just compensation." Agreement with this argument would, of course, invalidate not just New York City's law, but all comparable landmark legislation in the Nation. We find no merit in it.

■ ■ ■

Rejection of appellants' broad arguments is not, however, the end of our inquiry, for all we thus far have established is that the New York City law is not rendered invalid by its failure to provide "just compensation" whenever a landmark owner is restricted in the exploitation of property interests, such as air rights, to a greater extent than provided for under applicable zoning laws. We now must consider whether the interference with appellants' property is of such a magnitude that "there must be an exercise of eminent domain and compensation to sustain [it]." That inquiry may be narrowed to the question of the severity of the impact of the law on appellants' parcel, and its resolution in turn requires a careful assessment of the impact of the regulation on the Terminal site.

[T]he New York City law does not interfere in any way with the present uses of the Terminal. Its designation as a landmark not only permits but contemplates that appellants may continue to use the property precisely as it has been used for the past 65 years: as a railroad terminal containing office space and concessions. So the law does not interfere with what must be regarded as Penn Central's primary expectation concerning the use of the parcel. More importantly, on this record, we must regard the New York City law as permitting Penn Central not only to profit from the Terminal but also to obtain a "reasonable return" on its investment.

Justice REHNQUIST, with whom The Chief Justice [BURGER] and Justice STEVENS join, dissenting.

In August 1967, Grand Central Terminal was designated a landmark over the objections of its owner Penn Central. Immediately upon this designation, Penn Central, like all owners of a landmark site, was placed under an affirmative duty, backed by criminal fines and penalties, to keep "exterior portions" of the landmark "in good repair." Even more burdensome, however, were the strict limitations that were thereupon imposed on Penn Central's use of its property. At the time Grand Central was designated a landmark, Penn Central was in a precarious financial condition. In an effort to increase its sources of revenue, Penn Central had entered into a lease agreement with appellant UGP Properties, Inc., under which UGP would construct and operate a multistory office building cantilevered above the Terminal building. During the period of construction, UGP would pay Penn Central $1 million per year. Upon completion, UGP would rent the building for 50 years, with an option for another 25 years, at a guaranteed minimum rental of $3 million per year. The record is clear that the proposed office building was in full compliance with all New York zoning laws and height limitations. Under the Landmarks Preservation Law, however, appellants could not construct the proposed office building unless appellee Landmarks Preservation Commission issued either a "Certificate of No Exterior Effect" or a "Certificate of Appropriateness." Although appellants' architectural plan would have preserved the facade of the Terminal, the Landmarks Preservation Commission has refused to approve the construction.

■ ■ ■

As early as 1887, the Court recognized that the government can prevent a property owner from using his property to injure others without having to compensate the owner for the value of the forbidden use.

The nuisance exception to the taking guarantee is not coterminous with the police power itself. The question is whether the forbidden use is dangerous to the safety, health, or welfare of others.

Appellees are not prohibiting a nuisance. The record is clear that the proposed addition to the Grand Central Terminal would be in full compliance with zoning, height limitations, and other health and safety requirements. Instead, appellees are seeking to preserve what they believe to be an outstanding example of beaux-arts architecture. Penn Central is prevented from further developing its property basically because too good a job was done in designing and building it. The city of New York, because of its unadorned admiration for the design, has decided that the owners of the building must preserve it unchanged for the benefit of sightseeing New Yorkers and tourists.

Unlike land-use regulations, appellees' actions do not merely *prohibit* Penn Central from using its property in a narrow set of noxious ways. Instead, appellees have placed an *affirmative* duty on Penn Central to maintain the Terminal in its present state and in "good repair." Appellants are not free to use their property as they see fit within broad outer boundaries but must strictly adhere to their past use except where appellees conclude that alternative uses would not detract from the landmark. . . .

Even where the government prohibits a noninjurious use, the Court has ruled that a taking does not take place if the prohibition applies over a broad cross section of land and thereby "secure[s] an average reciprocity of advantage." It is for this reason that zoning does not constitute a "taking." While zoning at times reduces *individual* property values, the burden is shared relatively evenly and it is reasonable to conclude that on the whole an individual who is harmed by one aspect of the zoning will be benefited by another.

Here, however, a multimillion dollar loss has been imposed on appellants; it is uniquely felt and is not offset by any benefits flowing from the preservation of some 400 other "landmarks" in New York City. Appellees have imposed a substantial cost on less than one one-tenth of one percent of the buildings in New York City for the general benefit of all its people. It is exactly this imposition of general costs on a few individuals at which the "taking" protection is directed.

QUESTIONS FOR DISCUSSION

1. Why does Locke think there is a right to private property? What is the connection between property and labor?

2. Contrast the utilitarian and natural rights arguments for a right to private property. Which do you think is stronger? Why?

3. What was taken away from the Penn Central company? What did they get to keep? Do you think they have been deprived of their property?

4. Consider the following description of the facts in *Lucas v. South Carolina Coastal Council,* 112 S.Ct. 2886 (1992):

In 1986, petitioner David H. Lucas paid $975,000 for two residential lots on the Isle of Palms in Charleston County, South Carolina, on which he intended to build single family homes. In 1988, however, the South Carolina Legislature enacted the Beachfront Management Act, which had the direct effect of barring petitioner from erecting any permanent habitable structures on his two parcels.

South Carolina's expressed interest in intensively managing development activities in the so-called "coastal zone" dates from 1977 when, in the aftermath of Congress's passage of the federal Coastal Zone Management Act of 1972, the legislature enacted a Coastal Zone Management Act of its own. In its original form, the South Carolina Act required owners of coastal zone land that qualified as a "critical area" (defined in the legislation to include beaches and immediately adjacent sand dunes) to obtain a permit from the newly created South Carolina Coastal Council (respondent here) prior to committing the land to a "use other than the use the critical area was devoted to on [September 28, 1977]."

In the late 1970's, Lucas and others began extensive residential development of the Isle of Palms, a barrier island situated eastward of the City of Charleston. Toward the close of the development cycle for one residential subdivision known as "Beachwood East," Lucas in 1986 purchased the two lots at issue in this litigation for his own account. No portion of the lots, which were located approximately 300 feet from the beach, qualified as a "critical area" under the 1977 Act; accordingly, at the time Lucas acquired these parcels, he was not legally obliged to obtain a permit from the Council in advance of any development activity. His intention with respect to the lots was to do what the owners of the immediately adjacent parcels had already done: erect single-family residences. He commissioned architectural drawings for this purpose.

The Beachfront Management Act brought Lucas's plans to an abrupt end. Under that 1988 legislation, the Council was directed to establish a "baseline" connecting the landward-most "point[s] of erosion . . . during the past forty years." [The] Council fixed this baseline landward of Lucas's parcels. That was significant, for under the Act construction of occupable improvements was flatly prohibited seaward of a line drawn 20 feet landward of [the] baseline. The Act provided no exceptions.

B. Lucas promptly filed suit in the South Carolina Court of Common Pleas, contending that the Act's [complete] extinguishment of his property's value entitled him to compensation regardless of whether the legislature had acted in furtherance of legitimate police power objectives. Following a bench trial, the court agreed. Among its factual determinations was the finding that "at the time Lucas purchased the two lots, both were zoned for single-family residential construction and . . . there were no restrictions imposed upon such use of the property by either the State of South Carolina, the County of Charleston, or the Town of the Isle of Palms." The trial court further found that the Act decreed a permanent ban on construction insofar as Lucas's lots were concerned, and that this prohibition "deprive[d] Lucas of any reasonable economic use of the lots, . . . eliminated the unrestricted right of use, and render[ed] them valueless." The court thus concluded that Lucas's properties had been "taken" by operation of the Act, and [ordered] "just compensation" in the amount of $1,232,387.50.

> The Supreme Court of South Carolina reversed. It found dispositive what it described as Lucas's concession "that the Beachfront Management Act [was] properly and validly designed to preserve . . . South Carolina's beaches." [The] court believed itself bound to accept the "uncontested . . . findings" of the South Carolina legislature that new construction in the coastal zone [threatened] this public resource. The Court ruled that when a regulation respecting the use of property is designed "to prevent serious public harm," no compensation is owing [regardless] of the regulation's effect on the property's value.

a. As a matter of justice, independent of questions about the positive law, do you think South Carolina should have restricted Lucas' use of his land? If they did, do you think they should have to pay him compensation?

b. Independent of the question of precedent, do you think that the Fifth Amendment's requirement of "just compensation" when there is a "taking" requires South Carolina to pay compensation to Lucas?

c. Do you think that, under *Penn Central*, South Carolina is required to pay compensation to Lucas?

SUGGESTIONS FOR FURTHER READING

Good surveys of arguments about property rights are Alan Ryan, *Property* (Minneapolis: University of Minnesota Press, 1987); Lawrence Becker, *Property Rights* (London: Routledge & Kegan Paul, 1977). Two important and comprehensive analyses of the idea of property rights are Steven Munzer, *A Theory of Property* (Cambridge: Cambridge University Press, 1986); Jeremy Waldron, *The Right to Private Property* (Oxford: Clarendon Press, 1988). Robert Nozick's defense of a natural right to property is in *Anarchy, State, and Utopia* (New York: Basic Books, 1974). A spirited argument for a very strong interpretation of the "takings" clause of the Constitution is Richard Epstein, *Takings* (Cambridge: Harvard University Press, 1988). Also worth consulting is Allan Gibbard, "Natural Property Rights," in R. Stewart, ed., *Readings in Social and Political Philosophy* (New York: Oxford University Press, 1986). A good collection of perspectives is J. Roland Pennock and John W. Chapman, eds., *Property* (NOMOS XXII) (New York: New York University Press, 1980). More historical perspectives can be found in Stephen Buckle, *Natural Law and the Theory of Property: Grotius to Hume* (Oxford: Clarendon Press, 1991); and A. John Simmons, *The Lockean Theory of Rights* (Princeton: Princeton University Press, 1992).

CHAPTER 5

JUSTICE AND EQUALITY

WHAT IS JUSTICE? 5.1

INTRODUCTION

Justice and equality lie at the center of some of the most heated controversies in contemporary society. Recent debates about the health care system in the United States often hinge on the question of whether that system distributes medical care fairly or justly. When some people argue that the United States cannot afford to continue funding social security and entitlement programs, others respond that it would be unjust to discontinue or cut back on these programs. Tax cuts for the wealthy are rejected out of hand by people who see them as unjust. And, of course, recent disputes about affirmative action, about feminism, and about homosexuals in the military all raise deep issues of justice.

One reason why justice is cited so often is that so much value is attached to justice. Since the time of Plato and Aristotle in ancient Greece, it has been common to rank justice as the highest virtue. This means that, if an act or program or law is unjust, no other virtue or advantage can make it acceptable; and if it is required by justice, no other disadvantage can make it unacceptable. A strong sense of justice is present in almost everyone, even children. If one child gets a larger piece of pie, the parents can count on hearing, "But that's not fair." Later in life, students get upset if their bookstore charges forty dollars for a book that sells elsewhere for thirty dollars, even if these students would be willing to pay forty dollars if that were the normal price. But people seem willing to accept much greater losses (for example, in gambling) as long as they feel that they have not been treated unjustly.

Despite its applications outside law, the notion of justice has been closely associated with law. Some legal theorists claim that unjust laws are not really laws at all. (See Aquinas in Section 1.1.) Others seem to identify what is unjust with what is or ought to be illegal. (See Mill in Section 5.2.) And many others see justice as the main test of whether a law is acceptable. Because of these connections between law and justice, it is especially important to understand justice when studying the philosophy of law.

Various claims about justice cannot be understood until we have some idea of what justice is. In particular, it is important to realize that the term "justice" is applied to different qualities at different levels of generality.

As Aristotle said, "justice in [the widest] sense . . . is complete virtue; virtue, however, not unqualified but in relation to somebody else."[1] Even today, people sometimes call an act unjust when they mean nothing more specific than that the act is morally wrong considering *all* morally relevant factors concerning one's relations to other people.

Often, however, "justice" refers to only *part* of virtue. In this narrower sense, Aristotle argues, a person displays another vice, but not injustice, when he "through cowardice throws away his shield, or through bad temper uses abusive language, or through illiberality refuses financial help." Conversely, a person displays injustice but not these other vices when he "takes more than his share." So "there is another kind of injustice which is part of universal injustice."[2]

Aristotle is here mainly concerned with justice in individuals, but our focus is justice in laws and legal systems. Still, justice in law is also usually seen as a particular virtue that contrasts with other virtues, such as efficiency and benevolence, that are also important in legal systems. (See Rawls in Section 5.2.) And, just as justice is seen as the highest virtue in individuals, so justice is also seen as the most important, or one of the most important, standards for judging laws and legal systems.

Which virtue of a legal system is the particular virtue of justice? In order to see what is common to all cases of justice, we need first to distinguish different areas of justice.

One kind of justice is *formal.* A system of criminal law, for example, is formally just when courts follow specified uniform procedures, people who are convicted of violating laws that call for punishment are punished, and people who are not so convicted are not punished. In short, people who are equal in the eyes of the law are treated equally under the law. This kind of justice is so basic that Lon Fuller argued (in Chapter 1) that formal justice is necessary for any system to be a legal system at all.

Formal justice is often subsumed under a broader notion of *procedural* justice, which requires not only formal justice but also certain court procedures (see Chapter 8). For example, it is unjust not to allow all criminal defendants to collect evidence, select jurors, call and cross-examine witnesses, and so on. But procedural justice still does not ensure that the laws themselves are just. A law that requires escaped slaves to be returned to their masters is unjust, even if it is applied in the same way to every runaway slave, and even if fair procedures are followed to the letter. This shows that formal and procedural justice are not all there is to justice.

The area of justice that concerns whether laws themselves are just can be called *substantive* justice. Aristotle usefully divides substantive justice into three main parts:

> One kind of particular justice . . . is that which is shown in the distribution of honour or money or such other assets as are divisible among the members of the

---

[1] Aristotle, *Nicomachean Ethics* 1129b25. Here and below I use Tredennick's revision of Thomson's translation in The Ethics of Aristotle (New York: Penguin 1976).

[2] Aristotle, *Nicomachean Ethics* 1130a17–22.

community . . . ; and another kind [is that] which rectifies the conditions of a transaction. This latter kind has two parts, because some transactions are voluntary and others involuntary.[3]

Correspondingly, there are also three kinds of injustice, depending on whether what is unjust is a distribution or a rectification of one of the two kinds of transaction.

Aristotle's divisions apply as well to modern legal systems. The first kind of rectificatory justice concerns what Aristotle calls involuntary transactions, which today are usually called crimes. Crimes are the subject of what is now called *retributive* justice, which asks when, how, and how much to punish. For example, is it ever just to punish someone for an accident? Is capital punishment ever just? Would life imprisonment be too much punishment for rape? Such questions will be discussed in Chapters 6–7.

Voluntary transactions include typical private contracts, such as when one person sells, leases, or lends money or property to another person. For example, when a company develops a new drug (such as AZT) and then distributes it to sick people who need it desperately, how much should the patients be required to pay in order to rectify (or make right) this transaction? And when, if ever, is it just to require someone to fulfill a contract that was signed on the basis of misinformation? This problem area can be called *private* justice, for lack of a better term.

Both of these kinds of rectificatory justice contrast with distributive justice. When the government or another institution decides whether to adopt some program (such as a tax or a training program), its decision takes goods away from some people or gives goods to others, thereby affecting the distribution of wealth, income, honor (or social status), and other resources in society. The question of whether the resulting distribution of goods is just is a question of distributive justice.

These kinds of justice can now be diagrammed like this:

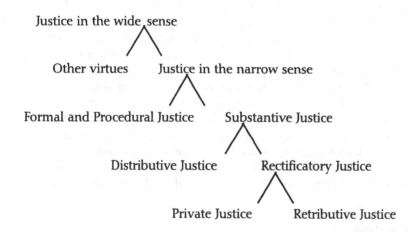

_____
[3]Aristotle, *Nicomachean Ethics* 1130a30–1131a2.

Despite their differences, these areas of justice are not completely separate. Punishment affects distribution by taking goods away from criminals, so retributive justice can be seen as part of distributive justice. Some private voluntary exchanges seem unjust because of how they affect the distribution of social goods, and then private justice seems to be based on distributive justice. Which distributions of social goods are just sometimes depends partly on past contracts and crimes, and then distributive justice is based on private justice and retributive justice. Despite these interactions, this division of justice is still fairly common, and it helps to display the variety of questions that arise about justice.

This chapter will focus on distributive justice in the law, but it is still useful to ask: What is common to all of the areas of justice that makes them all areas of justice? Aristotle's answer appears simple: "All men think justice to be a sort of equality," and "equals ought to have equality," but he immediately adds, "there still remains a question: equality or inequality of what?"[4] In the area of distributive justice, Aristotle says that a distribution of goods is just when "there will be the same equality between the shares as between the persons, because the shares will be in the same ratio to one another as the persons."[5] This does not mean that everyone gets the same share. Instead, Aristotle measures persons by their merit. "Everyone agrees that justice in distribution must be in accordance with merit in some sense, but they do not all mean the same kind of merit: the democratic view is that the criterion is free birth; the oligarchic that it is wealth or good family; the aristocratic that it is excellence."[6] Thus, Aristotle is not committed to egalitarianism in the modern sense of wanting every person to have an equal share of economic, social, or political goods. Indeed, he favored slavery and a lower status for women, and he did not even assign the same moral and political rank to all free men. But even such an elitist can require equality at an abstract level.

Under Aristotle's influence, it has become common to view justice in terms of equality. This has come to mean that it is just to treat people equally when they are equal in relevant respects and to treat people unequally when they are not equal in relevant respects. It is also seen as unjust to treat people unequally when they are equal in relevant respects and to treat people equally when they are unequal in relevant respects. Of course, a great deal hangs on which respects are relevant, but the abstract principles can gain general agreement because they can accommodate different views about which respects are relevant or important.

Despite the apparent gains from seeing justice as equality, Peter Westen, a law professor at the University of Michigan, argues (in the reading in this section) that equality is so malleable that it is empty. A concept lacks any force or content if it has no limits on its use. This is the problem with equality, according to Westen. Appeals to equality can be effective rhetoric, but they are based on illusion. What makes something unjust is not that one person receives less goods than other people, but instead that one person receives too little–less than what that person deserves or has a right to. Injustice is then determined not by com-

---

[4]Aristotle *Politics* 1282b22-3.

[5]Aristotle, *Nicomachean Ethics* 1131a20-22.

[6]Aristotle, *Nicomachean Ethics* 1131a25-7.

parisons among people but by each separate person's right to receive certain goods. If a person does not deserve or have a right to more goods than she has, there is nothing unjust about her having less goods than other people. And when a person's rights are violated, it does not add anything to say that this person is not treated equally to other people. If Westen is correct, justice is better understood not in terms of equality but directly in terms of rights and desert.

It does seem that many debates about equality are really about rights and desert, but Westen's critics can respond that equality still sometimes has some force independent of rights. Anthony D'Amato, in the reading after Westen, discusses a system of gasoline rationing that seems unjust because people do not get equal access to gasoline even though nobody has a prior right to any gasoline. And D'Amato suggests that his point generalizes to other kinds of cases. The challenge for Westen is to explain such judgments about justice without depending on any notion of equality. If such inequalities among people are unjust even if they do not violate any right other than a right to equality, then Westen is wrong, and equality does have an independent moral force. Moreover, even if demands for equality do not create any new constraints in addition to rights, it still might be useful theoretically or practically to view disputes about rights in terms of equality. If so, the force of equality remains at least an open question, despite Westen's arguments.

THE EMPTY IDEA OF EQUALITY

PETER WESTEN

Equality is commonly perceived to differ from rights and liberties. Rights are diverse; equality is singular. Rights are complicated; equality is simple. Rights are noncomparative in nature, having their source and their justification in a person's individual well-being; equality is comparative, deriving its source and its limits from the treatment of others. Rights are concerned with absolute deprivation; equality is concerned with relative deprivation. Rights mean variety, creativity, differentiation; equality means uniformity. Rights are individualistic; equality is social. Or so it is said.

These perceived differences are reflected in a certain ebb and flow between the ideal of equality, on one hand, and the ideal of rights and liberties, on the other. When the framers of the United States Constitution came to define the relationship between the central government and the people, they spoke in a bill of rights; when the victors of the Civil War reconstructed the relationship between the people and the states three-quarters of a century later, they spoke in the language of "equality." Fifty years ago equality was dismissed as a legal argument of "last resort," one to be eschewed

Peter Westen, "The Empty Idea of Equality," *Harvard Law Review*, vol. 95 (1982), pp. 537–96.

until all available "rights" had been tried and rejected; today equality is becoming the argument of first choice, one that threatens to swallow "rights" that once ranked far above it.

The juxtaposition of "rights" and "equality" also has led to a perceived tension between them. Equality is sometimes said to be flourishing at the expense of rights, just as rights are sometimes said to be flourishing at the expense of equality. Each is also said to be more important than the other. Thus, rights are often said to be the source of equality, while equality is often said to be the root or source of all rights.

I believe that this contrasting of rights and equality is fundamentally misconceived. It is based on a misunderstanding, both in law and in morals, about the role of equality in ethical discourse. To avoid possible misunderstanding, let me emphasize what I mean by equality and rights. By "equality" I mean the proposition in law and morals that "people who are alike should be treated alike" and its correlative, that "people who are unalike should be treated unalike." Equality thus includes all statements to the effect that the reason one person should be treated in a certain way is that he is "like" or "equal to" or "similar to" or "identical to" or "the same as" another who received such treatment. "Rights," by contrast, means all claims that can justly be made by or on behalf of an individual or group of individuals to some condition or power–except claims that "people who are alike be treated alike." The right may be a "liberty," "prerogative," "privilege," "power," "exemption," or "immunity." The right may have its source in law or morals or custom; it may be comparative or noncomparative;[14] it may consist of a principle or a policy; it may be absolute or defeasible. The only claims that do not qualify as "rights" are claims that "likes should be treated alike."

I try in this Article to establish two propositions: (1) that statements of equality logically entail (and necessarily collapse into) simpler statements of rights; and (2) that the additional step of transforming simple statements of rights into statements of equality not only involves unnecessary work but also engenders profound conceptual confusion. Equality, therefore, is an idea that should be banished from moral and legal discourse as an explanatory norm. . . .

I. EQUALITY IN MORALS

The study of equality begins with Plato and Aristotle, the first to proclaim that likes should be treated alike and to give equality its prominence in law and morals. Aristotle, building on the work of Plato, said two things about equality that have dominated Western thought ever since:

> (1) Equality in morals means this: things that are alike should be treated alike, while things that are unalike should be treated unalike in proportion to their unalikeness.[18] (2) Equality and justice are synonymous; to be just is to be equal, to be unjust is to be unequal.[19]

These propositions raise two questions for discussion. First, what is the connection between the fact that two things are alike and the moral inference that they should be treated alike? Second, what is the justification for equating justice and equality?

A. The Connection Between Being Alike and Being Entitled to Be Treated Alike

The proposition that "likes should be treated alike" is said to be a universal moral truth–a truth that can "be intuitively known with perfect clearness and certainty." Why? What is the connection between the fact that people are alike and the normative conclusion that they ought to be treated alike? How can one move from an "is" to an "ought"?

The answer can be found in the component parts of the equality formula. The formula "people who are alike should be treated alike" involves two components: (1) a determination that two people are alike; and (2) a moral judgment that they ought to be treated alike. The determinative component is the first. Once one determines that two people are alike for purposes of the equality principle, one knows how they ought to be treated. To understand why this is so—that is, to understand how (1) works—one must understand what kind of determination (1) is. One must know precisely what it means to say for purposes of equality that two persons are alike.

First, "people who are alike" might mean people who are alike in every respect. The trouble is that no two people are alike in every respect. The only things that are completely alike in every respect are immaterial symbols and forms, such as ideal numbers and geometric figures, which are not themselves the subject of morals.

Second, "people who are alike" may mean people, who, though not alike in every respect, are alike in some respects. Unfortunately, while the previous definition excludes every person in the world, the present definition includes every person and thing because all people and things are alike in some respect; and one is left with the morally absurd proposition that "all people and things should be treated alike."

Third, "people who are alike" may refer to people who are morally alike in a certain respect. The latter interpretation successfully avoids the philosophical hurdle of deriving an "ought" from an "is." It starts with a normative determination that two people are alike in a morally significant respect and moves to a normative conclusion that the two should be treated alike. Instead of deriving an "ought" from an "is," it derives an "ought" from an "ought." However, categories of morally alike objects do not exist in nature; moral alikeness is established only when people define categories. To say that people are morally alike is therefore to articulate a moral standard of treatment—a standard or rule specifying certain treatment for certain people—by reference to which they are, and thus are to be treated, alike.

Now that we understand what it means to be alike, it should be easy to understand what it means to be treated alike. Oddly enough, some commentators take it to mean that if a moral standard prescribes some uniform treatment for all members of a class (for instance, that all

Rhodes Scholars shall receive fellowships to Magdalen College, Oxford), equal treatment is achieved by either uniformly granting or uniformly denying that treatment to all members of the class. Thus, they would say, although it would not be just to deny all Rhodes Scholars fellowships, it would be equal.

This interpretation of like treatment, whatever else it may be, is certainly not empty. On the contrary, it instructs people to do what they would otherwise know they should not do—that is, to give people who are "alike" by one standard the treatment that is alike by that standard or by its converse. The real trouble with the concept is not that it is empty, but that it is patently absurd. Indeed, it is so preposterous a moral proposition that, if it were what equality really meant, no one would give it a moment's thought. To say "likes should be treated alike" is to make an "ought" statement—a statement of what people are morally enjoined to do. Yet if the statement directs people in countless cases to do what they concededly ought not to do (for instance, either award or deny fellowships to Rhodes Scholars), the statement itself cannot be true. Hence, if "likes should be treated alike" is to be taken seriously as a moral proposition—if it is to be accepted as true or just or lasting (as Aristotle and all the proposition's subsequent students have taken it to be)—"like treatment" cannot plausibly carry the foregoing meaning.

As the reader may have noticed, a more natural view of "like treatment" is suggested by the way "people who are alike" was interpreted. Just as no categories of "like" people exist in nature, neither do categories of "like" treatment exist; treatments can be alike only in reference to some moral rule. Thus, to say that people who are morally alike in a certain respect "should be treated alike" means that they should be treated in accord with the moral rule by which they are determined to be alike. Hence "likes should be treated alike" means that people for whom a certain treatment is prescribed by a standard should all be given the treatment prescribed by the standard. Or, more simply, people who by a rule should be treated alike should by the rule be treated alike.

So there it is: equality is entirely "[c]ircular." It tells us to treat like people alike; but when we ask who "like people" are, we are told they are "people who should be treated alike." Equality is an empty vessel with no substantive moral content of its own. Without moral standards, equality remains meaningless, a formula that can have nothing to say about how we should act. With such standards, equality becomes superfluous, a formula that can do nothing but repeat what we already know. As Bernard Williams observed, "when the statement of equality ceases to claim more than is warranted, it rather rapidly reaches the point where it claims less than is interesting."[32]

The recognition that equality is tautological explains several things. It explains why people who are alike should therefore be treated alike; why equality expresses a universal moral truth; why equality is taken to be a "law of thought"; and why this one aspect of Aristotle's moral views remains indisputable today, as it was 2,500 years ago. Equality is an undeniable and unchangeable moral truth because it is a simple tautology. This should come as no surprise; as an a priori moral truth, equality could scarcely be anything else.

B. The Connection Between Equality and Rights

. . . Relationships of equality (and inequality) are derivative, secondary relationships; they are logically posterior, not anterior, to rights. To say that two persons are the same in a certain respect is to presuppose a rule—a prescribed standard for treating them—that both fully satisfy. Before such a rule is established, no standard of comparison exists. After such a rule is established, equality between them is a "logical consequence" of the established rule. They are then "equal" in respect of the rule because that is what equal means: "Equally" means "'according to one and the same rule.'" They are also then entitled to equal treatment under the rule because that is what possessing a rule means. . . .

To say that two people are "equal" and entitled to be treated "equally" is to say that they both fully satisfy the criteria of a governing rule of treatment. It says nothing at all about the content or wisdom of the governing rule. . . .

It is sometimes said that two very different sorts of rules are at work in equality and rights cases. Equality differs from rights, it is said, because equality presupposes comparison, while rights do not. Substantive rights, such as the right of free speech and the right to counsel, can be described without reference to a person's relationship to other rightsholders. To decide whether a person's speech rights are violated, one juxtaposes the state's general duty of behavior against the state's particular treatment of the person to determine whether the state treats the person in accord with its prescribed duty. Equality, in contrast, is comparative in nature; it involves "comparative rights."[50] rights that cannot be assessed without ascertaining a person's relationship to others. In more precise terms, the contrast is between "noncomparative rights" on one hand and equality on the other; equality and comparative rights are taken to be identical.

This equation of comparative rights and equality is fundamentally misconceived. For one thing, some rights entail comparison without any suggestion of equality. Consider, for example, the right of secured creditors to absolute preference over unsecured creditors; or the right of veterans of foreign wars or physically handicapped persons or women or members of racial minorities to preferential treatment of certain kinds over other groups; or the right of certain applicants for competitive positions to be selected on the basis of relative exam scores. In each case, to determine whether the claimant's substantive rights are satisfied one must first ascertain his relationship to others.

Conversely, just as rights can be comparative, claims of equality can be noncomparative in nature. Again, it all depends on the content of the particular right that substantiates the equality claim. Consider such equality claims as the right of persons qua persons not to be tortured or their right to basic economic subsistence. To decide whether a person has been tortured or denied basic subsistence, one need not know how anyone else has been treated. One can assess each person's claim solely by reference to the particulars of his treatment, without the necessity of referring to others. . . .

To conclude, any noncomparative right—such as the claim of persons to basic economic subsistence or their right not to be tortured—can be stated either indirectly in terms of equality or directly as a right. The same is true of any comparative right, such as the claim of blacks to preferential admission. The distinction, therefore, is not between equality and some contrary notion of substantive justice, but between rights that cannot be determined independently of a person's relationship to others and rights that can. Moreover, the comparison entailed in rights that cannot be determined independently of a person's relation to others differs from the comparison entailed by framing rights in terms of equality.

C. The Connection Between Equality and Justice

"Justice" means "giving every person his due." What then is the relationship between "giving persons their due" and "treating like persons alike"? Are the two formulas equivalent, as Aristotle thought them to be? Or are they two separate (although related) principles, as others think them to be? Can something be just and yet unequal? Or, alternatively, can something be equal and yet unjust?

The answers, once again, can be found in the structure of the two moral propositions. The idea of justice, like the idea of equality, is entirely formal. It requires that persons be given their due but does not itself define what is their "due." To render justice meaningful, one must look beyond the proposition that every person should be given his due to the substantive moral or legal standards that determine what is one's "due."

One way to decide whether the two concepts are interchangeable is to determine whether each can be reduced linguistically to a statement of the other. Consider first the idea of justice:

(1) To "give persons their due" entails giving them the treatment they deserve;
(2) To give persons the treatment they deserve entails treating them in accordance with moral rules;
(3) To treat persons in accord with moral rules entails: (a) determining whether they possess those criteria determined to be morally significant by the rules; and (b) according those who possess the criteria the treatment prescribed by the rules, while not according such treatment to those who do not possess the criteria;
(4) To accord those who possess the criteria the treatment prescribed by the rules, while not according that treatment to those who do not possess the criteria, entails treating alike those who are alike in the morally significant respects while treating unalike those who are unalike in the morally significant respects; and
(5) To treat alike those who are alike in the morally significant respects while treating unalike those who are unalike in the morally significant respects entails "treating likes alike" and "treating unlikes unalike."

In short, to say that "every person should be given his due" means "persons who are alike should be treated alike" and "persons who are unalike should be treated unalike."

Just as justice can be reduced to equality, equality can be reduced to a statement of justice; one simply reverses the sequence of steps set forth in the previous paragraph. After all, to say that two people are "alike" and hence must be treated alike is to presuppose substantive principles of right and wrong, principles that render it "right" to treat them alike and "wrong" to treat them unalike. To speak of right and wrong regarding the treatment of people is to define what is "due" them under the circumstances. That is why philosophers from the time of Aristotle to the present have said that treating people equally means "giving every person his due." . . .

One recalls the phrase in stone over the entrance to the United States Supreme Court: "Equal Justice Under Law." Would the phrase mean less if it said "Justice Under Law"? Or

"Equality Under Law"? Is anything gained, then, by using four words instead of three—anything, that is, besides redundancy and obfuscation?

NOTES

[14]A "comparative" right is a right of a person that is "determinable only by reference to his relations to other persons," while a "noncomparative" right is one that can be "determined independently of that of other people." Feinberg, *Noncomparative Justice*, 83 PHIL. REV. 297, 298 (1974)....

[18]Aristotle, *Ethica Nicomachea* V.3.1131a–1131b (W. Ross trans. 1925); *see also* Aristotle, *Metaphysica* I.5.1055b–1056b (W. Ross trans. 2d ed. 1928)....

[19]Aristotle, *Ethica Eudemia* VII.9.1241b (W. Ross ed. 1925); Aristotle, *Ethica Nicomachea* V.3.1131a–1131b (W. Ross trans. 1925); Aristotle, *Politics* III.9.1280a, III.12.1282b– 1283a, V.1.1301a–1301b (B. Jowett trans. 1921).

[32]Williams, *The Idea of Equality*, in PHILOSOPHY, POLITICS AND SOCIETY 110, 111 (P. Laslett & W. Runciman eds. 1962).

[50]For the distinction between "comparative" and "non-comparative" rights, see *supra* note 14.

QUESTIONS FOR DISCUSSION

1. What exactly does Westen mean when he claims that the idea of equality is empty? What arguments does Westen give for this claim? Do you agree? Why or why not?

2. Does Westen's argument apply only to formal justice (equality under the law) or does it apply also to substantive justice? To retributive justice (for example, to the claim that a punishment should "equal" the crime)? To distributive justice (for example, to the idea that everyone should get an "equal" vote)?

IS EQUALITY A TOTALLY EMPTY IDEA?

ANTHONY D'AMATO

Professor Peter Westen's essay asserting that the concept of equality has no substantive content whatsoever usefully brushes aside much of the equal-protection rhetoric that, as Westen carefully explains, appropriately belongs to substantive due process. However, his absolutist position is open to challenge. I would like to posit one hypothetical case that I used in my classes when I taught Constitutional Law that I think contradicts Professor Westen's thesis. If it

does, then there will be other cases as well, and his position cannot stand as the logically tight construct that he repeatedly asserts that it is.

1. A HYPOTHETICAL CASE

Let us suppose that a state legislature decides to restrict motorists' use of gasoline by enacting a statute allowing drivers to purchase gasoline only on weekdays if their license plate is odd numbered and only on weekends if their license

Anthony D'Amato, "Is Equality a Totally Empty Idea?", *Michigan Law Review*, vol. 81, no. 3 (January 1983), pp. 600–603.

plate is even-numbered. The even-numbered drivers, constituting about half the motorists in the state, will thus effectively be restricted to purchasing gasoline on Saturdays [assuming that gas stations are closed on Sundays], or in other words will have one fifth the opportunity to purchase of the drivers who have odd-numbered plates. We can assume that this statute is not an attempt to reduce lines at service stations (actual statutes have done this by, for example, allowing odd-numbered plates to purchase gasoline on odd-numbered days), but rather to cut down on total gasoline consumption. We can further assume that the legislature calculated that the great difficulty of purchase now imposed upon even-numbered drivers will reduce total gasoline consumption by the desired amount in that state.

Suppose now that the even-numbered drivers bring a class-action suit to declare the statute unconstitutional. Have they been denied substantive due process? No, because the means selected by the legislature to reduce gasoline consumption is rationally related to its goal. In fact, it is probably cheaper than the alternative of issuing ration points to all drivers. Moreover, since the legislature could have stopped the sale of gasoline in the state entirely, cutting back on sales by the means chosen was well within the legislature's power.

Instead, the only real complaint that the even-numbered drivers have is that they have not been treated equally with the odd-numbered drivers. Here one can imagine Professor Westen saying, "But they are not equal—they are different in precisely the difference articulated by the legislature, namely, that they possess license plates that are divisible by 2 whereas the other drivers do not possess such plates." To be sure, this is, logically speaking, a difference. But the fact is that the "difference" selected by the legislature was a random one; it was arbitrary.[2] If people are subject to arbitrary classifications, they are not being treated equally. Only if the classifications are nonarbitrary can we agree with Professor Westen that the "equality"

rhetoric falls out, because then the classification *defines* the relevant difference such that the two groups should now be treated "unalike."

If the foregoing example contradicts Professor Westen's thesis, then elaborating it along his lines will worsen the situation and demonstrate the consequences of his mode of analysis. Accordingly, let us elaborate upon the hypothetical case by positing some legislative history that explains why the even-numbered drivers were relegated to the weekends. Suppose that a bill proposing a statute such as the one that was passed was circulated among members of the legislature, and suppose further that those members of the legislature who owned automobiles were split among even-numbered and odd-numbered license-plate owners. Sensing that a bill may be passed in the next session of the legislature, the solons whose plates are even-numbered apply to the Registry of Motor Vehicles for new, odd-numbered plates. When all of them have received their new plates, so that now all legislators have odd-numbered plates, the bill is enacted into law. Now we have a real reason for the difference between odd and even. According to Professor Westen, such a reason is the key to why equality analysis is purely formal, since it explains that this legislative classification, like all others, defines the differences between people. But this is precisely what is wrong with his analysis. For while this is an explanation, it does not help take the case out of the Equal Protection Clause. Rather, it puts it even more solidly within that clause.[4]

NOTES

[2]Of course, not all random or arbitrary statutes are violative of substantive due process, for example, a statewide lottery allowing gasoline purchases to the lucky numbers drawn out of a hat, with all motorists having an equal chance.

[4]It is not a violation of substantive due process for the legislators to favor themselves; suppose the statute exempted all legislators (because of the public nature of their duties) from the odd-even restrictions. Thus, in my hypothetical, the reason the legislators voted for the odd numbers was sufficient but not necessary.

QUESTIONS FOR DISCUSSION

1. Explain and evaluate D'Amato's response to Westen. How could Westen best respond to D'Amato's example? Do you think that equality is empty in this example? Why or why not?

2. Does D'Amato's example show why other kinds of inequality are unjust? Why, and which kinds, or why not?

3. If it would not be unjust to forbid anyone under 21 to drink 3.2% beer, would it be unjust to forbid only men but not women between 18 and 21 to drink 3.2% beer, on the grounds that men of this age are more likely to drive while drunk? Why or why not? What would Westen say about this case? See Craig v. Boren in Section 4.1.

4. If Amy has much more income than Betty, what should be equal: (a) the absolute amount that each must pay in taxes, or (b) the percentage of income that each must pay, or (c) the personal sacrifice that each must make in order to pay taxes (for example, assuming that, in order to pay 10 percent of her income, Betty would have to give up her car and walk to work each day, but Amy would only have to give up her pleasure boat), or (d) something else? Why is this answer just in this case?

5. About 8,000 Americans a year need hemodialysis (artificial blood filtration) as a treatment for kidney failure. This therapy normally costs $10,000–$30,000 per year. If there are not enough machines for everyone to get dialysis, is it just to choose the people who get the treatment on the basis of: (a) how much they can pay, (b) their chances of survival or of benefit from the treatment, (c) their merit or value to the community, (d) their age (preference for the oldest or the youngest?), (e) a lottery, or (f) something else? Why?

6. Is it unjust for Vermont and New York to have the same number of senators? Why or why not? Is it unjust if none of a state's representatives in Congress come from a minority group that composes 30 percent of the state's electorate but is not a majority in any district? Why or why not?[7]

SUGGESTIONS FOR FURTHER READING

For more on Aristotle's theory of justice, see his *Nicomachean Ethics*, Book V. Westen's skeptical views are developed further in the rest of the article excerpted here and in *Speaking of Equality* (Princeton: Princeton University Press, 1990). See also criticisms of Westen by Erwin Chemerisky and Westen's response to Chemerisky and D'Amato in *Michigan Law Review*, vol. 81, no. 3 (January 1983), pp. 575–663. It is revealing to compare Westen's views to similar views of Bernard Williams, "The Idea of Equality," in Peter Laslett and W. G. Runciman, eds., *Philosophy, Politics, and Society*, Series II (Oxford: Basil Blackwell, 1962), pp. 110–31.

[7]See Lani Guinier, *The Tyranny of the Majority* (New York: Free Press, 1994).

THEORIES OF JUSTICE 5.2

INTRODUCTION

If the concept of justice is based on equality, all substantive theories of justice require equality of some kind. That is what makes them theories of justice instead of some other subject. What competing theories of justice disagree about is the respects in which people must be equal. So we can compare theories of justice by asking which kind of equality is required by each theory.

One classic theory of justice is utilitarianism. Utilitarians claim that one morally ought to do an act if and only if that act creates the greatest good for the greatest number. This theory incorporates justice at one level by requiring that equal amounts of good count equally, no matter when or where those goods occur. For example, pain or freedom for one hour on Monday counts just as much as an equal pain or freedom for one hour on Tuesday. Furthermore, the good of one person counts equally with the good of anyone else. My pain or freedom counts just as much as an equal amount of your pain or freedom. In the slogan of Jeremy Bentham (1748-1842), a British philosopher and legal reformer, "Everybody to count for one, nobody for more than one."[8]

Utilitarianism runs into trouble if it considers only the total good and not the distribution of goods among different people. Suppose a large number of people would be happier if a much smaller number of people were enslaved. Even if each slave loses more than any master gains, if the masters outnumber the slaves by enough, the total and average happiness will be higher with slavery than without slavery. But slavery still seems unjust even in these special circumstances. So this utilitarianism seems too simple to comprehend justice.

A more complicated utilitarian theory of justice is defended in this section by John Stuart Mill (1806–1873), a child prodigy student of Bentham. On Mill's account, an act is unjust when it both is morally wrong and also violates a moral right of some assignable individual. An act is morally wrong when "a person ought to be punished in some way or other for doing it." (p. 512) An individual has a right to something when society ought to defend the individual's possession of it. So what is unjust depends on what ought to be punished or defended. And what ought to be punished or defended depends on what it maximizes utility to punish or defend. (That is why Mill's theory is still utilitarian.) Thus, an act is unjust roughly when it maximizes utility to punish people who do it and to

---

[8]Bentham sometimes calls justice a "phantom" or an "imaginary instrument," but only insofar as it is contrasted with utility. He also says that, "the dictates of justice are nothing more than a part of the dictates of benevolence." *Principles of Morals and Legislation*, Chapter X, Note 115.

defend people from it. Mill uses this theory to explain why it is unjust to deprive people of certain "essentials of well-being," such as freedom, since it maximizes utility to defend individual freedom and to punish people who interfere with freedom. Mill also infers that "society should treat all equally well who have deserved equally well of it" (p. 516). If Mill is right, utilitarianism supports more equality than just equal weight for each person's good.

But does Mill's modified utilitarianism explain why slavery is unjust? In the above example where slavery maximizes utility, it might not maximize utility for society to punish people who keep slaves or to defend slaves' rights to freedom. But slavery still seems unjust. Utilitarians often respond that this counterexample is unrealistic. One reason is that slaveholders will have to waste a lot of resources on stopping slaves from revolting. Another reason is that small amounts of goods (such as food, money, or freedom) will benefit slaves much more than their masters, because of a law of diminishing marginal utility. Because of such problems, slavery will always create less utility in the long run than some other alternative, such as a free labor market, according to utilitarians. Even if so, critics insist that this response misses the factors that really make slavery unjust, namely, the basic rights of the slaves and the inequalities between slaves and masters.

In order to guarantee rights against social utility, John Rawls, a Harvard University philosophy professor, turns to a contractarian theory. The reading from Rawls in this section argues that rational people under conditions of impartiality would agree to two principles, and that this hypothetical social contract justifies those principles. Rawls' first principle requires the greatest equal basic liberty. This principle is lexically ranked first, which means that it cannot be violated for the sake of other goods, including utility, in lower ranked principles. That explains why it is unjust to deprive slaves of equal basic liberties, even if it maximizes utility to do so. Once equality in basic liberty is ensured, Rawls' second principle allows social and economic inequalities to be just when and only when they are both "to the greatest benefit of the least advantaged" and also "attached to positions and offices open to all" (p. 521). This second principle allows many inequalities, but it is still at least moderately egalitarian, since it rules out economic and social inequalities that do not benefit the worst off, as well as all unfair inequalities in opportunity. In addition to this equality in the distribution of goods, Rawls also says that his system requires equality at a more "fundamental" level: "equality as it applies to the respect which is owed to persons irrespective of their social position."[9]

Some of the egalitarian implications of Rawls' theory are criticized in this chapter in a selection by Robert Nozick, another professor of philosophy at Harvard. In Nozick's central example, Wilt Chamberlain uses his basketball skill, bargaining power, and cunning to make a lot more money than anyone else. Nozick argues that the resulting inequality is not unjust, even though it is not to the greatest benefit of the least advantaged, and not everyone has an equal opportu-

---

[9]John Rawls, *A Theory of Justice* (Cambridge: Harvard University Press, 1971), p. 511. Rawls' claim is explained and expanded by Ronald Dworkin in *Taking Rights Seriously* (Cambridge: Harvard University Press, 1977), p. 180 and elsewhere.

nity to attain Chamberlain's economic position. If so, Nozick's example poses a serious problem for Rawls' second principle.

Nozick's alternative theory of justice is historical in the sense that he sees any pattern of distribution as just if it has the right kind of history. Essentially, a distribution is just if and only if everyone is entitled to the goods they possess in that distribution; and one is entitled to a certain good if and only if either one acquired that good before anyone else in a just way or one acquired that good in a just transfer from someone else who was entitled to that good. On this theory, it is not unjust for Chamberlain to have much more than anyone else, since Chamberlain did not coerce or defraud anyone in the process of becoming rich. Nozick's basic point is that Chamberlain and others should have the liberty to make any free bargains they want, regardless of the effects on the distribution of goods. That is why this kind of theory is often described as libertarian.

Although this theory has attractions for many, its implications are extreme. Suppose that over time Chamberlain acquires billions of dollars while most people fall into poverty. If there is nothing unjust in this situation, as Nozick and other libertarians suggest, then how could it be just for the government to force Chamberlain to pay taxes to support welfare, health care, and public education for the poor and their children? Some libertarians simply say that such taxation is unjust, and there should be no public schools or welfare, regardless of how poor or rich anyone is, but their opponents feel that something is lacking in any theory of justice with such implications.

A theory that puts this much emphasis on liberty might seem to have nothing to do with equality. However, Nozick does insist that everyone has an equal right to acquire goods first, to transfer goods, and not to be coerced or defrauded. Libertarians also insist on equality under the law. Indeed, libertarianism can be seen as a version of Rawls' first principle, which requires the greatest amount of liberty compatible with the same liberty for all. The difference between Rawls and libertarians is that libertarians do not accept anything like Rawls' second principle, because they see his first principle as implying rights that rule out the kinds of redistribution that Rawls brings in under his second principle. This limited kind of equality will not satisfy critics of libertarianism, but it does show that libertarians do not deny the importance of equality. All they do is to restrict the kinds of rights that must be equal.

Libertarianism, Rawlsian liberalism, and utilitarianism have all come under fire recently from communitarians, such as Michael Sandel, a Harvard government professor (a selection from whom also appears in this section). According to communitarians, these traditional theories of justice overlook the importance of community and depend on a false view of persons as isolated individuals. Communitarians insist that societies and governments should aim at a common good, so they should pass laws against activities that break down the common life of the community. Sandel's examples are laws to restrict pornography and disruptive industrial change. Critics claim that such laws violate individual rights, and that a government should not impose its own version of the common good on people who do not share that vision. But communitarians respond that this objection presupposes the atomistic view of persons that communitarians reject.

Communitarianism might, again, not seem to base justice on equality. If a common good is imposed by law, individuals might not seem to have an equal right to choose their own lives. But communitarians could respond that, if the majority of a community votes to restrict pornography in order to achieve a common life, then everyone has an equal say in choosing that common life. Once the community chooses a common life, communitarians can also insist that everyone has an equal right to participation in that common life. Sandel suggests as much, for example, when he justifies the civil rights movement "in the name of recognizing the full membership of fellow citizens wrongly excluded from the common life of the nation" (p. 539). Another communitarian, John Finnis, has argued for a requirement "of fundamental impartiality among the human subjects who are or may be partakers of those [basic] goods."[10] These kinds of equality are basic to justice even for communitarians.

There are many other theories of justice: radical egalitarian, Marxist, feminist, and so on. Another recent debate has arisen among advocates of equality of welfare, equality of resources, equality of capability, and equality of opportunity. These other theories and debates are fascinating and important, but they cannot all be included here. The important point for now is that they all see justice as requiring equality in some respects and not in others. Thus, in order to decide among these theories, we need to ask a series of questions: Which equalities are important? Why are they important? How important are they (that is, what costs in efficiency and liberty are worth paying for that kind of equality)? All of these questions must be answered before one can face the crucial practical question: Which laws are just?

[10]John Finnis, *Natural Law and Natural Rights* (Oxford: Clarendon Press, 1980), p. 107.

ON THE CONNECTION BETWEEN JUSTICE AND UTILITY

JOHN STUART MILL

In all ages of speculation one of the strongest obstacles to the reception of the doctrine that utility or happiness is the criterion of right and wrong, has been drawn from the idea of *justice*. The powerful sentiment and apparently clear perception, which that word recalls with a ra-

John Stuart Mill, *Utilitarianism*, Chapter 5

pidity and certainty resembling an instinct, have seemed to the majority of thinkers to point to an inherent quality in things; to show that the just must have an existence in nature as something absolute, generically distinct from every variety of the expedient, and, in idea, opposed to it, though (as is commonly acknowledged) never, in the long run, disjoined from it in fact. . . .

To throw light upon this question, it is necessary to attempt to ascertain what is the distinguishing character of justice or of injustice: what is the quality, or whether there is any quality, attributed in common to all modes of conduct designated as unjust (for justice, like many other moral attributes, is best defined by its opposite), and distinguishing them from such modes of conduct as are disapproved, but without having that particular epithet of disapprobation applied to them. If in everything which men are accustomed to characterize as just or unjust, some one common attribute or collection of attributes is always present, we may judge whether this particular attribute or combination of attributes would be capable of gathering round it a sentiment of that peculiar character and intensity by virtue of the general laws of our emotional constitution, or whether the sentiment is inexplicable, and requires to be regarded as a special provision of Nature. If we find the former to be the case, we shall, in resolving this question, have resolved also the main problem; if the latter, we shall have to seek for some other mode of investigating it.

To find the common attributes of a variety of objects, it is necessary to begin by surveying the objects themselves in the concrete. Let us therefore advert successively to the various modes of action and arrangements of human affairs which are classed, by universal or widely spread opinion, as just or as unjust. The things well known to excite the sentiments associated with those names are of a very multifarious character. I shall pass them rapidly in review, without studying any particular arrangement.

In the first place, it is mostly considered unjust to deprive anyone of his personal liberty, his property, or any other thing which belongs to him by law. Here, therefore, is one instance of the application of the terms just and unjust in a perfectly definite sense, namely, that it is just to respect, unjust to violate, the *legal rights* of anyone. But this judgment admits of several exceptions, arising from the other forms in which the notions of justice and injustice present themselves. For example, the person who suffers the deprivation may (as the phrase is) have *forfeited* the rights which he is so deprived of: a case to which we shall return presently. But also,

Secondly, the legal rights of which he is deprived, may be rights which *ought* not to have belonged to him; in other words, the law which confers on him these rights, may be a bad law. When it is so, or when (which is the same thing for our purpose) it is supposed to be so, opinions will differ as to the justice or injustice of infringing it. Some maintain that no law, however bad, ought to be disobeyed by an individual citizen; that his opposition to it, if shown at all, should only be shown in endeavoring to get it altered by competent authority. This opinion (which condemns many of the most illustrious benefactors of mankind, and would often protect pernicious institutions against the only weapons which, in the state of things existing at the time, have any chance of succeeding against them) is defended, by those who hold it, on grounds of expediency; principally on that of the importance, of the common interest of mankind, of maintaining inviolate the sentiment of submission to law. Other persons, again, hold the directly contrary opinion, that any law, judged to be bad, may blamelessly be disobeyed, even though it be not judged to be unjust, but only inexpedient; while others would confine the license of disobedience to the case of unjust laws: but again, some say that all laws which are inexpedient are unjust; since every law imposes some restriction on the natural liberty of mankind, which restriction is an injustice, unless legitimated by tending to their good. Among these diversities of opinion, it seems to be universally admitted that there may be unjust laws, and that law, consequently, is not the ultimate criterion of justice, but may give to one person a benefit, or impose on another an evil, which justice condemns. When, however, a law is thought to be unjust, it seems always to be regarded as being so in the same way in which a breach of law is unjust, namely, by infringing somebody's right; which, as it cannot in this case be a legal right, receives a different appellation, and is called a moral right. We may say, therefore, that a second case of injustice consists in taking or withholding from any person that to which he has a *moral right*.

Thirdly, it is universally considered just that each person should obtain that (whether good or evil) which he *deserves*, and unjust that he should obtain a good, or be made to undergo an evil, which he does not deserve. This is, perhaps, the clearest and most emphatic form in which the idea of justice is conceived by the general mind. As it involves the notion of desert, the question arises, what constitutes desert? Speaking in a general way, a person is understood to deserve good from those to whom he does or has done good, and evil from those to whom he does or has done evil. The precept of returning good for evil has never been regarded as a case of the fulfillment of justice, but as one in which the claims of justice are waived, in obedience to other considerations.

Fourthly, it is confessedly unjust to *break faith* with anyone: to violate an engagement, either express or implied, or disappoint expectations raised by our own conduct, at least if we have raised those expectations knowingly and voluntarily. Like the other obligations of justice already spoken of, this one is not regarded as absolute, but as capable of being overruled by a stronger obligation of justice on the other side; or by such conduct on the part of the person concerned as is deemed to absolve us from our obligation to him, and to constitute a *forfeiture* of the benefit which he has been led to expect.

Fifthly, it is, by universal admission, inconsistent with justice to be *partial;* to show favor or preference to one person over another, in matters to which favor and preference do not properly apply. Impartiality, however, does not seem to be regarded as a duty in itself, but rather as instrumental to some other duty; for it is admitted that favor and preference are not always censurable, and indeed the cases in which they are condemned are rather the exception than the rule. A person would be more likely to be blamed than applauded for giving his family or friends no superiority in good offices over strangers, when he could do so without violating any other duty; and no one thinks it unjust to seek one person in preference to another as a friend, connection, or companion. Impartiality where rights are concerned is of course obligatory, but this is involved in the more general obligation of giving to everyone his right. A tribunal, for example, must be impartial, because it is bound to award, without regard to any other consideration, a disputed object to the one of two parties who has the right to it. There are other cases in which impartiality means, being solely influenced by desert; as with those who, in the capacity of judges, preceptors, or parents, administer reward and punishment as such. There are cases, again, in which it means, being solely influenced by consideration for the public interest; as in making a selection among candidates for a government employment. Impartiality, in short, as an obligation of justice, may be said to mean, being exclusively influenced by the considerations which it is supposed ought to influence the particular case in hand; and resisting solicitation of any motives which prompt to conduct different from what those considerations would dictate.

Nearly allied to the idea of impartiality is that of *equality;* which often enters as a component part both into the conception of justice and into the practice of it, and, in the eyes of many persons, constitutes its essence. But in this, still more than in any other case, the notion of justice varies in different persons, and always conforms in its variations to their notion of utility. Each person maintains that equality is the dictate of justice, except where he thinks that expediency requires inequality. The justice of giving equal protection to the rights of all, is maintained by those who support the most outrageous inequality in the rights themselves. Even in slave countries it is theoretically admitted that the rights of the slave, such as they are, ought to be as sacred as those of the master; and that a tribunal which fails to enforce them with equal strictness is wanting in justice; while, at the same time, institutions which leave to the slave scarcely any rights to enforce, are not deemed unjust, because they are not deemed inexpedient. Those who think that utility requires distinctions of rank, do not consider it unjust that riches and social privileges should be unequally dispensed; but those who think this inequality inexpedient, think it unjust also. Whoever thinks that government is necessary, sees no injustice in as much inequality as is constituted by giving to the magistrate powers not granted to other people. Even among those who hold leveling doctrines, there are as many questions of justice as there are differences of opinion about expediency. Some communists consider it unjust that the produce of the labor of the community should be shared on any other principle than that of exact equality; others think it just that those should receive most whose wants are greatest; while others hold that those who work harder, or who produce more, or whose services are more valuable to the community, may justly claim a larger quota in the division of the produce. And the sense of natural justice may be plausibly appealed to in behalf of every one of these opinions.

Among so many diverse applications of the term "justice," which yet is not regarded as ambiguous, it is a matter of some difficulty to seize the mental link which holds them together, and on which the moral sentiment adhering to the term essentially depends. Perhaps, in this embarrassment, some help may be derived from the history of the word, as indicated by its etymology.

In most, if not in all, languages, the etymology of the word which corresponds to 'just,' points distinctly to an origin connected with the ordinances of law. *Justum* is a form of *jussum*, that which has been ordered. *Dikaion* comes directly from *dikē*, a suit at law. *Recht*, from which came right and righteous, is synonymous with law. The courts of justice, the administration of justice, are the courts and the administration of law. *La justice*, in French, is the established term for judicature. I am not committing the fallacy imputed with some show of truth to Horne Tooke, of assuming that a word must still continue to mean what it originally meant. Etymology is slight evidence of what the idea now signified is, but the very best evidence of how it sprang up. There can, I think, be no doubt that the *idée mère*, the primitive element, in the formation of the notion of justice, was conformity to law. It constituted the entire idea among the Hebrews, up to the birth of Christianity; as might be expected in the case of a people whose laws attempted to embrace all subjects on which precepts were required, and who believed those laws to be a direct emanation from the Supreme Being. But other nations, and in particular the Greeks and Romans, who knew that their laws had been made originally, and still continued to be made, by men, were not afraid to admit that those men might make bad laws: might do, by law, the same things, and from the same motives, which if done by individuals without the sanction of law, would be called unjust. And hence the sentiment of injustice came to be attached, not to all violations of law, but only to violations of such laws as ought to exist, including such as *ought* to exist, but do not; and to laws themselves, if supposed to be contrary to what ought to be law. In this manner the idea of law and of its injunctions was still predominant in the notion of justice, even when the laws actually in force ceased to be accepted as the standard of it.

It is true that mankind consider the idea of justice and its obligations as applicable to many things which neither are, nor is it desired that they should be, regulated by law. Nobody desires that laws should interfere with the whole detail of private life; yet everyone allows that in all daily conduct a person may and does show himself to be either just or unjust. But even here, the idea of the breach of what ought to be law, still lingers in a modified shape. It would always give us pleasure, and chime in with our feelings of fitness, that acts which we deem unjust should be punished, though we do not always think it expedient that this should be done by the tribunals. We forego that gratification on account of incidental inconveniences. We should be glad to see just conduct enforced and injustice repressed, even in the minutest details, if we were not, with reason, afraid of trusting the magistrate with so unlimited an amount of power over individuals. When we think that a person is bound in justice to do a thing, it is an ordinary form of language to say that he ought to be compelled to do it. We should be gratified to see the obligation enforced by anybody who had the power. If we see that its enforcement by law would be inexpedient, we lament the impossibility, we consider the impunity given to injustice as an evil, and strive to make amends for it by bringing a strong expression of our own and the public disapprobation to bear upon the offender. Thus the idea of legal constraint is still the generating idea of the notion of justice, though undergoing several transformations before that notion, as it exists in an advanced state of society, becomes complete.

The above is, I think, a true account, as far as it goes, of the origin and progressive growth of the idea of justice. But we must observe that it contains as yet nothing to distinguish that obligation from moral obligation in general. For the truth is, that the idea of penal sanction, which is the essence of law, enters not only into the conception of injustice, but into that of any kind of wrong. We do not call anything wrong unless we mean to imply that a person ought to be punished in some way or other for doing it: if not by law, by the opinion of his fellow-creatures; if not by opinion, by the reproaches of his own conscience. This seems the real turning point of the distinction between morality and simple expediency. It is a part of the notion of duty in every one of its forms, that a person may rightfully be compelled to fulfil it. Duty is a thing which may be *exacted* from a person, as one exacts a debt. Unless we think that it may be exacted from him, we do not call it his duty. Reasons of prudence, or the interest of other people, may militate against actually exacting it; but the person himself, it is clearly understood, would not be entitled to complain. There are other things, on the contrary, which we wish that people should do, which we like or admire them for doing, perhaps dislike or despise them for not doing, but yet admit that they are not bound to do it: it is not a case of moral obligation; we do not blame them, that is, we do not think that they are proper objects of punishment. How we come by these ideas of deserving and not deserving punishment, will appear, perhaps, in the sequel; but I think there is no doubt that this distinction lies at the bottom of the notions of right and wrong: that we call any conduct wrong, or employ, instead, some other term of dislike or disparagement, according as we think that the person ought, or ought not, to be punished for it; and we say, it would be right to do so and so, or merely that it would be desirable or laudable, according as we would wish to see the person whom it concerns, compelled, or only persuaded and exhorted, to act in that manner.

This, therefore, being the characteristic difference which marks off, not justice, but morality in general, from the remaining provinces of expediency and worthiness; the character is still to be sought which distinguishes justice from other branches of morality. Now it is known that ethical writers divide moral duties into two classes, denoted by the ill-chosen expressions, duties of perfect and of imperfect obligation; the latter being those in which, though the act is obligatory, the particular occasions of performing it are left to our choice—as in the case of charity or beneficence, which we are indeed bound to practice, but not towards any definite person, nor at any prescribed time. In the more precise language of philosophic jurists, duties of perfect obligation are those duties in virtue of which a correlative *right* resides in some person or persons; duties of imperfect obligation are those moral obligations which do not give birth to any right. I think it will be found that this distinction exactly coincides with that which exists between justice and the other obligations of morality. In our survey of the various popular acceptations of justice, the term appeared generally to involve the idea of a personal right—a claim on the part of one or more individuals, like that which the law gives when it confers a proprietary or other legal right. Whether the injustice consists in depriving a person of a possession, or in breaking faith with him, or in treating him worse than he deserves, or worse than other people who have no greater claims, in each case the supposition implies two things—a wrong done, and some assignable person who is wronged. Injustice may also be done by treating a person better than others; but the wrong in this case is to his competitors, who are also assignable persons. It seems to me that this feature in the case—a right in some person, correlative to the moral obligation—constitutes the specific difference between justice, and generosity or beneficence. Justice implies something which is not only right to do, and wrong not to do, but which some individual person can claim from us as his moral right. No one has a moral right to our generosity or beneficence, because we are not morally bound to practice those virtues towards any given individual. And it will be found with respect to this

as to every correct definition, that the instances which seem to conflict with it are those which most confirm it. For if a moralist attempts, as some have done, to make out that mankind generally, though not any given individual, have a right to all the good we can do them, he at once, by that thesis, includes generosity and beneficence within the category of justice. He is obliged to say that our utmost exertions are *due* to our fellow-creatures, thus assimilating them to a debt; or that nothing less can be a sufficient *return* for what society does for us, thus classing the case as one of gratitude; both of which are acknowledged cases of justice. Whenever there is a right, the case is one of justice, and not of the virtue of beneficence; and whoever does not place the distinction between justice and morality in general, where we have now placed it, will be found to make no distinction between them at all, but to merge all morality in justice. . . .

When we call anything a person's right, we mean that he has a valid claim on society to protect him in the possession of it, either by the force of law, or by that of education and opinion. If he has what we consider a sufficient claim, on whatever account, to have something guaranteed to him by society, we say that he has a right to it. If we desire to prove that anything does not belong to him by right, we think this done as soon as it is admitted that society ought not to take measures for securing it to him, but should leave him to chance, or to his own exertions. Thus a person is said to have a right to what he can earn in fair professional competition, because society ought not to allow any other person to hinder him from endeavoring to earn in that manner as much as he can. But he has not a right to three hundred a year, though he may happen to be earning it; because society is not called on to provide that he shall earn that sum. On the contrary, if he owns ten thousand pounds three per cent stock, he *has* a right to three hundred a year; because society has come under an obligation to provide him with an income of that amount.

To have a right, then, is, I conceive, to have something which society ought to defend me in the possession of. If the objector goes on to ask why it ought, I can give him no other reason than general utility. If that expression does not seem to convey a sufficient feeling of the strength of the obligation, nor to account for the peculiar energy of the feeling, it is because there goes to the composition of the sentiment, not a rational only, but also an animal element, the thirst for retaliation; and this thirst derives its intensity, as well as its moral justification, from the extraordinarily important and impressive kind of utility which is concerned. The interest involved is that of security, to everyone's feelings the most vital of all interests. All other earthly benefits are needed by one person, not needed by another; and many of them can, if necessary, be cheerfully foregone, or replaced by something else; but security no human being can possibly do without; on it we depend for all our immunity from evil, and for the whole value of all and every good beyond the passing moment; since nothing but the gratification of the instant could be of any worth to us, if we could be deprived of anything the next instant by whoever was momentarily stronger than ourselves. Now this most indispensable of all necessaries after physical nutriment, cannot be had unless the machinery for providing it is kept unintermittedly in active play. Our notion, therefore, of the claim we have on our fellow-creatures to join in making safe for us the very groundwork of our existence, gathers feelings around it so much more intense than those concerned in any of the more common cases of utility, that the difference in degree (as is often the case in psychology) becomes a real difference in kind. The claim assumes that character of absoluteness, that apparent infinity, and incommensurability with all other considerations, which constitute the distinction between the feeling of right and wrong and that of ordinary expediency and inexpediency. The feelings concerned

are so powerful, and we count so positively on finding a responsive feeling in others (all being alike interested), that *ought* and *should* grow into *must*, and recognized indispensability becomes a moral necessity, analogous to physical, and often not inferior to it in binding force.

If the preceding analysis, or something resembling it, be not the correct account of the notion of justice; if justice be totally independent of utility, and be a standard *per se*, which the mind can recognize by simple introspection of itself; it is hard to understand why that internal oracle is so ambiguous, and why so many things appear either just or unjust, according to the light in which they are regarded. . . .

To take [an] example from a subject already once referred to. In a co-operative industrial association, is it just or not that talent or skill should give a title to superior remuneration? On the negative side of the question it is argued that whoever does the best he can, deserves equally well, and ought not in justice to be put in a position of inferiority for no fault of his own; that superior abilities have already advantages more than enough, in the admiration they excite, the personal influence they command, and the internal sources of satisfaction attending them, without adding to these a superior share of the world's goods; and that society is bound in justice rather to make compensation to the less favored for this unmerited inequality of advantages, than to aggravate it. On the contrary side it is contended that society receives more from the more efficient laborer; that his services being more useful, society owes him a larger return for them; that a greater share of the joint result is actually his work, and not to allow his claim to it is a kind of robbery; that if he is only to receive as much as others, he can only be justly required to produce as much, and to give a smaller amount of time and exertion, proportioned to his superior efficiency. Who shall decide between these appeals to conflicting principles of justice? Justice has in this case two sides to it, which it is impossible to bring into harmony, and the two disputants have chosen opposite sides; the one looks to what it is just that the individual should receive, the other to what it is just that the community should give. Each, from his own point of view, is unanswerable; and any choice between them, on grounds of justice, must be perfectly arbitrary. Social utility alone can decide the preference.

How many, again, and how irreconcilable, are the standards of justice to which reference is made in discussing the repartition of taxation. One opinion is, that payment to the State should be in numerical proportion to pecuniary means. Others think that justice dictates what they term graduated taxation; taking a higher percentage from those who have more to spare. In point of natural justice a strong case might be made for disregarding means altogether, and taking the same absolute sum (whenever it could be got) from everyone—as the subscribers to a mess, or to a club, all pay the same sum for the same privileges, whether they can all equally afford it or not. Since the protection (it might be said) of law and government is afforded to, and is equally required by all, there is no injustice in making all buy it at the same price. It is reckoned justice, not injustice, that a dealer should charge to all customers the same price for the same article, not a price varying according to their means of payment. This doctrine, as applied to taxation, finds no advocates, because it conflicts so strongly with man's feelings of humanity and social expediency; but the principle of justice which it invokes is as true and as binding as those which can be appealed to against it. Accordingly it exerts a tacit influence on the line of defense employed for other modes of assessing taxation. People feel obliged to argue that the State does more for the rich than for the poor, as a justification for its taking more from them: though this is in reality not true, for the rich would be far better able to protect themselves, in the absence of law or government,

than the poor, and indeed would probably be successful in converting the poor into their slaves. Others, again, so far defer to the same conception of justice, as to maintain that all should pay an equal capitation tax for the protection of their persons (these being of equal value to all), and an equal tax for the protection of their property, which is unequal. To this others reply that the all of one man is as valuable to him as the all of another. From these confusions there is no other mode of extrication than the utilitarian.

Is, then, the difference between the just and the expedient a merely imaginary distinction? Have mankind been under a delusion thinking that justice is a more sacred thing than policy, and that the latter ought only to be listened to after the former has been satisfied? By no means. The exposition we have given of the nature and origin of the sentiment, recognizes a real distinction: and no one of those who profess the most sublime contempt for the consequences of actions as an element in their morality, attaches more importance to the distinction than I do. While I dispute the pretensions of any theory which sets up an imaginary standard of justice not grounded on utility, I account the justice which is grounded on utility to be the chief part, and incomparably the most sacred and binding part, of all morality. Justice is a name for certain classes of moral rules which concern the essentials of human well-being more nearly, and are therefore of more absolute obligation, than any other rules for the guidance of life; and the notion which we have found to be of the essence of the idea of justice, that of a right residing in an individual, implies and testifies to this more binding obligation.

The moral rules which forbid mankind to hurt one another (in which we must never forget to include wrongful interference with each other's freedom) are more vital to human well-being than any other maxims, however important, which only point out the best mode of managing some department of human affairs. They have also the peculiarity, that they are the main element in determining the whole of the social feelings of mankind. It is their observance which alone preserves peace among human beings: if obedience to them were not the rule, and disobedience the exception, everyone would see in everyone else an enemy, against whom he must be perpetually guarding himself. What is hardly less important, these are the precepts which mankind have the strongest and the most direct inducements for impressing upon one another. By merely giving to each other prudential instruction or exhortation, they may gain, or think they gain, nothing; in inculcating on each other the duty of positive beneficence they have an unmistakable interest, but far less in degree: a person may possibly not need the benefits of others, but he always needs that they should not do him hurt. Thus the moralities which protect every individual from being harmed by others, either directly or by being hindered in his freedom of pursuing his own good, are at once those which he himself has most at heart, and those which he has the strongest interest in publishing and enforcing by word and deed. It is by a person's observance of these that his fitness to exist as one of the fellowship of human beings is tested and decided; for on that depends his being a nuisance or not to those with whom he is in contact. Now it is these moralities primarily which compose the obligations of justice. The most marked cases of injustice, and those which give the tone to the feeling of repugnance which characterizes the sentiment, are acts of wrongful aggression, or wrongful exercise of power over someone; the next are those which consist in wrongfully withholding from him something which is his due: in both cases, inflicting on him a positive hurt, either in the form of direct suffering, or of the privation of some good which he had reasonable ground, either of a physical or of a social kind, for counting upon. . . .

That first of judicial virtues, impartiality, is an obligation of justice, partly . . . as being a necessary condition of the fulfillment of the other obligations of justice. But this is not the only source of the exalted rank, among human obligations, of those maxims of equality and impartiality which, both in popular estimation and in that of the most enlightened, are included among the precepts of justice. In one point of view, they may be considered as corollaries from the principles already laid down. If it is a duty to do to each according to his deserts, returning good for good as well as repressing evil by evil, it necessarily follows that we should treat all equally well (when no higher duty forbids) who have deserved equally well of us, and that society should treat all equally well who have deserved equally well of it, that is, who have deserved equally well absolutely. This is the highest abstract standard of social and distributive justice; towards which all institutions, and the efforts of all virtuous citizens, should be made in the utmost possible degree to converge. But this great moral duty rests upon a still deeper foundation, being a direct emanation from the first principle of morals, and not a mere logical corollary from secondary or derivative doctrines. It is involved in the very meaning of utility, or the greatest happiness principle. That principle is a mere form of words without rational signification, unless one person's happiness, supposed equal in degree (with the proper allowance made for kind), is counted for exactly as much as another's. Those conditions being supplied, Bentham's dictum, "everybody to count for one, nobody for more than one," might be written under the principle of utility as an explanatory commentary. The equal claim of everybody to happiness in the estimation of the moralist and of the legislator, involves an equal claim to all the means of happiness, except in so far as the inevitable conditions of human life, and the general interest, in which that of every individual is included, set limits to the maxim; and those limits ought to be strictly construed. As every other maxim of justice, so this is by no means applied or held applicable universally;

on the contrary, as I have already remarked, it bends to every person's ideas of social expediency. But in whatever case it is deemed applicable at all, it is held to be the dictate of justice. All persons are deemed to have a right to equality of treatment, except when some recognized social expediency requires the reverse. And hence all social inequalities which have ceased to be considered expedient, assume the character not of simple inexpediency, but of injustice, and appear so tyrannical, that people are apt to wonder how they ever could have been tolerated; forgetful that they themselves perhaps tolerate other inequalities under an equally mistaken notion of expediency, the correction of which would make that which they approve seem quite as monstrous as what they have at last learnt to condemn. The entire history of social improvement has been a series of transitions, by which one custom or institution after another, from being a supposed primary necessity of social existence, has passed into the rank of a universally stigmatized injustice and tyranny. So it has been with the distinctions of slaves and freemen, nobles and serfs, patricians and plebeians; and so it will be, and in part already is, with the aristocracies of color, race, and sex.

It appears from what has been said that justice is a name for certain moral requirements which, regarded collectively, stand higher in the scale of social utility, and are therefore of more paramount obligation, than any others; though particular cases may occur in which some other social duty is so important, as to overrule any one of the general maxims of justice. Thus, to save a life, it may not only be allowable but a duty to steal or take by force the necessary food

or medicine, or to kidnap and compel to officiate the only qualified medical practitioner. In such cases, as we do not call anything justice which is not a virtue; we usually say, not that justice must give way to some other moral principle, but that what is just in ordinary cases is, by reason of that other principle, not just in the particular case. By this useful accommodation of language, the character of indefeasibility attributed to justice is kept up, and we are saved from the necessity of maintaining that there can be laudable injustice.

The considerations which have now been adduced resolve, I conceive, the only real difficulty in the utilitarian theory of morals. It has always been evident that all cases of justice are also cases of expediency: the difference is in the peculiar sentiment which attaches to the former, as contradistinguished from the latter. If this characteristic sentiment has been sufficiently accounted for; . . . and if this feeling not only does but ought to exist in all the classes of cases to which the idea of justice corresponds: that idea no longer presents itself as a stumbling-block to the utilitarian ethics. Justice remains the appropriate name for certain social utilities which are vastly more important, and therefore more absolute and imperative, than any other are as a class (though not more so than others may be in particular cases); and which, therefore, ought to be, as well as naturally are, guarded by a sentiment not only different in degree, but also in kind; distinguished from the milder feeling which attaches to the mere idea of promoting human pleasure or convenience, at once by the more definite nature of its commands, and by the sterner character of its sanctions.

QUESTIONS FOR DISCUSSION

1. Can Mill adequately explain what is unjust about slavery? How or why not? Be sure to consider different kinds of slavery.

2. Is Mill's overall theory really a version of utilitarianism? Why or why not?

A THEORY OF JUSTICE

JOHN RAWLS

THE ROLE OF JUSTICE

Justice is the first virtue of social institutions, as truth is of systems of thought. A theory however elegant and economical must be rejected or revised if it is untrue; likewise laws and institutions no matter how efficient and well-arranged must be reformed or abolished if they are unjust. Each person possesses an inviolability founded on justice that even the welfare of society as a whole cannot override. For this reason justice denies that the loss of freedom for some is made right by a greater good shared by others. It does not allow that the sacrifices imposed on a few are outweighed by the larger sum of advantages enjoyed by many. Therefore in a just society the liberties of equal citizenship are taken as settled; the rights secured by justice are not subject to political bargaining or to the calculus of social interests. The only thing that permits us to acquiesce in an erroneous theory is the lack of a better one; analogously, an injustice is tolerable only when it is necessary to avoid an even greater injustice. Being first virtues of human activities, truth and justice are uncompromising.

These propositions seem to express our intuitive conviction of the primacy of justice. No doubt they are expressed too strongly. In any event I wish to inquire whether these contentions or others similar to them are sound, and if so how they can be accounted for. To this end it is necessary to work out a theory of justice in the light of which these assertions can be interpreted and assessed. I shall begin by considering the role of the principles of justice. Let us assume, to fix ideas, that a society is a more or less self-sufficient association of persons who in their relations to one another recognize cer-

tain rules of conduct as binding and who for the most part act in accordance with them. Suppose further that these rules specify a system of cooperation designed to advance the good of those taking part in it. Then, although a society is a cooperative venture for mutual advantage, it is typically marked by a conflict as well as by an identity of interests. There is an identity of interests since social cooperation makes possible a better life for all than any would have if each were to live solely by his own efforts. There is a conflict of interests since persons are not indifferent as to how the greater benefits produced by their collaboration are distributed, for in order to pursue their ends they each prefer a larger to a lesser share. A set of principles is required for choosing among the various social arrangements which determine this division of advantages and for underwriting an agreement on the proper distributive shares. These principles are the principles of social justice: they provide a way of assigning rights and duties in the basic institutions of society, and they define the appropriate distribution of the benefits and burdens of social cooperation. . . .

THE MAIN IDEA OF THE THEORY OF JUSTICE

My aim is to present a conception of justice which generalizes and carries to a higher level of abstraction the familiar theory of the social contract as found, say, in Locke, Rousseau, and Kant.[4] In order to do this we are not to think of the original contract as one to enter a particular society or to set up a particular form of government. Rather, the guiding idea is that the principles of justice for the basic structure of society are the object of the original agree-

John Rawls, *A Theory of Justice* (Cambridge: Harvard University Press, 1971)

ment. They are the principles that free and rational persons concerned to further their own interests would accept in an initial position of equality as defining the fundamental terms of their association. These principles are to regulate all further agreements; they specify the kinds of social cooperation that can be entered into and the forms of government that can be established. This way of regarding the principles of justice I shall call justice as fairness.

Thus we are to imagine that those who engage in social cooperation choose together, in one joint act, the principles which are to assign basic rights and duties and to determine the division of social benefits. Men are to decide in advance how they are to regulate their claims against one another and what is to be the foundation charter of their society. Just as each person must decide by rational reflection what constitutes his good, that is, the system of ends which it is rational for him to pursue, so a group of persons must decide once and for all what is to count among them as just and unjust. The choice which rational men would make in this hypothetical situation of equal liberty, assuming for the present that this choice problem has a solution, determines the principles of justice.

In justice as fairness the original position of equality corresponds to the state of nature in the traditional theory of the social contract. This original position is not, of course, thought of as an actual historical state of affairs, much less as a primitive condition of culture. It is understood as a purely hypothetical situation characterized so as to lead to a certain conception of justice. Among the essential features of this situation is that no one knows his place in society, his class position or social status, nor does any one know his fortune in the distribution of natural assets and abilities, his intelligence, strength, and the like. I shall even assume that the parties do not know their conceptions of the good or their special psychological propensities. The principles of justice are chosen behind a veil of ignorance. This ensures that no one is advantaged or disadvantaged in the choice of principles by the

outcome of natural chance or the contingency of social circumstances. Since all are similarly situated and no one is able to design principles to favor his particular condition, the principles of justice are the result of a fair agreement or bargain. For given the circumstances of the original position, the symmetry of everyone's relations to each other, this initial situation is fair between individuals as moral persons, that is, as rational beings with their own ends and capable, I shall assume, of a sense of justice. The original position is, one might say, the appropriate initial status quo, and thus the fundamental agreements reached in it are fair. This explains the propriety of the name "justice as fairness": it conveys the idea that the principles of justice are agreed to in an initial situation that is fair. The name does not mean that the concepts of justice and fairness are the same, any more than the phrase "poetry as metaphor" means that the concepts of poetry and metaphor are the same.

Justice as fairness begins, as I have said, with one of the most general of all choices which persons might make together, namely, with the choice of the first principles of a conception of justice which is to regulate all subsequent criticism and reform of institutions. Then, having chosen a conception of justice, we can suppose that they are to choose a constitution and a legislature to enact laws, and so on, all in accordance with the principles of justice initially agreed upon. Our social situation is just if it is such that by this sequence of hypothetical agreements we would have contracted into the general system of rules which defines it. Moreover, assuming that the original position does determine a set of principles (that is, that a particular conception of justice would be chosen), it will then be true that whenever social institutions satisfy these principles those engaged in them can say to one another that they are cooperating on terms to which they would agree if they were free and equal persons whose relations with respect to one another were fair. They could all view their arrangements as meeting the stipulations which they would acknowledge in an initial situation that embodies widely accepted and reasonable constraints on the choice of principles. The general recognition of this fact would provide the basis for a public acceptance of the corresponding principles of justice. No society can, of course, be a scheme of cooperation which men enter voluntarily in a literal sense; each person finds himself placed at birth in some particular position in some particular society, and the nature of this position materially affects his life prospects. Yet a society satisfying the principles of justice as fairness comes as close as a society can to being a voluntary scheme, for it meets the principles which free and equal persons would assent to under circumstances that are fair. In this sense its members are autonomous and the obligations they recognize self-imposed.

One feature of justice as fairness is to think of the parties in the initial situation as rational and mutually disinterested. This does not mean that the parties are egoists, that is, individuals with only certain kinds of interests, say in wealth, prestige, and domination. But they are conceived as not taking an interest in one another's interests. They are to presume that even their spiritual aims may be opposed, in the way that the aims of those of different religions may be opposed. Moreover, the concept of rationality must be interpreted as far as possible in the narrow sense, standard in economic theory, of taking the most effective means to given ends. I shall modify this concept to some extent. . . , but one must try to avoid introducing into it any controversial ethical elements. The initial situation must be characterized by stipulations that are widely accepted.

In working out the conception of justice as fairness one main task clearly is to determine which principles of justice would be chosen in the original position. To do this we must describe this situation in some detail and formulate with care the problem of choice which it presents. . . . It may be observed, however, that once the principles of justice are thought of as arising from an original agreement in a situation of equality, it is an open question whether the principle of utility would be acknowledged. Offhand it hardly seems likely that persons who view themselves as equals, entitled to press their claims upon one another, would agree to a principle which may require lesser life prospects for some simply for the sake of a greater sum of advantages enjoyed by others. Since each desires to protect his interests, his capacity to advance his conception of the good, no one has a reason to acquiesce in an enduring loss for himself in order to bring about a greater net balance of satisfaction. In the absence of strong and lasting benevolent impulses, a rational man would not accept a basic structure merely because it maximized the algebraic sum of advantages irrespective of its permanent effects on his own basic rights and interests. Thus it seems that the principle of utility is incompatible with the conception of social cooperation among equals for mutual advantage. It appears to be inconsistent with the idea of reciprocity implicit in the notion of a well-ordered society. Or, at any rate, so I shall argue.

I shall maintain instead that the persons in the initial situation would choose two rather different principles: the first requires equality in the assignment of basic rights and duties, while the second holds that social and economic inequalities, for example inequalities of wealth and authority, are just only if they result in compensating benefits for everyone, and in particular for the least advantaged members of society. These principles rule out justifying institutions on the grounds that the hardships of some are offset by a greater good in the aggregate. It may be expedient but it is not just that some should have less in order that others may prosper. But there is no injustice in the greater benefits earned by a few provided that the situation of persons not so fortunate is thereby improved. The intuitive idea is that since everyone's well-being depends upon a scheme of cooperation without which no one could have a satisfactory life, the division of advantages should be such as to draw forth the willing cooperation of everyone taking part in it, including those less well situated. Yet this can be expected only if reasonable terms are proposed. The two principles mentioned seem to be a fair agreement on the basis of which those better endowed, or more fortunate in their social position, neither of which we can be said to deserve, could expect the willing cooperation of others when some workable scheme is a necessary condition of the welfare of all. Once we decide to look for a conception of justice that nullifies the accidents of natural endowment and the contingencies of social circumstance as counters in quest for political and economic advantage, we are led to these principles. They express the result of leaving aside those aspects of the social world that seem arbitrary from a moral point of view.

The problem of the choice of principles, however, is extremely difficult. I do not expect the answer I shall suggest to be convincing to everyone. It is, therefore, worth noting from the outset that justice as fairness, like other contract views, consists of two parts: (1) an interpretation of the initial situation and of the problem of choice posed there, and (2) a set of principles which, it is argued, would be agreed to. One may accept the first part of the theory (or some variant thereof), but not the other, and conversely. The concept of the initial contractual situation may seem reasonable although the particular principles proposed are rejected. To be sure, I want to maintain that the most appropriate conception of this situation does lead to principles of justice contrary to utilitarianism and perfectionism, and therefore that the contract doctrine provides an alternative to these views. Still, one may dispute this contention even though one grants that the contractarian method is a useful way of studying ethical theories and of setting forth their underlying assumptions. . . .

TWO PRINCIPLES OF JUSTICE

I shall now state in a provisional form the two principles of justice that I believe would be chosen in the original position. In this section I wish to make only the most general comments, and therefore the first formulation of these principles is tentative. . . .

The first statement of the two principles reads as follows.

First: each person is to have an equal right to the most extensive basic liberty compatible with a similar liberty for others.

Second: social and economic inequalities are to be arranged so that they are both (a) reasonably expected to be to everyone's advantage, and (b) attached to positions and offices open to all. . . .

By way of general comment, these principles primarily apply, as I have said, to the basic structure of society. They are to govern the assignment of rights and duties and to regulate the distribution of social and economic advantages. As their formulation suggests, these principles presuppose that the social structure can be divided into two more or less distinct parts, the first principle applying to the one, the second to the other. They distinguish between those aspects of the social system that define and secure the equal liberties of citizenship and those that specify and establish social and economic inequalities. The basic liberties of citizens are, roughly speaking, political liberty (the right to vote and to be eligible for public office) together with freedom of speech and assembly; liberty of conscience and freedom of thought; freedom of the person along with the right to hold (personal) property; and freedom from arbitrary arrest and seizure as defined by the concept of the rule of law. These liberties are all required to be equal by the first principle, since citizens of a just society are to have the same basic rights.

The second principle applies, in the first approximation, to the distribution of income and wealth and to the design of organizations that make use of differences in authority and responsibility, or chains of command. While the distribution of wealth and income need not be equal, it must be to everyone's advantage, and at the same time, positions of authority and offices of command must be accessible to all. One applies the second principle by holding positions open, and then, subject to the constraint, arranges social and economic inequalities so that everyone benefits.

These principles are to be arranged in a serial order with the first principle prior to the second. This ordering means that a departure from the institutions of equal liberty required by the first principle cannot be justified by, or compensated for, by greater social and economic advantages. The distribution of wealth and income, and the hierarchies of authority, must be consistent with both the liberties of equal citizenship and equality of opportunity.

It is clear that these principles are rather specific in their content, and their acceptance rests on certain assumptions that I must eventually try to explain and justify. A theory of justice depends upon a theory of society in ways that will become evident as we proceed. For the present, it should be observed that the two principles (and this holds for all formulations) are a special case of a more general conception of justice that can be expressed as follows:

> All social values—liberty and opportunity, income and wealth, and the bases of self-respect—are to be distributed equally unless an unequal distribution of any, or all, of these values is to everyone's advantage.

Injustice, then, is simply inequalities that are not to the benefit of all. Of course, this conception is extremely vague and requires interpretation.

As a first step, suppose that the basic structure of society distributes certain primary goods, that is, things that every rational man is presumed to want. These goods normally have a use whatever a person's rational plan of life. For simplicity, assume that the chief primary goods at the disposition of society are rights and liberties, powers and opportunities, income and wealth. . . . These are the social primary goods.

Other primary goods such as health and vigor, intelligence and imagination, are natural goods; although their possession is influenced by the basic structures, they are not so directly under its control. Imagine, then, a hypothetical initial arrangement in which all the social primary goods are equally distributed: everyone has similar rights and duties, and income and wealth are evenly shared. This state of affairs provides a benchmark for judging improvements. If certain inequalities of wealth and organizational powers would make everyone better off than in this hypothetical starting situation, then they accord with the general conception.

Now it is possible, at least theoretically, that by giving up some of their fundamental liberties men are sufficiently compensated by the resulting social and economic gains. The general conception of justice imposes no restrictions on what sort of inequalities are permissible; it only requires that everyone's position be improved. We need not suppose anything so drastic as consenting to a condition of slavery. Imagine instead that men forego certain political rights when the economic returns are significant and their capacity to influence the course of policy by the exercise of these rights would be marginal in any case. It is this kind of exchange which the two principles as stated rule out; being arranged in serial order they do not permit exchanges between basic liberties and economic and social gains. The serial ordering of principles expresses an underlying preference among primary social goods. When this preference is rational so likewise is the choice of these principles in this order. . . .

Another thing to bear in mind is that when principles mention persons, or require that everyone gain from an inequality, the reference is to representative persons holding the various social positions, or offices, or whatever, established by the basic structure. Thus in applying the second principle I assume that it is possible to assign an expectation of well-being to representative individuals holding these positions. This expectation indicates their life prospects as viewed from their social station. In general, the expectations of representative persons depend upon the distribution of rights and duties throughout the basic structure. When this changes, expectations change. I assume, then, that expectations are connected: by raising the prospects of the representative man in one position we presumably increase or decrease the prospects of representative men in other positions. Since it applies to institutional forms, the second principle (or rather the first part of it) refers to the expectations of representative individuals.... [N]either principle applies to distributions of particular goods to particular individuals who may be identified by their proper names. The situation where someone is considering how to allocate certain commodities to needy persons who are known to him is not within the scope of the principles. They are meant to regulate basic institutional arrangements. We must not assume that there is much similarity from the standpoint of justice between an administrative allotment of goods to specific persons and the appropriate design of society. Our common sense intuitions for the former may be a poor guide to the latter.

Now the second principle insists that each person benefit from permissible inequalities in the basic structure. This means that it must be reasonable for each relevant representative man defined by this structure, when he views it as a going concern, to prefer his prospects with the inequality to his prospects without it. One is not allowed to justify differences in income or organizational powers on the ground that the disadvantages of those in one position are outweighed by the greater advantages of those in another. Much less can infringements of liberty be counterbalanced in this way. Applied to the basic structure, the principle of utility would have us maximize the sum of expectations of representative men (weighted by the number of persons they represent, on the classical view); and this would permit us to compensate for the losses of some by the gains of others. Instead, the two principles require

that everyone benefit from economic and social inequalities. It is obvious, however, that there are indefinitely many ways in which all may be advantaged when the initial arrangement of equality is taken as a benchmark. How then are we to choose among these possibilities? The principles must be specified so that they yield a determinate conclusion. I now turn to this problem.

INTERPRETATIONS OF THE SECOND PRINCIPLE

... The first interpretation ... I shall refer to as the system of natural liberty.... I assume in all interpretations that the first principle of equal liberty is satisfied and that the economy is roughly a free market system, although the means of production may or may not be privately owned. The system of natural liberty asserts, then, that a basic structure satisfying the principle of efficiency [that is, which it is impossible to change so as to make some persons better off without at the same time making other persons worse off] and in which positions are open to those able and willing to strive for them will lead to a just distribution. Assigning rights and duties in this way is thought to give a scheme which allocates wealth and income, authority and responsibility, in a fair way whatever this allocation turns out to be. The doctrine includes an important element of pure procedural justice which is carried over to the other interpretations....

In the system of natural liberty the initial distribution is regulated by the arrangements implicit in the conception of careers open to talents.... These arrangements presuppose a background of equal liberty (as specified by the first principle) and a free market economy. They require a formal equality of opportunity in that all have at least the same legal rights of access to all advantaged social positions. But since there is no effort to preserve an equality, or similarity, of social conditions, except insofar as this is necessary to preserve the requisite background institutions, the initial distribution of assets for any period of time is strongly influenced by natural and social contingencies. The existing distribution of income and wealth, say, is the cumulative effect of prior distributions of natural assets—that is, natural talents and abilities—as these have been developed or left unrealized, and their use favored or disfavored over time by social circumstances and such chance contingencies as accident and good fortune. Intuitively, the most obvious injustice of the system of natural liberty is that it permits distributive shares to be improperly influenced by these factors so arbitrary from a moral point of view.

The liberal interpretation, as I shall refer to it, tries to correct for this by adding to the requirement of careers open to talents the further condition of the principle of fair equality of opportunity. The thought here is that positions are to be not only open in a formal sense, but that all should have a fair chance to attain them. Offhand it is not clear what is meant, but we might say that those with similar abilities and skills should have similar life chances. More specifically, assuming that there is a distribution of natural assets, those who are at the same level of talent and ability, and have the same willingness to use them, should have the same prospects of success regardless of their initial place in the social system, that is, irrespective of the income class into which they are born. In all sectors of society there should be roughly equal prospects of culture and achievement for everyone similarly motivated and endowed. The expectations of those with the same abilities and aspirations should not be affected by their social class.

The liberal interpretation of the two principles seeks, then, to mitigate the influence of social contingencies and natural fortune on distributive shares. To accomplish this end it is necessary to impose further basic structural conditions on the social system. Free market arrangements must be set within a framework of political and legal institutions which regulates the overall trends of economic events and preserves the social conditions necessary for fair equality of opportunity. The elements of this framework are familiar enough, though it may be worthwhile to recall the importance of preventing excessive accumulations of property and wealth and of maintaining equal opportunities of education for all. Chances to acquire cultural knowledge and skills should not depend upon one's class position, and so the school system, whether public or private, should be designed to even out class barriers.

While the liberal conception seems clearly preferable to the system of natural liberty, intuitively it still appears defective. For one thing, even if it works to perfection in eliminating the influence of social contingencies, it still permits the distribution of wealth and income to be determined by the natural distribution of abilities and talents. Within the limits allowed by the background arrangements, distributive shares are decided by the outcome of the natural lottery; and this outcome is arbitrary from a moral perspective. There is no more reason to permit the distribution of income and wealth to be settled by the distribution of natural assets than by historical and social fortune. Furthermore, the principle of fair opportunity can be only imperfectly carried out, at least as long as the institution of the family exists. The extent to which natural capacities develop and reach fruition is affected by all kinds of social conditions and class attitudes. Even the willingness to make an effort, to try, and so to be deserving in the ordinary sense is itself dependent upon happy family and social circumstances. It is impossible in practice to secure equal chances of achievement and culture for those similarly endowed, and therefore we may want to adopt a principle which recognizes this fact and also mitigates the arbitrary effects of the natural lottery itself. That the liberal conception fails to do this encourages one to look for another interpretation of the two principles of justice. . . .

The democratic interpretation . . . is arrived at by combining the principle of fair equality of opportunity with the difference principle. This principle . . . singl[es] out a particular position from which the social and economic inequalities of the basic structure are to be judged. Assuming the framework of institutions required by equal liberty and fair equality of opportunity, the higher expectations of those better situated are just if and only if they work as part of a scheme which improves the expectations of the least advantaged members of society. The intuitive idea is that the social order is not to establish and secure the more attractive prospects of those better off unless doing so is to the advantage of those less fortunate. . . .

To illustrate the difference principle, consider the distribution of income among social classes. Let us suppose that the various income groups correlate with representative individuals by reference to whose expectations we can judge the distribution. Now those starting out as members of the entrepreneurial class in property-owning democracy, say, have a better prospect than those who begin in the class of unskilled laborers. It seems likely that this will be true even when the social injustices which now exist are removed. What, then, can possibly justify this kind of initial inequality in life prospects? According to the difference principle, it is justifiable only if the difference in expectation is to the advantage of the representative man who is worse off, in this case the representative unskilled worker. The inequality in expectation is permissible only if lowering it would make the working class even more worse off. Supposedly, given the rider in the second principle concerning open positions, and the principle of liberty generally, the greater expectations allowed to entrepreneurs encourages them to do things which raise the long-term prospects of laboring class. Their better prospects act as incentives so that the economic process is more efficient, innovation proceeds at a faster pace, and so on. Eventually the resulting material benefits spread throughout the system and to the least advantaged. I shall not consider how far these things are true. The point is that something of this kind must

be argued if these inequalities are to be just by the difference principle. . . .

THE REASONING LEADING TO THE TWO PRINCIPLES OF JUSTICE

In this . . . section . . . I take up the choice between the two principles of justice and the principle of average utility. Determining the rational preference between these two options is perhaps the central problem in developing the conception of justice as fairness as a viable alternative to the utilitarian tradition. I shall begin in this section by presenting some intuitive remarks favoring the two principles. I shall also discuss briefly the qualitative structure of the argument that needs to be made if the case for these principles is to be conclusive.

It will be recalled that the general conception of justice as fairness requires that all primary social goods be distributed equally unless an unequal distribution would be to everyone's advantage. No restrictions are placed on exchanges of these goods and therefore a lesser liberty can be compensated for by greater social and economic benefits. Now looking at the situation from the standpoint of one person selected arbitrarily, there is no way for him to win special advantages for himself. Nor, on the other hand, are there grounds for his acquiescing in special disadvantages. Since it is not reasonable for him to expect more than an equal share in the division of social goods, and since it is not rational for him to agree to less, the sensible thing for him to do is to acknowledge as the first principle of justice one requiring an equal distribution. Indeed, this principle is so obvious that we would expect it to occur to anyone immediately.

Thus, the parties start with a principle establishing equal liberty for all, including equality of opportunity, as well as an equal distribution of income and wealth. But there is no reason why this acknowledgement should be final. If there are inequalities in the basic structure that work to make everyone better off in comparison with the benchmark of initial equality, why not permit them? The immediate gain which a greater equality might allow can be regarded as intelligently invested in view of its future return. If, for example, these inequalities set up various incentives which succeed in eliciting more productive efforts, a person in the original position may look upon them as necessary to cover the costs of training and to encourage effective performance. One might think that ideally individuals should want to serve one another. But since the parties are assumed not to take an interest in one another's interests, their acceptance of these inequalities is only the acceptance of the relations in which men stand in the circumstances of justice. They have no grounds for complaining of one another's motives. A person in the original position would, therefore, concede the justice of these inequalities. Indeed, it would be short-sighted of him not to do so. He would hesitate to agree to these regularities only if he would be dejected by the bare knowledge or perception that others were better situated; and I have assumed that the parties decide as if they are not moved by envy. In order to make the principle regulating inequalities determinate, one looks at the system from the standpoint of the least advantaged representative man. Inequalities are permissible when they maximize, or at least all contribute to, the long-term expectations of the least fortunate group in society.

Now this general conception imposes no constraints on what sorts of inequalities are allowed, whereas the special conception, by putting the two principles in serial order (with the necessary adjustments in meaning), forbids exchanges between basic liberties and economic and social benefits. I shall not try to justify this ordering here. . . . But roughly, the idea underlying this ordering is that if the parties assume that their basic liberties can be effectively exercised, they will not exchange a lesser liberty for an improvement in economic well-being. It is only when social conditions do not allow the effective establishment of these rights that one can concede their limitation; and

these restrictions can be granted only to the extent that they are necessary to prepare the way for a free society. The denial of equal liberty can be defended only if it is necessary to raise the level of civilization so that in due course these freedoms can be enjoyed. Thus in adopting a serial order we are in effect making a special assumption in the original position, namely, that the parties know that the conditions of their society, whatever they are, admit the effective realization of the equal liberties. The serial ordering of the two principles of justice eventually comes to be reasonable if the general conception is consistently followed. This lexical ranking is the long-run tendency of the general view. For the most part I shall assume that the requisite circumstances for the serial order obtain.

It seems clear from these remarks that the two principles are at least a plausible conception of justice. The question, though, is how one is to argue for them more systematically. Now there are several things to do. One can work out their consequences for institutions and note their implications for fundamental social policy. In this way they are tested by a comparison with our considered judgments of justice. . . . But one can also try to find arguments in their favor that are decisive from the standpoint of the original position. In order to see how this might be done, it is useful as a heuristic device to think of the two principles as the maximin solution to the problem of social justice. There is an analogy between the two principles and the maximin rule for choice under uncertainty. This is evident from the fact that the two principles are those a person would choose for the design of a society in which his enemy is to assign him his place. The maximin rule tells us to rank alternatives by their worst possible outcomes: we are to adopt the alternative the worst outcome of which is superior to the worst outcomes of the others. The persons in the original position do not, of course, assume that their initial place in society is decided by a malevolent opponent. . . . [T]hey should not reason from false premises. The veil of ignorance does not violate this idea, since an absence of information is not misinformation. But that the two principles of justice would be chosen if the parties were forced to protect themselves against such a contingency explains the sense in which this conception is the maximin solution. And this analogy suggests that if the original position has been described so that it is rational for the parties to adopt the conservative attitude expressed by this rule, a conclusive argument can indeed be constructed for these principles. Clearly the maximin rule is not, in general, a suitable guide for choices under uncertainty. But it is attractive in situations marked by certain special features. My aim, then, is to show that a good case can be made for the two principles based on the fact that the original position manifests these features to the fullest possible degree, carrying them to the limit, so to speak.

Consider the gain-and-loss table below. It represents the gains and losses for a situation which is not a game of strategy. There is no one playing against the person making the decision; instead he is faced with several possible circumstances which may or may not obtain. Which circumstances happen to exist does not depend upon what the person choosing decides or whether he announces his moves in advance. The numbers in the table are monetary values (in hundreds of dollars) in comparison with some initial situation. The gain (g) depends upon the individual's decision (d) and the circumstances (c). Thus $g = f(d, c)$. Assuming that there are three possible decisions and three possible circumstances, we might have this gain-and-loss table.

	Circumstances		
Decisions	c_1	c_2	c_3
d_1	–7	8	12
d_2	–8	7	14
d_3	5	6	8

The maximin rule requires that we make the third decision. For in this case the worst that can happen is that one gains five hundred dollars, which is better than the worst for the other actions. If we adopt one of these we may lose either eight or seven hundred dollars. Thus, the choice of d_3 maximizes $f(d,c)$ for that value of c, which for a given d, minimizes f. The term "maximin" means the *maximum minimorum*; and the rule directs our attention to the worst that can happen under any proposed course of action, and to decide in the light of that.

Now there appear to be three chief features of situations that give plausibility to this unusual rule. First, since the rule takes no account of the likelihoods of the possible circumstances, there must be some reason for sharply discounting estimates of these probabilities. Offhand, the most natural rule of choice would seem to be to compute the expectation of monetary gain for each decision and then to adopt the course of action with the highest prospect. . . . Thus it must be, for example, that the situation is one in which a knowledge of likelihoods is impossible, or at best extremely insecure. In this case it is unreasonable not to be skeptical of probabilistic calculations unless there is no other way out, particularly if the decision is a fundamental one that needs to be justified to others.

The second feature that suggests the maximin rule is the following: the person choosing has a conception of the good such that he cares very little, if anything, for what he might gain above the minimum stipend that he can, in fact, be sure of by following the maximin rule. It is not worthwhile for him to take a chance for the sake of a further advantage, especially when it may turn out that he loses much that is important to him. This last provision brings in the third feature, namely, that the rejected alternatives have outcomes that one can hardly accept. The situation involves grave risks. Of course these features work most effectively in combination. The paradigm situation for following the maximin rule is when all three features are realized to the highest degree. This rule does not, then, generally apply, nor of course is it self-evident. Rather, it is a maxim, a rule of thumb, that comes into its own in special circumstances. Its application depends upon the qualitative structure of the possible gains and losses in relation to one's conception of the good, all this against a background in which it is reasonable to discount conjectural estimates of likelihoods.

It should be noted, as the comments on the gain-and-loss table say, that the entries in the table represent monetary values and not utilities. This difference is significant since for one thing computing expectations on the basis of such objective values is not the same thing as computing expected utility and may lead to different results. The essential point though is that in justice as fairness the parties do not know their conception of the good and cannot estimate their utility in the ordinary sense. In any case, we want to go behind de facto preferences generated by given conditions. Therefore expectations are based upon an index of primary goods and the parties make their choice accordingly. The entries in the example are in terms of money and not utility to indicate this aspect of the contract doctrine.

Now, as I have suggested, the original position has been defined so that it is a situation in which the maximin rule applies. In order to see this, let us review briefly the nature of this situation with these three special features in mind. To begin with, the veil of ignorance excludes all but the vaguest knowledge of likelihoods. The parties have no basis for determining the probable nature of their society, or their place in it. Thus they have strong reasons for being wary of probability calculations if any other course is open to them. They must also take into account the fact that their choice of principles should seem reasonable to others, in particular their descendants, whose rights will be deeply affected by it. . . . [T]hese considerations are strengthened by the fact that

the parties know very little about the gain-and-loss table. Not only are they unable to conjecture the likelihoods of the various possible circumstances, they cannot say much about what the possible circumstances are, much less enumerate them and foresee the outcome of each alternative available. Those deciding are much more in the dark than the illustration by a numerical table suggests. It is for this reason that I have spoken of an analogy with the maximin rule.

Several kinds of arguments for the two principles of justice illustrate the second feature. Thus, if we can maintain that these principles provide a workable theory of social justice, and that they are compatible with reasonable demands of efficiency, then this conception guarantees a satisfactory minimum. There may be, on reflection, little reason for trying to do better. Thus much of the argument . . . is to show, by their application to the main questions of social justice, that the two principles are a satisfactory conception. These details have a philosophical purpose. Moreover, this line of thought is practically decisive if we can establish the priority of liberty, the lexical ordering of the two principles. For this priority implies that the persons in the original position have no desire to try for greater gains at the expense of the equal liberties. The minimum assured by the two principles in lexical order is not one that the parties wish to jeopardize for the sake of greater economic and social advantages. . . .

Finally, the third feature holds if we can assume that other conceptions of justice may lead to institutions that the parties would find intolerable. For example, it has sometimes been held that under some conditions the utility principle (in either form) justifies, if not slavery or serfdom, at any rate serious infractions of liberty for the sake of greater social benefits. We need not consider here the truth of this claim, or the likelihood that the requisite conditions obtain. For the moment, this contention is only to illustrate the way in which conceptions of justice may allow for outcomes which the parties may not be able to accept. And having the ready alternative of the two principles of justice which secure a satisfactory minimum, it seems unwise, if not irrational, for them to take a chance that these outcomes are not realized.

So much, then, for a brief sketch of the features of situations in which the maximin rule comes into its own and of the way in which the arguments for the two principles of justice can be subsumed under them. . . .

NOTE

[4]As the text suggests, I shall regard Locke's *Second Treatise of Government*, Rousseau's *The Social Contract*, and Kant's ethical works beginning with *The Foundations of the Metaphysics of Morals* as definitive of the contract tradition. For all of its greatness, Hobbes's *Leviathan* raises special problems. A general historical survey is provided by J. W. Gough, *The Social Contract*, 2nd ed. (Oxford, The Clarendon Press, 1957), and Otto Gierke, *Natural Law and the Theory of Society*, trans. with an introduction by Ernest Barker (Cambridge, The University Press, 1934). A presentation of the contract view as primarily an ethical theory is to be found in G. R. Grice, *The Grounds of Moral Judgment* (Cambridge, The University Press, 1967). . . .

QUESTIONS FOR DISCUSSION

1. Rawls uses a kind of hypothetical contract to argue for his principles, but not all hypothetical contracts have force, as Dworkin argues in the following passage:

Suppose I did not know the value of my painting on Monday; if you had offered me $100 for it then I would have accepted. On Tuesday, I discovered it was valuable. You cannot argue that it would be fair for the courts to make me sell it to you for $100 on Wednesday. It may be my good fortune that you did not ask me on Monday, but that does not justify coercion against me later.[11]

In what ways is this hypothetical contract similar to Rawls'? In what ways is it different? Does Rawls' hypothetical contract show that his principles are justified? Why or why not?

2. Rawls' difference principle (the first part of his second principle) gives priority to the least advantaged class in society. Is this fair to people in other classes? Is it unjust for rich people to make themselves even richer when this does not affect the lowest class at all? Is a program just if it hurts the lowest class very little but helps the middle class a great deal? Why or why not?

3. What tax rates would be just according to Rawls' difference principle (the first part of his second principle)? Do you agree that such taxes are just? Why or why not?

[11]Ronald Dworkin, *Taking Rights Seriously*, p. 152.

ANARCHY, STATE, AND UTOPIA

ROBERT NOZICK

The term "distributive justice" is not a neutral one. Hearing the term "distribution," most people presume that some thing or mechanism uses some principle or criterion to give out a supply of things. Into this process of distributing shares some error may have crept. So it is an open question, at least, whether redistribution should take place; whether we should do again what has already been done once, though poorly. However, we are not in the position of children who have been given portions of pie by someone who now makes last minute adjustments to rectify careless cutting. There is no central distribution, no person or group entitled to control all the resources, jointly deciding how they are to be doled out. What each person gets, he gets from others who give to him in exchange for something, or as a gift. In a free society, diverse persons control different resources, and new holdings arise out of the voluntary exchanges and actions of persons. There is no more a distributing or distribution of shares than there is a distributing of mates in a society in which persons choose whom they shall marry. The total result is the product of many individual decisions which the different individuals involved are entitled to make. Some uses of the term "distribution," it is true, do not imply a previous distributing appropriately judged by some criterion (for example, "probability distribution"); nevertheless, despite the title of this chapter, it would be best to use a terminology that clearly is neutral. We shall speak of people's holdings; a principle of justice in holdings describes (part of) what justice tells us (requires) about holdings. I shall state first what I take to be the correct view

about justice in holdings, and then turn to the discussion of alternate views.

THE ENTITLEMENT THEORY

The subject of justice in holdings consists of three major topics. The first is the *original acquisition of holdings*, the appropriation of unheld things. This includes the issues of how unheld things may come to be held, the process, or processes, by which unheld things may come to be held, the things that may come to be held by these processes, the extent of what comes to be held by a particular process, and so on. We shall refer to the complicated truth about this topic, which we shall not formulate here, as the principle of justice in acquisition. The second topic concerns the *transfer of holdings* from one person to another. By what processes may a person transfer holdings to another? How may a person acquire a holding from another who holds it? Under this topic come general descriptions of voluntary exchange, and gift and (on the other hand) fraud, as well as reference to particular conventional details fixed upon in a given society. The complicated truth about this subject (with placeholders for conventional details) we shall call the principle of justice in transfer. (And we shall suppose it also includes principles governing how a person may divest himself of a holding, passing it into an unheld state.)

If the world were wholly just, the following inductive definition would exhaustively cover the subject of justice in holdings.

1. A person who acquires a holding in accordance with the principle of justice in acquisition is entitled to that holding.

Robert Nozick, *Anarchy, State, and Utopia* (New York: Basic Books, 1974), pp. 148–164.

2. A person who acquires a holding in accordance with the principle of justice in transfer, from someone else entitled to the holding, is entitled to the holding.

3. No one is entitled to a holding except by (repeated) applications of 1 and 2.

The complete principle of distributive justice would say simply that a distribution is just if everyone is entitled to the holdings they possess under the distribution.

A distribution is just if it arises from another just distribution by legitimate means. The legitimate means of moving from one distribution to another are specified by the principle of justice in transfer. The legitimate first "moves" are specified by the principle of justice in acquisition. Whatever arises from a just situation by just steps is itself just. The means of change specified by the principle of justice in transfer preserve justice. As correct rules of inference are truth–preserving, and any conclusion deduced via repeated application of such rules from only true premises is itself true, so the means of transition from one situation to another specified by the principle of justice in transfer are justice-preserving, and any situation actually arising from repeated transitions in accordance with the principle from a just situation is itself just. The parallel between justice-preserving transformations and truth–preserving transformations illuminates where it fails as well as where it holds. That a conclusion could have been deduced by truth–preserving means from premises that are true suffices to show its truth. That from a just situation a situation *could* have arisen via justice-preserving means does *not* suffice to show its justice. The fact that a thief's victims voluntarily *could* have presented him with gifts does not entitle the thief to his ill–gotten gains. Justice in holdings is historical; it depends upon what actually has happened. We shall return to this point later.

Not all actual situations are generated in accordance with the two principles of justice in holdings: the principle of justice in acquisition and the principle of justice in transfer. Some people steal from others, or defraud them, or enslave them, seizing their product and preventing them from living as they choose, or forcibly exclude others from competing in exchanges. None of these are permissible modes of transition from one situation to another. And some persons acquire holdings by means not sanctioned by the principle of justice in acquisition. The existence of past injustice (previous violations of the first two principles of justice in holdings) raises the third major topic under justice in holdings: the rectification of injustice in holdings. If past injustice has shaped present holdings in various ways, some identifiable and some not, what now, if anything, ought to be done to rectify these injustices? What obligations do the performers of injustice have toward those whose position is worse than it would have been had the injustice not been done? Or, than it would have been had compensation been paid promptly? How, if at all, do things change if the beneficiaries and those made worse off are not the direct parties in the act of injustice, but, for example, their descendants? Is an injustice done to someone whose holding was itself based upon an unrectified injustice? How far back must one go in wiping clean the historical slate of injustices? What may victims of injustice permissibly do in order to rectify the injustices being done to them, including the many injustices done by persons acting through their government? I do not know of a thorough or theoretically sophisticated treatment of such issues. Idealizing greatly, let us suppose theoretical investigation will produce a principle of rectification. This principle uses historical information about previous situations and injustices done in them (as defined by the first two principles of justice and rights against interference), and information about the actual course of events that flowed from these injustices, until the present, and it yields a description (or descriptions) of holdings in the society. The principle of rectification presumably will make use of its best estimate of subjunctive information about what would have occurred (or a probability distribution over what might have occurred, using the expected value) if the injustice had not taken place. If the actual description of holdings turns out not to be one of the descriptions yielded by the principle, then one of the descriptions yielded must be realized.

The general outlines of the theory of justice in holdings are that the holdings of a person are just if he is entitled to them by the principles of justice in acquisition and transfer, or by the principle of rectification of injustice (as specified by the first two principles). If each person's holdings are just, then the total set (distribution) of holdings is just. To turn these general outlines into a specific theory we would have to specify the details of each of the three principles of justice in holdings: the principle of acquisition of holdings, the principle of transfer of holdings, and the principle of rectification of violations of the first two principles. I shall not attempt that task here. . . .

PATTERNING

The entitlement principles of justice in holdings that we have sketched are historical principles of justice [in that whether a distribution is just depends upon how it came about]. To better understand their precise character, we shall distinguish them from another subclass of historical principles. Consider, as an example, the principle of distribution according to moral merit. This principle requires that total distributive shares vary directly with moral merit; no person should have a greater share than anyone whose moral merit is greater. (If moral merit could be not merely ordered but measured on an interval or ratio scale, stronger principles could be formulated.) Or consider the principle that results by substituting "usefulness to society" for "moral merit" in the previous principle. Or instead of "distribute according to moral merit," or "distributed according to usefulness to society," we might

consider "distribute according to the weighted sum of moral merit, usefulness to society, and need," with the weights of the different dimensions equal. Let us call a principle of distribution *patterned* if it specifies that a distribution is to vary along with some natural dimension, weighted sum of natural dimensions, or lexicographic ordering of natural dimensions. And let us say a distribution is patterned if it accords with some patterned principle. (I speak of natural dimensions, admittedly without a general criterion for them, because for any set of holdings some artificial dimensions can be gimmicked up to vary along with the distribution of the set.) The principle of distribution in accordance with moral merit is a patterned historical principle, which specifies a patterned distribution. "Distribute according to I.Q." is a patterned principle that looks to information not contained in distributional matrices. It is not historical, however, in that it does not look to any past actions creating differential entitlements to evaluate a distribution; it requires only distributional matrices whose columns are labeled by I.Q. scores. The distribution in a society, however, may be composed of such simple patterned distributions, without itself being simply patterned. Different sectors may operate different patterns, or some combination of patterns may operate in different proportions across a society. A distribution composed in this manner, from a small number of patterned distributions, we also shall term "patterned." And we extend the use of "pattern" to include the overall designs put forth by combinations of end-state principles.

Almost every suggested principle of distributive justice is patterned: to each according to his moral merit, or needs, or marginal product, or how hard he tries, or the weighted sum of the foregoing, and so on. The principle of entitlement we have sketched is *not* patterned. There is no one natural dimension or weighted sum or combination of a small number of natural dimensions that yields the distributions generated in accordance with the principle of entitlement. The set of holdings that results when some persons receive their marginal products, others win at gambling, others receive a share of their mate's income, others receive gifts from foundations, others receive interest on loans, others receive gifts from admirers, others receive returns on investment, others make for themselves much of what they have, others find things, and so on, will not be patterned. Heavy strands of patterns will run through it; significant portions of the variance in holdings will be accounted for by pattern-variables. If most people most of the time choose to transfer some of their entitlements to others only in exchange for something from them, then a large part of what many people hold will vary with what they held that others wanted. More details are provided by the theory of marginal productivity. But gifts to relatives, charitable donations, bequests to children, and the like, are not best conceived, in the first instance, in this manner. Ignoring the strands of pattern, let us suppose for the moment that a distribution actually arrived at by the operation of the principle of entitlement is random with respect to any pattern. Though the resulting set of holdings will be unpatterned, it will not be incomprehensible, for it can be seen as arising from the operation of a small number of principles. These principles specify how an initial distribution may be transformed into others (the principle of transfer of holdings). The process whereby the set of holdings is generated will be intelligible, though the set of holdings itself that results from this process will be unpatterned. . . .

To think that the task of a theory of distributive justice is to fill in the blank in "to each according to his _____" is to be predisposed to search for a pattern; and the separate treatment of "from each according to his _____" treats production and distribution as two separate and independent issues. On an entitlement view these are *not* two separate questions. Whoever makes something, having bought or contracted for all other held resources used in the process (transferring some of his holdings for these cooperating factors), is entitled to it. The situation is *not* one of something's getting made, and there being an open question of who is to get it. Things come into the world already attached to people having entitlements over them. From the point of view of the historical entitlement conception of justice in holdings, those who start afresh to complete "to each according to his _____" treat objects as if they appeared from nowhere, out of nothing. A complete theory of justice might cover this limit case as well; perhaps here is a use for the usual conceptions of distributive justice.

So entrenched are maxims of the usual form that perhaps we should present the entitlement conception as a competitor. Ignoring acquisition and rectification, we might say:

> From each according to what he chooses to do, to each according to what he makes for himself (perhaps with the contracted aid of others) and what others choose to do for him and choose to give him of what they've been given previously (under this maxim) and haven't yet expended or transferred.

This, the discerning reader will have noticed, has its defects as a slogan. So as a summary and great simplification (and not as a maxim with any independent meaning) we have:

> *From each as they choose, to each as they are chosen.*

HOW LIBERTY UPSETS PATTERNS

It is not clear how those holding alternative conceptions of distributive justice can reject the entitlement conception of justice in holdings. For suppose a distribution favored by one of these nonentitlement conceptions is realized. Let us suppose it is your favorite one and let us call this distribution D_1; perhaps everyone has an equal share, perhaps shares vary in accordance with some dimension you treasure. Now suppose that Wilt Chamberlain is greatly in demand by basketball teams, being a great gate attraction. (Also suppose contracts run only for a year, with players being free agents.) He signs the following sort of contract with a team: In each home game, twenty-five cents from the price of each ticket of admission goes to him. (We ignore the questions of whether he is "gouging" the owners, letting them look out for themselves.) The season starts, and people cheerfully attend his team's games; they buy their tickets, each time dropping a separate twenty-five cents of their admission price into a special box with Chamberlain's name on it. They are excited about seeing him play; it is worth the total admission price to them. Let us suppose that in one season one million persons attend his home games, and Wilt Chamberlain winds up with $250,000, a much larger sum than the average income and larger even than anyone else has. Is he entitled to this income? Is this new distribution D_2, unjust? If so, why? There is *no* question about whether each of the people was entitled to the control over the resources they held in D_1; because that was the distribution (your favorite) that (for the purposes of argument) we assumed was acceptable. Each of these persons *chose* to give twenty-five cents of their money to Chamberlain. They could have spent it on going to the movies, or on candy bars, or on copies of *Dissent* magazine, or of *Monthly Review*. But they all, at least one million of them, converged on giving it to Wilt Chamberlain in exchange for watching him play basketball. If D_1 was a just distribution, and people voluntarily moved from it to D_2, transferring parts of their shares they were given under D_1 (what was it for if not to do something with?), isn't D_2 also just? If the people were entitled to dispose of the resources to which they were entitled (under D_1), didn't this include their being entitled to give it to, or exchange it with, Wilt Chamberlain? Can anyone else complain on grounds of justice? Each other person already has his legitimate share under D_1. Under D_1, there is nothing that

anyone has that anyone else has a claim of justice against. After someone transfers something to Wilt Chamberlain, third parties *still* have their legitimate shares; *their* shares are not changed. By what process could such a transfer among two persons give rise to a legitimate claim of distributive justice on a portion of what was transferred, by a third party who had no claim of justice on any holding of the others *before* the transfer? To cut off objections irrelevant here, we might imagine the exchanges occurring in a socialist society, after hours. After playing whatever basketball he does in his daily work, or doing whatever other daily work he does, Wilt Chamberlain decides to put in *overtime* to earn additional money. (First his work quota is set; he works time over that.) Or imagine it is a skilled juggler people like to see, who puts on shows after hours.

Why might someone work overtime in a society in which it is assumed their needs are satisfied? Perhaps because they care about things other than needs. I like to write in books that I read, and to have easy access to books for browsing at odd hours. It would be very pleasant and convenient to have the resources of Widener Library in my back yard. No society, I assume, will provide such resources close to each person who would like them as part of his regular allotment (under D_1). Thus, persons either must do without some extra things that they want, or be allowed to do something extra to get some of these things. On what basis could the inequalities that would eventuate be forbidden? Notice also that small factories would spring up in a socialist society, unless forbidden. I melt down some of my personal possessions (under D_1) and build a machine out of the material. I offer you, and others, a philosophy lecture once a week in exchange for your cranking the handle on my machine, whose products I exchange for yet other things, and so on. (The raw materials used by the machine are given to me by others who possess them under D_1, in exchange for hearing lectures.) Each person might participate to gain things over and above their allotment under D_1. Some persons even might want to leave their job in socialist industry and work full time in this private sector. . . . [Thus,] private property even in means of production would occur in a socialist society that did not forbid people to use as they wished some of the resources they are given under the socialist distribution D_1. The socialist society would have to forbid capitalist acts between consenting adults.

The general point illustrated by the Wilt Chamberlain example and the example of the entrepreneur in a socialist society is that no [unhistorical] principle or distributional patterned principle of justice can be continuously realized without continuous interference with people's lives. Any favored pattern would be transformed into one unfavored by the principle, by people choosing to act in various ways; for example, by people exchanging goods and services with other people, or giving things to other people, things the transferrers are entitled to under the favored distributional pattern. To maintain a pattern one must either continually interfere to stop people from transferring resources as they wish to, or continually (or periodically) interfere to take from some persons resources that others for some reason chose to transfer to them. (But if some time limit is to be set on how long people may keep resources others voluntarily transfer to them, why let them keep these resources for *any* period of time? Why not have immediate confiscation?) It might be objected that all persons voluntarily will choose to refrain from actions which would upset the pattern. This presupposes unrealistically (1) that all will most want to maintain the pattern (are those who don't, to be "reeducated" or forced to undergo "self-criticism"?), (2) that each can gather enough information about his own actions and the ongoing activities of others to discover which of his actions will upset the pattern, and (3) that diverse and far-flung persons can coordinate their actions to dove-tail into the pattern. Compare the manner in which the market is neutral among persons' desires, as it reflects and transmits widely scattered information via prices, and coordinates persons' activities.

It puts things perhaps a bit too strongly to say that every patterned (or [unhistorical]) principle is liable to be thwarted by the voluntary actions of the individual parties transferring some of their shares they receive under the principle. For perhaps some *very* weak patterns are not so thwarted. Any distributional pattern with any egalitarian component is overturnable by the voluntary actions of individual persons over time; as is every patterned condition with sufficient content so as actually to have been proposed as presenting the central core of distributive justice. Still, given the possibility that some weak conditions or patterns may not be unstable in this way, it would be better to formulate an explicit description of the kind of interesting and contentful patterns under discussion, and to prove a theorem about their instability. Since the weaker the patterning, the more likely it is that the entitlement system itself satisfies it, a plausible conjecture is that any patterning either is unstable or is satisfied by the entitlement system.

QUESTIONS FOR DISCUSSION

1. How could Rawls best respond to Nozick's Wilt Chamberlain example?

2. Is there any inequality that is unjust even though it arose in a way that meets Nozick's principles? Why or why not?

3. What kinds of taxes are just according to Nozick's theory?

MORALITY AND THE LIBERAL IDEAL

MICHAEL J. SANDEL

Liberals often take pride in defending what they oppose—pornography, for example, or unpopular views. They say the state should not impose on its citizens a preferred way of life, but should leave them as free as possible to choose their own values and ends, consistent with a similar liberty for others. This commitment to freedom of choice requires liberals constantly to distinguish between permission and praise, between allowing a practice and endorsing it. It is one thing to allow pornography, they argue, something else to affirm it.

Conservatives sometimes exploit this distinction by ignoring it. They charge that those who would allow abortions favor abortions, that opponents of school prayer oppose prayer, that those who defend the rights of communists sympathize with their cause. And in a pattern of argument familiar in our politics, liberals reply by invoking higher principles; it is not that they dislike pornography less, but rather that they value toleration, or freedom of choice, or fair procedures more.

But in contemporary debate, the liberal rejoinder seems increasingly fragile, its moral basis increasingly unclear. Why should toleration and freedom of choice prevail when other important values are also at stake? Too often the answer implies some version of moral relativism, the idea that it is wrong to "legislate morality" because all morality is merely subjective. "Who is to say what is literature and what is filth? That is a value judgment, and whose values should decide?"

Relativism usually appears less as a claim than as a question. "Who is to judge?" But it is a question that can also be asked of the values

that liberals defend. Toleration and freedom and fairness are values too, and they can hardly be defended by the claim that no values can be defended. So it is a mistake to affirm liberal values by arguing that all values are merely subjective. The relativist defense of liberalism is no defense at all.

What, then, can be the moral basis of the higher principles the liberal invokes? Recent political philosophy has offered two main alternatives—one utilitarian, the other Kantian. The utilitarian view, following John Stuart Mill, defends liberal principles in the name of maximizing the general welfare. The state should not impose on its citizens a preferred way of life, even for their own good, because doing so will reduce the sum of human happiness, at least in the long run; better that people choose for themselves, even if, on occasion, they get it wrong. "The only freedom which deserves the name," writes Mill in *On Liberty*, "is that of pursuing our own good in our own way, so long as we do not attempt to deprive others of theirs, or impede their efforts to obtain it." He adds that his argument does not depend on any notion of abstract right, only on the principle of the greatest good for the greatest number. "I regard utility as the ultimate appeal on all ethical questions; but it must be utility in the largest sense, grounded on the permanent interests of man as a progressive being."

Many objections have been raised against utilitarianism as a general doctrine of moral philosophy. Some have questioned the concept of utility, and the assumption that all human goods are in principle commensurable. Others have objected that by reducing all values to

Michael Sandel, "Morality and the Liberal Ideal," *The New Republic*, May 7, 1984, pp. 15–17.

preferences and desires, utilitarians are unable to admit qualitative distinctions of worth, unable to distinguish noble desires from base ones. But most recent debate has focused on whether utilitarianism offers a convincing basis for liberal principles, including respect for individual rights.

In one respect, utilitarianism would seem well suited to liberal purposes. Seeking to maximize overall happiness does not require judging people's values, only aggregating them. And the willingness to aggregate preferences without judging them suggests a tolerant spirit, even a democratic one. When people go to the polls we count their votes, whatever they are.

But the utilitarian calculus is not always as liberal as it first appears. If enough cheering Romans pack the Coliseum to the watch the lion devour the Christian, the collective pleasure of the Romans will surely outweigh the pain of the Christian, intense though it be. Or if a big majority abhors a small religion and wants it banned, the balance of preferences will favor suppression, not toleration. Utilitarians sometimes defend individual rights on the grounds that respecting them now will serve utility in the long run. But this calculation is precarious and contingent. It hardly secures the liberal promise not to impose on some the values of others. As the majority will is an inadequate instrument of liberal politics—by itself it fails to secure individual rights—so the utilitarian philosophy is an inadequate foundation for liberal principles.

The case against utilitarianism was made most powerfully by Immanuel Kant. He argued that empirical principles, such as utility, were unfit to serve as basis for the moral law. A wholly instrumental defense of freedom and rights not only leaves rights vulnerable, but fails to respect the inherent dignity of persons. The utilitarian calculus treats people as means to the happiness of others, not as ends in themselves worthy of respect.

Contemporary liberals extend Kant's argument with the claim that utilitarianism fails to take seriously the distinction between persons. In seeking above all to maximize the general welfare, the utilitarian treats society as a whole as if it were a single person; it conflates our many, diverse desires into a single system of desires. It is indifferent to the distribution of satisfactions among persons, except insofar as this may affect the overall sum. But this fails to respect our plurality and distinctness. It uses some as means to the happiness of all, and so fails to respect each as an end in himself.

In the view of modern-day Kantians, certain rights are so fundamental that even the general welfare cannot override them. As John Rawls writes in his important work, *A Theory of Justice*, "Each person possesses an inviolability founded on justice that even the welfare of society as a whole cannot override. . . . The rights secured by justice are not subject to political bargaining or to the calculus of social interests."

So Kantian liberals need an account of rights that does not depend on utilitarian considerations. More than this, they need an account that does not depend on any particular conception of the good, that does not presuppose the superiority of one way of life over others. Only a justification neutral about ends could preserve the liberal resolve not to favor any particular ends, or to impose on its citizens a preferred way of life. But what sort of justification could this be? How is it possible to affirm certain liberties and rights as fundamental without embracing some vision of the good life, without endorsing some ends over others? It would seem we are back to the relativist predicament—to affirm liberal principles without embracing any particular ends.

The solution proposed by Kantian liberals is to draw a distinction between the "right" and the "good"—between a framework of basic rights and liberties, and the conceptions of the good that people may choose to pursue within the framework. It is one thing for the state to support a fair framework, they argue, something else to affirm some particular ends. For example, it is one thing to defend the right to free speech so that people may be free to form their own opinions and choose their own ends, but something else to support it on the grounds that a life of political discussion is inherently worthier than a life unconcerned with public affairs, or on the grounds that free speech will increase the general welfare. Only the first defense is available in the Kantian view, resting as it does on the ideal of a neutral framework.

Now, the commitment to a framework neutral with respect to ends can be seen as a kind of value—in this sense the Kantian liberal is no relativist—but its value consists precisely in its refusal to affirm a preferred way of life or conception of the good. For Kantian liberals, then, the right is prior to the good, and in two senses. First, individual rights cannot be sacrificed for the sake of the general good; and second, the principles of justice that specify these rights cannot be premised on any particular vision of the good life. What justifies the rights is not that they maximize the general welfare or otherwise promote the good, but rather that they comprise a fair framework within which individuals and groups can choose their own values and ends, consistent with a similar liberty for others.

Of course, proponents of the rights-based ethic notoriously disagree about what rights are fundamental and about what political arrangements the ideal of the neutral framework requires. Egalitarian liberals support the welfare state, and favor a scheme of civil liberties together with certain social and economic rights—rights to welfare, education, health care, and so on. Libertarian liberals defend the market economy, and claim that redistributive policies violate peoples' rights; they favor a scheme of civil liberties combined with a strict regime of private property rights. But whether egalitarian or libertarian, rights-based liberalism begins with the claim that we are separate, individual persons, each with our own aims, interests, and conceptions of the good; it seeks a framework of rights that will enable us to re-

alize our capacity as free moral agents, consistent with a similar liberty for others.

Within academic philosophy, the last decade or so has seen the ascendance of the rights-based ethic over the utilitarian one, due in large part to the influence of Rawls's *A Theory of Justice.* The legal philosopher H. L. A. Hart recently described the shift from the "the old faith that some form of utilitarianism must capture the essence of political morality" to the new faith that "the truth must lie with a doctrine of basic human rights, protecting specific basic liberties and interests of individuals. . . . Whereas not so long ago great energy and much ingenuity of many philosophers were devoted to making some form of utilitarianism work, latterly such energies and ingenuity have been devoted to the articulation of theories of basic rights."

But in philosophy as in life, the new faith becomes the old orthodoxy before long. Even as it has come to prevail over its utilitarian rival, the rights-based ethic has recently faced a growing challenge from a different direction from a view that gives fuller expression to the claims of citizenship and community than the liberal vision allows. The communitarian critics, unlike modern liberals, make the case for a politics of the common good. Recalling the arguments of Hegel against Kant, they question the liberal claim for the priority of the right over the good, and the picture of the freely choosing individual it embodies. Following Aristotle, they argue that we cannot justify political arrangements without reference to common purposes and ends, and that we cannot conceive of ourselves without reference to our role as citizens, as participants in a common life.

This debate reflects two contrasting pictures of the self. The rights-based ethic, and the conception of the person it embodies, were shaped in large part in the encounter with utilitarianism. Where utilitarians conflate our many desires into a single system of desire, Kantians insist on the separateness of persons. Where the utilitarian self is simply defined as the sum of its desire, the Kantian self is a choosing self, independent of the desires and ends it may have at any moment. As Rawls writes, "The self is prior to the ends which are affirmed by it; even a dominant end must be chosen from among numerous possibilities."

The priority of the self over its ends means I am never defined by my aims and attachments, but always capable of standing back to survey and assess and possibly to revise them. This is what it means to be a free and independent self, capable of choice. And this is the vision of the self that finds expression in the ideal of the state as a neutral framework. On the rights-based ethic, it is precisely because we are essentially separate, independent selves that we need a neutral framework, a framework of rights that refuses to choose among competing purposes and ends. If the self is prior to its ends, then the right must be prior to the good.

Communitarian critics of rights-based liberalism say we cannot conceive ourselves as independent in this way, as bearers of selves wholly detached from our aims and attachments. They say that certain of our roles are partly constitutive of the person we are—as citizens of a country, or members of a movement, or partisans of a cause. But if we are partly defined by the communities we inhabit, then we must also be implicated in the purposes and ends characteristic of those communities. As Alasdair MacIntyre writes in his book, *After Virtue,* "What is good for me has to be the good for one who inhabits these roles." Open-ended though it be, the story of my life is always embedded in the story of those communities from which I derive my identity—whether family or city, tribe or nation, party or cause. In the communitarian view, these stories make a moral difference, not only a psychological one. They situate us in the world and give our lives their moral particularity.

What is at stake for politics in the debate between unencumbered selves and situated ones? What are the practical differences between a politics of rights and politics of the common good? On some issues, the two theories may produce different arguments for similar policies. For example, the civil rights movement of the 1960s might be justified by liberals in the name of human dignity and respect for persons, and by communitarians in the name of recognizing the full membership of fellow citizens wrongly excluded from the common life of the nation. And where liberals might support public education in hopes of equipping students to become autonomous individuals, capable of choosing their own ends and pursuing them effectively, communitarians might support public education in hopes of equipping students to become good citizens, capable of contributing meaningfully to public deliberations and pursuits.

On other issues, the two ethics might lead to different policies. Communitarians would be more likely than liberals to allow a town to ban pornographic bookstores, on the grounds that pornography offends its way of life and the values that sustain it. But a politics of civic virtue does not always part company with liberalism in favor of conservative policies. For example, communitarians would be more willing than some rights-oriented liberals to see states enact laws regulating plant closings, to protect their communities from the disruptive effects of capital mobility and sudden industrial change. More generally, where the liberal regards the expansion of individual rights and entitlements as unqualified moral and political progress, the communitarian is troubled by the tendency of liberal programs to displace politics from smaller forms of association to more comprehensive ones. Where libertarian liberals defend the private economy and egalitarian liberals defend the welfare state, communitarians worry about the concentration of power in both the corporate economy and the bureaucratic state, and the erosion of those intermediate forms of community that have at times sustained a more vital public life.

Liberals often argue that a politics of the common good, drawing as it must on particular loyalties, obligations, and traditions, opens the way to prejudice and intolerance. The modern nation-state is not the Athenian polls, they point out; the scale and diversity of modern life have rendered the Aristotelian political ethic nostalgic at best and dangerous at worst. Any attempt to govern by a vision of the good is likely to lead to a slippery slope of totalitarian temptations.

Communitarians reply, rightly in my view, that intolerance flourishes most where forms of life are dislocated, roots unsettled, traditions undone. In our day, the totalitarian impulse has sprung less from the convictions of confidently situated selves than from the confusions of atomized, dislocated, frustrated selves, at sea in a world where common meanings have lost their force. As Hannah Arendt has written, "What makes mass society so difficult to bear is not the number of people involved, or at least not primarily, but the fact that the world between them has lost its power to gather them together, to relate and to separate them." Insofar as our public life has withered, our sense of common involvement diminished, we lie vulnerable to the mass politics of totalitarian solutions. So responds the party of the common good to the party of rights. If the party of the common good is right, our most pressing moral and political project is to revitalize those civic republican possibilities implicit in our tradition but fading in our time.

QUESTIONS FOR DISCUSSION

1. What exactly is the individualistic view of the self that Sandel claims is shared by liberals, libertarians, and utilitarians? Do these theories really depend on this view of the self? Is this view of the self inaccurate? Why or why not?

2. Do you agree with communitarians that politics should be based on the common good? Why or why not?

3. What are the implications of this view for laws that restrict pornography and plant closings? Would communitarians disagree with Rawls or Nozick on any other specific policies or laws?

4. In your opinion, which kinds of equality are required for justice? Why those? Why not others?

5. How, if at all, can the above theories of justice be applied to the distribution of housework in a family? To the distribution of wealth among nations?

SUGGESTIONS FOR FURTHER READING

A variety of readings are collected with a clear introduction and further bibliography in *Justice: Alternative Political Perspectives*, 2nd ed., edited by James P. Sterba (Belmont, California: Wadsworth, 1992). Sterba also discusses the main theories of justice and tries to reconcile them in his *How to Make People Just* (Totowa, New Jersey: Rowman and Littlefield, 1988). A good commentary on Mill is David Lyons, "Mill's Theory of Justice" in *Values and Morals*, edited by A. I. Goldman and J. Kim (Dordrecht: Reidel, 1978), pp. 1–20. For Rawls' more recent views, see his *Political Liberalism* (New York: Columbia

University Press, 1993). Three good collections of articles on Rawls are *Reading Rawls*, edited by Norman Daniels (Stanford: Stanford University Press, 1989); *John Rawls' Theory of Social Justice: An Introduction*, edited by H. Gene Blocker and Elizabeth H. Smith (Athens: Ohio University Press, 1980); and "Symposium on Rawlsian Theory of Justice: Recent Developments," *Ethics*, vol. 99, no. 4 (July 1989), which includes Rawlsian responses to communitarianism. Another prominent liberal theory of justice is presented by Ronald Dworkin, *A Matter of Principle* (Cambridge: Harvard University Press, 1985), Chapters 8–10, whose theories of law we encountered in Chapters 1 and 2. Some essays on Nozick's theory are in *Reading Nozick*, edited by Jeffrey Paul (Totowa, New Jersey: Rowman and Allanheld, 1981), especially Part IV. More libertarian views can be found in *The Libertarian Reader*, edited by Tibor Machan (Totowa, New Jersey: Rowman and Littlefield, 1982). Sandel develops his communitarianism in *Liberalism and the Limits of Justice* (Cambridge: Cambridge University Press, 1982). A different version of communitarianism is Michael Walzer, *Spheres of Justice* (New York: Basic Books, 1983). Arguments for and against communitarianism can be found in *Communitarianism and its Critics*, by Daniel Bell (New York: Oxford University Press, 1993); and *The Liberalism-Communitarianism Debate*, edited by C. F. Delaney (Totowa, New Jersey: Rowman, 1994). For a feminist critique of traditional theories of justice, see Susan Okin, *Justice, Gender, and the Family* (New York: Basic Books, 1989). For a more radical version of egalitarianism, see Kai Nielsen, *Equality and Liberty* (Totowa, New Jersey: Rowman and Allanheld, 1985). Excellent commentary on and bibliography for the recent debate on equality of welfare vs. resources vs. capabilities vs. opportunity can be found in Amartya Sen, *Inequality Reexamined* (Cambridge: Harvard University Press, 1992.

5.3 DISCRIMINATION

INTRODUCTION

The ability to discriminate among letters is a test of good eyesight. Here discrimination is simply the ability to tell one letter from another. People are also sometimes praised for having discriminating taste in food or art. Here discrimination is the ability to judge relative quality in food or art. In contrast, to call a law discriminatory is almost always a criticism. Most or even all laws distinguish among cases. Driving laws distinguish people who exceed the speed limit from those who do not, and people who are too young for a license from those who are old enough. Voting laws allow residents but not visitors to vote in local elections. However, such distinctions are not usually labelled *discrimination* unless they are seen as unjustified and thus unjust in some way.

The real disputes, then, are about which particular acts and laws are unjust discrimination. Even here there is much agreement. Criminals are punished, but innocent people are not. Poor people are given welfare, but rich people are not. Many important disputes remain, but nobody argues that it is *always* unjust to treat different people differently.

There is also much agreement that certain distinctions are unjust. Despite their profound differences, all of the theories of justice in Section 5.2 would agree that it is morally wrong to deny African–Americans or Asian–Americans the same basic rights (such as rights to vote, to own property, and to a criminal trial) that are granted to European–Americans. This consensus has not always existed, as the history of slavery shows, but some kinds of legal discrimination are almost universally condemned today.

Despite these agreements, people disagree in many other cases about whether a practice is unjust discrimination. There are serious disputes about schools and fraternities that admit men only or heterosexuals only. There are also important questions about how far the law can and should go to fight unjust discrimination. Should it be illegal for private clubs to exclude African–Americans or homosexuals? The challenge in writing laws against discrimination is to rule out the practices that everyone sees as unjust enough for government intervention, without ruling out practices that are clearly not unjust, and to deal somehow with the controversial cases in the middle.

This challenge has shaped law in the United States. The most basic law against discrimination in the United States is the Equal Protection Clause of the Fourteenth Amendment, which was passed in 1868, just after the Civil War brought an end to slavery. This clause reads simply: "No State shall . . . deny to any person within its jurisdiction the equal protection of the laws."[12] But what does "equal protection" mean? The words are very general. The amendment does not mention any particular group or any particular area of concern. The intent was more specific. The Fourteenth Amendment was intended to protect the newly emancipated slaves in some ways. It was clearly not intended to do away with all differences, since, for example, former slaves were not given enough money to bring them up to economic equality with their former masters. Of course, whether the words or the original intent matters is a controversial issue, as we saw in Section 2.1.

Which kinds of inequality are ruled out by the Equal Protection Clause? This question can be divided into three parts: Which areas or kinds of rights are covered? Which actions count as state actions? What, if anything, can justify unequal treatment?

First, which areas or kinds of rights are covered? The Equal Protection Clause was not seen as intended to rule out all differences, even in basic political rights. This is suggested by the fact that only two years later the Fifteenth Amendment was passed to guarantee voting rights to former slaves. Arguably, this new amendment would have been unnecessary if the Equal Protection Clause had already ruled out inequalities in voting rights. But then which rights were covered by the Fourteenth Amendment? This issue had to be decided by the courts. In *Strauder v. West Virginia* (1880),[13] a law that made blacks ineligible for jury duty was struck down on the grounds that the Equal Protection Clause prohibits discrimination in civil rights. In *Yick Wo v. Hopkins* (1886),[14] the Court extended the Equal Protection Clause to discrimination in granting permits for businesses. *Yick Wo* also established that the Equal Protection Clause protects not only African-Americans but also other groups (such as Chinese), and laws that do not explicitly mention racial or ethnic groups can violate the Equal Protection Clause if they are applied unequally in practice. However, the Court refused to extend the Equal Protection Clause to what it saw as social rights in *Plessy v. Ferguson* (1896),[15] which upheld a Louisiana statute enforcing racial segregation in public transportation. This decision wrote into law the infamous doctrine of separate but equal.

Racial segregation in schools, transportation, and even beaches and bathrooms continued to be lawful until 1954, when *Plessy* was overturned in effect by *Brown v. Board of Education* (excerpted in this section). The *Brown* decision encountered great opposition, but the courts still went on to strike down other forms of segregation and sometimes to mandate busing, when resistance stifled other attempts to eliminate the effects of segregation. The U.S. Congress then passed Civil Rights Acts in 1957, 1960, and 1964. Title VI of the Civil Rights Act of 1964 reads in part:

[12]This clause was interpreted to apply to the federal government as well in *Bolling v. Sharpe*, 347 U.S. 497 (1954).

[13]*Strauder v. West Virginia*, 100 U.S. 303 (1880).

[14]*Yick Wo v. Hopkins*, 118 U.S. 356 (1886).

[15]*Plessy v. Ferguson*, 163 U.S. 537 (1896).

No person in the United States shall, on the ground of race, color, or national origin, be excluded from participation in, be denied the benefits of, or be subjected to discrimination under any program or activity receiving Federal financial assistance.

Title VII reads in part:

. . . it shall be unlawful employment practice for an employer (1) to fail or refuse to hire or to discharge any individual, or otherwise to discriminate against any individual with respect to his compensation, terms, conditions, or privileges of employment, because of such individual's race, color, religion, sex, or national origin; or (2) to limit, segregate, or classify his employees or applicants for employment in any way which would deprive or tend to deprive any individual of employment opportunities or otherwise adversely affect his status as an employee, because of such individual's race, color, religion, sex, or national origin.

These and other new statutes specified which groups were protected and which treatments had to be equal in which areas.

They also partly answered our second question: Which actions count as state actions? The Fourteenth Amendment explicitly refers only to the equal protection *of the laws*, but governments do many things besides passing laws. Police officers arrest lawbreakers, clerks grant permits, courts enforce contracts, and so on. Does the Equal Protection Clause rule out discrimination in these areas?[16] What about discrimination by privately owned universities or companies with government grants or contracts? What about discrimination by individuals or clubs with no special government contacts? If these kinds of discrimination are not state actions, they are not forbidden by the Equal Protection Clause. But they still might be prohibited by civil rights laws. The crucial issue then is how far laws against discrimination should reach into the private sphere.

Our third question asks what, if anything, can justify unequal treatment by the state. Most or all state actions treat people differently in some ways, so it is crucial to determine which differences in treatment are justified. Of course, when legislatures treat people differently, they believe that they are justified. It is traditional for judges—who are often not elected, for example, in federal courts—to defer to elected legislators. So the courts decided early on that it was not their business, according to the accepted separation of powers, to examine the details of legislation to make sure that the laws were as equitable as possible. Instead, the court initially saw laws as violating the Equal Protection Clause only when they failed what became known as the *rational relation test*. This test required only that the law have some legitimate goal and that it not be unreasonable to believe that unequal treatment would serve that goal. It was taken for granted that a law could be *under-inclusive* (in the sense that it would not apply to some people who were involved in the harm that it was intended to prevent) and also *over-inclusive*

---

[16]Police actions were at issue in *U.S. v. Cruikshank*, 92 U.S. 542 (1875). Permits were at issue in *Yick Wo v. Hopkins*, 118 U.S. 356 (1886). Exclusive contracts were at issue in *Shelley v. Kraemer* (discussed by Fiss in this section, p. 555).

(in the sense that it would apply to some people who were not involved in the harm that it was intended to prevent). For example, if the purpose of a 65 miles per hour speed limit is to prevent unsafe driving, then the speed limit is under-inclusive to the extent that it fails to penalize drivers who are dangerous even below 65 miles per hour, and it is over-inclusive to the extent that it penalizes drivers who drive safely even above 65 miles per hour (see Tussman and ten-Broek below). The rational relation test put limits on over-inclusiveness and under-inclusiveness, but these limits were very wide. The only laws that fail this test are laws that are obviously arbitrary, so very few laws were found to violate the Equal Protection Clause under this test.

The rational relation test remained basically unchanged until the 1940s: During World War II, the Supreme Court had to decide whether it was constitutional to relocate Japanese-Americans away from Pacific ports. In *Korematsu v. United States* (1944),[17] the Supreme Court announced that

> [A]ll legal restrictions which curtail the rights of a single racial group are immediately suspect. That is not to say that all such restrictions are unconstitutional. It is to say that the courts must subject them to the most rigid scrutiny.

It is ironic that the Court did not strike down the Japanese relocation orders, but cases about these relocations established a new interpretation of equal protection that eventually greatly increased the power of the courts to strike down discriminatory laws.

This new interpretation of the Equal Protection Clause was codified in the classic article by Joseph Tussman (1914–), a philosophy professor, and Jacobus tenBroek (1911–), a law professor, both at the University of California at Berkeley (included in this section). Under their interpretation, most laws still need to pass only the rational relation test, but three features of a law are *triggers* of strict scrutiny. A law must pass *strict scrutiny* if the law either: (1) employs a *forbidden or suspect classification* or (2) has a *discriminatory motive* or (3) restricts a *fundamental right*. A classification is suspect if it concerns race, religion, or national origin, and other kinds of classifications could be added. Discriminatory motives involve hostility or prejudice. Fundamental rights include rights to vote, to own property, and to procreate, and other rights could be added.

These triggers do not always make laws unconstitutional, as *Korematsu* shows, but laws with these features must carry a heavy burden of proof, encapsulated in the *strict scrutiny* test. In order to pass strict scrutiny, the state has to show that: (1) its action serves a *legitimate* and *compelling* state interest, and also that (2) it does so in the *least intrusive* way possible. Which state interests are compelling is left up to judges, but a central example of a compelling interest is the protection of other people's fundamental rights. The intrusiveness of a state action is related to its over-inclusiveness, that is, the degree to which the state action restricts or hurts people who were not involved in the harm that the state action was intended to prevent.

---

[17]*Korematsu v. United States*, 323 U.S. 214, 216 (1944).

This whole framework—allowing suspect classifications and fundamental rights violations only when there is no less over-inclusive way to serve a compelling goal—is labelled "the anti–discrimination model" by Owen Fiss, a Yale law professor (in the reading in this section).

Because the strict scrutiny test is so hard for the government to pass, this new interpretation of the Equal Protection Clause gave the courts much more power to overturn legislative actions. One important example is *Brown v. Board of Education* (included in this section), which concerned segregation in public schools. Segregation clearly uses a suspect classification, and the court also emphasized that "the opportunity of an education . . . is a *right* which must be available to all on equal terms" (p. 563 below, our emphasis). The *Brown* opinion argues that segregated public schools violate this right, and it assumes that this triggers the strict scrutiny test, which segregation fails. "Separate but equal" was thus found unconstitutional in education and later in other areas as well.

In addition to being useful, this anti–discrimination model is also attractive to many because of its individualism. The triggers of suspect classifications and discriminatory motive seem to rule out acts that do not treat people as individuals, and fundamental rights are usually rights of individuals.

Despite its attractions, this anti–discrimination model is not beyond question. After all, the notions of suspect classifications, strict scrutiny, and so on, go far beyond the actual words and original intention of the Equal Protection Clause. Conservative critics argue that the anti–discrimination model gives too much power to judges, who decide which rights are fundamental, which interests are compelling, and how much intrusiveness is too much.

Other critics object that the anti–discrimination model is too individualistic. The purpose of the Equal Protection Clause was to prevent certain harms to disadvantaged groups, but those groups can be harmed by state actions without any suspect classification, violation of a fundamental right, or provable discriminatory motive. Examples of private restrictive covenants and facially innocent criteria are described by Owen Fiss.[18] The anti–discrimination model, according to Fiss, not only cannot prevent such inequalities, but also cannot provide any adequate analysis of whether such state actions violate the Equal Protection Clause.

Fiss claims that these problems can be solved by interpreting the Equal Protection Clause directly so as to rule out state actions with disparate adverse impact on disadvantaged groups. The notion of a group is admittedly vague, but Fiss tries to define it clearly enough to make it workable. He also argues that the anti–discrimination model depends on groups, for example, when it picks which classifications to make suspect. If the supposed advantages of the anti–discrimination model are illusory, and if Fiss' group-disadvantaging model provides a better account of facially innocent laws that cause group inequalities, then it is not clear why courts should not adopt Fiss' new interpretation of the Equal Protection Clause. Nonetheless, his proposal remains very controversial.

---

[18]Fiss also argues that the anti-discrimination model makes it too difficult to justify preferential treatment, but that part of his article is omitted here because preferential treatment will be discussed in Section 5.4.

THE EQUAL PROTECTION OF
THE LAWS

JOSEPH TUSSMAN AND JACOBUS TENBROEK

The injunction that no state "shall deny to any person with its jurisdiction the equal protection of the laws" might appear at first glance to be simply a demand for administrative fairness, the historically familiar assertion that all men must stand equal before the law, that justice must be blind to wealth or color, to rank or privilege. But early in its career, the equal protection clause received a formulation which strongly suggested that it was to be more than a demand for fair or equal enforcement of laws; it was to express the demand that the law itself be "equal." In *Yick Wo v. Hopkins*, Mr. Justice Matthews said that "The equal protection of the laws is a pledge of the protection of equal laws."[5] This has been frequently cited with approval and has never been challenged by the Court. It is a statement that makes it abundantly clear that the quality of legislation as well as the quality of administration comes within the purview of the clause.

The subsequent career of the equal protection clause as a standard for the criticism of legislation has moved along several lines. First, it has operated as a limitation upon permissible legislative classification. This is its most familiar role. Second, it is used to oppose "discriminatory" legislation. And third, it shares with due process the task of imposing "substantive" limits upon the exercise of the police power.

1. EQUAL PROTECTION AND CLASSIFICATION

a. *The Problem*

... It is clear that the demand for equal protection cannot be a demand that laws apply universally to all persons. The legislature, if it is to

act at all, must impose special burdens upon or grant special benefits to special groups or classes of individuals.

We thus arrive at the point at which the demand for equality confronts the right to classify. For it is the classification which determines the range of persons affected by the special burden or benefit of a law which does not apply to "all persons." "It is of the essence of classification," said Mr. Justice Brewer in 1898, "that upon the class are cast ... burdens different from those resting upon the general public. ... Indeed, the very idea of classification is that of inequality. ..."[8]

Here, then, is a paradox: The equal protection of the laws is a "pledge of the protection of equal laws." But laws may classify. And "the very idea of classification is that of inequality." In tackling this paradox the Court has neither abandoned the demand for equality nor denied the legislative right to classify. It has taken a middle course. It has resolved the contradictory demands of legislative specialization and constitutional generality by a doctrine of reasonable classification.

The essence of that doctrine can be stated with deceptive simplicity. The Constitution does not require that things different in fact be treated in law as though they were the same. But it does require, in its concern for equality, that those who are similarly situated be similarly treated. The measure of the reasonableness of a classification is the degree of its success in treating similarly those similarly situated. The difficulties concealed in this proposition will be analyzed in the following section.

Joseph Tussman and Jacobus tenBroek, "The Equal Protection of the Laws," *California Law Review*, vol. 37 (1949), pp. 341–381

b. *Reasonable Classification*

We begin with an elementary proposition: To define a class is simply to designate a quality or characteristic or trait or relation, or any combination of these, the possession of which, by an individual, determines his membership in or inclusion within the class. A legislature defines a class, or "classifies," when it enacts a law applying to "all aliens ineligible for citizenship," or "all persons convicted of three felonies," or "all citizens between the ages of 19 and 25" or "foreign corporations doing business within the state. . . ."

Turning now to the reasonableness of legislative classifications, the cue is to be taken from our earlier reference to the requirement that those similarly situated be similarly treated. A reasonable classification is one which includes all who are similarly situated and none who are not. The question is, however, what does that ambiguous and crucial phrase, "similarly situated" mean? And in answering this question we must first dispose of two errors into which the Court has sometimes fallen.

First, "similarly situated" cannot mean simply "similar in the possession of the classifying trait." All members of any class are similarly situated in this respect and consequently, any classification whatsoever would be reasonable by this test. . . .

The second error in the interpretation of the meaning of similarly situated arises out of the notion that some classes are unnatural or artificial. That is, a classification is sometimes held to be unreasonable if it includes individuals who do not belong to the same "natural" class. We call this an error without pausing to fight the ancient controversy about the natural status of classes. All legislative classifications are artificial in the sense that they are artifacts, no matter what the defining traits may be. And they are all real enough for the purposes of law, whether they be the class of American citizens of Japanese ancestry, or the class of makers of margarine, or the class of stockyards receiving more than one hundred head of cattle per day, or the class of feeble-minded confined to institutions.

The issue is not whether, in defining a class, the legislature has carved the universe at a natural joint. If we want to know if such classifications are reasonable, it is fruitless to consider whether or not they correspond to some "natural" grouping or separate those who naturally belong together.

But if we avoid these two errors, where are we to look for the test of similarity of situation which determines the reasonableness of a classification? The inescapable answer is that we must look beyond the classification to the purpose of the law. A reasonable classification is one which includes all persons who are similarly situated with respect to the purpose of the law.

The purpose of a law may be either the elimination of a public "mischief" or the achievement of some positive public good. To simplify the discussion we shall refer to the purpose of a law in terms of the elimination of mischief, since the same argument holds in either case. We shall speak of the defining character or characteristics of the legislative classification as the trait. We can thus speak of the relation of the classification to the purpose of the law as the relation of the Trait to the Mischief.

A problem arises at all because the classification in a law usually does not have as its defining Trait the possession of or involvement with the Mischief at which the law aims. For example, let us suppose that a legislature proposes to combat hereditary criminality—an admitted mischief—and that the sterilization of transmitters of hereditary criminality is a permissible means to that end. Now if the legislature were to pass a law declaring that for the purpose of eliminating hereditary criminality, all individuals who are tainted with inheritable criminal tendencies are to be sterilized, and if it provided for proper administrative identification of transmitters of hereditary criminality, our problem would largely disappear. The class, being defined directly in terms of the Mischief, automatically includes all who are similarly situated with respect to the purpose of the law.

This procedure requires, however, delegation of considerable discretion to administrators to determine which individuals to sterilize. Legislators, reluctant to confer such discretion, tend to classify the Traits which limit the range of administrative freedom. Suppose then, that they pass a law providing for the sterilization of all persons convicted of three felonies. The "reasonableness" of this classification depends upon the relation between the class of three-time felons and the class of hereditary criminals.

In other words, we are really dealing with the relation of two classes to each other. The first class consists of all individuals possessing the defining Trait; the second class consist of all individuals possessing, or rather, tainted by, the Mischief at which the law aims. The former is the legislative classification; the latter is the class of those similarly situated with respect to the purpose of the law. We shall refer to these two classes as T and M respectively.

Now, since the reasonableness of any class T depends entirely upon its relation to a class M, it is obvious that it is impossible to pass judgment on the reasonableness of a classification without taking into consideration, or identifying, the purpose of the law. That the Court has erred seriously in attempting to do this will be shown subsequently.

There are five possible relationships between the class defined by the Trait and the class defined by the Mischief. These relationships can be indicated by the following diagrams:

1. (M T) : All T's are M's and all M's are T's

2. (T) (M) : No T's are M's

3. (M/T) : All T's are M's but some M's are not T's

4. : All M's are T's but some T's are not M's

5. (T (M) : Some T's are M's; some T's are not M's; and some M's are not T's

One of these five relationships holds in fact in any case of legislative classification, and we will consider each from the point of view of its "reasonableness."

The first two situations represent respectively the ideal limits of reasonableness and unreasonableness. In the first case, the classification in the law coincides completely with the class of those similarly situated with respect to the purpose of the law. It is perfectly reasonable. In the second case, no member of the class defined in the law is tainted with the mischief at which the law aims. The classification is, therefore, perfectly unreasonable. These two situations need not detain us.

Classification of the third type may be called "under-inclusive." All who are included in the class are tainted with the mischief, but there are others also tainted whom the classification does not include. Since the classification does not include all who are similarly situated with respect to the purpose of the law, there is a prima facie violation of the equal protection requirement of reasonable classification.

But the court has recognized the very real difficulties under which legislatures operate—difficulties arising out of both the nature of the legislative process and of the society which legislation attempts perennially to reshape—and it has refused to strike down indiscriminately all legislation embodying the classificatory inequality here under consideration. . . .

The fourth type of classification imposes a burden upon a wider range of individuals than are included in the class of those tainted with the mischief at which the law aims. It can thus be called "over-inclusive." Herod, ordering the death of all male children born on a particular day because one of them would some day bring about his downfall, employed such a classification. It is exemplified by the quarantine and the dragnet. The wartime treatment of American citizens of Japanese ancestry is a striking recent instance of the imposition of burdens upon a large class of individuals because some of them were believed to be disloyal.

The prima facie case against such departures from the ideal standards of reasonable classification is stronger than the case against under-inclusiveness. For in the latter case, all who are included in the class are at least tainted by the mischief at which the law aims; while over-inclusive classifications reach out to the innocent bystander, the hapless victim of circumstance or association.

It should be noted that such classifications fly squarely in the face of our traditional antipathy to assertions of mass guilt and guilt by association. Guilt, we believe, is individual, and to act otherwise is to deprive the individual of due process of law. But while the courts have preferred to deal with this situation in due process terms, the reasonable classification requirement of the equal protection clause is also violated.

But in spite of the flagrant injustice of over-inclusive classifications, there are circumstances in which legislation of this character has been, and perhaps must be, sustained. The circumstances are those of emergency, which must be grave and imminent if the impositions are harsh and onerous—as in the case of the wartime evacuations of Japanese-Americans—or less grave but still "emergency" if the impositions are relatively mild—as in the case of a police roadblock. The problem for the court is simply whether there exists or existed a genuine emergency situation calling for emergency measures and whether there was "good faith" in the attempt to deal with it.

The nature of this justification for sustaining over-inclusion classification suggests a further consideration. A genuine emergency will usually involve the exercise of emergency power by some non-legislative agency. The legislative process is not particularly designed for dealing with emergencies. We would expect to find, therefore, very few cases of legislative classification which can successfully plead emergency justification, and it may well be held that the initial presumption, in the case of legislation, should run against the emergency plea.

The final situation to be considered is one in which the previously discussed factors of under-inclusiveness and over-inclusiveness are both present. While it may seem paradoxical to assert that a classification can be at once over-inclusive and under-inclusive, many classifications do, in fact, fall into this category, that is, they can be challenged separately on both grounds.

For example, in the *Hirabayashi*[18] case, the classification of "American citizens of Japanese ancestry" for the purpose of meeting the dangers of sabotage can be challenged both on the grounds that it is under-inclusive, since others—American citizens of German or Italian ancestry—are equally under the strain of divided loyalties, and that it is over-inclusive, since it is not supposed that all American citizens of Japanese ancestry are disloyal. The sustaining of this classification, therefore, requires both the finding of sufficient emergency to justify the imposition of a burden upon a larger class than is believed tainted with the Mischief and the establishment of "fair reasons" for failure to extend the operation of the law to a wider class of potential saboteurs.

No problems that have not already been discussed, however, arise in connection with classifications of this type.

Thus far we have spoken of reasonable classification in its bearing upon legislative activity. But it is obvious that the analysis extends to administrative action also. This is true not only because there is delegation of legislative power to non-legislative agencies, but because in the execution of legislatively determined policy there is a considerable range of classificatory discretion remaining in administrative hands. The exercise of that discretion can be judged reasonable or unreasonable by the same criteria as are relevant to the judgment of legislative activity. The reasonable classification requirement applies, in fact, to any classificatory activity involving "state action." Some interesting possibilities are suggested by the discernible tendency to broaden the meaning of "state action."

c. Forbidden Classification

The bearing of the equal protection clause on the problem of classification is not exhausted by the reasonable classification requirement. The assertion of human equality is closely associated with the denial that differences in color or creed, birth or status, are significant or relevant to the way in which men should be treated. These factors, the egalitarian asserts, are irrelevant accidents in the face of our common humanity. To these differences in the supplicants before her bar, Justice must be blind. Laws which classify men by color or creed or blood accordingly, are repugnant to the demand for equality, and therefore, such traits should not be made the basis for the classification of individuals in laws. Speaking of "indigence," for example, Mr. Justice Jackson has said, "The mere state of being without funds is a neutral fact—constitutionally an irrelevance, like race, creed, or color."[19]

"Constitutionally an irrelevance"! How much can be made of this phrase? Does it not suggest that there are some differences between men which cannot constitutionally be recognized, that classifications based upon such irrelevancies are repugnant to the Constitution? The analysis in the previous section has shown that classifying traits must have a reasonable relation to the purpose of a law. We now suggest the possibility that there are some traits which can never be made the basis of a constitutional classification. . . .

Perhaps the chief value of the doctrine would lie in its possible use as the basis for a frontal judicial attack upon segregation laws. Such laws have avoided the condemnation of the equal protection clause under the stubbornly persistent "separate but equal" doctrine. The forbidden classification doctrine would offer a way out. Segregation laws of all types, based upon racial, religious, or other such "constitutionally irrelevant" traits would fall by reason of the employment of those traits alone, and no "separate but equal" argument could save them.

Tempting as this possibility appears to those who are concerned with the perennial struggle for equality, the doctrine also presents difficulties. Chief among these, perhaps, is the problem of determining which traits to treat as forbidden. Candidates for this position today might be designated with relative ease—race, alienage, color, creed. Some of these might be challenged and others offered as candidates. One would hesitate to close the list arbitrarily and foreclose the future. Another epoch might discover constitutional irrelevancies of which we are unaware. . . .

d. Suspect Classification

If the forbidden classification doctrine seems too extreme to give promise of further judicial development, there is a milder form of that doctrine which is in effect. It is the doctrine which established a presumption of unconstitutionality against a law employing certain classifying traits.

Speaking for the Court in the *Korematsu* case, Mr. Justice Black said, "It should be noted, to begin with, that all legal restrictions which curtail the civil rights of a single racial group are immediately suspect. That is not to say that all such restrictions are unconstitutional. It is to say that the courts must subject them to the most rigid scrutiny."[24]

Presumably, this "rigid scrutiny" is also called for by classifications other than those which curtail the civil rights of any single racial group. But an attempt at an exhaustive listing of suspect classifications would be pointless. It suffices to say that this is of necessity a rather loose category. Its content, at any particular time, will depend upon the area in which the principle of equality is struggling against the recurring forms of claims to special and unequal status—whether along racial, religious, economic, or even political, lines.

But if there are "suspect" classifications requiring "rigid scrutiny," of what are they suspect and for what are they rigidly scrutinized? The answer leads in two directions. On the one hand, the reasonable relation test must be strictly applied. On the other hand, the Court must satisfy itself on the question of the discriminatory character of the regulation. The first of these has already been discussed. The problem of discriminatory legislation will be considered in the following section.

2. DISCRIMINATORY LEGISLATION

The equal protection clause has been used by the courts chiefly as a basis for the criticism of legislative classification. In this capacity the clause, while it has required the identification of the "purpose" of the law, has not involved or required a criticism of that purpose. But the court has gone beyond the use of the equal protection clause as a classification requirement. It has interpreted the clause as a ban against "discriminatory" legislation, and thus has become involved in the criticism of legislative purpose.

. . . [T]he prohibition against discriminatory legislation is a demand for purity of motive. It erects a constitutional barrier against legislative motives of hate, prejudice, vengeance, hostility, or, alternatively, of favoritism, and partiality. The imposition of special burdens, the granting of special benefits, must always be justified. They can only be justified as being directed at the elimination of some social evil, the achievement of some public good. When and if the proscribed motives replace a concern for the public good as the "purpose" of the law, there is a violation of the equal protection prohibition against discriminatory legislation.[36]

But only to state or clarify the meaning of the discriminatory legislation doctrine in these terms is to understand the Court's reluctance to use this doctrine freely. Whenever it does so it is in the unenviable position of calling into question the integrity of legislative motive. . . .

But more than a reluctance to question the integrity of legislative motive is at stake. To become involved in the search for motives, in the analysis or psychoanalysis of legislative behavior, is a task any sensible mortal might well shun in the easiest of circumstances. Add the fact that we are dealing with a sizeable body of men and the task becomes virtually hopeless. For it cannot be taken for granted that any particular law is the product of a common [motive] rather than the resultant of conflicting motives.

Moreover, the very demand for a non-partisan and impartial attitude on the part of legislators meets with opposition from the widespread view that a disinterested legislator is in fact betraying the special interests of his constituents, which it is his chief function to promote.

Finally, the consideration of motive is complicated by the fact that it is altogether possible for a law which is the expression of a forbidden motive to be a good law. What is to be done with a law which, passed with the most questionable of motives, still makes a positive contribution to the public good? Suppose the legislature decides to "get" Standard Oil, or Lovett, or Petrillo, but does so through a law which hits all monopolies, all government employees, or all labor unions. Does the forbidden motive vitiate a law that may operate generally and to the public advantage?

That, in the face of these difficulties, we can still speak of a judicial prohibition against discriminatory legislation is a minor miracle. . . .

3. SUBSTANTIVE EQUAL PROTECTION

The final doctrinal development of the equal protection clause to be considered may well be called its substantive development. The parallel with due process suggested by this term is deliberate and appropriate. This is not only because the equal protection clause is being used to preclude the attainment of certain results by the exercise of the police power but also because the results prohibited, or rather, the very rights guaranteed by the equal protection clause have, in the past, been considered as part of the guarantee of substantive due process. . . .

Whatever the reasons, . . . the substantive use of the equal protection clause is a fact. In this role it takes under its protection certain rights and prohibits their infringement. Thus the rights of white sellers and Negro buyers may not be interfered with [as in municipal restrictive covenant ordinances], and it is no answer to say that the rights of Negro sellers and white buyers are equally interfered with. The equal protection clause is held to be violated simply by the invasion of this substantive right no matter how "equally" the invasion is conducted.

It should be noted, of course, that shifting a right from the protection of due process to the protection of the equal protection clause neither clarifies or simplifies the problem of the "absolute" character of a right nor eases the problem of determining what particular rights are to be regarded as enjoying this absolute protection.

The transference of substantive rights to the equal protection clause by shifting the emphasis from equality to protection has implications for the Federal System. It undermines the doctrine that the Fourteenth Amendment forbids only state action. If the clause guarantees substantive rights, then it requires their protection by the state. The failure of the state to supply that protection is accordingly a violation of the clause. Hence, by the Fifth Section of the Fourteenth Amendment, congressional power to enforce the Amendment by appropriate legislation can fill the gap left by state inaction. What happens then to the court's oft reiterated assertion that the Fourteenth Amendment did not disturb the existing division of power between the states and the Nation? . . .

NOTES

[5]118 U.S. 356, 369 (1886).

[8]*Atchison, Topeka & S. F. R R v. Matthews*, 174 U.S. 96, 106 (1899).

[18]*Hirabayashi v. United States*, 320 U.S. 81 (1943).

[19]*Edwards v. California*, 314 U.S. 160, 184 (1941).

[24]*Korematsu v. United States*, 323 U.S. 214, 216 (1944).

[36]The fact that the Court sometimes speaks of laws as discriminatory in "result" does not really broaden the discriminatory legislation category beyond the field of motive. For this situation is generally one in which . . . the challenged statute on its face is quite innocuous. Only its application reveals the result that the classification falls along lines of race or consanguinity. This result raises the question of whether the classification, treated as "suspect," meets the reasonable relation test or whether it is the expression of a discriminatory motive. It is thus, apart from the classification problem, purely a question of motive.

QUESTIONS FOR DISCUSSION

1. Which is worse: under-inclusiveness, over-inclusiveness, or sometimes one and sometimes the other? Why? Give examples either way.

2. What exactly is it about race and ethnicity that justify treating them as suspect classifications that trigger strict scrutiny? Which other classifications should be suspect in your opinion?

3. When fundamental rights are used to trigger strict scrutiny, is the concept of equality as empty as Westen claimed (in Section 5.1)?

GROUPS AND THE EQUAL PROTECTION CLAUSE

OWEN M. FISS

This is an essay about the structure and limitations of the antidiscrimination principle, the principle that controls the interpretation of the Equal Protection Clause. To understand the importance of that principle in constitutional adjudication a distinction must first be drawn between two different modes of interpretation.

Under one mode the constitutional text is taken pure—the primary decisional touchstone is the actual language of the Constitution. The text of the Constitution is viewed as providing an intelligible rule of decision and that text, rather than any gloss, is the primary referent; at most, disagreement may arise as to how much weight should be given to one or two words and what the words mean. This is a plausible—arguable, though far from persuasive—approach to the Free Speech Clause. It is the approach associated with Justice Black.

The second mode of constitutional interpretation deemphasizes the text. Primary reliance is instead placed on a set of principles—which I call *mediating* because they "stand between" the courts and the Constitution—to give meaning and content to an ideal embodied in the text. These principles are offered as a paraphrase of the particular textual provision, but in truth the relationship is much more fundamental. They give the provision its only meaning as a guide for decision. So much so, that over time one often loses sight of the artificial status of these principles—they are not "part of" the Constitution, but instead only a judicial gloss, open to reevaluation and redefinition in a way that the text of the Constitution is not.

The Equal Protection Clause has generally been viewed in this second way. The words—no state shall "deny to any person within its jurisdiction the equal protection of the laws"—do not state an intelligible rule of decision. In that sense the text has no meaning. The Clause contains the word "equal" and thereby gives constitutional status to the ideal of equality, but that ideal is capable of a wide range of meanings. This ambiguity has created the need for a mediating principle, and the one chosen by courts and commentators is the antidiscrimination principle. When asked what the Equal Protection Clause means, an informed lawyer—even one committed to Justice Black's textual approach to the First Amendment—does not repeat the words of the Clause—a denial of equal protection. Instead, he is likely to respond that the Clause prohibits discrimination.

One purpose of this essay is simply to underscore the fact that the antidiscrimination principle is not the Equal Protection Clause, that it is nothing more than a mediating principle. I want to bring to an end the identification of the Clause with the antidiscrimination principle. But I also have larger ambitions. I want to suggest that the antidiscrimination principle embodies a very limited conception of equality, one that is highly individualistic and confined to assessing the rationality of means. I also want to outline another mediating principle—the group-disadvantaging principle—one that has as good, if not better, claim to represent the ideal of equality, one that takes a fuller account of social reality, and one that

Owen Fiss, "Groups and the Equal Protection Clause," *Philosophy and Public Affairs*, vol. 5 (1976), pp. 107–77 more clearly focuses the issues that must be decided in equal protection cases.

I. THE STRUCTURE OF THE ANTIDISCRIMINATION PRINCIPLE

The construction of the antidiscrimination principle proceeds in three steps. The first is to reduce the ideal of equality to the principle of equal treatment—similar things should be treated similarly. The second step is to take account of the fact that even the just state must make distinctions, must treat some things differently from others; for example, even the most noncontroversial criminal statute distinguishes between people on the basis of their conduct. Recognition of the inevitability and indeed the justice of some line–drawing makes the central task of equal protection theory one of determining which lines or distinctions are permissible. Not all discriminations can be prohibited; the word "to discriminate," once divested of its emotional connotation, simply means to distinguish or to draw a line. The mediating principle of the Equal Protection Clause therefore must be one that prohibits only "arbitrary" discrimination. The Clause does not itself tell us which distinctions are arbitrary, and as the third step in this process a general method is posited for determining the rationality and thus the permissibility of the lines drawn. The method chosen by the Supreme Court, and the one that generally goes under the rubric of the antidiscrimination principle, has two facets: (a) the identity of the discrimination is determined by the criterion upon which it is based, and (b) the discrimination is arbitrary if the criterion upon which it is based is unrelated to the state purpose. . . .

III. THE LIMITATIONS OF THE ANTI- DISCRIMINATION PRINCIPLE

Nondiscriminatory State Action

The antidiscrimination principle has created several gaps in the coverage of the Equal Protection Clause. The principle purports to be universalistic in terms of the persons protected, and yet it turns out to be far from universalistic in terms of the state practices proscribed. The gaps in coverage arise from the fact that not all objectionable state conduct is discriminatory. Discrimination involves a choice among persons and, as I said, an antidiscrimination principle operates by prohibiting government from making that choice arbitrarily. But there are government enactments or practices where no choice is made among persons and of these it does not make sense to ask whether there is "arbitrary" discrimination. I am not complaining of the fact that the antidiscrimination principle leaves standing state conduct that should be invalidated; but rather that it provides no frame of reference for assessing certain types of state conduct and for that reason is incomplete.

This gap in part accounts for the difficulty the Supreme Court has had with some of the classic state action cases. One such case is *Shelley v. Kraemer.*[44] The Court there invalidated a state policy of enforcing racially restrictive covenants and although that result seems right, on the analytic level *Shelley v. Kraemer* is generally deemed to be an extraordinarily difficult case—the Finnegans Wake of constitutional law. The difficult question was not, in the judgment, whether the state judges who enforced the restrictive covenant were acting as representatives of the "state." True, that issue was discussed by the Court, but it hardly seemed of any moment. Rather the troublesome question arose in trying to determine whether the state's action was the kind of "action" prohibited by the Equal Protection Clause. The Clause was viewed as prohibiting (racial) discrimination, and only that. The state asserted that its policy was not in any way discriminatory—restrictive covenants would be enforced against blacks and whites alike.

The basis of the Court's rejection of this defense remains a mystery to me to this day. Only a couple of sentences in the opinion purport to be responsive. In one the Court mentions the factual assertions of plaintiffs that, by and large, these racially restrictive covenants are used against blacks, rather than whites. The Court seemed willing to assume the truthfulness of this assertion as a factual matter, but it was hesitant to conclude much from it. That seemed a sound instinct, provided the Court was confined to the antidiscrimination principle and wanted to invalidate the policy, rather than its application; as long as the state stands ready to, and in fact would, enforce a racially restrictive covenant against whites this state policy cannot itself be deemed a form of racial discrimination. The other response is the well-known passage of *Shelley v. Kraemer* declaring that the Equal Protection Clause protects individual rights.[46] But I fail to see why this is responsive to the state's defense—there is no discrimination by the state. The more appropriate response to the state would be to reject its premise as to the kind of state action prohibited by the Clause. Why, I would ask, must the action of the state be discriminatory before it is deemed a violation of the Equal Protection Clause? . . .

The Problem of Facially Innocent Criteria

The classic state action cases . . . reveal the inability of the antidiscrimination principle to deal adequately with state conduct that does not discriminate among persons. Another problem area arises from state conduct that does in fact discriminate among persons, but not on the basis of a suspect criterion. The discrimination is based on a criterion that seems innocent on its face and yet nonetheless has the effect of disadvantaging blacks (or other minorities). For example, when the state purports to choose employees or college students on the basis of performance on standardized tests, and it turns out that the only persons admitted or hired are white.

As originally conceived—both by Tussman and tenBroek and by the Supreme Court in the important formative period of the 1940s and 1950s—the antidiscrimination principle promised

to evolve a small, finite list of suspect criteria, such as race, religion, national origin, wealth, sex. These would be presumptively impermissible. The great bulk of other criteria may ultimately be deemed arbitrary in some particular instances because of ill-fit, but they would be presumptively valid. For these criteria—which I call *facially innocent*—the mere rational-relation test would suffice, and the probability would be very high that the statute or administrative action incorporating or utilizing such criteria would be sustained.

In some instances the presumption of validity may be dissolved, and the contrary presumption created, through the use of the concept of the real criterion. The plaintiffs can charge cheating: while the state says that it is selecting on the basis of an innocent criterion (such as performance on a written test), in truth the selection is being made on the basis of a suspect criterion (race). The substantiation of this charge confronts the plaintiffs with enormous evidentiary burdens. No one can be expected to admit to charges of cheating, and rarely is the result so striking (for example, the twenty-eight-sided voting district of *Gomillion v. Lightfoot*[54] or no blacks on the work force) as to permit only one inference—discrimination on the basis of a suspect criterion. But if the charge could be substantiated (perhaps with an assist from the reallocation of the burdens of proofs when the criterion had almost the same effect as a suspect one), then there would be no problem of using the strict-scrutiny branch of the antidiscrimination principle: the real criterion, as opposed to the stated criterion, is a suspect one, and there the court should insist upon a very tight fit between purpose and criterion. The troublesome cases arise, however, when the charge of cheating cannot be substantiated, where, for example, the court finds that in truth the jobs were allocated or students selected on the basis of academic performance. What then?

One possible response is, of course, to apply the mere rational-relation test and validate the practice: there is certainly some connection between the state's purposes and these criteria. The fit may not be perfect, but perfection is not required. But the courts have balked. They have been troubled by the fact that the practice is particularly injurious to a disadvantaged group and for that reason have scrutinized state conduct with the greatest of care. The judicial inclination is all toward invalidation. This impulse seems correct as a matter of substantive justice, and yet is difficult to reconcile treatment of the facially innocent criteria with the original, modest conception of the antidiscrimination principle. . . .

IV. THE GROUP-DISADVANTAGING PRINCIPLE

The Shift from Classification to Class: Integrating the Concept of a Disadvantaged Group into the Law

In attempting to formulate another theory of equal protection, I have viewed the clause primarily, but not exclusively, as a protection for blacks. In part, this perspective stems from the original intent—the fact that the Clause was viewed as a means of safeguarding blacks from hostile state action. . . .

Starting from this perspective, a distinctively racial one, it strikes me as odd to build a general interpretation of the Equal Protection Clause, as Tussman and tenBroek did, on the rejection of the idea that there are natural classes, or social groups, in American society and blacks are such a group. Blacks are viewed as a group; they view themselves as a group; their identity is in large part determined by membership in the group; their social status is linked to the status of the group; and much of our action, institutional and personal, is based on these perspectives.

I use the term "group" to refer to a social group, and for me, a social group is more than a collection of individuals, all of whom, to use a polar example, happen to arrive at the same street corner at the same moment. A social group, as I use the term, has two other characteristics. (1) It is an *entity* (though not one that

has a physical body). This means that the group has a distinct existence apart from its members, and also that it has an identity. It makes sense to talk about the group (at various points of time) and know that you are talking about the same group. You can talk about the group without reference to the particular individuals who happen to be its members at any one moment. (2) There is also a condition of *interdependence*. The identity and well-being of the members of the group and the identity and well-being of the group are linked. Members of the group identify themselves—explain who they are—by reference to their membership in the group; and their well-being or status is in part determined by the well-being or status of the group. That is why the free blacks of the antebellum period—the Dred Scotts—were not really free, and could never be so long as the institution of Negro slavery still existed. Similarly, the well-being and status of the group is determined by reference to the well-being and status of the members of the group. The emancipation of one slave—the presence of one Frederick Douglass—may not substantially alter the well-being or status of the group; but if there were enough Frederick Douglasses, or if most blacks had his status, then surely the status of blacks as a social group would be altered. That is why the free black posed such a threat to the institution of slavery. Moreover, the identity and existence of the group as a discrete entity is in part determined by whether individuals identify themselves by membership in the group. If enough individuals cease to identify themselves in terms of their membership in a particular group (as occurs in the process of assimilation), then the very identity and separate existence of the group—as a distinct entity—will come to an end.

I would be the first to admit that working with the concept of a group is problematic, much more so than working with the concept of an individual or criterion. It is "messy." For example, in some instances, it may be exceedingly difficult to determine whether particular individuals are members of the group; or whether a particular collection of persons constitutes a social group. I will also admit that my definition of a social group, and in particular the condition of interdependence, compounds rather than reduces, these classificatory disputes. But these disputes do not demonstrate the illegitimacy of this category of social entity nor deny the validity or importance of the idea. They only blur the edges. Similarly, the present reality of the social groups should not be obscured by a commitment to the ideal of a "classless society" or the individualistic ethic—the ideal of treating people as individuals rather than as members of groups. Even if the Equal Protection Clause is viewed as the means for furthering or achieving these individualistic ideals (and I am not sure why it should be), there is no reason why the Clause—as an instrument for bringing about the "good society"—must be construed as though it is itself governed by that ideal or why it should be assumed that the "good society" had been achieved in 1868, or is so now.

The conception of blacks as a social group is only the first step in constructing a mediating principle. We must also realize they are a very special type of social group. They have two other characteristics as a group that are critical in understanding the function and reach of the Equal Protection Clause. One is that blacks are very badly off, probably our worst-off class (in terms of material well-being second only to the American Indians), and in addition they have occupied the lowest rung for several centuries. In a sense, they are America's perpetual underclass. . . .

It is not just the socioeconomic status of blacks as a group that explains their special position in equal protection theory. It is also their political status. The power of blacks in the political arena is severely limited. For the last two centuries the political power of this group was circumscribed in most direct fashion—disenfranchisement. The electoral strength of

blacks was not equal to their numbers. That has changed following the massive enfranchisement of the Voting Rights Act of 1965, but structural limitations on the political power of blacks still persist. These limitations arise from three different sources, which can act either alternatively or cumulatively and which, in any event, are all interrelated. One source of weakness is their numbers, the fact that they are a numerical minority; the second is their economic status, their position as the perpetual underclass; and the third is that, as a "discrete and insular" minority, they are the object of "prejudice"—that is, the subject of fear, hatred, and distaste that make it particularly difficult for them to form coalitions with others (such as the white poor) and that make it advantageous for the dominant political parties to hurt them—to use them as a scapegoat.

Recently, in some localities, such as large cities, the weakness of the group derived from their number has been eliminated; indeed in certain of these localities blacks may no longer be in the minority. The blacks may have a majority of a city council, or there may even be a black mayor. It would be wrong, however, to generalize from these situations. They are the exception, not the rule, and therefore should not control the formulation of a general theory of the Equal Protection Clause. Moreover, these black-dominated political agencies—the black city council or the black mayor—must be placed in context. One facet of their context is the white domination of those extra-political agencies such as the banks, factories, and police, that severely circumscribe the power of the formal political agencies. Another facet is the persistent white domination of the national political agencies, such as the Congress and presidency, agencies that have become the critical loci of political power in American society.

Hence, despite recent demographic shifts in several large cities, I think it appropriate to view blacks as a group that is relatively powerless in the political arena and in my judgment that political status of the group justifies a special judicial solicitude on their behalf. When the product of a political process is a law that hurts blacks, the usual countermajoritarian objection to judicial invalidation—the objection that denies those "nine men" the right to substitute their view for that of "the people"—has little force. For the judiciary could be viewed as amplifying the voice of the powerless minority; the judiciary is attempting to rectify the injustice of the political process as a method of adjusting competing claims. The need for this rectification turns on whether the law is deemed one that harms blacks—a judgment that is admittedly hard to make when the perspective becomes a group one, for that requires the aggregation of interests and viewpoints, many of which are in conflict. It is important to emphasize, however, that the need for this rectification does not turn on whether the law embodies a classification, racial or otherwise; it is sufficient if the state law simply has the *effect* of hurting blacks. Nor should the rectification, once triggered by a harmful law, be confined to questions of fit—the judicial responsibility is more extensive than simply one of guarding against the risk of imprecise classifications by the political agencies. The relative powerlessness of blacks also requires that the judiciary strictly scrutinize the choice of ends; for it is just as likely that the interests of blacks as a group will not be adequately taken into account in choosing ends or goals. Maximizing goals such as reducing transportation costs (a goal that might account for the neighborhood-school plan) or having the most brilliant law students (a goal that might account for requiring a 650 on the LSAT) are constitutionally permissible goals in the sense that there is no substantive constitutional provision (or implied purpose lying behind some provision) that deny them to the state. On the other hand, these maximizing goals are obviously not in any sense constitutionally compelled goals and there is a chance—a most substantial one—that

they would not be chosen as the goals (without any modification) if the interests of the blacks as a group were adequately taken into account—if the goal-choosers paid sufficient attention to the special needs, desires, and views of this powerless group.

The injustice of the political process must be corrected, and perhaps as a last resort, that task falls to the judiciary. But this claim does not yield any basis for specifying what the corrected process would look like, or what the court should say when it amplifies the voice of the powerless minority. A just political process would be one in which blacks would have "more" of a voice than they in fact do, but not necessarily one in which they would "win." In a sense there is a remedial lacuna; a pure process claim cannot determine substantive outcomes. (At the very most, it could yield those substantive outcomes that would tend to enhance the position of this group in the political process—such as favoring an increase in the numbers of black lawyers given the pivotal role lawyers play in the political process or favoring electoral districting that enhances the power of blacks as a group.) But this processual theory focusing on the relative powerlessness of blacks in the political arena need not stand alone. The substantive standards can be supplied by the other critical characteristics of this social group—perpetual subordination. The political status of the group justifies the institutional allocations—our willingness to allow those "nine men" to substitute their judgment (about ends as well as means) for that of "the people." The socioeconomic position of the group supplies an additional reason for the judicial activism and also determines the content of the intervention—improvement of the status of that group.

I would therefore argue that blacks should be viewed as having three characteristics that are relevant in the formulation of equal protection theory: (a) they are a social group; (b) the group has been in a position of perpetual subordination; and (c) the political power of the group is severely circumscribed. Blacks are what might be called a specially disadvantaged group, and I would view the Equal Protection Clause as a protection for such groups. Blacks are the prototype of the protected group, but they are not the only group entitled to protection. There are other social groups, even as I have used the term, and if these groups have the same characteristics as blacks—perpetual subordination and circumscribed political power—they should be considered specially disadvantaged and receive the same degree of protection. What the Equal Protection Clause protects is specially disadvantaged groups, not just blacks. A concern for equal treatment and the word "person" appearing in the Clause permit and probably require this generality of coverage.

Some of these specially disadvantaged groups can be defined in terms of characteristics that do not have biological roots and that are not immutable; the Clause might protect certain language groups and aliens. Moreover, in passing upon a claim to be considered a specially disadvantaged group, the court may treat one of the characteristics entitling blacks to that status as a sufficient but not a necessary condition; indeed the court may even develop variable standards of protection—it may tolerate disadvantaging practices that would not be tolerated if the group was a "pure" specially disadvantaged group. Jews or women might be entitled to less protection than American Indians, though nonetheless entitled to some protection. Finally, these judicial judgements may be time-bound. Through the process of assimilation the group may cease to exist, or even if the group continues to retain its identity, its socioeconomic and political positions may so improve so as to bring to an end its status as specially disadvantaged. . . .

V. THE CHOICE OF PRINCIPLE

In many situations it will not make a great deal of difference whether the court operates under the antidiscrimination principle or the group-disadvantaging one. An example of such a situation—which I would like to call "first-order"—would be one in which the state excludes blacks from public institutions. In these first-order situations, which were the focus of judicial attention up to the late 1940s, and the following decade or two, the same result is likely to flow from either principle. I would still prefer the group-disadvantaging principle on the ground of frankness—it more accurately captures the intellectual process that should go on in the mind of the judge. It is nevertheless hard to believe much turns on the choice of principle.

Today, however, we find ourselves beyond these first-order situations. A new situation arises when the court is confronted with challenges to nondiscriminatory state action . . . and with challenges to the state use of facially innocent criteria (such as test performance for allocating jobs or college places). With these second-order situations, there is more than frankness to recommend the group-disadvantaging principle. I believe this principle will frame matters in such a way as to expose the real issues and thus be more likely to lead to the correct decision—invalidation of those state practices that aggravate the subordinate position of the specially disadvantaged groups. It is, of course, possible that under the antidiscrimination principle a court willing to stretch and strain could reach the same result as it would under the group-disadvantaging principle; but that seems either to be a fortuity, or to require such a modification of the antidiscrimination principle—as evidenced by the "past discrimination," "de facto discrimination," or "fundamental right" offshoots—as to deprive the principle of any intellectual coherence and transform it into something it was never intended to be. In these situations, the group-disadvantaging principle should be preferred because it has a degree of coherence and completeness that can never be achieved with the antidiscrimination principle. . . .

I am willing to assume that the group–disadvantaging strategy will strain the resources, the imagination and even the patience of the judiciary. From the perspective of "mechanical jurisprudence" the group-disadvantaging principle offers no advantages. But I doubt whether these institutional considerations ought to be the bases for the choice between principles. For one thing, . . . this image of what judicial life will be under the antidiscrimination principle—no value judgments, sharp lines and no factual judgments—is largely illusory. The court must make determinations about whether the purpose served by the classification is "legitimate," which classifications are "suspect," what rights are "fundamental," what purposes are special or ordinary, whether it is permissible to take one step at a time, and whether the "fit" is sufficient. The quantitative ring to the terms "fit," "overinclusion," and "underinclusion" is decidedly an illusion. . . .

In any event, even if it can (somehow) be demonstrated that the antidiscrimination principle is more conducive to the traditional ideals of the craft, it still remains to be seen why these ideals—the ideals of "mechanical jurisprudence"—should be preserved at all or at least at the expense of substantive results deemed just. It is understandable why judges will choose that strategy most in accord with the ideal of their craft but that hardly makes it just, nor, for the self-conscious judge, inevitable. The redistributive aims served by the group-disadvantaging principle—the elevation of at least one group that has spent two centuries in this country in a position of subordination—may simply override these supposed institutional advantages. . . .

NOTES

[44]334 U.S. 1 (1948).

[46]The text reads: "The rights created by the first section of the Fourteenth Amendment are, by its terms, guaranteed to the individual. The rights established are personal rights." 334 U.S., at 22. A clever lawyer might have asserted that the discrimination was not between whites and blacks, but rather between two classes of sellers—those who sell land burdened with a restrictive covenant and those who sell unencumbered land. But if that were the challenged distinction, we have moved beyond the realm of suspect classifications and thus might have to operate under a minimum scrutiny inquiry. The Court did not seem willing to operate at that level; for them it was a racial case—a wrong to blacks. It is interesting to note that Tussman and tenBroek did not see *Shelley v. Kraemer* as resting on the "reasonable classification" (or antidiscrimination) principle. They did not view the case as a racial one, but rather as a matter of "substantive due process"—interference with the liberty to sell—though recognizing, given the bad taste left by that doctrine, that it might have to be called "substantive equal protection."

[54]364 U.S. 339 (1960).

QUESTIONS FOR DISCUSSION

1. What are the most important differences between Tussman and tenBroek's anti-discrimination model and Fiss' group-disadvantaging model? In your opinion, which provides the best interpretation of the Equal Protection Clause? Why?

2. Explain Fiss' definition of a group. Is this definition precise enough to answer the criticisms of his opponents? Why or why not? Should all groups be protected against discrimination? All disadvantaged groups? Any groups? Why or why not?

3. How could a defender of the anti-discrimination model best handle the cases of restrictive covenants and facially innocent criteria that Fiss describes?

BROWN V. BOARD OF EDUCATION

347 U.S. 483 (1954)

MR. CHIEF JUSTICE WARREN delivered the opinion of the Court.

These cases come to us from the States of Kansas, South Carolina, Virginia, and Delaware. They are premised on different facts and different local conditions, but a common legal question justifies their consideration together in this consolidated opinion.

In each of the cases, minors of the Negro race, through their legal representatives, seek the aid of the courts in obtaining admission to the public schools of their community on a nonsegregated basis. In each instance, they had been denied admission to schools attended by white children under laws requiring or permitting segregation according to race. This segregation was alleged to deprive the plaintiffs of the equal protection of the laws under the Fourteenth Amendment. In each of the cases other than the Delaware case, a three-judge federal district court denied relief to the plaintiffs on the so-called "separate but equal" doctrine announced by this Court in *Plessy v. Ferguson.* Under that doctrine, equality of treatment is accorded when the races are provided substantially equal facilities, even though these facilities be separate. In the Delaware case, the Supreme Court of Delaware adhered to that doctrine, but ordered that the plaintiffs be admitted to the white schools because of their superiority to the Negro schools.

The plaintiffs contend that segregated public schools are not "equal" and cannot be made "equal," and that hence they are deprived of the equal protection of the laws. Because of the obvious importance of the question presented, the court took jurisdiction. Argument was heard in the 1952 Term, and reargument was heard this Term on certain questions propounded by the Court.

Reargument was largely devoted to the circumstances surrounding the adoption of the Fourteenth Amendment in 1868. It covered exhaustively consideration of the Amendment in Congress, ratification by the states, then existing practices in racial segregation, and the views of proponents and opponents of the Amendment. This discussion and our own investigation convince us that, although these sources cast some light, it is not enough to resolve the problem with which we are faced. At best, they are inconclusive. The most avid proponents of the post-War Amendments undoubtedly intended them to remove all legal distinctions among "all persons born or naturalized in the United States." Their opponents, just as certainly, were antagonistic to both the letter and the spirit of the Amendments and wished them to have the most limited effect. What others in Congress and the state legislatures had in mind cannot be determined with any degree of certainty.

An additional reason for the inconclusive nature of the Amendment's history, with respect to segregated schools, is the status of public education at that time. In the South, the movement toward free common schools, supported by general taxation, had not yet taken hold. Education of white children was largely in the hands of private groups. Education of Negroes was almost nonexistent, and practically all of the race were illiterate. In fact, any education of Negroes was forbidden by law in some states. Today, in contrast, many Negroes have achieved outstanding success in the arts and sciences as well as in the business and professional world. It is true that public school education at the time of the Amendment had advanced further in the North, but the effect of the Amendment on northern states was generally ignored in the congressional debates. Even in the North, the conditions of public education did not approximate those existing today. The curriculum was usually rudimentary; ungraded schools were common in rural areas; the school term was but three months a year in many states; and compulsory school attendance was virtually unknown. As a consequence, it is not surprising that there should be so little in the history of the Fourteenth Amendment relating to its intended effect on public education.

In the first cases in this Court construing the Fourteenth Amendment, decided shortly after its adoption, the Court interpreted it as proscribing all state-imposed discriminations against the Negro race. The doctrine of "separate but equal" did not make its appearance in this Court until 1896 in the case of *Plessy v. Ferguson* involving not education but transportation. American courts have since labored with the doctrine over half a century. In this Court, there have been six cases involving the "separate but equal" doctrine in the field of public education. In *Cumming v. County Board of Education* and *Gong Lum v. Rice* the validity of the doctrine itself was not challenged. In more recent cases, all on the graduate school level, inequality was found in that specific benefits enjoyed by white students were denied to Negro students of the same educational qualifications. In none of these cases was it necessary to re-examine the doctrine to grant relief to the Negro plaintiff. And in *Sweatt v. Painter* the Court expressly reserved decision on the question whether *Plessy v. Ferguson* should be held inapplicable to public education.

In the instant cases, that question is directly presented. Here, unlike *Sweatt v. Painter*, there are findings below that the Negro and white schools involved have been equalized, or are being equalized, with respect to buildings,

curricula, qualifications and salaries of teachers, and other "tangible" factors. Our decision, therefore, cannot turn on merely a comparison of these tangible factors in the Negro and white schools involved in each of the cases. We must look instead to the effect of segregation itself on public education.

In approaching this problem, we cannot turn the clock back to 1868 when the Amendment was adopted, or even to 1896 when *Plessy v. Ferguson* was written. We must consider public education in the light of its full development and its present place in American life throughout the Nation. Only in this way can it be determined if segregation in public schools deprives these plaintiffs of the equal protection of the laws.

Today, education is perhaps the most important function of state and local governments. Compulsory school attendance laws and the great expenditures for education both demonstrate our recognition of the importance of education to our democratic society. It is required in the performance of our most basic public responsibilities, even service in the armed forces. It is the very foundation of good citizenship. Today it is a principal instrument in awakening the child to cultural values, in preparing him for later professional training, and in helping him to adjust normally to his environment. In these days, it is doubtful that any child may reasonably be expected to succeed in life if he is denied the opportunity of an education. Such an opportunity, where the state has undertaken to provide it, is a right which must be made available to all on equal terms.

We come then to the question presented: Does segregation of children in public schools solely on the basis of race, even though the physical facilities and other "tangible" factors may be equal, deprive the children of the minority group of equal educational opportunities? We believe that it does.

In *Sweatt v. Painter* in finding that a segregated law school for Negroes could not provide them equal educational opportunities, this

Court relied in large part on "those qualities which are incapable of objective measurement but which make for greatness in a law school." In *McLaurin v. Oklahoma State Regents* the Court, in requiring that a Negro admitted to a white graduate school be treated like all other students, again resorted to intangible considerations: ". . . his ability to study, to engage in discussions and exchange views with other students, and, in general, to learn his profession." Such considerations apply with added force to children in grade and high schools. To separate them from others of similar age and qualifications solely because of their race generates a feeling of inferiority as to their status in the community that may affect their hearts and minds in a way unlikely ever to be undone. The effect of this separation on their educational opportunities was well stated by a finding in the Kansas case by a court which nevertheless felt compelled to rule against the Negro plantiffs:

Segregation of white and colored children in public schools has a detrimental effect upon the colored children. The impact is greater when it has the sanction of the law; for the policy of separating the races is usually interpreted as denoting the inferiority of the Negro group. A sense of inferiority affects the motivation of a child to learn. Segregation with the sanction of law, therefore, has a tendency to [retard] the education and mental development of Negro children and to deprive them of some of the benefits they would receive in a racial[ly] integrated school system.

Whatever may have been the extent of psychological knowledge at the time of *Plessy v. Ferguson*, this finding is amply supported by modern authority. Any language in *Plessy v. Ferguson* contrary to this finding is rejected.

We conclude that in the field of public education the doctrine of "separate but equal" has no place. Separate educational facilities are inherently unequal. Therefore, we hold that the plantiffs and others similarly situated for whom the actions have been brought are, by reason of the segregation complained of, deprived of the equal protection of the laws guaranteed by the Fourteenth Amendment. . . .

QUESTIONS FOR DISCUSSION

1. Does the argument in *Brown* depend on the claim that education is a fundamental right in modern society? If so, can the argument in *Brown* be extended to racial segregation in public transportation? On golf courses?

2. Given *Brown* as a precedent, is it unconstitutional for public high schools to be segregated by gender? Is it unconstitutional for sports in public high schools to be segregated by gender? Why or why not?

3. Imagine that the only two public high schools in a city have equal budgets, facilities, and faculties. Every student is allowed to go to the public high school of his or her choice. Every student chooses the school that is closest to home. Because of segregation in housing, all of the African-American students choose one school and all of the other students choose a different school. Does this violate the Equal Protection Clause? Why or why not? If so, what should the courts do about it?

4. If African-Americans who kill European-Americans are much more likely to be sentenced to death than European-Americans who kill African-

Americans in similar circumstances, does this show that capital punishment violates the Equal Protection Clause? Why or why not? See *McCleskey v. Kemp* in Section 6.6.

5. Suppose that a small shoe store advertises for a salesperson. Only two people apply. The first has two years of experience, a successful record, and good recommendations. The second applicant has ten years of experience, an even more successful record, and even better recommendations. The second applicant, however, is African–American. If the owner of the store has good reason to believe that most of his customers are so prejudiced that they will not buy shoes from an African–American, should it still be illegal for the owner to hire the first applicant instead of the second? Would hiring the first applicant instead of the second violate the Equal Protection Clause or Title VII of the Civil Rights Act of 1964? Why or why not?

6. Should it be illegal or unconstitutional for a private club to refuse to admit anyone from a certain race or ethnic group? Why or why not? (Compare *Moose Lodge v. Irvis*, 407 U.S. 163 (1972), where Pennsylvania granted a liquor license to a private club that refused to serve African–Americans, and some African–Americans complained that they were deprived because only a limited number of liquor licenses were available.)

7. Would libertarians, such as Nozick (Section 5.2), approve of laws against racial and ethnic discrimination in employment and housing? Why or why not?

8. Is anti–discrimination law a kind of legal moralism? (See Section 4.2)

SUGGESTIONS FOR FURTHER READING

A readable history of anti–discrimination law through Brown is Richard Kluger, *Simple Justice* (New York: Vintage, 1975). A clear introduction with documents and further bibliography are in Kent Greenawalt, *Discrimination and Reverse Discrimination* (New York: Knopf, 1983). Criticisms of anti–discrimination laws from the perspectives of libertarianism and of economics can be found in Richard Epstein, "Two Conceptions of Civil Rights," *Social Philosophy and Policy*, vol. 8 (1989), pp. 38–59; and more extensively in his *Forbidden Grounds: The Case Against Employment Discrimination Laws* (Cambridge: Harvard University Press, 1992). For a revision of Tussman and tenBroek, see Kenneth Simons, "Overinclusion and Underinclusion: A New Model", *U.C.L.A. Law Review*, vol. 36 (1989), pp. 447–528.

5.4 PREFERENTIAL TREATMENT

INTRODUCTION

After *Brown*, the Supreme Court struck down segregation in many areas (transportation, parks, beaches, libraries, golf courses, and so on) as well as laws against racial intermarriage. Another string of decisions required school systems to use busing as a means to end segregation. The Court also required some employers to hire or promote minimum percentages of minorities because those employers had illegally discriminated in the past. In response to these court decisions, some schools and companies voluntarily took steps to overcome what they saw as the effects of past discrimination.

One such program was adopted by the University of California at Davis. When its medical school opened in 1968, the first class had no African–American, Mexican–American, or Native–American students, so Davis created a special admissions program in 1970 that set aside sixteen spots for disadvantaged minorities in each class of 100. As a result, some non–minority applicants, such as Allan Bakke (in the case later in this section), were rejected even though they had higher scores on admissions tests than some minority members who were admitted under the special program.

Similar programs were adopted by private companies. One was Kaiser Aluminum Company in Gramercy, Louisiana, whose craftworkers were only 2.2 percent African–American, even though the local labor force was 39 percent African–American. After some pressure from federal agencies and bargaining with the United Steelworkers of America union, Kaiser adopted a program that "reserves for black employees 50 percent of the openings in an in–plant craft-training program until the percentage of black craftworkers in the plant is commensurate with the percentage of blacks in the local labor force."[19] As a result, some white plant workers, such as Brian Weber, were not admitted into the training program, even though they had more seniority than some African–Americans in the training program.

These kinds of programs were and still are so controversial that people even argue about what to call them. Their opponents describe them as "reverse discrimination." Their defenders call them "affirmative action."[20] A more neutral description, which we will use, is "preferential treatment."

What is preferential treatment? Its name suggests that preferential treatment occurs whenever someone is treated better because of a preference. But some

[19]*United Steelworkers of America v. Weber*, 443 U.S. 193 (1979).

[20]Such uses of evaluative labels are analyzed by Charles L. Stevenson, "Persuasive Definitions," *Mind*, XLVII (July 1938).

programs of this general kind are not so controversial. Schools and businesses often go to great lengths to recruit minority or women applicants. They seek them out, fly them in, feed them, and shower them with attention. If they are offered positions, they might be given more financial aid, salary, or benefits to get them to enter the school or take the job. These kinds of special treatment do not raise the same legal and moral issues if minority and women candidates still must compete on the same basis as everyone else for admission or hiring or promotion. The controversy is also greater when such programs are voluntary. If a court finds a business guilty of illegal discrimination, and then orders the business to undo the effects of that discrimination by using racial or sexual classifications in hiring, few question the legality of the program. So, in order to focus on the deepest legal issues, we will describe a program as preferential treatment only if it involves voluntary racial, ethnic, or sexual classifications in the methods or standards for admissions, hiring, or promotion.

Even this narrow class includes great variety. Education and employment are different. Preferential treatment programs can be private or public. Some programs are limited in time; others are not. Some programs give preference to certain groups only to break rough ties, but other programs admit or hire candidates who are somewhat less qualified in other respects than candidates in non-preferred groups. Some programs aim at rough goals, whereas other programs set specific quotas of candidates from the preferred groups to be hired or admitted. So many variations make it hard to generalize about all preferential treatment.

Nonetheless, there are three main ways to argue for preferential treatment in general. The first kind of argument focuses on the past. Great injustices were done to certain groups or members of those groups, so compensation is supposed to be owed to those groups or their members. Preferential treatment is an appropriate form of compensation when it corrects the present effects of past injustice. The conclusion is not just that affirmative action is morally permitted. This argument is supposed to show that affirmative action is morally required, because a failure to institute affirmative action would violate the rights of disadvantaged people to compensation for past injustices.

Opponents respond, however, that compensation is owed only *by* the individuals who acted unjustly and only *to* the individuals whom they treated unjustly. If I run into your car, I owe you compensation for the damage. But I do not owe you compensation when some other professor runs into your car. And I do not owe compensation to someone else who is a member of the same student group as you. Analogously, compensation for past racial discrimination is owed by individuals who discriminated in the past and to individuals who suffered discrimination in the past. The problem is that preferential treatment programs often:

1. harm[21] individuals (such as Bakke and Weber) who did not (as far as we know) discriminate in the past,

---

[21]Those who think Bakke has no right to medical school admission might argue that the Davis program causes him no legally relevant harm, but the program still makes him worse off than he otherwise would have been, and that is the point here.

and

   2. do not directly harm individuals who did discriminate in the past (such as the legislators who passed segregation laws).

Also, preferential treatment programs often

   3. benefit privileged individuals who suffered little, if any, discrimination in the past,

and

   4. do not directly benefit those minority members and women who have been most discriminated against in the past (since those individuals rarely apply for jobs and schools that offer preferential treatment).

In technical terms, preferential treatment programs are often both over-inclusive and under-inclusive with respect to both their harms and their benefits (see Tussman and tenBroek in Section 5.3).

   Defenders of the argument from compensation can point out that individual guilt is not always necessary for compensation to be owed. Imagine that my father gives me a used car, and I drive it until it is so old that it falls apart. Only then do I find out that my father stole the car from you. If I do not pay compensation to you, then I benefit from my father's injustice, and you suffer from it. But if I compensate you for the value to me of using your car, then I do not lose anything overall, and you suffer less from my father's injustice. So it seems reasonable to shift the costs of injustice by requiring me to compensate you, even though I did nothing unjust.

   Compensation can also be owed by and to groups. The United States government, for example, compensated Japanese-Americans who were imprisoned unjustly in World War II, even though the compensation came from taxes paid by some individuals who were not even alive during World War II. This case is not exactly like preferential treatment. One difference is that all taxpayers shared the costs of compensating the Japanese-Americans, but preferential treatment programs impose much larger costs on some individuals, like Bakke and Weber, than on others. Critics of preferential treatment will also point out that the Japanese-Americans who were compensated were the very individuals who were treated unjustly, whereas the minorities and women who are compensated by preferential treatment are not always the ones who suffered most from past injustice. Probably all minorities and women in the United States have suffered from some discrimination, which might justify some compensation. And preferential treatment might indirectly benefit even minorities and women who are not admitted or hired under preferential treatment programs. Nonetheless, if more compensation is owed to those who suffered more injustice, then preferential treatment programs do not distribute the burdens or the benefits of compensation in an ideal way.

   The second kind of argument for preferential treatment focuses on the present. In a common analogy, a track race is not fair if only one runner has hurdles in his lane, regardless of who put the hurdles in the way. Similarly, if past injustices create hurdles that put minorities and women at a competitive disadvantage in the present, then it is not fair to require them to compete on the same terms as advantaged white males. Moreover, even if white males today did not commit the past injustices, they still benefit now from those injustices. If those injustices had not been committed, minorities and women would have taken more of the jobs, and would have developed more skills and more seniority. The past injustices thus decrease competition from minorities and women. This decrease in competition benefits white males by increasing their chances of getting into the schools and jobs of their choice.

Preferential treatment is a natural way to restore fair competition, if it gives an advantage to the very people who would have been admitted or hired if there had been no past discrimination. And those advantaged individuals who would have been admitted or hired if there had been no preferential treatment program seem to have little ground for complaint, if they also would not have been hired if there had been no past injustice. So this argument from fair competition seems to avoid some of the problems of over-inclusiveness and under-inclusiveness that plague the argument from compensation.

Nonetheless, opponents of preferential treatment respond that this argument depends on speculation. How can one tell who would have been admitted or hired if there had been no past injustices? Some of the excluded individuals suffered injustices of their own, and some individuals who benefit from preferential treatment come from privileged backgrounds. These uncertainties and variations show that justice can be obtained only by looking at individuals as individuals rather than as members of groups, according to Supreme Court Justice Powell in his opinion in *Bakke* and Carl Cohen, philosophy professor at the University of Michigan at Ann Arbor and former member of the Board of Directors of the American Civil Liberties Union (see *Bakke* and the reading from Cohen later in this section).

The third main argument for preferential treatment focuses on future consequences. Preferential treatment promises many benefits to society. It is supposed to: (1) provide role models who will motivate other members of their groups to seek and achieve more for themselves and for others, (2) reduce racial stereotypes and tensions by making other people aware of how much minorities and women can achieve, and (3) bring economic success and professional services to groups who most need them. Some cite such good consequences as reasons why our society will be better off overall with preferential treatment than without.

This argument from consequences runs into several problems. First, it is not clear that preferential treatment really does have the benefits that are claimed for it. Second, even if preferential treatment does have benefits, opponents claim that it also has serious costs. Preferential treatment sometimes seems to increase tensions between races and sexes, to perpetuate myths of inferiority, and to create self-doubts in those who are treated preferentially. And some argue that hiring or admitting people who are less qualified by normal standards will decrease quality and productivity in our schools and in our economy.

Defenders of preferential treatment must understand these problems in order to fashion preferential treatment programs so as to minimize tensions, stereotypes, self-doubts, and quality losses. Nonetheless, preferential treatment can still be defended if its benefits outweigh its costs. The crucial claim is not just that preferential treatment has better consequences overall than if nothing is done to help disadvantaged groups. Advocates of preferential treatment need to argue that preferential treatment is better than other ways to help disadvantaged groups. Other possible methods include vigorous recruitment, inducements, and improvements in welfare, early education, and health services for disadvantaged communities. If these other programs can achieve the benefits of preferential treatment without as many costs, then everyone should want them. But if these other programs do not work well enough or take too long to work, then preferential treatment might be justified by its consequences.

It is important to realize that this argument need not depend on a simple version of utilitarianism that totals up all desires of everyone. The point can be that preferential treatment brings about a more just distribution of goods in society. In this form, the argument cannot be refuted simply by bringing up standard counterexamples to utilitarianism.

Still, arguments from consequences are always open to doubt. One reason is that there are so many kinds of preferential treatment. Diversity in colleges can contribute a great deal to the education of every student, but it is not so clear that diversity is as important in factories. The level of stereotyping and of resentment by excluded individuals also varies greatly from one area to another. This makes it very difficult to determine the overall consequences of particular preferential treatment programs.

Such uncertainty might seem to speak against preferential treatment in some cases. As Carl Cohen points out (later in this section), when the benefits are uncertain, it makes a big difference who has the power to decide when to use preferential treatment. Should private companies like Kaiser be allowed to adopt preferential treatment whenever they want?

It is more common to criticize arguments from consequences by appealing to rights that are supposed to be violated by preferential treatment programs. It is inherent in the notion of a right, or at least in our tradition of rights, that rights put limits on the ways in which governments may seek social goals (see Section 4.1). Even very good consequences are not enough to justify preferential treatment if it violates rights of individuals.

But does preferential treatment violate any real rights? Opponents claim that preferential treatment violates a right to be judged on one's merit, a right to be judged as an individual, and a right not to be excluded because of one's race or sex. These claims are criticized by Ronald Dworkin in the reading later in this section. Even if Dworkin does refute these particular claims, his opponents might try to reformulate the right that preferential treatment is supposed to violate. If they can find any right that is violated by preferential treatment, then no simple argument from consequences can be adequate to justify preferential treatment. However, if preferential treatment does not violate any real rights, and if preferential treatment really does improve society, then it is morally justified.

Whether preferential treatment is *morally* permitted does not settle the issue of whether it is *legally* permitted. (See Chapters 1–2.) The legal issues depend on precedents, statutes, and the Constitution. These legal sources might forbid preferential treatment, even if it is morally just. And the law might allow or require preferential treatment, even if it is morally unjust. So we need to ask: does preferential treatment violate any statutes or the Constitution?

That depends on how the statutes and Constitution are interpreted. On the traditional anti-discrimination model, any state action that uses a racial or ethnic classification violates the Equal Protection Clause unless there is no less intrusive way to serve a legitimate and compelling state interest. This model makes it very difficult to justify preferential treatment programs, since they use racial and ethnic classifications, and it is hard to prove that no possible alternative is better. It is easier to argue for the constitutionality of preferential treatment on other interpretations of the Equal Protection Clause. For example, Owen Fiss' group–disadvantaging model raises fewer questions for preferential treatment programs, since he would not subject them to any special scrutiny as long as they do not adversely affect any disadvantaged group (see Section 5.3).

This battle of interpretations was fought in the case of *Regents of the University of California v. Bakke*. Bakke's application was rejected by the medical school of the University of California at Davis, even though his scores on admissions tests were higher than the scores of some minority members admitted under a special admissions program. Bakke claimed that this admissions program violated the Equal Protection Clause of the U.S. Constitution, the California Constitution, and Title VI of the Civil Rights Act of 1964 (see Section 5.3).

In the Supreme Court, four Justices (Burger, Stevens, Stewart, and Rehnquist) agreed with Bakke that the Davis program and any other consideration of race in school admissions violate both Title VI and the California Constitution. They did not reach the question of whether such programs violate the U.S. Constitution. On the other side, four Justices (Brennan, Marshall, Blackmun, and White) held that the Davis program and consideration of race do *not* violate either Title VI or the California Constitution or the U.S. Constitution. So the deciding vote belonged to Justice Powell. Powell argued for a compromise. Powell agreed with the first four Justices that *quotas* as in the Davis program violate Title VI and the California Constitution, and he added the U.S. Constitution. But Powell agreed with the second four Justices that these laws are not violated by *goals* as in the Harvard admissions program (described on pp. 589–90). Powell's argument was based on the anti–discrimination model. The Davis and Harvard programs use racial classifications, so Powell subjected them to strict scrutiny. He found that consideration of race does serve a compelling state interest (educational diversity), but he also held that goals are less intrusive than quotas, so quotas cannot pass strict scrutiny, although goals can.

In contrast, Brennan argued that strict scrutiny should not be applied when the state uses a racial classification to serve a benign, remedial purpose; that is, when nobody is stigmatized and when the racial classification is necessary to prevent a disadvantaged group from suffering differential impact due to past discrimination in society. Under these conditions, according to Brennan, the courts should apply a less exacting *middle level scrutiny* test, which requires the state to show that the legislation is substantially related to a legitimate and important state interest. Brennan's argument assumes that, to show a substantial relation, the state must show that there is no significantly less intrusive means to the interest. Brennan then argues that the difference between the Davis and Harvard programs is not significant, because both produce the same result for those who are excluded.

The heart of the controversy concerns the conditions under which to apply middle level scrutiny. Powell criticizes Brennan's conditions on the grounds that the notion of stigma is too vague and that discrimination in society at large is not enough to justify exclusion as long as neither Davis nor Bakke had been found guilty of any particular discrimination. Powell's basic claim is that the Equal Protection Clause protects individuals rather than groups.

The *Bakke* decision did not end the disputes. The very next year, the Supreme Court upheld a preferential treatment quota in employment in *United Steelworkers of America v. Weber*.[22] This program is criticized by Carl Cohen (later in this section). More recently, the court struck down a quota by a city in *Richmond v. Croson*[23] but then upheld a preferential treatment program by the federal government in *Metro Broadcasting v. FCC* (later in this section). These shifts show that no decision can settle the law once and for all. The legal and moral debates are still alive today.

---

[22]*United Steelworkers of America v. Weber*, 443 U.S. 193 (1979).

[23]*City of Richmond v. J. A. Croson Co.*, 488 U.S. 469 (1989).

WHY BAKKE HAS NO CASE

RONALD DWORKIN

On October 12, 1977, the Supreme Court heard oral argument in the case of *The Regents of the University of California v. Allan Bakke*. No lawsuit has ever been more widely watched or more thoroughly debated in the national and international press before the Court's decision. Still, some of the most pertinent facts set before the Court have not been clearly summarized.

The medical school of the University of California at Davis has an affirmative action program (called the "task force program") designed to admit more black and other minority students. It sets sixteen places aside for which only members of "educationally and economically disadvantaged minorities" compete. Allan Bakke, white, applied for one of the remaining eighty-four places; he was rejected but, since his test scores were relatively high, the medical school has conceded that it could not prove that he would have been rejected if the sixteen

Ronald Dworkin, "Why Bakke Has No Case," *New York Review of Books*, vol. 24, no. 18 (November 10, 1977), pp. 11–15

places reserved had been open to him. Bakke sued, arguing that the task force program deprived him of his constitutional rights. The California Supreme Court agreed, and ordered the medical school to admit him. The university appealed to the Supreme Court.

The Davis program for minorities is in certain respects more forthright (some would say cruder) than similar plans now in force in many other American universities and professional schools. Such programs aim to increase the enrollment of black and other minority students by allowing the fact of their race to count affirmatively as part of the case for admitting them. Some schools set a "target" of a particular number of minority places instead of setting aside a flat number of places. But Davis would not fill the number of places set aside unless there were sixteen minority candidates it considered clearly qualified for medical education. The difference is therefore one of administrative strategy and not of principle.

So the constitutional question raised by *Bakke* is of capital importance for higher education in the United States, and a large number of universities and schools have entered briefs *amicus curiae* urging the Court to reverse the California decision. They believe that if they are not free to use explicit racial criteria in their admissions programs, they will be unable to fulfill what they take to be their responsibilities to the nation.

It is often said that affirmative action programs aim to achieve a racially conscious society divided into racial and ethnic groups, each entitled as a group to some proportionable share of resources, careers, or opportunities. That is a perverse description. American society is currently a racially conscious society; this is the inevitable and evident consequence of a history of slavery, repression, and prejudice. Black men and women, boys and girls, are not free to choose for themselves in what roles—or as members of which social groups—others will characterize them. They are black, and no other

feature of personality or allegiance or ambition will so thoroughly influence how they will be perceived and treated by others, and the range and character of the lives that will be open to them.

The tiny number of black doctors and other professionals is both a consequence and a continuing cause of American racial consciousness, one link in a long and self-fueling chain reaction. Affirmative action programs use racially explicit criteria because their immediate goal is to increase the number of members of certain races in these professions. But their long-term goal is to reduce the degree to which American society is overall a racially conscious society.

The programs rest on two judgments. The first is a judgment of social theory: that the United States will continue to be pervaded by racial divisions as long as the most lucrative, satisfying, and important careers remain mainly the prerogative of members of the white race, while others feel themselves systematically excluded from a professional and social elite. The second is a calculation of strategy: that increasing the number of blacks who are at work in the professions will, in the long run, reduce the sense of frustration and injustice and racial self-consciousness in the black community to the point at which blacks may begin to think of themselves as individuals who can succeed like others through talent and initiative. At that future point the consequences of nonracial admissions programs, whatever these consequences might be, could be accepted with no sense of racial barriers or injustice.

It is therefore the worst possible misunderstanding to suppose that affirmative action programs are designed to produce a balkanized America, divided into racial and ethnic subnations. They use strong measures because weaker ones will fail; but their ultimate goal is to lessen, not to increase, the importance of race in American social and professional life.

According to the 1970 census, only 2.1 percent of American doctors were black. Affirmative action programs aim to provide more black doctors to serve black patients. This is not because it is desirable that blacks treat blacks and whites treat whites, but because blacks, through no fault of their own, are now unlikely to be well served by whites, and because a failure to provide the doctors they trust will exacerbate rather than reduce the resentment that now leads them to trust only their own. Affirmative action tries to provide more blacks as classmates for white doctors, not because it is desirable that a medical school class reflect the racial makeup of the community as a whole, but because professional association between blacks and whites will decrease the degree to which whites think of blacks as a race rather than as people, and thus the degree to which blacks think of themselves that way. It tries to provide "role models" for future black doctors, not because it is desirable for a black boy or girl to find adult models only among blacks, but because our history has made them so conscious of their race that the success of whites, for now, is likely to mean little or nothing for them.

The history of the campaign against racial injustice since 1954, when the Supreme Court decided *Brown v. Board of Education,* is a history in large part of failure. We have not succeeded in reforming the racial consciousness of our society by racially neutral means. We are therefore obliged to look upon the arguments for affirmative action with sympathy and an open mind. Of course, if Bakke is right that such programs, no matter how effective they may be, violate his constitutional rights, then they cannot be permitted to continue. But we must not forbid them in the name of some mindless maxim, like the maxim that it cannot be right to fight fire with fire, or that the end cannot justify the means. If the strategic claims for affirmative action are cogent, they cannot be dismissed on the ground that racially explicit tests are distasteful. If such tests are distasteful, it

can only be for reasons that make the underlying social realities the programs attack more distasteful still.

It is said that, in a pluralistic society, membership in a particular group cannot be used as a criterion of inclusion or exclusion from benefits. But group membership is, as a matter of social reality rather than formal admission standards, part of what determines inclusion or exclusion for us now. If we must choose between a society that is in fact liberal and an illiberal society that scrupulously avoids formal racial criteria, we can hardly appeal to the ideals of liberal pluralism to prefer the latter.

Archibald Cox of Harvard Law School, speaking for the University of California in oral argument, told the Supreme Court that this is the choice the United States must make. As things stand, he said, affirmative action programs are the only effective means of increasing the absurdly small number of black doctors. The California Supreme Court, in approving Bakke's claim, had urged the university to pursue that goal by methods that do not explicitly take race into account. But that is unrealistic. We must distinguish, Cox said, between two interpretations of what the California Court's recommendation means. It might mean that the university should aim at the same immediate goal, of increasing the proportion of black and other minority students in the medical school, by an admissions procedure that on the surface is not racially conscious.

That is a recommendation of hypocrisy. If those who administer the admissions standards, however these are phrased, understand that their immediate goal is to increase the number of blacks in the school, then they will use race as a criterion in making the various subjective judgments the explicit criteria will require, because that will be, given the goal, the only right way to make those judgments. The recommendation might mean, on the other hand, that the school should adopt some nonracially conscious goal, like increasing the number of disadvantaged students of all races, and then hope that that goal will produce an increase in the number of blacks as a by-product. But even if that strategy is less hypocritical (which is far from plain), it will almost certainly fail because no different goal, scrupulously administered in a non-racially conscious way, will significantly increase the number of black medical students.

Cox offered powerful evidence for that conclusion, and it is supported by the recent and comprehensive report of the Carnegie Council on Policy Studies in Higher Education. Suppose, for example, that the medical school sets aside separate places for applicants "disadvantaged" on some racially neutral test, like poverty, allowing only those disadvantaged in that way to compete for these places. If the school selects those from that group who scored best on standard medical school aptitude tests, then it will take almost no blacks, because blacks score relatively low even among the economically disadvantaged. But if the school chooses among the disadvantaged on some basis other than test scores, just so that more blacks will succeed, then it will not be administering the special procedure in a nonracially conscious way.

So Cox was able to put his case in the form of two simple propositions. A racially conscious test for admission, even one that sets aside certain places for qualified minority applicants exclusively, serves goals that are in themselves unobjectionable and even urgent. Such programs are, moreover, the only means that offer any significant promise of achieving these goals. If these programs are halted, then no more than a trickle of black students will enter medical or other professional schools for another generation at least.

If these propositions are sound, then on what ground can it be thought that such programs are either wrong or unconstitutional? We must notice an important distinction between two different sorts of objections that might be made. These programs are intended, as I said, to decrease the importance of race in the United States in the long run. It may be objected, first, that the programs will harm that goal more than they will advance it. There is no way now to prove that that is not so. Cox conceded in his argument that there are costs and risks in these programs.

Affirmative action programs seem to encourage, for example, a popular misunderstanding, which is that they assume that racial or ethnic groups are entitled to proportionate shares of opportunities, so that Italian or Polish ethnic minorities are, in theory, as entitled to their proportionate shares as blacks or Chicanos or American Indians are entitled to the shares the present programs give them. That is a plain mistake: the programs are not based on the idea that those who are aided are entitled to aid, but only on the strategic hypothesis that helping them is now an effective way of attacking a national problem. Some medical schools may well make that judgment, under certain circumstances, about a white ethnic minority. Indeed it seems likely that some medical schools are even now attempting to help white Appalachian applicants, for example, under programs of regional distribution.

So the popular understanding is wrong, but so long as it persists it is a cost of the program because the attitudes it encourages tend to a degree to make people more rather than less conscious of race. There are other possible costs. It is said, for example, that some blacks find affirmative action degrading; they find that it makes them more rather than less conscious of prejudice against their race as such. This attitude is also based on a misperception, I think, but for a small minority of blacks at least it is a genuine cost.

In the view of the many important universities which have such programs, however, the gains will very probably exceed the losses in reducing racial consciousness overall. This view is hardly so implausible that it is wrong for these universities to seek to acquire the experience that will allow us to judge whether they are right. It would be particularly silly to forbid these experiments if we know that the failure to try will mean, as the evidence shows, that the status quo will almost certainly continue. In any case, this first objection could provide no argument that would justify a decision by the Supreme Court holding the programs unconstitutional. The Court has no business substituting its speculative judgment about the probable consequences of educational policies for the judgment of professional educators.

So the acknowledged uncertainties about the long-term results of such programs could not justify a Supreme Court decision making them illegal. But there is a second and very different form of objection. It may be argued that even if the programs are effective in making our society less a society dominated by race, they are nevertheless unconstitutional because they violate the individual constitutional rights of those, like Allan Bakke, who lose places in consequence. In the oral argument Reynold H. Colvin of San Francisco, who is Bakke's lawyer, made plain that his objection takes this second form. Mr. Justice White asked him whether he accepted that the goals affirmative action programs seek are important goals. Colvin acknowledged that they were. Suppose, Justice White continued, that affirmative action programs are, as Cox had argued, the only effective means of seeking such goals. Would Colvin nevertheless maintain that the programs are unconstitutional? Yes, he insisted, they would be, because his client has a constitutional right that the programs be abandoned, no matter what the consequences.

Colvin was wise to put his objections on this second ground; he was wise to claim that his client has rights that do not depend on any judgment about the likely consequences of affirmative action for society as a whole, because if he sustains that claim, the Court must give him the relief he seeks.

But can he be right? If Allan Bakke has a constitutional right so important that the urgent goals of affirmative action must yield, then this must be because affirmative action violates some fundamental principle of political morality. This is not a case in which what might be called formal or technical law requires a decision one way or the other. There is no language in the Constitution whose plain meaning forbids affirmative action. Only the most naive theories of statutory construction could argue that such a result is required by the language of any earlier Supreme court decision or of the Civil Rights Act of 1964 or of any other congressional enactment. If Colvin is right, it must be because Allan Bakke has not simply some technical legal right but an important moral right as well.

What could that right be? The popular argument frequently made on editorial pages is that Bakke has a right to be judged on his merit. Or that he has a right to be judged as an individual rather than as a member of a social group. Or that he has a right, as much as any black man, not to be sacrificed or excluded from any opportunity because of his race alone. But these catch phrases are deceptive here, because, as reflection demonstrates, the only genuine principle they describe is the principle that no one should suffer from the prejudice or contempt of others. And that principle is not at stake in this case at all. In spite of popular opinion, the idea that the *Bakke* case presents a conflict between a desirable social goal and important individual rights is a piece of intellectual confusion.

Consider, for example, the claim that individuals applying for places in medical school should be judged on merit, and merit alone. If that slogan means that admissions committees should take nothing into account but scores on some particular intelligence test, then it is arbitrary and, in any case, contradicted by the long-standing practice of every medical school. If it means, on the other hand, that a medical school should choose candidates that it supposes will make the most useful doctors, then everything turns on the judgment of what factors make different doctors useful. The Davis medical school assigned to each regular applicant, as well as to each minority applicant, what it called a "benchmark score." This reflected not only the results of aptitude tests and college grade averages, but a subjective evaluation of the applicant's chances of functioning as an effective doctor, in view of society's present needs for medical service. Presumably the qualities deemed important were different from the qualities that a law school or engineering school would seek, just as the intelligence tests a medical school might use would be different from the tests these other schools would find appropriate.

There is no combination of abilities and skills and traits that constitutes "merit" in the abstract; if quick hands count as "merit" in the case of a prospective surgeon, this is because quick hands will enable him to serve the public better and for no other reason. If a black skin will, as a matter of regrettable fact, enable another doctor to do a different medical job better, then that black skin is by the same token "merit" as well. That argument may strike some as dangerous; but only because they confuse its conclusion—that black skin may be a socially useful trait in particular circumstances—with the very different and despicable idea that one race may be inherently more worthy than another.

Consider the second of the catch phrases I have mentioned. It is said that Bakke has a right to be judged as an "individual," in deciding whether he is to be admitted to medical school and thus to the medical profession, and not as a member of some group that is being judged as a whole. What can that mean? Any admissions procedure must rely on generalizations about groups that are justified only statistically. The regular admissions process at Davis, for example, set a cutoff figure for college grade-point average. Applicants whose averages fell below that figure were not invited to any interview, and therefore rejected out of hand.

An applicant whose average fell one point below the cutoff might well have had personal qualities of dedication or sympathy that would have been revealed at an interview, and that would have made him or her a better doctor than some applicant whose average rose one point above the line. But the former is excluded from the process on the basis of a decision taken for administrative convenience and grounded in the generalization, unlikely to hold true for every individual, that those with grade averages below the cutoff will not have other qualities sufficiently persuasive. Even the use of standard Medical College Aptitude Tests (MCAT) as part of the admissions procedure requires judging people as part of groups, because it assumes that test scores are a guide to medical intelligence, which is in turn a guide to medical ability. Though this judgment is no doubt true statistically, it hardly holds true for every individual.

Allan Bakke was himself refused admission to two other medical schools, not because of his race but because of his age: these schools thought that a student entering medical school at the age of thirty-three was likely to make less of a contribution to medical care over his career than someone entering at the standard age of twenty-one. Suppose these schools relied, not on any detailed investigation of whether Bakke himself had abilities that would contradict the generalization in his specific case, but on a rule of thumb that allowed only the most cursory look at applicants over (say) the age of thirty. Did these two medical schools violate his right to be judged as an individual rather than as a member of a group?

The Davis medical school permitted whites to apply for the sixteen places reserved for members of "educationally or economically disadvantaged minorities," a phrase whose meaning might well include white ethnic minorities. In fact several whites have applied, though none has been accepted, and the California Court found that the special committee charged with administering the program had decided, in advance, against admitting any. Suppose that decision had been based on the following administrative theory: it is so unlikely that any white doctor can do as much to counteract racial imbalance in the medical professions as a well-qualified and trained black doctor can do that the committee should for reasons of convenience proceed on the presumption no white doctor could. That presumption is, as a matter of fact, more plausible than the corresponding presumption about medical students over the age of thirty, or even the presumption about applicants whose grade–point averages fall below the cutoff line. If the latter presumptions do not deny the alleged right of individuals to be judged as individuals in an admissions procedure, then neither can the former.

Colvin, in oral argument, argued the third of the catch phrases I mentioned. He said that his client had a right not to be excluded from medical school because of his race alone, and this as a statement of constitutional right sounds more plausible than claims about the right to be judged on merit or as an individual. It sounds plausible, however, because it suggests the following more complex principle. Every citizen has a constitutional right that he not suffer disadvantage, at least in the competition for any public benefit, because the race or religion or sect or region or other natural or artificial group to which he belongs is the object of prejudice or contempt.

That is a fundamentally important constitutional right, and it is that right that was systematically violated for many years by racist exclusions and anti-Semitic quotas. Color bars and Jewish quotas were not unfair just because they made race or religion relevant or because they fixed on qualities beyond individual control. It is true that blacks or Jews do not choose to be blacks or Jews. But it is also true that those

who score low in aptitude or admissions tests do not choose their levels of intelligence. Nor do those denied admission because they are too old, or because they do not come from a part of the country underrepresented in the school, or because they cannot play basketball well, choose not to have the qualities that made the difference.

Race seems different because exclusions based on race have historically been motivated not by some instrumental calculation, as in the case of intelligence or age or regional distribution or athletic ability, but because of contempt for the excluded race or religion as such. Exclusion by race was in itself an insult, because it was generated by and signaled contempt.

Bakke's claim, therefore, must be made more specific than it is. He says he was kept out of medical school because of his race. Does he mean that he was kept out because his race is the object of prejudice or contempt? That suggestion is absurd. A very high proportion of those who were accepted (and, presumably, of those who run the admissions program) were members of the same race. He therefore means simply that if he had been black he would have been accepted, with no suggestion that this would have been so because blacks are thought more worthy or honorable than whites.

That is true: no doubt he would have been accepted if he were black. But it is also true, and in exactly the same sense, that he would have been accepted if he had been more intelligent, or made a better impression in his interview, or, in the case of other schools, if he had been younger when he decided to become a doctor. Race is not, in *his* case, a different matter from these other factors equally beyond his control. It is not a different matter because in his case race is not distinguished by the special character of public insult. On the contrary, the program presupposes that his race is still widely if wrongly thought to be superior to others.

In the past it made sense to say that an excluded black or Jewish student was being sacrificed because of his race or religion; that meant that his or her exclusion was treated as desirable in itself, not because it contributed to any goal in which he as well as the rest of society might take pride. Allan Bakke is being "sacrificed" because of his race only in a very artificial sense of the word. He is being "sacrificed" in the same artificial sense because of his level of intelligence, since he would have been accepted if he were more clever than he is. In both cases he is being excluded not by prejudice but because of a rational calculation about the socially most beneficial use of limited resources for medical education.

It may now be said that this distinction is too subtle, and that if racial classifications have been and may still be used for malign purposes, then everyone has a flat right that racial classifications not be used at all. This is the familiar appeal to the lazy virtue of simplicity. It supposes that if a line is difficult to draw, or might be difficult to administer if drawn, then there is wisdom in not making the attempt to draw it. There may be cases in which that is wise, but those would be cases in which nothing of great value would as a consequence be lost. If racially conscious admissions policies now offer the only substantial hope for bringing more qualified black and other minority doctors into the profession, then a great loss is suffered if medical schools are not allowed voluntarily to pursue such programs. We should then be trading away a chance to attack certain and present injustice in order to gain protection we may not need against speculative abuses we have other means to prevent. And such abuses cannot, in any case, be worse than the injustice to which we would then surrender.

We have now considered three familiar slogans, each widely thought to name a constitutional right that enables Allan Bakke to stop programs of affirmative action no matter how effective or necessary these might be. When we inspect these slogans, we find that they can stand for no genuine principle except one. This is the important principle that no one in our society should suffer because he is a member of a group thought less worthy of respect, as a group, than other groups. We have different aspects of that principle in mind when we say that individuals should be judged on merit, that they should be judged as individuals, and that they should not suffer disadvantages because of their race. The spirit of that fundamental principle is the spirit of the goal that affirmative action is intended to serve. The principle furnishes no support for those who find, as Bakke does, that their own interests conflict with that goal.

It is regrettable when any citizen's expectations are defeated by new programs serving some more general concern. It is regrettable, for example, when established small businesses fail because new and superior roads are built; in that case people have invested more than Bakke has. And they have more reason to believe their businesses will continue than Bakke had to suppose he could have entered the Davis medical school at thirty-three, even without a task force program.

There is, of course, no suggestion in that program that Bakke shares in any collective or individual guilt for racial injustice in the United States; or that he is any less entitled to concern or respect than any black student accepted in the program. He has been disappointed, and he must have the sympathy due that disappointment, just as any other disappointed applicant—even one with much worse test scores who would not have been accepted in any event—must have sympathy. Each is disappointed because places in medical schools are scarce resources and must be used to provide what the more general society most needs. It is not Bakke's fault that racial justice is now a special need—but he has no right to prevent the most effective measures of securing that justice from being used.

QUESTIONS FOR DISCUSSION

1. Does preferential treatment violate any individual rights? Which rights or why not?

2. Dworkin argues that black skin can sometimes be a kind of merit. What does Dworkin mean by this? Is he right? What are the proper standards of merit in admission to medical school? Law school? College? Employment? Why is merit important in choosing students or employees?

3. Are any legal or moral rights violated when private colleges that get federal grants give preference in admissions to children of alumni? To very rich applicants? To athletes? To veterans? Why or why not?

4. In an earlier article,[24] Dworkin distinguishes two rights: "The first is a right to equal treatment, which is the right to an equal distribution of some opportunity or resource or burden. . . . The second is the right to treatment as an equal, which is the right . . . to be treated with the same respect and concern as anyone else." Dworkin uses the following example to show that the right to treatment as an equal is more "fundamental": "If I have two children, and one is dying from a disease that is making the other uncomfortable, I do not show equal concern if I flip a coin to decide who should have the remaining dose of a drug." Dworkin goes on to argue that preferential treatment does not violate the right to treatment as an equal, and that there is no right to equal treatment in this kind of case. Do you agree? Why or why not?

[24]Ronald Dworkin, "Reverse Discrimination," in *Taking Rights Seriously*, Chapter 9 The following quotations are from p. 227.

WHY RACIAL PREFERENCE IS ILLEGAL AND IMMORAL

CARL COHEN

The role of race in assuring social justice is again squarely before the Supreme Court in a case whose full and revealing name is *Kaiser Aluminum & Chemical Corporation and United Steelworkers of America, AFL-CIO, v. Brian F. Weber,* individually and on behalf of all other persons similarly situated.

Carl Cohen, "Why Racial Preference is Illegal and Immoral," *Commentary,* vol. 67, no. 6 (June 1979), pp. 40–52

Weber, a white unskilled steelworker, is Bakke's analogue. . . . In *Bakke* a racially preferential admission system at the University of California Medical School at Davis was struck down, but attention to race in the admissions process was there held permissible within certain very narrow limits: to advance the diversity of an entering class, or to remedy the condition of specific persons who had been discriminated against by the school using the racial instrument. *Weber* is in many important respects different. Here the factor of diversity does not enter; here matters pertaining to intellectual qualifications are replaced by matters pertaining to seniority. Here the stakes are greater and the underlying moral issues are presented more cleanly.

I

This is what happened. Kaiser (Kaiser Aluminum & Chemical Corporation) and the union (United Steelworkers of America, AFL-CIO) sought to increase the number of minority workers in the skilled crafts at Kaiser's Gramercy, Louisiana, plant. To this end, in a 1974 collective-bargaining agreement, they changed the system whereby employees would enter on-the-job training for craft positions. Prior craft experience was eliminated as a requirement, and entrance ratios, by race, were established for acceptance in the job-training program. For each white worker admitted one minority worker would be admitted, until the percentage of minority craft workers in the Gramercy plant roughly approximated the percentage of the minority population in the surrounding area, then about 40 per cent. Dual seniority lists were established, one black and one white, and each two vacancies filled with the persons at the top of the two racially distinct lists.

It was an inevitable result of this system that some employees would be favored because of their race, and some would be injured because of theirs. Brian Weber was refused admission to the job-training program although

his seniority was higher than some employees from the other racial list who were admitted. Weber sued on his own behalf and on behalf of all non-minority employees who applied for on-the-job training at the Gramercy plant after that labor agreement was signed. A racially preferential scheme for allocating on-the-job training opportunities, he argues, is a clear violation of the Federal Civil Rights Act.

One portion of Title VII of that Act deals explicitly with on-the-job training programs. That portion (subsection (d) of Sec. 703) reads as follows:

> It shall be an unlawful employment practice for any employer, labor organization, or joint labor-management committee controlling apprenticeship or other training or retraining, *including on-the-job training programs*, to discriminate against any individual because of his race, color, religion, sex, or national origin in admission to, or employment in, any program established to provide apprenticeship or other training [42 U.S. Codes 2000e-2 (d) (1970); emphasis added].

Was it prescience that caused the Congress to formulate this ban with language so precisely and indubitably covering the case at hand? Not at all. Title VII had as its purpose the elimination of all ethnic favoritism in employment; there had been, at the time of its adoption, plenty of experience of the ways in which racial prejudice can be given effect—one of the commonest being in job-training programs. In that form as in all forms, said the Congress in effect, racial discrimination in employment is no longer permissible.

How can Kaiser and the union (and the U.S. Department of Justice) reasonably argue that such a scheme is indeed lawful or fair? They contend that the law, properly interpreted, does not forbid this variety of racial preference, which they think justified by our history of discrimination. They contend that if the pursuit of pressing social objectives now imposes incidental costs on individuals, Weber and his like are the right persons to bear those costs. . . . I examine these arguments in turn.

II

"Kaiser and the union [the first argument begins] reached an agreement that was fully in accord with the spirit of Title VII. Theirs was a voluntary effort to bring a greater number of minority workers into the skilled crafts. Congress never intended to forbid such voluntary efforts. If now the product of such agreements, reached through collective bargaining, is struck down, the cause of racial justice will have been dealt a devastating blow.

"We must [this argument continues] permit management and labor to join, as in this case, to correct a racially unbalanced situation flowing from the historical and social realities of American life. Blacks have been discriminated against, cruelly and consistently, by industry and by unions. Now an effort is being made to give redress. It is an ironic inversion of the Civil Rights Act to use that Act to forbid the only instruments that may effectively achieve its own intended result.

"It is true [the argument proceeds] that Title VII specifies that preferential treatment of racial minorities is not required [Section 703 (j)]. But that is not to say it is forbidden. When its aim is precisely that of the Act itself, it must not be forbidden. Weber relies upon the narrowest construction of the words and misses—inadvertently or deliberately—the remedial spirit of the law and of the Kaiser program here in question."

The main pillar of Weber's opposition comes to this: "If the court agrees that racial quotas such as this one are discriminatory, we will be kept from doing what many of us think it is necessary to do, and do quickly, in the interest of long-term justice. Let it be understood, therefore [the argument concludes], that this quota, although it does of course distinguish by race, and does, admittedly, give favor by race, does not 'discriminate' by race in the bad sense that the law condemns. When we come to

realize that some plans for racial balance, while they may have adverse effects upon some white workers, are nevertheless justified by pressing societal needs, we will also see what interpretation of the law is required by justice."

To put the argument plainly is to see both its earnestness and its frailty. The requirements of the Civil Rights Act, which in turn were intended to give concrete meaning to the constitutional demand that no citizen be denied the equal protection of the laws, were aimed at bringing to a final halt all formal discrimination on the basis of race—and color, religion, sex, and national origin. It certainly was not intended, and it obviously was not formulated, to forbid only such racial discrimination as employers and unions thought objectionable, while permitting any racially discriminatory schemes that employers and unions might by agreement find worthy or convenient. What the employer and the union happen to prefer, whether their motives be honorable or crass, has absolutely no weight, says the law in effect, against the right of each individual citizen to be dealt with, in matters pertaining to employment, without regard to race, religion, or national origin.

III

"But that cannot be the correct interpretation of the law," answer Kaiser and the union in chorus, "because the Supreme Court has several times, in the years since, recognized the lawfulness and wisdom of racially preferential employment schemes. Indeed, our federal courts have *ordered* the imposition of such racial preference in some cases! So it is clearly false that *all* racial preference has been forbidden. If that is so, then it is not obviously true that *this* scheme for racial preference has been forbidden."

This rejoinder brings us to the core, legal and moral, of the controversy in *Weber*. What kind of attention to race does the Civil Rights Act (and, indirectly, the Constitution) permit?

And what should it permit? In the *Bakke* case, this question was complicated by the entry of First Amendment considerations pertaining to the robust exchange of ideas in the classroom; the holding in *Bakke* was tangled by the fact that Justice Powell's pivotal opinion, although condemning racial favoritism, permits attention to race to advance diversity among an entering school class. Here, in *Weber*, such First Amendment considerations are totally absent. What, if anything, remains to justify race–conscious employment practices?

There is a clear and honorable answer to this question, given forcefully by federal courts at every level. Title VII of the Civil Rights Act forbids all deliberate discrimination by race, save only in cases where racial classification is absolutely essential to give redress to *identifiable persons* injured by racial discrimination *and where the injury done them was done by the same party upon whom the numerical program is imposed.* One purpose only may justify numerical schemes using racial categories: the *making whole* of those to whom redress for racial injury is specifically owed, by those who owe it.

For example: the known victims of racial discrimination by a trucking company have been held entitled, as a remedy, to a place in the seniority lists of that company that would have been theirs if they had not been so victimized. To put them now in as good a place as they would have been in but for the discriminatory employment practice from which they can be shown to have suffered, it may be necessary to attend to race. Only in that way can the victims be made whole; they would otherwise remain subordinate to persons who, had it not been for racial discrimination in that company, would now be their subordinates. (See *Franks v. Bowman Transportation Co.* 424 U.S. 747 [1976].) In such cases, the racially oriented remedy cannot be refused on the ground that the effect on other employees is adverse because, although the employees who suffer from the imposition of the plan are very possibly innocent themselves, they have clearly benefited,

in seniority, from the specific discriminatory practice for which remedy is being given. Race-conscious remedies for the victims of illegal discrimination are lawful, consistent with Title VII, only in such circumstances.

Weber and Kaiser Aluminum are in no such circumstances. Upon examining the facts, the Federal District court found that Kaiser had not been guilty of any discriminatory hiring or promotion at its Gramercy plant. Kaiser's industrial–relations superintendent at that plant testified that, prior to 1974, Kaiser had vigorously sought trained black craftsmen from the general community. Advertising in periodicals and newspapers that were published primarily for black subscribers, Kaiser found it very difficult to attract black craftsmen. The evidence established two key facts:

1. Kaiser had a serious, operational, no-discrimination hiring policy at its Gramercy plant from the day of that plant's opening in 1958.

2. Not one of the black employees who were offered on–the-job training opportunities over more senior white employees (pursuant to the 1974 Labor Agreement) had been subject to any prior employment discrimination by Kaiser.

From these facts it is an inescapable conclusion that the quota system at Kaiser's Gramercy plant was not an instrument for the specific redress of persons injured by racial discrimination there; it was unabashed racial preference aimed at numerical proportions having nothing to do with past conduct in that plant. Such preference Title VII outlaws. The distinction, between impermissible racial preference and permissible remedy for past discrimination, is put eloquently by the Circuit Court of Appeals in affirming Weber's rights:

If employees who have been arbitrarily favored are deprived of benefits capriciously conferred on them in order that those who were arbitrarily deprived may receive what they should, in fairness, have had to begin with, no law is violated. This is so even if both the class whose rights are restored and the class required to "move over" are defined by race—if the original arbitrariness was defined in that manner. And the reason is that no one is being favored or disfavored, advantaged or injured, under these circumstances *because* of race; rather, those who have been unjustly deprived receive their due and those who have been arbitrarily favored surrender some of the largesse capriciously conferred on them. That these consequences end by race is a mere incident of the fact that they began that way.*

But those who were favored by race at Weber's expense were admittedly not the victims of such original arbitrariness. The Circuit Court's support of Weber is therefore categorical: "[U]nless a preference is enacted to restore employees to their rightful places within a particular employment scheme it is strictly forbidden by Title VII" (p. 225).

IV

Since it is clear that the beneficiaries of this racial program were not victims of Kaiser's previous discrimination, and equally clear that the use of dual seniority lists is an explicit effort to favor blacks over whites, the defenders of this program are compelled to resort to a different justification—past "societal discrimination."

"We cannot deny [say the defenders in effect] that the two-list system deliberately favors one race over another. But we do deny that favoring this race at this time in this country is unfair. We contend that, in view of the historical discrimination against blacks (and other minorities), the racially preferential device now before us is entirely justifiable. It is justifiable not only because blacks have been so long oppressed, but because, as a corollary, whites have been unfairly *advantaged* by a race prejudice. The white employees of Kaiser who are passed over by this plan may indeed be innocent of any racial discrimination themselves, but they have been and are the beneficiaries of racial discrimination by others. This is the heart of our justifi-

cation. Favor to blacks now is just because of the favor whites have enjoyed until now."

This is the principled argument by which many without selfish interests in these programs are persuaded that they are fair. One might have expected the American Civil Liberties Union, for example, to spring to the defense of the rights of an almost defenseless individual. Instead it joins the forces against Weber because the ACLU has convinced itself that his rights have not really been infringed on, even though he suffers from deliberate disadvantage because of race. How can that be?

"Racial preference in employment is justified [the argument proceeds] when it is a response to the morally legitimate demand that the *lingering effects* of past racial discrimination be remedied. The lingering effects of historical oppression include the continuing losses of decent employment, together with the money and status that it brings. But the same historical race prejudice that has systematically blocked minorities from access to decent jobs has conferred an involuntary benefit upon whites because, while the number of desirable jobs remains roughly constant, the elimination of competition by minority workers results in the availability of desirable jobs for whites in generous disproportion to their numbers. This benefit is conferred even upon those whites who may, in fact, deplore the prejudice from which they gain. Yet they did gain. Now, with racial quotas favoring blacks, they lose. Their present loss is morally justified by their earlier gain. The primary target of racially preferential programs should be those guilty of past unlawful discrimination, of course. But where those guilty parties simply cannot be identified or are no longer available to make restitution, a secondary but legitimate target is the unjust enrichment attributable to that racial discrimination. Quota plans, like the one devised by Kaiser and the union, seek to redistribute that unjust enrichment. Seen in this light, their fairness—the moral rightness of racial preference for societal rebalancing—cannot be denied," so reasons the ACLU explicitly, and many other honest citizens implicitly, in giving pained approval to race quotas.

The argument fails utterly upon inspection. It relies upon a premise that is clearly and admittedly false in the *Weber* case and like cases. And were all its premises true, they could still not justify the racial preference here in question.

Consider the premises first. The adverse impact on Weber is held justifiable by his unjust enrichment resulting from the bad conduct of others. But if Weber were in any way the beneficiary of past discrimination, he certainly was not unjustly enriched by employment discrimination in the Gramercy plant. In that plant, it is agreed by advocates of the quota and by the courts, there had been no refusal to hire or promote blacks or other minorities, no racial discrimination from which Weber benefited. But the injustice done to Weber is manifested in the loss of entitlement he earned by ten years of work *in that plant*—not in the Kaiser Corporation or in the workforce at large. His entitlement in this matter cannot have been acquired as the result of the historical misconduct of others. Long before Weber came to work at that plant, blacks and whites received equal employment treatment there—so the claim that simply by virtue of his having the seniority that he did in the Gramercy plant Weber was enjoying an unjust enrichment is simply false. That false premise cannot justify "redistribution." The Circuit Court put the matter crisply: "Whatever other effects societal discrimination may have, it has had—by the specific finding of the court below—*no effect* on the seniority of any party here. It is therefore inappropriate to meddle with any party's seniority or with any perquisites attendant upon it, since none has obtained any unfair seniority advantage at the expense of any other" (p. 226).

But suppose *arguendo* (what is not true) that Weber had been unfairly enriched by past racial discrimination. What would follow? The enrichment thus identified might then be a target for redistribution. Among whom? To take

from Weber and give to another because Weber got his seniority "unjustly" could conceivably be justified (if ever) *only* if those to whom the redistribution were made were the same persons from whom the spoils had been taken in the first instance. The appealing argument by which so many are persuaded makes the faulty supposition that, if X has gained fortuitously but undeservedly from some unidentifiable Y, we are morally justified in taking from him and giving to a wholly different Z who suffered no loss to X's benefit, but who happens to be of the same *race* as that injured but unidentifiable Y. Buried in this reasoning process is the mistaken premise that the distribution of goods or opportunities is rightly made by racial categories. Z, the person now given preference over X because of race, has a right to get from him (this premise supposes) because Z is black, and blacks have been so long oppressed. But rights do not and cannot inhere in skin-color groups. Individuals have rights, not races. It is true, of course, that many persons have been cruelly deprived of rights simply because of their blackness. Whatever the remedy all such persons deserve, it is deserved by those injured and because of their injury; nothing is deserved because of the color of one's skin. This is the philosophical nub of the *Weber* case.

V

So long-lasting and self-perpetuating have been the damages done to many blacks and others by discrimination that some corrective steps must be undertaken. The moral anxiety created by this need for affirmative action accounts, in part, for the willingness of some to tolerate outright racial quotas. In the passion to make social restitution, sensitive and otherwise fair-minded people have gotten the moral claims of living persons badly confused. The head of the Office of Federal Contract Compliance (by whom, as we shall see, Kaiser was threatened) epitomizes this confusion: "Society is trying to correct an age-old problem, and

Weber is a victim of that process. There is nothing I can say to him. This is something that has to happen. The question is whether you give priority to a group that's been systematically deprived of opportunity while Brian Weber's parents and grandparents were not discriminated against. If someone has to bear the sins of the fathers, surely it has to be their children" (*New York Times Magazine*, February 25, 1979).

But deliberately visiting the sins of the fathers upon their innocent sons and grandsons, to the special advantage of persons not connected with the original sinning, is conduct neither lawful nor morally right. To suppose that both the beneficiaries of redress and those who are made to carry its burden are properly identified by race is, to be plain, racism. It is ethical racism because supposed with good will. It is simplistic because, on this view, race by itself—without consideration of the nature or degrees of past injuries, present advantages, or future pains—is sufficient to trigger the preferential device. The mistaken view in question is therefore properly entitled *simplistic ethical racism.*

Injuries are suffered in fact, claims made and burdens carried, by individual persons. Civil society is constituted to protect the rights of individuals; the sacrifice of fundamental individual rights cannot be justified by the desire to advance the well-being of any ethnic group. Precisely such justification is precluded by the Fourteenth Amendment of our Constitution, whose words—no state "shall deny to any person within its jurisdiction the equal protection of the laws"—express no mere legalism but a philosophical principle of the deepest importance. Explicating the clause, in a now famous passage, the Supreme Court wrote: "The rights created by the first section of the Fourteenth Amendment are, by its terms, guaranteed to the individual. The rights established are personal rights. . . . Equal protection of the laws is not advanced through indiscriminate imposition of inequalities" (*Shelley v. Kraemer* 334 U.S. 1, 22 [1948]).

The nature and degree of the injury done to many Americans because they were black or brown or yellow varies greatly from case to case. Some such injuries may justify compensatory advantage now to those injured. But the calculation of who is due what from whom is a very sticky business; compensatory instruments are likely to compound injustice unless the individual circumstances of all involved—those who were originally hurt, those who benefit now, and those who will bear the cost—are carefully considered. Whatever compensatory advantage may be given—in employment or elsewhere—it must be given to all and only those who have suffered like injury, without regard to their race. What we may not do, constitutionally or morally, is announce in effect: "No matter that you, X, were innocent and gained no advantage; you are white and therefore lose points. No matter whether you, Z, were damaged or not; you are black and therefore gain points." If the moral ground for compensatory affirmative action is the redress of injury, the uninjured have no claim to it, and all those individuals of whatever ethnic group who have suffered the injury in question have equal claim to it.

Racially based numerical instruments have this grave and unavoidable defect: they cannot make the morally crucial distinctions between the blameworthy and the blameless, between the deserving and the undeserving. As compensatory devices that are under-inclusive in failing to remedy the same damage when it has been done to persons of the non-favored races; they are over-inclusive in benefiting some in the favored categories who are without claims, often at substantial cost to innocent persons. Except in those cases where the discriminatory policy of the employer is established, and the identity of injured applicants or employees determinable, racial preference in employment is intolerably blunt, incapable of respecting the rights of individuals. . . .

IX

The reality of the evils flowing from racial instruments introduces one of the most intriguing aspects of the *Weber* case. A dispute arises between the District and the Circuit Court beneath which lies a momentous philosophical issue. Numerical remedies based on race do damage, the two courts agree; they further agree that this is a case in which the imposition of such a numerical remedy cannot be justified because there has been, in fact, no previous unlawful discrimination by the employer here. However, in those cases in which such remedy might prove justifiable (previous discriminatory practice in that setting being alleged), the following question arises: may that numerical instrument of redress be devised and executed on the authority of the employer and union acting jointly? Or is a racial quota permissible as remedy only on the express authority of the judiciary? The District Court not only found the remedy unjustifiable, but held in addition that such painful remedies would in no case be in the province of unions and management to impose. The Circuit Court, agreeing on the first point, did not agree on the second. Voluntary remedial action (said they) is preferable to court action; therefore, to insist upon judicial imposition of remedies would interfere unduly with reasonable private amelioration. The underlying issue here is the locus of authority in resolving questions of justice. Which court is the wiser?

In permitting numerical remedies to be imposed (if at all) only by the judiciary, the District Court, I submit, is deeply right. The reasons for this are several and complicated.

First, the question of whether the circumstances are such as to justify the imposition of a numerical remedy (a question that must be answered affirmatively if any such remedy is to be lawful) is precisely the kind of question that cannot be answered fairly by employers and unions acting in their joint interests. Individuals will bear the burden; if the case were of a kind to justify the imposition of that burden on Weber and his like, past discrimination by that employer in that context must be proved or admitted. No employer is likely to make that admission. To do so would invite a host of very expensive lawsuits in behalf of those injured. Employers will therefore enter such agreements only with the understanding that no past discrimination has been proved or admitted. That

very understanding (however arguable it may be) on which an employer might be willing to enter an agreement with a union to give racial preference to minorities is precisely the understanding which, if reflecting the facts truly, shows that racial preference unjustly injurious and unlawful.

This peculiar feature of "voluntary" racial instruments is admitted—even emphasized, ironically—by the UAW, the NEA, and other assorted unions. If (they argue) voluntary racial preference is permissible only when the employer's past conduct would be found in violation of Title VII, there will be no voluntary race-conscious action. For, as they agree: "[I]t is usually difficult to predict whether or not [previous] discrimination would be found" (associated unions, brief *amici,* p. 13). Indeed! For this reason precisely it is a question of such a kind that no answer to it reached as part of a labor-management agreement could be trusted.

The aggregated unions continue: "Moreover, the employer would, by taking voluntary action, put itself in a no-win situation in a suit such as this. Either its past conduct will be determined to be unlawful, thereby inviting litigation by discriminatees, or the remedial action will be found unlawful, and liability to white employees will exist" (*ibid*). Just so! But the authors of this candid statement apparently do not see where their argument leads. They would like the courts to conclude that, since the present standard (that "voluntary" racial quotas suppose the same finding of unlawful discrimination which alone might justify court-imposed remedies) effectively precludes "voluntary" quotas altogether, we should permit the introduction of a new standard, one that would allow "voluntary" quotas under some factual circumstances that— as they admit—would not justify a court in imposing them! What could serve as such a standard? The lone dissenting judge of the Circuit Court, pursuing the same line, is driven to propose an astounding answer: A "voluntary" quota plan should be upheld, he suggests, if it is "a *reasonable remedy* for an *arguable violation* of Title VII" (p. 230, emphasis added).

This standard is neither feasible in practice, nor morally acceptable if it were. As a practical matter, such notions as "reasonable remedy" and "arguable violation" have virtually no objective content. Only the courts could resolve, on a case-by-case basis, disputed claims about "arguable violations" and about the reasonableness of remedy. Endless litigation could not be avoided—but it is the elimination of time-consuming litigation that is alleged to be the great merit of "voluntary" racial instruments. The increase in court involvement that would result undercuts any proposed justification of "voluntary" quotas on grounds of efficiency.

More important than its inefficiency, however, is the fact that the proposed standard (that a voluntary quota plan should be upheld if it is "a reasonable remedy for an arguable violation of Title VII") is morally unacceptable. Just remedies presuppose some determinable wrongs for which they give redress and by which they are justified. It is confusion of mind to propose a *remedy* for an *arguable* violation; one cannot put right what might prove on more judicious examination to have been no wrong at all.

All "voluntary" quotas (i.e., those introduced without court imposition) presuppose reliance upon some standard that must encounter essentially the same problem. The philosophical dimensions of the dispute between the two courts here emerge. The Circuit Court's position exhibits irremediable moral defect: by permitting racially preferential programs without the backing of judicial authority, it permits the delegation of questions of justice to private hands that are neither equipped, nor disposed, nor authorized to resolve them fairly.

To resolve a matter of individual right the bargaining process between labor and management is almost the worst imaginable tool. The impartial determination of facts without regard to interest, and the honest application of principles without regard to advantage, are essential in adjudicating questions of right—but the elimination of regard for self-interest and advantage is precisely what is impossible at the bargaining table.

Even if the needed impartiality were possible there, it would be inappropriate, uncommon, and surely could not be relied upon. Union and management bargainers are duty-bound to press for the advantage of the units they represent. The process is designed to deal with issues of pay and working conditions, not with the protection of individual rights. Justice entails giving to each his due—whether or not he or others can negotiate for it successfully.

Most important, the authority to resolve questions of justice cannot lie in a labor-management bargain. Individual rights *may not*—as a matter of law or morals—be bargained away. As a matter of constitutional principle . . . the courts have repeatedly held that, in compromising with an employer, a union may not take race into account. Programs like the one at issue in Weber explicitly take race into account. The conclusion of this syllogism is inescapable.

XIV

The villain of the piece—here, in *Bakke*, wherever it raised its head—is preference by race. The *Weber* case provides an opportunity to reaffirm the moral and constitutional commitment to govern ourselves without preference to any by reason of color, or religion, or national origin. If we undermine that commitment—even though it be in an honest effort to do good—we will reap the whirlwind.

NOTE

*653 F. 2d 216, 225 (1977); page references below refer to this decision. The Supreme Court has agreed. In a case arising from a plan devised to give remedy to school employees within a previously discriminatory system, the Supreme Court declined review of a decision that, in view of the source and nature of that earlier injury, a minority worker may there be entitled to preferential treatment "not because he is black, but because, and only to the extent that, he has been discriminated against," *Chance v. Board of Examiners*, 534 F. 2d 993, 999 (1976); cert. denied 431 U.S. 965 (1977).

QUESTIONS FOR DISCUSSION

1. How would Cohen respond to Dworkin's arguments that Bakke and Weber do not have a right to be judged as individuals or without regard to race?

2. Whereas Dworkin discussed a case of preferential treatment in school admissions, Cohen focuses on a case of preferential treatment in employment. Does this make a difference? In your opinion, is preferential treatment more or less justified in admissions than in hiring or promotion? Why or why not?

3. Cohen argues that private companies, such as Kaiser, should not be given the power to decide when preferential treatment is needed. Do you agree? Why or why not?

REGENTS OF UNIVERSITY OF CALIFORNIA V. BAKKE

438 U.S. 268 (1978)

SUMMARY BY THE REPORTER OF DECISIONS:

[The Medical School of the University of California at Davis (hereinafter Davis) had two admissions programs for the entering class of 100 students—the regular admissions program and the special admissions program. Under the regular procedure, candidates whose overall undergraduate grade point averages fell below 2.5 on a scale of 4.0 were summarily rejected. About one out of six applicants was then given an interview, following which he was rated on a scale of 1 to 100 by each of the committee members (five in 1973 and six in 1974), his rating being based on the interviewers' summaries, his overall grade point average, his science courses grade point average, and his Medical College Admissions Test (MCAT) scores, letters of recommendation, extracurricular ac-

tivities, and other biographical data, all of which resulted in a total "benchmark score." The full admissions committee then made offers of admission on the basis of their review of the applicant's file and his score, considering and acting upon applications as they were received. The committee chairman was responsible for placing names on the waiting list and had discretion to include persons with "special skills." A separate committee, a majority of whom were members of minority groups, operated the special admissions program. The 1973 and 1974 application forms, respectively, asked candidates whether they wished to be considered as "economically and/or educationally disadvantaged" applicants and members of a "minority group" (blacks, Chicanos, Asians, American Indians). If an applicant of a minority group was found to be "disadvantaged," he would be rated in a manner similar to the one employed by the general admissions committee. Special candidates, however, did not have to meet the 2.5 grade point cut-off and were not ranked against candidates in the general admissions process. About one-fifth of the special applicants were invited for interviews in 1973 and 1974, following which they were given benchmark scores, and the top choices were then given to the general admissions committee, which could reject special candidates for failure to meet course requirements or other specific deficiencies. The special committee continued to recommend candidates until 16 special admission selections had been made. During a four-year period 63 minority students were admitted to Davis under the special program and 44 under the general program. No disadvantaged whites were admitted under the special program, though many applied.

Respondent, a white male, applied to Davis in 1973 and 1974, in both years being considered only under the general admissions program. Though he had a 468 out of 500 score in 1973, he was rejected since no general applicants with scores less than 470 were being accepted after respondent's application, which was filed late in the year, had been processed and completed. At that time four special admission slots were still unfilled. In 1974 respondent applied early, and though he had a total score of 549 out of 600, he was again rejected. In neither year was his name placed on the discretionary waiting list. In both years special applicants were admitted with significantly lower scores than respondent's. After his second rejection, respondent filed this action in state court for mandatory injunctive and declaratory relief to compel his admission to Davis, alleging that the special admissions program operated to exclude him on the basis of his race in violation of the Equal Protection Clause of the Fourteenth Amendment, a provision of the California Constitution, and §601 of Title VI of the Civil Rights Act of 1964. . . .

EXCERPTS FROM JUSTICE POWELL'S OPINION:
III

Racial and ethnic classifications . . . are subject to stringent examination without regard to . . . additional characteristics. We declared as much in the first cases explicitly to recognize racial distinctions as suspect: ". . . [All] legal restrictions which curtail the rights of a single racial group are immediately suspect. That is not to say that all such restrictions are unconstitutional. It is to say that courts must subject them to the most rigid scrutiny" (*Korematsu*, 323 U.S. at 216). The Court has never questioned the validity of those pronouncements. Racial and ethnic distinctions of any sort are inherently suspect and thus call for the most exacting judicial examination. . . .

Petitioner urges us to adopt for the first time a more restrictive view of the Equal Protection Clause and hold that discrimination against members of the white "majority" cannot be suspect if its purpose can be characterized as "benign." The clock of our liberties, however, cannot be turned back to 1868. It is far too late to argue that the guarantee of equal protection to all persons permits the recognition of special wards entitled to a degree of protection greater than that accorded others.

Moreover, there are serious problems of justice connected with the idea of preference itself. First, it may not always be clear that a so-called preference is in fact benign. Courts may be asked to validate burdens imposed upon individual members of particular groups in order to advance the group's general interest. . . . Nothing in the Constitution supports the notion that individuals may be asked to suffer otherwise impermissible burdens in order to enhance the societal standing of their ethnic groups. Second, preferential programs may only reinforce common stereotypes holding that certain groups are unable to achieve success without special protection based on a factor having no relationship to individual worth. . . . Third, there is a measure of inequity in forcing innocent persons in respondent's position to bear the burdens of redressing grievances not of their making.

Petitioner contends that on several occasions this Court has approved preferential classifications without applying the most exacting scrutiny. . . . But we have never approved preferential classifications in the absence of proven constitutional or statutory violations. . . . When a classification denies an individual opportunities or benefits enjoyed by others solely because of his race or ethnic background, it must be regarded as suspect. . . .

IV

We have held that in "order to justify the use of a suspect classification, a State must show that its purpose or interest is both constitutionally permissible and substantial, and that its use of the classification is 'necessary . . . to the accomplishment' of its purpose or the safeguarding of its interest." The special admissions program purports to serve the purposes of: (i) "reducing the historic deficit of traditionally disfavored minorities in medical schools and the medical profession"; (ii) countering the effects of societal discrimination; (iii) increasing the number of physicians who will practice in communities currently underserved; and (iv) obtaining the educational benefits that flow from an ethnically diverse student body. It is necessary to decide which, if any, of these purposes is substantial enough to support the use of a suspect classification. . . .

If petitioner's purpose is to assure within its student body some specified percentage of a particular group merely because of its race or ethnic origin, such a preferential purpose must be rejected not as insubstantial but as facially invalid. Preferring members of any one group for no reason other than race or ethnic origin is discrimination for its own sake. This the Constitution forbids. . . .

The State certainly has a legitimate and substantial interest in ameliorating, or eliminating, where feasible, the disabling effects of identified discrimination. The line of school de-segregation cases, commencing with *Brown,* attests to the importance of this state goal and the commitment of the judiciary to affirm all lawful means towards its attainment. In the school cases, the States were required by court order to redress the wrongs worked by specific instances of racial discrimination. That goal was far more focused than the remedying of the effects of "societal discrimination," an amorphous concept of injury that may be ageless in its reach into the past.

We have never approved a classification that aids persons perceived as members of relatively victimized groups at the expense of other innocent individuals in the absence of judicial, legislative or administrative findings of constitutional or statutory violations. . . . After such findings have been made, the governmental interest in preferring members of the injured groups at the expense of others is substantial, since the legal rights of the victims must be vindicated. . . . Without such findings of constitutional or statutory violations, it cannot be said that the government has any greater interest in helping one individual than in refraining from harming another. Thus, the government has no compelling justification for inflicting such harm.

Petitioner does not purport to have made, and is in no position to make, such findings. Its broad mission is education, not the formulation of any legislative policy or the adjudication of particular claims of illegality. . . . Hence, the purpose of helping certain groups whom the faculty of the Davis Medical School perceived as victims of "societal discrimination" does not justify a classification that imposes disadvantages upon persons like respondent, who bear no responsibility for whatever harm the beneficiaries of the special admissions program are thought to have suffered.

Petitioner identifies, as another purpose of its program, improving the delivery of health care services to communities currently underserved. It may be assumed that in some situations a State's interest in facilitating the health care of its citizens is sufficiently compelling to support the use of a suspect classification. But there is virtually no evidence in the record indicating that petitioner's special admissions program is either needed or geared to promote that goal. The court below addressed this failure of proof: "The University concedes it cannot assure that minority doctors who entered under the program, all of whom express an 'interest' in participating in a disadvantaged community, will actually do so. . . ." [Thus, the petitioner] simply has not carried its burden of demonstrating that it must prefer members of particular ethnic groups over all other individuals in order to promote better health care delivery to deprived citizens. Indeed, petitioner has not shown that its preferential classification is likely to have any significant effect on the problem. . . .

The fourth goal asserted by petitioner is the attainment of a diverse student body. This clearly is a constitutionally permissible goal for an institution of higher education. Academic freedom, though not a specifically enumerated constitutional right, long has been viewed as a special concern of the First Amendment. The freedom of a university to make its own judgments as to education includes the selection of its student body. . . . Thus, in arguing that its universities must be accorded the right to select those students who will contribute the most to the "robust exchange of ideas," petitioner invokes a countervailing constitutional interest, that of the First Amendment. In this light, petitioner must be viewed as seeking to achieve a goal that is of paramount importance in the fulfillment of its mission. . . .

It may be assumed that the reservation of a specified number of seats in each class for individuals from the preferred ethnic groups would contribute to the attainment of considerable ethnic diversity in the student body. But petitioner's argument that this is the only effective means of serving the interest of diversity is seriously flawed. In a most fundamental sense the argument misconceives the nature of the state interest that would justify consideration of race or ethnic background. It is not an interest in simple ethnic diversity, in which a specific percentage of the student body is in effect guaranteed to be members of selected ethnic groups, with the remaining percentage an undifferentiated aggregation of students. The diversity that furthers a compelling state interest encompasses a far broader array of qualifications and characteristics of which racial or ethnic origin is but a single though important element. Petitioner's special admissions program, focused *solely* on ethnic diversity, would hinder rather than further attainment of genuine diversity.

The experience of other university admissions programs, which take race into account in achieving the educational diversity valued by the First Amendment, demonstrates that the assignment of a fixed number of places to a minority group is not a necessary means toward that end. An illuminating example is found in the Harvard College program:

> In recent years Harvard College has expanded the concept of diversity to include students from disadvantaged economic, racial and ethnic groups. Harvard College now recruits not only Californians or Louisianans but also blacks and Chicanos and other minority students.
>
> In practice, this new definition of diversity has meant that race has been a factor in some admission decisions. When the Committee on Admissions reviews the large middle group of applicants who are 'admissible' and deemed capable of doing good work in their courses, the race of an applicant may tip the balance in his favor just as geographic origin or a life spent on a farm may tip the balance in other candidates' cases. A farm boy from Idaho can bring something to Harvard College that a Bostonian cannot offer. Similarly, a black student can usually bring something that a white person cannot offer. . . .
>
> In Harvard college admissions the Committee has not set target-quotas for the

number of blacks, or of musicians, football players, physicists or Californians to be admitted in a given year. . . . But that awareness [of the necessity of including more than a token number of black students] does not mean that the Committee sets the minimum number of blacks or of people from west of the Mississippi who are to be admitted. It means only that in choosing among thousands of applicants who are not only 'admissible' academically but have other strong qualities, the Committee, with a number of criteria in mind, pays some attention to distribution among many types and categories of students. (Brief for Columbia University, Harvard University, Stanford University, and the University of Pennsylvania, as *Amici Curiae*, App. 2, 3.)

In such an admissions program, race or ethnic background may be deemed a "plus" in a particular applicant's file, yet it does not insulate the individual from comparison with all other candidates for the available seats. The file of a particular black applicant may be examined for his potential contribution to diversity without the factor of race being decisive when compared, for example, with that of an applicant identified as an Italian-American if the latter is thought to exhibit qualities more likely to promote beneficial educational pluralism. Such qualities could include exceptional personal talents, unique work or service experience, leadership potential, maturity, demonstrated compassion, a history of overcoming disadvantage, ability to communicate with the poor, or other qualifications deemed important. In short, an admissions program operated in this way is flexible enough to consider all pertinent elements of diversity in light of the particular qualifications of each applicant, and to place them on the same footing for consideration, although not necessarily according them the same weight. Indeed, the weight attributed to a particular quality may vary from year to year depending upon the "mix" both of the student body and the applicants for the incoming class.

This kind of program treats each applicant as an individual in the admissions process. The applicant who loses out on the last available seat to another candidate receiving a "plus" on the basis of ethnic background will not have been foreclosed from all consideration for that seat simply because he was not the right color or had the wrong surname. It would mean only that his combined qualifications, which may have included similar nonobjective factors, did not outweigh those of the other applicant. His qualifications would have been weighed fairly and competitively, and he would have no basis to complain of unequal treatment under the Fourteenth Amendment.

It has been suggested than an admissions program which considers race only as one factor is simply a subtle and more sophisticated—but no less effective—means of according racial preference than the Davis program. A facial intent to discriminate, however, is evident in petitioner's preference program and not denied in this case. No such facial infirmity exists in an admissions program where race or ethnic background is simply one element—to be weighed fairly against other elements—in the selection process. "A boundary line," as Mr. Justice Frankfurter remarked in another connection, "is none the worse for being narrow." And a Court would not assume that a university, professing to employ a facially nondiscriminatory admissions policy, would operate it as a cover for the functional equivalent of a quota system. In short, good faith would be presumed in the absence of a showing to the contrary in the manner permitted by our cases.

In summary, it is evident that the Davis special admission program involves the use of an explicit racial classification never before countenanced by this Court. It tells applicants who are not Negro, Asian, or "Chicano" that they are totally excluded from a specific percentage of the seats in an entering class. No matter how strong their qualifications, quantitative and extracurricular, including their own potential for contribution to educational diversity, they are never afforded the chance to compete with applicants from the preferred groups for the special admission seats. At the same time, the preferred applicants have the opportunity to compete for every seat in the class.

The fatal flaw in petitioner's preferential program is its disregard of individual rights as guaranteed by the Fourteenth Amendment. Such rights are not absolute. But when a State's distribution of benefits or imposition of burdens hinges on the color of a person's skin or ancestry, that individual is entitled to a demonstration that the challenged classification is necessary to promote a substantial state interest. Petitioner has failed to carry this burden. For this reason, that portion of the California court's judgment holding petitioner's special admissions program invalid under the Fourteenth Amendment must be affirmed.

EXCERPTS FROM JUSTICE BRENNAN'S OPINION:

The assertion of human equality is closely associated with the proposition that differences in color or creed, birth or status, are neither significant nor relevant to the way in which persons should be treated. Nonetheless, the position that such factors must be "[c]onstitutionally an irrelevance," summed up by the shorthand phrase "[o]ur Constitution is color-blind," has never been adopted by this Court as the proper meaning of the Equal Protection Clause. Indeed, we have expressly rejected this proposition on a number of occasions.

We conclude, therefore, that racial classifications are not per se invalid under the Fourteenth Amendment. Accordingly, we turn to the problem of articulating what our role should be in reviewing state action that expressly classifies by race. . . .

Respondent argues that racial classifications are always suspect and, consequently, that this Court should weigh the importance of the objectives served by Davis' special admissions program to see if they are compelling. In addition, he asserts that this Court must in-

quire whether, in its judgment, there are alternatives to racial classifications which would suit Davis' purposes. Petitioner, on the other hand, states that our proper role is simply to accept petitioner's determination that the racial classifications used by its program are reasonably related to what it tells us are its benign purposes. We reject petitioner's view, but, because our prior cases are in many respects inapposite to that before us now, we find it necessary to define with precision the meaning of the inexact term, "strict scrutiny." . . .

Unquestionably we have held that a government practice or statute which restricts "fundamental rights" or which contains "suspect classifications" is to be subjected to "strict scrutiny" and can be justified only if it furthers a compelling government purpose and, even then, only if no less restrictive alternative is available. . . . But no fundamental right is involved here. . . . Nor do whites as a class have any of the "traditional indicia of suspectness; the class is not saddled with such disabilities, or subjected to such a history of purposeful unequal treatment, or relegated to such a position of political powerlessness as to command extraordinary protection from the majoritarian political process."

[The] fact that this case does not fit neatly into our prior analytic framework for race cases does not mean that it should be analyzed by applying the very loose rational-basis standard of review that is the very least that is always applied in equal protection cases. "'[T]he mere recitation of a benign, compensatory purpose is not an automatic shield which protects against any inquiry into the actual purposes underlying a statutory scheme.'" Instead, a number of considerations—developed in gender discrimination cases but which carry even more force when applied to racial classifications—lead us to conclude that racial classifications designed to further remedial purposes "'must serve important governmental objectives and must be substantially related to achievement of those objectives.'"

First, race, like "gender-based classifications too often [has] been inexcusably utilized to stereotype and stigmatize politically powerless segments of society." While a carefully tailored statute designed to remedy past discrimination could avoid these vices, we nonetheless have recognized that the line between honest and thoughtful appraisal of the effects of past discrimination and paternalistic stereotyping is not so clear and that a statute based on the latter is patently capable of stigmatizing all women with a badge of inferiority. State programs designed ostensibly to ameliorate the effects of past racial discrimination obviously create the same hazard of stigma, since they may promote racial separatism and reinforce the views of those who believe that members of racial minorities are inherently incapable of succeeding on their own.

Second, race, like gender and illegitimacy, is an immutable characteristic which its possessors are powerless to escape or set aside. While a classification is not per se invalid because it divides classes on the basis of an immutable characteristic, it is nevertheless true that such divisions are contrary to our deep belief that "legal burdens should bear some relationship to individual responsibility or wrongdoing," and that advancement sanctioned, sponsored, or approved by the State should ideally be based on individual merit or achievement, or at the least on factors within the control of an individual. . . .

In sum, because of the significant risk that racial classifications established for ostensibly benign purposes can be misused, causing effects not unlike those created by invidious classifications, it is inappropriate to inquire only whether there is any conceivable basis that might sustain such a classification. Instead, to justify such a classification an important and articulated purpose for its use must be shown. In addition, any statute must be stricken that stigmatizes any group or that singles out those least well represented in the political process to bear the brunt of a benign program. Thus our review under the Fourteenth Amendment should be strict—not "'strict' in theory and fatal in fact," because it is stigma that causes fatality—but strict and searching nonetheless. . . .

Davis' articulated purpose of remedying the effects of past societal discrimination is, under our cases, sufficiently important to justify the use of race-conscious admissions programs where there is a sound basis for concluding that minority underrepresentation is substantial and chronic, and that the handicap of past discrimination is impeding access of minorities to the medical school.

[In the school desegregation cases, the Court] held both that courts could enter desegregation orders which assigned students and faculty by reference to race, *Swann v. Charlotte-Mecklenberg Board of Ed.*, 402 U.S. 1 (1971), and that local school boards could *voluntarily* adopt desegregation plans which made express reference to race if this was necessary to remedy the effects of past discrimination. *McDaniel v. Barresi* [402 U.S. 39] (1971). Moreover, we stated that school boards, even in the absence of a judicial finding of past discrimination, could voluntarily adopt plans which assigned students with the end of creating racial pluralism by establishing fixed ratios of black and white students in each school. *Charlotte-Mecklenberg*, supra, at 16. In each instance, the creation of unitary school systems, in which the effects of past discrimination had been "eliminated root and branch," . . . was recognized as a compelling social goal justifying the overt use of race.

These cases cannot be distinguished simply by the presence of judicial findings of discrimination, for race-conscious remedies have been approved where such findings have not been made. *McDaniel v. Barresi*, supra. . . . Indeed, the requirement of a judicial determination of a constitutional or statutory violation as a predicate for race-conscious remedial actions would be self-defeating. Such a requirement would severely undermine efforts to achieve voluntary compliance with the requirements of law. And, our society and jurisprudence have always stressed the value of voluntary efforts to further the objectives of the law. Judicial intervention is a last resort to achieve cessation of illegal conduct or the remedying of its effects rather than a prerequisite to action. . . .

Moreover, the presence or absence of past discrimination by universities or employers is largely irrelevant to resolving respondent's constitutional claims. The claims of those burdened by the race-conscious actions of a university or employer who has never been adjudged in violation of an antidiscrimination law are not any more or less entitled to deference than the claims of the burdened nonminority workers in *Franks v. Bowman*, 424 U.S. 747 (1976), in which the employer had violated Title VII, for in each case the employees are innocent of past discrimination.

Properly construed, therefore, our prior cases unequivocally show that a state government may adopt race-conscious programs if the purpose of such programs is to remove the disparate racial impact its actions might otherwise have and if there is reason to believe that the disparate impact is itself the product of past discrimination, whether its own or that of society at large. There is no question that Davis' program is valid under this test.

Certainly, on the basis of the undisputed factual submissions before this Court, Davis had a sound basis for believing that the problem of underrepresentation of minorities was substantial and chronic and that the problem was attributable to handicaps imposed on minority applicants by past and present racial discrimination. Until at least 1973, the practice of medicine in this country was, in fact, if not in law, largely the prerogative of whites. In 1950, for example, while Negroes comprised 10% of the total population, Negro physicians constituted only 2.2% of the total number of physicians. The overwhelming majority of these, moreover, were educated in two predominantly Negro medical schools, Howard and Meharry. By 1970, the gap between the proportion of Negroes in medicine and their proportion in the population had widened: The number of Negroes employed in medicine remained frozen at 2.2% while the Negro population had increased to 11.1%. The number of Negro admittees to predominantly white medical schools, moreover, had declined in absolute numbers during the years 1955 to 1964.

Moreover, Davis had a very good reason to believe that the national pattern of underrepresentation of minorities in medicine would be perpetuated if it retained a single admissions standard. For example, the entering classes in 1968 and 1969, the years in which such a standard was used, included only one Chicano and two Negroes out of 100 admittees. Nor is there any relief from this pattern of underrepresentation in the statistics for the regular admissions program in later years.

Davis clearly could conclude that the serious and persistent underrepresentation of minorities in medicine depicted by these statistics is the result of handicaps under which minority applicants labor as a consequence of a background of deliberate, purposeful discrimination against minorities in education and in society generally, as well as in the medical profession. . . .

The second prong of our test—whether the Davis program stigmatizes any discrete group or individual and whether race is reasonably used in light of the program's objectives—is clearly satisfied by the Davis program.

It is not even claimed that Davis' program in any way operates to stigmatize or single out any discrete and insular, or even any identifiable, nonminority group. Nor will harm comparable to that imposed upon racial minorities by exclusion or separation on grounds of race be the likely result of the program. It does not, for example, establish an exclusive preserve for minority students apart from and exclusive of whites. Rather, its purpose is to overcome the effects of segregation by bringing the races together. True, whites are excluded from participation in the special admissions program, but this fact only operates to reduce the number of whites to be admitted in the regular admissions program in order to permit admission of a reasonable percentage—less than their proportion of the California population—of otherwise underrepresented qualified minority applicants.

Nor was Bakke in any sense stamped as inferior by the Medical School's rejection of him. . . . Unlike discrimination against racial minorities, the use of racial preferences for remedial purposes does not inflict a pervasive injury upon individual whites in the sense that wherever they go or whatever they do there is a significant likelihood that they will be treated as second-class citizens because of their color. This distinction does not mean that the exclusion of a white resulting from the preferential use of race is not sufficiently serious to require justification; but it does mean that the injury inflicted by such a policy is not distinguishable from disadvantages caused by a wide range of government actions, none of which has ever been thought impermissible for that reason alone.

In addition, there is simply no evidence that the Davis program discriminates intentionally or unintentionally against any minority group which it purports to benefit. The program does not establish a quota in the invidious sense of a ceiling on the number of minority applicants to be admitted. Nor can the program reasonably be regarded as stigmatizing the program's beneficiaries or their race as inferior. The Davis program does not simply advance less qualified applicants; rather, it compensates applicants, whom it is uncontested are fully qualified to study medicine, for educational disadvantage which it was reasonable to conclude was a product of state-fostered discrimination. Once admitted, these students must satisfy the same degree requirements as regularly admitted students; they are taught by the same faculty in the same classes; and their performance is evaluated by the same standards by which regularly admitted students are judged. Under these circumstances, their performance and degrees must be regarded equally with the regularly admitted students with whom they compete for standing. Since minority graduates cannot justifiably be regarded as less well qualified than nonminority graduates by virtue of the special admissions program, there is no reasonable basis to conclude that minority graduates at schools using such programs would be stigmatized as inferior by the existence of such programs.

Finally, Davis' special admissions program cannot be said to violate the Constitution simply because it has set aside a predetermined number of places for qualified minority applicants rather than using minority status as a positive factor to be considered in evaluating the applications of disadvantaged minority applicants. For purposes of constitutional adjudication, there is no difference between the two approaches. In any admissions program which accords special consideration to disadvantaged racial minorities, a determination of the degree of preference to be given is unavoidable, and any given preference that results in the exclusion of a white candidate is no more or less constitutionally acceptable than a program such as that at Davis. Furthermore, the extent of the preference inevitably depends on how many minority applicants the particular school is seeking to admit in any particular year so long as the number of qualified minority applicants exceeds that number. There is no sensible, and certainly no constitutional, distinction between, for example, adding a set number of points to the admissions rating of disadvantaged minority applicants as an expression of the preference with the expectation that this will result in the admission of an approximately determined number of qualified minority applicants and setting a fixed number of places for such applicants as was done here.

Accordingly, we would reverse the judgment of the Supreme Court of California holding the Medical School's special admissions program unconstitutional and directing respondent's admission, as well as that portion of the judgment enjoining the Medical School from according any consideration to race in the admissions process.

QUESTIONS FOR DISCUSSION

1. How do quotas (as in the Davis program) differ from goals (as in the Harvard program)? Do these differences make quotas unconstitutional? Unjust? Why or why not?

2. Compare Powell's arguments against quotas with Cohen's arguments. How are they similar? How are they different?

3. Compare Brennan's arguments with Fiss' group-disadvantaging model in Section 5.3. How are they similar? How are they different?

4. Do you agree with Brennan that preferential treatment should be subjected to less than strict scrutiny? Why or why not?

METRO BROADCASTING, INC. V. FCC

497 U.S. 547 (1990)

BRENNAN, J., delivered the opinion of the Court, in which WHITE, MARSHALL, BLACKMUN, and STEVENS, JJ., joined.

The issue in these cases, consolidated for decision today, is whether certain minority preference policies of the Federal Communications Commission violate the equal protection component of the Fifth Amendment. . . . The policies in question are (1) a program awarding an enhancement for minority ownership in comparative proceedings for new licenses, and (2) the minority "distress sale" program, which permits a limited category of existing radio and television broadcast stations to be transferred only to minority-controlled firms. We hold that these policies do not violate equal protection principles.

I

A

The policies before us today can best be understood by reference to the history of federal efforts to promote minority participation in the broadcasting industry. . . . Although for the past two decades minorities have constituted at least one-fifth of the United States population, during this time relatively few members of minority groups have held broadcast licenses. In 1971, minorities owned only 10 of the approximately 7,500 radio stations in the country and none of the more than 1,000 television stations . . . ; in 1978, minorities owned less than 1 percent of the Nation's radio and television stations . . . ; and in 1986, they owned just 2.1 percent of the more than 11,000 radio and television stations in the United States. . . . Moreover, these statistics fail to reflect the fact that, as late entrants who often have been able to obtain only the less valuable stations, many minority broadcasters serve geographically limited markets with relatively small audiences.

The Commission has recognized that the viewing and listening public suffers when minorities are underrepresented among owners of television and radio stations. . . . The Commission has therefore worked to encourage minority participation in the broadcast industry. . . . [T]he FCC adopted in May 1978 its Statement of Policy on Minority Ownership of Broadcasting Facilities . . . [which] outlined two elements of a minority ownership policy.

First, the Commission pledged to consider minority ownership as one factor in comparative proceedings for new licenses. . . . The "plus" is awarded only to the extent that a minority owner actively participates in the day-to-day management of the station.

Second, the FCC outlined a . . . "distress sale" policy . . . [which] allow[s] a broadcaster whose license has been designated for a revocation hearing, or whose renewal application has been designated for hearing, to assign the license to an FCC-approved minority enterprise. . . . The assignee must meet the FCC's basic qualifications, and the minority ownership must exceed 50 percent or be controlling. The buyer must purchase the license before the start of the revocation or renewal hearing, and the price must not exceed 75 percent of fair market value. These two Commission minority ownership policies are at issue today.

B

. . . [P]etitioner Metro Broadcasting, Inc. (Metro), challenges the Commission's policy awarding preferences to minority owners in comparative licensing proceedings. Several applicants, including Metro and Rainbow Broadcasting (Rainbow), were involved in a comparative proceeding to select among three mutually exclusive proposals to construct and operate a new UHF television station in the Orlando, Florida, metropolitan area. . . . [T]he Commission's Review Board . . . proceeded to consider Rainbow's comparative showing and found it superior to Metro's. In so doing, the Review Board awarded Rainbow a substantial enhancement on the ground that it was 90 percent Hispanic owned, whereas Metro had only one minority partner who owned 19.8 percent of the enterprise. The Review Board found that Rainbow's minority credit outweighed Metro's local residence and civic participation advantage. . . .

II

It is of overriding significance in these cases that the FCC's minority ownership programs have been specifically approved—indeed, mandated—by Congress. In *Fullilove v. Klutznick,* 448 U.S. 448 (1980), Chief Justice Burger, writing for himself and two other Justices, observed that although "[a] program that employs racial or ethnic criteria . . . calls for close examination," when a program employing a benign racial classification is adopted by an administrative agency at the explicit direction of Congress, we are "bound to approach our task with appropriate deference to the Congress, a co-equal branch charged by the Constitution with the power to 'provide for the . . . general Welfare of the United States' and 'to enforce, by appropriate legislation,' the equal protection guarantees of the Fourteenth Amendment". . .

Our decision last term in *Richmond v. J. A. Croson Co.,* 488 U.S. 469 (1989), concerning a minority set-aside program adopted by a municipality, does not prescribe the level of scrutiny to be applied to a benign racial classification employed by Congress. As Justice Kennedy noted, the question of congressional action was not before the Court . . . , and so *Croson* cannot be read to undermine our decision in *Fullilove.* In fact, much of the language and reasoning in *Croson* reaffirmed the lesson of *Fullilove* that race-conscious classifications adopted by Congress to address racial and ethnic discrimination are subject to a different standard than such classifications prescribed by state and local governments. . . .

We hold that the FCC minority ownership policies pass muster under the test we announce today. First, we find that they serve the important governmental objective of broadcast diversity. Second, we conclude that they are substantially related to the achievement of that objective.

A

Congress found that "the effects of past inequities stemming from racial and ethnic discrimination have resulted in a severe under-representation of minorities in the media of mass communications." . . . Congress and the Commission do not justify the minority ownership policies strictly as remedies for victims of this discrimination, however. Rather, Congress and the FCC have selected the minority ownership policies primarily to promote programming diversity, and they urge that such diversity is an important governmental objective that can serve as a constitutional basis for the preference policies. We agree. . . . Just as a "diverse student body" contributing to a "'robust exchange of ideas'" is a "constitutionally permissible goal" on which a race-conscious university admissions program may be predicated, *Regents of University of California v. Bakke* (opinion of Powell, J.), the diversity of views and information on the airwaves serves important First Amendment values. . . . The benefits of such diversity are not limited to the members of minority groups who gain access to the broadcasting industry by virtue of the ownership policies; rather, the benefits redound to all members of the viewing and listening audience. As Congress found, "the American public will benefit by having access to a wider diversity of information sources." . . .

B

We also find that the minority ownership policies are substantially related to the achievement of the Government's interest. One component of this inquiry concerns the relationship between expanded minority ownership and greater broadcast diversity; both the FCC and Congress have determined that such a relationship exists. Although we do not "'defer' to the judgment of the Congress and the Commission on a constitutional question," . . . we must pay close attention to the expertise of the Commission and the factfinding of Congress when analyzing the nexus between minority ownership and programming diversity. . . .

C

The judgment that there is a link between expanded minority ownership and broadcast diversity does not rest on impermissible stereotyping. Congressional policy does not assume that in every case minority ownership and management will lead to more minority-oriented programming or to the expression of a discrete "minority viewpoint" on the airwaves. Neither does it pretend that all programming that appeals to minority audiences can be labeled "minority programming" or that programming that might be described as "minority" does not appeal to nonminorities. Rather, both Congress and the FCC maintain simply that expanded minority ownership of broadcast outlets will, in the aggregate, result in greater broadcast diversity. . . .

D

. . . Finally, we do not believe that the minority ownership policies at issue impose impermissible burdens on nonminorities. Although the nonminority challengers in these cases concede that they have not suffered the loss of an already-awarded broadcast license, they claim that they have been handicapped in their ability to obtain one in the first instance. But just as we have determined that "[a]s part of this Nation's dedication to eradicating racial discrimination, innocent persons may be called upon to bear some of the burden of the remedy," we similarly find that a congressionally mandated, benign, race-conscious program that is substantially related to the achievement of an important governmental interest is consistent with equal protection principles so long as it does not impose undue burdens on nonminorities. . . .

Respondent Shurberg insists that because the minority distress sale policy operates to exclude nonminority firms completely from consideration in the transfer of certain stations, it is a greater burden than the comparative hearing preference for minorities, which is simply a "plus" factor considered together with other characteristics of the applicants. . . . We disagree that the distress sale policy imposes an undue burden on nonminorities. By its terms, the policy may be invoked at the Commission's discretion only with respect to a small fraction of broadcast licenses—those designated for revocation or renewal hearings to examine basic qualification issues—and only when the licensee chooses to sell out at a distress price rather than to go through with the hearing. The distress sale policy is not a quota or fixed quantity set-aside. Indeed, the nonminority firm exercises control over whether a distress sale will ever occur at all, because the policy operates only where the qualifications of an existing licensee to continue broadcasting have been designated for hearing and no other applications for the station in question have been filed with the Commission at the time of the designation. . . . Thus, a nonminority can prevent the distress sale procedures from ever being invoked by filing a competing application in a timely manner. . . .

III

The Commission's minority ownership policies bear the imprimatur of longstanding congressional support and direction and are substantially related to the achievement of the important governmental objective of broadcast diversity. The judgment is affirmed. . . .

JUSTICE O'CONNOR, with whom THE CHIEF JUSTICE, JUSTICE SCALIA, and JUSTICE KENNEDY join, dissenting.

At the heart of the Constitution's guarantee of equal protection lies the simple command that the Government must treat citizens "as individuals, not 'as simply components of a racial, religious, sexual or national class.'" . . . Social scientists may debate how peoples' thoughts and behavior reflect their background, but the Constitution provides that the Government may not allocate benefits and burdens among individuals based on the assumption that race or ethnicity determines how they act or think. To uphold the challenged programs, the Court departs from these fundamental principles and from our traditional requirement that racial classifications are permissible only if necessary and narrowly tailored to achieve a compelling interest. This departure marks a renewed toleration of racial classifications and a repudiation of our recent affirmation that the Constitution's equal protection guarantees extend equally to all citizens. The Court's application of a lessened equal protection standard to congressional actions finds no support in our cases or in the Constitution. I respectfully dissent.

I

As we recognized last Term, the Constitution requires that the Court apply a strict standard of scrutiny to evaluate racial classifications such as those contained in the challenged FCC distress sale and comparative licensing policies. . . . "Strict scrutiny" requires that, to be upheld, racial classifications must be determined to be necessary and narrowly tailored to achieve a compelling state interest. The Court abandons this traditional safeguard against discrimination for a lower standard of review, and in practice applies a standard like that applicable to routine legislation. Yet the Government's different treatment of citizens according to race is no routine concern. This Court's precedents in no way justify the Court's marked departure from our traditional treatment of race classifications and its conclusion that different equal protection principles apply to these federal actions. . . .

Nor does the congressional role in prolonging the FCC's policies justify any lower level of scrutiny. As with all instances of judicial review of federal legislation, the Court does not lightly set aside the considered judgment of a coordinate branch. Nonetheless, the respect due a coordinate branch yields neither less vigilance in defense of equal protection principles nor any corresponding diminution of the standard of review. . . .

This dispute regarding the appropriate standard of review may strike some as a lawyers' quibble over words, but it is not. The standard of review establishes whether and when the Court and Constitution allow the Government to employ racial classifications. A lower standard signals that the Government may resort to racial distinctions more readily. The Court's departure from our cases is disturbing enough, but more disturbing still is the renewed toleration of racial classifications that its new standard of review embodies.

II

Our history reveals that the most blatant forms of discrimination have been visited upon some members of the racial and ethnic groups identified in the challenged programs. Many have lacked the opportunity to share in the Nation's wealth and to participate in its commercial enterprises. It is undisputed that minority participation in the broadcasting industry falls markedly below the demographic representation of those groups . . . , and this shortfall may be traced in part to the discrimination and the patterns of exclusion that have widely affected our society. As a Nation we aspire to create a society untouched by that history of exclusion, and to ensure that equality defines all citizens' daily experience and opportunities as well as the protection afforded to them under law.

For these reasons, and despite the harms that may attend the Government's use of racial classifications, we have repeatedly recognized that the Government possesses a compelling interest in remedying the effects of identified race discrimination. . . . Yet it is equally clear that the policies challenged in these cases were not designed as remedial measures and are in no sense narrowly tailored to remedy identified discrimination. The FCC appropriately concedes that its policies embodied no remedial purpose . . . , and has disclaimed the possibility that discrimination infected the allocation of licenses. The congressional action at most simply en-dorsed a policy designed to further the interest in achieving diverse programming. . . .

III

Under the appropriate standard, strict scrutiny, only a compelling interest may support the Government's use of racial classifications. Modern equal protection doctrine has recognized only one such interest: remedying the effects of racial discrimination. The interest in increasing the diversity of broadcast viewpoints is clearly not a compelling interest. It is simply too amorphous, too insubstantial, and too unrelated to any legitimate basis for employing racial classifications. The Court does not claim otherwise. Rather, it employs its novel standard and claims that this asserted interest need only be, and is, "important." . . .

An interest capable of justifying race-conscious measures must be sufficiently specific and verifiable, such that it supports only limited and carefully defined uses of racial classifications. . . . The FCC and the majority of this Court understandably do not suggest how one would define or measure a particular viewpoint that might be associated with race, or even how one would assess the diversity of broadcast viewpoints. Like the vague assertion of societal discrimination, a claim of insufficiently diverse broadcasting viewpoints might be used to justify equally unconstrained racial preferences, linked to nothing other than proportional representation of various races. . . .

The FCC's extension of the asserted interest in diversity of views in these cases presents, at the very least, an unsettled First Amendment issue. The FCC has concluded that the American broadcasting public receives the incorrect mix of ideas and claims to have adopted the challenged policies to supplement programming content with a particular set of views. Although we have approved limited measures designed to increase information and views generally, the Court has never upheld a broadcasting measure designed to amplify a distinct set of views or the views of a particular class of speakers. Indeed, the Court has suggested that the First Amendment prohibits allocating licenses to further such ends. . . .

IV

Our traditional equal protection doctrine requires, in addition to a compelling state interest, that the Government's chosen means be necessary to accomplish, and narrowly tailored to further, the asserted interest. . . . This element of strict scrutiny is designed to "ensur[e] that the means chosen 'fit' [the] compelling goal so closely that there is little or no possibility that the motive for the classification was illegitimate racial prejudice or stereotype." . . . The chosen means, resting as they do on stereotyping and so indirectly furthering the asserted end, could not plausibly be deemed narrowly tailored. The Court instead finds the racial classifications to be "substantially related" to achieving the Government's interest . . . , a far less rigorous fit requirement. The FCC's policies fail even this requirement.

1

. . . The FCC assumes a particularly strong correlation of race and behavior. The FCC justifies its conclusion that insufficiently diverse viewpoints are broadcast by reference to the percentage of minority owned stations. This assumption is correct only to the extent that minority owned stations provide the desired additional views, and that stations owned by individuals not favored by the preferences cannot, or at least do not, broadcast underrepresented programming. Additionally, the FCC's focus on ownership to improve programming assumes that preferences linked to race are so strong that they will dictate the owner's behavior in operating the station, overcoming the owner's personal inclinations and regard for the market. . . .

[E]ven if the Court's equation of race and programming viewpoint has some empirical basis, equal protection principles prohibit the Government from relying upon that basis to employ racial classifications. . . . This reliance on the "aggregate" and on probabilities confirms that the Court has abandoned heightened scrutiny, which requires a direct rather than approximate fit of means to ends. We would not tolerate the Government's claim that hiring persons of a particular race leads to better service "in the aggregate," and we should not accept as legitimate the FCC's claim in this case that members of certain races will provide superior programming, even if "in the aggregate." The Constitution's text, our cases, and our Nation's history foreclose such premises.

2

Our equal protection doctrine governing intermediate review indicates that the Government may not use race and ethnicity as "a 'proxy for other, more germane bases of classification.'" . . . The FCC has used race as a proxy for whatever views it believes to be underrepresented in the broadcasting spectrum. This reflexive or unthinking use of a suspect classification is the hallmark of an unconstitutional policy. . . . The ill fit of means to ends is manifest. The policy is overinclusive: Many members of a particular racial or ethnic group will have no interest in advancing the views the FCC believes to be underrepresented, or will find them utterly foreign. The policy is underinclusive: It awards no preference to disfavored individuals who may be particularly well versed in and committed to presenting those views. The FCC has failed to implement a case-by-case determination, and that failure is particularly unjustified when individualized hearings already occur, as in the comparative licensing process. . . .

Moreover, the FCC's programs cannot survive even intermediate scrutiny because race-neutral and untried means of directly accomplishing the governmental interest are readily available. The FCC could directly advance its interest by requiring licensees to provide programming that the FCC believes would add to diversity. The interest the FCC asserts is in programming diversity, yet in adopting the challenged policies, the FCC expressly disclaimed having attempted any direct efforts to achieve its asserted goal. . . .

4

Finally, the Government cannot employ race classifications that unduly burden individuals who are not members of the favored racial and ethnic groups. . . . The challenged policies fail this independent requirement, as well as the other constitutional requirements. The comparative licensing and distress sale programs provide the eventual licensee with an exceptionally valuable property and with a rare and unique opportunity to serve the local community. The distress sale imposes a particularly significant burden. The FCC has at base created a specialized market reserved exclusively for minority controlled applicants. There is no more rigid quota than a 100% set-aside. This fact is not altered by the observation . . . that the FCC and the seller have some discretion over whether stations may be sold through the distress program. For the would-be purchaser or person who seeks to compete for the station, that opportunity depends entirely upon race or ethnicity. The Court's argument that the distress sale allocates only a small percentage of all license sales . . . also misses the mark. This argument readily supports complete preferences and avoids scrutiny of particular programs. It is

no response to a person denied admission at one school, or discharged from one job, solely on the basis of race, that other schools or employers do not discriminate.

The comparative licensing program, too, imposes a significant burden. The Court's emphasis on the multifactor process should not be confused with the claim that the preference is in some sense a minor one. It is not. The basic non-race criteria are not difficult to meet, and, given the sums at stake, applicants have every incentive to structure their ownership arrangement to prevail in the comparative process. Applicants cannot alter their race, of course, and race is clearly the dispositive factor in a substantial percentage of comparative proceedings. . . .

In sum, the FCC has not met its burden even under the Court's test that approves of racial classifications that are substantially related to an important governmental objective. Of course, the programs even more clearly fail the strict scrutiny that should be applied. The Court has determined, in essence, that Congress and all federal agencies are exempted, to some ill-defined but significant degree, from the Constitution's equal protection requirements. This break with our precedents greatly undermines equal protection guarantees and permits distinctions among citizens based on race and ethnicity which the Constitution clearly forbids. I respectfully dissent. . . .

QUESTIONS FOR DISCUSSION

1. Do you think that preferential treatment by the federal government should be subjected to a lower level of scrutiny than preferential treatment by city governments? State governments? Why or why not?

2. Do the FCC policies in Metro violate the freedom of speech clause of the First Amendment? Why or why not?

3. Is the "distress sale" policy of the FCC a quota? Is it less justified than the preference given to minority owners in licensing? Why or why not?

4. How is preferential treatment similar to discrimination against members of disadvantaged groups? How is it different? Are the similarities or the differences more important? Why?

5. When is it just for the government to require one person to pay compensation for an injustice done to another person?

6. How can you tell whether a competition is fair?

7. In your experience, does preferential treatment create or sustain stereotypes about African-Americans? Does preferential treatment cause more or less harm overall to African-Americans in general? To society in general?

8. Which of the arguments for preferential treatment of African-Americans can be extended to women? To homosexuals? To the handicapped? To poor people? To other groups?

9. Robert Nozick asks, "If the woman who later became my wife rejected another suitor . . . would the rejected less intelligent and less handsome suitor have a legitimate complaint about unfairness . . . ?"[25] How is choosing one's spouse like choosing an employee or student? How are they different? Are the similarities or the differences more important? Why? Does this analogy show that businesses and schools should have the right to give preferential treatment to whomever they want?

10. *Morton v. Mancari*[26] upheld a federal statute that gave members of federally recognized tribes a preference in employment in the Bureau of Indian Affairs. Is this preferential treatment constitutional? Legal? Just? Why or why not? Would it be unconstitutional, illegal, or unjust to refuse to hire anyone other than members of federally recognized tribes in the Bureau of Indian Affairs? Answer the same question about preferential treatment for veterans in the Veterans Administration.

11. What kinds of preferential treatment programs are used for admission into your own school? Are these programs justified? Would other kinds of preferential treatment be justified in your school? Why or why not?

12. In Detroit in 1992, city officials proposed that a certain high school be reserved for black males only. Assuming that this school really would help to solve chronic problems among black male youths, would it be just or constitutional to exclude women and white males? Why or why not?

SUGGESTIONS FOR FURTHER READING

Some of the best philosophical writings on affirmative action are collected in *Equality and Preferential Treatment*, eds. M. Cohen, T. Nagel, and T. Scanlon (Princeton: Princeton University Press, 1977). See also B. Gross, ed., *Reverse Discrimination* (Buffalo: Prometheus Books, 1977) and W. T. Blackstone and R. D. Heslep, eds., *Social Justice and Preferential Treatment* (Athens: University of Georgia Press, 1977). Important legal documents are collected with a clear introduction and further bibliography in Kent Greenawalt,

---

[25]*Anarchy, State, and Utopia* (New York: Basic Books, 1984), pp. 237–38.

[26]*Morton v. Mancari*, 417 U.S. 535 (1974).

Discrimination and Reverse Discrimination (New York: Knopf, 1983). Good philosophical monographs include Alan H. Goldman, *Justice and Reverse Discrimination* (Princeton: Princeton University Press, 1979) (generally critical of preferential treatment); and Robert K. Fullinwider, *The Reverse Discrimination Controversy* (Totowa, New Jersey: Rowman and Littlefield, 1980) (mainly supportive of preferential treatment). More recent monographs include Michael Rosenfeld, *Affirmative Action and Justice* (New Haven: Yale University Press, 1991); and Gertrude Ezorsky, *Racism and Justice: The Case for Affirmative Action* (Ithaca: Cornell University Press, 1991), a short, clear work that also includes useful documents. Recent African-American critics of affirmative action include Stephen Carter, *Reflections of an Affirmative Action Baby* (New York: Basic Books, 1991); and Shelby Steele, *The Content of Our Character* (New York: St. Martin's, 1990). For a response, see Cornel West, *Race Matters* (Boston: Beacon Press, 1993), Chapters 4–5. Quotas and goals are compared by Mary Anne Warren, "Secondary Sexism and Quota Hiring," *Philosophy and Public Affairs*, vol. 6, no. 3 (Spring 1977), pp. 240–261; and Michael Davis, "Racial Quotas, Weights, and Real Possibilities," *Social Theory and Practice*, vol. 7, no. 1 (Spring 1981), pp. 49–84.

EQUALITY FOR WOMEN 5.5

INTRODUCTION

The Equal Protection Clause was originally intended to prevent discrimination on the basis of race. It was not intended to ensure equality for women. But the actual words of the Equal Protection Clause mention neither race nor sex. The amendment reads simply, "No State shall . . . deny to any person within its jurisdiction the equal protection of the law." The normal meanings of these words suggest that the equal protection clause guarantees equality for women as much as for any other persons. (Again, it is controversial whether original intent or word meanings should govern interpretation. See Section 2.1.)

In any case, the U.S. Supreme Court has not applied the Equal Protection Clause to gender discrimination in the same way as it has applied the clause to racial discrimination. Courts have allowed laws that prevented women from entering certain professions (such as law), that set maximum hours and maximum loads for women but not for men, and that kept women in the military from getting combat assignments. And, of course, women did not gain the right to vote until the Nineteenth Amendment was ratified in 1920. Such laws keep some women from doing things that they want to do and that men are allowed to do.

Other legal distinctions between women and men do not seem to restrict women. Women were not subject to military drafts, were eligible for alimony, and were given preference in child custody disputes. Wives of deceased or disabled male workers automatically received benefits that did not go as easily to the husbands of deceased or disabled female workers. These laws did not prevent women from doing anything or force them to do anything. Women were not required to join the military or to seek alimony, custody, or benefits, but they could if they wanted. Such laws contrast with laws that discriminate against African-Americans. Nonetheless, even laws that apparently benefit women might have reinforced stereotypes about women, such as that women cannot fight in the military, are dependent on their husbands, and should take care of children.

As gender discrimination encountered opposition, legislatures and courts acted to reduce gender distinctions in law, but not in as many areas as racial distinctions. For example, in the Civil Rights Act of 1964 (discussed in Section 5.3), Title VII bars discrimination in employment on the basis of sex as well as race. In contrast, Title III prohibits discrimination in public accommodation on the basis of race but not on the basis of sex, and Title VI prohibits race discrimination but not sex discrimination in "any program receiving Federal financial assistance." Even Title VII allows exceptions when sex is a "bona fide occupational qualification."

Starting in the early 1970s, the Supreme Court began to use the Equal Protection Clause against some gender classifications, but it also did not give as much protection to women as to racial and ethnic minorities. The Supreme Court struck down laws that gave preference to males over females as administrators of estates,[27] that made it more difficult for women in the military to claim their husbands as dependents than for men in the military to claim their wives as dependents,[28] and that allowed women but not men between the ages of 18 and 21 to buy 3.2 percent beer.[29] The Court did not, however, apply strict scrutiny to gender classifications as it did to racial classifications. Instead, the Court developed a middle level of scrutiny that requires only that gender classifications "must serve important governmental objectives and must be substantially related to the achievement of those objectives."[30] Because this test is less strict, courts have approved gender classifications in some areas where they would not allow racial classifications, such as in laws that exclude women from combat and require draft registration only for males. It is also interesting to ask whether preferential treatment for women is easier to justify legally if gender classifications are not subject to as much scrutiny as racial classifications.

The pinnacle of opposition to gender discrimination occurred when Congress proposed a Twenty-seventh Amendment to the U.S. Constitution in 1971–72. The so-called Equal Rights Amendment reads in full:

> Section 1. Equality of rights under the law shall not be denied or abridged by the United States or by any state on account of sex.
> Section 2. The Congress shall have the power to enforce, by appropriate legislation, the provisions of this article.

This amendment was ratified by thirty-five states, but it fell three states short of passage when the extended deadline arrived in 1982. The amendment's backers said that it was not intended to prohibit all sex classifications, such as separate bathrooms, but its opponents argued that its wording was too general and did not adequately specify what it would forbid. Would the ERA, for example, rule out single-sex sports in public schools? Would it deprive women of the legal and economic benefits mentioned above? Some opponents also feared that the ERA would break down the traditional family structure.

Without the ERA, women's groups could still fight against sex inequality in particular areas. Probably the most prominent example is the movement for pay equity. By 1986, fourteen states had statutes requiring equal pay for equal worth. Opponents argue that it is often hard to determine when the worth of two jobs is equal or comparable. Does equity depend on training? Skills? Effort? Responsibility? Desirability? Supply of workers? Demand for the service? It is also argued that government interference in private business will be inefficient and will restrict the liberty of workers and employers to make the agreements they want. Because of such problems, many of the statutes that require equal pay for equal

---

[27]*Reed v. Reed*, 404 U.S. 71 (1971).

[28]*Frontiero v. Richardson*, 411 U.S. 677 (1973).

[29]*Craig v. Boren*, 429 U.S. 190 (1976) (excerpted in Section 4.1).

[30]*Craig v. Boren*, at 197. This is the same test that Brennan later supported in cases of preferential treatment.

worth are limited in their applicability, and similar statutes have been rejected in many states. The average pay for women continues to lag behind that for men.

Instead of opposing all laws that treat men and women differently, many women's groups support laws that recognize the differences between men and women and laws that oppose the domination of women by men. For example, some want laws that require employers to grant pregnancy leaves and to include pregnancy costs in health care plans, even though men would not benefit as much as women. Others fight for new laws against pornography, sexual harassment, and violence to women. And, of course, many women's groups demand that abortion remain legal and become more accessible. All of these laws are said to be necessary for women to have an equal opportunity to succeed in employment and in life. Catharine MacKinnon, professor of law at the University of Michigan, argues for many of these measures in the following reading. Her point is that law collaborates in sex inequality in many ways, including by, in effect, permitting violence against women, so that sex equality cannot be achieved simply by doing away with gender classifications. The law must change in all areas that affect women's lives if equality is to be achieved.

On the other side, Richard Epstein, professor of law at the University of Chicago (also in this section), argues not only that government should not get involved in promoting equality, but also that there should not even be laws against sex discrimination in employment, so he opposes Title VII of the Civil Rights Act of 1964. His argument is based on a libertarian theory of justice and on the methods of the law and economics movement. In other parts of his book, Epstein even uses the same basic kinds of arguments against laws that forbid racial discrimination in employment. Whatever you think of his conclusions, his arguments deserve careful attention, and his position shows that equality between the sexes remains deeply complex and controversial.

REFLECTIONS ON SEX EQUALITY UNDER LAW

CATHARINE MACKINNON

I

... The first step in these legal attempts to advance women was to demand women's inclusion on the same terms as men. Laws that had provided "special protections" for women were to be avoided. The point was to apply existing

Catharine MacKinnon, "Reflections on Sex Equality Under Law", *Yale Law Journal*, vol. 100, no. 5 (March 1991)

law to women as if women were citizens—as if the doctrine was not gendered to women's disadvantage, as if the legal system had no sex, as if women were gender-neutral persons temporarily trapped by law in female bodies. The women's movement claimed women's control over their procreative lives from intercourse to child care. In legal translation, this became state nonintervention in reproductive decisions under the law of privacy. The women's movement demanded an end to the sexual plunder of rapists, meaning to include an end to intercourse under conditions of unequal power on the basis of sex. In legal translation, this became the argument that rape had nothing to do with sexuality or with women and must be considered a gender-neutral crime of violence like any other. The women's movement exposed and documented the exploitation and subordination of women by men economically, socially, culturally, sexually, and spiritually. Legal initiatives in the name of this movement called for an end to legal classifications on the basis of sex.

Equality, in this approach, merely had to be applied to women to be attained. Inequality consisted in not applying it. *The content of the concept of equality itself was never questioned.* As if there could be no other way of thinking about it, the courts adopted that content from Aristotle's axiom that equality meant treating likes alike and unlikes unalike, an approach embodied in the Constitution's "similarly situated" requirement which under Title VII became the more tacit requirement of comparability. Inequality is treating someone differently if one is the same, the same if one is different. Unquestioned is how difference is socially created or defined, who sets the point of reference for sameness, or the comparative empirical approach itself. Why should anyone have to be like white men to get what they have, given that white men do not have to be like anyone except each other to have it? Since men have defined women as different to the extent they are female, can women be entitled to equal treatment only to the extent they are not women? Why is equality as

consistent with systematic advantage as with systematic disadvantage, so long as both correlate with differences? Wouldn't this support Hitler's Nuremberg laws? Why doesn't it matter if the differences are created by social inequality? Never mind that Aristotle defended slavery and lived in a society in which prostitution—the buying and selling of women for sex—thrived, and in which no women were citizens.

Rather than designing an indigenous solution to the problem of sex inequality, the early feminist legal view was, implicitly, that if equality meant being the same as men—and being different from men meant either no rights at all or sex-based deprivation circumscribed and rigidified by inadequate and patronizing compensation—women would be the same as men. Embarrassments to this analysis such as pregnancy, insurance, women's schools, and women-only prisons were minimized as unimportant or lone exceptions or problems to be treated under some other rubric. Sexual assault and reproductive control were not considered legal issues of sex inequality at all, not in the doctrinal sense.

The essentially assimilationist approach fundamental to this legal equality doctrine—be like us and we will treat you like we treat each other—was adopted in sex cases wholesale from the cases on racial discrimination. The judicial interpretation of sex equality, like its predicates the Fourteenth Amendment and Title VII, has been built on the racial analogy. So not only must women be like men, sexism must be like racism, or nothing can be done. Where the analogy seems to work, that is, where the sexes are reasonably fungible and the inequalities can be seen to function similarly—as in some elite employment situations, for example—equality law can work for sex. Where the sexes are different, and sexism does not readily appear to work like racism—as with sexual abuse and reproductive control, for example—discrimination as a legal theory does not even come up. Along with these issues, the reality of inequality for those women for whom racism and sexism are too inseparable to be subject to a relation of analogy—those who are apparently too both to be regarded as fully either—has also been obscured. . . .

II

The inequality of women to men deserves a theory of its own. The status of women resembles other bases for inequality, but, like every inequality, is also particular and unique. Women's situation combines unequal pay with allocation to disrespected work; sexual targeting for rape, domestic battering, sexual abuse as children, and systematic sexual harassment; depersonalization, demeaned physical characteristics, and use in denigrating entertainment; deprivation of reproductive control and forced prostitution. These abuses have occurred, in one form or another, for a very long time in a context characterized by disenfranchisement, preclusion from property ownership, ownership and use as object, exclusion from public life, sex-based poverty, degraded sexuality, and a devaluation of women's human worth and contributions throughout society. Like other inequalities, but in its own way, the subordination of women is socially institutionalized, cumulatively and systematically shaping access to human dignity, respect, resources, physical security, credibility, membership in community, speech, and power. Composed of all its variations, the group women has a collective social history of disempowerment, exploitation, and subordination extending to the present. To be treated like a woman is to be disadvantaged in these ways as an incident of being assigned to the female sex. To speak of social treatment "as a woman" is thus not to invoke any universal essence or homogeneous generic or ideal type, but to refer to this diverse material reality of social meanings and practices such that to be a woman "is not yet the name of a way of being human."

In this context, the failure of the law of sex equality to address sexual abuse and reproductive exploitation stands out. The law typically considers these abuses, cardinal experiences of sex inequality, to be crimes or privacy violations, not acts of sex discrimination. Equality doctrine does not seem to fit them. Equality law privileges recognition of facial classifications, in which the group descriptor is the legal inequality, because such devices have enforced much racial inequality. For the most part, the laws of sexual assault and reproductive control do not mention women or men, not any more. Yet these laws are not exactly neutral with an adverse impact either, at least not in the usual sense. They are too gendered to be neutral, and any law on rape or pregnancy affects the sexes differentially, without necessarily being discriminatory.

Existing legal equality templates utterly fail to capture the particular way in which the legal system organizes its participation in the subordination of women. Consider whether the law of sex classification has the same relation to the realities of women's subordination as the law of racial classifications has to the realities of racial subordination. Does a law preferring men as administrators of estates[88] have the same relation to women's subjection as a law prescribing "white only" railway cars has to racial subordination? Does a law prohibiting eighteen- to twenty-year-old boys in Oklahoma from drinking 3.2% beer while permitting it to girls[89] have the same relation to sex inequality as a law requiring black children in Kansas to attend racially segregated schools has to racial inequality? I mention the two seminal sex discrimination cases to suggest that facial sex classifications may be relatively peripheral to women's inequality, including by law. For claims based on sex, what the constitutional inequality net is made to catch has always been relatively rare and is now virtually extinct, while sex inequality, including through law, remains predatory and flourishing.

Much sex inequality is successfully accomplished in society without express legal enforcement and legitimation. Yet the law is deeply implicated in it. Law actively engages in sex inequality by apparently prohibiting abuses it largely permits, like rape, and by hiding the deprivations it imposes beneath ostensibly gender-neutral terms, like abortion. In the areas of sexual assault and reproductive control specifically, these legal concepts have been designed and applied from the point of view of the accused rapist and the outsider/impregnator respectively, and in the absence of the point of view of the sexually assaulted or pregnant woman. Most of the sexual assaults women experience do not fit the legal model of the ideal violation. Most rapes are by familiars not strangers, by members of one's own ethnic group not others, at home not on the street. The notion of consent here, the law's line between intercourse and rape, is so passive that a dead body could satisfy it. The law of rape is designed so that rape is what somebody else does and what almost never happens: so that what is done all the time, presumably including by those who design and interpret and enforce the laws, can be done. . . .

Women are sexually assaulted because they are women: not individually or at random, but on the basis of sex, because of their membership in a group defined by gender. Forty-four percent of women in the United States have been or will be victims of rape or attempted rape at least once in their lives.[99] Women of color experience disproportionately high incidence rates.[100] In one random sample study, only 7.5% of American women reported encountering no sexual assault or harassment at any time in their lives.[101] Females—adults and children—make up the overwhelming population of victims of sexual assault. The perpetrators are, overwhelmingly, men. Men do this to women and to girls, boys, and other men, in that order. Women hardly ever do this to men.

Sexual violation symbolizes and actualizes women's subordinate social status to men. It is both an indication and a practice of inequality between the sexes, specifically of the low status of women relative to men. Availability for aggressive intimate intrusion and use at will for pleasure by another defines who one is socially taken to be and constitutes an index of social worth. To be a means to the end of the sexual pleasure of one more powerful is, empirically, a degraded status and the female position. In social reality, rape and fear of rape operate cross-culturally as a mechanism of terror to control women. To attempt to avoid it, women are constrained in moving about in the world and walk down the street with their eyes averted.[102] Rape is an act of dominance over women that works systemically to maintain a gender-stratified society in which women occupy a disadvantaged status as the appropriate victims and targets of sexual aggression.[103]

Sexual aggression by men against women is normalized. In traditional gender roles, male sexuality embodies the role of aggressor, female sexuality the role of victim, and some degree of force is romanticized as acceptable.[104] Sexual assaults frequently occur in the context of family life or everyday social events, often perpetrated by an assailant who is known to the victim.[105] In one study, one-third of American men in the sample say they would rape a woman if assured they would not get caught. The figure climbs following exposure to commonly available aggressive pornography.[106] Pornography, which sexualizes gender inequality, is a major institution of socialization into these roles. The evidence suggests that women are targeted for intimate assault because the degradation and violation and domination of women is eroticized, indeed defines the social meaning of female sexuality in societies of sex inequality. Sexual assault thus becomes a definitive act of sexualized power and masculinity under male supremacy.

Only a fraction of rapes is reported, the most frequently mentioned reason for nonreporting being fear of the criminal justice system. Women of color fear its racism particularly. Only a fraction of reported rapes is prosecuted. Many rapes are "unfounded," an active verb describing the police decision not to believe that a rape happened as reported. Only a fraction of prosecuted rapes results in convictions. Rape sentences are often short. Most rapists therefore continue to live in society either undetected or unpunished and unrehabilitated. In many instances, one must suppose that they remain unaware that they did anything even potentially culpable. Perhaps these data are viewed with complacency on the unconscious belief that sexual assault is inevitable or a constant that cannot be taken seriously because it is so common.

Seen in this way, sexual assault in the United States today resembles lynching prior to its recognition as a civil rights violation. It is a violent humiliation ritual with sexual elements in which the victims are often murdered. It could be done to members of powerful groups but hardly ever is. When it is done, it is as if it is what the victim is for; the whole target population cringes, withdraws, at once identifies and disidentifies in terror. The exemplary horror keeps the group smaller, quieter, more ingratiating. The legal system is dominated by members of the same group engaged in the aggression. The practice is formally illegal but seldom found to be against the law. The atrocity is de jure illegal but de facto permitted.

Unlike the law of murder, however, before the rape law is administered, it is biased on its face. Rape is typically defined as intercourse with force against one's will. Apparently this is not considered redundant, implying that women consent to sex with force all the time. Given this sadomasochistic definition of sex at the line between intercourse and rape, it is no wonder the legal concept of consent can coexist with a lot of force. Crystallizing in doctrine a norm that animates the rape law more generally, the defense of "mistaken belief in consent" defines whether a rape occurred from the perspective of the accused rapist, not from the perspective of the victim or even based on a social standard of unacceptable force or of mutuality. To a degree unlike any other crime to the person, the credibility of the victim is the issue on which turns whether any harm was done. Only in sexual assault cases is it believed,

against the victim's statement to the contrary, that she may have consented to forced acts against her. The view that women seek out and enjoy forced sex is pure special pleading for the accused. This is the perspective the law has taken.

A major exception in application has been accusations by white women of sexual assault by African American men—a relatively rare type of rape. Here the usual presumption that the woman consented turns to the opposite on racist grounds: because the man is Black, she could not have wanted it. The possibility exists that prosecutions under such conditions can be successful independent of whether a rape occurred or of whether the particular defendant was the perpetrator. At the same time, women of color, overwhelmingly the victims of the sexual assaults men of color do perpetrate, are often faced with the necessity of siding with men of color on grounds of community self-preservation. Statistically, such a legal posture makes it more possible to convict when a sexual assault is less likely to have occurred, and next to impossible to convict when one is more likely to have occurred. It is not in women's interest to have men convicted of rape who did not do it, any more than it is in women's interest not to have men convicted of rape who did. Not only the law, but the credibility of women—that rare commodity—is undermined.

Women and men are not similarly situated with regard to sexual assault in the sense that they are not equally subject to it or equally subjected to it. But this is the inequality that indicts it, not the difference that exonerates it or exempts it from equality scrutiny. . . .

[EDITOR'S NOTE: MacKinnon's intervening discussion of the law of reproductive control is excerpted in Section 4.4.]

III

. . . Inequality, as analyzed here, is not a bad attitude that floats in the sky but an embodied particular that walks on the ground. It is first concrete, historical, present, and material, only derivatively generic, and never abstract. Social inequality does not first exist in the abstract, in search of a basis or polarization or natural joint to carve or asymmetry to which to attach. It exists in the social rarity of its particulars, such as the social dominance of men through which women are subjected. Sex equality as a norm comes into being through the resistance of women as a people to their subjection. The equality principle, in this approach, is properly comprised of the practical necessities for ending inequality in each of its real forms.

Such an analysis does not generate abstractly fungible categories. Inequality is not conceptually reversible, only concretely changeable. To be "similarly situated," a test which relies on and produces abstract counter-hierarchical comparisons as the essence of equality reasoning, thus cannot remain the threshold for access to equality guarantees. If inequality is concrete, no man is ever in the same position a woman is, because he is not in it as a woman. That does not mean a man cannot be recognized as discriminated against on the basis of sex. It does mean that it is no measure of virtue for an equality theory to accord the same solicitude to dominant groups as to subordinate ones, all the while ignoring who is who.[184] If the point of equality law is to end group-based dominance and subordination, rather than to recognize sameness or accommodate difference, a greater priority is placed on rectifying the legal inequality of groups that are historically unequal in society, and less solicitude is accorded pure legal artifacts or reversals of social fortune. Although such a substantive interpretation is technically possible, indeed compelled, under existing law, the passage of an Equal Rights Amendment could help provide a political and textual basis for this rectification of constitutional emphasis.

Law furthering this equality norm would develop a new relation to society. In societies governed by the rule of law, law is typically a status quo instrument; it does not usually guarantee rights that society is predicated on denying. In this context equality law is unusual: social equality does not exist, yet a legal guarantee of equality does. If law requires equality, in a society that is structurally and pervasively unequal, and the social status quo were no longer to be maintained through the abstract equality model, then equality law could not even be applied without producing social change. For example, it is generally thought that nondiscrimination and affirmative action are two different things. Under the equality approach argued here, there is no difference between them. Equality law becomes a distinct species of law, in need of its own norms for its distinct relation to an unequal society.

One part of developing the jurisprudence of such law is creating new doctrine. Here, the laws of sexual assault and abortion are argued to constitute facially sex-discriminatory state action. While existing state action doctrine readily accommodates these obvious forms, and existing discrimination law provides a basis for this recognition, the larger implications of this exposed interface between the state and women's everyday lives suggests the need for more commodious notions of both discrimination and state action. On a continuum of examples, denial of access to abortion, the marital rape exclusion, failure to enforce laws against domestic violence, the mistaken belief in consent defense in rape, and state protection of pornography[185] are all gendered acts of government. Are they facial discrimination? From the standpoint of a woman being injured by them, are they state action? If not, are the concepts gender biased?

These forms of discrimination look like much of it: perhaps less provably purposeful than the existing model for intentional, but far from facially neutral and massively disparate in impact, they show a supportive interaction between government permission or omission and male aggression. More explicitly invidious than the neutral, but less superficially intentional than existing requirements for motive, such discriminations have social markers of sex written all over them and would arguably happen very differently if the stance of the government were different. Such laws and practices are simply biased, their one-sidedness diagnosable from subordinate group disadvantage, provable from invidious social meaning and damaging material consequences. Failure to see the state's hand in these examples would miss much of the way law insinuates itself into social life, intruding on and structuring relations between the sexes, institutionalizing male dominance. . . .

NOTES

[88]*Reed v. Reed,* 404 U.S. 71 (1971).

[89]*Craig v. Boren,* 429 U.S. 190 (1976).

[99]D. Russell, *Sexual Exploitation* (1984), at 35.

[100]The following percentages of women report being victimized at least once by rape or attempted rape: white (non–Jewish), 45%; Jewish, 50%; Black, 44%; Latins, 30%; Asian, 17%; Filipina, 17%; Native American, 55%; other, 28%. Note that these figures refer to the proportions of women victimized and say nothing of the number of times they were victimized. D. Russell, *Sexual Exploitation* (1984) at 84; see also Wyatt, "The Sexual Abuse of Afro–American and White–American Women in Childhood," *9 Child Abuse & Neglect* 507 (1985) (57% of African American women and 67% of white American women report at least one incident of sexual abuse before age 18).

[101]Diana Russell made this calculation on her data base at my request.

[102]M. Gordon & S. Riger, *The Female Fear* (1989).

[103]S. Brownmiller, *Against Our Will* (1976) at 15; Sanday, "The Socio–Cultural Context of Rape: A Cross–Cultural Study," 37 J. Soc. Issues 5 (1981).

[104]D. Scully, *Understanding Sexual Violence* 47–50, 59–92 (1990) (rape as "normal deviance" for men); J. Stoltenberg, *Refusing to be a Man* 15 (1989) (rape central to masculinity); Check & Malamuth, "An Empirical Assessment of Some Feminist Hypothesis About Rape," 8 *Int'l J. Women's Stud.* 414 (1985) (rape and forced sex widespread and largely acceptable).

[105]D. Russell, Rape in *Marriage* (1990) at 64–68; see also P. Sanday, *Fraternity Gang Rape* (1990).

[106]Malamuth, Rape "Proclivity Among Males," 37 *J. Soc. Issues* 138 (1981); Malamuth & Check, "The Effects of Mass Media Exposure on Acceptance of Violence Against Women: A Field Experiment," 15 *J. Res. Personality* 436 (1981); Malamuth, "Aggression Against Women: Cultural and Individual Causes," in *Pornography and Sexual Aggression* 23–23 (1984); Malamuth & Check, "The Effects of Aggressive Pornography on Beliefs in Rape Myths: Individual Differences," 19 *J. Res. Personality* 299 (1985); Check & Guloien, "Reported Proclivity for Coercive Sex Following Repeated Exposure to Sexually Violent Pornography, Nonviolent Dehumanizing Pornography, and Erotica," in *Pornography: Research Advances and Polity Considerations* (1989); see also Linz, "Exposure to Sexually Explicit Materials and Attitudes Toward Rape: A Comparison of Study Results," 26 *J. Sex Res.* 50 (1989); Russell, "Pornography and Rape: A Causal Model," 9 *Pol. Psychology* 41, 43–45 (1988). Pornography is also implicated in the domestic battering of women. Sommers & Check, "An Empirical Investigation of the Role of Pornography in the Verbal and Physical Abuse of Women," 2 *Violence & Victims* 189 (1987).

[184]Useful texts urging an approach consistent with the one advanced here are Fiss, "Groups and the Equal Protection Clause," 5 *Phil. & Pub. App.* 107 (1976), and Strauss, "The Myth of Colorblindness," 1986 *Sup. Ct. Rev.* 99.

[185]For an illustration of this last category of gendered law, see *American Booksellers Ass'n v. Hudnut,* 771 F.2d 323 (7th Cir. 1985), *summarily aff'd,* 475 U.S. 1001 (1986).

QUESTIONS FOR DISCUSSION

1. Describe the traditional theory of sex equality under law. Why does MacKinnon oppose it? Do you agree with her criticisms? Why or why not?

2. Why does MacKinnon say that the law of sexual assault is an issue of sex equality? Do you agree? What kinds of laws governing sexual assault are justified in order to achieve equality between the sexes?

3. One version of the recent Violence against Women Act increases punishments for violence against women and sees this kind of crime as discriminatory and thus a violation of women's civil rights. Do you support such laws? Why or why not? You might consider how this law fits into different theories of punishment in Chapter 6.

4. Must pornography be made illegal in order for women to achieve justice and equality in our society? Why or why not? (See Section 4.3).

FORBIDDEN GROUNDS: THE CASE AGAINST EMPLOYMENT DISCRIMINATION LAWS

RICHARD A. EPSTEIN

RACE AND SEX DISCRIMINATION: A MISLEADING PARALLEL

The basic provisions of the Civil Rights Act link race and sex as parallel grounds on which it is impermissible to discriminate against employees. This statutory parallelism could easily lead to the belief that the same basic issues are at stake in the two types of cases, and that the received learning in race cases explains what happens in sex cases as well. The substantive theories developed by the courts reinforce this apparent basic symmetry. Disparate treatment and disparate impact theories apply to cases of both sex and race discrimination, and their similarity could lead to the mistaken conclusion that the two can easily be yoked into a single harness.

A moment's reflection, however, should reveal that the differences between the cases are as great as their similarities, and in some ways even come to dominate the comparison. The simplest way to capture the distinction is to note that the phrase "separate but equal" rightfully carries with it odious connotations in race cases, but it generates far more ambivalent responses when carried over to sex cases. In both the public and the private sphere there is a sense that systematic differences between the sexes matter in a way that differences among races do not. Wholly apart from the commands of Title VII, many employers have no use for policies that take race into account in any way, shape, or form, but they regard it as vitally necessary to take sex differences into account in making certain employment decisions. Pregnancy, parenthood, medical coverage, rest room facilities, and job descriptions and classifications are all areas in which some differentiation of contract terms by sex is routinely considered and routinely practiced. . . .

RESPONDING TO SEX DIFFERENCES IN PRACTICE

The differences between sex discrimination and race discrimination enter into the law in many contexts that exist wholly independently of Title

Richard Epstein, *Forbidden Grounds: The Case Against Employment Discrimination Laws* (Cambridge: Harvard University Press, 1992), Chapters 13–14

VII. Historically as well as analytically one sees the constant tension between race and sex discrimination cases. The distinction between race and sex runs through the length and breadth of the law, and becomes especially vivid on the critical issue of separate but equal accommodations. In race relations the label "separate but equal" carries with it the heavy opprobrium of segregated washrooms and drinking fountains, of being sent to the back of the bus. Yet in the area of male–female relations, separate but equal captures a large portion of what is desired by the champions of the antidiscrimination principle, and of feminists more generally. The goal is not unisex bathrooms in airports or single-sex locker rooms. Rather, the goal, never seriously contested, is to ensure that men and women have access to accommodations that offer equal quality and comfort. In this context the reason for the shift is quite clear. Providing separate but equal public accommodations is a strategy that advances the welfare of men and women simultaneously. . . .

If the public accommodation question seems easy, the program of separate but equal faces more complex tastes in other settings—from athletics, dance, and gambling to business, mathematics, and the arts—where again differences between men and women, such as those related to risk taking, do matter, and are likely to remain critical no matter what government policy is introduced. The hard problem is to disentangle the relative effects of social and biological influences. But often it seems best to make peace with natural differences instead of railing against them. No program of weightlifting or socialization will ever make women equal in strength with men, and there is no reason to try. Nor is there any possibility that a set of adroit exercises will allow men to dance on pointe, and no reason why ballet should forfeit its charm by forbidding women to do so as well. And there is no reason to ban boxing or football for women, because women on the whole do not choose to participate in those sports.

The sources of the differences between men and women, however, do not have to be sorted out with precision to prove that they count. With athletic facilities, separate but equal is widely regarded as unacceptable on grounds of race, but at some level it is virtually required on grounds of sex. Feminist authors such as Catharine MacKinnon will at least broach the subject, even if MacKinnon provides no insight on how to respond to it.[15] And judges are overtly hostile toward efforts by men to invoke constitutional principles of equal protection to secure male plaintiffs a place on women's volleyball teams.[16] It is difficult to insist that any university, for example, should field only one tennis or basketball team whose membership is determined by open competition without regard to sex. That formula would be a recipe for all-male teams in a large number of sports, or for mixed teams run by quotas. Either way, athletic programs would be impoverished. Unisex competition would distort the dynamics in other sports such as gymnastics, where men and women participate in different events, again to the benefit of neither women nor men. The separation of the two sexes in competitive sports is therefore rightly understood as a way to advance the welfare of both men and women. . . .

SEX DIFFERENCES AND TITLE VII

The relevance of biological differences has influenced the development of Title VII, a statute deriving its moral force from the consensus on the question of race. Sex discrimination was almost an afterthought. The statutory prohibition was added to Title VII while the bill was on the floor of the House of Representatives as a ploy by the bill's opponents, who hoped to make the entire bill unpalatable to some of its wavering supporters.[20] . . . In political terms, the opponents of the Civil Rights Act made a fatal miscalculation: the dare was taken up, and the statute passed with its broader coverage. . . .

Once sex discrimination was covered under Title VII, however, it generated a new source of legal obligation to which first the disparate treatment and then, eventually, the disparate impact theory applied. But from the first, the antidiscrimination principle was more contestable and more ambiguous in matters of sex than of race. The disparate treatment cases illustrate the difference. Within the area of racial discrimination Title VII works on an overwhelming, virtually conclusive presumption that disparate treatment is, and ought to be, illegal. The conviction undergirding the act (apart from issues of affirmative action) is that the relevant differences between white and black, for example, are so trivial that they should almost never be the grounds for explicit distinctions in treatment. There are of course extreme cases to test this proposition. A white man would not be a good undercover narcotics agent in a black neighborhood, and a black man could not work as a CIA agent trying to pass himself off as a Swedish businessman vacationing in London. But these extreme cases show how far from ordinary jobs one has to deviate in order to find a viable exception to the rule, once the basic antidiscrimination principle is accepted. On matters of race the dominant inquiry under the Civil Rights Act is instrumental: what steps are best able to root out all forms of disparate treatment at acceptable social cost? The hardest task facing the legal system is to determine whether facially legitimate and race–neutral reasons for passing over blacks in favor of whites are pretexts for some underlying bias.

The disparate treatment cases in regard to sex do not share that logic at all. Again the contrasting responses to the slogan "separate but equal" in race and sex cases hold the key. There are many instances in which employers have defended explicit sex classifications that were in common use before the statute and had been subject to no moral criticism. It is also worth recalling that the bona fide occupational qualification exception to the antidiscrimination principle applies to sex but not to race. It follows, therefore, that when we turn to the specific context of employment, we should expect to see some serious debate over the proper reach of the antidiscrimination principle. More concretely, we should also expect to see a shift in emphasis on matters of relative importance. In race cases few defendants have offered any justification for the disparate treatment of blacks and whites. The race cases thus tend to focus on motives and impact. But with sex cases the dominant question is whether these explicit differences in treatment are justifiable. . . .

STATUTORY FRAMEWORK

The Civil Rights Act has, since its inception, contained an exception to the basic antidiscrimination norm that is directed to sex but not to race. The act reads:

> Notwithstanding any other provision of this title, (1) it shall not be an unlawful employment practice for an employer to hire and employ employees . . . on the basis of . . . religion, sex, or national origin in those certain instances where religion, sex, or national origin is a bona fide occupational qualification reasonably necessary to the normal operation of that particular business or enterprise.[1]

To the untutored this provision looks to be a substantial qualification of the basic nondiscrimination principle, one which recognizes that differences in sex (as well as religion and national origin) are matters that people could, and would, on some occasions at least, regard as relevant to private decision making. The exclusion of race from this section reflects the strong intuition that racial discrimination is always impermissible. The difficult question of statutory construction is to determine the extent to which the bona fide occupational qualification (BFOQ) authorizes a deviation from this categorical norm in sex discrimination cases. . . .

In order to analyze both how a BFOQ might work and why neither it nor the basic provisions of Title VII are needed, I shall consider three types of problems that arise under the current interpretation of the BFOQ. The first problem concerns cost differentials. The second asks whether firms should be allowed to take into account the preferences of customers, suppliers, or co-workers. The third involves the interaction between the BFOQ and asserted health justifications for explicit discrimination between male and female employees.

LEGITIMATE COST DIFFERENTIALS

Let us begin with work rules adopted voluntarily by firms before the passage of Title VII which were designed to reduce the total set of employer costs, of which wage payments were only one albeit significant part. For example, many employers had rules that restricted women from certain positions that required them to lift heavy objects, weighing, say, over fifty pounds, or to engage in strenuous physical activity. In a world of freedom of contract these terms are as valid as any other. The employer may choose to cut itself off from a certain source of labor. If (but only if) its decision is erroneous, the firm will have to pay the price, since other firms will ignore those self-imposed restrictions and be able to provide goods and services at lower cost. The mechanisms of self-correction are powerful, and the demands on the courts are slight. With freedom of contract, therefore, the legal system judges only those contractual offers that are made and accepted. Thereafter, competition within the economic system, and not government fiat, determines which hiring strategy is superior.

Within the market setting we should expect some sex-specific classifications to endure. The obvious line of defense is that sex-based limitations work at low cost to distinguish those workers who are likely to be injured on the job from those who are not. The fit be-

tween the rule and its objective is, of course, not perfect, but the positive correlation is still better than random association. Sex classifications, at least the ones that endure, thus operate like other types of tests or qualifications by providing some useful information for making decisions at reasonable cost. As long as they generate net improvements, they will be used—at least by some firms some of the time.

Under Title VII, however, any reliance on market judgment and self-correction is misplaced, for now there has to be some "objective" showing of the relation of the explicit requirement to the job at hand. The attack on these rough-and-ready classifications is familiar: individual case-by-case judgments about strength are possible, and should therefore be preferred to broad classifications, which may or may not be accurate. But the same reply should be decisive: the object of the firm is not to minimize the costs of error alone, which perfect individuation might do, but to minimize the sum of the twin costs of error and administration. At this point two sets of considerations enter. First, the case-by-case analysis may be less accurate than the per se rule. If only a small percentage of men or women qualify for a certain job, the tests may not be able to identify them. If, for example, under a perfect test 95 out of 100 qualifiers would be women, a test that has a 10 percent error rate is inferior to the per se rule that says hire only women, for the per se rule makes only 5 percent errors. The case-by-case rule, even if it appoints 5 men and 95 women, may cut the wrong 5 women and hire the wrong 5 men. The error costs may not be reduced to an acceptable rate even if the level of precaution taken is very high. The ideal solution to finding the *right* 5 men and the *right* 95 women is unattainable in a world with positive transaction costs.

Second, the costs of administration are relevant to any overall calculation. The use of sex-based rules of thumb is consistent with minimizing the sum of administrative and error costs, so the firm that adopts the so-called stereotype (read: accurate statistical generalization) may well flourish in competition with a firm that chooses to abandon it in favor of tests that are perhaps both more costly and less reliable. In principle, employers should easily be able to demonstrate that case-by-case individuation costs a good deal of money but has little predictive power. After all, the EEOC is the leading skeptic on facially neutral job-related standards for all forms of testing. The relevant trade-off, moreover, is sufficiently pervasive that it seems pointless to require much proof in individual cases. Per se rules are always cheaper to design and administer than complex balancing tests.

The attack on the BFOQ exception does not rest, however, solely on the insufficient ground that sex classifications are imperfect. In addition, there have been arguments based on individual liberty—that the weight and work restrictions, for example, represent a misguided form of paternalism. Perhaps the most influential statement of that position is found in the well-known decision of *Weeks v. Southern Bell Telephone & Telegraph Co.*,[12] where just such weight requirements for a telephone switchman were held not to fall within the BFOQ exception:

> Title VII rejects just this type of romantic paternalism as unduly Victorian and instead vests individual women with the power to decide whether or not to take on unromantic tasks. Men have always had the right to determine whether the incremental increase in remuneration for strenuous, dangerous, obnoxious, boring or unromantic tasks is worth the candle. The promise of Title VII is that women are now to be on equal footing.[13]

Thus the language of freedom of choice is pressed into service to justify the narrow construction given to the BFOQ exception. Rhetorically *Weeks* appeals to the market-enforcing

impetus behind the antidiscrimination acts by posting an outcome that increases the scope of individual choice and gives women parity in terms of the "rights" long held and enjoyed by men. On matters of contracting choice, Title VII, we are told, enacts Mr. Herbert Spencer's Social Statics after all.

Yet the antipaternalist defense of Title VII is wrong in one vital respect. The ability of men to undertake strenuous, risky, or boring work has always been contingent on the willingness of an employer, male or female, corporate or individual, to offer that work to them. There is nothing paternalistic about a legal rule that says that workers may not take risks for employers who do not wish to hire them or to provide them with the demanded compensation. The market baseline made it perfectly clear that risk-preferring men could not foist themselves on employers, and the same rule does, and should, apply to women now that the nineteenth-century limitations on contractual capacity have happily been lifted. The equal footing of men and women in a marketplace gives both groups the right to *offer* their labor to the highest bidder on whatever terms and conditions they choose. It does not give either group the right to conscript employers to provide them with the identical wages and positions that are offered to members of the opposite sex, regardless of the losses to those employers. *Weeks* did not strike down legally imposed barriers to entry that prevent women from competing with men. It addressed only the case of a private employer who chose not to hire for reasons it found sufficient. . . .

The issue can be placed in a somewhat broader perspective. The antidiscrimination statute imposes an implicit tax that employers will try to resist, an observation that explains much of the foot-dragging evasions and ill-concealed hostility that develop when Title VII is invoked to insert women into, say, heavy manufacturing or the construction industry. A law would be regarded as both unfair and inefficient if it enabled a person to make a hapless buyer pay $100 for a good that he values at only $50. The same principle applies when Title VII coerces employers into hiring workers worth on net $50 for $100 in wages. The losing contract forced on an employer by Title VII operates as the thin edge of the wedge for a regime of inefficient state confiscation. Given the evident size of the displacement, the overall efficiency losses are substantial. The total number of employment opportunities for both men and women necessarily *shrinks* as a result of the reduced level of economic activity. The de facto obliteration of the BFOQ requirement thus works synergistically with the mistaken mandatory features of the workers' compensation statute by denying the employer any sensible leeway in selecting workers whose anticipated accident rates are lower than other applicants'.

Weeks, then, badly misfires when it seeks to justify public coercion on antipaternalistic grounds. In practice the case sanctions a massive interference with market forces. Nonetheless, the decision has been widely accepted not only for determining workers' compensation costs but also for setting other costs that may be higher for women than for men or vice versa—for example, when new facilities have to be provided in the switch from a single-sex to a dual-sex work force. As one textbook writer in the field has written: "The thrust of the BFOQ defense is on the inability of an employee to perform. Additional costs cannot be a defense because they do not affect an employee's performance."[19] The law in effect ignores the total level of employer benefit and the total level of employer cost. Title VII systematically disregards those factors most relevant to the operation of a sensible market. . . .

CUSTOMER PREFERENCES AND FORGONE BENEFITS

The BFOQ serves double duty. In addition to its potential application to the cost side of the equation, it also has relevance to the benefit side: that is, may the employer rely on the BFOQ to offer men and women different wages and terms of employment when the benefits they provide to the employer differ systematically by sex? A ski resort I visited proudly advertised that it provided male or female instructors at the preference of the customer. Yet any employer that allows women skiers to match themselves with women instructors appears to be in flat violation of Title VII, at least as construed by the EEOC, whose guidelines provide in no uncertain terms that employers cannot take into account "the preferences of coworkers, the employer, clients or customers," save in exceptionally rare cases.[26] Its position is that the only question that matters is the ability to perform a particular job, taken in isolation from the environment in which the work is done, or the value of the performance tendered. In a sense its view is almost preordained. If the employer is not permitted to take into account the collateral costs of hiring certain classes of employees (such as accident or life insurance), there is no particular reason to allow it to take into account preferences of customers or co-workers either. "Reasonably necessary for the normal operation of the business" hardly gives a preferred status to dealing with customers as opposed to controlling internal costs. Indeed, in light of *Weeks* the result here is in a sense inexorable. Once the preferences of other people are taken into account, the BFOQ exception becomes large enough to engulf Title VII's prohibition against sex discrimination, for many, if not all, employers can use this argument to take refuge in the BFOQ and thus gut Title VII's prohibition against sex discrimination.

This argument is, however, a two-edged sword. If the number of cases that properly falls within this exception is large, then the basic prohibition against sex-based discrimination is flawed and should be repealed, precisely because there are widely shared social beliefs that differences between the sexes do matter in all sorts of ways. Employers are far more responsive to customer demands than the defenders of the "contract of adhesion" view of the world will admit. But arguments based on the efficiency of market mechanisms are too powerful for interpreting the BFOQ exception, in light of the central purpose of Title VII. Rather, the criticism of the EEOC guidelines in the context of the statute takes another form. Not being able to take customers' and co-workers' preferences into account is wholly inconsistent with the effort to find a middle ground which is characteristic of any statute that relies on the twin tests of "bona fide" and "reasonably necessary." The task, therefore, is to try to find some way in which to distinguish between the informed and honest preferences of the vast majority of well-meaning people and the intensely irrational or invidious preferences of the bigoted few. It is in essence a matter of articulating an objective standard to determine which subjective preferences should prevail.

At this point the inquiry becomes cautious and factually dense. It is very hard to formulate any a priori judgment as to the types of subjective preferences that should be vindicated or the frequency of their occurrence. Instead, the employer should be allowed to introduce proof of the pervasive nature of a given practice, or of the unsuccessful efforts to replace it with a sex-blind policy. Evidence from the EEOC could be used to show that other firms have succeeded without relying on the sex-based practice, or that other low-cost precautions, such as good marketing programs, can reduce the level of consumer dissatisfaction. Of course, all this trouble could be avoided by repealing Title VII. But the problems are only magnified by its remorseless application. . . .

SAFETY CONCERNS AS A JUSTIFICATION FOR DISPARATE TREATMENT

The legislative debates over Title VII did not anticipate the most controversial question about the BFOQ: To what extent must the business necessity test be bent in order to take into account concerns, ostensible or real, about the safety of employees? That issue came to a head in the critical 1991 Supreme Court decision, *International Union, UAW v. Johnson Controls, Inc.*,[40] on the vexing question of fetal vulnerability. The relevant company rule applied to the battery division of Johnson Controls, whose work necessarily exposes employees to levels of lead high enough to cause potentially serious damage to unborn children. In response to this risk, Johnson Controls (actually a predecessor company) in the late 1960s instituted internal tests to monitor workers for lead exposure and installed an extensive $15 million control system to minimize that exposure. In 1977 the company issued a warning to women that they should not work in the battery division, citing the cumulative evidence of the impact of lead poisoning in the early stages of fetal development. But it stopped short of excluding women from taking jobs in the division. By 1982 the company had concluded that it was "medically necessary" to bar women from working in the battery division except for those whose inability to bear children was "medically documented." It was this last decision that was challenged under Title VII and defended successfully as a BFOQ when the Seventh Circuit, sitting en banc, affirmed the defendant's motion for summary judgment by a seven-to-four-vote. . . .

The Supreme Court unanimously reversed the decision of the Seventh Circuit and awarded the summary judgment for the plaintiff.[44] The first step in its analysis is uncontroversial; Johnson Controls adopted a policy that did discriminate on its face between men and women. The entire case therefore turns on the issue of justification. On this second issue the Court is on far weaker ground when it construes the business necessity standard so narrowly that it becomes *always* improper for employers for reasons of sex to take into account the risks to employees or their offspring, wholly apart from the question of overbreadth. The firm could not impose a fetal vulnerability policy even if *all* women (or their offspring) were exposed to a manifest risk of injury when no men were subject to that risk. Overbreadth does not matter. All that matters is the work that women do, not the risks to which they are exposed. . . .

The basic argument here should have a familiar ring. First, the employment discrimination laws sweep away all protection regulation with sex–specific orientation, no matter what the magnitude of the risk. If women were certain to die from a class of exposures harmless to men, Title VII would preclude any state intervention by the employer. The same Court that is suspicious of freedom of choice in a thousand other industrial contexts adopts it here, but for only one side of the contractual relationship. In addition, the Court notes that there is still some residual risk—small in probability but potentially large in magnitude. That risk follows the usual pattern under Title VII: firms must take the residual losses, which the court then proceeds to understate. Initially the Court ignores the possible claims of its female employees under the workers' compensation laws, in which recovery depends not on proof of negligence but on accidents or occupational diseases arising out of and in the scope of employment. It then understates the relevant tort exposure to suits by offspring. It is often unnecessary to show negligence under modern products liability law.[50] In addition, it is far more difficult to protect oneself by warnings than the Court perceives. "Full disclosure" in products cases is a term of art, and state courts often impose disclosure requirements that are far stricter than those that the reassuring words "full disclosure" might suggest.[51] Even if warnings were found adequate, the offspring of a worker might well maintain a tort action on the ground that the defendant should have taken steps to reduce the level of exposure below what it in fact was, even if it already met the stringent standards imposed by OSHA.

It is a familiar story. Costs that are speculative and uncertain may also be large. But whether large or small, they are now borne by an employer. The implicit subsidies worked by the employment discrimination laws are again explicitly ratified by the Supreme Court. There are surely many delicate judgments that must be made about sex roles in the workplace, but a decent respect for differences in judgment and taste, both of employers and employees, makes it imperative that these judgments be made in the workplace, and not in the halls of Congress or the courts.

NOTES

[15]See, e.g., for endless repetition of the theme of differences, Catharine MacKinnon, *Feminism Unmodified* 123 (1986); "Given what I have said about women's physicality, women's point of view on athletics, and its connections with sexuality and the subordination of women generally, *now* let's ask, what about separate teams? What about separate programs? What about separate institutions?" MacKinnon does not answer the questions she raises, but surely they could not even be asked today in the context of race.

[16]*Clark v. Arizona Interscholastic Association*, 886 F.2d 1191 (9th Cir. 1989), noting that "due to physiological differences, males would displace females to a substantial extent if they were allowed to compete for positions on the volleyball team." Id. at 1193.

[20]See, e.g., Francis J. Vaas, "Title VII: Legislative History," 7 *Bost. C. Ind. & Comm. L. Rev.* 431, 441 (1966).

[1]Civil Rights Act of 1964 §703(e).

[11]See Chapters 2 and 3. A parallel case is made in Fuchs, *Women's Quest*, at 35–38.

[12]408 F.2d 228 (5th Cir. 1969).

[13]*Id.* at 236.

[19]Mack A. Player, *Employment Discrimination Law* 288 (1988).

[26]29 C.F.R. §1604.2(a)(iii) (1989).

[40]886 F.2d 871 (7th Cir. 1989), rev'd, 111 Sup. Ct. 1196 (1991).

[44]*International Union, UAW v. Johnson Controls*, 111 S.Ct. 1196 (1991).

[50]See Restatement (Second) of Torts §402A (1965).

[51]See, e.g., *MacDonald v. Ortho Pharmaceutical Corp.*, 394 Mass. 131, 475 N.E.2d 65 (1985).

QUESTIONS FOR DISCUSSION

1. What are the main differences between race discrimination and sex discrimination, according to Epstein? Why does he think these differences are important to the law? Do you agree? Why or why not? Would MacKinnon agree? Why or why not?

2. How would you determine when sex is a BFOQ (bona fide occupational qualification)? If possible, give several examples where sex is a BFOQ and where it is not.

3. Should it be illegal for ski resorts to offer male or female instructors at the preference of the customer? Should it be illegal for universities to allow students to choose whether to study math or philosophy with a male or a female professor? Why or why not?

4. Is it unjust or illegal for Johnson Controls to exclude all women from their battery division? Why or why not? Be sure to consider Epstein's arguments about this case.

CALIFORNIA FEDERAL SAVINGS & LOAN ASSN. ET AL. V. GUERRA, DIRECTOR, DEPARTMENT OF FAIR EMPLOYMENT AND HOUSING, ET AL.

479 U.S. 272 (1987)

JUSTICE MARSHALL delivered the opinion of the Court.

The question presented is whether Title VII of the Civil Rights Act of 1964, as amended by the Pregnancy Discrimination Act of 1978, preempts a state statute that requires employers to provide leave and reinstatement to employees disabled by pregnancy.

I

California's Fair Employment and Housing Act (FEHA) . . . is a comprehensive statute that prohibits discrimination in employment and housing. In September 1978, California amended the FEHA to proscribe certain forms of employment discrimination on the basis of pregnancy. . . . Subdivision (b)(2) [of Section

12945]—the provision at issue here—is the only portion of the statute that applies to employers subject to Title VII. It requires these employers to provide female employees an unpaid pregnancy disability leave of up to four months. . . .

Title VII of the Civil Rights Act of 1964 . . . also prohibits various forms of employment discrimination, including discrimination on the basis of sex. However, in *General Electric Co. v. Gilbert*, 429 U.S. 125 (1976), the Court ruled that discrimination on the basis of pregnancy was not sex discrimination under Title VII. In response to the Gilbert decision, Congress passed the Pregnancy Discrimination Act of 1978 (PDA). . . . The PDA specifies that sex discrimination includes discrimination on the basis of pregnancy.[1]

II

Petitioner California Federal Savings & Loan Association (Cal Fed) is a federally chartered savings and loan association based in Los Angeles; it is an employer covered by Title VII and §12945(b)(2). Cal Fed has a facially neutral leave policy that permits employees who have completed three months of service to take unpaid leaves of absence for a variety of reasons, including disability and pregnancy. Although it is Cal Fed's policy to try to provide an employee taking unpaid leave with a similar position upon returning, Cal Fed expressly reserves the right to terminate an employee who has taken a leave of absence if a similar position is not available.

Lillian Garland was employed by Cal Fed as a receptionist for several years. In January 1982, she took a pregnancy disability leave. When she was able to return to work in April of that year, Garland notified Cal Fed, but was informed that her job had been filled and that there were no receptionist or similar positions available. Garland filed a complaint with respondent Department of Fair Employment and Housing, which issued an administrative accusation against Cal Fed on her behalf. Respondent charged Cal Fed with violating §12945(b)(2)

of the FEHA. Prior to the scheduled hearing before respondent Fair Employment and Housing Commission, Cal Fed . . . sought a declaration that §12945(b)(2) is inconsistent with and preempted by Title VII and an injunction against enforcement of the section. The District Court granted petitioners' motion for summary judgment. . . .

The United States Court of Appeals for the Ninth Circuit reversed. . . . [W]e now affirm.

III
B

Petitioners argue that the language of the federal statute itself [PDA] unambiguously rejects California's "special treatment" approach to pregnancy discrimination, thus rendering any resort to the legislative history unnecessary. They contend that the second clause of the PDA forbids an employer to treat pregnant employees any differently than other disabled employees. Because "'[the] purpose of Congress is the ultimate touchstone'" of the pre-emption inquiry . . . , however, we must examine the PDA's language against the background of its legislative history and historical context. . . .

It is well established that the PDA was passed in reaction to this Court's decision in *General Electric Co. v. Gilbert*. . . . By adding pregnancy to the definition of sex discrimination prohibited by Title VII, the first clause of the PDA reflects Congress' disapproval of the reasoning in *Gilbert*. . . . Rather than imposing a limitation on the remedial purpose of the PDA, we believe that the second clause was intended to overrule the holding in Gilbert and to illustrate how discrimination against pregnancy is to be remedied. . . . Accordingly, subject to certain limitations, we agree with the Court of Appeals' conclusion that Congress intended the PDA to be "a floor beneath which pregnancy disability benefits may not drop—not a ceiling above which they may not rise". . . .

Title VII, as amended by the PDA, and California's pregnancy disability leave statute share a common goal. The purpose of Title VII is "to achieve equality of employment opportunities and remove barriers that have operated in the past to favor an identifiable group of . . . employees over other employees." . . . Rather than limiting existing Title VII principles and objectives, the PDA extends them to cover pregnancy. As Senator Williams, a sponsor of the Act, stated: "The entire thrust . . . behind this legislation is to guarantee women the basic right to participate fully and equally in the workforce, without denying them the fundamental right to full participation in family life". . .

C

Moreover, even if we agreed with petitioners' construction of the PDA, we would nonetheless reject their argument that the California statute requires employers to violate Title VII. . . . Section 12945(b)(2) does not compel California employers to treat pregnant workers better than other disabled employees; it merely establishes benefits that employers must, at a minimum, provide to pregnant workers. Employers are free to give comparable benefits to other disabled employees, thereby treating "women affected by pregnancy" no better than "other persons not so affected but similar in their ability or inability to work." Indeed, at oral argument, petitioners conceded that compliance with both statutes "is theoretically possible". . .

IV

Thus, petitioners' facial challenge to §12945(b)(2) fails. The statute is not pre-empted by Title VII, as amended by the PDA, because it is not inconsistent with the purposes of the federal statute, nor does it require the doing of an act which is unlawful under Title VII.

The judgment of the Court of Appeals is Affirmed.

JUSTICE WHITE, with whom THE CHIEF JUSTICE and JUSTICE POWELL join, dissenting.

I disagree with the Court that Cal. Govt. Code Ann. §12945(b)(2) . . . is not preempted by the Pregnancy Discrimination Act of 1978 (PDA) . . . and §708 of Title VII. . . . Title VII . . . forbids discrimination in the terms of employment on the basis of race, color, religion, sex, or national origin. The PDA gave added meaning to discrimination on the basis of sex:

> "The terms 'because of sex' or 'on the basis of sex' [in §703(a) of this Title] include, but are not limited to, because of or on the basis of pregnancy, childbirth or related medical conditions; and women affected by pregnancy, childbirth, or related medical conditions shall be treated the same for all employment-related purposes, including receipt of benefits under fringe benefit programs, as other persons not so affected but similar in their ability or inability to work. . . ."

The second clause quoted above could not be clearer: it mandates that pregnant employees "shall be treated the same for all employment-related purposes" as nonpregnant employees similarly situated with respect to their ability or nonability to work. This language leaves no room for preferential treatment of pregnant workers. . . .

Contrary to the mandate of the PDA, California law requires every employer to have a disability leave policy for pregnancy even if it has none for any other disability. An employer complies with California law if it has a leave policy for pregnancy but denies it for every other disability. On its face, §12945(b)(2) is in square conflict with the PDA and is therefore pre-empted. . . .

The majority nevertheless would save the California law on two grounds. First, it holds that the PDA does not require disability from pregnancy to be treated the same as other disabilities; instead, it forbids less favorable, but permits more favorable, benefits for pregnancy disability. The express command of the PDA is unambiguously to the contrary, and the legislative history casts no doubt on that mandate.

The legislative materials reveal Congress' plain intent not to put pregnancy in a class by itself within Title VII, as the majority does with its "floor . . . not a ceiling" approach. . . . The Senate Report clearly stated:

"By defining sex discrimination to include discrimination against pregnant women, the bill rejects the view that employers may treat pregnancy and its incidents as sui generis, without regard to its functional comparability to other conditions. Under this bill, the treatment of pregnant women in covered employment must focus not on their condition alone but on the actual effects of that condition on their ability to work. Pregnant women who are able to work must be permitted to work on the same conditions as other employees; and when they are not able to work for medical reasons, they must be accorded the same rights, leave privileges and other benefits, as other workers who are disabled from working."

The House Report similarly stressed that the legislation did not mark a departure from Title VII principles. . . .

The Court's second, and equally strange, ground is that even if the PDA does prohibit special benefits for pregnant women, an employer may still comply with both the California law and the PDA: it can adopt the specified leave policies for pregnancy and at the same time afford similar benefits for all other disabilities. This is untenable. California surely had no intent to require employers to provide general disability leave benefits. . . . The text of the PDA does not speak to this question but it is clear from the legislative history that Congress did not intend for the PDA to impose such burdens on employers. As recognized by the majority, opposition to the PDA came from those concerned with the cost of including pregnancy in health and disability benefit plans. . . . The House Report acknowledged these concerns and explained that the bill "in no way requires the institution of any new programs where none currently exist." The Senate Report gave a similar assurance. In addition, legislator after legislator stated during the floor debates that the PDA would not require an employer to institute a disability benefits program if it did not already have one in effect. Congress intended employers to be free to provide any level of disability benefits they wished—or none at all—as long as pregnancy was not a factor in allocating such benefits. The conjunction of §12945(b)(2) and the PDA requires California employers to implement new minimum disability leave programs. Reading the state and federal statutes together in this fashion yields a result which Congress expressly disavowed. . . .

In sum, preferential treatment of pregnant workers is prohibited by Title VII, as amended by the PDA. Section 12945(b)(2) of the California Government Code, which extends preferential benefits for pregnancy, is therefore pre-empted. . . .

NOTE

[1] The PDA added subsection (k) to . . . the definitional section of Title VII. Subsection (k) provides, in relevant part: "The terms 'because of sex' or 'on the basis of sex' include, but are not limited to, because of or on the basis of pregnancy, childbirth, or related medical conditions; and women affected by pregnancy, childbirth, or related medical conditions shall be treated the same for all employment-related purposes, including receipt of benefits under fringe benefit programs, as other persons not so affected but similar in their ability or inability to work, and nothing in section 703(h) of this title shall be interpreted to permit otherwise."

QUESTIONS FOR DISCUSSION

1. In your opinion, should all employers be legally required to grant an unlimited number of pregnancy leaves to female employees? Should the law require that pregnancy leaves be paid leaves? Why or why not?

2. If Epstein wrote an opinion in *Cal Fed*, what would he say?

3. If MacKinnon wrote an opinion in *Cal Fed*, what would she say?

MERITOR SAVINGS BANK
V. VINSON ET AL.

477 U.S. 57 (1986)

JUDGES: REHNQUIST, J., delivered the opinion of the Court, in which BURGER, C. J., and WHITE, POWELL, STEVENS, and O'CONNOR, JJ., joined. MARSHALL, J., filed an opinion concurring in the judgment, in which BRENNAN, BLACKMUN, and STEVENS, JJ., joined.

OPINION BY: REHNQUIST

This case presents important questions concerning claims of workplace "sexual harassment" brought under Title VII of the Civil Rights Act of 1964. . . .

I

In 1974, respondent Mechelle Vinson met Sidney Taylor, a vice president of what is now petitioner Meritor Savings Bank (bank) and manager of one of its branch offices. When respondent asked whether she might obtain employment at the bank, Taylor gave her an application, which she completed and returned the next day; later that same day Taylor called her to say that she had been hired. With Taylor as her supervisor, respondent started as a teller-trainee, and thereafter was promoted to teller, head teller, and assistant branch manager. She worked at the same branch for four years, and it is undisputed that her advancement there was based on merit alone. In September 1978, respondent notified Taylor that she was taking sick leave for an indefinite period. On November 1, 1978, the bank discharged her for excessive use of that leave.

Respondent brought this action against Taylor and the bank, claiming that during her four years at the bank she had "constantly been subjected to sexual harassment" by Taylor in violation of Title VII. She sought injunctive relief, compensatory and punitive damages against Taylor and the bank, and attorney's fees.

At the 11-day bench trial, the parties presented conflicting testimony about Taylor's behavior during respondent's employment. Respondent testified that during her probationary period as a teller-trainee, Taylor treated her in a fatherly way and made no sexual advances. Shortly thereafter, however, he invited her out to dinner and, during the course of the meal, suggested that they go to a motel to have sexual relations. At first she refused, but out of what she described as fear of losing her job she eventually agreed. According to respondent, Taylor thereafter made repeated demands upon her for sexual favors, usually at the branch, both during and after business hours; she estimated that over the next several years she had intercourse with him some 40 or 50 times. In addition, respondent testified that Taylor fondled her in front of other employees, followed her into the women's restroom when she went there alone, exposed himself to her, and even forcibly raped her on several occasions. These activities ceased after 1977, respondent stated, when she started going with a steady boyfriend.

Respondent also testified that Taylor touched and fondled other women employees of the bank, and she attempted to call witnesses to support this charge. But while some supporting testimony apparently was admitted without objection, the District Court did not allow her "to present wholesale evidence of a pattern and practice relating to sexual advances to other female employees in her case in chief, but advised her that she might well be able to present such evidence in rebuttal to the defendants' cases." . . . Respondent did not offer such evidence in rebuttal. Finally, respondent testified that because she was afraid of Taylor she never reported his harassment to any of his supervisors and never attempted to use the bank's complaint procedure.

Taylor denied respondent's allegations of sexual activity, testifying that he never fondled her, never made suggestive remarks to her, never engaged in sexual intercourse with her, and never asked her to do so. He contended instead that respondent made her accusations in response to a business-related dispute. The bank also denied respondent's allegations and asserted that any sexual harassment by Taylor was unknown to the bank and engaged in without its consent or approval.

The District Court denied relief, but . . . [t]he Court of Appeals for the District of Columbia Circuit reversed. We . . . now affirm but for different reasons.

II

Title VII of the Civil Rights Act of 1964 makes it "an unlawful employment practice for an employer . . . to discriminate against any individual with respect to his compensation, terms, conditions, or privileges of employment, because of such individual's race, color, religion, sex, or national origin."

Respondent argues, and the Court of Appeals held, that unwelcome sexual advances that create an offensive or hostile working environment violate Title VII. Without question, when a supervisor sexually harasses a subordinate because of the subordinate's sex, that supervisor "discriminate[s]" on the basis of sex. Petitioner apparently does not challenge this proposition. It contends instead that in prohibiting discrimination with respect to "compensation, terms, conditions, or privileges" of employment, Congress was concerned with what petitioner describes as "tangible loss" of "an economic character," not "purely psychological aspects of the workplace environment." In support of this claim petitioner observes that in both the legislative history of Title VII and this Court's Title VII decisions, the focus has been on tangible, economic barriers erected by discrimination.

We reject petitioner's view. First, the language of Title VII is not limited to "economic" or "tangible" discrimination. The phrase "terms, conditions, or privileges of employment" evinces a congressional intent "'to strike at the entire spectrum of disparate treatment of men and women'" in employment. . . . Petitioner has pointed to nothing in the Act to suggest that Congress contemplated the limitation urged here.

Second, in 1980 the EEOC issued Guidelines specifying that "sexual harassment," as there defined, is a form of sex discrimination prohibited by Title VII. . . . In defining "sexual harassment," the Guidelines first describe the kinds of workplace conduct that may be actionable under Title VII. These include "[unwelcome] sexual advances, requests for sexual favors, and other verbal or physical conduct of a sexual nature." . . . Relevant to the charges at issue in this case, the Guidelines provide that such sexual misconduct constitutes prohibited "sexual harassment," whether or not it is directly linked to the grant or denial of an economic quid pro quo, where "such conduct has the purpose or effect of unreasonably interfering with an individual's work performance or creating an intimidating, hostile, or offensive working environment." . . .

[T]he District Court's conclusion that no actionable harassment occurred might have rested on its earlier "finding" that "[if] [respondent] and Taylor did engage in an intimate or sexual relationship . . . , that relationship was a voluntary one." . . . But the fact that sex-related conduct was "voluntary," in the sense that the complainant was not forced to participate against her will, is not a defense to a sexual harassment suit brought under Title VII. The gravamen of any sexual harassment claim is that the alleged sexual advances were "unwelcome." ... While the question whether particular conduct was indeed unwelcome presents difficult problems of proof and turns largely on credibility determinations committed to the trier of fact, the District Court in this case erroneously focused on the "voluntariness" of respondent's participation in the claimed sexual episodes. The correct inquiry is whether respondent by her conduct indicated that the alleged sexual advances were unwelcome, not whether her actual participation in sexual intercourse was voluntary.

Petitioner contends that even if this case must be remanded to the District Court, the Court of Appeals erred in one of the terms of its remand. Specifically, the Court of Appeals stated that testimony about respondent's "dress and personal fantasies," ... which the District Court apparently admitted into evidence, "had no place in this litigation." ... To the contrary, such evidence is obviously relevant. The EEOC Guidelines emphasize that the trier of fact must determine the existence of sexual harassment in light of "the record as a whole" and "the totality of circumstances, such as the nature of the sexual advances and the context in which the alleged incidents occurred." ... Respondent's claim that any marginal relevance of the evidence in question was outweighed by the potential for unfair prejudice is the sort of argument properly addressed to the District Court. ... While the District Court must carefully weigh the applicable considerations in deciding whether to admit evidence of this kind, there is no per se rule against its admissibility.

III

Although the District Court concluded that respondent had not proved a violation of Title VII, it nevertheless went on to consider the question of the bank's liability. Finding that "the bank was without notice" of Taylor's alleged conduct, and that notice to Taylor was not the equivalent of notice to the bank, the court concluded that the bank therefore could not be held liable for Taylor's alleged actions. The Court of Appeals took the opposite view, holding that an employer is strictly liable for a hostile environment created by a supervisor's sexual advances, even though the employer neither knew nor reasonably could have known of the alleged misconduct. ... We ... decline the parties' invitation to issue a definitive rule on employer liability, but we do ... hold that the Court of Appeals erred in concluding that employers are always automatically liable for sexual harassment by their supervisors.

... Finally, we reject petitioner's view that the mere existence of a grievance procedure and a policy against discrimination, coupled with respondent's failure to invoke that procedure, must insulate petitioner from liability. While those facts are plainly relevant, the situation before us demonstrates why they are not necessarily dispositive. Petitioner's general nondiscrimination policy did not address sexual harassment in particular, and thus did not alert employees to their employer's interest in correcting that form of discrimination. ... Moreover, the bank's grievance procedure apparently required an employee to complain first to her supervisor, in this case Taylor. Since Taylor was the alleged perpetrator, it is not altogether surprising that respondent failed to invoke the procedure and report her grievance to him. Petitioner's contention that respondent's failure should insulate it from liability might be substantially stronger if its procedures were better calculated to encourage victims of harassment to come forward.

IV

In sum, we hold that a claim of "hostile environment" sex discrimination is actionable under Title VII, that the District Court's findings were insufficient to dispose of respondent's hostile environment claim, and that the District Court did not err in admitting testimony about respondent's sexually provocative speech and dress. As to employer liability, we conclude that the Court of Appeals was wrong to entirely disregard agency principles and impose absolute liability on employers for the acts of their supervisors, regardless of the circumstances of a particular case.

Accordingly, the judgment of the Court of Appeals reversing the judgment of the District Court is affirmed, and the case is remanded for further proceedings consistent with this opinion.

It is so ordered.

QUESTIONS FOR DISCUSSION

1. In your opinion, should there be laws against sexual harassment on the job? In public schools? What kinds of laws?

2. Do sexual harassment laws violate the right to free speech if they prevent fellow workers or students from saying what they want to say about and to women? Why or why not? (See Section 4.3.)

3. Is it unjust for schools to provide more funding for men's sports than for women's sports? Why or why not?

4. Is it unjust for a government to exclude women from combat service? Why or why not?

5. Some argue that women cannot achieve equal opportunity in employment unless governments provide or support affordable quality day care. Do you agree? Is it unjust for governments to refuse to provide or support this service? Why or why not?

6. In his opinion in *Bakke*, Justice Powell argues that strict scrutiny should not be applied to gender classifications in the same way as it is applied to racial classifications in preferential treatment programs. He gives his reasons in the following passage. Explain Powell's arguments. Do you agree? Why or why not?

Gender-based distinctions are less likely to create the analytical and practical problems present in preferential programs premised on racial or ethnic criteria. With respect to gender there are only two possible classifications. The incidence of the burdens imposed by preferential classifications is clear. There are no rival groups who can claim that they, too, are entitled to preferential treatment. Classwide questions as to the group suffering previous injury and groups which fairly can be burdened are relatively manageable for reviewing courts. . . . More importantly, the perception of racial classifications as inherently odious stems from a lengthy and tragic history that gender-based classifications do not share. In sum, the Court has never viewed such classification as inherently suspect or as comparable to racial or ethnic classifications for the purpose of equal–protection analysis.[51]

---

[51]*Regents of the University of California v. Bakke*, 438 U.S. 268 at 302–03 (1978).

7. Preferential treatment for women is less justified than for African-Americans, according to George Sher. He summarizes his reasons in the following passage. Do you agree? Why or why not?

. . . [E]ven if it is granted without question that cultural bias and absence of suitable role-models do have some direct and pervasive effect upon women, it is not clear that this effect must take the form of a reduction in women's *abilities* to do the jobs men do. A more likely outcome would seem to be a reduction in women's *inclinations* to do these jobs—a result whose proper compensation is not preferential treatment of those women who have sought the jobs in question, but rather the encouragement of others to seek those jobs as well. . . . Moreover, and conclusively, since there is surely the same dearth of role-models for blacks as for women, whatever psychological disadvantages accrue to women because of this will beset blacks as well. Since blacks, but not women, must also suffer the privations associated with poverty, it follows that they are the group more deserving of reverse discrimination.[32]

SUGGESTIONS FOR FURTHER READING

Classic articles on sex equality are collected in Jane English, ed., *Sex Equality* (Englewood Cliffs, New Jersey: Prentice-Hall, 1977). More recent work on law and bibliography can be found in Katherine Bartlett and Rosanne Kennedy, eds., *Feminist Legal Theory* (Boulder, Colorado: Westview Press, 1991), Part One; and D. Kelley Weisberg, *Feminist Legal Theory: Foundations* (Philadelphia: Temple University Press, 1993), especially Chapters 2–3. For more historical background, see Deborah L. Rhode, *Justice and Gender* (Cambridge: Harvard University Press, 1989). MacKinnon's other works include *Toward a Feminist Theory of the State* (Cambridge: Harvard University Press, 1989); *Feminism Unmodified* (Cambridge: Harvard University Press, 1980); and *Sexual Harassment of Working Women: A Case of Sex Discrimination* (New Haven: Yale University Press, 1979), which is criticized by Ellen Paul, "Sexual Harassment as Sex Discrimination: A Defective Paradigm," *Yale Law and Policy Review*, vol. 8 (1990), pp. 33 ff. For a different model that MacKinnon criticizes, see Martha Minow, *Making All the Difference* (Ithaca: Cornell University Press, 1990). An insightful commentary on this debate is Christine A. Littleton, "Reconstructing Sexual Equality," *California Law Review*, vol. 75 (1987), pp. 1279 ff. Many more arguments against various sex discrimination laws, such as those about pensions and pregnancy, can be found in the rest of Epstein's *Forbidden Grounds*, Chapters 13–16. "Equal pay for equal worth" is discussed by Heidi Hartmann, "Pay Equity for Women," and Mark Killingsworth, "The Economics of Comparable Worth," both in *The Moral Foundations of Civil Rights*, ed. Robert Fullinwider and Claudia Mills (Totowa, New Jersey: Rowman and Littlefield, 1986). Arguments for preferential treatment of women can be found in Mary Anne Warren, "Secondary Sexism and Quota Hiring," *Philosophy and Public Affairs*, vol. 6, no. 3 (Spring 1977), pp. 240–261; and L. W. Sumner, "Positive Sexism," *Social Philosophy and Policy*, vol. 5, no. 1 (Autumn 1987), pp. 204–222. For an argument against extending preferential treatment to women, see George Sher, "Justifying Reverse Discrimination in Employment," *Philosophy and Public Affairs*, vol. 4, no. 2 (Winter 1975), pp. 159–90.

[32]George Sher, "Justifying Reverse Discrimination in Employment," *Philosophy and Public Affairs*, vol. 4, no. 2 (Winter 1975), pp. 159–90.

EQUALITY FOR
HOMOSEXUALS

INTRODUCTION

Discrimination against homosexuals (lesbians and gay men, as well as bisexuals) takes many of the same forms as discrimination against women and African-Americans. Homosexuals are fired from jobs or not hired, denied housing and membership in organizations, and physically attacked because of their sexual orientation. Nonetheless, many people argue that the law should not protect homosexuals in all of the ways that it protects African-Americans, women, and ethnic minorities, because sexual orientation is different from these other classifications in ways that are relevant to the law.

First, many people still believe that sodomy and other acts that are closely associated with homosexuality are immoral, often for religious reasons. Moreover, these acts are illegal in twenty-five states and the District of Columbia (as of 1992). Only eight states limit their statutes to same-sex couples. Nobody today believes that it is immoral to be African-American or female, and no act so closely associated with being African-American or female is illegal.

Second, many people believe that homosexuality is at least partly a matter of choice. Even if sexual orientation (or propensity for sexual attraction to a certain sex) is genetic and thus not a matter of choice, people can still choose not to perform any sexual acts at all, so the sexual acts associated with homosexuality are a matter of choice. Such choices have no exact parallel in race or sex.

Third, many people deny that homosexuals are a disadvantaged group, because the average economic, educational, and social status of homosexuals is above the national average. This is notoriously not the case with African-Americans. Some argue that women as a group are not economically disadvantaged, because many women are in wealthy families, but it is also well-known that women are paid lower average wages than men, even for similar work. Homosexuals are not seen as disadvantaged as much in these ways.

One reason might be that homosexuals can often hide their sexual orientation, whereas African-Americans and females cannot hide their race or sex, except in unusual cases. The demand that homosexuals hide their sexual orientation while heterosexuals can freely declare their sexual orientation strikes many as a form of discrimination itself. Nonetheless, others argue that homosexuals need and deserve no special protection from the government, because they are able to protect themselves from discrimination simply by not openly admitting their sexual orientation.

In response, those who want laws to protect homosexuals against discrimination deny that these differences are relevant. A common comparison is with religion. People are and should be protected against discrimination on the basis of religion, even when people are able to hide their religion, religious acts are a matter of choice, and some religious groups are above the national average in income, education, and social status. If this analogy holds, then none of these features shows that a group does not deserve protection against discrimination.

Much of the argument then comes down to the fact that, whereas religion is protected explicitly in the First Amendment, homosexuality is not protected explicitly in the Constitution, and some homosexual acts even violate laws such as those that were found constitutional in *Bowers v. Hardwick* (1986). However, homosexuals and their defenders respond that the law should not enforce controversial or religion-based moral beliefs (see Section 4.5) and that the Constitution includes a right to privacy (see Section 4.4). If so, *Bowers* was a mistake, and laws against sodomy and other homosexual acts should be found unconstitutional. They can also respond that, even if laws against sodomy are constitutional, discrimination against homosexuals is based on sexual orientation rather than on illegal acts. Such discrimination occurs even where sodomy is not illegal, and even against homosexuals who never commit sodomy or any other illegal act. If discrimination against homosexuals is justified by the criminality of homosexual acts, then homosexuals should be innocent and free of discrimination until they are proven guilty, but people who fire or refuse to rent housing to homosexuals do not wait until their victims are convicted.

Despite, or because of, such arguments for protecting homosexuals against discrimination, a few states recently had referenda on proposed state constitutional amendments that explicitly deny legal protection to homosexuals. One prominent example is Colorado's Proposition 2, which reads:

> Neither the State of Colorado, through any of its branches or departments, nor any of its agencies, political subdivisions, municipalities or school districts, shall enact, adopt or enforce any statute, regulation, ordinance or policy whereby homosexual, lesbian or bisexual orientation, conduct, practices or relationships shall constitute or otherwise be the basis of, or entitle any person or class of persons to have, any claims of minority status, quota preferences, protected status or claim of discrimination.

This amendment to the state constitution was ratified by 53 percent of Colorado's voters on November 3, 1992. However, on December 14, 1993, a federal district court in Colorado found the amendment unconstitutional and ordered that a preliminary injunction (which had kept the amendment from taking effect) be made permanent. Higher court decisions are yet to come.

Under Proposition 2, homosexuals could not make any "claim of discrimination" if their employers or landlords fire or evict them simply because of their sexual orientation. Many people find this unjust. However, some of these people still see homosexuality as relevant in other areas. Should local school boards be allowed to fire elementary school teachers for being openly homosexual? Should heterosexuals be given preference in custody disputes? Should homosexuals be allowed to adopt the children of their partners?[33] Should homosexual couples be allowed to adopt children together? Should homosexual couples be allowed to marry?[34] If not, should homosexual partners be allowed to gain the legal and economic benefits of marriage, such as inclusion under a partner's insurance plan, in some other ways? These questions create controversy even among people who oppose other forms of sexual orientation discrimination, such as Ernest van den Haag, a Distinguished Scholar at the Heritage Foundation (see the reading in this section).

Such issues become even more complex because of real or imagined associations between male homosexuality and HIV or AIDS (acquired immune deficiency syndrome). Although this deadly disease strikes many people who are not homosexual, it also strikes a greater percentage of homosexuals; so discrimination against people with HIV or AIDS is often discrimination against people who happen to be homosexual. Moreover, many people think of AIDS whenever they think of male homosexuality. When insurers believe that male homosexuals are more likely to get AIDS, with its high medical costs, they sometimes refuse coverage or charge higher rates for those people. Such insurers claim that higher rates are not unjust, because insurers always use statistical correlations to adjust rates to their expected costs. Critics respond, however, that such rate hikes will be unfair to those male homosexuals who are not more likely to get AIDS, and will sometimes have devastating effects on male homosexuals who have AIDS or are at risk of AIDS.

A final issue, which has received a great deal of attention recently, is the role of homosexuals in the United States military. Traditionally, homosexuality has been grounds for dismissal from the armed forces mainly on the argument that the presence of known homosexuals will harm morale, unit cohesiveness, and thus effectiveness. Opponents point out that many homosexuals (such as Sergeant Perry Watkins) have served with great distinction in the military and that many of the arguments against homosexuals in the military are similar to arguments that were used to segregate African-Americans in the military in the 1940s. These arguments are discussed in *Watkins v. U. S. Army* and by Richard Mohr, philosophy professor at the University of Illinois at Urbana-Champaign (later in this section).[35]

The prohibition on homosexuals in the military was changed by President Bill Clinton in 1993. The new policy is often known as "Don't ask, don't tell, don't pursue":

> Applicants for military service will not be asked or required to reveal their sexual orientation. Applicants will be informed of accession and separation policy. Service-

[33]The lesbian partner of a child's biological mother was allowed to adopt the child as a "second parent" in *Adoption of Tammy*, 619 N.E.2d 315 (Mass. 1993). Other adoption attempts by homosexuals still fail.

[34]Prohibition of homosexual marriage was approved in *Baker v. Nelson*, 191 N.W. 2d 185 (Minn. 1971). More recently, in *Baehr v. Lewin*, 852 P.2d 44 (Haw. 1993), the Hawaii Supreme Court held that excluding homosexuals from marriage violates the state constitution, because it is a form of sex discrimination.

[35]See also *Steffan v. Aspin*, 8 F.3d 57 (D.C. Circuit 1993) and *Cammermeyer v. Aspin*, 850 F. Supp. 910 (W.D. Wash. 1994), both of which involved successful claims by officers who had been discharged for admitting their homosexuality. Further court decisions in these cases are expected.

members will be separated for homosexual conduct. . . . Homosexual conduct is a homosexual act, a statement by the servicemember that demonstrates a propensity or intent to engage in homosexual acts, or a homosexual marriage or attempted marriage. . . . A homosexual act includes any bodily contact, actively undertaken or passively permitted, between members of the same sex for the purpose of satisfying sexual desires or any bodily contact which a reasonable person would understand to demonstrate a propensity or intent to engage in homosexual acts. . . . Service-members will not be asked or required to reveal their sexual orientation. Commanders and investigating agencies will not initiate inquiries or investigations solely to determine a member's sexual orientation. However, commanders will continue to initiate inquiries or investigations, as appropriate, when there is credible information that a basis for discharge or disciplinary action exists.[36]

The policy guidelines give same-sex "handholding and kissing in most circumstances" as examples of what "will be sufficient to initiate separation." They add that investigations will not be initiated on the sole basis of "association with known homosexuals, presence at a gay bar, possessing or reading homosexual publications, or marching in a gay rights rally in civilian clothes."

Defenders of this new policy argue that it is necessary to serve military needs and also to protect the rights of homosexuals. Some opponents respond that this compromise is unfair and unconstitutional, partly because it restricts free speech, so they want homosexuals to be allowed to serve openly in the military. Other opponents agree in rejecting the Clinton policy, but they want to go back to excluding homosexuals from military service. These issues are not settled yet.

---

[36]From a memo from the Secretary of Defense on July 19, 1993. The last three sentences have been reordered for clarity.

GAY RIGHTS

RICHARD MOHR

In this paper I will suggest that there are no good moral reasons for exempting gays as a class from the protections which the 1964 Civil Rights Act affords racial, gender, ethnic and religious classes. These protections bar discrimination in private employment, housing and public accommodations.[1]

I shall assume that it is a reasonable government function to eliminate arbitrariness regarding with whom we make contracts dealing

Richard Mohr, "Gay Rights," *Social Theory and Practice*, vol. 8 (1982), pp. 31–41

with employment, housing and public accommodations. The reasons for this are diverse,[2] and I shall not discuss them here. All but the most hardened of libertarians would accept this, and even hardened libertarians are likely to hold that consistency demands that if some classes are afforded such protections, all relevantly similar classes should also be afforded such protections. And I take it that it is not in general the claim that one's sexual orientation is dissimilar in relevant respects to one's protected properties (race, religion) that forms the core of possible reasonable objections to the inclusion of gays within the protections of the Civil Rights Act. For on the one hand, if sexual orientation is something over which an individual has virtually no control, either for genetic or psychological reasons, then sexual orientation becomes relevantly similar to race, gender, and ethnicity. Discrimination on these grounds is deplorable because it holds a person accountable without regard for anything *he himself* has done. And to hold a person accountable for that over which he has no control is one form of prejudice. A similar argument from nonprejudicial consistency would seem persuasive for also including the physically and mentally challenged within the reach of the Civil Rights Act.

On the other hand, if one's sexual orientation is a matter of individual choice, it would seem relevantly similar to religion, which is a protected category. We would say that such a personal moral choice is not a reasonable ground for discrimination *even when* the private belief in and practice of it has very public manifestations, as when a religious person becomes involved in politics with a religious motive and a religious intent. And to claim that gay sex is in some sense immoral will not suffice to establish a relevant dissimilarity here. For the nonreligious and the religious may consider each other immoral in this same sense and various religious sects will consider each other immoral, and yet all religious belief is protected.

Now a sufficient moral reason for the protection of private morality from discrimination

in the public sphere is the following. In religious and sexual behavior as well as in other types of behavior, like excretory behavior, there is in our society a presumption of an *obligation* that they be carried out in private, even when there is virtually universal acceptance of the behavior, for example non-gay sex in missionary position for the sake of procreation; and this obligation in turn generates a right to privacy for these same practices. For society cannot consistently claim that these activities must be carried out in private (despite their manifest public consequences, like population growth) and yet retain a claim to investigate such activity and so make it *pro tanto* public behavior.[5] And by giving up the right to investigate such matters, *a fortiori* society gives up the right to discriminate based on them.

So I take it that there is a *prima facie* case for including sexual orientation within the ambit of the 1964 Civil Rights Act, since sexual orientation is relevantly similar to either race or religion. Now the Civil Rights Act reasonably enough has an exemption clause which allows for discrimination on the basis of a protected category when the discrimination against an otherwise protected category represents a "bona fide occupational qualification." This is a reasonable ground for exemption since it means that the discrimination ceases to be whimsical or arbitrary. Such discrimination would be discrimination in good faith. Two obvious examples of good faith discrimination are the following. It seems to me reasonable that a Chinese restaurant, for the sake of ambience, should choose to hire only orientals. Further, it is good faith discrimination for the director of the movie "The Life of Martin Luther King, Jr." to consider only black actors for the title role.

Now I take it that the possibly reasonable attempt to argue that gays should not be afforded Civil Rights protections is that in the case of gays such exemptions swallow the rule, that is, that pretty much all discrimination against gays is discrimination in good faith, so that it would be disingenuous to include gays within the compass of protected classes. What I wish to argue in the rest of this paper is that virtually all attempts to justify discrimination against gays as discrimination in good faith fail, and therefore that there is nothing remotely approaching a general case to be made for exemptions of gays from Civil Rights protections. I shall take as my examples discriminations in the public sector, where, thanks to the 14th Amendment's equal protection clause, there is already a general presumption against discrimination against gays and where such discrimination is permissible only if it is rationally related to a legitimate government concern.[4]

In trying to give an account of what constitutes good faith discrimination, we enter murky territory. In current practice there is no widely recognized and accepted taxonomy of what constitutes good faith discrimination, nor is there any obvious sufficient set of general principles governing what constitutes a good faith discrimination. Is it, for instance, a good faith discrimination for the new management of a bar that has gone gay to fire all the non-gay union employees of the former management, claiming that only gay waiters will make the bar's new clientele feel comfortable? This is an actual case that occurred recently in Toronto. The outcome of a legal challenge to the firings was that the same court which had ruled earlier that the new management of what was to become an Irish bar could fire all the previous non–Irish employees, ruled against the new gay management, claiming that "being gay is not as substantially different as being Irish." So stated, we seem to have bad grammar, dubious metaphysics, and liberal condescension all masking bigotry; but, I suggest that, for whatever bad reasons the court came up with this ruling, it was the correct ruling.

For I suggest that the following is a valid general principle governing the establishment of good faith discriminations. The principle is that simply citing the current existence of prejudice, bigotry or discrimination in a society against some group or citing the obvious consequences of such prejudice, bigotry, or discrimination can never constitute a good reason in trying to establish a good faith discrimination against that group.[5] Let us call this principle alfred dreyfus. Dreyfus tells us that stigmas which are entirely socially induced shall not play a part in our rational moral deliberations. I suggest, for instance, that a community could not legitimately claim that a by-law banning blacks from buying houses in the community was a good faith discrimination on the grounds that whenever blacks move into a heretofore white area, property values plummet. This is illegitimate, since it is only the current bigotry in the society that causes property values to drop, as the result of white flight and the subsequent reduction in size of the purchasing market.

In general, the *fact* that people discriminate can never be cited as a good reason for institutionalizing discrimination.[6] But even more clearly, the current existence of discrimination cannot ethically ground the continuance of the discrimination, when there are reasonable *prima facie* claims against discrimination.

If dreyfus is intuitively obvious (once attention is drawn to it) it has a direct bearing on almost every case where people try to justify discrimination against gays as discrimination in good faith. For one of its obvious ranges of application is cases where some joint project is a necessary part of a job. It is in this category of cases that good faith discriminations against gays are most often attempted.

Bans against gays in the armed forces and on police forces are classic cases of the attempt to establish such good faith discrimination against gays. The armed forces, after recently losing a series of court cases, have abandoned the strategy that gays make incompetent soldiers as the basis for the systematic discrimination against gays. In light of the Matlovich case, the Beller case, and others in which gay soldiers were shown to have sterling performance records, the armed forces no longer rest their policy on such contentions as the claims that all faggots have limp wrists; limp wrists cannot fire M16s; and therefore gays reduce combat readiness. Instead the Pentagon has placed renewed emphasis on the contention that gays cause a drop in morale and for this reason reduce combat readiness. As of January 16, 1981, the Pentagon has seven, official, articulated reasons for banning gays:

> The presence of such members adversely affects the ability of the armed forces 1) to maintain discipline, good order and morale, 2) to foster mutual trust and confidence among servicemen, 3) to insure the integrity of the system of rank and command, 4) to facilitate assignment and worldwide deployment of servicemembers who frequently must live and work under close conditions affording minimal privacy, 5) to recruit and retain members of the armed forces, 6) to maintain the public acceptability of military service, and 7) to prevent breaches of security.[7]

Claims 1) through 6) form a group. I will discuss 7) in a separate context below. What all the first six claims have negatively in common is that none of them is based on the ability of gay soldiers to fulfill the duties of their stations. More generally, none of the claims is based on gays *doing* anything at all. So whatever else may be said for the policy, it lacks the virtue of being a moral stance, since it is a minimal requirement of a moral stance that people are judged and held culpable only for *actions* of their own doing. What the six reasons have positively in common is that their entire force relies exclusively on current widespread bigoted attitudes against gays. They appeal to the bigotry and consequent disruptiveness of non-gay soldiers (reasons 1, 2, 3, & 5) who apparently are made "up-tight" by the mere presence of gay soldiers and officers, and so claim that they cannot work effectively in necessary joint projects with gay soldiers. The reasons appeal to the anti-gay prejudices of our own society (reason 6), especially that segment of it which constitutes potential recruits (reason 5), and to the anti-gay prejudices of other societies (reason 4). No reasons other than currently existing widespread prejudice and bigotry of others are appealed to here in order to justify a discriminatory policy. So all six reasons violate dreyfus and are illegitimate.

Gay soldiers are being discriminated against on current Pentagon policy simply because currently existing bigotry and prejudice are counted as good reasons in trying to establish a good faith discrimination. To accept such a reasoning process as sound is to act like a right-wing terrorist who produces social disorder through indiscriminate bombings and then claims that what is needed is a police state. Clearly the social problem created by the bigoted soldiers and the terrorist is not solved by society acceding to their demands. It is soldiers who do not cease to be bigoted, not gay soldiers, who should be thrown out of the armed forces. Practically, of course, the solution to the problem is for the armed forces to re-educate its bigots and to expel those who are incorrigible. It should be remembered that until 1948 the U.S. armed forces were racially segregated on exactly the same grounds as those adduced now for barring gays, and especially on the ground that whites could not work with blacks. That year the forces were racially integrated and the skies did not fall. The West German armed forces have been gay/non-gay integrated in non-commissioned ranks and the skies have not fallen there either.

It is perhaps worthy of note that the current Pentagon policy on gays is simply a mirror image of the long-standing anti-gay policy of the International Association of Chiefs of Police, a policy which for the same reasons is equally illegitimate. That policy reads:

> Whereas, the life-style of homosexuals is abhorrent to most members of the society we serve, identification with this life-style destroys trust, confidence and esteem so necessary in both fellow workers and the general public for a police agency to operate efficiently and effectively; now, therefore, be it resolved, that the IACP . . . endorses a no hire policy for homosexuals in law enforcement.[8]

Despite the bogus appeal to "life-style," gays are here again being discriminated against not for anything they *do,* or on the basis of their ability to carry out police duties, but solely on the basis of the bigoted attitudes of others. If, as is quite possibly the case, the majority of society lacks trust and confidence in and finds abhorrent blacks, latinos, women, and jews as police officers, the argument would hold equally well against these groups, and yet the argument only singles out gays. So aside from being a bad argument, based entirely on violations of dreyfus, the policy fails to treat relevantly similar cases similarly.

I wish to give three other, I hope now obvious, examples of bad faith parading as good faith. The U.S. Civil Service has ceased as a matter of policy to discriminate against gays, but discrimination against gays is still systematic in the State Department, the CIA, the FBI, and the armed forces, on the alleged good faith discrimination that gays are security risks, since they are, it is claimed, subject to blackmail. That gays are subject to blackmail, though, is simply the result of currently existing prejudices and bigotries in the society, some of which are enshrined in law and government practice; so this argument violates dreyfus. Further, since it is the fact that one will be thrown out of the CIA (or any of the other organizations cited above) if exposed, that leads to the potential for blackmail, the argument also looks as though it is verging on being circular; for the government policy establishes the situation the government is trying to avoid, and then the government uses this situation as a reason for its policy. The practical solution is for the President to issue an executive order banning discrimination on the basis of sexual orientation in all branches of the government.[9]

Take as another example of bad faith discrimination the arguments used in lesbian child custody cases. Never has there been an area where socially endorsed stereotyping has been so flatfootedly appealed to in forming social policy as in child custody cases. In nearly all jurisdictions, there is a strong presumption in favor of giving custody to the mother, *unless* the mother is a lesbian, in which case the presumption of parental fitness shifts sharply in the direction of the father. Sometimes the argument for this sharp shift is merely a statement of bigotry. It runs: lesbians are evil; lesbians cause their children to be lesbians; and therefore, lesbians cause their children to be evil. When the shift is attempted to be justified as a good faith discrimination, the argument runs as follows: there is nothing inherently evil about mother or child being lesbian, but nevertheless, since, while the child is growing, there will be strong social recrimination from peers and other parents against the child as it becomes known in the community that the mother is a lesbian, only by discriminating against lesbian mothers are their children spared unnecessary suffering.[10] This argument, I take it, is an obvious violation of dreyfus. Currently existing bigotry and its consequences are cited as the only reason for perpetrating and institutionalizing discrimination. Note that if one does not think such discrimination is illegitimate *exactly because* it violates dreyfus, one would seem equally obliged to argue for the sterilization of inter-racial couples; for, only as such are their "progeny" spared the needless suffering created by the strong social recrimination which is directed against mixed-race children in current society.

Another bad faith argument is the widely held *Time* magazine (January 8, 1979) argument for discriminating against gay teachers.[11] It runs as follows: though openly gay teachers do not cause their students to become gay, nevertheless an openly gay teacher might (inadvertently or not) cause a closeted gay student to become openly gay; the life of an openly gay person is a life of misery and suffering; therefore, openly gay teachers must be fired, since they promote misery and suffering. It seems that the second premise, life of misery, if true in some way peculiar to gays, is so as the result of currently existing bigotry and discrimination in society of the very sort which the argument tries to enshrine into school board policy. So the argument violates dreyfus. But further, one cannot try to justify a social policy based on the consequences it is supposed to have, then attach negative sanctions or punishments to violations of the policy, and then say one was obviously correct in establishing the policy, citing as evidence that only behavior in conformity with the policy is producing good consequences. Stated more formally: it is illegitimate to give a rule–utilitarian rationale for a law, attach sanctions to the law and then show that one was correct in one's moral ground for the law by observing the consequence of implementing the sanctioned law. Sanctions make rule–utilitarian justifications self-fulfilling prophecies. If one passes sanctions against openly gay people, then obviously if one observes openly gay people beset by these sanctions one is going to claim one wouldn't want one's children to live that way. The solution, though, is to eliminate the sanctions which turn discriminations, based on alleged consequences of being openly gay, into self-fulfilling prophecies.

It should be noted that "purely moral" or religious claims to the effect that gays are wicked seem to bear no weight at all in establishing good faith discriminations. For what sort of job is being a non–sinner an essential job qualification? Nevertheless, most jurisdictions do require "good moral standing" for state and city licensing for a vast number of professional jobs ranging from doctors and lawyers to hairdressers and morticians. How these requirements are held to be reasonable or even desirable qualifications for these jobs is unclear. One wants as a lawyer someone who is shrewd, not someone who is pious. I suspect that eventually the courts will rule that these sorts of moral qualifications are so *vague* as to be incapable of fair application and so violate the due process clause of the Constitution. In the meanwhile, these requirements are abused in the most outrageous ways against gays. For in states which do not have consenting adult

laws,[12] gays are selectively discriminated against as systematically violating the laws and so, allegedly, as necessarily lacking in good moral character.[13] Now I think this application of such qualifications against gays should also count as a violation of dreyfus. The claim that violating some law was the ground for a good faith discrimination would be legitimate, I suggest, only if the moral ground of the law turned out to be, independently of the enshrinement of the law, a good ground for a good faith discrimination. And on examination arguments against consenting adult laws turn out to be mere statements of prudery or merely religious or aesthetic claims.[14]

My hunch is that all anti-gay arguments that are cast as good faith discriminations violate dreyfus or are circular or are illegitimate self-fulfilling prophecies, but I do not presume to outguess human ingenuity in coming up with rationalizations for its hatreds and fears.

NOTES

[1]A version of this paper was read to the Society for the Philosophy of Sex and Love at the meetings of the Eastern Division of the American Philosophical Association, December 1981. Many people have read and offered useful comments on earlier drafts of the paper. I would especially like to thank Professor Lee Rice of Marquette University and my colleague, Professor James Wallace for their comments.

[2]In unanimously finding the 1964 Civil Rights Act constitutional, the Supreme Court cited the Act's promotion of "personal dignity" as its most noteworthy justification for state action (*Heart of Atlanta Motel v. U.S.* 379 US 241 [1964]).

[3]The legal correlate of this moral principle is that the mere presence of a police agent in an action that would otherwise be private or personal does not make the action a public action. This correlate has led the Massachusetts Supreme Court to rule on procedural due process grounds that the state's sodomy laws are unenforceable, without actually ruling the laws unconstitutional on substantive due process grounds (*Commonwealth v. Sefranka* Mass. 414 N.E. 2d 602 [Dec. 1980]).

[4]This "rational relation" test was established for gays in the public sphere generally and the Civil Service specifically by *Norton v. Macy* 417 F.2d 1161 (D.C.Cir.

1969). The test for good faith discrimination in the Civil Rights Act is in fact a more stringent test. For "bona fide occupational qualification" is elaborated as that which is "reasonably necessary to the normal operation" of a business. "Reasonably necessary" is a judicial oxymoron. For in equal protection cases, a rational relation or reasonable relation is simply a relation to a legitimate government concern, while a necessary relation is one which is *essential* to a *compelling* state interest. The tension of the phrase "reasonably necessary" notwithstanding, the courts have tended to interpret the Civil Rights Act as establishing a "business necessity test" (*Diaz v. Pan American Airways* 442 F.2d 385 [5th Cir. 1971]). If I can establish my claims operating with the weaker test, *a fortiori* my argument will hold for the more stringent test.

[5] I take prejudice to be a species of bigotry. A bigot is an adult capable of reason who is willing to act on his moral opinions and who has no reason for his opinion, *or* who has a reason but it is prejudicial, is a rationalization, is merely a personal emotional response or is merely a parroting of someone *else's* reason, *or* who is unwilling to apply consistently the ethical principles which inform and give substance to his reason, once the relevant principles are pointed out to him, *or* whose principles themselves are so specialized as to be arbitrary.

[6] See Ronald Dworkin, *Taking Rights Seriously* (Cambridge, Mass.; Harvard University Press, 1977), pp. 248–54.

[7] San Francisco Sentinel, January 23, 1981. These regulations are published in the *Federal Register*, vol. 46, no. 19, Jan. 29, 1981, pp. 9571–8. They were largely constructed out of the holdings of the extremely anti-gay Beller case (*Beller v. Middendorf*, 632 F.2d 788 [9th Cir. 1980] denied US cert.). For a military case, though, which ended in a gay re-instatement see *benShalom v. Sec'y of Army* 22 F.E.P. 1396 (U.S. D.Ct. E.D. Wis. 1980). This case is important, for in it the court recognized that the Army had violated the plaintiff's First Amendment rights and rights to substantive due process, in particular the right to privacy. In fact, the court recognized a constitutional right to sexual preference within the right to privacy.

[8] San Francisco *Sentinel*, October 3, 1980.

[9] In military cases and others where "security risk" is adduced as a reason for dismissal, the government has not once brought forth a case where a gay was blackmailed into disclosing secrets. This means that gays are being judged on the basis of stereotypes which have no factual basis. In sex discrimination cases, claims based on stereotypes and unsubstantiated fears and apprehensions have been given no weight in attempts to establish bona fide occupational qualifications (*Weeks v. Southern Bell Telephone* 408 F.2d 228).

[10] In fact it would seem that children in the custody of lesbian mothers do not suffer. On this subject allow me to recommend the movie on lesbian child custody cases. *In the Best Interest of the Children* (Iris Films/Iris Feminist Collective, Berkeley 1977). For a fairly recent discussion of gay parent custody cases see Donna Hitchens, "Social Attitudes, Legal Standards, and Personal Trauma in Child Custody Cases," in Homosexuality and the Law, ed. Donald Knutson (NY: Haworth Press, 1980) = *Journal of Homosexuality*, 5 (Fall 1979–Winter 1980): 89–95.

[11] The current judicial status of discrimination against gay teachers is turbid. For an important and generally pro-gay case, see *Acanfora v. Bd. of Educ.* 491 F.2d 498 (4th Cir. 1974). For a recent anti-gay holding based on religious morality see *Gaylord v. Tacoma School Dist. #10* Wash. 559 P.2d 1340 (1981) denied US cert.

[12] Approximately 65% of the US population now lives in states with consenting adult laws. Twenty-two states have revoked their sodomy laws through legislative means: Alaska, California, Colorado, Connecticut, Delaware, Hawaii, Illinois, Indiana, Iowa, Maine, Nebraska, New Hampshire, New Jersey, New Mexico, North Dakota, Ohio, Oregon, South Dakota, Vermont, Washington, West Virginia, and Wyoming. In addition, the highest courts of Pennsylvania and New York have, on the basis of the right to privacy, declared unconstitutional their states' statutes prohibiting private, consensual sodomy between unmarried adults (*Commonwealth v. Bonadio* 490 Pa 91, 415 A.2d 47 [1980]; *People v. Onofre* 434 N.Y.S. 2d 947, 51 NY 2d 476, 415 N.E. 2d 936 [1980] denied US cert.).

[13] A recent landmark gay naturalization case will, it is to be hoped, clear up this area of administrative law: *Nemetz v. Immigration and Naturalization Service* 647 F.2d 432 (4th Cir. April 1981). This case ruled 1) that in cases of laws which are national in nature discriminations based on "moral turpitude" cannot be achieved merely by citing the violation of statutes which are peculiarly local, and even more importantly ruled 2) that determinations of good moral character or moral turpitude can only be made by appealing to public morality and that private sexual acts are not a matter of public morals: "The appropriate test in such cases is whether the act is harmful to the public or is offensive merely to a personal morality. Only those acts harmful to the public will be appropriate bars to a finding of good moral character" (at 436).

[14] Anyone who doubts the truth of this claim might usefully read the floor debate surrounding H.Res. 208 (*Congressional Record-House* 6737–62, Oct. 1, 1981), by which the House by a nearly three-to-one margin quashed consenting adult laws which had been passed unanimously by the D.C. City Council.

QUESTIONS FOR DISCUSSION

1. What is the principle that Mohr calls "alfred dreyfus"? Do you agree with Mohr's principle? Why or why not? What kinds of discrimination against African-Americans or women would Mohr's principle rule out? Does his principle really rule out the kinds of discrimination against homosexuals that he opposes? Why or why not?

2. Mohr argues that a heterosexual father should not be given any preference over a lesbian mother in child custody after a divorce. What is his argument? Is his argument affected if the father is homosexual and the mother is heterosexual? Do you agree with Mohr's claims? Why or why not?

3. Should homosexual couples be allowed to adopt children or to serve as foster parents? Why or why not?

SODOM AND BEGORRAH

ERNEST VAN DEN HAAG

Notwithstanding the old joke that an Irish homosexual is a man who prefers women to drink, a group of Irish gays and lesbians applied this year for an official presence in the St. Patrick's Day parade in New York. Resistance was interpreted by liberal politicians like Mayor David Dinkins as bigotry. It is better understood as instinctive resentment at being asked to bestow moral approval on the practice of homosexuality.

The St. Patrick's Day parade celebrates not only Irishness but Catholicism, which frowns on homosexuality. No doubt many of the marchers privately do things incompatible with Catholicism, or merely irrelevant to it. But they do not seek to march behind banners such as "Irish Adulterers" or "Irish Stamp Collectors." Does homosexuality have any more to do with being Irish, than stamp collecting or adultery?

The St. Patrick's Day controversy indicates that the demand for "gay rights" is essentially a demand for respect and approval rather than for rights. And it begins with numbers.

By some current estimates about 10 per cent of the male population in the Western world is homosexual. Homosexual groups tend to cite the higher figure; presumably because that makes homosexuality seem more acceptable. Other estimates go as low as 5 or 3 per cent. However, these are no more than guesses; and they refer to an average: the proportion in San Francisco may be higher; elsewhere it may be lower. About female homosexuality not enough is known even for a guess. Little is known as well about homosexuality in the non-Western world, or in the past. Further, homosexuality is vaguely defined: do we include only persons who have sexual activity with

Ernest van den Haag, "Sodom and Begorrah," *National Review* (April 29, 1991), pp. 35–38

others of the same sex exclusively, or also those who do so preponderantly or just occasionally? (Perhaps the label "bisexual" better suits the last category.)

Has the proportion of homosexuals in the U.S. population increased recently? They certainly have become more visible. It is not possible, however, to determine whether the same number of homosexuals has become more visible, owing to recently lessened legal and social pressures, or whether the number has actually increased. Less pressure might lead some to activate homosexual inclinations which previously they did not avow even to themselves. There may be more homosexual activity, then, or just more open homosexual activity, or both.

Whatever its size, a homosexual minority is known to have existed in all societies throughout history. At times that minority was fully accepted; at other times merely tolerated, or even ferociously suppressed. Suppression reduces visibility; it also leads some to give up homosexual activity. Still, the most ferocious suppression, including the death penalty, has never stamped out homosexuality altogether.

CAUSES AND EFFECTS

What causes homosexuality? And what causes the hostility of many heterosexuals? The simplest and, among homosexuals, the most popular theory explains that homosexuality is just as genetic as heterosexuality. There is indeed some evidence for genetic inheritance: identical twins separated at birth tend both to be either homosexual or heterosexual; babies with a homosexual natural father, adopted by heterosexual families, tend to become homosexual. This suggests a degree of genetic disposition, which, in some cases, seems to be sufficient to produce homosexuality. But the genetic disposition does not seem to be necessary or sufficient. Homosexuality occurs in families that have not known it before, and heterosexuality occurs in children of homosexuals.

If homosexuality were altogether genetic, its frequency would diminish over time. Homosex-

uals have fewer children than heterosexuals. Thus, the proportion of homosexuals in the population would diminish, if homosexuality were produced solely, or even mainly, by genetic factors. However, there is no indication of a smaller proportion of homosexuals. One must conclude that homosexual behavior depends partly on environmental influences, even if genetic dispositions play an as yet unquantified role.

We know very little about the early intrafamilial and later extrafamilial factors that may contribute to homosexual behavior. Theories abound, some quite plausible, but none fully demonstrated. A goodly proportion of homosexuality may be caused by very early imprinting in babies. But this is a possibility rather than a certainty. The most widely accepted theories postulate an unacceptable paternal figure, who is either too weak, or too punitively dominating, or too distant, combined with an overly possessive maternal figure on whom the infant comes to depend excessively for emotional support. There are many such constellations, but they are not found in all cases. Nor are narcissism or unconscious castration fears.

The American Psychiatric Association used to list homosexuality as a disease, although homosexuality does not shorten life, is not painful, and does not impair desired functions—which is what diseases do, by definition. The listing was a thinly disguised moral judgment. The recent delisting expressed a change in moral judgment. But it is justified also because there never was any clinical evidence for the disease listing. Psychiatrists should not make moral judgments disguised as medical ones.

Similarly, what is now called homophobia—namely, the dislike of homosexuals—is scarcely a phobia, i.e., a pathological fear. A phobic person suffers great anxiety in the presence of the object of his phobia, which he will try to avoid. Now, people who dislike homosexuals may be unsure of their own sexual identity, or may have made an adverse moral judgment on homosexuality, or may have an irrational prejudice against it. None of this is phobic. "Homophobia" is also an illiterate coinage, which literally means fear of one's own kind, e.g., fear of homosexuals by homosexuals or of heterosexuals by heterosexuals, but not fear of the former by the latter.

Is homosexuality associated specifically with promiscuity? Some homosexuals have stable relations with each other just as married heterosexuals do. Others are moderately or extremely promiscuous. The most promiscuous homosexuals are the most highly visible, but seem also to constitute a higher proportion of homosexuals than of heterosexuals.

Highly promiscuous behavior is usually a symptom of a personality disturbance, most often compulsiveness. Some promiscuous persons hate their own behavior. Others make it the center of their life. Since homosexuality is not a disease, it need not and cannot be "cured." However, when homosexual behavior is symptomatic of an underlying personality disturbance, treatment of that disturbance may lead to a change, including a change of the sexual object. In other cases, treatment may lead to the patient's fuller acceptance, with less conflict of some homosexual pattern.

GOD'S WILL

Judaic and Christian Scriptural tradition condemns homosexuality as contrary to God's will (there are some, rather strained, dissenting interpretations). Thus, the view of traditional believers is preordained: homosexual acts are sinful. Other traditions (including most legal ones) condemn homosexuality as contrary to nature. However, nature makes homosexuality possible (else there would be no problem) and can acquire the prescriptive authority ascribed to it only if it is believed to reveal the divine will. Thus "contrary to nature" is not essentially different from "contrary to God's will." This won't do for unbelievers; nor for a society legislating according to non-revealed secular principles.

Our Constitution is mute on homosexuality. The idea that we can read into it whatever is reasonable or fashionable, by interpreting "ema-

nations," is unconvincing. Thus, if states prohibit sodomy they may be silly, but the Constitution does not prohibit silliness. We should vote against such prohibitions, however. Prohibition is unlikely to be effective, and consensual sodomy by adults at worst harms the participants, who ought to be free to harm themselves.

Admittedly, anal intercourse brings a high risk of infection with the AIDS virus. But this sexual practice is not always, nor exclusively, engaged in by homosexuals. Nor is it the only way in which the virus is transmitted. Homosexuals do, however, take the risk of anal intercourse more often than heterosexuals, and thus are more vulnerable to the disease. Nonetheless, AIDS is not a specific homosexual disease.

In short, society has no compelling interest that justifies prohibiting or even legislating about homosexuality. But this is only a partial answer to the question: How should we deal with homosexuals?

Homosexual groups demand "gay rights." To be sure, homosexuals should have the same civil rights as heterosexuals, which currently they do not in some instances. The military won't accept known homosexuals, contending that they would be disruptive, and that sexual liaisons would undermine discipline. Yet history suggests that homosexuals can make excellent soldiers. And the admission of women soldiers undermines the sexual rationale for excluding them. Hence there are no longer solid grounds for the exclusionary policy and it should be changed—not by the courts (constitutional grounds are doubtful) but by the executive or Congress.

Should there be, however, legal intervention to prohibit private discrimination? What about discrimination in employment or housing? Here, the question is one of need. There was good reason in the past for protecting blacks from discrimination. They often had to live in segregated areas, with little access to education and to desirable jobs. Their average income was low. But none of this applies to homosexuals. They do well in education, the professions, in business and the arts. They do not have to live in segregated areas. Their income is not below average. To protect them by law against discrimination—as we currently do in New York—is not just unnecessary, but harmful. Legislation makes it harder to fire homosexuals for whatever reason, because they can claim illegal discrimination. Employers, therefore, will hesitate to hire them. Similarly, landlords will hesitate to rent to them. Most antidiscrimination legislation has such unintended effects. It is more advantageous to lawyers and politicians than to those it supposedly benefits.

The exclusion of homosexuals from some private institutions is justifiable. If a church regards homosexuality as sinful, one should not demand that it hire practicing homosexuals. However, in non-religious institutions of higher learning, the sexual disposition of teachers and students is irrelevant to the educational tasks involved. College students should be adult enough not to be affected by the sexual inclinations of their teachers. Hence the exclusion of homosexuals is not justified, unless the college belongs to an exclusionary denomination.

Many colleges currently subsidize homosexual clubs and organizations. Instead, colleges should make sure that homosexuals can join the organizations for which they would ordinarily qualify. Subsidies should be available exclusively to organizations which cultivate the interests colleges exist to foster, such as science, literature, philosophy, etc. Sexual interests should be a private matter. It seems silly to make them one's main interest in life, even while in college, and even more silly for colleges to subsidize such distortions. However, purely social organizations ought to be allowed to be as selective as they wish. Freedom of association implies freedom of dissociation.

In primary and secondary education the situation is different. There is no evidence that homosexual teachers seduce minors more often than heterosexuals do. But teachers not only teach, but also serve as models for children. Therefore, parents should be able to exclude teachers whose conduct they regard as immoral. Consider a competent mathematics teacher who, in her free time, is known to work as a prostitute, in a state in which prostitution is legal. Parents will object, because they do not want their children to be taught by someone whose known sexual activities would make her unwelcome in their homes and who, they fear, may somehow influence their children by giving respectability to activities they regard as wrong. The case of the homosexual teacher does not seem to be all that different.

Courts have held, however, that a teacher is entitled to his job regardless of his sexual behavior outside the school. I think the courts are wrong. The right of parents not to have their children taught by persons whose conduct they abhor, and who they think will set a bad example for their children, ought to take precedence over anyone's right to be employed in a school. Reasonable parents may not always want to exercise their right. But they should retain it.

Activists occasionally complain that heterosexuals can marry each other, while homosexuals cannot. They see this as a disadvantage particularly with respect to inheritance and pensions of survivors. But marriage is a heterosexual institution, which exists largely to provide for the upbringing of the couple's children. Homosexual "marriage" would be an entirely different institution. Society simply does not have as great an interest in keeping homosexual couples together as it does in maintaining a stable family life for children.

Pensions for survivors exist to protect widows unaccustomed to gainful employment and their minor children. None of this applies to homosexual couples. As for inheritance, homosexual partners can make wills and leave whatever they wish to one another. ("Ah," the activist may object, "but not the apartment." However, homosexuals can bequeath their shared apartment to the surviving partner—if they own it—just as heterosexuals can. What if they just rent the apartment? A rented apartment belongs to the landlord. The tenant cannot leave it to anyone, because it is not his. To be sure, rent-control legislation often treats rented apartments as the property of the tenant and allows tenants to leave them to surviving spouses. That unwarranted discrimination against landlords should not be available to homosexual or heterosexual tenants.)

NOT-SO-HIDDEN AGENDA

But the campaign for "gay rights" aims at more than rectification of specific forms of discrimination. The attempt to increase legal protection for homosexuals reflects a not-so-hidden agenda: to compel everybody to regard homosexuals as morally equal to heterosexuals, homosexuality as no less legitimate than heterosexuality. Can any laws accomplish this? Should they?

Homosexuality is not a disease (nor can it be labeled a preference; preferences are voluntary and homosexuality rarely is). Yet homosexuality is perceived by the majority of people as a defect. There is no way of showing that perception to be wrong. Compare homosexuality to a limp, acquired or inborn. The limping person may be a brilliant mathematician, philosopher, artist, politician, businessman, or physician. He may be charming as well. Still, he will not do for baseball games and some other sports; nor will

he be a good companion on long walks. For those to whom these things matter, his defect matters. Even for others it will matter at times, particularly when they are young.

Homosexuality is certainly not a physical defect. But in the eyes of most heterosexuals, it is a psychological one. Most if not all males, at the beginning of their sexual careers, are intimidated, by, even fearful of, women. In time they overcome much of that fear. Heterosexuals feel that somehow homosexuals do not; and that they take the easy way out by turning to their own sex. There may be some truth to this vague and half-conscious theory, though it may explain more about heterosexual attitudes than about homosexual behavior.

At any rate, the belief does not mean that homosexuals are less good than heterosexuals. Despite his limp, a man may be a much better person than another who does not limp. However, the heterosexual belief means that in the eyes of most heterosexuals, homosexuality is a psychological defect. Nothing will persuade heterosexuals to believe that homosexuality is psychologically or morally as legitimate as their own heterosexuality. They cannot be shown to be wrong, and they should not be compelled by law to act as if they were.

QUESTIONS FOR DISCUSSION

1. Explain why van den Haag compares homosexuality to a limp. Is this comparison fair? Why or why not?

2. Is discrimination against homosexuals more or less justified if homosexuality is genetic? Why or why not?

3. Van den Haag argues against laws that protect homosexuals from discrimination in housing and employment. What are his arguments? Do you agree? Why or why not? In the case of housing, does it matter whether the landlord is a large, distant corporation or a small family renting a room in its home?

4. Explain and evaluate van den Haag's argument that parents should be able to exclude known homosexual teachers from public primary and secondary schools. What kind of theory of justice does this argument assume? How would Mohr respond?

SERGEANT PERRY WATKINS V. UNITED STATES ARMY

847 F.2d 1329 (9th Cir. 1988)

NORRIS, Circuit Judge:

In August 1967, at the age of 19, Perry Watkins enlisted in the United States Army. In filling out the Army's pre-induction medical form, he candidly marked "yes" in response to a question whether he had homosexual tendencies. The Army nonetheless considered Watkins "qualified for admission" and inducted him into its ranks. Watkins served fourteen years in the Army, and became, in the words of his commanding officer, "one of our most respected and trusted soldiers." . . .

Even though Watkins' homosexuality was always common knowledge, . . . the Army has never claimed that his sexual orientation or behavior interfered in any way with military functions. To the contrary, an Army review board found "there is no evidence suggesting that his behavior has had either a degrading effect upon unit performance, morale or discipline, or upon his own job performance." . . .

In 1981 the Army promulgated new regulations which mandated the disqualification of all homosexuals from the Army without regard to the length or quality of their military service. Pursuant to these new regulations, the Army notified Watkins that he would be discharged and denied reenlistment because of his homosexuality. In this federal court action, Watkins challenges the Army's actions and new regulations on various statutory and constitutional grounds. . . .

II

Almost all of Watkins' arguments can be rejected without reaching their merits. . . . We are left, then, with Watkins' claim that the Army's regulations deny him equal protection of the laws in violation of the Fifth Amendment.[9] Specifically, Watkins argues that the Army's regulations constitute an invidious discrimination based on sexual orientation. To address this claim we must engage in a three-stage inquiry. First, we must decide whether the regulations in fact discriminate on the basis of sexual orientation. Second, we must decide which level of judicial scrutiny applies by asking whether discrimination based on sexual orientation burdens a suspect or quasi-suspect class, which would make it subject, respectively, to strict or intermediate scrutiny. . . . Finally, we must decide whether the challenged regulations survive the applicable level of scrutiny. . . .

III

We now turn to the threshold question raised by Watkins' equal protection claim: Do the Army's regulations discriminate based on sexual orientation? The portion of the Army's reenlistment regulation that bars homosexuals from reenlisting states in full:

Applicants to whom the disqualifications below apply are ineligible for RA [Regular Army] reenlistment at any time and requests for waiver or exception to policy will not be submitted. . . .

c. Persons of questionable moral character and a history of antisocial behavior, sexual perversion or homosexuality. A person who has committed homosexual acts or is an admitted homosexual but as to whom there is no evidence that they have engaged in homosexual acts either before or during military service is included. (See note 1). . . .

k. persons being discharged under AR 635-200 for homosexuality. . . .

Note: Homosexual acts consist of bodily contact between persons of the same sex, actively undertaken or passively permitted, with the intent of obtaining or giving sexual satisfaction, or any proposal, solicitation, or attempt to perform such an act. Persons who have been involved in homosexual acts in an apparently isolated episode, stemming solely from immaturity, curiousity [sic], or intoxication, and in the absence of other evidence that the person is a homosexual, normally will not be excluded from reenlistment. A homosexual is a person, regardless of sex, who desires bodily contact between persons of the same sex, actively undertaken or passively permitted, with the intent to obtain or give sexual gratification. Any official, private, or public profession of homosexuality, may be considered in determining whether a person is an admitted homosexual.

. . . Although worded in somewhat greater detail, the Army's regulation mandating the separation of homosexual soldiers from service (discharge) . . . is essentially the same in substance.

We conclude that these regulations, on their face, discriminate against homosexuals on the basis of their sexual orientation. Under the regulations any homosexual act or statement of homosexuality gives rise to a presumption of homosexual orientation, and anyone who fails to rebut that presumption is conclusively barred from Army service. In other words, the regulations target homosexual orientation itself. The homosexual acts and statements are merely relevant, and rebuttable, indicators of that orientation. . . .

The Army [responds] that the Supreme Court's decision in *Bowers v. Hardwick* . . . forecloses Watkins' equal protection challenge to

its regulations. In *Hardwick,* the court rejected a claim by a homosexual that a Georgia statute criminalizing sodomy deprived him of this liberty without due process of law in violation of the Fourteenth Amendment. More specifically, the Court held that the constitutionally protected right to privacy . . . does not extend to acts of consensual homosexual sodomy. . . . The Court's holding was limited to this due process question. The parties did not argue and the court explicitly did not decide the question whether the Georgia sodomy statute might violate the equal protection clause.

The Army nonetheless argues that it would be "incongruous" to hold that its regulations deprive gays of equal protection of the laws when *Hardwick* holds that there is no constitutionally protected privacy right to engage in homosexual sodomy. . . . We disagree. First, while *Hardwick* does indeed hold that the due process clause provides no substantive privacy protection for acts of private homosexual sodomy, nothing in *Hardwick* suggests that the state may penalize gays for their sexual orientation. . . .

Second, although *Hardwick* held that the due process clause does not prevent states from criminalizing acts of homosexual sodomy, . . . nothing in *Hardwick* actually holds that the state may make invidious distinctions when regulating sexual conduct. Unlike the Army's regulations, the Georgia sodomy statute at issue in *Hardwick* was neutral on its face, making anal and oral intercourse a criminal offense whether engaged in by partners of the same or opposite sex. . . .

The Army also argues that *Hardwick's* concern "about the limits of the court's role in carrying out its constitutional mandate," . . . should prevent courts from holding that equal protection doctrine protects homosexuals from discrimination. . . . These concerns have little relevance to equal protection doctrine. The right to equal protection of the laws has a clear basis in the text of the Constitution. This principle of equal treatment, when imposed against majoritarian rule, arises from the Constitution itself, not from judicial fiat. . . .

V

We now address the merits of Watkins' claim that we must subject the Army's regulations to strict scrutiny because homosexuals constitute a suspect class under equal protection jurisprudence. The Supreme Court has identified several factors that guide our suspect class inquiry.

The first factor the Supreme Court generally considers is whether the group at issue has suffered a history of purposeful discrimination. . . . As the Army concedes, it is indisputable that "homosexuals have historically been the object of pernicious and sustained hostility." . . . Homosexuals have been the frequent victims of violence and have been excluded from jobs, schools, housing, churches, and even families. . . . In any case, the discrimination faced by homosexuals in our society is plainly no less pernicious or intense than the discrimination faced by other groups already treated as suspect classes, such as aliens or people of a particular national origin. . . .

The second factor that the Supreme Court considers in suspect class analysis is difficult to capsulize and may in fact represent a cluster of factors grouped around a central idea—whether the discrimination embodies a gross unfairness that is sufficiently inconsistent with the ideals of equal protection to term it invidious. Considering this additional factor makes sense. After all, discrimination exists against some groups because the animus is warranted—no one could seriously argue that burglars form a suspect class. . . . In giving content to this concept of gross unfairness, the Court has considered (1) whether the disadvantaged class is defined by a trait that "frequently bears no relation to ability to perform or contribute to society" . . . ; (2) whether the class has been saddled with unique disabilities because of prejudice or inaccurate stereotypes; and (3) whether the trait defining the class is immutable. . . . We consider these questions in turn.

Sexual orientation plainly has no relevance to a person's "ability to perform or contribute to society." Indeed, the Army makes no claim that homosexuality impairs a person's ability to perform military duties. Sergeant Watkins' exemplary record of military service stands as a testament to quite the opposite. . . . Moreover, as the Army itself concluded, there is not a scintilla of evidence that Watkins' avowed homosexuality "had either a degrading effect upon unit performance, morale or discipline, or upon his own job performance."

This irrelevance of sexual orientation to the quality of a person's contribution to society also suggests that classifications based on sexual orientation reflect prejudice and inaccurate stereotypes—the second indicia of a classification's gross unfairness. . . . The Army does not dispute the hard fact that homosexuals face enormous prejudice. Nor could it, for the Army justifies its regulations in part by asserting that straight soldiers despise and lack respect for homosexuals and that popular prejudice against homosexuals is so pervasive that their presence in the Army will discourage enlistment and tarnish the Army's public image. . . . Instead, the Army suggests that the public opprobrium directed towards gays does not constitute prejudice in the pejorative sense of the word, but rather represents appropriate public disapproval of persons who engage in immoral behavior. The Army equates homosexuals with sodomists and justifies its regulations as simply reflecting a rational bias against a class of persons who engage in criminal acts of sodomy. In essence, the Army argues that homosexuals, like burglars, cannot form a suspect class because they are criminals.

The Army's argument, essentially adopted by the dissent, rests on two false premises. First, the class burdened by the regulations is defined by the sexual *orientation* of its members, not by their sexual conduct. . . . To our knowledge, homosexual orientation itself has never been criminalized in this country. Moreover, any attempt to criminalize the status of an individual's sexual orientation would present grave constitutional problems. . . .

Second, little of the homosexual *conduct* covered by the regulations is criminal. The regulations reach many forms of homosexual conduct other than sodomy such as kissing, hand-holding, caressing, and hand–genital contact. Yet, sodomy is the only consensual adult sexual conduct that Congress has criminalized. . . .

Finally, we turn to immutability as an indicator of gross unfairness. The Supreme Court has never held that only classes with immutable traits can be deemed suspect. . . . We nonetheless consider immutability because the Supreme Court has often focused on immutability. . . .

Although the Supreme Court considers immutability relevant, it is clear that by "immutability" the Court has never meant strict immutability in the sense that members of the class must be physically unable to change or mask the trait defining their class. People can have operations to change their sex. Aliens can ordinarily become naturalized citizens. The status of illegitimate children can be changed. People can frequently hide their national origin by changing their customs, their names, or their associations. Lighter skinned blacks can sometimes "pass" for white, as can Latinos for Anglos, and some people can even change their racial appearance with pigment injections. . . . At a minimum, then, the Supreme Court is willing to treat a trait as effectively immutable if changing it would involve great difficulty, such as requiring a major physical change or a traumatic change of identity. Reading the case law in a more capacious manner, "immutability" may describe those traits that are so central to a person's identity that it would be abhorrent for government to penalize a person for refusing to change them, regardless of how easy that change might be physically. Racial discrimination, for example, would not suddenly become constitutional if medical science developed an easy, cheap, and painless method of changing one's skin pigment. . . .

Under either formulation, we have no trouble concluding that sexual orientation is immutable for the purposes of equal protection doctrine. Although the causes of homosexuality are not fully understood, scientific research in-

dicates that we have little control over our sexual orientation and that, once acquired, our sexual orientation is largely impervious to change. . . . Scientific proof aside, it seems appropriate to ask whether heterosexuals feel capable of changing their sexual orientation. . . .

The final factor the Supreme Court considers in suspect class analysis is whether the group burdened by official discrimination lacks the political power necessary to obtain redress from the political branches of government. . . . Courts understandably have been more reluctant to extend heightened protection under equal protection doctrine to groups fully capable of securing their rights through the political process. . . .

[T]he social, economic, and political pressures to conceal one's homosexuality commonly deter many gays from openly advocating pro–homosexual legislation, thus intensifying their inability to make effective use of the political process. . . . Even when gays overcome this prejudice enough to participate openly in politics, the general animus towards homosexuality may render this participation wholly ineffective. Elected officials sensitive to public prejudice may refuse to support legislation that even appears to condone homosexuality. . . . These barriers to political power are underscored by the underrepresentation of avowed homosexuals in the decisionmaking bodies of government and the inability of homosexuals to prevent legislation hostile to their group interests. . . .

In sum, our analysis of the relevant factors in determining whether a given group should be considered a suspect class for the purposes of equal protection doctrine ineluctably leads us to the conclusion that homosexuals constitute such a suspect class. We find not only that our analysis of each of the relevant factors supports our conclusion, but also that the principles underlying equal protection doctrine—the principles that gave rise to these factors in the first place—compel us to conclude that homosexuals constitute a suspect class. . . .

VI

Having concluded that homosexuals constitute a suspect class, we must subject the Army's regulations facially discriminating against homosexuals to strict scrutiny. Consequently, we may uphold the regulations only if "'*necessary* to promote a compelling governmental interest.'" . . .

[E]ven granting special deference to the policy choices of the military, we must reject many of the Army's asserted justifications because they illegitimately cater to private biases. For example, the Army argues that it has a valid interest in maintaining morale and discipline by avoiding hostilities and "'tensions between known homosexuals and other members [of the armed services] who despise/detest homosexuality.'" . . . The Army also expresses its "'doubts concerning a homosexual officer's ability to command the respect and trust of the personnel he or she commands'" because many lower-ranked heterosexual soldiers despise and detest homosexuality. . . . Finally, the Army argues that the presence of gays in its ranks "might well be a source of ridicule and notoriety, harmful to the Army's recruitment efforts" and to its public image.

These concerns strike a familiar chord. For much of our history, the military's fear of racial tension kept black soldiers separated from whites. . . . As recently as World War II both the Army chief of staff and the Secretary of the Navy justified racial segregation in the ranks as necessary to maintain efficiency, discipline, and morale. . . . Today, it is unthinkable that the judiciary would defer to the Army's prior "professional" judgment that black and white soldiers had to be segregated to avoid interracial tensions. Indeed, the Supreme Court has decisively rejected the notion that private prejudice against minorities can ever justify official discrimination, even when those private prejudices create real and legitimate problems. . . .

The Army's defense of its regulations, however, goes beyond its professed fear of prejudice in the ranks. Apparently, the Army believes that its regulations rooting out persons with certain sexual tendencies are not merely a response to prejudice, but are also grounded in legitimate moral norms. In other words, the Army believes that its ban against homosexuals simply codifies society's moral consensus that homosexuality is evil. Yet, even accepting *arguendo* this proposition that anti–homosexual animus is grounded in morality (as opposed to prejudice masking as morality), equal protection doctrine does not permit notions of majoritarian morality to serve as compelling justification for laws that discriminate against suspect classes. . . .

Conclusion

We hold that the Army's regulations violate the constitutional guarantee of equal protection of the laws because they discriminate against persons of homosexual orientation, a suspect class, and because the regulations are not necessary to promote a legitimate compelling governmental interest. We thus reverse the district court's rulings denying Watkins's motion for summary judgment and granting summary judgment in favor of the Army, and remand with instructions to enter a declaratory judgment that the Army Regulations AR 635–200, Chapter 15, and 601–280, ¶ 2–21(c), are constitutionally void on their face, and to enter an injunction requiring the Army to consider Watkins' reenlistment application without regard to his sexual orientation. . . .

REINHARDT, Circuit Judge, dissenting.

With great reluctance, I have concluded that I am unable to concur in the majority opinion. Like the majority, I believe that homosexuals have been unfairly treated both historically and in the United States today. Were I free to apply my own view of the meaning of the Constitution and in that light to pass upon the validity of the Army's regulations, I too would conclude that the Army may not refuse to enlist homosexuals. I am bound, however, as a circuit judge to apply the Constitution as it has been interpreted by the Supreme Court and our own circuit, whether or not I agree with those interpretations. Because of this requirement, I am sometimes compelled to reach a result I believe to be contrary to the proper interpretation of constitutional principles. This is, regrettably, one of those times.

I.

In this case we consider the constitutionality of a regulation which bars homosexuals from enlisting in the Army. Sergeant Perry Watkins challenges that regulation under the Equal Protection Clause. The majority holds that homosexuals are a suspect class, and that the regulation cannot survive strict scrutiny. Because I am compelled by recent Supreme Court and Ninth Circuit precedent to conclude first, that homosexuals are not a suspect class and second, that the regulation survives both rational and intermediate level scrutiny, I must dissent.

Bowers v. Hardwick . . . is the landmark case involving homosexual conduct. In *Hardwick*, the Supreme Court decided that homosexual sodomy is not protected by the right to privacy, and thus that the states are free to criminalize that conduct. Because Hardwick did not challenge the Georgia sodomy statute under the Equal Protection Clause, and neither party presented that issue in its briefs or at oral argument, the Court limited its holding to due process and properly refrained from reaching any direct conclusion regarding an equal protection challenge to the statute. . . . However, the fact that *Hardwick* does not address the equal protection question directly does not mean that the case is not of substantial significance to such an inquiry. . . .

In my opinion, *Hardwick* must be read as standing precisely for the proposition the majority rejects. To put it simply, I believe that after *Hardwick* the government may outlaw homosexual sodomy even though it fails to regulate the private sexual conduct of heterosexuals. In *Hardwick* the Court took great care to make clear that it was saying only that *homosexual* sodomy is not constitutionally protected, and

not that all sexual acts—both heterosexual and homosexual—that fall within the definition of sodomy can be prohibited. . . .

II.

The majority opinion concludes that under the criteria established by equal protection case law, homosexuals must be treated as a suspect class. . . . Were it not for *Hardwick* (and other cases discussed *infra*), I would agree, for in my opinion the group meets all the applicable criteria. . . . However, after *Hardwick*, we are no longer free to reach that conclusion.

The majority opinion treats as a suspect class a group of persons whose defining characteristic is their desire, predisposition, or propensity to engage in conduct that the Supreme Court has held to be constitutionally unprotected, an act that the states can—and approximately half the states have—criminalized. Homosexuals are different from groups previously afforded protection under the equal protection clause in that homosexuals are defined by their conduct—or, at the least, by their desire to engage in certain conduct. With other groups, such as blacks or women, there is no connection between particular conduct and the definition of the group. When conduct that plays a central role in defining a group may be prohibited by the state, it cannot be asserted with any legitimacy that the group is specially protected by the Constitution. . . .

The decision in *Hardwick* has not affected my firm belief that the Constitution, properly interpreted, does afford homosexuals the same protections it affords other groups that are historic victims of invidious discrimination. Nevertheless, for the reasons I have already stated, it is my obligation to follow *Hardwick* as long as it has precedential force—and for now it does. . . .

IV.

Because we are not free to hold that homosexuals are a suspect class, we can not apply strict scrutiny to the Army's regulations. At the most the regulations must pass intermediate scrutiny—and in *Hatheway* [641 F.2d 1376 (9th Cir. 1981)] we decided that the military's singling out of homosexual conduct for special adverse treatment survives that level of review: applying intermediate level scrutiny we concluded that prosecutions by the military on the basis of sexual preference bear "a substantial relationship to an important government interest." . . . We then upheld the Army's discriminatory treatment of Hatheway. We are bound by *Hatheway* to conclude that military "[c]lassifications which are based solely on sexual preference" survive an intermediate level of review. . . .

Courts must give special deference when adjudicating matters involving the military. . . . In rejecting the Army's justifications for the regulation, the majority fails to give proper deference to the Army's determinations. . . . Although I see no merit in the Army's ideas about homosexuals, its beliefs about the consequences of allowing homosexuals to serve in the Army, and its pandering to negative stereotypes of homosexuals, . . . we are not permitted to substitute our views for the Army's "considered professional judgment" as to what kind of person should be barred from enlisting in order to ensure a disciplined fighting force. . . .

Conclusion

As the majority points out, Sgt. Watkins has every reason to feel aggrieved. His homosexuality has been well known for many years. During that entire period, his army service has been exemplary. Those who have worked with him, including his supervisors, are anxious to see him continue with his military career. Yet, under the Supreme Court's (and our own circuit's) interpretation of the Constitution, the Army is free to terminate that career solely because he is a homosexual. There are only three entities which have the authority to afford Sgt. Watkins the relief which I, like the majority, believe a proper interpretation of the Constitution would require. First, the Supreme Court could undo the damage to the Constitution wrought by *Hardwick*; it could overrule that precedent directly or implicitly. Second, the Army could voluntarily abandon its unfair and discriminatory regulation (or, I would assume, the Department of Defense could direct it to do so). Third, the Congress could enact appropriate legislation prohibiting the armed services from excluding homosexuals. I recognize that from a practical standpoint the existence of these forums may offer Sgt. Watkins little solace. Nevertheless, I do not believe that a panel of the Ninth Circuit may, consistent with its duty to apply precedent properly, afford him the relief he seeks.

For the above reasons, I must reluctantly dissent.

[EDITOR'S NOTE: When the Ninth Circuit later considered this case en banc, the *Watkins* panel opinion was vacated, although the result was affirmed on technical grounds.]

NOTE

[9]The equal protection component of the Fifth Amendment imposes precisely the same constitutional requirements on the federal government as the equal protection clause of the Fourteenth Amendment imposes on state governments. . . .

QUESTIONS FOR DISCUSSION

1. In what ways is Judge Norris' argument in *Watkins* similar to Mohr's arguments against bans on homosexuals in the military? In what ways are they different?

2. Do Norris's arguments apply as well to the 1993 policy of the Clinton administration (pp. 635–6)? Why or why not?

3. Reinhardt argues that *Bowers v. Hardwick* (Section 4.2) rules out making sexual orientation a suspect classification under the Equal Protection Clause. Do you agree? Why or why not? How does Norris respond?

4. Norris outlines several factors that determine whether a classification is suspect. Do you agree with the factors on his list? Is his list complete?

5. Is it unjust for the government to allow heterosexual couples but not homosexual couples to get married? Is it sex discrimination to allow Pat to marry a man if Pat is female but not if Pat is male? How are laws that forbid same-sex marriage similar to and different from laws that forbid interracial marriage? If homosexual couples are not allowed to marry, should they be allowed to gain the legal advantages of marriage in some other way? Why and how, or why not?

6. Like many employers, New York City provides health benefits and other benefits not only to employees but also to their spouses and children. In a settlement in 1993, New York City agreed to extend exactly the same benefits to employees' homosexual partners and their partners' children. Would it have been unjust for New York to refuse to extend these benefits? Why or why not? Should all employers be required by law to extend all spousal benefits to homosexual partners? Why or why not? Is it unjust to extend benefits to unmarried homosexual couples but not to unmarried heterosexual couples? Why or why not?

7. What kinds of discrimination against homosexuals are unjust according to a communitarian theory of justice? According to a utilitarian theory? According to Rawls' theory? According to a libertarian theory? (See Section 5.2.)

SUGGESTIONS FOR FURTHER READING

Mohr develops his views in *Gays/Justice* (New York: Columbia University Press, 1988) and in *A More Perfect Union: Why Straight America Must Stand Up For Gay Rights* (Boston: Beacon Press, 1994). Jeffrey Rosen, "Sodom and Demurrer," *The New Republic* (November 29, 1993), pp. 16–19, argues for judicial restraint on gay rights. An excellent survey of laws affecting homosexuals is *Sexual Orientation and the Law*, by the Editors of the *Harvard Law Review* (Cambridge: Harvard University Press, 1990) (originally published in *Harvard Law Review* (May 1989)). For a communitarian perspective, see Michael J. Sandel, "Moral Argument and Liberal Toleration: Abortion and Homosexuality," *California Law Review*, vol. 77 (1989).

5.7 OTHER KINDS OF DISCRIMINATION

INTRODUCTION

Racial and ethnic minorities, women, and homosexuals are not the only groups that suffer discrimination. Other common targets of discrimination include elderly people, disabled people, poor people, followers of some religions, immigrants, illegal aliens, and so on. In order to fight some of these other kinds of discrimination, courts and Congress have taken various steps.

One example is the Age Discrimination in Employment Act,[37] which Congress passed in 1967. Here are some key sections:

> §2 (b) It is . . . the purpose of this Act to promote employment of older persons based on their ability rather than age; to prohibit arbitrary age discrimination in employment; to help employers and workers find ways of meeting problems arising from the impact of age on employment. . . .

> §4 (a) It shall be unlawful for an employer—
> (1) to fail or refuse to hire or to discharge any individual or otherwise discriminate against any individual with respect to his compensation, terms, conditions, or privileges of employment, because of such individual's age;
> (2) to limit, segregate, or classify his employees in any way which would deprive or tend to deprive any individual of employment opportunities or otherwise adversely affect his status as an employee, because of such individual's age; or
> (3) to reduce the wage rate of any employee in order to comply with this Act. . . .
> (f) It shall not be unlawful for an employer, employment agency, or labor organization—
> (1) to take any action otherwise prohibited under subsection (a) . . . where age is a bona fide occupational qualification reasonably necessary to the normal operation of the particular business, or where the differentiation is based on reasonable factors other than age, or . . .
> (2) to take any action otherwise prohibited under subsection (a) . . . — (A) to observe the terms of a bona fide seniority system that is not intended to evade the purposes of this Act . . . ; or (B) to observe the terms of a bona fide employee benefit plan . . .

> §12 (a) The prohibitions in this chapter shall be limited to individuals who are at least 40 years of age. . . .

---

[37] 29 U.S.C. §621, et seq.

(c) (1) Nothing in this chapter shall be construed to prohibit compulsory retirement of any employee who has attained 65 years of age and who, for the 2–year
period immediately before retirement, is employed in a bona fide executive or
high policymaking position if such an employee is entitled to an immediate non-
forfeitable annual retirement benefit from a pension, profit sharing, savings, or
deferred compensation plan, or any combination of such plans, of the employer
of such employee, which equals in the aggregate, at least $44,000.
(d) Nothing in this chapter shall be construed to prohibit compulsory retirement
of any employee who has attained 70 years of age and who is serving under a
contract of unlimited tenure . . . at an institution of higher education. [Effective
until December 31, 1993.]

It is striking that section §12 (a) allows discrimination against people on the basis
of their young age, even though the act is supposed to rule out discrimination
against people on the basis of their age.[38]

A more recent example of anti–discrimination legislation by Congress is the
Americans with Disabilities Act of 1990.[39] This is a very complex bill, but here are
a few selected passages:

Title I—Employment
Section 102
(a) No covered entity shall discriminate against a qualified individual with a disability because of the disability of such individual in regard to job application
procedures, the hiring, advancement, or discharge of employees, employee compensation, job training, and other terms, conditions and privileges of employment.
(b) As used in subsection (a), the term "discriminate" includes— . . . (5) (A) not
making reasonable accommodations to the known physical or mental limitations
of an otherwise qualified individual with a disability who is an applicant or employee, unless such covered entity can demonstrate that the accommodation
would impose an undue hardship on the business of such covered entity; or
(B) denying employment opportunities to a job applicant or employee who is an
otherwise qualified individual with a disability, if such denial is based on the
need of such covered entity to make reasonable accommodation to the physical
or mental impairments of the employee or applicant.

Of course, there will be disagreements about which accommodations are "reasonable" and which hardships are "undue." Some guidelines are spelled out in the
rest of the act, but much is still left for courts to decide as cases arise.

As we said, there are many other kinds of discrimination and many laws governing them. We cannot discuss them all here. Each kind of discrimination raises
somewhat different issues, so each must be considered separately. The difficult
task is to develop a general theory of justice in law that specifies which kinds of
legal distinctions are just, which are unjust, which should be illegal, and why.
Such a theory can be constructed only by comparing all of the different kinds of
discrimination.

---

[38]Cf. *Massachusetts Board of Retirement v. Murgia*, 427 U.S. 307 (1976).
[39]42 U.S.C. §12101, et seq.

QUESTIONS FOR DISCUSSION

1. Is it ever just to force an otherwise qualified person to retire because of his or her age? To refuse to hire an otherwise qualified person because he or she is close to retirement? Should all such acts be illegal? Why or why not?

2. Should there be any age limit on driver's licenses? Should people over a certain age be required to have their driving ability tested more often than younger people? Why or why not?

3. Since there are laws protecting old people from discrimination, should there be similar laws protecting young people from discrimination? Should it be illegal, for example, to refuse to hire an otherwise qualified individual because of his or her youth? Are minimum ages for buying alcohol unjust discrimination? Why or why not?

4. Suppose there are two candidates for a job. One is slightly more qualified but has a disability such that reasonable accommodation would cost the company the equivalent of one year's salary. Is it just for the company to hire the candidate without the disability? Should this be illegal? Why or why not?

5. Should a local school be required to provide a sign language interpreter for a deaf student who can partially read lips but would learn more in school with the interpreter? Why or why not?

6. Should obesity count as a disability under the Americans with Disabilities Act? Should it be illegal to refuse to hire a person as a salesperson or receptionist or flight attendant because that person is 200 pounds overweight? Why or why not?

7. If a disabled person is responsible for his or her own disability, does this make it just to discriminate against him or her in employment? Why or why not?

8. The common practice of funding local schools through local property taxes often results in much lower budgets for schools in areas of poverty where property is less valuable. This results in a lower quality of education for poor people. Is this just? Does it violate the Equal Protection Clause? Why or why not?[40]

9. Should it be illegal for employers to refuse to hire someone because that person is homeless? Why or why not?

SUGGESTIONS FOR FURTHER READING

Strong arguments for rights of disabled people can be found in Gregory Kavka, "Disability and the Right to Work," *Social Philosophy and Policy*, vol. 9 (1992), pp. 262–290; and Susan Wendell, "Toward a Feminist Theory of Disability," *Hypatia*, vol. 4, no. 2 (Summer 1989). Richard Epstein argues against the Americans with Disabilities Act in *Forbidden Grounds* (Cambridge: Harvard University Press, 1992), Chapter 22. On equality for the poor, see John Arthur and William Shaw, *Justice and Economic Distribution* (Englewood Cliffs, New Jersey: Prentice-Hall, 1978).

---

[40]Compare *San Antonio Independent School District v. Rodriguez*, 411 U.S. 1 (1973).

CHAPTER 6

PUNISHMENT

INTRODUCTION

Imagine that your 12–year–old son just hit your 10–year–old daughter. What would you do about it? Some parents would spank their son. Others would ground him. A few would just tell him not to hit her again and maybe also explain to him why hitting her is wrong. An even smaller number would offer him a reward if he can go a week without hitting her again. Which reaction is best? Such questions are not easy for parents. Loving parents hate to hurt their children, but even loving parents might have to punish their son in order protect their daughter. On the other hand, angry parents sometimes punish too often, too much, or in the wrong way, and this can cause resentment and regression.

Issues of punishment are even more difficult for governments. Although parents usually love their sons, governments are not so fond of criminals. Of course, a government might also lack the concern for the victim that a parent has towards a daughter. So there is reason to fear that governments might be too harsh or too lenient.

The complexity of government also creates problems. Parents can punish swiftly and efficiently. Modern governments, in contrast, rarely punish (or do anything else) as quickly or as efficiently as anyone wishes. This increases the expense of punishment and often reduces its effectiveness, which raises questions about whether and when punishment is worth its costs.

Punishment is also problematic for governments because of the nature of law. Criminal laws are general: all acts of a certain kind are to be punished in a certain way. Even when such a generality is fully justified as a general rule, there will still be particular cases where the prescribed punishment is too harsh or too lenient for the special circumstances. The solution might seem to lie in individualized sentencing, but that makes it hard for people to predict how they will be treated, and it allows judges to enforce their prejudices. One way to avoid such problems is to have general rules about punishment even if those general rules lead astray in some particular cases.[1]

---

[1]Compare the discussion of rules in Chapter 2, and Lloyd E. Ohlin and Frank J. Remington, eds., *Discretion in Criminal Justice* (Albany; State University of New York Press, 1993).

Which rules should govern punishment? Since legal punishment is administered in a complex institution, we need many rules at many levels to answer many questions:

1. *Who should punish?* Should private citizens, including victims, ever be allowed to administer punishments? When the government punishes, which branch and level of government should administer or control punishment in which cases?

2. *For what should they punish?* Which acts should be grounds for punishment? Should people be punished for anything other than an act (such as a state of being addicted to a drug)? Should people be punished for failures to act? Should people be punished for mistakes and accidents?

3. *Whom should they punish?* Should they punish everyone who has broken a criminal law? Should they punish anyone who has not broken a criminal law?

4. *How much should they punish?* Should rape receive two years or ten or twenty? Should rapists receive more or less punishment than robbers or murderers? Should repeat offenders receive more punishment than first-time offenders? Should criminals receive more punishment if they are motivated by hate or prejudice? Do unsuccessful attempts warrant less punishment than successful attempts?

5. *How should they punish?* Should they use imprisonment or death or corporal punishments, such as whipping or amputation? What about allowing convicted rapists to choose chemical or physical castration in place of prison?

There are also procedural questions about how we should go about deciding these issues and applying our general rules to particular cases. All of these questions must be answered in order for a theory of punishment to be complete.

These questions are normative. It is also interesting to ask who, how, and how much our judicial system does *in fact* punish. But the theories to be studied here will be primarily about which kinds of laws we *should* have.

How can such normative questions be answered? One crucial factor is our purposes. In order to determine what kind of car we should buy, we need to know why we want to buy a car. If we want to take children to school, we should buy a different car than if we want to race at Indianapolis. Similarly, it is common to determine what kind of punishment we should have by asking a more basic question: why should we punish in the first place? This question asks for a justification of punishment.

Of course, we cannot determine why we should do something unless we know what it is. If someone asks why we should play, we first need to know what counts as playing: playing a game or playing a theatrical role or playing the stock market or just playing around. Similarly, if we do not know which treatments count as punishments, we cannot even begin to say anything precise or useful about why or when punishment is justified. So we have to begin with a more fundamental question: *what is punishment?*

THE NATURE OF **6.1**
PUNISHMENT

INTRODUCTION

Although boxers are sometimes said to punish their opponents, and hangovers can be seen as punishments for drinking too much, theories of punishment are *not* about boxing or hangovers. To see what theories of punishment *are* about, a good place to start is the definition of punishment by H.L.A. Hart, a professor of jurisprudence at the University of Oxford (1907–1993) (see Section 1.2). Hart says that, in order for an act to be a central case of punishment:

i. It must involve pain or other consequences normally considered unpleasant.

ii. It must be for an offence against legal rules.

iii. It must be of an actual or supposed offender for his offense.

iv. It must be intentionally administered by human beings other than the offender.

v. It must be imposed and administered by an authority constituted by a legal system against which the offense is committed.[2]

Hart admits that this definition excludes many acts that would normally be called "punishment," but he wants his definition to capture what is most important to the clearest cases of legal punishment.

The main purpose of clause (i) is to distinguish punishments from rewards. To pay someone money for killing is not to punish him but to reward him. Even a neutral treatment, such as writing his name on a list of killers, is not a punishment if it causes no harm to him. Still, some criminals might want their punishments. A classic story tells of a homeless person who throws a brick through a window of the police station every November so that he will be sentenced to stay in the jail for the winter. The prisoner might not feel any pain, and he might be better off overall in jail than on the cold streets. But imprisonment still deprives him of freedom, and this deprivation is *normally* considered unpleasant. Similarly, some modern prisons include many facilities (even golf courses) that take much of the pain out of punishment, and some alternatives to imprisonment (such as ankle bracelets that keep track of released convicts) also do not seem painful. But

[2]*Punishment and Responsibility* (New York; Oxford University Press, 1968), pp. 4–5.

such treatments still include a loss of freedom, and that is what makes them punishment. (Whether or not they are justified is a different issue.)

Clause (ii) ensures that not all harmful acts are punishments. Suppose that someone with an infectious disease is locked in a prison in order to stop the spread of the disease. (Cuba reportedly does this to AIDS patients.) This quarantine is not punishment, according to (ii), because the person is not imprisoned *for* any legal offense. Clause (ii) might seem too narrow when it restricts punishment to violations of "legal" rules. But Hart is simply assuming that the "central" cases of punishment are legal punishments, and these are also our main concern.

Clauses (iv) and (v) focus on the person doing the punishment. Suppose that a teenage boy gets drunk and rapes his girlfriend. The victim's friends then verbally or even physically assault the rapist, so much that he cannot safely leave his house for months before the trial. He has not yet been punished. Even if he feels so much remorse that he locks himself in his room and tries to commit suicide in a way that leaves him scarred for life, he still has not been punished in the literal sense. That is why, when he is convicted, he cannot argue that he has already served part of his sentence. That is also why Hart's definition needs clauses (iv) and (v).

The most controversial clause is (iii). Suppose that a policeman hears about yet another drive-by shooting and becomes so frustrated and angry that he hits an innocent bystander. This act inflicts harm, is a reaction to an offense, and is done by an authority, but it is still not punishment, because the act is not directed towards any offender. Clause (iii) is needed to exclude such cases. But what about people who are really innocent but are thought to be guilty? Hart discusses an example where "in order to avert some social catastrophe, officials of the system fabricate evidence on which he is charged, tried, convicted, and sent to prison or death."[3] In this case, the officials do not suppose that their victim is an offender, so sending him to prison or death would not count as punishment on a narrow interpretation of clause (iii). Nonetheless, other people do suppose that the victim is an offender who is punished for his offense. That is the point of the fraud. Consequently, sending this victim to prison or death does count as punishment on a wider interpretation of clause (iii) such that a "supposed offender" is anyone who is generally supposed to be an offender. Hart can thus include fraudulent punishment as punishment, if he wants.

Clause (iii) might seem less plausible in cases of *vicarious* punishment. Suppose that a government imprisons the family of a known dissident in order to force the dissident to recant. This would not count as punishment on Hart's definition if the family is not treated this way because *they* violated a legal rule. Yet it might seem natural to say that the family is being punished for the crime of the dissident. Hart responds that these cases are not "central" cases of punishment, but one might wonder whether any important issues are affected by dismissing such common cases as "secondary."

---

[3]*Punishment and Responsibility*, p. 11; compare McCloskey's example, pp. 670–1; and Carritt's example in Rawls, p. 686.

Despite some problems, many people think that Hart's definition is generally on the right track. However, Joel Feinberg, a professor of philosophy at the University of Arizona, argues that Hart's definition misses a crucial feature that distinguishes punishments from mere penalties. Penalties in the law include, for example, fines for filing income tax forms late and parking fines when these are seen as no more than fees for parking in certain areas. (This might not apply to all parking fines.) In contrast, prison is much more than a fee to be paid for burglary or assault. According to Feinberg:

> At its best, in civilized and democratic countries, punishment surely expresses the community's strong *disapproval* of what the criminal did. Indeed, it can be said that punishment expresses the *judgment* (as distinct from any emotion) of the community that what the criminal did was wrong. I think it is fair to say of our community, however, that punishment generally expresses more than judgments of disapproval; it is also a symbolic way of getting back at the criminal, of expressing a kind of vindictive resentment.[4]

These symbolic and expressive functions of punishment must be made part of the *definition* of punishment, according to Feinberg, in order to understand some roles of punishment in our society, such as its showing that the government does not condone certain acts and that the government really meant what it said when it made those acts illegal. The expressive function of punishment is also useful insofar as people who want to avoid social disapproval will want to avoid punishment.

These disputes about the definition of punishment are important, because one cannot determine when punishment is justified or which theories are sufficient to justify punishment until one specifies which elements are essential to the punishment that is to be justified. If Feinberg is right, a complete justification of a punishment will need to justify not only the harm caused by the punishment but also the condemnation inherent in the punishment, so punishment cannot be justified except in cases where the offender deserves such condemnation. This definitional issue thus affects many of the substantive positions to be discussed later (see especially Sections 6.4, 7.4, and 7.5).

QUESTIONS FOR DISCUSSION

1. Do you agree with Feinberg that punishment always or typically expresses disapproval? If not, why not? If so, should this expressive function be built into the definition of punishment? In what ways is the expressive function of punishment similar to and different from an individual expressing anger to someone who hurt her?

---

[4]Joel Feinberg, "The Expressive Function of Punishment," in *Doing and Deserving* (Princeton; Princeton University Press, 1970), p. 100.

2. Is it a punishment when legislatures deny prisoners the right to vote? When they deny felons the right to practice law or medicine after release? Why or why not? If not, what kinds of limitations on prisoners' privileges would count as punishments?

3. In Florida, some convicted drunk drivers were required to put bumper stickers on their cars that read, "I was convicted of DWI." Is this a punishment? Why or why not?

4. On November 14, 1981, Debbie Black Barrett, then 27, of Artesia, New Mexico, shot her husband. After conviction, District Judge Harvey Fort sentenced her to a probation that required her to attend Eastern New Mexico State University and maintain a "C" average. He pointed out that college is cheaper than prison. Even so, is college a punishment in this case? Why or why not?

5. In *People v. Levy*,[5] Levy already had at least one prior misdemeanor sex conviction when, in 1954, he pleaded guilty to the misdemeanor of annoying and molesting a child under the age of 18. After further observation and hearings, the superior court found Levy to be a sexual psychopath and ordered him committed for an indeterminate period to the Department of Mental Hygiene for placement in the Atascadero State Hospital. Eighteen months later there was no change in his condition, and the court "concluded that [Levy] would not be benefited by further hospitalization, found that he was still a menace to the health and safety of others and that he was predisposed to the commission of sexual offenses, and committed him 'for an indeterminate period to the department of Mental Hygiene, for placement in an Institutional Unit for the treatment of Sexual Psychopaths in a facility in the Department of Corrections, namely: The California State Prison at San Quentin.'" Levy complained that confining him in San Quentin subjected him to double jeopardy and thus violated the Fifth Amendment of the Constitution. The Court responded, "The emphasis that [Levy] places on the fact that he was originally convicted of a misdemeanor, and now finds himself in San Quentin, possibly for life, is misplaced. This argument would be sound only were his confinement punishment. As we have already seen, the purpose of the confinement is to protect society and to try and cure the accused." Roughly, the court argues that the *purpose* of a confinement determines whether it is punishment, and Levy argues that the *place* of confinement determines whether it is punishment. In your opinion, is Levy's confinement to San Quentin a punishment? Does it violate the constitutional prohibition on double jeopardy? Should Levy be sent back to a hospital, as he wants?

6. McKinney was convicted of murder and assigned to a cell with another inmate who smoked five packs of cigarettes a day. He sued on the grounds that the health risk posed by involuntary exposure to environmental to-

[5]311 P.2d 897 (Cal. App. 1957).

bacco smoke (E.T.S.) violates the Eighth Amendment prohibition of cruel and unusual punishment. In *Helling v. McKinney*,[6] the majority of the Supreme Court held that McKinney had a cause of action under the Eighth Amendment if prison officials "have, with deliberate indifference, exposed [the inmate] to levels of E.T.S. that pose an unreasonable risk of serious damage to his future health." In his dissenting opinion, Justice Clarence Thomas argued that, "To state a claim under the cruel and unusual punishments clause, a party must prove not only that the challenged conduct was both cruel and unusual, but also that it constitutes punishment. The text and history of the Eighth Amendment, together with pre-Estelle [v. Gamble, 1976] precedent, raise substantial doubts in my mind that the Eighth Amendment proscribes a prison deprivation that is not inflicted as part of a sentence." Do you agree with the majority or with Thomas? Why? What if McKinney's cellmates had serious infectious diseases? What about violent cellmates or overcrowding that can lead to violence? What if McKinney had been convicted of a lesser crime?

7. Some opponents of affirmative action programs see those programs as a form of punishment. Accordingly, they object that those programs harm people who are not guilty of any crime and have not been given the benefit of the criminal procedures that are usually required before punishment. However, these procedures might not be required if inflicting these harms does not count as punishment. So, in your opinion, in what ways is affirmative action like punishment? In what ways is it different? (See Section 5.4.)

SUGGESTIONS FOR FURTHER READING

H.L.A. Hart presents his standard definition of punishment in "Prolegomenon to the Principles of Punishment" in *Punishment and Responsibility* (New York: Oxford University Press, 1968). Criticisms of definitions like Hart's can be found in Kurt Baier, "Is Punishment Retributive?", *Analysis*, vol. 16 (1955), pp. 25–32; and Ted Honderich, *Punishment: The Supposed Justifications*, rev. ed. (Harmondsworth: Penguin, 1976), which also provides a concise overview of theories of punishment. Joel Feinberg argues for an alternative definition in "The Expressive Function of Punishment" in *Doing and Deserving* (Princeton: Princeton University Press, 1970). Feinberg's account is criticized by R.A. Duff in *Trials and Punishments* (New York: Cambridge University Press, 1986), pp. 235–45. Duff goes on to develop a different kind of expressive theory. See also Michael Davis, "Punishment as Language: Misleading Analogy for Desert Theorists," *Law and Philosophy*, vol. 10 (August 1991), pp. 310–22. The quest for a single definition of punishment is questioned by H. J. McCloskey, "The Complexity of the Concepts of Punishment," *Philosophy*, vol. 37 (1962).

---

[6]113 S.Ct. 2475 (1993).

6.2 THEORIES OF PUNISHMENT

INTRODUCTION

The nature of punishment raises serious questions about its justification. By definition, punishment causes harm to the punished person, and the person doing the punishing intends to cause that harm. Yet intentionally causing harm is usually a paradigm of immorality. So *why* should we punish criminals instead of leaving them alone? And if punishment includes moral condemnation, then we also need to ask *why* we should punish criminals instead of just penalizing them without condemning them.

The two most common answers to such questions are complete opposites. Roughly, *retributivists* say that punishment is justified because the punished person is guilty of a past crime. *Utilitarians*, in contrast, claim that punishment is justified because the act of punishing has good future consequences for society, such as reducing crime. Retributivists focus on the past, whereas utilitarians focus on the future. Retributivists focus on the act of the criminal, whereas utilitarians focus on the act of punishment.

These general justifications of punishment are also often used as the basis for answers to the other main questions about punishment.

Whom should we punish? The simple answer is that one should punish a person if and only if punishing that person will serve the basic purpose of punishment. Retributivists then claim that one should punish those and only those who are guilty. In contrast, utilitarians claim that we should punish a person if and only if punishing that person has better consequences than not punishing that person.

How much should we punish? The simple answer is: as much and no more than is justified by the original reason to punish at all. This means that retributivists claim that we should punish to and only to a degree proportionate to the guilt of the punished person. And utilitarians claim that we should punish to the degree that brings about the best consequences overall.

How should we punish? As before: in whatever way best serves the general goal of punishment. So retributivists think that we should punish in a manner that corresponds best with the guilt of the punished person. And utilitarians think that we should punish in whatever way has the best consequences overall.

Although it is simpler to answer all questions about punishment by reference to its basic justification, this is not the only possibility. One could consistently give a retributivist answer to one question (such as, whom should one punish?) but a utilitarian answer to another question (such as, how much should we punish?). One also might combine utilitarian and retributivist elements in one's answer to a single question (such as, why should we punish?). Such mixed positions are difficult to formulate and defend, since one needs to show how the various elements fit together, and one also needs an argument for including each of the elements in the theory. But such mixed theories are still important, because they remind us to look separately at each of the main questions about punishment.

Nonetheless, we will focus initially on purely utilitarian theories and purely retributivist theories. These pure views seem relatively simple, but we will see that actual retributivists and utilitarians are much more subtle, sophisticated, and divided than these rough initial formulations suggest.

6.3 UTILITARIAN THEORIES OF PUNISHMENT

INTRODUCTION

Utilitarianism is not only a theory of punishment. We already saw utilitarian theories of civil disobedience in Chapter 3 and of justice in Chapter 5. Indeed, utilitarianism is a general moral theory and even a general theory of how to live. According to utilitarianism, *whenever* you choose, you ought (to try) to make the world a better place. It is irrational to try to change the past. Let bygones be bygones. And it is selfish to attach more importance to your own good than to the good of others. Everyone should count equally. So what you ought to do is, in John Stuart Mill's phrase, what creates the greatest good for the greatest number. More precisely, utilitarianism is the claim that an act is right if and only if it causes at least as great a balance of good effects over bad effects for everyone as any alternative. An act is then wrong if and only if it is not right; that is, if and only if there is any incompatible alternative that produces more good overall.

The overall good is a function of all good and bad effects on all people. But which effects are good or bad? One answer is *hedonism*, which is the view that only pleasure is intrinsically good and only pain is intrinsically bad. Everything else is good or bad only insofar as it causes pleasure and pain. Hedonism was accepted by Jeremy Bentham, a nineteenth–century British philosopher (in the reading in this section). Most contemporary utilitarians, however, are not hedonists. Some see an effect as good or bad insofar as it fulfills or frustrates a person's desire or preference (whether or not it causes pleasure or pain). Others think that some things (such as freedom) are good and other things (such as death) are bad independently of whether they cause any pleasure or pain, or fulfill or frustrate any desire. These disputes about value do not greatly affect punishment, since most punishments cause and are supposed to prevent things that are bad on all common theories. So the important question here is whether punishments do enough good to override the harm that they do.

How much good is enough? To apply this theory, we need to know how to compare and total up benefits and harms. Bentham's method is his *hedonic calculus*, which considers extent (how many people are affected), intensity (how much they are affected), duration (how long they are affected), and certainty (how probable each effect is).[7] Subtract all of the harms from all of the benefits, and the act with

---

[7]Bentham also mentions propinquity (or temporal distance), fecundity (the extent to which pain leads to pain and pleasure to pleasure), and purity (the extent to which pain leads to pleasure and pleasure to pain), but these three factors are redundant, since propinquity matters only insofar as it affects probability, and fecundity and purity are already considered if one sums all of the benefits and harms.

the highest total is the one that ought to be done. Bentham realizes that this procedure cannot be completed before every act. His point is that a mistake can result from overlooking any one of these factors. One should not, for example, overemphasize a large harm or benefit if it is extremely improbable. Mistakes also often result from overlooking small harms or benefits to many people for a long time.

This theory is supposed to apply to every action. Punishment is just another kind of action, so punishment also is right when and only when it maximizes the good. This might seem simple, but it becomes complex because every punishment has many effects on many people. The main benefit of punishment is to reduce crime, but punishment can reduce crime in many ways.

One way in which punishment reduces crime is by *general deterrence* or the fear of a threatened punishment. If the law threatens drug dealers with ten years in prison, then whether a person deals drugs depends on that person's beliefs about how much he will make as a dealer, how likely conviction is, and how bad prison is. Prison brings not only a loss of freedom but many other dangers and discomforts. Social stigma can also remove opportunities after release from prison. And a prisoner's family and friends often suffer along with the prisoner. When these harms are seen as severe enough and probable enough, people will choose not to commit crimes.

Of course, the mere threat of punishment is often not enough. Some people commit crimes despite the risks. Their actual punishment can then make the threatened harms of punishment more vivid to them as well as to others. This *special deterrence* is another way that punishment can scare people away from crime.

Deterrence is not the only way that punishment reduces crime. Punishment also reduces crime by *incapacitation*. Usually, there are no cars to steal in prison, and prisoners cannot assault people on the streets. The death penalty also takes away a criminal's capacity to commit crimes.

Another benefit of prison is the opportunity for *rehabilitation*. Some people commit crimes because they do not have any lawful way to make a decent living or because they suffer from treatable mental illnesses. If time in prison is used to equip the criminal for a better life after release, then the criminal is supposed to be less likely to commit crimes after release.

Other effects of punishment work on law–abiding citizens. When a legislature attaches a punishment to a certain kind of act, this can make people believe that this kind of act is immoral, and this belief can lead people not to do that kind of act. This kind of *moral education* seems to be part of the point of laws against sexual harassment and marital rape. Some people did not see such acts as wrong, but changes in the law convinced them not to do such acts even apart from any fear of punishment. (See rule 11 in the reading from Bentham.)

In all of these ways, punishment can reduce crime. Punishment can also have other benefits. Bentham even lists the pleasure that victims and others get from seeing the guilty suffer. But punishment also has costs. Not only is harm inflicted on the criminal, but the criminal's family often suffers, even when family members are completely innocent. Moreover, courts and prisons are neither cheap nor safe.

Overall, utilitarians have to weigh all of the benefits of punishment against all of its costs. They also have to weigh the benefits and costs of alternatives to punishment. On their view, then, we are justified in punishing a person when doing so produces at least as great a balance of benefits over costs as any alternative. When this condition is *not* met, punishing a person is *not* justified, according to utilitarianism. Bentham argues that punishment is "unmeet" or unjustified when it is: (1) groundless, (2) inefficacious, (3) unprofitable, and (4) needless (see the reading in this section).

Bentham also shows how utilitarianism can answer another question: *how much* should we punish? He gives thirteen "rules of proportionality," but with regard to deterrence his system boils down to a simple formula. To deter crime, the harm of the punishment to the criminal must be greater than the expected profit of each offense divided by the perceived probability of punishment, that is:

<table>
<tr><td>The harm of
the punishment</td><td></td><td>the expected profit of each offense
———————————————————
the perceived probability of punishment</td></tr>
</table>

This means that the punishment must be increased when the expected profit increases, and it must also be increased as the perceived probability of punishment decreases.

To see how this works, imagine a car thief who believes that he can get rich quickly by stealing cars. He is also convinced by movies or the media that he can get away with crime, because the police are incompetent, prosecutors will bargain down to a minimal plea, and judges will let him off on technicalities. Even if these beliefs are false, the expected profit is high, and the perceived probability of punishment is low, so the punishment will have to be very high to deter the crime. There is no way to determine exactly how much punishment is necessary to deter car thefts. In fact, deterrence comes in degrees, and more or less punishment will deter more or less car thefts. So what governments need to do is experiment with different punishments and different strategies for catching car thieves in order to arrive at a level of deterrence that seems acceptable.

Despite their plausibility, Bentham's rules of proportionality do lead to some anomolies. Consider car theft as above, where news reports make the police seem incompetent. If this reduces the perceived probability of punishment by half, and if the punishment for car theft was five years, then the punishment will have to be increased to ten years in order to get the same deterrent effect. But this means that a car thief might be required to serve an additional five years just because the police are seen as incompetent and not because the thief did anything different than before. This kind of result is unjust according to retributivists who think that punishment should be proportionate to the guilt of the criminal and not to the reputation of the police.

The most common objection to utilitarianism concerns another question: *whom* should we punish? Even apart from punishment, many object that utilitarianism can justify violations of individual rights. The relevant instance of this general problem is that utilitarianism seems to justify punishing an innocent person in some cases. In one classic example, "a sheriff fram[es] an innocent Negro in order to stop a series of lynchings which he knew would occur if the guilty person were not immediately found, or believed to have been found."[8] If ten innocent people would be lynched in the absence of framing and hanging one innocent person, then utilitarianism seems to imply that the sheriff should frame and hang the innocent one. But most people think that this would be wrong.

The point is that three propositions are inconsistent:

1. Agents always ought to do whatever maximizes utility.
2. Agents never ought to punish innocent people.
3. Sometimes it maximizes utility to punish an innocent person.

Since these three claims are inconsistent, every consistent theory must deny at least one of them. But which one?

One response is to stick with the utilitarian principle (1) and the claim (2) but deny (3). The sheriff example is supposed to establish (3). However, utilitarians can respond that, in order to know that hanging the innocent person maximizes utility, the sheriff would have to know that there is no less harmful or dangerous way to prevent the lynchings (such as getting a volunteer to wait in jail until the judge comes). The sheriff will also have to know that hanging the innocent person will succeed in stopping the lynchings (and will not lead to even more lynchings or counter-reactions). And the sheriff will also have to know that the deception will not soon be discovered (since then the sheriff will probably be punished and the lynchings might occur anyway). And so on. Utilitarians can plausibly claim that no real person could know all of this in any realistic situation.

Nonetheless, the example is still possible in principle. There is nothing contradictory in supposing that the sheriff knows all that he needs to know in order to know that hanging an innocent person is necessary and sufficient to maximize utility. Thus, *if* moral theories must handle all possible situations, no matter how unrealistic, then utilitarians cannot avoid the problem by denying (3).

Another possible response is to deny (2). Most people accept (2), but few can justify (2) except by saying that it seems wrong to punish innocent people. So utilitarians can respond by asking: why should we trust our common moral beliefs or intuitions in cases that are this unrealistic? Our moral intuitions are formed from our experiences and from the experiences of those who taught us, so we should expect our intuitions to reflect the most common kinds of situations that we and others actually have experienced. To trust our moral intuitions in unrealistic situations is no better than to trust Newtonian mechanics when studying subatomic particles.[9]

However, many people still find it difficult to give up the belief that it is morally wrong to punish innocent people. Even if there are some extreme emergencies where it is permissible to hang an innocent person, a slight increase in overall utility does not seem to be enough to justify such hanging, especially when the goal is achieved by means of deception and intentional harm. Such beliefs are

[8]H. J. McCloskey, "A Non-Utilitarian Approach to Punishment," *Inquiry* vol. 8 (1965), pp. 249–263 at 255. Compare the quotation from Carritt in Rawls, p. 686 in this section.

[9]For this response, see T. L. S. Sprigge, "A Utilitarian Reply to Dr. McCloskey," *Inquiry* vol. 8 (1965), pp. 264–91.

so deeply ingrained and seem so obvious that many people want to find another solution to this problem.

The final way to escape the above inconsistency is to deny (1), the principle of utility. Retributivists do this, but it is also possible to stay within a broadly utilitarian framework[10] and yet modify (1) so as to condemn hanging innocent people. That is the move made by *rule utilitarians*.

John Austin, a nineteenth–century British philosopher, expressed rule utilitarianism by saying, "The probable *specific* consequences of doing that single act, of forebearing from that single act, or of omitting that single act, are not the objects of the inquiry. The question to be solved is this—If acts of the *class* were *generally* done, or *generally* foreborne or omitted, what would be the probable effect on the general happiness or good?"[11] For example, when a sheriff hangs an innocent person, one must not ask whether this single act maximizes utility. Instead, one must ask what would happen if acts of this kind were done generally. If this general pattern of action would not maximize utility, then the individual act of hanging an innocent person is morally wrong.

This theory is encapsulated in the common question: "What would happen if everybody did that?" But this question quickly leads to another: "What is *that?*" The description of the act is crucial, because whether an individual act is wrong, according to rule utilitarianism, depends on the general class it is in. This problem can be illustrated by the example of the sheriff hanging an innocent person to stop lynchings. One class of acts is (a) hangings of innocent people. It clearly does not maximize utility to hang innocent people generally. However, another class of acts is (b) hangings of innocent people that prevent a series of lynchings. It would maximize utility to do acts of *this* class generally, that is, to hang innocent people when (and only when) this is necessary and sufficent to prevent a series of lynchings. Rule utilitarianism so far gives us no reason to focus on class (a) instead of class (b), so it does not tell us definitively whether or not it is wrong to hang an innocent person in the sheriff example.

One common solution to this problem is to require *publicity*. This approach is described but not endorsed by John Rawls in the reading in this section. Rawls writes, "One must describe more carefully what the *institution* is which his example suggests, and then ask oneself whether or not it is likely that having this institution would be for the benefit of society in the long run." (pp. 686–7) Later, he adds, "It is essential to the notion of a practice that the rules are publicly known and understood as definitive."[12] This theory then has two steps. First, a general practice is justified if it would maximize utility for everyone to follow that practice publicly. Second, a particular act is morally wrong if it violates a rule of a practice that is justified.

---

[10]We have been using and will continue to use the term "utilitarianism" to include only act utilitarianism unless otherwise indicated. Rule utilitarianism is a different kind of theory, even though it is similar in some ways. Rawls argues that classical utilitarians were rule utilitarians, but, even if so, that does not affect the points in the text.

[11]John Austin, *The Province of Jurisprudence Determined* (New York: The Noonday Press, 1954), p. 38. There is a selection from Austin in Chapter 1 above.

[12]"Two Concepts of Rules," *Philosophical Review* vol. 44 (1955), p. 24. This passage is not in the selection by Rawls that follows.

It might seem artificial and arbitrary to split a moral theory into two stages in this way. If consequences are what matter, why not just apply the principle of utility directly to individual acts? This criticism is forceful in some areas, but Rawls argues that punishment is special because its very definition:

> refers to such things as the normal rights of a citizen, rules of law, due process of law, trials and courts of law, statutes, etc., none of which can exist outside the elaborate stage setting of a legal system. It is also the case that many of the actions for which people are punished presuppose practices. For example, one is punished for stealing, for trespassing, and the like, which presuppose the institution of property. It is impossible to say what punishment is, or to describe a particular instance of it, without referring to offices, actions, and offenses, specified by practices.[13]

If practices are so essential to punishment, it seems natural to judge particular acts of punishment in terms of the general practices that they follow or violate.

To see how this helps utilitarianism, we need to apply it to our example. What would happen if it were publicly known that sheriffs and judges are allowed to hang innocent people when they believe that doing so will maximize utility? Rawls argues that this practice would have many disadvantages. Such officials are likely to misuse their power through prejudice or mistake. The useful public condemnation of criminals would also diminish if the public believed that those who are punished might be innocent pawns in an official social strategy. And every one of us would have reason to fear being the next innocent person to be hanged. These are only some of the many disadvantages to publicly allowing punishment of innocent people. Thus, the practice that maximizes utility would seem to be one that rules out punishment of anyone who is innocent. For rule utilitarians, that makes it wrong to punish an innocent person even in special circumstances where doing so would maximize utility.

Although this seems plausible, there are also advantages to publicly allowing officials to punish innocent people. Even if judges and sheriffs sometimes make mistakes, they often get things right. Consider a practice of allowing some officials to frame and hang innocent people as long as they have very strong reasons to believe that this is the only way to prevent very many more killings of equally innocent people. This practice would make innocent people more likely to be hanged, but it would also make innocent people less likely to be lynched. And if the public knows that it is rare for innocent people to be hanged, their attitudes towards criminals might not change. If so, utility might be maximized by some practice that allows punishing innocent people in very limited circumstances, and then hanging innocent people might sometimes be allowed even by rule utilitarians.

This produces several reactions. Some rule utilitarians might accept that it is not morally wrong to hang an innocent person in some clear and extreme emergencies. Other rule utilitarians, however, will stick by their intuition that it is *always* wrong to

---

[13]"Two Concepts of Rules," p. 31. This passage is not in the selection that follows. Rawls also claims that hanging innocent people would not be punishment, but see the discussion of fraudulent punishment in Section 6.2.

hang innocent people. They must then either deny that any practice could maximize utility if it ever allowed innocent people to be punished or look for another formulation of rule utilitarianism that explains why punishing innocent people is always wrong. Yet another possible reaction is to turn to a completely different kind of theory, such as retributivism.

AN INTRODUCTION TO THE PRINCIPLES OF MORALS AND LEGISLATION

JEREMY BENTHAM

CHAPTER I. OF THE PRINCIPLE OF UTILITY.

I. *Mankind governed by pain and pleasure.* Nature has placed mankind under the governance of two sovereign masters, *pain* and *pleasure.* It is for them alone to point out what we ought to do, as well as to determine what we shall do. On the one hand the standard of right and wrong, on the other the chain of causes and effects, are fastened to their throne. They govern us in all we do, in all we say, in all we think: every effort we can make to throw off our subjection, will serve but to demonstrate and confirm it. In words a man may pretend to abjure their empire: but in reality he will remain subject to it all the while. The *principle of utility* recognises this subjection, and assumes it for the foundation of that system, the object of which is to rear the fabric of felicity by the hands of reason and of law. Systems which attempt to question it, deal in sounds instead of sense, in caprice instead of reason, in darkness instead of light.

But enough of metaphor and declamation: it is not by such means that moral science is to be improved.

II. *Principle of utility, what.* The principle of utility is the foundation of the present work: it will be proper therefore at the outset to give an explicit and determinate account of what is meant by it. By the principle of utility is meant that principle which approves or disapproves of every action whatsoever, according to the tendency which it appears to have to augment or diminish the happiness of the party whose interest is in question: or, what is the same thing in other words, to promote or to oppose that happiness. I say of every action whatsoever; and therefore not only of every action a private individual, but of every measure of government. . . .

CHAPTER XIII. CASES UNMEET FOR PUNISHMENT.

§ 1. *General view of cases unmeet for punishment.*

I. *The end of law is, to augment happiness.* The general object which all laws have, or ought to have, in common, is to augment the total happiness of the community; and therefore, in the first place, to exclude, as far as may be, everything that tends to subtract from that happiness: in other words, to exclude mischief.

Jeremy Bentham, *An Introduction to the Principles of Morals and Legislation,* Chapter I (Sections I–II), and Chapters XIII–XIV (complete)

II. *But punishment is an evil.* But all punishment is mischief: all punishment in itself is evil. Upon the principle of utility, if it ought at all to be admitted, it ought only to be admitted in as far as it promises to exclude some great evil.[155]

III. *Therefore ought not to be admitted;* It is plain, therefore, that in the following cases punishment ought not to inflicted.

1. *Where groundless.* Where it is *groundless:* where there is no mischief for it to prevent; the act not being mischievous upon the whole.

2. *Inefficacious.* Where it must be *inefficacious:* where it cannot act so as to prevent the mischief.

3. *Unprofitable.* Where it is *unprofitable,* or too *expensive:* where the mischief it would produce would be greater than what it prevented.

4. *Or needless.* Where it is *needless:* where the mischief may be prevented, or cease of itself, without it: that is, at a cheaper rate.

§ 2. *Cases in which punishment is groundless.*
These are,

IV. 1. *Where there has never been any mischief: as in the case of consent.* Where there has never been any mischief: where no mischief has been produced to any body by the act in question. Of this number are those in which the act was such as might, on some occasions, be mischievous or disagreeable, but the person whose interest it concerns gave his consent to the performance of it. This consent, provided it be free, and fairly obtained, is the best proof that can be produced, that, to the person who gives it, no mischief, at least no immediate mischief, upon the whole, is done. For no man can be so good a judge as the man himself, what it is gives him pleasure or displeasure.

V. 2. *Where the mischief was outweighed: as in precaution against calamity, and the exercise of powers.* Where the mischief was *outweighed:* although a mischief was produced by that act, yet the same act was necessary to the production of a benefit which was of greater value than the mischief. This may be the case with any thing that is done in the way of precaution against instant calamity, as also with any thing that is done in the exercise of the several sorts of powers necessary to be established in every community, to wit, domestic, judicial, military, and supreme.

VI. 3. *—or will, for a certainty be cured by compensation.* Where there is a certainty of an adequate compensation: and that in all cases where the offence can be committed. This supposes two things: 1. That the offence is such as admits of an adequate compensation: 2. That such a compensation is sure to be forthcoming. Of these suppositions, the latter will be found to be a merely ideal one: a supposition that cannot, in the universality here given to it, be verified by fact. It cannot, therefore, in practice, be numbered amongst the grounds of absolute impunity. It may, however, be admitted as a ground for an abatement of that punishment, which other considerations, standing by themselves, would seem to dictate.

§ 3. *Cases in which punishment must be inefficacious.*
These are,

VII. 1. *Where the penal provision comes too late: as in, 1. An ex-post-facto law, 2. An ultra-legal sentence.* Where the penal provision is *not established* until after the act is done. Such are the cases, 1. Of an *ex-post-facto* law; where the legislator himself appoints not a punishment till after the act is done. 2. Of a sentence beyond the law; where the judge, of his own authority, appoints a punishment which the legislator had not appointed.

VIII. 2. *Or is not made known: as in a law not sufficiently promulgated.* Where the penal provision, though established is *not conveyed* to the notice of the person on whom it seems intended that it should operate. Such is the case where the law has omitted to employ any of the expedients which are necessary, to make sure that every person whatsoever, who is within the reach of the law, be apprized of all the cases whatsoever, in which (being in the station of life he is in) he can be subjected to the penalties of the law.

IX. 3. *Where the will cannot be deterred from* any *act: as in,* Where the penal provision, though it were conveyed to a man's notice, *could produce no effect* on him, with respect to the preventing him from engaging in any act of the *sort* in question. Such is the case, 1. In extreme *infancy;* where a man has not yet attained that state or disposition of mind in which the prospect of evils so distant as those which are held forth by the law, has the effect of influencing his conduct. 2. In *insanity;* where the person, if he has attained to that disposition, has since been deprived of it through the influence of some permanent though unseen cause. 3. In *intoxication;* where he has been deprived of it by the transient influence of a visible cause: such as the use of wine, or opium, or other drugs, that act in this manner on the nervous system: which condition is indeed neither more nor less than a temporary insanity produced by an assignable cause.[161]

X. 4. *Or not from the individual act in question, as in,* Where the penal provision (although, being conveyed to the party's notice, it might very well prevent his engaging in acts of the sort in question, provided he knew that it related to those acts) could not have this effect, with regard to the *individual* act he is about to engage in: to wit, because he knows not that it is of the number of those to which the penal provision relates. This may happen, 1. In the case of *unintentionality;* where he intends not to engage, and thereby knows not that he is about to engage, in the *act* in which eventually he is about to engage. 2. In the case of *unconsciousness;* where, although he may know that he is about to engage in the *act* itself, yet, from not knowing all the material *circumstances* attending it, he knows not of the *tendency* it has to produce that mischief, in contemplation of which it has been made penal in most instances. 3. In the case of *missupposal;* where, although he may know of the tendency the act has to produce that degree of mischief, he supposes it, though mistakenly, to be attended with some circumstance, or set of circumstances, which, if it had been attended with, it would either not have been productive of that mischief, or have been productive of such a greater degree of good, as has determined the legislator in such a case not to make it penal.

XI. 5. *Or is acted on by an opposite superior force: as by,* Where, though the penal clause might exercise a full and prevailing influence, were it to act alone, yet by the *predominant* influence of some opposite cause upon the will, it must necessarily be ineffectual; because the evil which he sets himself about to undergo, in the case of his *not* engaging in the act, is so great, that the evil denounced by the penal clause, in case of his engaging in it, cannot appear greater. This may happen, 1. In the case of *physical danger;* where the evil is such as appears likely to be brought about by the unassisted powers of *nature.* 2. In the case of a *threatened mischief;* where it is such as appears likely to be brought about through the intentional and conscious agency of *man.*

XII. 6. —*or the bodily organs cannot follow its determination: as under* Where (though the penal clause may exert a full and prevailing influence over the *will* of the party) yet his *physical faculties* (owing to the predominant influence of some physical cause) are not in a condition to follow the determination of the will: insomuch that the act is absolutely *involuntary.* Such is the case of physical *compulsion* or *restraint,* by whatever means brought about; where the man's hand, for instance, is pushed against some object which his will disposes him *not* to touch; or tied down from touching some object which his will disposes him to touch.

§ 4. *Cases where punishment is unprofitable.*
These are,

XIII. 1. *Where, in the sort of case in question, the punishment would produce more evil than the offence would.* Where, on the one hand, the nature of the offence, on the other hand, that of the punishment, are, *in the ordinary state of things,* such, that when compared together, the evil of the latter will turn out to be greater than that of the former.

XIV. *Evil producible by a punishment—its four branches—viz.* Now the evil of the punishment divides itself into four branches, by which so many different sets of persons are affected. 1. The evil of *coercion* or *restraint:* or the pain which it gives a man not to be able to do the act, whatever it be which by the apprehension of the punishment he is deterred from doing. This is felt by those by whom the law is *observed.* 2. The evil of *apprehension:* or the pain which a man, who has exposed himself to punishment, feels at the thoughts of undergoing it. This is felt by those by whom the law has been *broken,* and who feel themselves in *danger* of its being executed upon them. 3. The evil of *sufferance:* or the pain which a man feels, in virtue of the punishment itself, from the time when he begins to undergo it. This is felt by those by whom the law is broken, and upon whom it comes actually to be executed. 4. The pain of sympathy, and the other *derivative* evils resulting to the persons who are in *connection* with the several classes of original sufferers just mentioned. Now of these four lots of evil, the first will be greater or less according to the nature of the act from which the party is restrained: the second and third according to the nature of the punishment which stands annexed to that offence.

XV. (*The evil of the offence being different, according to the nature of the offence, cannot be represented here.*) On the other hand, as to the evil of the offence, this will also, of course, be greater or less, according to the nature of each offence. The proportion between the one evil and the other will therefore be different in the case of each particular offence. The cases, therefore, where punishment is unprofitable on this ground, can by no other means be discovered, than by an examination of each particular offence; which is what will be the business of the body of the work.

XVI. 2. —*or in the* individual *case in question:* *by reason of* Where, although in the *ordinary state* of things, the evil resulting from the punishment is not greater than the benefit which is likely to result from the force with which it op-

erates, during the same space of time, towards the excluding the evil of the offences, yet it may have been rendered so by the influence of some *occasional circumstances.* In the number of these circumstances may be, 1. *The multitude of delinquents.* The multitude of delinquents at a particular juncture; being such as would increase, beyond the ordinary measure, the *quantum* of the second and third lots, and thereby also of a part of the fourth lot, in the evil of the punishment. 2. *The value of a delinquent's service.* The extraordinary value of the services of some one delinquent; in the case where the effect of the punishment would be to deprive the community of the benefit of those services. 3. *The displeasure of the people.* The displeasure of the *people;* that is, of an indefinite number of the members of the *same* community, in cases where (owing to the influence of some occasional incident) they happen to conceive, that the offence or the offender ought not to be punished at all, or at least ought not to be punished in the way in question. 4. *The displeasure of foreign powers.* The displeasure of foreign powers; that is, of the governing body, or a considerable number of the members of some *foreign* community or communities, with which the community in question is connected.

§ 5. *Cases where punishment is needless.*
These are,

XVII. 1. *Where the mischief is to be prevented at a cheaper rate;* as, Where the purpose of putting an end to the practice may be attained as effectually at a cheaper rate: by instruction, for instance, as well as by terror: by informing the understanding; as well as by exercising an immediate influence on the will. *By instruction.* This seems to be the case with respect to all those offences which consist in the disseminating pernicious principles in matters of *duty;* of whatever kind the duty be; whether political, or moral, or religious. And this, whether such principles be disseminated *under,* or even *without,* a sincere persuasion of their being beneficial. I say, even *without:* for though in such a case it is not instruction that can prevent the writer from endeavouring to inculcate his principles, yet it may the readers from adopting them: without which, his endeavouring to inculcate them will do no harm. In such a case, the sovereign will commonly have little need to take an active part: if it be the interest of *one* individual to inculcate principles that are pernicious, it will as surely be the interest of *other* individuals to expose them. But if the sovereign must needs take a part in the controversy, the pen is the proper weapon to combat error with, not the sword.

CHAPTER XIV. OF THE PROPORTION BETWEEN PUNISHMENTS AND OFFENCES.

I. *Recapitulation.* We have seen that the general object of all laws is to prevent mischief; that is to say, when it is worth while; but that, where there are no other means of doing this than punishment, there are four cases in which it is not worth while.

II. *Four objects of punishment.* When it *is* worth while, there are four subordinate designs or objects, which, in the course of his endeavours to compass, as far as may be, that one general object, a legislator, whose views are governed by the principle of utility, comes naturally to propose to himself.

III. 1. *1st Object—to prevent all offences.* His first, most extensive, and most eligible object, is to prevent, in as far as it is possible, and worth while, all sorts of offences whatsoever:[167] in other words, so to manage, that no offence whatsoever may be committed.

IV. 2. *2d Object—to prevent the worst.* But if a man must needs commit an offence of some kind or other, the next object is to induce him to commit an offence *less* mischievous, *rather* than one *more* mischievous: in other words, to choose always the *least* mischievous, of two offences that will either of them suit his purpose.

V. 3. *3d Object—to keep down the mischief.* When a man has resolved upon a particular offence, the next object is to dispose him to do *no more* mischief than is *necessary* to his purpose: in

other words, to do as little mischief as is consistent with the benefit he has in view.

VI. 4. *4th Object—to act at the least expense.* The last object is, whatever the mischief be, which it is proposed to prevent, to prevent it at as *cheap* a rate as possible.

VII. *Rules of proportion between punishments and offences.* Subservient to these four objects, or purposes, must be the rules or canons by which the proportion of punishments to offences is to be governed.

VIII. Rule 1. *Outweigh the profit of the offence.* The first object, it has been seen, is to prevent, in as far as it is worth while, all sorts of offences; therefore,

The value of the punishment must not be less in any case than what is sufficient to outweigh that of the profit[169] of the offence.

If it be, the offence (unless some other considerations, independent of the punishment, should intervene and operate efficaciously in the character of tutelary motives) will be sure to be committed notwithstanding: the whole lot of punishment will be thrown away: it will be altogether *inefficacious.*

IX. *The propriety of taking the strength of the temptation for a ground of abatement, no objection to this rule.* The above rule has been often objected to, on account of its seeming harshness: but this can only have happened for want of its being properly understood. The strength of the temptation, *cæteris paribus*, is as the profit of the offence: the quantum of the punishment must rise with the profit of the offence: *cæteris paribus*, it must therefore rise with the strength of the temptation. This there is no disputing. True it is, that the stronger the temptation, the less conclusive is the indication which the act of delinquency affords of the depravity of the offender's disposition. So far then as the absence of any aggravation, arising from extraordinary depravity of disposition, may operate, or at the utmost, so far as the presence of a ground of extenuation, resulting from the innocence or beneficence of the offender's disposition, can operate, the strength of the temptation may operate in abatement of the demand for punishment. But it can never operate so far as to indicate the propriety of making the punishment ineffectual, which it is sure to be when brought below the level of the apparent profit of the offence.

The partial benevolence which should prevail for the reduction of it below this level, would counteract as well those purposes which such a motive would actually have in view, as those more extensive purposes which benevolence ought to have in view: it would be cruelty not only to the public, but to the very persons in whose behalf it pleads: in its effects, I mean, however opposite in its intention. Cruelty to the public, that is cruelty to the innocent, by suffering them, for want of an adequate protection, to lie exposed to the mischief of the offence: cruelty even to the offender himself, by punishing him to no purpose, and without the chance of compassing that beneficial end, by which alone the introduction of the evil of punishment is to be justified.

X. Rule 2. *Venture more against a great offence than a small one.* But whether a given offence shall be prevented in a given degree by a given quantity of punishment, is never any thing better than a chance; for the purchasing of which, whatever punishment is employed, is so much expended in advance. However, for the sake of giving it the better chance of outweighing the profit of the offence,

The greater the mischief of the offence, the greater is the expense, which it may be worth while to be at, in the way of punishment.[175]

XI. Rule 3. *Cause the least of two offences to be preferred.* The next object is, to induce a man to choose always the least mischievous of two offences; therefore

Where two offences come in competition, the punishment for the greater offence must be sufficient to induce a man to prefer the less.

XII. Rule 4. *Punish for each particle of the mischief.* When a man has resolved upon a particular offence, the next object is, to induce him to do no more mischief than what is necessary for his purpose: therefore

The punishment should be adjusted in such manner to each particular offence, that for every part of the

mischief there may be a motive to restrain the offender from giving birth to it.[177]

XIII. Rule 5. *Punish in no degree without special reason.* The last object is, whatever mischief is guarded against, to guard against it at as cheap a rate as possible: therefore

The punishment ought in no case to be more than what is necessary to bring it into conformity with the rules here given.

XIV. Rule 6. *Attend to circumstances influencing sensibility.* It is further to be observed, that owing to the different manners and degrees in which persons under different circumstances are affected by the same exciting cause, a punishment which is the same in name will not always either really produce, or even so much as appear to others to produce, in two different persons the same degree of pain: therefore

That the quantity actually inflicted on each individual offender may correspond to the quantity intended for similar offenders in general, the several circumstances influencing sensibility ought always to be taken into account.

XV. *Comparative view of the above rules.* Of the above rules of proportion, the four first, we may perceive, serve to mark out the limits on the side of diminution; the limits *below* which a punishment ought not to be *diminished*: the fifth, the limits on the side of increase; the limits *above* which it ought not to be *increased.* The five first are calculated to serve as guides to the legislator: the sixth is calculated, in some measure, indeed, for the same purpose; but principally for guiding the judge in his endeavours to conform, on both sides, to the intentions of the legislator.

XVI. *Into the account of the value of a punishment must be taken its deficiency in point of certainty and proximity.* Let us look back a little. The first rule, in order to render it more conveniently applicable to practice, may need perhaps to be a little more particularly unfolded. It is to be observed, then, that for the sake of accuracy, it was necessary, instead of the word *quantity* to make use of the less perspicuous term *value.* For the word *quantity* will not properly include the circumstances either of certainty or proximity: circumstances which, in estimating the value of a lot of pain or pleasure, must always be taken into the account. Now, on the one hand, a lot of punishment is a lot of pain; on the other hand, the profit of an offence is a lot of pleasure, or what is equivalent to it. But the profit of the offence is commonly more *certain* than the punishment, or, what comes to the same thing, *appears* so at least to the offender. It is at any rate commonly more *immediate*. It follows, therefore, that, in order to maintain its superiority over the profit of the offence, the punishment must have its value made up in some other way, in proportion to that whereby it falls short in the two points of *certainty* and *proximity*. Now there is no other way in which it can receive any addition to its *value*, but by receiving an addition in point of magnitude. Wherever then the value of the punishment falls short, either in point of *certainty*, or of *proximity*, of that of the profit of the offence, it must receive a proportionable addition in point of *magnitude*.[180]

XVII. *Also, into the account of the mischief, and profit of the offence, the mischief and profit of other offences of the same habit.* Yet farther. To make sure of giving the value of the punishment the superiority over that of the offence, it may be necessary, in some cases, to take into the account the profit not only of the *individual* offence to which the punishment is to be annexed, but also of such *other* offences of the *same sort* as the offender is likely to have already committed without detection. This random mode of calculation, severe as it is, it will be impossible to avoid having recourse to, in certain cases: in such, to wit, in which the profit is pecuniary, the chance of detection very small, and the obnoxious act of such a nature as indicates a habit: for example, in the case of frauds against the coin. If it be *not* recurred to, the practice of committing the offence will be sure to be, upon the balance of the account, a gainful practice. That being the case, the legislator will be absolutely sure of *not* being able to suppress it, and the whole punishment that is bestowed upon it will be

thrown away. In a word (to keep to the same expressions we set out with) that whole quantity of punishment will be *inefficacious*.

XVIII. Rule 7. *Want of certainty must be made up in magnitude.* These things being considered, the three following rules may be laid down by way of supplement and explanation to Rule 1.

To enable the value of the punishment to outweigh that of the profit of the offence, it must be increased, in point of magnitude, in proportion as it falls short in point of certainty.

XIX. Rule 8. (*So also want of proximity.*) *Punishment must be further increased in point of magnitude, in proportion as it falls short in point of proximity.*

XX. Rule 9. (*For acts indicative of a habit punish as for the habit.*) *Where the act is conclusively indicative of a habit, such an increase must be given to the punishment as may enable it to outweigh the profit not only of the individual offence, but of such other like offences as are likely to have been committed with impunity by the same offender.*

XXI. *The remaining rules are of less importance.* There may be a few other circumstances or considerations which may influence, in some small degree, the demand for punishment but as the propriety of these is either not so demonstrable, or not so constant, or the application of them not so determinate as that of the foregoing, it may be doubted whether they be worth putting on a level with the others.

XXII. Rule 10. (*For the sake of quality, increase in quantity.*) *When a punishment, which in point of quality is particularly well calculated to answer its intention, cannot exist in less than a certain quantity, it may sometimes be of use, for the sake of employing it, to stretch a little beyond that quantity which, on other accounts, would be strictly necessary.*

XXIII. Rule 11. (*Particularly for a moral lesson.*) *In particular, this may sometimes be the case, where the punishment proposed is of such a nature as to be particularly well calculated to answer the purpose of a moral lesson.*[181]

XXIV. Rule 12. *Attend to circumstances which may render punishment unprofitable.* The tendency of the above considerations is to dictate an augmentation in the punishment: the following rule operates in the way of diminution. There are certain cases (it has been seen) in which, by the influence of accidental circumstances, punishment may be rendered unprofitable in the whole: in the same cases it may chance to be rendered unprofitable as to a part only. Accordingly,

In adjusting the quantum of punishment, the circumstances, by which all punishment may be rendered unprofitable, ought to be attended to.

XXV. Rule 13. *For simplicity's sake, small disproportions may be neglected.* It is to be observed, that the more various and minute any set of provisions are, the greater the chance is that any given article in them will not be borne in mind: without which, no benefit can ensue from it. Distinctions, which are more complex than what the conceptions of those whose conduct it is designed to influence can take in, will even be worse than useless. The whole system will present a confused appearance: and thus the effect, not only of the proportions established by the articles in question, but of whatever is connected with them, will be destroyed. To draw a precise line of direction in such case seems impossible. However, by way of memento, it may be of some use to subjoin the following rule.

Among provisions designed to perfect the proportion between punishments and offences, if any occur, which, by their own particular good effects, would not make up for the harm they would do by adding to the intricacy of the Code, they should be omitted. . . .

NOTES

[155]. . . A very few words . . . concerning the *ends* of punishment can scarcely be dispensed with. The immediate principal end of punishment is to control action. This action is either that of the offender, or of others: that of the offender it controls by its influence, either on his will, in which case it is said to operate in the way of *reformation;* or on his physical power, in which case it is said to operate by *disablement:* that of others it can influence no otherwise than by its influence over their wills; in which case it is said to operate in the way of *example.* A kind of collateral end, which it has a natural tendency to answer, is that of affording a pleasure or satisfaction to the party injured, where there is one, and, in general, to parties whose ill–will, whether on a self-regarding account, or on the account of sympathy or antipathy, has been excited by the offence. This purpose, as far

as it can be answered *gratis,* is a beneficial one. But no punishment ought to be allotted merely to this purpose, because (setting aside its effects in the way of control) no such pleasure is ever produced by punishment as can be equivalent to the pain. The punishment, however, which is allotted to the other purpose, ought, as far as it can be done without expense, to be accommodated to this. Satisfaction thus administered to a party injured, in the shape of a dissocial pleasure . . . , may be styled a vindictive satisfaction or compensation: as a compensation, administered in the shape of a self-regarding profit, or stock of pleasure, may be styled a lucrative one. . . . Example is the most important end of all, in proportion as the *number* of the persons under temptation to offend is to *one.*

[161]*In infancy and intoxication the case can hardly be proved to come under the rule.* Notwithstanding what is here said, the cases of infancy and intoxication (as we shall see hereafter) cannot be looked upon in practice as affording sufficient grounds for absolute impunity. But this exception in point of practice is no objection to the propriety of the rule in point of theory. The ground of the exception is neither more nor less than the difficulty there is of ascertaining the matter of fact: viz. whether at the requisite point of time the party was actually in the state in question; that is, whether a given case comes really under the rule. Suppose the matter of fact capable of being perfectly ascertained, without danger or mistake, the impropriety of punishment would be as indubitable in these cases as in any other.

[167]By *offences* I mean, at present, acts which appear to him to have a tendency to produce mischief.

[169]*Profit may be of any other kind, as well as pecuniary.* By the profit of an offence, is to be understood, not merely the pecuniary profit, but the pleasure or advantage, of whatever kind it be, which a man reaps, or expects to reap, from the gratification of the desire which prompted him to engage in the offence. . . .

[175]*Example—Incendiarism and coining.* For example, if it can ever be worth while to be at the expense of so horrible a punishment as that of burning alive, it will be more so in the view of preventing such a crime as that of murder or incendiarism, than in the view of preventing the uttering of a piece of bad money.

[177]*Example—In blows given and money stolen.* If any one have any doubt of this, let him conceive the offence to be divided into as many separate offences as there are distinguishable parcels of mischief that result from it. Let it consist, for example, in a man's giving you ten blows, or stealing from you ten shillings. If then, for giving you ten blows, he is punished no

more than for giving you five, the giving you five of these ten blows is an offence for which there is no punishment at all: which being understood, as often as a man gives you five blows, he will be sure to give you five more, since he may have the pleasure of giving you these five for nothing. In like manner, if for stealing from you ten shillings, he is punished no more than for stealing five, the stealing of the remaining five of those ten shillings is an offence for which there is no punishment at all. This rule is violated in almost every page of every body of laws I have ever seen. . . .

[180]It is for this reason, for example, that simple compensation is never looked upon as sufficient punishment for theft or robbery.

[181]*A punishment applied by way of moral lesson, what.* A punishment may be said to be calculated to answer the purpose of a moral lesson, when, by reason of the ignominy it stamps upon the offence, it is calculated to inspire the public with sentiments of aversion towards those pernicious habits and dispositions with which the offence appears to be connected; and thereby to inculcate the opposite beneficial habits and dispositions.

Example.—In simple corporal injuries. It is this, for example, if any thing, that must justify the application of so severe a punishment as the infamy of a public exhibition, hereinafter proposed, for him who lifts up his hand against woman, or against his father.

Example.—In military laws. It is partly on this principle, I suppose, that military legislators have justified to themselves the inflicting [of] death on the soldier who lifts up his hand against his superior officer.

QUESTIONS FOR DISCUSSION

1. Bentham claims that punishment is "inefficacious" in cases of insanity and intoxication. What exactly does he mean? Is he right? Why or why not?

2. Some legislators propose that we punish a bartender who sells more drinks to a person who is already drunk and plans to drive, if that person has an accident while she is driving drunk. Should utilitarians favor this proposal? What if the bartender did not know that the customer was drunk or that she planned to drive? Be sure to consider the difficulty of proving what the bartender knew. Is utilitarianism plausible in this case? (Compare Section 7.4 on strict liability.)

3. Use Bentham's rules of proportionality to determine the best punishments for (a) an arrogant car thief who believes that there is only one chance in a million that he will be punished, and that he can become rich quickly and then live off his profits; and (b) a hardened professional thief who knows and weighs the actual risks, which are much greater. Are different punishments appropriate? Why or why not?

4. Should we punish armed robbery more severely than unarmed robbery, according to utilitarianism? Why or why not? Which of Bentham's rules applies?

5. If rape were punished with death, some rapists would have no motive not to kill their victims, and they would have a motive to kill their victims if this helps them get away with it.[14] Does this show that utilitarians should oppose the death penalty for rape? Which of Bentham's rules applies?

[14]This argument is discussed in *Coker v. Georgia* 433 U.S. 485 (1977).

TWO CONCEPTS OF RULES

JOHN RAWLS

In this paper I want to show the importance of the distinction between justifying a practice[1] and justifying a particular action falling under it, and I want to explain the logical basis of this distinction and how it is possible to miss its significance. While the distinction has frequently been made,[2] and is now becoming commonplace, there remains the task of explaining the tendency either to overlook it altogether, or to fail to appreciate its importance.

To show the importance of the distinction I am going to defend utilitarianism against those objections which have traditionally been made against it in connection with punishment. . . . I hope to show that if one uses the distinction in question then one can state utilitarianism in a way which makes it a much better explication of our considered moral judgments than these traditional objections would seem to admit.[3] Thus the importance of the distinction is shown by the way it strengthens the utilitarian view regardless of whether that view is completely defensible or not. . . .

I

The subject of punishment, in the sense of attaching legal penalties to the violation of legal rules, has always been a troubling moral question.[4] The trouble about it has not been that people disagree as to whether or not punishment is justifiable. Most people have held that, freed from certain abuses, it is an acceptable institution. Only a few have rejected punishment entirely, which is rather surprising when one considers all that can be said against it. The difficulty is with the justification of punishment: various arguments for it have been given by moral philosophers, but so far none

of them has won any sort of general acceptance; no justification is without those who detest it. I hope to show that the use of the aforementioned distinction enables one to state the utilitarian view in a way which allows for the sound points of its critics.

For our purposes we may say that there are two justifications of punishment. What we may call the retributive view is that punishment is justified on the grounds that wrongdoing merits punishment. It is morally fitting that a person who does wrong should suffer in proportion to his wrongdoing. That a criminal should be punished follows from his guilt, and the severity of the appropriate punishment depends on the depravity of his act. The state of affairs where a wrongdoer suffers punishment is morally better than the state of affairs where he does not; and it is better irrespective of any of the consequences of punishing him.

What we may call the utilitarian view holds that on the principle that bygones are bygones and that only future consequences are material to present decisions, punishment is justifiable only by reference to the probable consequences of maintaining it as one of the devices of the social order. Wrongs committed in the past are, as such, not relevant considerations for deciding what to do. If punishment can be shown to promote effectively the interest of society it is justifiable, otherwise it is not.

I have stated these two competing views very roughly to make one feel the conflict between them: one feels the force of *both* arguments and one wonders how they can be reconciled. From my introductory remarks it is obvious that the resolution which I am going

John Rawls, "Two Concepts of Rules," *Philosophical Review*, vol. 64 (1955), pp. 3–13

to propose is that in this case one must distinguish between justifying a practice as a system of rules to be applied and enforced, and justifying a particular action which falls under these rules; utilitarian arguments are appropriate with regard to questions about practices, while retributive arguments fit the application of particular rules to particular cases.

We might try to get clear about this distinction by imagining how a father might answer the question of his son. Suppose the son asks, "Why was J put in jail yesterday?" The father answers, "Because he robbed the bank at B. He was duly tried and found guilty. That's why he was put in jail yesterday." But suppose the son had asked a different question, namely, "Why do people put other people in jail?" Then the father might answer, "To protect good people from bad people" or "To stop people from doing things that would make it uneasy for all of us; for otherwise we wouldn't be able to go to bed at night and sleep in peace." There are two very different questions here. One question emphasizes the proper name: it asks why J was punished rather than someone else, or it asks what he was punished for. The other question asks why we have the institution of punishment: why do people punish one another rather than, say, always forgiving one another?

Thus the father says in effect that a particular man is punished, rather than some other man, because he is guilty, and he is guilty because he broke the law (past tense). In his case the law looks back, the judge looks back, the jury looks back, and a penalty is visited upon him for something he did. That a man is to be punished, and what his punishment is to be, is settled by its being shown that he broke the law and that the law assigns that penalty for the violation of it.

On the other hand we have the institution of punishment itself, and recommend and accept various changes in it, because it is thought by the (ideal) legislator and by those to whom the law applies that, as a part of a system of law

impartially applied from case to case arising under it, it will have the consequence, in the long run, of furthering the interests of society.

One can say, then, that the judge and the legislator stand in different positions and look in different directions: one to the past, the other to the future. The justification of what the judge does, *qua* judge, sounds like the retributive view; the justification of what the (ideal) legislator does, *qua* legislator, sounds like the utilitarian view. Thus both views have a point (this is as it should be since intelligent and sensitive persons have been on both sides of the argument); and one's initial confusion disappears once one sees that these views apply to persons holding different offices with different duties, and situated differently with respect to the system of rules that make up the criminal law.[5]

One might say, however, that the utilitarian view is more fundamental since it applies to a more fundamental office, for the judge carries out the legislator's will so far as he can determine it. Once the legislator decides to have laws and to assign penalties for their violation (as things are there must be both the law and the penalty) an institution is set up which involves a retributive conception of particular cases. It is part of the concept of the criminal law as a system of rules that the application and enforcement of these rules in particular cases should be justifiable by arguments of a retributive character. The decision whether or not to use law rather than some other mechanism of social control, and the decision as to what laws to have and what penalties to assign, may be settled by utilitarian arguments; but if one decides to have laws then one has decided on something whose working in particular cases is retributive in form.[6]

The answer, then, to the confusion engendered by the two views of punishment is quite simple: one distinguishes two offices, that of the judge and that of the legislator, and one distinguishes their different stations with respect to the system of rules which make up the law; and then one notes that the different sorts of considerations which would usually be offered as reasons for what is done under the cover of these offices can be paired off with the competing justifications of punishment. One reconciles the two views by the time-honored device of making them apply to different situations.

But can it really be this simple? Well, this answer allows for the apparent intent of each side. Does a person who advocates the retributive view necessarily advocate, as an *institution*, legal machinery whose essential purpose is to set up and preserve a correspondence between moral turpitude and suffering? Surely not.[7] What retributionists have rightly insisted upon is that no man can be punished unless he is guilty, that is, unless he has broken the law. Their fundamental criticism of the utilitarian account is that, as they interpret it, it sanctions an innocent person's being punished (if one may call it that) for the benefit of society.

On the other hand, utilitarians agree that punishment is to be inflicted only for the violation of law. They regard this much as understood from the concept of punishment itself.[8] The point of the utilitarian account concerns the institution as a system of rules: utilitarianism seeks to limit its use by declaring it justifiable only if it can be shown to foster effectively the good of society. Historically it is a protest against the indiscriminate and ineffective use of the criminal law.[9] It seeks to dissuade us from assigning to penal institutions the improper, if not sacrilegious, task of matching suffering with moral turpitude. Like others, utilitarians want penal institutions designed so that, as far as humanly possible, only those who break the law run afoul of it. They hold that no official should have discretionary power to inflict penalties whenever he thinks it for the benefit of society; for on utilitarian grounds an institution granting such power could not be justified.[10]

The suggested way of reconciling the retributive and the utilitarian justifications of punishment seems to account for what both sides have wanted to say. There are, however, two further questions which arise, and I shall devote the remainder of this section to them.

First, will not a difference of opinion as to the proper criterion of just law make the proposed reconciliation unacceptable to retributionists? Will they not question whether, if the utilitarian principle is used as the criterion, it follows that those who have broken the law are guilty in a way which satisfies their demand that those punished deserve to be punished? To answer this difficulty, suppose that the rules of the criminal law are justified on utilitarian grounds (it is only for laws that meet his criterion that the utilitarian can be held responsible). Then it follows that the actions which the criminal law specifies as offenses are such that, if they were tolerated, terror and alarm would spread in society. Consequently, retributionists can only deny that those who are punished deserve to be punished if they deny that such actions are wrong. This they will not want to do.

The second question is whether utilitarianism doesn't justify too much. One pictures it as an engine of justification which, if consistently adopted, could be used to justify cruel and arbitrary institutions. Retributionists may be supposed to concede that utilitarians *intend* to reform the law and to make it more humane; that utilitarians do not *wish* to justify any such thing as punishment of the innocent; and that utilitarians may appeal to the fact that punishment presupposes guilt in the sense that by punishment one understands an institution attaching penalties to the infraction of legal rules, and therefore that it is logically absurd to suppose that utilitarians in justifying *punishment* might also have justified punishment (if we may call it that) of the innocent. The real question, however, is whether the utilitarian, in justifying punishment, hasn't used arguments which commit him to accepting the infliction of suffering on innocent persons if it is for the good of society (whether or not one calls this punishment). More generally, isn't the utilitarian committed in principle to accepting many practices which he, as a morally sensitive person, wouldn't want to accept? Retributionists are inclined to hold that there is no way to stop the utilitarian principle from justifying too much except by adding to it a principle which distributes certain rights to individuals. Then the amended criterion is not the greatest benefit of society *simpliciter*, but the greatest benefit of society subject to the constraint that no one's rights may be violated. Now while I think that the classical utilitarians proposed a criterion of this more complicated sort, I do not want to argue that point here.[11] What I want to show is that there is *another* way of preventing the utilitarian principle from justifying too much, or at least of making it much less likely to do so: namely, by stating utilitarianism in a way which accounts for the distinction between the justification of an institution and the justification of a particular action falling under it.

I begin by defining the institution of punishment as follows: a person is said to suffer punishment whenever he is legally deprived of some of the normal rights of a citizen on the ground that he has violated a rule of law, the violation having been established by trial according to the due process of law, provided that the deprivation is carried out by the recognized legal authorities of the state, that the rule of law clearly specifies both the offense and the attached penalty, that the courts construe statutes strictly, and that the statute was on the books prior to the time of the offense.[12] This definition specifies what I shall understand by punishment. The question is whether utilitarian arguments may be found to justify institutions widely different from this and such as one would find cruel and arbitrary.

This question is best answered, I think, by taking up a particular accusation. Consider the following from Carritt:

. . . the utilitarian must hold that we are justified in inflicting pain always and only to prevent worse pain or bring about greater happiness. This, then, is all we need to consider in so-called punishment, which must be purely preventive. But if some kind of very cruel crime becomes common, and none of the criminals can be caught, it might be highly expedient, as an example, to hang an innocent man, if a charge against him could be so framed that he were universally thought guilty; indeed this would only fail to be an ideal instance of utilitarian 'punishment' because the victim himself would not have been so likely as a real felon to commit such a crime in the future; in all other respects it would be perfectly deterrent and therefore felicific.[13]

Carritt is trying to show that there are occasions when a utilitarian argument would justify taking an action which would be generally condemned; and thus that utilitarianism justifies too much. But the failure of Carritt's argument lies in the fact that he makes no distinction between the justification of the general systems of rule which constitutes penal institutions and the justification of particular applications of these rules to particular cases by the various officials whose job it is to administer them. This becomes perfectly clear when one asks who the "we" are of whom Carritt speaks. Who is this who has a sort of absolute authority on particular occasions to decide that an innocent man shall be "punished" if everyone can be convinced that he is guilty? Is this person the legislator, or the judge, or the body of private citizens, or what? It is utterly crucial to know who is to decide such matters, and by what authority, for all of this must be written into the rules of the institution. Until one knows these things one doesn't know what the institution is whose justification is being challenged; and as the utilitarian principle applies to the institution one doesn't know whether it is justifiable on utilitarian grounds or not.

Once this is understood it is clear what the countermove to Carritt's argument is. One must describe more carefully what the *institution* is which his example suggests, and then ask oneself whether or not it is likely that having this institution would be for the benefit of society in the long run. One must not content oneself with the vague thought that, when it's a question of *this* case, it would be a good thing if *somebody* did something even if an innocent person were to suffer.

Try to imagine, then, an institution (which we may call "telishment") which is such that the officials set up by it have authority to arrange a trial for the condemnation of an innocent man whenever they are of the opinion that doing so would be in the best interests of society. The discretion of officials is limited, however, by the rule that they may not condemn an innocent man to undergo such an ordeal unless there is, at the time, a wave of offenses similar to that with which they charge him and telish him for. We may imagine that the officials having the discretionary authority are the judges of the higher courts in consultation with the chief of police, the minister of justice, and a committee of the legislature.

Once one realizes that one is involved in setting up an *institution*, one sees that the hazards are very great. For example, what check is there on the officials? How is one to tell whether or not their actions are authorized? How is one to limit the risks involved in allowing such systematic deception? How is one to avoid giving anything short of complete discretion to the authorities to telish anyone they like? In addition to these considerations, it is obvious that people will come to have a very different attitude towards their penal system when telishment is adjoined to it. They will be uncertain as to whether a convicted man has been punished or telished. They will wonder whether or not they should feel sorry for him. They will wonder whether the same fate won't at any time fall on them. If one pictures how such an institution would actually work, and the enormous risks involved in it, it seems clear that it would serve no useful purpose.

A utilitarian justification for this institution is most unlikely.

It happens in general that as one drops off the defining features of punishment one ends up with an institution whose utilitarian justification is highly doubtful. One reason for this is that punishment works like a kind of price system: by altering the prices one has to pay for the performance of actions it supplies a motive for avoiding some actions and doing others. The defining features are essential if punishment is to work in this way; so that an institution which lacks these features, e.g., an institution which is set up to "punish" the innocent, is likely to have about as much point as a price system (if one may call it that) where the prices of things change at random from day to day and one learns the price of something after one has agreed to buy it.[14]

If one is careful to apply the utilitarian principle to the institution which is to authorize particular actions, then there is *less* danger of its justifying too much. Carritt's example gains plausibility by its indefiniteness and by its concentration on the particular case. His argument will only hold if it can be shown that there are utilitarian arguments which justify an institution whose publicly ascertainable offices and powers are such as to permit officials to exercise that kind of discretion in particular cases. But the requirement of having to build the arbitrary features of the particular decision into the institutional practice makes the justification much less likely to go through. . . .

NOTES

[1] I use the word "practice" throughout as a sort of technical term meaning any form of activity specified by a system of rules which defines offices, roles, moves, penalties, defenses, and so on, and which gives the activity its structure. As examples one may think of games and rituals, trials and parliaments.

[2] The distinction is central to Hume's discussion of justice in *A Treatise of Human Nature*, bk. III, pt. II, esp. secs. 2–4. It is clearly stated by John Austin in the second lecture of *Lectures on Jurisprudence* (4th ed.; London, 1873), I, 116ff. (1st ed., 1832). Also it may be argued that J. S. Mill took it for granted in *Utilitarianism*;

on this point cf. J. O. Urmson, "The Interpretation of the Moral Philosophy of J. S. Mill," *Philosophical Quarterly*, vol. III (1953). In addition to the arguments given by Urmson there are several clear statements of the distinction in *A System of Logic* (8th ed.; London, 1872), bk. VI, ch. xii pars. 2, 3, 7. The distinction is fundamental to J. D. Mabbott's important paper, "Punishment," *Mind*, n.s., vol. XLVIII (April, 1939). More recently the distinction has been stated with particular emphasis by S. E. Toulmin in *The Place of Reason in Ethics* (Cambridge, 1950), see esp. ch. xi, where it plays a major part in his account of moral reasoning. Toulmin doesn't explain the basis of the distinction, nor how one might overlook its importance, as I try to in this paper, and in my review of his book (*Philosophical Review*, vol. LX [October, 1951]), as some of my criticisms show, I failed to understand the force of it. See also, H. D. Aiken, "The Levels of Moral Discourse," *Ethics*, vol. LXII (1952), A. M. Quinton, "Punishment," *Analysis*, vol. XIV (June, 1954), and P. H. Nowell-Smith, *Ethics* (London, 1954), pp. 236–239, 271–273.

³On the concept of explication see the author's paper *Philosophical Review*, vol. LX (April, 1951).

⁴While this paper was being revised, Quinton's appeared; footnote 2 supra. There are several respects in which my remarks are similar to his. . . .

⁵Note the fact that different sorts of arguments are suited to different offices. One way of taking the differences between ethical theories is to regard them as accounts of the reasons expected in different offices.

⁶In this connection see Mabbott, *op. cit.*, pp. 163–64.

⁷On this point see Sir David Ross, *The Right and the Good* (Oxford, 1930), pp. 57–60.

⁸See Hobbes's definition of punishment in *Leviathan*, ch. xxviii; and Bentham's definition in *The Principle of Morals and Legislation*, ch. xii, par. 36, ch. xv, par. 28, and in *The Rationale of Punishment*, (London, 1830), bk. I, ch. i. They could agree with Bradley that: "Punishment is punishment only when it is deserved. We pay the penalty, because we owe it, and for no other reason; and if punishment is inflicted for any other reason whatever than because it is merited by wrong, it is a gross immorality, a crying injustice, an abominable crime, and not what it pretends to be." *Ethical Studies* (2nd ed.; Oxford, 1927), pp. 26–27. Certainly by definition it isn't what it pretends to be. The innocent can only be punished by mistake; deliberate "punishment" of the innocent necessarily involves fraud.

⁹Cf. Leon Radzinowicz, *A History of English Criminal Law: The Movement for Reform 1750–1833* (London, 1948), esp. ch. xi on Bentham.

¹⁰Bentham discusses how corresponding to a punitory provision of a criminal law there is another provision which stands to it as an antagonist and which needs a name as much as the punitory. He calls it, as one might expect, the *anaetiosostic*, and of it he says: "The punishment of guilt is the object of the former one: the preservation of innocence that of the latter." In the same connection he asserts that it is never thought fit to give the judge the option of deciding whether a thief (that is, a person whom he believes to be a thief, for the judge's belief is what the question must always turn upon) should hang or not, and so the law writes the provision: "The judge shall not cause a thief to be hanged unless he have been duly convicted and sentenced in course of law" (*The Limits of Jurisprudence Defined*, ed. C. W. Everett [New York, 1945], pp. 238–239).

¹¹By the classical utilitarians I understand Hobbes, Hume, Bentham, J.S. Mill and Sidgwick.

¹²All these features of punishment are mentioned by Hobbes; cf. *Leviathan*, ch. xxviii.

¹³*Ethical and Political Thinking* (Oxford, 1947), p. 65.

¹⁴The analogy with the price system suggests an answer to the question how utilitarian considerations insure that punishment is proportional to the offense. It is interesting to note that Sir David Ross, after making the distinction between justifying a penal law and justifying a particular application of it, and after stating that utilitarian considerations have a large place in determining the former, still holds back from accepting the utilitarian justification of punishment on the grounds that justice requires that punishment be proportional to the offense, and that utilitarianism is unable to account for this. Cf. *The Right and the Good*, pp. 61–62. I do not claim that utilitarianism can account for this requirement as Sir David might wish, but it happens, nevertheless, that if utilitarian considerations are followed penalties will be proportional to offenses in this sense: the order of offenses according to seriousness can be paired off with the order of penalties according to severity. Also the absolute level of penalties will be as low as possible. This follows from the assumption that people are rational (i.e., that they are able to take into account the "prices" the state puts on actions), the utilitarian rule that a penal system should provide a motive for preferring the less serious offense, and the principle that punishment as such is an evil. All this was carefully worked out by Bentham in *The Principles of Morals and Legislation*, chs. xiii–xv.

QUESTIONS FOR DISCUSSION

1. In the rule utilitarianism that Rawls describes, retributivism applies to judges and utilitarianism applies to legislators. Is this right? May judges ever consider the consequences of their particular decisions? (See Posner in Section 2.1.) Should legislators consider only consequences when they decide the appropriate punishments for crimes?

2. Does rule utilitarianism give an adequate explanation of why we should not punish innocent people? Why or why not?

3. Suppose a terrorist is convicted of bombing the World Trade Center, but other members of his group threaten to bomb another building for each month that he spends in prison. They show that they are serious by bombing another building. Should the terrorist be kept in prison, according to an act utilitarian? According to a rule utilitarian? According to you? Why or why not?

4. After a six-year study, Peter Greenwood of the Rand Corporation concluded, "Shorter sentences for most robbers and longer terms for the active few could reduce the robbery rate by 15 percent while reducing the number of jailed robbers by 5 percent."[15] Who would get longer sentences? "High-rate offenders," defined as those who fit four or more of seven variables: "imprisonment for more than half the two years previous to the current arrest; a previous conviction for the same crime; a conviction before the age of 16; commitment to a juvenile facility; heroin or barbiturate use in the preceding two years; heroin or barbiturate use as a juvenile; and unemployment for more than half of the preceding two years." Would act utilitarians justify longer sentences for high-rate offenders? Would rule utilitarians? Do you think that this proposal is fair? Why or why not?

5. Some politicians support a recent proposal popularly known as "three strikes and you're out." In one form, anyone convicted of three felonies (or three violent felonies or three felonies of the same kind) would receive a sentence of life in prison without chance of parole. Would act utilitarians support this proposal? Would rule utilitarians? Would you? Why or why not?

6. Some advocacy groups have argued that severe punishments for rape lead juries to acquit people who committed rape. Assuming this is true, would utilitarians favor less severe punishments for rape? Would you? Why or why not?

SUGGESTIONS FOR FURTHER READING

A clear overview of arguments for and against utilitarian theories of punishment can be found in Igor Primoratz, *Justifying Legal Punishment* (Atlantic Highlands, New Jersey:

[15]The *New York Times*, October 6, 1982, p. A16.

Humanities Press, 1989), Chapters 2–3. Several essays for and against rule utilitarianism and utilitarian theories of punishment are collected in *Contemporary Utilitarianism*, ed. Michael Bayles (Garden City, New York: Doubleday, 1968). A version of rule utilitarianism is defended by Richard Brandt in *Ethical Theory* (Englewood Cliffs, New Jersey: Prentice-Hall, 1959), with applications to punishment in Chapter 19. The most detailed discussion of rule utilitarianism is David Lyons, *Forms and Limits of Utilitarianism* (Oxford: Clarendon Press, 1965). A recent defense of an act utilitarian theory of punishment can be found in J.J.C. Smart, "Utilitarianism and Punishment," *Israel Law Review*, vol. 25, nos. 3–4 (Summer–Autumn 1991), pp. 360–75.

RETRIBUTIVISMS **6.4**

INTRODUCTION

The most popular alternative to utilitarianism is retributivism. This theory is often misunderstood. Many retributivists themselves describe retributivism simply as the view that the government ought to take "an eye for an eye."[16] But they usually do not really favor poking out eyes. Their opponents often associate retributivism with hatred and desire for revenge for its own sake. But retributivism need not be based simply on emotions or desires. Retributivism is a complex and sophisticated theory of punishment.

The distinguishing feature of retributivism is its focus on the past and on acts by the punished person. It is guilt for a past act that retributivists use to answer the main questions about punishment. Why should we punish? Because the punished person is guilty. Whom should we punish? Those and only those who are guilty. How much should we punish? In proportion to the person's guilt.

These answers still allow numerous variations within the general framework of retributivism. There are many kinds of guilt and many possible relations between guilt and punishment.

One important distinction is between legal guilt and moral guilt. Most retributivists base punishment on moral guilt, but some base it on legal guilt. J. D. Mabbott is in the latter camp. He argues, first, that someone who does an act that is morally wrong but not legally wrong should not be punished:

> It takes two to make a punishment, and for a moral or social wrong I can find no punisher. . . . If I see a man ill-treating a horse in a country where cruelty to animals is not a legal offence, and I say to him, "I shall now punish you," he will reply, rightly, "What has it to do with you? Who made you a judge and a ruler over me?"[17]

Mabbott also argues that someone who does an act that is legally wrong but not morally wrong should (or may) be punished:

> I was myself for some time disciplinary officer of a college whose rules included a rule compelling attendance at chapel. Many of those who broke this rule broke it on principle. I punished them. I certainly did not want to reform them; I respected

---

[16]Exodus 21:24. This formula is supposed to have originally been meant to stop private avengers from taking more than an eye for an eye.

[17]J. D. Mabbott, "Punishment", *Mind* vol. 48 (1939), pp. 150–67 at 154. The following quotation is from p. 155.

their characters and their views. I certainly did not want to drive others into chapel through fear of penalties. Nor did I think there had been a wrong which merited retribution. I wished I could have believed that I would have done the same myself. My position was clear. They had broken a rule; they knew it and I knew it. Nothing more was necessary to make punishment proper.

Although this example involves institutional rules rather than laws, Mabbott's point can easily be extended to the wider legal arena. If someone commits an act of civil disobedience (see Section 3.2), such as by violating a law compelling African–Americans to sit at the back of the bus, Mabbott would claim that the person still deserves punishment because he broke the law, even if his act is not morally wrong at all, not even prima facie. This legalistic retributivism might not be obviously right, but it is also not obviously wrong, so it deserves serious consideration.

Nonetheless, most retributivists base punishment on *moral* guilt. This moralistic form of retributivism suggests that people should not be punished when they perform acts that are illegal but not immoral and that people should be punished when they perform acts that are immoral but not illegal. Also, if morality concerns our mental lives, as is often assumed, then a person should be punished "in proportion to his *inner wickedness*," (p. 703 in this section) in the words of Immanuel Kant, a German philosopher (1724–1804). Inner wickedness is absent when a person honestly and reasonably believes that his acts are harmless or justified. This is supposed to explain why reasonable mistakes preclude punishment. A focus on moral guilt also seems natural because the basic question asks when punishment is morally permitted, not when it is legally permitted.

Whichever kind of guilt one focuses on, there are still several possible relations between guilt and punishment.[18] These relations can be presented as answers to the question: who should be punished?

The most common claim is that guilt is necessary in order for punishment to be permitted. In other words,

1. It is always morally wrong for the state to punish a person who is not guilty.

This is usually called "minimal retributivism." (1) is the common claim that we already met as an objection to utilitarianism. It rules out punishing the innocent.

A much stronger claim is that guilt is sufficient in order for punishment to be required. In other words,

2. It is always morally wrong for the state not to punish a person who is guilty.

This claim can be called "maximal retributivism." Instead of ruling out punishment, it rules out mercy. For example, suppose that a car thief is paralyzed in an

---

[18]The following trichotomy is derived from J. L. Mackie, "Morality and the Retributive Emotions" in his *Persons and Values* (Oxford: Clarendon Press, 1985), pp. 206–219.

accident while trying to escape. He is unable to steal cars again, and his paralysis is as likely to deter car thefts as any punishment. But he has not yet been punished, since his accident does not fit the definition of punishment. So maximal retributivism implies that this person still has to be punished, because he is guilty of stealing the car, even if punishing him would have no good effects.

Between minimal and maximal retributivism lies the claim that guilt is sufficient in order for punishment to be permitted. In other words,

3. It is never morally wrong for the state to punish a person who is guilty.

This claim can be called "permissive retributivism." It is suggested when people say that a criminal owes "a debt to society." For most debts, the person to whom the debt is owed is permitted to forgive the debt and also is permitted to demand payment. If punishment is fully analogous, then society is permitted to punish the guilty but is also permitted to show mercy and pardon. Because permissive retributivism does not rule out pardons, it is different from maximal retributivism. Permissive retributivism also differs from minimal retributivism, because permissive retributivism says that punishing the guilty is always morally permitted, regardless of whether it does any good, whereas minimal retributivism is compatible with the claim that punishing the guilty is sometimes morally wrong, possibly when it does more harm than good.

Maximal, minimal, and permissive retributivism represent only three of the many possible relations between guilt and punishment. Some others fall in the empty boxes of the following diagram:

	One who is guilty	**One who is not guilty**
It is always wrong to punish		(1) minimal retributivism
It is always wrong not to punish	(2) maximal retributivism	
It is never wrong to punish	(3) permissive retributivism	
It is never wrong not to punish		

It would be fascinating to explore these other possibilities, but we will focus on minimal, maximal, and permissive retributivism, since these have been and are the most common forms of retributivism.

These versions of retributivism answer the question: who should be punished? There is also a similar array of answers to the question, how much should we punish?

(1*) It is morally wrong for the state to punish a person more than is proportionate to that person's guilt.

(2*) It is morally wrong for the state to punish a person less than is proportionate to that person's guilt.

(3*) It is not morally wrong for the state to punish a person as much as is proportionate to that person's guilt.

Notice that minimal retributivism (1) can be seen as an instance of (1*) where the person has no moral guilt at all. Similarly, maximal retributivism (2) and permissive retributivism (3) can be seen as instances of (2*) and (3*) where the person has some moral guilt.

Why should any of these retributivist claims be accepted? Many arguments have been given for them, but some of these arguments are better than others, and different arguments support different claims within retributivism.

MINIMAL RETRIBUTIVISM

Let's begin with minimal retributivism, the claim that it is always wrong to punish someone who is not guilty. Some philosophers argue that this is true by the very definition of punishment, since hanging or imprisoning someone does not count as punishment if the person is not guilty. But that is not right. Punishment is not limited to actual offenders. It is limited to "supposed" offenders, as in condition (iii) of Hart's definition (see Section 6.1). If someone is falsely believed to be guilty, either by the person who does the punishing or by society in general, then hanging or imprisoning would count as punishment. Furthermore, even if nothing we did to an innocent person would count as punishment, this would not settle the normative issue of whether the kinds of treatment that usually count as punishment should be used against people who are not guilty. Since it is this treatment that minimal retributivists want to oppose, the definition of punishment cannot be used to support minimal retributivism.

A better argument for minimal retributivism comes from Kant. In his general moral theory, Kant argued roughly that murder, theft, lying, and promise breaking are all morally wrong when and because they involve treating a person as a means only. Kant then applies this general moral theory to punishment:

> Punishment by a court . . . can never be inflicted merely as a means to promote some other good for the criminal himself or for civil society. It must always be inflicted upon him only *because he has committed a crime.* For a man can never be treated merely as a means to the purposes of another. (p. 702)

There are many disputes about exactly what Kant means by treating a person as a *means* and *merely* as a means. One natural interpretation seems to make sense in the sheriff example (discussed in Section 6.3). If the state hangs an innocent person in order to stop a series of lynchings, then the state is using the innocent victim as a means to achieve the state's goal of stopping the riots. The state is using the victim *merely* as a means because the state disregards the victim's own goals and the victim's own ability to decide whether or not to commit a crime. For these reasons, to punish an innocent person is always to treat the victim as a means only, which is the very essence of immorality, according to Kant.

This theory seems plausible to most people, but utilitarians have a response. Since utilitarians count everyone's good, they count the victim's good, even when it is outweighed by the good of others. This suggests that the victim is not really treated *merely* as a means. Utilitarians can also respond that, when hanging an innocent person really is necessary and sufficient to prevent many lynchings, then to refuse to do so would be to disregard the welfare of those who would be lynched, so this refusal itself might treat these other people merely as means.

Kantians would claim that such utilitarians misunderstand what it is to treat someone merely as a means. But then Kantians owe us a better account of when a person is treated merely as a means. This issue takes us deep into moral theory, so it cannot be resolved here. In any case, the point of minimal retributivism is to rule out punishing one person solely for the sake of others, so minimal retributivism will be attractive to anyone who thinks that individual rights should not be sacrificed in this way to social goals.

None of this supports maximal retributivism or even permissive retributivism. Minimal retributivism tells us when we *may not* punish, but permissive retributivism tells us when we *may* punish, and maximal retributivism tells us when we *must* punish. Minimal retributivism does not imply these other claims, so they require separate arguments.

PERMISSIVE RETRIBUTIVISM

The most common argument for permissive retributivism is based on choice. Since the criminal chooses to commit the crime, and the punishment is known, the criminal chooses to be punished. But a person cannot be wronged by giving him what he himself chooses. So punishment of the guilty can't be wrong. The problem with this argument is that criminals do *not* choose to be punished. When people choose to drive their cars, they know that they might have an accident, but this does not mean that they choose to have an accident. Instead, they do their best to avoid an accident. Analogously, criminals accept the risk of being punished, but they do not choose to be punished, as is shown by their efforts to avoid punishment.

Permissive retributivists often respond that what matters is not real choice but some kind of hypothetical choice. Jeffrie Murphy, a philosophy professor at Arizona State University, presents this argument forcefully:

> Respecting a man's autonomy, at least on one view, is not respecting what he now happens, however uncritically, to desire; rather it is to respect what he desires (or would desire) as a rational man. . . . On this theory, a man may be said to rationally will X if, and only if, X is called for by a rule that the man would necessarily have adopted in the original position of choice—i.e., in a position of coming together with others to pick rules for the regulation of their mutual affairs. . . . Thus, I can be said to will my own punishment if, in an antecedent position of choice, I and my fellows would have chosen institutions of punishment as the most rational means of dealing with those who might break the other generally

beneficial rules that had been adopted. . . . Coercion and autonomy are thus reconciled, at least apparently.[19]

On this view, to punish a criminal is to respect her true autonomy and her rational will, so it cannot be wrong to the criminal.

This hypothetical theory faces several problems. First, it is hard to project what criminals would choose if they were rational and impartial. Under such circumstances, they might not even be criminals. Second, permissions are granted only by actual choice and not by hypothetical choice. If I choose to enter a boxing match with you, then it is not wrong for you to hit me. But that does not mean that you are permitted to hit me when I do not actually consent to the match, even if you can show that I would enter the match if I were rational and impartial. Third, even if a criminal did actually consent to be punished, this would not be enough by itself to show that it cannot ever be wrong to punish that criminal. Consent and guilt might show that punishment cannot do a wrong *to the criminal,* but what about other people? If a democratic government chooses to punish the criminal, everyone in that society might consent indirectly to the punishment. This might seem to show that nobody else in the society is wronged. But that does not follow. A punishment can be wrong if it harms too many innocent people. For example, suppose that a single parent with five children loses her job and then, out of frustration with her financial situation, shoplifts some new clothes for herself. She later gets a new job and regrets what she did, but then the police track her down, and she is convicted of theft. The normal punishment is one year in prison, but this punishment would not hurt her alone. Her children would suffer a great deal as well, although they are innocent. If her crime is minor enough, and the harm to her children would be large enough, then some would claim that punishing the mother would be unfair to the children. If so, it is sometimes wrong to punish a guilty person. This claim might be questioned, but, until it is refuted, the argument for permissive retributivism is not conclusive.

MAXIMAL RETRIBUTIVISM

Even if minimal and permissive retributivism are accepted, it takes more than that to establish maximal retributivism. Many strange things have been said to support maximal retributivism. Kant said that the state has to punish the guilty in order that "blood guilt does not cling to the people" (p. 703 in this section). But this can't be right, if taken literally. Neither the people nor the judge nor the jury becomes guilty of car theft just because a car thief is shown mercy or let off on a technicality. Similarly, F. H. Bradley, a philosophy professor at Oxford (1846–1924), claimed that punishment is required in order that "we annihilate the wrong."[20] This is false, if taken literally. Once a murder or rape has been committed, there is no way to remake the world as if it never happened. The wrongful will of the

---

[19]Jeffrie G. Murphy, "Marxism and Retribution," *Philosophy and Public Affairs* vol. 2 (1973), pp. 218–243. Murphy's "original position of choice" is related to Rawls' theory of justice described in Section 5.2.

[20]F. H. Bradley, *Ethical Studies,* 2nd ed. (Oxford; Clarendon Press, 1927), p. 28.

criminal can be changed in some cases, but many criminals leave prison even more bent on crime, and that does not show that their punishment was pointless. Finally, G. W. F. Hegel, a German idealist (1770–1831), said, "punishment is regarded as containing the criminal's right and hence by being punished he is honoured as a rational being."[21] However, a right to be punished would be a very strange right, since most criminals would choose not to exercise that right, but they are not given that choice. It also does not seem much of an "honor" to be thrown in prison or executed. These pronouncements might be more plausible when interpreted more charitably, but that remains to be shown.

Other common claims on behalf of maximal retributivism make more sense. For example, it seems that criminals deserve punishment and that the state must give people what they deserve. Normally it would be wrong to refuse to give a prize to the winner who deserves it. But this is only because the winner demands the prize. If the winner does not want the prize, then it does not seem wrong to give him what he wants: nothing. And criminals, of course, usually do not demand what they deserve, namely, punishment. So it is still not clear why it is always wrong not to punish a criminal, as maximal retributivism claims.

It is also common to say that punishment expresses society's disapproval of crime, and not to express disapproval would be to approve, but society must not approve of crime, so society must punish. But this does not follow. Even though punishment is one way to express disapproval, it is not clear that punishment is always the best way. It is also not clear that we should always give in to our desire to express outrage. Maximal retributivism implies that criminals must be punished even if punishment would lead to more crime, but that would lead to more outrage. Why would it be more important to express our outrage in every case than to reduce the number of cases that create outrage?

The most general argument for maximal retributivism is based on equality. Kant wrote, "But what kind and what amount of punishment is it that public justice makes its principle and measure? None other than the principle of equality (in the position of the needle on the scale of justice), to incline no more to one side than to the other" (p. 702 in this section). At other places, Kant makes the same point in terms of "proportionality" or "equilibrium." All of these terms refer to relations between two "sides," but *which* two "sides"? What exactly has to be equal to what?

The first version of this argument requires equality between the punishment for one person and the punishment for another person: "the retributive theory . . . is a particular application of a general principle of justice, namely, that equals should be treated equally and unequals unequally."[22] This seemingly simple principle applies in many ways. Why is it wrong to punish the innocent? Because we do not punish all innocent people, so, if we punish some innocent people and not others, then we are treating the punished ones differently from the unpunished

---

[21] G. W. F. Hegel, *The Philosophy of Right*, trans. T. M. Knox (London; Oxford University Press, 1969), section 100.

[22] H. J. McCloskey, "A Non-Utilitarian Approach to Punishment," pp. 249–263 at 260.

ones, even though both groups are equally innocent. Furthermore, we do punish guilty people, so, if we also punish some innocent people, then we are treating those innocent people the same as guilty people, even though the two groups are different. This is supposed to support minimal retributivism. The same principles can be used to support maximal retributivism. Why is it wrong not to punish the guilty? Because we do punish some guilty people, so, if we punish some guilty people and not others, then we are treating the punished ones differently from the unpunished ones, even though both groups are equally guilty. Furthermore, we do not punish innocent people, so, if we also do not punish some guilty people, then we are treating those guilty people the same as innocent people, even though they are different. Thus, the only way to ensure equality is to punish all guilty people and no innocent people. These arguments about whom we should punish can also be extended to determine how much we should punish.

All such arguments assume that like cases should be treated alike and different cases should be treated differently. These principles might seem plausible in the abstract, but it is hard to tell when cases really are alike or different in relevant respects. Recall the car thief who was paralyzed in an accident while trying to get away. Or consider a drug dealer who is not punished in order to get him to testify against his supplier. These people are not like other guilty people who are not paralyzed and do not testify, so we do not fail to treat like cases alike when we do not punish them. We do fail to treat all guilty people the same, but opponents of maximal retributivism simply claim that not all guilty people are similar in *all* relevant respects. Even if two people are guilty of the same crime with the same degree of responsibility, these are not the only factors relevant to punishment, according to non-retributivists. If maximal retributivists claim otherwise, they need a separate argument to show which likenesses matter. (See also Section 5.1.)

A second argument from equality refers instead to equality or proportionality between the harm caused by the crime and the harm caused by the punishment for the crime. In the case of a "verbal injury," for example, Kant says that the punishment should harm the offender in a degree (and manner) similar to "the outrage he has done to someone's love of honor" (p. 702 in this section). Kant also applies this principle when he insists that death is the only proportionate punishment for criminals who cause death by murdering.

This kind of theory can be complicated so as to account for degrees of responsibility as well as degrees of harm. Robert Nozick, for example, argues that, "The punishment deserved depends on the magnitude H of the wrongness of the act, and the person's degree of responsibility r for the act, and is equal in magnitude to their product, $r \times H$."[25] The degree of responsibility is supposed to vary from 0 to 1, so someone who is only partly responsible for a larger harm should be punished the same amount as someone who is fully responsible for a smaller harm. Regardless of such refinements, this version of retributivism runs into serious problems. One problem is that many crimes cause no harm at all. For example, suppose that a would-be assassin aims at the president and pulls the trigger of

---

[25]Robert Nozick, *Philosophical Explanations* (Cambridge: Harvard University Press, 1981), p. 363. Nozick is a philosophy professor at Harvard University. His general theory of justice is discussed in Section 5.2.

his gun. Fortunately, his gun has no bullets and no firing mechanism. Nobody is harmed or even in danger. Yet punishment still seems justified. So the purpose of punishment cannot be to counterbalance the harm caused by the crime. The same problem arises for many more crimes, such as conspiracy, solicitation, and failure to report a bribe (discussed by Davis in the reading in this section).

Maximal retributivists can respond that many crimes still do cause harm, and in these cases criminals should never be punished less than the harm that they cause to their victims. Most people do find it inadequate to punish a criminal only a little when the criminal caused a great harm to the victim, assuming the criminal was fully responsible. We still need to know *why* this is inadequate, but this limited claim at least seems plausible. However, there are still problems. Even for crimes that cause harm, there can sometimes be reasons not to inflict a punishment as great as the harm. Suppose that a single parent of five loses his job, becomes depressed, gets drunk, and assaults a stranger in the bar. In the morning, he feels great remorse, so he joins Alcoholics Anonymous and finds a new and better job. Although his victim was harmed, proportionately punishing this father would do almost no good and would lead to greater harm to his children, who are innocent. It is hard to see why the state is always required to cause this greater harm in order to avenge a smaller harm. Furthermore, this position seems *ad hoc* unless it is generally true that punishments for crimes should be proportional to the harms caused by the crimes. But this is not always true. If a thief steals $100 from a rich person, this will cause much less harm than if another thief steals the same amount from a poor person. Still, the latter thief does not deserve more punishment, nor the former less. So even when crimes do cause harm, their punishments need not always equal the harms they cause.

A third and final argument from equality focuses not on harms to victims but on benefits to criminals. Virtuous people should be happy, and vicious people should be unhappy. This is not the way things are when criminals benefit from their crimes. So, some argue, criminals should be harmed enough to make them as bad off as their acts were bad. This seems to be what Kant means when he says that "justice has been done" when punishment restores "the proportion between welfare and well-doing."[24]

There are serious problems for this position. One is that many criminals "may well be persons who are more sinned against than sinning, and may be, quite apart from our intervention [in punishment], already enjoying less happiness than a perfectly fair distribution would allow them."[25] Imagine a very good person who has spent her life helping others. Then she steals a car. The car is worth something, but she was so poor that she still remains far below the overall level of well-being of many people who are morally far worse than she. To punish her would not move her overall level of well-being closer to the level that her overall virtue deserves.

One might respond that, even if we cannot make happiness match virtue, punishment can still bring the criminal back to the level that he or she was at before

---

[24]Immanuel Kant, *Critique of Practical Reason*, trans. L. W. Beck (New York: Bobbs Merrill, 1956), Part 1, book 1, ch. 2, p. 63.

[25]W. D. Ross, *The Right and the Good* (Oxford; Oxford University Press, 1930), p. 59.

the crime. This will be accomplished if the punishment inflicts enough harm to counterbalance what the criminal gains from the crime. But this view also runs into problems. If the punishment is equal only to the gain of the crime, then the punishment will not be enough to deter future crimes, since criminals will usually believe that they have a good chance of not being punished at all, so crime will be in their expected interest. (See Section 6.3 on deterrence.) Moreover, some criminals seem to gain little, if anything, from their crimes. Imagine that a man loves his wife, but she threatens to leave, and he becomes so enraged that he kills her. He might suffer tremendous remorse when he recalls how much he really did love her. And he might not gain anything to compensate for his loss. But he still deserves to be punished. So it does not seem that punishment must always be equal to the gain by the criminal. Maximal retributivists might respond that the punishment still must never be less than the gain by the criminal, but it is hard to see any argument for this in the absence of the more general principle that requires punishment to be neither more nor less than the criminal's gain.

All of these objections depend on construing the criminal's gain in terms of material and psychological goods. If retributivists shift to a different conception of the criminal's gain, then they might be able to hold on to their claim that punishment must equal the criminal's gain. One such conception was suggested by Herbert Morris, a philosophy and law professor at the University of California, Los Angeles, when he wrote:

> . . . it is just to punish those who have violated the rules and caused the unfair distribution of benefits and burdens. A person who violates the rules has something others have—the benefits of the system—but by renouncing what others have assumed, the burdens of self-restraint, he has acquired an unfair advantage. Matters are not even until this advantage is in some way erased. Another way of putting it is that he owes something to others, for he has something that does not rightfully belong to him. Justice—that is punishing such individuals—restores the equilibrium of benefits and burdens by taking from the individual what he owes, that is, exacting the debt.[26]

The crucial point is that, even if the criminal gains neither material goods nor happiness from the crime, the criminal still gains the advantage of renouncing "the burdens of self-restraint." That is what enables Morris to respond to the above objections. Morris' theory can also explain why we should not punish the innocent: they restrained themselves and did not unfairly gain any advantage over others. And Morris can explain why we should not punish people who break laws but have excuses, such as that they were coerced or reasonably mistaken or insane: such people did not renounce the burden of self-restraint.

This kind of theory is developed and defended by Michael Davis, a philosopher at the Center for the Study of Ethics in the Professions at the Illinois Institute of Technology. Davis shows how Morris' approach can be used to answer the ques-

---

[26]Herbert Morris, "Persons and Punishment," *The Monist* vol. 52, 4 (October 1968), pp. 475–501 at 478. It is not clear whether Morris is arguing for permissive retributivism or for maximal retributivism, but the main issue here is whether Morris' argument can support maximal retributivism.

tion: how much should we punish? Retributivists often answer this question by arranging crimes in order of wickedness, arranging punishments in order of severity, and then aligning the lists so that the worst crimes get the most punishment. Here is a short example of such a list:

Crimes	Punishments
first degree murder	death
second degree murder	15–20 years in prison
rape	10–15 years in prison
armed robbery	5–10 years in prison
unarmed robbery	3–5 years in prison

This simplistic example shows that just setting up lists is not enough by itself. One needs some reason for the order of the crimes on the list. One must also determine which punishment to put at the top of the list. Why put death instead of life imprisonment or 30 years? Then one must determine the separation between punishments. Why put 15–20, 10–15, 5–10 and 3–5 years on the list instead of 20–25, 5–10, 3–4, and 1–2 years?

Davis answers these questions by postulating a market for licenses to commit crimes. No government would ever really sell such licenses, but this hypothetical model is still supposed to reveal the amount of unfair advantage gained in particular crimes. Since punishment should be proportionate to unfair advantage, according to Davis, the punishment for each crime should equal the price that one would be willing to pay for a license to commit that crime. Davis does not claim to be able to tell exactly how much each license would cost, and it is not clear how to apply his theory to some examples. Nonetheless, Davis at least provides an outline of a method for assigning punishments to particular crimes. Whether his method is fully defensible remains to be seen.

ON THE RIGHT TO PUNISH

IMMANUEL KANT

The *right to punish* is the right a ruler has against a subject to inflict pain upon him because of his having committed a crime. The head of a state can therefore not be punished; one can only withdraw from his dominion. A transgression of public law that makes someone who

Immanuel Kant, "On the Right to Punish," in *The Metaphysics of Morals* (Cambridge: Cambridge University Press, 1991), pp. 140–144

commits it unfit to be a citizen is called a *crime* simply (*crimen*) but is also called a public crime (*crimen publicum*); so the first (private crime) is brought before a civil court, the latter before a criminal court. *Embezzlement*, that is, misappropriation of money or goods entrusted for commerce, and fraud in buying and selling, when committed in such a way that the other could detect it, are private crimes. On the other hand, counterfeiting money or bills of exchange, theft and robbery, and the like are public crimes, because they endanger the commonwealth and not just an individual person. They can be divided into crimes arising from a *mean* character (*idolis abiectae*) and crimes arising from a *violent* character (*indolis violentae*).

Punishment by a court (*poena forensis*)—this is distinct from *natural punishment* (*poena naturalis*), in which vice punishes itself and which the legislator does not take into account—can never be inflicted merely as a means to promote some other good for the criminal himself or for civil society. It must always be inflicted upon him only *because he has committed a crime*. For a man can never be treated merely as a means to the purposes of another or be put among the objects of rights to things: His innate personality protects him from this, even though he can be condemned to lose his civil personality. He must previously have been found punishable before any thought can be given to drawing from his punishment something of use for himself or his fellow citizens. The principle of punishment is a categorical imperative, and woe to him who crawls through the windings of eudaemonism in order to discover something that releases the criminal from punishment or even reduces its amount by the advantage it promises, in accordance with the Pharisaical saying, "It is better for one man to die than for an entire people to perish." For if justice goes, there is no longer any value in men's living on the earth. What, therefore, should one think of the proposal to preserve the life of a criminal sentenced to death if he agrees to let dangerous experiments be made on him and is lucky

enough to survive them, so that in this way physicians learn something new of benefit to the commonwealth? A court would reject with contempt such a proposal from a medical college, for justice ceases to be justice if it can be bought for any price whatsoever.

But what kind and what amount of punishment is it that public justice makes its principle and measure? None other than the principle of equality (in the position of the needle on the scale of justice), to incline no more to one side than to the other. Accordingly, whatever undeserved evil you inflict upon another within the people, that you inflict upon yourself. If you insult him, you insult yourself; if you steal from him, you steal from yourself; if you strike him, you strike yourself; if you kill him, you kill yourself. But only the *law of retribution* (*ius talionis*)—it being understood, of course, that this is applied by a court (not by your private judgment)—can specify definitely the quality and the quantity of punishment; all other principles are fluctuating and unsuited for a sentence of pure and strict justice because extraneous considerations are mixed into them. Now it would indeed seem that differences in social rank would not allow the principle of retribution, of like for like; but even when this is not possible in terms of the letter, the principle can always remain valid in terms of its effect if account is taken of the sensibilities of the upper classes. A fine, for example, imposed for a verbal injury has no relation to the offense, for someone wealthy might indeed allow himself to indulge in a verbal injury on some occasion; yet the outrage he has done to someone's love of honor can still be quite similar to the hurt done to his pride if he is constrained by judgment and Right not only to apologize publicly to the one he has insulted but also to kiss his hand, for instance, even though he is of a lower class. Similarly, someone of high standing given to violence could be condemned not only to apologize for striking an innocent citizen socially inferior to himself but also to undergo a solitary confinement involving hardship; in addition to the discomfort he undergoes, the offender's vanity would be painfully affected, so that through his shame like would be fittingly repaid with like. But what does it mean to say, "If you steal from someone, you steal from yourself"? Whoever steals makes the property of everyone else insecure and therefore deprives himself (by the principle of retribution) of security in any possible property. He has nothing and can also acquire nothing; but he still wants to live, and this is now possible only if others provide for him. But since the state will not provide for him free of charge, he must let it have his powers for any kind of work it pleases (in convict or prison labor) and is reduced to the status of a slave for a certain time, or permanently if the state sees fit. If, however, he has committed murder he must *die.* Here there is no substitute that will satisfy justice. There is no *similarity* between life, however wretched it may be, and death, hence no likeness between the crime and the retribution unless death is judicially carried out upon the wrongdoer, although it must still be freed from any mistreatment that could make the humanity in the person suffering it into something abominable. Even if a civil society were to be dissolved by the consent of all its members (e.g., if a people inhabiting an island decided to separate and disperse throughout the world), the last murderer remaining in prison would first have to be executed, so that each has done to him what his deeds deserve and blood guilt does not cling to the people for not having insisted upon this punishment; for otherwise the people can be regarded as collaborators in this public violation of justice.

This fitting of punishment to the crime, which can occur only by a judge imposing the death sentence in accordance with the strict law of retribution, is shown by the fact that only by this is a sentence of death pronounced on every criminal in proportion to his *inner wickedness* (even when the crime is not murder but another crime against the state that can be paid for only by death). Suppose that some (such as Balmerino and others) who took part in the re-

cent Scottish rebellion believed that by their uprising they were only performing a duty they owed the House of Stuart, while others on the contrary were out for their private interests; and suppose that the judgment pronounced by the highest court had been that each is free to make the choice between death and convict labor. I say that in this case the man of honor would choose death, and the scoundrel convict labor. This comes along with the nature of the human mind; for the man of honor is acquainted with something that he values even more highly than life, namely *honor,* while the scoundrel considers it better to live in shame than not to live at all (*animam praeferre pudori;* Iuvenal [Satires III, 8, 83]). Since the man of honor is undeniably less deserving of punishment than the other, both would be punished quite proportionately if all alike were sentenced to death; the man of honor would be punished mildly in terms of his sensibilities and the scoundrel severely in terms of his. On the other hand, if both were sentenced to convict labor the man of honor would be punished too severely and the other too mildly for his vile action. And so here too, when sentence is pronounced on a number of criminals united in a plot, the best equalizer before public justice is *death.* Moreover, one has never heard of anyone who was sentenced to death for murder complaining that he was dealt with too severely and therefore wronged; everyone would laugh in his face if he said this. If his complaint were justified it would have to be assumed that even though no wrong is done to the criminal in accordance with the law, the legislative authority of the state is still not authorized to inflict this kind of punishment and that, if it does so, it would be in contradiction with itself.

Accordingly, every murderer—anyone who commits murder, orders it, or is an accomplice in it—must suffer death; this is what justice, as the Idea of judicial authority, wills in accordance with universal laws that are grounded a priori. If, however, the number of accomplices (*correi*) to such a deed is so great that the state, in order to have no such criminals in it, could soon find itself without subjects; and if the state still does not want to dissolve, that is, to pass over into the state of nature, which is far worse because there is no external justice at all in it (and if it especially does not want to dull the people's feeling by the spectacle of a slaughter-house), then the sovereign must also have it in his power, in this case of necessity (*casus necessitatis*), to assume the role of judge (to represent him) and pronounce a judgment that decrees for the criminals a sentence other than capital punishment, such as deportation, which still preserves the population. This cannot be done in accordance with public law, but it can be done by an executive decree, that is, by an act of the right of majesty which, as clemency, can always be exercised only in individual cases.

In opposition to this the Marchese Beccaria, moved by overly compassionate feelings of an affected humanity (*compassibilitas*), has put forward his assertion that any capital punishment is wrongful because it could not be contained in the original civil contract; for if it were, everyone in a people would have to have consented to lose his life in case he murdered someone else (in the people), whereas it is impossible for anyone to consent to this because no one can dispose of his own life. This is all sophistry and juristic trickery.

No one suffers punishment because he has willed it but because he has willed a *punishable* action; for it is no punishment if what is done to someone is what he wills, and it is impossible to will to be punished. Saying that I will to be punished if I murder someone is saying nothing more than that I subject myself together with everyone else to the laws, which will naturally also be penal laws if there are any criminals among the people. As a colegislator in dictating the penal law, I cannot possibly be the same person who, as a subject, is punished in accordance with the law; for as one who is punished, namely as a criminal, I cannot possibly have a voice in legislation (the legislator is holy). Consequently, when I draw up a penal law against myself as a criminal, it is pure reason in me (*homo noumenon*), legislating with regard to rights, which subjects me, as someone capable of crime and so as another person (*homo phaenomenon*), to the penal law, together with all others in a civil union. In other words, it is not the people (each individual in it) that dictates capital punishment but rather the court (public justice), and so another than the criminal; and the social contract contains no promise to let oneself be punished and so to dispose of oneself and one's life. For if the authorization to punish had to be based on the offender's promise, on his willing to let himself be punished, it would also have to be left to him to find himself punishable and the criminal would be his own judge. The chief point of error (πρῶτον ψε υδος) in this sophistry consists in its confusing the criminal's own judgment (which must necessarily be ascribed to his reason) that he has to forfeit his life with a resolve on the part of his will to take his own life, and so in representing as united in one and the same person the judgment upon a right [*Rechtsbeurteilung*] and the realization of that right [*Rechtsvollziehung*]. . . .

QUESTIONS FOR DISCUSSION

1. Was Kant a minimal retributivist, a permissive retributivist, and/or a maximal retributivist (as defined on pp. 692–3)? Find specific passages in the reading to support your interpretation.

2. Kant asks, "What, therefore, should one think of the proposal to preserve the life of a criminal sentenced to death if he agrees to let dangerous experi-

ments be made on him and is lucky enough to survive them, so that in this way physicians learn something new of benefit to the commonwealth?" (p. 702) What is Kant's answer? What arguments does he suggest for this answer? Do you agree with his position and his arguments? Why or why not?

3. What would Kant think of plea bargaining (for example, letting a drug dealer plead guilty to a lesser charge of drug possession if he agrees to testify against his supplier)?

4. What must punishment be proportionate to, according to Kant? Why?

5. Why does Kant support the death penalty? Does he think that it is required for all murders? For any other crimes? Why or why not? Do you agree with his position on the death penalty? Why or why not?

HARM AND RETRIBUTION

MICHAEL DAVIS

Recently, a respected legal theorist, Hugo Bedau, was asked to evaluate a proposed revision of Pennsylvania's penal code. He began by noting: "The classification [of crimes and punishments] . . . has been assumed to be fundamentally retributive, and so its penalty schedule must be based on two basic retributive principles: (1) the severity of the punishment must be proportional to the gravity of the offense, and (2) the gravity of the offense must be a function of fault in the offender and harm caused the victim."[1] These two "basic principles" (or part of them) are often referred to as "*lex talionis.*"

What interests me here are two of Bedau's three uses of "must." Because the classification of crimes and punishments is retributive, it *must*, Bedau says, be based on *lex talionis.* And, for the same reason, the penalties provided

must be a function of fault in the offender and harm done the victim (and, except in special cases, nothing else). My thesis is that there is no "must" about either.

Some retributivists, most notably F. H. Bradley, may seem to have argued something similar.[2] But the upshot of their arguments was that retribution needs a utilitarian principle to proportion punishment to crime. Those retributivists defended a compromised retributivism. I shall not. I shall not because there is, I believe, a better *retributive* principle for proportioning punishment to crime. That principle proportions punishment to the unfair advantage the criminal takes just by committing his crime. Let us call it "the unfair-advantage principle."

The unfair-advantage principle superficially resembles *lex talionis* enough that, as far as I can tell, no one has clearly distinguished

Michael Davis, "Harm and Retribution," *Philosophy and Public Affairs,* vol. 15 (Summer 1986), pp. 236–266

them. Yet the differences are important. Or, at least, that is what I shall try to show. I proceed in this way. First, I distinguish *lex talionis* from the unfair-advantage principle. Second, I show that the unfair-advantage principle can explain a variety of criminal laws better than *lex talionis* can. Third, I show that *lex talionis* is virtually unusable in large areas of criminal law while the unfair-advantage principle should be equally usable everywhere. . . .

I shall not explain (or defend) the unfair advantage principle more than necessary to make clear how it differs from *lex talionis*. Space forbids me to do here what has already been done elsewhere.[3]

My thesis, if proved, should be important to retributivists in at least three ways. First, it should help to establish that the unfair-advantage approach to punishment is significantly different from other forms of (uncompromised) retributivism (since it gives up *lex talionis* while other forms do not). Second, given the problems of *lex talionis*, the argument here should help to establish the superiority of the unfair-advantage approach over other forms of retributivism. And third, because critics of (uncompromised) retributivism tend to treat *lex talionis* as retributivism's chief weakness,[4] my argument should also help to dissuade such critics from treating it as a weakness of retributivism as such. They would have to treat *lex talionis* merely as weakness of some forms of retributivism. If they still chose to reject retributivism categorically, it would have to be for reasons independent of *lex talionis*.

While this article is supposed to be a contribution to retributive theory, much of what is said should also be relevant to "utilitarian" (or "consequentialist") theories of punishment in which desert limits what may be done to the criminal. Such "mixed" theories need not interpret "desert" as requiring proportion between punishment and the harm the criminal did.

But (I should add) this article is not supposed to be relevant only to theory. Retributivism is not merely a subject for theorists. As Bedau's commentary on the proposed revision of Pennsylvania's penal code should suggest, retributivism is again a principle helping to shape and justify the way punishment is in fact administered. So, what I say here should be useful to legislators, criminologists, and others who are concerned to make punishment as just as possible.

I. WHAT IS *LEX TALIONIS*?

Lex talionis (or *jus talionis*) may once have referred unequivocally to a certain principle defining or limiting the right of retaliation, but it has long since become equivocal. *Lex talionis* may now refer either to a general principle of corrective justice or to a particular principle of criminal law. As a general principle of corrective justice, *lex* requires the wrongdoer to suffer as much as (but no more than) he has wrongfully made others suffer. This principle is more at home in the mountains of Corsica or in a schoolyard fight than in the criminal law. ("He hit you once, so you should hit him just once in return.")[5] This is not the *lex talionis* that concerns me. My concern is a principle of criminal law, one that is supposed to explain what statutory penalties and judicial sentences must be to be justified as acts of a relatively just legal system. Whatever light that principle sheds on natural justice, poetic justice, divine justice, or the like is, while welcome, gratuitous.

Lex talionis, understood as a principle of criminal law, is still equivocal. It may be understood either "formally" or "materially." Understood formally, it is the first of Bedau's "two basic principles," that is, the principle that punishment should be proportioned to the gravity of the offense or otherwise made to "fit the crime." This *lex talionis* is simply a reminder that criminal justice consists primarily in punishing violations of the criminal law, not in punishing faults of character, deterring antisocial behavior, or doing other sorts of good. Other good may be done as well, of course, but doing it is secondary, not to be achieved by punishment greater than the crime deserves (however desert happens to be measured). Bedau was certainly right to include that principle among the "basic principles" of retributivism. So understood, *lex talionis*, is essential to any retributive theory.[6] Differences among retributivist theories are largely in how to measure desert, not in whether desert is what punishment should be measured against. For example, some retributivists have held that deserved punishment is determined by the moral wrong the criminal did when he broke the law; others, that it is the special moral wrong involved in breaking a particular criminal law as such.

Lex talionis may also be understood "materially," that is, as a principle requiring punishment to be proportioned (in part at least) to harm done (or, perhaps, to be limited by the harm done). This is Bedau's second "basic principle." Different retributive theories differ concerning what shall count as harm (and how important harm is for determining punishment). But, any theory for which *lex talionis* is not purely formal will have to understand "harm" as existing *independent of a particular criminal statute*. Harm will have to be something a statute can protect against by forbidding (or requiring) certain acts. The loss of an eye is an example of such a harm. For most retributivists, the invasion of a right would be another. What else may be is controversial.

Lex talionis is so often invoked as the principle that requires an eye for an eye, a tooth for a tooth, that it may be worth a moment to point out that even those among its defenders who talk that way, do not mean what they seem to say. For example, Kant states the "law of retribution" as "any undeserved evil that you inflict on someone else among the people is one that you do to yourself."[7] Yet, his examples of retribution include apology followed by solitary confinement as punishment for attacking a social inferior without just cause, penal servitude as punishment for theft, and death as punishment for treason. Accompanying each example is an explanation of how the suggested punishment would satisfy the "spirit," if not the letter, of *lex talionis*.[8] Plainly, even Kant

understood *lex talionis* to require an *equivalent* "evil," not the *same* "evil."

Of course, retributivists *are* divided on whether *lex talionis* requires the punishment to *be* equivalent or merely specifies equivalence as the *most* justice will allow. Kant left little room for clemency. For him, justice generally required a certain punishment and the sovereign had no right to do more or less. Most modern retributivists would reject Kant's rigorism. But that need not concern us. Now we may complete our explanation of *lex talionis* by contrasting it with the unfair-advantage principle.

The unfair-advantage principle assumes that each criminal law (or perhaps the criminal law as a whole) creates a system of cooperation. Some people forbear doing what they would otherwise do because the law has given them reasonable assurance that others will do the same (and everyone will be better off if everyone abstains). Such a system imposes burdens insofar as people do forbear doing what they would otherwise do. Anyone who breaks a law does not bear the same burden the rest do. Unless he is punished, he will, in effect, have gotten away with doing less than others. He will have an advantage they do not.

According to the unfair-advantage principle, it is this advantage the criminal law is supposed to take back by punishing the criminal for his crime. The advantage bears no necessary relation to the harm the criminal actually did. For example, he may have done great damage and only committed theft; or no damage at all even though he tried to commit murder. According to the unfair-advantage principle, the damage a criminal actually does is between him and his victim, a private matter to be settled by civil suit (or the moral equivalent). His *crime* consists only in the unfair advantage he necessarily took over the law-abiding by breaking the law in question. The measure of punishment due is the relative value of *that* unfair advantage. The greater the advantage, the greater the punishment should be. The focus of the unfair-advantage principle is on what the *criminal* gained; the focus of *lex talionis*, on what *others* lost.[9]

In one respect, however, the two principles are alike. Neither the unfair-advantage principle nor *lex talionis* distinguishes sharply between laying down rules for punishment and applying those rules to particular cases. Under either principle, a legislature has little or no discretion concerning *how much* the crime should be punished (though it may have wide discretion concerning the form of that punishment). That a legislature requires a certain penalty for a certain crime does not mean that the criminal deserves it for the crime in question or that it would be just for a judge to impose it even under an otherwise just procedure. The principle of punishment, whether *lex talionis* or unfair-advantage principle, determines that. From the perspective of either principle, there is only one continuous process of proportioning punishment to crime once a legislature has made an act criminal. The judge completes whatever the legislature has left undone.

The rule-act distinction seems to belong to utilitarian, rather than to retributive, theories of punishment. I shall say nothing more of it here. For retributivists, the important distinction seems to be between (a) the legislative decision to make a class of acts criminal, (b) the legislative or judicial decision that a certain crime deserves (no more than) a certain punishment, and (c) the judicial decision that the actual sentence should be such and such (the judge taking into account the criminal as well as his crime to determine whether the sentence should be less than what the crime itself deserves).[10]

II. HARM, "HARM," AND NO "HARM"

Harm is the engine of *lex talionis*. To determine how much (or how little) *lex talionis* can help us understand the criminal law, we must consider the place of harm in the criminal law. Is it the right place for *lex talionis* to provide an adequate theory of how much to punish?

I suggest that, while trying to answer that question, we confine ourselves to the criminal law as we know it. This limitation is not meant to foreclose the possibility that a retributive theory might provide a criticism of practice.[11] Rather, it serves to remind us of the practice we are trying to understand. We may wish to criticize some of it, perhaps all of it. But criticism not founded on understanding will hardly convince. So, whether our ultimate aim is understanding or reform, we should begin with the criminal law as it is.

Harm certainly has a significant place in the criminal law even if "harm" is understood strictly as physical injury to some person or physical damage to some thing. Many common crimes do harm in this sense. Murder and mayhem require that some individual suffer physical injury: arson and wanton destruction of property, that some property be damaged.

But many common crimes do no harm—if "harm" is understood that strictly. Kidnapping, robbery, theft, burglary, and perhaps even battery may leave no mark on any person or reduce the value of anything. Such crimes do harm, if they do harm, only in a looser sense of "harm." They invade the *right* of some individual. A kidnapper must deprive his victim of liberty, for example, by carrying the victim off against his will. A robber must deprive her victim of property by force. And so on. The rights in question (liberty, property, or the like) are rights existing independent of the particular criminal statute. They would be enforceable by civil suit whether or not protected by criminal statute. So, extending "harm" to include what such crimes do is certainly consistent with *lex talionis*.[12]

But, extended only in this way, "harm" is still not broad enough for anything like a full theory of deserved punishment. Some serious crimes do not seem to be an invasion of anyone's right but merely a beneficial restraint on commerce. For example, a blackmailer may have a right (that is, a "liberty-right") to publish the information he uses to blackmail and a similar right to accept payment for silence. What right (what "claim-right") could one have (all else equal) to the helpful silence of another if one is not willing to pay for it? What right not to be given an opportunity to pay for it?

The law—civil or criminal—is ordinarily not concerned to prevent publication of the sort of (truthful) information a blackmailer uses, nor is it generally concerned with people receiving money to keep silent. The blackmail statute simply forbids a blackmailer's volunteering to sell his silence. Here, it seems, if we are still to talk of "harm," we must understand "harm" as violating a (preexisting) *interest*, that is, an interest in not having someone force you to choose between paying for his silence and having your reputation blasted, not as violating a (preexisting) right. The point of prohibiting blackmail seems to be to remove a certain temptation to destroy the reputation of others. The law against blackmail may be said to protect an individual from the "harm of lost reputation," but that "harm" is to an interest, not (like the harms discussed earlier) harm that constitutes "breach of peace" or invades a right.

But extending "harm" to include protecting (some) interests of individuals still does not extend the concept enough to explain punishing all serious crimes. . . . Consider, for example, the crime of reckless driving. If I drive recklessly on an empty highway, I do not in fact invade anyone's interest in safety (since I endanger no one). I also do not invade any interest of government . . . (since what I do does not endanger the government . . .). What I do is *risk endangering* anyone who *might* be on the highway (even though it happens that no one is there). If we are to describe what I am doing in terms of preexisting interest, we shall have to say that I am violating the interest of all those who might have used the highway in not having me risk endangering them, or perhaps society's interest in not having people risk endangering each other. If the interests we have discussed so far may be described as "primary," this is a "secondary interest," that is, an

interest in not having a primary interest put at risk (where "risk" refers to the harm reasonably foreseeable given what the actor knows or, perhaps, should know, and "danger" refers to the harm reasonably foreseeable given—something like—full information).

Perhaps we can explain punishing attempts in the same way. By definition, an attempt does not do the harm the complete crime would have done. Some attempts violate no primary interest at all. For example, an attempted murder might consist of no more than putting sugar, believed to be poison, in the coffee of one's senile aunt or trying to shoot one's enemy from ambush with an empty gun believed to be loaded. While such crimes do not in fact endanger, they could, like reckless driving, endanger someone under other circumstances and, for all the actor knew, the other circumstances prevailed. So, it seems reasonable to say that attempts violate a secondary interest in not having our safety or control of property risked (whether it is in fact endangered or not).

There are, however, other crimes, some serious, that seem not to harm even a secondary interest. Consider, for example, the crime of conspiracy. A conspiracy may be no more than an agreement to attempt an ordinary crime, for example, robbery or murder. Two would-be criminals can be guilty of such a conspiracy if, having agreed to commit the crime, they buy rope or do some other (ordinarily) lawful act in preparation for carrying out the planned crime. They need not do anything amounting to an attempt. Since two would-be criminals cannot lawfully do some acts one would-be criminal can lawfully do, the "harm" of conspiracy seems to be harm in a sense different from that in which attempt does harm. It is, it seems, an invasion of the interest in not having people join together to undertake a criminal attempt. Perhaps we can call this a "tertiary interest."

If so, we shall have to talk of "fourth-degree interests" too. Consider the crime of solicitation. You commit this crime by (in effect) attempting to commit conspiracy, that is, by going about trying to get others to agree to attempt a crime for you. ("Try," because if you succeed, there is a conspiracy.) The "harm" done by solicitation seems very far from harm strictly so called. Of course, if solicitation of a certain sort were allowed, there might be more successful attempts of the corresponding primary crime. That possibility is something that rightly concerns a legislature. But, more than in conspiracy or attempt, it seems odd to talk about that sensible concern in terms of someone's (fourth-degree) interest a particular criminal harms by a particular solicitation. . . .

Here, it seems, *lex talionis* reveals disturbing prelegal roots the unfair-advantage principle does not have. According to *les talionis*, a law, even if itself not unjust, can*not* make an act punishable unless the act is "punishable" law or not, that is, unless it invades a (legitimate) interest existing independent of the criminal law in question. The criminal law cannot make a "harmless" act punishable because without harm there is, according to *lex talionis* nothing to measure deserved punishment against. Since it would be unjust to punish to any degree what cannot deserve punishment to any degree, for *lex talionis* prelegal conditions limit what the law can punish. The law cannot add to what deserves punishment, only select a subset of punishable acts to make punishable at law. *Lex talionis* is, in effect, a theory of legislation as well as a theory of how much to punish.

The unfair-advantage principle is not (or, at least, not to the same degree). The principle is consistent with any theory of what the criminal law should forbid or allow (provided the criminal law is conceived as part of a relatively just legal system). That is so because (ordinarily) any law within a relatively just legal system creates a cooperative scheme most departures from which would take unfair advantage. Of course, a particular departure for special reason may not amount to taking such advantage (for example, because the departure constitutes a "mere technical violation" or because enforcing

the law in that case would be discriminatory or otherwise unfair). In such cases, the unfair-advantage principle would provide the basis for excuse or justification. Such special cases, while an important problem for any adequate theory of criminal law, present a problem different from the one we are now considering. The category of excuse or justification presupposes that punishment for the crime in question is generally deserved. The problem we have been considering until now is whether *lex talionis* or the unfair-advantage principle better explains how punishment for various *sorts* of crime can be deserved.

Because the unfair-advantage principle is concerned with unfair advantage taken by disobeying the law rather than with harm done against the law, the unfair-advantage principle automatically separates (most) questions of demarcation from those of proportion. Because separating such questions seems more judicious than implicitly supposing that what justifies making an act criminal will also provide the measure of punishment for doing the act once doing it is a crime, I take this difference between the unfair-advantage principle, and *lex talionis* to be an advantage of the unfair-advantage principle.[15]

IV. HARM AS THE MEASURE OF DESERT
The last two sections compared *lex talionis* and the unfair-advantage principle as explanations of *what* the criminal law punishes. We learned that *lex talionis* cannot make sense of certain kinds of criminal law the unfair-advantage principle can. We may now inquire which principle is better at helping us understand *how much* punishment a crime deserves. To be fair to *lex talionis*, we must, given the results of the last two sections, limit our inquiry to those crimes for which there is an identifiable harm (or invasion of interest). That, as we saw, is a significant limitation, but one about which we have said enough already.

Does the concept of harm give us insight into how much punishment a criminal deserves for what he did? The answer seems to be that it certainly does—sometimes. For example, it seems only simple good sense to explain why murder deserves more punishment than battery by pointing out that the harm done by killing someone is greater than the harm done by hitting him. The simpler the legal system, the more likely it is that the relation among crimes will be like that, one crime differing from another only in the seriousness of harm done. Perhaps this explanation's good sense has something to do with the enduring appeal of *lex talionis*.

Unfortunately, modern systems of criminal law are not simple. They include many laws differing from one another in more than harm. . . . [S]o long as one depends on *lex talionis*, [w]hat we need is some way to weigh a variety of considerations (at least four kinds of interest and several kinds of *mens rea* including purposefulness, intention, recklessness, and negligence). The problem bears an unpleasant likeness to that which a utilitarian theory of punishment faces. We could, for example, think of the weight of a certain secondary interest as equal to the product of the primary interest threatened and the probability of that threat being realized. So, if I attempt a crime with a fifty-fifty chance of success, my attempt would (all else equal) be half as bad as the complete crime. But, thinking in such terms requires cardinal numbers (or something very like them). *Lex talionis* would have to be arithmetic and so, to apply it, we would have to find some way to assign cardinal numbers to the various primary harms. We would, for example, have to be able to say how much worse is being killed than being disfigured by acid. Fifty percent worse? Two hundred percent worse? Or what? And we would have to be able to do the same for kinds of *mens rea* as well. Is intentionally committing a certain crime twice as bad as committing it recklessly?

The absurdity of such questions suggests either a deeper absurdity in any version of retributivism assuming *lex talionis* or a mistake in

our understanding of *lex talionis*. My view is that it reveals a deeper absurdity. But, to be fair, let us assume that defenders of *lex talionis* can work out the mathematics necessary to handle comparison of different kinds of interest and different mental states, and then examine *lex talionis* under the most favorable conditions, that is, holding *mens rea* and kind of interest constant. Intentional crime will be compared with intentional crime, complete crime with complete crime, and so on.

Consider two crimes in which *mens rea* and kind of interest seem identical. For example, Illinois distinguishes between (ordinary) involuntary manslaughter and what is often called "vehicular homicide" (though Illinois calls it "reckless homicide"). While vehicular homicide is a class-4 felony (one to three years imprisonment), involuntary manslaughter is a class-3 felony (two to five years imprisonment).[21] Does *lex talionis* help us to understand why these two kinds of manslaughter are punished as they are? It *seems* not. Manslaughter, whether "involuntary" or "vehicular," requires exactly the same *mens rea*, "recklessness," and the same harm, death. So, how can the defenders of *lex talionis* defend against what seems to be a clear counterexample to their version of retributivism?

They have at least three strategies open to them. One is to dismiss the distinction between "involuntary manslaughter" and "vehicular homicide" as an "anomaly," that is, as an indefensible distinction. The second strategy is to show that the two crimes, contrary to all appearances, violate different interests. The third strategy is to show that our example is not as "clean" as it should be, that is, that there is in it another factor *lex talionis* recognizes as relevant.

The first strategy would be tempting if Illinois were alone (or almost alone) in distinguishing between involuntary manslaughter and vehicular homicide. Unfortunately, the distinction has long been part of the criminal law of many jurisdictions, both American and foreign. So, dismissing the distinction as an anomaly would appear *ad hoc* without a powerful argument. That argument cannot (on pain of begging the question) rest on the principle that, all else equal, punishment should be proportioned to harm done. And it is hard to see on what other ground it could rest. So, the strategy of dismissal looks uninviting.

If the first strategy looks uninviting, so does the second. It is hard to guess what interest (ordinary) involuntary manslaughter violates that vehicular homicide would not violate as well. Death by automobile is seldom pretty and is often as painful as death by any means by which involuntary manslaughter is commonly committed. Still, with enough ingenuity, perhaps we could find some way to distinguish the interest harmed by involuntary manslaughter from the interest harmed by vehicular homicide. But the ingenuity required signals another problem with the second strategy. The greater the ingenuity required, the less intuitive what we find is likely to be.

That leaves the third strategy, showing the example not to be as "clean" as it seems. The strategy has some promise. It seems that, as soon as cars became common, juries began to refuse to convict of involuntary manslaughter drivers who recklessly caused death. Legislatures responded by creating a less serious crime of which juries were willing to convict drivers. Whether juries were reluctant to convict drivers of involuntary manslaughter because they thought, "There but for the grace of God go I," or because they considered driving to constitute a partial excuse for manslaughter, a cousin of duress or extreme temptation, or because of some other reason, is open to debate. It is, however, easy to see why juries might have thought driving a partial excuse. Living would be far less convenient if we did not drive, yet driving puts us in circumstances where it is easier to be reckless with life than it is in (ordinary) involuntary manslaughter. Since this is a general feature of conduct, it should be recognized by law as other such excuses are, not left to the discretion of the judge when sentencing.

This third strategy is not as *ad hoc* as it may seem. Legal theorists have long explained the distinction between ("second degree") murder and *voluntary* manslaughter in just this way. Voluntary manslaughter differs from murder neither in the harm caused, death, nor in the intention to kill. An intentional killing is voluntary manslaughter rather than murder if there are certain extenuating circumstances. In Illinois, for example, a killer commits voluntary manslaughter if he kills "under a sudden and intense provocation" or because he "wrongly believes himself to be acting in self-defense."[22]

Though obviously promising, the third strategy is not without problems. One problem is that thinking of voluntary manslaughter as partially excused murder seems more informative than thinking of vehicular homicide as partially excused involuntary manslaughter. "Provocation" or "mistake of fact" sounds more like an excuse than does "driving a vehicle" (or even "the convenience and difficulty of driving"). A more substantial problem is simply an extension of one discussed earlier. It now seems that *lex talionis* cannot be applied without a theory of excuses. Since that is so, we have a new layer of complexity in the setting of statutory penalties. We must weigh not only various kinds of interests and various kinds of *mens rea* but also partial excuses if likely to be widely shared by those doing the harm in question (all this without any guidance on how to weigh such things). The problem would be even more complex for a judge imposing sentence if the legislature left him with full discretion.

Any theory upon which intelligent people have long labored is likely to have the resources to answer almost any objection. The objections made here are probably no exception. But, if each answer is bought at the cost of new complexity, the theory may become too expensive to hold, at least if there is a simpler alternative available. So, it would be useful to contrast the complexity to which *lex talionis* has already driven us here with the *relative* simplicity with which the unfair-advantage principle handles the same examples.

The unfair-advantage principle does not require us to distinguish harm, *mens rea*, and excuse in a statute like that prohibiting vehicular homicide. To find *what*, according to the unfair-advantage principle, we are to proportion punishment to, we need only determine the unfair advantage the criminal would take by violating the statute in question. One way to do that is to formulate a license that would pardon in advance one instance of that crime. Ordinarily, the formula of the license will be a simple paraphrase of the statute itself. Having formulated the license, we can determine *how much* unfair advantage the crime takes by comparing the value of licenses pardoning similar crimes (for example, with the value of a license pardoning involuntary manslaughter). That would place the crime in question (in our case, vehicular homicide) in a ranking of crimes.

But how (it may be asked) are we to compare the advantages such licenses represent without the same arithmetic *lex talionis* requires? The answer is simple. *Lex talionis* requires cardinal numbers because it requires us to agree (at least approximately) on both the degree we would assign each harm, *mens rea*, and excuse and the weight we would assign these factors relative to one another. The *lex talionis* presupposes a single point of view from which all this can be done. The unfair-advantage principle presupposes no such thing. Instead, it provides guidance on how to *construct* such a point of view (or, rather, its equivalent). Unfair advantage is, of course, a function of physical act, degree of *mens rea*, and so on just as harm (and fault) are in *lex talionis*. But, under the unfair-advantage principle, these factors can be weighed differently by different people (just as people may have widely different views about the relative value of houses and apartments) and yet provide the basis for agreement on what punishment is deserved (just as people can agree on what "the going rate" for this house or that apartment would be). How much unfair advantage an act takes is primarily a function of the social circumstances in which the act is committed (just as market price is). One way to represent that function, one I have found useful elsewhere, is as the result of auc-

tioning pardons in advance for the relevant crimes under circumstances otherwise as close as possible to those of the society in question, consistent with getting a reasonable result. The procedure permits comparison (to the degree necessary) of relative seriousness of crimes without use of any numbers beyond what is necessary to indicate ordinal rank.[25]

Consider again the problem of explaining why vehicular homicide is punished less than involuntary manslaughter. According to the unfair-advantage principle, we can solve that problem by explaining why a license to commit the crime would be worth less than a license to commit similar crimes ranked above it. So, to explain why vehicular homicide should be punished less than involuntary manslaughter, we need only explain why a license to commit vehicular manslaughter would not be worth as much as a license to commit involuntary manslaughter. The explanation is obvious if we think of vehicular homicide as a special case of involuntary manslaughter (that is, as involuntary manslaughter with the "partial excuse" of "done with a vehicle"). A license to commit involuntary manslaughter would be more valuable than a license to commit vehicular homicide because (and just insofar as) a license to commit involuntary manslaughter in any way whatever is more useful than a license to commit it in only one way, by use of a vehicle. The unfair-advantage principle does not need a theory of excuses to reach this result (that is, a theory of what should count as an excuse). Whatever lowers the value of a license is relevant, whether it fits the general category of excuse or not. For example, the requirement that the involuntary manslaughter be done with a vehicle would reduce the value of a license to do involuntary manslaughter because committing involuntary manslaughter with a vehicle is inherently more risky than committing it in the other ways in which it is commonly committed (for example, by failure to provide one's patient with adequate medical attention or by careless use of a rifle). A rational person choosing between various acts of recklessness would, all else equal, prefer to be reckless in some way other than driving. If that is so, licenses for reckless driving would, all else equal, be worth less than licenses to kill by other means (even if a substantial portion of drivers did not share that preference). That being so, vehicular manslaughter would, according to the unfair advantage principle, deserve less punishment than (ordinary) involuntary manslaughter (all else equal).

I have, it should be noticed, framed the problem as one of comparing a general license to commit manslaughter with a special license to commit a certain kind of manslaughter. This frame fits one statutory scheme, that is, the one in which a reckless driver who has killed someone could be charged under either the involuntary manslaughter statute or the vehicular homicide statute. This is not the only statutory scheme. Another scheme expressly excludes vehicular homicide from coverage under the involuntary manslaughter statute. I have not framed the problem to fit that scheme because doing so would have meant an argument more complicated than necessary for my limited purpose here. The argument I have given, whatever its faults, is enough to show how much easier to use than *lex talionis* the unfair-advantage principle can be. The argument also shows that the two principles are quite different in the way they work. We would not, for example, expect *lex talionis* to be as sensitive to the details of a statutory scheme as the unfair-advantage principle here seems to be. . . .

My frequent appeal to economics may suggest another objection to the unfair-advantage principle. That principle cannot (it might be said) be the principle implicit in the criminal law as we know it because the economic models appealed to seem to require more information than legislators usually have and more mathematical sophistication than they have had at their command until quite recently. The objection is correct insofar as it rejects the possibility that legislators (and judges) could explicitly engage in the sort of reasoning our auction involves. But I do not claim otherwise. All I claim is that such models provide a way of picturing their (and our) conception of criminal desert in much the way that economic models help us to understand why prices are what they are. I have elsewhere set out the procedures I think legislators (and judges) actually follow.[27] These correspond to the very rough-and-ready way most of us decide what price to pay for this or that. They do not require the sort of information my auction requires. But they also do not contribute to our understanding of what we do in the way that a model can, even if the model requires assuming that in practice we have information (or other resources) we can at best only approximate. Interestingly, *lex talionis* seems never to have suggested any model, only regulative metaphors like "an eye for an eye."

I conclude that retributivists should give up *lex talionis* for the unfair-advantage principle.

NOTES

[1]H. A. Bedau, "Classification-Based Sentencing: Some Conceptual and Ethical Problems," *NOMOS XXVII: Criminal Justice* (1985): 102.

[2]F. H. Bradley, *Ethical Studies*, 2d ed. (London: Oxford University Press, 1962). pp. 26–27. (Whether Bradley meant to make such a compromise is another question. My impression is that he has been misread.) Cf. B. Bosanquet, *The Philosophical Theory of the State*, 4th ed. (London: Macmillan, 1965), p. 212; and Bedau, p. 103.

[3]See, for example, Herbert Morris, "Persons and Punishment," *Monist* 52 (1968): 475–501 (to whom the recent popularity of the principle seems to be due). For a defense of the principle against the utilitarian charge that it is incapable of giving content to the concept of proportion, see Michael Davis, "How to Make the Punishment Fit the Crime," *Ethics* 93 (1983): 726–52.

[4]See, for example, Michael H. Mitias, "Is Retribution Inconsistent Without *Lex Talionis*?" *Rivista internazionale di filosofia del diritto* 56 (1983): 211–30.

[5]For a recent, extensive, and highly sophisticated discussion of this principle of morality, see Robert Nozick, *Philosophical Explanations* (Cambridge, MA: Harvard University Press, Belknap Press, 1981), pp. 363–93.

[6]And not only to retributive theories. John Rawls makes the point that utilitarian theories such as Bentham's also include (something like) the formal ver-

sion of *lex talionis*. "Two Concepts of Rules," in (among other places) *The Philosophy of Punishment*, ed. H. B. Acton (London: Macmillan, 1969), p. 114n.

[7]Immanuel Kant, *The Metaphysical Elements of Justice*, trans. John Ladd (Indianapolis: Liberal Arts Library, 1965), pp. 101–102 (VI, 332–33) and pp. 132–33 (VI, 363–67).

[8]Ibid.

[9]Cf. Davis, "How to Make the .Punishment Fit the Crime," pp. 736–46.

[10]Cf. ibid., pp. 750–52; and Michael Davis, "Sentencing: Must Justice Be Even-Handed? *Law and Philosophy* 1 (1982): 77–117.

[11]Indeed, I have elsewhere provided examples of the critical power of retributivism. See, for example, "Setting Penalties: What Does Rape Deserve?" *Law and Philosophy* 3 (1984): 62–111; and "Guilty But Insane?" *Social Theory and Practice* 10 (1984): 1–23.

[12]See W. D. Ross, *The Right and The Good* (London: Oxford University Press, 1930), pp. 62–63, for an example of someone who expressly limits justified punishment to the vindication of rights.

[15]For those who see no advantage in separating those questions, I would suggest considering the advantages of separation as illustrated in my "Why Attempts Deserve Less Punishment than Complete Crimes," *Law and Philosophy*, forthcoming, and "Strict Liability: Deserved Punishment for Faultless Conduct," also forthcoming.

[21]*Ill. Rev. Statutes*, Ch. 38, sec. 9–3 (and sec. 1005–8–1).

[22]*Ill. Rev. Statutes*, Ch. 38, sec. 9–2 (and sec. 1005–8–1).

[25]For examples of this, see papers cited above on rape, recidivism, attempts, and strict liability.

[27]"How to Make the Punishment Fit the Crime," esp. pp. 736–42.

QUESTIONS FOR DISCUSSION

1. Explain and evaluate Davis' arguments against the *lex talionis*. How would Kant respond? How does the *lex talionis* differ from Davis' own theory?

2. Can anyone determine what people would pay for licenses to commit certain crimes? If so, when and how? If not, why not?

3. Davis claims that vehicular homicide should receive less punishment than involuntary manslaughter, because one would pay more for a license to commit involuntary manslaughter (p. 713). What is his argument for this claim? Do you agree? Why or why not?

4. Would poor people pay more or less for a license to rob houses than rich people would pay? Why or why not? Does this show that poor people should be punished more or less for burglary than rich people, according to Davis? According to you? Why or why not?

5. Would homosexuals pay more or less for a license to commit sodomy than heterosexuals? Does this show that homosexuals should be punished more or less than heterosexuals for sodomy, according to Davis? According to you? Why or why not?

6. Consider a former Nazi prison commander who obeyed all German laws of the time. Fifty years later, he has fully renounced his former views and now spends all of his time helping the poor. Punishing him will prevent him from doing his good work, and it is doubtful that his punishment will deter future Nazis or war criminals. Would punishment in this case be justified by a legalistic retributivist? By a maximal moralistic retributivist? Are these theories plausible here? Why or why not?

7. Can you think of any wrong that really is annihilated by punishment, as Bradley claims (p. 696)? Be sure to consider what Morris says about self-restraint (p. 700) and what Davis says about unfair advantage.

8. Morris argues that Hegel was right to claim that criminals have a right to be punished, because they do have a right to be punished instead of being treated as if they were mentally ill. Is this a plausible interpretation of Hegel's claim? Can this claim be used to support maximal retributivism? Why or why not?

9. Write down every crime you can think of, then list them in order of viciousness, and assign punishments so as to reflect this order. What kinds of problems do you run into?

10. Many people think that recidivists (criminals who repeat a crime after being punished for it) should be punished more severely than first-time offenders. Do you agree? Would retributivists agree? Would utilitarians agree? Why or why not? Be sure to consider various versions of retributivism and of utilitarianism.

SUGGESTIONS FOR FURTHER READING

On distinctions among kinds of retributivism, see J. L. Mackie, "Morality and the Retributive Emotions" in his *Persons and Values* (Oxford: Clarendon Press, 1985), pp. 206–219. Classic retributivist writings are collected in *Philosophical Perspectives on Punishment*, edited by Gertrude Ezorsky (Albany: State University of New York Press, 1972), Chapter 2, Section 2. Michael Davis develops his retributivism, applies it to cases (recidivism, attempts, and strict liability), and responds to criticisms in *To Make the Punishment Fit the Crime* (Boulder, Colorado: Westview Press, 1992). For criticisms, see Don Scheid, "Davis and the Unfair-Advantage Theory of Punishment: A Critique," *Philosophical Topics* (Spring 1990), pp. 143–70; and Davis' response, "Criminal Desert and Unfair Advantage: What's the Connection?" *Law and Philosophy*, vol. 12 (May 1993), pp. 133–156. Views like Davis' can be found in Herbert Morris, *On Guilt and Innocence* (Berkeley: University of California Press, 1976) and Jeffrie G. Murphy, *Retribution, Justice, and Therapy* (Dordrecht: Reidel, 1979) and *Retribution Reconsidered* (Boston: Kluwer, 1992). A more traditional version of retributivism is developed by Robert Nozick in *Philosophical Explanations* (Cambridge: Harvard University Press, 1980), Part 4, Chapter III, pp. 363–397. For criticisms of retributivism, see Ted Honderich, *Punishment: The Supposed Justifications*, rev. ed. (Harmondsworth: Penguin, 1976), Chapter 1; and John Braithwaite and Philip Pettit, *Not Just Deserts* (Oxford: Clarendon Press, 1990), Chapters 8–9.

COMBINATIONS AND 6.5 ALTERNATIVES

INTRODUCTION

After studying utilitarianism and retributivism, many students conclude that neither theory is completely adequate by itself. This leaves two main options. Some try to combine utilitarian considerations with retributivist considerations. Others try to find a new kind of theory that is neither retributivist nor utilitarian.

We already saw one attempt to combine retributivist and utilitarian considerations. Rawls, in the reading in Section 6.3, writes, ". . . the decision as to what laws to have and what penalties to assign, may be settled by utilitarian arguments; but if one decides to have laws, then one has decided on something whose working in particular cases is retributive in form." (p. 684)[27] The former decision is made by legislators, but the latter work is done by judges, so different theories apply to different offices.

However attractive this reconciliation would be, it is too simple. If legislators consider only utility, they might pass laws that overlook personal responsibility, and they might use heavy punishments to prevent minor crimes, as we saw. Also, if judges are guided solely by (maximal) retributivism, they will punish in cases where inflicting harm is useless or even counterproductive. If these results are unacceptable, then neither judges nor legislators should look solely to one kind of consideration.

But how can legislators or judges coherently consider both utilitarian and retributive considerations? One possibility is to let retributivism govern some areas of criminal law, but let utilitarianism govern other areas. Crimes such as theft, rape, and murder are traditionally called *mala in se* (wrongs in themselves), because they are immoral independent of any law. Retributivist demands for moral condemnation and proportionate punishment seem appealing in this area. Other crimes, such as insider trading, driving without a license, and draft evasion, are called *mala prohibita* (wrongs by prohibition), because they would not be immoral if they were not prohibited by law. Since laws against such acts are based mainly on social and economic considerations, utilitarianism seems the natural theory for determining punishments in this area.[28] This division of tasks has its attractions, but pure retributivists will still object that utilitarianism will allow punishments that

---

[27]A similar distinction was made by W. D. Ross, *The Right and the Good* (Oxford: Clarendon Press, 1930), pp. 61–64.

[28]Hart describes but does not endorse this bifurcation in *Punishment and Responsibility*, p. 236.

are too harsh for crimes that are *mala prohibita,* and pure utilitarians will object that retributivism will allow useless punishment for crimes that are *mala in se.*

Another possibility is to keep the *minimal* retributivist claim that we should never punish innocent people, but, once someone is guilty, use utilitarianism to determine how much and how to punish. Bradley suggests this when he says, "Having once the right to punish, we may modify the punishment according to the useful and the pleasant; but these are external to the matter, they cannot give us a right to punish, and nothing can do that but criminal desert."[29] But so far this would allow us to punish beyond what is proportionate to the criminal's guilt, which would be unacceptable to most retributivists.

Another possibility is that retributivism also sets an *upper* bound to the amount of punishment that is permissible.[30] It is then wrong to punish more than is proportionate to the criminal's guilt. This explains why we should never punish the innocent, since they are not guilty at all. As long as we stay below this upper bound, we may use utility to determine how much to punish. This will satisfy some retributivists, but maximal retributivists will object that this mixture is too weak, because it would allow or even require us to let off reformed Nazis and paralyzed car thieves without any punishment at all, if it would do no good to punish them.

One might respond by saying that guilt also sets a *lower* bound to punishment, that is, that we should never punish less than a certain amount, which is also determined by guilt. Utility could then be used to determine the degree of punishment as long as it remains between the upper limit and the lower limit set by retributivism. But how could there be any room at all between these limits if both limits are set by proportionality to guilt? And some will still find it objectionable to require punishment in cases where punishment does more harm than good. There are other ways to combine retributivist and utilitarian considerations, but the problems for these attempts show that mixed theories will not be easy to formulate and defend.

Another reaction to the shortcomings of pure utilitarianism and retributivism is to move outside both traditional camps. One way to do this is to limit the relevant consequences. Utilitarians insist that we should add up *all* harms and benefits to everyone. One might argue, instead, that only *some* consequences are relevant to the justification of punishment. For example, some philosophers claim that punishment is justified only insofar as it promotes a kind of moral education of the criminal.[31] Another possibility is to emphasize benefits to the victims of a crime, which might lead to programs of restitution and community service in place of traditional punishments.[32]

If none of these theories of punishment seems adequate, you might try to develop your own justification for punishment. But you also might reach the radical

---

[29]Bradley, *Ethical Studies,* p. 27.

[30]See, for example, K. G. Armstrong, "The Retributivist Hits Back," *Mind* vol. 70 (1961), pp. 471–90 at 486–87

[31]See Jean Hampton, "The Moral Education Theory of Punishment," *Philosophy and Public Affairs,* vol. 13 (1984), pp. 208–38.

[32]See Barnett's works in the Suggestions for Further Reading at the end of this section.

conclusion that punishment simply cannot be justified in any way. Then you will need to find some other solution to the problem of crime. Crime might be reduced by some combination of aid, job training, prevention, moral education, and so on. These programs might be used alongside punishment, but one also might consider using them in place of punishment. It is hard to know how much crime could be reduced by such programs alone. They might work adequately against some crimes even if not all. Since this approach has never been tried in a systematic way, the possibility of reducing crime without any punishment at least remains open.

QUESTIONS FOR DISCUSSION

1. Is there any completely adequate way to combine utilitarian and retributivist considerations in a theory of punishment in your opinion? If not, why not? If so, what is it?

2. When, if ever, should other ways to prevent crime be substituted for punishment? Why then? Why not in other cases?

SUGGESTIONS FOR FURTHER READING

Attempts to combine utilitarianism and retributivism are collected in Gertrude Ezorsky, ed., *Philosophical Perspectives on Punishment* (Albany: State University of New York Press, 1972), Chapter II, Section 3; and discussed by Igor Primoratz in *Justifying Legal Punishment* (Atlantic Highlands, New Jersey: Humanities Press, 1989), Chapter 6. The most prominent mixed theory is probably H.L.A. Hart, *Punishment and Responsibility* (New York: Oxford University Press, 1968), Chapter I, "Prolegomena to the Principles of Punishment." Other mixed theories include Andrew von Hirsch, *Doing Justice* (New York: Hill and Wang, 1976); and C. L. Ten, *Crime, Guilt, and Punishment* (Oxford: Clarendon Press, 1987). On moral education theories, see Jean Hampton, "The Moral Education Theory of Punishment," *Philosophy and Public Affairs*, vol. 13 (1984), pp. 208–238. Randy Barnett presents a restitution theory in "Restitution: A New Paradigm of Criminal Justice," *Ethics*, vol. 87 (1977), pp. 279–301; and develops it further in his essays in *Assessing the Criminal: Restitution, Retribution, and the Legal Process*, ed. Randy E. Barnett and John Hagel III (Cambridge: Ballinger, 1977). Richard Dagger surveys criticisms of Barnett's work and argues for a modified version of restitution theory in "Restitution: Pure or Punitive?" *Criminal Justice Ethics*, vol. 10, no. 2 (Summer/Fall 1991), pp. 29–39. Other promising alternative theories of punishment are presented by Warren Quinn in "The Right to Threaten and the Right to Punish," *Philosophy and Public Affairs*, vol. 14, no. 4 (Fall, 1985), pp. 327–373 (with criticisms by Richard Brook and a reply by Quinn in *Philosophy and Public Affairs*, vol. 17, no. 3 (Summer 1988), pp. 235–247); and John Braithwaite and Philip Pettit, *Not Just Deserts: A Republican Theory of Criminal Justice* (Oxford: Clarendon Press, 1990). Alternatives to punishment are discussed in Jeffrie G. Murphy, ed., *Punishment and Rehabilitation*, 2nd ed. (Belmont, California: Wadsworth, 1985), Part III; and Gertrude Ezorsky, ed., *Philosophical Perspectives on Punishment*, Chapter V.

6.6 CAPITAL PUNISHMENT

INTRODUCTION

So far we have focused on two main questions: *whom* should we punish and *how much* should we punish? Another important question is: *how* should we punish? The most dramatic issue of how to punish concerns capital punishment or the death penalty. This issue can also be used to test the theories of punishment we have discussed. A general theory of punishment is inadequate if it does not yield plausible results in particular cases, such as capital punishment.

The issue of capital punishment arises at many levels. Courts must ask whether or not capital punishment violates the U.S. Constitution. Even if capital punishment is constitutional, that does not necessarily mean that states should threaten or perform executions. Capital punishment still might be morally wrong in ways that are not recognized in the Constitution or in any other law. Consequently, legislators still need to ask whether capital punishment is morally permissible, and whether they want it in their jurisdiction. We will begin with the moral question and return later to the constitutional issue.

The death penalty has been attached to many crimes. Long ago in England, one could be executed for driving sheep over Westminster Bridge. Today, some propose capital punishment for rape, hijacking, treason, and drug dealing. Others want to reserve execution for the most horrendous murders, which involve torture or multiple victims, or for murders of children, police officers, or other officials. The most common question, however, is whether the death penalty is morally permissible under present circumstances for premeditated murders.

MORAL ARGUMENTS FOR CAPITAL PUNISHMENT

There are many moral arguments for capital punishment, but they share a common structure. Every argument for capital punishment must show that it is better than any alternative. The main alternative to the death penalty is life imprisonment, possibly without chance of parole. So the question is: why isn't life imprisonment enough?

The first argument for the death penalty is based on "an eye for an eye." This slogan is often associated with retributivism, but it is important to remember that many retributivists do not accept it (see Section 6.4). Still, some do, and those who accept this slogan often use it to argue for capital punishment. "An eye for an eye" suggests that the punishment must be similar in some way to the crime. Kant (in Section 6.4) and others then claim that no punishment other than death is similar in the required way to murder. Even life imprisonment without parole allows the murderer to live, unlike the murderer's victim, who is dead.

However, the slogan "an eye for an eye" runs into several problems. First, it is often not so easy to find an acceptable punishment that resembles the crime. Retributivists can be inventive about some cases. Kant wrote, "The punishment for rape and pederasty is castration (like that of a white or black eunuch in a Seraglio), that for bestiality, permanent expulsion from civil society, since the criminal has made himself unworthy of human society."[33] However, few people today approve of such punishments, and other punishments that resemble crimes are even less acceptable. We should not torture murderers before executing them, even if they tortured their victims before murdering them. In other cases, there is *no* punishment that could resemble the crime. When someone is convicted of bribery, it doesn't make sense to punish him by bribing him or anyone else. What punishment would be similar to prostitution? insider trading? drunk driving? conspiracy? Because of such problems, contemporary retributivists rarely claim that punishments must always match the manner of the crime. And if retributivists do not defend this principle in general, it would be *ad hoc* to use it to argue for capital punishment.

In addition, not all murderers are equal. Consider the case of John Spenkelink. He walked out of a minimum security prison in 1972. In Nebraska, he picked up a hitchhiker, Joe Szymankiewicz, who stayed with Spenkelink for several weeks. Then, according to Spenkelink, the 230-pound Szymankiewicz stole $8,000 from him, forced him at gunpoint to perform fellatio, and made him play Russian roulette. Szymankiewicz was found the next morning bludgeoned and shot twice from behind. It is not clear whether Spenkelink told the truth, but, if so, his acts were not unprovoked. Yet, in 1979, Spenkelink became the first person executed involuntarily in the United States in twelve years. The point is not to feel sorry for Spenkelink or any murderer. The point is that some murders are worse than others. If we want to reserve capital punishment for the worst crimes, we do not want capital punishment for all murderers, so the principle of "an eye for an eye" is again too simple.

Other versions of retributivism might provide better arguments for capital punishment. Robert Nozick can use degrees of responsibility to show why Spenkelink deserves less punishment than other murderers.[34] And neither Nozick nor Davis requires punishments to resemble crimes, so the problems with "an eye for an eye" do not infect their forms of retributivism (see Section 6.4). If one of these more sophisticated forms of retributivism can be developed and defended, and if it supports the death penalty over every alternative punishment, then it might provide a retributivist argument for the death penalty.

A simpler view underlies more common retributivist arguments for capital punishment. Many people (not only retributivists) feel the need to express strong disapproval of horrible murders. Capital punishment expresses disapproval in a particularly strong way. However, it is not so clear that capital punishment is the only way or the best way to express our disapproval strongly enough, or that we

---

[33]*The Metaphysics of Morals*, trans. Mary Gregor (New York: Cambridge University Press, 1991), p. 169

[34]Robert Nozick, *Philosophical Explanations*, pp. 363 ff. See Section 6.4.

should express our disapproval in such a strong way. Many people think so, but it is hard to build this view into a general theory.

The second main argument for the death penalty is *utilitarian*. Utilitarians consider all effects, including various ways to prevent crime, but the focus is usually on deterrence. It seems obvious to many people that capital punishment deters. Most people fear death, even if some people are willing to risk it. However, the people who need to be deterred are a very special class, specifically, those who would not commit a murder if they thought that they might get the death penalty, but who would commit a murder if they thought that the most they could get would be life imprisonment without parole. Unless you are in this deterrable class, it is hard to see why you should trust your intuitions about the minds of people who are in this class.

Whom can we trust? It is natural to ask criminals themselves. The Los Angeles Police Department reported that many apprehended robbers told police that they had used toy guns or empty guns "rather than take a chance on killing someone and getting the gas chamber."[35] If so, the threat of death really did affect their behavior and did make their crimes less dangerous. However, prisoners are not always honest. They usually try to tell the police what the police want to hear. Furthermore, if life imprisonment were the punishment for killing during robbery, then the robbers might have said that they used toy guns "rather than taking a chance on getting life imprisonment." Criminals want to avoid whatever happens to be the worst punishment. So this study does not prove that capital punishment deters more than life imprisonment.

The same problems cast doubt on another source. Police often claim to know from experience that capital punishment deters. But their relevant experience consists largely of their interactions with criminals. If we cannot trust what criminals say, and if the police base their views on what criminals say, then we cannot trust police officers' intuitions on this issue.

That is why we need other kinds of evidence, such as statistical analysis of large samples. Trends in murder rates might reveal the factors that really do affect criminal behavior. These murder rates reflect how all murderers behave, not only how they talk and not only the murderers who are caught. The murder rate should go down to the extent that capital punishment deters or incapacitates or teaches a moral lesson.

But statistics are not so simple. It might seem that all we need to do is compare the murder rates in jurisdictions that have the death penalty to the murder rates in jurisdictions that do not (or a jurisdiction at a time when it has the death penalty to the same jurisdiction at a time when it does not). Here are the average annual homicide rates per 100,000 population for 1940–1955 for some sets of contiguous states with (D) and without the death penalty at that time:[36]

[35]*Report of the California Senate on the Death Penalty* (1960), pp. 16–17.

[36]This information comes from table 4-2-1 of Hans Zeisel, "The Deterrent Effect of the Death Penalty: Facts v. Faith," in *The Death Penalty in America*, 3rd edition, ed. Hugo Adam Bedau (New York: Oxford University Press, 1982), p. 121.

Midwest		**New England**	
Michigan	3.5	Maine	1.5
Indiana (D)	3.5	New Hampshire (D)	0.9
Ohio (D)	3.5	Vermont (D)	1.0
Minnesota	1.4	Rhode Island	1.3
Wisconsin	1.2	Massachusetts (D)	1.2
Iowa (D)	1.4	Connecticut (D)	1.7
N. Dakota	1.0		
S. Dakota (D)	1.5		
Nebraska (D)	1.8		

If one compares Maine with New Hampshire and Vermont, or Rhode Island with Massachusetts, then one might conclude that the death penalty *lowers* the murder rate. But this would be too quick. If one compares North Dakota with South Dakota and Nebraska, or Rhode Island with Connecticut, then one might suspect that the death penalty *raises* the murder rate. And the comparison among Michigan, Indiana, and Ohio might seem to suggest that the death penalty has no effect at all. Since different comparisons point to incompatible conclusions, none of these comparisons is adequate evidence for any conclusion.

The problem is clear: *Other factors* besides the death penalty affect the murder rate, so we need to consider these other factors. Here are some factors for the three states in the first group above for 1960:[37]

	Michigan	Indiana	Ohio
Status of death penalty	. . .	D	D
Homicide rate (per 100,000)	4.3	4.3	3.2
Probability of apprehension	.75	.83	.85
Probability of conviction	.25	.55	.33
Labor force participation	54.9%	55.3%	54.9%
Unemployment rate	6.9%	4.2%	5.5%
Population aged 15–24	12.9%	13.4%	12.9%
Real per capita income	$1292	$1176	$1278
Non-white population	10.4%	6.2%	9.8%
Civilian population (thousands)	7811	4653	9690
Per capita government expenditures	$363	$289	$338
Per capita police expenditures	$11.3	$7.6	$9.0

[37]This information comes from table 4-2-2 of Zeisel in Bedau, *The Death Penalty in America*, p. 123.

What does this show? First consider police expenditures. Most people would suspect that a strong police force would reduce the murder rate. Michigan spends the most per capita, but Michigan has a higher murder rate than Ohio, and the same murder rate as Indiana, with the lowest police expenditures. This might seem to suggest that the death penalty is a less expensive way to reduce murder. But other comparisons suggest otherwise. Indiana has a much higher probability of conviction and a lower unemployment rate than Michigan. These factors tend to reduce the murder rate, and yet Indiana has the same murder rate as Michigan. This might seem to suggest that the death penalty is what keeps Indiana's murder rate high. Since different comparisons again point in opposite directions, none of this proves anything.

What we need is some way to determine *how much* each factor affects the murder rate. Then we can subtract the effects for other factors, and the remaining changes in the murder rate must be due to the death penalty. This is the goal of multiple regression analysis, a complex statistical technique applied to capital punishment by Isaac Ehrlich, a professor of economics at the State University of New York–Buffalo. Ehrlich compared homicide rates with execution rates for the whole country and concluded that "[A]n additional execution per year may have resulted in 7 or 8 fewer murders."[38] Such precision is impressive, and Ehrlich's study was very influential, but critics were quick to point out several flaws. In addition to some technical problems, Ehrlich's results depended on the time period that he picked. If the data from the last five years of his study were omitted, all evidence of deterrence disappeared. Moreover, the central challenge for multiple regression analysis is to come up with a complete list of factors that might affect murder rates. If even one factor is left out, that factor might explain the variations in murder rates that are attributed to capital punishment. Ehrlich's critics showed that the deterrent effect of capital punishment disappeared when other factors were introduced into his analysis.[39]

Some more recent studies even claim that, when more factors are considered, there is evidence that each execution "adds roughly three more to the number of homicides in the next nine months of the year after the execution."[40] This *counterdeterrence* strikes many people as odd, but it might be explained either because executions "brutalize" society by sending the message that it is acceptable to kill one's enemies or because some people kill as a way to commit suicide or to gain the publicity and pity that comes with the death penalty.

With some studies suggesting deterrence, others suggesting no effect, and still others suggesting counterdeterrence, it is hard to be confident about any conclu-

[38]Isaac Ehrlich, "The Deterrent Effect of Capital Punishment: A Question of Life and Death," *American Economic Review*, vol. 65 (1975), pp. 397–414. Originally published as Working Paper No. 18, National Bureau of Economic Research (1973).

[39]For an excellent survey of multiple regression analysis, Ehrlich's study, and criticisms of it, see Zeisel, "The Deterrent Effect of the Death Penalty," pp. 125–33.

[40]W. J. Bowers and G. L. Pierce, "Deterrence or Brutalization: What is the Effect of Executions?", *Crime and Delinquency* vol. 26 (1980), pp. 453–84. Cited by Bedau in *The Death Penalty in America*, p. 99.

sion. One reason for this uncertainty might be that deterrence and counterdeterrence cancel each other out. Another possible explanation is that capital punishment has recently been employed so rarely and so long after the crime that its deterrent effect has been lost. But the problem also might be just that the social situation is too complex to reach any definitive conclusion.

In the face of this *uncertainty*, what can we do? Decision theorists have developed several methods for choice under uncertainty, but none of the common principles is applicable to the death penalty.[41] Uncertainty might be manageable when there is a big enough difference between the values at stake. This approach is suggested by Ernest van den Haag, a Distinguished Scholar at the Heritage Foundation. Van den Haag argues in a reading later in this section that, whereas capital punishment gambles with the lives of convicted murderers, abolition gambles with the lives of potential innocent victims, and we ought to put more weight on the lives of potential innocent victims than on the lives of convicted murderers, so we ought to retain capital punishment (pp. 735 ff). However, even if murderers count less than their victims, execution is certain to cause death. If we have no adequate reason to believe that executions deter, our choice is between a certainty of a lesser loss and a lower probability of a greater loss. The right choice in such cases is just not clear. (Compare Reiman, p. 748.) It is also important to remember that capital punishment risks innocent lives as well, since it is almost certain that some innocent people will be executed in any actual practice of capital punishment.

Defenders of capital punishment point out that, even if capital punishment does not deter, capital punishment still prevents murders in other ways. The most obvious way is *incapacitation*. Dead murderers never murder again. In contrast, murderers who get life sentences are often paroled, some escape, and some murder again. But not many. Between 1965–75, 11,404 murderers were released in the United States. Only thirty-four were found to commit willful homicide during the first year after release.[42] There were almost certainly more murders after the first year and more murders by released lifers who were not caught, and even thirty-four murders is thirty-four too many. However, we have no reliable way of knowing which murderers are likely to murder again, so we would have had to execute all 11,404 murderers in order to be sure to prevent the repeat murders. The question is whether the gain is worth the carnage.

A special problem arises for murder *in prison*. Murderers who are already serving life sentences without any possibility of parole have little to lose by murdering guards and inmates. Capital punishment sometimes seems to be the only way to stop a killer. One example is Henry Brisbon, Jr., known as the I-51 killer. Brisbon was convicted of torturing and killing three people in 1973 in Illinois. Illinois had no death penalty, so Brisbon was sentenced to 1,000 to 3,000 years. In

---

[41]For three techniques (dominance, maximin, and disaster avoidance) and their limitations, see Gregory Kavka, *Moral Paradoxes of Nuclear Deterrence* (New York: Cambridge University Press, 1987), chapter 3. The analogies between deterrence of crime and deterrence of nuclear war are worth exploring.

[42]See table 4-5-2 in Bedau, *The Death Penalty in America*, p. 177

his first year in prison, he killed an inmate by stabbing him with the sharpened handle of a soup ladle. He also took part in fourteen other attacks on prisoners and guards, and he instigated at least one riot.[43] In such an extreme case, it is hard not to feel the need for the death penalty. (Brisbon did get the death penalty when Illinois reinstituted it in 1977.) Nonetheless, killers like Brisbon might be stopped by other measures, such as solitary confinement. Furthermore, studies have found no evidence that capital punishment reduces murders in prison.[44] So it is still not clear whether capital punishment is the best way to solve the general problem of prison murder.

Capital punishment is also supposed to reduce crime by teaching a *moral lesson*. When a legislature attaches the death penalty to a certain crime, it is often making a statement about how horrible that crime is. People who accept that message, and who want to avoid doing horrible crimes, will be less likely to commit that crime. This sounds plausible, but it is not clear that it works in practice. If the moral lesson of the death penalty really did prevent crimes, this should show up in the murder rates. But no such effect can be found. Furthermore, if capital punishment also brutalizes society by sending the conflicting message that it is permissible to kill people who do you wrong, then it might produce as many murders as it prevents by its intended moral message. This might explain why the statistics are so inconclusive.

The final argument for capital punishment is that it *saves money*. Some people find this argument trivial or even repulsive, but utilitarians should consider all of the consequences of alternative punishments. Prison is expensive, but studies have found that capital punishment is even more expensive. The *Miami Herald*, for example, reported that Florida taxpayers spend about $3,200,000 per execution compared to $515,964 to house an inmate in a maximum security prison for 40 years (although court costs must be added for a fair comparison). New York found that execution is overall about three times more expensive than life imprisonment.[45] Why? In capital cases, trials are longer, appeals are more common, prison security is greater, and convicted murderers usually spend years on death row before they are executed. If we tried to save money by limiting appeals and stays on death row, this would increase the chances of executing innocent people. So it is not clear that any acceptable death penalty system would save money.

MORAL ARGUMENTS AGAINST CAPITAL PUNISHMENT

What about arguments *against* capital punishment? A common one is that it is *uncivilized* (see Reiman in the reading in this section). Capital punishment is now used less often for a smaller range of crimes in fewer countries than a hundred

---

[43]*Time*, January 24, 1983, p. 30.

[44]See Wendy Phillips Wolfson, "The Deterrent Effect of the Death Penalty on Prison Murder," in Bedau, *The Death Penalty in America*, pp. 159–73.

[45]Reported in "Death Row Lawyers," by Claire Conway, in *Update on Law Related Education* (Winter 1989), p. 65. See also Barry Nakell, "The Cost of the Death Penalty" in Bedau, *The Death Penalty in America*, pp. 241–46.

years ago. In fact, it is the only corporal punishment still used in the United States. We don't whip or brand criminals anymore (although it is not clear why). Nonetheless, it is not clear how these trends support abolition. The rarity of corporal and capital punishment might be desirable even if capital punishment must be retained for a few cases. Its overuse in the past does not show that it should *never* be used in the present.

Capital punishment still strikes many people as *inhumane.* It is not just that execution is painful. Life imprisonment might cause even more pain over the long run, and some methods of execution, such as lethal injection, involve little pain. But there is something especially horrifying to most people about the mental anguish of years on death row awaiting execution. It is also often said that, whereas other punishments allow criminals to retain some rights, execution takes away all of one's rights (see Justice Brennan in *Furman,* p. 762). This is not completely true, since executed criminals have rights, for example, that their wills be probated. Still, there are many rights, such as the right to appeal, that are retained by prisoners but not by people after they are executed. Since lower animals do not have rights, this is supposed to show that execution denies criminals their "humanity" and treats them like lower animals.

Even if so, does this show that capital punishment is wrong? Defenders of capital punishment often see its horrors as attractive, when they are deserved. The point of capital punishment is to do horrible things to people who did horrible things. There are still limits. Defenders of capital punishment usually oppose torture. But then the issue is whether capital punishment is too horrible ever to be permitted, and that is not obvious to many people.

Some defenders of capital punishment have even argued that life imprisonment without hope of parole is crueler than capital punishment.[46] Life imprisonment lasts longer, involves more pain, and also treats criminals like animals. If capital punishment is like putting dogs to sleep, life imprisonment is like caging tigers. So the death penalty might be justified as a way to avoid the cruelty of life imprisonment without parole. Another alternative would be to let convicted murderers choose which of these two punishments they would prefer, but that alternative has never been tried, although it is not clear why. In any case, the horrors of capital punishment do not obviously show that it is always wrong.

Another distinguishing feature of capital punishment is its *irrevocability.* Mistaken executions cannot be taken back. Admittedly, if someone spends ten years in prison because of a mistaken conviction, nobody can give back those years. But at least the innocent prisoner can be released and given some compensation, however inadequate. Release cannot restore everything, but it is better than execution. Just ask prisoners who have been released. With execution, there is a moment after which nothing at all can be done. This problem came out dramatically in the execution of Robert Streetman.[47] At 3:19 a.m. on January 7, 1988, lethal

---

[46]For example, Jacques Barzun, "In Favor of Capital Punishment," *The American Scholar* vol. 31, no. 2 (Spring 1962), pp. 181–91.

[47]*The New York Times,* Sunday, January 17, 1988.

drugs were pumped into his veins. He was pronounced dead seven minutes later. As the drugs did their job, the Texas governor's office called to ask "where we were in the process," because the governor was considering whether to stop the execution in order to give Streetman's attorney time to file a new motion. The governor's call might have come before the execution began if Streetman's lawyer had not been put on hold while pleading with the governor on the telephone. Of course, the motion might have failed, and Streetman might have been executed anyway, but we will never know. That shows why irrevocability makes the death penalty problematic.

Of course, the permanence of capital punishment is attractive to its defenders. Murderers serving life sentences might get out to murder again, but executed criminals are incapacitated forever. Nonetheless, even if permanence is attractive sometimes, it is still a problem when an execution was a mistake.

In order to assess the seriousness of this problem, we need to ask how often *mistakes* occur. In the most extensive study so far, Bedau and Radelet claim that the defendant was later found innocent in twenty-three executions out of 7,092 between 1900 and 1985, for an error rate of 0.32 percent.[48] Defenders of capital punishment will point out that fewer than one in 300 of those executed were found innocent. However, people usually stop looking for evidence after an execution, so we don't know how many more of those executed were innocent. The number of errors is probably small, especially in more recent years; and we can take steps to reduce the risk; but errors cannot be avoided completely. The question, then, is whether capital punishment has enough advantages to override the inevitable errors that will occur.

In addition to errors, abolitionists also object to caprice and discrimination in the distribution of capital punishment. *Caprice* occurs when one murderer is sentenced to death and another is not, even though there is no difference between them that is adequate to justify this difference in their sentences. Such cases do occur in our system. If two people take equal part in a single murder, they can be tried separately and receive different sentences, because they face different prosecutors, judges, and jurors, each of whom has discretion in determining punishments. Caprice is not error, because neither criminal is innocent, but there still seems to be something wrong with distributing capital punishment arbitrarily.

The most objectionable kind of caprice is *discrimination*. There is ample evidence that even now African-Americans who killed European-Americans are much more likely to receive the death penalty than European-Americans who killed African-Americans. Although such discrimination might be reduced, there is no way to prevent discrimination entirely. As long as there are prejudices in society, these prejudices are bound to affect when prosecutors seek the death penalty, when the best lawyers take cases, when judges grant motions, and when juries find guilt or enough guilt for the death penalty.

---

[48]Hugo Adam Bedau and Michael L. Radelet, "Miscarriages of Justice in Potentially Capital Cases," *Stanford Law Review* 40, 1 (November, 1987), pp. 21–179 at 73. Only two of the errors were made after 1945, but there were also fewer executions during that period.

Even though this discrimination is indefensible, it is not clear that it makes capital punishment wrong. First, discrimination and caprice run throughout our whole system, but they do not show that we should do away with all punishments. In order to argue against the death penalty in particular, abolitionists need to show why discrimination is more rampant or more objectionable when it affects the death penalty. Stephen Nathanson develops this argument and Ernest van den Haag criticizes it in the readings that follow in this section.

Second, discrimination in the overall *system* does not show either that a *particular* death sentence was due to discrimination or that a particular murderer does not deserve to be executed. Even if some murderers get off too often, it is not clear why this makes it wrong to execute an individual who is guilty of a horrible murder (see the majority opinion in *McCleskey* in this section).

This response raises larger questions about the relation between a particular case and its institutional setting. If one focuses on a particular case, capital punishment will seem justified to many people. What else can we do with the I–51 killer? But one will be less inclined to support the death penalty if one focuses on the general institution, which is necessary for any execution to be lawful, and which inevitably leads to discrimination and even errors. Even if there is less discrimination now than in the past, there is still too much. Just as we do not trust the government to restrict free speech even when some speech deserves to be restricted, so, some would argue, we also should not trust the government to execute criminals even when some criminals deserve to be executed. The basic question concerns when we should give the government a power that it needs in some cases but will misuse in others. This is a deep issue that capital punishment shares with many other areas of law.

CONSTITUTIONALITY

So far we have focused on the moral issue of whether states should have capital punishment, but there are also important questions about whether capital punishment is even allowed by the U.S. Constitution. Abolitionists sometimes use the above moral arguments to show that capital punishment is "cruel and unusual punishment" as prohibited by the Eighth Amendment or that it denies "equal protection of the laws" as guaranteed by the Fourteenth Amendment (see Section 5.3 on equal protection). Defenders of capital punishment often respond that these clauses were not originally intended to exclude capital punishment, since it was used widely in those times, and that a majority of U.S. citizens still support it (see Section 2.1 on original intention). Retentionists also often argue that courts should defer to legislatures except when laws are clearly unconstitutional, but capital punishment is at least not clearly unconstitutional, so courts should not prevent legislatures from using capital punishment.

These methodological and substantive issues have been at the center of recent cases about capital punishment. In *Furman v. Georgia* (1973), excerpted in this section, the majority of the Supreme Court overruled a death penalty statute. Justices Brennan and Marshall opposed every death penalty, but the majority depended on Justices Douglas, Stewart, and White, who opposed the death penalty because the statutes in this case allowed discrimination and other kinds of caprice in violation of the Equal Protection Clause of the Fourteenth Amendment.

After *Furman*, many states rewrote their statutes in order to reduce discrimination by specifying the conditions when capital punishment is allowed. For example, the new Georgia statute did not allow a death sentence unless the jury found at least one aggravating factor on an official list. Most statutes also provided automatic appeal for any death sentence. These safeguards were supposed to reduce the room for discrimination. There was also new evidence of public support for capital punishment, as many legislatures passed new capital punishment statutes. Finally, there was new evidence of deterrence in Ehrlich's studies (discussed earlier). These developments explain why the majority of the Supreme Court upheld the new Georgia statute in *Gregg v. Georgia* (1976), excerpted in this section.

However, new studies soon revealed that significant discrimination remained even after the new statutes.[49] On this basis, the Georgia statute was challenged again in *McCleskey v. Kemp* (1986), also excerpted in this section. This time, a five-Justice majority of the Supreme Court held that a particular death sentence does not violate the Equal Protection Clause unless the decision makers in this particular case acted with a discriminatory purpose. Critics of *McCleskey* object that it is too hard to prove discrimination in a particular case, so the *McCleskey* decision makes it practically impossible to overturn death sentences on grounds of discrimination.[50] (Compare Section 8.2 below on statistical evidence.)

Another kind of challenge to the death penalty arose in *Herrera v. Texas* (1993), excerpted in this section. Ten years after receiving a death sentence, Herrera came up with new affidavits testifying to his innocence. He asked for a new trial, so a jury could decide whether this new evidence created a reasonable doubt of his guilt. A majority of the Supreme Court denied Herrera a new trial, because they found that the evidence was not strong enough. They also argued that the system could not function if every prisoner could obtain a new trial by coming up with new evidence. Here the Supreme Court uses general institutional needs to justify its decision in a particular case.

This line of cases as a whole suggests that the Court will allow capital punishment, but only for certain crimes, only if imposed by certain kinds of statutes, and only if certain procedures are followed. Although restricted, executions will go on, so total abolitionists will not be satisfied, but they can continue to fight against the death penalty in legislatures, in individual court cases, and in moral debates outside the courts. This kind of compromise and continuing discussion is a common result in our legal system.

---

[49]See the Baldus study discussed in *McCleskey v. Kemp*; and William J. Bowers and Glenn L. Pierce, "Racial Discrimination and Criminal Homicide under Post-*Furman* Statutes," in Bedau, *The Death Penalty in America*, pp. 206–24.

[50]A proposal to allow courts to use the same kind of statistical evidence that *McCleskey* ruled out was originally part of the crime bill before Congress in 1994.

THE COLLAPSE OF THE CASE AGAINST CAPITAL PUNISHMENT

ERNEST VAN DEN HAAG

Three questions about the death penalty so overlap that they must each be answered. I shall ask seriatim: Is the death penalty constitutional? Is it useful? Is it morally justifiable?

I. THE CONSTITUTIONAL QUESTION

The Fifth Amendment states that no one shall be "deprived of life, liberty, or property without due process of law," implying a "due process of law" to deprive persons of life. The Eighth Amendment prohibits "cruel and unusual punishment." It is unlikely that this prohibition was meant to supersede the Fifth Amendment, since the amendments were simultaneously enacted in 1791.[1]

The Fourteenth Amendment, enacted in 1868, reasserted and explicitly extended to the states the implied authority to "deprive of life, liberty, or property" by "due process of law." Thus, to regard the death penalty as unconstitutional one must believe that the standards which determine what is "cruel and unusual" have so evolved since 1868 as to prohibit now what was authorized then, and that the Constitution authorizes the courts to overrule laws in the light of *new* moral standards. What might these standards be? And what shape must their evolution take to be constitutionally decisive?

Consensus. A moral consensus, intellectual or popular, could have evolved to find execution "cruel and unusual." It did not. Intellectual opinion is divided. Polls suggest that most people would vote for the death penalty. Congress recently has legislated the death penalty for skyjacking under certain conditions. The representative assemblies of two-thirds of the states did re-enact capital punishment when previous laws were found constitutionally defective.[2]

If, however, there were a consensus against the death penalty, the Constitution expects the political process, rather than judicial decisions, to reflect it. Courts are meant to interpret the laws made by the political process and to set constitutional limits to it—not to replace it by responding to a presumed moral consensus. Surely the "cruel and unusual" phrase was not meant to authorize the courts to become legislatures.[3] Thus, neither a consensus of moral opinion nor a moral discovery by judges is meant to be disguised as a constitutional interpretation. Even when revealed by a burning bush, new moral norms were not meant to become constitutional norms by means of court decisions.[4] To be sure, the courts in the past have occasionally done away with obsolete kinds of punishment—but never in the face of legislative and popular opposition and re-enactment. Abolitionists constantly press the courts now to create rather than to confirm obsolescence. That courts are urged to do what so clearly is for voters and lawmakers to decide suggests that the absence of consensus for abolition is recognized by the opponents of capital punishment. What then can the phrase "cruel and unusual punishment" mean today?

"Cruel" may be understood to mean excessive—punitive without, or beyond, a rational-utilitarian purpose. Since capital punishment excludes rehabilitation and is not needed for incapacitation, the remaining rational-utilitarian purpose would be deterrence, the reduction of the rate at which the crime punished is

Ernest van den Haag, "The Collapse of the Case Against Capital Punishment," *National Review* (March 31, 1978), pp. 395–407.

committed by others. I shall consider this reduction below. Here I wish to note that, if the criterion for the constitutionality of any punishment were an actual demonstration of its rational-utilitarian effectiveness, all legal punishments would be in as much constitutional jeopardy as the death penalty. Are fines for corporations deterrent? rehabilitative? incapacitative? Is a jail term for marijuana possession? Has it ever been established that ten years in prison are doubly as deterrent as five, or at least sufficiently more deterrent? (I don't pretend to know what "sufficiently" might mean: whether 10 percent or 80 percent added deterrence would warrant 100 percent added severity.)

The Constitution certainly does not require a demonstration of rational–utilitarian effects for any punishment. Such a demonstration so far has not been available. To demand it for one penalty—however grave—and not for others, when it is known that no such demonstration is available, or has been required hitherto for any punishment, seems unjustified. Penalties have always been regarded as constitutional if they can be plausibly intended (rather than demonstrated) to be effective (useful), and if they are not grossly excessive, i.e., unjust.

Justice, a rational but non–utilitarian purpose of punishment, requires that it be proportioned to the felt gravity of the crime. Thus, constitutional justice authorizes, even calls for, a higher penalty the graver the crime. One cannot demand that this constitutionally required escalation stop short of the death penalty unless one furnishes positive proof of its irrationality by showing injustice, i.e., disproportionality (to the felt gravity of the crime punished or to other punishments of similar crimes), as well as ineffectiveness, i.e., uselessness in reducing the crime rate. There is no proof of cruelty here in either sense.

"*Unusual*" is generally interpreted to mean either randomly capricious and therefore unconstitutional, or capricious in a biased, discriminatory way, so as particularly to burden specifiable groups, and therefore unconstitutional. (Random arbitrariness might violate the Eighth, biased arbitrariness the Fourteenth Amendment, which promises "the equal protection of the laws.") Apart from the historical interpretation noted above (Footnote 1), "unusual" seems to mean "unequal" then. The dictionary equivalent—"rare"—seems to be regarded as relevant only inasmuch as it implies "unequal." Indeed it is hard to see why rarity should be objectionable otherwise.

For the sake of argument, let me grant that either or both forms of capriciousness prevail[5] and that they are less tolerable with respect to the death penalty than with respect to milder penalties—which certainly are not meted out less capriciously. However prevalent, neither form of capriciousness would argue for abolishing the death penalty. Capriciousness is not inherent in that penalty, or in any penalty, but occurs in its distribution. Therefore, the remedy lies in changing the laws and procedures which distribute the penalty. It is the process of distribution which is capable of discriminating, not that which it distributes.

Unavoidable capriciousness. If capricious distribution places some convicts, or groups of convicts, at unwarranted disadvantage,[6] can it be remedied enough to satisfy the Eighth and Fourteenth Amendments? Some capriciousness is unavoidable because decisions of the criminal justice system necessarily rest on accidental factors at many points, such as the presence or absence of witnesses to an act; or the cleverness or clumsiness of police officers who exercise their discretion in arresting suspects and seizing evidence. All court decisions must rest on the available and admissible evidence for, rather than the actuality of, guilt. Availability of evidence is necessarily accidental to the actuality of whatever it is that the evidence is needed for. Accident is the capriciousness of fate.

Now, if possible without loss of other desiderata, accident and human capriciousness should be minimized. But, obviously, discretionary judgments cannot be avoided altogether. The Framers of the Constitution were certainly aware of the unavoidable elements of discretion which affect all human decisions, including those of police officers, of prosecutors, and of the courts. Because it always was unavoidable, discretion no more speaks against the constitutionality of the criminal justice system or of any of the penalties now than it did when the Constitution was written—unless something has evolved since, to make unavoidable discretion, tolerable before, intolerable now, at least for the death penalty. I know of no such evolution; and I would think it was up to the legislative branch of government to register it had it occurred.

The Constitution, though it enjoins us to minimize capriciousness, does not enjoin a standard of unattainable perfection or exclude penalties because that standard has not been attained.[7] Actually, modern legislative trends hitherto have favored enlargement of discretion in the judicial process. I have always thought that enlargement to be excessive, immoral, irrational, and possibly unconstitutional—even when not abused for purposes of discrimination. Yet though we should not enlarge it *praeter necessitatem*, some discretion is unavoidable and even desirable, and no reason for giving up any punishment.

Avoidable capriciousness. Capriciousness should be prevented by abolishing penalties capriciously distributed only in one case: when it is so unavoidable and so excessive that penalties are randomly distributed between the guilty and the innocent. When that is not the case, the abuses of discretion which lead to discrimination against particular groups of defendants or convicts certainly require correction, but not abolition of the penalty abused by maldistribution.

II. PRELIMINARY MORAL ISSUES

Justice and equality. Regardless of constitutional interpretation, the morality and legitimacy of the abolitionist argument from capriciousness, or discretion, or discrimination, would be more persuasive if it were alleged that those selectively executed are not guilty. But the argument merely maintains that some other guilty but more favored persons, or groups, escape the death penalty. This is hardly sufficient for letting anyone else found guilty escape the penalty. On the contrary, that some guilty persons or groups elude it argues for extending the death penalty to them. Surely "due process of law" is meant to do justice; and "the equal protection of the law" is meant to extend justice equally to all. Nor do I read the Constitution to command us to prefer equality to justice. When we clamor for "equal justice for all" it is justice which is to be equalized and extended, and which therefore is the prior desideratum, not to be forsaken and replaced by equality but rather to be extended.

Justice requires punishing the guilty—as many of the guilty as possible, even if only some can be punished—and sparing the innocent—as many of the innocent as possible, even if not all are spared. Morally, justice must always be preferred to equality. It would surely be wrong to treat everybody with equal injustice in preference to meting out justice at least to some. Justice then cannot ever permit sparing some guilty persons, or punishing some innocent ones, for the sake of equality—because others have been unjustly spared or punished. In practice, penalties never could be applied if we insisted that they cannot be inflicted on any guilty person unless we can make sure that they are equally applied to all other guilty persons. Anyone familiar with law enforcement knows that punishments can be inflicted only on an unavoidably capricious, at best a random, selection of the guilty. I see no more merit in the attempt to persuade the courts to let all capital-crime defendants go free of capital punishment because some have wrongly escaped it than I see in an attempt to persuade the courts to let all burglars go because some have wrongly escaped imprisonment.

Although it hardly warrants serious discussion, the argument from capriciousness looms large in briefs and decisions because for the last seventy years courts have tried—unproductively—to prevent errors of procedure, or of evidence collection, or of decision-making, by the paradoxical method of letting defendants go free as a punishment, or warning, or deterrent, to errant law enforcers. The strategy admittedly never has prevented the errors it was designed to prevent—although it has released countless guilty persons. But however ineffective it be, the strategy had a rational purpose. The rationality, on the other hand, of arguing that a penalty must be abolished because of allegations that some guilty persons escape it, is hard to fathom—even though the argument was accepted by some Justices of the Supreme Court.

The essential moral question. Is the death penalty morally just and/or useful? This is the essential moral, as distinguished from constitutional, question. Discrimination is irrelevant to this moral question. If the death penalty were distributed quite equally and uncapriciously and with superhuman perfection to all the guilty, but was morally unjust, it would remain unjust in each case. Contrariwise, if the death penalty is morally just, however discriminatorily applied to only some of the guilty, it does remain just in each case in which it is applied. Thus, if it were applied exclusively to guilty males and never to guilty females, the death penalty, though unequally applied, would remain just. For justice consists in punishing the guilty and sparing the innocent, and its equal extension, though desirable, is not part of it. It is part of equality, not of justice (or injustice), which is what equality equalizes. The same consideration would apply if some benefit were distributed only to males but not equally to deserving females. The inequality would not argue against the benefit, or against distribution to deserving males, but rather for distribution to equally deserving females. Analogously, the nondistribution of the death penalty to guilty females would argue for applying it to them as well, and not against applying it to guilty males.

The utilitarian (political) effects of unequal justice may well be detrimental to the social fabric because they outrage our passion for equality, particularly for equality before the law. Unequal justice is also morally repellent. Nonetheless unequal justice is justice still. What is repellent is the incompleteness, the inequality, not the justice. The guilty do not become innocent or less deserving of punishment because others escaped it. Nor does any innocent deserve punishment because others suffer it. Justice remains just, however unequal, while injustice remains unjust, however equal. However much each is desired, justice and equality are not identical. Equality before the law should be extended and enforced, then—but not at the expense of justice.

Maldistribution among the guilty: a sham argument. Capriciousness, at any rate, is used as a sham argument against capital punishment by all abolitionists I have ever known. They would oppose the death penalty if it could be meted out without any discretion whatsoever. They would oppose the death penalty in a homogeneous country without racial discrimination. And they would oppose the death penalty if the incomes of those executed and of those spared were the same. Abolitionists oppose the death penalty, not its possible maldistribution. They should have the courage of their convictions.

Maldistribution between the guilty and the innocent: another sham argument. What about persons executed in error? The objection here is not that some of the guilty get away, but that some of the innocent do not—a matter far more serious than discrimination among the guilty. Yet, when argued by abolitionists, this too is a sham argument, as are all distributional arguments. For abolitionists are opposed to the death penalty for the guilty as much as for the innocent. Hence, the question of guilt, if at all relevant to their position, cannot be decisive for them. Guilt is decisive only to those who urge the death penalty for the guilty. They must worry about distribution—part of the justice they seek.

Miscarriages of justice. The execution of innocents believed guilty is a miscarriage of justice which must be opposed whenever detected. But such miscarriages of justice do not warrant abolition of the death penalty. Unless the moral drawbacks of an activity or practice, which include the possible death of innocent bystanders, outweigh the moral advantages which include the innocent lives that might be saved by it, the activity is warranted. Most human activities—construction, manufacturing, automobile and air traffic, sports, not to speak of wars and revolutions—cause the death of some innocent bystanders. Nevertheless, if the advantages sufficiently outweigh the disadvantages, human activities, including those of the penal system with all its punishments, are morally justified: Consider now the advantages in question.

III. DETERRENCE

New evidence. Is there evidence for the usefulness of the death penalty in securing the life of the citizens? Researchers in the past found no statistical evidence for the effects sought: i.e., marginal deterrent effects, deterrent effects over and above those of alternative sanctions. However, in the last few years new and more sophisticated research has led, for instance, Professor Isaac Ehrlich to conclude that over the period 1933–1969, "an additional execution per year . . . may have resulted on the average in seven or eight fewer murders."[8] Other investigators have confirmed Ehrlich's tentative results. Not surprisingly, refutations have been attempted, and Professor Ehrlich has answered them. He has also published a new cross-sectional analysis of the data which confirms the conclusions of his original (time–series) study.[9] The matter will remain controversial for some time,[10] but two tentative conclusions can be drawn with some confidence by now. First, Ehrlich has shown that previous investigations, which did not find deterrent effects of the death penalty, suffer from fatal defects. Second, there is now some likelihood—much more than

hitherto—of demonstrating marginal deterrent effects statistically.

The choice. Thus, with respect to deterrence, we must choose 1) to trade the certain shortening of the life of a convicted murderer for the survival of between seven and eight innocent victims whose future murder by others may be less likely if the convicted murderer is executed. Or 2) to trade the certain lengthening of the life of a convicted murderer for the possible loss of the lives of between seven and eight innocent victims, who may be more likely to be murdered by others because of our failure to execute the convicted murderer.[11]

If we were certain that executions have a zero marginal effect, they could not be justified in deterrent terms. But even the pre–Ehrlich investigations never did demonstrate this. They merely found that an above–zero effect cannot be demonstrated statistically. While we do not know at present the degree of confidence with which we can assign an above–zero marginal deterrent effect to executions, we can be more confident than in the past. It seems morally indefensible to let convicted murderers survive at the probable—even at the merely possible—expense of the lives of innocent victims who might have been spared had the murderers been executed.

Non-deterrence as a sham argument. Most of the studies purporting to show that capital punishment produces no added deterrence, or that it cannot be shown to do so, were made by abolitionists, such as Professor Thorsten Sellin. They were used to show the futility of the death penalty. Relying on their intuition as well as on these studies, many abolitionists still are convinced that the death penalty is no more deterrent than life imprisonment. And they sincerely believe that the failure of capital punishment to produce additional deterrence argues for abolishing it. However, the more passionate and committed abolitionists use the asserted ineffectiveness of the death penalty as a deterrent as a sham argument—just as they use alleged capriciousness and maldistribution in application. They use the argument for debating purposes—but actually would abolish the death penalty even if it were an effective deterrent, just as they would abolish the death penalty if it were neither discriminatorily nor otherwise maldistributed.

Professors Charles Black (Yale Law School) and Hugo Adam Bedau (Tufts, Philosophy) are both well known for their public commitment to abolition of the death penalty, attested to by numerous writings. At a symposium held on October 15, 1977 at the Arizona State University at Tempe, Arizona, they were asked to entertain the hypothesis—whether or not contrary to fact—that the death penalty is strongly deterrent over and above alternative penalties: Would they favor abolition in the face of conclusive proof of a strong deterrent effect over and above that of alternative penalties? Both gentlemen answered affirmatively. They were asked whether they would still abolish the death penalty if they knew that abolition (and replacement by life imprisonment) would increase the homicide rate by 10 percent, 20 percent, 50 percent, 100 percent, or 1,000 percent. Both gentlemen continued to answer affirmatively.

I am forced to conclude that Professors Black and Bedau think the lives of convicted murderers (however small their number) are more worth preserving than the lives of an indefinite number of innocent victims (however great their number). Or, the principle of abolition is more important to them than the lives of any number of innocent murder victims who would be spared if convicted murderers were executed.

I have had occasion subsequently to ask former Attorney General Ramsey Clark the same question; he answered as Professors Black and Bedau did, stressing that nothing could persuade him to favor the death penalty—however deterrent it might be. (Mr. Clark has kindly permitted me to quote his view here.)

Now, Professors Black and Bedau and Mr. Clark do *not* believe that the death penalty adds deterrence. They do not believe therefore—regardless of the evidence—that abolition would cause an increase in the homicide rate. But the question they were asked, and which—after some dodging—they answered forthrightly, had nothing to do with the acceptance or rejection of the deterrent effect of the death penalty. It was a hypothetical question: If it were deterrent, would you still abolish the death penalty? Would you still abolish it if it were very deterrent, so that abolition would lead to a quantum jump in the murder rate? They answered affirmatively.

These totally committed abolitionists, then, are not interested in deterrence. They claim that the death penalty does not add to deterrence only as a sham argument. Actually, whether or not the death penalty deters is, to them, irrelevant. The intransigence of these committed humanitarians is puzzling as well as inhumane. Passionate ideological commitments have been known to have such effects. These otherwise kind and occasionally reasonable persons do not want to see murderers executed ever—however many innocent lives can be saved thereby. *Fiat injustitia, pereat humanitas.*

Experiments? In principle one could experiment to test the deterrent effect of capital punishment. The most direct way would be to legislate the death penalty for certain kinds of murder if committed on weekdays, but never on Sunday. Or, on Monday, Wednesday, and Friday, and not on other days; on other days, life imprisonment would be the maximum sentence. (The days could be changed around every few years to avoid possible bias.) I am convinced there will be fewer murders on death-penalty than on live-imprisonment days. Unfortunately the experiment faces formidable obstacles.[12]

The burden of proof of usefulness. Let me add a common-sense remark. Our penal system rests on the proposition that more severe penalties are more deterrent than less severe penalties. We assume, rightly, I believe, that a $5 fine deters rape less than a $500 fine, and that the threat of five years in prison will deter more than either fine.[13] This assumption of the penal system rests on the common experience that, once aware of them, people learn to avoid natural dangers the more likely these are to be injurious and the more severe the likely injuries. Else the survival of the human race would be hard to explain. People endowed with ordinary common sense (a class that includes a modest but significant number of sociologists) have found no reason why behavior with respect to legal dangers should differ from behavior with respect to natural dangers. Indeed, it doesn't. Hence, all legal systems proportion threatened penalties to the gravity of crimes, both to do justice and to achieve deterrence in proportion to that gravity.

But if, *ceteris paribus*, the more severe the penalty the greater the deterrent effect, then the most severe available penalty—the death penalty—would have the greatest deterrent effect. Arguments to the contrary assume either that capital crimes never are deterrable (sometimes merely because not all capital crimes have been deterred), or that, beyond life imprisonment, the deterrent effect of added severity is necessarily zero. Perhaps. But the burden of proof must be borne by those who presume to have located the point of zero marginal returns before the death penalty.

The threat of death needed in special circumstances. Another common-sense observation. Without the death penalty, we necessarily confer immunity on just those persons most likely to be in need of deterrent threats: thus, prisoners serving life sentences can kill fellow prisoners or guards with impunity. Prison wardens are unlikely to be able to prevent violence in prisons as long as they give humane treatment to inmates and have no serious threats of additional punishment available for the murderers among them who are already serving life sentences. I cannot see the moral or utilitarian reasons for giving permanent immunity to homicidal life prisoners, thereby endangering the other prisoners and the guards, in effect preferring the life prisoners to their victims who *could* be punished if they murdered.

Outside prison an offender who expects a life sentence for his offense may murder his victim, or witnesses, or the arresting officer, to improve his chances of escaping. He could not be threatened with an additional penalty for his, additional crime—an open invitation. Only the death penalty could deter in such cases.[14] If there is but a possibility that it will, we should retain it. But I believe there is a *probability* that the threat of the death penalty will deter.

Reserved for the worst crimes. However, effective deterrence requires that the threat of the ultimate penalty be reserved for the worst crime from which the offender may be deterred by that threat. Hence, the extreme punishment should not be prescribed when the offender, because already threatened by it, might feel he can add further crimes with impunity. Thus, rape, or kidnapping, should not incur the death penalty, while killing the victim of either crime should.[15] (The death penalty for rape may actually function as an incentive to murder the victim/witness.) This may not stop an Eichmann after his first murder; but it will stop most people before. To be sure, an offender not deterred from murdering one victim by the threat of execution is unlikely to be deterred from additional murders by further threats. The range of effective punishments is not infinite; on the contrary, it is necessarily more restricted than the range of possible crimes. Some offenders cannot be deterred by any threat. But most people can be; and most people respond to the size of the threat addressed to them. Since death is the ultimate penalty—the greatest threat available—it must be reserved for the ultimate crime even though it cannot always prevent it.

IV. SOME POPULAR ARGUMENTS

Consider now some popular arguments against capital punishment.

Barbarization. According to Beccaria, with the death penalty the "laws which punish homicide

. . . themselves commit it," thus giving "an example of barbarity." Those who speak of "legalized murder" use an oxymoronic phrase to echo this allegation. However, punishments—fines, incarcerations, or executions—although often physically identical to the crimes punished, are neither crimes, nor their moral equivalent. The difference between crimes and lawful acts, including punishments, is not physical, but legal: crimes differ from other acts by being unlawful. Driving a stolen car is a crime, though not physically distinguishable from driving a car lawfully owned. Unlawful imprisonment and kidnapping need not differ physically from the lawful arrest and incarceration used to punish unlawful imprisonment and kidnapping. Finally, whether a lawful punishment gives an "example of barbarity" depends on how the moral difference between crime and punishment is perceived. To suggest that its physical quality, *ipso facto*, morally disqualifies the punishment is to assume what is to be shown.

It is quite possible that all displays of violence, criminal or punitive, influence people to engage in unlawful imitations. This seems one good reason not to have public executions. But it does not argue against executions. Objections to displaying on TV the process of violently subduing a resistant offender do not argue against actually subduing him.[16] Arguments against the public display of vivisections, or of the effects of painful medications, do not argue against either. Arguments against the public display of sexual activity do not argue against sexual activity. Arguments against public executions, then, do not argue against executions.[17] The deterrent effect of punishments depends on their being known. But it does not depend on punishments' being carried out publicly. The threat of imprisonment deters, but incarcerated persons are not on public display.

Crimes of passion. Abolitionists often maintain that most capital crimes are "acts of passion" which a) could not be restrained by the threat of the death penalty, and b) do not de-

serve it morally even if other crimes might. It is not clear to me why a crime motivated by, say, sexual passion is morally less deserving of punishment than one motivated by passion for money. Is the sexual passion morally more respectable than others? or more gripping? or just more popular? Generally, is violence in personal conflicts morally more excusable than violence among people who do not know each other? A precarious case might be made for such a view, but I shall not attempt to make it.

Perhaps it is true, however, that many murders are irrational "acts of passion" which cannot be deterred by the threat of the death penalty. Either for this reason or because "crimes of passion" are thought less blameworthy than other homicides, most "crimes of passion" are not punishable by death now.[18]

But if most murders are irrational acts, it would therefore seem that the traditional threat of the death penalty has succeeded in deterring most rational people, or most people when rational, from committing murder, and that the fear of the penalty continues to deter all but those who are so irrational that they cannot be deterred by any threat. Hardly a reason for abolishing the death penalty. Indeed, that capital crimes are committed mostly by irrational persons and only by some rational ones would suggest that more rational persons might commit these crimes if the penalty were lower. This hardly argues against capital punishment. Else we would have to abolish penalties whenever they succeed in deterring people. Yet abolitionists urge that capital punishment be abolished because capital crimes are most often committed by the irrational—as though deterring the rational is not quite enough.

Samuel Johnson. Finally, some observations on an anecdote reported by Boswell and repeated ever since *ad nauseam.* Dr. Johnson found pickpockets active in a crowd assembled to see one of their number hanged. He concluded that executions do not deter. His conclusion does not follow from his observation.

1. Since the penalty Johnson witnessed was what pickpockets had expected all along, they had no reason to reduce their activities. Deterrence is expected to increase (i.e., crime is expected to decrease) only when penalties do. It is unreasonable to expect people who entered a criminal occupation—e.g., that of pickpocket—fully aware of the risks, to be subsequently deterred by those risks if they are not increased. They will not be deterred unless the penalty becomes more severe, or is inflicted more often.

2. At most, a public execution could have had the deterrent effect on pickpockets expected by Dr. Johnson because of its visibility. But visibility may also have had a contrary effect: the spectacle of execution was probably more fascinating to the crowd than other spectacles; it distracted attention from the activities of pickpockets and thereby increased their opportunities more than other spectacles would. Hence, an execution crowd might have been more inviting to pickpockets than other crowds. (As mentioned before, deterrence depends on knowledge, but does not require visibility.)

3. Even when the penalty is greatly increased, let alone when it is unchanged, the deterrent effect of penalties is usually slight with respect to those already engaged in criminal activities.[19] Deterrence is effective in the main by restraining people not as yet committed to a criminal occupation from entering it. This point bears some expansion.

The risk of penalty is the cost of crime offenders expect. When this cost (the penalty multiplied by the risk of suffering it) is high enough, relative to the benefit the crime is expected to yield, the cost will deter a considerable number of people who would have entered a criminal occupation had the cost been lower. When the net benefit is very low, only those who have no other opportunities at all, or are irrationally attracted to it, will want to engage in an illegal activity such as picking pockets. In this respect the effects of the cost of crime are not different from the effects of the cost of automobiles or movie tickets, or from the effects of the cost (effort, risks, and other disadvantages) of any activity relative to its benefits. When (comparative) net benefits decrease because of cost increases, so does the flow of new entrants. But those already in the occupation usually continue. *Habits, law-abiding or criminal, are less influenced by costs than habit formation is.* That is as true for the risk of penalties as for any other cost.

Most deterrence studies disregard the fact that the major effect of the legal threat system is on habit formation rather than on habits formed. It is a long-run rather than a short-run effect. By measuring only the short-run effects (on habits already formed) rather than the far more important long-run (habit-forming) effects of the threat system, such studies underrate the effectiveness of the deterrence.

4. Finally, Dr. Johnson did not actually address the question of the deterrent effect of execution in any respect whatever. To do so he would have had to compare the number of pocket-picking episodes in the crowd assembled to witness the execution with the number of such episodes in a similar crowd assembled for some other purpose. He did not do so, probably because he thought that a deterrent effect occurs only if the crime is altogether eliminated. That is a common misunderstanding. But crime can only be reduced, not eliminated. However harsh the penalties there are always non-deterrables. Many, perhaps most, people can be deterred, but never all.

V. THE FINAL MORAL CONSIDERATIONS

The motive of revenge. One objection to capital punishment is that it gratifies the desire for revenge, regarded as morally unworthy. The Bible has the Lord declare: "Vengeance is mine" (Romans 12:19). He thus legitimized vengeance and reserved it to Himself, probably because it would otherwise be disruptive. But He did not deprecate the desire for vengeance.

Indeed Romans 12:19 barely precedes Romans 13:4, which tells us that the ruler "beareth not the sword in vain: for he is the minister of God, a revenger to execute wrath upon him that doeth evil." It is not unreasonable to interpret Romans 12:19 to suggest that revenge is to be delegated by the injured to the ruler, "the minister of God" who is "to execute wrath." The Bible also enjoins, "the murderer shall surely be put to death" (Numbers 35:16–18), recognizing that the death penalty can be warranted—whatever the motive. Religious tradition certainly suggests no less. However, since religion expects justice and vengeance in the world to come, the faithful may dispense with either in this world, and with any particular penalties—though they seldom have. But a secular state must do justice here and now—it cannot assume that another power, elsewhere, will do justice where its courts did not.

The motives for the death penalty may indeed include vengeance. Vengeance is a compensatory and psychologically reparatory satisfaction for an injured party, group, or society. I do not see wherein it is morally blameworthy. When regulated and controlled by law, vengeance is also socially useful: legal vengeance solidifies social solidarity against lawbreakers and probably is the only alternative to the disruptive private revenge of those who feel harmed. Abolitionists want to promise murderers that what they did to their victims will never be done to them. That promise strikes most people as psychologically incongruous. It is.

At any rate, vengeance is irrelevant to the function of the death penalty. It must be justified independently, by its purpose, whatever the motive. An action, a rule, or a penalty cannot be justified or discredited by the motive for it. No rule should be discarded or regarded as morally wrong (or right) because of the motive of those who support it. Actions, rules, or penalties are justified not by the motives of supporters but by their purpose and by their effectiveness in achieving it without excessively impairing other objectives.[20] Capital punishment is warranted if it achieves its purpose—doing justice and deterring crime—regardless of whether or not it is motivated by vengeful feelings.

Characteristics. Before turning to its purely moral aspects, we must examine some specific characteristics of capital punishment. It is feared above all punishments because 1) it is not merely irreversible, as most other penalties are, but also irrevocable; 2) it hastens an event which, unlike pain, deprivation, or injury, is unique in every life and never has been reported on by anyone. Death is an experience that cannot actually be experienced and that ends all experience. Actually, being dead is no different from not being born—a (non) experience we all had before being born. But death is not so perceived. The process of dying, a quite different matter, is confused with it. In turn, dying is feared mainly because death is anticipated—even though death is feared because confused with dying. At any rate, the fear of death is universal and is often attached to the penalty that hastens it—as though without that penalty death would not come. 3) However, the penalty is feared for another reason as well. When death is imposed as a deliberate punishment by one's fellow men, it signifies a complete severing of human solidarity. The convict is explicitly and dramatically rejected by his fellow humans, found unworthy of their society, of sharing life with them. The rejection exacerbates the natural separation anxiety of those who expect imminent death, the fear of final annihilation. Inchoate as these characteristics are in most minds, the specific deterrent effect of executions depends on them, and the moral justification of the death penalty, above and beyond the deterrent effect, does no less.

Methodological aside. Hitherto I have relied on logic and fact. Without relinquishing either, I must appeal to plausibility as well, as I turn to questions of morality unalloyed by other issues. For, whatever ancillary service facts and logic can render, what one is persuaded to accept as morally right or wrong depends on what appears to be plausible in the end. Outside the realm of morals one relies on plausibility only in the beginning.

The value of life. If there is nothing for the sake of which one may be put to death, can there ever be anything worth risking one's life for? If there is nothing worth dying for, is there any moral value worth living for? Is a life that cannot be transcended by—and given up, or taken, for—anything beyond itself more valuable than one that can be transcended? Can it be that existence, life itself, is the highest moral value, never to be given up, or taken, for the sake of anything? And, psychologically, does a social value system in which life itself, however it is lived, becomes the highest of goods enhance the value of human life or cheapen it? I shall content myself here with raising these questions.[21]

Homo homini res sacra. "The life of each man should be sacred to each other man," the ancients tell us. They unflinchingly executed murderers.[22] They realized it is not enough to proclaim the sacredness and inviolability of human life. It must be secured as well, by threatening with the loss of their own life those who violate what has been proclaimed as inviolate—the right of innocents to live. Else the inviolability of human life is neither credibly proclaimed nor actually protected. No society can profess that the lives of its members are secure if those who did not allow innocent others to continue living are themselves allowed to continue living—at the expense of the community. To punish a murderer by incarcerating him as one does a pickpocket cannot but cheapen human life. Murder differs in quality from other crimes and deserves, therefore, a punishment that differs in quality from other punishments. There is a discontinuity. It should be underlined, not blurred.

If it were shown that no punishment is more deterrent than a trivial fine, capital punishment for murder would remain just, even if

not useful. For murder is not a trifling offense. Punishment must be proportioned to the gravity of the crime, if only to denounce it and to vindicate the importance of the norm violated. Wherefore all penal systems proportion punishments to crimes. The worse the crime the higher the penalty deserved. Why not then the highest penalty—death—for the worst crime—wanton murder? Those rejecting the death penalty have the burden of showing that no crime ever deserves capital punishment[23]—a burden which they have not so far been willing to bear.

Abolitionists insist that we all have an imprescriptible right to live to our natural term: if the innocent victim had a right to live, so does the murderer. That takes egalitarianism too far for my taste. The crime sets victim and murderer apart; if the victim did, the murderer does not deserve to live. If innocents are to be secure in their lives murderers cannot be. The thought that murderers are to be given as much right to live as their victims oppresses me. So does the thought that a Stalin, a Hitler, an Idi Amin should have as much right to live as their victims did.

Failure of nerve. Never to execute a wrongdoer, regardless of how depraved his acts, is to proclaim that no act can be so irredeemably vicious as to deserve death—that no human being can be wicked enough to be deprived of life. Who actually can believe that? I find it easier to believe that those who affect such a view suffer from a failure of nerve. They do not think themselves—and therefore anyone else—competent to decide questions of life and death. Aware of human frailty, they shudder at the gravity of the decision and refuse to make it. The irrevocability of a verdict of death is contrary to the modern spirit that likes to pretend that nothing ever is definite, that everything is open-ended, that doubts must always be entertained and revisions must always remain possible. Such an attitude may be helpful to the reflections of inquiring philosophers and scientists; but it is not proper for courts. They must make final judgments beyond a reasonable doubt. They must decide. They can evade decisions on life and death only by giving up their paramount duties: to do justice, to secure the lives of the citizens, and to vindicate the norms society holds inviolable.

One may object that the death penalty either cannot actually achieve the vindication of violated norms or is not needed for it. If so, failure to inflict death on the criminal does not belittle the crime, or imply that the life of the criminal is of greater importance than the moral value he violated or the harm he did to his victim. But it is not so. In all societies the degree of social disapproval of wicked acts is expressed in the degree of punishment threatened.[24] Thus, punishments both proclaim and enforce social values according to the importance given to them. There is no other way for society to affirm its values. There is no other effective way of denouncing socially disapproved acts. To refuse to punish any crime with death is to suggest that the negative value of a crime can never exceed the positive value of the life of the person who committed it. I find that proposition quite implausible.

NOTES

This a greatly revised version of a paper first delivered at a symposium sponsored by the Graduate School of Criminal Justice and the Criminal Justice Research Center of Albany, N.Y. in April 1977.

[1]Apparently the punishment must be both—else cruel or unusual would have done. Historically it appears that punishments were prohibited if unusual in 1791 *and* cruel: the Framers did want to prohibit punishments, even cruel ones, only if already unusual in 1791; they did prohibit new (unusual) punishments if cruel. The Eighth Amendment was not meant to apply to the death penalty in 1791 since it was not unusual then; nor was the Eighth Amendment intended to be used against capital punishment in the future, regardless of whether it may have come to be considered cruel: it is neither a new penalty nor one unusual in 1791.

[2]These may be a consensus against the death penalty among the college educated. If so, it demonstrates a) the power of indoctrination wielded by sociologists;

b) the fact that those who are least threatened by violence are most inclined to do without the death penalty. College graduates are less often threatened by murder than the uneducated.

[3]See Chief Justice Burger dissenting in *Furman:* "In a democratic society legislatures not courts are constituted to respond to the will and consequently the moral values of the people."

[4]The First Amendment might be invoked against such sources of revelation. When specific laws do not suffice to decide a case, courts, to be sure, make decisions based on general legal principles. But the death penalty (as distinguished from applications) raises no serious legal problem.

[5]Attention should be drawn to John Hagan's "Extralegal Attributes and Criminal Sentencing" (*Law and Society Review*, Spring 1974), which throws doubt on much of the discrimination which sociologists have found.

[6]I am referring throughout to discrimination among those already convicted of capital crimes. That discrimination can be tested. However, the fact that a higher proportion of blacks, or poor people, than of whites, or rich people, are found guilty of capital crimes does not *ipso facto* indicate discrimination, any more than does the fact that a comparatively high proportion of blacks or poor people become professional baseball players or boxers.

[7]Although this is the burden of Charles Black's *Capital Punishment: The Inevitability of Caprice and Mistake* (Norton, 1974). *Codex ipsus loquitur.*

[8]"The Deterrent Effect of Capital Punishment: A Question of Life and Death." *American Economic Review*, June 1975. In the period studied capital punishment was already infrequent and uncertain. Its deterrent effect might be greater when more frequently imposed for capital crimes, so that a prospective offender would feel more certain of it.

[9]See *Journal of Legal Studies*, January 1977; *Journal of Political Economy*, June 1977; and (this is the cross-sectional analysis) *American Economic Review*, June 1977.

[10]*Per contra* see Brian Forst in *Minnesota Law Review*, May 1977, and *Deterrence and Incapacitation* (National Academy of Sciences, Washington, D.C., 1978). By now statistical analyses of the effects of the death penalty have become a veritable cottage industry. This has happened since Ehrlich found deterrent effects. No one much bothered when Thorsten Sellin found none. Still, it is too early for more than tentative conclusions. The two papers mentioned above are replied to, more than adequately in my view, in Isaac Ehrlich's "Fear of Deterrence," *Journal of Legal Studies*, June 1977.

[11]I thought that prudence as well as morality commanded us to choose the first alternative even when I believed that the degree of probability and the extent of deterrent effects might remain unknown. (See my "On Deterrence and the Death Penalty," *Journal of Criminal Law, Criminology, and Police Science,* June 1969.) That probability is more likely to become known now and to be greater than was apparent a few years ago.

[12]Though it would isolate deterrent effects of the punishment from incapacitating effects, and also from the effect of Durkheimian "normative validation" when it does not depend on threats. Still, it is not acceptable to our sense of justice that people guilty of the same crime would deliberately get different punishments and that the difference would be made to depend deliberately on a factor irrelevant to the nature of the crime or of the criminal.

[13]As indicated before, demonstrations are not available for the exact addition to deterrence of each added degree of severity in various circumstances, and with respect to various acts. We have coasted so far on a sea of plausible assumptions. (It is not contended, of course, that the degree of severity alone determines deterrent effects. Other factors may reinforce or offset the effect of severity, be it on the motivational [incentive] side, or as added costs and risks).

[14]Particularly since he, unlike the person already in custody, may have much to gain from his additional crime (see Footnote 18).

[15]The Supreme Court has decided that capital punishment for rape (at least of adults) is "cruel and unusual" (*Coker v. Georgia,* 1977). For the reasons stated in the text, I welcome the decision—but not the justification given by the Supreme Court. The penalty may indeed be as excessive as the court feels it is, but not in the constitutional sense of being irrationally or extravagantly so, and thus contrary to the Eighth Amendment. The seriousness of the crime of rape and the appropriateness of the death penalty for it are matters for political rather than judicial institutions to decide. I should vote against the death penalty for rape—and not only for the reasons stated in the text above; but the Court should have left the matter to vote of the citizens.

The charge of racially discriminatory application was most often justified when the penalty was inflicted for rape. Yet I doubt that the charge will be dropped, or that the agitation against the death penalty will stop, once it is no longer inflicted for rape. Discrimination never was more than a pretext used by abolitionists.

[16]There is a good argument here against unnecessary public displays of violence. (See my "What to Do about TV Violence," *The Alternative* August/September 1976.)

[17]It may be noted that in Beccaria's time executions were regarded as public entertainments. *Tempora mutantur et nos mutamur in illis.*

[18]I have reservations on both these counts, being convinced that many crimes among relatives, friends, and associates are as blameworthy and as deterrable as crimes among strangers. Thus, major heroin dealers in New York are threatened with life imprisonment. In the absence of the death penalty they find it advantageous to have witnesses killed. Such murders surely are not acts of passion in the classical sense, though they occur among associates. They are, in practice, encouraged by the present penal law in New York.

[19]The high degree of uncertainty and arbitrariness of penalization in Johnson's time may also have weakened deterrent effects. Witnessing an execution cannot correct this defect.

[20]Different motives (the reason why something is done) may generate the same action (what is done), purpose, or intent, just as the same motive may lead to different actions.

[21]Insofar as these questions are psychological, empirical evidence would not be irrelevant. But it is likely to be evaluated in terms depending on moral views.

[22]Not always. On the disastrous consequences of periodic failure to do so, Sir Henry Maine waxes eloquent with sorrow in his *Ancient Law* (pp. 408–9).

[23]One may argue that some crimes deserve more than execution and that the above reasoning would justify punitive torture as well. Perhaps. But torture, unlike death, is generally rejected. Therefore penalties have been reduced to a few kinds—fines, confinement, and execution. The issue is academic because, unlike the death penalty, torture has become repulsive to us. (Some reasons for this public revulsion are listed in Chapter 17 of my *Punishing Criminals,* Basic Books, 1975.) As was noted above (p. 404) the range of punishments is bound to be more limited than the range of crimes. We do not accept some punishments, however much deserved they may be.

[24]Social approval is usually not unanimous, and the system of rewards reflects it less.

QUESTIONS FOR DISCUSSION

1. Are van den Haag's arguments for capital punishment mainly retributivist, utilitarian, or a mixture? Can they all fit under a single coherent theory of punishment? Why or why not? Does this matter?

2. *Which* crimes should receive the death penalty, according to van den Haag's arguments? Why these? Why not others?

3. Van den Haag argues that "the threat of death [is] needed in special circumstances." (p. 737) What exactly are these special circumstances? Why do they create a need for the death penalty, according to van den Haag? Do you agree? Why or why not?

4. Explain van den Haag's response to Beccaria's argument from barbarization. Is his response adequate? Why or why not?

JUSTICE, CIVILIZATION, AND THE DEATH PENALTY

JEFFREY REIMAN

On the issue of capital punishment, there is as clear a clash of moral intuitions as we are likely to see. Some (now a majority of Americans) feel deeply that justice requires payment in kind and thus that murderers should die; and others (once, but no longer, nearly a majority of Americans) feel deeply that the state ought not be in the business of putting people to death.[1] Arguments for either side that do not do justice to the intuitions of the other are unlikely to persuade anyone not already convinced. And, since, as I shall suggest, there is truth on both sides, such arguments are easily refutable, leaving us with nothing but conflicting intuitions and no guidance from reason in distinguishing the better from the worse. In this context, I shall try to make an argument for the abolition of the death penalty that does justice to the intuitions on both sides. I shall sketch out a conception of retributive justice that accounts for the justice of executing murderers, and then I shall argue that *though the death penalty is a just punishment for murder*, abolition of the death penalty is part of the civilizing mission of modern states. . . .

III. CIVILIZATION, PAIN, AND JUSTICE

As I have already suggested, from the fact that something is justly deserved, it does not automatically follow that it should be done, since there may be other moral reasons for not doing it such that, all told, the weight of moral

Jeffrey Reiman, "Justice, Civilization, and the Death Penalty," *Philosophy and Public Affairs*, vol. 14, no. 2 (Spring, 1985), pp. 115, 134–148

reasons swings the balance against proceeding. The same argument that I have given for the justice of the death penalty for murderers proves the justice of beating assaulters, raping rapists, and torturing torturers. Nonetheless, I believe, and suspect that most would agree, that it would not be right for us to beat assaulters, rape rapists, or torture torturers, *even though it were their just deserts*—and even if this were the only way to make them suffer as much as they had made their victims suffer. Calling for the abolition of the death penalty, though it be just, then, amounts to urging that as a society we place execution in the same category of sanction as beating, raping, and torturing, and treat it as something it would also not be right for us to do to offenders, *even if it were their just deserts.*

To argue for placing execution in this category, I must show what would be gained therefrom; and to show that, I shall indicate what we gain from placing torture in this category and argue that a similar gain is to be had from doing the same with execution. I select torture because I think the reasons for placing it in this category are, due to the extremity of torture, most easily seen—but what I say here applies with appropriate modification to other severe physical punishments, such as beating and raping. First, and most evidently, placing torture in this category broadcasts the message that we as a society judge torturing so horrible a thing to do to a person that we refuse to do it even when it is deserved. Note that such a judgment does not commit us to an absolute prohibition on torturing. No matter how horrible we judge something to be, we may still be justified in doing it if it is necessary to prevent something even worse. Leaving this aside for the moment, what is gained by broadcasting the public judgment that torture is too horrible to inflict even if deserved?

I think the answer to this lies in what we understand as civilization. In *The Genealogy of Morals*, Nietzsche says that in early times "pain did not hurt as much as it does today."[23] The truth in this puzzling remark is that progress in civilization is characterized by a lower tolerance for one's own pain and that suffered by others. And this is appropriate, since, via growth in knowledge, civilization brings increased power to prevent or reduce pain and, via growth in the ability to communicate and interact with more and more people, civilization extends the circle of people with whom we empathize. If civilization is characterized by lower tolerance for our own pain and that of others, then publicly refusing to do horrible things to our fellows both signals the level of our civilization *and, by our example, continues the work of civilizing.* And this gesture is all the more powerful if we refuse to do horrible things to those who deserve them. I contend then that the more things we are able to include in this category, the more civilized we are and the more civilizing. Thus we gain from including torture in this category, and if execution is especially horrible, we gain still more by including it. . . .

To complete the argument, however, I must show that execution is horrible enough to warrant its inclusion alongside torture. Against this it will be said that execution is not especially horrible since it only hastens a fate that is inevitable for us. I think that this view overlooks important differences in the manner in which people reach their inevitable ends. I contend that execution is especially horrible, and it is so in a way similar to (though not identical with) the way in which torture is especially horrible. I believe we view torture as especially awful because of two of its features, which also characterize execution: intense pain and the spectacle of one human being completely subject to the power of another. This latter is separate from the issue of pain since it is something that offends us about unpainful things, such as slavery (even voluntarily entered) and prostitution (even voluntarily chosen as an occupation). Execution shares this separate feature, since killing a bound and defenseless human being enacts the total subjugation of that person to his fellows. I think, incidentally, that this accounts for the general uneasiness with which execution by lethal injection has been greeted. Rather than humanizing the event, it seems only to have purchased a possible reduction in physical pain at the price of increasing the spectacle of subjugation—with no net gain in the attractiveness of the death penalty. Indeed, its net effect may have been the reverse.

In addition to the spectacle of subjugation, execution, even by physically painless means, is also characterized by a special and intense psychological pain that distinguishes it from the loss of life that awaits us all. Interesting in this regard is the fact that although we are not terribly squeamish about the loss of life itself, allowing it in war, self-defense, as a necessary cost of progress, and so on, we are, as the extraordinary hesitance of our courts testifies, quite reluctant to execute. I think this is because execution involves the most psychologically painful features of deaths. We normally regard death from human causes as worse than death from natural causes, since a humanly caused shortening of life lacks the consolation of unavoidability. And we normally regard death whose coming is foreseen by its victim as worse than sudden death, because a foreseen death adds to the loss of life the terrible consciousness of that impending loss.[31] As a humanly caused death whose advent is foreseen by its victim, an execution combines the worst of both.

Thus far, by analogy with torture, I have argued that execution should be avoided because of how horrible it is to the one executed. But there are reasons of another sort that follow from the analogy with torture. Torture is to be avoided not only because of what it says about what we are willing to do to our fellows, but also because of what it says about us who are willing to do it. To torture someone is an awful spectacle not only because of the intensity of pain imposed, but because of what is required to be able to impose such pain on one's fellows. The tortured body cringes, using its full exertion to escape the pain imposed upon it—it literally begs for relief with its muscles as it does with its cries. To torture someone is to demonstrate a capacity to resist this begging, and that in turn demonstrates a kind of hardheartedness that a society ought not parade.

And this is true not only of torture, but of all severe corporal punishment. Indeed, I think this constitutes part of the answer to the puzzling question of why we refrain from punishments like whipping, even when the alternative (some months in jail versus some lashes) seems more costly to the offender. Imprisonment is painful to be sure, but it is a reflective pain, one that comes with comparing what is to what might have been, and that can be temporarily ignored by thinking about other things. But physical pain has an urgency that holds body and mind in a fierce grip. Of physical pain, as Orwell's Winston Smith recognized, "you could only wish one thing: that it should stop."[32] Refraining from torture in particular and corporal punishment in general, we both refuse to put a fellow human being in this grip *and* refuse to show our ability to resist this wish. The death penalty is the last corporal punishment used officially in the modern world. And it is corporal not only because administered via the body, but because the pain of foreseen, humanly administered death strikes us with the urgency that characterizes intense physical pain, causing grown men to cry, faint, and lose control of their bodily functions. There is something to be gained by refusing to endorse the hardness of heart necessary to impose such a fate.

By placing execution alongside torture in the category of things we will not do to our fellow human beings even when they deserve them, we broadcast the message that totally subjugating a person to the power of others and confronting him with the advent of his own humanly administered demise is too horrible to be done by civilized human beings to their fellows even when they have earned it: too horrible to do, and too horrible to be capable of doing. And I contend that broadcasting this message loud and clear would in the long run contribute to the general detestation of murder and be, to the extent to which it worked itself into the hearts and minds of the populace, a deterrent. In short, refusing to execute murderers though they deserve it both reflects and continues the taming of the human species that we call civilization. Thus, I take it that the abolition of the death penalty, though it is a just punishment for murder, is part of the civilizing mission of modern states.

IV. CIVILIZATION, SAFETY, AND DETERRENCE

[J]udging a practice too horrible to do even to those who deserve it does not exclude the possibility that it could be justified if necessary to avoid even worse consequences. Thus, were the death penalty clearly proven a better deterrent to the murder of innocent people than life in prison, we might have to admit that we had not yet reached a level of civilization at which we could protect ourselves without imposing this horrible fate on murderers, and thus we might have to grant the necessity of instituting the death penalty.[35] But this is far from proven. The available research by no means clearly indicates that the death penalty reduces the incidence of homicide more than life imprisonment does. Even the econometric studies of Isaac Ehrlich, which purport to show that each execution saves seven or eight potential murder victims, have not changed this fact, as is testified to by the controversy and objections from equally respected statisticians that Ehrlich's work has provoked.[34]

Conceding that it has not been proven that the death penalty deters more murders than life imprisonment, van den Haag has argued that neither has it been proven that the death penalty does not deter more murders, and thus we must follow common sense which teaches that the higher the cost of something, the fewer people will choose it, and therefore at least some potential murderers who would not be deterred by life imprisonment will be deterred by the death penalty. Van den Haag writes:

> . . . our experience shows that the greater the threatened penalty, the more it deters.
>   . . . Life in prison is still life, however unpleasant. In contrast, the death penalty does not just threaten to make life unpleasant— it threatens to take life altogether. This difference is perceived by those affected. We find that when they have the choice between life in prison and execution, 99% of all prisoners under sentence of death prefer life in prison. . . .
>   From this unquestioned fact a reasonable conclusion can be drawn in favor of the superior deterrent effect of the death penalty. Those who have the choice in practice . . . fear death more than they fear life in prison. . . . If they do, it follows that the threat of the death penalty, all other things equal, is likely to deter more than the threat of life in prison. One is most deterred by what one fears most. From which it follows that whatever statistics fail, or do not fail, to show, the death penalty is likely to be more deterrent than any other. [Pp. 68–69][36]

Those of us who recognize how common-sensical it was, and still is, to believe that the sun moves around the earth, will be less willing than Professor van den Haag to follow common sense here, especially when it comes to doing something awful to our fellows. Moreover, there are good reasons for doubting common sense on this matter. Here are four:

1. From the fact that one penalty is more feared than another, it does not follow that the more feared penalty will deter more than the less feared, unless we know that the less feared penalty is not fearful enough to deter everyone who can be deterred—and this is just what we don't know with regard to the death penalty. Though I fear the death penalty more than life in prison, I can't think of any act that the death penalty would deter me from that an equal likelihood of spending my life in prison wouldn't deter me from as well. Since it seems

to me that whoever would be deterred by a given likelihood of death would be deterred by an *equal* likelihood of life behind bars, I suspect that the common-sense argument only seems plausible because we evaluate it unconsciously assuming that potential criminals will face larger likelihoods of death sentences than of life sentences. If the likelihoods were equal, it seems to me that where life imprisonment was improbable enough to make it too distant a possibility to worry much about, a similar low probability of death would have the same effect. After all, we are undeterred by small likelihoods of death every time we walk the streets. And if life imprisonment were sufficiently probable to pose a real deterrent threat, it would pose as much of a deterrent threat as death. And this is just what most of the research we have on the comparative deterrent impact of execution versus life imprisonment suggests.

2. In light of the fact that roughly 500 to 700 suspected felons are killed by the police in the line of duty every year, and the fact that the number of privately owned guns in America is substantially larger than the number of households in America, it must be granted that anyone contemplating committing a crime *already* faces a substantial risk of ending up dead as a result. It's hard to see why anyone *who is not already deterred by this* would be deterred by the addition of the more distant risk of death after apprehension, conviction, and appeal. Indeed, this suggests that people consider risks in a much cruder way than van den Haag's appeal to common sense suggests—which should be evident to anyone who contemplates how few people use seatbelts (14% of drivers, on some estimates), when it is widely known that wearing them can spell the difference between life (outside prison) and death.

3. Van den Haag has maintained that deterrence doesn't work only by means of cost-benefit calculations made by potential criminals. It works also by the lesson about the wrongfulness of murder that is slowly learned in a society that *subjects murderers to the ultimate punishment* (p. 63). But if I am correct in claiming that the refusal to execute even those who deserve it has a civilizing effect, then the refusal to execute also teaches a lesson about the wrongfulness of murder. My claim here is admittedly speculative, but no more so than van den Haag's to the contrary. And my view has the added virtue of accounting for the failure of research to show an increased deterrent effect from executions *without having to deny the plausibility of van den Haag's common-sense argument that at least some additional potential murderers will be deterred by the prospect of the death penalty*. If there is a deterrent effect from not executing, then it is understandable that while executions will deter some murderers, this effect will be balanced out by the weakening of the deterrent effect of not executing, such that no net reduction in murders will result. And this, by the way, also disposes of van den Haag's argument that, in the absence of knowledge one way or the other on the deterrent effect of executions, we should execute murderers rather than risk the lives of innocent people whose murders might have been deterred if we had. If there is a deterrent effect of not executing, it follows that we risk innocent lives either way. And if this is so, it seems that the only reasonable course of action is to refrain from imposing what we know is a horrible fate.

4. Those who still think that van den Haag's common-sense argument for executing murderers is valid will find that the argument proves more than they bargained for. Van den Haag maintains that, in the absence of conclusive evidence on the relative deterrent impact of the death penalty versus life imprisonment, we must follow common sense and assume that if one punishment is more fearful than another, it will deter some potential criminals not deterred by the less fearful punishment. Since people sentenced to death will almost universally try to get their sentences changed to life in prison, it follows that death is more fearful than life imprisonment, and

thus that it will deter some additional murderers. Consequently, we should institute the death penalty to save the lives these additional murderers would have taken. But, since people sentenced to be tortured to death would surely try to get their sentences changed to simple execution, the same argument proves that death-by-torture will deter still more potential murderers. Consequently, we should institute death-by-torture to save the lives these additional murderers would have taken. Anyone who accepts van den Haag's argument is then confronted with a dilemma: Until we have conclusive evidence that capital punishment is a greater deterrent to murder than life imprisonment, he must grant *either* that we should not follow common sense and not impose the death penalty; *or* we should follow common sense and torture murderers to death. In short, either we must abolish the electric chair or reinstitute the rack. Surely, this is the *reductio ad absurdum* of van den Haag's common-sense argument.

CONCLUSION: HISTORY, FORCE, AND JUSTICE

I believe that, taken together, these arguments prove that we should abolish the death penalty though it is a just punishment for murder. Let me close with an argument of a different sort. When you see the lash fall upon the backs of Roman slaves, or the hideous tortures meted out in the period of the absolute monarchs, you see more than mere cruelty at work. Surely you suspect that there is something about the injustice of imperial slavery and royal tyranny that requires the use of extreme force to keep these institutions in place. That is, . . . we take the amount of force a society uses against its own people as an inverse measure of its justness. And though no more than a rough measure, it is a revealing one nonetheless, because when a society is limited in the degree of force it can use against its subjects, it is likely to have to be a juster society since it will have to gain its subjects' cooperation by offering them

fairer terms than it would have to, if it could use more force. From this we cannot simply conclude that reducing the force used by our society will automatically make our society more just—but I think we can conclude that it will have this tendency, since it will require us to find means other than force for encouraging compliance with our institutions, and this is likely to require us to make those institutions as fair to all as possible. Thus I hope that America will pose itself the challenge of winning its citizens' cooperation by justice rather than force, and that when future historians look back on the twentieth century, they will find us with countries like France and England and Sweden that have abolished the death penalty, rather than with those like South Africa and the Soviet Union and Iran that have retained it—with all that this suggests about the countries involved.

NOTES

[1]Asked, in a 1981 Gallup Poll, "Are you in favor of the death penalty for persons convicted of murder?" 66.25% were in favor, 25% were opposed, and 8.75% had no opinion. Asked the same question in 1966, 47.5% were opposed, 41.25% were in favor, and 11.25% had no opinion (Timothy J. Flanagan, David J. van Alstyne, and Michael R. Gottfredson, eds., *Sourcebook of Criminal Justice Statistics—1981*, U.S. Department of Justice, Bureau of Justice Statistics [Washington, D.C.: U.S. Government Printing Office, 1982], p. 209).

[23]Friedrich Nietzsche, *The Birth of Tragedy and The Genealogy of Morals* (New York: Doubleday, 1956), pp. 199–200.

[31]This is no doubt partly due to modern skepticism about an afterlife. Earlier peoples regarded a foreseen death as a blessing allowing time to make one's peace with God. . . .

[32]George Orwell, *1984* (New York: New American Library, 1983; originally published in 1949), p. 197.

[33]I say "might" here to avoid the sticky question of just how effective a deterrent the death penalty would have to be to justify overcoming our scruples about executing. It is here that the other considerations often urged against capital punishment—discrimination, irrevocability, the possibility of mistake, and so on—would play a role. Omitting such qualifications, however, my position might crudely be

stated as follows: *Just desert limits what a civilized society may do to deter crime, and deterrence limits what a civilized society may do to give criminals their just deserts.*

[34]Isaac Ehrlich, "The Deterrent Effect of Capital Punishment: A Question of Life or Death," *American Economic Review* 65 (June 1975): 397–417. . . . Much of the criticism of Ehrlich's work focuses on the fact that he found a deterrence impact of executions in the period from 1933–1969, which includes the period of 1963–1969, a time when hardly any executions were carried out and crime rates rose for reasons that are

arguably independent of the existence or nonexistence of capital punishment. When the 1963–1969 period is excluded, no significant deterrent effect shows. . . .

[36][Page references in the text are to Ernest van den Haag and John P. Conrad, *The Death Penalty: A Debate* (New York; Plenum Press, 1983).] An alternative formulation of this "common-sense argument" is put forth and defended by Michael Davis in "Death, Deterrence, and the Method of Common Sense," *Social Theory and Practice* 7, no. 2 (Summer 1981): 145–77. . . .

QUESTIONS FOR DISCUSSION

1. Why does Reiman think that the death penalty is uncivilized? Do you agree? Why or why not?

2. In what respects is the death penalty similar to and different from torture, according to Reiman? Do you agree?

3. Reiman gives four criticisms of van den Haag's argument that the death penalty deters. Explain each of Reiman's criticisms. How would van den Haag respond? Who is right?

DOES IT MATTER IF THE DEATH PENALTY IS ARBITRARILY ADMINISTERED?

STEPHEN NATHANSON

I

In this article, I will examine the argument that capital punishment ought to be abolished because it has been and will continue to be imposed in an arbitrary manner.

This argument has been central to discussions of capital punishment since the Supreme

Court ruling in the 1972 case *Furman v. Georgia.* In a 5-4 decision, the Court ruled that capital punishment as then administered was unconstitutional. Although the Court issued several opinions, the problem of arbitrariness is widely seen as having played a central role in the Court's thinking. As Charles Black, Jr., has put it,

Stephen Nathanson, "Does It Matter if the Death Penalty is Arbitrarily Administered?" *Philosophy and Public Affairs*, vol. 14, no. 2 (Spring, 1985), pp. 149–164

. . . The decisive ground of the 1972 Furman case anti–capital punishment ruling—the ground persuasive to the marginal justices needed for a majority—was that, out of a large number of persons "eligible" in law for the punishment of death, a few were selected as if at random, by no stated (or perhaps statable) criteria, while all the rest suffered the lesser penalty of imprisonment.[1]

Among those justices moved by the arbitrariness issue, some stressed the discriminatory aspects of capital punishment, the tendency of legally irrelevant factors like race and economic status to determine the severity of sentence, while others emphasized the "freakish" nature of the punishment, the fact that it is imposed on a miniscule percentage of murderers who are not obviously more deserving of death than others.

Although the Supreme Court approved new death penalty laws in *Gregg v. Georgia* (1976), the reasoning of *Furman* was not rejected. Rather, a majority of the Court determined that Georgia's new laws would make arbitrary imposition of the death penalty much less likely. By amending procedures and adding criteria which specify aggravating and mitigating circumstances, Georgia had succeeded in creating a system of "guided discretion," which the Court accepted in the belief that it was not likely to yield arbitrary results.

The *Gregg* decision has prompted death penalty opponents to attempt to show that "guided discretion" is an illusion. This charge has been supported in various ways. Charles Black has supported it by analyzing both the legal process of decision making in capital cases and the legal criteria for determining who is to be executed. He has argued that, appearances to the contrary, there are no meaningful standards operating in the system. Attacking from an empirical angle, William Bowers and Glenn Pierce have tried to show that even after *Furman* and under new laws, factors like race and geographic location of the trial continue to

play a large role and that the criteria which are supposed to guide judgment do not separate those sentenced into meaningfully distinct groups. Perhaps the most shocking conclusion of Bowers and Pierce concerns the large role played by the race of the killer and the victim, as the chances of execution are by far the greatest when blacks kill whites and least when whites kill blacks.[2]

The upshot of both these approaches is that "guided discretion" is not working and, perhaps, cannot work. If this is correct and if the argument from arbitariness is accepted, then it would appear that a return from *Gregg* to *Furman* is required. That is, the Court should once again condemn capital punishment as unconstitutional.

I have posed these issues in terms of the Supreme Court's deliberations. Nonetheless, for opponents of the death penalty, the freakishness of its imposition and the large role played by race and other irrelevant factors are a moral as well as a legal outrage. For them, there is a fundamental moral injustice in the practice of capital punishment and not just a departure from the highest legal and constitutional standards.

II

The argument from arbitrariness has not, however, been universally accepted, either as a moral or a constitutional argument. Ernest van den Haag, an articulate and longtime defender of the death penalty, has claimed that the Supreme Court was wrong to accept this argument in the first place and thus that the evidence of arbitrariness presented by Black, Bowers and Pierce and others is beside the point. In his words:

. . . the abolitionist argument from capriciousness, or discretion, or discrimination, would be more persuasive if it were alleged that those selectively executed are not guilty. But the argument merely maintains that some other guilty but more favored persons, or groups, escape the death penalty.

This is hardly sufficient for letting anyone else found guilty escape the penalty. On the contrary, that some guilty persons or groups elude it argues for extending the death penalty to them.[3]

Having attacked the appeal to arbitrariness, van den Haag goes on to spell out his own conception of the requirements of justice. He writes:

> Justice requires punishing the guilty—as many of the guilty as possible, even if only some can be punished—and *sparing* the innocent—as many of the innocent as possible, even if not all are spared. It would surely be wrong to treat everybody with equal injustice in preference to meting out justice at least to some. . . . [I]f the death penalty is morally just, however discriminatorily applied to only *some of the guilty*, it does remain just *in each case* in which it is applied. (emphasis added)[4]

Distinguishing sharply between the demands of justice and the demands of equality, van den Haag claims that the justice of individual punishments depends on individual guilt alone and not on whether punishments are equally distributed among the class of guilty persons.

Van den Haag's distinction between the demands of justice and the demands of equality parallels the distinction drawn by Joel Feinberg between "noncomparative" and "comparative" justice.[5] Using Feinberg's terminology, we can express van den Haag's view by saying that he believes that the justice of a particular punishment is a *noncomparative* matter. It depends solely on what a person deserves and not on how others are treated. For van den Haag, then, evidence of arbitrariness and discrimination is irrelevant, so long as those who are executed are indeed guilty and deserve their punishment.

There is no denying the plausibility of van den Haag's case. In many instances, we believe it is legitimate to punish or reward deserving individuals, even though we know that equally deserving persons are unpunished or unrewarded. Consider two cases:

A. A driver is caught speeding, ticketed, and required to pay a fine. We know that the percentage of speeders who are actually punished is extremely small, yet we would probably regard it as a joke if the driver protested that he was being treated unjustly or if someone argued that no one should be fined for speeding unless all speeders were fined.

B. A person performs a heroic act and receives a substantial reward, in addition to the respect and admiration of his fellow citizens. Because he deserves the reward, we think it just that he receive it, even though many equally heroic persons are not treated similarly. That most heroes are unsung is no reason to avoid rewarding this particular heroic individual.

Both of these instances appear to support van den Haag's claim that we should do justice whenever we can in individual cases and that failure to do justice in all cases is no reason to withhold punishment or reward from individuals.

III

Is the argument from arbitrariness completely unfounded then? Should we accept van den Haag's claim that "unequal justice is justice still"?

In response to these questions, I shall argue that van den Haag's claim is not as strong as it looks and that the argument from arbitrariness can be vindicated.

As a first step in achieving this, I would like to point out that there are in fact several different arguments from arbitrariness. While some of these arguments appeal to the random and freakish nature of the death penalty, others highlight the discriminatory effects of legally irrelevant factors. Each of these kinds of arbitrariness raises different sorts of moral and legal issues.

For example, though we may acknowledge the impossibility of ticketing all speeding drivers and still favor ticketing some, we will not find every way of determining which speeders are ticketed equally just. Consider the policy of ticketing only those who travel at extremely high speeds, as opposed to that of ticketing every tenth car. Compare these with the policy of giving tickets only to speeders with beards and long hair or to speeders whose cars bear bumper stickers expressing unpopular political views. While I shall not pursue this point in detail, I take it to be obvious that these different selection policies are not all equally just or acceptable.

A second difference between versions of the argument from arbitrariness depends on whether or not it is granted that we can accurately distinguish those who deserve to die from those who do not. As van den Haag presents the argument, it assumes that we are able to make this distinction. Then, the claim is made that from this class of people who deserve to die, only some are selected for execution. The choice of those specific persons who deserve to die is held to be arbitrary.

Van den Haag neglects a related argument which has been forcefully defended by Charles Black. Black's argument is that the determination of who deserves to die—the first step—is itself arbitrary. So his claim is not merely that arbitrary factors determine who among the deserving will be executed. His point is that the determination of who deserves to die is arbitrary. His main argument is that

> the official choices—by prosecutors, judges, juries, and governors—that divide those who are to die from those who are to live are on the whole not made, and cannot be made, under standards that are consistently meaningful and clear, but that they are often made, and in the foreseeable future will continue often to be made, under no standards at all or under pseudo-standards without discoverable meaning.[6]

According to Black, even the most conscientious officials could not make principled judg-

ments about desert in these instances, because our laws do not contain clear principles for differentiating those who deserve to die from those who do not. While I shall not try to summarize Black's analysis of the failures of post-*Furman* capital punishment statutes, it is clear that if van den Haag were to meet this argument, he would have to provide his own analysis of these laws in order to show that they do provide clear and meaningful standards. Or, he would have to examine the actual disposition of cases under these laws to show that the results have not been arbitrary. Van den Haag does not attempt to do either of these things. This seems to result from a failure to distinguish (a) the claim that judgments concerning *who deserves* to die are arbitrarily made, from (b) the claim that judgments concerning *who among the deserving shall be executed* are arbitrarily made.

Van den Haag may simply assume that the system does a decent job of distinguishing those who deserve to die from those who do not, and his assumption gains a surface plausibility because of his tendency to oversimplify the nature of the judgments which need to be made. In contrast to Black, who stresses the complexity of the legal process and the complexity of the judgments facing participants in that process, van den Haag is content to say simply that "justice requires punishing the guilty . . . and sparing the innocent." This maxim makes it look as if officials and jurors need only divide people into two neat categories, and if we think of guilt and innocence as *factual* categories, it makes it look as if the only judgment necessary is whether a person did or did not kill another human being.

In fact, the problems are much more complicated than this. Not every person who kills another human being is guilty of the same crime. Some may have committed no crime at all, if their act is judged to be justifiable homicide. Among others, they may have committed first-degree murder, second-degree murder, or some form of manslaughter. Furthermore, even if we limit our attention to those who are convicted of first-degree murder, juries must consider aggravating and mitigating circumstances in order to judge whether someone is guilty enough to deserve the death penalty. It is clear, then, that simply knowing that someone is factually guilty of killing another person is far from sufficient for determining that he deserves to die, and if prosecutors, juries, and judges do not have criteria which enable them to classify those who are guilty in a just and rational way, then their judgments about who deserves to die will necessarily be arbitrary and unprincipled.

Once we appreciate the difficulty and complexity of the judgments which must be made about guilt and desert, it is easier to see how they might be influenced by racial characteristics and other irrelevant factors. The statistics compiled by Bowers and Pierce show that blacks killing whites have the greatest chance of being executed, while whites killing blacks have the least chance of execution. What these findings strongly suggest is that officials and jurors think that the killing of a white by a black is a more serious crime than the killing of a black by a white. Hence, they judge that blacks killing whites deserve a more serious punishment than whites killing blacks. Given the bluntness of our ordinary judgments about desert and the complexity of the choices facing jurors and officials, it may not be surprising either that people find it difficult to make the fine discriminations required by law or that such judgments are influenced by deep-seated racial or social attitudes.

Both legal analysis and empirical studies should undermine our confidence that the legal system sorts out those who deserve to die from those who do not in a nonarbitrary manner. If we cannot be confident that those who are executed in fact deserve to die, then we ought not to allow executions to take place at all.

Because van den Haag does not distinguish this argument from other versions of the argument from arbitrariness, he simply neglects it. His omission is serious because this argument is an independent, substantial argument against the death penalty. It can stand even if other versions of the argument from arbitrariness fall.

IV

I would like now to turn to the form of the argument which van den Haag explicitly deals with and to consider whether it is vulnerable to his criticism. Let us assume that there is a class of people whom we know to be deserving of death. Let us further assume that only some of these people are executed and that the executions are arbitrary in the sense that those executed have not committed worse crimes than those not executed. This is the situation which Justice Stewart described in *Furman*. He wrote:

> These death sentences are cruel and unusual in the same way that being struck by lightning is cruel and unusual. For of all the people convicted of rapes and murders in 1967 and 1968, *many just as reprehensible as these,* the petitioners are among *a capriciously selected random handful* upon whom the sentence of death has in fact been imposed. (emphasis added)[7]

What is crucial here (and different from the argument previously discussed) is the assumption that we can judge the reprehensibility of both the petitioners and others convicted of similar crimes. Stewart does not deny that the petitioners deserve to die, but because other equally deserving people escape the death penalty for no legally respectable reasons, the executions of the petitioners, Stewart thought, would violate the Eighth and Fourteenth Amendments.

This is precisely the argument van den Haag rejected. We can sum up his reasons in the following rhetorical questions: How can it possibly be unjust to punish someone if he deserves the punishment? Why should it matter whether or not others equally deserving are punished?

I have already acknowledged the plausibility of van den Haag's case and offered the examples of the ticketed speeder and the rewarded hero as instances which seem to confirm his view. Nonetheless, I think that van den Haag is profoundly mistaken in thinking that the justice of a reward or punishment depends solely on whether the recipient deserves it.

Consider the following two cases which are structurally similar to A and B (given above) but which elicit different reactions:

C. I tell my class that anyone who plagiarizes will fail the course. Three students plagiarize papers, but only one receives a failing grade. The other two, in describing their motivation, win my sympathy, and I give them passing grades.

D. At my child's birthday party, I offer a prize to the child who can solve a particular puzzle. Three children, including my own, solve the puzzle. I cannot reward them all, so I give the prize to my own child.

In both cases, as in van den Haag's, only some of those deserving a reward or punishment receive it. Unlike cases A and B, however, C and D do not appear to be just, in spite of the fact that the persons rewarded or punished deserve what they get. In these cases, the justice of giving them what they deserve appears to be affected by the treatment of others.

About these cases I am inclined to say the following. The people involved have not been treated justly. It was unjust to fail the single plagiarizer and unjust to reward my child. It would have been better—because more just— to have failed no one than to have failed the single student. It would have been better to have given a prize to no one than to give the prize to my child alone.

The unfairness in both cases appears to result from the fact that the reasons for picking out those rewarded or punished are irrelevant and hence that the choice is arbitrary. If I have a stated policy of failing students who plagiarize, then it is unjust for me to pass students with whom I sympathize. Whether I am sym-

pathetic or not is irrelevant, and I am treating the student whom I do fail unjustly because I am not acting simply on the basis of desert. Rather, I am acting on the basis of desert plus degree of sympathy. Likewise, in the case of the prize, it appears that I am preferring my own child in giving out the reward, even though I announced that receipt of the award would depend only on success in solving the puzzle.

This may be made clearer by varying the plagiarism example. Suppose that in spite of my stated policy of failing anyone who plagiarizes, I am regularly lenient toward students who seem sufficiently repentant. Suppose further that I am regularly more lenient with attractive female students than with others. Or suppose that it is only redheads or wealthy students whom I fail. If such patterns develop, we can see that whether a student fails or not does not depend simply on being caught plagiarizing. Rather, part of the explanation of a particular student's being punished is that he or she is (or is not) an attractive female, redheaded or wealthy. In these instances, I think the plagiarizers who are punished have grounds for complaint, even though they were, by the announced standards, clearly guilty and deserving of punishment.

If this conclusion is correct, then doing justice is more complicated than van den Haag realizes. He asserts that it would be "wrong to treat everybody with equal injustice in preference to meting out justice at least to some." If my assessment of cases C and D is correct, however, it is better that everyone in those instances be treated "unjustly" than that only some get what they deserve. Whether one is treated justly or not depends on how others are treated and not solely on what one deserves.[8]

In fact, van den Haag implicitly concedes this point in an interesting footnote to his essay. In considering the question of whether capital punishment is a superior deterrent, van den Haag mentions that one could test the deterrent power of the death penalty by allowing executions for murders committed on Monday, Wednesday, and Friday, while setting life imprisonment as the maximum penalty for murders committed on other days. In noting the obstacles facing such an experiment, he writes:

> . . . it is not acceptable to our sense of justice that *people guilty of the   same crime would get different punishments* and that the difference would be made to depend deliberately on *a factor irrelevant to the nature of the crime* or of the criminal. (emphasis added)[9]

Given his earlier remarks about the argument from arbitrariness, this is a rather extraordinary comment, for van den Haag concedes that the justice of a punishment is not solely determined by what an individual deserves but is also a function of how equally deserving persons are treated in general.

In his case, what he finds offensive is that there is no difference between what the Monday, Wednesday, Friday murderers deserve and what the Tuesday, Thursday, Saturday, and Sunday murderers deserve. Yet the morally irrelevant factor of date is decisive in determining the severity of the punishment. Van den Haag (quite rightly) cannot swallow this.

Yet van den Haag's example is exactly parallel to the situation described by opponents of the death penalty. For, surely, the race of the criminal or victim, the economic or social status of the criminal or victim, the location of the crime or trial and other such factors are as irrelevant to the gravity of the crime and the appropriate severity of the punishment as is the day of the week on which the crime is committed. It would be as outrageous for the severity of the punishment to depend on these factors as it would be for it to depend on the day of the week on which the crime was committed.

In fact, it is more outrageous that death sentences depend on the former factors because a person can control the day of the week on which he murders in a way in which he cannot control his race or status. Moreover, we are committed to banishing the disabling effects of race and economic status from the law. Using the day of the week as a critical factor is at least not invidiously discriminatory, as it neither favors nor disfavors previously identifiable or disadvantaged groups.

In reply, one might contend that I have overlooked an important feature of van den Haag's example. He rejected the deterrence experiment not merely because the severity of punishment depended on irrelevant factors but also because the irrelevant factors were *deliberately* chosen as the basis of punishment. Perhaps it is the fact that irrelevant factors are deliberately chosen which makes van den Haag condemn the proposed experiment.

This is an important point. It certainly makes matters worse to decide deliberately to base life and death choices on irrelevant considerations. However, even if the decision is not deliberate, it remains a serious injustice if irrelevant considerations play this crucial role. Individuals might not even be aware of the influence of these factors. They might genuinely believe that their judgments are based entirely on relevant considerations. It might require painstaking research to discover the patterns underlying sentencing, but once they are known, citizens and policymakers must take them into consideration. Either the influence of irrelevant factors must be eradicated or, if we determine that this is impossible, we may have to alter our practices more radically.

This reasoning, of course, is just the reasoning identified with the *Furman* case. As Justice Douglas wrote:

> A law that stated that anyone making more than $50,000 would be exempt from the death penalty would plainly fall, as would a law that in terms said that blacks, those who never went beyond the fifth grade in school, those who make less than $3,000 a year, or those who were unpopular or unstable should be the only people executed. A law which in the overall view reaches the same result in practice has no more sanctity than a law which in terms provides the same.[10]

The problem, in Douglas's view, was that the system left life and death decisions to the "uncontrolled discretion of judges or juries," leading to the unintended but nonetheless real result that death sentences were based on factors which had nothing to do with the nature of the crime.

What I want to stress here is that the arbitrariness and discrimination need not be purposeful or deliberate. We might discover, as critics allege, that racial prejudice is so deeply rooted in our society that prosecutors, juries, and judges cannot free themselves from prejudice when determining how severe a punishment for a crime should be. Furthermore, we might conclude that these tendencies cannot be eradicated, especially when juries are called upon to make subtle and complex assessments of cases in the light of confusing, semi-technical criteria. Hence, although no one *decides* that race will be a factor, we may *predict* that it will be a factor, and this knowledge must be considered in evaluating policies and institutions.

If factors *as irrelevant* as the day of the crime determine whether people shall live or die and if the influence of these factors is ineradicable, then we must conclude that we cannot provide a just system of punishment and even those who are guilty and deserving of the most severe punishments (like the Monday killers in van den Haag's experiment) will have a legitimate complaint that they have been treated unjustly.

I conclude, then, that the treatment of *classes* of people is relevant to determining the justice of punishments for *individuals* and van den Haag is wrong to dismiss the second form of the argument from arbitrariness. That argument succeeds in showing that capital punishment is unjust and thus provides a powerful reason for abolishing it.

V

Supporters of the death penalty might concede that serious questions of justice are raised by the influence of arbitrary factors and still deny that this shows that capital punishment ought to be abolished. They could argue that some degree of arbitrariness is present throughout the system of legal punishment, that it is unreasonable to expect our institutions to be perfect, and that acceptance of the argument from arbitrariness would commit us to abolishing all punishment.

In fact, van den Haag makes just these points in his essay. He writes:

> The Constitution, though it enjoins us to minimize capriciousness, does not enjoin a standard of unattainable perfection or exclude penalties because that standard has not been attained. . . . I see no more merit in the attempt to persuade the courts to let all capital-crime defendants go free of capital punishment because some have wrongly escaped it than I see in an attempt to persuade the courts to let all burglars go because some have wrongly escaped imprisonment.[11]

It is an important feature of this objection that it could be made even by one who conceded the injustice of arbitrarily administered death sentences. Rather than agreeing that capital punishment should be abolished, however, this objection moves from the premise that the flaws revealed in capital punishment are shared by all punishments to the conclusion that we must either (a) reject all punishments (because of the influence of arbitrary factors on them) or (b) reject the idea that arbitrariness provides a sufficient ground for abolishing the death penalty.

Is there a way out of this dilemma for death penalty opponents?

I believe that there is. Opponents of the death penalty may continue to support other punishments, even though their administration also involves arbitrariness. This is not to suggest, of course, that we should be content with arbitrariness or discrimination in the imposition of any punishment.[12] Rather the point is to emphasize that the argument from arbitrariness counts against the death penalty with special force. There are two reasons for this.

First, death is a much more severe punishment than imprisonment. This is universally acknowledged by advocates and opponents of the death penalty alike. It is recognized in the law by the existence of special procedures for capital cases. Death obliterates the person, depriving him or her of life and thereby, among other things, depriving him or her of any further rights of legal appeal, should new facts be discovered or new understandings of the law be reached. In this connection, it is worth recalling that many people were executed and are now dead because they were tried and sentenced under the pre-*Furman* laws which allowed the "uncontrolled discretion of judges and juries."

Second, though death is the most severe punishment in our legal system, it appears to be unnecessary for protecting citizens, while punishments generally are thought to promote our safety and well-being. The contrast between death and other punishments can be brought out by asking two questions. What would happen if we abolished all punishments? And, what would happen if we abolished the death penalty?

Most of us believe that if all punishments were abolished, there would be social chaos, a Hobbesian war of all against all. To do away with punishment entirely would be to do away with the criminal law and the system of constraints which it supports. Hence, even though the system is not a just one, we believe that we must live with it and strive to make it as fair as possible. On the other hand, if we abolish capital punishment, there is reason to believe that nothing will happen. There is simply no compelling evidence that capital punishment prevents murders better than long-term prison sentences. Indeed, some evidence even suggests that capital punishment increases the number of murders. While I cannot review the various empirical studies of these questions here, I think it can plausibly be asserted that the results of abolishing punishment generally would be disastrous, while the results of abol-

ishing capital punishment are likely to be insignificant.[13]

I conclude then that the argument from arbitrariness has special force against the death penalty because of its extreme severity and its likely uselessness. The arbitrariness of other punishments may be outweighed by their necessity, but the same cannot be said for capital punishment.

VI

In closing, I would like to comment briefly on one other charge made by van den Haag, the charge that the argument from arbitrariness is a "sham" argument because it is not the real reason why people oppose the death penalty. Those who use this argument, van den Haag claims, would oppose capital punishment even if it were not arbitrarily imposed.

At one level, this charge is doubly fallacious. The suggestion of dishonesty introduced by the word "sham" makes the argument into an *ad hominem*. In addition, the charge suggests that there cannot be more than one reason in support of a view. There are many situations in which we offer arguments and yet would not change our view if the argument were refuted, not because the argument is a sham, but because we have additional grounds for what we believe.

Nonetheless, van den Haag's charge may indicate a special difficulty for the argument from arbitrariness, for the argument may well strike people as artificial and legalistic. Somehow, one may feel that it does not deal with the real issues—wrongness of killing, deterrence, and whether murderers deserve to die.

Part of the problem, I think, is that our ordinary moral thinking involves specific forms of conduct or general rules of personal behavior. The argument from arbitrariness deals with a feature of an *institution*, and thinking about institutions seems to raise difficulties for many people. Believing that an individual murderer deserves to die for a terrible crime, they infer that there ought to be capital punishment, without attending to all of the implications for other individuals which will follow from setting up this practice.

The problem is similar to one that John Stuart Mill highlighted in *On Liberty*. For many people, the fact that an act is wrong is taken to be sufficient ground for its being made illegal. Mill argued against the institutionalization of all moral judgments, and his argument still strikes many people as odd. If the act is wrong, they ask, shouldn't we do everything in our power to stop it? What they fail to appreciate, however, are all of the implications of institutionalizing such judgments.

Likewise, people ask, If so and so deserves to die, shouldn't we empower the state to execute him? The problem, however—one of many problems—is that institutionalizing this judgment about desert yields a system which makes neither moral nor legal sense. Moreover, it perpetuates and exacerbates the liabilities and disadvantages which unjustly befall many of our fellow citizens. These are genuine and serious problems, and those who have raised them in the context of the capital punishment debate have both exposed troubling facts about the actual workings of the criminal law and illuminated the difficulties of acting justly. Most importantly, they have produced a powerful argument against authorizing the state to use death as a punishment for crime.

NOTES

[1]*Capital Punishment: The Inevitability of Caprice and Mistake,* 2d ed. (New York: W. W. Norton & Co., 1981), p. 20.

[2]Ibid., *passim*; W. Bowers and G. Pierce, "Arbitrariness and Discrimination under Post-*Furman* Capital Statutes," *Crime & Delinquency* 26 (1980): 563–635. Reprinted in *The Death Penalty in America*, 3d ed., ed. Hugo Bedau (New York: Oxford University Press, 1982), pp. 206–24.

[3]"The Collapse of the Case Against Capital Punishment," *National Review*, 31 March 1978: 397 [p. 733 above]. A briefer version of this paper appeared in the *Criminal Law Bulletin* 14 (1978): 51–68 and is reprinted in Bedau, pp. 323–33.

[4]Ibid.

[5]"Noncomparative Justice," in *Rights, Justice, and the Bounds of Liberty: Essays in Social Philosophy* (Princeton, N.J.: Princeton University Press, 1980); originally published in the *Philosophical Review* 83 (1974): 297–338.

[6]Black, *Capital Punishment*, p. 29.

[7]Reprinted in Bedau, pp. 263–64.

[8]Using Feinberg's terminology, these can be described as cases in which the criteria of comparative and noncomparative justice conflict with one another. I am arguing that in these instances, the criteria of comparative justice take precedence. Although Feinberg does discuss such conflicts, it is unclear to me from his essay whether he would agree with this claim.

[9]Van den Haag, "The Collapse of the Case Against Capital Punishment," p. 403, n. 12 [p. 743 above]. (This important footnote does not appear in the shorter version of the paper.)

[10]Reprinted in Bedau, pp. 255–56.

[11]Van den Haag, "The Collapse of the Case Against Capital Punishment," p. 397 [p. 733 above].

[12]For a discussion of the role of discrimination throughout the criminal justice system and recommendations for reform, see American Friends Service Committee, *Struggle for Justice* (New York: Hill and Wang, 1971).

[13]In support of the superior deterrent power of the death penalty, van den Haag cites I. Ehrlich, "The Deterrent Effect of Capital Punishment: A Question of Life and Death," *American Economic Review* 65 (1975): 397–417. Two reviews of the evidence on deterrence, both of which criticize Ehrlich at length, are Hans Zeisel, "The Deterrent Effect of the Death Penalty: Facts v. Faith," and Lawrence Klein et al., "The Deterrent Effect of Capital Punishment: An Assessment of the Evidence." (Both of these articles appear in Bedau.) The thesis that executions increase the number of homicides is defended by W. Bowers and G. Pierce in "Deterrence or Brutalization: What is the Effect of Executions?," *Crime & Delinquency* 26 (1980): 453–84.

My thanks are due to Hugo Bedau, William Bowers, Richard Daynard, and Ernest van den Haag for reactions to my thinking about the death penalty. I would especially like to thank Ursula Bentele for helpful discussions and access to unpublished research, Nelson Lande for spirited comments (both philosophical and grammatical), and John Troyer, whose keen and persistent criticisms of my views forced me to write this article.

QUESTIONS FOR DISCUSSION

1. In his Section III, Nathanson distinguishes two arguments from arbitrariness. Explain the difference between these arguments. How could van den Haag best respond to the particular argument that Nathanson discusses in his Section III?

2. Do you agree with Nathanson that it would have been better not to fail anyone in his case C and not to give anyone a prize in his case D than to do what was done in those cases (p. 755)? Why or why not? What is this analogy supposed to show about capital punishment? Does the analogy show this? Why or why not?

3. Nathanson argues that van den Haag's own example of giving capital punishment for murders committed on Mondays, Wednesdays, and Fridays, but at most life imprisonment for murders committed on other days, "is exactly parallel to the situation described by opponents of the death penalty" (p. 756). Do you agree? Why or why not? What is this analogy supposed to show about capital punishment? Does the analogy show this? Why or why not?

4. A common objection to the argument from discrimination against capital punishment is that the same argument would rule out all punishments. How does Nathanson respond to this objection? Is his response adequate? Why or why not?

5. If the overall system of capital punishment is applied in a discriminatory manner, does that make it morally wrong for states to execute individuals who are guilty of murder when there was no discrimination in their particular trial? Why or why not? What would Nathanson say?

6. Can the moral problem of discrimination be solved by making the death penalty mandatory for all crimes of certain kinds? Why or why not?[51]

---

[51]Mandatory death penalties were declared unconstitutional in *Woodson v. North Carolina* 428 U.S. 280 (1976), but the above question is moral.

FURMAN V. GEORGIA

408 U.S. 238 (1972)

Mr. Justice BRENNAN, concurring.

. . . We have very little evidence of the Framers' intent in including the Cruel and Unusual Punishments Clause among those restraints upon the new Government enumerated in the Bill of Rights. . . . [T]he Framers were well aware that the reach of the Clause was not limited to the proscription of unspeakable atrocities. Nor did they intend simply to forbid punishments considered "cruel and unusual" at the time. The "import" of the Clause is, indeed, "indefinite," and for good reason. A constitutional provision "is enacted, it is true, from an experience of evils, but its general language should not, therefore, be necessarily confined to the form that evil had theretofore taken. Time works changes, brings into existence new conditions and purposes. Therefore a principle to be vital must be capable of wider application than the mischief which gave it birth." . . .

There are, then, four principles by which we may determine whether a particular punishment is "cruel and unusual." The primary principle, which I believe supplies the essential predicate for the application of the others, is that a punishment must not by its severity be degrading to human dignity. The paradigm violation of this principle would be the infliction of a torturous punishment of the type that the Clause has always prohibited. Yet "[i]t is unlikely that any State at this moment in history," would pass a law providing for the infliction of such a punishment. Indeed, no such punishment has ever been before this Court. The same may be said of the other principles. It is unlikely that this Court will confront a severe punishment that is obviously inflicted in wholly arbitrary fashion; no State would engage in a reign of blind terror. Nor is it likely that this Court will be called upon to review a severe punishment that is patently unnecessary; no State today would inflict a severe punishment knowing that there was no reason whatever for doing so. In short, we are unlikely to have occasion to determine that a punishment is fatally offensive under any one principle. . . .

The test, then, will ordinarily be a cumulative one: If a punishment is unusually severe, if there is a strong probability that it is inflicted arbitrarily, if it is substantially rejected by contemporary society, and if there is no reason to believe that it serves any penal purpose more effectively than some less severe punishment, then the continued infliction of that punishment violates the command of the Clause that the State may not inflict inhuman and uncivilized punishments upon those convicted of crimes.

. . . I will analyze the punishment of death in terms of the principles set out above and the cumulative test to which they lead: It is a denial of human dignity for the State arbitrarily to subject a person to an unusually severe punishment that society has indicated it does not regard as acceptable, and that cannot be shown to serve any penal purpose more effectively than a significantly less drastic punishment. Under these principles and this test, death is today a "cruel and unusual" punishment.

I.

Death is a unique punishment in the United States. In a society that so strongly affirms the sanctity of life, not surprisingly the common view is that death is the ultimate sanction. This natural human feeling appears all about us. . . .

The only explanation for the uniqueness of death is its extreme severity. Death is today an unusually severe punishment, unusual in its pain, in its finality, and in its enormity. No other existing punishment is comparable to death in terms of physical and mental suffering. . . .

The unusual severity of death is manifested most clearly in its finality and enormity. Death, in these respects, is in a class by itself. . . . The calculated killing of a human being by the State involves, by its very nature, a denial of the executed person's humanity. The contrast with the plight of a person punished by imprisonment is evident. An individual in prison does not lose "the right to have rights." A prisoner retains, for example, the constitutional rights to the free exercise of religion, to be free of cruel and unusual punishments, and to treatment as a "person" for purposes of due process of law and the equal protection of the laws. A prisoner remains a member of the human family. Moreover, he retains the right of access to the courts. His punishment is not irrevocable. Apart from the common charge, grounded upon the recognition of human fallibility, that the punishment of death must inevitably be inflicted upon innocent men, we know that death has been the lot of men whose convictions were unconstitutionally secured in view of later, retroactively applied, holdings of this Court. The punishment itself may have been unconstitutionally inflicted, . . . yet the finality of death precludes relief. An executed person has indeed "lost the right to have rights." . . .

In comparison to all other punishments today, then, the deliberate extinguishment of human life by the State is uniquely degrading to human dignity. I would not hesitate to hold, on that ground alone, that death is today a "cruel and unusual" punishment, were it not that death is a punishment of longstanding usage and acceptance in this country. I therefore turn to the second principle—that the State may not arbitrarily inflict an unusually severe punishment.

II.

The outstanding characteristic of our present practice of punishing criminals by death is the infrequency with which we resort to it. . . . Although there are no exact figures available, we know that thousands of murders and rapes are committed annually in States where death is an authorized punishment for those crimes. However the rate of infliction is characterized—as "freakishly" or "spectacularly" rare, or simply as rare—it would take the purest sophistry to deny that death is inflicted in only a minute fraction of these cases. How much rarer, after all, could the infliction of death be?

When the punishment of death is inflicted in a trivial number of cases in which it is legally available, the conclusion is virtually inescapable that it is being inflicted arbitrarily. Indeed, it smacks of little more than a lottery system. The States claim, however, that this rarity is evidence not of arbitrariness, but of informed selectivity: Death is inflicted, they say, only in "extreme" cases.

Informed selectivity, of course, is a value not to be denigrated. Yet presumably the States could make precisely the same claim if there were ten executions per year, or five, or even if there were but one. That there may be as many as 50 per year does not strengthen the claim. When the rate of infliction is at this low level, it is highly implausible that only the worse criminals or the criminals who commit the worst crimes are selected for this punishment. No one has yet suggested a rational basis that could differentiate in those terms the few who die from the many who go to prison. . . .

Furthermore, our procedures in death cases, rather than resulting in the selection of "extreme" cases for this punishment, actually sanction an arbitrary selection. For this Court has held that juries may, as they do, make the decision whether to impose a death sentence wholly unguided by standards governing that decision. . . . In other words, our procedures are not constructed to guard against the totally capricious selection of criminals for the punishment of death.

III.

. . . The progressive decline in, and the current rarity of, the infliction of death demonstrate that our society seriously questions the appropriateness of this punishment today. The States point out that many legislatures authorize death as the punishment for certain crimes and that substantial segments of the public, as reflected in opinion polls and referendum votes, continue to support it. Yet the availability of this punishment through statutory authorization, as well as the polls and referenda, which amount simply to approval of that authorization, simply underscores the extent to which our society has in fact rejected this punishment. When an unusually severe punishment is authorized for wide-scale application but not, because of society's refusal, inflicted save in a few instances, the inference is compelling that there is a deepseated reluctance to inflict it. Indeed, the likelihood is great that the punishment is tolerated only because of its disuse. The objective indicator of society's view of an unusually severe punishment is what society does with it, and today society will inflict death upon only a small sample of the eligible criminals. Rejection could hardly be more complete without becoming absolute. At the very least, I must conclude that contemporary society views this punishment with substantial doubt.

IV.

The final principle to be considered is that an unusually severe and degrading punishment may not be excessive in view of the purposes for which it is inflicted. This principle, too, is related to the others. When there is a strong probability that the State is arbitrarily inflicting an unusually severe punishment that is subject to grave societal doubts, it is likely also that the punishment cannot be shown to be serving any penal purpose that could not be served equally well by some less severe punishment.

The States' primary claim is that death is a necessary punishment because it prevents the commission of capital crimes more effectively than any less severe punishment. . . . We are not presented with the theoretical question whether under any imaginable circumstances the threat of death might be a greater deterrent to the commission of capital crimes than the threat of imprisonment. We are concerned with the practice of punishing criminals by death as it exists in the United States today. Proponents of this argument necessarily admit that its validity depends upon the existence of a system in which the punishment of death is invariably and swiftly imposed. Our system, of course, satisfies neither condition. A rational person contemplating a murder or rape is confronted, not with the certainty of a speedy death, but with the slightest possibility that he will be executed in the distant future. The risk of death is remote and improbable; in contrast, the risk of long-term imprisonment is near and great. In short, whatever the speculative validity of the assumption that the threat of death is a superior deterrent, there is no reason to believe that as currently administered the punishment of death is necessary to deter the commission of capital crimes. . . .

There is, however, another aspect to the argument that the punishment of death is necessary for the protection of society. The infliction of death, the States urge, serves to manifest the community's outrage at the commission of the crime. It is, they say, a concrete public expression of moral indignation that inculcates respect for the law and helps assure a more peaceful community. Moreover, we are told, not only does the punishment of death exert this widespread moralizing influence upon community values, it also satisfies the popular demand for grievous condemnation of abhorrent crimes and thus prevents disorder, lynching, and attempts by private citizens to take the law into their own hands.

The question, however, is not whether death serves these supposed purposes of punishment, but whether death serves them more effectively than imprisonment. There is no evidence whatever that utilization of imprisonment rather than death encourages private blood feuds and other disorders. Surely if there were such a danger, the execution of a handful of criminals each year would not prevent it. The assertion that death alone is a sufficiently emphatic denunciation for capital crimes suffers from the same defect. If capital crimes require the punishment of death in order to provide moral reinforcement for the basic values of the community, those values can only be undermined when death is so rarely inflicted upon the criminals who commit the crimes. Furthermore, it is certainly doubtful that the infliction of death by the States does in fact strengthen the community's moral code; if the deliberate extinguishment of human life has any effect at all, it more likely tends to lower our respect for life and brutalize our values. That, after all, is why we no longer carry out public executions. . . .

There is, then, no substantial reason to believe that the punishment of death, as currently administered, is necessary for the protection of society. The only other purpose suggested, one that is independent of protection for society, is retribution. . . . Obviously, concepts of justice change; no immutable moral order requires death for murderers and rapists. The claim that death is a just punishment necessarily refers to the existence of certain public beliefs. The claim must be that for capital crimes death alone comports with society's notion of proper punishment. As administered today, however, the punishment of death cannot be justified as a necessary means of exacting retribution from criminals. When the overwhelming number of criminals who commit capital crimes go to prison, it cannot be concluded that death serves the purpose of retribution more effectively than imprisonment. The asserted public belief that murderers and rapists deserve to die is flatly inconsistent with the execution of a random few. As the history of the punishment of death in this country shows, our society wishes to prevent crime; we have no desire to kill criminals simply to get even with them.

In sum, the punishment of death is inconsistent with all four principles: Death is an unusually severe and degrading punishment; there is a strong probability that it is inflicted arbitrarily; its rejection by contemporary society is virtually total; and there is no reason to believe that it serves any penal purpose more effectively than the less severe punishment of imprisonment. The function of these principles is to enable a court to determine whether a punishment comports with human dignity. Death, quite simply, does not. . . .

Mr. Justice STEWART, concurring.

. . . [T]wo of my Brothers have concluded that the infliction of the death penalty is constitutionally impermissible in all circumstances under the Eighth and Fourteenth Amendments. Their case is a strong one. But I find it unnecessary to reach the ultimate question they would decide. . . .

Instead, the death sentences now before us are the product of a legal system that brings them, I believe, within the very core of the Eighth Amendment's guarantee against cruel and unusual punishments. . . . These death sentences are cruel and unusual in the same way that being struck by lightning is cruel and unusual. For, of all the people convicted of rapes and murders in 1967 and 1968, many just as reprehensible as these, the petitioners are among a capriciously selected random handful upon whom the sentence of death has in fact been imposed. My concurring Brothers have demonstrated that, if any basis can be discerned for the selection of these few to be sentenced to die, it is the constitutionally impermissible basis of race. . . . But racial discrimination has not been proved, and I put it to one side. I simply conclude that the Eighth and Fourteenth Amendments cannot tolerate the infliction of a sentence of death under legal systems that permit this unique penalty to be so wantonly and so freakishly imposed. . . .

GREGG V. GEORGIA

428 U.S. 153 (1976)

Judgment of the Court, and opinion of Mr. Justice STEWART, Mr. Justice POWELL, and Mr. Justice STEVENS, announced by Mr. Justice STEWART.

II

. . . The Georgia statute, as amended after our decision in *Furman v. Georgia*, . . . retains the death penalty for six categories of crime: murder, kidnapping for ransom or where the victim is harmed, armed robbery, rape, treason, and aircraft hijacking. . . . The capital defendant's guilt or innocence is determined in the traditional manner, either by a trial judge or a jury, in the first stage of a bifurcated trial. . . .

In the assessment of the appropriate sentence to be imposed the judge is required to consider or to include in his instructions to the jury "any mitigating circumstances or aggravating circumstances otherwise authorized by law and any of statutory aggravating circumstances which may be supported by the evidence. . . ." The scope of the nonstatutory aggravating or mitigating circumstances is not delineated in the statute. Before a convicted defendant may be sentenced to death, however, except in cases of treason or aircraft hijacking, the jury, or the trial judge in cases tried without a jury, must find beyond a reasonable doubt one of the 10 aggravating circumstances specified in the statute.[1] The sentence of death may be imposed only if the jury (or judge) finds one of the statutory aggravating circumstances and then elects to impose that sentence. . . .

In addition to the conventional appellate process available in all criminal cases, provision is made for special expedited direct review by the Supreme Court of Georgia of the appropriateness of imposing the sentence of death in the particular case. . . .

III

We now consider specifically whether the sentence of death for the crime of murder is a *per se* violation of the Eighth and Fourteenth Amendments to the Constitution. We note first that history and precedent strongly support a negative answer to this question.

The imposition of the death penalty for the crime of murder has a long history of acceptance both in the United States and in England. . . .

It is apparent from the text of the Constitution itself that the existence of capital punishment was accepted by the Framers. At the time the Eighth Amendment was ratified, capital punishment was a common sanction in every State. Indeed, the First Congress of the United States enacted legislation providing death as the penalty for specified crimes. . . . The Fifth Amendment, adopted at the same time as the Eighth, contemplated the continued existence of the capital sanction by imposing certain limits on the prosecution of capital cases:

> No person shall be held to answer for a capital, or otherwise infamous crime, unless on a presentment or indictment of a Grand Jury . . . ; nor shall any person be subject for the same offense to be twice put in jeopardy of life or limb; . . . nor be deprived of life, liberty, or property, without due process of law. . . .

And the Fourteenth Amendment, adopted over three–quarters of a century later, similarly contemplates the existence of the capital sanction in providing that no State shall deprive any person of "life, liberty, or property" without due process of law.

For nearly two centuries, this Court, repeatedly and often expressly, has recognized that capital punishment is not invalid *per se*. . . .

Four years ago, the petitioners in *Furman* and its companion cases predicated their argument primarily upon the asserted proposition that standards of decency had evolved to the point where capital punishment no longer could be tolerated. . . . The petitioners in the capital cases before the Court today renew the "standards of decency" argument, but developments during the four years since *Furman* have undercut substantially the assumptions upon which their argument rested. Despite the continuing debate, dating back to the nineteenth century, over the morality and utility of capital punishment, it is now evident that a large proportion of American society continued to regard it as an appropriate and necessary criminal sanction.

The most marked indication of society's endorsement of the death penalty for murder is the legislative response to *Furman*. The legislatures of at least 35 States have enacted new statutes that provide for the death penalty for at least some crimes that result in the death of another person. And the Congress of the United States, in 1974, enacted a statute providing the death penalty for aircraft piracy that results in death. . . .

In the only statewide referendum occurring since *Furman* and brought to our attention, the people of California adopted a constitutional amendment that authorized capital punishment. . . .

The jury also is a significant and reliable objective index of contemporary values because it is so directly involved. . . . It may be true that evolving standards have influenced juries in recent decades to be more discriminating in imposing the sentence of death. But the relative infrequency of jury verdicts imposing the death sentence does not indicate rejection of capital punishment *per se*. Rather, the reluctance of juries in many cases to impose the sentence may well reflect the humane feeling that this most irrevocable of sanctions should be reserved for a small number of extreme cases. . . . Indeed, the actions of juries in many States since *Furman* is fully compatible with the legislative judgments, reflected in the new statutes, as to the continued utility and necessity of capital punishment in appropriate cases. At the close of 1974 at least 254 persons had been sentenced to death since *Furman*, and by the end of March 1976, more than 460 persons were subject to death sentences.

As we have seen, however, the Eighth Amendment demands more than that a challenged punishment be acceptable to contemporary society. The Court also must ask whether it comports with the basic concept of human dignity at the core of the Amendment. Although we cannot "invalidate a category of penalties because we deem less severe penalties adequate to serve the ends of penology," . . . the sanction imposed cannot be so totally without penological justification that it results in the gratuitous infliction of suffering. . . .

The death penalty is said to serve two principal social purposes; retribution and deterrence of capital crimes by prospective offenders.

In part, capital punishment is an expression of society's moral outrage at particularly offensive conduct. This function may be unappealing to many, but it is essential in an ordered society that asks its citizens to rely on legal processes rather than self-help to vindicate their wrongs.

> The instinct for retribution is part of the nature of man, and channeling that instinct in the administration of criminal justice serves an important purpose in promoting the stability of a society governed by law. When people begin to believe that organized society is unwilling or unable to impose upon criminal offenders the punishment they "deserve," then there are sown the seeds of anarchy—of self-help, vigilante justice, and

lynch law. Furman v. Georgia, supra, at 308 (Stewart, J., concurring).

"Retribution is no longer the dominant objective of the criminal law," . . . but neither is it a forbidden objective nor one inconsistent with our respect for the dignity of men. . . . Indeed, the decision that capital punishment may be the appropriate sanction in extreme cases is an expression of the community's belief that certain crimes are themselves so grievous an affront to humanity that the only adequate response may be the penalty of death.

Statistical attempts to evaluate the worth of the death penalty as a deterrent to crimes by potential offenders have occasioned a great deal of debate. The results simply have been inconclusive. . . . Although some of the studies suggest that the death penalty may not function as a significantly greater deterrent than lesser penalties, there is no convincing empirical evidence either supporting or refuting this view. We may nevertheless assume safely that there are murderers, such as those who act in passion, for whom the threat of death has little or no deterrent effect. But for many others, the death penalty undoubtedly is a significant deterrent. There are carefully contemplated murders, such as murder for hire, where the possible penalty of death may well enter into the cold calculus that precedes the decision to act. And there are some categories of murder, such as murder by a life prisoner, where other sanctions may not be adequate.

The value of capital punishment as a deterrent of crime is a complex factual issue the resolution of which properly rests with the legislatures, which can evaluate the results of statistical studies in terms of their own local conditions and with a flexibility of approach that is not available to the courts. . . . Indeed, many of the post-*Furman* statutes reflect just such a responsible effort to define those crimes and those criminals for which capital punishment is most probably an effective deterrent.

In sum, we cannot say that the judgment of the Georgia legislature that capital punishment may be necessary in some cases is clearly wrong. Considerations of federalism, as well as respect for the ability of a legislature to evaluate, in terms of its particular State, the moral consensus concerning the death penalty and its social utility as a sanction, require us to conclude, in the absence of more convincing evidence, that the infliction of death as a punishment for murder is not without justification and thus is not unconstitutionally severe.

Finally, we must consider whether the punishment of death is disproportionate in relation to the crime for which it is imposed. There is no question that death as a punishment is unique in its severity and irrevocability. . . . When a defendant's life is at stake, the Court has been particularly sensitive to insure that every safeguard is observed. . . . But we are concerned here only with the imposition of capital punishment for the crime of murder, and when a life has been taken deliberately by the offender, we cannot say that the punishment is invariably disproportionate to the crime. It is an extreme sanction, suitable to the most extreme of crimes.

We hold that the death penalty is not a form of punishment that may never be imposed, regardless of the circumstances of the offense, regardless of the character of the offender, and regardless of the procedure followed in reaching the decision to impose it. . . .

IV

While *Furman* did not hold that the infliction of the death penalty *per se* violates the Constitution's ban on cruel and unusual punishments, it did recognize that the penalty of death is different in kind from any other punishment imposed under our system of criminal justice. Because of the uniqueness of the death penalty, *Furman* held that it could not be imposed under sentencing procedures that created a substantial risk that it would be inflicted in an arbitrary and capricious manner. . . .

Furman mandates that where discretion is afforded a sentencing body on a matter so grave as the determination of whether a human life should be taken or spared, that discretion must be suitably directed and limited so as to minimize the risk of wholly arbitrary and capricious action. . . . While some have suggested that standards to guide a capital jury's sentencing deliberations are impossible to formulate, the fact is that such standards have been developed. . . . While such standards are by necessity somewhat general, they do provide guidance to the sentencing authority and thereby reduce the likelihood that it will impose a sentence that fairly can be called capricious or arbitrary. Where the sentencing authority is required to specify the factors it relied upon in reaching its decision, the further safeguard of meaningful appellate review is available to ensure that death sentences are not imposed capriciously or in a freakish manner.

In summary, the concerns expressed in *Furman* that the penalty of death not be imposed in an arbitrary or capricious manner can be met by a carefully drafted statute that ensures that the sentencing authority is given adequate information and guidance. . . .

The basic concern of *Furman* centered on those defendants who were being condemned to death capriciously and arbitrarily. Under the procedures before the Court in that case, sentencing authorities were not directed to give attention to the nature or circumstances of the crime committed or to the character or record of the defendant. Left unguided, juries imposed the death sentence in a way that could only be called freakish. The new Georgia sentencing procedures, by contrast, focus the jury's attention on the particularized nature of the crime and the particularized characteristics of the individual defendant. While the jury is permitted to consider any aggravating or mitigating circumstances, it must find and identify at least one statutory aggravating factor before it may impose a penalty of death. In this way the jury's decision is channeled. No longer can a jury wantonly and freakishly impose the death sentence; it is always circumscribed by the legislative guidelines. In addition, the review function of the Supreme Court of Georgia affords additional assurance that the concerns that prompted our decision in *Furman* are not present to any significant degree in the Georgia procedure applied here.

For the reasons expressed in this opinion, we hold that the statutory system under which Gregg was sentenced to death does not violate the Constitution. Accordingly, the judgment of the Georgia Supreme Court is affirmed.

NOTES

[1]The statute provides in part:

(a) The death penalty may be imposed for the offenses of aircraft hijacking or treason, in any case.

(b) In all cases of other offenses for which the death penalty may be authorized, the judge shall consider, or he shall include in his instructions to the jury for it to consider, any mitigating circumstances or aggravating circumstances otherwise authorized by law and any of the following statutory aggravating circumstances which may be supported by the evidence:

(1) The offense of murder, rape, armed robbery, or kidnapping was committed by a person with a prior record of conviction for a capital felony, or the offense of murder was committed by a person who has a substantial history of serious assaultive criminal convictions.

(2) The offense of murder, rape, armed robbery, or kidnapping was committed while the offender was engaged in the commission of another capital felony, or aggravated battery, or the offense of murder was committed while the offender was engaged in the commission of burglary or arson in the first degree.

(3) The offender by his act of murder, armed robbery, or kidnapping knowingly created a great risk of death to more than one person in a public place by means of a weapon or device which would normally be hazardous to the lives of more than one person.

(4) The offender committed the offense of murder for himself or another, for the purpose of receiving money or any other thing of monetary value.

(5) The murder of a judicial officer, former judicial officer, district attorney or solicitor or for-

mer district attorney or solicitor was committed during or because of the exercise of his official duty.

(6) The offender caused or directed another to commit murder or committed murder as an agent or employee of another person.

(7) The offense of murder, rape, armed robbery, or kidnapping was outrageously or wantonly vile, horrible or inhuman in that it involved torture, depravity of mind, or an aggravated battery to the victim.

(8) The offense of murder was committed against any peace officer, corrections employee or fireman while engaged in the performance of his official duties.

(9) The offense of murder was committed by a person in, or who has escaped from, the lawful custody of a peace officer or place of lawful confinement.

(10) The murder was committed for the purpose of avoiding, interfering with, or preventing a lawful arrest or custody in a place of lawful confinement, of himself or another.

(c) The statutory instructions as determined by the trial judge to be warranted by the evidence shall be given in charge and in writing to the jury for its deliberation. The jury, if its verdict be a recommendation of death, shall designate in writing, signed by the foreman of the jury, the aggravating circumstance or circumstances which it found beyond a reasonable doubt. In non-jury cases the judge shall make such designation. Except in cases of treason or aircraft hijacking, unless at least one of the statutory aggravating circumstances enumerated in section 27-2534.1(b) is so found, the death penalty shall not be imposed. . . .

The Supreme Court of Georgia . . . recently held unconstitutional the portion of the first circumstance encompassing persons who have a "substantial history of serious assaultive criminal convictions" because it did not set "sufficiently 'clear and objective standards.'"

MCCLESKEY V. KEMP, SUPERINTENDENT GEORGIA DIAGNOSTIC AND CLASSIFICATION CENTER

481 U.S. 279 (1986)

Justice POWELL delivered the opinion of the Court, in which REHNQUIST, C. J., and WHITE, O'CONNOR, and SCALIA, JJ., joined.

This case presents the question whether a complex statistical study that indicates a risk that racial considerations enter into capital sentencing determinations proves that petitioner McCleskey's capital sentence is unconstitutional under the Eighth or Fourteenth Amendment.

I

McCleskey, a black man, was convicted of two counts of armed robbery and one count of murder in the Superior Court of Fulton County, Georgia, on October 12, 1978. McCleskey's convictions arose out of the robbery of a furniture store and the killing of a white police officer during the course of the robbery. The evidence at trial indicated that McCleskey and three accomplices planned and carried out the robbery. All four were armed. McCleskey entered the front of the store while the other three entered the rear. McCleskey secured the front of the store by rounding up the customers and forcing them to lie face down on the floor. The other three rounded up the employees in the rear and tied them up with tape. The manager was forced at gunpoint to turn over the store receipts, his watch, and $6. During the course of the robbery, a police officer, answering a silent alarm, entered the store through the front door. As he was walking down the center aisle of the store, two shots were fired. Both struck the officer. One hit him in the face and killed him.

Several weeks later, McCleskey was arrested in connection with an unrelated offense. He confessed that he had participated in the furniture store robbery, but denied that he had shot the police officer. At trial, the State introduced evidence that at least one of the bullets that struck the officer was fired from a .38 caliber Rossi revolver. This description matched the description of the gun that McCleskey had carried during the robbery. The State also introduced the testimony of two witnesses who had heard McCleskey admit to the shooting.

The jury convicted McCleskey of murder. At the penalty hearing, the jury heard arguments as to the appropriate sentence. Under Georgia law, the jury could not consider imposing the death penalty unless it found beyond a reasonable doubt that the murder was accompanied by one of the statutory aggravating circumstances. . . . The jury in this case found two aggravating circumstances to exist beyond a reasonable doubt: the murder was committed during the course of an armed robbery. . . ; and the murder was committed upon a peace officer engaged in the performance of his duties. . . . McCleskey offered no mitigating evidence. The jury recommended that he be

sentenced to death on the murder charge and to consecutive life sentences on the armed robbery charges. The court followed the jury's recommendation and sentenced McCleskey to death.

On appeal, the Supreme Court of Georgia affirmed the convictions and the sentences. . . .

McCleskey next filed a petition for a writ of habeas corpus in the Federal District Court for the Northern District of Georgia. His petition raised 18 claims, one of which was that the Georgia capital sentencing process is administered in a racially discriminatory manner in violation of the Eighth and Fourteenth Amendments to the United States Constitution. In support of his claim, McCleskey proffered a statistical study performed by Professors David C. Baldus, Charles Pulaski, and George Woodworth (the Baldus study) that purports to show a disparity in the imposition of the death sentence in Georgia based on the race of the murder victim and, to a lesser extent, the race of the defendant. The Baldus study is actually two sophisticated statistical studies that examine over 2,000 murder cases that occurred in Georgia during the 1970's. The raw numbers collected by Professor Baldus indicate that defendants charged with killing white persons received the death penalty in 11% of the cases, but defendants charged with killing blacks received the death penalty in only 1% of the cases. The raw numbers also indicate a reverse racial disparity according to the race of the defendant: 4% of the black defendants received the death penalty, as opposed to 7% of the white defendants.

Baldus also divided the cases according to the combination of the race of the defendant and the race of the victim. He found that the death penalty was assessed in 22% of the cases involving black defendants and white victims; 8% of the cases involving white defendants and white victims; 1% of the cases involving black defendants and black victims; and 3% of the cases involving white defendants and black victims. Similarly, Baldus found that prosecutors sought the death penalty in 70% of the cases involving black defendants and white victims; 32% of the cases involving white defendants and white victims; 15% of the cases involving black defendants and black victims; and 19% of the cases involving white defendants and black victims.

Baldus subjected his data to an extensive analysis, taking account of 230 variables that could have explained the disparities on nonracial grounds. One of his models concludes that, even after taking account of 39 nonracial variables, defendants charged with killing white victims were 4.3 times as likely to receive a death sentence as defendants charged with killing blacks. According to this model, black defendants were 1.1 times as likely to receive a death sentence as other defendants. Thus, the Baldus study indicates that black defendants, such as McCleskey, who kill white victims have the greatest likelihood of receiving the death penalty.

The District Court . . . denied the petition insofar as it was based upon the Baldus study. . . . The Court of Appeals affirmed the denial. . . . We . . . now affirm.

II

McCleskey's first claim is that the Georgia capital punishment statute violates the Equal Protection Clause of the Fourteenth Amendment.[1] He argues that race has infected the administration of Georgia's statute in two ways: persons who murder whites are more likely to be sentenced to death than persons who murder blacks, and black murderers are more likely to be sentenced to death than white murderers. As a black defendant who killed a white victim, McCleskey claims that the Baldus study demonstrates that he was discriminated against because of his race and because of the race of his victim. In its broadest form, McCleskey's claim of discrimination extends to every actor in the Georgia capital sentencing process, from the prosecutor who sought the death penalty and the jury that imposed the

sentence, to the State itself that enacted the capital punishment statute and allows it to remain in effect despite its allegedly discriminatory application. We agree with the Court of Appeals, and every other court that has considered such a challenge, that this claim must fail.

A

Our analysis begins with the basic principle that a defendant who alleges an equal protection violation has the burden of proving "the existence of purposeful discrimination." . . . Thus, to prevail under the Equal Protection Clause, McCleskey must prove that the decisionmakers in his case acted with discriminatory purpose. He offers no evidence specific to his own case that would support an inference that racial considerations played a part in his sentence. Instead, he relies solely on the Baldus study. McCleskey argues that the Baldus study compels an inference that his sentence rests on purposeful discrimination. McCleskey's claim that these statistics are sufficient proof of discrimination, without regard to the facts of a particular case, would extend to all capital cases in Georgia, at least where the victim was white and the defendant is black.

The Court has accepted statistics as proof of intent to discriminate in certain limited contexts. First, this Court has accepted statistical disparities as proof of an equal protection violation in the selection of the jury venire in a particular district. . . . Second, this Court has accepted statistics in the form of multiple-regression analysis to prove statutory violations under Title VII of the Civil Rights Act of 1964. . . .

But the nature of the capital sentencing decision, and the relationship of the statistics to that decision, are fundamentally different from the corresponding elements in the venire-selection or Title VII cases. Most importantly, each particular decision to impose the death penalty is made by a petit jury selected from a properly constituted venire. Each jury is unique in its composition, and the Constitution requires that its decision rest on consideration of innumerable factors that vary according to the characteristics of the individual defendant and the facts of the particular capital offense. . . . Thus, the application of an inference drawn from the general statistics to a specific decision in a trial and sentencing simply is not comparable to the application of an inference drawn from general statistics to a specific venire-selection or Title VII case. In those cases, the statistics relate to fewer entities, and fewer variables are relevant to the challenged decisions. . . .

Because discretion is essential to the criminal justice process, we would demand exceptionally clear proof before we would infer that the discretion has been abused. The unique nature of the decisions at issue in this case also counsels against adopting such an inference from the disparities indicated by the Baldus study. Accordingly, we hold that the Baldus study is clearly insufficient to support an inference that any of the decisionmakers in McCleskey's case acted with discriminatory purpose.

B

McCleskey also suggests that the Baldus study proves that the State as a whole has acted with a discriminatory purpose. He appears to argue that the State has violated the Equal Protection Clause by adopting the capital punishment statute and allowing it to remain in force despite its allegedly discriminatory application. But "'discriminatory purpose' . . . implies more than intent as volition or intent as awareness of consequences. It implies that the decisionmaker, in this case a state legislature, selected or reaffirmed a particular course of action at least in part 'because of,' not merely 'in spite of,' its adverse effects upon an identifiable group." . . . For this claim to prevail, McCleskey would have to prove that the Georgia Legislature enacted or maintained the death penalty statute because of an anticipated racially discriminatory effect. In Gregg v. Georgia, . . . this Court found that the Georgia capital sentencing

system could operate in a fair and neutral manner. There was no evidence then, and there is none now, that the Georgia Legislature enacted the capital punishment statute to further a racially discriminatory purpose. . . . Nor has McCleskey demonstrated that the legislature maintains the capital punishment statute because of the racially disproportionate impact suggested by the Baldus study. . . .

Accordingly, we reject McCleskey's equal protection claims.

NOTE

[1] Although the District Court rejected the findings of the Baldus study as flawed, the Court of Appeals assumed that the study is valid and reached the constitutional issues. Accordingly, those issues are before us. As did the Court of Appeals, we assume the study is valid statistically without reviewing the factual findings of the District Court. . . .

Justice BRENNAN, with whom Justice MARSHALL joins, and with whom Justice BLACKMUN and Justice STEVENS join in all but Part I, dissenting.

III

A

It is important to emphasize at the outset that the Court's observation that McCleskey cannot prove the influence of race on any particular sentencing decision is irrelevant in evaluating his Eighth Amendment claim. Since Furman v. Georgia, . . . the Court has been concerned with the risk of the imposition of an arbitrary sentence, rather than the proven fact of one. . . . This emphasis on risk acknowledges the difficulty of divining the jury's motivation in an individual case. In addition, it reflects the fact that concern for arbitrariness focuses on the rationality of the system as a whole, and that a system that features a significant probability that sentencing decisions are influenced by impermissible considerations cannot be regarded as rational. . . . As we said in Gregg v. Georgia . . ., "the petitioner looks to the sentencing system as a whole (as the Court did in Furman and we do today)": a constitutional violation is established if a plaintiff demonstrates a "pattern of arbitrary and capricious sentencing." . . .

Defendants challenging their death sentences thus never have had to prove that impermissible considerations have actually infected sentencing decisions. We have required instead that they establish that the system under which they were sentenced posed a significant risk of such an occurrence. McCleskey's claim does differ, however, in one respect from these earlier cases: it is the first to base a challenge not on speculation about how a system might operate, but on empirical documentation of how it does operate.

The Court assumes the statistical validity of the Baldus study, and acknowledges that McCleskey has demonstrated a risk that racial prejudice plays a role in capital sentencing in Georgia. . . . Nonetheless, it finds the probability of prejudice insufficient to create constitutional concern. . . . Close analysis of the Baldus study, however, in light of both statistical principles and human experience, reveals that the risk that race influenced McCleskey's sentence is intolerable by any imaginable standard.

B

The Baldus study indicates that, after taking into account some 230 nonracial factors that might legitimately influence a sentencer, the jury more likely than not would have spared McCleskey's life had his victim been black. The study distinguishes between those cases in which (1) the jury exercises virtually no discretion because the strength or weakness of aggravating factors usually suggests that only one outcome is appropriate; and (2) cases reflecting an "intermediate" level of aggravation, in which the jury has considerable discretion in choosing a sentence. McCleskey's case falls into the intermediate range. In such cases, death is imposed in 34% of white-victim crimes and 14% of black-victim crimes, a difference of 139% in the rate of imposition of the death penalty. . . . In other words, just

under 59%—almost 6 in 10—defendants comparable to McCleskey would not have received the death penalty if their victims had been black. . . .

Of the more than 200 variables potentially relevant to a sentencing decision, race of the victim is a powerful explanation for variation in death sentence rates—as powerful as nonracial aggravating factors such as a prior murder conviction or acting as the principal planner of the homicide. . . .

C

Evaluation of McCleskey's evidence cannot rest solely on the numbers themselves. We must also ask whether the conclusion suggested by those numbers is consonant with our understanding of history and human experience. Georgia's legacy of a race-conscious criminal justice system, as well as this Court's own recognition of the persistent danger that racial attitudes may affect criminal proceedings, indicates that McCleskey's claim is not a fanciful product of mere statistical artifice. . . .

IV

The Court cites four reasons for shrinking from the implications of McCleskey's evidence: the desirability of discretion for actors in the criminal justice system, the existence of statutory safeguards against abuse of that discretion, the potential consequences for broader challenges to criminal sentencing, and an understanding of the contours of the judicial role. While these concerns underscore the need for sober deliberation, they do not justify rejecting evidence as convincing as McCleskey has presented.

The Court maintains that petitioner's claim "is antithetical to the fundamental role of discretion in our criminal justice system.". . . It states that "where the discretion that is fundamental to our criminal process is involved, we decline to assume that what is unexplained is invidious." . . . Reliance on race in imposing capital punishment, however, is antithetical to the very rationale for granting sentencing discretion. Discretion is a means, not an end. It is bestowed in order to permit the sentencer to "trea[t] each defendant in a capital case with that degree of respect due the uniqueness of the individual." . . . Considering the race of a defendant or victim in deciding if the death penalty should be imposed is completely at odds with this concern that an individual be evaluated as a unique human being. . . .

The Court also declines to find McCleskey's evidence sufficient in view of "the safeguards designed to minimize racial bias in the [capital sentencing] process.". . . [T]he Court cannot rely on the statutory safeguards in discounting Mc-Cleskey's evidence, for it is the very effectiveness of those safeguards that such evidence calls into question. While we may hope that a model of procedural fairness will curb the influence of race on sentencing, "we cannot simply assume that the model works as intended; we must critique its performance in terms of its results." . . .

The Court next states that its unwillingness to regard petitioner's evidence as sufficient is based in part on the fear that recognition of McCleskey's claim would open the door to widespread challenges to all aspects of criminal sentencing. . . . Taken on its face, such a statement seems to suggest a fear of too much justice. . . . In fairness, the Court's fear that McCleskey's claim is an invitation to descend a slippery slope also rests on the realization that any humanly imposed system of penalties will exhibit some imperfection. Yet to reject Mc-Cleskey's powerful evidence on this basis is to ignore both the qualitatively different character of the death penalty and the particular repugnance of racial discrimination, considerations which may properly be taken into account in determining whether various punishments are "cruel and unusual." Furthermore, it fails to take account of the unprecedented refinement and strength of the Baldus study. . . .

Finally, the Court justifies its rejection of McCleskey's claim by cautioning against usurpation of the legislatures' role in devising and monitoring criminal punishment. The Court is, of course, correct to emphasize the gravity of constitutional intervention and the importance that it be sparingly employed. The fact that "capital punishment is now the law in more than two thirds of our States," . . . however, does not diminish the fact that capital punishment is the most awesome act that a State can perform. The judiciary's role in this society counts for little if the use of governmental power to extinguish life does not elicit close scrutiny. . . . Those whom we would banish from society or from the human community itself often speak in too faint a voice to be heard above society's demand for punishment. It is the particular role of courts to hear these voices, for the Constitution declares that the majoritarian chorus may not alone dictate the conditions of social life. The Court thus fulfills, rather than disrupts, the scheme of separation of powers by closely scrutinizing the imposition of the death penalty, for no decision of a society is more deserving of "sober second thought." . . .

LEONEL TORRES HERRERA, PETITIONER V. JAMES A. COLLINS, DIRECTOR, TEXAS DEPARTMENT OF CRIMINAL JUSTICE, INSTITUTIONAL DIVISION

113 S. Ct. 853 (1993)

Chief Justice REHNQUIST delivered the opinion of the Court, in which O'CONNOR, SCALIA, KENNEDY, and THOMAS, JJ., joined. [JUSTICE WHITE filed a concurring opinion.]

Petitioner Leonel Torres Herrera was convicted of capital murder and sentenced to death in January 1982. He unsuccessfully challenged the conviction on direct appeal and state collateral proceedings in the Texas state courts, and in a federal habeas petition. In February 1992—10 years after his conviction—he urged in a second federal habeas petition that he was "actually innocent" of the murder for which he was sentenced to death, and that the Eighth Amendment's prohibition against cruel and unusual punishment and the Fourteenth Amendment's guarantee of due process of law therefore forbid his execution. He supported this claim with affidavits tending to show that his now-dead brother, rather than he, had been the perpetrator of the crime. Petitioner urges us to hold that this showing of innocence entitles him to relief in this federal habeas proceeding. We hold that it does not.

Shortly before 11 p.m. on an evening in late September 1981, the body of Texas Department of Public Safety Officer David Rucker was found by a passerby on a stretch of highway about six miles east of Los Fresnos, Texas, a few miles north of Brownsville in the Rio Grande Valley. Rucker's body was lying beside his patrol car. He had been shot in the head.

At about the same time, Los Fresnos Police Officer Enrique Carrisalez observed a speeding vehicle traveling west towards Los Fresnos, away from the place where Rucker's body had been found, along the same road. Carrisalez, who was accompanied in his patrol car by Enrique Hernandez, turned on his flashing red lights and pursued the speeding vehicle. After the car had stopped briefly at a red light, it signaled that it would pull over and did so. The patrol car pulled up behind it. Carrisalez took a flashlight and walked toward the car of the speeder. The driver opened his door and exchanged a few words with Carrisalez before firing at least one shot at Carrisalez' chest. The officer died nine days later.

Petitioner Herrera was arrested a few days after the shootings and charged with the capital murder of both Carrisalez and Rucker. He was tried and found guilty of the capital murder of Carrisalez in January 1982, and sentenced to death. In July 1982, petitioner pleaded guilty to the murder of Rucker.

At petitioner's trial for the murder of Carrisalez, Hernandez, who had witnessed Carrisalez' slaying from the officer's patrol car, identified petitioner as the person who had wielded the gun. A declaration by Officer Carrisalez to the same effect, made while he was in the hospital, was also admitted. Through a license plate check, it was shown that the speeding car involved in Carrisalez' murder was registered to petitioner's "live-in" girlfriend. Petitioner was known to drive this car, and he had a set of keys to the car in his pants pocket when he was arrested. Hernandez identified the car as the vehicle from which the murderer had emerged to fire the fatal shot. He also testified that there had been only one person in the car that night.

The evidence showed that Herrera's Social Security card had been found alongside Rucker's patrol car on the night he was killed. Splatters of blood on the car identified as the vehicle involved in the shootings, and on petitioner's blue jeans and wallet were identified as type A blood—the same type which Rucker had. (Herrera has type O blood.) Similar evidence with respect to strands of hair found in the car indicated that the hair was Rucker's and not Herrera's. A handwritten letter was also found on the person of petitioner when he was arrested, which strongly implied that he had killed Rucker.

Petitioner appealed his conviction and sentence, arguing, among other things, that Hernandez' and Carrisalez' identifications were unreliable and improperly admitted. The Texas Court of Criminal Appeals affirmed . . . , and we denied certiorari. . . . Petitioner's application for state habeas relief was denied. . . . Petitioner then filed a federal habeas petition, again challenging the identifications offered against him at trial. This petition was denied . . . , and we again denied certiorari. . . .

Petitioner next returned to state court and filed a second habeas petition, raising, among other things, a claim of "actual innocence" based on newly discovered evidence. In support of this claim petitioner presented the affidavits of Hector Villarreal, an attorney who had represented petitioner's brother, Raul Herrera,

Sr., and of Juan Franco Palacious, one of Raul Sr.'s former cellmates. Both individuals claimed that Raul Sr., who died in 1984, had told them that he—and not petitioner—had killed Officers Rucker and Carrisalez. The State District Court denied this application, finding that "no evidence at trial remotely suggested that anyone other than [petitioner] committed the offense." . . . The Texas Court of Criminal Appeals affirmed, . . . and we denied certiorari. . . .

In February 1992, petitioner lodged the instant habeas petition—his second—in federal court, alleging, among other things, that he is innocent of the murders of Rucker and Carrisalez, and that his execution would thus violate the Eighth and Fourteenth Amendments. In addition to proffering the above affidavits, petitioner presented the affidavits of Raul Herrera, Jr., Raul Sr.'s son, and Jose Ybarra, Jr., a schoolmate of the Herrera brothers. Raul Jr. averred that he had witnessed his father shoot Officers Rucker and Carrisalez and petitioner was not present. Raul Jr. was nine years old at the time of the killings. Ybarra alleged that Raul Sr. told him one summer night in 1983 that he had shot the two police officers. Petitioner alleged that law enforcement officials were aware of this evidence, and had withheld it. . . .

Petitioner asserts that the Eighth and Fourteenth Amendments to the United States Constitution prohibit the execution of a person who is innocent of the crime for which he was convicted. This proposition has an elemental appeal. . . . But the evidence upon which petitioner's claim of innocence rests was not produced at his trial, but rather eight years later. In any system of criminal justice, "innocence" or "guilt" must be determined in some sort of a judicial proceeding. Petitioner's showing of innocence, and indeed his constitutional claim for relief based upon that showing, must be evaluated in the light of the previous proceedings in this case, which have stretched over a span of 10 years.

A person when first charged with a crime is entitled to a presumption of innocence, and may insist that his guilt be established beyond a reasonable doubt. . . . In capital cases, we have required additional protections because of the nature of the penalty at stake. . . . All of these constitutional safeguards, of course, make it more difficult for the State to rebut and finally overturn the presumption of innocence which attaches to every criminal defendant. But we have also observed that "due process does not require that every conceivable step be taken, at whatever cost, to eliminate the possibility of convicting an innocent person." . . . To conclude otherwise would all but paralyze our system for enforcement of the criminal law.

Once a defendant has been afforded a fair trial and convicted of the offense for which he was charged, the presumption of innocence disappears. Here, it is not disputed that the State met its burden of proving at trial that petitioner was guilty of the capital murder of Officer Carrisalez beyond a reasonable doubt. Thus, in the eyes of the law, petitioner does not come before the Court as one who is "innocent," but on the contrary as one who has been convicted by due process of law of two brutal murders. . . .

The dissent would place the burden on petitioner to show that he is "probably" innocent. . . . Were petitioner to satisfy the dissent's "probable innocence" standard, therefore, the District Court would presumably be required to grant a conditional order of relief, which would in effect require the State to retry petitioner 10 years after his first trial, not because of any constitutional violation which had occurred at the first trial, but simply because of a belief that in light of petitioner's new found evidence a jury might find him not guilty at a second trial.

Yet there is no guarantee that the guilt or innocence determination would be any more exact. To the contrary, the passage of time only diminishes the reliability of criminal adjudications. . . . We may assume, for the sake of argument in deciding this case, that in a capital case a truly persuasive demonstration of "actual innocence" made after trial would render the execution of a defendant unconstitutional, and warrant federal habeas relief if there were no state avenue open to process such a claim. But because of the very disruptive effect that entertaining claims of actual innocence would have on the need for finality in capital cases, and the enormous burden that having to retry cases based on often stale evidence would place on the States, the threshold showing for such an assumed right would necessarily be extraordinarily high. The showing made by petitioner in this case falls far short of any such threshold.

Petitioner's newly discovered evidence consists of affidavits. In the new trial context, motions based solely upon affidavits are disfavored because the affiants' statements are obtained without the benefit of cross-examination and an opportunity to make credibility determinations. . . . Petitioner's affidavits are particularly suspect in this regard because, with the exception of Raul Herrera, Jr.'s, affidavit, they consist of hearsay. Likewise, in reviewing petitioner's new evidence, we are mindful that defendants often abuse new trial motions "as a method of delaying enforcement of just sentences." . . . Although we are not presented with a new trial motion per se, we believe the likelihood of abuse is as great—or greater—here.

This is not to say that petitioner's affidavits are without probative value. Had this sort of testimony been offered at trial, it could have been weighed by the jury, along with the evidence offered by the State and petitioner, in deliberating upon its verdict. Since the statements in the affidavits contradict the evidence received at trial, the jury would have had to decide important issues of credibility. But coming 10 years after petitioner's trial, this showing of innocence falls far short of that which would have to be made in order to trigger the sort of constitutional claim which we have assumed, arguendo, to exist.

The judgment of the Court of Appeals is affirmed.

JUSTICE BLACKMUN, with whom JUSTICE STEVENS and JUSTICE SOUTER join with respect to Parts I–IV, dissenting.

III

. . . I agree with the majority that "in state criminal proceedings the trial is the paramount event for determining the guilt or innocence of the defendant." . . . I also think that "a truly persuasive demonstration of 'actual innocence' made after trial would render the execution of a defendant unconstitutional." . . . The question is what "a truly persuasive demonstration" entails, a question the majority's disposition of this case leaves open. . . .

I would hold that, to obtain relief on a claim of actual innocence, the petitioner must show that he probably is innocent. This standard is supported by several considerations. First, new evidence of innocence may be discovered long after the defendant's conviction. Given the passage of time, it may be difficult for the State to retry a defendant who obtains relief from his conviction or sentence on an actual-innocence claim. The actual-innocence proceeding thus may constitute the final word on whether the defendant may be punished. In light of this fact, an otherwise constitutionally valid conviction or sentence should not be set aside lightly. Second, conviction after a constitutionally adequate trial strips the defendant of the presumption of innocence. . . . When a defendant seeks to challenge the determination of guilt after he has been validly convicted and sentenced, it is fair to place on him the burden of proving his innocence, not just raising doubt about his guilt. . . .

A prisoner raising an actual-innocence claim in a federal habeas petition is not entitled to discovery as a matter of right. . . . The district court retains discretion to order discovery, however, when it would help the court make a reliable determination with respect to the prisoner's claim. . . .

It should be clear that the standard I would adopt would not convert the federal courts into "'forums in which to relitigate state trials.'" . . . A prisoner raising an actual-innocence claim in a federal habeas petition is not entitled to discovery as a matter of right. . . . The district court retains discretion to order discovery, however, when it would help the court make a reliable determination with respect to the prisoner's claim. . . .

IV

I do not understand why the majority so severely faults petitioner for relying only on affidavits. . . . It is common to rely on affidavits at the preliminary-consideration stage of a habeas proceeding. The opportunity for cross-examination and credibility determinations comes at the hearing, assuming that the petitioner is entitled to one. It makes no sense for this Court to impugn the reliability of petitioner's evidence on the ground that its credibility has not been tested when the reason its credibility has not been tested is that petitioner's habeas proceeding has been truncated by the Court of Appeals and now by this Court. In its haste to deny petitioner relief, the majority seems to confuse the question whether the petition may be dismissed summarily with the question whether petitioner is entitled to relief on the merits of his claim.

QUESTIONS FOR DISCUSSION

1. In a note, Justice Brennan describes what Furman did: "The victim surprised Furman in the act of burglarizing the victim's home in the middle of the night. While escaping, Furman killed the victim with one pistol shot fired through the closed kitchen door from the outside. At the trial, Furman gave his version of the killing: 'They got me charged with murder and I admit, I admit going to these folks' home and they did caught me in there and I was coming back out, backing up and there was a wire down there on the floor. I was coming out backwards and fell back and I didn't intend to kill nobody. I didn't know they was behind the door. The gun went off and I didn't know nothing about no murder until they arrested me, and the gun went off when I was down on the floor and I got up and ran. That's all to it.' . . . The Georgia Supreme Court accepted that version." Assuming these facts, do you think that Furman deserved the death penalty? (Compare Section 7.4 on felony murder.) Does this matter to the constitutional issues in *Furman v. Georgia*? Why or why not?

2. Which theory of constitutional interpretation is assumed by Brennan's argument in *Furman*? By Stewart's argument in *Gregg*? (See Section 2.1.)

3. How, if at all, is popular opinion about the death penalty relevant to its constitutionality according to the Supreme Court? According to you? Justice Marshall claims, "the American people are largely unaware of the information critical to a judgment on the morality of the death penalty" and "if they were better informed they would consider it shocking, unjust, and unacceptable" (from his dissent in *Gregg*). If these claims are true, does this show that actual public opinion does not matter to constitutionality? Does it matter what people would believe if they were fully informed? Why or why not?

4. Should statistical evidence of racial discrimination in the application of the death penalty in a jurisdiction be relevant to a particular legal case? (Compare Section 8.2.) Should defendants be required to prove discrimination in their own particular cases before their convictions are overturned on the basis of the Equal Protection Clause? Why or why not? (Compare Section 5.3.)

5. The Supreme Court gives priority to the individual case in *McCleskey v. Kemp*, but they argue partly from the needs of the overall system in *Herrera v. Texas*. Are these two decisions compatible? Are they both correct? Why or why not?

6. If you were on the Supreme Court, would you have voted to give Herrera a new trial? Why or why not?

7. In one of his last opinions before retirement, Justice Harry Blackmun dissented in *Callins v. Collins* (No. 93–7054, 1994). He wrote, "From this day forward, I no longer shall tinker with the machinery of death. For more than 20 years I have endeavored—indeed, I have struggled, along with the majority of this

court—to develop procedural and substantive rules that would lend more than the mere appearance of fairness to the death penalty endeavor. . . . I feel morally and intellectually obligated simply to concede that the death penalty experiment has failed. It is virtually self-evident to me now that no combination of procedural rules or substantive regulations ever can save the death penalty from its inherent constitutional deficiencies. . . . The problem is that the inevitability of factual, legal and moral error gives us a system that we know must wrongly kill some defendants, a system that fails to deliver the fair, consistent and reliable sentences of death required by the Constitution. . . . In my view, the proper course when faced with irreconcilable constitutional commands is not to ignore one or the other, nor to pretend that the dilemma does not exist, but to admit the futility of the effort to harmonize them. This means accepting the fact that the death penalty cannot be administered in accord with our Constitution." In light of the above cases, do you agree with Blackmun? Why or why not?

8. Do you think that Spenkelink deserved the death penalty? What about Henry Brisbon, the I–51 killer? Why or why not? (Both cases are described in the introduction to this section.)

9. Should there be a death penalty for rape under any circumstances? Why or why not?[52]

10. Does Davis' version of retributivism (Section 6.4) support the death penalty? Is his theory plausible in this case? Why or why not?

11. How do you make choices in your everyday life when you are uncertain about consequences? Are your methods applicable to the question of whether the death penalty deters? Why or why not?

12. Which is more humane: execution or life imprisonment without parole? Why? Should convicted murderers be given a choice between these punishments? Why or why not?

13. Who should decide whether to have capital punishment in a society: courts or legislatures or the people (in referenda)? Why?

SUGGESTIONS FOR FURTHER READING

The best collection of readings on capital punishment is still Hugo Bedau, *The Death Penalty in America*, 3rd edition (New York: Oxford University Press, 1982). For arguments against capital punishment, see Bedau's own articles in *Death Is Different* (Boston: Northeastern University Press, 1987); and Stephen Nathanson, *An Eye for an Eye?: The Morality of Punishing by Death* (Totowa, New Jersey: Rowman & Littlefield, 1987). Van den Haag defends capital punishment at length against criticisms by John P. Conrad in *The Death*

---

[52] The Supreme Court addressed this issue in *Coker v. Georgia* 433 U.S. 485 (1977). See also Bentham's rule 4 in Section 6.3.

Penalty: A Debate (New York: Plenum Press, 1983). For a retributivist defense of capital punishment, see Walter Berns, *For Capital Punishment* (New York: Basic Books, 1979), excerpted in Bedau, *The Death Penalty in America*. On deterrence and uncertainty, see David A. Conway, "Capital Punishment and Deterrence: Some Considerations in Dialogue Form," *Philosophy and Public Affairs*, vol. 3, no. 4 (Summer 1974); Michael Davis, "Death, Deterrence and the Method of Common Sense," *Social Theory and Practice*, vol. 7 (Summer 1981), pp. 145–78; and Jeffrey Reiman, "The Death Penalty, Deterrence, and Horribleness; Reply to Michael Davis," *Social Theory and Practice*, vol. 16, no. 2 (Summer 1990), pp. 261–72. On irrevocability, see Michael Davis, "Is the Death Penalty Irrevocable?" *Social Theory and Practice*, vol. 10 (Summer 1984), pp. 143–56. On discrimination, see Charles Black, *Capital Punishment: The Inevitability of Caprice and Mistake* (New York: Norton, 1974); and Gregory Russell, *The Death Penalty and Racial Bias* (Westport, Connecticut: Greenwood Press, 1994). On constitutionality, see Mark Tushnet, *The Death Penalty* (New York: Facts on File, 1994).

CHAPTER 7

RESPONSIBILITY

INTRODUCTION

Imagine that I drive drunk, but *you* are imprisoned for what I did. Or I park illegally, but you are fined. Or I drive over my neighbor's prize flower bed, but you are forced to pay for the damage. In all of these cases, you would probably be upset (and bewildered). What would upset you is not just that you do not want to go to prison or pay money, although you don't want that. You would feel especially cheated, because you were not responsible for the acts or harms for which you are punished or fined or forced to pay compensation. Of course, the government often forces you to pay taxes that are used to relieve harms (such as hurricane damage) for which you are not responsible. But it still seems wrong for courts to punish people or fine them or force them to pay compensation when those people are not responsible.

When is a person responsible? The preceding cases were clear if you had no significant relation to me. But many cases are not so clear. If Ann is Bill's parent or spouse, should Ann have to pay Bill's parking fines? If Casey tells Dan to run over a neighbor's flower bed, and that is why Dan does it, should Casey be forced to pay for the damage? If Esther knows that Dan is about to run over the flower bed, but Esther does nothing to stop him, should Esther be liable for civil damages? If Dan parks his car without putting on the brake, and his car rolls over the flower bed, should he have to pay compensation? What if Dan puts on the brake, but it slips? What if Dan's car runs over a person instead of a flower bed? Should he be criminally liable? Such a threat of punishment would give Dan a strong incentive to check his brakes carefully, but would it be unjust? To answer such questions, we need, first, to determine what responsibility is.

7.1 WHAT IS RESPONSIBILITY?

INTRODUCTION

The nature of responsibility is anything but simple. One reason for this is that there are many kinds of responsibility, which are easily confused.[1]

First, people often have special responsibilities when they occupy special roles. In my role as a parent, I have responsibilities to my children, and you do not. What this means is that I have a duty to take care of my children—to feed, clothe, and shelter them, among other things—and you do not have this duty. Similarly, lawyers are supposed to have professional responsibilities to their clients, which means that lawyers are required to do some things for their clients. This kind of responsibility is basically a duty derived from a role, so it is usually called a *role responsibility*. Although role responsibilities are very important and common, a special role is not always necessary for punishment, fines, or damages to be justified, so the earlier questions were not about role responsibilities.

Another kind of responsibility is *causal responsibility*. Some people say things like "The drought was responsible for the famine," when all they mean is that the drought caused the famine. But even if a person causes harm, this might be an accident that could not have been avoided, and then the agent need not be responsible in any way that justifies punishment, fines, or damages. So causal responsibility is not the notion that we are looking for here.

The kind of responsibility that is our topic here is described by the late H. L. A. Hart and his then–Oxford colleague Tony Honoré as follows:

> Usually in discussion of the law and occasionally in morals, to say that someone is responsible for some harm means that in accordance with legal rules or moral principles it is at least permissible, if not mandatory, to blame or punish or exact compensation from him.

This definition makes it obvious why responsibility is necessary to justify certain reactions to harmful acts. To say that one is responsible in this sense is just another way of saying that one may be blamed or penalized. ("Penalty" and its cognates will be used broadly to include punishments, fines, and forced compensation.)

But what do "may" and "permissible" mean here? The view seems to be that a person is responsible whenever blaming or penalizing that person is not wrong

---

[1]The following distinctions among kinds of responsibility are derived from H. L. A. Hart, *Punishment and Responsibility* (New York: Oxford University Press, 1968), pp. 211–30.

in that it does not violate any moral principle or legal rule. There might be special circumstances where blame and penalties are not worth the trouble, or where they can be inflicted only by some unjust means, such as by coercing a confession. But Hart and Honoré can still say that someone is responsible in the relevant way if and only if it would not violate any legal rule or moral principle to blame or penalize that person, at least if doing so were not too costly and did not require improper procedures.[2]

It is crucial that Hart and Honoré's account includes both moral and legal responsibility. When moral principles permit us to blame people, then they are *morally responsible*. When legal principles permit the government to penalize people (that is, punish, fine, or exact compensation from them), then they are *legally responsible*. Many of the most important and fascinating issues about responsibility concern the relation between moral responsibility and legal responsibility.

It seems clear that people can be morally responsible when they are not legally responsible. For example, if a friend does me a favor, but I refuse to thank him, I might be morally responsible for hurting him. Nonetheless, I am not legally responsible, because my friend cannot successfully sue me or get me fined or punished. (See Section 4.1 on cases where it is morally wrong to do what one has a legal right to do.)

There can also be cases of legal responsibility without moral responsibility. Suppose that Fred parks his car on a hill, but the brake slips, and his car rolls into an illegal parking spot. If Fred took every reasonable precaution to prevent his car from moving, then he is not morally responsible, for it would be wrong to blame him. Nonetheless, Fred still might be legally responsible under applicable laws. He might be forced to pay a fine for parking illegally, possibly because it is too hard to prove whether he really did pull the parking brake hard enough. And if Fred's car rolls into another car, Fred might be forced to pay compensation to the owner of the other car, possibly because it would not be fair to make the other car's owner suffer the loss. Some legal systems might not allow fines or compensation in such cases, and maybe none should, but the point here is that it is possible for laws to hold people legally responsible when they are not morally responsible.

The greatest controversy arises in *criminal* cases where someone is *punished* without being morally responsible. Lack of moral responsibility often seems to preclude justified punishment. If Fred's car rolled over and killed a pedestrian, most people would think that Fred should not be found guilty of any crime, since he did everything that could reasonably be expected of him to prevent his car from rolling. Other cases are not so clear. Suppose Fred shoots at cans in his yard, and a bullet ricochets and kills a passerby. Fred intended to hit a can and not a man. But even if he is not morally responsible for the death (which is not obvious), should

---

[2]One can also be responsible for something good, in which case one deserves credit, gratitude, praise, or even a reward. So the general notion of responsibility seems to be that someone is responsible for something good (or bad) when and only when that person deserves good (or bad) treatment if it is not too costly and does not require improper procedures. I focus on responsibility for bad things only because that is what most interests the law.

Fred be found legally guilty of homicide or manslaughter? In other cases, such as felony murder, some laws do allow people to be punished even when they do not seem to be morally responsible in a relevant way. The arguments for and against such laws will be discussed in Section 7.4. The point here is just that we cannot even formulate these substantive issues unless we distinguish moral responsibility from legal responsibility. Even if people ideally *should* not be punished when they are not morally responsible, the laws can be written in such a way that people actually *are* punished within the law when they are not morally responsible. That shows that legal responsibility and legal liability to punishment are different from moral responsibility.

It is also important not to confuse the question of whether someone *is* legally responsible with the separate question of whether someone *should be* legally responsible. Suppose a lawyer advises a client not to open a bungee jumping school because the client will be legally responsible for some harmful mishaps. The lawyer is probably applying actual laws at the time in the jurisdiction. It is a separate question whether these laws are good or should be followed or maintained. These other questions determine whether a person should be legally responsible, but, when actual laws are not as they should be, people can actually *be* legally responsible when they *should not* be legally responsible. That is what some people think when, for example, battered wives are punished for killing their husbands. Conversely, someone might *not* actually be legally responsible when ideally they *should* be legally responsible. For example, if a defective product causes harm but existing laws do not allow the manufacturer to be held responsible (criminally or at all), then critics might argue that the laws should be changed so that the manufacturer can be held responsible (criminally or at least civilly). Whichever side one takes, such issues cannot be understood without distinguishing actual legal responsibility from ideal legal responsibility. Admittedly, judges often interpret laws and precedents so as to bring actual legal responsibility closer to what the judges take to be ideal (see Chapter 2). Nonetheless, as long as *some* laws in this area *might* be bad, we can distinguish the circumstances when people are legally responsible from the circumstances when people should be legally responsible.

Our main topic will be the normative one: when should people be held legally responsible? Nonetheless, we will approach this topic in the usual way, which is to describe the circumstances under which people actually are held legally responsible in a typical legal system, and then ask whether these laws make people legally responsible in the right circumstances, that is, when they should be legally responsible.

Perhaps the most common structure occurs when a law says that anyone who does a certain kind of act with a certain mental condition will be liable to a punishment, fine, or forced compensation. In addition to the penalty, then, the crucial elements of a crime or tort are the act (or *actus reus*) and the mental condition (or *mens rea*). These two elements are not always separable, but they still provide a good starting point.

First, a law has to specify the kind of act that is prohibited or required. This is not as easy as one might think. For example, imagine writing a law against passing bad checks. What exactly must a person do to pass a bad check? First, the person must try to cash the check or use it to pay a bill. This requires physical movements, such as handing over the check or putting it in the mail. In addition, the check must be bad, because the funds in the account are insufficient. So certain circumstances are also necessary. Finally, if the law is not to penalize honest mistakes, it should apply only when the person knows or should know that the check is bad. So some kind of mental condition is necessary. There are many other complications, but the main point is that the crime of passing a bad check, like many other crimes, cannot be defined adequately without referring to physical movements, circumstances, and mental conditions.

It is also important that the crime of passing a bad check is *not* defined by its consequences. Handing a teller a check that one knows to be bad counts as passing a bad check, even if the teller is not fooled, no money changes hands, and nobody else is harmed. Other crimes and torts, in contrast, are defined by harms. Typical cases of legal responsibility for a harm occur when a person does an act that causes a harm. One simple case is murder: an act is normally not a murder unless it causes a death. Causation of harm is also essential to many torts or civil wrongs that bring civil liability for damage.

A law that prohibits acts defined by their effects must first specify a certain kind of harm that is caused by that particular crime. An act is not murder if it causes only a property loss, and an act is not theft if it causes only death. The kind of harm determines the kind of crime. The system of laws also must specify which kinds of harms can trigger liability at all. For example, if I cut down trees on my property close to your house, this might make your house less attractive and less valuable, but I still need not be legally responsible for this kind of loss. Unless I somehow violate your property rights, you might not be able to get any compensation for your loss.

Even if the right kind of harm occurs after an act, that is usually not enough to make the actor responsible for the harm. Normally, you cannot be guilty of murder just because John dies; you have to *cause* John's death. In most cases, you also cannot be guilty of murder when someone else causes John's death; *you* have to cause John's death. The same is true for many civil laws. You usually are not liable for damages just because John's flowers die or just because someone else kills John's flowers; you have to kill John's flowers. Thus, for many important crimes and civil wrongs or torts,[3] causation of harm by a person is necessary for that person to be legally responsible for the harm. And it also seems that this should be the case.

In addition to one's causing harm, some kind of mental condition is also often required for legal responsibility. Suppose Ken buys a bottle of soda at his usual grocery store and pours Larry a drink from the bottle. Because of an undetectable manufacturing problem, this bottle contains poison, so Larry dies as soon

---

[3]Exceptions might include vicarious responsibility for acts by another person (such as one's child or an accomplice) or thing (such as one's dog or runaway car). However, if the harm in such cases is caused by one person's failure to control the other person or thing, then these are cases of responsibility for omissions (see Section 7.3).

as he drinks it. Larry would not have died if Ken had not poured Larry a drink from this bottle, but Ken still might not be legally responsible, because Ken did not intend to kill Larry, did not know that the drink would kill Larry, and had no way of knowing that the drink would kill Larry (so Ken was not negligent). In such cases, it seems that a certain mental condition is and should be necessary for legal responsibility.

A person is then not legally responsible in such cases without a certain kind of act, harm, causal relation, and mental condition. Looked at from the other side, a person who is accused of such a crime can give several different defenses. The accused might deny that he did any act at all or any act of the kind that is prohibited. The accused might deny that there was any harm at all or any harm of the specified kind. The accused might deny that his act caused the harm. The accused might deny that he had the necessary mental condition. As we will see later, the accused might even deny that he was sane.

Although this general framework is standard, the devil is in the details. Deep puzzles arise when we look more carefully at causation, acts, intentions, sanity, and so on. Philosophers and legal scholars have also argued for exceptions to each requirement for legal responsibility. The rest of this chapter explores each of these requirements in turn. The next section (7.2) looks at the causation requirement. The following section (7.3) inspects an instance of the act requirement. The penultimate section (7.4) discusses the mental condition requirement. And the final section (7.5) debates the sanity requirement. Together these sections should fill out the picture of legal responsibility.

LEGAL CAUSATION 7.2

INTRODUCTION

When people will be held legally responsible if their acts cause harms, it is crucial to ask: when exactly does an act *cause* a harm?

One natural answer is that an act causes a harm when the act is sufficient for the harm to occur. One event is *sufficient* for another event if and only if, whenever the first event occurs, the second event also occurs. For example, pulling the trigger of a gun is not sufficient to cause a death, since the gun might not be loaded or aimed at anyone. But pulling the trigger of a large, loaded, working gun pointed directly at the nearby, unprotected brain of a live person is sufficient to cause that person's death, since every time someone pulls the trigger of a large, loaded, working gun pointed directly at the nearby, unprotected brain of a live person, that person dies. If the person does not die, then the gun must not have worked, or it must not have been large enough, or it must not have been loaded (with real bullets), or it must not have been aimed directly at the person's brain (at the time of firing), or the person's brain must have been protected or too far away, or the person must have already been dead. The list could go on, but the point is that a sufficient condition must rule out all possibilities within the laws of nature of the effect not occurring.

It is not clear, however, that causes must always be sufficient conditions. This comes out in *People v. Kibbe.*[4] After seeing George Stafford very drunk and flashing money in a bar, Kibbe and the other defendants befriended Stafford, took him for a ride in Kibbe's car, robbed him, and left him on the side of the road without his eyeglasses on a cold, windy night. About twenty–five minutes later, Michael Blake was driving his truck at about 50 m.p.h. in blowing snow when he saw Stafford sitting in the middle of the road with his hands up in the air. Blake tried to stop, but it was too late, and Stafford was killed. The court held that the acts by Kibbe and the other defendants caused Stafford's death. But their acts were not sufficient for Stafford's death. The defendants could have done exactly what they did without Stafford dying if Stafford had not walked onto the highway or if Blake had not been driving as he was. Thus, if the defendants should be legally responsible for Stafford's death, and if legal responsibility in this case should require causation, then causes should not always have to be sufficient conditions.

The main alternative is to see causes as necessary conditions. One event is *necessary* for another event if and only if, whenever the first event does *not* occur, the second event also does *not* occur. In other words, the second event will never

---

[4]35 N.Y.2d 407 (1974).

occur unless the first event occurs or, as lawyers sometimes say, the second event would not occur "but for" the first event, or the first event was a *sine qua non* of the second event. For example, Xavier puts rat poison in Yancy's glass, and then a waiter brings the glass to Yancy, who drinks it and dies. Xavier's act seems to be a cause of Yancy's death, but why? Xavier's act is *not* a sufficient condition of Yancy's death, since Yancy still would not have died if the waiter had not brought that glass to Yancy, or if he had cleaned it first, or if Yancy had not taken a drink. But Xavier's act *is* a necessary condition of Yancy's death, since Yancy would not have died as he did if Xavier had not put poison in the drink (assuming that nobody else would put in poison if Xavier didn't). That is supposed to be why Xavier's act is the cause of Yancy's death, and why Xavier is responsible and liable to punishment.

This can't be the whole story. Yancy would not have died in the way he did if Xavier had not been born, and Xavier would not have been born if his parents had never had sexual intercourse, so Xavier's parents' sexual acts were also necessary for Yancy to die in the way he did. Still, Xavier's parents' sexual acts were not causes of Yancy's death. The same goes for Yancy's parents. So not all necessary conditions are causes.

Like Yancy's death, every event has many necessary conditions, and each of these has many necessary conditions, and so on. So every event has a branching *chain* or a spreading *cone* of necessary conditions reaching far back in time. We then pick out only some necessary conditions as causes.

Which? That depends. Suppose that, in a drive-by shooting, a gang member shoots an innocent bystander, who is rushed to a hospital. The bullet does not enter the victim's heart, but it is so close to her heart that even the best doctor is very likely to slip while taking it out. Unfortunately, the doctor does slip, and his instrument pierces the wall of the heart. The patient bleeds a lot, but she could still be saved if the hospital had the right equipment. Unfortunately, the hospital does not have this equipment, so the patient dies. The question is: what was the cause of her death? The coroner would probably say that her death was caused by massive bleeding. This is a *scientific* answer that explains why she died. In contrast, a hospital administrator might say that the patient's death was caused by the lack of proper equipment. This is a *practical* answer that points to a way for the hospital to save more lives. Third, a prosecutor would say that the cause of her death was the drive-by shooting. This is a *legal* answer that specifies a person to hold responsible. Thus, which necessary condition one picks out as "the cause" depends on the purpose for which (or the perspective from which) one picks out the cause.[5]

This makes it misleading to say that an act creates responsibility for a harm only when the act is "the cause" of the harm. The shooting is not "the cause" of death from the coroner's perspective, but that does not show that the shooter is not legally responsible for the death. What, if anything, is required for legal responsibility is only that the act be a necessary condition and also be picked out by a legally relevant test—in short, that the act be "the legal cause." An act is (or

---

[5]Our trichotomy is derived from the three criteria for causal citations in Joel Feinberg, *Doing and Deserving* (Princeton: Princeton University Press, 1970), pp. 202–07; cf. pp. 158–66.

should be) the legal cause of a harm if and only if the agent of the act is (or should be) legally responsible for that harm if the other conditions of legal responsibility are met.

The term "cause" is then used ascriptively. In legal contexts, to say that an act causes a harm is not just to *describe* the facts of the case but is also to *ascribe* legal responsibility when other conditions of responsibility are met. So what we need to ask is: which of the necessary conditions of a harm is (or should be) the focus of legal responsibility and liability?

The best known answer to this question is by Hart and Honoré (in the reading that follows). Their basic idea is that acts rarely cause harm immediately, so we need to look at what happens between the act and the harm. For example, when the gang member shoots the bystander, his act of pulling the trigger is necessary for the gun to fire, which is necessary for the bullet to enter the victim's chest, which is necessary for the doctor to need to operate, which is necessary for the doctor to slip during the operation, which is necessary for the victim to die as she did. According to Hart and Honoré, the shooter's act (pulling the trigger) is the legal cause of the harm (death) only if the causal chain between the act and the harm is not broken. More generally, the causal chain from an act to a harm looks like this:

act ➡ first ➡ second ➡ third ➡ ... ➡ harm
     intervening   intervening   intervening
     event   event   event

Whether the act is the cause of the harm depends on the nature of the intervening events. Hart and Honoré claim that causal chains are broken by and only by two kinds of intervening events: voluntary and coincidental. Thus, they claim that an act is the legal cause of a harm if and only if there is no voluntary or coincidental intervention in the chain of necessary conditions between the act and the harm.

This theory becomes more complicated when Hart and Honoré specify more precisely what count as coincidental interventions and voluntary interventions. They define coincidences roughly as unlikely, uncontrived, and significant conjunctions of independent events (p. 798). Their example is an aggressor who knocks down a victim and then a tree happens to fall on the victim. This does not mean that effects are always foreseeable. One reason is that Hart and Honoré emphasize that coincidences do not include conjunctions of an event with a background condition. For example, "A innocently gives B a tap over the head of a normally quite harmless character, but because B is then suffering from some rare disease [called 'eggshell skull'] the tap has, as we say, 'fatal results'. In this case, A caused B's death though unintentionally." (p. 799) B's disease is unlikely, uncontrived, significant, and independent of A's tap, so the conjunction of A's tap with B's disease would be a coincidence except that Hart and Honoré see B's disease as "an abnormal *condition* existing at the time of a human intervention" (p. 799), rather than as an event. That is why there is no coincidence between A's tap and B's death, so A's tap is the cause of B's death. This distinction between events and background conditions is tricky, but Hart and Honoré argue that it is essential in order to put a limit on the coincidental interventions that break causal chains.

Voluntary acts by other agents also seem to break causal chains. When a salesperson sells a kitchen knife to a customer who uses the knife to kill someone, the salesperson is not the cause of the death, because the customer's voluntary act of killing comes between the selling and the death in the chain of necessary conditions. Hart and Honoré emphasize that the intervening act must be fully voluntary in order to break the causal chain. If Mary forces or misleads Nancy into doing something harmful, then Nancy's act is not fully voluntary, so it does not keep Mary's act from being the cause of the harm. Moreover, a person is often seen as a cause of the harm when he or she provides or creates a reason for someone else to cause the harm. Chris might entice Pat with rewards for doing an act or coerce Pat with threats for failure to do the act ("Your money or your life!"). Even if Chris does not know Hilary, if Chris provides an opportunity for Hilary to steal, such as by leaving a house or car unlocked in a dangerous neighborhood, then Chris is sometimes seen as a cause of the loss and as legally responsible. In such cases, Hilary's act is voluntary, and Hilary is also responsible, but Hilary's act still does not break the causal chain or remove responsibility from Chris (possibly because Chris still controls the risk of harm in some ways).

When these qualifications are added, Hart and Honoré claim that their theory captures the concept of causation that is employed by actual courts, and they also defend its coherence and plausibility. And this theory does seem plausible in many cases. However, several problems remain (see the Questions for Discussion that follow).

One kind of problem arises when a causal chain is *not* broken according to Hart and Honoré's definitions, but the initial act still does *not* seem to be the cause of the harm. One famous example is *Palsgraf* (selections follow). In that case, as a train pulled out of the station, a man with a package jumped on a car, a guard pushed him in, and his package fell. Although there was no way to tell, the package contained fireworks, which exploded when they fell. The explosion knocked down some scales about twenty-five feet away, and the falling scales hit Mrs. Palsgraf, who then sued the railroad company. The question is whether the guard's act, which caused the package to fall, also caused Palsgraf's injuries. The causal chain between the act by the guard and the harm to Palsgraf does not contain any voluntary intervention, but does it contain a coincidental intervention? It does not seem to be a coincidence, and it also does not fit Hart and Honoré's definition. The fact that the package contained fireworks was "very unlikely," but this fact was not an event, and Hart and Honoré emphasize that a coincidence must be a conjunction of events. It was also unlikely that the explosion would affect scales so far away, but the explosion and the falling scales were not "independent" because the explosion caused the falling. So it seems that the guard's act did cause Palsgraf's injuries, according to Hart and Honoré's theory.

However, Justice Benjamin Cardozo (1870–1938), who was later a Supreme Court Justice, argued that the railroad company should not be held legally responsible, because:

The conduct of the [railroad company's] guard, if wrong in its relation to the holder of the package, was not a wrong in relation to [Mrs. Palsgraf], standing far away. Relatively to her it was not negligence at all. Nothing in the situation gave notice that the falling package had in it the potency of peril to persons thus removed. (p. 803)

This argument does not deny that the guard caused harm to Mrs. Palsgraf. Instead, Cardozo said, "the law of causation, remote or proximate, is . . . foreign to the case before us. The question of liability is always anterior to the question of the measure of the consequences that go with liability (p. 805)." His point is that, if the guard was not negligent with respect to the harm to Mrs. Palsgraf, then it does not matter whether the guard caused the harm to her.

Nonetheless, others see this case in terms of *proximate* causation. (See Justice Andrews' dissent in *Palsgraf.*) That means that if the harm is too distant in some way from the initial act, then the initial act is not and should not be the legal cause of the harm. It is not clear how to measure "proximity," nor is it clear whether the guard's act was too far from the harm in the actual case. But what if the falling scales had not hit Mrs. Palsgraf, but had instead hit a cart that rolled fifty feet into a pile of packages that fell over, waking a stray dog that ran into the street under a horse that reared up and kicked Mrs. Palsgraf in the face? This chain of events would probably be too long for legal causation or responsibility, according to those who restrict legal causation to proximate causation. But Hart and Honoré put no limit on the length or complexity of the chain between a cause and its effect. If there is such a limit, then Hart and Honoré's theory must be modified in some way.

CAUSATION IN THE LAW

H. L. A. HART AND TONY HONORÉ

I. RESPONSIBILITY IN LAW AND MORALS

. . . In the moral judgments of ordinary life, we have occasion to blame people because they have caused harm to others, and also, if less frequently, to insist that morally they are bound to compensate those to whom they have caused harm. These are the moral analogues of more precise legal conceptions; for, in all legal systems, liability to be punished or to make compensation frequently depends on whether actions (or omissions) have caused harm. Moral blame is not of course confined to such cases of causing harm. We blame a man who cheats or lies or breaks promises, even if no one has suffered in the particular case: this has its legal counterpart in the punishment of abortive attempts to commit crimes, and of offences constituted by the unlawful possession of certain kinds of weapons, drugs, or materials, for example, for counterfeiting currency.

H. L. A. Hart and Tony Honoré, *Causation in the Law,* 2nd edition (Oxford: Clarendon Press, 1985)

When the occurrence of harm is an essential part of the ground for blame the connection of the person blamed with the harm may take any of the forms of causal connection we have examined. His action may have initiated a series of physical events dependent on each other and culminating in injury to persons or property, as in wounding and killing. These simple forms are the paradigms for the lawyer's talk of harm 'directly' caused. But we blame people also for harm which arises from or is the consequence of their neglect of common precautions; we do this even if harm would not have come about without the intervention of another human being deliberately exploiting the opportunities provided by neglect. The main legal analogue here is liability for 'negligence'. The wish of many lawyers to talk in this branch of the law of harm being 'within the risk of' rather than 'caused by' the negligent conduct manifests appreciation of the fact that a different form of relationship is involved in saying that harm is the consequence, on the one hand, of an explosion and, on the other, of a failure to lock the door by which a thief has entered. Again, we blame people for the harm which we say is the consequence of their influence over others, either exerted by non-rational means or in one of the ways we have designated 'interpersonal transactions'. To such grounds for responsibility there correspond many important legal conceptions: the instigation of crimes ('commanding' or 'procuring') constitutes an important ground of criminal responsibility and the concepts of enticement and of inducement (by threats or misrepresentation) are an element in many civil wrongs as well as in criminal offences.

The law, however, especially in matters of compensation, goes far beyond these causal grounds for responsibility in such doctrines as the vicarious responsibility of a master for his servant's civil wrongs and that of the responsibility of an occupier of property for injuries suffered by passers-by from defects of which the occupier had no knowledge and which he had no opportunity to repair. There is a recognition, perhaps diminishing, of this non-causal ground of responsibility outside the law; responsibility is sometimes admitted by one person or group of persons, even if no precaution has been neglected by them, for harm done by persons related to them in a special way, either by family ties or as members of the same social or political association. Responsibility may be simply 'placed' by moral opinion on one person for what others do. The simplest case of such vicarious moral responsibility is that of a parent for damage done by a child; its more complex (and more debatable) form is the moral responsibility of one generation of a nation to make compensation for their predecessors' wrong, such as the Germans admitted in payment of compensation to Israel.

At this point it is necessary to issue a caveat about the meaning of the expression 'responsible' if only to avoid prejudicing a question about the character of *legal* determinations of causal connection with which we shall be much concerned. . . . Usually in discussion of the law and occasionally in morals, to say that someone is responsible for some harm means that in accordance with legal rules or moral principles it is at least permissible, if not mandatory, to blame or punish or exact compensation from him. In this use[1] the expression 'responsible for' does not refer to a factual connection between the person held responsible and the harm but simply to his liability under the rules to be blamed, punished, or made to pay. The expressions 'answerable for' or 'liable for' are practically synonymous with 'responsible for' in *this* use, in which there is no implication that the person held responsible actually *did* or *caused* the harm. In this sense a master is (in English law) responsible for the damage done by his servants acting within the scope of their authority and a parent (in French and German law) for that done by his children; it is in this sense that a guarantor or surety is responsible for the debts or the good behaviour of other persons and an insurer for losses sustained by the insured. Very often, however, especially in discussion of morals, to say that someone is responsible for some harm is to assert (*inter alia*) that he *did* the harm or *caused* it, though such a statement is perhaps rarely confined to this for it usually also carries with it the implication that it is at least permissible to blame or punish him. This double use of the expression no doubt arises from the important fact that doing or causing harm constitutes not only the most usual but the primary type of ground for holding persons responsible in the first sense. We still speak of inanimate or natural causes such as storms, floods, germs, or the failure of electricity supply as 'responsible for' disasters; this mode of expression, now taken only to mean that they caused the disasters, no doubt originated in the belief that all that happens is the work of spirits when it is not that of men. Its survival in the modern world is perhaps some testimony to the primacy of causal connection as an element in responsibility and to the intimate connection between the two notions.

We shall consider later an apparent paradox which interprets in a different way the relationship between cause and responsibility. Much modern thought on causation in the law rests on the contention that the statement that someone has caused harm either means no more than that the harm would not have happened without ('but for') his action or where (as in normal legal usage and in all ordinary speech), it apparently means more than this, it is a disguised way of asserting the 'normative' judgment that he is responsible in the first sense, i.e. that it is proper or just to blame or punish him or make him pay. On this view to say that a person caused harm is not really, though ostensibly it is, to give a *ground* or *reason* for holding him responsible in the first sense; for we are only in a position to say that he has caused harm when we have decided that he is responsible. Pending consideration of the theories of legal causation which exploit this point of view we shall use the expression 'responsible for' only in the first of the two ways explained, i.e. without any implication as to the type of factual connection between the person held responsible and the harm; and we shall provisionally, though without prejudicing the issue, treat statements that a person caused harm as one sort of non-tautologous ground or reason for saying that he is responsible in this sense.

If we may provisionally take what in ordinary life we say and do at its face value, it seems that there coexist in ordinary thought, apart from the law though mirrored in it, several different types of connection between a person's action and eventual harm which render him responsible for it; and in both law and morals the various forms of causal connection between act or omission and harm are the most obvious and least disputable reasons for holding anyone responsible. Yet, in order to understand the extent to which the causal notions of ordinary thought are used in the law, we must bear in mind the many factors which must differentiate moral from legal responsibility in spite of their partial correspondence. The law is not only not bound to follow the moral patterns of attribution of responsibility but, even when it does, it must take into account, in a way which the private moral judgment need not and does not, the general social consequences which are attached to its judgments of responsibility; for they are of a gravity quite different from those attached to moral censure. The use of the legal sanctions of imprisonment, or enforced monetary compensation against individuals, has such formidable repercussions on the general life of society that the fact that individuals have a type of connection with harm which is adequate for moral censure or claims for compensation is only *one* of the factors which the law must consider, in defining the kinds of connection between actions and harm for which it will hold individuals legally responsible. Always to follow the private moral judgment here would be far too expensive for the law; not only in the crude sense that it would entail a vast machinery of courts and officials, but in the more important sense that it would inhibit or discourage too many other valuable activities of society. To limit the *types* of harm which the law will recognize is not enough; even if the types of harm are limited it would still be too much for any society to punish or exact compensation from individuals whenever their connection with harm of such types would justify moral censure. Conversely, social needs may require that compensation should be paid and even (though less obviously) that punishment be inflicted where no such connection between the person held responsible and the harm exists.

So causing harm of a legally recognized sort or being connected with such harm in any of the ways that justify moral blame, though vitally important and perhaps basic in a legal system, is not and should not be either always necessary or always sufficient for legal responsibility. All legal systems in response either to tradition or to social needs both extend responsibility and cut it off in ways which diverge from the simpler principles of moral blame. In England a man is not guilty of murder if the victim of his attack does not die within a year and day. In New York a person who negligently starts a fire is liable to pay only for the first of several houses which it destroys.[2] These limitations imposed by legal policy are prima facie distinguishable from limitations due to the frequent requirement of legal rules that responsibility be limited to harm caused by wrongdoing. Yet a whole school of thought maintains that this distinction does not exist or is not worth drawing.

Apart from this, morality can properly leave certain things vague into which a legal system must attempt to import some degree of precision. Outside the law nothing requires us, when we find the case too complex or too strange, to say whether any and, if so, which of the morally significant types of connection between a person's action and harm exists; we can simply say the case is too difficult for us to pass judgment, at least where moral condemnation of others is concerned. No doubt we evade less easily our questions about our own connection with harm, and the great novelists have often described, sometimes in language very like the lawyers, how the conscience may be still tortured by uncertainties as to the *character* of a part in the production of harm, even when all the facts are known. The fact that there is no precise system of punishments or rewards for common sense to administer, and so there are no 'forms of action' or 'pleadings' to define precise heads of responsibility for harm, means that the principles which guide common-sense attributions of responsibility give precise answers only in relatively simple types of case.

II. TRACING CONSEQUENCES

'To consequences no limit can be set': 'Every event which would not have happened if an earlier event had not happened is the consequence of that earlier event.' These two propositions are not equivalent in meaning and are not equally or in the same way at variance with ordinary thought. They have, however, both been urged sometimes in the same breath by the legal theorist[4] and the philosopher: they are indeed sometimes said by lawyers to be 'the philosophical doctrine' of causation. It is perhaps not difficult even for the layman to accept the first proposition as a truth about certain physical events; an explosion may cause a flash of light which will be propagated as far as the outer nebulae; its effects or consequences continue indefinitely. It is, however, a different matter to accept the view that whenever a man is murdered with a gun his death was the consequence of (still less an 'effect' of or 'caused by') the manufacture of the bullet. The first tells a perhaps unfamiliar tale about unfamiliar events; the second introduces an unfamiliar, though, of course, a possible way of speaking about familiar events. It is not that this unrestricted use of 'consequence' is unintelligible or never found; it is indeed used to refer to bizarre or fortuitous connections or coincidences: but the point is that the various causal notions employed for the purposes of explanation, attribution of responsibility, or the assessment of contributions to the course of history carry with them implicit limits which are similar in these different employments.

It is, then, the second proposition, defining consequence in terms of 'necessary condition', with which theorists are really concerned. This proposition is the corollary of the view that, if we look into the past of any given event, there is an infinite number of events, each of which is a necessary condition of the given event and so, as much as any other, is its cause. This is the 'cone'[5] of causation, so called because, since any event has a number of simultaneous conditions, the series fans out as we go back in time. The justification, indeed only partial, for calling this 'the philosophical doctrine' of causation is that it resembles Mill's doctrine that 'we have no right to give the name of cause to one of the conditions exclusive of the others of them'. It differs from Mill's view in taking the essence of causation to be 'necessary condition' and not 'the sum total'[6] of the sufficient conditions of an event.

Legal theorists have developed this account of cause and consequence to show what is 'factual', 'objective', or 'scientific' in these notions: this they call 'cause in fact' and it is usually stressed as a preliminary to the doctrine that any more restricted application of these terms in the law represents nothing in the facts or in the meaning of causation, but expresses fluctuating legal policy or sentiments of what is just or convenient. . . .

No short account can be given of the limits thus placed on 'consequences' because these limits vary, intelligibly, with the variety of causal connection asserted. Thus we may be tempted by the generalization that consequences must always be something intended or foreseen or at least foreseeable with ordinary care: but counterexamples spring up from many types of context where causal statements are made. If smoking is shown to cause lung cancer this discovery will permit us to describe past as well as future cases of cancer as the effect or consequence of smoking even though no one foresaw or had reasonable grounds to suspect this in the past. What is common and commonly appreciated and hence foreseeable certainly controls the scope of consequences in certain varieties of causal statement but not in all. Again the voluntary intervention of a second person very often constitutes the limit. If a guest sits down at a table laid with knife and fork and plunges the knife into his hostess's breast, her death is not in any context other than a contrived one[8] thought of as caused by, or the effect or result of the waiter's action in laying the table; nor would it be linked with this action as its consequence for any of the purposes, explanatory or attributive, for which we employ causal notions. Yet as we have seen there are many other types of case where a voluntary action or the harm it does are naturally treated as the consequence of some prior neglect of precaution. Finally, we may think that a simple answer is already supplied by Hume and Mill's doctrine that causal connection rests on general laws asserting regular connection; yet, even in the type of case to which this important doctrine applies, reference to it alone will not solve our problem. For we often trace a causal connection between an antecedent and a consequent which themselves very rarely go together: we do this when the case can be broken down into intermediate stages, which themselves exemplify different generalizations, as when we find that the fall of a tile was the cause of someone's death, rare though this be. Here our problem reappears in the form of the question: When can generalizations be combined in this way?

We shall examine first the central type of case where the problem is of this last-mentioned form. Here the gist of the causal connection lies in the general connection with each other of the successive stages; and is not dependent on the special notions of one person providing another with reasons or exceptional opportunities for actions. This form of causal connection may exist between actions and events, and between purely physical events, and it is in such cases that the words 'cause' and 'causing' used of the antecedent action or event have their most obvious application. It is convenient to refer to cases of the first type where the consequence is harm as cases of 'causing harm', and to refer to cases where harm is the consequence of one person providing another with reasons or opportunities for doing harm as cases of 'inducing' or 'occasioning' harmful acts. In cases of the first type a voluntary act, or a conjunction of events amounting to a coincidence, operates as a limit in the sense that events subsequent to these are not attributed to the antecedent action or event as its consequence even though they would not have happened without it. Often such a limiting action or coincidence is thought of and described as 'intervening': and lawyers speak of them as 'superseding' or 'extraneous' causes 'breaking the chain of causation'. To see what these metaphors rest on (and in part obscure) and how such factors operate as a limit we shall consider the detail of three simple cases.

(i) A forest fire breaks out, and later investigation shows that shortly before the outbreak *A* had flung away a lighted cigarette into the bracken at the edge of the forest, the bracken caught fire, a light breeze got up, and fanned the flames in the direction of the forest. If, on discovering these facts, we hesitate before saying that *A*'s action caused the forest fire this would be to consider the alternative hypothesis that in spite of appearances the fire only succeeded *A*'s action in point of time, that the bracken flickered out harmlessly and the forest fire was caused by something else. To dispose of this it may be necessary to examine in further detail the process of events between the ignition of the bracken and the outbreak of fire in the forest and to show that these exemplified certain types of continuous change. If this is shown, there is no longer any room for doubt: *A*'s action *was* the cause of the fire, whether he intended it or not. This seems and is the simplest of cases. Yet it is important to notice that even in applying our general knowledge to a

case as simple as this, indeed in regarding it as simple, we make an implicit use of a distinction between types of factor which constitute a limit in tracing consequences and those which we regard as mere circumstances 'through' which we trace them. For the breeze which sprang up after *A* dropped the cigarette, and without which the fire would not have spread to the forest, was not only subsequent to his action but entirely independent of it: it was, however, a common recurrent feature of the environment, and, as such, it is thought of not as an 'intervening' force but as merely part of the circumstances in which the cause 'operates'. The decision so to regard it is implicitly taken when we combine our knowledge of the successive stages of the process and assert the connection.

It is easy here to be misled by the natural metaphor of a causal 'chain', which may lead us to think that the causal process consists of a series of single events each of which is dependent upon (would not have occurred without) its predecessor in the 'chain' and so is dependent upon the initiating action or event. In truth in any causal process we have at each phase not single events but complex sets of conditions, and among these conditions are some which are not only subsequent to, but independent of the initiating action or event. Some of these independent conditions, such as the evening breeze in the example chosen, we classify as mere conditions in or on which the cause operates; others we speak of as 'interventions' or 'causes'. To decide how such independent elements shall be classified is also to decide how we shall combine our knowledge of the different general connections which the successive stages exemplify, and it is important to see that nothing *in* this knowledge itself can resolve this point. We may have to go to science for the relevant general knowledge before we can assert with proper confidence that *A*'s action did cause the fire, but science, though it tells us that an air current was required, is silent on the difference between a current in the form of an evening breeze and one produced by someone who deliberately fanned the flames as they were flickering out in the bracken. Yet an air current in this deliberately induced form is not a 'condition' or 'mere circumstance' through which we can trace the consequence; its presence would force us to revise the assertion that A caused the fire. Conversely if science helped us to identify as a necessary factor in producing the fire some condition or element of which we had previously been totally ignorant, e.g. the persistence of oxygen, this would leave our original judgment undisturbed if this factor were a common or pervasive feature of the environment or of the thing in question. There is thus indeed an important sense in which it is true that the distinction between cause and conditions is not a 'scientific' one. It is not determined by laws or generalizations concerning connections between events. . . .

(ii) A throws a lighted cigarette into the bracken which catches fire. Just as the flames are about to flicker out, B, who is not acting in concert with A, deliberately pours petrol on them. The fire spreads and burns down the forest. A's action, whether or not he intended the forest fire, was not the cause of the fire: B's was.

The voluntary intervention of a second human agent, as in this case, is a paradigm among those factors which preclude the assimilation in causal judgments of the first agent's connection with the eventual harm to the case of simple direct manipulation. Such an intervention displaces the prior action's title to be called the cause and, in the persistent metaphors found in the law, it 'reduces' the earlier action and its immediate effects to the level of 'mere circumstances' or 'part of the history'. B in this case was not an 'instrument' through which A worked or a victim of the circumstances A has created. He has, on the contrary, freely exploited the circumstances and brought about the fire without the co-operation of any further agent or any chance coincidence. Compared with this the claim of A's action to be ranked the cause of the fire fails. That this and not the moral appraisal of the two actions is the point of comparison seems clear. If

A and B both intended to set the forest on fire, and this destruction is accepted as something wrong or wicked, their moral wickedness, judged by the criterion of intention, is the same. Yet the causal judgment differentiates between them. If their moral guilt is judged by the outcome, this judgment though it would differentiate between them cannot be the source of the causal judgment; for it presupposes it. The difference just is that B has caused the harm and A has not. Again, if we appraise these actions as good or bad from different points of view, this leaves the causal judgments unchanged. A may be a soldier of one side anxious to burn down the enemy's hide-out: B may be an enemy soldier who has decided that his side is too iniquitous to defend. Whatever is the moral judgment passed on these actions by different speakers it would remain true that A had not caused the fire and B had.

There are, as we have said, situations in which a voluntary action would not be thought of as an intervention precluding causal connection in this way. These are the cases discussed further below where an opportunity commonly exploited for harmful actions is negligently provided, or one person intentionally provides another with the means, the opportunity, or a certain type of reason for wrongdoing. Except in such cases a voluntary intervention is a limit past which consequences are not traced. By contrast, actions which in any of a variety of different ways are less than fully voluntary are assimilated to the means by which or the circumstances in which the earlier action brings about the consequences. Such actions are not the outcome of an informed choice made without pressure from others, and the different ways in which human action may fall short in this respect range from defective muscular control, through lack of consciousness or knowledge, to the vaguer notions of duress and of predicaments, created by the first agent for the second, in which there is no 'fair' choice. . . .

(iii) The analogy with single simple actions which guides the tracing of consequences may be broken by certain kinds of conjunctions of physical events. *A* hits *B* who falls to the ground stunned and bruised by the blow; at that moment a tree crashes to the ground and kills *B*. *A* has certainly caused *B*'s bruises but not his death: for though the fall of the tree was, like the evening breeze in our earlier example, independent of and subsequent to the initiating action, it would be differentiated from the breeze in any description in causal terms of the connection of *B*'s death with *A*'s action. It is to be noticed that this is not a matter which turns on the intention with which *A* struck *B*. Even if *A* hit *B* inadvertently or accidentally his blow would still be the cause of *B*'s bruises: he would have caused them, though unintentionally. Conversely even if *A* had intended his blow to kill, this would have been an attempt to kill but still not the cause of *B*'s death, unless *A* knew that the tree was about to fall just at that moment. On this legal and ordinary judgments would be found to agree; and most legal systems would distinguish for the purposes of punishment an attempt with a fatal upshot, issuing by such chance or anomalous events, from 'causing death'—the terms in which the offences of murder and manslaughter are usually defined.

Similarly the causal description of the case does not turn on the moral appraisal of *A*'s action or the wish to punish it. *A* may be a robber and a murderer and *B* a saint guarding the place *A* hoped to plunder. Or *B* may be a murderer and *A* a hero who has forced his way into *B*'s retreat. In both cases the causal judgment is the same. *A* had caused the minor injuries but not *B*'s death, though he tried to kill him. *A* may indeed be praised or blamed but not for causing *B*'s death. However intimate the connection between responsibility and causation, it does not determine causal judgments in this simple way. Nor does the causal judgment turn on a refusal to attribute grave consequences to actions which normally have less serious results. Had *A*'s blow killed *B* outright and the tree, falling on his body, merely

smashed his watch we should still treat the coincidental character of the fall of the tree as determining the form of causal statement. We should then recognize *A*'s blow as the cause of *B*'s death but not the breaking of the watch.

The connection between *A*'s action and *B*'s death in the first case would naturally be described in the language of *coincidence*. 'It was a coincidence: it just happened that, at the very moment when *A* knocked *B* down, a tree crashed at the very place where he fell and killed him.' The common legal metaphor would describe the fall of the tree as an 'extraneous' cause. This, however, is dangerously misleading, as an analysis of the notion of coincidence will show. It suggests merely an event which is subsequent to and independent of some other contingency, and of course the fall of the tree has both these features in relation to *A*'s blow. Yet in these respects the fall of the tree does not differ from the evening breeze in the earlier case where we found no difficulty in tracing causal connection.[15] The full elucidation of the notion of a coincidence is a complex matter for, though it is very important as a limit in tracing consequences, causal questions are not the only ones to which the notion is relevant. The following are its most general characteristics. We speak of coincidence whenever the conjunction of two or more events in certain spatial or temporal relations (1) is very unlikely by ordinary standards and (2) is for some reason significant or important, provided (3) that they occur without human contrivance and (4) are independent of each other. It is therefore a coincidence if two persons known to each other in London meet without design in Paris on their way to separate independently chosen destinations; or if two persons living in different places independently decide to write a book on the same subject. The first is a coincidence of time and place ('It just happened that we were at the same place at the same time'), and the second a coincidence of time only ('It just happened that they both decided to write on the subject at the same time').

Use of this general notion is made in the special case when the conjunction of two or more events occurs in temporal and/or spatial relationships which are significant, because, as our general knowledge of causal processes shows, this conjunction is required for the production of some given further event. In the language of Mill's idealized model, they form a necessary part of a complex set of jointly sufficient conditions. In the present case the fall of the tree just as B was struck down within its range satisfies the four criteria for a coincidence which we have enumerated. First, though neither event was of a very rare or exceptional kind, their conjunction would be rated very unlikely judged by the standards of ordinary experience. Secondly, this conjunction was causally significant for it was a necessary part of the process terminating in B's death. Thirdly, this conjunction was not consciously designed by A; had he known of the impending fall of the tree and hit B with the intention that he should fall within its range B's death would not have been the result of any coincidence. A would certainly have caused it. The common-sense principle that a contrived conjunction cannot be a coincidence is the element of truth in the legal maxim (too broadly stated even for legal purposes) that an intended consequence cannot be too 'remote'. Fourthly, each member of the conjunction in this case was independent of the other; whereas if B had fallen against the tree with an impact sufficient to bring it down on him, this sequence of physical events, though freakish in its way, would not be a coincidence and in most contexts of ordinary life, as in the law, the course of events would be summarized by saying that in this case, unlike that of the coincidence, A's act was the cause of B's death, since each stage is the effect of the preceding stage. Thus, the blow forced the victim against the tree, the effect of this was to make the tree fall and the fall of the tree killed the victim.

One further criterion in addition to these four must be satisfied if a conjunction of events is to rank as a coincidence and as a limit when the consequences of the action are traced. This further criterion again shows the strength of the influence which the analogy with the case of the simple manipulation of things exerts over thought in causal terms. An abnormal *condition* existing at the time of a human intervention is distinguished both by ordinary thought and, with a striking consistency, by most legal systems from an abnormal event or conjunction of events subsequent to that intervention; the former, unlike the latter, are not ranked as coincidences or 'extraneous' causes when the consequences of the intervention come to be traced. Thus A innocently gives B a tap over the head of a normally quite harmless character, but because B is then suffering from some rare disease the tap has, as we say, 'fatal results'. In this case A has caused B's death though unintentionally. The scope of the principle which thus distinguishes contemporaneous abnormal conditions from subsequent events is unclear; but at least where a human being initiates some physical change in a thing, animal, or person, abnormal physical states of the object affected, existing at the time, are ranked as part of the circumstances in which the cause 'operates'. In the familiar controlling imagery these are part of 'the stage already set' before the 'intervention'.

Judgments about coincidences, though we often agree in making them, depend in two related ways on issues incapable of precise formulation. One of these is patent, the other latent but equally important. Just how unlikely must a conjunction be to rank as a coincidence, and in the light of what knowledge is likelihood to be assessed? The only answer is: 'very unlikely in the light of the knowledge available to ordinary men'. It is, of course, the indeterminacies of such standards, implicit in causal judgments, that make them inveterately disputable, and call for the exercise of discretion or choice by courts. The second and latent indeterminacy of these judgments depends on the fact that the things or events to which they relate do not have pinned to them some uniquely correct description always to be used in assessing likelihood. It is an important pervasive feature of all our empirical judgments that there is a constant possibility of more or less specific description of any event or thing with which they are concerned. The tree might be described not simply as a 'tree' but as a 'rotten tree' or as a 'fir tree' or a 'tree sixty feet tall'. So too its fall might be described not as a 'fall' but as a fall of a specified distance at a specified velocity. The likelihood of conjunctions framed in these different terms would be differently assessed. The criteria of appropriate description like the standard of likelihood are supplied by consideration of common knowledge. Even if the scientist knew the tree to be rotten and could have predicted its fall with accuracy, this would not change the judgment that its fall at the time when B was struck down within its range was a coincidence; nor would it make the description 'rotten tree' appropriate for the assessment of the chances involved in this judgment. There are other controls over the choice of description derived from the degree of specificity of our interests in the final outcome of the causal process. We are concerned with the fall of an object sufficient to cause 'death' by impact and the precise force or direction which may account for the detail of the wounds is irrelevant here.

OPPORTUNITIES AND REASONS

Opportunities. The discrimination of voluntary interventions as a limit is no longer made when the case, owing to the commonness or appreciable risk of such harmful intervention, can be brought within the scope of the notion of providing an opportunity, known to be commonly exploited for doing harm. Here the limiting principles are different. When A leaves the house unlocked the range of consequences to be attributed to this neglect, as in any other case where precautions are omitted, depends primarily on the way in which such opportunities are commonly exploited. An alternative

formulation of this idea is that a subsequent intervention would fall within the scope of consequences if the likelihood of its occurring is one of the reasons for holding A's omission to be negligent.

It is on these lines that we would distinguish between the entry of a thief and of a murderer; the opportunity provided is believed to be sufficiently commonly exploited by thieves to make it usual and often morally or legally obligatory not to provide it. Here, in attributing consequences to prior actions, causal judgments are directly controlled by the notion of the risk created by them. Neglect of such precautions is both unusual and reprehensible. For these reasons it would be hard to separate the two ways in which such neglect deviates from the 'norm'. Despite this, no simple identification can be made of the notion of responsibility with the causal connection which is a ground for it. This is so because the provision of an opportunity commonly taken by others is ranked as the cause of the outcome independently of the wish to praise or blame. The causal judgment may be made simply to assess a contribution to some outcome. Thus, whether we think well or ill of the use made of railways, we would still claim that the greater mobility of the population in the nineteenth century was a consequence of their introduction.

It is obvious that the question whether any given intervention is a sufficiently common exploitation of the opportunity provided to come within the risk is again a matter on which judgments may differ, though they often agree. The courts, and perhaps ordinary thought also, often describe those that are sufficiently common as 'natural' consequences of the neglect. They have in these terms discriminated the entry of a thief from the entry of a man who burnt the house down, and refused to treat the destruction of the house as a 'natural' consequence of the neglect.[18]

We discuss later . . . the argument that this easily intelligible concept of 'harm within the risk', overriding as it does the distinctions between voluntary interventions and others, should be used as the general test for determining what subsequent harm should be attributed for legal purposes to prior action. The merits of this proposal to refashion the law along these simple lines are perhaps considerable, yet consequences of actions are in fact often traced both in the law and apart from it in other ways which depend on the discrimination of voluntary interventions from others. We distinguish, after all, as differing though related grounds of responsibility, causing harm by one's own action and providing opportunities for others to do harm, where the guiding analogy with the simple manipulation of things, which underlies causal thought, is less close. When, as in the examples discussed above, we trace consequences through the non-voluntary interventions of others our concern is to show that certain stages of the process have a certain type of connection with the preceding stages, and not, as when the notion of risk is applied, to show that the ultimate outcome is connected in some general way with the initiating action. Thus, when A's shot makes B start and break a glass it is the causal relationship described by the expression 'made B start' that we have in mind and not the likelihood that on hearing a shot someone may break a glass. Causal connection may be traced in such cases though the initiating action and the final outcome are not contingencies that commonly go together.

Apart from these conceptual reasons for distinguishing these related grounds for responsibility, it is clear that both in the law . . . and apart from it we constantly treat harm as caused by a person's action though it does not fall 'within the risk'. If, when B broke the glass in the example given above, a splinter flew into C's eye, blinding him, A's action is indeed the cause of C's injury though we may not always blame him for so unusual a consequence.

Reasons. In certain varieties of interpersonal transactions, unlike the case of coercion, the second action is quite voluntary. A may not threaten B but may bribe or advise or persuade him to do something. Here, A does not 'cause' or 'make' B do anything: the strongest words we should use are perhaps that he 'induced' or 'procured' B's act. Yet the law and moral principles alike may treat one person as responsible for the harm which another free agent has done 'in consequence' of the advice or the inducements which the first has offered. In such cases the limits concern the range of those actions done by B which are to rank as the consequence of A's words or deeds. In general this question depends on A's intentions or on the 'plan of action' he puts before B. If A advises or bribes B to break in and steal from an empty house and B does so, he acts in consequence of A's advice or bribe. If he deliberately burns down the house this would not be treated as the consequence of A's bribe or advice, legally or otherwise, though it may in some sense be true that the burning would not have taken place without the advice or bribe. Nice questions may arise, which the courts have to settle, where B diverges from the detail of the plan of action put before him by A.

NOTES

[1]Cf. *OED sub tit.* Responsible: Answerable, accountable (*to* another *for* something); liable to be called to account: 'being responsible to the King for what might happen to us', 1662; Hart, 'Varieties of Responsibility' (1967) 83 *LQR* 346, reprinted with additions as 'Responsibility and Retribution' in Hart, *Punishment and Responsibility* (Oxford, 1968), chap. IX.

[2]The rule is defended on the ground that, most houseowners being insured, it promotes efficient loss distribution. Harper and James, *Torts* [Boston, 1956], s. 20.6 n. 1.

[4]Lawson, *Negligence in the Civil Law* [Oxford, 1950], p. 53.

[5]Glanville Williams, *Joint Torts and Contributory Negligence* [London, 1951], p. 239.

[6]Mill [*A System of Logic*, 8th ed. (London, 1886)], Book III, chap. v, s. 2.

[8]e.g. if the guest was suspected of being a compulsive stabber and the waiter had therefore been told to lay only a plastic knife in his place.

[15]Above, pp. [798] ff.

[18]*Bellows v. Worcester Storage Co.* (1937) 297 Mass. 188, 7 NE 2d 588.

QUESTIONS FOR DISCUSSION

1. Explain the need for each condition in Hart and Honoré's definition of a co-incidence.

2. Why do Hart and Honoré think that an agent should not be legally responsible for a harm when a coincidence intervenes between that agent's act and the harm? Do you agree? Why or why not?

3. In the drive–by shooting example (p. 790), suppose that the victim could be saved only by a certain kind of medical equipment. The hospital has two pieces of equipment of this kind, but both happen to break down, so the victim dies. Does this meet the conditions in Hart and Honoré's definition of a coincidental intervention? Should the gang member who shot the by-stander be held legally responsible for causing the death? How could Hart and Honoré best respond to this example?

4. State precisely and completely the kinds of acts that are voluntary interventions according to Hart and Honoré.

5. Why do Hart and Honoré think that an agent should not be legally responsible for a harm when such a voluntary act intervenes between that agent's act and the harm? Do you agree? Why or why not?

6. One proposed counterexample to Hart and Honoré's account of voluntary interventions is Joel Feinberg's *foolhardy bank teller*: "Jones, a depositor in the defendant's bank, was standing in line before the depositor's window when a bank robber entered, drew his gun, and warned 'If anyone moves, I'll shoot.' The teller immediately grabbed something and dived to the floor. The bandit shot at him, and the ricocheting bullet struck Jones, still waiting in line, causing him severe injury. Jones then sued the bank (a more likely defendant than the impecunious bandit), charging that the teller's violation of the bandit's order created an unreasonable risk of harm to the customers and that the teller's thoughtless act was thus the cause of Jones's injury."[6] Feinberg argues that the teller's movement should count as a legal cause, so the wounded customer should get compensation from the bank: "The perti-nent principle here is that the more expectable human behavior is, whether voluntary or not, the less likely it is to 'negative causal connection'; and when the stakes are high, as in our bank robbery example, consequences will be traced right back through a voluntary act providing only that in ret-rospect it seems 'not highly extraordinary' that it intervened."[7] Now, does the robber's shot meet Hart and Honoré's conditions for a voluntary inter-vention between the teller's movement and the customer's wounding? Should the teller or the bank be held partly responsible for the customer's wounding? Why or why not? How could Hart and Honoré best respond to this example?

[6]"Causing Voluntary Actions," in *Doing and Deserving*, pp. 155–6.
[7]"Causing Voluntary Actions," pp. 166–7, notes omitted.

PALSGRAF V. THE LONG ISLAND RAILROAD CO.

248 N.Y. 339 (New York Court of Appeals, 1928)

CARDOZO, CH. J.

Plaintiff was standing on a platform of defendant's railroad after buying a ticket to go to Rockaway Beach. A train stopped at the station, bound for another place. Two men ran forward to catch it. One of the men reached the platform of the car without mishap, though the train was already moving. The other man, carrying a package, jumped aboard the car, but seemed unsteady as if about to fall. A guard on the car, who had held the door open, reached forward to help him in, and another guard on the platform pushed him from behind. In this act, the package was dislodged, and fell upon the rails. It was a package of small size, about fifteen inches long, and was covered by a newspaper. In fact it contained fireworks, but there was nothing in its appearance to give notice of its contents. The fireworks when they fell exploded. The shock of the explosion threw down some scales at the other end of the platform, many feet away. The scales struck the plaintiff, causing injuries for which she sues.

The conduct of the defendant's guard, if a wrong in its relation to the holder of the package, was not a wrong in its relation to the plaintiff, standing far away. Relatively to her it was not negligence at all. Nothing in the situation gave notice that the falling package had in it the potency of peril to persons thus removed. Negligence is not actionable unless it involves in the invasion of a legally protected interest, the violation of a right. "Proof of negligence in the air, so to speak, will not do.". . . "Negligence is the absence of care, according to the circumstances.". . . The plaintiff as she stood upon the platform of the station might claim to be protected against intentional invasion of her bodily security. Such invasion is not charged. She might claim to be protected against unintentional invasion by conduct involving in the thought of reasonable men an unreasonable hazard that such invasion would ensue. These, from the point of view of the law, were the bounds of her immunity, with perhaps some rare exceptions, survivals for the most part of ancient forms of liability, where conduct is held to be at the peril of the actor. . . . If no hazard was apparent to the eye of ordinary vigilance, an act innocent and harmless, at least to outward seeming, with reference to her, did not take to itself the quality of a tort because it happened to be a wrong, though apparently not one involving the risk of bodily insecurity, with reference to some one else. "In every instance, before negligence can be predicated of a given act, back of the act must be sought and found a duty to the individual complaining, the observance of which would have averted or avoided the injury." . . . "The ideas of negligence and duty are strictly correlative." . . . The plaintiff sues in her own right for a wrong personal to her, and not as the vicarious beneficiary of a breach of duty to another.

A different conclusion will involve us, and swiftly too, in a maze of contradictions. A guard stumbles over a package which has been left upon a platform. It seems to be a bundle of newspapers. It turns out to be a can of dynamite. To the eye of ordinary vigilance, the bundle is abandoned waste, which may be kicked or trod on with impunity. Is a passenger at the other end of the platform protected by the law against the unsuspected hazard concealed beneath the waste? If not, is the result to be any different, so far as the distant passenger is concerned, when the guard stumbles over a valise which a truckman or a porter has left upon the walk? The passenger far away, if the victim of a wrong at all, has a cause of action, not derivative, but original and primary. His claim to be protected against invasion of his bodily security is neither greater nor less because the act resulting in the invasion is a wrong to another far removed. In this case, the rights that are said to have been violated, the interests said to have been invaded, are not even of the same order. The man was not injured in his person nor even put in danger. The purpose of the act, as well as its effect, was to make his person safe. If there was a wrong to him at all, which may very well be doubted, it was a wrong to a property interest only, the safety of his package. Out of this wrong to property, which threatened injury to nothing else, there has passed, we are told, to the plaintiff by derivation or succession a right of action for the invasion of an interest of another order, the right to bodily security. The diversity of interests emphasizes the futility of the effort to build the plaintiff's right upon the basis of a wrong to some one else. The gain is one of emphasis, for a like result would follow if the interests were the same. Even then, the orbit of the danger as disclosed to the eye of reasonable vigilance would be the orbit of the duty. One who jostles one's neighbor in a crowd does not invade the rights of others standing at the outer fringe when the unintended contact casts a bomb upon the ground. The wrongdoer, as to them is the man who carries the bomb, not the one who explodes it without suspicion of the danger. Life will have to be made over, and human nature transformed, before prevision so extravagant can be accepted as the norm of conduct, the customary standard to which behavior must conform.

The argument for the plaintiff is built upon the shifting meanings of such words as "wrong" and "wrongful," and shares their instability. What the plaintiff must show is "a wrong" to herself, i. e., a violation of her own right, and not merely a wrong to some one else, nor conduct "wrongful" because unsocial, but not "a wrong" to any one. We are told that one who drives at reckless speed through a crowded city street is guilty of a negligent act and, therefore, of a wrongful one irrespective of the consequences. Negligent the act is, and wrongful in the sense that it is unsocial, but wrongful and unsocial in relation to other travelers, only because the eye of vigilance perceives the risk of damage. If the same act were to be committed on a speedway or a race course, it would lose its wrongful quality. The risk reasonably to be perceived defines the duty to be obeyed, and risk imports relation; it is risk to another or to others within the range of apprehension. . . . This does not mean, of course, that one who launches a destructive force is always relieved of liability if the force, though known to be destructive, pursues an unexpected path. It was not necessary that the defendant should have had notice of the particular method in which an accident would occur, if the possibility of an accident was clear to the ordinarily prudent eye. . . . Some acts, such as shooting, are so imminently dangerous to any one who may come within reach of the missile, however unexpectedly, as to impose a duty of prevision not far from that of an insurer. Even today, and much oftener in earlier stages of the law, one acts sometimes at one's peril. . . . Under this head, it may be, fall certain cases of what is known as transferred intent, an act willfully dangerous to A resulting by misadventure in injury to B. . . . These cases aside, wrong is defined in terms of the natural or probable, at least when unintentional. . . . The range of reasonable apprehension is at times a question for the court, and at times, if varying inferences are possible, a question for the jury. Here, by concession, there was nothing in the situation to suggest to the most cautious mind that the parcel wrapped in newspaper would spread wreckage through the station. If the guard had thrown it down knowingly and willfully, he would not have threatened the plaintiff's safety, so far as appearances could warn him. His conduct would not have involved, even then, an unreasonable probability of invasion of her bodily security. Liability can be no greater where the act is inadvertent.

Negligence, like risk, is thus a term of relation. Negligence in the abstract, apart from things related, is surely not a tort, if indeed it is understandable at all. . . . Negligence is not a tort unless it results in the commission of a wrong, and the commission of a wrong imports the violation of a right, in this case, we are told, the right to be protected against interference with one's bodily security. But bodily security is protected, not against all forms of interference or aggression, but only against some. One who seeks redress at law does not make out a cause of action by showing without more that there has been damage to his person. If the harm was not willful, he must show that the act as to him had possibilities of danger so many and apparent as to entitle him to be protected against the doing of it though the harm was unintended. Affront to personality is still the keynote of the wrong. Confirmation of this view will be found in the history and development of the action on the case. Negligence as a basis of civil liability was unknown to mediaeval law. . . . For damage to the person, the sole remedy was trespass, and trespass did not lie in the absence of aggression, and that direct and personal. . . . Liability for other damage, as where a servant without orders from the master does or omits something to the damage of another, is a plant of later growth. . . . When it emerged out of the legal soil, it was thought of as a variant of trespass, an offshoot of the parent stock. This appears in the form of action, which was known as trespass on the case. . . . The victim does not sue derivatively, or by right of subrogation, to vindicate an interest invaded in the person of another. Thus to view his cause of action is to ignore the fundamental difference between tort and crime. . . . He sues for breach of a duty owing to himself.

The law of causation, remote or proximate, is thus foreign to the case before us. The question of liability is always anterior to the question of the measure of the consequences that go with liability. If there is no tort to be redressed, there is no occasion to consider what damage might be recovered if there were a finding of a tort. We may assume, without deciding, that negligence, not at large or in the abstract, but in relation to the plaintiff, would entail liability for any and all consequences, however novel or extraordinary. . . . There is room for argument that a distinction is to be drawn according to the diversity of interests invaded by the act, as where conduct negligent in that it threatens an insignificant invasion of an interest in property results in an unforeseeable invasion of an interest of another order, as e.g, one of bodily security. Perhaps other distinctions may be necessary. We do not go into the question now. The consequences to be followed must first be rooted in a wrong.

The judgment of the Appellate Division and that of the Trial Term should be reversed, and the complaint dismissed, with costs in all courts.

ANDREWS, J. (dissenting).

Assisting a passenger to board a train, the defendant's servant negligently knocked a package from his arms. It fell between the platform and the cars. Of its contents the servant knew and could know nothing. A violent explosion followed. The concussion broke some scales standing a considerable distance away. In falling they injured the plaintiff, an intending passenger.

Upon these facts may she recover the damages she has suffered in an action brought against the master? The result we shall reach depends upon our theory as to the nature of negligence. Is it a relative concept—the breach of some duty owing to a particular person or to particular persons? Or where there is an act which unreasonably threatens the safety of others, is the doer liable for all its proximate consequences, even where they result in injury to one who would generally be thought to be outside the radius of danger? This is not a mere dispute as to words. We might not believe that to the average mind the dropping of the bundle would seem to involve the probability of harm to the plaintiff standing many feet away whatever might be the case as to the owner or to one so near as to be likely to be struck by its fall. If, however, we adopt the second hypothesis we have to inquire only as the relation between cause and effect. We deal in terms of proximate cause, not of negligence.

Negligence may be defined roughly as an act or omission which unreasonably does or may affect the rights of others, or which unreasonably fails to protect oneself from the dangers resulting from such acts. Here I confine myself to the first branch of the definition. Nor do I comment on the word "unreasonable." For present purposes it sufficiently describes that average of conduct that society requires of its members.

There must be both the act or the omission, and the right. It is the act itself, not the intent of the actor, that is important. . . . In criminal law both the intent and the result are to be considered. Intent again is material in tort actions, where punitive damages are sought, dependent on actual malice—not on merely reckless conduct. But here neither insanity nor infancy lessens responsibility. . . .

As has been said, except in cases of contributory negligence, there must be rights which are or may be affected. Often though injury has occurred, no rights of him who suffers have been touched. A licensee or trespasser upon my land has no claim to affirmative care on my part that the land be made safe. . . . Where a railroad is required to fence its tracks against cattle, no man's rights are injured should he wander upon the road because such fence is absent. . . . An unborn child may not demand immunity from personal harm. . . .

But we are told that "there is no negligence unless there is in the particular case a legal duty to take care, and this duty must be one which is owed to the plaintiff himself and not merely to others." . . . This, I think too narrow a conception. Where there is the unreasonable act, and some right that may be affected there is negligence whether damage does or does not result. That is immaterial. Should we drive down Broadway at a reckless speed, we are negligent whether we strike an approaching car or miss it by an inch. The act itself is wrongful. It is a wrong not only to those who happen to be within the radius of danger but to all who might have been there—a wrong to the public at large. Such is the language of the street. Such the language of the courts when speaking of contributory negligence. Such again and again their language in speaking of the duty of some defendant and discussing proximate cause in cases where such a discussion is wholly irrelevant on any other theory. . . . As was said by Mr. Justice Holmes many years ago, "the measure of the defendant's duty in determining whether a wrong has been committed is one thing, the measure of liability when a wrong has been committed is another." . . . Due care is a duty imposed on each one of us to protect society from unnecessary danger, not to protect *A*, *B* or *C* alone.

It may well be that there is no such thing as negligence in the abstract. "Proof of negligence in the air, so to speak, will not do." In an empty world negligence would not exist. It does involve a relationship between man and his fellows. But not merely a relationship between man and those whom he might reasonably expect his act would injure. Rather, a relationship between him and those whom he does in fact injure. If his act has a tendency to harm some one, it harms him a mile away as surely as it does those on the scene. We now permit children to recover for the negligent killing of the father. It was never prevented on the theory that no duty was owing to them. A husband may be compensated for the loss of his wife's services. To say that the wrongdoer was negligent as to the husband as well as to the wife is merely an attempt to fit facts to theory. An insurance company paying a fire loss recovers its payment of the negligent incendiary. We speak of subrogation—of suing in the right of the insured. Behind the cloud of words is the fact they hide, that the act, wrongful as to the insured, has also injured the company. Even if it be true that the fault of father, wife or insured will prevent recovery, it is because we consider the original negligence not the proximate cause of the injury. . . .

In the well-known *Polemis Case* . . . , Scrutton, L. J., said that the dropping of a plank was negligent for it might injure "workman or cargo or ship." Because of either possibility the owner of the vessel was to be made good for his loss. The act being wrongful the doer was liable for its proximate results. Criticized and explained as this statement may have been, I think it states the law as it should be and as it is. . . .

The proposition is this. Every one owes to the world at large the duty of refraining from those acts that may unreasonably threaten the safety of others. Such an act occurs. Not only is he wronged to whom harm might reasonably be expected to result, but he also who is in fact injured, even if he be outside what would generally be thought the danger zone. There needs be duty due the one complaining but this is not a duty to a particular individual because as to him harm might be expected. Harm to some one being the natural result of the act, not only that one alone, but all those in fact injured may complain. We have never, I think, held otherwise. Indeed in the *Di Caprio* case we said that a breach of a general ordinance defining the degree of care to be exercised in one's calling is evidence of negligence as to every one. We did not limit this statement to those who might be expected to be exposed to danger. Unreasonable risk being taken, its consequences are not confined to those who might probably be hurt.

If this be so, we do not have a plaintiff suing by "derivation or succession." Her action is original and primary. Her claim is for a breach of duty to herself—not that she is subrogated to any right of action of the owner of the parcel or of a passenger standing at the scene of the explosion.

The right to recover damages rests on additional considerations. The plaintiff's rights must be injured, and this injury must be caused by the negligence. We build a dam, but are negligent as to its foundations. Breaking, it injures property down stream. We are not liable if all this happened because of some reason other than the insecure foundation. But when injuries do result from our unlawful act we are liable for the consequences. It does not matter that they are unusual, unexpected, unforeseen and unforeseeable. But there is one limitation. The damages must be so connected with the negligence that the latter may be said to be the proximate cause of the former.

These two words have never been given an inclusive definition. What is a cause in a legal sense, still more what is a proximate cause, depend in each case upon many considerations, as does the existence of negligence itself. Any philosophical doctrine of causation does not help us. A boy throws a stone into a pond. The ripples spread. The water level rises. The history of that pond is altered to all eternity. It will be altered by other causes also. Yet it will be forever the resultant of all causes combined. Each one will have an influence. How great only omniscience can say. You may speak of a chain, or if you please, a net. An analogy is of little aid. Each cause brings about future events. Without each the future would not be the same. Each is proximate in the sense it is essential. But that is not what we mean by the word. Nor on the other hand do we mean sole cause. There is no such thing.

Should analogy be thought helpful, however, I prefer that of a stream. The spring, starting on its journey, is joined by tributary after tributary. The river, reaching the ocean, comes from a hundred sources. No man may say whence any drop of water is derived. Yet for a time distinction may be possible. Into the clear creek, brown swamp water flows from the left. Later, from the right comes water stained by its clay bed. The three may remain for a space, sharply divided. But at last, inevitably no trace of separation remains. They are so commingled that all distinction is lost.

As we have said, we cannot trace the effect of an act to the end, if end there is. Again, however, we may trace it part of the way. A murder at Sarajevo may be the necessary antecedent to an assassination in London twenty years hence. An overturned lantern may burn all Chicago. We may follow the fire from the shed to the last building. We rightly say the fire started by the lantern caused its destruction.

A cause, but not the proximate cause. What we do mean by the word "proximate" is, that because of convenience, of public policy, of a rough sense of justice, the law arbitrarily declines to trace a series of events beyond a certain point. This is not logic, it is practical politics. Take our rule as to fires. Sparks from my burning haystack set on fire my house and my neighbor's. I may recover from a negligent railroad. He may not. Yet the wrongful act as directly harmed the one as the other. We may regret that the line was drawn just where it was, but drawn somewhere it had to be. We said the act of the railroad was not the proximate cause of our neighbor's fire. Cause it surely was. The words we used were simply indicative of our notions of public policy. Other courts think differently. But somewhere they reach the point where they cannot say the stream comes from any one source.

Take the illustration given in an unpublished manuscript by a distinguished and helpful writer on the law of torts. A chauffeur negligently collides with another car which is filled with dynamite, although he could not know it. An explosion follows. A, walking on the sidewalk nearby, is killed. B, sitting in a window of a building opposite, is cut by flying glass. C, likewise sitting in a window a block away, is similarly injured. And a further illustration. A nursemaid, ten blocks away, startled by the noise, involuntarily drops a baby from

her arms to the walk. We are told that C may not recover while A may. As to B it is a question for court or jury. We will all agree that the baby might not. Because, we are again told, the chauffeur had no reason to believe his conduct involved any risk of injuring either C or the baby. As to them he was not negligent.

But the chauffeur, being negligent in risking the collision, his belief that the scope of the harm he might do would be limited is immaterial. His act unreasonably jeopardized the safety of any one who might be affected by it. C's injury and that of the baby were directly traceable to the collision. Without that, the injury would not have happened. C had the right to sit in his office, secure from such dangers. The baby was entitled to use the sidewalk with reasonable safety.

The true theory is, it seems to me, that the injury to C, if in truth he is to be denied recovery, and the injury to the baby is that their several injuries were not the proximate result of the negligence. And here not what the chauffeur had reason to believe would be the result of his conduct, but what the prudent would foresee, may have a bearing. May have some bearing, for the problem of proximate cause is not to be solved by any one consideration.

It is all a question of expediency. There are no fixed rules to govern our judgment. There are simply matters of which we may take account. We have in somewhat different connection spoken of "the stream of events." We have asked whether that stream was deflected—whether it was forced into new and unexpected channels. . . . This is rather rhetoric than law. There is in truth little to guide us other than common sense.

There are some hints that may help us. The proximate cause, involved as it may be with many other causes, must be, at the least, something without which the event would not happen. The court must ask itself whether there was a natural and continuous sequence between cause and effect. Was the one a substantial factor in producing the other? Was there a direct connection between them, without too many intervening causes? Is the effect of cause on result not too attenuated? Is the cause likely, in the usual judgment of mankind, to produce the result? Or by the exercise of prudent foresight could the result be foreseen? Is the result too remote from the cause, and here we consider remoteness in time and space? . . . Clearly we must so consider, for the greater the distance either in time or space, the more surely do other causes intervene to affect the result. When a lantern is overturned the firing of a shed is a fairly direct consequence. Many things contribute to the spread of the conflagration—the force of the wind, the direction and width of street, the character of intervening structures, other factors. We draw an uncertain and wavering line, but draw it we must as best we can.

Once again, it is all a question of fair judgment, always keeping in mind the fact that we endeavor to make a rule in each case that will be practical and in keeping with the general understanding of mankind.

Here another question must be answered. In the case supposed it is said, and said correctly, that the chauffeur is liable for the direct effect of the explosion although he had no reason to suppose it would follow a collision. "The fact that the injury occurred in a different manner than that which might have been expected does not prevent the chauffeur's negligence from being in law the cause of the injury." But the natural results of a negligent act—the results which a prudent man would or should foresee—do have a bearing upon the decision as to proximate cause. We have said so repeatedly. What should be foreseen? No human foresight would suggest that a collision itself might injure one a block away. On the contrary, given an explosion, such a possibility might be reasonably expected. I think the direct connection, the foresight of which the courts speak, assumes prevision of the explosion, for the immediate results of which, at least, the chauffeur is responsible.

It may be said this is unjust. Why? In fairness he should make good every injury flowing from his negligence. Not because of tenderness toward him we say he need not answer for all that follows his wrong. We look back to the catastrophe, the fire kindled by the spark, or the explosion. We trace the consequences—not indefinitely, but to a certain point. And to aid us in fixing that point we ask what might ordinarily be expected to follow the fire or the explosion.

This last suggestion is the factor which must determine the case before us. The act upon which defendant's liability rests is knocking an apparently harmless package onto the platform. The act was negligent. For its proximate consequences the defendant is liable. If its contents were broken, to the owner; if it fell upon and crushed a passenger's foot, then to him. If it exploded and injured one in the immediate vicinity, to him also as to A in the illustration. Mrs. Palsgraf was standing some distance away. How far cannot be told from the record—apparently twenty-five or thirty feet. Perhaps less. Except for the explosion, she would not have been injured. We are told by the appellant in his brief "it cannot be denied that the explosion was the direct cause of the plaintiff's injuries." So it was a substantial factor in producing the result—there was here a natural and continuous sequence—direct connection. The only intervening cause was that instead of blowing her to the ground the concussion smashed the weighing machine which in turn fell upon her. There was no remoteness in time, little in space. And surely, given such an explosion as here it needed no great foresight to predict that the natural result would be to injure one on the platform at no greater distance from its scene than was the plaintiff. Just how no one might be able to predict. Whether by flying fragments, by broken glass, by wreckage of machines or structures no one could say. But injury in some form was most probable.

Under these circumstances I cannot say as a matter of law that the plaintiff's injuries were not the proximate result of the negligence. That is all we have before us. The court refused to so charge. No request was made to submit the matter to the jury as a question of fact, even would that have been proper upon the record before us.

The judgment appealed from should be affirmed, with costs.

POUND, LEHMAN and KELLOGG, JJ., concur with CARDOZO, CH. J.; ANDREWS, J., dissents in opinion in which CRANE and O'BRIEN, JJ., concur.

Judgment reversed, etc.

QUESTIONS FOR DISCUSSION

1. Justice Cardozo says, "the conduct of the guard . . . was not a wrong in relation to" Mrs. Palsgraf (p. 803). What does he mean? Why does he think this? Can an act create legal responsibility for a harm in any case where the act is not wrong in relation to the person harmed? Why or why not?

2. Justice Cardozo wrote, "The law of causation, remote or proximate, is . . . foreign to the case before us. (p. 805)" What does he mean? Why does he think this? Do you agree? Why or why not?

3. What arguments does Justice Andrews give in his dissent to Cardozo's position? How could Cardozo best respond? Would you have voted with the majority or the dissent? Why?

4. What does Justice Andrews mean by a "proximate" cause? Should legal responsibility be limited to causes that are proximate in this sense? Why or why not?

5. In what kinds of cases would Cardozo and Andrews disagree about whether someone is legally responsible for a harm? Give examples.

6. Should the guard or the railroad be legally responsible in a case just like *Palsgraf* except that the guard knew that the passenger was carrying fireworks? What if Mrs. Palsgraf was hurt by bottle rockets that flew straight from the fallen package into her eye? If these variations on the facts make a difference, why? If not, why not?

7. In *People v Kibbe* (p. 789), did Kibbe's act cause Stafford's death? Should Kibbe be legally responsible for the death? Why or why not? Be sure to consider whether Kibbe's act was a sufficient condition of Stafford's death (given the circumstances), whether Stafford's act of walking into the road was a voluntary intervention for Hart and Honoré, and whether Blake's driving into Stafford was a voluntary intervention or a coincidental intervention for Hart and Honoré.

8. According to Mr. and Mrs. Joseph Ault, their 21-year-old daughter, Linda Ault, "failed to return home from a dance in Tempe [Arizona] Friday night. On Saturday she admitted she had spent the night with an Air Force lieutenant. The Aults decided on a punishment that would 'wake Linda up.' They ordered her to shoot the dog she had owned for two years. On Sunday, the Aults and Linda took the dog into the desert near their home. They had the girl dig a shallow grave. Then Mrs. Ault grasped the dog between her hands, and Mr. Ault gave his daughter a .22-caliber pistol and told her to shoot the dog. Instead, the girl put the pistol to her right temple and shot herself. The police said that there were no charges that could be filed against the parents except possibly cruelty to animals." After Linda's death, however, her grief-stricken father said, "I killed her. I killed her. It's just like I killed her myself. . . . I handed her the gun. I didn't think she would do anything like that."[8] Did her parents cause Linda's death, according to Hart and Honoré's theory? (Be sure to consider whether her parents gave her reasons and opportunity to shoot herself.) Do you think that Mr. and Mrs. Ault should be held legally responsible for Linda's death? Why or why not?

9. The question of whether a cause must be a necessary condition is raised by cases where a harm is *overdetermined* in the sense that two or more conditions are each sufficient for the harm, so neither is necessary for the harm. For example, in *Corey v. Havener*,[9] "It appeared that the plaintiff [Corey] . . . was driving slowly in a wagon along Shrewsbury Street, a public street and main thoroughfare in Worcester; that the defendants came up from behind and passed [Corey] at a high rate of speed one on each side; that each defendant was mounted on a motor tricycle with a gasoline engine making a loud noise and emitting steam. . . . The plaintiff testified that his horse took fright when the defendant first passed but was under control and guidance until he overtook the defendants, and that running between them the horse shied and he then lost control. His wagon wheel struck another wagon going in the same direction, and the injuries to the wagon and to himself occurred." Assuming that either noisy motorcycle by itself would have been sufficient to frighten the horse out of control, was either individual motorcyclist a cause of the harm? Should either one be legally responsible for the harm? Should either one be forced to pay compensation for the damage? For how much of the damage? Why?

10. Should cigarette manufacturers be held legally responsible for cancer in their customers? How does this case fit into Hart and Honoré's theory? Be sure to consider time periods both before and after it could have been known that smoking causes cancer.

11. Suppose that ten companies dump their waste into the same stream, so it has to be cleaned up in order to avoid health problems for the people who use the stream. Consider one of the companies: the Sludge Company. The stream would not have become polluted to unacceptable levels if the Sludge Company had been the only one to dump waste in the stream, so the Sludge Company's dumping was not sufficient for the harm. The Sludge Company's dumping was also not necessary for the harm, since the stream would have become too polluted if any six of the companies had dumped their waste into the stream, even if the Sludge Company had

---

[8]*The New York Times*, February 7, 1968.
[9]65 N.E. 69 (Mass. 1902).

dumped nothing. Now, did the Sludge Company cause the pollution? Why or why not? Should the Sludge Company be forced to pay part of the cleanup costs? Why or why not?

12. Under what circumstances, if ever, should one be held legally responsible for a harm that one did not cause? Why?

SUGGESTIONS FOR FURTHER READING

Two useful collections of philosophical writings on causation are *The Nature of Causation*, ed. Myles Brand (Urbana: University of Illinois Press, 1976) and *Causation and Conditionals*, ed. Ernest Sosa (New York: Oxford University Press, 1975). A clearly written monograph that discusses both philosophical and legal issues of causation is J. L. Mackie, *The Cement of the Universe* (New York: Oxford University Press, 1974). On legal causation in particular, the classic is H. L. A. Hart and Tony Honoré, *Causation in the Law*, 2nd edition (New York: Oxford University Press, 1985). Different views can be found in Richard Epstein, "A Theory of Strict Liability," *Journal of Legal Studies*, vol. 2 (1973), pp. 151 ff.; and Robert E. Keeton, *Legal Cause in the Law of Torts* (Columbus: Ohio State University Press, 1963). Joel Feinberg argues that not all voluntary acts break causal chains in "Causing Voluntary Actions" in *Doing and Deserving* (Princeton: Princeton University Press, 1970), pp. 152–86; and he further develops his views in "Instigating the Unpredisposed: Bad Luck in Law and Life," in *Modality, Morality, and Belief*, ed. W. Sinnott-Armstrong, D. Raffman, and N. Asher (New York: Cambridge University Press, 1994). The importance of requiring causation is discussed in Judith Jarvis Thomson, "Remarks on Causation and Liability," *Philosophy and Public Affairs*, vol. 13 (Spring 1984), pp. 101–33. For discussion of Thomson's article, see John Martin Fischer and Robert H. Ennis, "Causation and Liability"; Shelly Kagan, "Causation, Liability, and Internalism"; and Judith Jarvis Thomson, "A Note on Internalism," all in *Philosophy and Public Affairs*, vol. 15 (Winter 1986), pp. 33–66. On the related issue of whether pornography causes violence to women, see Frederick Schauer, "Causation Theory and the Causes of Sexual Violence," *American Bar Foundation Research Journal*, vol. 1987 (1987), pp. 737–70.

RESPONSIBILITY FOR OMISSIONS

INTRODUCTION

It is often assumed that people should be held responsible only for what they do—for their actions. Part of what this means is that people should not be punished or fined or forced to pay civil damages simply because of who they are or what they are—for their status. This principle was applied in *Robinson v. California*[10] when the Supreme Court held that a California statute that made it a criminal offense to "be addicted to the use of narcotics" violated the Eighth Amendment prohibition of cruel and unusual punishment. The majority opinion argued in part that addiction is a status rather than an action, so people should be held responsible not for being addicted but only for using or buying or selling or transporting illegal narcotics.

This same principle raises questions about whether people should be held legally responsible for what they do *not* do. If action is necessary for responsibility, how can inaction create responsibility? If Adam fills up a swimming pool, throws in a baby, and the baby drowns, Adam murdered the baby. But what if the baby crawls by itself into the pool after the pool is filled? Bruce sees the baby crawl in, and he can tell that the baby is too young to swim or climb out, and there is nobody else to save it. If Bruce does not save it, the baby will drown. Bruce can easily save the baby at little or no cost to anyone. But Bruce watches the baby drown. Should Bruce be held responsible for the baby's death?[11]

WHAT ARE OMISSIONS?

In order to understand this issue, we need to distinguish positive acts from negative acts. This is not as easy as it might seem. Adam performs a positive act of killing, and Bruce does not. But what if the baby crawls in while Carl is filling up the pool, and Carl just keeps filling it up? What if Carl fills up the pool, then his accomplice throws in the baby, and both watch the baby drown? What if Carl filled up the pool because he knew that the baby would be tempted to crawl in? What if Carl thought only that the baby had some chance of crawling in? In such cases, it is not clear whether Carl performs a positive act (of killing) or just a negative act (of not saving). Although such cases are fascinating, we will try to stick to clear examples.

---

[10]*Robinson v. California*, 370 U.S. 660 (1962)

[11]If you think that this hypothetical case is unrealistic, see the similar actual case of *Handiboe v. McCarthy*, 151 S.E.2d 905 (1966).

Even within clearly negative acts, it is crucial to distinguish several kinds. Compare three people's relations to the drowning. Debra is a stranger on the far side of town. She is not aware of the baby drowning, and that is why she does *not* save the child. Still, Debra does not fail to save the child, since she does not try to save the child, and she has no special duty to save it. Second, Emily is tied to a chair as she watches the baby drown. She tries to get loose, but she can't. So Emily *fails* to save the child. Similarly, if Frances promises to take care of the baby but falls asleep, she fails to save the baby, even if she never tries to save it. But Emily and Frances do not refrain from saving the child, since their failures do not result from their decisions. Finally, Grace sees the child drowning, and could save the child, but consciously chooses not to get involved. Grace does not save the child, and she fails to save it. In addition, Grace *refrains* from saving the child. She also *omits* saving the child, since refrainings seem to be what many people have in mind when they talk about omissions. There are many other possible classifications, but the important point is that there is much more to many negative acts than merely not doing something.

BAD SAMARITAN LAWS

The main question is: which, if any, negative acts should create legal liability? There is no doubt that *some* negative acts do and should create legal liability. If you fail to file an income tax form or to report all of your income on the form, when you are required to do so, then you may be fined or even punished. It also seems clear that people are and should be held responsible for harms that they fail to prevent when they have special obligations to prevent the harms. A lifeguard on duty who refrains from saving a drowning swimmer when she could save him easily at no cost should be held responsible in some way. The controversial issue is whether people should be held legally responsible for harms because of what they refrain from doing when they have no special obligation to prevent the harm.

People with no special obligation to prevent a harm can be called *bystanders*. Bystanders who prevent the harm are called *good samaritans*, after the parable in the New Testament of the Bible (Luke 10:29–37). Bystanders who refrain from preventing a harm when they could do so easily at little cost can then be called *bad samaritans*.

There are two main kinds of laws about bystanders. *Good samaritan laws* apply when someone is a good samaritan. In particular, good samaritan laws might guarantee rewards for good samaritans, or ensure that they will be repaid for any costs incurred in the course of preventing the harm, or limit the liability of people who accidentally cause harm while trying to prevent harm. In contrast, *bad samaritan laws* apply to bad samaritans. These laws impose punishments, fines, or civil liability on bystanders who refrain from preventing harm under certain conditions. Bad samaritan laws are what many people have in mind when they refer to good samaritan laws in a broader sense (as in the readings below), but we will distinguish bad samaritan laws from good samaritan laws, because they raise different issues.

Bad samaritan laws are common on the European continent, but they are rejected in most of England and the United States. This trend is partly due to the influence of Lord Macaulay, an English statesman (1800–1859), who formulated his position as follows:[12]

> What we propose is this, that where acts are made punishable on the ground that they have caused, or have been intended to cause, or have been known to be likely to cause, a certain evil effect, omissions which have caused, which have been intended to cause, or which have been known to be likely to cause the same effect, shall be punishable in the same manner, provided that such omissions were, on other grounds, illegal.

Macaulay gives several illustrations, including the following:

> A omits to give Z food, and by that omission voluntarily causes Z's death. Is this murder? Under our rule it is murder if A was Z's gaoler, directed by law to furnish Z with food. It is murder if Z was the infant child of A, and had, therefore, a legal right to sustenance, which right a Civil Court would enforce against A. It is murder if Z was a bedridden invalid, and A a nurse hired to feed Z. It is murder if A was detaining Z in unlawful confinement and had thus contracted . . . a legal obligation to furnish Z, during the continuance of the confinement, with necessities. It is not murder if Z is a beggar, who has no other claim on A than that of humanity.

Although Macaulay allows some responsibility for omissions, what is most striking is what Macaulay says about when we should *not* hold a person responsible. He allows responsibility for omissions *only* when they are illegal on independent grounds, such as when they violate a contract or a legal duty of parents to their children. Less restrictive opponents of bad samaritan laws might allow responsibility for omissions in some cases of special obligations that are not otherwise recognized by law. One example is *Farwell v. Keaton* (excerpts follow). Siegrist and Farwell were friends who had gone out for the evening together when Farwell was beaten up. Siegrist took some steps to help Farwell but eventually left him in a car where he died. Farwell's parents then sued not only the assailants, including Keaton, but also Siegrist. Such cases raise important issues about which relations are sufficient to create a duty to rescue, and about who counts as a bystander.

Still, all opponents of bad samaritan laws agree that a person should not be held legally responsible for failing to help another person when the two people have no special relation at all to each other. On this view, if Grace has no special obligation to the baby in the example above, Grace should not be punished (or fined or liable in civil damages) if she watches the baby drown when she alone could easily save it at no cost to anyone.

---

[12]Thomas Babington Macaulay, "Notes on the Indian Penal Code," in *Works of Lord Macaulay*, ed. Sir George Otto Trevelyan, vol. 7 (1866), pp. 493–7

ARGUMENTS FOR BAD SAMARITAN LAWS

This doctrine might seem strange. There seem to be plenty of reasons to punish Grace in this situation. One reason is that Grace is immoral. As Macaulay admits, she is morally worse than many people who are punished severely. The question of whether we should have bad samaritan laws can then be viewed as another instance of the general question of when, if ever, the law should be used to enforce morality or moral beliefs. Legal moralists claim that we should punish people who do positive acts that are morally wrong, so legal moralists might also want to punish people who do negative acts that are morally bad or who refrain from doing positive acts that are morally good. We already saw some objections to legal moralism in general (Section 4.2). However, the main objections were to laws against harmless immoralities, but harm does occur when people refrain from preventing it. So some version of legal moralism limited to harmful immoralities still might be used to argue for bad samaritan laws.

Some kinds of retributivism also might support bad samaritan laws. If one consciously chooses not to prevent harm to another person when one could easily prevent it, then many people would view one as morally guilty in just the way that ought to be punished according to traditional retributivism. More recent versions of retributivism justify punishment as a way to prevent unfair advantages (see Davis in Section 6.4). That justification also seems to apply to bad samaritan laws. People who refuse to help others seem to gain an unjust advantage both over the people whom they refuse to help and also over people who do help others and suffer losses in the process. This imbalance can be redressed by imposing punishments, fines, or civil liability on people who refrain from helping others. Of course, there are objections to such versions of retributivism (also discussed earlier), but, if those views can be defended, they might provide a justification for bad samaritan laws.

Utilitarian arguments emphasize that bad samaritan laws make more people prevent more harm.[13] Fewer babies drown if people save them because these people fear punishment or civil liability for refraining from saving them. Bad samaritan laws also might change people's moral beliefs so that they would begin to view it as more wrong not to help someone in need, and these new moral beliefs might even spill over into other areas of life so as to lead people to help each other even in situations where the bad samaritan laws do not apply. These mechanisms are analogous to the ways in which punishment prevents positive criminal acts by means of deterrence and moral education (see Section 6.3). Citizens also benefit from the greater security that comes when they believe that they and their loved ones will be more likely to be saved when they are in trouble. A sense of community is also valuable, but it is hard to feel community with someone who would not rescue you from serious harm even at no cost. So bad samaritan laws are also supposed to strengthen bonds of community (compare Sandel in Section 5.2). In addition, bad samaritan laws might be needed to build respect for the law. If someone suffers harm because another person refuses to help, even

[13]For example, Jeremy Bentham, *Introduction to the Principles of Morals and Legislation*, edited by J. Burns and H. L. A. Hart (London: Athlone Press 1970), pp. 292–3.

though he or she could help easily at no cost, but the law does nothing, then the law seems to take the side of people who are morally reprehensible. We have a lot to lose if respect for the law is undermined in this way, so avoiding this loss seems to be yet another benefit of bad samaritan laws.

ARGUMENTS AGAINST BAD SAMARITAN LAWS

If bad samaritan laws have so many benefits, why shouldn't legislatures pass them? Many reasons have been given.

Slippery Slopes: Probably the most famous argument against bad samaritan laws comes again from Lord Macaulay. Just after he states his rule against punishing bystanders who fail to help (quoted earlier), he says:

> We are sensible that in some of the cases which we have put, our rule may appear too lenient; but we do not think that it can be made more severe without disturbing the whole order of society. It is true that a man who, having abundance of wealth, suffers a fellow creature to die of hunger at his feet, is a bad man, a worse man, probably, than many of those for whom we have provided very severe punishment. But we are unable to see where, if we make such a man legally punishable, we can draw the line. If the rich man who refuses to save the beggar's life at the cost of a little copper is a murderer, is the poor man just one degree above beggary also to be a murderer if he omits to invite the beggar to partake his hard-earned rice? Again, if the rich man is a murderer for refusing to save the beggar's life at the cost of a little copper, is he also to be a murderer if he refuses to save the beggar's life at the cost of a thousand rupees? . . . The distinction between a legal and an illegal omission is perfectly plain and intelligible; but the distinction between a large and a small sum of money is very far from being so, not to say that a sum which is small to one man is large to another.[14]

As Macaulay points out, the same kind of argument applies as well to other costs of helping others. Not only is there a problem of how much money a person should be required to spend to help others. There are also problems of how much time a person should be required to spend, how much distance a person should be required to cross, how much effort a person should be required to exert, how much discomfort a person should be required to suffer, how much risk a person should be required to run, and so on. Such costs lie on a continuum. Macaulay argues that there is only one acceptable way to draw a line on this continuum: limiting government intervention to failures that are otherwise illegal. Beyond these cases, there is no acceptable way to draw a line between the cases where the government should punish failures to help and the cases where the government should not.

This is a classic slippery slope argument.[15] Like many slippery slopes, there are two ways to understand the argument. One is *practical.* Macaulay's claim might

---

[14]Macaulay, "Notes on the Indian Penal Code," pp. 493–7.

[15]See Frederick Schauer, "Slippery Slopes," *Harvard Law Review,* vol. 99 (1985), pp. 361–83; and Douglas Walton, *Slippery Slope Arguments* (Oxford: Clarendon Press, 1992).

be that, as a matter of fact, if legislators punish people for omissions that are not otherwise illegal, they might start with people who refrain from helping others when they could easily help at no cost, but they or others will be tempted to go further and also punish people for failing to help even when helping is not so easy or cheap. Eventually the government will punish people for all failures to help others. Since there are so many people to help, the government will then control how we spend most of our lives. Thus ends freedom and individuality.

Such an end to freedom and individuality would be horrible. However, it is not clear why anything so bad has to result from a few limited bad samaritan laws. Bad samaritan laws might be the start of a road that ends in a swamp, but not everyone who starts on the road has to drive all the way into the swamp. Admittedly, some governments will go too far. There is a real danger here. But there are also benefits, as we saw, so the basic question is whether the real dangers outweigh the benefits. That issue cannot be settled just by pointing out a potential slippery slope.

The other way to interpret Macaulay's argument is *conceptual*. If the government is allowed to require a rich person to spend a dollar to save a life, why isn't the government also allowed to require the same person to spend ten dollars or a hundred or a thousand or ten thousand? The government might not actually go so far in practice, but it is still unsatisfying to allow bad samaritan laws if there is no way in theory to say how far the government should go or be allowed to go, and why.

The main way to respond to this conceptual argument is to write a law that shows which bystanders to hold responsible and why. One of the rare attempts in the United States is from Vermont:[16]

> (a) A person who knows that another is exposed to grave physical harm shall, to the extent that the same can be rendered without danger or peril to himself or without interference with important duties owed to others give reasonable assistance to the exposed person unless that assistance or care is being provided by others.
> (b) A person who provides reasonable assistance in compliance with subsection (a) of this section shall not be liable in civil damages unless his acts constitute gross negligence or unless he will receive or expects to receive remuneration. Nothing contained in this subsection shall alter existing law with respect to tort liability of a practitioner of the healing arts for acts committed in the ordinary course of his practice.
> (c) A person who willfully violates subsection (a) of this section shall be fined not more than $100.

This law does not specify a number of dollars or minutes that constitutes "reasonable assistance" or a level of risk that counts as "grave physical harm" or as "danger or peril." Opponents object that such phrases are vague, and vagueness is troublesome, since it will be hard for people to predict whether they might be

---

[16]Vermont Title 12, §519 (1967). See also Good Samaritan Law, ch. 319, 1983 Minn. Sess. Law Serv. 2329 (West).

fined for failures in some situations. However, there are also clear cases. The Vermont law is clearly violated if someone who is alone does not even shout a warning as he watches a blind person walk into a deep hole. Many other cases will not be so clear, but many laws are vague, and our system has a standard way of dealing with vagueness, namely, juries. If twelve impartial people all agree about what is "grave," "reasonable," and a "danger," then the case is probably clear enough. Admittedly, juries can be erratic, so one has to weigh the likelihood of bad decisions against the benefits of bad samaritan laws. But juries are trusted in other areas of equal importance, and the proper level of trust cannot be settled simply by pointing out a slippery slope.

Causation and Responsibility: The second main argument against bad samaritan laws claims that they violate individual rights, so they are unacceptable even in clear cases and even if they benefit society. Most people agree that people have a right not to be punished for something for which they are not responsible. That is why we should not punish innocent people. (See minimal retributivism in Section 6.4.) It is also common to assume that bystanders are not legally responsible for a harm unless they cause it. So, if negative acts can't cause harms, negative acts should never create legal responsibility for harms.

But why couldn't negative acts cause harms? Most people think that negative acts cause harm all the time. My failure to give someone a birthday present can hurt her or him deeply. My failure to brake my car can cause an accident.

However, when viewed more closely, the claim that a negative act is a legal cause of harm seems to produce a dilemma.[17] Suppose that Grace sees the baby drowning; she could save it, but she decides not to. We might say that it was the fact that Grace did not save the baby that caused its death. This might seem plausible, because the baby would not have died if Grace had saved it. However, the causal story can't be that simple. Everyone else in town, including Debra, who knew nothing about the baby, also did not save the baby. But Debra did not cause the baby's death. So the mere fact that someone did not save the baby cannot show that that person caused the baby's death.

Of course, Grace did not do nothing. She did *something else* instead of saving the baby. She walked away. So one might think that this act of walking away, or the fact that she did walk away, was what caused the baby's death. But that can't be right. There were lots of other things that she might have done that would not have saved the baby. She might have just stood still. Or she could have walked closer to get a better look. Thus, her act of walking away was not necessary for . the baby's death, so that substitute act could not have been the cause of the baby's death, assuming that causes must be necessary conditions, as on most accounts of legal causation (see Section 7.2).

Maybe it was Grace's *decision* not to save the baby that caused the baby's death. But that also seems problematic. If Grace had not known or believed anything

[17]The following discussion is derived from Eric Mack, "Bad Samaritanism and the Causation of Harm," *Philosophy and Public Affairs*, vol. 9 (1980), pp. 230–59

about the baby, then she would not have made any decision about the baby, but she still would not have saved it, and it still would have died. In fact, if Grace had not been aware of the baby, she might have moved her body in exactly the same way as she did, and the baby might have died in exactly the same way as it did. Thus, it seems that Grace's decision not to save the baby is not necessary for the baby to die in the way it did, so Grace's decision cannot be part of the cause of the baby's death, if causes have to be necessary conditions, as is usually assumed.

One might respond that Grace's decision really is necessary *under the circumstances* for the baby's death. The circumstances here include the facts that Grace knows that the baby is drowning and that Grace is able to save the baby if she decides to. Given these circumstances, it might seem that the baby really will not die unless Grace decides not to save it. If so, her decision not to save it is necessary under the circumstances for the baby's death. However, there are other ways in which Grace might not save the baby. Grace might get distracted and forget about the baby, or she might deliberate so long about whether or not to save the baby that she never gets around to deciding one way or the other. This again seems to show that Grace's decision not to save the baby is not necessary for her not to save the baby, or for the baby to drown. Defenders of the causal claim can respond as before that the circumstances include the facts that Grace will neither get distracted nor deliberate too long. Any such claim of necessity can be defended by building enough facts into the circumstances. But if too much has to be built into the circumstances to make her decision necessary for the baby's death, this seems to make it empty to claim that her decision is necessary for the baby's death.

Another kind of response is that causal claims are complex, because two conditions are necessary for X to be the legal cause of Y. First, X must be necessary for Y. Second, X must be the proper subject of the attention of the law. The first condition might be met by the fact that Grace did not save the baby, since that is necessary for the baby to die. The second condition might be met by the fact that Grace chooses not to save the baby, since the law should not inflict penalties on her if she did not choose not to save the baby. The two conditions are met jointly, then, only if Grace does not save the baby because she chooses not to. That conjunction is what it means to say that she refrains from saving the baby. So her refraining from saving the baby is what legally causes the baby's death.

However, this response faces its own problems. One is that it seems to beg the question. To say that Grace is the proper subject of legal attention and penalties is just another way of saying that Grace should be legally responsible. So this response seems to require us to figure out whether Grace should be legally responsible before we can figure out whether she causes the baby's death. But we were trying to figure out whether Grace should be held legally responsible, by asking whether she causes the baby's death. It is not clear whether this circle is vicious, but it is at least problematic.

There's another way to go. We have been assuming that causation is a necessary condition of legal responsibility in such cases. If that assumption is discarded, one can claim that Grace is responsible for the baby's death even though her omission does not cause the baby's death. This move will not be attractive to those who see Grace as just like a murderer. Nonetheless, even if Grace does not cause the baby's death, Grace still does *control* whether the baby lives or dies, and that control might be enough to show that she is responsible for the baby's death. If so, bad samaritan laws can impose punishments for omissions that do not cause harm without violating anyone's right not to be punished without responsibility.

A Right to be Rescued? Even if omissions do cause harms, this is not enough to justify punishing people for causing those harms. Many acts that harm other people are not subject to punishment. When a business wins a contract, this can cause great harm to its competitor, but that is no reason to punish the winner. Why? Because the loser had no right to get the contract. This suggests that punishment is justified only when someone causes harm in a way that violates some right of the person who is harmed. If so, bad samaritan laws are not justified unless the person who is harmed has a right to be helped.

Some opponents of bad samaritan laws deny that anyone has a right to be helped. They can admit that everyone has negative rights, such as the right not to be robbed or killed. They can even admit that a baby has a positive right to be fed and to be saved by its parents or its babysitter. But they deny that a bystander violates the baby's right if she lets it drown, even if she could easily save it at no cost.

One argument against the baby's right to be saved is that saving the baby would merely confer a benefit on it, but the baby has no right that any bystander give it a benefit. However, it is not clear whether saving the baby really does benefit it. To *benefit* someone is normally to raise that person's level of welfare above what it was at some earlier time. Someone who saves a drowning baby does increase its welfare above what it was when it was about to drown. But after the baby is saved it is still no better off than it was before it started to drown. Thus, which time one takes as the baseline determines whether a rescuer is seen as benefiting the person rescued. This makes it hard to see how the notion of benefit can be used to argue either way.[18]

The more important question is whether someone who fails to prevent a harm causes or is responsible for the harm. If the failure to save the baby causes its death, then the person who fails to save the baby actually lowers the baby's welfare to a level below what it was before it started to drown, and even below what it was when it was drowning, since then it still had at least a chance to live. People do seem to have a right that other people not cause their deaths, so, if failures to save can cause deaths, they do violate the rights of those who are not saved.

Opponents of bad samaritan laws can respond that causing someone's death is still not enough to violate that person's right. If you will die without a certain medicine, and I own the only dose of that medicine, I still do not violate or even infringe your rights if I take the sole dose in order to save myself. So some acts

---

[18]This point derives from Joel Feinberg, *Harm to Others* (New York: Oxford, 1984), pp. 130–50.

that cause deaths do not seem to violate rights, even if others do. The basic question is whether omissions can cause deaths in a way that violates rights of the person who is not saved. Opponents of bad samaritan laws claim that they cannot, unless the victim had some independent legal right to be saved. Defenders of bad samaritan laws think that people do have rights to be saved by bystanders. It is hard to see how to resolve this debate without some general theory of rights or some independent argument for why we should or should not impose legal responsibility in such cases.

Side Effects: Other common arguments against bad samaritan laws claim that they have harmful side effects that override their benefits. The most obvious is that bad samaritan laws take away freedom. If there is no law requiring her to save the baby, then Grace is free to choose what to do. But if a bad samaritan law threatens her with punishment if she does not save the baby, then Grace is no longer free to choose whether or not to get involved. The freedom to choose should not be underrated. However, every law that imposes a duty reduces freedom. Laws against murder take away our freedom to murder. Such laws are accepted because people have a right not to be murdered, but defenders of bad samaritan laws think that people also have a right to be rescued. So we need more of an argument to show why the freedom to watch the baby drown is especially important to Grace.

One reason might be that helping others is morally good in a positive way that merely not murdering is not. Some people argue that, if bad samaritan laws force Grace to save the baby, they take away her opportunity to be *morally good*, because she gets no credit if she saves the baby because she is threatened with punishment if she does not save it. But this does not follow. Even if she is threatened with punishment for failure, it still might be true that she saves the baby because she cares for it, and that she would have saved the baby even if she had not been threatened with punishment for failure. Bad samaritan laws aim to affect the behavior of people who would not help others if not for the laws. For people who would help others anyway, these laws do not affect their behavior or the credit and praise that they are due. So bad samaritan laws need not cause any loss of moral virtue.

Bad samaritan laws still might make people less likely to form dispositions to help others *freely*. When people are forced to do something, they sometimes lose the inclination to do it in other circumstances where they are not forced to do it. It is not clear, however, that bad samaritan laws really do make people less likely to help others freely. People often learn good habits initially by being forced to act in good ways. And even if bad samaritan laws do cause some loss in freely given assistance, this loss must be weighed against the benefits of bad samaritan laws.

Bad samaritan laws are also supposed to make people less *self-reliant*. If they know that they will be saved when they are in trouble if anyone can save them easily, then they might be less inclined to avoid trouble and also to learn how to get out of trouble by themselves. But again it is not clear that bad samaritan laws really do have this effect. If bystanders are punished only when they could save someone easily at little cost, then there will be almost as much incentive to avoid danger, because nobody can count on the presence of a bystander who can easily prevent the harm at little cost. So people will still need to learn how to take care of themselves. And even if there is some loss in self-reliance, this loss will have to be weighed against the benefits of bad samaritan laws.

In all arguments regarding consequences, the challenge is to write laws so as to maximize benefits and minimize costs—to induce people to help others without taking away their valuable inclinations to help others freely, to be self-reliant, and so on. It is still an open question whether such laws can be written well enough.

Alternatives: Even if bad samaritan laws do have greater benefits than costs, opponents still might object that there are better means of gaining those benefits. There are many private ways to encourage people to help others, such as religious and moral education, which do not involve the government at all. Moreover, the government can use some kind of *good* samaritan laws, that is, laws that provide incentives or take away disincentives for people to prevent harms and be good samaritans. Which kind of good samaritan law works best depends on why people don't help others in need.

If people don't help others because they ask, "What's in it for me?" then the law could get them to help others by ensuring rewards to people who do help. These rewards might be given by the people who are rescued, by the insurance companies who save money when their clients are rescued, by the government, or by some combination.

If people don't help others because they fear the costs of helping others, then the law could guarantee people who do help that they will be compensated for any reasonable losses or injuries incurred. For example, it costs a great deal of time and money to rescue fallen rock climbers. If private rescuers are forced to bear these expenses, they will be less likely to undertake rescues, so it might even be in the expected interest of rock climbers to require the climbers or their insurance companies to repay rescuers for all expenses, including medical bills when a rescuer is injured. We might even want to force rescued people to pay for rescues by public officials, such as in national parks, on the grounds that it is unfair for cautious taxpayers to foot the bill for other people's dangerous hobbies.

Another reason why some people decide not to help others in need is that they are afraid of being sued or even punished if their rescue attempt fails or if they injure the person who is rescued. If Karen is choking and you apply the Heimlich maneuver too hard, then you might break her ribs or even her back, and Karen might sue you. Even if you were not negligent, this legal battle will cost time and money, and you might have to settle out of court in order to avoid the risk of a greater loss. Given these dangers, people will be more likely to rescue others if the law limits rescuers' liability for harms they cause during attempts to rescue, possibly by allowing damages only when the rescuer was grossly negligent. (See Section (b) in the Vermont law, p. 820.)

These kinds of *good* samaritan laws probably increase the number of people who help others in need. If they increase it enough, then they seem preferable to *bad* samaritan laws, since bad samaritan laws have costs that are not shared by good samaritan laws. In particular, bad samaritan laws impose fines, punishments, or civil liability, which take away people's freedom to choose whether or not to get involved. This freedom is not affected by rewards, repayment for rescue costs, or limits on liability. Consequently, bad samaritan laws are not justified if good samaritan laws are enough to achieve an acceptable level of harm prevention.

However, it is not clear how much good samaritan laws can accomplish. If they alone do not work well enough to satisfy our desire for security, community, and avoidance of harm, then bad samaritan laws might still be justified in addition to good samaritan laws. This is presumably what Vermont legislators thought when they added the bad samaritan law in Section (a) to its good samaritan law in Section (b). Whether one sees such an addition as justified depends on how much one wants people to prevent harm to others and what price one is willing to pay.

The following readings expand on these arguments. Richard Epstein, a professor of law at the University of Chicago, opposes bad samaritan laws for many reasons. Ernest Weinrib, a professor of law at the University of Toronto, then argues in favor of bad samaritan laws.

A THEORY OF STRICT LIABILITY

RICHARD A. EPSTEIN

I. A CRITIQUE OF NEGLIGENCE

The development of the common law of tort has been marked by the opposition between two major theories. The first [theory, that of negligence,] holds that a plaintiff should be entitled, prima facie, to recover from a defendant who has caused him harm only if the defendant intended to harm the plaintiff or failed to take reasonable steps to avoid inflicting the harm. The alternative theory, that of strict liability, holds the defendant prima facie liable for the harm caused whether or not either of the two further conditions relating to negligence and intent is satisfied. . . .

II. AN ANALYSIS OF CAUSATION

Under the orthodox view of negligence, the question of causation is resolved by a two-step process. The first part of the inquiry concerns the "cause in fact" of the plaintiff's injury. The usual test to determine whether or not the plaintiff's injury was in fact caused by the negligence of the defendant is to ask whether, "but for the negligence of the defendant, the plaintiff would not have been injured." But this complex proposition is not in any sense the semantic equivalent of the assertion that the defendant caused the injury to the plaintiff. The former expression is in counterfactual form

Richard A. Epstein, "A Theory of Strict Liability," *Journal of Legal Studies*, vol. 2 (January 1973)

and requires an examination of what *would have* been the case if things had been otherwise. The second expression simply asks in direct indicative form what in fact *did* happen. The change in mood suggests the difference between the two concepts.

The "but for" test does not provide a satisfactory account of the concept of causation if the words "in fact" are taken seriously. A carelessly sets his alarm one hour early. When he wakes up the next morning he has ample time before work and decides to take an early morning drive in the country. While on the road he is spotted by B, an old college roommate, who becomes so excited that he runs off the road and hurts C. But for the negligence of A, C would never have been injured, because B doubtless would have continued along his uneventful way. Nonetheless, it is common ground that A, even if negligent, is in no way responsible for the injury to C, caused by B.

Its affinity for absurd hypotheticals should suggest that the "but for" test should be abandoned as even a tentative account of the concept of causation.

The pages the follow are designed to show that the concept of causation, as it applies to cases of physical injury, can be analyzed in a matter that both renders it internally coherent and relevant to the ultimate question who shall bear the loss. There will be no attempt to give a single semantic equivalent to the concept of causation. Instead, the paper will consider in succession each of four distinct paradigm cases covered by the proposition "A caused B harm." These paradigms are not the only way in which we can talk about torts cases. They do, however, provide modes of description which best capture the ordinary use of causal language. Briefly put, they are based upon notions of force [when A hit B], fright [when A frightened B], compulsion [when A compelled B to hit C], and dangerous conditions [when A created dangerous conditions that resulted in harm to either person or property]. . . .

III. THE PROBLEM OF THE GOOD SAMARITAN

The first two portions of this paper have compared the common law rules of negligence with those of strict liability in cases where the defendant has harmed the plaintiff's person or property. If that analysis is sound, then the rules of liability should be based upon the harm in fact caused and not upon any subsequent determination of the reasonableness of the defendant's conduct. The question of liability is thereby severed from both general cost-benefit analysis of the defendant's conduct and a moral examination of his individual worth. In the cases of affirmative action, the rules of strict liability avoid both the unfairness and complications created when negligence, in either its economic or moral sense, is accepted as the basis of the tort law.

The purpose of this section is to show that these conclusions are capable of extension to areas in which the law has traditionally not allowed recovery. The theories of strict liability explain and justify, as the rules of reasonableness cannot, the common law's refusal to extend liability in tort to cases where the defendant has not harmed the plaintiff by his affirmative action.[91] The problem arises in its starkest form in the case of the good Samaritan. A finds himself in a perilous situation which was not created by B, as when A is overwhelmed by cramps while swimming alone in a surging sea. B, moreover, is in a position where he could, without any danger of injury to himself, come to A's assistance with some simple and well-nigh costless steps, such as throwing a rope to the plaintiff. The traditional common law position has been that there is no cause of action against B solely because B, in effect, permitted A to drown.

It is important to note the manner in which such cases should be decided under a negligence system. In the verbal formulation of the law of negligence, little attention is paid to the distinction between those cases in which the defendant acted and those cases in which he did not act, failed to act, or omitted to act. "Negligence is the *omission* to do something which a reasonable man guided upon those considerations which ordinarily regulate the conduct of human affairs, would do, or doing something which a prudent and reasonable man would not do."[92] . . .

Thus, if one considers the low costs of prevention to *B* of rescuing *A*, and the serious, if not deadly, harm that *A* will suffer if *B* chooses not to rescue him, there is no reason why . . . the general rules of negligence should not require, under pain of liability, the defendant to come to the aid of the plaintiff. Nonetheless, the good Samaritan problem receives special treatment even under the modern law of torts. The reasons for the special position of this problem are clear once the theories of strict liability are systematically applied. Under these rules, the act requirement has to be satisfied in order to show that the defendant in a given lawsuit caused harm to the plaintiff. Once that is done, the private predicament of the defendant, his ability to take precautions against the given risk, and the general economic rationality of his conduct are all beside the point. Only the issue of causation, of what *the defendant did*, is material to the statement of the prima facie case. The theory is not utilitarian. It looks not to the consequences of alternate course of conduct but to what was done. When that theory with its justification is applied to the problem of the good Samaritan, it follows in the case just put that *A* should not be able to recover from *B* for his injuries. No matter how the facts are manipulated, it is not possible to argue that *B* caused *A* harm in any of the senses of causation which were developed in the earlier portions of the article when he failed to render assistance to *A* in his time of need. In typical negligence cases, all the talk of avoidance and reasonable care may shift attention from the causation requirement, which the general "but for" test distorts beyond recognition. But its importance is revealed by its absence in the good Samaritan cases where the presence of all those

elements immaterial to tortious liability cannot, even in combination, persuade judges who accept the negligence theory to apply it in the decisive case. . . .

There is a . . . class of exceptions to the good Samaritan rule, motivated by . . . judicial distaste for the doctrine, which . . . cannot be rationalized by an appeal to the theories of strict liability. Consider the case where the defendant gratuitously takes steps to aid the plaintiff only to discontinue his efforts before the plaintiff is moved to a position of comparative safety. For example, *A* sees *B* lying unconscious on the public street. Immediately, he runs to the phone, dials an emergency room, and then hangs up the receiver. Or, in the alternative, he picks *B* up and places him in his automobile, only to return him to his original position on the sidewalk when he thinks, for whatever reason, better of the involvement.

It has often been argued that the good Samaritan doctrine in these situations is of no application on the ground that once the defendant undertakes to assist the plaintiff in distress, he can no longer claim that his conduct amounted to a "simple nonfeasance," no longer maintain that the two were still strangers in the eyes of the law. The general refusal of the law to require one man to come to aid another is only a consequence of the act requirement in the law of tort. But once the defendant dials the phone or moves the plaintiff, the act requirement is satisfied; and once satisfied, the defendant cannot disregard the welfare of a plaintiff whom he has taken into his charge.

This position must be rejected. The act requirement in the law of tort is but a combination of the volition and the causation requirements already discussed. The law of tort cannot be invoked simply because the defendant has done something; it must be shown that the act in question has caused harm to the plaintiff. Where the defendant has dialed the phone only to put the receiver back on the hook, he has acted, but those acts have not caused harm. The theories of force, fright, compulsion, and dangerous condition are inapplicable, either alone or in combination, to the facts as described. The same result applies even where the defendant has moved the plaintiff's body. It is true that there is a technical trespass in that case, but unless it could be shown that the plaintiff was worse off afterward because he was moved, the causation requirement has not been satisfied even if there was more than simple nonfeasance by the plaintiff.

Properly conceived, these situations should be discussed together with other forms of gratuitous undertakings and the obligations they generate. The common law has never found a home for such obligations. They should not be part of the law of tort because they do not satisfy the causation requirement; and the unfortunate doctrine of consideration prevents their easy inclusion in the law of contracts. But even though the obligations attached to gratuitous undertakings stand in need of systematic examination, it is still in general the case that a defendant should not be compelled to complete a gratuitous undertaking against his will even where he has made an express promise to do so. And that result applies even if the defendant has taken steps to discharge his promise. A bare promise to pay $1000 does not become enforceable simply because the plaintiff has written a check for that amount; delivery is still required. Nor does the payment of $100 as the first of ten gratuitous installments obligate the donor to pay the other $900. In the case just put where the plaintiff is unconscious, there cannot of course be any question of an express promise. But it is only appropriate to hold that once a defendant begins to help a plaintiff in distress, he should be in no worse a position than a defendant who had made an express promise to assist. Even if the defendant has been of a partial assistance to the plaintiff, that does not of itself obligate the defendant to provide him with still further benefits. It follows that the defendant can discontinue his efforts at will and escape all liability unless he has caused harm to the plaintiff in one of the senses developed above.[104]

The common law position on the good Samaritan question does not appeal to our highest sense of benevolence and charity, and it is not at all surprising that there have been many proposals for its alteration or abolition. Let us here examine but one of these proposals. After concluding that the then (1908) current position of the law led to intolerable results, James Barr Ames argued that the appropriate rule should be that:

> One who fails to interfere to save another from impending death or great bodily harm, when he might do so with little or no inconvenience to himself, and the death or great bodily harm follows as a consequence of his inaction, shall be punished criminally and shall make compensation to the party injured or to his widow and children in case of death.[109]

. . . Under Ames' good Samaritan rule, a defendant in cases of affirmative acts would be required to take only those steps that can be done "with little or no inconvenience." But if the distinction between causing harm and not preventing harm is to be disregarded, why should the difference in standards between the two cases survive the reform of the law? The only explanation is that the two situations are regarded at bottom as raising totally different issues, even for those who insist upon the immateriality of this distinction. Even those who argue, as Ames does, that the law is utilitarian must in the end find some special place for the claims of egoism which are an inseparable byproduct of the belief that individual autonomy—individual liberty—is a good in itself not explainable in terms of its purported social worth. It is one thing to *allow* people to act as they please in the belief that the "invisible hand" will provide the happy congruence of the individual and the social good. Such a theory, however, at bottom must regard individual autonomy as but a means to some social end. It takes a great deal more to assert that men are *entitled* to act as they choose (within the limits of strict liability) even though it is certain that there will be cases where individual welfare will be in conflict with the social good.[110] Only then is it clear that even freedom has its costs: costs revealed in the acceptance of the good Samaritan doctrine.

But are the alternatives more attractive? Once one decides that as a matter of statutory or common law duty, an individual is required under some circumstances to act at his own cost for the exclusive benefit of another, then it is very hard to set out in a principled manner the limits of social interference with individual liberty. Suppose one claims, as Ames does, that his proposed rule applies only in the "obvious" cases where everyone (or almost everyone) would admit that the duty was appropriate: to the case of the man upon the bridge who refuses to throw a rope to a stranger drowning in the waters below. Even if the rule starts out with such modest ambitions, it is difficult to confine it to those limits. Take a simple case first. X as a representative of a private charity asks you for $10 in order to save the life of some starving child in a country ravaged by war. There are other donors available but the number of needy children exceeds that number. The money means "nothing" to you. Are you under a legal obligation to give the $10? Or to lend it interest-free? Does $10 amount to a substantial cost or inconvenience within the meaning of Ames' rule? It is true that the relationship between the gift to charity and the survival of an unidentified child is not so apparent as is the relationship between the man upon the bridge and the swimmer caught in the swirling seas. But lest the physical imagery govern, it is clear in both cases that someone will die as a consequence of your inaction in both cases. Is there a duty to give, or is the contribution a matter of charity?

Consider yet another example where services, not cash, are in issue. Ames insists that his rule would not require the only surgeon in India capable of saving the life of a person with a given affliction to travel across the sub-continent to perform an operation, presumably because the inconvenience and cost would be substantial. But how would he treat the case if some third person were willing to pay him for all of his efforts? If the payment is sufficient to induce the surgeon to act, then there is no need for the good Samaritan doctrine at all. But if it is not, then it is again necessary to compare the costs of the physician with the benefits to his prospective patient. It is hard to know whether Ames would require the forced exchange under these circumstances. But it is at least arguable that under his theory forced exchanges should be required, since the payment might reduce the surgeon's net inconvenience to the point where it was trivial.

Once forced exchanges, regardless of the levels of payment, are accepted, it will no longer be possible to delineate the sphere of activities in which contracts (or charity) will be required in order to procure desired benefits and the sphere of activity in which those benefits can be procured as of right. Where tests of "reasonableness"—stated with such confidence, and applied with such difficulty—dominate the law of tort, it becomes impossible to tell where liberty ends and obligation begins; where contract ends, and tort begins. In each case, it will be possible for some judge or jury to decide that there was something else which the defendant should have done, and he will decide that on the strength of some cost-benefit formula that is difficult indeed to apply. These remarks are conclusive, I think, against the adoption of Ames' rule by judicial innovation, and they bear heavily on the desirability of the abandonment of the good Samaritan rule by legislation as well. It is not surprising that the law has, in the midst of all the clamor for reform, remained unmoved in the end, given the inability to form alternatives to the current position.

But the defense of the common law rule on the good Samaritan does not rest solely upon a criticism of its alternatives. Strong arguments can be advanced to show that the common law position on the good Samaritan problem is in the end consistent with both moral and economic principles.

The history of Western ethics has been marked by the development of two lines of belief. One line of moral thought emphasizes the importance of freedom of the will. It is the intention (or motive) that determines the worth of the act; and no act can be moral unless it is performed free from external compulsion. Hence the expansion of the scope of positive law could only reduce the moral worth of human action. Even if positive law could insure conformity to the appropriate external standards of conduct, it, like other forms of external constraints, destroys the moral worth of the act. Hence the elimination of the positive law becomes a minimum condition for moral conduct, even if it means that persons entitled to benefits (in accordance with some theory of entitlements respected but not enforced) will not receive them if their fellow men are immoral.

On the other hand there are those theories that concern themselves not with the freedom of the will, but with the external effects of individual behavior. There is no room for error, because each act which does not further the stated goals (usually, of the maximization of welfare) is in terms of these theories a bad act. Thus a system of laws must either require the individual to act, regardless of motive, in the socially desired manner, or create incentives for him to so behave. Acceptance of this kind of theory has as its corollary the acceptance, if necessary, of an elaborate system of legal rules to insure compliance with the stated goals of maximization even if individual liberty (which now only counts as a kind of satisfaction) is sacrificed in the effort.

At a common sense level, neither of these views is accepted in its pure form. The strength of each theory lays bare the weaknesses of the other. Preoccupation with the moral freedom of a given actor ignores the effects of his conduct upon other persons. Undue emphasis upon the conformity to external standards of behavior entails a loss of liberty. Hence, most systems of conventional morality try to distinguish between those circumstances in which a person should be compelled to act for the benefit of his fellow man, and those cases where he should be allowed to do so only if prompted by the appropriate motives. To put the point in other terms, the distinction is taken between that conduct which is required and that which, so to speak, is beyond the call of duty. If that distinction is accepted as part of a common morality, then the argument in favor of the good Samaritan rule is that it, better than any possible alternatives, serves to mark off the first class of activities from the second. Compensation for harm caused can be demanded in accordance with the principles of strict liability. Failure to aid those in need can invoke at most moral censure on the ground that the person so accused did not voluntarily conform his conduct to some "universal" principle of justice. The rules of causation, which create liability in the first case, deny it in the second. It may well be that the conduct of individuals who do not aid fellow men is under some circumstances outrageous, but it does not follow that a legal system that does not enforce a duty to aid is outrageous as well.

The defense of the good Samaritan rule in economic terms takes the same qualified form. The cost–benefit analysis has in recent literature been regarded as the best means for the solution of all problems of social organization in those cases where market transactions are infeasible. On that view, the basic principles of economics become a most powerful instrument for the achievement of social justice. But there is another strand of economic thought—more skeptical in its conclusions—which emphasizes the limitations of economic theory for the solution of legal problems.

Most economics textbooks accept that the premises of economic theory do not permit so-called interpersonal comparisons of utility. Thus Kenneth Arrow states: "The viewpoint will be taken here that interpersonal comparison of utilities has no meaning and, in fact, that there is no meaning relevant to welfare comparisons in the measurability of individual utility."[114] In effect, all attempts to compare costs and benefits between different persons require in the end some noneconomic assumption to measure trade-offs in utility between them. Where no noneconomic assumptions are made, it follows that, in strict theory, an economist can make utility comparisons between alternative social arrangements only under a very restricted set of conditions. One social arrangement can be pronounced superior to a second alternative only if (1) it can be shown that everybody is at least as well off under the first alternative as he is under the second, and (2) at least one person is better off under the first system than he is under the second. If these conditions are respected, then no strictly economic judgment can be made between alternative social states where one person under the allegedly preferred state is worse off than he is under the next best alternative. Yet it is precisely that kind of situation that is involved whenever there is a legal dispute. In economic terms, the resolution of every dispute requires a trade-off between the parties, for no one has yet found a way in which both parties could win a lawsuit. In order to decide the case of the good Samaritan, therefore, we must make the very kind of interpersonal comparisons of utility which economic theory cannot make in its own terms.

There is one possible escape from this problem. It could be argued that the defendant should be held liable because if the parties had the opportunity to contract between themselves, they doubtless would have agreed that the defendant should assume the obligation to save the plaintiff in his time of distress. Thus one could argue that (in the absence of externalities) an agreement between two persons can only have favorable welfare effects since each person will be better off on account of the voluntary exchange. On this view the function of the law of tort is to anticipate those contractual arrangements which parties would have made had the transactions costs been low enough to permit direct negotiations.

This position, however, is subject to objections. The courts have struggled for years to determine the content of incomplete and ambiguous contracts which were actually negotiated by the parties. There at least they could look to, among other things, the language of the relevant documents, the custom of the trade, and the history of the prior negotiations. In the good Samaritan context, there are no documents, no customs, and no prior negotiations. The courts have only the observation that the parties would have contracted to advance their mutual interests. Given the infinite variation in terms (what price? what services?) that we could expect to find in such contracts, it is difficult to believe that that theoretical observation could enable us to determine or even approximate any bargain which the parties might have made if circumstances had permitted. It is for good reason that the courts have always refused to make contracts for the parties.

But there is a further point. We are concerned with the enforcement of a contract by private action when one of the parties objects to its performance. It no longer seems possible to argue that both parties are better off on account of the contract since one party has indicated his desire to repudiate it. Even though the theory of the underlying action is shifted from tort to some extended form of contract, the difficulties raised by the rule that forbids interpersonal comparison of utilities still remain. At the time of the enforcement, one party argues not for an *exchange* which makes both parties better off, but for a *transfer* of wealth which makes him better off. Again we must find some way—some theory of fairness—which can explain which of them is to be made better off. Welfare economics cannot provide the answer because it cannot accommodate the trade-offs which are part and parcel of legal decisions.

Even after these arguments are made many people will be concerned with the social costs of a system of rules which does not purport to have an economic base. But in a social sense it should be clear that people will act in a manner to minimize their losses, regardless of the legal rules adopted. Once people know that others are not obliged to assist them in their time of peril, they will on their own take steps to keep from being placed in a position where they will need assistance where none may be had. These precautions may not eliminate losses in the individual case, but they should reduce the number of cases in which such losses should occur.

In addition, the incentive effects created by the absence of a good Samaritan rule must be examined in the context of other rules of substantive law. Thus it is critical to ask about the incentives which are created by rules which permit a rescuer to bring an action against the person he saved on quasi-contractual theories. It is also important to ask what modifications of behavior could be expected if the scope of this kind of action were expanded, and important, too, to know about the possible effects of systems of public honors and awards for good Samaritans. None of these arguments is designed to show that the common law approach can be justified on economic grounds, but they do show how perilous it is to attempt to justify legal rules by the incentives that they create. . . .

But it is a mistake to dwell too long upon questions of cost, for they should not be decisive in the analysis of the individual cases. Instead it is better to see the law of torts in terms of what might be called its political function. The arguments made here suggest that the first task of the law of torts is to define the boundaries of individual liberty. To this question the rules of strict liability based upon the twin notions of causation and volition provide a better answer than the alternative theories based upon the notion of negligence, whether explicated in moral or economic terms. In effect, the principles of strict liability say that the liberty of one person ends when he causes harm to another. Until that point he is free to act as he chooses, and need not take into account the welfare of others.

But the law of tort does not end with the recognition of individual liberty. Once a man

causes harm to another, he has brought himself within the boundaries of the law of tort. It does not follow, however, that he will be held liable in each and every case in which it can be showed that he caused harm, for it may still be possible for him to escape liability, not by an insistence upon his freedom of action, but upon a specific showing that his conduct was either excused or justified. Thus far in this paper we have only made occasional and unsystematic references to the problems raised by both pleas of excuse and justification. Their systematic explication remains crucial to the further development of the law of tort. That task, however, is large enough to deserve special attention of its own.

NOTES

[91]I put aside here all those cases in which there are special relationships between the plaintiff and the defendants: parent and child, invitor and invitee, and the like.

[92]Blyth v. Birmingham Waterworks, 11 Exch. 781, 784, 156 Eng. Rep. 1047, 1049 (1856) (emphasis added).

[104]The hardest case of this sort arises where the defendant places the plaintiff in a position where he is no longer able to get help from others who might wish to aid him. Under those circumstances it is proper to hold the defendant liable, even though it is difficult to establish whether the help from some third party would indeed be forthcoming. See Zelenko v. Gimbel Bros., 158 Misc. 904, 287 N.Y. S. 134 (Sup. Ct. 1935). "Defendant *segregated* this plaintiff's intestate where such aid could not be given and then left her alone." *Id.* at 905, 287 N.Y.S. 135 (emphasis added). *The act requirement is satisfied in this statement of the cause of action.*

[109]James Barr Ames, ["Law and Morals," 22 Harv. L.R. 97 (1908)] at 113. . . .

[110]"Each person possesses an inviolability founded on justice that even the welfare of society as a whole cannot override. For this reason justice denies that the loss of freedom for some is made right by a greater good shared by others. It does not allow that the sacrifices imposed on a few are outweighed by the larger sum of advantages enjoyed by many." John Rawls, *A Theory of Justice* 3–4 (1971).

[114]Kenneth Arrow, *Social Choice and Individual Values* 9 (2d ed. 1963).

QUESTIONS FOR DISCUSSION

1. According to Epstein, what exactly is the common law position on good and bad samaritans?

2. An apparent exception to the common law position discussed by Epstein is a case where "A sees B lying unconscious on the public street. . . . [H]e picks B up and places him in an automobile, only to return him to his original position on the sidewalk when he thinks, for whatever reason, better of the involvement." (p. 828) Should A be penalized at all in this case, according to Epstein? Why or why not? How would Epstein's opponents criticize his position? How could he best respond?

3. What kinds of arguments does Epstein use against alternatives to the common law position on bad samaritans? How could his opponents best respond?

4. Explain how Epstein uses freedom of the will to argue for the common law position. Do you agree with his argument? Why or why not?

5. Explain how Epstein uses economics to argue for the common law position. Do you agree with his argument? Why or why not?

THE CASE FOR A DUTY TO RESCUE

ERNEST J. WEINRIB

IV. PHILOSOPHICAL FOUNDATIONS FOR A DUTY OF EASY RESCUE

. . . [This] section of the article puts forth arguments for the adoption of [a legal duty of easy rescue]. To this end, the section attempts to give philosophical specificity to the moral sentiment that condemns a failure to effect an easy rescue. Attention is devoted to the two traditions of moral philosophy represented by Kant and by Bentham, for those traditions have dominated efforts of the last two centuries to explicate and systematize our moral notions. If the law is to be "the witness and external deposit of our moral life,"[122] the demonstration that both traditions provide support for a duty of easy rescue implies that the absence of a duty to rescue at common law is an aberration that should be corrected.

Consideration of the utilitarian approach towards rescue must begin with Jeremy Bentham's thought on the problem. "[I]n cases where the person is in danger," he asked, "why should it not be made the duty of every man to save another from mischief, when it can be done without prejudicing himself . . . ?"[123] Bentham supported the implicit answer to this question with several illustrations: using water at hand to quench a fire in a woman's head-

Ernest J. Weinrib, "The Case for a Duty to Rescue," *Yale Law Journal*, vol. 90 (1980)

dress; moving a sleeping drunk whose face is in a puddle; warning a person about to carry a lighted candle into a room strewn with gunpowder. Bentham clearly had in mind a legal duty that would be triggered by the combination of the victim's emergency and the absence of inconvenience to the rescuer—that is, by the features of most of the proposed reforms requiring rescue. Unfortunately, the rhetorical question was the whole of Bentham's argument for his position. With this question, Bentham appealed directly to his reader's moral intuition; he did not show how his proposed duty can be derived through his distinctive felicific calculus.

Can one supply the Benthamite justification that Bentham himself omitted? Because the avoidance of injury or death obviously contributes to the greatest happiness of the greatest number, the difficulties revolve not around the basic requirement of rescue but around the limitations placed upon that requirement by the notions of emergency and absence of inconvenience. Those limitations have no parallel with respect to participation in putting others at risk; they apply only in cases of nonfeasance. Indeed, Bentham's comments come in a section of his *Introduction to the Principles of Morals and Legislation* that distinguishes beneficence (increasing another's happiness) from probity (forbearing to diminish another's happiness). Yet Bentham had earlier contended that the distinction between acts of omission and acts of commission was of no significance. The utilitarian's only concern is that an individual bring about a situation that results in a higher surplus of pleasure over pain than would any of the alternative situations that his actions could produce. Consequences are important; how they are reached is not. The distinction between nonfeasance and misfeasance has no place in this theory, and neither would the rescue duty's emergency or convenience limitations, which apply only after that distinction is made.

One solution to the apparent inconsistency between the rescue limitations and Benthamite theory's regard only for consequences is to drop the conditions of emergency and convenience as limitations on the duty to rescue. The position could be taken that there is an obligation to rescue whenever rescuing would result in greater net happiness than not rescuing. This principle, it is important to observe, cannot really be a principle about rescuing as that concept is generally understood. As a matter of common usage, a rescue presupposes the existence of an emergency, of a predicament that poses danger of greater magnitude and imminence than one ordinarily encounters. The proposed principle, however, requires no emergency to trigger a duty to act. The principle, in fact, is one of beneficence, not rescue, and should be formulated more generally to require providing aid whenever it will yield greater net happiness than not providing aid.

Eliminating the limitations regarding emergency and convenience might transform a requirement of rescue conceived along utilitarian lines into a requirement of perfect and general altruism. This demand of perfect altruism would be undesirable for several reasons. First, it would encourage the obnoxious character known to the law as the officious intermeddler. Also, its imposition of a duty of continual saintliness and heroism is unrealistic. Moreover, it would overwhelm the relationships founded on friendship and love as well as the distinction between the praiseworthy and the required; it would thereby obscure some efficient ways, in the utilitarian's eyes, of organizing and stimulating beneficence. Finally, and most fundamentally, it would be self-defeating. The requirement of aid assumes that there is some other person who has at least a minimal core of personhood as well as projects of his own that the altruist can further. In a society of perfect and general altruism, however, any potential recipient of aid would himself be an altruist, who must, accordingly, subordinate the pursuit of his own projects to the rendering of aid to others. No one could claim for his own projects the priority that would provide others with a stable object of their altruistic ministrations. Each person would continually find himself obligated to attempt to embrace a phantom.

Although the utilitarian principle that requires the provision of aid whenever it will result in greater net happiness than failure to aid easily slips into the pure–altruism duty, it need not lead to so extreme a position. The obvious alternative interpretation of the principle is that aid is not obligatory whenever the costs to one's own projects outweigh the benefits to the recipient's. This interpretation avoids the embracing–of–phantoms objection to pure altruism, but it is subject to all the other criticisms of the purer theory. Because the cost–benefit calculus is so difficult to perform in particular instances, the duty would remain ill–defined. In many cases, therefore, it would encourage the officious intermeddler, seem unrealistically to require saintliness, overwhelm friendship and love, and obliterate the distinction between the praiseworthy and the required. Moreover, the vagueness of the duty would lead many individuals unhappily and inefficiently to drop their own projects in preference for those of others.

A different formulation of the rescue duty is needed to harness and temper the utilitarian impulses toward altruism and to direct them more precisely toward an intelligible goal. One important weakness of a too–generally beneficent utilitarianism is that it tempts one to consider only the immediate consequences of particular acts, and not the longer term consequences, the most important of which are the expectations generated that such acts will continue. If, as the classical utilitarians believed, the general happiness is advanced when people engage in productive activities that are of value to others, the harm done by a duty of general beneficence, in either version discussed above, would override its specific benefits. The deadening of industry resulting from both reliance on beneficence and devotion to beneficence would in the long run be an evil greater than the countenancing of individual instances of unfulfilled needs or wants. "In all cases of helping," wrote John Stuart Mill, in a passage concerned only with the reliance costs,

there are two sets of consequences to be considered: the consequences of the assistance and the consequences of relying on the assistance. The former are generally beneficial, but the latter, for the most part, injurious. . . . There are few things for which it is more mischievous that people should rely on the habitual aid of others than for the means of subsistence, and unhappily there is no lesson which they more easily learn.[132]

Utilitarianism can use the notion of reliance to restrict the requirement of beneficence. If an act of beneficence would tend to induce reliance on similar acts, it should be avoided. If the act of beneficence does not have this tendency, it should be performed as long as the benefit produced is greater than the cost of performance. In the latter case, there are no harmful effects on industry flowing from excessive reliance to outweigh the specific benefits. This rule can account for Bentham's restriction of the duty to rescue to situations of emergency. People do not regularly expose themselves to extraordinary dangers in reliance on the relief that may be available if the emergency materializes, and only a fool would deliberately court a peril because he or others had previously been rescued from a similar one. As Sidgwick put it, an emergency rescue "will have no bad effect on the receiver, from the exceptional nature of the emergency."[133] Furthermore, an emergency is not only a desperate situation; it is also a situation that deviates from society's usual pattern. The relief of an emergency is therefore unlikely to induce reliance on the assistance of others in normal conditions. The abnormality of emergencies also means that rescuers can confidently pursue their own projects under normal circumstances. The motive for industry that Bentham located in each person's needs is not undermined by extraordinary and isolated events.

The role of emergency in the utilitarian obligation to rescue corresponds to, and illuminates, the definition of a legal duty to rescue by reference to the absence of contract values. Utilitarian philosophy and the concept of the market are closely related. Both regard individuals as maximizers of their own happiness, and both see the use of contracts to acquire and to exchange property as conducive to the public good. Contract law's refusal to enforce certain transactions sets them apart from the usual structure of relationships, in which the satisfaction of the parties' needs and desires can legitimately serve as a stimulus to exchange. The person who sees a member of his own family in difficulty and the police officer who notices a hazard on the highway may not act as ordinary members of the market with respect to those endangered. Those pockets of contractual nonenforcement are sufficiently isolated that they are unlikely to be generalized: they will not generate a widespread reliance on assistance or sense of obligation to assist in settings where market exchanges are permitted and common.

An emergency is similar. Contract values are absent in such a situation because the assistance required is of such a kind that it cannot be purchased on ordinary commercial terms. Suspension of contract values in an emergency will not result in a general deadening of individual industry; the utilitarian can therefore confine his calculus to the specific consequences of the rescue. The denial of relief to the Southwark squatters[135] is a case in point. The desperate situation there was a consequence of poverty and not an extraordinary condition that deviated from the ordinary pattern of contemporary existence. The utilitarian must be concerned in that situation that judicially coercing individual assistance to the poor will generate a reliance whose harmful effects will, in the long run and across society as a whole, outweigh the benefits of the specific assistance.

Bentham's intuitive restriction of beneficence to situations of emergency can thus be supported on utilitarian grounds. Is the same true of the inconvenience limitation? As with the emergency restriction, finding utilitarian support requires looking behind the specific

action to its social and legal context. For the utilitarian, the enforcement of a duty through legal sanctions is always an evil, which can be justified only to avoid a greater evil. If the sanction is applied, the offender suffers the pain of punishment. If the prospect of the sanction is sufficient to deter conduct, those deterred suffer the detriment of frustrated preferences. Moreover, the apparatus of enforcement siphons off social resources from other projects promoting the general happiness.

Accordingly, a utilitarian will be restrained and circumspect in the elaboration of legal duties. In particular, he will not pitch a standard of behavior at too high a level: the higher the standard, the more onerous it will be to the person subjected to it, the greater the pleasure that he must forego in adhering to it, and the greater his resistance to its demands. A high standard entails both more severe punishment and a more elaborate apparatus of detection and enforcement. Applied to the rescue situation, this reasoning implies that some convenience restriction should be adopted as part of the duty. Compelling the rescuer to place himself in physical danger, for instance, would be inefficacious, to use Bentham's terminology, because such coercion cannot influence the will: "the evil, which he sees himself about to undergo . . . is so great that the evil denounced by the penal clause . . . cannot appear greater."[136] Limiting the duty of rescue to emergency situations where the rescue will not inconvenience the rescuer—as judicial decisions would elaborate that limitation and thus give direction to individuals—minimizes both the interference with the rescuer's own preferences and the difficulties of enforcement that would result from recalcitrance. Bentham's second limitation can thus also be supported on a utilitarian basis.

The utilitarian arguments for the duty to rescue and for the limitations on that duty rest primarily on administrative considerations. The arguments focus not so much on the parties and their duties as persons as on the difficulties that might be created throughout the whole range of societal interactions. The elements of the duty are evaluated in terms of their likely consequences, no matter how remote. In the convenience limitation, for instance, whether the rescuer *ought* to feel aggrieved at the requirements of a high standard is of no concern. The likelihood that he *will* feel aggrieved is all that matters: for the Benthamite utilitarian, general happiness is the criterion of evaluation and not itself an object of evaluation. Moreover, recalcitrance necessitates more costly enforcement, and that consequence must also enter the calculus. The same is true for the emergency limitation. The argument for that limitation focused on the possibility that a particular instance of assistance would, by example, induce socially detrimental general reliance or beneficence. This use of example does not explore either the fairness of singling out particular persons for particular treatment or the consistency and scope of certain principles. Rather, the argument examines the cumulative consequences of repetition, and decides whether a particular person should perform a particular act on the basis of the act's implications for the entire society's market arrangements.

At least one philosopher has argued that administrative considerations of this sort are not moral ones at all, or that they are moral only in a derivative sense. In this view, the administrative and enforcement considerations on which the utilitarian account of rescue rests are irrelevant to the individual's obligations as a moral agent. The individual should ask what he ought to do, not how others can compel him to fulfill his duty. The merit of this view is its observation that any utilitarian version of a duty to rescue has nuances that do not ring true to the moral contours of the situation. The person in need of rescue stands in danger of serious physical injury or loss of life, harms not quite comparable by any quantitative measure to other losses of happiness. Health and life are not merely components of the aggregate of goods that an individual enjoys. Rather, they are constitutive of the individual, who partakes of them

in a unique and intimate way; they are the preconditions for the enjoyment of other goods. Moreover, there is something false in viewing an act of rescue as a contribution to the greatest happiness of the greatest number. If there is an obligation to rescue, it is owed to particular persons rather than to the greatest number. Any such duty would require the rescuing not only of the eminent heart surgeon but also of the hermit bachelor; and even the duty to rescue the heart surgeon would be owed primarily to him, not to his present or prospective patients.

Because the utilitarian account of rescue thus appears to lack an important moral ingredient, and because utilitarianism is not the law's only important philosophical tradition, it is worth attempting to outline a non-utilitarian version of the obligation to rescue. Although the two approaches support the same conclusion, the arguments are different in texture. In particular, the non-utilitarian argument recognizes the distinctive importance of avoiding physical injury or death; it resists the assimilation of health and life to other goods. This attention to the centrality of the person avoids the utilitarian dilemma of either demanding excessive beneficence or having recourse to administrative considerations, which shifts the focus away from the rescuer's obligation to a particular endangered individual. In the non-utilitarian argument, of course, administrative considerations are not ignored; to do so would be impossible in elaborating an argument that attempts to provide an ethical foundation for a judicially enforced duty to rescue. Nonetheless, the non-utilitarian's use of administrative considerations differs from the utilitarian's. The utilitarian weaves the fabric of the duty to rescue out of administrative strands; the cost of administration and enforcement are relevant to the very existence of the duty. The non-utilitarian, by contrast, justifies a legal duty to rescue independently of the administrative costs; the mechanisms of enforcement are invoked only to structure and to coordinate the operation of the duty.

The deontological argument begins with the observation that the idea of an individual's being under a moral duty is intimately related to the notion that health and life are of distinctive importance. The concept of duty applies only to an individual endowed with the capacity to make choices and to set ends for himself. Further, the person, as a purposive and choosing entity, does not merely set physical integrity as one of his ends; he requires it as a precondition to the accomplishment of the purposes that his freedom gives him the power to set. As Kant put it, physical integrity is "the basic *stuff* (the matter) in man without which he could not realize his ends."[144]

A person contemplating the ethical exercise of his freedom of action must impose certain restrictions on that freedom. Because morality is something he shares with all humanity, he cannot claim a preferred moral position for himself. Any moral claim he makes must, by its very nature as a moral claim, be one to which he is subject when others can assert it. Acting on the basis of his own personhood therefore demands recognition of the personhood of others. This recognition, however, cannot be elaborated in the first instance in terms of the enjoyment of ordinary material goods. Because no conception of happiness is shared by everyone and is constant throughout any individual's life, the universal concept of personhood cannot be reflected in a system of moral duties directed at the satisfaction of unstable desires for such goods. Physical integrity, by contrast, is necessary for the accomplishment of any human aim, and so is an appropriate subject for a system of mutually restraining duties.

An individual contemplating his actions from a moral point of view must recognize that all others form their projects on a substratum of physical integrity. If he claims the freedom to pursue his projects as a moral right, he cannot as a rational and moral agent deny to others the same freedom. Because his claim to that freedom implies a right to the physical integrity that is necessary to its exercise, he must concede to others the right to physical integrity that he implicitly and inevitably claims for himself.

This conception of the right to life and health derives from the notion of personhood that is presupposed by the concept of moral action. So too do the right's natural limitations. The duty of beneficence exacted by this right need not collapse into a comprehensive and self-defeating altruism. Respect for another's physical security does not entail foregoing one's own.[148] The right to life and health, seen to give content to the universal concept of personhood, must be ascribed not only to others, but also to oneself. As Kant put it,

> since all *other* men with the exception of myself would not be *all* men, and the maxim would then not have the universality of a law, as it must have in order to be obligatory, the law prescribing the duty of benevolence will include myself, as the object of benevolence, in the command of practical reason.[149]

Moreover, the universalizing process radiates outward from the actor: it is only one's desire to act that makes necessary the exploration of the action's implicit claims and thus of the rights that he must rationally concede to others. The priority of the actor is thus embedded in the structure of the argument and should be reflected in the concrete duties that the argument yields.

This outline of deontological analysis can be applied to examine the standard suggestion that the common law should recognize a duty to effect an easy rescue. Such a duty would be the judicial analogue of the moral obligation to respect the person of another and to safeguard his physical integrity, which is necessary for whatever aims he chooses to pursue. The emergency and convenience limitations also fit quite readily into the analysis. An emergency is a particularly imminent threat to physical security, and the convenience limitation reflects the rescuer's entitlement to the priority of his own physical security over that of the endangered person. Although the proposed legal duty fits comfortably within the deontological moral duty of beneficence, however, the two are not coextensive. Emergencies are not the only circumstances in which life and health are threatened; disease, starvation, and poverty can affect the physical substratum of personhood on a routine basis. If legal duties must reflect moral ones, should not a legal duty to rescue be supplemented by a legal duty to alleviate those less isolated abridgments of physical security?

The convenience limitation on the rescue duty might similarly be loosened in a deontological analysis. One tempting extension would be very far-reaching: if the physical substratum is the "basic *stuff* (the matter) in man without which he could not realize his ends,"[151] and if we are under a duty to safeguard that substratum in others as in ourselves, the priority that the rescuer can legitimately grant to himself can be only with respect to his physical integrity. Under this extension, a rescuer could—indeed would be obligated to—abstain from acting only if the act would place him in physical danger; if it would not put him in danger, he would be required to attempt a rescue, no matter what the disruption of his life. In Macaulay's famous example, the surgeon would have to travel from Calcutta to Meerut to perform an operation that only he could perform, because the journey, though inconvenient, would not be dangerous. Indeed, he would have to make the trip even if he were about to leave for Europe or to greet members of his family arriving on an incoming ship. The patient's right to physical security would rank ahead of the satisfaction of the surgeon's contingent desires.

The deontological approach to rescue does not compel such a drastic extension. Although every moral person must value physical integrity, its protection is not an end in itself. Rather, physical security is valued because it allows individuals to realize their own projects and purposes. Whatever the reach of the right to physical integrity, therefore, it must allow the rescuer to satisfy his purposes in a reason-

ably coherent way. Still, though the extension of the moral duty cannot be so drastic as to require the sacrifice of all of a person's projects, it can be substantial. It can require the rescuer to undergo considerable inconvenience short of fundamental changes in the fabric of his life. The deontological duty relaxes both the emergency and convenience limitations of the duty of easy rescue in emergencies: it applies not only in emergencies but whenever physical integrity is threatened, and it applies even when the rescuer might have to undergo considerable inconveniences. The duty might, after all, obligate Macaulay's surgeon to travel from Calcutta to Meerut. Would it also require the wealthy to use at least some of their resources to alleviate the plight of the starving and the afflicted? For those concerned about the possibility of setting principled limits to a duty of rescue, the question is critical.

The objection to an affirmative answer to the question rests on the premises that even the wealthy are under no obligation to be charitable and that the afflicted have no right to receive charity. Under the deontological theory, those premises are incorrect. The duty of beneficence derives from the concept of personhood; it is therefore not properly called charity, for the benefactor's performance of this duty is no reason for self-congratulation. Although the duty is an imperfect one—"since no determinate limits can be assigned to what should be done, the duty has in it a play-room for doing more or less,"[156] as Kant said—it is nonetheless a duty to the performance of which the recipient is entitled.

The extent of the duty of beneficence, of course, can still be troubling. It is the indeterminateness of the duty, the "play-room," that is particularly relevant to this problem. Kant meant by this expression that the form and the amount of the benefaction would vary, depending on the resources of the benefactor, the identity of the recipient, and the recipient's own conception of happiness. The indeterminateness, however, applies not only to the form of the benefaction but also to the linking of particular benefactors to particular beneficiaries. Why should any particular person be singled out of the whole group of potential benefactors, and why should the benefit be conferred on one rather than another person in need? If a duty "may be *exacted* from a person, as one exacts a debt,"[158] it is a debt that leaves unclear the precise terms of discharge as well as the identities of obligor and obligee.

The proper response to this indeterminacy is not to deny that there is a duty. What is required is to set up social institutions to perform the necessary tasks of coordination and determination. Those institutions would ensure that no person is singled out unfairly either for burdens or for benefits, and that the forms of benefaction correlate both with the resources of those who give and with the needs of those who receive. In fact, all Western democracies undertake to perform this task through programs for social assistance. The institutions they establish, however, are primarily legislative and administrative; precisely because a general duty of beneficence is imperfect, it cannot be judicially enforced. The traditional claim–settling function of courts does not permit the transfer of a resource from one person to another solely because the former has it and the latter needs it. Such judicial action would unfairly prefer one needy person over others and unfairly burden one resourceful person over others. Because the duty of beneficence is general and indeterminate, it does not, in the absence of legislative action that specifies and coordinates, yield judicially enforceable moral claims by individuals against others.

The significant characteristic of the emergency and convenience limitations is that, in combination, they eliminate the "play–room" inherent in the duty of beneficence, thus providing a principled response to Kant and to Epstein and rendering the narrower duty to rescue appropriate for judicial enforcement. An emergency marks a particular person as physically endangered in a way that is not general or routine throughout the society. An imminent peril cannot await assistance from the appropriate social institutions. The provision of aid to an emergency victim does not deplete the social resources committed to the alleviation of more routine threats to physical integrity. Moreover, aid in such circumstances presents no unfairness problems in singling out a particular person to receive the aid. Similarly, emergency aid does not unfairly single out one of a class of routinely advantaged persons; the rescuer just happens to find himself for a short period in a position, which few if any others share, to render a service to some specific person. In addition, when a rescue can be accomplished without a significant disruption of his own projects, the rescuer's freedom to realize his own ends is not abridged by the duty to preserve the physical security of another. In sum, when there is an emergency that the rescuer can alleviate with no inconvenience to himself, the general duty of beneficence that is suspended over society like a floating charge is temporarily revealed to identify a particular obligor and obligee, and to define obligations that are specific enough for judicial enforcement. . . .

NOTES

[122]Holmes, *The Path of the Law* 10 Harv. L. Rev. 457, 459 (1897).

[125]J. Bentham, [*Introduction to the Principles of Morals and Legislation*] at 293; *see* J. Bentham, *The Principles of Legislation* 85–86 (R. Hildreth ed. 1840).

[132]J. S. Mill, *The Principles of Political Economy* 967 (W. Ashley ed. 1923).

[133]H. Sidgwick, [*The Methods of Ethics* (7th ed. 1907)] at 437.

[135]London Borough of Southwark v. Williams, [1971] 2 All E.R. 175 (C.A.).

[136]J. Bentham [*Introduction to the Principles of Morals and Legislation*] at 162 (footnote omitted).

[144]J. Kant, [*The Metaphysical Principles of Virtue* (M. Gregor trans. 1964)], at 112.

[148]*See* I. Kant, *supra* note 144, at 53, 122.

[149]*Id.* at 118.

[151]I. Kant, *supra* note 144, at 112.

[156]*See* I. Kant, *supra* note 144, at 121.

[158]J.S. Mill, [*Utilitarianism* (1888)], at 232–33.

QUESTIONS FOR DISCUSSION

1. What is the best way for a utilitarian to argue for a duty to rescue, according to Weinrib? Do you find this argument persuasive? Why or why not?

2. What is the best way for a Kantian to argue for a duty to rescue, according to Weinrib? Do you find this argument persuasive? Why or why not?

3. How would Epstein criticize Weinrib's arguments? How could Weinrib best respond?

4. Does Weinrib's argument depend on any objectionable kind of legal moralism? (See Section 4.2.) Why or why not?

FARWELL V. KEATON

240 N.W. 2d 217 (Mich. 1976)

LEVIN, Justice.

On the evening of August 26, 1966, Siegrist and Farwell drove to a trailer rental lot to return an automobile which Siegrist had borrowed from a friend who worked there. While waiting for the friend to finish work, Siegrist and Farwell consumed some beer.

Two girls walked by the entrance to the lot. Siegrist and Farwell attempted to engage them in conversation; they left Farwell's car and followed the girls to a drive-in restaurant down the street.

The girls complained to their friends in the restaurant that they were being followed. Six boys [including Keaton] chased Siegrist and Farwell back to the lot. Siegrist escaped unharmed, but Farwell was severely beaten. Siegrist found Farwell underneath his automobile in the lot. Ice was applied to Farwell's head. Siegrist then drove Farwell around for approximately two hours, stopping at a number of drive-in restaurants. Farwell went to sleep in the back seat of his car. Around midnight Siegrist drove the car to the home of Farwell's grandparents, parked it in the driveway, unsuccessfully attempted to rouse Farwell, and left. Farwell's grandparents discovered him in the car the next morning and took him to the hospital. He died three days later of an epidural hematoma.

At trial, plaintiff [Farwell's father] contended that had Siegrist taken Farwell to the hospital, or had he notified someone of Farwell's condition and whereabouts, Farwell would not have died. A neurosurgeon testified that if a person in Farwell's condition is taken to a doctor before, or within half an hour after, consciousness is lost, there is an 85 to 88 per cent chance of survival. Plaintiff testified that Siegrist told him that he knew Farwell was badly injured and that he should have done something.

The jury returned a verdict for plaintiff and awarded $15,000 in damages. The Court of

Appeals reversed, finding that Siegrist had not assumed the duty of obtaining aid for Farwell and that he neither knew nor should have known of the need for medical treatment. . . .

Siegrist contends that he is not liable for failure to obtain medical assistance for Farwell because he had no duty to do so.

Courts have been slow to recognize a duty to render aid to a person in peril. Where such a duty has been found, it has been predicated upon the existence of a special relationship between the parties; in such a case, if defendant knew or should have known of the other person's peril, he is required to render reasonable care under all the circumstances. . . .

Farwell and Siegrist were companions on a social venture. Implicit in such a common undertaking is the understanding that one will render assistance to the other when he is in peril if he can do so without endangering himself. Siegrist knew or should have known when he left Farwell, who was badly beaten and unconscious, in the back seat of his car that no one would find him before morning. Under these circumstances, to say that Siegrist had no duty to obtain medical assistance or at least to notify someone of Farwell's condition and whereabouts would be "shocking to humanitarian considerations" and fly in the face of "the commonly accepted code of social conduct." "[C]ourts will find a duty where, in general, reasonable men would recognize it and agree that it exists."

Farwell and Siegrist were companions engaged in a common undertaking; there was a special relationship between the parties. Because Siegrist knew or should have known of the peril Farwell was in and could render assistance without endangering himself he had an affirmative duty to come to Farwell's aid.

FITZGERALD, Justice (dissenting).

The unfortunate death of Richard Farwell prompted this wrongful death action brought by his father against the defendant, David Siegrist, a friend who had accompanied Farwell during the evening in which the decedent received injuries which ultimately caused his death three days later. The question before us is whether the defendant, considering his relationship with the decedent and the activity they jointly experienced on the evening of August 26–27, 1966, by his conduct voluntarily or otherwise assumed, or should have assumed, the duty of rendering medical or other assistance to the deceased. We find that defendant had no obligation to assume, nor did he assume, such a duty. . . .

Defendant did not voluntarily assume the duty of caring for the decedent's safety. Nor did the circumstances which existed on the evening of August 26, 1966, impose such a duty. Testimony revealed that only a qualified physician would have reason to suspect that Farwell had suffered an injury which required immediate medical attention. The decedent never complained of pain and, in fact, had expressed a desire to retaliate against his attackers. Defendant's inability to arouse the decedent upon arriving at his grandparents' home does not permit us to infer, as does plaintiff, that defendant knew or should have known that the deceased was seriously injured. While it might have been more prudent for the defendant to insure that the decedent was safely in the house prior to leaving, we cannot say that defendant acted unreasonably in permitting Farwell to spend the night asleep in the back seat of his car.

The close relationship between defendant and the decedent is said to establish a legal duty upon defendant to obtain assistance for the decedent. No authority is cited for this proposition other than the public policy observation that the interest of society would be benefited if its members were required to assist one another. This is not the appropriate case to establish a standard of conduct requiring one to legally assume the duty of insuring the safety of another. Recognizing that legal commentaries have expressed moral outrage at those decisions which permit one to refuse aid to another whose life may be in peril, we cannot say that, considering the relationship between these two parties and the existing circumstances, defendant acted in an unreasonable manner.

Plaintiff believes that a legal duty to aid others should exist where such assistance greatly benefits society and only a reasonable burden is imposed upon those in a position to help. He contends further that the determination of the existence of a duty must rest with the jury where questions of foreseeability and the relationship of the parties are primary considerations.

It is clear that defendant's nonfeasance, or the "passive inaction or a failure to take steps to protect [the decedent] from harm" is urged as being the proximate cause of Farwell's death. We must reject plaintiff's proposition which elevates a moral obligation to the level of a legal duty where, as here, the facts within defendant's knowledge in no way indicated that immediate medical attention was necessary and the relationship between the parties imposes no affirmative duty to render assistance. . . . The posture of this case does not permit us to create a legal duty upon one to render assistance to another injured or imperiled party where the initial injury was not caused by the person upon whom the duty is sought to be imposed.

QUESTIONS FOR DISCUSSION

1. Do you think that Siegrist should be punished for failing to help Farwell? Should Siegrist be forced to pay civil damages? Why or why not?

2. If Farwell and Siegrist had not gone out together but had instead met at a bar only shortly before the attack, but everything else had happened just as in the real case, should Siegrist be forced to pay civil damages? Why or why not?

3. If Farwell had been hurt not by any person but by a tree limb that fell in the wind, should Siegrist be forced to pay civil damages? Why or why not?

4. If Farwell had not died but had suffered more as a result of not being brought quickly to a doctor, should Siegrist then be forced to pay civil damages for the extra suffering? Why or why not?

5. Several diseases leave people unable to survive for long without a bone marrow transplant. A bone marrow transplant is no guarantee of life or cure but will give these patients varying chances of survival. A bone marrow donor usually feels slight to moderate pain over a few days. If only one potential donor is available, should that person be physically forced to donate her bone marrow? If that person refuses to donate, should she be punished, fined, or civilly liable? Why or why not?[19]

6. If one person has good reason to believe that a second person is going to kill a third person, should the first person have a legal duty to warn the third person or the police? What if the first person is the second person's

[19]See *McFall* v. *Shimp* 10 Pa D & C 3rd 90 (Allegheny County Court, 1978) and *Curran* v. *Bosze* 141 III.2d 473, 566 N.E.2d 1319 (Supreme Court of Illinois, 1990).

psychiatrist? If the psychiatrist does tell the police, should the patient be able to recover damages from the psychiatrist for breach of confidentiality?[20] What if the first person is a doctor who knows that the second person is HIV–positive (that is, has the AIDS virus) but plans to have unprotected sex with the third person without telling the third person?

7. When, if ever, should hospitals be required to treat patients who cannot pay?[21]

8. How could Vermont's samaritan law (p. 820) be rewritten to make it less vague? Would these changes make it a better law? Why or why not?

9. The most notorious failure to rescue might be the case of Kitty Genovese. In a courtyard in front of her apartment, she was attacked repeatedly for over thirty minutes. Thirty–eight people watched, but nobody called the police until after she was dead, reportedly because they did not want to get in-volved. Should any of these people be subject to any legal action at all? Why or why not? If only one person had witnessed the attack, should that person be held responsible in any way for not helping or seeking help? Why or why not? This case raises the more general problem of what to do when there are many people who fail to rescue. How should bad samaritan statutes be written to deal with multiple offenders?

SUGGESTIONS FOR FURTHER READING

Clear overviews of issues surrounding bad samaritan laws can be found in Joel Fein-berg, *Harm to Others* (New York: Oxford University Press, 1984), pp. 126–86; and Michael A. Menlowe, "The Philosophical Foundations of a Duty to Rescue," in Michael A. Men-lowe and Alexander McCall Smith, eds., *The Duty to Rescue: The Jurisprudence of Aid* (Brook-field, Vermont: Dartmouth Publishing Co., 1993), pp. 5–54. Feinberg and Menlowe support some bad samaritan laws, as do John Harris, "The Marxist Conception of Vio-lence," *Philosophy and Public Affairs*, vol. 3 (1974); John Kleinig, "Good Samaritanism," *Phi-losophy and Public Affairs*, vol. 5 (1976); R.J. Lipkin, "Beyond Good Samaritans and Moral Monsters: An Individualistic Justification of the Duty to Rescue," *University of California, Los Angeles, Law Review*, vol. 31 (1983), pp. 252–93; and Alison McIntyre, "Guilty By-standers," *Philosophy and Public Affairs*, vol. 23 (1994), pp. 157–91. For opposition to bad samaritan laws, on the grounds that omissions cannot cause harm, see Eric Mack, "Bad Samaritanism and the Causation of Harm," *Philosophy and Public Affairs*, vol. 9 (1980), pp. 230–59. For distinctions among various kinds of good and bad samaritan laws, see A.M. Honoré, "Law, Morals, and Rescue," in J.M. Ratcliffe, ed., *The Good Samaritan and the Law* (Garden City, New Jersey: Doubleday, 1966). This collection also includes many other important articles.

---

[20]See *Tarasoff* v. *University of California*, 17 Cal.3d 425 (1976).

[21]See *O'Neill* v. *Montefiore Hospital*, 202 N.Y.S.2d 436 (Appellate Division, New York 1960).

7.4 *MENS REA AND STRICT LIABILITY*

INTRODUCTION

Someone who does a positive act that causes harm still might not be responsible for the harm. In Hart and Honoré's example (Section 7.2), someone gives a normally harmless tap on the head to a victim with an eggshell skull, who then dies. This tap is a positive act. It also causes death. However, if the tapper had no way of knowing that this tap would cause death, and if he would not have tapped this person on the head if he had known what would happen, then most people would say that the tapper should not be held responsible for the victim's death. If so, then act and causation together are still not enough for responsibility, at least in this case. More is needed, namely, some kind of mental condition or *mens rea*.

This mental requirement also seems to apply when what would make an act illegal is not its effects alone but also its internal nature or the circumstances in which it is done. For example, suppose that Frances' husband, George, goes on a very dangerous mission in a war, and several eyewitnesses report that he was killed. Frances grieves for years, but she finally falls in love with Harry and has sex with him. Then George comes back from a prisoner of war camp. Frances might not have harmed George, if he did not care about what she did, but the question is whether Frances is guilty of adultery. If not, adultery requires more than that she had sex with one person under the circumstance of being married to another person; some kind of mental condition is also necessary.[22]

It is traditional to say that people are liable when they perform a certain *actus reus* with a certain *mens rea*. The *mens rea* of an offense is the mental condition that is required for an act to violate that law and count as that offense. This is too simple, however, since an agent can have different mental conditions with respect to different aspects of a single act. In the earlier example, Frances knew that she had sex with someone other than George. What she did not know was just that George was alive. When such circumstances or aspects of an act are essential for the act to count as an offense, they are *material elements* of that offense. Frances was aware that her act had some of the material elements of adultery, but she had no way of knowing that her act had another material element of adultery, namely,

---

[22]Mental conditions have not always been required in such cases. See *Commonwealth v. Elwell*, 43 Mass. 190 (1840), where a man was convicted of adultery with a woman reasonably believed to be unmarried. Compare *Commonwealth v. Mash*, 48 Mass. 472 (1844), where a person was convicted of bigamy even though he reasonably believed that his first wife was dead.

the circumstance that she had a live spouse. Many people would say that the lack of this single element should be enough to keep Frances from being legally responsible. If so, legal responsibility should require a certain mental condition not just with respect to one material element but with respect to every material element that is essential to the offense.

LEVELS OF LIABILITY

Which mental conditions are and should be required for legal responsibility? The answer depends on the material element and on the kind of case, and mental conditions vary almost continuously along a spectrum. Nonetheless, the ends of the spectrum can be characterized simply. Some laws apply only to acts that are done intentionally or on purpose. Other laws impose strict liability, which means that they do not require any specific mental condition at all. The arguments for and against such laws will be discussed below, but first we need to know what the options are, so we need to distinguish more precisely among various mental conditions and levels of liability.

The class of mental conditions can be divided in many ways, but a common and useful framework is provided by the Model Penal Code of the American Law Institute.[25] According to the Model Penal Code,

> A person acts *purposely* with respect to a material element of an offense when: (i) if the element involves the nature of his conduct or a result thereof, it is his conscious object to engage in conduct of that nature or to cause such a result; and (ii) if the element involves the attendant circumstances, he is aware of the existence of such circumstances or he believes or hopes that they exist.

For example, if a butcher sells tainted meat to a customer just because he wants to kill the customer, and the customer dies as a result, then the butcher kills purposely. In contrast, a second butcher knows that his meat is tainted and deadly but sells it just to make money. He has nothing against his customer, but the customer dies. This second butcher does not kill the customer purposely but does kill the customer knowingly. In general, according to the Model Penal Code,

> A person acts *knowingly* with respect to a material element of an offense when: (i) if the element involves the nature of his conduct or the attendant circumstances, he is aware that his conduct is of that nature or that such circumstances exist; and (ii) if the element involves a result of his conduct, he is aware that it is practically certain that his conduct will cause such a result.

Now these different mental conditions can be used to distinguish levels of liability. When a law can be violated only by someone who acts purposely with respect to a material element of an offense, then that law imposes *purpose liability* with respect to that element. When a law can be violated by a person who acts either knowingly

---

[25](Philadelphia: The American Law Institute, 1956), Section 2.02.

or purposely with respect to a material element of an offense, then that law imposes *knowledge liability* with respect to that element. So the second butcher violates a law that imposes knowledge liability but not a law that imposes purpose liability. The difference between purpose and knowledge might make a difference to the kind of crime (such as between first and second degree murder) or to the sentence. However, the difference between what one does purposely and what one does knowingly rarely affects whether one is subject to any punishment or fine at all. Both butchers, for example, would and should be punished.

People often do not believe or know that their acts *will* cause harms, but still do know that their acts create a *risk* of harm. Such people meet the Model Penal Code's third mental condition:

> A person acts *recklessly* with respect to a material element of an offense when he consciously disregards a substantial and unjustifiable risk that the material element exists or will result from his conduct. The risk must be of such a nature and degree that, considering the nature and purpose of the actor's conduct and the circumstances known to him, its disregard involves a gross deviation from the standard of conduct that a law–abiding person would observe in the actor's situation.

For example, suppose a third butcher does not know that his meat is tainted, but he does know that there is a good chance that his meat is tainted and deadly, since he knows that the freezer that housed the meat broke down for many days. Despite knowledge of this risk, this butcher does not check the meat, because it would cost too much money if the meat turned out to be tainted, so he just goes ahead and sells the meat. Customers die as a result, so this butcher kills them recklessly, although neither purposely nor knowingly.

This third mental condition yields a third level of liability. A law imposes *recklessness liability* with respect to an element of an offense if and only if the law can be violated only by a person who acts either recklessly or knowingly or purposely with respect to that element. Laws that impose recklessness liability are not violated unless the agent believes both that there is a risk and that the risk is substantial, but it is not so clear that the agent must also believe that the risk is unjustifiable. It seems natural to call people reckless when they believe that there is a substantial risk and *should* believe that this risk is unjustifiable, but consciously disregard it and don't even consider whether it is justifiable.

Sometimes people are not aware of any substantial risk just because they don't think about it. When such people should be more careful, they have the Model Penal Code's fourth mental condition:

> A person acts *negligently* with respect to a material element of an offense when he should be aware of a substantial and unjustifiable risk that the material element exists or will result from his conduct. The risk must be of such a nature and degree that the actor's failure to perceive it, considering the nature and purpose of his conduct and the circumstances known to him, involves a gross deviation from the standard of care that a reasonable person would observe in the actor's situation.

To illustrate this condition, suppose that a fourth butcher does not ever check to see whether the meat freezer fails. This butcher is not consciously aware of a risk that the meat is poisoned or dangerous, but reasonable butchers check their equipment and would be aware of the risk if a freezer did fail, so this butcher should also be aware of the risk. If customers die as a result, then this butcher kills them negligently, although neither recklessly nor knowingly nor purposely.

Negligence differs from the preceding conditions in an important way. Whereas someone must have a positive mental state in order to act purposely or knowingly or recklessly, negligence does not require any positive mental state. Instead, people act negligently when they lack a mental state that they should have. In short, negligence is negative. That is why we call these four categories "mental conditions" rather than "mental states."

Correspondingly, a law imposes *negligence liability* with respect to an element of an offense if and only if the law can be violated only by a person who acts either negligently or recklessly or knowingly or purposely with respect to that element. Since negligence was defined negatively, a law that imposes negligence liability can be violated even if an agent never had any positive thought that his act had any chance of causing harm or breaking a law. Negligence liability thus imposes an objective standard of care. Regardless of whether a person subjectively thinks about any risks, there are certain risks about which a person should think and be careful. When laws threaten people who are not careful enough, they impose negligence liability.

Finally, some laws seem to impose liability even when a person is as careful as any reasonable person would be. A law imposes *strict liability* with respect to an element of an offense if and only if the law is violated by anyone who engages in an act with that element (effect or nature). Such laws impose liability on agents who act neither intentionally nor knowingly nor recklessly nor negligently with respect to the material elements of the offense. No mental condition or *mens rea* at all is necessary to violate a strict liability law. All that is required is causation of harm or doing an act with the wrong nature or in the wrong circumstances. For example, if the butcher who sells tainted meat is liable even if he did everything humanly possible to make sure that the meat was not tainted, then the law imposes strict liability.

These mental conditions and levels of liability can be summarized in a diagram:

Is doing the act in this way enough for conviction?	Purpose Liability	Knowledge Liability	Recklessness Liability	Negligence Liability	Strict Liability
Purposely	Yes	Yes	Yes	Yes	Yes
Knowingly	No	Yes	Yes	Yes	Yes
Recklessly	No	No	Yes	Yes	Yes
Negligently	No	No	No	Yes	Yes
None of the above	No	No	No	No	Yes

These distinctions are, admittedly, not always so clear. A known effect might be part of one's goal, but only part: the butcher might want to make money and also to kill a certain customer, who has always bugged him. Then it is not clear whether the effect was brought about purposefully or just knowingly. And what if the butcher knows that the meat might be tainted but thinks that it will only make customers sick? Then is death caused recklessly or just negligently? Further problems arise because it is often not clear in real cases what the agent's mental condition was, or even what kind of evidence we would need to classify his mental condition into the above categories. Despite such problems, these classifications can still provide a useful framework for discussion.

WHICH LEVEL OF LIABILITY SHOULD BE IMPOSED?

These distinctions raise several questions. We can ask which levels of liability *are* actually imposed by various laws in a certain jurisdiction. That depends on how the laws are written, but it also depends on precedents and dominant methods of interpretation. These questions are interesting and important, but they will not be our main concern here.

Our main question will be normative: which level of liability *should* be imposed? This question still arises at two levels: with legislators and with judges. How should legislators write laws? How should judges interpret laws that appear to impose strict liability, for example, and should judges uphold the constitutionality of laws that impose strict criminal liability? We will focus on the question for legislators.

Which level of liability should legislators impose? Which mental condition, if any, should they require before conviction? It is impossible to answer these questions in the abstract. If someone asks you whether you favor strict liability, you probably should not answer simply "yes" or "no." Most people support strict liability in some cases but not in others. For example, if I reasonably mistake your coat for mine in a restaurant, and I take it home with me, I am still liable to be forced by law to return your coat to you, even if this costs me a fair amount of time and money. In contrast, few people would want to punish me, even if you were inconvenienced when your coat was missing.

In general, strict liability becomes more controversial as penalties become harsher. Many people are willing to impose strict liability in civil cases for parking violations, failures to fulfill small contracts, and other minor infractions, but there is more reluctance when violators must pay large amounts of money. Strict liability raises additional questions in criminal laws that inflict punishments, if punishment expresses moral condemnation (see Section 6.1).

Nonetheless, many laws do seem to impose strict liability when major penalties are involved. One important area concerns so-called *public welfare offenses*. Manufacturers have been forced to pay millions of dollars in compensation for damages due to defective products even though nobody showed that the company had any way of knowing that its product was defective. Drug merchants have been penalized heavily for selling or possessing drugs that were adulterated or improperly labelled, even though this was unknown to the merchant after normal inspection.

Other strict liability laws impose not only civil penalties but even *criminal punishments*. One well-known example of strict criminal liability is for statutory rape. Under the New Hampshire criminal code, for example, "A person is guilty of [aggravated felonious sexual assault] if he engages in sexual penetration . . . when the victim is less than thirteen years of age," and "a person is guilty of [felonious sexual assault] . . . if he engages in sexual penetration with a person other than his legal spouse who is thirteen years of age or older and under 16 years of age."[24] Punishments apply even if the perpetrator had a reasonable belief that the victim was older (and even if the victim consented). Another apparent example of strict criminal liability is felony murder, where a person can be found guilty of first-degree murder if a death occurs during a felony. In *Tison v. Arizona* (selections follow), one person was found guilty of felony murder, even though the death was caused by another person who was told not to kill anyone. It is not completely clear whether these laws and decisions really do impose strict liability, but, if they do, then strict liability is not confined to minor offenses and penalties.

Even if some laws do impose strict liability, and even if recent trends are towards more strict liability, as some claim, we still need to ask whether such laws are justified. Many legal scholars argue that our law is moving in exactly the wrong direction.

The main argument against strict criminal liability applies a kind of retributivism about the justification of punishment. Kant and some other retributivists hold that we should punish according to the "inner wickedness" of the criminal (Section 6.4). Many who reject such strong retributivism still hold that moral guilt is a necessary condition for justified punishment. Such theories rule out strict criminal liability, if a person who honestly and reasonably believes that he is not violating a law does not have any inner wickedness or moral guilt with respect to that law. The same argument might also speak against criminal liability for negligence, because negligence does not require any positive inner state, but only a lack of care. If inner wickedness is necessary for punishment to be justified, then the government should not punish someone without showing something about his inner mental states.

There are also utilitarian arguments against strict liability. (See Bentham on inefficacious punishment in Section 6.3.) A person who reasonably believes that she is not violating a law cannot be deterred by threats of punishment for violating that law. Since such reasonable mistakes are the only cases that would be punished under strict liability but not under negligence liability, strict liability is supposed to have no benefits in deterrence.

On the other side, however, there are also utilitarian arguments in favor of strict liability. Even if there is no way to deter people who never had any chance of avoiding the act that caused harm, strict liability laws still might prevent crimes in other ways.

One reason is that it is often very difficult to find good *evidence* of what a criminal was thinking during a crime. When a criminal swears under oath that he did not believe that his acts would cause harm, or that his act was illegal, this will seem to create a reasonable doubt in the absence of strong evidence to the contrary. Some juries will be gullible, so some guilty people will get off if laws do not impose strict liability. This will bother some retributivists. And utilitarians will

[24]Chapter 632-A, Sections 2–3.

worry that dangerous criminals who avoid prison by faking excuses will not be incapacitated from committing more crimes, and also that some potential criminals might commit crimes that they would not commit if they did not think that they could get off by faking some excuse that would not be allowed if the law imposed strict liability.

Strict liability can also reduce harm in other ways. If people know that they will be liable for causing harm, even if they do so by accident or by mistake, then they will probably be more careful not to have an accident or make a mistake, so they will be less likely to cause as much harm. Furthermore, if people know that they are likely to cause some harm if they engage in a certain dangerous activity, then strict liability will make them less inclined to engage in that activity in the first place. For example, if I know that I will be held strictly liable for any harm caused by firing a gun inside the city limits and outside a licensed target range, then I will be less likely to fire a gun at all in such a setting. Some people will still engage in dangerous activities when they see the benefits as worth the risks, but strict liability increases the risks and thereby decreases the number of people who engage in the dangerous activity. And even when people do engage in the dangerous activity, they will be more careful if they know that they will be held strictly liable for any harm that they cause. In these and other ways, strict criminal liability can reduce harms and crimes.

The same kinds of arguments are used to justify strict liability outside the criminal law. Those who favor strict liability for parking violations (and defective products) usually favor it because of difficulties of proving the mental conditions of drivers (and manufacturers) and because of the harms prevented by making them more careful. Those who think that the main purpose of the law is to prevent harm see these advantages as strong reasons to favor strict liability.

Opponents respond, however, that we should not achieve social goals, such as harm prevention, at the cost of freedom and justice for individuals. The most famous version of this argument is by H. L. A. Hart. Hart lists three main reasons for opposing strict criminal liability.

> The first concerns individual freedom. In a system in which proof of *mens rea* is no longer a necessary condition for conviction, the occasions for official interferences with our lives and for compulsion will be greatly increased. Take, for example, the notion of a criminal assault. If the doctrine of *mens rea* were swept away, every blow, even if it was apparent to a policeman that it was purely accidental or merely careless and therefore not, according to the present law a criminal assault, would be a matter for investigation under the new scheme.[25]

Hart's point is not only that official interferences would be more common but also that people would be "less able to predict" official interferences and thus less able to plan their lives in such a way as to avoid interference.

---

[25]H. L. A. Hart, "Changing Conceptions of Responsibility," p. 206. See also "Punishment and the Elimination of Responsibility," pp. 181-2. Both essays are reprinted in *Punishment and Responsibility* (New York and Oxford: Oxford University Press, 1968).

But how much does this show? It does seem to show that people should not be held strictly liable for hitting someone (although they still might be held liable for negligently hitting someone). However, this objection does not apply to strict liability for many other crimes. It is easy, for example, to plan your life so as to avoid convictions for felony murder. Just don't commit felonies. Then you will face no more "occasions for official interferences" if the law does include a felony murder rule than if it does not. Thus, Hart's first argument might show that some criminal laws should not impose strict liability, but it is hardly a reason for rejecting *all* strict criminal liability.

The same response can be given to another of Hart's arguments. Hart writes:

> . . . there are some socially harmful activities which are now and should always be treated as criminal offences which can only be identified by reference to intention or some other mental element. Consider the idea of an attempt to commit a crime. It is obviously desirable that persons who attempt to kill or injure or steal, even if they fail, should be brought before courts for punishment or treatment; yet what distinguishes an attempt which fails from an innocent activity is just the fact that it is a step taken with the intention of bringing about some harmful consequence.[26]

If this is right, there are conceptual reasons for requiring *mens rea* for attempts and some other crimes. However, this still does not show why *mens rea* should be required for all crimes, and in particular for statutory rape or felony murder convictions.

Hart's strongest argument is a dilemma that purports to show that strict criminal liability falls into one of two traps: it must be either immoral or counterproductive. In his words,

> . . . conviction by a court followed by a sentence of imprisonment is a public act expressing the odium, if not the hostility, of society for those who break the law. As long as these features attach to conviction and a sentence of imprisonment, the moral objection to their use on those who could not have helped doing what they did will remain. On the other hand, if they cease to attach, will not the law have lost an important element in its authority and deterrent force—as important perhaps for some convicted persons as the deterrent force of the actual measures which it administers.[27]

This argument might seem to depend on a false dichotomy. Punishment need not express full condemnation of all or no condemnation at all. Strict liability laws might make punishment express moral condemnation less strongly or in fewer cases. Nonetheless, Hart could respond that the law's ability to prevent crime will be reduced to the extent that punishment expresses less moral condemnation, and punishment is unfair to the extent that it expresses any moral condemnation of those who could not have helped doing what they did. So we need to look at these claims.

---

[26]"Changing Conceptions of Responsibility," p. 209.
[27]"Changing Conceptions of Responsibility," pp. 208–9

Hart is probably right that criminal laws would prevent fewer crimes if people did not morally condemn criminals who are punished. One of the most important ways in which law prevents crime is to teach a moral lesson about how wrong certain crimes are. This prevents some people from committing crimes even when they do not fear punishment. This power seems worth preserving.

It is not so clear, however, that strict criminal liability will reduce the tendency of people to condemn criminals who are punished. If every criminal law imposed strict liability, so that even accidental blows were prosecuted as assaults, this might make people feel sorry for some criminals, and this pity might spill over to other criminals. However, if strict liability is used sparingly for only a few crimes, it is not clear that there will be any loss at all. In particular, if strict criminal liability is justified by special difficulties in proving mental conditions, then most citizens might suppose that convicted criminals really committed their crimes knowingly or at least recklessly, so they might continue to morally condemn these criminals.

Hart can still turn to the second prong of his dilemma. To the extent that punishment continues to express moral condemnation (odium or hostility), it is unfair to punish "those who could not have helped doing what they did." As Hart puts it elsewhere, "unless a man has the capacity and a fair opportunity or chance to adjust his behavior to the law, its penalties ought not to be applied to him."[28] This makes a lot of sense in some cases. It does seem unfair in Hart's own example to punish someone who hits someone else completely accidentally.

However, it is not at all clear how well this point generalizes to other kinds of cases. Consider a statutory rape of a 12-year-old under the New Hampshire law (quoted earlier). Even if the perpetrator did not know that the victim was only 12, he still could have avoided committing statutory rape by not having sexual intercourse with her or with anyone who is even close to 12. This does not seem to ask too much, so the perpetrator seems to have had a fair opportunity to avoid his crime.

Similar considerations apply to felony murder, as in the case of *Furman v. Georgia* (Section 6.6). While burglarizing a home, Furman heard the owner, started out, and fell. His pistol went off and shot through a closed door, killing the owner. At the exact time of the killing, maybe Furman could not have helped tripping and killing the person behind the door. However, there is no reason to look only at that time. At earlier times Furman did have the capacity and opportunity not to commit burglary and not to carry a gun, and then he would not have killed anyone during a burglary. So Furman could have helped doing what he did.

Hart might respond that, if the criminal is already punished for the felony, it is unfair to add more punishment for the killing. But is this really unfair? Many people do not think so, particularly victims and their families. One thing that might make it seem unfair is that strict criminal liability makes punishment depend partly on luck: a burglar like Furman who is unlucky might be punished more than a burglar who is lucky enough not to kill anyone. However, luck also affects punishment in other areas, such as when failed attempts are punished less than successful attempts. And it is not clear that luck must always be avoided in the distribution of punishments. Indeed, such uses of luck might be the most efficient way to deter

---

[28]"Punishment and the Elimination of Responsibility," p. 181.

dangerous practices. If burglars know that they will be held strictly liable for harms that they cause during burglaries, this might make them more careful not to cause any harm. It might even convince some not to commit burglary at all, or not to carry a loaded gun during burglaries. If so, the law might achieve greater deterrence at less cost by giving greater punishments to the unlucky few who unintentionally cause more harm during their felonies. This greater efficiency might be a good enough reason to impose strict liability on felons who already lie beyond any threshold of wrongdoing that is necessary to justify punishment.

This argument does not apply to all cases. If athletes were held strictly liable for injuring opponents, this might discourage people from playing competitive sports. Unless one wants this result, one should not want strict liability in this area. In contrast, when one does want to discourage some activity, such as felonies or sex with young children, then strict criminal liability might be the most efficient means, and it might not seem unfair as long as the activity that is being discouraged already involves enough wrongdoing to justify some punishment.

It might, however, be preferable to find some other way to achieve the goals of strict liability without raising so many doubts. One possible means is *negligence* liability. Since negligence does not require any particular mental state to be proven, negligence liability might overcome the problems of evidence that motivate strict liability. Negligence liability should also make people careful, since they might be punished if they are not careful enough. And when we want to discourage people from engaging in a certain activity at all, we can raise the standards of care so high that almost anyone who would be strictly liable will also be liable for negligence. One could argue, for example, that burglars who carry loaded guns are not careful enough, so any harm that they cause is caused negligently. It might also be negligent to have sex with a girl who is close to 12 years old without doing extensive research on her age.

Nonetheless, negligence liability also has problems. It is very hard to formulate and justify the standards of care that must be followed in order to avoid negligence. One can instead talk about what a reasonable person would do, but it is just as hard to define in general what a reasonable person is, and it is often questionable what a reasonable person would do. There are some clear cases, and standards of care can sometimes be based on community practices that are public in the sense that any normal person in the community should know what the standards are. But there will still be many acts that seem reasonable to some and negligent to others. Moreover, people can be negligent even if they intend nothing but the best for everyone, even if they honestly believe that their acts create no risk of any harm, and even if it is not their fault that they lack the beliefs that a reasonable person would have. Such people have none of the inner wickedness that Kant and his followers take to be necessary for justified punishment, so these theorists will see negligence liability as no better than strict liability.

Such theorists might prefer *recklessness* liability. Recklessness does not require a belief that one's act will cause harm, but it does require a belief that one's act will create a substantial *risk* of harm. When an agent believes there will be a substantial risk but consciously disregards it and does the act anyway without adequate justification, then that agent has a kind of inner wickedness that might be enough to justify punishment for some Kantians. It also seems easier to prove belief in a risk, since any steps to avoid the risk will be evidence of belief in the risk. One could even hold that, if a reasonable person would be aware of a risk, then a defendant can be presumed to be aware of the risk in the absence of evidence to the contrary. In some such way, recklessness liability might avoid most of the problems of evidence that motivated strict liability. Finally, recklessness liability will make people more careful to avoid causing harm when they know that their acts create a substantial risk of harm, and that is when we want people to be more careful.

One problem with recklessness liability is that, if people are liable only when they are aware of a substantial risk, they could try to avoid liability by never considering risks at all. However, one cannot play this trick without already having some awareness that one's act creates a substantial risk. That awareness will make one's act reckless, so one will not escape recklessness liability after all. It still might seem odd not to punish someone who causes harm without thinking about risks, but to punish another person who causes harm after thinking about risks. The latter person might seem to be punished for thinking about risks. However, what that person is really punished for is consciously disregarding risks, and that does seem to be an appropriate thing to justify punishment.

Like all compromises, recklessness liability will not satisfy extremists on either side. It also will not fit every kind of case. Nonetheless, something like recklessness liability does seem attractive in criminal law to those who want to break the impasse between advocates of strict liability and their opponents who predicate liability on the agent's beliefs about what he or she does.

STRICT LIABILITY
IN THE CRIMINAL LAW

RICHARD A. WASSERSTROM

The proliferation of so-called "strict liability" offenses in the criminal law has occasioned the vociferous, continued, and almost unanimous criticism of analysts and philosophers of the law.[1] The imposition of severe criminal sanctions[2] in the absence of any requisite mental element has been held by many to be incompatible with the basic requirements of our Anglo-American, and, indeed, any civilized jurisprudence.

The Model Penal Code, for example, announces that its provisions for culpability make a "frontal attack" upon the notion of strict, or absolute, liability.[3] Francis B. Sayre, in his classic article on "Public Welfare Offenses," contends that since the real menace to society is the in-

Richard A. Wasserstrom, "Strict Liability in the Criminal Law," *Stanford Law Review*, vol. 12 (1960)

tentional commission of undesirable acts, evil intent must remain an element of the criminal law. "To inflict substantial punishment upon one who is morally entirely innocent, who caused injury through reasonable mistake or pure accident, would so outrage the feelings of the community as to nullify its own enforcement."[4] And Jerome Hall, perhaps the most active and insistent critic of such offenses, has consistently denounced the notion of strict liability as anathema to the coherent development of a rational criminal law: "It is impossible to defend strict liability in terms of or by reference to the only criteria that are available to evaluate the influence of legal controls on human behavior. What then remains but the myth that through devious, unknown ways some good results from strict liability in 'penal' law?"[5]

Without attempting to demonstrate that strict liability offenses are inherently or instrumentally desirable, one can question the force of the arguments which have been offered against them. It is not evident, for example, that strict liability statutes cannot have a deterrent effect greater than that of ordinary criminal statutes. Nor, is it clear that all strict liability statutes can most fruitfully be discussed and evaluated as members of a single class of criminality. The notion of "fault" is sufficiently ambiguous, perhaps, so as to obscure the sense or senses in which these statutes do impose liability "without fault." And finally, the similarities between strict liability and criminal negligence are such that it seems difficult to attack the former without at the same time calling the latter into comparable question. Issues of this kind are, then, the explicit subjects for examination here.

THE CONCEPT OF STRICT CRIMINAL LIABILITY

Neither the arguments against the imposition of strict criminal liability nor the justifications for such imposition can be evaluated intelligently until the meaning of the phrase "strict criminal liability" has been clarified. One possible approach—and the one selected here as appropriate for the scope of this analysis—is that of ostensive definition. That is to say, a small, but representative, sample of the kinds of offenses which are usually characterized as strict liability offenses can be described briefly so as to make the common characteristics of this class relatively obvious upon inspection.

At the outset, it is essential that strict liability offenses not be confused with Sayre's "public welfare" offenses, i.e., those which he defines as essentially regulative in function and punishable by fine rather than imprisonment.[6] This inquiry is concerned with those offenses which cannot be distinguished from other criminal conduct by virtue of the fact that the punishment involved is consistently less than imprisonment.[7] Thus, the cases here selected as exemplary of strict criminal liability are all cases in which the prescribed sentences are surely not minimal in degree or merely regulative in function.

The landmark case in American jurisprudence is undoubtedly *United States v. Balint.*[8] The defendant was indicted under a statute which made it unlawful to sell narcotics without a written order. The defendant claimed that the indictment was insufficient because it failed to allege that he had known that the drugs sold were narcotics. The United States Supreme Court held that his conviction did not deny due process.

Another classic example is *State v. Lindberg.*[9] The statute in question provided that "every director and officer of any bank . . . who shall borrow . . . any of its funds in an excessive amount . . . shall . . . be guilty of a felony"[10] The defendant contended that he had borrowed the money in question only after he had been assured by another official of the bank that the money had come from a bank other than his own. But the court held that the reasonableness of the defendant's mistake was not a defense.

The final case, *Regina v. Prince,*[11] is famous in both English and American jurisprudence. Prince was indicted under a statute which made it a misdemeanour to "unlawfully take . . . any unmarried Girl, being under the Age of Sixteen

Years, out of the Possession and against the Will of her Father or Mother. . . ."[12] One of the defenses which Prince sought to interpose rested upon the reasonableness of his belief that the girl in question was over sixteen years old. The majority of the court interpreted the statute to make the reasonableness of a belief as to the girl's age irrelevant, and found Prince guilty.

Assuming these cases to be representative,[13] strict liability offenses might be tentatively described (although not defined) as those in which the sole question put to the jury is whether the jury believes the defendant to have committed the act proscribed by the statute.[14] If it finds that he did the act, then it is obliged to bring in a verdict of guilty.[15] Whether this characterization of the above three cases is either precise or very helpful is a question which must await further discussion below. For the present, however, it is perhaps sufficient to observe that whatever it is that the concept of *mens rea* is thought to designate, it is this which needs not be shown to be predicable of the defendant.[16]

THE JUSTIFICATION OF STRICT LIABILITY

Before attempting to assess the arguments for and against the notion of strict criminal liability, it should be made clear that the author agrees with most of the critics in not finding many of the usual justifications of strict liability at all persuasive. The fact, for example, that slight penalties are usually imposed, or that *mens rea* would be peculiarly unsusceptible of proof in these cases, does not, either singly or in combination, justify the presence of these offenses in the criminal law. But to reject these and comparable arguments is not necessarily to prove that plausible justifications cannot be located. In fact, it is precisely when the "stronger" arguments of the opponents of strict liability are considered in detail that the case against strict liability is found to be less one-sided than the critics so unanimously suppose.

Critics of strict criminal liability usually argue that the punishment of persons in accordance with the minimum requirements of strict liability (1) is inconsistent with any or all of the commonly avowed aims of the criminal law; and (2) runs counter to the accepted standards of criminal culpability which prevail in the community. They assert that the imposition of criminal sanctions in a case in which—conceivably—the defendant acted both reasonably and with no intention to produce the proscribed events cannot be justified by an appeal to the deterrent, the rehabilitative, or the incarcerative functions of punishment.[17] And, in fact, they assert the practical effect of strict liability offenses is simply to create that anomalous situation in which persons not morally blamed by the community are nevertheless branded criminal.[18] Although the two lines of criticism are intimately related, for purposes of discussion they will be treated somewhat separately.

The notion that strict liability statutes can be defended as efficacious deterrents has been consistently rejected. It has been proposed, for example, that strict liability offenses cannot be a deterrent simply because they do not proscribe the kind of activity which is obviously incompatible with the moral standards of the community. Thus Gerhard Mueller argues that the substance of common law *mens rea* is the "awareness of evil, the *sense of doing something which one ought not.* . . ."[19] Since all common–law crimes involved the commission of some act which was known by all the members of the community to be morally wrong, there was, he suggests, no problem in finding the presence of *mens rea* in cases of common–law criminal acts. Such, he insists, is not true of strict liability offenses. They do not punish those activities which a person would know to be wrong independently of the existence of a particular statute. Thus strict liability statutes are to be condemned because they necessarily imply that a person might be punished even though he could not have appealed to that one certain indicia of criminality—the moral laws of the community—to decide whether he was doing something which would violate the law.

If I understand Mr. Mueller's argument correctly, then it clearly proves too much to be of any special significance as a criticism of strict liability offenses. The argument rests upon the obviously sound premise that a person cannot be deterred if he does not know or have reason to believe that his intended action will violate the law. And if this theory about common-law *mens rea* is correct, it only demonstrates that everyone either knew or should have known that certain kinds of activity would be legally punishable. These two points, however, at best imply that ignorance of the law ought—on deterrent grounds—to be always admitted as a complete defense to any criminal prosecution founded upon a statute which does not incorporate an express moral rule or practice into the criminal law.[20] Concomitantly, if a person knew of the existence and import of a statute of this kind, it seems wholly irrelevant to distinguish strict liability statutes from those requiring some greater "mental element." It is just as possible to know that one might be violating a strict liability statute as it is to know that one might be violating some other kind of criminal statute. Thus, unless special reasons exist for believing that strict liability offenses are not effective deterrents, Mr. Mueller's argument leaves them undifferentiated from many other statutory crimes which do not incorporate the moral law of the community.[21]

Just such special reasons for rejecting the deterrent quality of *strict* liability offenses are offered by Jerome Hall, among others. He rejects the argument that a strict liability statute is a more efficacious deterrent than an ordinary criminal statute for at least two reasons: (*a*) It is not plausible to suppose that the "strictness" of the liability renders it more of a deterrent than the liability of ordinary criminal statutes; and (*b*) persons are not, as a matter of fact, deterred by those penalties usually imposed for the violation of a strict liability offense.[22]

The first of these objections is, it is submitted, inconclusive. For there seem to be at least two respects in which strict liability statutes might have a greater deterrent effect than "usual" criminal statutes. In the first place, it should be noted that Hall's first proposition is just as apt to be false as to be true. That is to say, it might be the case that a person engaged in a certain kind of activity would be more careful precisely because he knew that this kind of activity was governed by a strict liability statute. It is at least plausible to suppose that the knowledge that certain criminal sanctions will be imposed if certain consequences ensue might induce a person to engage in that activity with much greater caution than would be the case if some lesser standard prevailed.

In the second place (and this calls Hall's second premise into question as well), it seems reasonable to believe that the presence of strict liability offenses might have the added effect of keeping a relatively large class of persons from engaging in certain kinds of activity.[23] A person who did not regard himself as capable of conducting an enterprise in such a way so as not to produce the deleterious consequences proscribed by the statute might well refuse to engage in that activity at all. Of course, if the penalties for violation of the statute are minimal—if payment of fines is treated merely as a license to continue in operation—then unscrupulous persons will not be deterred by the imposition of this sanction. But this does not imply that unscrupulous persons would be quite so willing to engage in these activities if the penalties for violation were appreciably more severe. In effect, Hall's second argument, if it proves anything, shows only that stronger penalties are needed if strict liability statutes are to be effective.

If the above analysis of the possible deterrent effect of strict liability offenses is plausible, then one of the results of their continued existence and enforcement might very well be that few if any persons would be willing to engage in certain kinds of conduct. The presence of statutes such as that in the *Lindberg* case might have the effect of inducing persons not to engage in banking as an occupation since the risks, one might suppose, are just too great to be compensated by the possible rewards. More plausibly, such a statute might merely have the effect of discouraging bankers from borrowing money—or possibly only from borrowing money from banks. But these effects, too, might conceivably make banking a less attractive occupation, although they would probably not cause the disappearance of banking as an institution ' in society. However, if we assume the strongest of all results—that a statute of this kind would lead to the disappearance of the institution involved—what conclusions are to be drawn?

The case of socially undesirable activity is easy. If the operation of the felony murder rule has the effect of inducing persons to refuse to commit felonies, there are surely few if any persons who would object to this consequence.[24] Where socially beneficial activities, such as banking and drug distribution[25] are concerned, the case is more troublesome. If it is further assumed that at least some of the strict liability statutes in these areas have been rigidly enforced, it is also to be noted that these institutions have not disappeared from the society. One possible conclusion to be drawn is that these strict liability offenses have been deemed to impose a not unreasonable risk. The fact that banking is still considered an extremely attractive endeavor (despite the possibility of a prison sentence for borrowing money from one's own bank) might be interpreted as evidence that people believe they can be successful bankers without violating this or a comparable strict liability statute. They believe, in other words, that they can operate with sufficient care so as not to violate the statute. Admittedly, the evidence in support of this thesis is not particularly persuasive. Perhaps most people who have gone into banking never even knew of the existence of the statute. Perhaps there is no such statute in most jurisdictions. Perhaps they knew of the statute but believed it would never attach to their conduct. And perhaps they took the statute into account incorrectly and should have been deterred by the statute. In part, the difficulty stems from the fact that there is so little empirical evidence available. It is suggested only that the above interpretation of the extant evidence is just as plausible as are the contrary inferences so often drawn.

The fact that strict liability statutes might cause the disappearance of socially desirable undertakings raises, in a specific context, one important feature of the kind of justification which might be offered for these statutes. If it is conceded that strict liability statutes have an additional deterrent effect, then a fairly plausible utilitarian argument can be made for their perpetuation.

To the extent to which the function of the criminal law is conceived to be that of regulating various kinds of conduct, it becomes relevant to ask whether this particular way of regulating conduct leads to more desirable results than possible alternative procedures. The problem is not peculiar to strict liability statutes but is endemic to the legal system as a whole. Consider, for instance, one such justification of the present jury system. In order to prevent the conviction of persons who did not in fact commit the crimes of which they are accused, it is required that a unanimous jury of twelve persons find, among other things, that they believe the accused did the act in question. Perhaps if the concern were solely with guaranteeing that no innocent man be convicted, a twenty or thirty man jury in which unanimous consent was required for conviction would do a better job. But such is not the sole concern of the criminal law; there is also the need to prevent too many guilty persons from going free. Here, a twelve man jury is doubtless more effective than a thirty man jury. Requiring unanimous vote for acquittal would be a still more efficacious means of insuring that every guilty man be convicted. The decision to have a twelve man jury which must be unanimous for conviction can be justified, in other words, as an attempt to devise an adjudicatory procedure (perhaps it is unsuccessful) which will yield a greater quantity of desirable results than would any of the alternatives.

Precisely the same kind of analysis can be made of strict liability offenses. One of the ways to prevent the occurrence of certain kinds of consequences is to enact strict liability offenses, since, *ex hypothesi*, these will be an added deterrent. One of the deleterious consequences of strict liability offenses is the possibility that certain socially desirable institutions will be weakened or will disappear. The problem is twofold: first one must decide whether the additional deterrent effect of the strict liability statutes will markedly reduce the occurrence of those events which the statute seeks quite properly to prevent. And second, one must decide whether this additional reduction in undesirable occurrences is more beneficial to society than the possible deleterious effects upon otherwise desirable activities such as banking or drug distribution. For even if it be conceded that strict liability offenses may have the additionally undesirable effect of holding as criminal some persons who would not on other grounds be so regarded, strict liability could be supported on the theory that the need to prevent certain kinds of occurrences is sufficiently great so as to override the undesirable effect of punishing those who might in some other sense be "innocent."

I do not urge that either or both of these arguments for strict liability offenses are either irrefutable or even particularly convincing. But I do submit that this is a perfectly plausible kind of argument which cannot be met simply by insisting either that strict liability is an inherently unintelligible concept or that the legislative judgment of the desirability of strict criminal liability is necessarily irrational.[26] It is one thing to attack particular legislative evaluations on the grounds that they have misconstrued either the beneficial effects of strict liability or its attendant deleterious consequences, but it is quite another thing to attack the possible rationality of any such comparative determination.[27]

As was observed earlier, the second of the two major kinds of criticism directed against strict criminal liability is that punishment of persons in accordance with the minimal requirements of strict liability—the punishment of persons in the absence of *mens rea*—is irreconcilable with those fundamental, long extant standards of criminal culpability which prevail in the community. As usually propounded the thesis is a complex one; it is also considerably more ambiguous than many of its proponents appear to have noted. One possible, although less interesting, implication concerns the notion of criminal culpability. The claim is made that the imposition of strict liability is inconsistent with the concept of criminal culpability— criminal culpability being defined to mean "requiring *mens rea*." But unless the argument is to be vacuous it must be demonstrated that independent reasons exist for selecting just this definition which precludes strict liability offenses from the class of actions to which the criminal sanctions are to attach.[28]

A more troublesome and related question is whether the proposition is presented as a *descriptive or prescriptive* assertion. It is not clear whether the imposition of strict liability is thought to be incompatible with the accepted values of society or whether the prevalence of strict liability is inconsistent with what ought to be accepted values.

As an empirical assertion the protest against strict liability on the grounds that it contravenes public sentiment is, again, at best an open hypothesis. Those who seek to substantiate its correctness turn to the fact that minimal penalties are often imposed. They construe this as indicative of the felt revulsion against the concept of strict criminal liability. That judges and juries often refuse to impose those sanctions which would be imposed in the comparable cases involving the presence of *mens rea*, is taken as additional evidence of community antipathy.

The evidence is, however, no less (and probably no more) persuasive on the other side. The fact that most strict liability offenses are creatures of statute has already been alluded to. While few persons would seriously wish to maintain that the legislature is either omniscient or a wholly adequate reflection of general or popular sentiment, the fact that so many legislatures have felt such apparently little compunction over enacting such statutes is surely indicative of the presence of a comparable community conviction. Strict liability offenses, as the critics so persistently note, are not mere sports, mere sporadic legislative oversights or anomalies. They are, again as the critics note, increasing in both number and scope. It may very well be the case that strict liability offenses ought to be condemned by the community; it is much more doubtful that they are presently held in such contumely.

"MENTAL" REQUIREMENTS, STRICT LIABILITY, AND NEGLIGENCE

The arguments against strict liability offenses which remain to be examined go to what is conceived to be the very heart of a strict liability offense; namely, the imposition of criminal sanctions in the absence of any *fault* on the part of the actor.

> Since that liability [strict liability] is meaningful only in its complete exclusion of fault, it is patently inconsistent to assert, e.g., that a business man is honest, exercises care and skill; and also, if a misbranded or adulterated package of food somehow, unknown to anyone, is shipped from his establishment, that he should be punished or coercively educated to increase his efficiency.[29]

The actor has, *ex hypothesi*, lacked precisely those mental attributes upon which fault is properly predicated—indeed, proof of his state of mind is irrelevant. Thus, the argument concludes, the vicious character of convictions founded upon strict liability is revealed. Intelligent understanding and evaluation of this objection must await, however, the clarification of several critically ambiguous notions. In particular, the ways in which a strict liability offense may fail to take the defendant's state of mind into account are far from clearly delineated. More seriously, still, there seem to be a variety

of alternative meanings of "fault" which should be explored and discriminated.

That certain offers of proof concerning the defendant's state of mind might not be irrelevant even in the case of a putative violation is apparent. Quite apart from the ambiguous meaning of the word "act,"[30] there are several other questions about the defendant's mental state which might be permitted in a strict liability prosecution. For example, suppose the defendant in the *Lindberg* case were to offer to prove that he had never intended to become a director or officer of the bank and that he reasonably believed that he was merely becoming an employee. Is it clear that this offer would be rejected as irrelevant? Or, suppose the offer of proof was that the defendant had never intended to borrow any money and reasonably believed that he was receiving a bonus. Would this statement be excluded? Thus, it can be argued that if strict liability statutes are to be characterized as "strict" because of their failure to permit inquiry as to the defendant's state of mind, this description is too broad. More appropriately, each criminal statute must be examined to determine in what respects it is "strict."

The ambiguity in the notion of "fault" can be illustrated by a hypothetical situation. Consider a statute which reads: "If a bank director borrows money in excess of [a certain amount] from the bank of which he is director, then the directors of any other bank shall be punishable by not more than ten years in the state prison." Suppose that there is no connection between the various banks in the jurisdiction, that a director of bank A had borrowed money in excess of the statutory amount from his own bank, and that a director of bank B, a wholly unrelated bank, was accused and convicted. This, it is submitted, would be a case of "stricter" liability. The example is surely chimerical; the point is not. It serves to illustrate the way in which ordinary strict liability statutes do require "fault."

If the notion of fault requires that there be some sort of causal relationship between the accused and the act in question, it is arguable that the *Lindberg* case takes account of such a relationship. The defendant in the *Lindberg* case by virtue of his position *qua* officer of the bank had considerable control over the affairs of that bank. And he had even greater control over his own borrowing activities. If the element of control is sufficient to permit some kind of a causal inference as to events occurring within that control, then a finding of fault in this sense does not seem arbitrary in the same manner in which a finding of fault in the hypothetical clearly would be.

Admittedly, there is a second, more restricted sense of "fault" which was clearly not present in the *Lindberg* case. This would require that the actor intended to have the particular act—borrowing money *from his own bank*—occur. And yet, there was a conscious intent to engage in just that activity—banking—which the defendant knew or should have known to be subject to criminal sanctions under certain specified circumstances. Strict liability offenses can be interpreted as legislative judgments that persons who intentionally engage in certain activities and occupy some peculiar or distinctive position of control are to be held accountable for the occurrence of certain consequences.

It is entirely possible that such a characterization of fault might still be regarded as unsatisfactory.[31] The mere fact that there was control over the general activity may be insufficient to justify a finding of fault in every case in which certain results ensue. The kind of fault which must be present before criminal sanctions ought to be imposed, so the argument might continue, is one which is predicated upon some affirmative state of mind with respect to the particular act or consequence.

There may be good reasons why this more restrictive concept of fault ought to be insisted upon in the criminal law. Indeed, I think such reasons exist and are persuasive. Furthermore, "deontological" arguments, which rest upon analysis of what ought to be entailed by concepts of justice, criminal guilt, and culpability might support the more restrictive definition. Ar-

guments of this nature will not be challenged here, for to a considerable extent this article is written in the hope that others will feel the need to articulate these contentions more precisely. However, there remains one final thesis which must be questioned. That is, that a person who accepts this more restrictive notion of fault can consistently believe that negligent acts ought to be punished by the criminal law.[32]

If the objection to the concept of strict liability is that the defendant's state of mind is irrelevant, then a comparable objection seems to lie against offenses founded upon criminal negligence. For the jury in a criminal negligence prosecution asks only whether the activity of the defendant violated some standard of care which a reasonable member of the community would not have violated.[33] To the extent that strict liability statutes can be interpreted as legislative judgments that conduct which produces or permits certain consequences is unreasonable, strict criminal liability is similar to a jury determination that conduct in a particular case was unreasonable.

There are, of course, important differences between the two kinds of offenses. Precisely because strict liability statutes require an antecedent judgment of *per se* unreasonableness, they necessarily require a more general classification of the kind of activity which is to be regulated. They tend, and perhaps inherently so, to neglect many features which ought to be taken into account before such a judgment is forthcoming. Criminal negligence, on the other hand, demands an essentially *a posteriori* judgment as to the conduct in the particular case. As such, it surely provides more opportunity for the jury to consider just those factors which are most significant in determining whether the standard of care was observed.

In spite of these important distinctions, insofar as strict liability statutes are condemned because they fail to require a mental element, negligence as a category of criminality ought to be likewise criticized. There may be independent reasons for urging the retention or rejection of the category of criminal negligence—just as there may be such reasons for accepting or disallowing strict liability offenses. But the way in which the two kinds of criminal liability are similar must be kept in mind whenever they are evaluated.

CONCLUSION

It is readily conceded that many strict liability statutes do not perform any very meaningful or desirable social function. It is admitted too, that legislatures may have been both negligent and unwise in their selection of strict criminal liability as the means by which to achieve certain ends. But until the issues raised in the preceding discussion have been considered more carefully and precisely, it will *not* be immediately evident that all strict liability statutes are inherently vicious and irrational legislative or judicial blunders.

NOTES

[1] The history of those strict liability offenses which are of legislative origin is of quite recent date. One of the first cases in which a statute was interpreted as imposing strict criminal liability was *Regina v. Woodrow*, 15 M. & W. 404, 153 Eng. Rep. 907 (1846). For an exhaustive account of the earlier history of these statutory offenses see Sayre, "Public Welfare Offenses," 33 *Colum. L. Rev.* 55, 56–66 (1933).

[2] "Severe criminal sanctions" refer to imprisonment as opposed to the mere imposition of a fine.

[3] Model Penal Code §2.05, comment (Tent. Draft No. 4, 1955).

[4] Sayre, *supra* note 1, at 56.

[5] Hall, *General Principles of Criminal Law* 304–5 (1947). See also Williams, *Criminal Law* §§70–76 (1953); Hart, "The Aims of Criminal Law," 23 *Law & Contemp. Prob.* 401, 422–25 (1958).

[6] Sayre, *supra* note 1, at 83.

[7] If the offenses were always punishable by something less than imprisonment then it would surely be relevant to ask in what sense they were penal in anything but name. This appears in part to be Hall's criticism of Sayre's article. See Hall, op. cit. *supra* note 5, at 279.

[8] 258 U.S. 250 (1922).

[9] 125 Wash. 51, 215 Pac. 41 (1923).

[10] Wash. Comp. Stat. § 3259 (Remington 1922).

[11] 13 Cox Crim. Cas. 138 (1875).

[12] Offenses Against the Person Act, 1861, 24 & 25 Vict., c. 100, § 55.

[13] Exhaustive enumerations of leading strict liability cases can be found in Sayre, "Public Welfare Offenses," 33 *Colum. L. Rev.* 55 (1933).

[14] Jackson, "Absolute Prohibition in Statutory Offences," 6 *Camb. L.J.* 83, 88 (1938).

[15] There is, of course, a sense in which the notion of having "committed an act" is far from unambiguous. Depending upon how "act" is defined, it may or may not be true that the sole question is whether the defendant committed the act. The fact that the defendant was sleepwalking or insane at the time might be treated as bearing upon the issue of whether the "act" was committed. There is an obvious sense in which even this determination requires some inquiry into the defendant's state of mind.

[16] This would be true whether *mens rea* is interpreted as requiring only that the person "intend" to do the act, or as requiring that the person intend to do something which is morally wrong. The latter interpretation is advanced in Mueller, "On Common Law Mens Rea," 42 *Minn. L. Rev.* 1043 (1958).

[17] One author has suggested that the question of whether a crime has been committed ought to be determined solely by deciding whether the defendant committed the specific act proscribed by the statute. The actor's mental state would be relevant to the separate question of the actor's punishment. Levitt, "Extent and Function of the Doctrine of Mens Rea," 17 *Ill. L. Rev.* 578 (1923). This bifurcation is unobjectionable insofar as it recognizes that one of the factors to be considered in the sentencing of an individual is his mental state at the time of the crime. The author seems to imply that in the absence of a finding of the requisite mental element it would be proper for the court not to punish the defendant at all. This, too, is perhaps in itself unobjectionable. The question remains then whether it makes any sense to speak of this defendant as having committed a crime.

[18] Hall, *General Principles of Criminal Law* 302–3 (1947); Williams, *Criminal Law* § 76, at 269 (1953); Sayre, "Public Welfare Offenses," 33 *Colum. L. Rev.* 55, 56 (1933).

[19] Mueller, op. cit. *supra* note 16, at 1060.

[20] Mueller cites the recent case of *Lambert v. California*, 355 U.S. 225 (1957) as implicitly attacking all strict liability statutes on this ground. Such a reading of the case seems plainly incorrect. At *most*, the reasoning of the court can be construed as suggesting that strict li-

ability statutes of which the defendant neither had nor ought to have had notice might violate due process. More plausibly, the court struck down the conviction in *Lambert* because the statute there reached a very general kind of activity which the defendant could not reasonably have supposed to be regulated by statute at all: namely, the mere fact that the defendant came into a city and failed to register with the sheriff as an ex-convict. Surely, it is reading too much into the opinion to find a disposition on the part of the Court to group all strict liability statutes in this class.

[21]It is assumed throughout the remainder of this article that knowledge of the relevant strict liability statutes is possessed or is readily capable of being possessed by those subject to the statutes.

[22]"There is, first, the opinion of highly qualified experts that the present rules are regarded by unscrupulous persons merely 'as a license fee for doing an illegitimate business.'" Hall, op. cit., *supra* note 18, at 301.

[23]Glanville Williams concedes both of these points. Williams, op. cit. *supra* note 18, § 73, at 258. But he argues in part that this kind of deterrent places an "undesirable restraint on proper activities." Ibid. Yet, to a considerable extent, this only succeeds in raising the precise point at issue: namely, whether the restraint which is imposed upon activity is undesirable. The legislature might believe that for certain kinds of activity, at least, the restraint was less undesirable than the production of those consequences proscribed by the statute.

[24]Nor do there appear to be any very serious undesirable societal consequences in discouraging persons from having intercourse with females who may be around the age of sixteen. See *Regina v. Prince*, 13 Cox Crim. Cas. 138 (1875).

[25]See the more recent federal case, *United States v. Dotterweich*, 320 U.S. 277 (1943), where the defendant, president of a drug company, was indicted and convicted under the Federal Food, Drug, and Cosmetic Act, 52 Stat. 1040 (1938), 21 U.S.C. §§ 301-92 (1938) for shipping misbranded and adulterated drugs in interstate commerce. There was no showing that Dotterweich personally was either negligently or intentionally engaged in the proscribed conduct. It was sufficient that he was the president of the company.

[26]In this connection, it has been suggested that there is little evidence that legislatures consciously intend criminal statutes to be strict liability statutes. The most exhaustive examination of this issue is in a recent study conducted by the Wisconsin Law Review, 1956 *Wis. L. Rev.* 625. And while it seems clear that there is little affirmative evidence on this score, what evidence is available seems to indicate that at times the legislature has consciously intended the statute to be a strict criminal liability statute. Cf. id. at 644. Additionally, Glanville Williams argues that Parliament seems to have intended to retain strict liability in the statute interpreted by the court in the *Prince* case. See Williams, op. cit. *supra* note 18, §73, at 259–60.

[27]Cf. Note, 74 *L.Q. Rev.* 321, 343 (1958). "It must always be remembered that the primary purpose of the criminal law is to prevent the commission of certain acts which it regards as being against the public interest and not to punish or to reform a wrongdoer. It may, therefore, be necessary to provide for strict liability when this is the only practical way to guard against the commission of the harmful act."

While I do not feel committed to the view that the primary function of the criminal law is that of the prevention of certain acts, the writer of the Note seems correct in suggesting that if an essentially utilitarian view of the criminal law is adopted, then the justification of many strict liability offenses becomes increasingly plausible

[28]Cf. p. 743 *infra*.

[29]Hall, op. cit. *supra* note 18, at 304.

[30]See note 15 *supra*.

[31]Hall, op. cit. *supra* note 18, at 304, clearly regards such a definition as unsatisfactory.

[32]The Model Penal·Code §§ 2.02, 2.05 (Tent. Draft No. 4, 1955) appears to take this approach.

[33]I find highly unpersuasive, attempts to treat negligence as in fact requiring *mens rea*. It has been argued that "in the case of negligence . . . the law operates with an objective standard which, based upon experience, closely approximates that under which the defendant must have operated in fact. In my opinion, therefore, we are here confronted with the use of a schematic and crude way of establishing the *mens rea*, but one which nevertheless evidences the law's concern for the mental attitude of the defendant." Mueller, *supra* note 16, at 1063–64.

If Mueller is suggesting merely that when certain kinds of consequences occur in certain kinds of situations it is reasonable to infer that the defendant in fact had a certain state of mind, then I find nothing objectionable about his claim. But, of course, *mutatis mutandis*, the same can be said for many strict liability offenses. If, on the other hand, he is suggesting that negligence in fact requires the jury to make a determination as to the presence or absence of the defendant's *mens rea*, then I do not understand in what sense this is accurate.

QUESTIONS FOR DISCUSSION

1. Explain Wasserstrom's criticisms of Hall. How could Hall best respond? Are his best responses good enough to satisfy you? Why or why not?

2. What is the best positive reason for strict criminal liability according to Wasserstrom? Do you agree? Why or why not?

3. Is someone convicted of a strict liability offense at fault, according to Wasserstrom? Why or why not? Do his claims apply equally well to all kinds of strict criminal liability? Why or why not?

4. Wasserstrom argues that strict liability and negligence liability are so similar that "it seems difficult to attack the former without at the same time calling the latter into comparable question." (p. 857) Explain his arguments for this claim. Do you agree? Why or why not?

TISON V. ARIZONA

481 U.S. 137 (1986)

O'CONNOR, J., delivers the opinion of the Court in which REHNQUIST, C. J., and WHITE, POWELL, and SCALIA, JJ., joined.

The question presented is whether the petitioners' participation in the events leading up to and following the murder of four members of a family makes the sentences of death imposed by the Arizona courts constitutionally permissible although neither petitioner specifically intended to kill the victims and neither inflicted the fatal gunshot wounds. . . .

Gary Tison was sentenced to life imprisonment as the result of a prison escape during the course of which he had killed a guard. After he had been in prison a number of years, Gary Tison's wife, their three sons Donald, Ricky, and Raymond, Gary's brother Joseph, and other relatives made plans to help Gary Tison escape again. . . .

On July 30, 1978, the three Tison brothers entered the Arizona State Prison at Florence carrying a large ice chest filled with guns. The Tisons armed [Randy] Greenawalt and their father, and the group, brandishing their weapons, locked the prison guards and visitors present in a storage closet. The five men fled the prison grounds in the Tisons' Ford Galaxy automobile. No shots were fired at the prison.

After leaving the prison, the men abandoned the Ford automobile and proceeded on to an isolated house in a white Lincoln automobile that the brothers had parked at a hospital near the prison. At the house, the Lincoln automobile had a flat tire; the only spare tire was pressed into service. After two nights at the house, the group drove toward Flagstaff. As the group traveled on back roads and secondary highways through the desert, another tire blew out. The group decided to flag down a passing motorist and steal a car. Raymond stood out in front of the Lincoln; the other four armed themselves and lay in wait by the side of the road. One car passed by without stopping, but a second car, a Mazda occupied by John Lyons, his wife Donnelda, his 2-year-old son Christopher, and his 15-year-old niece, Theresa Tyson, pulled over to render aid.

As Raymond showed John Lyons the flat tire on the Lincoln, the other Tisons and Greenawalt emerged. The Lyons family was forced into the backseat of the Lincoln. Raymond and Donald drove the Lincoln down a dirt road off the highway and then down a gas line service road farther into the desert; Gary Tison, Ricky Tison, and Randy Greenawalt followed in the Lyons' Mazda. The two cars were parked trunk to trunk and the Lyons family was ordered to stand in front of the Lincoln's headlights. . . .

The petitioners' statements diverge to some extent, but it appears that both of them went back towards the Mazda, along with Donald, while Randy Greenawalt and Gary Tison stayed at the Lincoln guarding the victims. . . . In any event, petitioners agree they saw Greenawalt and their father brutally murder their four captives with repeated blasts from their shotguns. Neither made an effort to help the victims, though both later stated they were surprised by the shooting. The Tisons got into the Mazda and drove away, continuing their flight. Physical evidence suggested that Theresa Tyson managed to crawl away from the bloodbath, severely injured. She died in the desert after the Tisons left.

Several days later the Tisons and Greenawalt were apprehended after a shootout at a police roadblock. Donald Tison was killed. Gary Tison escaped into the desert where he subsequently died of exposure. Raymond and Ricky Tison and Randy Greenawalt were captured and tried jointly for the crimes associated with the prison break itself and the shootout at the roadblock; each was convicted and sentenced.

The State then individually tried each of the petitioners for capital murder of the four victims as well as for the associated crimes of armed robbery, kidnaping, and car theft. The capital murder charges were based on Arizona felony-murder law providing that a killing occurring during the perpetration of robbery or kidnaping is capital murder, . . . and that each participant in the kidnaping or robbery is legally responsible for the acts of his accomplices. . . . Each of the petitioners was convicted of the four murders under these accomplice liability and felony-murder statutes. . . . [T]he Judge sentenced both petitioners to death.

On direct appeal, the Arizona Supreme Court affirmed. . . .

We granted certiorari in order to consider the Arizona Supreme Court's application of *Enmund.* . . .

II

In *Enmund v. Florida,* this Court reversed the death sentence of a defendant convicted under Florida's felony-murder rule. Enmund was the driver of the "getaway" car in an armed robbery of a dwelling. The occupants of the house, an elderly couple, resisted and Enmund's accomplices killed them. The Florida Supreme Court found the inference that Enmund was the person in the car by the side of the road waiting to help his accomplices escape sufficient to support his sentence of death. . . .

This Court, citing the weight of legislative and community opinion, found a broad societal consensus, with which it agreed, that the death penalty was disproportional to the crime of robbery-felony murder "in these circumstances." . . . The Court noted that although 32 American jurisdictions permitted the imposition of the death penalty for felony murders under a variety of circumstances, Florida was 1 of only 8 jurisdictions that authorized the death penalty "solely for participation in a robbery in which another robber takes life." . . . Enmund was, therefore, sentenced under a distinct minority regime, a regime that permitted the imposition of the death penalty for felony murder *simpliciter.* . . .

Against this background, the Court undertook its own proportionality analysis. Armed robbery is a serious offense, but one for which the penalty of death is plainly excessive; the imposition of the death penalty for robbery, therefore, violates the Eighth and Fourteenth Amendments' proscription "'against all punishments which by their excessive length or severity are greatly disproportioned to the offenses charged.'" . . . Furthermore, the Court found that Enmund's degree of participation in *the murders* was so tangential that it could not be said to justify a sentence of death. It found that neither the deterrent nor the retributive purposes of the death penalty were advanced by imposing the death penalty upon Enmund. The *Enmund* Court was unconvinced "that the threat that the death penalty will be imposed for murder will measurably deter one who does not kill and has no intention or purpose that life will be taken." . . . In reaching this conclusion, the Court relied upon the fact that killing only rarely occurred during the course of robberies, and such killing as did occur even more rarely resulted in death sentences if the evidence did not support an inference that the defendant intended to kill. The Court acknowledged, however, that "[i]t would be very different if the likelihood of a killing in the course of a robbery were so substantial that one should share the blame for the killing if he somehow participated in the felony." . . .

That difference was also related to the second purpose of capital punishment, retribution. The heart of the retribution rationale is that a criminal sentence must be directly related to the personal culpability of the criminal offender. . . . Since Enmund's own participation in the felony murder was so attenuated and since there was no proof that Enmund had any culpable mental state, . . . the death penalty was excessive retribution for his crimes.

Enmund explicitly dealt with two distinct subsets of all felony murders in assessing whether Enmund's sentence was disproportional under the Eighth Amendment. At one pole was Enmund himself: the minor actor in an armed robbery, not on the scene, who neither intended to kill nor was found to have had any culpable mental state. Only a small minority of States even authorized the death penalty in such circumstances and even within those jurisdictions the death penalty was almost never exacted for such a crime. The Court held that capital punishment was disproportional in these cases. *Enmund* also clearly dealt with the other polar case: the felony murderer who actually killed, attempted to kill, or intended to kill. The Court clearly held that the equally small minority of jurisdictions that limited the death penalty to these circumstances could continue to exact it in accordance with local law when the circumstances warranted. The Tison brothers' cases fall into neither of these neat categories.

Petitioners argue strenuously that they did not "intend to kill" as that concept has been generally understood in the common law. We accept this as true. . . .

On the other hand, it is equally clear that petitioners also fall outside the category of felony murderers for whom *Enmund* explicitly held the death penalty disproportional: their degree of participation in the crimes was major rather than minor, and the record would support a finding of the culpable mental state of reckless indifference to human life. We take the facts as the Arizona Supreme Court has given them to us. . . .

Raymond Tison brought an arsenal of lethal weapons into the Arizona State Prison which he then handed over to two convicted murderers, one of whom he knew had killed a prison guard in the course of a previous escape attempt. By his own admission he was prepared to kill in furtherance of the prison break. He performed the crucial role of flagging down a passing car occupied by an innocent family whose fate was then entrusted to the known killers he had previously armed. He robbed these people at their direction and then guarded the victims at gunpoint while they considered what next to do. He stood by and watched the killing, making no effort to assist the victims before, during, or after the shooting. Instead, he chose to assist the killers in their continuing criminal endeavors, ending in a gun battle with the police in the final showdown.

Ricky Tison's behavior differs in slight details only. . . .

These facts not only indicate that the Tison brothers' participation in the crime was anything but minor; they also would clearly support a finding that they both subjectively appreciated that their acts were likely to result in the taking of innocent life. The issue raised by this case is whether the Eighth Amendment prohibits the death penalty in the intermediate case of the defendant whose participation is major and whose mental state is one of reckless indifference to the value of human life. *Enmund* does not specifically address this point. We now take up the task of determining whether the Eighth Amendment proportionality requirement bars the death penalty under these circumstances.

Like the *Enmund* Court, we find the state legislatures' judgment as to proportionality in these circumstances relevant to this constitutional inquiry. . . . Th[e] substantial and recent legislative authorization of the death penalty for the crime of felony murder regardless of the absence of a finding of an intent to kill powerfully suggests that our society does *not* reject the death penalty as grossly excessive under these circumstances. . . .

A critical facet of the individualized determination of culpability required in capital cases is the mental state with which the defendant commits the crime. Deeply ingrained in our legal tradition is the idea that the more purposeful is the criminal conduct, the more serious is the offense, and therefore, the more severely it ought to be punished. . . . A narrow focus on the question of whether or not a given defendant "intended to kill," however, is a highly unsatisfactory means of definitively distinguishing the most culpable and dangerous of murderers. Many who intend to, and do, kill are not criminally liable at all—those who act in self-defense or with other justification or excuse. Other intentional homicides, though criminal, are often felt undeserving of the death penalty—those that are the result of provocation. On the other hand, some nonintentional murderers may be among the most dangerous and inhumane of all—the person who tortures another not caring whether the victim lives or dies, or the robber who shoots someone in the course of the robbery, utterly indifferent to the fact that the desire to rob may have the unintended consequence of killing the victim as well as taking the victim's property. This reckless indifference to the value of human life may be every bit as shocking to the moral sense as an "intent to kill." . . .

We will not attempt to precisely delineate the particular types of conduct and states of mind warranting imposition of the death penalty here. Rather, we simply hold that major participation in the felony committed, combined with reckless indifference to human life, is sufficient to satisfy the *Enmund* culpability requirement. The Arizona courts have clearly found that the former exists; we now vacate the judgments below and remand for determination of the latter in further proceedings not inconsistent with this opinion. . . .

JUSTICE BRENNAN, with whom JUSTICE MARSHALL joins and with whom JUSTICE BLACKMUN and JUSTICE STEVENS join as to Parts I through IV–A, dissenting.

The murders that Gary Tison and Randy Greenawalt committed revolt and grieve all who learn of them. When the deaths of the

Lyons family and Theresa Tyson were first reported, many in Arizona erupted "in a towering yell" for retribution and justice. Yet Gary Tison, the central figure in this tragedy, the man who had his family arrange his and Greenawalt's escape from prison, and the man who chose, with Greenawalt, to murder this family while his sons stood by, died of exposure in the desert before society could arrest him and bring him to trial. The question this case presents is what punishment Arizona may constitutionally exact from two of Gary Tison's sons for their role in these events. Because our precedents and our Constitution compel a different answer than the one the Court reaches today, I dissent. . . .

II

The facts on which the Court relies are not sufficient, in my view, to support the Court's conclusion that petitioners acted with reckless disregard for human life. But even if they were, the Court's decision to restrict its vision to the limited set of facts that "the Arizona Supreme Court has given . . . to us" . . . is improper. . . .

The evidence in the record overlooked today regarding petitioners' mental states with respect to the shootings is not trivial. For example, while the Court has found that petitioners made no effort prior to the shooting to assist the victims, the uncontradicted statements of both petitioners are that just prior to the shootings they were attempting to find a jug of water to give to the family. While the Court states that petitioners were on the scene during the shooting and that they watched it occur, Raymond stated that he and Ricky were still engaged in repacking the Mazda after finding the water jug when the shootings occurred. Ricky stated that they had returned with the water, but were still some distance ("farther than this room") from the Lincoln when the shootings started, . . . and that the brothers then turned away from the scene and went back to the Mazda. . . . Neither stated that they anticipated that the shootings would occur, or that they could have done anything to prevent them or to help the victims afterward. Both, however, expressed feelings of surprise, helplessness, and regret. This statement of Raymond's is illustrative:

"Well, I just think you should know when we first came into this we had an agreement with my dad that nobody would get hurt because we [the brothers] wanted no one hurt. And when this [killing of the kidnap victims] came about we were not expecting it. And it took us by surprise as much as it took the family [the victims] by surprise because we were not expecting this to happen. And I feel bad about it happening. I wish we could [have done] something to stop it, but by the time it happened it was too late to stop it. And it's just something we are going to live with the rest of our lives. It will always be there." . . .

III

Notwithstanding the Court's unwarranted observations on the applicability of its new standard to this case, the basic flaw in today's decision is the Court's failure to conduct the sort of proportionality analysis that the Constitution and past cases require. Creation of a new category of culpability is not enough to distinguish this case from *Enmund*. The Court must also establish that death is a proportionate punishment for individuals in this category. In other words, the Court must demonstrate that major participation in a felony with a state of mind of reckless indifference to human life deserves the same punishment as intending to commit a murder or actually committing a murder. The Court does not attempt to conduct a proportionality review of the kind performed in past cases raising a proportionality question, . . . but instead offers two reasons in support of its view.

A

One reason the Court offers for its conclusion that death is proportionate punishment for persons falling within its new category is that limiting the death penalty to those who intend to kill "is a highly unsatisfactory means of definitively distinguishing the most culpable and dangerous of murderers." . . . [A]n exception to the requirement that only intentional murders be punished with death might be made for persons who actually commit an act of homicide; *Enmund*, by distinguishing from the accomplice case "those who kill," clearly reserved that question. But the constitutionality of the death penalty for those individuals is no more relevant to this case than it was to *Enmund*, because this case, like *Enmund*, involves accomplices *who did not kill*. Thus, although some of the "most culpable and dangerous of murderers" may be those who killed without specifically intending to kill, it is considerably more difficult to apply that rubric convincingly to those who not only did not intend to kill, but who also have not killed. . . .

The person who chooses to act recklessly and is indifferent to the possibility of fatal consequences often deserves serious punishment. But because that person has not chosen to kill, his or her moral and criminal culpability is of a different degree than that of one who killed or intended to kill.

The importance of distinguishing between these different choices is rooted in our belief in the "freedom of the human will and a consequent ability and duty of the normal individual to choose between good and evil." To be faithful to this belief, which is "universal and persistent in mature systems of law," the criminal law must ensure that the punishment an individual receives conforms to the choices that individual has made. Differential punishment of reckless and intentional actions is therefore essential if we are to retain "the relation between criminal liability and moral culpability" on which criminal justice depends. . . .

B

The Court's second reason for abandoning the intent requirement is based on its survey of state statutes authorizing the death penalty

for felony murder, and on a handful of state cases. On this basis, the Court concludes that "[o]nly a small minority *of those jurisdictions imposing capital punishment for felony murder* have rejected the possibility of a capital sentence absent an intent to kill, and we do not find this minority position constitutionally required.". . . The Court would thus have us believe that "the majority of American jurisdictions clearly authorize capital punishment" in cases such as this. . . . This is not the case. First, the Court excludes from its survey those jurisdictions that have abolished the death penalty and those that have authorized it only in circumstances different from those presented here. When these jurisdictions are included, and are considered with those jurisdictions that require a finding of intent to kill in order to impose the death sentence for felony murder, one discovers that approximately three-fifths of American jurisdictions do not authorize the death penalty for a nontriggerman absent a finding that he intended to kill. Thus, contrary to the Court's implication that its view is consonant with that of "the majority of American jurisdictions,". . . the Court's view is itself distinctly the minority position.

Second, it is critical to examine not simply those jurisdictions that authorize the death penalty in a given circumstance, but those that actually *impose* it. Evidence that a penalty is imposed only infrequently suggests not only that jurisdictions are reluctant to apply it but also that, when it is applied, its imposition is arbitrary and therefore unconstitutional. Thus, the Court in *Enmund* examined the relevant statistics on the imposition of the death penalty for accomplices in a felony murder. The Court found that of all executions between 1954 and 1982, there were "*only 6 cases out of 362 where a nontriggerman felony murderer was executed. All six executions took place in 1955.*". . . This evidence obviously militates against imposing the death penalty on petitioners as powerfully as it did against imposing it on Enmund. . . .

QUESTIONS FOR DISCUSSION

1. If you had been on the Supreme Court, would you have voted with the majority in *Enmund v. Florida*? Why or why not?

2. If you had been on the Supreme Court, would you have voted with the majority or with the dissent in *Tison*? Why? If your answer to this question is different from your answer to question (1), explain why.

3. Would a conviction for felony murder in *Tison* be more justified if the defendants had not been sentenced to death but only to life imprisonment, even if this is still more punishment than they would have received if nobody had died? Why or why not?

4. If two people commit burglary together, and one intentionally kills the owner, should the other burglar be found guilty of felony murder if this other burglar did not know that the killer was armed? Why or why not?

5. If two people rob a bank together, the police catch them in the act, and a policeman is killed in a shootout with both robbers, should the bank robber who did not kill the policeman be found guilty of felony murder? If the only person killed in the shootout is one of the bank robbers, and he is shot by a policeman, then should the other bank robber be found guilty of felony murder? Explain and justify your answers.

6. In *Furman v. Georgia* (Section 6.6), Furman testified that he was burglarizing a home when he heard the owner, so he started backing out, but he tripped over a wire, and his gun went off and shot the owner, who was standing behind a door. The Georgia Supreme Court accepted these facts, but Furman was still found guilty of first-degree murder and sentenced to death, because he caused death while committing a felony. Was his sentence fair? Why or why not?

7. Suppose that a truck driver runs over a cardboard box in the middle of the road, just because it is too much trouble to avoid it. Unfortunately, a child is playing in the box, and the child is killed. The truck driver had no way of knowing that anything was in the box. Should the truck driver be found guilty of murder or manslaughter? What if the truck was stolen or contained illegal cargo, so the truck driver was committing a felony at the time? Then should the driver be found guilty of murder or manslaughter? Why or why not?

◼ Case Study—Liability for Rape

LORDS' DECISION ON
THE LAW OF RAPE

GLANVILLE WILLIAMS

EDITORS' NOTE: This letter to the Editor of the London *Times* was written in response to *Director of Public Prosecutions v. Morgan.* For a description of the facts of that case, see the second paragraph of the reading by Susan Estrich, which follows Williams' letter.

SIR:

There has been a good deal of misunderstanding of the recent decision of the law lords in the rape case, which merely applied established principles.

(1) With a few exceptions, which need not be considered (and ought not to exist), serious crimes require a mental element (an intention to do the act or to produce the result, and knowledge of the facts, or at least conscious recklessness).

(2) Rape is a serious crime, involving sexual intercourse with a woman without her consent.

(3) Therefore rape requires the mental element that the man must know that the woman does not consent.

This was the simple point decided by their lordships, and the decision is warmly to be welcomed. The opposing view was that a man could be convicted of rape although he honestly believed that the woman was consenting, if he was stupid (unreasonable) in forming that belief. To convict the stupid man would be to convict him for what lawyers call inadvertent

negligence—honest conduct which may be the best that this man can do but that does not come up to the standard of the so-called reasonable man. People ought not to be punished for negligence except in some minor offences established by statute. Rape carries a possible sentence of imprisonment for life, and it would be wrong to have a law of negligent rape.

Further, it is unnecessary. Except perhaps in one situation to be mentioned in a moment, it is virtually inconceivable that even a stupid man would fail to realise that a woman with whom he has sexual intercourse does not consent. Let me try to clear away some misconceptions.

(a) Many charges of rape fail because of a clash of evidence; if there is a doubt, the jury have to give the man the benefit of it. This difficulty is inherent in the situation. It would make almost no difference even if rape were turned by statute into an offence of strict liability (not requiring a mental element or other fault on the man's part); there would still be conflicts of evidence on whether the man had intercourse with the woman or whether the woman consented. For the purpose of any further discussion of the problem we must assume that the jury have found that the act took place and that the woman did not consent.

(b) What further difficulty does the prosecution face in proving that the man knew that the woman did not consent? Virtually none. If a man procures a woman's submission to sexual intercourse by threats, it is rape. If he is a stranger and an intruder, the jury will very readily believe that he used threats. No one who uses threats against a woman will be heard to say that he thought she consented. If the man does not use threats, even by implication, the only way that anyone can tell whether the woman consents or not is by her words or behaviour. It is no use her saying afterwards that she did not really consent, if she did nothing to indicate this at the time. If she protests, the man is bound to know it. There is nothing in the Lords' decision to prevent a judge directing the jury that if anyone would have realised from what the woman said and did that she was not consenting, then they are entitled to conclude that the defendant realised it, unless there are some other facts to raise a doubt in their minds. What the judge must not tell the jury, on a charge of rape or any other serious crime, is that they can convict the defendant although he did not know that the vital facts existed and was not reckless as to those facts, if he was stupid in not realising that they existed.

Critics of the recent decision should note not only that the jury convicted the defendants but that the House of Lords affirmed the conviction on the ground that any jury properly instructed would have convicted. The only type of case in which an insistence on the mental element in rape is likely to give any opening to the defence is where the defendant claims that he was so intoxicated that he did not realise that the woman was resisting, although any sober person would have realised it.

Two remarks may be made about this. First, there is no reported instance of the defence of intoxication having been set up in a rape case in this country, and before becoming alarmed about it we might wait to see if it ever succeeds. A sensible jury may take the view that a man who is sober enough to perform is sober enough to realise that the woman is resisting. Secondly, the question of intoxication in relation to the mental element in crime is a general one, and one that certainly needs legislative attention, though not particularly in relation to rape. Proposals on the subject are being considered by one of the committees considering the reform of the criminal law.

Yours faithfully,
GLANVILLE WILLIAMS

QUESTIONS FOR DISCUSSION

1. What arguments does Williams suggest against rape convictions when the defendant was merely negligent?

2. Williams suggests that "conscious recklessness" is enough of a mental element for a conviction of a serious crime. What is the difference between recklessness and negligence with regard to rape? Do you agree that recklessness is enough for a conviction for rape? Why or why not?

3. Williams claims that, if the prosecution can prove that the woman did not consent, then the prosecution will have "virtually" no difficulty proving that the man knew that the woman did not consent. Why does he think this? Do you agree? What further evidence, if any, would be necessary to prove the man's knowledge?

REAL RAPE

SUSAN ESTRICH

Until very recently, if any rape case was included in a basic criminal law casebook, it was likely to be the 1975 decision of the British House of Lords in *Director of Public Prosecutions v. Morgan.*[1] *Morgan* stands for the proposition that if a man believes that a woman is consenting to sex, he cannot be convicted of rape, no matter how unreasonable his belief may be.

The four co-defendants in *Morgan* had been drinking together; when they failed in their efforts to "find some women," Mr. Morgan invited them home to have intercourse with his wife. According to these three, Morgan told them not to be surprised if his wife struggled, since she was "kinky" and this was the only way she could get "turned on." All four were convicted, Mr. Morgan for aiding and abetting, and their convictions were affirmed by the intermediate Court of Appeals.[2] The question posed to the House of Lords, the highest British court, was: "Whether in rape the defendant can properly be convicted notwithstanding that he in fact believed that the woman consented, if such a belief was not based on reasonable grounds."[3] In other words, is it enough for a rape conviction that the man's belief in consent was unreasonable (what the law terms "negligence"), or is it necessary that he himself also have known, or at least known the risk, of nonconsent.

The majority of the House of Lords answered that negligence would not do; if a man believed, honestly but foolishly, in consent, he could not be convicted. According to Lord Hailsham:

Once one has accepted, what seems to me abundantly clear, that the prohibited act in rape is non-consensual sexual intercourse, and that the guilty state of mind is an intention to commit it, it seems to me to follow as a matter of inexorable logic that there is no room either for a "defence" of honest belief or mistake, or for a defence of honest and reasonable belief and mistake. Either the prosecution proves that the accused had the requisite intent, or it does not. In the former case it succeeds, and in the latter it fails. Since honest belief clearly negatives intent, the reasonableness of that belief can only be evidence for or against the view that the belief and therefore the intent was actually held.[4]

Whether the decision followed "as a matter of inexorable logic" was a matter of some dispute. The London *Times* attacked *Morgan* as "unduly legalistic" and not in accord with "common sense,"[5] while the academic community sprang to the defense of the House of Lords decision as, in Professor J. C. Smith's view, "a victory for common sense so far as intention in the criminal law is concerned."[6] A special committee was created in the wake of the controversy to review the decision. The committee's recommendation, ultimately enacted in 1976, retained the *Morgan* approach in requiring that at the time of intercourse the man "knows that she does not consent to the intercourse or he is reckless as to whether she consents to it," but provided that the reasonableness of the man's belief "is a matter to which the jury is to have regard, in conjunction with any other relevant matters, in considering whether he so believed."[7]

In *Morgan* itself the House of Lords, although holding that negligence was not sufficient to

Susan Estrich, *Real Rape* (Cambridge: Harvard University Press, 1987), Chapter 6

establish liability for rape, also upheld the convictions on the ground that no jury, properly instructed in the circumstances of that case, could have concluded that the defendants honestly believed that their victim was consenting. Yet that is precisely what happened in an English case decided shortly after *Morgan*. On facts substantially similar (a husband procuring a buddy to engage in sex with his crying wife), an English jury concluded that the defendant had been negligent in believing, honestly but unreasonably, in the wife's consent. On the authority of *Morgan*, the court held that he deserved acquittal.[8] Because the later case involved not three buddies but one, it was, by the definition of this book, a "simple" rape, not an aggravated one. In the simple rape, the rule of *Morgan* made a determinative difference.

While the matter of the requisite intent for rape was hotly debated in England and the Commonwealth countries, it was barely mentioned in American cases. In the older opinions there is some discussion of intent with respect to attempted rape—where the essence of the crime is criminal intent. But in completed rapes, questions of intent or mistake are rarely even mentioned. That is not surprising: the man who jumps from the bushes could hardly be expected to persuade anyone that he thought the woman was consenting; and in more "appropriate" circumstances, the doctrines of consent and force provide far more comprehensive protection against any mistake as to consent.

A number of recent American cases have gone so far as to say explicitly that there is no intent requirement at all for rape. The Maine Supreme Judicial Court has stated that there is no requirement of a culpable mental state for rape: "The legislature, by carefully defining the sex offenses in the criminal code, and by making no reference to a culpable state of mind for rape, clearly indicated that rape compelled by force or threat requires no culpable state of mind."[9]

In Pennsylvania the Superior Court held in 1982 that even a reasonable belief as to the victim's consent would not exculpate a defendant charged with rape:

> defendant contends that the court should have instructed the jury that if the defendant reasonably believed that the prosecutrix had consented to his sexual advances that this would constitute a defense to the rape and involuntary deviate sexual intercourse charge. Defendant relies on [an] obscure Alabama case . . . for this proposition. The charge requested by the defendant is not now and has never been the law of Pennsylvania. . . . If the element of the defendant's belief as to the victim's state of mind is to be established as a defense to the crime of rape then it should be done by our legislature which has the power to define crimes and offenses. We refuse to create such a defense.[10]

Similarly, in South Dakota, the state supreme court has held that "evidence of other alleged rapes cannot be deemed to be admissible because it shows intent for the reason that intent is simply not one of the elements of the crime charged."[11]

In Massachusetts the Supreme Judicial Court in 1982 left open the question whether it would recognize a defense of *reasonable* mistake of fact as to consent, while rejecting out of hand the defendant's suggestion that any mistake, reasonable or unreasonable, would be sufficient to negate the required intent to rape; such a claim was treated by the court as bordering on the ridiculous.[12] The following year the court went on to hold that a specific intent that intercourse be without consent was not an element of the crime of rape. That decision has since been construed to mean that there is no intent requirement at all as to consent in rape cases.[13]

To say that what the defendant knew or should have known about the victim's consent is irrelevant to his liability might sound like a stand favorable to the prosecution of simple rapes and to the women who are their victims.

Not necessarily. Refusing to inquire into intent leaves two possibilities: turning rape into a strict liability offense, where the man may be guilty of rape regardless of whether he (or anyone) would have recognized nonconsent in the circumstances; or defining the crime in a fashion so limited that it effectively excludes simple rapes which present any risk that the man could have been unaware or mistaken as to nonconsent. In fact, the latter approach has been employed in all of the older, and many of the newer, American cases. In virtually every case cited as rejecting an intent requirement for rape, the only reason the defendant was even arguing intent seems to be because his case would have been utterly hopeless on the issues of actual consent or resistance or force. It is not that the American courts have been more willing to expose foolish and mistaken men to conviction than their English counterparts. Rather, it is that they have provided protection for men who find themselves in these potentially ambiguous situations through the doctrines of consent, defined as nonresistance, and force, measured by resistance.

This alternative to intent is troubling for a number of reasons. First, it means that the trial focuses almost entirely on the woman, not the man. Her intent, not his, is disputed. And since her state of mind is key, her sexual history may be considered relevant, even though utterly unknown to him. Considering consent from *his* perspective, by contrast, substantially undermines the relevance of her sexual history, at least where it was unknown to him.[14]

Second, the issue to be determined is not whether the man is a rapist, but whether the woman was raped. A verdict of acquittal does more than signal that the prosecution has failed to prove the defendant guilty beyond a reasonable doubt; it signals that the prosecution has failed to prove the woman's sexual violation—her innocence—beyond a reasonable doubt. Thus, as one of the dissenters in *Rusk* put it, in disagreeing with the judgment of rape: "The court today declares the innocence

of an at best distraught young woman."[15] Presumably the dissent thought her guilty.

Third, the resistance requirement is an overbroad substitute for intent. Both can be used to enforce a male perspective on the crime and to exclude the simple rape from punishment; but although intent might be justified as protecting the individual defendant who has not made a blameworthy choice, the resistance standard requires women to risk injury to themselves in cases where there is no doubt as to the man's knowledge or his blameworthiness. The application of the resistance requirement is not limited to cases where there is uncertainty as to what the man thought, knew, or intended; it has been fully applied in cases like *Goldberg* and *Evans* where there is no question that the man's intent was to engage in intercourse regardless of nonconsent.[16] To use resistance as a substitute for intent unnecessarily and unfairly immunizes those men whose victims are afraid enough or intimidated enough, or frankly smart enough not to take the risk of resisting physically.

In short, even if the results in cases were exactly the same, it would be better if they were reached through inquiry into the man's blameworthiness instead of the woman's. In some cases the different approach might lead to a different result.

I would go even further. The key question is not simply whose intent should govern, but what we should expect and demand of men in the "appropriate" and "ambiguous" situations where rape has been most narrowly defined. It is not unfair, *Morgan* notwithstanding, to demand that men behave "reasonably" and to impose criminal penalties when they do not. Even more important, the reasonable man in the 1980s should be one who understands that a woman's word is deserving of respect, whether she is a perfect stranger or his own wife.

The traditional argument against negligence liability is that punishment should be limited to cases of choice, that it is unjust to punish a man for his stupidity and ineffective in deterrence terms. According to this view, a man should be held responsible only for what he does knowingly, or purposely, or at least aware of the risks involved. As one of *Morgan's* most respected defenders put it: "to convict the stupid man would be to convict him for what lawyers call inadvertent negligence—honest conduct which may be the best that this man can do but that does not come up to the standard of the so-called reasonable man. People ought not to be punished for negligence except in some minor offences established by statute. Rape carries a possible sentence of imprisonment for life, and it would be wrong to have a law of negligent rape."[17]

If inaccuracy or indifference to consent is "the best that this man can do" because he lacks the capacity to act reasonably, then it might well be unjust and ineffective to punish him for it.[18] But such men will be rare, at least so long as /voluntary drunkenness is not equated with inherent lack of capacity. More common is the case of the man who could have done better but did not; could have paid attention, but did not; heard her refusal or saw her tears, but decided to ignore them. The man who has the inherent capacity to act reasonably but fails to has, through that failure, made a blameworthy choice for which he can justly be punished. The law has long punished unreasonable action which leads to the loss of human life as manslaughter—a lesser crime than murder, but a crime nonetheless. By holding out the prospect of punishment for negligence, the Model Penal Code commentators point out, the law provides an additional motive to men to "take care before acting, to use their faculties and draw on their experience in gauging the potentialities of contemplated conduct."[19] The injury of sexual violation is sufficiently great, the need to provide that additional incentive pressing enough, to justify negligence liability for rape as for killing.

The real significance of saying that negligence is enough—or that unreasonable mistakes will not exculpate—will depend on how we define what is reasonable. If the "reasonable" attitude to which a male defendant is held is defined according to a "no means yes" philosophy that celebrates male aggressiveness and female passivity and limits the "tools of coercion" to physical violence, little is accomplished for women by expanding liability to negligence and requiring that mistakes be reasonable. Simple rapes would still be easy to exclude from the prohibitions of the law. On the other hand, if the reasonable man is the one who in the 1980s understands that "no means no" and that extortion for sex is no more justifiable than extortion for money, a great deal may be accomplished.

In holding a man to a higher standard of reasonableness, the law would signify that it considers a woman's consent to sex significant enough to merit a man's reasoned attention and respect. It would recognize that being sexually penetrated without consent is a grave harm; and that being treated like an object whose words are not even worthy of consideration adds insult to injury. In effect, the law would impose a duty on men to open their eyes and use their heads before engaging in sex—not to read a woman's mind, but to give her credit for knowing it herself when she speaks it, regardless of their relationship.

One night a few years ago, three doctors and a nurse met at a party in Boston. The four left the party and drove to a summer house on the shore north of Boston. The nurse was carried by one of the doctors into the car, and later into the house. She testified that she was pulled into the car, that in the car she told the doctors she wanted to go home but was ignored. The doctors testified that she went with them voluntarily and enjoyed the "piggyback" ride. Once inside the summer home the four smoked some marijuana; the nurse testified that she then went into the master bedroom to admire an antique. The men joined her there and began to disrobe. She testified that she said, "what are you doing" and "this is crazy" and "stop." Then they were all over her; each had intercourse with her. She was finally led to an upstairs bedroom and ultimately fell asleep. The next morning they drove back to Boston, on the way stopping for breakfast at a local restaurant. She was driven to her car; one of the doctors gave her his phone number and told her to call if she felt like seeing him again. When she got home, she told her roommate she had been raped; later she went to the hospital, and the next day to the police.

The three men were charged with kidnapping and rape. In their defense they testified that the nurse had gone with them voluntarily and engaged in sexual intercourse with each of them willingly and consensually. The fact that three men were involved, rather than only one, takes this case, like *Morgan*, out of the category of a simple rape. My sense, and certainly that of the defense attorneys, is that the numbers were critical to the result.[20]

The jury acquitted on the kidnapping charge, but convicted each of nonaggravated rape, defined by Massachusetts law to punish "whoever has sexual intercourse or unnatural sexual intercourse with a person and compels such person to submit by force and against his will." The convictions were affirmed by the state courts on appeal; a challenge brought in federal court for further review is pending.[21]

One of the key issues in the case has been the judge's refusal to instruct the jury that, to convict of rape they must find that the defendants themselves knew the victim was not consenting. The trial judge considered the defendants' attitude toward consent irrelevant: in refusing so to instruct the jury, he explained that they should "not look at [the case] from the point of view of the defendant's perceptions . . . I don't think that's the law."[22] The defendants have claimed that the trial judge was wrong as a matter of Massachusetts law and that, in upholding him, the Massachusetts courts unconstitutionally expanded the crime of rape after the fact.

Whether the defendants are right or not as to Massachusetts law is a close question. So long as the Massachusetts statute required ac-

tual force and was not satisfied even by proof of threats, the question of intent did not arise, since the use of such force was unlikely to be accidental. At least one noted commentator has pointed to this case as an example of one in which both victim and defendants may have, essentially, been telling the truth: she did not consent; they thought that she had.[23] Under existing Massachusetts law, this may be enough for acquittal. If so, Massachusetts law needs to be changed.

If the woman is believed at all—and the jury clearly did credit her testimony—these men were at least negligent by my definition. In the 1980s it should not be reasonable as a matter of law to assume that "stop" means "go," and that if the woman does not "actually resist"—a point frequently emphasized by the defendants in their court papers—consent can fairly be presumed. If their mistake as to consent was honest, it was nonetheless unreasonable, and that ought to be enough. If Massachusetts law is not clear on this, they may well have some claim for reversal for lack of fair warning. But it is high time that it was made clear.

The constitutional mandate of fair warning in the criminal law requires that people be told, or be capable of ascertaining, their obligations. It does not mean that new obligations cannot be imposed in future cases to prevent injuries which have been ignored for too long.

In advocating this change of understanding, I recognize that the law did not invent the "no means yes" philosophy that it has enforced for so long. Women as well as men have viewed male aggressiveness as desirable and forced sex as an expression of love.[24] Women as well as men have been taught and come to believe that if a woman "encourages" a man, he is entitled to sexual satisfaction.[25] Or, as Ann Landers put it in 1985, "the woman who 'repairs to some private place for a few drinks and a little shared affection' has, by her acceptance of such a cozy invitation, given the man reason to believe she is a candidate for whatever he might have in mind."[26] From sociological surveys to prime-time television, one can find ample support in our society and culture for even the broadest notions of seduction enforced by the most traditional judges.[27]

But the evidence is not entirely one-sided. College men and women may think that the typical male is forward and primarily interested in sex, but they no longer conclude that he is the desirable man.[28] Older sex manuals may have lauded male sexual responses as automatic and uncontrollable,[29] but some of the newer ones no longer see men as machines and even advocate sensitivity as seductive.[30] Date rape is beginning to be thought of as just that, by its women victims and by those in positions of authority on college campuses.

We live in a time of changing sexual mores, and we are likely to for some time to come. In such times the law can bind us to the past or help push us into the future. It can continue to enforce traditional views of male aggressiveness and female passivity, continue to uphold the "no means yes" philosophy as reasonable, continue to exclude the simple rape from its understanding of force and coercion and nonconsent—until change overwhelms us. That is not a neutral course. In taking it, the law (judges, legislators, or prosecutors) not only reflects the views of (a part of) society, but legitimates and reinforces those views.

Or we can use the law to push forward. It may be impossible—and unwise—to try to use the criminal law to articulate any of our ideal visions of male-female relationships. But recognition of the limits of the criminal sanction need not be taken to justify the status quo. As for choosing between reinforcing the old and the new in a world of changing norms, it is not necessarily more legitimate or neutral to choose the old. There are lines to be drawn short of the ideal. The challenge we face in thinking about rape is to use the legitimatizing power of law to reinforce what is best, not what is worst, in our changing sexual mores.

In the late eighteenth and early nineteenth centuries the judges of England waged a suc-cessful campaign against dueling. Although the "attitude of the law" was clear in its stance that killing in a duel was murder, the problem was that, for some, accepting a challenge remained a matter of honor and juries would therefore not convict. As one noted commentator describes it: "Some change in the public attitude toward duelling, coupled with the energy of judges directing juries in strong terms, eventually brought about convictions, and it was not necessary to hang many gentlemen of quality before the understanding became general that duelling was not required by the code of honour."[32]

There has been "some change in the public attitude" about the demands of manhood in heterosexual relations, as in dueling. If the "attitude of the law" toward simple rape is made clearer—and that is what this book is about—then it may not be necessary to prosecute too many "gentlemen of quality" before the understanding becomes general that manly honor need not be inconsistent with female autonomy.

Many feminists would argue that so long as women are powerless, relative to men, viewing a "yes" as a sign of true consent is misguided. For myself, I am quite certain that many women who say yes to men they know, whether on dates or on the job, would say no if they could. I have no doubt that women's silence sometimes is the product not of passion and desire but of pressure and fear. Yet if yes may often mean no, at least from a woman's perspective, it does not seem so much to ask men, and the law, to respect the courage of the woman who does say no and to take her at her word.

In the nineteenth century and on into the twentieth courts celebrating female chastity in the abstract were so suspicious of the women who actually complained of simple rape that they adopted rules that effectively presumed consent. I have heard the same response justified in the 1980s by those who would seize on women's liberation as a basis to celebrate female unchastity. I could not disagree more. If in the 1980s more women do feel free to say yes, that provides more reason—not less—to credit the word of those who say no. The issue is not chastity or unchastity, but freedom and respect. What the law owes us is a celebration of our autonomy, and an end at long last to the distrust and suspicion of women victims of simple rape that has been the most dominant and continuing theme in the cases and commentary.

"Consent" should be defined so that no means no. The "force" or "coercion" that negates consent ought to be defined to include extortionate threats and misrepresentations of material fact. As for intent, unreasonableness as to consent, understood to mean ignoring a woman's words, should be sufficient for liability. Reasonable men should be held to know that no means no; and unreasonable mistakes, no matter how honestly claimed, should not exculpate. Thus, the threshold of liability—whether phrased in terms of "consent," "force," and "coercion" or some combination of the three—should be understood to include at least those nontraditional rapes where the woman *says* no or submits only in response to lies or threats which would be prohibited were money sought instead.

The crime I have described may be a lesser offense than the aggravated rape in which life is threatened or bodily injury inflicted (most state statutes today have at least two degrees of rape), but it is a serious offense that should be called "rape." In sentencing a man who pled guilty to the aggravated rape of his fourteen-year-old stepdaughter in exchange for the dismissal of charges of sexual assault on his twelve-year-old stepson, a Michigan trial judge in 1984 commented:

> On your behalf, there are many things that you are not. You are not a violent rapist who drags women and girls off the street and into the bushes or into your car from a parking lot, and I have had a lot of these in my courtroom . . . You are not a child chaser, one whose obsession with sex causes him to seek neighborhood children or children in parks or in playgrounds, and we see these people in court. You are a man who has warm personal feelings for your stepchildren, but you

let them get out of hand, and we see a number of people like you in our courts.[33]

The judge is absolutely wrong. What makes both the "violent rapist" and the stepfather whose feelings "get out of hand" different and more serious offenders than those who commit assault or robbery is the injury to personal integrity involved in forced sex. That injury is the reason that forced sex should be considered a serious crime even where there is no weapon or beating. Whether one adheres to the "rape as sex" school or the "rape as violence" school, the fact remains that what makes rape, whether "simple" or "aggravated," different from other crimes is that rape is a sexual violation—a violation of the most personal, most intimate, and most offensive kind.

Conduct is labeled criminal "to announce to society that these actions are not to be done and to secure that fewer of them are done."[34] It is time—long past time—to announce to society our condemnation of simple rape, and to enforce that condemnation "to secure that fewer of them are done." The message of the law to men, and to women, should be made clear. Simple rape is real rape.

NOTES

[1][1975] 2 W.L.R. 923 (H.L.).

[2]*Regina v. Morgan*, [1975] 2 W.L.R. 913 (C.A.).

[3]Ibid., p. 922.

[4]*Director of Public Prosecutions v. Morgan*, [1975] 2 W.L.R. 923, 937 (H.L.).

[5]*The Times* (London), May 5, 1975, p. 15.

[6]Ibid., May 7, 1975, p. 17; see also ibid., May 8, 1975, p. 15, letter of Professor Glanville Williams. Compare ibid., May 12, 1975, p. 15, letter of Jack Ashley, M.P.

[7]Sexual Offences (Amendment) Act, 1976, ch. 82, sec. 1. See generally J. C. Smith, "The Heilbronn Report," *Criminal Law Review*, 1976 (February 1976): 97–106.

[8]*Regina v. Cogan*, [1975] 3 W.L.R. 316 (C.A.).

[9]*State v. Reed*, 479 A.2d 1291, 1296 (Me. 1984).

[10]*Commonwealth v. Williams*, 294 Pa. Super. 93, 439 A.2d 765, 769 (Pa. Super. Ct. 1982).

[11]*State v. Houghton*, 272 N.W.2d 788, 791 (S.D. 1977). . . .

[12]*Commonwealth v. Sherry*, 386 Mass. 682, 437 N.E.2d 224 (1982).

[13]See *Commonwealth v. Grant*, 391 Mass. 645, 649 (1984). . . .

[14]A defendant obviously enjoys no constitutional right to present irrelevant evidence; to the extent that the legal issue is framed in terms of his intent, rather than hers, her reputation and her history which was unknown to him is far less relevant and thus far more easily excluded in a balance of probative value and prejudice and a recognition of the strong public policy grounds favoring exclusion of such evidence. See Vivian Berger, "Man's Trial, Woman's Tribulation: Rape Cases in the Courtroom," *Columbia Law Review*, 77 (1977): 1–103, including in her model statute a distinction based on the defendant's knowledge.

[15]*State v. Rusk*, 289 Md. 230, 424 A.2d 720, 733 (1981) (Cole, J., dissenting).

[16]See, for example, *Goldberg v. State*, 41 Md. App. 58, 395 A.2d 1213 (Md. Ct. Spec. App. 1979); *People v. Evans*, 85 Misc.2d 1088, 379 N.Y.S.2d 912 (N.Y. Sup. Ct. 1975), *aff'd*, 55 A.D.2d 858, 390 N.Y.S.2d 768 (N.Y. App. Div. 1976).

[17]Glanville Williams in a Letter to *The Times* (London), May 8, 1975, p. 15. See also Glanville Williams, *Criminal Law: The General Part*, 2nd ed. (London: Stevens and Sons, 1961), pp. 122–123.

[18]See H. L. A. Hart, *Punishment and Responsibility: Essays in the Philosophy of Law* (New York; Oxford University Press, 1968), pp. 152–154. Professor Hart argues that what is critical to just punishment is not the defendant's awareness of the risks of his conduct, but "that those whom we punish should have had, when they acted, the normal capacities, physical and mental, for doing what the law requires and abstaining from what it forbids, and a fair opportunity to exercise these capacities."

[19]*Model Penal Code and Commentaries* (Philadelphia: American Law Institute, 1980), sec. 2.02, Comment 4, p. 243. The Model Penal Code commentators thus recognized the deterrence rationale of negligence liability in justifying its inclusion as a potential basis for

criminal liability (albeit for a limited number of crimes, not including rape).

[20]See Art Jahnke, "The Jury Said Rape," *Boston Magazine*, October 1981, p. 186.

[21]See *Commonwealth v. Sherry*, 386 Mass. 682, 437 N.E.2d 224 (1982); *Commonwealth v. Lefkowitz*, 20 Mass. App. Ct. 513, 481 N.E.2d 227 (Mass. App. Ct. 1985); *Lefkowitz v. Fair*, Civ. Action No. 82-1917-K (D. Mass.).

[22]See *Commonwealth v. Lefkowitz*, 20 Mass. App. 513, 481 N.E.2d 227, 230 (Mass. App. 1985).

[23]See Jahnke, "The Jury Said Rape," p. 186, quoting Harvard Law School professor Alan Dershowitz.

[24]See T. L. Ruble, "Sex Stereotypes: Issues of Change in the 1970's," *Sex Roles*, 9 (1983): 400; K. Kelley, C. T. Miller, D. Byrne, and P. A. Bell, "Facilitating Sexual Arousal via Anger, Aggression, or Dominance," *Motivation and Emotion*, 7 (1983): 200. . . .

[25]See M. R. Burt, "Cultural Myths and Supports for Rape," *Journal of Personality and Social Psychology*, 38 (1980): 229; N. M. Malamuth, "Rape Proclivity among Males," *Journal of Social Issues*, 37 (Fall 1981): 143–144.

[26]*Boston Globe*, July 29, 1985, p. 9.

[27]See sources cited, notes 24–25 supra. . . .

[28]See Ruble, "Sex Stereotypes," *Sex Roles*, 9 (1983): 400.

[29]See Alex Comfort, ed., *The Joy of Sex: A Cordon Bleu Guide to Lovemaking* (New York: Simon and Schuster, 1972).

[30]See Radlove, "Sexual Response and Gender Roles," in Elizabeth W. Allgeier, ed., *Changing Boundaries: Gender Roles and Sexual Behaviour* (Palo Alto: Mayfield, 1983), pp. 87, 102. . . .

[32]Glanville Williams, "Consent and Public Policy," *Criminal Law Review*, 1962 (February–March 1962): 77.

[33]The defendant was sentenced to probation, conditional on his receiving experimental drug treatment with Depo–Provera. Both the defendant and the state appealed, and the sentence was reversed on appeal. *People v. Gauntlett*, 134 Mich. App. 737, 352 N.W.2d 310, 313 (Mich. Ct. App. 1984).

[34]Hart, *Punishment and Responsibility*, p. 6.

QUESTIONS FOR DISCUSSION

1. Do you agree with the decision in *Director of Public Prosecutions v. Morgan*? Why or why not?

2. What are Estrich's main arguments for rape convictions in cases of negligence? How could Williams best respond? Would her concerns be satisfied by recklessness liability in rape cases? Why or why not?

3. What problems does Estrich see in defining rape in terms of the victim's consent without regard to the rapist's *mens rea*? Do you agree with her arguments? Why or why not?

4. What should a person be required to do to avoid being negligent regarding the consent of a sexual partner? Should a man be required to ask the woman explicitly whether she consents? Is a man ever justified in believing that a woman consents when she says that she does not want to have sex? If a woman is drunk, should her consent count as valid? If the man has economic or social power over the woman, is her consent ever valid? If so, when? If not, why not?

COMMONWEALTH V. EUGENE SHERRY

437 N.E.2d 224 (Mass., 1982)

LIACOS, Justice.

Each defendant was indicted on three charges of aggravated rape . . . and one charge of kidnapping. . . . A jury acquitted the defendants of kidnapping and convicted them of so much of each of the remaining three indictments as charged the lesser included offense of rape without aggravation. . . .

There was evidence of the following facts. The victim, a registered nurse, and the defendants, all doctors, were employed at the same hospital in Boston. The defendant Sherry, whom the victim knew professionally, with another doctor was a host at a party in Boston for some of the hospital staff on the evening of September 5, 1980. The victim was not acquainted with the defendants Hussain and Lefkowitz prior to this evening.

According to the victim's testimony, she had a conversation with Hussain at the party,

during which he made sexual advances toward her. Later in the evening, Hussain and Sherry pushed her and Lefkowitz into a bathroom together, shut the door, and turned off the light. They did not open the door until Lefkowitz asked them to leave her in peace. At various times, the victim had danced with both Hussain and Sherry.

Some time later, as the victim was walking from one room to the next, Hussain and Sherry grabbed her by the arms and pulled her out of the apartment as Lefkowitz said, "We're going to go up to Rockport." The victim verbally protested but did not physically resist the men because she said she thought that they were just "horsing around" and that they would eventually leave her alone. She further testified that once outside, Hussain carried her over his shoulder to Sherry's car and held her in the front seat as the four drove to Rockport. En route, she engaged in superficial conversation with the defendants. She testified that she was not in fear at this time. When they arrived at Lefkowitz's home in Rockport, she asked to be taken home. Instead, Hussain carried her into the house.

Once in the house, the victim and two of the men smoked some marihuana, and all of them toured the house. Lefkowitz invited them into a bedroom to view an antique bureau, and, once inside, the three men began to disrobe. The victim was frightened. She verbally protested, but the three men proceeded to undress her and maneuver her onto the bed. One of the defendants attempted to have the victim perform fellatio while another attempted intercourse. She told them to stop. At the suggestion of one of the defendants, two of the defendants left the room temporarily. Each defendant separately had intercourse with the victim in the bedroom. The victim testified that she felt physically numbed and could not fight; she felt humiliated and disgusted. After this sequence of events, the victim claimed that she was further sexually harassed and forced to take a bath.

Some time later, Lefkowitz told the victim that they were returning to Boston because Hussain was on call at the hospital. On their way back, the group stopped to view a beach, to eat breakfast, and to get gasoline. The victim was taken back to where she had left her car the prior evening, and she then drove herself to an apartment that she was sharing with another woman.

The defendants testified to a similar sequence of events, although the details of the episode varied significantly. According to their testimony, Lefkowitz invited Sherry to accompany him from the party to a home that his parents owned in Rockport. The victim was present when this invitation was extended and inquired as to whether she could go along. As the three were leaving, Sherry extended an invitation to Hussain. At no time on the way out of the apartment, in the elevator, lobby, or parking lot did the victim indicate her unwillingness to accompany the defendants.

Upon arrival in Rockport, the victim wandered into the bedroom where she inquired about the antique bureau. She sat down on the bed and kicked off her shoes, whereupon Sherry entered the room, dressed only in his underwear. Sherry helped the victim get undressed, and she proceeded to have intercourse with all three men separately and in turn. Each defendant testified that the victim consented to the acts of intercourse.

Motions for a required finding of not guilty. At the close of the commonwealth's case, the defendants moved for a required finding of not guilty on each of the indictments. The defendants argued that there was no evidence of force or threat of bodily injury, a required element of the crime of rape. The defendants also argued that aggravating circumstances, i.e., kidnapping or rape by joint enterprise, had not been proved. The judge denied their motions.

The defendants contend that, at the close of the Commonwealth's case, . . . the evidence was insufficient to persuade a rational trier of fact of each of the elements of the crime charged beyond a reasonable doubt. . . . The essence of the crime of rape, whether aggravated or unaggravated, is sexual intercourse with another compelled by force and against the victim's will or compelled by threat of bodily injury. . . . At the close of the Commonwealth's case, the evidence viewed in the light most favorable to the Commonwealth established the following. The victim was forcibly taken from a party by the three defendants and told that she would accompany them to Rockport. Despite her verbal protestations, the victim was carried into an automobile and restrained from leaving until the automobile was well on its way. Notwithstanding her requests to be allowed to go home, the victim was carried again and taken into a house. The three defendants undressed and began to undress the victim and to sexually attack her in unison over her verbal protestations. Once they had overpowered her, each in turn had intercourse with her while the others waited nearby in another room.

The evidence was sufficient to permit the jury to find that the defendants had sexual intercourse with the victim by force and against her will. The victim is not required to use physical force to resist; any resistance is enough when it demonstrates that her lack of consent is "honest and real.". . . The jury could well consider the entire sequence of events and acts of all three defendants as it affected the victim's ability to resist. . . . There was no error in the denial of the defendants' motions. . . .

Exclusion of victim's prior out-of-court statements. Defense counsel sought a pretrial ruling regarding the admissibility of two out-of-court statements of the victim. A voir dire was conducted, during which one Cheryl Rowley testified that the victim had made statements at a rape crisis seminar. Rowley testified that the victim stated at the seminar "that she had been raped in the past, and that she had had a couple of occasions where she was almost raped. And she told us about different ways that she got out of being raped—the times that she did." Rowley testified further that "[t]he one that I remembered the most was that she had been taken to a sand pit by some man, and he was attempting to rape her, and she said that she got out of it by what she said, 'Jerking the guy off.'" The trial judge ruled that this evidence would not be admitted.

The defendants argue that the judge erred. . . . There was no error. There was no showing that the statements were false or even an exaggeration of the truth. . . . Without evidence of falsity, the statements become irrelevant to any issue in the case, including the credibility of the complainant. . . .

The trial judge, in his sound discretion, may exclude evidence if the danger of confusion, unfair prejudice, or undue consumption of time in trial of collateral issues outweighs the probative worth of the evidence offered. . . . In the circumstances of this case, we cannot say that the judge abused his discretion. . . .

Instructions to the jury. The defendants next contend that because the judge failed to give two instructions exactly as requested, the judge's jury charge, considered as a whole, was inadequate and the cause of prejudicial error. . . .

To the extent the defendants, at least as to the first requested instruction, appear to have been seeking to raise a defense of good faith mistake on the issue of consent, the defendants' requested instruction would have required the jury to "find beyond a reasonable doubt that the accused had *actual knowledge* of [the victim's] lack of consent" (emphasis added). The defendants, on appeal, argue that mistake of fact, negating criminal intent is a defense to the crime of rape. The defense of mistake of fact, however, requires that the accused act in good faith and with reasonableness. . . . Whether a reasonable good faith mistake of fact as to the fact of consent is a defense to the crime of rape has never, to our knowledge, been decided in this Commonwealth. We need not reach the issue whether a reasonable and honest mistake to the fact of consent would be a defense, for even if we assume it to be so, the defendants did not request a jury instruction based on a reasonable good faith mistake of fact. We are aware of no American court of last resort that recognizes mistake of fact, without consideration of its reasonableness as a defense; nor do the defendants cite such authority. There was no error. . . .

QUESTIONS FOR DISCUSSION

1. Given the evidence in the reading, if you had been on the jury, would you have voted to convict the defendants in *Sherry* of rape? Why or why not? If the evidence is inadequate, what more evidence would you need, and why?

2. In your opinion, did the defendants make a "mistake of fact" about the victim's consent? Did they make a "reasonable mistake of fact"? Should either kind of mistake remove their criminal liability? Why or why not?

3. When, if ever, is strict liability justified in civil law (where violators are not punished but only fined or forced to pay compensation)? Is strict liability more justifiable in civil law than in criminal law? Why or why not?

4. Can the rule "ignorance of the law is no excuse" lead to strict liability or something like it? If not, why not? If so, when? Is this rule justified? Why or why not?

5. Would Michael Davis' version of retributivism (Section 6.4) justify strict criminal liability?[29]

6. One case that seems to impose strict liability, and that also raises questions about responsibility for omissions, is *In re Yamashita* 327 U.S. 1 (1945). Yamashita was the Commanding General of the Fourteenth Army Group of the Imperial Japanese Army in the Philippine Islands. Between October 1944 and September 1945, members of Yamashita's forces committed various war crimes, including brutal mistreatment and killing of more than 25,000 unarmed noncombatant civilians. Laws of war hold that a commander is "responsible for his subordinates" (Article 1 of the Fourth Hague Convention) and "must see that the above articles are carried out" (Article 19 of the Tenth Hague Convention) and must "provide for the details of execution of the foregoing articles, as well as for unforeseen cases" (Article 26 of the Geneva Red Cross Convention of 1929). On this basis, the government charged that Yamashita "unlawfully disregarded and failed to discharge his duty as commander to control the operations of the members of his command, permitting them to commit brutal atrocities and other high crimes" (at 13–4). Yamashita was convicted and executed. However, when the case was considered by the U.S. Supreme Court, Justice Murphy's dissent argued that Yamashita "was not charged with personally participating in the acts of atrocity or with ordering or condoning their commission. Not even knowledge of these crimes was attributed to him" (at 28). In your opinion, should Yamashita be held legally responsible for his failure to control his troops? When, if ever, should a military commander be held legally responsible for acts of his troops? Is strict liability justified in such cases?

SUGGESTIONS FOR FURTHER READING

A classic debate is that between Lady Barbara Wootton, who defends strict liability in *Social Science and Social Pathology* (London: Allen and Unwin, 1959), Chapter 8, and *Crime and the Criminal Law* (London: Stevens, 1963); and H. L. A. Hart, who criticizes Wootton

[29]See Michael Davis, To Make the Punishment Fit the Crime (Boulder, Colorado: Westview, 1992), Chapter 7, pp. 149–72.

in *Punishment and Responsibility* (New York: Oxford University Press, 1968), pp. 158–209. A more recent exchange with more emphasis on American law is that between Mark Kelman, "Strict Liability: An Unorthodox View," and Phillip E. Johnson, "Strict Liability: The Prevalent View," both in *Encyclopedia of Crime and Justice,* edited by Sanford Kadish (New York: Macmillan, 1983), pp. 1512–21. Other good recent discussions include Michael Davis, *To Make the Punishment Fit the Crime* (Boulder, Colorado: Westview, 1992), Chapter 7; Hyman Gross, *A Theory of Criminal Justice* (New York: Oxford University Press, 1979), especially pp. 342–74 and 414–9; and Larry Alexander, "Reconsidering the Relationship Among Voluntary Acts, Strict Liability, and Negligence in Criminal Law," *Social Philosophy and Policy,* vol. 7 (1990), pp. 84–104, as well as other essays in the same issue of *Social Philosophy and Policy.* On recklessness, see R. A. Duff, *Intention, Agency, and Criminal Liability* (Oxford: Basil Blackwell, 1990), Chapter 7, pp. 139–79. Many more aspects of rape are discussed in the rest of Susan Estrich, *Real Rape* (excerpted earlier), with more legal details in her "Rape," *Yale Law Journal,* vol. 95 (1986), pp. 1087–1184. An excellent discussion of levels of liability for rape is E. M. Curley, "Excusing Rape," *Philosophy and Public Affairs,* vol. 5 (1976), pp. 325–60; which is discussed by Leigh Bienen, "Mistakes," *Philosophy and Public Affairs,* vol. 7 (1978), pp. 224–45.

7.5 THE INSANITY DEFENSE

INTRODUCTION

In 1843, Daniel M'Naghten believed that the Tories, including Prime Minister Robert Peel, were plotting to destroy him, and that the only way to defend himself was to kill the Prime Minister first. So M'Naghten shot into the Prime Minister's carriage and killed the passenger, who turned out to be the Prime Minister's private secretary, Edward Drummond. M'Naghten seems to meet all of the conditions of responsibility that we have considered so far. M'Naghten clearly caused harm: he killed. M'Naghten also clearly intended to cause harm: he plotted. M'Naghten did think that his act was justified as self-defense, but he had no good reason to think this, so he could not cite self-defense as an excuse. Nonetheless, the House of Lords did not find him guilty. They found him not guilty by reason of insanity. The Lords held that action, harm, causation, and intent together are still not enough for legal responsibility. More is needed, namely, sanity. M'Naghten's lack of sanity is what kept him from being criminally responsible. He was committed for the rest of his life to a mental institution, but he did not have to go to prison.

This verdict outraged many people, just as it did when John Hinckley was found not guilty by reason of insanity after shooting President Ronald Reagan in 1981. Such (in)famous cases create the impression that political assassins can get off just by pleading insanity. However, most insanity pleas are not successful. In 1963, Jack Ruby pleaded insanity but was convicted of shooting Lee Harvey Oswald, the presumed assassin of President John Fitzgerald Kennedy. In 1968, Sirhan Sirhan pleaded "diminished responsibility" but was convicted of first-degree murder for killing Robert Kennedy. In 1972, Arthur Bremer pleaded insanity but was convicted of shooting Alabama Governor George Wallace. So the insanity defense is not a free ticket home.

Another reason why the insanity defense is not a free ticket home is that people who are found not guilty by reason of insanity are not sent home. They are sent to mental institutions with bars, and they sometimes spend more time in these mental institutions than they would spend in prison if they had been found guilty.[30]

Still, successful insanity defenses are often controversial. When someone is well known to have caused a death intentionally, it is hard for some people to understand how the killer could be found not guilty, even if only by reason of insanity. Defenders of the insanity defense respond, however, that we have no

---

[30]See *Jones v. United States*, 463 U.S. 354 (1983), where the Supreme Court held that someone who was found not guilty by reason of insanity could be held indefinitely even though he had only been charged with attempted shoplifting, which had a maximum sentence of one year.

business condemning or punishing people who have no control over being insane or over what they do as a result of being insane.

In order to understand these controversies, we need to ask, first, what is insanity? It is common to think that insanity is a medical concept. However, psychiatrists almost never describe their patients as "insane" or "sane." They say instead that their patients have a psychosis or a paranoid delusion or a borderline personality disorder or kleptomania or schizophrenia. Such diagnostic categories are what doctors use to decide how to treat their patients. It would not help in diagnosis or treatment to ask which patients are insane. Instead, it is judges and lawyers who have to decide which mental conditions make someone insane. The law classifies some people as sane and others as insane in order to determine who should be held criminally responsible or competent to stand trial or capable of handling their financial affairs or capable of living without supervision. In this way, insanity is a legal concept, much like causation (Section 7.2). Just as scientists determine which events are necessary conditions of a harm, and then lawmakers decide which of the necessary conditions is a legal cause that creates legal responsibility; so psychiatrists determine a person's mental condition, and then law-makers decide whether that mental condition removes legal responsibility or legal competence.

Where the law draws the line between sanity and insanity depends on particular contexts and purposes. The law might draw one line between those who are competent to stand trial and those who are not, but a different line between those who need to be committed to mental institutions and those who do not. Our concern here is responsibility and punishment. So what we need to ask is, what kinds of mental conditions remove criminal responsibility?

FORMULATIONS

Probably the most influential answer to that question was given by the judges in M'Naghten's case in 1843:

> To establish a defense on the grounds of insanity, it must be conclusively proved that, at the time of committing the act, the party accused was laboring under such a defect of reason, from disease of the mind, as not to know the nature and quality of the act he was doing; or, if he did know it, that he did not know that what he was doing was wrong.[31]

This rule refers to two kinds of knowledge. An extreme example of someone who lacks the first kind, because he does not know "the nature and quality of the act," is someone who strangles his spouse while believing that he is squeezing juice out of a lemon. The second kind is knowledge that the act is wrong, but it is not clear whether "wrong" here refers to legal or moral wrongness. The difference comes out in Hadfield's case.[32] Hadfield shot in the direction of King George, because Hadfield believed himself to be another Christ. He wanted the King to crucify him, so he

---

[31]*Regina v. M'Naghten*, 8 Eng. Rep 718 (1843).
[32]27 Howell 1281 (1800).

could save the world. Hadfield knew that his act was illegal, but he did not believe that his act was morally wrong. In contrast, someone who believes that he is the supreme ruler might believe that his act of killing is legally permitted but still recognize his act as morally wrong. The first agent is excused, but the second is not, *if* the M'Naghten rule requires only knowledge of moral wrongness. In contrast, the second agent is excused, and the first is not, *if* the M'Naghten rule requires only knowledge of legal wrongness. Possibly either lack of knowledge is sufficient, and then both agents would be excused. Anyway, legal and moral wrongness go together in most cases, so many versions of the M'Naghten rule do not bother to specify which kind of wrongness must be known.

It is also not clear why the M'Naghten test refers to "a defect of reason." On one interpretation, mere lack of knowledge does not remove responsibility, especially if the agent *should* know what he is doing. Someone who does not know that there is poison in a glass might still be responsible if he was negligent—that is, if he should have known or should have checked to see whether there was poison in the glass. What removes responsibility on the M'Naghten test, and what counts as a defect of reason, seems to be a lack of the capacity to know what one is doing or what is wrong. M'Naghten's belief that the Prime Minister was out to get him was probably resistant to contrary evidence: no matter how much one argued with him, he would still believe the falsehood. People who suffer from paranoia are like that. They are not able to correct their beliefs in light of reasons. That seems to be why they are said to suffer "a defect of reason."

Of course, not every aspect of the act is relevant and important. If someone is deluded into believing that he is the father of his victim, that does not remove his responsibility. For this reason, the Lords added a further requirement that the delusion also had to be such that the accused would not be responsible "if the facts with respect to which the delusion exists were real." A murderer would then not be excused even if he had a delusion that his victim was his brother, since he would not be justified in killing his brother. However, this qualification might seem to rule out too much. If a murderer today has a delusion that he is Jack the Ripper, he would not be justified in killing even if his delusion turned out to be real, but this seems to be the very kind of delusion that is supposed to remove responsibility, according to proponents of the insanity defense.

Another problem in the M'Naghten rule led to later modifications. The original formulation covers diseases that affect cognition or knowledge (cognitive diseases), but it does not cover all diseases that affect people's abilities to choose and act (volitional diseases). For example, some kleptomaniacs steal items that they could easily afford, even when they know that there is a significant chance that they will be caught. These kleptomaniacs are not like regular thieves who believe that it is in their self-interest to steal, since they think they can get away with it. Kleptomaniacs often know that they are likely to be caught and that the punishment is many times worse than anything they might gain by stealing. They still can't stop themselves. Their mental diseases are then much like being addicted to a drug, except that they usually did nothing to create their disabilities.

When it became clear how many mental diseases are not cognitive, many states modified the M'Naghten rule so as to excuse people whose crimes resulted from volitional diseases. One way was to add an "irresistible impulse" test, on which a person is not criminally responsible if he was:

> impelled to do the act by an irresistible impulse, which means before it will justify a verdict of acquittal that his reasoning powers were so dethroned by his diseased mental condition as to deprive him of the will power to resist the insane impulse to perpetrate the deed, though knowing it to be wrong.[35]

This test seems to view mental disease like physical force that overcomes the agent's ability to resist either because the force is too strong or the agent is too weak or both.

The notion of an impulse suggests suddenness, but many volitional diseases do not operate quickly. Just as someone can be addicted to cigarettes over a long period of time without feeling any sudden impulses to smoke immediately, so some volitional diseases display themselves in long-term patterns of behavior rather than in temporary states. A kleptomaniac might not feel any sudden rush to steal, but still might be unable to stop himself from stealing for any extended period of time.

Moreover, many volitional diseases are not completely overwhelming. A kleptomaniac might be able to keep himself from stealing when he knows that a policeman is standing at his elbow but still not able to stop himself when he knows that a policeman is likely to be watching from the other side of the room. Or he might be able to go for a week without stealing, but still unable to refrain for a whole month. Such incomplete incapacities do not guarantee that the person will steal under all circumstances, but they still affect the person's behavior in many circumstances of everyday life.

These kinds of cases are excused from criminal responsibility by some "loss of control" tests. One leading case, *Parsons v. State*,[34] held that a person who knows what he is doing and that it is wrong,

> may nevertheless not be legally responsible, if the following two conditions concur: (1) if, by reason of the duress or such mental disease, he had so far lost the power to choose between the right and wrong, and to avoid doing the act in question, as that his free agency was at the time destroyed; (2) and if, at the same time, the alleged crime was so connected with such mental disease, in the relation of cause and effect, as to have been the product of it solely.

This Parsons rule does not require a sudden impulse or a complete loss of power, for the loss need go only "so far."

Once partial loss of control is seen as excusing, it becomes natural to wonder about partial loss of knowledge. Imagine a mother who stands on her newborn child. We ask, "Did you know that this would hurt your child?" She answers, "Yes." We ask, "Did you know that it was wrong to hurt the child?" She answers, "Yes."

---

[35] *Smith v. U.S.*, 36 F.2d 548 (D.C. Cir., 1929).
[34] *Parsons v. State*, 81 Ala. 577, 597 (1887).

We ask, "Why did you do it?" She answers, "I just felt like standing on him." She is able to give some right answers, but such a person does not seem to appreciate fully what she is saying or doing. It is then not clear whether she really does know right from wrong, and it is not clear whether such people should be excused from criminal responsibility. Those who do want to excuse such cases sometimes formulate the insanity defense so that legal responsibility requires not only formal knowledge but also emotional appreciation of the wrongness of the act.

Another new element in the Parsons rule is causation. The M'Naghten rule excused only for mental disease "at the time of committing the act." Someone who murders this year does not escape responsibility just because he suffered from mental disease last year. And if a murderer goes insane after committing murder, he would still be responsible for the murder, even if he is now incompetent to stand trial. However, this temporal requirement is not enough to ensure that the mental disease is relevant to the crime. Even if someone does suffer from kleptomania at the time of his crime, this should not prevent legal responsibility if his crime was rape. In order to remove responsibility, the mental disease must cause the crime in some way. That is what the Parsons rule requires.

All of these modifications were brought together by the American Law Institute in its Model Penal Code,[35] which said:

> A person is not responsible for criminal conduct if at the time of such conduct as a result of mental disease or defect he lacks substantial capacity either to appreciate the criminality (or wrongfulness) of his conduct or to conform his conduct to the requirements of the law.

This rule says "criminality (or wrongfulness)" because the American Legal Institute was just recommending this rule to states, so it wanted states to adopt the rule with either wording. The Model Penal Code also added a restriction:

> the terms 'mental disease or defect' do not include an abnormality manifested only by repeated criminal or otherwise anti-social conduct.

This restriction was added so that contract killers and sociopaths would not be found not guilty by reason of insanity just because they committed so many crimes. On this test, mental disease removes legal responsibility only if some evidence for the mental disease is distinct from the crimes themselves.

This complex rule requires simultaneity, causation, and appreciation, but not complete loss of control, so it excuses all of the kinds of mental disease discussed above. By 1980, the Model Penal Code rule or some close relative was adopted in twenty-eight states and the District of Columbia, and some modified version of the M'Naghten rule was used in every other state except New Hampshire.

Despite its popularity, the Model Penal Code rule has problems. The selections from the transcript of John Hinckley's trial (included in this section) show how hard it is to apply the Model Penal Code rule to actual cases, although many

---

[35](Philadelphia: The American Law Institute, 1956), Tentative Draft No. 4, Art. 2, Sec. 4.01, p. 27

cases are much easier than Hinckley. In addition, some opponents argued that such detailed rules tie the hands of juries and expert witnesses, including psychiatrists. Many psychiatrists resist classifying their patients under the legal terms of specific rules. Others insist that patients should be viewed as wholes without subdividing their minds into parts, such as knowledge, emotional appreciation, and capacity to conform. Such psychiatrists and their supporters often favor a simpler rule that does not specify the kind of mental disease that removes legal responsibility.

Although there was precedent in New Hampshire,[36] the main recent example of this approach is the Durham rule, which says:

> An accused is not criminally responsible if his unlawful conduct was the product of mental disease or mental defect.[37]

This simple test requires only two elements: mental disease or defect and a causal connection with the act.

The main problem for the Durham rule stems from its very point. This rule gives psychiatrists the freedom to testify as they want, and it gives juries the freedom to consider what they want, but it also gives them no guidance in testifying or reaching decisions. When tough decisions had to be made, courts felt forced to clarify the terms of the Durham rule.

The first question is whether a mental disease causes an act when it is a necessary condition or a sufficient condition of the act. It might seem that only a sufficient condition would excuse, since, if a mental disease is not sufficient for the act, the person might have been able to avoid doing the act. However, following general theories of legal causation (see Section 7.2), the main decision on the causal prong of the Durham test requires the mental disease to be a necessary condition: An unlawful act is the product of mental disease if "the accused would not have committed the act he did if he had not been diseased as he was."[38]

The next question asks what counts as a mental disease. It might seem tempting to say just that "mental disease" in the Durham rule means the same as the medical term "psychosis." However, this interpretation would give great legal powers to psychiatrists, since psychiatrists decide which conditions to label "psychoses," and such classifications are not always based on legal purposes. Partly for this reason, a leading decision held that:

> [A] mental disease or defect includes any abnormal condition of the mind which substantially affects mental or emotional processes and substantially impairs behavior controls.[39]

[36]*State v. Pike* 49 New Hamp. 399 (1870). Cf. also The British Royal Commission on Capital Punishment (1953).

[37]*Durham v. U.S.*, 214 F.2d 862 (D.C. Cir., 1954).

[38]*Carter v. United States*, 252 F.2d 608 (D.C. Cir., 1957).

[39]*McDonald v. United States*, 312 F.2d 847 at 851 (D.C. Cir., 1962).

With this definition, the Durham rule came back towards the M'Naghten tradition. This fusion was recognized when many courts gave up the Durham rule and adopted the Model Penal Code rule.[40]

A different reconceptualization of the insanity defense has been proposed by some philosophers,[41] who emphasize that mentally ill people typically act irrationally. Different proponents of this general approach disagree about the nature of irrationality, but they agree that insanity should be understood in terms of irrationality of some kind. However, we need to look carefully at the kind of irrationality that is supposed to remove responsibility. When an angry person kicks a wall, this act is irrational insofar as it hurts his foot and harms the wall for no good reason. But the kicker still seems responsible for any damage to the wall. He seems just as responsible if what he kicks is a child. As long as he has the ability to think things through and realize that he has no reason to kick the child and many reasons not to, as well as the ability to act on his reasons, then he should be required to use these abilities. This shows that it is not simply irrationality that removes responsibility. What removes responsibility, if anything, is a lack of the *capacity* to be rational. People lack this capacity if they cannot form rational beliefs, or cannot appropriately consider the criminality or wrongfulness of their acts, or cannot act according to the reasons they have. These are exactly the lacks that remove responsibility, according to the Model Penal Code rule. Consequently, it is not clear that these philosophical revisionists are so far from the Model Penal Code rule after all.

The notion of rationality still might add a lot to the Model Penal Code approach. It might enable us to understand what "substantial capacity" is. It might also reveal an underlying unity among defenses involving mental incapacities, such as insanity, mental retardation, intoxication, sleepwalking, hypnosis, and more. And it might help us to apply the Model Penal Code rule and other rules more accurately to concrete situations. If so, the notion of rationality will contribute not only theoretically but also practically.

ARGUMENTS PRO AND CON

Partly because of the problems in defining insanity, there are serious doubts about whether our laws should recognize insanity as a separate defense at all. People whose criminal acts are due to mental disease can sometimes be found not guilty on the basis of other, less controversial conditions of responsibility, such as that the agent lacks the specific *mens rea* for the crime. So the real question is about those insane people who would not be excused on any other ground. Why shouldn't we hold them responsible?

The main argument for the insanity defense is that insanity removes moral responsibility. (See the reading by Richard Bonnie following.) If punishment expresses moral condemnation, punishment seems wrong when the person is not

---

[40]For example, *United States v. Brawner*, 471 F.2d 969 (D.C. Cir., 1972).

[41]See references in Suggestions for Further Reading at the end of this section.

morally responsible. People are normally not seen as morally responsible for acts that they could not avoid doing. For example, an epileptic is not responsible for hitting someone during a seizure. Analogously, if mental diseases make people unable to avoid breaking the law, then those mental diseases should preclude responsibility and make it wrong to punish those people.

This seems to be the point behind most traditional formulations of the insanity defense. Suppose someone is eating steak in a restaurant. If she is so deluded that she cannot know whether what she is cutting is a steak or a person, then she cannot avoid cutting people who sit next to her. And if she cannot know that it is wrong to cut people, then she cannot choose her acts so as to avoid doing what is wrong. Even if she knows that it is wrong to cut people, she still might lack the capacity to conform to this norm, because she just can't stop herself from cutting her neighbors. Thus, the clauses in traditional tests of insanity seem tailored to capture the conditions under which a person cannot avoid doing illegal acts. If so, and if the ability to do otherwise is necessary for moral responsibility, and if moral responsibility is necessary for justified punishment, then we should not punish people who are insane by the traditional tests.

Of course, there are degrees of ability to do otherwise. It is harder for some people than for others to obey the law. And some insane people can avoid breaking the law by seeking treatment during their lucid periods or by avoiding situations where they will end up doing harm. Nonetheless, if we can define insanity so as to ensure that insane people are not morally responsible, then this is one reason why those insane people should be excused.

Some utilitarians give a different argument for the insanity defense. (See Bentham in Section 6.3.) If someone really is insane in a way that removes the ability to avoid doing illegal acts, then threats of punishment will not deter this person from breaking the law. Thus, if the purpose of punishment is to deter crime, punishing such an insane person might seem pointless. Similarly, if the purpose of punishment is moral education of criminals, and if an insane person cannot know what is wrong, then punishing the insane person does not serve its purpose. And insofar as the purpose of punishment is to reform criminals, if hospitalization could cure a person's mental disease, but punishment would make that person even more sick and dangerous, as many claim, then punishing the insane seems counterproductive.

Nonetheless, other utilitarians argue that the insanity defense reduces the ability of punishment to prevent crime. Even if punishment cannot deter or morally educate or reform some insane people, other potential criminals can be affected in other ways.

First, threats of punishment can deter *some* mentally ill criminals. Even if fully insane people cannot be deterred or taught moral lessons, those who are only partially incapacitated can be affected by threats of punishment. Even someone as extreme as Jeffrey Dahmer, who raped, killed, and ate many young boys, still might harm fewer people if he fears punishment than if there were no threat of punishment.

The insanity defense also might weaken deterrence of sane criminals by allowing them to fake insanity. A few criminals have reported that they considered in advance the possibility of faking insanity if they were caught.[42] There is no reliable evidence of how often this happens, but the insanity defense interferes with deterrence to some extent if there are any criminals who commit crimes that they would not commit if they did not think that they could avoid punishment by faking insanity. This is just one instance of the general point that, whenever the law allows another way to avoid punishment, this decreases the chances of punishment and thus the power of deterrence.

Opponents of the insanity defense also argue that a verdict of not guilty by reason of insanity creates the impression that a criminal "got away with it." After millions of television viewers watched Hinckley shoot President Reagan in 1981, then heard that he was found not guilty by reason of insanity, many people thought that he got off at least partly because he was rich and had tricky lawyers and psychiatrists on his side. Whether or not this is true, the impression that rich, tricky people get away with crimes can decrease people's respect for the law and thereby their motivation to obey the law.

Finally, many opponents of the insanity defense fear that dangerous people are incapacitated for less time in mental institutions than in jails. This was not true in the nineteenth century, when people committed to mental institutions often stayed there for the rest of their lives. But today new drugs and new requirements for involuntary commitment combine to make release seem easier and quicker. If so, the insanity defense might result in less incapacitation of potential criminals and thereby less prevention of crime.

Some of these arguments against the insanity defense depend on the fundamental problem of knowing whether a particular defendant really is insane under ·any of the tests. In many cases, psychiatrists testify on both sides, and juries don't know which experts to believe. In addition, psychiatrists themselves often admit that, even if they can determine what a person intended to do, they cannot determine whether a particular defendant had the ability to do otherwise. It is not even clear what kind of evidence could support claims about such abilities and counterfactuals. These difficulties lead to apparently arbitrary results in the actual administration of the insanity defense. Some convicted criminals in prisons have more serious psychiatric problems than others who were found not guilty by reason of insanity. These practical problems are often seen as additional reasons to change the insanity defense, as well as some of the procedures surrounding it.

PROPOSED REFORMS

Since there are powerful arguments both for and against the insanity defense, it is reasonable to try to give each side its due. The main goals are then to minimize the risk of punishing people who are not morally responsible and to maximize the prevention of crime through deterrence, moral education, and the incapacitation of dangerous people. These goals are supposed to be furthered in varying degrees by the various reforms that have been proposed.

---

[42]Cf. Senator Orrin Hatch, "The Insanity Defense Is Insane," *Reader's Digest* (October 1982).

The most radical proposal is to *abolish* the insanity defense entirely. The case
for abolition is argued by Norval Morris, a professor of law at the University of
Chicago (in the reading that follows). Even if the insanity defense is abolished, defendants can still be found not guilty if they lack a mental condition (such as intent or knowledge) required for a crime. Insanity also might reduce a crime, say,
from first–degree murder to manslaughter under doctrines of *diminished responsibility*. Still, people who commit crimes because of insanity would often be punished
to some degree if the insanity defense is abolished.

A less radical approach is to *narrow* the insanity defense by reducing the
number of mental conditions that preclude guilt. The most prominent proposal of
this kind is championed by Richard Bonnie, a professor of law at the University
of Virginia (in the reading that follows), and has been adopted by the American
Bar Association and the American Psychiatric Association. Bonnie's proposal is to
drop the "volitional prong" of the Model Penal Code rule which excuses defendants who lack substantial capacity to conform their conduct to the law. Without
this clause, the only people who would be found not guilty by reason of insanity
are those who cannot know either what they are doing or that it is wrong, as in
the original M'Naghten rule. This proposal is motivated not only by a desire to
reduce the number of insanity verdicts but also by supposedly special difficulties
in determining whether an individual who *did not* conform to law still *could* have
conformed to law. The main problem with this proposal is that people who know
what is wrong but really are incapable of conforming to the law do not seem
morally responsible, so it seems wrong to punish them. If the reason why cognitive incapacities remove responsibility is that they make one unable to avoid
breaking the law, then it is hard to see why volitional incapacities would not also
remove responsibility for the same reason.[43]

There are also other ways to narrow the Model Penal Code rule. One could
drop the word "substantial" so that only a complete lack of the capacity to appreciate the wrong or to conform to the law would remove responsibility. One could
also change the word "appreciate" back to "know" so that lack of emotional appreciation of the wrongfulness would not remove responsibility. It is not clear,
however, how much difference such changes in wording would make in practice,
since it is not clear how much attention juries pay to the precise wording of the
insanity defense in concrete cases.

Another proposed reform is a new *verdict*, usually called "guilty but mentally
ill" (GBMI). This verdict might replace "not guilty by reason of insanity" (NGRI), or
it might be allowed in addition to "not guilty by reason of insanity," so that juries
can decide between these two verdicts. Separate rules would then have to be formulated for the different verdicts. There might even be separate trials with different procedures for determining guilt and insanity. However this new verdict is
handled, the point is to allow juries to label someone as "guilty" in such cases.
This is supposed to reduce the impression that a criminal "got away with it." In
addition, people who are found "guilty but mentally ill" are sometimes required

[43]For Bonnie's response to this objection, see "Debate: Should the Insanity Defense Be Abolished?"
Journal of Law and Health, vol. 1 (1986–7), pp. 117–40 at 133.

to serve out their sentences in prison if they are released from a mental institution before a certain period. This reduces the chances that dangerous people will return to the streets too soon, and it also takes away much of the incentive to fake insanity. However, opponents of such proposals argue that if someone really was insane when she committed the crime, then she was not morally responsible, so sending her to prison after she is cured amounts to punishing an innocent person.

Restrictions on *evidence* have also been proposed. One possibility is to limit defense testimony about the background and emotional history of the defendant. Some critics claim that sad stories of a defendant's childhood can stir up emotions that distort verdicts. If all that matters is the defendant's mental condition at the time of the crime, it might seem irrelevant to talk about his life at other times, much less how his parents treated him when he was young. However, psychiatrists often respond that a person's mental condition cannot be understood in isolation from circumstances that gave rise to it. If so, juries need to know the defendant's background in order to reach a justified verdict.

Other restrictions on evidence are also possible. If problems arise when psychiatrists are forced to use legal language, then the law could prohibit psychiatric experts from saying anything directly about the legal issues. Or, if insanity trials are ruined by battles between defense and prosecution experts, then the court could assign its own impartial panel of experts. This panel might testify in addition to the experts of both sides or the court might not allow either side to call its own expert witnesses who are not on the panel. However, such restrictions on evidence fly in the face of a strong tradition of allowing great leeway to defendants in presenting their cases. Without such leeway, defendants will be at the mercy of judges who can select experts known to be unsympathetic to defendants.

Possibly the most popular reform is to shift the *burden of proof* (compare Section 8.1). Normally the prosecution is required to prove "beyond a reasonable doubt" that the defendant is sane if the defendant raises the issue of sanity. This burden is often hard to carry because insanity is obscure and experts conflict. It also seems natural to presume that people are sane in the absence of any evidence to the contrary. For such reasons, revisionists have proposed lightening the burden of proof on the prosecution so as to require only "clear and convincing evidence" or even just "a preponderance of evidence," which is the normal burden of proof in civil cases. A more radical proposal is to shift the burden to the defense to prove insanity with some level of evidence, as in the original M'Naghten rule. However, such shifts do seem to conflict with the traditional view that every element necessary for someone to be guilty must be proven by the state beyond a reasonable doubt. This stringent requirement is usually justified by the dangers of convicting innocent people who cannot prove their innocence. Reducing the burden on the prosecution or shifting the burden to the defense might increase the chance of punishing people who are not guilty, if insane people really are not guilty.

Finally, those who fear that the insanity defense lets dangerous people get back on the streets too soon often propose stricter requirements for *release* from mental institutions. Whereas the government is now usually required to show that involuntary mental patients are dangerous to themselves or to others, some reformers want people who are found not guilty by reason of insanity to be confined until the patients themselves show that they are not dangerous any more. One could also require approval by a judge or a panel before release, and some even suggest that the victim or relatives of the victim be reserved a place on the panel. All of this would create longer stays for those found not guilty by reason of insanity. However, opponents object again that these people are not truly guilty, so the government should not take away their freedom if the government cannot show that they are dangerous, just as in other cases of involuntary confinement.

Each of these proposals has benefits as well as costs. If too many people are found not guilty by reason of insanity, and if they are released too early, there is a real danger that they will harm again. On the other hand, if we make it too hard to be found not guilty by reason of insanity, or too hard to be released after such a verdict, there is a real danger that innocent people will be punished, or that guilty people will be punished too much. And on any approach it will be hard to know whether a particular person is insane or dangerous. The proper course then seems to depend on how many mistakes of each kind are likely to be made and on the importance of the different kinds of mistakes.

MADNESS AND THE CRIMINAL LAW

NORVAL MORRIS

THE ABOLITION OF THE SPECIAL DEFENSE OF INSANITY

. . . In accordance with the thesis of separation of the mental health law and the criminal–law powers to incarcerate, I propose the abolition of the special defense of insanity. . . . The argument will be presented in broad perspective, the nuances of difference between the competing defenses of insanity being glossed over. The sequence will be (a) the general argument for abolition, (b) an analysis of how the law would operate under the proposed abolition, and (c) a consideration and repudiation of the main criticisms of the abolition proposal.

The problem is to cut through the accumulated cases, commentaries, and confusions to the issues of principle underlying the responsibility of the mentally ill for conduct otherwise criminal. The issues are basically legal, moral, and political, not medical or psychological, though,

Norval Morris, *Madness and the Criminal Law* (Chicago: University of Chicago Press, 1982) Chapter Two, Section III.

of course, the developing insights of psychiatry and psychology are of close relevance to those legal, moral, and political issues. . . .

Hence we are brought to the central issue—the question of fairness, the sense that it is unjust and unfair to stigmatize the mentally ill as criminals and to punish them for their crimes. The criminal law exists to deter and to punish those who would or who do choose to do wrong. If they cannot exercise choice, they cannot be deterred and it is a moral outrage to punish them.[60] The argument sounds powerful but its premise is weak.

Choice is neither present nor absent in the typical case where the insanity defense is currently pleaded; what is at issue is the degree of freedom of choice on a continuum from the hypothetically entirely rational to the hypothetically pathologically determined—in states of consciousness neither polar condition exists.

The moral issue sinks into the sands of reality. Certainly it is true that in a situation of total absence of choice it is outrageous to inflict punishment; but the frequency of such situations to the problems of criminal responsibility becomes an issue of fact in which tradition and clinical knowledge and practice are in conflict. The traditions of being possessed of evil spirits, of being bewitched, confront the practices of a mental health system which increasingly fashions therapeutic practices to hold patients responsible for their conduct. And suppose we took the moral argument seriously and eliminated responsibility in those situations where we thought there had been a substantial impairment of the capacity to choose between crime and no crime (I set aside problems of strict liability and of negligence for the time being). Would we not have to, as a matter of moral fairness, fashion a special defense of gross social adversity? The matter might be tested by asking which is the more criminogenic, psychosis or serious social deprivation? In an article in 1968 on this topic I raised the question of whether there should be a special defense of dwelling in a black ghetto.[61] Some

literal-minded commentators castigated me severely for such a recommendation, mistaking a form of argument, the *reductio ad absurdum*, for a recommendation. But let me again press the point. If one were asked how to test the criminogenic effect of any factor in man or in the environment, the answer would surely follow empirical lines. One would measure and try to isolate the impact of that factor on behavior, with particular reference to criminal behavior. To isolate genetic pressure toward crime one might pursue twin studies or cohort studies, one might look at patterns of adoption and the criminal behavior of natural fathers and adoptive fathers and see whether they were related to the criminal behavior of their children.[62] Somewhat similar measuring techniques would be followed if one were trying to search out the relationship between unemployment and criminality, or a Bowlby-like study of the effects of maternal separation or maternal deprivation on later criminal behavior. Our answers to the question of the determining effects of such conditions would be found empirically and not in a priori arguing about their relationships to crime, though there may be ample room for argument involved in the empirical studies.

Hence, at first blush, it seems a perfectly legitimate correlational and, I submit, causal inquiry, whether psychosis, or any particular type of psychosis, is more closely related to criminal behavior than, say, being born to a one-parent family living on welfare in a black inner-city area. And there is no doubt of the empirical answer. Social adversity is grossly more potent in its pressure toward criminality, certainly toward all forms of violence and street crime as distinct from white-collar crime, than is any psychotic condition. As a factual matter, the exogenous pressures are very much stronger than the endogenous.

But the argument feels wrong. Surely there is more to it than the simple calculation of criminogenic impact. Is this unease rationally based? I think not, though the question certainly merits further consideration. As a rational matter it is hard to see why one should be more responsible for what is done to one than for what one is. Yet major contributors to jurisprudence and criminal-law theory insist that it is necessary to maintain the denial of responsibility on grounds of mental illness to preserve the moral infrastructure of the criminal law.[63] For many years I have struggled with this opinion by those whose work I deeply respect, yet I remain unpersuaded. Indeed, they really don't try to persuade, but rather affirm and reaffirm with vehemence and almost mystical sincerity the necessity of retaining the special defense of insanity as a moral prop to the entire criminal law.

And indeed I think that much of the discussion of the defense of insanity is the discussion of a myth rather than of a reality. It is no minor debating point that in fact we lack a defense of insanity as an operating tool of the criminal law other than in relation to a very few particularly heinous and heavily punished offenses. There is not an operating defense of insanity in relation to burglary or theft, or the broad sweep of index crimes generally; the plea of not guilty on the ground of insanity is rarely to be heard in city courts of first instance which handle the grist of the mill of the criminal law—though a great deal of pathology is to be seen in the parade of accused and convicted persons before these courts. As a practical matter we reserve this defense for a few sensational cases where it may be in the interest of the accused either to escape the possibility of capital punishment (though in cases where serious mental illness is present, the risk of execution is slight) or where the likely punishment is of a sufficient severity to make the indeterminate commitment of the accused a preferable alternative to a criminal conviction. Operationally the defense of insanity is a tribute, it seems to me, to our hypocrisy rather than to our morality.

To be less aggressive about the matter and to put aside anthropomorphic allegations of hypocrisy, the special defense of insanity may

properly be indicted as producing a morally unsatisfactory classification on the continuum between guilt and innocence. It applies in practice to only a few mentally ill criminals, thus omitting many others with guilt-reducing relationships between their mental illness and their crime; it excludes other powerful pressures on human behavior, thus giving excessive weight to the psychological over the social. It is a false classification in the sense that if a team of the world's most sensitive and trained psychiatrists and moralists were to select from all those found guilty of felonies and those found not guilty by reason of insanity any given number who should not be stigmatized as criminals, very few of those found not guilty by reason of insanity would be selected. How to offer proof of this? The only proof, I regret, is to be found by personal contact with a flow of felony cases through the courts and into the prisons. No one of serious perception will fail to recognize both the extent of mental illness and retardation among the prison population and the overwhelming weight of adverse social circumstances on criminal behavior. This is, of course, not an argument that social adversities should lead to acquittals; they should be taken into account in sentencing. And the same is true of the guilt and sentencing of those pressed by psychological adversities. The special defense is thus a morally false classification. And it is a false classification also in the sense that it does not select from the prison population those most in need of psychiatric treatment.

It may help to resolve these moral complexities to consider briefly how the law would work in practice were the special defense abolished. . . . Were the special defense abolished, mental illness would remain relevant and admissible on the question of the *actus reus* of crime. . . . [T]he criminal law can seek to control only voluntary acts and not those achieved in fugue states. Manifestly, the epileptic in a *grand mal* whose clonic movements strike and injure another commits no crime; but we need no special defense of insanity to reach that result, well-established *actus reus* doctrines suffice.

The *mens rea* question is more complex though the principle is easy to state: evidence of mental illness is admissible to show that the accused lacked the prohibited *mens rea*. For states of mind defined as "purpose" or "intent" there is no analytic difficulty. For "recklessness," insofar as a definition of "recklessness" requires that it be shown that the accused in fact foresaw the risk of this type of harm, there is again no analytic difficulty; but when "recklessness" may be achieved by "gross negligence," by failure to live up to an objective standard of care, then difficulties do come in the abolition position which will be addressed later in this chapter. But in the broad run of cases, certainly in those where the special defense is now pleaded, ordinary *mens rea* principles can well carry the freight. . . .

There remain for consideration three lines of criticism of these recommendations which have not been adequately presented or responded to so far in this chapter, namely, (a) mental illness and the lesser degrees of *mens rea*; (b) the trial as a public morality play; and (c) the constitutionality of abolition.

Mental illness and the lesser degrees of mens rea. When the criminal law embraces negligence liability and strict liability, the message to the accused is that he must fall for the common good. Clearly one cannot lapse into moral fault by failure to recognize the existence of a risk of injury to another or to property; the argument for conviction in these cases is opportunistic not moral: The processes of the law cannot stay to test the difficult question of whether the accused did or did not recognize the risk. The injury has occurred. In negligence liability the average person would have recognized the risk and that for us satisfies his liability; in strict liability the prohibited event has occurred, and that suffices for his liability if he indeed did it, whether he knew about it or not.

There are both a considerable literature and many cases supportive of negligence and strict liability in the criminal law. Problems of proof of higher degrees of criminal intent are often intractable, and when the circumstances of the prohibited event are peculiarly within the cognizance of the accused and the public injury is substantial, a case can be made for both these degrees of *mens rea* as sufficient to support criminal liability.

Does the mentally ill accused stand in any different situation in relation to his liability for crimes of negligence and of strict liability? Some have argued that *mens rea* doctrines can achieve justice for the mentally ill in crimes requiring purpose or intent, which involve proof of subjective prescription of the prohibited harm, but not for lesser degrees of *mens rea*. It is an awkward as distinct from a difficult argument to meet. That the mentally ill are in no worse situation than others who, because of stupidity or because of preoccupation with matrimonial conflict or because of a wide variety of distractions, have failed to live up to the assumed norm of perception and care is an accurate if curt reply and should suffice; there is equality in injustice.

The truth is that there should be neither negligence liability nor strict liability in the criminal law, whatever the social injury risked and whatever the modesty of the penalty imposed. A rational system, considerate of the need to use the great engine of criminal guilt and punishment parsimoniously and with moral sensitivity, would manipulate the onus and burden of proof in these cases to allow the accused who had fallen below statutorily imposed norms of care to explain that failure and the law would define what would be satisfactory explanations. But that is neither the rule nor the practice in a busy world and it is hard to see why a special rule to that effect should be made for the mentally ill if it is not available to other "innocents" convicted of crimes of negligence or strict liability.

One might argue that negligence and strict liability of the mentally ill are *de minimis* problems best solved by police and prosecutorial discretion. But that view is less confidently taken in relation to certain problems of reckless liability, in particular, reckless homicide. Whenever recklessness statutorily or by common law suffices for manslaughter and includes what has come to be called "gross negligence," that is to say, a substantial departure from an acceptable standard of care in which it is not necessary (as it is under those codes which follow the ALI's Model Penal Code definition of recklessness) to prove that the accused in fact recognized the risk and persisted in running it, the mentally ill are at risk for manslaughter convictions which many would think unjust.

The point was nicely made in a debate between Chief Justice Weintraub of New Jersey and Professor Herbert Wechsler in a conference of the Federal Second Circuit.[73] Chief Justice Weintraub had advanced an argument for the abolition of the special defense of insanity; Professor Wechsler, the major architect of the Model Penal Code, took a contrary view. He sought to tear at the heartstrings of the assembled judges by asking them to suppose their arteriosclerotic father were in a hospital. The father experiences a delusion and in his anguish knocks over a lamp, causing a fire and killing an attendant. Are the judges really ready to accept that the father should in these circumstances be convicted of a homicide?

It was stimulating material for a conference, but surely consciously convoluted pleading by the leading American theoretician of the criminal law. Without reflection, it is clear that the offense is not murder. Can there be a manslaughter conviction? If the hypothetical events occurred in a state where manslaughter requires Model Penal Code recklessness as its minimum *mens rea*, then there can be no manslaughter conviction. If they occurred in a jurisdiction where gross negligence suffices, then there can be a conviction since there is considerable and compelling authority that abnormalities of mind cannot be included in weighing the negligence equation. In such a

jurisdiction the elderly hypothetical father of the Second Circuit judges may be so convicted, his mental condition being taken into account in sentencing him. It is a grave injustice even though the accused is morally indistinguishable from others who would similarly be unjustly convicted though suffering deficiencies of intelligence, adversities of social circumstance which have led to overswift reactions, and a variety of other ills to which the flesh and life of man is prey. But the solution to this difficulty of mental illness and the lesser degrees of *mens rea* is, as I say, awkward rather than difficult, since it is clearly to be found in the general processes of reform of the substantive criminal law and of its supportive rules of evidence. Of course, in the interim, the problem is easily solved by a sensible use of prosecutorial discretion.

The trial as a public morality play. The whole argument for abolition of the insanity defense is misconceived, it might be argued. These trials have little to do with the accused; he is highly likely to be protractedly incarcerated whatever the outcome and it doesn't matter much where. The thesis is disingenuous, the criticism would continue; it fails to appreciate the larger function of the sensational trials of mad murderers and insane assassins. They are the modern "Everyman"; they are public morality plays, spectacles, moral circuses for the masses to educate them in virtue and in moral sensitivity. For mass consumption they distinguish the mad from the bad, even though on close analysis that is a philosophically impossible trick to perform.

It is not easy to respond to such high-flying rhetoric except to reject it as a prescription. As a description it has truth but I doubt strongly that community moral values are in any way strengthened by the more publicized insanity defenses. At the time of writing, John Hinckley, who shot President Reagan and most seriously injured James Brady, is about to go to trial, the announced defense being that of insanity. One wonders what social purposes are to be served by what will indeed be a massively publicized performance. The reputations of several psychiatrists and lawyers will be made, their fee scales enhanced. Passionate and ill-informed discussion will engulf dinner tables throughout the country. Hinckley will not be at large for many years. He clearly planned and intended to shoot the President. His need for psychiatric assistance may or may not be real and lasting; if it is, we should see that he gets it. But the interstitial orgy of psychiatric moralizing seems of no social utility.

Lurking within this rhetorically overblown argument may be a more subtle and difficult point. It may be argued that, in addition to deterrent purposes, criminal trials and convictions have another important purpose, that of dramatically and formally affirming minimum standards of moral conduct, of stigmatizing the wicked and only the wicked. Seen thus, the criminal justice system is a name-calling, stigmatizing, community-superego-reinforcing system—a system which should not be used against the mentally ill. They are mad, not bad, sick not wicked; it is important that we should not misclassify them.

Again, in my view, practice casts down theory. We fail in this classificatory effort and are doomed to failure no matter how we try since the distinction surpasses our moral and intellectual capacities. And, in any event, we do not stigmatize the insane killer (who is at the heart of the argument about the special defense) or other psychologically disturbed persons who commit serious criminal acts as *either* bad or mad; in practice, we stigmatize them as *both* bad and mad.

This double stigmatization of the subjects of our inquiry can be seen by anyone who visits a prison containing mentally ill prisoners or a mental hospital holding the unfit to plead or those found not guilty by reason of insanity. Prison authorities regard their inmates in the facilities for the psychologically disturbed, no matter how they got there, as both criminal and insane, as bad and mad; mental hospital authorities regard their patients who have been arrested and charged with a crime as both insane and criminal, mad and bad. And it is a regrettable fact that conditions in both types of institutions are often adjusted adversely to the inmate to accommodate the larger political risks that would flow from his escape because of that double stigmatization.

And as a final sad point on this question: it is not only the public and those working in prisons and mental hospitals who doubly rather than alternatively stigmatize in these cases, the patient-inmates in my experience also see themselves as both bad and mad, though it is a tribute to divine mercy and the human spirit that processes of repentance and cognitive dissonance help them to fashion some sort of a life despite that miserable, doubly blemished self-image.

The *constitutionality of abolition.* In 1970, in *In re Winship*, the Supreme Court stressed that the due process clause of the Fourteenth Amendment "protects the accused against conviction except upon proof beyond a reasonable doubt of every fact necessary to constitute the crime with which he is charged",[74] it is my view that the abolition of the special defense of insanity would not conflict with the adjuration.

Predicting decisions of the Supreme Court of the United States is a popular though high risk occupation, a professional hazard of legal scholarship. To take the risks and to try to cut through a substantial body of case law and commentary, let me confidently affirm the constitutional validity of a statute abolishing the special defense of insanity, provided, of course, it left in place basic common-law requirements of *actus reus* and *mens rea* for the conviction of a crime.

The several lines of authority supporting this conclusion are clear enough once it is appreciated that the *actus reus* would still need to be shown to be a "voluntary" act if the accused is to be convicted and that mental illness would be admissible on the question of whether or not the accused had the prohibited *mens rea* at the time of the alleged crime.

Decisions of the Supreme Court on the burden of proof of the special defense of insanity and of an affirmative defense of "extreme emotional disturbance," in particular *Leland v. Oregon* [76] and *Patterson v. New York*[77] respectively, have made clear that these defenses do not go to the underlying facts necessary to be established by the prosecution for a constitutionally acceptable, due process conviction.

Another possible constitutional barrier is to be found in the Eighth Amendment. Would the abolition of the special defense of insanity lead to the infliction of constitutionally unacceptable cruel and unusual punishment? The decisions and much dicta in *Robinson v. California*[78] and *Powell v. Texas*[79] compel, it seems to me, an answer in the negative. Mr. Justice Black in *Powell* was express on the issue:

A form of the insanity defense would be a constitutional requirement throughout the Nation, should the Court now hold it cruel and unusual to punish a person afflicted with any mental disease whenever his conduct was part of the pattern of his disease and occasioned by a compulsion symptomatic of the disease.[80]

The Court in *Powell* adopted the view that the statute did not violate the Eighth Amendment even if alcoholism was a disease, since it punished an act and not the mere status of being an alcoholic. By similar analysis, it would be cruel and unusual punishment to convict a criminal defendant of being mentally ill, but it would not be cruel and unusual punishment to convict a mentally ill person of a crime other than that of being mentally ill if the state proved beyond a reasonable doubt that he had possessed the *mens rea* of the crime of which he was charged.

Abolition of the defense of insanity would thus neither deprive a defendant of his Fourteenth Amendment right to due process nor impinge upon the Eighth Amendment proscription against cruel and unusual punishment. . . .

NOTES

[60]Arguments for the retention of the special defense of insanity as a moral foundation of the criminal law are offered by Herbert Wechsler (see, for example, 37 F.R.D. 365 (2d Cir. 1964)) and by Sanford Kadish ("The Decline of Innocence," 26 *Camb. L. J.* 273 (1968)). A more cautious support of retention is advanced by Francis A. Allen (*Law, Intellect and Education*, at 114–18 (1979)). Contrary views, generally supporting the abolitionist position taken in this chapter, are advanced by H. L. A. Hart, Chief Justice Weintraub, Lady Barbara Wooton, Joel Feinberg, Dr. Seymour Halleck, and Dr. Thomas Szasz. (Their views are summarized in the appendix to N. Morris, "Psychiatry and the Dangerous Criminal," 41 *S. Cal. L. Rev.* 514 (1968), prepared by Gary Lowenthal; see n.13 of that article). . . .

[61]Morris, note 60 *supra.*

[62]Mednick & Volovka, "Biology and Crime," in 2 *Crime and Justice* (N. Morris & M. Tonry, eds., 1980).

[63]See note 60 *supra.*

[73]37 F.R.D. 365 at 381 (2d Cir. 1964).

[74]97 U.S. 358, 364 (1970).

[76]343 U.S. 790 (1952).

[77]432 U.S. 197 (1977).

[78]370 U.S. 660 (1962).

[79]392 U.S. 514 (1968).

[80]*Id.* at 545.

QUESTIONS FOR DISCUSSION

1. Morris claims, "Social adversity is grossly more potent in its pressure towards criminality . . . than is any psychotic condition. (p. 900)" Do you agree? Why or why not? Assuming he is right about this, does it show that people who commit crimes because of social adversity should not be legally responsible if people commit crimes because of psychosis are not legally responsible? Why or why not? Should people who commit crimes because of social adversity be legally responsible? Why or why not?

2. Morris claims, "in practice, we stigmatize [insane killers] as *both* mad and bad." (p. 904) Do you agree? Is this unfair? Is this a good reason to abolish the insanity defense? Why or why not?

3. Would it be constitutional to abolish the insanity defense? Why or why not?[44]

[44]On March 28, 1994, without comment or dissent, the Supreme Court declined to review the constitutionality of a criminal conviction of a schizophrenic man in Montana, which had abolished the insanity defense in 1979

THE MORAL BASIS OF
THE INSANITY DEFENSE

RICHARD BONNIE

Two fundamentally distinct questions are intertwined in discussions of the insanity defense. One concerns the moral issue of responsibility, a question looking backward to the offender's mental condition at the time of the offense. The other is essentially dispositional and looks forward in time: what should be done with mentally disordered offenders, including those who are acquitted by reason of insanity, to minimize the risk of future recidivism?

This article addresses the issue of responsibility. Sweeping proposals to abolish the insanity defense should be rejected in favor of proposals to narrow it and shift the burden of proof to the defendant. The moral core of the defense must be retained, in my opinion, because some defendants afflicted by severe mental disorder who are out of touch with reality and are unable to appreciate the wrongfulness of their acts cannot justly be blamed

and do not therefore deserve to be punished. The insanity defense, in short, is essential to the moral integrity of the criminal law.

But there are several observations to be made about the dispositional issues now receiving legislative attention.

First, the present dissatisfaction with the insanity defense is largely rooted in public concern about the premature release of dangerous persons acquitted by reason of insanity. Increased danger to the public, however, is not a necessary consequence of the insanity defense. The public can be better protected than is now the case in many states by a properly designed dispositional statute that assures that violent offenders acquitted by reason of insanity are committed for long-term treatment, including a period of post-discharge supervision or "hospital parole."

Second, a separate verdict of "guilty but mentally ill," which has been enacted in several

Richard Bonnie, "The Moral Basis of the Insanity Defense," *ABA Journal*, vol. 69 (February 1983)

states, is an ill-conceived way of identifying prisoners who are amenable to psychiatric treatment. It surely makes no sense for commitment procedures to be triggered by a jury verdict based on evidence concerning the defendant's past rather than present mental condition and need for treatment. Decisions concerning the proper placement of incarcerated offenders should be made by correctional and mental health authorities, not by juries or trial judges. Of course, the "guilty but mentally ill verdict" may not reflect dispositional objectives so much as it does a desire to afford juries a "compromise" verdict in cases involving insanity pleas. If so, it should be rejected as nothing more than moral sleight of hand.

Third, it is often said that the participation of mental health professionals in criminal proceedings should be confined to the sentencing stage. Clinical expertise is likely to be the most useful on dispositional rather than on responsibility questions, and, indeed, most clinical participation in the criminal process now occurs at the sentencing stage. Expert witnesses, however, cannot be excluded from the guilt stage so long as the defendant's mental condition is regarded as morally relevant to his criminal liability.

This brings the inquiry back to the issue of criminal responsibility.

The historical evolution of the insanity defense has been influenced by the ebb and flow of informed opinion concerning scientific understanding of mental illness and its relation to criminal behavior. But it is well to remember that, at bottom, the debate about the insanity defense and the idea of criminal responsibility raises fundamentally moral questions, not scientific ones. As Lord Hale observed three centuries ago, in *History of Pleas of the Crown*, the ethical foundations of the criminal law are rooted in beliefs about human rationality, deterrability, and free will. But these are articles of moral faith rather than scientific fact.

Some critics of the insanity defense believe that mentally ill persons are not substantially

less able to control their behavior than normal persons and that, in any case, a decent respect for the dignity of those persons requires that they be held accountable for their wrongdoing on the same terms as everyone else. On the other hand, proponents of the defense, among whom I count myself, believe that it is fundamentally wrong to condemn and punish a person whose rational control over his or her behavior was impaired by the incapacitating effects of severe mental illness.

Few would dispute this as a moral claim. The question is how best to describe the moral criterion of irresponsibility and to minimize the number of cases in which the defense is successfully invoked by persons who should properly be punished.

CRIMINAL RESPONSIBILITY: THE OPTIONS

Putting aside details concerning the drafting of various tests, there are, in principle, three approaches to the insanity defense.

1. The Model Penal Code. One option is to leave the law as it now stands in a majority of the states and, by judicial ruling, in all of the federal courts. Apart from technical variations, this means the test proposed by the American Law Institute in its Model Penal Code. Under this approach, a person whose perceptual capacities were sufficiently intact that he had the criminal "intent" or mens rea required in the definition of the offense nonetheless can be found "not guilty by reason of insanity" if, by virtue of mental disease or defect, he lacked substantial capacity either to understand or appreciate the legal or moral significance of his actions, or to conform his conduct to the requirements of law. In other words, a person may be excused if his thinking was severely disordered—the so-called cognitive prong of the defense—or if his ability to control his behavior was severely impaired—the so-called volitional prong of the defense.

2. Revival of M'Naghten. The second option is to retain the insanity defense as an independent exculpatory doctrine—independent, that is, of mens rea—but to restrict its scope by eliminating the volitional prong. This approach would revive the M'Naghten test as the sole basis for exculpation on ground of insanity. This is the approach I favor, although I would modify the language used by the House of Lords in 1843 in favor of modern terminology that is simpler and has more clinical meaning. M'-Naghten is now distinctly the minority position in this country. Fewer than one third of the states use this approach, although it is still the law in England.

3. Abolition: the mens rea approach. The third option is the "mens rea" approach, which has been adopted in two states and has been endorsed by the Reagan administration. Its essential substantive effect is to abolish any criterion of exculpation, based on mental disease, that is independent of the mens rea elements of particular crimes. Instead, mentally ill (or retarded) defendants would be treated like everyone else.

CASE AGAINST THE MENS REA APPROACH

If the insanity defense were abolished, the law would not take adequate account of the incapacitating effects of severe mental illness. Some mentally ill defendants who were psychotic and grossly out of touch with reality may be said to have "intended" to do what they did but nonetheless may have been so severely disturbed that they were unable to understand or appreciate the significance of their actions. These cases do not arise frequently, but when they do a criminal conviction, which signifies the societal judgment that the defendant deserves to be punished, would offend the basic moral intuitions of the community. Judges and juries would be forced either to return a verdict of conviction, which they would regard as morally obtuse, or to acquit the defendant in defiance of the law. They should be spared that moral embarrassment.

The moral difficulty with the mens rea approach is illustrated by a case involving Joy Baker, a 31-year-old woman who shot and killed her aunt. According to her account—which no one has ever doubted—she became increasingly agitated and fearful during the days before the shooting; she was worried that her dogs, her children (ages eight and 11), and her neighbors were becoming possessed by the devil and that she was going to be "annihilated." On the morning of the shooting, after a sleepless night, she ran frantically around the house clutching a gun to her breast. Worried about what the children might do to her if they became demonically "possessed" and about what she might to do them to defend herself, she made them read and reread the 23d Psalm. Suddenly her aunt arrived unexpectedly. Unable to open the locked front door, and ignoring Mrs. Baker's frantic pleas to go away, the aunt came to the back door. When she reached through the broken screening to unlock the door, Mrs. Baker shot her.

The aunt then fell backward into the mud behind the porch, bleeding profusely, "Why, Joy?" she asked. "Because you're the devil, and you came to hurt me," Joy answered. Her aunt said, "Honey, no, I came to help you." At this point, Mrs. Baker said, she became very confused and "I took the gun and shot her again just to relieve the pain she was having because she said she was hurt."

All the psychiatrists who examined Mrs. Baker concluded that she was acutely psychotic at the time she killed her aunt. The police who arrested her and others in the small rural community agreed that she must have been crazy because there was no rational explanation for her conduct. She was acquitted. Yet, had there been no insanity defense, she could have been acquitted only in defiance of the law. Although she was clearly out of touch with reality and unable to understand the wrongfulness of her conduct, she had the "criminal intent" or mens rea required for some form of criminal homicide. If we look only at her conscious motivation for the second shot and do not take into account her highly regressed and disorganized emotional condition, she was technically guilty of murder (euthanasia being no justification, of course). Moreover, even if the first shot had been fatal, she probably would have been guilty of manslaughter because her delusional belief that she was in imminent danger of demonic annihilation was, by definition, unreasonable.

These technical points, of course, may make little practical difference in the courtroom. If the expert testimony in Joy Baker's case were admitted [only] to disprove mens rea, juries might ignore the law and decide, very bluntly, whether the defendant was "too crazy" to be convicted. The cause of rational criminal law reform, however, is not well served by designing rules of law in the expectation that they will be ignored or nullified when they appear unjust in individual cases.

THE CASE FOR NARROWING THE DEFENSE

While I do not favor abolition of the "cognitive" prong of the insanity defense, I agree with critics who believe the risks of fabrication and "moral mistakes" in administering the defense are greatest when the experts and the jury are asked to speculate whether the defendant had the capacity to "control" himself or whether he could have "resisted" the criminal impulse. I favor narrowing the defense by eliminating its so-called volitional prong or control test.

Few people would dispute the moral predicate for the control test—that a person who "cannot help" doing what he did is not blameworthy. Unfortunately, however, there is no scientific basis for measuring a person's capacity for self-control or for calibrating the impairment of that capacity. There is, in short, no objective basis for distinguishing between offenders who were undeterrable and those who were merely undeterred, between the impulse that was irresistible and the impulse not resisted, or between substantial impairment of capacity and some lesser impairment. Whatever the precise terms of the volitional test, the question is unanswerable, or it can be answered only by "moral guesses." To ask it at all

invites fabricated claims, undermines equal administration of the penal law, and compromises its deterrent effect.

Sheldon Glueck of the Harvard Law School observed in *Mental Disorder and the Criminal Law* (1925) that the 19th century effort to establish irresistible impulse as a defense met judicial resistance because "much less than we know today was known of mental disease." He predicted "that with the advent of a more scientific administration of the law—especially with the placing of expert testimony upon a neutral, unbiased basis and in the hands of well-qualified experts—much of the opposition to judicial recognition of the effect of disorders of the . . . impulses should disappear." He added that "expert, unbiased study of the individual case will aid judge and jury to distinguish cases of pathological irresistible impulse from those in which the impulse was merely unresisted."

The opposition to the control test did not disappear in Professor Glueck's generation. In 1955, when the Model Penal Code was being drafted, *M'Naghten* still constituted the exclusive test of insanity in two thirds of the states. Advances in clinical understanding of mental illness in the 1940s and 1950s, however, inspired a new era of optimism about the potential contributions of psychiatry to a progressive and humane penal law. This renewed optimism was reflected in the model code's responsibility test that included "substantial" volitional impairment as an independent ground of exculpation.

The Model Penal Code has had an extraordinary impact on criminal law. For this we should be thankful, but I believe the code approach to criminal responsibility should be rejected. Psychiatric concepts of mental abnormality remain fluid and imprecise, and most academic commentary within the last ten years continues to question the scientific basis for assessment of volitional incapacity.

The volitional inquiry probably would be manageable if the insanity defense were permitted only in cases involving psychotic disorders. When the control test is combined with a loose or broad interpretation of the term "mental disease," however, the inevitable result is unstructured clinical speculation regarding the "causes" of criminal behavior in any case in which a defendant can be said to have a personality disorder, an impulse disorder, or any other diagnosable abnormality.

For example, it is clear enough in theory that the insanity defense is not supposed to be a ground for acquittal of persons with weak behavior controls, who misbehave because of anger, jealousy, fear, or some other strong emotion. These emotions may account for a large proportion of all homicides and other assaultive crimes. Many crimes are committed by persons who are not acting "normally" and who are emotionally disturbed at the time. It is not uncommon to say that they are temporarily "out of their minds." But this is not what the law means or should mean by "insanity." Because the control test, as now construed in most states, entitles defendants to insanity instructions on the basis of these claims, I am convinced that the test involves an unacceptable risk of abuse and mistake.

It might be argued, of course, that the risk of mistake should be tolerated if the volitional prong of the defense is morally necessary. The question may be put this way: Are there clinically identifiable cases involving defendants whose behavior controls were so pathologically impaired that they ought to be acquitted although their ability to appreciate the wrongfulness of their actions was [un]impaired? I do not think so. The most clinically compelling cases of volitional impairment involve the so-called impulse disorders—pyromania, kleptomania, and the like. These disorders involve severely abnormal compulsions that ought to be taken into account in sentencing, but the exculpation of pyromaniacs would be out of touch with commonly shared moral intuitions.

A PROPOSED TEST

The sole test of legal insanity should be whether the defendant, as a result of severe mental disease, was unable "to appreciate the wrongfulness of his conduct." My statute would read:

"Defense of [Insanity] [Nonresponsibility Due to Mental Disease].

"A. A person charged with a criminal offense shall be found [not guilty by reason of insanity] [not guilty only by reason of insanity] [guilty of a criminal act but not responsible due to mental disease] if he proves, by the greater weight of the evidence, that, as a result of mental disease or mental retardation, he was unable to appreciate the wrongfulness of his conduct at the time of the offense,

"B. As used in this section, the terms mental disease or mental retardation include only those severely abnormal mental conditions that grossly and demonstrably impair a person's perception or understanding of reality and that are not attributable primarily to the voluntary ingestion of alcohol or other psychoactive substances."

This language, drawn from the Model Penal Code, uses clinically meaningful terms to ask the same question posed by the House of Lords in *M'Naghten* 150 years ago. It is a necessary and sufficient test of criminal responsibility. During the past ten years we have evaluated hundreds of cases at our clinic. Only a handful have involved what I would regard as morally compelling claims of irresponsibility, and all of these would be comprehended by the proposed formulation. This test is fully compatible with the ethical premises of the penal law. Results reached by judges and juries in particular cases ordinarily would be congruent with the community's moral sense.

Some clinicians have argued that the volitional prong of the defense is morally necessary to take adequate account of psychotic deterioration, especially in cases involving affective disorders like manic-depressive illness. My view is that a test of insanity that focuses exclusively on the defendant's ability to "appreciate the wrongfulness of his conduct" is broad enough to encompass all cases of severe psychotic deterioration. This is because the term "appreciate" is designed to encompass "affective" dimensions of major mental illness.

BURDEN OF PERSUASION

Much has been said about the proper allocation of the burden of proof since the Hinckley trial. This issue does not arise under the mens rea option, because the prosecution clearly must bear the burden of proving all elements of the crime beyond a reasonable doubt. If the insanity defense is retained as an independent basis of exculpation, the argument may be put that the defendant should bear the burden of persuading the fact-finder of the truth or sufficiency of his claim.

Some commentators have argued that the prosecution should bear the burden of persuading the fact-finder, beyond a reasonable doubt, of all facts regarded as necessary to establish an ethically adequate predicate for criminal liability. When so-called defenses are concerned, the question is whether a just penal law could fail to give exculpatory effect to the claim. Consider entrapment and self-defense, for example. If the law need not recognize the defense at all—as is true for claims of entrapment, I submit—it is entirely proper to recognize it only if the defendant bears the risk of nonpersuasion. If exculpation is morally required if certain facts exist—as is true for claims of self-defense, I would argue—then, as a general rule, the prosecution should bear the risk and be required to negate the existence of those facts beyond a reasonable doubt.

The issue in the present context is whether the insanity defense presents any special considerations that warrant departure from the general rule disfavoring burden shifting on ethically essential predicates for liability. This is a close question, but on balance, I think the answer is yes. In defenses of justification (self-defense) and situational excuses (duress), the defendant's claim must be linked to external realities and can be tested against ordinary experience, thereby reducing the likelihood of successful fabrication or jury confusion. A defendant's claim that he had a mental disorder that disabled him from functioning as a normal person, however, is not linked to the external world and by definition cannot be tested against ordinary experience. The concept of knowing, understanding, or appreciating the legal or moral significance of one's actions also is more fluid and less precise than many aspects of the elements of the penal law.

PUBLIC CONCERNS SATISFIED

The insanity defense, as I have defined it, should be narrowed, not abandoned, and the burden of persuasion may properly be shifted to the defendant. Like the mens rea proposal, this approach adequately responds to public concern about possible misuse of the insanity defense. Unlike the mens rea proposal, it is compatible with the basic doctrines and principles of Anglo-American penal law.

QUESTIONS FOR DISCUSSION

1. Bonnie argues that abolition of the insanity defense would lead to the wrong result in the case of Joy Baker (p. 908). In your opinion, should Joy Baker be found guilty of murder? Would she be found guilty of murder if there were no special insanity defense, so her only defense would be lack of *mens rea*? How would Morris respond to this case?

2. Bonnie argues that the insanity defense should not have any volitional prong, because this prong "invites fabricated claims, undermines equal administration of the penal law, and compromises its deterrent effect." (p. 909)

Do you agree? Why or why not? Does removing this prong solve the most serious problems for the insanity defense in your view? Why or why not?

3. Bonnie argues that the burden of persuasion (or proof) should be shifted to the defendant when the defendant pleads insanity. Do you agree? Why or why not?

THE TRANSCRIPT OF JOHN HINCKLEY'S TRIAL

Background: John Hinckley had almost no friends as an adolescent and as a student at Texas Tech University, which he entered in 1973. In 1976, he dropped out of college and went to Hollywood to become a songwriter. There he watched "Taxi Driver" about 15 times. In the movie, Travis Bickle becomes interested in Betsy but is rejected, so Bickle attempts to assassinate the presidential candidate for whom Betsy works. When his attempt fails, Bickle rescues Iris, a young prostitute played by Jodie Foster. After watching "Taxi Driver," Hinckley began to imitate Bickle, and he developed a strong interest in Jodie Foster. He returned to Texas Tech but did not do well and had no real career plans, which led to intense conflicts with his parents. Hinckley became depressed, bought a gun, and apparently played Russian Roulette at least twice in late 1979. In 1980, at his parents' request, Hinckley saw a physician and a psychologist about his problems. He then decided to enroll in a writing program at Yale University, but his main purpose was apparently to establish contact with Jodie Foster who was then attending Yale. He called her twice, taped the calls, and left her letters and poems, but she showed no interest in him. Hinckley then stalked President Jimmy Carter in Washington, D.C., and Dayton, Ohio, for three days, but he never attempted to shoot. While following Carter on October 9 in Nashville, Tennessee, airport security staff detected and confiscated his guns, but he soon bought more. He went home to Denver, Colorado, and saw a psychiatrist for several months, and he continued to write to Foster. His parents insisted that he get a job by February, but he did not, and he continued to travel around the country, including one trip on November 30 to Washington, D.C., where then President-elect Reagan was staying. When Hinckley returned to Denver on March 7, 1981, his father did not permit him to come home. He stayed in motels until March 25, then he went again to Hollywood to sell songs. After only one day, he took a bus to Washington, D.C. He arrived on March 29. The next day, he shot President Reagan.

A. HINCKLEY'S MENTAL DISORDER

Defense Witness, Dr. William T. Carpenter Direct Examination by Defense Attorney Vincent Fuller

Q. [C]an you describe as you understand from Mr. Hinckley his activities of the evening of March 29th and early March 30th?

A. Yes, when he checked into the Park Central Hotel, he of course was fatigued from

---

Based on selections in Peter W. Low, John Calvin Jeffries, Jr., and Richard Bonnie, *The Trial of John W. Hinckley, Jr.: A Case Study in the Insanity Defense* (Mineola, New York: The Foundation Press, 1986).

the many things, including [the bus ride]. He attempted to rest and sleep during that afternoon, was not able to fall asleep and spent the time reading and watching TV. [He] went out for dinner at a nearby fast-food restaurant, came back to the room and watched TV and then fell asleep that night; that would have been Sunday night, the 29th. [He] described it as a restless fitful sleep that night.

[He] woke up the next morning still feeling fatigued. [He] went out again from the hotel to a nearby fast-food place to get breakfast, picked up a newspaper, returned to his room and in the course of reading the newspaper, he came across itineraries, including President Reagan's itinerary for the day. [He] saw that [the President] was going to be at the Hilton, decided to go to the Hilton and attempt to assassinate President Reagan.

He showered, wrote some material, wrote a letter to Jodie Foster, otherwise prepared himself for . . . the plan . . . to go to the Hilton. He was not sure [what he would do] in part because there had been a number of other times when he had gone to a place to shoot someone and had been unable to do it. He wasn't sure what the outcome of the trip to the Hilton would be, but he did load his gun.

He had a .22 pistol, loaded his gun, left for the Hilton.

At that point in his mind was the possibility that he might be able to see President Reagan, might be able to attempt the assassination, the possibility that he might proceed that day on to New Haven. . . . He entertained the possibility he might have to stay another night in Washington and then go to New Haven, so in the course of going to the Hilton, there are still these several possibilities, which includes the possibility of making an assassination attempt.

MR. FULLER: Your Honor, I hand the witness what has been marked Exhibit N-15. . . . Can you identify that document, Doctor?

A. Yes. The document, N-15, is a letter that John Hinckley wrote to Jodie Foster when he was in his hotel room. . . .

Q. Without reading the letter, can you just summarize the substance of it?

A. Yes. He says to her that he is going to assassinate President Reagan, that there is a definite possibility that he will be killed in his attempt to do that. He describes to her how he has tried to gain her attention and affection. . . . That time is running out on him. That he is not able to wait any longer to make her understand the importance of this and that he hopes in sacrificing his own life or his own freedom in what he refers to as an "historic deed" that he will finally gain her respect and love.

Q. Is there a time written on that document, N-15?

A. The date is 3/30/81, and the time is 12:45 p.m.

Q. And shortly after that, Mr. Hinckley left for the Hilton Hotel?

A. Yes.

Q. And have you reviewed with Mr. Hinckley his thought processes that he was experiencing when he arrived at the Hilton Hotel up to and through the actual shooting?

A. Yes, I have.

Q. . . . First, recite what you learned from Mr. Hinckley regarding his thought processes.

A. Yes. Picking up then after he has prepared the letter, has loaded his weapon, he goes to the Hilton. What is on his mind is to see if he can in fact make an assassination attempt on Reagan; not knowing that that is possible, to decide whether or not to stay overnight again in Washington before going to New Haven or going on to New Haven then.

He is seeing two possible outcomes both now and in the immediate future, either the outcome of the assassination attempt and what happens to him in that process or, and what he assumes to be at least a termination of his freedom and a wish for termination of his life, and the other outcome being to proceed on to New Haven, which has been his primary plan during this period of time, to either kill himself or to kill Jodie Foster and himself. So those are the things that are on his mind.

When he arrives at the Hilton he said that he was surprised at how easy it was to get in the vicinity of where President Reagan would be. He had a sense there was something lapsed about the security, but was able to get in the vicinity, and when President Reagan arrived was fairly close to him as he went into the Hilton.

He said that, on his way in, . . . President Reagan looked at him and smiled and waved and his own interpretation of that was something highly personal, that he felt that President Reagan was looking at him and smiling and waving.

President Reagan went on into the Hilton. John Hinckley left, left that location, walked up into the lobby of the Hilton and spent some time resting, trying to decide what to do.

He at that point assumed that President Reagan would be . . . there for 45 minutes or an hour or so, some period of time, and he was debating whether to wait and see if he could get close to him as he departed, [or] whether he should go back to the hotel. There was still this issue about whether to go to New Haven, whether to stay overnight in Washington.

He walks back out of the hotel in what he estimates to be about 15 minutes later, goes back to the spot where he had been before and would have been, as he describes it, one or two minutes, but in a very quick period of time he is surprised that President Reagan's party is coming out again and as he comes out he has the experience of time moving very quickly, that is that there is only a moment before President Reagan [will] walk to his limousine and be out of the area, that he is there, is able to do it. [He] feels that President Reagan is about to turn again in his direction, and before the President has an opportunity to do that, he beings shooting.

Q. Doctor, how do you interpret Mr. Hinckley's mental state in those moments, those few moments before the actual shooting?

A. Well, his mental state is predominantly one of despair, depression, and a sense of the end of things. In terms of his own, as he can weigh and value things, the thing that is most important to him is to terminate his own existence and to find a way to do that. The suicidal aspects and self-destructiveness of this are foremost in his mind.

At the same time the wish for realization of this relationship with Jodie Foster is on his mind in terms of how his doing this act will unite him with Jodie Foster.

These are the primary things that are on his mind. There is a quickening of the time perspective at the moment that President Reagan is coming out and the sense of something highly personal in the encounter between the two. . . .

[A]s Mr. Hinckley described it, his experience of that opportunity for assassination was different from some earlier opportunities that he had had. He had been in situations on previous occasions where he could have shot at President-elect Reagan in early December and other high level officials when he was in town stalking. He feels that he was unable to act at those times in part because he would see them and there would be too long a period of time, whatever it would take to kind of provoke him into action, prompt action would take place, the timing of it was not sufficient. Some months before that he had tried to psych himself up when he was stalking President Carter because he wanted to make the act, but wasn't able to get himself to do it.

So that I think both the highly personalized quality in his experience and the rapid time frame became important and why this particular assassination attempt actually got taken to action while in earlier occasions when he had attempted to pull off some acts, he had been unable to act, but that was the mental state at the time.

Q. Doctor, you included in your description of his mental state [a] suicidal motive?

A. Yes, the primary, I mean his primary purpose in all of this is to terminate his own experience, his own existence so that is the predominant mental motivation that he is experiencing.

Cross Examination by Assistant U.S. Attorney Roger Adelman

Q. You have heard, have you not, the tapes of Mr. Hinckley talking to Jodie Foster; right?

A. Yes.

Q. Now, Mr. Hinckley told you that he went up there because he admired Miss Foster, he was interested in her; right?

A. Well, those two things are true. That doesn't quite capture what was on his mind about Miss Foster, but it is true that part of what was on his mind included admiration and an interest.

Q. Right. And he was in a way obsessed with her?

A. He was more than obsessed. I mean he was obsessed with her.

Q. Was he delusional about her?

A. Yes; he had developed delusional expectations of that relationship by that time.

Q. Now wait a minute. Are you telling this jury then that when Mr. Hinckley was up there on the telephone with Miss Foster and her roommates, that he was delusional?

A. He had delusions at that time, yes.

Q. What delusion did he have during the telephone calls that this jury heard? Name those delusions for us, please.

A. Oh, the whole, the basis of being there, including making the telephone calls, was based on delusional formation that he had in relationship to Jodie Foster. . . .

He, by then, had come to believe that the only salvation that he had, the only way he could extricate himself from this life was through union with her.

He had come to believe that a union with her was in some sense ordained, that he was being propelled in that direction. He had taken it as a message to him that a number of her films had been shown on television during the time prior to that as the purpose—the purpose of that was a personal purpose, to spur him onward to activity in this regard.

He believed if he could make contact with her, that they could become an extraordinary couple.

He believed that he had some responsibilities toward her in terms of protecting her.

He believed that he could be made whole again in some sense in terms of the wretched existence and experiences that he was having.

[All] of these things . . . are called a delusion because there are many components of false belief, and they are false beliefs that could not be readily shaken by evidence to the contrary, and they are beliefs upon which he is basing his activity, his plans, his actions.

In pursuing them he then makes telephone calls, and the delusions that are present during that whole period of time, including the telephone calls, are the type of thing I am saying.

This type of delusional formation would not [be expected] to interfere with ordinary activities like purchasing tickets or purchasing food or being able to make telephone calls.

There is considerable evidence that he did not have the kind of incoherence of thinking, the scattering of thoughts . . . that can be an aspect of schizophrenia, and lead in certain periods of time during a person's life to much more incoherent activity. Those have never been present, to my knowledge, in John Hinckley. . . .

The delusional formation—and of course this is very common to process schizophrenia—people can have long-term delusional formations at the same time they can be going to work everyday. They can be conducting their life outside of hospitals. They can be looking after families. So it is not an incompatibility with many areas of functioning that appears ordinary and accomplishes ordinary tasks, but the whole basis for [his] being there and making the telephone calls is [his] delusions. . . .

Q. What you are saying is that nobody, including you, has ever found any observable delusions in this person, Mr. Hinckley; right?

A. Say that again.

Q. You are telling us in that long response there that nobody observed active delusions in Mr. Hinckley, right? Or manifestations?

A. A delusion is a mental process and it is not possible to have direct access to observe it. . . .

You learn about delusions from learning about the person, what their beliefs are, and then by trying to see whether or not there are behaviors and impacts and effects on the person's life that are consistent with those beliefs. . . .

Government Witness,
Dr. Park Elliott Dietz
Direct Examination by Mr. Adelman

Q. Can you determine from all of your evaluation of the case, including interviews of Mr. Hinckley, as to whether, in fact, he had a delusion as to Miss Foster?

A. I made such a determination.

Q. What did you determine? . . .

A. In my opinion he did not have a delusion about Miss Foster.

Q. What is the reason or reasons that you say that? What is the evidence?

A. Well, let me tell you the evidence.

First of all, the development of his interest in Miss Foster took a perfectly natural course. He had seen her in movies. He saw her on television. He saw more of her movies. He became interested in her through that medium, and this is the first time he had become interested that way in a movie star. There was nothing special about the way he regarded seeing her in the movies. It is just that he was attracted to her and thought she would be a good person.

When he narrates his efforts to contact Jodie Foster by telephone, Mr. Hinckley has consistently narrated them to me in a manner indicating he understood that she was not really available to him. For example, in the very first interview we had with him, this is on May 30th, he said he felt that part of his fascination with Jodie Foster is that she was unattainable, out of reach, unapproachable.

He speculated that he knew all along that it wasn't going to work out, and that even when he went to New Haven, intending to introduce himself to her, he knew it wouldn't work.

Q. Why does that show it was not a delusion in your opinion?

A. Well, part of what would make this kind of belief system a delusion—and it is not even a belief system—what would render these ideas delusional would be a fixed false belief.

Q. Did he have a fixed false belief?

A. No, he didn't have a fixed belief, and it is hard to find evidence that he had a false belief. He had unrealistic hopes.

Q. What is that called besides—

A. That is called being a dreamer.

Q. Is being a dreamer a manifestation of serious mental disorder?

A. No, it isn't.

Q. Can you continue to tell us the evidence that you pointed to regarding the question whether this young lady, Miss Foster, was a delusion for Mr. Hinckley?

A. I will give you another example of what he said. He said, "She probably doesn't know what to make of me. I am probably just an aberration to her, but you know, she is getting a lot of publicity out of this and she is an actress and not exactly publicity shy. I am probably the best thing that ever happened to her career."

Q. How does that show he didn't have a delusional view of her?

A. Well, this is a rationalization after the fact, one way or the other, and I think that idea was actually an imitation of something Dr. Carpenter suggested to him. I think Dr. Carpenter's notes earlier than that date indicate that this was something he had suggested to Mr. Hinckley.

Q. What else do you have there regarding the question of delusions or not with regard to Jodie Foster?

A. In the first interview, Mr. Hinckley said that he had been—this is the first interview at which I was present—that he had been at Jodie Foster's door, but that he didn't knock or make an effort to introduce himself in person, and when asked why he hadn't, he said: "just basically shyness and insecurity. I mean, she was a pretty famous movie star and there I was, Mr. Insignificant himself."

Q. What does that show with respect to whether or not he had a delusion?

A. Well, it shows that he understood the reality of the situation, that she was a movie star and he wasn't. . . .

[Q] Did you learn in the course of your evaluation of Mr. Hinckley's goals for that day [of the assassination attempt]?

A. Yes, I did.

Q. Can you tell us what they were and what significance each of them has as far as your evaluation of his criminal responsibility is concerned?

A. [D]uring the first interview that I had occasion to speak to Mr. Hinckley personally, . . . Mr. Hinckley was asked if he had thought that after he carried out his plan of assassination, that Jodie Foster would know about him, and his response on that date was to smile and to say "Yeah, it worked."

Q. Now, have you explored that with him either then or [in] other interviews?

A. Yes. I will give you other examples of exploring that question.

On June 7, 1981, I interviewed Mr. Hinckley, and I asked him if he had been trying to impress Jodie Foster, and he said, "Well, it is a combination of things: To impress her, almost to traumatize her. That is the best word. To link myself with her for almost the rest of history, if you want to go that far."

I asked how he thought Jodie Foster would view him. He said, "I would have preferred for her to feel good about me, but going this way it is kind of hard for her to feel good about me."

I then asked him if he had been trying to communicate something to Jodie Foster, and he said that he had been trying to communicate something to the effect of, "Now you will appreciate how much I cared for you. I went to this extent. Now do you appreciate it?" . . . I asked a follow-up to that, which was whether he thought he had accomplished that goal, and he said, "You know, actually, I accomplished everything I was going for there. Actually I should feel good that I accomplished everything on a grand scale." I asked him if he really

meant that because that statement struck me as an extraordinary one, and he said, "Actually, I accomplished exactly what I wanted to accomplish, without exception."

Q. . . . Does the fact that he had this particular goal show he suffered from a particular mental disorder?

A. That fact does not show that, no.

Q. Explain that to the jury.

A. Well, this goal certainly seems like a very odd one, and when I first heard that that was the goal—prior to my involvement in this case—I was impressed with what an odd and, in the lay sense, "crazy" thing such a goal would be.

After having the opportunity to evaluate Mr. Hinckley; to interview all of these other people, to review all of the facts, that goal makes sense. He had felt rejected by Jodie Foster as early as September, after his first efforts to contact her, and, as he later described, he was angry about what she had done, that is, that she had not responded to his calls as he hoped. To win her attention, to be able to impress upon her, here is John Hinckley who loves her, to make her remember him, was a goal for which he was willing to sacrifice a great deal. But it was not entirely a sacrifice, as I will show, because in addition to winning her attention, he wished to have fame and notoriety.

Q. Is that a separate goal?

A. Well, they are linked in this way, but it is a goal that I will show separate evidence for.

Q. All right. Do you have anything more to say about the goal insofar as it relates to a serious mental disorder?

A. Only to say that my first impression without the facts was that that could well reflect a serious mental disorder.

Q. Where do you stand today?

A. That it does not.

Q. Why?

A. Because I have had the opportunity to obtain the facts, to speak with him, and to determine that indeed that was a goal that developed out of his experiences in life and which he feels he has accomplished. . . .

Q. You mentioned the goal of—I believe it is—fame?

A. He displayed a considerable concern with the media, . . . [a]nd he indicated his interest in assassination through not only the things I have referred to already, but comparisons he made between himself and other assassins.

Q. Does the fact he had the goal or purpose or whatever of fame show that he had a serious mental disorder?

A. No, the goal of becoming famous is not limited to those who are mentally disordered. In Mr. Hinckley's case, it does relate to [the] narcissistic personality disorder that I have diagnosed.

Q. Briefly, why is that?

A. That is because with narcissistic personality disorders, the view of one's self as special and more important than others may translate itself into a concern with becoming both the center of attention and famous to the extent of wanting to be in the media, wanting to be in history books. . . .

Cross Examination by Mr. Fuller

Q. You . . . discussed yesterday, doctor, a motive on Mr. Hinckley's part that you described as a desire for fame, is that correct?

A. That is correct.

Q. And . . . is it not so that you have identified that feature as one which you observed in Mr. Hinckley as supporting your diagnosis of his suffering from a narcissistic personality disorder?

A. Yes, it is. Of course it is also the case that part of his concern with fame may have nothing to do with personality disorder. It is hard to know how much of that concern comes from this personality feature and how much of it is independent of it.

Q. And is it fair to characterize this idea of fame . . . [as] an idea of grandiosity?

A. Well, it is a grandiose concern and a grandiose preoccupation if one continues it to the point of fantasizing unlimited success, unlimited fame, and so on. It is not a grandiose delusion, which is another matter altogether.

Q. If it were a grandiose delusion, it then, of course, would it not, become a personality feature associated with the disease of schizophrenia?

A. Yes. Well, yes. Grandiose delusions are often found in schizophrenia as well as in other disorders, and that is when a person believes that they already are successful or famous or has a delusion—of being Napoleon or Jesus Christ—examples of grandiose delusions.

Q. Well, there are other grandiose delusions short of thinking you are Napoleon, are there not?

A. Yes, there are.

Q. . . . There is quite an array of the delusions that might go into delusions of grandiosity?

A. Yes, indeed. I have heard many of them.

B. HINCKLEY'S CAPACITY TO APPRECIATE WRONGFULNESS

Defense Witness, Dr. Carpenter
Direct Examination by Mr. Fuller

Q. Doctor, have you an opinion whether at the time of the shooting on March 30, 1981, the defendant, as a result of the mental disease you have described, lacked substantial capacity to appreciate the wrongfulness of his conduct?

A. Yes, I do have an opinion on that. . . .

Q. Would you please tell us what that opinion is?

A. Yes, that I do think that he had—lacked substantial capacity to appreciate the wrongfulness of his conduct.

Q. Would you in your own terms elaborate on that and explain to the jury what you mean when you say he "lacked capacity to appreciate the wrongfulness of his conduct"?

A. Yes. In forming an opinion about his ability to appreciate wrongfulness, I tried to look at three components of that, the components in real life that are merged together, but found it useful to try to think of each separately.

The first was whether there was a purely intellectual understanding that what he did was illegal. And it is my opinion on a purely intellectual level . . . that he had that knowledge, that those were illegal acts.

The ability to reason that is implied in appreciation: I think appreciation of wrongfulness would mean that a person had an ability to reason about it, to think about it, to understand the consequences, to draw inferences about the acts and their meaning. And reasoning processes, which involve both the intellectual component and the emotional component. It is part of what goes together in our reasoning about any issue. That in this regard I believe Mr. Hinckley lacked substantial capacity to appreciate.

The reason for this opinion is that it is an understanding of the very reasoning process he was going through in preparation for and in carrying out the acts, that in his own mind, his own reasoning, the predominant reasoning had to do with two major things, the first of which was the termination of his own existence; the second of which was to accomplish this union with Jodie Foster through death, after life, whatever. But these were the major things that were dominating his reasoning about it. The magnitude of importance to him in weighing and in his reasoning of accomplishing these aims was far greater than the magnitude of the events per se. And in that regard it was not only his mind. He was not able to—he was not reasoning about the legality issue itself.

On the more emotional side of appreciation, which would have to do with some—with the feelings, the emotional appreciation or understanding of the nature of the events, the consequences, he also had an impairment in that regard. And the impairment there was that the emotional consequences of the acts that he conducted were in his experience solely in terms of the inner world he had constructed. The meaning of this to the victims of the act was not on his mind. I don't mean to be crass about this, but in his mental state the effect of this on the President [and] on any other victims was trivial,

that they—in his mental state they were bit players who were there in a way to help him to accomplish the two major roles [on] which his reasoning was taking place and were not in and of themselves important to this.

So that I do think that he had a purely intellectual appreciation that it was illegal. Emotionally he could give no weight to that because other factors weighed far heavier in his emotional appreciation.

And as these two things come together in his reasoning process, his reasoning processes were dominated by the inner state—by the inner drives that he was trying to accomplish in terms of the ending of his own life and in terms of the culminating relationship with Jodie Foster.

It was on that basis that I concluded that he did lack substantial capacity to appreciate the wrongfulness of his acts.

Q. In considering his cognitive awareness, doctor, does that include an element of reason as well?

A. . . . You see, reason is where the purely emotional and purely cognitive parts don't take place independent of each other. They come together and that is around the reasoning.

The cognitive part, just for clarity of thinking about it, [consider an] analogy that might help explain what I am thinking about there. If one were in a medical emergency, rushing someone to the hospital and you asked the true/false question . . . "Are you aware that the speed you are going is breaking the law?" there would be a cognitive appreciation, but in their reasoning around what they are doing, because of the emotional importance of what is going on, this cognitive appreciation would not be having a major impact on their reasoning about what they are doing.

So in my view the purely intellectual and purely emotional doesn't exist independent of each other, but they come together in the reasoning. And it is the impact on his reasoning that I have tried to describe predominantly in understanding his impairment in his ability to appreciate wrongfulness.

MR. FULLER: I have no further questions, Your Honor.

Cross Examination by Mr. Adelman

Q. What was the planning that he undertook [before going to the Hilton on March 30]?

A. The planning was to get dressed, load the gun and to get himself over to the Hilton.

Q. I take it the planning also included wearing a jacket so that the gun wouldn't be seen. Would you add that to it?

A. Yes. The gun was concealed, yes.

Q. He did that because he knew it is illegal to carry a gun in Washington and he would be arrested if he were seen carrying it in his hand up [to] the Hilton, right?

A. Right.

Q. And again he did that because he knew that the Secret Service, as other people, would know it is wrong for a man to come up and stand with a gun in his hand right at the President's side, right?

A. He did it because he knew that if they saw him, they would interfere with what he was going to do and that he wouldn't achieve his aims.

Q. True, but he also realized that it was wrong.

A. Well, you are asking me why he did certain things and he did, he concealed the gun, concealed this so that there wouldn't be an interference of his carrying out his plan. He didn't—it was not utmost in his mind [that he didn't] want to be caught doing something illegal. What was uppermost in his mind was terminating his existence.

Q. But whether it was uppermost or not, it was in his mind?

A. The terminating of his existence was in his mind. He wasn't spending time thinking about whether this breaks the law or not. He was spending time pursuing his major goal at that point.

Q. Well, whether it was a major goal or not a major goal, he knew that carrying a gun

going to the Hilton and doing what he planned to do was wrong?

A. He would have had that knowledge, yes.

Q. And you would agree with me that from the time he had this thought of shooting the President until he did it, he did not reveal to anybody his intent . . .

A. That is correct.

Q. . . . except in that letter [to Jodie Foster]?

A. Well, he wrote it in the letter, but this, of course, didn't get to anybody else.

Q. He was able then, in other words, to conceal his intent from the third parties who might interfere with his plan?

A. Yes, he was.

Prosecution Witness, Dr. Dietz
Direct Examination by Mr. Adelman

Q. . . . [L]et me ask you . . . whether at the time of the criminal conduct on March 30, 1981, the defendant, as a result of mental disease or defect, lacked substantial capacity to appreciate the wrongfulness of his conduct?

A. . . . [He] did not. . . .

Q. Can you tell us [t]he evidence that you have evaluated and set forth that indicates that Mr. Hinckley was on that day able to appreciate the wrongfulness of his conduct?

A. The answer is yes, I can provide some of the evidence. . . .

When we get closer to the events of March 30th his decision on that day to, as he put it, "check out the scene" and to see how close he could get at the Hilton Hotel indicates that his decision to go to the Hilton Hotel reflected his thoughts about committing assassination on that day.

He wanted to know how close he could get. Could he get within range? Could he get a clear shot?

He wrote a letter, having made his decision, to Jodie Foster, and we discussed that today already. In that letter to Jodie Foster, he indicated he was going to attempt to get Reagan and he indicates his knowledge that he could be killed by the Secret Service in the attempt. That is an indication that he understood and appreciated the wrongfulness of his plans because the Secret Service might well shoot someone who attempted to kill the President.

His decision to load his revolver with exploding ammunition before he left room 312 at the Park Central Hotel: Again, decisionmaking reflecting a choice of the use of explodable bullets which would have maximum effect on the victim, and understanding of the wrongfulness of his behavior, and understanding of the damage that he might bring upon other people.

His concealment of his revolver in his right pocket because he shoots right-handed: A decision to have his revolver where he could quickly draw it and understanding that the purpose of taking the revolver with him was to shoot.

His waiting until he had a clear shot at the President before drawing his gun: He didn't draw his gun when the President first arrived at the Hilton Hotel, as I have indicated before, because he didn't have a clear shot when the presidential motorcade first arrived. The limousine was farther away, and there was a curve in the wall between Mr. Hinckley and where the President entered the building. His waiting until the President came within his accurate range before drawing his gun reflects an appreciation of the behavior he was about to engage in and its purpose: its purpose was to shoot the President of the United States.

His reflection about his decision to draw the gun: I have referred before to his saying that he thought to himself "Should I?" reflecting on a moral decision he was to make.

And his decision to draw the gun at the very moment he did because of the circumstances which at that time favored a successful assassination: He viewed the situation as having poor security. He saw that the range was close and within the distance with which he was accurate, and at the precise moment that he chose to draw his revolver there was a diversion of attention from him. The Secret Service and the others in the presidential entourage looked the other way just as he was pulling the gun.

Finally, his decision to proceed to fire, thinking that others had seen him, as I have mentioned before, indicates his awareness that others seeing him was significant because others recognized that what he was doing and about to do were wrong.

These are examples of the evidence that he appreciated the wrongfulness on March 30.

Cross-Examination by Mr. Fuller

Q. Is it not fair to say that the qualities of emotional coldness, aloofness, cruelness—cruelty, indifference to the feelings of others are features which would go into the whole constellation of features that would bear on the question of one's ability to appreciate the wrongfulness of his conduct? . . .

A. My answer to that is no, these are not features that relate to the ability of a defendant to appreciate wrongfulness of his conduct. Indeed, these are features that—the ones you mentioned—that are characteristic of sexual sadists who, while they know it is wrong to mutilate their victims, to remove their viscera, to eat parts of the body, may do so anyway. They do that for other reasons. They enjoy that, and they do it coldly and cruelly.

This issue of emotional coldness is not one that can be translated into a legal concern with appreciation for wrongfulness.

C. HINCKLEY'S CAPACITY TO CONFORM

Defense Witness, Dr. Carpenter
Direct Examination by Mr. Fuller

Q. [B]ased upon your diagnosis of Mr. Hinckley's mental existence—of the mental disease of Mr. Hinckley on March 30, 1981, do you have an opinion whether at the time of the shooting, which occurred on that date, Mr. Hinckley, as a result of mental disease lacked substantial capacity to [conform] his conduct to the requirements of the law?

A. Yes, I have an opinion about that.

Q. Would you please tell us what that opinion is?

A. Yes. The fact that he had, in my opinion, that he had the illness that I have described to you does not indicate whether at any particular moment he would have had a substantial incapacity to conform his conduct to the requirements of the law. I reach, in my own opinion, I reach the conclusion that he did have a substantial incapacity at that time. The basis for that view deals, of course, with the whole background of psychotic development in his illness that I have described.

And then, more particularly for the point of time in question, was the driven quality to his experiences, the frantic activity that he had become involved in, his determination to end his own life, to terminate this existence that he was experiencing made, foremost in his own mind, actions that would terminate his own life. He experienced the lack of the anchoring, the two anchors that I described [his effort to get psychiatric help and his relationship with his parents], potentially holding him somewhat in contact with reality, so that by the time March 30th had arrived he was so dominated, in my opinion, by the inner state that he had developed over a period of time that his actions and the requirement for actions were so extensively determined by this inner state that he was, in my opinion, not able to [conform] his conduct to the outside requirements, to the legal requirements or social requirements of conduct, so that things at that point were completely out of balance for him and it was the driven quality of his inner state that was foremost in determining [his] actions.

And for that reason I reach the opinion that he did have a substantial incapacity in his ability to conform his conduct to the requirements of the law.

Cross-Examination by Mr. Adelman

Q. When he got up on the morning of March 30 down at the Park Central Hotel, was he out of control, driven by these internal forces that you have described?

A. These inner forces are driving him to this whole series of behavior that he is now in.

Q. Well, I am asking a particularized question. When he got out of bed that day, when he woke, up, was he out of control, under the compulsion of these inner forces?

A. He was under the compulsion of these inner forces.

Q. In the morning?

A. Throughout this whole period of time.

Q. Okay. Now he woke up roughly at eight o'clock in the morning, didn't he?

A. I think it was about something like that. He had had a fitful night's sleep so he had been awake many times during the night, so it was about eight or so he was getting up.

Q. Nevertheless even though he was under control and being driven by these forces at eight o'clock in the morning, he didn't load his gun and go outside and shoot then?

A. It is not that sort of thing.

Q. He didn't do that?

A. No, he did not do that.

THE COURT: Do you want to explain it, doctor? You say it is "not that sort of thing."

THE WITNESS: Yes. What I am describing is a process, the very fact he is in Washington waking up has to do with this inner drive and these forces, so that it is a process that is taking place over time. At that moment he thinks he is most likely to end in New Haven and some relationship with Jodie Foster and his own death, but there is an inner state. The inner state doesn't come for a second [leading one to ask] why did everything happen then?

It is a process that has been developing over time and it is dominant throughout this. In a process like that, you don't expect that every moment there is going to be a catastrophic act or that the actual barriers of control will come apart. . . . The process is present throughout this period of time, but he did not go out and shoot anybody . . .

Q. Fine.

A. . . . at eight o'clock that morning. . . .

Q. Now during the time that he was writing a letter, loading the gun and preparing himself at the hotel, was he under the same compulsion that you have described he was when he actually pulled the trigger?

A. Well, some other things I described that happened at the time that I think played a role in his being able to fully pull the trigger, but the underlying compulsion and drive was present.

Q. Now was he under the same compulsion when he took the taxicab from the Hotel Park Central up to the Hilton?

A. Yes.

Q. Are you aware that he arrived at the Hilton about 1:45 p.m., correct?

A. Yes, about that or maybe a few minutes before that, 1:30 or 1:45.

Q. You are aware that he positioned himself close to where the President's limousine would eventually appear, right?

A. Yes.

Q. When the President prepared to make an entry into the hotel, was Mr. Hinckley with the gun in his pocket under the same compulsion that he was when he fired the shots?

A. Well, things—again basically the same compulsion was there. When President Reagan came out of the car, there was a change to some extent in the intensity of it when he had—had that highly personalized experience of feeling that the President was waving and smiling at him.

There was an additional factor that may have played a role in why he was able to take action on this occasion, so things were changing some. Also being in that setting, realized how close he was, how easy it might be to do it. All of these things tend to stir up emotions and to give a different emotional tone.

The basic drive, the basic scenario that he is playing out again is consistent throughout this period of time.

Q. Let me ask you to focus on the moment when President Reagan leaves the limousine and walks into the hotel. Okay?

A. Yes.

Q. Mr. Hinckley was there with the gun, right?

A. Yes.

Q. And he could have shot him if he wanted to, right?

A. Yes.

Q. But he elected not to shoot him because he didn't have a good shot right?

A. No, he did not act on that impulse at that moment.

Q. Well, if the impulse was overwhelming, why didn't he shoot him when he first saw him at 1:45 when he walked into the hotel?

A. It was the same sort of thing why he didn't shoot himself at the Dakota, why he didn't shoot Reagan early in December and why he didn't shoot Carter. This whole balance of drive and impulse and the thing that makes one hesitate—I think the ability to hesitate has become sharply eroded and I think that personalized experience as Mr. Reagan comes out of the limousine is a further erosion in that, but he did not pull the gun out and fire at that time.

Q. If the ability to hesitate was eroded when the President got out and waved, why didn't Mr. Hinckley with his ability to hesitate eroded shoot him then?

A. Because it is not one way or the other and this is the balancing of many factors and there is no way to give you a precise, emphatic answer to why he didn't shoot then, and shot when he came out.

I can describe the alterations that are taking place in his mental state as best I can discern them during that time.

Q. You mentioned a balancing of factors that means that Mr. Hinckley was considering several options at that particular point?

A. No, no, no, the balancing, this is part of the entire kind of mind at work. It is not a few things that are isolated out from the rest of one's experience around which they are now weighing out their options the way one might weigh if they are trying to buy a used car and decide if the price is right or not.

It is not a highly reasonable rational, logical "Will I weigh this option against that option?"

This is an experience that is taking place. It is happening and it has many, many components, many of which would not be in the conscious mind, his awareness and he is not playing a rational, logical balancing this out.

It is a process that is taking place with many, many components and cannot be isolated to a couple of intellectual decisions about "Do I shoot now" or "Do I hang around a few minutes and shoot later?"

Q. Look at it this way objectively. He has as an objective matter, the opportunity to shoot the President when he got out of the car, or not to shoot him, correct? He had that option?

A. Yes.

Q. And he exercised and made the decision not to shoot him at that point, right?

A. He did not shoot him at that point.

Q. And he didn't shoot him because he made, for whatever reason, some decision not to shoot him, right?

A. Well, maybe I should ask you to define decision. I mean, it is not that he is standing there making decisions. It is like if someone suicides how could you explain why he didn't suicide five minutes ago. He could have done it five minutes ago as well as now. It is not a clear decisionmaking process that one can isolate then give highly satisfying answers to why did it happen five minutes later instead of then.

He is not there going through decisionmaking processes. He did fire a few minutes later.

Q. Doctor, it is fair to say that you, Dr. Carpenter, can't explain why Mr. Hinckley didn't shoot at that point? Is that what your testimony is?

A. No. I think I could try to give a good deal of information that could help to develop an understanding of why he was there, why the shooting would have taken place and why he was vulnerable to acting on that impulse at that time. I do not have a satisfactory explanation for why did it happen precisely when it did instead of five seconds later [or] instead of 15 minutes before. [It is not possible to give a]

precise explanation for why at that moment, not five minutes before, not ten seconds later—[but] I do think that I can give a good deal of information that is relevant to a consideration of why the shooting took place.

Q. But for that question you have no definitive answer, right?

A. For why it took place at precisely the moment it did rather than a few seconds earlier or later or rather than a few seconds earlier or later or rather than ten minutes before? I think it could have taken place before and it didn't. I think he could have found himself unable to act and gone on to New Haven and what, in fact, happened is that he shot as Reagan was leaving the building.

Prosecution Witness, Dr. Dietz
Direct Examination by Mr. Adelman

Q. . . . [L]et me ask you formally, if you determined whether at the time of the criminal conduct on March 30, 1981, the defendant Hinckley, as a result of mental disease or defect, lacked substantial capacity to conform his conduct to the requirements of the law?

A. I did make such a determination.

Q. What determination did you make?

A. That on March 30, 1981, as a result of mental disease or defect, Mr. Hinckley did not lack substantial capacity to conform his conduct to the requirements of the law.

Q. . . . Can you give us the evidence, some of the evidence which underlies your answer?

A. Yes, I can. . . . Among the reasons, the pieces of evidence, for my opinion that Mr. Hinckley was able to conform his conduct on March 30, 1981, are, again, the background. I have reviewed for you some of the evidence that he was capable of deliberation, of planning, that he had backed out in the past despite his efforts to "psych himself up."

This background indicates that in the past he had conformed his behavior, that he had had the ability to do so and had, in fact, done so. He hadn't drawn a gun in Dayton, perhaps because he didn't carry one with him. He hadn't drawn a gun in Nashville, and at Blair House in Washington he hadn't shot. He says he thought to himself on those occasions that he could do it another time. His ability to control his conduct on those dates to conform to the requirements of the law is part of the background for how it is that we know that he had that ability on March 30th.

At no point has Mr. Hinckley stated to me that he had a compulsion or a drive to assassinate or to commit other crimes.

Now, specific examples of evidence:

First of all, his decisionmaking ability itself was [intact] on March 30th. He was able to make other decisions on that date. He decided where to go for breakfast, what to eat. He decided to buy a newspaper, to shower. He made personal decisions of that sort. He was not a man incapable on that day of making decisions about his life, about which of these relatively minor things to do.

He deliberated and made a decision to survey the scene at the Hilton Hotel. There was no voice commanding him to do that. There was no drive within him pushing him to do that. He decided, as he tells us, to go to the Hilton to check out the scene to see how close he could get.

We know from the facts that he chose his bullets, that he loaded his revolver. He has never said that a voice commanded him to choose the shiniest bullets or that he had, for some other reason, to choose these. He indicated that he chose them randomly. And we know that is not so. He chose the exploding [Devastator] bullets. This reflects decisionmaking and choice. He is controlling his conduct, is taking the time to write the "Jodie letter" to explain that one of his goals for the assassination attempt, and to explain that he had a deliberate reason for carrying it out. A man driven by passion, by uncontrollable forces, is not often inclined to take the time to write a letter to explain what this is about. He did. And he claims he spent 20 to 35 minutes writing that letter.

He concealed the weapon not only from Mrs. Kondeah [the maid at the hotel], but from people in the hotel lobby, from taxi drivers, from people at the scene at the Hilton, until the moment he chose to draw his weapon. That ability to conceal his weapon is further evidence of his conforming his conduct, that is, he recognized that [w]aving a gun would be behavior likely to attract attention, and did not wave the gun. He concealed it.

His ability to wait, when he did not have a clear shot of the President on the president's way into the Hilton is further evidence of his ability to conform his behavior. A man driven, a man out of control, would not have the capacity to wait at that moment for the best shot.

His lack of desperation that day, and his recognition that he had other options: I haven't told you all the evidence of that yet, but he has indicated on a number of occasions what some of his options were. He considered going to New Haven, Connecticut. He considered going back to his hotel and going to sleep. These are options. He chose which option to carry out.

His ability to wait in the crowd until the entourage exited the Hilton: now, he waited inside, he says, and then exited taking up the spot he had occupied previously. He went back to the same place outside the Hilton Hotel and indicates that he didn't have very long to wait there. But he did go back out, he had waited 'til that point, and he went outside, and he waited again until the President came out.

He says that he gave consideration to not firing after he had pulled the gun, and of course he said that he deliberated whether to pull the gun.

These choices, his description of deliberation, of decisionmaking, indicate that he was conforming his conduct to his own wishes, that he had the ability to control, to think, to decide, and that he did so. He controlled his conduct. He decided what to do, and he carried out his goals.

His having waited for the very moment to pull his gun and seizing that moment to fire the six shots, again indicates not a man who is willed, but a man who chooses the precise moment when his opportunity for assassination is best.

He took aim at the President, not, as he says, not aiming. He is seen in the videotapes in a combat crouch with a two-handed hold on the gun, the gun pointed toward the President, tracking the President's movements. These are organized acts. These are not disorganized random motions. These are specifically designed, organized acts.

Those are examples of the evidence supporting Mr. Hinckley having had the capacity to conform his conduct on March 30.

Cross Examination by Mr. Fuller

Q. Now, it is accurate, is it not, Doctor, that a psychotic condition is not indispensable to a finding that an accused's ability to [conform] his conduct to the requirements of the law is impaired?

A. It is correct that a person need not be found psychotic for a Court to find that . . . the individual has substantially impaired capacity to conform. . . .

Q. Is it not accurate that you concluded, you and your colleagues, referring to the be-havior of Mr. Hinckley which eventuated in the shootings of March 30, 1981, "it is quite clear that these are not the reasonable acts of a completely rational individual?"

A. We did conclude that. That is correct.

Q. And that, going on, your "opinion about the legal question of criminal responsibility—and it is only an opinion, for the final determination is for the jury—does not hinge on psychiatric diagnoses or speculations?"

A. That is absolutely correct, that our opinion is just our opinion—it is for the jury to determine—and that our opinion isn't based on psychiatric diagnoses or speculation.

Q. And that you indicated Mr. Hinckley's history is clearly indicative of a person who did not function in a usual reasonable manner?

A. That's right. That is why we have diagnosed him as having these disorders.

Q. And you go on to say, "However, there is no evidence that he was so impaired that he could not appreciate the wrongfulness of his conduct or conform his conduct to the requirements of the law," is that correct?

A. Yes, it is. . . .

QUESTIONS FOR DISCUSSION

1. On the basis of the testimony that you have read, if you were a juror in Hinckley's case, would you find that he suffered from a delusion? That he lacked substantial capacity to appreciate wrongfulness? That he lacked substantial capacity to conform to the law? Why or why not?

2. Would Hinckley have been guilty under a different formulation of the insanity defense, such as the M'Naghten rule (p. 889) or the Durham rule (p. 893)? Under a different burden of proof? Why or why not?

3. Does the transcript of this part of Hinckley's trial support or undermine Morris' call for abolition? Bonnie's compromise position? Why?

4. If insane people are excused for what they do because they are unable to conform to law, should people also be excused when they cannot conform to law because of mental retardation? Intoxication? Drug addiction? Hypnosis? Sleepwalking? Extreme emotion? Reasonable mistakes? Unreasonable mistakes? Hormonal influences? Why or why not?

5. Lorena Bobbitt was found not guilty by reason of (temporary) insanity, after she cut off her husband's penis with a kitchen knife while he slept on June 23, 1993. "The defense argued—and the jury, after slightly more than six hours of deliberation, apparently agreed—that Mrs. Bobbitt, flooded with nightmarish images of her husband's abuse and suffering from a variety of mental illnesses, snapped psychologically after her husband raped her, and yielded to an 'irresistible impulse' to strike back. In testimony, Mrs. Bobbitt said she had not realized what she had done until later when she fled their home and was in her car." The prosecution argued that this testimony "was belied by more credible statements" in which she did refer to memories of her act only hours after she did it. "Three doctors from the hospital in Petersburg, and two forensic psychologists and a psychiatrist appointed by the court last fall [1993] to examine Mrs. Bobbitt all concluded that she was a battered woman. They also concluded that she was seriously depressed when she maimed her husband; two held that she was suffering from post-traumatic stress disorder. But all rejected the diagnosis of a defense expert that Mrs. Bobbitt suffered a 'brief reactive psychosis,' one that left her defenseless when the thought of dismembering her husband came to her. Her actions, they concluded, were too purposeful and 'goal-oriented' to meet the definition of 'irresistible impulse,' which impels random attacks on friend or foe alike without regard to consequences. At the insistence of the defense, Judge Herman A. Whisenant's charge to jurors on irresistible impulse was considerably less stringent, requiring only that they find that Mrs. Bobbitt's mind 'was so impaired by disease that she was unable to resist the impulse to commit the crime.' The jury wrestled with the language of the charge, asking Judge Whisenant at one point whether they could use the doctors' broader definition. He told them they could not; moments later, they returned with their verdict."[45] Assuming these facts (or others that you know), should Mrs. Bobbitt have been found not guilty by reason of insanity? If you don't know, what further evidence would you need in order to convince you one way or the other?

6. Should anyone ever be found not guilty by reason of temporary insanity, that is, where their mental condition lasts only a few hours or days? Why or why not? How and how long should such people be treated?

SUGGESTIONS FOR FURTHER READING

Various legal tests of insanity are discussed in detail by Herbert Fingarette in *The Meaning of Criminal Insanity* (Berkeley: University of California Press, 1972). Fingarette's views are developed further in *Mental Disabilities and Criminal Responsibility*, co-authored with Ann Fingarette Hasse (Berkeley and Los Angeles: University of California Press, 1979).

[45]*The New York Times*, January 22, 1994, pp. 1. and 7

For excellent rationality–based analyses of mental disease and disability from a psychiatric perspective, see Bernard Gert and Charles Culver, *Philosophy in Medicine* (New York: Oxford University Press, 1982), Chapters 5–6. Others who interpret insanity in terms of irrationality are Joel Feinberg, "What is so Special about Mental Illness?" in *Doing and Deserving* (Princeton: Princeton University Press, 1970); and Michael Moore, *Law and Psychiatry* (Cambridge: Cambridge University Press, 1974). These attempts to assimilate insanity and irrationality are criticized by Walter Sinnott-Armstrong, "Insanity vs. Irrationality," *Public Affairs Quarterly*, vol. 1 (1987), pp. 1–21. The most prominent advocates of abolition are Norval Morris (excerpted in this section) and Thomas Szasz, *Law, Liberty, and Psychiatry* (New York: Collier-Macmillan, 1963). Richard Bonnie and Norval Morris criticize each other's views in "Debate: Should the Insanity Defense be Abolished?" *Journal of Law and Health*, vol. 1 (1986–7), pp. 117–40. On various reforms, see James M. Varga, "Due Process and the Insanity Defense; Examining Shifts in the Burden of Persuasion," *Notre Dame Lawyer*, vol. 53 (1977), pp. 123–40; Scott Leigh Sherman, "Guilty but Mentally Ill: A Retreat from the Insanity Defense," *American Journal of Law and Medicine*, vol. 7 (1981), pp. 237–64; Michael Davis, "Guilty But Insane?" *Social Theory and Practice*, vol. 10 (Spring 1984), pp. 1–23; and David Louisell and Geoffrey C. Hazard, Jr., "Insanity as a Defense: The Bifurcated Trial," *California Law Review*, vol. 49 (1961), pp. 805–30. More of the transcript of Hinckley's trial with commentary can be found in Peter Low, John Calvin Jeffries, Jr., and Richard J. Bonnie, *The Trial of John W. Hinckley Jr.: A Case Study in the Insanity Defense* (Mineola, New York: The Foundation Press, 1986). Original articles from various perspectives are collected in *The Insanity Defense*, edited by Richard Moran (Beverly Hills: Sage Publications, 1985).

CHAPTER 8

LEGAL PROCEDURE AND EVIDENCE

INTRODUCTION

In Chapters 1 and 2 we considered a contrast between two different accounts of the distinctiveness of legal decision making. While few theorists contend that legal decision making is no different from other forms of decision making, there is still a debate over just how much the decision–making devices of law differ from those found elsewhere. Thus on one side of this division we found the Legal Realists as well as many members of the Critical Legal Studies Movement. Those holding these perspectives typically see legal decision making as less different from other sorts of decision making than has traditionally been supposed. Although these "skeptics" do acknowledge the ways in which the law and its decision–making forms might differ from those of, say, legislative politics, they believe the similarities to be often more important than the differences.

It would be misleading to reduce Legal Realism to the slogan, "Law is policy," and just as misleading to reduce Critical Legal Studies to the slogan, "Law is politics." But the slogans capture something important about the perspectives with which they are associated, something designed to challenge a traditional picture of law as a quite different form of decision making. Indeed, in some respects Ronald Dworkin has points of contact with these perspectives. His challenge to legal positivism is largely a challenge to the view that legal decision making uses sources not used by non–legal decision makers. For Dworkin, good legal decision making is less different from good moral decision making than many of the legal positivists had imagined.

By contrast, many of the legal positivists whose views we considered stressed the distinction between legally recognized sources and other kinds of sources. In focusing on this distinction, these positivists emphasized the ways in which not every important social value could or should find its way into the legal system. Thus, one version of contemporary legal positivism focuses on the rule–based nature of legal decision making. When, for example, Justice Antonin Scalia of the U.S. Supreme Court writes that the "rule of law is a law of rules,"[1] he asserts

[1]Antonın Scalia, "The Rule of Law as a Law of Rules," *University of Chicago Law Review*, vol. 56 (1989), pp. 1175 ff.

(although very controversially) that forms of decision making that involve great discretion for the decision maker, or that require the decision maker to consider and *balance* all conceivably relevant factors, are not the forms of decision making that belong in the legal system. For Justice Scalia, legal decision making is *special*, and the only justification for having unelected officials make important decisions about public policy and about people's lives is that the way the judges do so is different from and more constrained than the decision-making methods of legislative, executive, administrative, and other political policymakers.

Closely related to this debate over the distinctiveness of law's decision-making methods is the "internal morality" of Lon Fuller. Recall that Fuller offered his theory as a version of natural law. But unlike some other natural law theorists, Fuller did not claim that compliance with substantive moral standards of justice was a necessary condition for the existence of something properly called "law." He did claim, however, that various features of decision making—promulgation, generality, and nonretroactivity, for example—were necessary for that decision making to deserve the label "law." Some critics argued that these procedural requirements were not really the kinds of things properly called "moral," and claimed as well that there was such a difference between Fuller's perspective and that of Aquinas and others in the natural law tradition that it was misleading to think of Fuller's approach as even a version of natural law. Still, whether we call Fuller's version "natural law" or not, and whether we call this internal morality a "morality" or not, the fact remains that Fuller thought that *legal* decision making was different, and he thought so because of his list of features of decision making without which a system of decision making or a system of social control did not deserve to be called *law*.

That these various debates have even existed, however, shows the persistent force of the belief that legal systems are different from other social systems, that legal decision making is different from other kinds of decision making, and that there are things that lawyers do that are in important ways different from the things that other people do. Although part of the difference is often thought to have something to do with a different kind of *reasoning*, the subject of Chapter 2, part of the difference has also always been thought to have something to do with the idea of *procedure*. The idea is that lawyers are the ones particularly concerned with process and procedure, and that courts proceed in a more formal and systematic way than many other decision-making bodies. When courts make decisions, they are constantly concerned not only with *substantive* rules, like the rule that possession of heroin is prohibited, or the rule that doctors who injure people by negligent medical practice are liable in damages to those they have injured. Courts are also concerned, more than many other decision-making bodies, with *procedural* rules, determining who speaks first, controlling what kind of evidence can be heard, and allowing the parties to make various motions throughout the proceeding in order to keep the proceedings close to a set of formal rules specified in advance.

We cannot in this chapter hope to address all of the issues of legal procedure that are of particular philosophical interest. Still, there are some procedural issues that have generated much philosophical attention, in part because they touch closely on many of the most enduring questions of epistemology. A trial, after all, is a proceeding devoted in part to gaining knowledge. Accordingly, any procedure for gaining knowledge will be designed in light of a host of assumptions about what knowledge is, and about how we come by it. If a trial is a search for truth, assumptions about what truth is are embedded into trials themselves and into the rules and procedures by which those trials are conducted.

Consider, for example, the institution of the jury. In the United States the defendant in a criminal trial has the right to be tried by a jury. Typically this is a jury of twelve, picked at random from the population at large. People likely to have personal knowledge of the facts are excluded from jury duty, as are those with strong views in advance about the issues involved. Someone whose house has been burgled eight times and thinks that burglars should be given very heavy sentences is unlikely to wind up as a juror in a burglary case, nor is a person who thinks that the police are bad people whose word can never be trusted. In addition, there can be no conviction in a criminal case, ordinarily, without a unanimous vote of the jurors. Various rules of evidence, moreover, significantly limit the amount of information that the jury receives. Information likely to prejudice or inflame the jurors—such as gruesome pictures of the victim, or information about the defendant's previous criminal record—is likely to be kept from the jury even though it might, in theory, be relevant to the determination of the questions the jury is asked to decide.

Now let us reflect briefly on the assumptions embedded in the process of trial by jury. One is that a very good way of discovering truth is through an adversarial process, one in which the two sides present their best cases and try to tear down the cases of the other side. This might be a good way to discover truth, but perhaps it is not. Maybe a better way of discovering truth would be to find experts in the issues and have these experts conduct their own investigations, in the same way that police detectives try to determine what happened. Or perhaps it would be better to find as decision makers those most, rather than least, likely to have personal knowledge of the particular facts. Indeed, when the institution of the jury as we know it first developed in fifteenth-century England, jurors were picked precisely because they were members of the community likely to know all of the participants. This was thought particularly useful because the jurors were expected and encouraged to go out into the community to conduct their own investigations. But whatever the answer to the question of whether there are decision-making procedures better than the jury system as we know it, it is clear that any answer to that question makes assumptions about what truth is and what is a good way to discover it, just the kind of questions that have engaged philosophers as well as lawyers and scientists.

Questions of legal procedure not only touch the enduring issues of epistemology, but also the associated questions of social and moral philosophy that pertain to issues of knowledge. This intersection between questions of epistemology and questions of moral, political, and social philosophy is a new area of philosophical inquiry often called *social epistemology*. When we take up social epistemology, we consider the ways in which questions of truth and its determination may intersect closely with normative factors. Suppose we thought, not unreasonably, that a jury was a worse way of discovering the truth in a criminal case than a panel of judges, which is the procedure used in France and many other countries with civil law (as opposed to common law) origins. We might think jurors drawn from the public at large were more likely to base their decisions on emotions than facts, at least as compared to a trained judge. We might think, as well, that citizen jurors would be less likely to understand the law, even when carefully instructed by the judge. If we thought these things, would we want to eliminate the institution of jury, and follow the French model rather than the English model we have?[2] Perhaps the answer would be yes, because we would want the process to achieve the greatest accuracy. But perhaps not. Perhaps it is important that people be tried by their *peers*, even if that is not the most accurate procedure. Perhaps trial by a jury of one's peers is the greatest insurance against governmental tyranny, even if trial by jury is a cumbersome, expensive, and often inaccurate process when tyranny is not on the immediate horizon.

We cannot hope to answer these questions here, but we can suggest that answering them again requires recourse to philosophy, broadly speaking, and to the kinds of issues with which moral, political, and social philosphers are closely concerned. That is true with the three topics—burden of proof, probability and the law of evidence, and the exclusionary rule—that form the bulk of this chapter. Each of these topics is about procedural devices characteristic of decision making within the legal system, but each of these topics demonstrates quite clearly the way in which issues about legal procedure depend on and connect with issues both of epistemology and of moral, social, and political philosophy.

[2]Although the American jury is modelled on the English, the jury is paradoxically more prevalent now in the United States than it is in Great Britain. Great Britain has no written constitution, at least nothing that looks like a single constitutional document. Thus the British have felt free, for various reasons, to cut back on the use of the jury. Although the jury is still a central part of British *criminal* practice, juries have been almost totally eliminated (libel is a prominent exception) in civil cases. In the United Statest however, not only is the right to trial by jury in criminal cases protected by the Sixth Amendment to the Constitution, but also the right to trial by jury in civil cases whose "amount in controversy" is greater than twenty dollars is protected by the Seventh Amendment. Although this pertains only to trials in federal courts, all of the states except Louisiana (whose legal system is of French and not English origin) have similar provisions in their state constitutions. The result is that civil juries remain common in the United States, although they are all but gone in the very country in which they were originated.

THE BURDEN OF PROOF

INTRODUCTION

In law, as in life, we can rarely be sure of what happened. Indeed, uncertainty about what happened may be an especially prominent feature of legal decision making, particularly at trials. Witnesses tell conflicting stories, and jurors are asked to decide between them about events that may have taken place a long time ago and about which the jurors have no knowledge of their own. The prosecuting attorney tries to prove that the defendant murdered the victim, and the defendant claims he was somewhere else at the time. Witnesses tell stories that support one version or another of accounts that are, in the end, mutually exclusive. In many cases the defendant either did it or he did not.

On television, but only on television, these issues are usually resolved when, under intense cross-examination by the lawyer, one of the witnesses breaks down and confesses to the crime. In real life, however, this almost never happens. Liars stick to their lies even under cross-examination by clever lawyers, and often the existence of incompatible accounts is less a matter of some witness lying than of conflicting perceptions and conflicting understandings by well-meaning (and possibly self-interested) people. In the end, then, decision makers, whether judge or jury, have to make decisions under conditions of uncertainty, under conditions in which they simply cannot be *sure* or *certain* that one account is the correct one.

Once we are short of absolute certainty, it becomes very important to specify what the law refers to as *the burden of proof*, just how strong the evidence must be, just how confident a decision maker must be, before reaching a certain conclusion. When the risk of a mistake is the risk that an innocent person may go to jail, we see the common standard that the prosecution in a criminal case must prove its case *beyond a reasonable doubt*. If the jury decides that the prosecution has not met this burden of proof, then the defendant will be acquitted and go free.

Yet we certainly would not want to have the same very high burden of proof that we have in criminal cases in all civil cases. Suppose you are crossing the street and you are hit by a car. The driver of the car says you ran out in front of his car while he was driving through a green light. You say that the driver ran a red light and hit you while you were in the crosswalk. There are no witnesses. If the jury is instructed to award you damages—make the driver pay for your injuries—only if it believes your version *beyond a reasonable doubt*, the jury will in effect be told to worry far more about a mistaken award of damages against the driver than it will be worried about not giving you damages when you have in fact been injured by someone else's negligence. Yet in a civil case we do not normally think that one kind of mistake is worse than another. We ordinarily believe that it is just as much of a mistake to fail to compensate someone who deserves compensation as it is to compel compensation from someone who has done no wrong. Because we do not think that one kind of error is worse than another, the typical burden of proof in a civil lawsuit is the *preponderance of the evidence*. If the plaintiff's case is more believable than the defendant's, however slightly, then the plaintiff will win. If the defendant's case is more believable than the plaintiff's, again however slightly, then the defendant will win.

Things are rarely this simple, however, and the issues get even more complicated when we move out of the courtroom. The materials that follow will start by exploring the question of burden of proof as a question of non–legal epistemology, for the burden of proof is part of the decisions we make in everyday life, as when we decide to believe or not believe rumors about the misconduct of one of our acquaintances. After considering this question of burden of proof outside the courtroom, we will then turn to philosophical issues about the burden of proof in various legal settings. In considering these materials, try to be attentive to what values are served by choosing one burden of proof over another, and whether and when the selection of a burden of proof is based on considerations other than simply trying to maximize the times in which the conclusion that is reached is actually correct.

DECISION THEORY AND THE
FACTFINDING PROCESS

JOHN KAPLAN

Whether we like it or not we must realize that in no criminal case can one be sure to a mathematical certainty that the accused is guilty: eyewitnesses may be lying or mistaken; the accused may confess, even in open court, because of deep psychological compulsions to protect someone or because his will has been overborne; the most damning circumstantial and testimonial evidence might be the product of a number of illogical and unlikely but nonetheless conceivable coincidences, or even of a perjurious conspiracy. The impossibility of absolute certainty does not mean that we cannot make our factfinding apparatus substantially better than it is. It does mean that no matter how fine we make it, it will be fallible. It would be comforting to be able to say that in all cases of doubt we would acquit rather than chance convicting an innocent man. But because no case is doubt free, unless we decide to avoid trying anyone, we will, if we try enough people, inevitably convict an innocent man. Moreover, we cannot avoid this by trying only a small number of defendants. Since the chance of error, however small, is random, we may convict an innocent man, not only in the long run but in our very first trial.

Granting, then, that we are going to apply our decision process to some defendants, we must consider the utilities attached to the two

John Kaplan, "Decision Theory and the Factfinding Process," *Stanford Law Review*, vol. 20 (1968), pp. 1065 ff. Kaplan (1929–90) was Professor of Law at Stanford Law School.

possible decisions, guilt and innocence. For convenience we will deal not directly with utilities but with disutilities, since the problem is more easily phrased in terms of avoiding certain consequences than in terms of achieving others. Thus, we can represent the disutility of convicting an innocent man by D_i and the disutility of acquitting a guilty man by D_g. Decision theory teaches that in order to convict, the jury must feel that the expected disutility of a decision to acquit is greater than that of a decision to convict. For this to be true, the jury must be convinced that the probability of guilt is at least P, where PD_g is greater than $(I - P)D_i$. Assuming that $D_i + D_g > 0$, P can then be expressed in terms of the different disutilities:

$$P > \frac{I}{I + \frac{D_g}{D_i}}$$

I. *Civil cases.*

Inspecting the above formula, we note that where D_g and D_i are equal, that is, where the consequences of an error in one direction are just as serious as the consequences of an error in the other, $\frac{D_g}{D_i} = I$ and, therefore, P need only be greater than 1/2 to allow a verdict for the plaintiff. This is the preponderance-of-the-evidence test in civil cases, where the jury must merely be satisfied that the probability is greater than 50 percent—in other words, that it is more likely than not that the plaintiff has a right to recover.

The assumption that an erroneous verdict in favor of the defendant is no more serious than one in favor of the plaintiff is, of course, open to question. Indeed, as we tend more and more to the view that compensation, not fault, is the primary stuff of tort law—a view demonstrated in the progression toward compensating the victims of our industrial society regardless of fault—this assumption becomes increasingly dubious. Perhaps it is because jurors tend,

dimly, to appreciate this that they frequently disregard the judges and substitute their own values for the judge-decreed utilities.

The assumption of equal disutilities that the preponderance-of-the-evidence test reflects does not completely pervade our noncriminal law, however. In certain cases we typically require that a party demonstrate certain facts to a higher degree of probability. Thus, where the defendant is accused of fraud, a finding against him may do more than merely cost him money. Since he loses reputation as well, the disutility of an erroneous judgment against him may be greater than that of an erroneous judgment against the plaintiff; as a result we demand that the plaintiff prove his case to a higher probability—clear-and-convincing evidence. The clear-and-convincing-evidence requirement is applied in two other situations, each of which is explainable on somewhat similar reasoning. In denaturalization proceedings, even though they are technically civil in nature, the harshness of the result for one deprived of his citizenship requires us at least to move nearer to the criminal standard. And in attempts to upset certain types of regular and common transactions, for example by showing that a deed in form is really a mortgage, clear-and-convincing evidence is often required because of the disutility of calling into question a whole range of apparently settled arrangements.

2. *Criminal cases.*

Probably the best illustration of the effect of the disutilities on the requirements of proof is the criminal case. One of the fundamental feelings of our society is that it is far more serious to convict an innocent man than to let a guilty man go free. In other words, D_i is much larger than D_g. This attitude explains the criminal law's insistence that in order to convict, the jury must be convinced of the defendant's guilt "beyond a reasonable doubt."

We are here assuming that the defendant, if he is not guilty, is not guilty because he did not commit the act in question or because even though he did do so he did not have the requisite state of mind. In both these situations the disutility of convicting him is clear (although more so in the former case). What, however, if the defendant is not guilty because he committed the crime in another state or because the statute of limitations has run? In these cases the disutility (of the action if not the rule) is much less clear. Here, interestingly enough, we do not require proof beyond a reasonable doubt, but are satisfied with proof by the preponderence-of-the-evidence standard.

The very indefiniteness of the term "reasonable doubt" raises a number of issues. In civil cases where the preponderance test is used, the finder of fact is often instructed in some detail on the burden of proof; yet in criminal cases there is no such specification, even though "reasonable doubt" is a far more indefinite term. Nor do judges appear at all interested in the likelihood that reasonable doubt might be much more comprehensible if expressed in quantitative terms. After all, we can understand much better "a 2–out–of–3 chance" than we can "pretty probable." Similarly, we can understand 999 out of 1,000 more precisely and even intuitively than we can understand the concept of overwhelming probability.

Several reasons explain this policy. First and most obvious, if we tell the jury that they must be 99.5-percent certain of the guilt of the accused before they convict him, we are telling them that they will and indeed are expected to convict 1 innocent man in each 200 guilty verdicts. We recoil from admitting that the imperfection of knowledge and of human beings makes it inevitable that we convict some defendants who are innocent, though of course this is the case.

Probably the most important reason why we do not attempt to express reasonable doubt in terms of quantitative odds, however, is that in any rational system the utilities (or disutilities) that determine the necessary probability of guilt will vary with the crime for which the defendant is being tried, and indeed with the particular defendant. In a criminal trial, as in any decision process, we must consider the utilities associated with differing decisions of the particular case at issue—not just the average utilities over many disparate types of criminal cases. Thus the rational factfinder should consider the disadvantages of convicting *this* defendant of *this* crime if he is innocent as compared with those of acquitting him if he is guilty. It is obviously far less serious to society, for instance, to acquit an embezzler, who, in any event, may find it very difficult to be placed again in a position of trust, than it would be to acquit a child molester, since the latter crime is one that tends to be repeated. The utilities, particularly D_g, will vary then, not only with the seriousness of the offense, but with the danger of its repetition.

Similarly we might rationally weigh D_i, the disutility of convicting an innocent man, differently in different cases. The better the reputation of the defendant, the greater the tragedy of his fall from grace, and hence perhaps the greater disutility of convicting him should he be innocent. If so, we perhaps have an explanation of the relatively powerful effect of character testimony on behalf of a criminal defendant. In addition to the usual justification—that the evidence of the good character of the defendant makes it less likely that he in fact committed the crime—we have a second reason: that by raising the disutility of convicting the defendant should he be innocent, we raise P, the quantum of proof or probability of guilt necessary to convict. Converse reasoning makes clear a very important reason for excluding evidence of previous convictions from the prosecution's case in chief. Not only may such evidence lead the jurors to the wholly rational conclusion that if the defendant has committed previous crimes he is more likely to be guilty of this one; it may also lead them to the perhaps rational but clearly undesirable conclusion that because of his earlier convictions, D_i, the disutility of convicting the defendant should he be innocent, is minimal. Obviously, in a system of justice that regards it as crucial that the defendant be found guilty only of the crime specifically charged, we cannot permit a mistaken factual judgment to be made either on the theory that even if the defendant did not commit the crime charged he probably committed others, or on the theory that since the defendant has been convicted several times before it is not very important to him or to society that he is convicted one more time.

Character testimony is not the only facet of evidence that can be examined from a decision-theoretic view. We would expect that since the disutility of convicting an innocent man increases with the severity of the sentence he will receive, the likely sentence would be a matter greatly affecting the decision of a rational trier of fact. In the most extreme situation—the capital case—we can argue that we obtain convictions at least in part by the drastic expedient of disqualifying possible factfinders with too "extreme" a view of this disutility. In one somewhat more common type of case—that involving a mandatory prison sentence—the consequences for the defendant of conviction might be clear, yet this important determinant of the utilities is kept from the jury. It is hard to defend this on a decision-theoretic view. It is one thing to say that the psychological and sociological data relevant to the likely sentence are kept from the jury and made available only to the sentencing judge because the jury might not be equal to the complex task of predicting the actual sentence, and might use this type of data for a less desirable purpose. It is quite another thing to argue that an important determinant of the utilities, in itself easy to understand and not likely to be abused, should be kept from the factfinder.

Returning now to the formula expressing the probability of guilt necessary for conviction,

$$P > \frac{I}{I + \frac{D_g}{D_i}}$$ it is clear that as D_g, becomes lower,

or D_i, becomes higher, the probability of guilt necessary for conviction drops. Thus the observed high rate of conviction in the South of Negroes for crimes against white persons may be explained not only by the typical white Southern juror's view that the white complainant is always telling the truth, but also by his low estimate of D_i, the disutility of convicting an innocent Negro, and his high estimate of D_g, the disutility of letting a guilty Negro "get away" with something.

An especially interesting application of this type of consideration comes from a quasi-criminal proceeding—the decision process in the loyalty-security hearing. One can argue that aside from the hysteria and maladministration of the McCarthy era, a basic cause of unfairness in employee discharge cases was a genuine misapprehension of the utilities. First, most of those passing on such cases, as well as the public at large, overestimated the disutility of allowing even a serious security risk to hold a nonsensitive government post. Conversely, and probably more important, there was a great underestimation of the disutility of "convicting" one who might be innocent. A discharge on security grounds was asserted by many to be no more serious than one attributable to a reduction in force caused by budget difficulties—despite the facts that the pervasiveness of the security apparatus made it possible for a discharge on security grounds to effectively prevent a worker in some fields from engaging in his occupation at all and that such a discharge, in view of the temper of the country, was a badge of infamy that restricted opportunity in fields completely unrelated to national security.

We have thus far treated D_i and D_g as if they must always be positive numbers—as if there must always be a net disutility in acquitting a guilty person or in convicting an innocent one. This, however, is far from obvious.

We can readily see that under various circumstances a rational factfinder might believe it better to acquit a defendant who he felt was certainly guilty than to convict him. Such a view might be based on the conclusion that the defendant would not commit any other crimes, that a conviction would serve no deterrent function, and that the punishment to be imposed would be so harsh that even should the defendant be guilty there would be a disutility in subjecting him to that punishment. In such a case we would have to conclude that D_g would be a negative quantity; that therefore, applying our equation (which remains valid so long as $D_i \neq 0$, and $D_g + D_i > 0$), the necessary probability of guilt would have to be greater than one—an impossibility. All the above means is that in some cases the rational factfinder should acquit regardless of how certain is the guilt of the defendant. Interestingly enough, although we give our factfinder this prerogative in criminal cases, it is, according to the most complete study on the issue, not often used. The jury, feeling itself bound by the court's instructions, more often reserves its power to acquit for those cases where the factual guilt of the defendant is not crystal-clear.

The problem of controlling the jury's rationality becomes a much more serious one where the jury might be led to the view that D_i is negative. This can occur where the jury believes either that, although the accused may not be guilty of the crime charged, he is guilty of something else, or that he is so dangerous that he should be convicted regardless of his guilt. Nor is this the only type of case where the jury might see an advantage in convicting an innocent man. If the jury took seriously the deterrent purposes of the criminal law, it might conclude that the deterrent value of convicting the defendant was sufficient to outweigh the fact that he was innocent. As long as it could not be shown publicly that the defendant was innocent, the deterrent effect of conviction would be essentially the same as if he were guilty.

The problem in some sense lies with differing views of the rationality to be exhibited by the trier of fact. Rational behavior can only be defined in terms of its goals; and the goals of our criminal system as a whole may not only be somewhat unclear, but may also on occasion be at odds with one another. Thus, while it might be rational for a jury whose goal was the diminishing of crime to convict a man felt to be innocent of the crime charged, it might well be irrational for a criminal system oriented toward diminishing crime, preserving a wide ambit of individual freedom, and decreasing fear of improper conviction to act in the same way.

Indeed, the problem arises not only where a negative D_i requires a guilty verdict, but in all cases where the jury's view of the D_g and D_i might lead it to convict where the probability of guilt was quite low. The basic problem presented by both situations is that our legal system has as a fundamental tenet that it is better that an undetermined number of guilty men (but clearly more than one) should go free rather than that one innocent man be convicted. The difficulty of giving effect to this tenet in the determination of the jury verdict is one of the basic dilemmas of our criminal system. Although a trial judge can prevent a case from reaching the jury if the evidence will not support a guilty verdict, in the majority of cases it is the jurors who must weigh the evidence, and their mixed decision about the evidence and the utilities is extremely difficult to review. Nonetheless, we do attempt to assure ourselves that the jury is using a reasonably high value for P. First, and most important, we exclude insofar as possible the types of evidence that we feel would cause the jury to reach too high a value for D_g and (even more important) too low a value for D_i. Of course this is not an easy matter. In many cases evidence bearing strongly on the issues and hence perfectly admissible under the rules of evidence may be sufficient to convince a rational juror that the disutility of convicting the innocent defendant would be virtually nonexistent, or even negative, and that, guilty or not, society would be better off for his conviction.

Next, we hope that the jury will be able to discern practical arguments for adhering to a high value of P. If a defendant is convicted with little regard for his guilt because of a supposed deterrent effect, we take the great chance that the truth will out sooner or later and thereby not only weaken deterrence for that crime but also cast a doubt upon the whole legal system. Similarly, we wish the jury to consider the fact that in addition to reducing crime, the criminal system should also weigh the waste of human and financial resources caused by improper convictions.

Finally, we hope that the jury—not because of a conclusion about what is rational from its own perspectives but because of the perspectives of the broader system—will adopt the role of one part of a complex system and hence confine itself to the consideration of the probabilities and the utilities within the established framework. To this end we instruct it, although not in very enlightening terms, on the content of "reasonable doubt."

ON THE DEGREE OF CONFIDENCE FOR ADVERSE DECISIONS

FREDERICK SCHAUER AND RICHARD ZECKHAUSER

A Vermont police officer was recently reinstated to his position after having been acquitted in court on charges of misdemeanor sexual harassment. His acquittal followed a trial in which the complaining witness, a police department employee, testified about the ways in which the defendant had physically and verbally harassed her over a period of several months. Four other witnesses, however, each prepared to offer similar testimony about the defendant's harassment of her, were not permitted to testify. The jury, limited therefore to hearing just one complaining witness, found that the state had not proved its case beyond a reasonable doubt, and so returned a verdict of not guilty. Immediately after the acquittal, the police department, which had suspended the officer when the criminal charges were brought against him, revoked the suspension and reinstated the officer. ´

This outcome was typical of a range of cases in which potentially adverse decisions in a social or professional context—here the decision whether to retain the officer—must be made in the face of uncertainty about whether the facts that would support an adverse decision are true. Embedded in this quite typical story are thus a host of issues of social epistemology, the domain in which normative issues of social justice play out in the context of questions of factual knowledge. One central issue pertains to the way in which the police department appears not only to have taken the result in a criminal trial as dispositive to its own decision whether to retain an employee, but also to have supposed that the probability of guilt necessary to secure a criminal conviction is also the probability of guilt to be employed by the department in deciding whether to continue the officer's employment.

Frederick Schauer and Richard Zeckhauser, "On the Degree of Confidence for Adverse Decisions," *Kennedy School of Government Working Paper* (1991)

In order to focus on the evidentiary question, we assume the relevance of the proposition whose truth we are trying to assess to the decision we are proposing to take. It is one thing to ask whether a proposition, if true, would be relevant to a decision; and quite another, our concern here, to ask what it is to take the proposition as true for the purposes of a decision. Indeed, failure to attend to this distinction generated great confusion in the commentary about the propriety of publishing the allegations about the sex life of then–candidate Bill Clinton. Almost all who either criticized or supported the subsequent decision by the mainstream press to publish allegations first printed in a supermarket tabloid commingled questions about the *validity* of the evidence with questions about the *relevance* of the charges, even if true, to Clinton's candidacy. Sorting out the confusion, we see that one issue is whether acts of marital infidelity, even if established to a virtual certainty, are relevant to assessing the qualifications of a presidential candidate. A quite different issue, however, is the determination of the standard of proof before, say, a national newspaper decides to print allegations about something conceded to be relevant if it is true. Here the dispute about the former inhibited clear thought about the latter, because most who questioned the reliability of the evidence also articulated doubts about the relevance of the facts charged.

To avoid this confusion, we limit our discussion to questions about acts which, if they in fact occurred, would with little controversy be relevant to the decision at hand. This limitation excludes cases like those involving charges of marital infidelity in a political context (although there might be less controversy about the same charges in a different context, such as selecting a marriage counselor, or a spouse), or that an applicant for a job committed a crime thirty years ago, or that a candidate for the Baseball Hall of Fame gambled on baseball games, all of which confusingly juxtapose relevance with epistemology.

We avoid this confusion if we think instead, for example, of charges that a candidate for state treasurer has recently embezzled corporate funds, that a prospective or sitting judge takes bribes, that a babysitter is a child molester, that a used car dealer turns back odometers, that a store employee pilfers from the inventory, or that a candidate for tenure plagiarized his publications. In each of these cases the charge, if true, would with little question justify taking some action adverse to the individual, action that would not have been taken were the charges untrue.

In many of these examples, the conduct is treated by the law as a crime, despite the fact that the pertinent decision is outside the context of the state's imposition of criminal penalties. But this fact prompts much of the confusion we address here. An act that is criminal is an act that, in at least one setting, requires proof beyond a reasonable doubt before sanctions may be imposed. Thus we see the common mistake of assuming that it is the nature of the *act* that occasions the stringent standard of proof, rather than the decisional context. Yet where the potential is something other than deprivation of physical liberty or imposition of a criminal fine, there is no reason to suppose that the standard of proof should be the same even though the underlying act is identical.

To further isolate the issue, therefore, we stress at the outset that criminality under the law is largely irrelevant to the epistemological question in settings other than a criminal trial. In some instances, the fact of criminality may be of only limited pertinence in assessing relevance. We can question whether committing larceny is disqualifying from being a quarterback, whether murderers should have their books published, or whether Presidents should be impeached for illegally disposing of toxic wastes without doubting the necessity of proscribing those acts. Conversely, many acts that are not criminal are in some contexts so plainly wrong that the issues are just the ones that concern us here. A bridge player who peeks at his opponent's hand, an orthodox rabbi who secretly eats pork chops, and a dinner guest who picks his nose during the meal have committed no crimes. Yet each of these charges would, if true, be relevant to a decision whether to ask the bridge player to be a fourth, to dismiss the rabbi, or to invite the guest to a dinner party. Thus, our assumption of non-controversial relevance does not depend on criminality; neither does it entail any conclusions about whether the alleged conduct would be wrong in any other context.

These examples illustrate the way in which some fact may be relevant to one decision but irrelevant to another. Outside of general moral assessment or imposition of penalties through the criminal law, the question is rarely whether conduct is good or bad independent of context, but instead whether it is desirable or undesirable relative to some position or decision. Doing a favor for one's friend is morally desirable in many contexts, but not if one is doing so as a judge. And even though deliberate deception is usually wrong and sometimes legally actionable, past successes at such deception would hardly be disqualifying—indeed, quite the opposite—if one were seeking to employ a professional poker player. So when we say that we seek to isolate the issue by focusing only on those charges which, if true, would without question be relevant, we mean only that they would without question be relevant to some particular decision to be made.

■ ■ ■

The legal system's choice among [different] standards of proof represents a straightforward exercise in trading off the harms flowing from two different types of error. When Blackstone wrote that "it is better that ten guilty persons escape, than that one innocent suffer," he was identifying the greater harm of one type of error (conviction of the innocent) than the other (non-conviction of the guilty). As long as one type of error is deemed more serious than another, an optimal decision procedure will seek not simply to minimize the number of errors, but will instead be willing to suffer some in-

crease in the total number of errors in order to decrease the number of errors of the more harmful kind. When applied to the criminal law, this principle generates a system that is tilted towards concluding innocence by incorporating a number of defendant-favoring procedural devices, of which the standard of proof beyond a reasonable doubt is among the most noteworthy. As long as a society believes that a wrongful deprivation of an individual's liberty is a harm far greater than the harms consequent upon non-punishment of those who deserve it, something like Blackstone's ratio will inform the selection of procedures in the context of the criminal law.

Conversely, where there is no reason to consider one type of error to be more harmful than the other, such a skewed standard of proof is inappropriate. The preponderance-of-the-evidence standard generally applied in civil litigation is grounded in the belief that there is no difference between failure to make an award to a deserving plaintiff and making an award of damages against a non-culpable defendant.

The standard of proof beyond a reasonable doubt is properly thought to represent a very high burden of proof, but if we look at it from another direction we can see that it sets a very low burden of proof for the defendant. If the defendant establishes a reasonable doubt as to his guilt, he will prevail. Say .95 quantifies the proof beyond a reasonable doubt standard; a defendant then establishes a reasonable doubt by establishing a .06 or greater likelihood that she did not commit the act charged. Thus, even if a defendant offers only slight evidence of her innocence, what would otherwise be a conclusion of guilt is cancelled as a consequence of the fact that society places much greater value on avoiding mistaken conviction than on avoiding mistaken acquittal.

If a probability of innocence of .06 is sufficient to justify an acquittal, it follows that equally low probabilities of guilt ought to govern in settings in which the stakes of the criminal process are reversed. If there is a reasonable possibility (the positive numerical equivalent of what "reasonable doubt" implies negatively) that an applicant for the job of school teacher is a sexual-harasser of students, then it seems intuitively plausible to believe that this .06 possibility would justify refraining from making an offer of employment that would otherwise have been made, just as the same probability would justify refraining from reaching a finding of guilt that would otherwise be reached.

■ ■ ■

The foregoing assumes that the consequences of denial are merely the loss of the position. In some cases that may be true, but in others the *reasons* for denial may have stigmatizing consequences (including a lessened ability to obtain similar positions) beyond the consequences of not having the relevant position.

If so, then the expected harm to the individual accused of a mistaken decision to deny becomes greater, while the expected harm of a mistaken decision to confirm might remain unchanged. As a result, the changed balance

of expected harms should elevate the standard of proof above what it would otherwise have been.

The stigmatization effect, like all reputation effects, is obviously a function of publicity, and thus less public decision-making processes, with less stigmatization worry, can, *ceteris paribus*, employ lower burdens of proof.

The upshot of this is that we can imagine the extreme case, an applicant for a competitive position involving great responsibility to third parties, charged with having committed acts going directly to the responsibilities of the position (which acts may not be criminal), and involving a great risk of harm if true, and in which the reasons for the denial would not be publicized, in which merely a slight possibility (say, .06 again) that the charges were true would be sufficient to withhold the making of what would otherwise be a positive decision. In other words, we can well imagine settings in which merely a slight chance of guilt would be sufficient for making a negative decision.

IN RE WINSHIP

397 U.S. 359 (1970)

JUSTICE BRENNAN

. . . This case presents the single, narrow question whether proof beyond a reasonable doubt is among the "essentials of due process and fair treatment" required during the adjudicatory stage when a juvenile is charged with an act which would constitute a crime if committed by an adult.

. . . The requirement that guilt of a criminal charge be established by proof beyond a reason-

able doubt dates at least from our early years as a Nation. The demand for a higher degree of persuasion in criminal cases was recurrently expressed from ancient times, though its crystallization into the formula 'beyond a reasonable doubt' seems to have occurred as late as 1798. It is now accepted in common law jurisdictions as the measure of persuasion by which the prosecution must convince the trier of all the essential elements of guilt. Although virtually unanimous adherence to the reasonable-doubt standard in common-law jurisdictions may not conclusively establish it as a requirement of due process, such adherence does reflect a profound judgment about the way in which law should be enforced and justice administered.

Expressions in many opinions of this Court indicate that it has long been assumed that proof of a criminal charge beyond a reasonable doubt is constitutionally required.

. . . The reasonable-doubt standard plays a vital role in the American scheme of criminal procedure. It is a prime instrument for reducing the risk of convictions resting on factual error. The standard provides concrete substance for the presumption of innocence—that bedrock axiomatic and elementary principle whose enforcement lies at the foundation of the administration of our criminal law. As the dissenters in the New York Court of Appeals observed, and we agree, "a person accused of a crime . . . would be at a severe disadvantage, a disadvantage amounting to a lack of fundamental fairness, if he could be adjudged guilty and imprisoned for years on the strength of the same evidence as would suffice in a civil case."

The requirement of proof beyond a reasonable doubt has this vital role in our criminal procedure for cogent reasons. The accused during a criminal prosecution has at stake interest of immense importance, both because of the possibility that he may lose his liberty upon conviction and because of the certainty that he would be stigmatized by the conviction. Accordingly, a society that values the good name and freedom of every individual should not condemn a man for commission of a crime when there is reasonable doubt about his guilt. As we said in Speiser v. Randall, "There is always in litigation a margin of error, representing error in factfinding, which both parties must take into account. Where one party has at stake an interest of transcending value—as a criminal defendant his liberty—this margin of error is reduced as to him by the process of placing on the other party the burden of . . . persuading the factfinder at the con-

clusion of the trial of his guilt beyond a reasonable doubt. Due process commands that no man shall lose his liberty unless the Government has borne the burden of . . . convincing the factfinder of his guilt."

Moreover, use of the reasonable-doubt standard is indispensable to command the respect and confidence of the community in applications of the criminal law. It is critical that the moral force of the criminal law not be diluted by a standard of proof that leaves people in doubt whether innocent men are being condemned. It is also important in our free society that every individual going about his ordinary affairs have confidence that his government cannot adjudge him guilty of a criminal offense without convincing a proper factfinder of his guilt with utmost certainty.

Lest there remain any doubt about the constitutional stature of the reasonable-doubt standard, we explicitly hold that the Due Process Clause protects the accused against conviction except upon proof beyond a reasonable doubt of every fact necessary to constitute the crime with which he is charged.

JUSTICE BLACK, dissenting

The Bill of Rights, which in my view is made fully applicable to the States by the Fourteenth Amendment, does by express language provide for, among other things, a right to counsel in criminal trials, a right to indictment, and the right of a defendant to be informed of the nature of the charges against him. And in two places the Constitution provides for trial by jury, but nowhere in that document is there any statement that conviction of crime requires proof of guilt beyond a reasonable doubt. The Constitution thus goes into some detail to spell out what kind of trial a defendant charged with crime should have, and I believe the Court has no power to add to or subtract from the procedures set forth by the Founders. I realize that it is far easier to substitute individual judges' ideas of "fairness" for the fairness prescribed by the Constitution, but I shall not at any time surrender my belief that that document itself should be our guide, not our own concept of what is fair, decent, and right. That this old "shock-the-conscience" test is what the Court is relying on, rather than the words of the Constitution, is clearly enough revealed by the reference of the majority to "fair treatment" and to the statement by the dissenting judges in the New York Court of Appeals that failure to require proof beyond a reasonable doubt amounts to a "lack of fundamental fairness." As I have said time and time again, I prefer to put my faith in the words of the written Constitution itself rather than to rely on the shifting, day-to-day standards of fairness of individual judges.

QUESTIONS FOR DISCUSSION

1. As Kaplan notes, William Blackstone said that "it is better that ten guilty persons escape, than that one innocent suffer." Do you think Blackstone was right? Why or why not? What moral, social, and political values are implicit in Blackstone's claim?

2. Schauer and Zeckhauser think there might be some cases in which a low probability, even less than a preponderance of the evidence, would be sufficient to take some adverse action. Why do they think this? Do you agree? In what kinds of settings, if any, might this be appropriate?

3. The *Winship* case talks about the "presumption of innocence." What is a presumption of innocence? How does a presumption of innocence relate to burden of proof?

4. When now–Justice Clarence Thomas of the U.S. Supreme Court was nominated by President George Bush to be a Supreme Court Justice, the confirmation hearings before the Senate Judiciary Committee were initially concerned with Thomas's views about various questions of constitutional law. Shortly after the hearings commenced, however, Anita Hill, a professor of law at the University of Oklahoma, charged that, when she had been an employee of Thomas' at the Equal Employment Opportunity Commission some years earlier, Thomas had committed various acts of sexual harassment. In particular, she charged that Thomas had made numerous inappropriate sexual remarks to her, and in other ways created an unlawful "hostile and intimidating" workplace environment. Thomas categorically denied the charges. Assume you are a United States Senator who must vote yes or no on the nomination. Assuming that the charges are now public, assuming that you had previously decided on the basis of all other factors to vote yes, and assuming that these charges, if true, would be sufficient for you to vote no, what burden of proof do you apply, and why?

SUGGESTIONS FOR FURTHER READING

On occasion, philosophers have used the legal ideas of burden of proof in making philosophical arguments. Two good examples are Roderick Chisholm, *Theory of Knowledge*, 2nd ed. (Englewood Cliffs, New Jersey: Prentice-Hall, 1977), Chapter 1, and Edna

Ullman–Margalit, "On Presumption," *Journal of Philosophy*, vol. 80 (1983), pp. 143 ff. Sophisticated analyses of the burden of proof in law include Ronald J. Allen, "The Nature of Juridical Proof," *Cardozo Law Review*, vol. 13 (1991), pp. 373 ff.; James Bell, "Decision Theory and Due Process: A Critique of the Supreme Court's Lawmaking for Burdens of Proof," *Journal of Criminal Law and Criminology*, vol, 78 (1987), pp. 557 ff.; Neil Cohen, "The Role of Evidential Weight in Criminal Proof," *Boston University Law Review*, vol. 66 (1986), pp. 635 ff.; R.J. Simon and L. Mahan, "Quantifying Burdens of Proof," *Law and Society Review*, vol. 5 (1971), pp. 319 ff.; William Twining, *Theories of Evidence: Bentham and Wigmore* (London: Weidenfeld and Nicolson, 1985).

PROBABILITY AND THE LAW OF EVIDENCE

INTRODUCTION

Suppose you are asked to buy a lottery ticket. The ticket costs $1, and in exchange for the $1 you get a one in 100 chance of winning $100? Should you buy the ticket? The answer, of course, is that there is no reason to buy the ticket, and no reason not to buy the ticket, at least if maximizing your monetary return is all you care about. A one in 100 chance of winning $100 is worth $1, and we reach this *expected value* by multiplying the chance of getting something (here .01) times what we would get if the chance turns out to occur. And since we are being asked to buy something worth exactly $1 for $1, there is no advantage to buying it, nor any disadvantage. If we were asked to pay more than $1 for a one in 100 chance of winning $100, we should say no, because the price of the ticket is now greater than its expected value. And if we were asked if we wanted to buy the ticket for less than $1, we should buy it, because now we are getting a bargain. We are paying less than $1 for something with an expected value of, and therefore worth, $1.

Although the idea of expected value is one of the most elementary applications of probability theory, it turns out that expected value and related theories of probability have less use in actual legal systems than we might think. Suppose you are a member of the jury. The plaintiff claims that the defendant defrauded her of $1 million. The defendant claims he did not do it. You and your fellow jurors are not sure. Suppose you all think that there is a 60 percent chance that the defendant committed fraud, and that the defendant's fraud damaged the plaintiff in the amount of $1 million. You might think that the rational thing to do would be to award the plaintiff $600,000, because there is a 60 percent chance that she is entitled to $1 million, and 60 percent of $1 million is $600,000.

However rational this might seem, it is not the way in which the legal system typically operates. Because all of the jurors in this case believe by a preponderance of the evidence (equal to or greater than .51, say) that the plaintiff is entitled to $1 million, the plaintiff will get $1 million. And by the same procedures, if all twelve jurors believed there was a 40 percent chance that the defendant was liable to the plaintiff in the amount of $1 million, the plaintiff would get not $400,000, but nothing at all. And finally, if six jurors were absolutely convinced that the plaintiff should be awarded $1 million, and six jurors were equally convinced that the plaintiff should be awarded nothing, the law prohibits the obvious solution—splitting the difference.[3]

---

[3]That the law prohibits splitting the difference does not mean that it never happens. Jury proceedings are generally secret, and it is likely that splitting the difference and other similar prohibited practices happen more than the the rules themselves might suggest.

Why in all of these cases is there a gap between what it seems most rational to do and what the legal system actually does? Is this because the legal system is irrational? Is it because the experience of the legal system casts doubt on the seeming rationality of the procedures just described? Or is it because the legal system might also be serving other values not captured in the simple decision theory model? In addition to the materials that follow, two cases—one real and one hypothetical—might further illustrate the issues and the problems.

Consider first a hypothetical case created by the Oxford philosopher L. Jonathan Cohen and described in his book *The Probable and the Provable.*[4] Cohen calls his case The Paradox of the Gatecrasher and it goes as follows:

> Consider . . . a case in which it is common ground that 499 people paid for admission to a rodeo, and that 1,000 are counted in the seats, of whom A is one. Suppose no tickets were issued and there can be no testimony as to whether A paid for admission or climbed over the fence. So by any plausible criterion of mathematical probability there is a .501 probability, on the admitted facts, that he did not pay. The mathematicist theory would apparently imply that in such circumstances the rodeo organizers are entitled to judgement against A for the admission-money, since the balance of probability [the preponderance of the evidence —eds.] . . . would lie in their favour. But it seems manifestly unjust that A should lose his case when there is an agreed mathematical probability of as high as .499 that he in fact paid for admission.

> Indeed, if the organizers were really entitled to judgement against A, they would presumably be equally entitled to judgement against each person in the same situation as A. So they might conceivably be entitled to recover 1,000 admission-moneys, when it was admitted that 499 had actually been paid. The absurd injustice of this suffices to show that there is something wrong somewhere. But where?

Unlike Cohen's hypothetical case, in which he assumes that it would be wrong to award judgment against A, there are a few real cases in which what Cohen calls the "mathematicist" theory has in fact been used. The most famous is a case called *Sindell v. Abbott Laboratories.*[5] In this case there was a class action lawsuit brought on behalf of all women who had been injured as a result of taking the drug DES (diethylstilbestrol), a drug designed to prevent miscarriages. The drug, however, was also shown to cause various cancerous and precancerous vaginal disorders. The problem, however, was that although there was strong evidence that DES caused certain conditions, it was almost impossible to link a particular manufacturer of the drug to particular consequences, especially because the drug was widely used between 1947 and 1971, and thus few records existed at the time of the lawsuit, and also because the drug, never having been patented, was manufactured by numerous companies.

[4]Oxford: Clarendon Press, 1977.

[5]607 P.2d 924 (California 1980).

Because there was no way to link a specific injury with a specific DES manufacturer, it seems, or at least it might seem to Cohen, that there could be no liability. The California courts, however, devised a novel solution. They were able to determine the percentage of the market (the "market share") that specific DES manufacturers had during the entire time of the product's availability. The courts then awarded judgment against *all* of the DES manufacturers, and ordered the manufacturers to contribute to a damages pool based on each manufacturer's market share. So if a company sold 40 percent of the DES, then it would be required to pay an amount equal to 40 percent of the total damage award. The pool made up of these market share contributions was then allocated among all of the women who had filed damages claims based on harms they suffered as a result of taking DES.

Is there a difference between this case and Cohen's gatecrasher case? If so, what might that difference be? In considering the materials that follow, consider how you would decide the gatecrasher case, and how you would have decided the DES case.

HUMAN INFORMATION PROCESSING
AND ADJUDICATION:
TRIAL BY HEURISTICS

MICHAEL J. SAKS AND ROBERT F. KIDD

While a trial is many things, it most surely is a social invention for deciding between disputed alternatives under conditions of uncertainty. The values this invention seeks to maximize may be manifold and contradictory, but one of the most important among them is accuracy or correctness. Through legal decision making we seek to avoid the classic errors of convicting an innocent defendant or acquitting a guilty one, or finding liability when there is none or failing to find liability when it is present. Whatever justice may be, surely it is not error.

Various commentators have proposed, and various advocates have sought to introduce at trial, mathematical or statistical tools to guide the trier of fact and to reduce the number of inevitable errors. A limited amount of sharply reasoned and intriguing debate has taken place over these issues both in law reviews and in appellate courts. Perhaps the most thorough critique of these proposals has been that of Lawrence Tribe in his article, "Trial by Mathematics: Precision and Ritual in the Legal Process" (1971). In that paper, Tribe seeks to per-

Michael J. Saks and Robert F. Kidd, "Human Information Processing and Adjudication: Trial By Heuristics," *Law and Society Review*, vol. 15 (1980), pp. 1 ff.

suade us that "the costs of attempting to integrate mathematics into the factfinding process of a legal trial outweigh their benefits."

Tribe does not object to the introduction of quantitative evidence, though he is decidedly wary of it and its aroma of certitude. What he advocates is that such data be used, if they must, in their most descriptive and raw form, that the judge or jury not be told how these data might be analyzed and what inferences might be drawn from the results of such analysis. The kinds of analysis and mathematical models used by all sorts of scientists, engineers, administrators, planners, and others in order to put questions to their data is what Tribe would ban from legal fact finding. His objections to such mathematizing of evidence are based on his opinion that it leads to imprecise estimates that are inevitably probabilistic, that soft variables are dwarfed in favor of more easily quantifiable variables, that it is difficult to apply background probability estimates to deciding specific instances, and that the trial process would be dehumanized. Tribe argues, in essence, that keeping a trial as intuitive, as elemental, as the Anglo-Saxon trial can be will preserve the symbolism and humanness, thereby best serving the courts and society.

In a fundamental criticism of using the somewhat more precise language and meaning of mathematics, Tribe eloquently defends the value of legal symbolism and the resulting mask of certainty.

The system does *not* in fact authorize the imposition of criminal punishment when the trier recognizes a quantifiable doubt as to the defendant's guilt. Instead, the system dramatically—if imprecisely—insists upon as close an approximation to certainty as seems humanly attainable in the circumstances. The jury is charged that any "reasonable doubt," of whatever magnitude, must be resolved in favor of the accused. Such insistence on the greatest certainty that seems reasonably attainable can serve at the trial's end, like the presumption of inno-

cence at the trial's start, to affirm the dignity of the accused and to display respect for his rights as a person—in this instance, by declining to put those rights in deliberate jeopardy and by refusing to sacrifice him to the interests of others.

In contrast, for the jury to announce that it is prepared to convict the defendant in the face of an acknowledged and numerically measurable doubt as to his guilt is to tell the accused that those who judge him find it preferable to accept the resulting risk of his unjust conviction than to reduce that risk by demanding any further or more convincing proof of his guilt.

. . . That some mistaken verdicts are inevitably returned even by jurors who regard themselves as "certain" is of course true but is irrelevant; such unavoidable errors are in no sense *intended,* and the fact that they must occur if trials are to be conducted at all need not undermine the effort, through the symbols of trial procedure, to express society's fundamental commitment to the protection of the defendant's rights as a person, as an end in himself. On the other hand, formulating an "acceptable" risk of error to which the trier is willing deliberately to subject the defendant would interfere seriously with this expressive role of the demand for certitude—however unattainable real certitude may be, and however clearly all may ultimately recognize its unattainability.

A trial may indeed be more than a search for the truth in a given matter; but surely it is not less. We will seek to demonstrate, contrary to Tribe, that while certain errors and harm may be inherent even in the proper use of probabilistic tools, even more harm may be inherent in not using them.

Most legal decision making, like that in many other areas of complex activity, is done under conditions of uncertainty. Events must be classified, predicted, or post-dicted in circumstances where the correct choice is more probable than zero but less probable than unity. If one wished to choose a given product with the lowest unit price, the fastest transit route between two cities, or which manner of calculating one's taxes results in the least liability, one could, through proper information gathering and analysis, identify the correct solution with certainty (or something bordering on certainty). Other problems, by virtue of their complexity, the limitations of available information, or the inadequacy of our conceptualizations for dealing with them, have best solutions that cannot be known with certainty to be correct. Judges and jurors are called upon, for example, to assess the likelihood that a witness's report is congruent with the actual event; the probability, given certain evidence, that a defendant committed an alleged offense; the risk of harm that reasonably should have been foreseen as associated with certain design features of a product; the probability that a pollutant caused certain damage; or the likelihood that a person in jeopardy of civil commitment is dangerous to self or others. Thus, the nature of the questions and the information available to judicial decision makers defines their task as an uncertain and probabilistic one.

Abundant evidence from psychological research, however, suggests that in many contexts decision makers' intuitive, common-sense judgments depart markedly and lawfully (in the scientific sense) from the actual probabilities. People use a number of simplifying operations, called "heuristics," to reduce the complexity of information which must be integrated to yield a decision. These simplifying strategies often lead to errors in judgment. Consider the following examples:

1. After observing three consecutive red wins, a group of people playing roulette start to switch their bets to black. After red wins on the fourth and fifth spins, more and more players switch to black, and they are increasingly surprised when the roulette wheel produces a red win the sixth, and then the seventh time. In actuality, on each spin the odds of a red win remain constant at 1:1. The shifting of bets to black was irrational, as was the strong subjective sense that after each successive red win, black became more likely.

2. One group of respondents was asked to estimate the probability that John is a lawyer rather than an engineer. Their median probability estimate was .95. Another group of respondents was asked the same question, except that they were first told that the group from which John was selected consisted of 30 lawyers and 70 engineers. The second group's median estimate of the likelihood that John is a lawyer was also .95. Information about the composition of the group from which John was selected logically should have affected the estimated probability, but it had no effect at all on the decision makers' judgment. Only at the extremes of the distributions, where the group approaches 100 lawyers and 0 engineers (or the converse) do the decision makers become sensitive to the information about group composition.

3. A cab was involved in a hit-and-run accident at night. Two cab companies, the green and the blue, operate in the city. A witness reports that the offending cab was blue, and legal action is brought against the blue cab company. The court learns that 85 percent of the city's cabs are green and 15 percent are blue. Further, the court learns that on a test of ability to identify cabs under appropriate visibility conditions, the witness is correct on 80 percent of the identifications and incorrect on 20 percent. Several hundred persons have been given this problem and asked to estimate the probability that the responsible cab was in fact a blue cab. Their typical probability response was .80. In actuality, the evidence given leads to a probability of .41 that the responsible cab was blue.

The first example illustrates the simplest and best known of errors in human probability judgment, the "Gambler's Fallacy." In a sequence of independent events, outcomes of prior events do not affect the probability of later events. Each event is independent of the other. On the seventh spin, the roulette wheel neither remembers nor cares what it did on the preceding six spins. People know that in the long run, half the wins will be red and half black. They err in believing that a small local sequence of events will be representative of the infinite sequence. "Chance is commonly viewed as a self-correcting process in which a deviation in one direction induces a deviation in the opposite direction to restore the equilibrium. In fact, deviations are not 'corrected' as a chance process unfolds, they are merely diluted." Although intuition in this context is out of harmony with reality, we all feel it compellingly, and continue to hear that baseball players who have not had a hit in some time are "due" for one, and that lightning will not strike twice in the same place. These common-sense judgments are, nevertheless, dead wrong.

The second example illustrates how human decision making tends to be insensitive to base rates when case-specific information is available. Given only the group base rates—30 lawyers: 70 engineers—people rely heavily on this information to make their judgments. They correctly say the probability is .30 that the person selected is a lawyer. When descriptive case-specific information is added, they tend to ignore the numerical base rate and rely instead on the degree to which the description of John is representative of their stereotype of lawyers. Subjects base their estimate of the probability that John is a lawyer on the degree of correspondence between his description and their stereotype of lawyers as argumentative, competitive, and politically aware. Given the base-rate data in this example, it is 5.44 times as likely that John is a lawyer when the group is composed of 70 lawyers and 30 engineers than when the opposite membership distribution holds.

The third example also demonstrates insensitivity to base-rate information, this time in a context where both the base-rate and the case-specific information are given numerically. The actual low probability that the cab is blue is due to the fact that the base rate for blue cabs is very low, and the witness is of dubious acuity. Indeed, the base rate is more extreme than the witness is credible. But, fact finders apparently are unable simultaneously to relate the color of the hit-and-run cab to two different concerns, namely, the sampling of cabs from the city's cab population and imperfect color identification by the witness. They ignore the base-rate information and treat the accuracy of the witness as equal to the probability of a correct identification.

These illustrations demonstrate the gap between the judgments people make intuitively and the probabilities yielded by explicit calculation (or by empirical observation of actual outcomes). People do not always err, but in particular decision making situations they tend predictably to be incorrect. Because these errors of intuition are systematic and lawful, they are called biases. Because these biases result from the simplifying strategies used by decision makers, whose cognitive capacities cannot otherwise efficiently process the information, they are known as heuristic biases.

As Tribe has argued, the trial is not only a search for truth, but also a social ritual which supports certain values and helps litigants and the society as a whole to accept the judgments of courts. Tribe goes so far as to argue that the more formal mathematical processing departs from intuition, the more it should be eschewed by the courts. As we have seen, under specifiable circumstances, intuition is a poor guide and may lead to incorrect conclusions. To accept the dilemma posed by Tribe and adopt his preference for intuition is to choose a comforting ritual over accurate decisions, much like a patient who would rather have a human physician make a wrong diagnosis than allow a computer to make a correct one. The discovery of heuristic decision processes sharpens this dilemma by clarifying the costs of truth seeking: the decision maker whose only tool is intuition will often err.

One may be unconvinced of this if we attend only to judicial proceedings, where the criterion of accuracy is permanently elusive. (If some ultimate truth were available against which to test the fact finder's accuracy, there would be little need for the trial.) In many other decision-making contexts, such as where medical diagnoses are testable against later and better evidence, or where psychiatric predictions are testable against future behavior, or where predictions about weather or economic behavior or the performance of physical materials are testable against easily observable criteria, it is possible to evaluate the intuitive decision maker's accuracy in comparison to other decision-making devices, notably formal decision models. It has been well established for some time now that when the same information is available to intuitive humans or a good mathematical model, the human's decisions are consistently less accurate. These studies have been conducted in a variety of decision-making contexts and we think it safe to generalize these processes to human judgment in legal settings.

We might ask how human decision making differs, if at all, in its processes or products, when contrasted to decision making by mathematical models. That differences exist seems universally accepted. Even when mathematical tools are modeled after human decision processes, the copy works better than the original. One can "capture the decision policies" of individuals, converting their choice behavior into a mathematical statement which links the input evidence to the decision. This "paramorphic linear representation" of the human decision maker can be directly compared with the individual's judgments. Consistently, the paramorphic linear representation of the human decision maker is more accurate than the decision maker, a phenomenon known as "bootstrapping." Even then, models using random weights do better than both the human or the human's model. One learns a few things about human information processing from such comparisons. The mathematical model of a person's own decision policies is more accurate than the person because it consistently applies the same logic, while the human decision maker fluctu-

ates, being over-influenced by fortuitous, attention-catching pieces of information that vary from time to time, and processing a too-limited set of variables. Unaided individuals tend to have great difficulty incorporating quantified variables, give excessive weight to bits and pieces that happen for whatever reason to be salient, base their decisions on less information (often the less useful information) than do mathematical models, and apply their decision policies inconsistently. This presents an interesting set of concerns about human decision making that contrasts with Tribe's concerns about mathematical decision making. The problems associated with drawing inferences from probability evidence, problems Tribe would like to see the courts avoid, are not avoided by dumping the data, quantitative as well as nonquantitative, into the mental laps of human decision makers, armed only with their intuition.

Moreover, the choice is not really between computers and people. It is between explicitly presented computing and subjective computing, or between more and less accurate computing. This is not to degrade humans. It is merely to recognize, on the one hand, our information processing limitations and, on the other, our capacity to invent tools that can do the job better. After all, many people trust their pocket calculators and the light meters in their cameras, whose workings they do not begin to comprehend; yet their faith is well placed, because these devices make decisions and judgments faster and more accurately than people do. The comparison is not between humans and mathematics, but between humans deciding alone and humans deciding with the help of a tool.

Our suggestion is modest, and most lawyers should find it comfortingly traditional. Namely, experts ought to be permitted to offer their data, their algorithms, and their Bayesian theorems. The errors that may be introduced will be subjected to adversarial cross-examination. Various formal mathematical models do have room for errors—variables omitted, poor measurements, and others that Tribe has cogently presented. But so do intuitive techniques. Properly employed and developed, the former can have fewer. It is up to opposing counsel to unmask the errors. Moreover, as a matter of developing and introducing new tools from what might be called decision-making technology, the identification of flaws does not imply that the tools ought not be used. The proper question is whether the tool, however imperfect, still aids the decision maker more than no tool at all.

LIABILITY AND INDIVIDUALIZED EVIDENCE

JUDITH JARVIS THOMSON

1. Cases like *Smith v. Rapid Transit, Inc.* present a problem to students of tort law. Here is a typical hypothetical case—I will call it *Smith v. Red Cab*—which presents the problem more cleanly than the actual case does. Mrs. Smith was driving home late one night. A taxi came towards her, weaving wildly from side to side across the road. She had to swerve to avoid it; her swerve took her into a parked car; in the crash, she suffered two broken legs. Mrs. Smith therefore sued Red Cab Company. Her evidence is as follows: She could see that it was a cab which caused her accident by weaving wildly across the road, and there are only two cab companies in town, Red Cab (all of whose cabs are red) and Green Cab (all of whose cabs are green), and of the cabs in town that night, six out of ten were operated by Red Cab. Why is that the only evidence she can produce against Red Cab? She says that although she could see that it was a cab which came at her, she could not see its color, and as it was late, there were no other witnesses to the accident— other than the driver himself, of course, but he has not come forward to confess.

If we believe Mrs. Smith's story, and are aware of no further facts that bear on the case, then we shall think it .6 probable that her accident was caused by a cab operated by Red Cab. I think it pays to spell this reasoning out; what follows is one way of doing so. If we believe Mrs. Smith's story, then we believe that a cab, indeed exactly one cab, caused the accident, so that there is such a thing as *the* cab which caused the accident; and we believe that it was a cab in town that night. Thus we believe:

(1) The cab which caused the accident was a cab in town that night.

If we believe Mrs. Smith's story, we also believe:

(2) 6 out of 10 of the cabs in town that night were operated by Red Cab.

Relative to the facts reported by (1) and (2),

(3) The probability that the cab which caused the accident was operated by Red Cab is .6

is true. But those are the only facts such that we are both aware of them and aware of their bearing on the question who operated the cab

Judith Jarvis Thomson, "Liability and Individualized Evidence," in *Rights, Restitution, and Risk* (Cambridge: Harvard University Press, 1986), Chapter 13

which caused the accident. (Perhaps we are aware that the accident took place on, as it might be, a Tuesday. Even so, we are not aware of any reason to think that fact bears on the question whose cab caused the accident.) Other facts whose relevance is clear might come out later: For example, a Green Cab driver might later confess. But as things stand, we have no more reason (indeed we have less reason) to think that any facts which later come out would support the hypothesis that the cab which caused the accident was operated by Green Cab than we have to think they would support the hypothesis that the cab which caused the accident was operated by Red Cab. We are therefore entitled to conclude that (3) is true—in fact, rationality requires us to conclude that (3) is true, for .6 is the degree of belief that, situated as we are, we ought to have in the hypothesis that the cab which caused the accident was operated by Red Cab.

Is it right that Mrs. Smith win her suit against Red Cab? The standard of proof in a tort suit is "more probable than not," which is plausibly interpretable as requiring only that the plaintiff establish a greater than .5 probability that the defendant (wrongfully) caused the harm. But most people feel uncomfortable at the idea of imposing liability on Red Cab on such evidence as Mrs. Smith here presents. Why? That is the problem.

2. *People v. Collins* and its typical descendant hypotheticals raise an analogous problem for the student of criminal law, but less cleanly, so let us set them aside for the time being. Consider, instead, a hypothetical case which I shall call *People v. Tice*. Two people, Tice and Simonson, both hated Summers and wished him dead. Summers went hunting one day. Tice followed with a shotgun loaded with ninety-five pellets. Quite independently, Simonson also followed, but *he* had loaded his shotgun with only five pellets, that being all he had on hand. Both caught sight of Summers at the same time, and both shot all their pellets at him. Independently: I stress that there was no plot or

plan. Only one pellet hit Summers, but that one was enough: It hit Summers in the head and caused his death. While it was possible to tell that the pellet which caused Summers's death came either from Tice's gun or from Simonson's gun, it was not possible to tell which. So what charges should be brought against Tice and Simonson? In the event, Simonson is charged with attempted murder, and in *People v. Tice*, Tice is charged with murder.

Well, why not? To win its case against Tice, the prosecution must show that it is beyond a reasonable doubt that the pellet which caused Summers's death was a pellet fired by Tice. But given the information in hand, that seems easy, for given the information in hand, we can say both:

(1') The pellet which caused Summers's death was a pellet fired at Summers

and

(2') Ninety-five out of the 100 pellets fired at Summers were fired by Tice. The facts these report are the only facts such that we are both aware of them and aware of their bearing on the question whose pellet caused Summers's death. We therefore may, indeed should, conclude that

(3') The probability that the pellet which caused Summers's death was fired by Tice is .95

is also true. And isn't a proposition beyond a reasonable doubt if it is .95 probable?

I hope you will feel at least as uncomfortable at the idea of convicting Tice of murder on such evidence as this that he caused the death as you feel at the idea of imposing liability on Red Cab in *Smith v. Red Cab*.

There are differences, of course. In *Smith v. Red Cab*, the information we have in hand gives no reason at all to think that both cab companies were at fault: It gives reason to think that one cab company was at fault, namely the one, whichever it was, that caused the accident. So if Mrs. Smith wins her suit, then Red Cab may be being held liable for her costs despite the fact that it not only did not cause her injury, but was entirely without fault.

By contrast, the information we have in hand in *People v. Tice* gives reason to think that both Tice and Simonson were at fault: It gives reason to think that both committed attempted murder. So if the people win their case against Tice, then while Tice may be being held liable for murder without having caused Summers's death, he was all the same gravely at fault, having at a minimum tried to bring that death about.

This difference brings in train yet another. If Tice did not cause Summers's death, then his failure to do so was—relative to the evidence we have in hand—just *luck*, good or bad luck according to the view you take of the matter. He did everything he could to cause the death, and if he did not cause it, well, that was certainly no credit to him. By contrast, if Red Cab did not cause Mrs. Smith's injury, that was a credit to Red Cab, for—relative to the evidence we have in hand—if Red Cab did not cause the accident, it was not at fault at all.

We could have eliminated these differences by altering the details of *People v. Tice* so as to make the evidence suggest only that one of the actors (Tice or Simonson) was at fault, the evidence that it was Tice who was at fault issuing from nothing other than the evidence that it was a pellet from Tice's gun which caused the death—just as the evidence that it was Red Cab that was at fault issues from nothing other than the evidence that it was one of Red Cab's cabs which caused Mrs. Smith's accident. It is not easy to alter the details in that way without introducing a measure of weirdness. But I think we ought to feel that there is no need to do so; that is, I think we ought not be moved by the differences I pointed to between *Smith v. Red Cab* and *People v. Tice*.

No doubt it was just luck for Tice if he did not cause Summers's death. But that does not justify convicting him of murder. Anyone who

attempts murder, and goes about things as carefully and well as he can, is just lucky (or unlucky) if he does not cause the death he wishes to cause, and that does not warrant holding him for murder. So also for Simonson, in fact. He too attempted murder, and it is also just luck for him if he did not cause Summers's death.

It is arguable that if a man attempts murder, and it is just luck for him that he does not cause the death he wishes to cause, then morally speaking he has acted as badly as he would have acted had he succeeded. Many of those who take this view regard it as morally suspect that the penalty for murder should be heavier than the penalty for attempted murder. (Perhaps they view it as flatly unacceptable that there is such a difference in penalty. Perhaps they think the difference is just barely acceptable in light of the fact that imposing the same penalty might give unsuccessful attempters a motive to try again, or in light of some other, or additional, considerations.) At all events, the penalty for murder is everywhere heavier than the penalty for attempted murder. Or at least so I suppose; and we can anyway assume this true in the jurisdiction in which Tice is to be tried. So it is not enough to justify the charge of murder against Tice that it is just luck for him if he did not cause the death: To warrant imposition of the heavier penalty the prosecution has positively to prove beyond a reasonable doubt *that* he caused it.

Well, isn't it beyond a reasonable doubt that Tice caused Summers's death? After all, it is .95 probable that he did.

3. It is often said that the kind of evidence available in *Smith v. Red Cab* and *People v. Tice* merely tells us the "mathematical chances" or the "quantitative probability" of the defendant's guilt. And it would be said that what is missing in those cases, the lack of which makes conviction suspect, is "real" "individualized" evidence against the defendant.

I strongly suspect that what people feel the lack of, and call individualized evidence, is evidence which is in an appropriate way causally connected with the (putative) fact that the defendant caused the harm.

Consider the evidence that it was Red Cab which caused the accident in *Smith v. Red Cab*: It consists entirely of Mrs. Smith's testimony that a cab caused her accident, and that six out of ten of the cabs in town that night were operated by Red Cab. If we believe her, we believe there are such facts as that a cab caused her accident, and that six out of ten of the cabs in town that night were operated by Red Cab. But those facts lack an appropriate causal connection with the (putative) fact that Red Cab caused the accident.

What sort of causal connection would be appropriate? Well, if a witness came forward to say he saw the accident, and that the cab which caused the accident looked red to him, *then* we would have what would be called individualized evidence against Red Cab; and my suggestion is that that is because the accident-causing cab's actually being red (and therefore being Red Cab's) would causally explain its looking red to that witness. We might call this "backward-looking individualized evidence" of the defendant's guilt because the bit of evidence (the witness' believing the cab looked red to him) points back toward the (putative) fact that Red Cab caused the accident.

Or if it turned out that Red Cab had given a party for its drivers on the evening of the accident, a party which turned into a drunken brawl, then too we would have what would be called individualized evidence against Red Cab; and my suggestion is that that is because the party would causally explain its having been a Red Cab which caused the accident. We might call this "forward-looking individualized evidence" of the defendant's guilt because the bit of evidence (the party) points forward towards the (putative) fact that Red Cab caused the accident.

Or more complicated (since it involves a common cause), if a red cab crashed into a parked car shortly after Mrs. Smith's accident, and four blocks past the place of it, the driver giving all signs of being drunk, then that too

would be called individualized evidence against Red Cab; and my suggestion is that that is because that driver's having been drunk would causally explain *both* his crashing into the parked car *and* his (and therefore Red Cab's) having caused Mrs. Smith's accident.

In the actual *Smith v. Red Cab*, no such further evidence came out. The facts available to us provide no forward-looking individualized evidence that Red Cab caused the accident, for they neither supply nor suggest any causal explanation of its having been a red cab which caused the accident. Moreover, the facts available to us neither supply nor suggest anything which might have been a common cause *both* of those facts available to us *and* of the (putative) fact that Red Cab caused the accident.

What is of interest is that we do have in the actual *Smith v. Red Cab* a piece of backward-looking individualized evidence for *a* hypothesis. Mrs. Smith says she could see it was a cab which came towards her, and its actually being a cab which came towards her would causally explain her believing this; so her saying she could see it was a cab which came towards her is backward-looking individualized evidence that it was a cab which caused her accident.

No one, of course, supposes that individualized evidence is (deductively valid) proof. In particular, our having backward-looking individualized evidence that a cab caused Mrs. Smith's accident is logically compatible with its not having been a cab which caused the accident.

Moreover, different bits of individualized evidence may differ in strength. For example, it is possible for a private car or bus or truck, or for all I know a gorilla, to be disguised as a cab, and the more noncabs there are on the roads that are disguised as cabs, the less weight we are entitled to place on the causal hypothesis that Mrs. Smith's believing it was a cab which caused her accident was caused by its being a cab which caused her accident, and thus the less weight her believing it was a cab which caused her accident lends to the causal hypothesis that it was a cab which caused her accident. Still, her believing it was a cab which caused her accident is backward-looking individualized evidence that it was a cab which caused her accident, for her having that belief would be causally explained by its having been a cab which caused her accident.

Mrs. Smith's believing it was a cab which caused her accident would also be causally explained by its having been a red cab which caused her accident. (Again, her believing it was a cab which caused her accident would also be causally explained by its having been a cab once ridden in by a Presbyterian minister which caused her accident.) That does not mean that her believing it was a cab which caused her accident is backward-looking individualized evidence for the hypothesis that it was a red cab which caused her accident (or for the hypothesis that it was a cab once ridden in by a Presbyterian minister which caused her accident). For there is no reason to think that the redness of a cab (or its past ridership) is causally relevant to its looking to a person like a cab. Mrs. Smith of course might be unusual in this respect: It might be that her retinas are so structured as to record cabbiness only when caused to do so by red-cabbiness. If we were given reason to think that that is true of her, we would thereby have been given reason to think her believing it was a cab which caused her accident *was* backward-looking individualized evidence that it was a red cab which caused her accident. But in the absence of reason to think her odd in some such respect as that, what we have is backward-looking individualized evidence only for the hypothesis that it was a cab which caused her accident.

For Red Cab to be guilty, the cab that came at Mrs. Smith (supposing it was a cab that came at her, as we do suppose if we believe her story) has to have had the features which distinguish Red Cab's cabs from the other cabs in town that night. Redness is one such feature, and no doubt there are indefinitely many others. But we have in hand no facts about the accident in

which the (putative) redness of the accident-causing cab, or its (putative) possession of some other feature which distinguishes Red Cab's cabs, can be assigned an appropriate causal role. The facts available to us, then, provide (backward-looking) individualized evidence that a cab caused Mrs. Smith's accident, but no individualized evidence that the cab that caused the accident was one of Red Cab's cabs.

The point, then, is not that the only evidence we actually have in hand in *Smith v. Red Cab* is numerical or statistical, for we do have in that case a piece of individualized evidence for the hypothesis that it was a cab that caused the accident.

More important, numerical or statistical evidence too can be causally connected in an appropriate way with the (putative) fact it is presented to support. Suppose a plaintiff alleges that he was refused a job with a certain organization on grounds of race; in evidence, he presents statistics showing that the racial composition of the organization's workforce diverges widely from that of the local population. Those data suggest a causal hypothesis, namely that the organization intends to discriminate in its hiring practices, and the organization's intending to discriminate in its hiring practices would causally explain *both* the existing divergence in racial composition, *and* the (putative) fact that it refused to hire the plaintiff on grounds of race. So that evidence too is individualized, although it is numerical or statistical.

If we had individualized evidence (and thus, on my hypothesis, appropriately causally connected evidence) against Red Cab, in addition to the evidence we already have in hand, then we would feel considerably less reluctant to impose liability on Red Cab. Why is that? That seems to me to be a very hard question to answer.

It cannot plausibly be said that the addition of individualized evidence against Red Cab would make us feel less reluctant to impose liability on it because the addition of individualized evidence against Red Cab would raise the probability that Red Cab caused the accident. Even in the absence of individualized evidence, the probability that Red Cab caused the accident is already .6, which on a plausible interpretation of the requirements of tort law is higher than it need be.

Friends of the idea that individualized evidence is required for conviction have not really made it clear why this should be thought true. That has encouraged their enemies to suppose they have the idea because they think that individualized evidence is uniquely highly probabilifying. The enemies have then found it easy to make mincemeat of the friends. The enemies draw attention to the fact (and it is a fact) that eyewitness testimony, for example, which is paradigm individualized evidence, may be quite unreliable, that is, may probabilify to a lower degree than would some pieces of purely numerical or statistical evidence. And they draw attention to the mistakes about probability (and they are mistakes) which have been studied by Tversky and Kahneman, in particular, those which issue from ignoring base rates.

But I think that is at best an ungenerous diagnosis of what is at work in the friends of individualized evidence. What is at work in them is not the thought that individualized evidence is uniquely highly probabilifying, but rather the feeling that it supplies something which nonindividualized evidence does not supply, which further something is not of value because it raises the probability of the hypothesis in question.

■ ■ ■

5. The jurors do not say "We know that the defendant is guilty" at the close of the trial, they say only "The defendant is guilty"; but in saying that they do something of great significance. It is not strong enough to say they declare the defendant guilty. If you and I have been watching the trial, I may say to you as we leave the courtroom "The defendant is guilty"; I have declared the defendant guilty, but have not done, because I am not so situated as to be able to do, what the jurors do when they say these words

at the close of the trial. The institution in which they are participating is so structured that their saying these words then is their imposing liability on the defendant—for if they say these words at that time, appropriate others will act on the supposition that he is guilty, which includes imposing the relevant penalty on him. So they do not merely invite reliance, they act in awareness that reliance will follow.

Under what conditions is it acceptable for the jurors to agree to say those words at the close of the trial? One thing which is perfectly plain is that their agreeing to say those words is not made acceptable by the mere fact that the defendant actually is guilty of what he is charged with. That what the jurors declare true turns out to have in fact been true does not by itself make it acceptable for them to have declared it true.

This point is obvious, but it pays to make its source explicit. Suppose that a jury is puzzled by the evidence which has been presented to it, and cannot arrive at a consensus as to its weight. "I know," says one juror, "let's decide by flipping a coin—heads we impose liability, tails we don't." They agree; they flip a coin, which comes up heads; so they return and say "The defendant is guilty." Their doing that is not made acceptable by the fact (supposing it a fact) that the defendant actually is guilty. If the defendant is guilty, then he deserves the penalty which this jury causes to be imposed on him; but that the defendant not suffer the relevant penalty unjustly is not all that matters to us. It matters to us, not just that a defendant not suffer a penalty unjustly, but also that the penalty not be imposed on him unjustly.

The defendant will suffer the penalty unjustly if he is not guilty, and so does not deserve the penalty; that means that it is unjust to impose liability on him, and thereby cause him to suffer the penalty, unless one believes one has good reason to believe that he is guilty, and therefore deserves the penalty. That being so, we can say, and we have an explanation of why we can say, that the jury I just described imposed liability unjustly: They imposed liability without believing they had good reason to believe that the defendant was guilty.

There is a second, and stronger, possible explanation of why we can say that that jury imposed liability unjustly: It was just luck for those jurors if what they declared true was true—just luck for them if it actually was the case that the defendant was guilty.

That *is* stronger. Consider the jury in the hypothetical case I called *People v. Tice* in section 3 above. Suppose it declares Tice guilty of murder, not on the ground that a coin was tossed and came up heads, but on the following two grounds. First, the evidence makes clear (perhaps Tice has even confessed) that he attempted to kill Summers. Second, Summers was killed by one of 100 pellets fired at him, and ninety-five of the pellets fired at him were fired by Tice. Then the jury imposes liability on Tice on the ground of what is on any view good reason to believe Tice guilty. (Its situation in respect of Tice's being guilty is exactly like Alfred's situation in respect of Bert's losing his lottery: In both cases, rationality requires believing the conclusion highly probable.) If it is required of a jury only that it not impose liability without good reason to believe the defendant guilty, then this jury does not impose liability unjustly. All the same, it is just luck for the jury if it actually was Tice who killed Summers, and thus if Tice committed murder. So if it is required of a jury that it not impose liability unless it has, not merely good reason, but reason of a kind which would make it not be just luck for the jury if its verdict is true, then this jury imposes liability unjustly.

On my view of them, what is at work in the friends of individualized evidence is precisely the feeling that just imposition of liability requires that this stronger requirement be met. They believe, as they say, that "mathematical chances" or "quantitative probability" is not by itself enough; on my view of them, that is because they feel, rightly, that if a jury declares a defendant guilty on the ground of nonindividualized evidence alone, then it is just luck for the jury if what it declares true is true—and they feel, not without reason, that it is unjust to impose liability where that is the case. I say "not without reason" because I feel in considerable sympathy with them.

SMITH V. RAPID TRANSIT, INC.

58 N.E.2d 754 (Mass. 1945)

SPALDING, Justice.

The decisive question in this case is whether there was evidence for the jury that the plaintiff was injured by a bus of the defendant that was operated by one of its employees in the course of his employment. If there was, the defendant concedes that the evidence warranted the submission to the jury of the question of the operator's negligence in the management of the bus. The case is here on the plaintiff's exception to the direction of a verdict for the defendant.

These facts could have been found: While the plaintiff at about 1:00 A.M. on February 6, 1941, was driving an automobile on Main Street, Winthrop, in an easterly direction toward Winthrop Highlands, she observed a bus coming toward her which she described as a "great big, long, wide affair." The bus, which was proceeding at about forty miles an hour, "forced her to turn to the right," and her automobile collided with a "parked car." The plaintiff was coming from Dorchester. The department of public utilities had issued a certificate of public convenience or necessity to the defendant for three routes in Winthrop, one of which included Main Street, and this was in effect in February, 1941. "There was another bus line in operation in Winthrop at that time but not on Main Street." According to the defendant's time-table, buses were scheduled to leave Winthrop Highlands for Maverick Square via Main Street at 12:10 A.M., 12:45 A.M., 1:15 A.M., and 2:15 A.M. The running time for this trip at that time of night was thirty minutes.

The direction of a verdict for the defendant was right. The ownership of the bus was a matter of conjecture. While the defendant had the sole franchise for operating a bus line on Main Street, Winthrop, this did not preclude private or chartered buses from using this street; the bus in question could very well have been one operated by someone other than the defendant. It was said in Sargent v. Massachusetts Accident Co. that it is "not enough that mathematically the chances somewhat favor a proposition to be proved; for example, the fact that colored automobiles made in the current year outnumber black ones would not warrant a finding that an undescribed automobile of the current year is colored and not black, nor would the fact that only a minority of men die of cancer warrant a finding that a particular man did not die of cancer." The most that can be said of the evidence in the instant case is that perhaps the mathematical chances somewhat favor the proposition that a bus of the defendant caused the accident. This was not enough. A proposition is proved by a preponderance of the evidence if it is made to appear more likely or probable in the sense that actual belief in its truth, derived from the evidence, exists in the mind or minds of the tribunal notwithstanding any doubts that may still linger there.

PEOPLE V. COLLINS

In *Collins*, an elderly woman walking home in an alley in the San Pedro area of Los Angeles was assaulted from behind and robbed. The victim said that she managed to see a young woman with blond hair run from the scene. Another witness said that a Caucasian woman with dark blond hair and a ponytail ran out of the alley and entered a yellow automobile driven by a male Negro with a mustache and beard. A few days later officers investigating the robbery arrested a couple on the strength of these descriptions, and charged them with the crime. At their trial, the prosecution called an instructor of mathematics at a state college in an attempt to establish that, assuming the robbery was committed by a Caucasian blond with a ponytail who left the scene in a yellow car accompanied by a Negro with a beard and mustache, the probability was overwhelming that the accused were guilty because they answered to this unusual description. The witness testified to the "product rule" of elementary

People v. Collins, 68 Cal.2d 319, 438 P.2d 33, 66 Cal. Rptr. 497 (1968), as described and analyzed in Michael Finkelstein and William Fairley, "A Bayesian Approach to Identification Evidence," *Harvard Law Review*, vol. 83 (1970), pp. 489 ff.

probability theory. This rule states that the probability of the joint occurrence of a number of mutually independent events equals the product of the individual probabilities of each of the events. The prosecutor then had the witness assume the following individual probabilities of the relevant characteristics:

Yellow automobile	1/10
Man with mustache	1/4
Girl with ponytail	1/10
Girl with blond hair	1/3
Negro man with beard	1/10
Interracial couple in car	1/1000

Applying the product rule to the assumed values, the prosecutor concluded that there would be but one chance in twelve million that a couple selected at random would possess the incriminating characteristics. The jury convicted. On appeal, the Supreme Court of California reversed, holding that the trial court should not have admitted the evidence pertaining to the mathematical theory of probability.

The Supreme Court objected to the expert's testimony on several grounds. First, the record was devoid of evidence to support any of the six assumed individual probabilities. This objection is clearly justified. Some evidence of those probabilities is surely required as a foundation for such testimony. However, evidence sufficient to support a finding that the probability estimates are likely to be greater than the true values should suffice. This is significant because it may often be possible to justify generous estimates of probabilities which cannot be determined exactly.

Second, the court found no proof that the six factors were statistically independent. Again the court was correct. If traits are not independent, but rather tend to occur together, then the multiplication of the individual probabilities of each factor usually yields a composite probability that is far too small, even if the individual probabilities are accurate. For example, given the hypothetical probabilities in *Collins*, if every Negro man with a beard also had a mustache then the chance of a Negro man with a beard

and mustache is one–tenth, not one–fortieth as indicated by the product rule. Either the mathematical method must take correlations into account, or there must be sufficient evidence of independence of the factors.

A first look at *Collins* thus reveals two requirements for the introduction of statistical analysis in evidence: the prosecutor must introduce evidence as to the probabilities of the individual factors and of the relations among them. The court also explored two obstacles to such proof. The first relates to the capacity of a jury to deal with statistical evidence, and will be discussed presently. The second, as to which the court's analysis was wrong, cuts much deeper.

Writing for the court, Justice Sullivan asserted that "no mathematical equation can prove beyond a reasonable doubt . . . that only *one* couple possessing those distinctive characteristics could be found in the entire Los Angeles area." He supported his conclusion with a mathematical demonstration purporting to show that even if a couple selected at random had only one chance in twelve million of bearing the incriminating characteristics, the expert witness could not conclude that the accused were probably guilty because it was quite possible (about a forty percent chance) that at least one other couple in the Los Angeles area had those same traits.

The court's argument is incorrect because the supporting mathematical demonstration was wrongly conceived. The court's proof begins with the probability of selecting a couple with the specified characteristics at random from the population. This is assumed, following the prosecution, to be one in twelve million. The court then proceeds to derive the probability that there are two or more such couples in the population. Because the court was dealing with an existing, finite population, the frequency with which couples with the identifying characteristics may be found in that population is identical to the probability of selecting one at random. Thus, the court's assumption that one in twelve million is a fair estimate of the probability of selecting such a couple at random necessarily implies that it is a fair estimate of the number of such couples in the population. The probability that couples with the fatal characteristics would appear more frequently could only have been determined by examining the precision of the estimate—an examination which neither the court nor the expert was able to make because the estimate was not the result of any statistically valid sampling procedure.

The court's formula would have been relevant if it were assumed that nothing were known about the actual population of Los Angeles and the only available information concerned some unknown process by which it had been created. If the one-in-twelve-million figure represented the probability that a couple when created would have the fatal characteristics, then out of all possible populations of Los Angeles that could be produced by this unknown process, forty percent of those with at least one such couple would have at least two such couples.

The objection to this approach in *Collins* is that the one-in-twelve-million figure was intended by the prosecution and by the court to describe the actual population of Los Angeles and not as a parameter for a "generational" probability model. It is not valid to use as a generational probability an estimate intended to reflect the actual population, and then assume that since nothing was known about the actual population, the probabilities of various populations could be computed by calculating the hypothetical outcomes of the creation process. Moreover, a generational model will not usually be useful in the problems discussed in this article because in most cases it will be far easier to gain knowledge of the actual population by sampling than to define in probabilistic terms the forces producing it.

The statistical problem of the *Collins* case is that of estimating the very figure which the court took as its assumption, namely the probability that a couple selected at random would have the characteristics of the accused. That

probability represents the frequency of couples meeting the description of the one placed at the crime. If a sufficiently precise estimate could be made that the frequency of such couples in the Los Angeles area was one in twelve million, it would be possible to state within reasonable margins for error that there was only one such couple in the Los Angeles area.

But as a practical matter the court was right to doubt that the prosecutor could show uniqueness. A derivation of such extraordinarily small probabilities with any useful degree of precision would be extremely difficult. In most cases, the estimate of the population frequency of evidentiary traces (of hair or incomplete fingerprints, for example) will have to be made on the basis of samples numbering at most a few thousand. As a result, probabilities of the magnitude involved in *Collins* would require an inference, based on a few thousand trials, that an event would occur once rather than more than once in millions of trials. Such an inference inevitably involves powerful assumptions which cannot be adequately supported without extensive data. Except in cases where the number of suspects is sharply limited, it will almost never be practically possible to gather enough data to sustain a conclusion of uniqueness with any confidence.

The approach in *Collins* thus makes the number of suspects critical. Determining this number, however, will usually involve wholly arbitrary decisions. Shall it include only those in the same neighborhood, the same county, the same city, state, or the entire country? The jury might be given a range of choices and the probability associated with each choice, but jurors cannot rationally choose when, as is usual, there is no evidence bearing on this issue. Setting a generous upper bound will usually defeat the proof: the incriminating characteristics will occur more than once in a sufficiently large population. Moreover, it is probably as difficult to decide intuitively how many "suspects" there are as to decide how many of the suspects have the incriminating characteristics.

We now turn to the court's second objection to the use of statistics. The court reversed the Collins' conviction because it felt that the powerful statistics would cow a jury into overlooking the possibility that the basis for the calculations could be in error. The court was obviously right. However, correct statistical methods will usually have an effect opposite to that feared by the *Collins* court. Findings based on such statistics should generally weaken nonquantitative testimony based on the same evidence. An expert's opinion that similarities between fragments (*e.g.,* of fingernails or hair) identify a defendant must rest on his limited experience with similar fragments. If to his knowledge no such similarities have been observed in fragments from different sources, he may testify flatly that the two fragments have a common origin. But proper statistical methods, by invoking an experience larger than any expert's, may well yield an estimate that a fragment occurs several times in a large population, even though the expert would conclude there were no duplicates. In addition, an expert witness may base his appraisal on a multitude of details imperfectly recognized and difficult to define or catalog—just as we know a face from a multitude of features. It is impossible statistically to take all such details into account. Statistical observation is of attributes that can be objectively measured; it cannot hope to have the richness of information involved in ordinary or educated recognition. For these reasons, the inference of identity from statistics will generally be weaker than expert judgment expressed in the usual way.

On its facts *Collins* was bizarre, and its pseudo–statistics scarcely can be taken seriously. But the method used in the case was entirely representative of more sophisticated efforts made in earlier cases in which the experts also applied the product rule to generate vanishingly small probabilities. The *Collins* court was right when it concluded that efforts to prove uniqueness usually will be futile. Few, if any, evidentiary traces can be demonstrated by statistical analysis to be unique to a defendant. There is, however, a class of traces, potentially useful as evidence, which could be shown to appear only infrequently, though not uniquely. What is the probative significance of such non-unique traces? We propose to show that non-unique traces generally deserve substantial evidentiary weight, and that by the explicit use of mathematical theory the data can be cast in a form permitting more effective use of this evidence by the jury.

QUESTIONS FOR DISCUSSION

1. Saks and Kidd are generally sympathetic to the use of statistical evidence. What is their argument? How do you think they would decide the Gatecrasher case? The *Rapid Transit* case? The *Collins* case?

2. What does Thomson mean by "individualized" and "nonindividualized" evidence? Do you agree with the distinction? Does Thomson distinguish between civil and criminal cases? Would you?

3. What is the difference between the actual *Smith* case and Thomson's hypothetical *Smith v. Red Cab*? Does the difference mean more than Thomson supposes? Why or why not?

4. If you had been a juror in the *Collins* case, and the judge had allowed the statistical evidence to be heard by a jury, would you have voted to convict or acquit? If you had been the judge, would you have allowed the statistical evidence to be heard by the jury?

SUGGESTIONS FOR FURTHER READING

A thorough analysis of the issues from a scholar of the law of evidence is Richard Eggleston, *Evidence, Proof and Probability* (London: Weidenfeld and Nicolson, 1978). Michael O. Finkelstein and William B. Fairley, "A Bayesian Approach to Identification Evidence," *Harvard Law Review*, vol. 83 (1970), pp. 489 ff., is sympathetic to the use of statistical evidence, when employed correctly, as are David Kaye, "The Paradox of the Gatecrasher and Other Stories," *Arizona State Law Journal*, vol. 1979, pp. 101 ff. and Daniel Shaviro, "Statistical–Probability Evidence and the Appearance of Justice," *Harvard Law Review*, vol. 103 (1989), pp. 530 ff. The more skeptical view, by someone well-versed in mathematics, is Laurence H. Tribe, "Trial by Mathematics: Precision and Ritual in the Legal Process," *Harvard Law Review*, vol. 84 (1971), pp. 1329 ff.

CRIMINAL PROCEDURE AND 8.3
THE EXCLUSIONARY RULE

INTRODUCTION

As the previous two sections have indicated, many of the important procedural issues in which legal and philosophical concerns are connected arise both in civil and in criminal cases. Even though the resolution of some of the questions raised might be different in one than they are in the other, the central issues of burden of proof and of statistical evidence are similar in both civil and criminal settings.

Some issues, however, are unique to the criminal process. In the typical civil case, the state assists in the adjudication of private disputes, but, in theory, the state is not an interested party. In criminal cases, however, things are different. As the very names of the cases—*Regina* (The Queen) versus someone, *State* versus someone, *People* versus someone—indicate, in a criminal case the government itself is not only operating the mechanism for adjudication, but is also seeking punishment against the defendant. Because of this dual role, and because it is in the context of the criminal law that the state often exercises its most massive power of punishment, special concerns of political and legal philosophy often arise, concerns that are simply not present in the typical civil case. We dealt with some of these in Chapter 6 when we took up the question of punishment, but there are others that are worthy of exploration as we look at a range of procedural questions.

Consider, for example, the privilege against self-incrimination, protected in the United States in the Fifth Amendment to the Constitution, which says that "No person . . . shall be compelled in any criminal case to be a witness against himself." What this means, as this provision has been interpreted, is that the defendant in a criminal trial cannot be called to the witness stand by the prosecution (although the defendant can voluntarily take the witness stand if he wishes, in which case he is subject to cross-examination by the prosecution); that the failure of the defendant to testify cannot be the subject of comment by the prosecution to the jury; that a suspect need not talk to the police if he does not want to; that a suspect must be informed of his Fifth Amendment rights at the time of arrest (the so-called *Miranda* warning, from the Supreme Court case of *Miranda v. Arizona*[6]); and that a person can refuse to answer questions in a civil case, or in hearings before Congress or other investigative bodies, if that person is afraid that the answers she might give would tend to incriminate her in some later criminal proceeding.

The obvious result of the privilege against self-incrimination is that the prosecution and the jury are denied access to what is often the best source of

---

[6]384 U.S. 436 (1966).

information. Moreover, the jury is instructed to ignore the quite ordinary and reasonable inference that people who are innocent usually take the witness stand in their own defense, and people who are guilty are more likely than those who are innocent to avoid cross-examination by the prosecution, and to avoid answering questions from the police. Yet however reasonable this inference might be, and however reasonable it might seem to allow the state to pursue what is often the best source of information, the criminal procedure of the United States and most other countries takes the privilege against self-incrimination seriously. Why is this so? Is it because state power is so potentially dangerous that it is important to erect special barriers against its misuse? Is it because there is something "unfair" about requiring a person to assist in his or her own imprisonment, or even death? If so, what exactly is the unfairness? Or does the privilege against self-incrimination relate to freedom of conscience, freedom of belief, freedom of religion, and the right to privacy, all in one way or another supporting the idea that there are some things that the individual is entitled to keep to herself? And the answer to these questions might help to determine just what kind of right the privilege against self-incrimination is. If it is of the same family as the right to privacy and freedom of conscience, then it may have a non-empirical basis and be the kind of strong and non-utilitarian right we discussed in Chapter 4. But if the privilege against self-incrimination is instead a strategic protection against state over-reaching, then the need for it may depend on empirical evidence, and may vary with time, with place, with context, and with the government against which we seek the protection.

Similar questions arise in the context of the exclusionary rule, the subject of the readings in this section. The exclusionary rule is again a rule of American criminal procedure that often gets in the way of maximum accuracy, and often produces what on the surface are anomalous results. The exclusionary rule prohibits the introduction at a trial of evidence that has been obtained illegally by the police. It is important, however, to distinguish two types of illegality. One goes to the evidentiary value of the evidence itself. Take, for example, a confession that is coerced, either physically, or by some form of psychological or related pressure. Such a confession is illegal under the Constitution, violating the privilege against self-incrimination in the Fifth Amendment, perhaps the right to a lawyer protected by the Sixth Amendment, and perhaps also the general right not to have one's life, liberty, or property taken without the due process of law, also protected by the Fifth Amendment, and by the Fourteenth as well. And in this case the very thing that makes the confession illegal also makes it unreliable as evidence. Sometimes people who are coerced confess to things they did not in fact do, and thus a coerced confession is less reliable than a confession given freely without coercion. When the exclusionary rule is applied to exclude evidence obtained in violation of the various rules against coerced confessions, therefore, the exclusionary rule simultaneously protects constitutional values and safeguards the accuracy of the process.

Compare this, however, to a different kind of illegal police behavior. The Fourth Amendment to the Constitution provides: "The right of the people to be secure in their persons, houses, papers, and effects, against unreasonable searches and seizures, shall not be violated, and no Warrants shall issue, but upon probable cause, supported by Oath or affirmation, and particularly describing the place to be searched, and the persons or things to be seized."

Now suppose that the police, without a warrant and without probable cause, break into a person's house, and then discover five pounds of cocaine, the possession of which is illegal. The homeowner is prosecuted for possession of narcotics and claims that the narcotics were seized illegally. In that the homeowner is correct, for the search without a warrant and without probable cause undoubtedly violates the Fourth Amendment. But unlike the case with the coerced confession, here the constitutional violation does not undercut the reliability of the evidence. The evidence may have been seized illegally and unconstitutionally, but the illegal and unconstitutional behavior does not detract from the fact that the narcotics were on the defendant's property, in the way that the coerced nature of a confession does undercut the reliability of the confession.

Because of this difference, many people who support the exclusionary rule for coerced confessions do not support it for violations of the Fourth Amendment. In any event, the difference raises questions about the purposes the exclusionary rule serves, and as with the rest of the material in this chapter, raises questions about the values other than maximum accuracy that may be served by the various rules used in trials, both criminal and civil.

THE EXCLUSIONARY RULE: COSTS AND VIABLE ALTERNATIVES

MALCOLM WILKEY

At the outset, let me emphasize the difference between my role as essayist and my role as active judge. As a judge on an appellate court, I faithfully apply the law—the Constitution and the statutes—as it has been interpreted by the Supreme Court. In doing this, I have become increasingly aware of the tremendously high cost to our entire system of justice of applying the exclusionary remedy for violations of the Fourth Amendment. I am not alone in that increased awareness, because during the twelve years I have been on the bench, more than half the justices on the Supreme Court have spoken, in opinions and elsewhere, of the high social cost of the exclusionary remedy. In assuming the role of commentator, I acquire the freedom to suggest what I think would be in the best interests of the administration of justice, while recognizing that only if such measures are adopted bv the Congress or by the High Court will I later be privileged to apply them as law.

Malcolm Wilkey, "The Exclusionary Rule: Costs and Viable Alternatives," *Criminal Justice Ethics*, vol. 1 (1982), pp. 16 ff.

Within the past year the United States Senate has taken important action in another context which illustrates dramatically the illogic and injustice of the exclusionary rule and, in contrast, the wisdom and fairness of proposed reforms. The exclusionary remedy has always been condemned—by Cardozo, Wigmore, and many others—for confusing two entirely separate inquiries: the guilt of the accused and the conduct of the investigating officer. The alternative remedies which I suggest in my monograph on the Fourth Amendment preserve the distinction between these lines of inquiry. And the Senate itself recognized the necessary logic of this in its recent dealing with Senator Harrison Williams.

Senator Williams contended that the Senate should inquire into the conduct of the Federal Bureau of Investigation at the same time that the Senate examined his own conduct, on the theory that the FBI's alleged misconduct would excuse his own. Senator Williams was thus, in fact, invoking the logic (or illogic) of the exclusionary rule. The Senate rejected this. It properly recognized that Senator Williams's fitness to sit in the Senate was an issue quite different from the conduct of the FBI. Hence, the Senate will examine the FBI's conduct, but this will be a separate inquiry, having no effect on Senator Williams. Whatever the FBI did could not alter what was shown of Senator Williams's actions on seven videotapes and thus could not alter the ultimate issue of Senator Williams's fitness to sit in the Senate.

Similarly, the conduct of an investigating officer can never alter the fact of material evidence found in a search and seizure. I submit, first, that the Senate, by its action in the Williams case, has already recognized the illogic and injustice of the exclusionary rule. Second, I would argue that each of my proposed alternative remedies to enforce the Fourth Amendment is designed to permit the courts to follow the same reasonable and fair procedures the Senate did by separating totally unrelated issues. Inquiries must be made into both the guilt of the accused and the conduct of the investigating officer, but these inquiries must be made independently of one another. The truth of the guilt of the accused is never altered by the conduct of the officer. That is exactly what the Senate has recently determined by the procedure it adopted in regard to Senator Williams. All I ask is that justice in the courts be administered on the same logical basis as justice in the United States Senate.

The time has come to abolish the exclusionary rule. This judicial creation has failed. Its alleged value has always hinged on the assumption, still unproven after seventy years, that it will deter police illegality. This doubtful gain is overwhelmed by the rule's horrible side effects, which are so destructive of the efficiency and integrity of our criminal justice system and whose costs are undeniable. Fourth Amendment suppression motions arise so frequently that, whether granted or not, they constitute the single issue most burdensome to the courts in criminal trials. And when a motion is granted the result is a manifest injustice—the exclusion of reliable evidence which may be essential to convicting the undeniably guilty. Moreover, the exclusionary rule perversely insures that the wrongdoer, the police officer who conducted the illegal search, escapes punishment as well. Under the rule's logic, two wrongs apparently make a right.

Abolition of the rule does not mean abolition of our constitutional rights. The exclusionary rule is not the Fourth Amendment, and it is not a constitutional necessity. It is clear from the way the rule originated in *Weeks v. United States* in 1914 that the Court was simply choosing a method of enforcing the Fourth Amendment. The search and seizure opinions of the Supreme Court for the last twenty years exhibit a reiteration by one Justice after another that this is *a* method of enforcing a constitutional protection, not necessarily *the* precise method commanded by the Constitution, but instead one chosen by the High Court. One can find support for this in opinions by Chief Justice

Burger, and Justices Stewart, White, Blackmun, Powell, and Rehnquist. The very manner in which they have spoken of the rule and its rationale of deterrence shows that they regard it as a chosen method, a method about which they are having increasing doubts. Other methods, if reasonably believed to be effective and equally or better suited to enforcing the Fourth Amendment, could be adopted. The Constitution prohibits unreasonable searches and seizures: It may mandate *a* remedy to enforce that prohibition, but nowhere does the Constitution mandate the exclusion of all other possible remedies.

Three workable legislative alternatives are available: an independent review board in the executive branch; a civil tort action against the government; and a minitrial separate from the main criminal trial. One alternative which should *not* be adopted is the "good faith" exception advocated by the Attorney General's Task Force on Violent Crime. Although appealing to the extent that it reduces the number of guilty criminals who go free, the good faith proposal perpetuates all the other evils of the exclusionary rule and adds new additional costs.

Of all the civilized countries in the world, only the United States applies this demonstrably illogical exclusionary remedy to illegal searches and seizures of material evidence. The Congress should act decisively to repudiate the absurd notion that the United States alone is incapable of using its executive, administrative, and judicial processes *directly* to control the conduct of its law enforcement officials.

Without going into a detailed description of each, well known to students of the exclusionary rule, let me enumerate the twelve undeniable costs for reference:

Cost 1: "The criminal is to go free because the constable has blundered."

Cost 2: Only the undeniably guilty benefit from the exclusionary rule, while innocent victims of illegal searches have neither protection nor remedy.

Cost 3: The exclusionary rule in any form vitiates all internal disciplinary efforts by law enforcement agencies.

Cost 4: The disposition of exclusionary rule issues constitutes an unnecessary and intolerable burden on the court system.

Cost 5: The exclusionary rule forces the judiciary to perform the executive branch's job of disciplining its employees.

Cost 6: The misplaced burden on the judiciary deprives innocent defendants of due process.

Cost 7: The exclusionary rule encourages perjury by the police.

Cost 8: The exclusionary remedy makes hypocrites out of judges.

Cost 9: The high cost of applying the exclusionary rule causes the courts to expand the scope of search and seizure for all citizens.

Cost 10: The exclusionary remedy is applied with no sense of proportion to the crime of the accused.

Cost 11: The exclusionary remedy is applied with no sense of proportion to the misconduct of the officer.

Cost 12: All of the above costs result inevitably in greatly diminished respect for the judicial process among lawyers and laymen alike. The sole rationale for preserving the rule is that it deters police misconduct. Efforts to resurrect other rationales, long since discarded by the Supreme Court, are a very revealing admission by even the rule's most ardent supporters that deterrence has *not* been proved by seventy years of experience, and such efforts arouse a sneaking suspicion that the supporters know deterrence is impossible to prove. While from *Weeks* to *Mapp* the rule was justified as protecting the privacy of the individual, the Supreme Court later downgraded this rationale:

The purpose of the exclusionary rule is not to redress F the injury to the privacy of the search victim: "The ruptured privacy of the victim's homes and effects cannot be restored." Reparation comes too late.

And while Justice Clark in *Mapp* did refer to "that judicial integrity so necessary in the true administration of justice," four years later he wrote for the court unequivocally:

> All of the cases since *Wolf* requiring the exclusion of illegal evidence have been based on the necessity for an effective deterrent to illegal police action.

More recently, Justice Powell for the Court reaffirmed this: "The rule's prime purpose is to deter future unlawful police conduct."

Because the effectiveness of deterrence is shown to be unproved and unprovable, it will not do for supporters of the rule to scurry back to the original but discarded rationales of privacy and judicial integrity. And the unequivocal refutation of alternative rationales comes not from the rule's critics but from the Supreme Court itself.

As Justice Blackmun remarked, "No empirical researcher, proponent or opponent of the rule, has yet been able to establish with any assurance whether the rule has a deterrent effect even in situations in which it is now applied." On this same point, Chief Justice Burger described the current situation:

> I do not question the need for some remedy to give meaning and teeth to the constitutional guarantees against unlawful conduct by government officials. . . . But the hope that this objective could be accomplished by the exclusion of reliable evidence from criminal trials was hardly more than a wistful dream. . . . There is no empirical evidence to support the claim that the rule actually deters illegal conduct of law enforcement officials. . . . We should view the suppression doctrine as one of the experimental steps in the great tradition of the common law and acknowledge its shortcomings. But in the same spirit we should be prepared to discontinue what the experience of over half a century has shown neither deters errant officers nor affords a remedy to the totally innocent victim of official misconduct.

It is highly significant that, in nearly seventy years of Supreme Court decisions on the exclusionary rule, the High Court itself has never cited empirical data to support its faith that the rule actually deters. Indeed, the fragmented nature itself of law enforcement and the pressures generated by the exclusionary rule may make it logically impossible for it to have any appreciable deterrent effect.

And even if there were shown to be *some* deterrent effect, supporters of the rule have never addressed what would seem to be a primary question: How much deterrence is necessary to outweigh the admitted cost of the rule?

The proponents of the exclusionary rule not only ignore the absence of any evidence that the rule deters at all, they not only ignore their own failure to weigh some quantum of deterrence versus the admitted high costs of the rule, they also ignore where the burden of proof lies on this critical issue. Nowhere else in our system of proof do we bar valid, probative, irrefutable, relevant, material evidence on some unproven nebulous theory of overall gain in the system. Those who want to bar this evidence never seem to realize that the *burden of proving* that some greater good will be gained is on them.

THE EXCLUSIONARY RULE: A PROSECUTOR'S DEFENSE

STEPHEN H. SACHS

I believe that the exclusionary rule, the *remedy* for a Fourth Amendment violation which suppresses its fruits and denies government the benefit of its unconstitutional conduct, is sound in theory and effective in practice.

The rule is also very fragile, especially in today's atmosphere of understandable public outrage at crime and at our perceived inability to do much about it. It is vulnerable to attack because its values are abstract while its costs are tangible. It frequently excludes hard evidence—the truth—from trial. It appears to reward the undeserving criminal, whom it sometimes frees because "the constable blundered." It seems to give aid and comfort only to the enemy in the war on crime. It makes almost no sense to citizens fed up with crime and impatient with legal "technicalities" who want to believe that crime would disappear if only courts would stop coddling criminals. That is why the rule, although it has plenty of responsible critics, has become a favorite whipping boy of anticrime rhetoricians.

My purpose in this essay is to bear witness to what my own experience and study have taught me:

1 the rule is of constitutional origin and beyond the reach of Congress;

2 it results in freeing guilty criminals in a relatively small proportion of cases;

3 it definitely deters police and prosecutor violations of constitutional rights to privacy;

4 it manifests our refusal to stoop to conquer, to convict lawbreakers by relying on official lawlessness, a vital demonstration of our commitment to the rule of law.

I can't offer statistical studies on the deterrent effect of the rule. What I can offer, however, is my testimony that I have watched the rule deter, routinely, throughout my years as a prosecutor. When an Assistant United States Attorney, for example, advises an FBI agent that he lacks probable cause to search for bank loot in a parked automobile unless he gets a better "make" on the car; or that the agent has a "staleness" problem with the probable cause to believe that the ski masks used in the robbery are still in the suspect's friend's apartment; or that he should apply for a search warrant from a magistrate and not rely on the "consent" of the suspect's sister to search his home—the rule is working. The principal, perhaps the only, reason those conversations occur is that the assistant and the agent want the search to stand up in court.

Episodes like these are commonplace. They are part of the routine of every federal prosecutor with whom I have worked. Although my present office has more limited criminal jurisdiction, such police–prosecutor consultation is customary in all of our cases when Fourth Amendment concerns arise. I strongly suspect that scenes like these are repeated daily throughout federal law enforcement and on homicide, narcotics, and gambling squads in cities throughout the country. In at least three Maryland jurisdictions, for example, prosecutors are on twenty-four hour call to field search and seizure questions presented by police officers.

These contacts do not occur because of some self-limiting controls in the police and prosecutors themselves. I hope and trust that most of us

Stephen H. Sachs, "The Exclusionary Rule: A Prosecutor's Defense," *Criminal Justice Ethics*, vol. 1, no. 2 (1982), pp. 28 ff.

in law enforcement are principled enough to avoid violating the clear constitutional rights of suspects. But in the heat of the chase, and in the absence of effective sanction, I believe that we would define those rights somewhat narrowly. Questions of adequate identification, "staleness" of information, and the need for a warrant will be answered differently by unchecked law enforcers than by judges. We are, after all, hunters stalking crime. It is simply too much to ask for objectivity in the midst of the hunt, especially when the quarry is in sight. This is precisely what the warrant requirement of the Fourth Amendment is about. As Justice Jackson once put it:

> The point of the Fourth Amendment, which often is not grasped by zealous officers, is not that it denies law enforcement support of the usual inferences which reasonable men draw from evidence. Its protection consists in requiring that those inferences be drawn by a neutral and detached magistrate instead of being judged by the officer engaged in the often competitive enterprise of ferreting out crime.

Exclusion from evidence is almost certainly the only effective deterrent in the vast majority of unconstitutional intrusions. Even critics of the rule are quick to acknowledge the severe limitations of police self-discipline or court damage actions as deterrents when crime-fighting police officers are in the dock. In rare cases involving especially gross misconduct, a police disciplinary board or a court or jury in a damage action might impose sanctions, at least if the victim of the trespass is innocent and the police misconduct truly outrageous.

But most of the suppression cases do not deal with such outrageous conduct. They deal with undramatic Fourth Amendment concerns—the sufficiency of "probable cause" in a given case, whether "exigent circumstances" excuse the necessity of a warrant, whether there is sufficient corroboration of the tip of an anonymous informer to justify intrusion into a suspect's apartment. These requirements are not the stuff to move police disciplinary boards, or judges and juries accustomed to awarding damages on the basis of "fault." But they are our constitutional rules of the road and only the suppression sanction, the exclusionary rule, will force prosecutors and police to obey them.

■ ■ ■

It is sometimes said that the exclusionary rule breeds disrespect for the law because it suppresses the truth and permits crime to go unpunished. I believe that abolition of the rule would be far more destructive of respect for law. When an American court admits evidence obtained in violation of the Constitution, it is not merely permitting the truth to be heard. It is inescapably condoning, validating, even welcoming, the illegality that produced it. It becomes part of that illegality. It paints a portrait of hypocrisy in a nation that professes to believe in the rule of law and whose courts, in the words of Madison, are to be the great "bulwarks" and "guardians" of our liberties. And the admission of such evidence is dangerous. As Justice Brandeis put it:

> In a government of laws, existence of the government will be imperilled if it fails to observe the law scrupulously. Our Government is the potent, the omnipresent teacher. For good or for ill, it reaches the whole people by its example. Crime is contagious. If the Government becomes a lawbreaker, it breeds contempt for law; it invites every man to become a law unto himself; it invites anarchy. To declare that in the administration of the criminal law the end justifies the means—to declare that the government may commit crimes in order to secure the conviction of a private criminal—would bring terrible retribution.

Law enforcement, in particular, needs public trust and respect for its authority in order to do its job effectively and safely. Official lawlessness destroys that trust, poisons police relations with the citizenry, and thus adds immeasurably to law enforcement's burdens.

It is easy to salute the liberties of the Bill of Rights in the abstract. But these freedoms have a price. It is difficult to remember, but we must never forget, that we cannot apply them selectively. Only insofar as we permit their effective exercise by the guilty will they remain strong protection for the innocent. Rights atrophy with disuse. They must be used not only in times of calm but in times of passion and fear as well.

In the play, *A Man for All Seasons,* an account of the martyrdom of Saint Thomas More,

More warns a zealot against "cut[ting] a great road through the law to get after the Devil."

"When the last law was down, and the Devil turned round on you, where would you hide," he asks, "the laws all being flat?" "Yes," More adds, "I'd give the Devil benefit of law, for my own safety's sake."

In this time of great passion about crime we should be extremely careful, for our own safety's sake, not to let our zeal to "get after the Devil" lead us to cut a great road through the Bill of Rights.

UNITED STATES V. LEON

467 U.S. 713 (1984)

Justice WHITE delivered the opinion of the Court.

This case presents the question whether the Fourth Amendment exclusionary rule should be modified so as not to bar the use in the prosecution's case in chief of evidence obtained by officers acting in reasonable reliance on a search warrant issued by a detached and neutral magistrate but ultimately found to be unsupported by probable cause. To resolve this question, we must consider once again the tension between the sometimes competing goals of, on the one hand, deterring official misconduct and removing inducements to unreasonable invasions of privacy and, on the other, establishing procedures under which criminal defendants are "acquitted or convicted on the basis of all the evidence which exposes the truth."

In August 1981, a confidential informant of unproven reliability informed an officer of the Burbank Police Department that two persons known to him as "Armando" and "Patsy" were selling large quantities of cocaine and methaqualone from their residence at 620 Price Drive in Burbank, Cal. The informant also indicated that he had witnessed a sale of methaqualone by "Patsy" at the residence approximately five months earlier and had observed at that time a shoebox containing a large amount of cash that belonged to "Patsy." He further declared that "Armando" and "Patsy" generally kept only small quantities of drugs at their residence and stored the remainder at another location in Burbank.

On the basis of this information, the Burbank police initiated an extensive investigation focusing first on the Price Drive residence and later on two other residences as well. Cars parked at the Price Drive residence were determined to belong to respondents Armando Sanchez, who had previously been arrested for possession of marihuana, and Patsy Stewart, who had no criminal record. During the course of the investigation, officers observed an automobile belonging to respondent Ricardo Del Castillo, who had previously been arrested for possession of 50 pounds of marihuana, arrive at the Price Drive residence. The driver of that car entered the house, exited shortly thereafter carrying a small paper sack, and drove away. A check of Del Castillo's probation records led the officers to respondent Alberto Leon, whose telephone number Del Castillo had listed as his employer's. Leon had been arrested in 1980 on drug charges, and a companion had informed the police at that time that Leon was heavily involved in the importation of drugs into this country. Before the current investigation began, the Burbank officers had learned that an informant had told a Glendale police officer that Leon stored a large quantity of methaqualone at his residence in Glendale. During the course of this investigation, the Burbank officers learned that Leon was living at 716 South Sunset Canyon in Burbank.

Subsequently, the officers observed several persons, at least one of whom had prior drug involvement, arriving at the Price Drive residence and leaving with small packages; observed a variety of other material activity at the two residences as well as at a condominium at 7902 Via Magdalena; and witnessed a variety of relevant activity involving respondents' automobiles. The officers also observed respondents Sanchez and Stewart board separate flights for Miami. The pair later returned to Los Angeles together, consented to a search of their luggage that revealed only a small amount of marihuana, and left the airport. Based on these and other observations summarized in the affidavit, App. 34, Officer Cyril Rombach of the Burbank Police Department, an experienced and well-trained narcotics investigator, prepared an application for a warrant to search 620 Price Drive, 716 South Sunset Canyon, 7902 Via Magdalena, and automobiles registered to each of the respondents for an extensive list of items believed to be related to respondents' drug-trafficking activities. Officer Rombach's extensive application was reviewed by several Deputy District Attorneys.

A facially valid search warrant was issued in September 1981 by a State Superior Court Judge. The ensuing searches produced large quantities of drugs at the Via Magdalena and Sunset Canyon addresses and a small quantity at the Price Drive residence. Other evidence was discovered at each of the residences and in Stewart's and Del Castillo's automobiles. Respondents were indicted by a grand jury in the District Court for the Central District of California and charged with conspiracy to possess and distribute cocaine and a variety of substantive counts.

The respondents then filed motions to suppress the evidence seized pursuant to the warrant. The District Court held an evidentiary hearing and, while recognizing that the case was a close one, granted the motions to suppress in part. It concluded that the affidavit was insufficient to establish probable cause, but did not suppress all of the evidence as to all of the respondents because none of the respondents had standing to challenge all of the searches. In response to a request from the Government, the court made clear that Officer Rombach had acted in good faith, but it rejected the Government's suggestion that the Fourth Amendment exclusionary rule should not apply where evidence is seized in reasonable, good-faith reliance on a search warrant.

If exclusion of evidence obtained pursuant to a subsequently invalidated warrant is to have any deterrent effect, therefore, it must alter the behavior of individual law enforcement officers or the policies of their departments. One could argue that applying the exclusionary rule in cases where the police failed to demonstrate probable cause in the warrant application deters future inadequate presentations or "magistrate shopping" and thus promotes the ends of the Fourth Amendment. Suppressing evidence obtained pursuant to a technically defective warrant supported by probable cause also might encourage officers to scrutinize more closely the form of the warrant and to point out suspected judicial errors. We find such arguments speculative and conclude that suppression of evidence obtained pursuant to a warrant should be ordered only on a case-by-case basis and only in those unusual cases in which exclusion will further the purposes of the exclusionary rule.

■ ■ ■

This is particularly true, we believe, when an officer acting with objective good faith has obtained a search warrant from a judge or magistrate and acted within its scope. In most such cases, there is no police illegality and thus nothing to deter. It is the magistrate's responsibility to determine whether the officer's allegations establish probable cause and, if so, to issue a warrant comporting in form with the requirements of the Fourth Amendment. In the ordinary case, an officer cannot be expected to question the magistrate's probable-cause determination or his judgment that the form of the warrant is technically sufficient. "[O]nce the warrant issues, there is literally nothing more the policeman can do in seeking to comply with the law." Penalizing the officer for the magistrate's error, rather than his own, cannot logically contribute to the deterrence of Fourth Amendment violations.

We conclude that the marginal or nonexistent benefits produced by suppressing evidence obtained in objectively reasonable reliance on a subsequently invalidated search warrant cannot justify the substantial costs of exclusion.

In so limiting the suppression remedy, we leave untouched the probable-cause standard and the various requirements for a valid warrant. Other objections to the modification of the Fourth Amendment exclusionary rule we consider to be insubstantial. The good-faith ex-

ception for searches conducted pursuant to warrants is not intended to signal our unwillingness strictly to enforce the requirements of the Fourth Amendment, and we do not believe that it will have this effect. As we have already suggested, the good-faith exception, turning as it does on objective reasonableness, should not be difficult to apply in practice. When officers have acted pursuant to a warrant, the prosecution should ordinarily be able to establish objective good faith without a substantial expenditure of judicial time.

In the absence of an allegation that the magistrate abandoned his detached and neutral role, suppression is appropriate only if the officers were dishonest or reckless in preparing their affidavit or could not have harbored an objectively reasonable belief in the existence of probable cause. Only respondent Leon has contended that no reasonably well trained police officer could have believed that there existed probable cause to search his house; significantly, the other respondents advance no comparable argument. Officer Rombach's application for a warrant clearly was supported by much more than a "bare bones" affidavit. The affidavit related the results of an extensive investigation and, as the opinions of the divided panel of the Court of Appeals make clear, provided evidence sufficient to create disagreement among thoughtful and competent judges as to the existence of probable cause. Under these circumstances, the officers' reliance on the magistrate's determination of probable cause was objectively reasonable, and application of the extreme sanction of exclusion is inappropriate.

QUESTIONS FOR DISCUSSION

1. Does Judge Wilkey's objection to the exclusionary rule rest on empirical evidence or assumptions? If so, which ones? Do you think they are correct?

2. Does Sachs rely on empirical facts to support his defense of the exclusionary rule? Could there be a defense of the exclusionary rule that did not rest on empirical facts? What would it look like?

3. Great Britain, Australia, New Zealand, and Israel are countries with no written bill of rights, and therefore with nothing resembling the American Fourth and Fifth Amendments. If you were a judge in one of these countries, would you support a privilege against self-incrimination? On what grounds? An exclusionary rule? If so, under what circumstances?

4. What does the Supreme Court mean by "good faith" in the *Leon* case? Does the *Leon* case substantially erode the force of the exclusionary rule, as many commentators argued at the time it was decided?

SUGGESTIONS FOR FURTHER READING

One of the most thorough defenses of the exclusionary rule, from a leading scholar of criminal procedure, is Yale Kamisar, "Does (Did) (Should) The Exclusionary Rule Rest on a 'Principled Basis' Rather than an 'Empirical Proposition'?", *Creighton Law Review*, vol. 16 (1983), pp. 565 ff. Other important articles include Dallin Oaks, "Studying the Exclusionary Rule in Search and Seizure," *University of Chicago Law Review*, vol. 37 (1970), pp. 665 ff.; Wayne LaFave, "'The Seductive Call of Expediency': United States v. Leon, Its Rationale and Ramifications," *University of Illinois Law Review*, vol. 1984, pp. 895 ff.

THE CONSTITUTION OF THE UNITED STATES OF AMERICA

We the People of the United States, in Order to form a more perfect Union, establish Justice, insure domestic Tranquility, provide for the common defence, promote the general Welfare, and secure the Blessings of Liberty to ourselves and our Posterity, do ordain and establish this Constitution for the United States of America.

ARTICLE I

Section 1. All legislative Powers herein granted shall be vested in a Congress of the United States, which shall consist of a Senate and House of Representatives.

Section 2. The House of Representatives shall be composed of Members chosen every second Year by the People of the several States, and the Electors in each State shall have the Qualifications requisite for Electors of the most numerous Branch of the State Legislature.

No Person shall be a Representative who shall not have attained to the Age of twenty five Years, and been seven Years a Citizen of the United States, and who shall not, when elected, be an Inhabitant of that State in which he shall be chosen.

Representatives and direct Taxes shall be apportioned among the several States which may be included within this Union, according to their respective Numbers, which shall be determined by adding to the whole Number of free Persons, including those bound to Service for a Term of Years, and excluding Indians not taxed, three fifths of all other Persons. The actual Enumeration shall be made within three Years after the first Meeting of the Congress of the United States, and within every subsequent Term of ten Years, in such Manner as they shall by Law direct. The Number of Representatives shall not exceed one for every thirty Thousand, but each State shall have at Least one Representative; and until such enumeration shall be made, the State of New Hampshire shall be entitled to chuse three; Massachusetts eight; Rhode Island and Providence Plantations one; Connecticut five; New York six; New Jersey four; Pennsylvania eight; Delaware one; Maryland six; Virginia ten;

North Carolina five; South Carolina five; and Georgia three.

When vacancies happen in the Representation from any State, the Executive Authority thereof shall issue Writs of Election to fill such Vacancies.

The House of Representatives shall chuse their Speaker and other Officers; and shall have the sole Power of Impeachment.

Section 3. The Senate of the United States shall be composed of two senators from each State, chosen by the Legislature thereof, for six Years; and each Senator shall have one Vote.

Immediately after they shall be assembled in Consequence of the first Election, they shall be divided as equally as may be into three Classes. The Seats of the Senators of the first Class shall be vacated at the Expiration of the second Year, of the second class at the Expiration of the fourth Year, and of the third Class at the Expiration of the sixth Year, so that one third may be chosen every second Year; and if Vacancies happen by Resignation, or otherwise, during the Recess of the Legislature of any State, the Executive thereof may make temporary Appointments until the next Meeting of the Legislature, which shall then fill such Vacancies.

No Person shall be a Senator who shall not have attained to the Age of thirty Years, and been nine Years a Citizen of the United States, and who shall not, when elected, be an Inhabitant of that State for which he shall be chosen.

The Vice President of the United States shall be President of the Senate, but shall have no Vote, unless they be equally divided.

The Senate shall chuse their other Officers, and also a President pro tempore, in the Absence of the Vice President, or when he shall exercise the Office of President of the United States.

The Senate shall have the sole Power to try all Impeachments. When sitting for that Purpose, they shall be on Oath or Affirmation.

When the President of the United States is tried, the Chief Justice shall preside: And no Person shall be convicted without the Concurrence of two thirds of the Members present.

Judgment in Cases of Impeachment shall not extend further than to removal from Office, and disqualification to hold and enjoy any Office of honor, Trust or Profit under the United States: but the Party convicted shall nevertheless be liable and subject to Indictment, Trial, Judgment and Punishment, according to law.

Section 4. The Times, Places and Manner of holding Elections for Senators and Representatives, shall be prescribed in each State by the Legislature thereof; but the Congress may at any time by Law make or alter such Regulations, except as to the Places of chusing Senators.

The Congress shall assemble at least once in every Year, and such Meeting shall be on the first Monday in December, unless they shall by Law appoint a different Day.

Section 5. Each House shall be the Judge of the Elections, Returns and Qualifications of its own Members, and a Majority of each shall constitute a Quorum to do Business; but a smaller Number may adjourn from day to day, and may be authorized to compel the Attendance of absent Members, in such Manner, and under such Penalties as each House may provide.

Each House may determine the Rules of its Proceedings, punish its Members for disorderly Behaviour, and, with the Concurrence of two thirds, expel a Member.

Each House shall keep a Journal of its Proceedings, and from time to time publish the same, excepting such Parts as may in their Judgment require Secrecy; and the Yeas and Nays of the Members of either House on any question shall, at the Desire of one fifth of those Present, be entered on the Journal.

Neither House, during the Session of Congress, shall, without the Consent of the other, adjourn for more than three days, nor to any other Place than that in which the two Houses shall be sitting.

Section 6. The Senators and Representatives shall receive a Compensation for their Services, to be ascertained by Law, and paid out of the Treasury of the United States. They shall in all Cases, except Treason, Felony and Breach of the Peace, be privileged from Arrest during their Attendance at the Session of their respective Houses, and in going to and returning from the same; and for any Speech or Debate in either House, they shall not be questioned in any other Place.

No Senator or Representative shall, during the Time for which he was elected, be appointed to any civil Office under the Authority of the United States, which shall have been created, or the Emoluments whereof shall have been encreased during such time; and no Person holding any Office under the United States, shall be a Member of either House during his Continuance in Office.

Section 7. All Bills for raising Revenue shall originate in the House of Representatives; but the Senate may propose or concur with Amendments as on other bills.

Every Bill which shall have passed the House of Representatives and the Senate shall, before it become a Law, be presented to the President of the United States; If he approve he shall sign it, but if not he shall return it, with his Objections to that House in which it shall have originated, who shall enter the Objections at large on their Journal, and proceed to reconsider it. If after such Reconsideration two thirds of that House shall agree to pass the Bill, it shall be sent, together with the Objections, to the other House, by which it shall likewise be reconsidered, and if approved by two thirds of that House, it shall become a Law. But in all such Cases the Votes of both Houses shall be determined by yeas and Nays, and the Names of the Persons voting for and against

the Bill shall be entered on the Journal of each House respectively. If any Bill shall not be returned by the President within ten Days (Sundays excepted) after it shall have been presented to him, the Same shall be a Law, in Manner as if he had signed it, unless the Congress by their Adjournment prevent its Return, in which Case it shall not be a Law.

Every Order, Resolution, or Vote to which the Concurrence of the Senate and House of Representatives may be necessary (except on a question of Adjournment) shall be presented to the President of the United States; and before the Same shall take Effect, shall be approved by him, or being disapproved by him shall be repassed by two thirds of the Senate and House of Representatives, according to the rules and Limitations prescribed in the Case of a Bill.

Section 8. The Congress shall have Power To lay and collect Taxes, Duties, Imposts and Excises, to pay the Debts and provide for the common Defence and general Welfare of the United States; but all Duties, Imposts and Excises shall be uniform throughout the United States;

To borrow Money on the credit of the United States;

To regulate Commerce with foreign Nations, and among the several States, and with the Indian Tribes;

To establish an uniform Rule of Naturalization, and uniform Laws on the subject of Bankruptcies throughout the United States;

To coin Money, regulate the Value thereof, and of foreign Coin, and fix the Standard of Weights and Measures;

To provide for the Punishment of counterfeiting the Securities and current Coin of the United States;

To establish Post Offices and Post Roads;

To promote the Progress of Science and useful Arts, by securing for limited Times to Authors and Inventors the exclusive Right to their respective Writings and Discoveries;

To constitute Tribunals inferior to the supreme Court;

To define and punish Piracies and Felonies committed on the high Seas, and Offences against the Law of Nations;

To declare War, grant Letters of Marque and Reprisal, and make Rules concerning Captures on Land and Water;

To raise and support Armies, but no Appropriation of Money to that Use shall be for a longer Term than two Years;

To provide and maintain a Navy;

To make Rules for the Government and Regulation of the land and naval Forces;

To provide for calling forth the Militia to execute the Laws of the Union, suppress Insurrections and repel Invasions;

To provide for organizing, arming, and disciplining, the Militia, and for governing such Part of them as may be employed in the Service of the United States, reserving to the States respectively, the Appointment of the Officers, and the Authority of training the Militia according to the discipline prescribed by Congress;

To exercise exclusive Legislation in all Cases whatsoever, over such District (not exceeding ten Miles square) as may, by Cession of particular States, and the Acceptance of Congress, become the Seat of the Government of the United States, and to exercise like Authority over all Places purchased by the consent of the Legislature of the State in which the Same shall be, for the Erection of Forts, Magazines, Arsenals, dock-Yards, and other needful Buildings;—And

To make all Laws which shall be necessary and proper for carrying into Execution the foregoing Powers, and all other Powers vested by this Constitution in the Government of the United States, or in any Department or Officer thereof.

Section 9. The Migration or Importation of such Persons as any of the States now existing shall think proper to admit, shall not be prohibited by the Congress prior to the Year one thousand eight hundred and eight, but a Tax or Duty may be imposed on such Importation, not exceeding ten dollars for each Person.

The Privilege of the Writ of Habeas Corpus shall not be suspended, unless when in Cases of Rebellion or Invasion the public Safety may require it.

No Bill of Attainder or ex post facto Law shall be passed.

No Capitation, or other direct, Tax shall be laid, unless in Proportion to the Census or Enumeration herein before directed to be taken.

No Tax or Duty shall be laid on Articles exported from any State.

No Preference shall be given by any Regulation of Commerce or Revenue to the Ports of one State over those of another: nor shall Vessels bound to, or from, one State, be obliged to enter, clear, or pay Duties in another.

No Money shall be drawn from the Treasury, but in Consequence of Appropriations made by Law, and a regular Statement and Account of the Receipts and Expenditures of all public Money shall be published from time to time.

No Title of Nobility shall be granted by the United States: And no Person holding any Office or Profit or Trust under them, shall, without the Consent of the Congress, accept of any present, Emolument, Office, or Title, of any kind whatever, from any King, Prince, or foreign State.

Section 10. No State shall enter into any Treaty, Alliance, or Confederation; grant Letters of Marque and Reprisal; coin Money; emit bills of Credit; make any Thing but gold and silver Coin a Tender in Payment of Debts; pass any Bill of Attainder, ex post facto Law, or Law impairing the Obligation of Contracts, or grant any Title of Nobility.

No state shall, without the Consent of the Congress, lay any Imposts or Duties on Imports or Exports, except what may be absolutely necessary for executing its inspection Laws: and the net Produce of all Duties and Imposts, laid by any State on Imports or Exports, shall be for the Use of the Treasury of the United States; and all such Laws shall be subject to the Revision and Controul of the Congress.

No State shall, without the Consent of Congress, lay any Duty of Tonnage, keep Troops, or Ships of War in time of peace, enter into any Agreement or Compact with another State, or with a foreign Power, or engage in War, unless actually invaded, or in such imminent Danger as will not admit of delay.

ARTICLE II

Section 1. The executive Power shall be vested in a President of the United States of America. He shall hold his Office during the Term of four Years, and together with the Vice President, chosen for the same Term, be elected, as follows:

Each State shall appoint, in such Manner as the Legislature thereof may direct, a Number of Electors, equal to the whole Number of Senators and Representatives to which the State may be entitled in the Congress: but no Senator or Representative, or Person holding an Office of Trust or Profit under the United States, shall be appointed an Elector.

The Electors shall meet in their respective States, and vote by Ballot for two Persons, of whom one at least shall not be an Inhabitant of the same State with themselves. And they shall make a List of all the Persons voted for and of the Number of Votes for each; which List they shall sign and certify, and transmit sealed to the Seat of the Government of the United States, directed to the President of the Senate. The President of the Senate shall, in the Presence of the Senate and House of Representatives, open all the Certificates, and the Votes shall then be counted. The Person having the greatest Number of votes shall be the President, if such Number be a Majority of the whole Number of Electors appointed; and if there

be more than one who have such Majority, and have an equal Number of Votes, then the House of Representatives shall immediately chuse by Ballot one of them for President; and if no Person have a Majority, then from the five highest on the List the said House shall in like Manner chuse the President. But in chusing the President, the Votes shall be taken by States, the Representation from each State having one Vote; A quorum for this Purpose shall consist of a Member or Members from two thirds of the States, and a Majority of all the States shall be necessary to a Choice. In every Case, after the Choice of the President, the Person having the greatest Number of Votes of the Electors shall be the Vice President. But if there should remain two or more who have equal Votes, the Senate shall chuse from them by Ballot the Vice President.

The Congress may determine the Time of chusing the Electors, and the Day on which they shall give their Votes; which Day shall be the same throughout the United States.

No Person except a natural born Citizen, or a Citizen of the United States, at the time of the Adoption of this Constitution, shall be eligible to the Office of President; neither shall any Person be eligible to that Office who shall not have attained to the Age of thirty five Years, and been fourteen Years a Resident within the United States.

In Case of the Removal of the President from Office, or of his Death, Resignation, or Inability to discharge the Powers and duties of the said Office, the Same shall devolve on the Vice President, and the Congress may by Law provide for the Case of Removal, Death, Resignation or Inability, both of the President and Vice President, declaring what Officer shall then act as President, and such Officer shall act accordingly, until the Disability be removed, or a President shall be elected.

The President shall, at stated Times, receive for his Services, a Compensation, which shall neither be encreased nor diminished during the Period for which he shall have been elected, and he shall not receive within that Period any other Emolument from the United States, or any of them.

Before he enter on the Execution of his Office, he shall take the following Oath or Affirmation:—"I do solemnly swear (or affirm) that I will faithfully execute the Office of President of the United States, and will to the best of my Ability, preserve, protect and defend the Constitution of the United States."

Section 2. The President shall be Commander in Chief of the Army and Navy of the United States, and of the Militia of the several States, when called into the actual Service of the United States; he may require the Opinion, in writing, of the principal Officer in each of the executive Departments, upon any Subject relating to the Duties of their respective Offices, and he shall have Power to grant Reprieves and Pardons for Offences against the United States, except in Cases of Impeachment.

He shall have Power, by and with the Advice and Consent of the Senate, to make Treaties, provided two thirds of the Senators present concur; and he shall nominate, and by and with the Advice and Consent of the Senate, shall appoint Ambassadors, other public Ministers and Consuls, Judges of the supreme Court, and all other Officers of the United States, whose Appointments are not herein otherwise provided for, and which shall be established by Law; but the Congress may by Law vest the Appointment of such inferior Officers, as they think proper, in the President alone, in the Courts of Law, or in the Heads of Departments.

The President shall have Power to fill up all Vacancies that may happen during the Recess of the Senate, by granting Commissions which shall expire at the End of their next Session.

Section 3. He shall from time to time give to the Congress Information of the State of the Union, and recommend to their Consideration such measures as he shall judge necessary and expedient; he may, on extraordinary Occasions, convene both Houses, or either of them, and in Case of Disagreement between them, with respect to the Time of Adjournment, he may adjourn them to such Time as he shall think proper; he shall receive Ambassadors and other public Ministers; he shall take Care that the Laws be faithfully executed, and shall Commission all the Officers of the United States.

Section 4. The President, Vice President and all civil Officers of the United States, shall be removed from Office on Impeachment for, and Conviction of, Treason, Bribery, or other high Crimes and Misdemeanors.

ARTICLE III

Section 1. The judicial Power of the United States, shall be vested in one supreme Court, and in such inferior Courts as the Congress may from time to time ordain and establish. The Judges, both of the supreme and inferior Courts, shall hold their Offices during good Behaviour, and shall, at stated Times, receive for their Services, a Compensation, which shall not be diminished during their Continuance in Office.

Section 2. The judicial Power shall extend to all Cases, in Law and Equity, arising under this Constitution, the Laws of the United States, and Treaties made, or which shall be made, under their Authority;—to all Cases affecting Ambassadors, other public Ministers and Consuls;—to all Cases of admiralty and maritime Jurisdiction;—to Controversies to which the United States shall be a Party;—to Controversies between two or more States;—between a State and Citizens of another State;—between Citizens of different States;—between Citizens of the same State claiming Lands under Grants of different States, and between a State, or the Citizens thereof, and foreign States, Citizens or Subjects.

In all Cases affecting Ambassadors, other public Ministers and Consuls, and those in which a State shall be Party, the supreme Court shall have original Jurisdiction. In all the other Cases before mentioned, the supreme Court shall have appellate Jurisdiction, both as to Law and Fact, with such Exceptions, and under such Regulations as the Congress shall make.

The Trial of all Crimes, except in Cases of Impeachment, shall be by Jury; and such Trial shall be held in the State where the said Crimes shall have been committed, but when not committed within any State, the trial shall be at such Place or Places as the Congress may by Law have directed.

Section 3. Treason against the United States, shall consist only in levying war against them, or in adhering to their Enemies, giving them aid and Comfort. No Person shall be convicted of Treason unless on the Testimony of two Witnesses to the same overt Act, or on confession in open Court.

The Congress shall have Power to declare the Punishment of Treason, but no Attainder of Treason shall work Corruption of Blood, or Forfeiture except during the Life of the Person attainted.

ARTICLE IV

Section 1. Full Faith and Credit shall be given in each State to the public Acts, Records, and judicial Proceedings of every other State. And the Congress may by general Laws prescribe the Manner in which such Acts, Records and Proceedings shall be proved, and the Effect thereof.

Section 2. The Citizens of each State shall be entitled to all Privileges and Immunities of Citizens in the several States.

A Person charged in any State with Treason, Felony, or other Crime, who shall flee from Justice, and be found in another State, shall on Demand of the executive Authority of the State from which he fled, be delivered up, to be removed to the State having Jurisdiction of the Crime.

No Person held to Service or Labour in one State, under the Laws thereof, escaping into another, shall, in Consequence of any Law or Regulation therein, be discharged from such Service or Labour, but shall be delivered up on Claim of the Party to whom such Service or Labour may be due.

Section 3. New States may be admitted by the Congress into this Union; but no new State shall be formed or erected within the Jurisdiction of any other State, nor any State be formed by the Junction of two or more States, or Parts of States, without the Consent of the Legislatures of the States concerned as well as of the Congress.

The Congress shall have Power to dispose of and make all needful Rules and Regulations respecting the Territory or other Property belonging to the United States; and nothing in this Constitution shall be so construed as to Prejudice any Claims of the United States, or of any particular State.

Section 4. The United States shall guarantee to every State in this Union a Republican Form of Government, and shall protect each of them against Invasion; and on Application of the Legislature, or of the Executive (when the Legislature cannot be convened) against domestic Violence.

ARTICLE V

The Congress, whenever two thirds of both Houses shall deem it necessary, shall propose Amendments to this Constitution, or, on the Application of the Legislatures of two thirds of the several States, shall call a Convention for proposing Amendments, which, in either Case, shall be valid to all Intents and Purposes, as Part of this Constitution, when ratified by the Legislatures of three fourths of the several States, or by Conventions in three fourths thereof, as the one or the other Mode of Ratification may be proposed by the Congress; Provided that no Amendment which may be made prior to the Year One thousand eight hundred and eight shall in any Manner affect the first and fourth Clauses in the Ninth Section of the first Article; and that no State, without its Consent, shall be deprived of its equal Suffrage in the Senate.

ARTICLE VI

All Debts contracted and Engagements entered into, before the Adoption of this Constitution, shall be as valid against the United States under this Constitution, as under the Confederation.

This Constitution, and the Laws of the United States which shall be made in Pursuance thereof; and all Treaties made, or which shall be made, under the Authority of the United States, shall be the supreme Law of the Land; and the Judges in every State shall be bound thereby, any Thing in the Constitution or Laws of any State to the Contrary notwithstanding.

The Senators and Representatives before mentioned, and the Members of the several State Legislatures, and all executive and judicial Officers, both of the United States and of the several States, shall be bound by Oath or Affirmation, to support this Constitution; but no religious Test shall ever be required as a Qualification to any Office or public Trust under the United States.

ARTICLE VII

The Ratification of the Conventions of nine States, shall be sufficient for the Establishment of this Constitution between the States so ratifying the Same. .

Done in convention by the Unanimous Consent of the States present the Seventeenth Day of September in the Year of our Lord one thousand seven hundred and Eighty seven and of the Independence of the United States of America the twelfth. In witness whereof We have hereunto subscribed our Names,

George Washington, President and deputy from Virginia

Attest: William Jackson, Secretary

New Hampshire
John Landon, Nicholas Gilman

Massachusetts
Nathaniel Gorham, Rufus King

Connecticut
Wm. Saml. Johnson, Roger Sherman

New York
Alexander Hamilton

New Jersey
Wil: Livingston, David Brearley, Wm. Paterson, Jona: Dayton

Pennsylvania
B. Franklin, Thomas Mifflin, Robt. Morris, Geo. Clymer, Thos FitzSimons, Jared Ingersoll, James Wilson, Gouv. Morris

Delaware
Geo: Read, Gunning Bedford Jun., John Dickinson, Richard Bassett, Jaco: Broom

Maryland
James McHenry, Daniel of Saint Thomas' Jenifer, Danl. Carroll

Virginia
John Blair, James Madison Jr.

North Carolina
Wm. Blount, Rich'd. Dobbs Spaight, Hugh Williamson

South Carolina
J. Rutledge, Charles Cotesworth Pinckney, Charles Pinckney, Pierce Butler

Georgia
William Few, Abr. Baldwin

AMENDMENTS TO THE UNITED STATES CONSTITUTION

(The first ten amendments are collectively known as the Bill of Rights.)

AMENDMENT I

Congress shall make no law respecting an establishment of religion, or prohibiting the free exercise thereof; or abridging the freedom of speech, or of the press; or the right of the people peaceably to assemble, and to petition the Government for a redress of grievances.

[effective December 15, 1791]

AMENDMENT II

A well regulated Militia, being necessary to the security of a free State, the right of the people to keep and bear Arms, shall not be infringed.

[December 15, 1791]

AMENDMENT III

No Soldier shall, in time of peace be quartered in any house, without the consent of the Owner, nor in time of war, but in a manner to be prescribed by law.

[December 15, 1791]

AMENDMENT IV

The right of the people to be secure in their persons, houses, papers, and effects, against unreasonable searches and seizures, shall not be violated, and no Warrants shall issue, but upon probable cause, supported by Oath or affirmation, and particularly describing the place to be searched, and the persons or things to be seized.

[December 15, 1791]

AMENDMENT V

No person shall be held to answer for a capital or otherwise infamous crime, unless on a presentment or indictment of a Grand Jury, except in cases arising in the land or naval forces, or in the Militia, when in actual service in time of War or public danger; nor shall any person be subject for the same offence to be twice put in jeopardy of life or limb; nor shall be compelled in any criminal case to be a witness against himself, nor be deprived of life, liberty, or property, without due process of law; nor shall private property be taken for public use, without just compensation.

[December 15, 1791]

AMENDMENT VI

In all criminal prosecutions, the accused shall enjoy the right to a speedy and public trial, by an impartial jury of the State and district wherein the crime shall have been committed, which district shall have been previously ascertained by law, and to be informed of the nature and cause of the accusation; to be confronted with the witnesses against him; to have compulsory process for obtaining witnesses in his favor, and to have the Assistance of Counsel for his defence.

[December 15, 1791]

AMENDMENT VII

In Suits at common law, where the value in controversy shall exceed twenty dollars, the right of trial by a jury shall be preserved, and no fact tried by a jury, shall be otherwise re-examined in any Court of the United States, than according to the rules of the common law.

[December 15, 1791]

AMENDMENT VIII

Excessive bail shall not be required, nor excessive fines imposed, nor cruel and unusual punishments inflicted.

[December 15, 1791]

AMENDMENT IX

The enumeration in the Constitution, of certain rights, shall not be construed to deny or disparage others retained by the people.

[December 15, 1791]

AMENDMENT X

The powers not delegated to the United States by the Constitution, nor prohibited by it to the States, are reserved to the States respectively, or to the people.

[December 15, 1791]

AMENDMENT XI

The Judicial power of the United States shall not be construed to extend to any suit in law or equity, commenced or prosecuted against one of the United States by citizens of another State, or by Citizens or Subjects of any foreign State.

[February 7, 1795]

AMENDMENT XII

The Electors shall meet in their respective States and vote by ballot for President and Vice-President, one of whom, at least, shall not be an inhabitant of the same State with themselves; they shall name in their ballots the person voted for as President, and in distinct ballots the person voted for as Vice-President, and they shall make distinct lists of all persons voted for as President, and of all persons voted for as Vice-President, and of the number of votes for each, which lists they shall sign and certify, and transmit sealed to the seat of the government of the United States, directed to the President of the Senate;—The President of the Senate shall, in the presence of the Senate and House of Representatives, open all the certificates and the votes shall then be counted;—The person having the greatest number of votes for President, shall be the President, if such number be a majority of the whole number of Electors appointed; and if no person have such majority, then from the persons having the highest numbers not exceeding three on the list of those voted for as President, the House of Representatives shall choose immediately, by ballot, the President. But in choosing the President, the votes shall be taken by states, the representation from each state having one vote; a quorum for this purpose shall consist of a member or members from two-thirds of the states, and a majority of all the states shall be necessary to a choice. And if the House of Representatives shall not choose a President whenever the right of choice shall devolve upon them, before the fourth day of March next following, then the Vice-President shall act as President, as in the case of the death or other constitutional disability of the President.—The person having the greatest number of votes as Vice-President, shall be the Vice-President, if such number be a majority of the whole number of Electors appointed, and if no person have a majority, then from the two highest numbers on the list, the Senate shall choose the Vice-President; a quorum for the purpose shall consist of two-thirds of the whole number of Senators, and a majority of the whole number shall be necessary to a choice. But no person constitutionally ineligible to the office of President shall be eligible to that of Vice-President of the United States.

[June 15, 1804]

AMENDMENT XIII

Section 1. Neither slavery nor involuntary servitude, except as a punishment for crime whereof the party shall have been duly convicted, shall exist within the United States, or any place subject to their jurisdiction.

Section 2. Congress shall have power to enforce this article by appropriate legislation.

[December 18, 1865]

AMENDMENT XIV

Section 1. All persons born or naturalized in the United States, and subject to the jurisdiction thereof, are citizens of the United States and of the State wherein they reside. No State shall make or enforce any law which shall abridge the privileges or immunities of citizens of the United States; nor shall any State deprive any person of life, liberty, or property, without due process of law; nor deny to any person within its jurisdiction the equal protection of the laws.

Section 2. Representatives shall be apportioned among the several States according to their respective numbers, counting the whole number of persons in each State, excluding Indians not taxed. But when the right to vote at any election for the choice of electors for President and Vice-President of the United States, Representatives in Congress, the Executive and Judicial officers of a State, or the members of the Legislature thereof, is denied to any of the male inhabitants of such State, being twenty-one years of age, and citizens of the United States, or in any way abridged, except for participation in rebellion, or other crime, the basis of representation therein shall be reduced in the proportion which the number of such male citizens shall bear to the whole number of male citizens twenty-one years of age in such State.

Section 3. No person shall be a Senator or Representative in Congress, or elector of President and Vice-President, or hold any office, civil or military, under the United States, or under any State, who, having previously taken an oath, as a member of Congress, or as an officer of the United States, or as a member of any State legislature, or as an executive or judicial officer of any State, to support the Constitution of the United States, shall have engaged in insurrection or rebellion against the same, or given aid or comfort to the enemies thereof. But Congress may by a vote of two-thirds of each House, remove such disability.

Section 4. The validity of the public debt of the United States, authorized by law, including debts incurred for payment of pensions and bounties for services in suppressing insurrection or rebellion, shall not be questioned. But neither the United States nor any State shall assume or pay any debt or obligation incurred in aid of insurrection or rebellion against the United States, or any claim for the loss or emancipation of any slave; but all such debts, obligations, and claims shall be held illegal and void.

Section 5. The Congress shall have the power to enforce, by appropriate legislation, the provisions of this article.

[July 28, 1868]

AMENDMENT XV

Section 1. The right of citizens of the United States to vote shall not be denied or abridged by the United States or by any State on account of race, color, or previous condition of servitude.

Section 2. The Congress shall have power to enforce this article by appropriate legislation.

[March 30, 1870]

AMENDMENT XVI

The Congress shall have power to lay and collect taxes on incomes, from whatever source derived, without apportionment among the several States, and without regard to any census or enumeration.

[February 25, 1913]

AMENDMENT XVII

The Senate of the United States shall be composed of two Senators from each State, elected by the people thereof, for six years;

and each Senator shall have one vote. The electors in each State shall have the qualifications requisite for electors of the most numerous branch of the State legislatures.

When vacancies happen in the representation of any State in the Senate, the executive authority of such State shall issue writs of election to fill such vacancies: *Provided,* That the legislature of any State may empower the executive thereof to make temporary appointments until the people fill the vacancies by election as the legislature may direct.

This amendment shall not be so construed as to affect the election or term of any Senator chosen before it becomes valid as part of the Constitution.

[May 31, 1913]

AMENDMENT XVIII

Section 1. After one year from the ratification of this article the manufacture, sale, or transportation of intoxicating liquors within, the importation thereof into, or the exportation thereof from the United States and all territory subject to the jurisdiction thereof for beverage purposes is hereby prohibited.

Section 2. The Congress and the several States shall have concurrent power to enforce this article by appropriate legislation.

Section 3. This article shall be inoperative unless it shall have been ratified as an amendment to the Constitution by the legislatures of the several States, as provided in the Constitution, within seven years from the date of the submission hereof to the States by the Congress.

[January 29, 1919; repealed December 5, 1933]

AMENDMENT XIX

The right of citizens of the United States to vote shall not be denied or abridged by the United States or by any State on account of sex.

Congress shall have power to enforce this article by appropriate legislation.

[August 26, 1920]

AMENDMENT XX

Section 1. The terms of the President and Vice President shall end at noon on the 20th day of January, and the terms of Senators and Representatives at noon on the 3d day of January, of the years in which such terms would have ended if this article had not been ratified; and the terms of their successors shall then begin.

Section 2. The Congress shall assemble at least once in every year, and such meeting shall begin at noon the 3d day of January, unless they shall by law appoint a different day.

Section 3. If, at the time fixed for the beginning of the term of the President, the President elect shall have died, the Vice President elect shall become President. If a President shall not have been chosen before the time fixed for the beginning of his term, or if the President elect shall have failed to qualify, then the Vice President elect shall act as President until a President shall have qualified; and the Congress may by law provide for the case wherein neither a President elect nor a Vice President elect shall have qualified, declaring who shall then act as President, or the manner in which one who is to act shall be selected, and such person shall act accordingly until a President or Vice President shall have qualified.

Section 4. The Congress may by law provide for the case of the death of any of the persons from whom the House of Representatives may choose a President whenever the right of choice shall have devolved upon them, and for the case of the death of any of the persons from whom the Senate may choose a Vice President whenever the right of choice shall have devolved upon them.

Section 5. Sections 1 and 2 shall take effect on the 15th day of October following the ratification of this article.

Section 6. This article shall be inoperative unless it shall have been ratified as an amendment to the Constitution by the legislatures of three-fourths of the several States within seven years from the date of its submission.

[January 23, 1933]

AMENDMENT XXI

Section 1. The eighteenth article of amendment to the Constitution of the United States is hereby repealed.

Section 2. The transportation or importation into any State, Territory, or possession of the United States for delivery or use therein of intoxicating liquors, in violation of the laws thereof, is hereby prohibited.

Section 3. This article shall be inoperative unless it shall have been ratified as an amendment to the Constitution by conventions in the several States, as provided in the Constitution, within seven years from the date of the submission hereof to the States by the Congress.

[December 5, 1933]

AMENDMENT XXII

Section 1. No person shall be elected to the office of the President more than twice, and no person who has held the office of President, or acted as President, for more than two years of a term to which some other person was elected President shall be elected to the office of the President more than once. But this Article shall not apply to any person holding the office of President when this Article was proposed by the Congress, and shall not prevent any person who may be holding the office of President, or acting as President, during the term within which this Article becomes operative from holding the office of President or acting as President during the remainder of such term.

Section 2. This article shall be inoperative unless it shall have been ratified as an amendment to the Constitution by the legislatures of three-fourths of the several States within seven years from the date of its submission to the States by the Congress.

[February 27, 1951]

AMENDMENT XXIII

Section 1. The district constituting the seat of Government of the United States shall appoint in such manner as the Congress may direct:

A number of electors of President and Vice President equal to the whole number of Senators and Representatives in Congress to which the District would be entitled if it were a State, but in no event more than the least populous State; they shall be in addition to those appointed by the States, but they shall be considered, for the purposes of the election of President and Vice President, to be electors appointed by a State; and they shall meet in the District and perform such duties as provided by the twelfth article of amendment.

Section 2. The Congress shall have power to enforce this article by appropriate legislation.

[March 29, 1961]

AMENDMENT XXIV

Section 1. The right of citizens of the United States to vote in any primary or other election for President or Vice President, for electors for President or Vice President, or for Senator or Representative in Congress, shall not be denied or abridged by the United States or any State by reason of failure to pay any poll tax or other tax.

Section 2. The Congress shall have power to enforce this article by appropriate legislation.

[January 23, 1964]

AMENDMENT XXV

Section 1. In case of the removal of the President from office or of his death or resignation, the Vice President shall become President.

Section 2. Whenever there is a vacancy in the office of the Vice President, the President shall nominate a Vice President who shall take office upon confirmation by a majority vote of both Houses of Congress.

Section 3. Whenever the President transmits to the President pro tempore of the Senate and the Speaker of the House of Representatives his written declaration that he is unable to discharge the powers and duties of his office, and until he transmits to them a written declaration to the contrary, such powers and duties shall be discharged by the Vice President as Acting President.

Section 4. Whenever the Vice President and a majority of either the principal officers of the executive department or of such other body as Congress may by law provide, transmit to the President pro tempore of the Senate and the Speaker of the House of Representatives their written declaration that the President is unable to discharge the powers and duties of his office, the Vice President shall immediately assume the powers and duties of the office of Acting President.

Thereafter, when the President transmits to the President pro tempore of the Senate and the Speaker of the House of Representatives his written declaration that no inability exists, he shall resume the powers and duties of his office unless the Vice President and a majority of either the principal officers of the executive department or of such other body as Congress may by law provide, transmit within four days to the President pro tempore of the Senate and the Speaker of the House of Representatives their written declaration that the President is unable to discharge the powers and duties of his office. Thereupon Congress shall decide the issue, assembling within forty-eight hours for that purpose if not in session. If the Congress, within twenty-one days after receipt of the latter written declaration, or, if Congress is not in session, within twenty-one days after Congress is required to assemble, determines by two-thirds vote of both Houses that the President is unable to discharge the powers and duties of his office, the Vice President shall continue to discharge the same as Acting President; otherwise, the President shall resume the powers and duties of his office.

[February 10, 1967]

AMENDMENT XXVI

Section 1. The right of citizens of the United States, who are eighteen years of age or older, to vote shall not be denied or abridged by the United States or by any State on account of age.

Section 2. The Congress shall have power to enforce this article by appropriate legislation.

[July 1, 1971]

AMENDMENT XXVII

No law, varying the compensation for the services of the Senators and Representatives, shall take effect, until an election of Representatives shall have intervened.

[May 7, 1992]

COPYRIGHTS AND ACKNOWLEDGMENTS

The authors are indebted to the following for permission to reprint from copyrighted material:

CHAPTER ONE

A. C. Pegis Estate. For the excerpt from *Basic Writings of St. Thomas Aquinas*, edited by Anton Pegis. Reprinted by permission of estate.

Oxford University Press. For the excerpt from *Natural Law and Natural Rights* (1980) by John Finnis. Copyright © John Finnis 1980. Reprinted by permission of Oxford University Press.

Yale University Press. For the excerpt from *The Morality of Law* by Lon Fuller. copyright © 1969 Reprinted by permission of the publisher.

Oxford University Press. For the excerpt from *The Concept of Law* (1961) by H. L. A. Hart. Copyright © 1961 Oxford University Press. Reprinted by permission of Oxford University Press.

Columbia Law Review. For the excerpt from "A Realistic Jurisprudence: The Next Step" by Karl Llewellyn which appeared in *Columbia Law Review*, vol. 30. Copyright © 1930 Columbia Law Review. Reprinted by permission.

Vanderbilt Law Review. For the excerpt from "Remarks on the Theory of Appellate Decision and The Rules or Canons About How Statutes Are To Be Construed" by Karl Llewellyn which appeared in *Vanderbilt Law Review* (1950). Reprinted by permission.

Journal of Legal Education. For the excerpt from "Freedom and Constraint in Adjudication: A Critical Phenomenology" by Duncan Kennedy. Reprinted by permission.

Ronald Dworkin. For the excerpt from *Taking Rights Seriously* by Ronald Dworkin. Copyright © 1977 Reprinted by permission of the author.

Harvard University Press. For the excerpt from *Law's Empire* by Ronald Dworkin, Cambridge, Mass.. Harvard University Press, Copyright © 1986 by Ronald Dworkin. Reprinted by permission of the publishers.

Frederick Schauer. For the excerpt from *Playing by the Rules* by Frederick Schauer. Copyright © 1991. Reprinted by permission of the author.

Yale University Press. For the excerpt from *Justice Accused* by Robert M. Cover. Copyright © 1975. Reprinted by permission of the publisher.

CHAPTER TWO

The Yale Law Journal Company. For the excerpt from "Formalism" by Frederick Schauer which appeared in *The Yale Law Journal*, vol. 97, pages 509–548. Reprinted by permission of The Yale Law Journal Company, Fred B. Rothman & Company, and the author.

Harvard University Press. For the excerpts from *Government by Judiciary* by Raoul Berger. Reprinted by permission of the author.

Simon & Schuster. For the excerpts from *The Tempting of America: The Political Seduction of the Law* by Robert H. Bork. Abridged with the permission of The Free Press, a Division of Simon & Schuster, Inc. Copyright © 1990 by Robert H. Bork.

The Boston University Law Review. For the excerpt from "The Misconceived Quest for the Original Understanding" by Paul Brest which appeared in *The Boston University Law Review*, vol. 60. Copyright © 1980. Reprinted by permission of the publisher.

University of Florida Law Review. For the excerpt from "Natural Law Revisited" by Ronald Dworkin which originally appeared in the *University of Florida Law Review* vol. 34. Copyright © 1982. Reprinted with the permission of the *University of Florida Law Review*.

Harvard Law Review Association. For the excerpt from "On Analogical Reasoning" by Cass Sunstein which appeared in the *Harvard Law Review*, vol. 106. Reprinted by permission of the publisher and the author.

Larry Alexander. For the excerpt from "Constrained by Precedent" by Larry Alexander. Reprinted by permission of the author.

The estate of Barbara Frank Kristein. For the excerpts from *Law and the Modern Mind* by Jerome Frank. Copyright 1963. Reprinted by permission of the estate.

Harvard Law Review Association. For the excerpt from "Follow the Rules Laid Down" by Mark Tushnet which appeared in the *Harvard Law Review*, vol. 96. Reprinted by permission of the publisher and the author.

Southern California Law Review. For the excerpt from "In Context" by Martha Minow and Elizabeth V Spelman which appeared in the *Southern California Law Review*, vol. 63. Copyright © 1990. Reprinted by permission.

CASE INDEX

SUBJECT AND NAME INDEX